# The Cambridge Handbook of Experimental Syntax

Experimental syntax is an area that is rapidly growing as linguistic research becomes increasingly focused on replicable language data, in both fieldwork and laboratory environments. The first of its kind, this handbook provides an in-depth overview of current issues and trends in this field, with contributions from leading international scholars. It pays special attention to sentence acceptability experiments, outlining current best practices in conducting tests, and pointing out promising new avenues for future research. Separate sections review research results from the past 20 years, covering specific syntactic phenomena and language types. The handbook also outlines other common psycholinguistic and neurolinguistic methods for studying syntax, comparing and contrasting them with acceptability experiments, and giving useful perspectives on the interplay between theoretical and experimental linguistics. Providing an up-to-date reference on this exciting field, it is essential reading for students and researchers in linguistics interested in using experimental methods to conduct syntactic research.

GRANT GOODALL is Professor of Linguistics at University of California, San Diego. He is the author of the influential 1987 book *Parallel Structures in Syntax* and of many important articles on syntactic phenomena in English, Spanish, and other languages. In recent years, he has been at the forefront of using experimental techniques to address longstanding questions in syntactic theory.

# The Cambridge Handbook of Experimental Syntax

Edited by

**Grant Goodall**

*University of California, San Diego*

CAMBRIDGE
UNIVERSITY PRESS

# CAMBRIDGE
## UNIVERSITY PRESS

University Printing House, Cambridge CB2 8BS, United Kingdom

One Liberty Plaza, 20th Floor, New York, NY 10006, USA

477 Williamstown Road, Port Melbourne, VIC 3207, Australia

314–321, 3rd Floor, Plot 3, Splendor Forum, Jasola District Centre,
New Delhi – 110025, India

103 Penang Road, #05–06/07, Visioncrest Commercial, Singapore 238467

Cambridge University Press is part of the University of Cambridge.

It furthers the University's mission by disseminating knowledge in the pursuit of
education, learning, and research at the highest international levels of excellence.

www.cambridge.org
Information on this title: www.cambridge.org/9781108474801
DOI: 10.1017/9781108569620

First published 2021

Printed in the United Kingdom by TJ Books Limited, Padstow, Cornwall

*A catalogue record for this publication is available from the British Library.*

*Library of Congress Cataloging-in-Publication Data*
Names: Goodall, Grant, editor.
Title: The Cambridge handbook of experimental syntax / edited by Grant Goodall.
Description: Cambridge ; New York, NY : Cambridge University Press, 2021. |
Includes bibliographical references and index.
Identifiers: LCCN 2021001515 (print) | LCCN 2021001516 (ebook) | ISBN
9781108474801 (hardback) | ISBN 9781108465496 (paperback) | ISBN
9781108569620 (ebook)
Subjects: LCSH: Grammar, Comparative and general – Syntax. | Acceptability
(Linguistics) | Linguistics – Methodology.
Classification: LCC P291 .C325 2021 (print) | LCC P291 (ebook) | DDC 415–dc23
LC record available at https://lccn.loc.gov/2021001515
LC ebook record available at https://lccn.loc.gov/2021001516

ISBN 978-1-108-47480-1 Hardback

# Contents

# Figures

# Tables

# Contributors

Markus Bader, Goethe University Frankfurt
Dustin A. Chacón, New York University Abu Dhabi
Wayne Cowart, University of Southern Maine
Brian Dillon, University of Massachusetts, Amherst
Gisbert Fanselow, University of Potsdam
Sam Featherston, University of Tübingen
Claudia Felser, University of Potsdam
Jerid Francom, Wake Forest University
Shin Fukuda, University of Hawai'i at Mānoa
Phoebe Gaston, University of Connecticut
Grant Goodall, University of California, San Diego
Timothy Gupton, University of Georgia
Chung-hye Han, Simon Fraser University
Jesse Harris, University of California, Los Angeles
Jana Häussler, Bielefeld University
Nick Huang, National University of Singapore
Tania Ionin, University of Illinois at Urbana-Champaign
Tom S. Juzek, Saarland University
Elsi Kaiser, University of Southern California
Vadim Kimmelman, University of Bergen
Robert Kluender, University of California, San Diego
Tania Leal, University of Nevada, Reno
William Matchin, University of South Carolina
Dana McDaniel, University of Southern Maine
Aya Meltzer-Asscher, Tel Aviv University
Shota Momma, University of Massachusetts, Amherst
Hanna Muller, University of Maryland
Colin Phillips, University of Maryland
William Snyder, University of Connecticut

Jon Sprouse, New York University Abu Dhabi
Arthur Stepanov, University of Nova Gorica
Rosalind Thornton, Macquarie University
Sandra Villata, University of Connecticut
Matthew W. Wagers, University of California, Santa Cruz
Thomas Weskott, University of Göttingen

# Introduction

Grant Goodall

The present volume is a handbook of experimental syntax, but what is "experimental syntax?" One could reasonably argue that all syntax is experimental, in the sense that traditional syntactic research is based on series of small, informal experiments where the syntactician asks whether particular sentences are acceptable in the language. Syntacticians may ask this of others, in the case of fieldwork with a native-speaking consultant, or of themselves, in the case of introspective "armchair" work, or through some combination of the two, but in any event, there is something clearly experimental about the approach. On the other hand, one might understand "experimental syntax" to refer to studies that use the tools and techniques of formal experiments, as in the tradition of experimental psychology, to explore linguistic behavior relevant to the structure of sentences. In this sense, much of psycholinguistics and neurolinguistics would be part of "experimental syntax."

In practice, though, the term "experimental syntax" is generally used to refer to the intersection of the traditional approach of informal experiments and the approach utilizing more formal experiments based on methods from experimental psychology. That is, the label "experimental syntax" is typically applied to studies that focus on the varying acceptability of particular sentence types and explore this by means of formal experiments. As a consequence, this handbook is devoted primarily to experimental syntax in this sense, focusing on the use of formal sentence acceptability experiments to study issues in syntactic theory. Nevertheless, this approach is built upon a tradition of experimental work in a broader sense, including the informal experiments used in syntactic research for many decades, and has many points of contact with the more conventionally experimental work of psycholinguists and neurolinguists, so these areas receive significant attention in the handbook as well.

The goal of the handbook is to review what we have learned in the area of experimental syntax, but also to make sense of what this new body of knowledge is telling us, understand how experimental studies relate to the study of syntax more broadly, and explore what type of work we should be doing as the field moves forward. Experimental syntax has exploded in popularity over the last several years, so a pause to reflect on what we have done and where we are going is sorely needed.

The handbook consists of 27 chapters, organized into four parts. Part I is devoted to sentence acceptability experiments as such: how to do them, how to interpret the results, and how they can be of use to syntacticians. This type of experiment presents many methodological challenges in terms of designing the stimuli, choosing participants, creating an appropriate response method for the participants, and making sense of the gradience in their responses, but it also leads to deep questions about the nature of acceptability and grammaticality, and the varying results that one can get across time and across languages.

Part II explores particular syntactic phenomena that have been studied in depth using acceptability experiments and related methods. For some of these phenomena, such as resumptive pronouns and the *that*-trace effect, to mention only two, experimental work has had such an impact that even "traditional" syntacticians now pay close attention, while for some other phenomena, the broader influence of experimental studies has been more limited. In all cases, though, a thorough review of what has been found so far and what remains to be investigated, as is provided in these chapters, should provide a necessary foundation for new work.

In Part III, the focus is on using techniques of experimental syntax to study specific populations of speakers and specific groups of languages. For studying the first language of young children and the second language of speakers of all ages, for instance, formal experiments have long been a mainstay, but these populations present special challenges that mean that the techniques used for adult native speakers cannot always be utilized as is. For better or worse, the fields of child language acquisition, second language acquisition, and experimental syntax have each developed their own experimental traditions relatively independently, but we are now in a position to reflect on this and look for the most productive path forward. With regard to experimental work on different languages, the situation is similar in the sense that each language (or language family) may present its own challenges, such as a need to use non-written stimuli or a lack of clarity as to who counts as a native speaker or signer of the language. In addition, specific sentence types in individual languages may be difficult to study experimentally for a variety of reasons. All of the chapters in Part III attempt to survey what experimental work has shown us for particular populations and language families, and to recommend areas for further research that could be fruitful.

While much of Parts I–III looks at acceptability experiments, Part IV examines other experimental approaches to the study of syntax. Many of the techniques examined are traditionally thought of as relevant mainly for psycholinguists, neurolinguists, or computational linguists, but the authors show they can address issues of interest to syntacticians of all stripes. This leads to broader questions about the relation between these types of experimental methods and the acceptability experiments that are discussed in many of the other chapters, and at an even broader level, the relation between "theoretical linguistics" and "experimental linguistics" in general.

It seems clear now that the methodological and conceptual silos in which linguists have operated for decades, with syntacticians relying on acceptability judgments gathered through fieldwork and introspection and psycholinguists and others relying on formal experiments, will soon be a thing of the past. The tradition of acceptability judgments has yielded a rich set of data and important insights, as has the tradition of experimentation, but some of the most interesting new work now comes from trying to integrate these two traditions, both in terms of methodology and in terms of theoretical concepts and mechanisms.

Though the methodological and conceptual silos may be in the process of being broken down, it is less clear what will emerge from this. A new way of doing syntax will take the sustained and thoughtful work of many researchers, and it is hoped that the present volume will provide a solid foundation for this work and inspiring ideas on how to move forward.

# Part I

# General Issues in Acceptability Experiments

# 1

# Sentence Acceptability Experiments: What, How, and Why

Grant Goodall

Sentence acceptability experiments have become increasingly common since Cowart (1997) first presented a detailed method for carrying them out, but there is still relatively little clarity among syntacticians about what goes into a well-designed experiment, how to perform one and interpret the results, and why one might want to do this in the first place. This chapter addresses these concerns, by providing recommendations and perspective on how experimental approaches to acceptability can be understood and put to use. Section 1.1 discusses the notion of acceptability in general and the role that it has played in linguistic research. Section 1.2 enters into the details of experimental design, giving an overview of the best practices in acceptability experiments that have emerged from the last two decades of research. Section 1.3 explores the variety of factors, both grammatical and extra-grammatical, that acceptability experiments seem to be able to detect, while Section 1.4 addresses the question of why one might undertake the effort of conducting acceptability experiments.

## 1.1 Acceptability

Any description of a language inevitably includes a description of what is possible, e.g., a listing of the phonemes, the allowable syllable structures, the preferred word order, etc. These are essentially descriptions of what is "acceptable" in the language, and such descriptions form the core of grammatical research in all traditions. By characterizing what is acceptable, such descriptions also make implicit claims about what is not acceptable. More explicit claims of unacceptability were occasionally included

I am grateful to the members of the Experimental Syntax Lab at UC San Diego and to research assistants Chengrui Zheng and Noah Hermansen for their valuable comments, discussion, and assistance in the preparation of this chapter.

in classical, Renaissance, and American structuralist grammars (see Householder 1973; Myers 2017), but with the advent of generative grammar in the mid-twentieth century, and its emphasis on explicitness in grammatical description, the distinction between acceptability and unacceptability became much more important. This distinction played a crucial role in Chomsky (1957), for instance, and was much more extensively discussed in Chomsky (1965).

The focus on acceptability vs. unacceptability also led to a more nuanced understanding of what these concepts mean. The most widespread view, proposed originally in Chomsky (1965), is that (un)acceptability may be influenced by a variety of factors, of which (un)grammaticality is only one. Under this view, then, "acceptability" and "grammaticality" are not synonyms, in that a sentence that is well-formed according to principles of the grammar, for instance, may turn out to be unacceptable due to parsing difficulties, etc. Both concepts are presumably gradient (i.e. acceptability and grammaticality are both "a matter of degree," in Chomsky's (1965) terms), but only acceptability is perceived directly. Grammaticality, like the other factors that contribute to acceptability, can only be inferred based on the evidence available.

Given this distinction between acceptability and grammaticality, it should be clear why one performs "acceptability experiments," but not "grammaticality experiments." Expressions such as "grammaticality judgments" are traditional, but as has often been pointed out, they are a misnomer (Schütze 2016; Myers 2017) and appear to be declining in frequency relative to "acceptability judgments" (Myers 2009).

Acceptability is assumed to be a percept that occurs when a speaker encounters a linguistic stimulus, and in an experiment, the speaker is typically asked to report on this percept (Schütze & Sprouse 2014). For example, speakers have a percept in response to *Girl the boy the saw* (presumably different from the percept they would have with *The girl saw the boy*) and can report on it. Referring to how this percept and the following report come to be has always been problematic, however. The term "introspection" is traditionally used, but this brings to mind introspectionist psychology and the idea that experiment participants can report on their internal cognitive mechanisms. Since no one assumes that the primary mechanisms underlying linguistic behavior are accessible to consciousness, this term can be misleading. Similarly, the term "intuition," rightly or wrongly, can give the impression that the process is capricious or unempirical. "Judgment" may avoid these unwanted implications, but it carries one of its own: it suggests that the process involves protracted and conscious deliberation on whether the sentence is acceptable or not, whereas in practice, the process appears to be virtually instantaneous.

The terms "introspection," "intuition," and "judgment," then, might all seem inadequate in one way or another, although all three are commonly used. As Schütze (2016) points out, terms like "sensation" or "reaction" come much closer to capturing the true nature of acceptability as a percept. Neither is currently in regular use for this purpose, but it is helpful to keep them in mind when designing and interpreting the results from acceptability experiments, because they allow us to think much more clearly about what these experiments are actually measuring. Acceptability is obviously different from other "sensations" that one might want to measure, such as pain or thirst, but there are also important similarities. Like pain, for instance, acceptability is a percept that one feels subjectively, without necessarily being aware of the causes or mechanisms behind it, and there is a clear sense of fine-grained gradience: a sentence may feel slightly more acceptable or less acceptable than another, just as pain can subtly increase or decrease. In addition, the most reliable way to measure either acceptability or pain is to rely on what the individual reports.[1]

Among the various experimental methods that are used in linguistics, acceptability is often categorized as being both "behavioral," meaning that participants' overt response to the stimulus is what is being measured, and "offline," meaning that the participants' response is untimed and comes once the stimulus is complete (Garrod 2006). Acceptability thus contrasts with methods that are neurolinguistic, where brain responses are measured directly, and/or "online," where participants' responses are timed and come while the stimulus is in progress, such as in self-paced reading or eye-tracking (see Chapters 23, 24, and 27). These distinctions are valuable, but the offline vs. online contrast in particular should not be exaggerated. In standard acceptability experiments, participants typically read the stimulus sentence, give their response, and move to the next stimulus within 5 seconds, suggesting that participants are registering an immediate sensation without much conscious deliberation.[2] The main difference, then, between online methods and acceptability seems to be when the response/measurement take place (while the sentence is in progress vs. after it is complete), rather than the extent to which the response might be influenced by conscious thought (see Phillips & Wagers 2007; Lewis & Phillips 2015).

## 1.2  Best Practices in Acceptability Experiments

At a bare minimum, an experiment that attempts to measure acceptability will need to present a stimulus sentence to a participant and give that

---

[1] In fact, pain is standardly measured in terms of a Visual Analog Scale (VAS; Carlsson 1983), which bears many similarities to the types of scales used for measuring acceptability, and the effectiveness of treatments is determined by calculating whether there is a statistically significant difference in VAS between the treatment group and a control group, in a way analogous to acceptability studies (though unlike acceptability studies, pain studies also deal with the question of whether a given statistically significant difference in VAS is clinically meaningful (e.g. Forouzanfar et al. 2003; Dworkin et al. 2008)).

[2] This time estimate is based on our observations of the amount of time that most participants need to finish an entire acceptability experiment.

participant a way to express the sensation that arises in response. Beyond that, though, several difficult questions about design and procedure must be addressed, and here I will present suggestions for doing this. I will follow the basic guidelines from Cowart (1997), supplemented with lessons learned in the subsequent decades of experimental practice.

### 1.2.1   Factorial Design

In general, presenting a single sentence in isolation to participants will be of little use. Most sentences will be neither 100 percent nor 0 percent acceptable, so their intermediate status will only be comprehensible in relation to other sentences. In addition, it is only the comparison to other sentences that can tell us what contributes to an increase or decrease in acceptability for a given sentence. For example, participants presented with a sentence like (1) will feel some degree of discomfort.

(1)    Who do you think that _ will hire Mary?

Without anything else to compare it to, we won't know whether this level of unacceptability is a lot or a little, and in any event, we won't know what to attribute the unacceptability to. To remedy this, we can compare acceptability in (1) and (2).

(2)    Who do you think _ will hire Mary?

(2) is exactly like (1) except that in (2), there is no overt complementizer. This is the well-known *that*-trace phenomenon (see Chapter 10, as well as Perlmutter (1971) and Pesetsky (2017)), so we expect that (2) will be of much higher acceptability than (1). Given these two data points, we can conclude that omission of *that* ameliorates extraction of an embedded subject, but we don't know how much of this effect might be due to the omission of *that* alone, which might affect acceptability even without extraction of the subject. To test for this, we can include control conditions to give us a baseline indication of the effect of *that* on acceptability. For example, we could consider the counterparts to (1) and (2) but with extraction of the object, as in (3) and (4).

(3)    Who do you think that Mary will hire _ ?

(4)    Who do you think Mary will hire _ ?

We could also use yes/no questions or declarative statements for this purpose; the crucial part is to get a baseline measure of the presence/absence of *that* independently of extraction of the embedded subject. The choice of which conditions count as controls is partly a matter of perspective: if we are testing subject vs. object extraction, such as (1) and (3), then (2) and (4) act as controls.

In our example so far, then, we are manipulating two factors, each with two levels: *that* (presence vs. absence) and extraction site (subject vs. object). This gives us the four conditions (1)–(4), as in Table 1.1.

This "factorial design" of our stimuli (Fisher 1935) allows us to measure each of the two factors on their own, but more importantly, it allows us to detect any interactions between them, i.e. cases where the effect of one factor differs depending on the level of the other factor. In cases like this, for example, researchers have generally found that the effect of *that* is much larger when the extraction site is the embedded subject than when it is the embedded object, and the effect of the extraction site is much larger when *that* is present than when it is not (see Chapter 10 for more details).

A factorial design bears many important similarities to minimal pairs/ sets as they are traditionally used in linguistics, and the use of the full set of four conditions in (1)–(4) to demonstrate the existence of an effect will be familiar even to syntacticians without backgrounds in experimentation. As with a minimal pair/set, the conditions in a factorial design are lexically matched to the extent possible, so that any differences found can be attributed to the factors being tested, rather than to random lexical differences across conditions. More so than with a traditional minimal pair/set, though, a factorial design allows one to examine the interaction of two factors with great care and precision. The robustness of the *that*-trace effect may obscure this point here, but it is not hard to imagine how in principle (and often in practice), the differences among conditions could be small enough that only a factorial experiment would be able to detect an interaction.

The example in Table 1.1 is known as a "2 × 2" design, because each of the two factors has two levels. It is of course possible to have more levels (e.g. 2 × 3) or more factors (e.g. 2 × 2 × 2), resulting in more conditions. This is sometimes justified, but it must be weighed against the disadvantages that come with a more complex design. Going beyond 2 × 2 can make lexically matched stimuli more difficult to construct, the statistical analysis more cumbersome, and the results more difficult to interpret. In addition, the more conditions in the design, the more stimuli in the experiment, so the amount of time that people can participate in the experiment without undue fatigue also sets an upper limit on the

Table 1.1 *A factorial design for measuring the* that*-trace effect*

| | | *that* | |
|---|---|---|---|
| | | + | − |
| Extraction Site | **subject** | (1) Who do you think that _ will hire Mary? | (2) Who do you think _ will hire Mary? |
| | **object** | (3) Who do you think that Mary will hire _? | (4) Who do you think Mary will hire _? |

complexity of the factorial design. With some other experimental techniques (e.g. self-paced reading), the relative difficulty of getting statistically significant contrasts can also discourage researchers from designing experiments with more than a 2 × 2 design. This is less of an issue in acceptability studies, where experiments finding significant contrasts among four to six conditions are not uncommon, but still, it should be kept in mind. Overall, then, 2 × 2 is generally the default design, with more complex designs recommended only when needed to test the hypothesis at hand and when the potential disadvantages have been carefully considered.

### 1.2.2   Lexicalizations

Having lexically matched stimuli as in Table 1.1 is an important first step in designing an experiment, since as we have seen, only true minimal sets like these allow us to know that differences in acceptability are due to differences in the factors. Running an experiment with only these four stimuli would not be a good idea, however. First, we would not know whether the results obtained were specific to these particular lexical items or were due to something more general about the structure. Since we are typically interested in the latter, it is advisable to abstract away from the effects of individual items by testing many different lexical versions of a set like Table 1.1, thus allowing any deeper structural effect to emerge. Second, presenting experiment participants with four such similar sentences could cause a number of problems. It could mean, for instance, that their experience of reading the first sentence, in which every word is new, will be different from their experience of reading the other sentences, in which the words are already familiar, that the ratings for one sentence could affect the ratings of the other, and that the monotony of the sentences could result in declining levels of attention among the participants as the experiment proceeds. Any of these consequences would be undesirable, since they could affect the results in unpredictable ways.

Given these considerations, we would ideally want each participant to see the four conditions of Table 1.1 in such a way that each condition is lexicalized differently. To make this possible, we need to construct four separate "lexicalization sets" of our factorial design; Table 1.1 already constitutes one such set. At a minimum, there must be as many lexicalization sets as there are conditions in the design. These sets need to be constructed by hand, so the potential for error is great (with potentially very bad consequences for the experiment). To avoid such errors, it is best to take one of the conditions from the factorial design and break the sample sentence into components in a table or spreadsheet (Cowart (1997)). Additional stimuli can then be created either by copying the component into the entire column, in cases where the component will

Table 1.2 *A table of components for Condition 1*

| | | | | | | |
|---|---|---|---|---|---|---|
| Who | do you | think | that | will hire | Mary | ? |
| Who | do they | suppose | that | might contact | Tom | ? |
| Who | did he | decide | that | should interview | Sophia | ? |
| Who | did she | imagine | that | could photograph | Ryan | ? |

be found in all lexicalizations of that condition, or by populating the other cells in that column with similar lexical items, in cases where each lexicalization for that component will be different. An example is shown in Table 1.2, where the first, fourth, and seventh columns are invariable, while the others change.

The other conditions can now be constructed simply by copying the table and then manipulating it. Deleting the fourth column, for instance, will create Condition 2, while Condition 3 can be constructed by reversing the order of the fifth and sixth columns. When this process is done, the table or spreadsheet can be converted to ordinary text. By following this procedure, a full set of 16 stimuli (4 lexicalization sets of 4 conditions each) can be created with only a minimal possibility of error.

### 1.2.3  Counterbalancing

Let us suppose that at this point, for each of the conditions in Table 1.1, we have a set of four lexicalizations as in Table 1.2. For the reasons given earlier, we do not want any participant to see a given lexicalization in more than one condition. We also do not want different lexicalizations of a given condition to be seen by different numbers of participants, since we don't want certain stimuli to be overrepresented in the results. These considerations are aspects of "counterbalancing," and the usual way to ensure counterbalancing of the stimuli is to perform a "Latin square" procedure (using either a spreadsheet or a script). This refers to distributing the stimuli into lists such that each list contains only one representative of each lexicalization and the same number of stimuli for each condition, as illustrated in Table 1.3, without any repetition of stimuli across lists.

Each list in Table 1.3 corresponds to what an individual participant would see in the experiment. In this example, each participant will see one example of each condition. If we want participants to see more than that, as we often do (see Section 1.2.6 below), the same principles and procedures apply, but we will need to create additional stimuli in order to achieve our counterbalancing goals. For example, if we want each participant to see 5 examples of each condition, then we need to create 20 lexicalization sets (5 examples × 4 conditions), or put differently, 20 rows in the equivalent of Table 1.2.

Table 1.3 *Counterbalanced lists of experimental stimuli using a Latin square design*

| List 1 | List 2 | List 3 | List 4 |
| --- | --- | --- | --- |
| Who do you think that will hire Mary? | Who do they suppose that might contact Tom? | Who did he decide that should interview Sophia? | Who did she imagine that could photograph Ryan? |
| Who did she imagine could photograph Ryan? | Who do you think will hire Mary? | Who do they suppose might contact Tom? | Who did he decide should interview Sophia? |
| Who did he decide that Sophia should interview? | Who did she imagine that Ryan could photograph? | Who do you think that Mary will hire? | Who do they suppose that Tom might contact? |
| Who do they suppose Tom might contact? | Who did he decide Sophia should interview? | Who did she imagine Ryan could photograph? | Who do you think Mary will hire? |

## 1.2.4 Order

Presenting the lists in Table 1.3 as they are introduces a confound: Condition 1 is always first, Condition 2 is always second, etc. This could influence the results in undesirable ways, so the obvious solution is to randomize the order in each list so that each participant sees the conditions in different orders. The lists in Table 1.3 are short enough that this could easily be done manually, but in most experiments, this is not practical. A common solution using a spreadsheet is to insert a column to the left of each list, insert a random number in each cell (using the RAND function in Excel, for instance), and then sort each list by the random number column. If there are multiple tokens of each condition in a list, then randomization will sometimes result in two such tokens being adjacent. Some researchers prefer to avoid this by performing "pseudo-randomization," in which such cases are manually separated after the regular randomization process is complete.

Counterbalancing for order is also advisable. This can be done by re-randomizing the lists in Table 1.3 or by reversing the randomized order already obtained. Either method will produce a new set of four lists.

## 1.2.5 Fillers

Even with experimental stimuli fully counterbalanced and randomized (or pseudo-randomized), participants will still see lists of sentences that are all structurally very similar. This could result in participants becoming desensitized to the distinctions we are interested in or beginning to speculate as to the structure being investigated, all of which could affect their judgments in unknown ways. "Filler" items (i.e. stimuli that are not part of the factorial design of the experiment) help avoid this outcome, in that they "cleanse the palate" between experimental items, while also disguising the purpose of the experiment.

Table 1.4 *Planning table for fillers assuming a factorial design as in Table 1.1, 6 tokens per condition, and a 2:1 filler–experimental ratio*

| Acceptability | Experimental items | Filler items | Total |
|---|---|---|---|
| High | 18 | 6 | 24 |
| Intermediate | 0 | 24 | 24 |
| Low | 6 | 18 | 24 |
| Total | 24 | 48 | 72 |

For filler items to serve their purpose, there should be at least a 1:1 ratio of fillers to experimental items. Having more fillers is better, though this has to be balanced against the need for the overall list to be of reasonable length. The filler–experimental ratio that we choose will tell us how many fillers need to be constructed, but knowing what type they should be requires doing an inventory of the anticipated acceptability levels of the experimental items. The reason for this is that the fillers should help create a list of stimuli that is roughly balanced in terms of acceptability, so that participants will use the full range of the response scale provided. Table 1.4 provides an example of such an inventory for an experiment with a factorial design as in Table 1.1. In that design, we can anticipate that Condition 1 will be of relatively low acceptability, but the other three will be relatively high. Table 1.4 assumes that we have chosen to have participants see 6 tokens of each condition, with a 2:1 filler–experimental ratio.

As Table 1.4 shows, fillers can be used to correct the imbalance in acceptability among the experimentals, so that the overall list of stimuli is distributed well across the full range of acceptability.

It would be counterproductive for participants to become aware of the filler–experimental distinction, so to the extent possible, most of the fillers should be superficially similar to the experimental items. Table 1.5 gives examples of possible fillers at three rough levels of acceptability for an experiment as in Table 1.1.

Having fillers of extremely high or extremely low acceptability can serve another purpose: They can guard against ceiling or floor effects with the experimental stimuli. Both of the "high" examples in Table 1.5, for example, would probably be of higher acceptability than the high-acceptability experimentals in Table 1.1, and conversely for the "low" examples in relation to the low-acceptability experimental. In addition, these fillers at the extremes of acceptability can be used to detect participants who are not attending to the task (see Section 1.2.8).

Another function of fillers is to act as practice items at the beginning of the experiment. These need not (and should not) be explicitly marked as such, but having the first 3–5 stimuli be fillers allows participants to

Table 1.5 *Example fillers for an experiment with a factorial design as in Table 1.1*

| | |
|---|---|
| High | Who says that it will rain tomorrow? |
| | What is the name of your dentist? |
| Intermediate | Who do you wonder whether anyone will approach? |
| | What do you believe that the man who you saw in the park ate? |
| Low | Who do thinks you that the birds are singing? |
| | What will they say about a cars are park on the street? |

become familiar with the task and the response scale before they start reacting to experimental items.

It is sometimes convenient to join two or more small experiments as sub-experiments of a larger experiment. In this instance, the experimentals from one sub-experiment can act as fillers for another, but because of counterbalancing in each sub-experiment, the fillers will not be uniform for all participants. Even in this case, though, an analysis as in Table 1.4 should be done and some true fillers created so that gross imbalances in acceptability across the stimuli are avoided.

### 1.2.6  Presentation of Stimuli to Participants

If stimuli are counterbalanced as in Section 1.2.3, the number of conditions in the factorial design will determine the minimum number of lists to be created. In a 2 × 3 design, for instance, there will need to be 6 lists (or a multiple of 6) in order for counterbalancing to be preserved. The number of lists, in turn, determines the ideal number of participants. With 6 lists, for instance, having 6 participants (or again, a multiple of 6) makes it possible to have the same number of participants for each list and thus maintain full counterbalancing. Small deviations from this ideal are unlikely to have a large effect on the results, but major deviations (e.g. having many more participants for one list than for others) should be avoided, since the resulting lack of counterbalancing could plausibly affect the outcome of the experiment.

Apart from counterbalancing, statistical power should also be taken into consideration when deciding on the number of experimental participants. Increasing the number of participants increases the statistical power, as does increasing the number of tokens of each condition that participants see. Sprouse and Almeida (2017) give some useful guidelines on this (see also Cowart 1997), but as a rough rule of thumb, two or three dozen participants are generally sufficient to yield useful results with most experimental designs. It is also often possible to have at least four or five tokens per condition without the overall experiment becoming too long.

In practice, presenting the stimuli in written form is by far the most common option. Having participants listen to the stimuli instead might seem preferable, but the amount of work required to record stimuli uniformly across all levels of acceptability discourages most researchers from doing this. Nonetheless, recorded stimuli have been used in some cases where oral presentation was particularly crucial (see Polinsky et al. 2013; Ritchart, Goodall, & Garellek 2016; Sedarous & Namboodiripad 2020).

In addition to the experiment itself, a consent form and a language background questionnaire are often also presented to participants. When possible, it is preferable to present the questionnaire after the experiment, to avoid the possibility that it might affect participant responses.

### 1.2.7  Response Method

As discussed in Section 1.1, acceptability is a kind of sensation experienced by speakers of the language after they have heard a linguistic stimulus, so if we are to measure this experimentally, we must provide the stimuli that will induce these sensations and a way for participants to record them. There are many such response methods (see Chapter 2 for detailed discussion), but a fixed numerical scale is very widely used, because it is easy to implement for researchers and easy to understand for participants (see also the detailed comparison between this method and others in Langsford et al. (2018)).

A fixed numerical scale, such as one going from 1 to 7, is technically an ordinal scale: there is a rank order among the elements (i.e. the numerals) on the scale (Stevens 1946). To interpret the results, however, it is helpful to be able to treat the scale as an interval scale, in which the difference between any two adjacent elements on the scale is the same. The use of numerals for the points on the scale implies this, but does not guarantee it. For whatever reason, participants might treat the difference between 1 and 2, for instance, as being smaller than the difference between 6 and 7, and in that case, we no longer have an interval scale. Fortunately, there are a number of steps the researcher can take to discourage participants from conceiving of the scale in this way. First, the numerals should be spread out evenly on the scale so that the amount of physical space between any two adjacent elements is always the same. Second, the extremes of the scale should be labeled (e.g. "good" and "bad"), but the intermediate points on the scale should not be. Such intermediate labels (e.g. "fair," "not very good," etc.) virtually ensure that participants will not treat the scale as an interval scale and may even discourage them from treating it as ordinal, thus making the results very difficult to interpret. Third, the numerals should all be similar in appearance and status so that participants do not perceive a "break" at any point along the scale. For this reason, scales including both single-digit and double-digit numbers, or both positive and negative numbers, should be avoided. Fourth, the scale should consist of an odd number of numerals, so that participants don't introduce an artificial break and divide them, consciously or unconsciously, into "good" and "bad" ones.

Scales that range from 1 to 5 or from 1 to 7 make it easy to satisfy the above constraints, so they are very frequently used. Because of the way that humans interact with left-to-right arrays and mentally represent numerical scales (see Natale et al. 1983; Davidson 1992; Dehaene et al. 1993; Zorzi et al. 2002; Harvey et al. 2013), it is best for the lowest number (i.e. 1) to correspond to lowest acceptability and be on the left, while the highest number (i.e. 5 or 7) should correspond to highest acceptability and be on the right. In other words, the numbers should be arranged in ascending order from left to right and from least acceptable to most acceptable (at least for languages in which that is the customary direction of text).

Participants of course need to be told what will happen and what they need to do in the experiment, but it appears that the exact form of these instructions does not crucially affect the results (Cowart (1997), though see Beltrama and Xiang (2016) for results perhaps suggesting otherwise). It is probably best to keep the instructions very short, as in (5), and place filler items representing a range of acceptability as the first several stimuli.

(5)    Sample instructions: Rate each sentence on a scale from 1 (bad) to 7 (good) based on how it sounds to you. Use only your sense as a speaker of the language. There are no correct or incorrect answers and you should not try to analyze the sentence.

The initial filler items give participants a better idea of what is being asked of them and should allow them to feel comfortable with the task by the time they get to any experimental items.

## 1.2.8    Analyzing the Results

Before the participants' numerical responses are analyzed, it is worth employing a screening procedure to eliminate any participants who appear not to have completed the task appropriately, which could occur because they do not actually speak the language being investigated, because they unintentionally inverted the "good" and "bad" labels on the scale, or because they chose not to follow the instructions for some reason (see Chapter 4 for further discussion). At its most basic level, screening can be done by visually inspecting the results to detect participants who gave the same rating to all sentences, but more involved procedures are worthwhile in most cases. There are a variety of ways to do this, but the basic idea is to look for participants who have many anomalous responses to the filler items. One could, for instance, select filler items that are especially good or especially bad (and for which one would thus expect responses on one side or another of the rating scale) and eliminate participants who exceed a certain threshold for "errors" on these items (where an "error" might be a rating of 3 or below on a seven-point scale for a sentence that is known to be highly acceptable, for instance). It is also possible to compute the group mean and standard deviation for each filler, note cases where a participant's ratings are more than two standard deviations away from the mean, and then eliminate participants who go beyond a certain number of such cases. If participants are eliminated in this way, they may need to be replaced by new participants if counterbalancing as in Section 1.2.6 is to be preserved.

Such screening procedures should be used cautiously and judiciously, of course, so as not to eliminate legitimate results, but they can be a useful way to remove some of the noise that inevitably arises in experiments of this type. Another potential source of noise stems from the fact that individual participants may choose to use the numerical scale for their responses in very different ways. One participant, for instance, might concentrate most responses around the center of the scale, while another might use the extremes much more readily, with the result that a response of "7" on a seven-point scale could mean different things for the two participants. Because of this type of variation, it is advisable to standardize the results by transforming them to z-scores. Each z-score shows how many standard deviations the participant's response is above or below that participant's mean for all items. Two participants might both have a z-score of 0 for a particular item, for instance, meaning that their responses for that item were the same as their overall mean, even though their raw ratings for that item were different. Any statistical analysis of the results should then be based on the z-scores (though doing a parallel analysis using the raw scores is also possible).

A basic analysis of the results using descriptive statistics should include the mean, standard deviation, and response distribution for each condition in the experimental design. Visualization of the results usually includes at least a bar or line graph showing the means and error bars for all conditions. Line graphs make interactions (or a lack of inter-action) more perspicuous and avoid giving the appearance that there is an absolute lower bound to acceptability (which there will not be if z-scores are being used). In addition to descriptive statistics, an analysis in terms of inferential statistics needs to be done in order to test for statistical significance. This has traditionally been done using a repeated-measures ANOVA, but is now more commonly done with a linear mixed-effects model.

## 1.3 What Acceptability Includes

Following an experimental procedure as outlined in Section 1.2 will very regularly result in statistically significant contrasts among conditions. In fact, it is not uncommon to be able to detect significant differences among three or four conditions, signifying three or four distinct levels of acceptability, in effect. Acceptability studies are more fine-grained in this sense than many other experimental methods for the study of syntax, such as self-paced reading or event-related brain potential (ERP) (see Chapters 23 and 24), where such multiple contrasts are unusual. Interpreting the contrasts that the experiment detects is not always a simple matter, however, since acceptability seems to be sensitive to a number of factors, including ones that the experimenter did not intend to investigate. In this section, we survey some of the main factors that are known to influence acceptability.

### 1.3.1  Grammaticality

Not surprisingly, acceptability experiments are sensitive to grammaticality, in that sentences that are generable by the postulated grammatical model are generally more acceptable than those that are not. Studies such as Sprouse and Almeida (2012) and Sprouse, Schütze, and Almeida (2013) have found that where linguists have traditionally claimed a difference in grammaticality, experimental work finds a difference in acceptability in over 90 percent of the cases. There are exceptions to this, and these are worth investigating, but as a general rule of thumb, one can expect that if there is a well-founded claim of a difference in grammaticality between two conditions, this difference will be detectable in an acceptability experiment.

Cowart (1997) shows this convincingly across an interesting range of phenomena. In terms of *wh*-extraction out of NPs, for instance, he finds (6b) to be significantly less acceptable than (6a), an effect that has been claimed to stem from grammatical constraints on extraction (Chomsky 1977; Fiengo & Higginbotham 1981). (6c) does not show this degradation, again in line with what grammatical accounts predict.

(6)      a. Who did the Duchess sell [a portrait [of __]] ?
          b. Who did the Duchess sell [Max's portrait [of __]] ?
          c. Who did the Duchess sell [Max's portrait] [to __] ?

For the four conditions in our earlier discussion of the *that*-trace effect as in (7) (repeated from (1)–(4) above), Cowart found that the contrasts predicted by grammatical accounts of the effect are easily detected in acceptability experiments.

(7)      a. Who do you think that __ will hire Mary?
          b. Who do you think __ will hire Mary?
          c. Who do you think that Mary will hire __ ?
          d. Who do you think Mary will hire __ ?

Specifically, (7a) is significantly less acceptable than any of the other conditions. Finally, with respect to the behavior of anaphors, Cowart finds that Binding Theory effects show up as significant contrasts in acceptability experiments (see Chapter 11 for further discussion). In (8)–(10), the anaphor has a local antecedent in the (a) examples, in accord with Principle A, but a remote antecedent in the (b) examples, in violation of Principle A.

(8)     a. Cathy's parents require that Paul support himself.
        b. Paul requires that Cathy's parents support himself.

(9)     a. Cathy's parents require that Paul support himself and the child.
        b. Paul requires that Cathy's parents support himself and the child.

(10)    a. Cathy's parents require that Paul support both himself and the child.
        b. Paul requires that Cathy's parents support both himself and the child.

In all three cases, Cowart shows experimentally that (a) is significantly more acceptable than (b), as predicted.

It may turn out that some or all of the contrasts in (6)–(10) are not ultimately due to the grammar per se, but are to be accounted for in other ways (see Phillips & Wagers (2007) for general discussion). Nonetheless, these cases show that the types of contrasts that syntacticians are typically interested in generally yield very robust distinctions when examined within an acceptability experiment. Beyond this, however, most acceptability experiments also uncover distinctions that are clearly not tied to standard notions of grammaticality, in that significant degradations are revealed experimentally that do not correspond to any expected declines in grammaticality.

This fact highlights the importance of the distinction between "acceptability" and "grammaticality" (see Section 1.1), and in Sections 1.3.2–1.3.4, we survey those factors beyond grammaticality that are thought to play a role in acceptability (see also Chapter 5 for more detailed discussion).

## 1.3.2 Presence of a Dependency

One of the most solid, well-replicated findings in the experimental literature is that the presence of a *wh*-dependency results in a sharp decline in acceptability relative to controls without such a dependency. In the experiments from Cowart (1997) sketched above, for instance, all of the sentences in (6) are significantly less acceptable than the control in (11).

(11)   Why did the Duchess sell a portrait of Max?

This is a striking finding because of the sentences in (6), (a) and (c) seem unobjectionable when presented in isolation and are standardly taken to be fully grammatical, on a par with (11). The difference, though, is that (6a)

and (c) involve a clear dependency between a *wh*-filler and a gap, whereas
(11) does not (either because there is no dependency or because there is no
subcategorized gap).[3]

Similar results are seen in Sprouse, Wagers, and Phillips (2012) and
much subsequent work, where sentences with a *wh*-dependency are significantly less acceptable than matched controls where there is only
a vacuous *wh*-dependency. (12a) is an example of such a control, in that
there is only a vacuous dependency, while (12b) is the type of sentence that
shows significant degradation, apparently because of the non-vacuous
dependency in this case.

(12)    a. Who __ thinks that John bought a car?
        b. What do you think that John bought __ ?

Both (12a) and (12b) are textbook examples of grammatical sentences, so
the difference observed experimentally does not seem to be attributable to
a difference in grammaticality.

Filler–gap dependencies such as those just seen have been studied
extensively in the experimental literature on acceptability, and the results
have been remarkably consistent: the presence of a non-vacuous dependency leads to significant degradation. Whether other types of syntactic
dependencies, such as binding, control, and A-dependencies (e.g. in passives, unaccusatives, etc.), show similar effects remains largely unexplored. Recent work by Dayoung Kim (Kim & Goodall 2018) found no
significant difference in acceptability between simple active and passive
sentences as in (13).

(13)    a. The director hugged the actress in the theater.
        b. The actress was hugged by the director in the theater.

In many analyses, there is a non-vacuous dependency in (13b) between *the
actress* and the object position in the clause, but this putative relation does
not seem to lead to the type of degradation seen with *wh*-dependencies
(though Kim does find an effect for the dependency when it spans more
than one clause). Overall, though, much work remains to be done on the
possible effects on acceptability of syntactic dependencies other than
traditional filler–gap dependencies.

### 1.3.3  Length of Dependency
In addition to the simple presence of a *wh*-dependency, the length of the
dependency also has an effect on acceptability, with greater distance (in
terms of syntactic structure) resulting in a larger degradation. This was

---

[3] Hofmeister, Culicover, and Winkler (2015) provide another very clear example of how the simple presence of a *wh*-dependency results in significant degradation, as do Omaki et al. (2020) with regard to the presence of a scrambling dependency in Japanese. See also Namboodiripad (2017).

first seen in cases where the dependency crosses an NP boundary. In the experiment from Cowart (1997) mentioned above, a significant difference is found between sentences like (14a), where an NP boundary is crossed, and (14b), where it is not.

(14)    a. Who did the Duchess sell [a portrait [of __]] ? (= (6a))
        b. Who did the Duchess sell [a portrait] [to __] ?

This results in significantly lower acceptability for (14a) relative to (14b).

Crossing clause boundaries seems to have a similar effect. Work by Bethany Keffala (reported in Keffala (2011); Keffala & Goodall (2011, 2013); Goodall (2017)), for instance, shows that placing the gap inside an embedded clause, such as in (15b) relative to (15a), significantly degrades acceptability, as seen in Figure 1.1 (results reported on an eleven-point scale).

(15)    a. These are the potatoes [that we prepared __].
        b. These are the potatoes [that we realized [that the chef prepared __]].
        c. These are the potatoes [that we inquired [how the chef prepared __]].
        d. These are the potatoes [that we spoke to the chef [that prepared __]].

(15c) and (15d) represent island violations (a *wh*-island and a relative clause island, respectively), so their low level of acceptability is expected, but the long extraction in (15b) occupies an intermediate position: less acceptable than a simple case of extraction as in (15a), but more acceptable than island violations as in (15c) and (15d). The degradation in (15b) could also be related to the fact that it simply has more words than (15a), but given the size of the effect, it seems likely that the length of the dependency is also playing a major role. Alexopoulou and Keller (2007) present similar results based on *wh*-questions, rather than relative clauses.

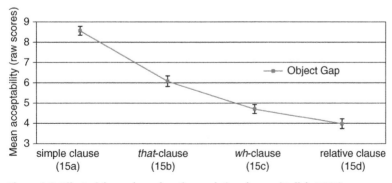

**Figure 1.1** Effect of dependency length on relative clauses (Keffala 2011)

Whether acceptability is sensitive to more fine-grained distinctions in dependency length is less clear. In cases where the number of NP and/or clause boundaries remains constant, for instance, one might expect that all other things being equal, dependencies with the gap in object position would be less acceptable than those with the gap in subject position. This expectation is not confirmed, however, in a number of studies of extraction from embedded clauses in English. In the experiment in Cowart (1997) mentioned above, for example, no significant difference is found between embedded subject and object gaps in *wh*-questions such as those in (16) (see also Fukuda et al. 2012).

(16)      a. Who do you think [_ will hire Mary] ? (= (7b))
          b. Who do you think [Mary will hire _] ? (= (7d))

### 1.3.4   Frequency

There are two types of frequency that might be relevant to acceptability: the relative frequency of the lexical items used and the relative frequency of the syntactic structure (see also Chapter 25). With regard to the first, it seems intuitively likely that sentences with high-frequency words, as in (17a), would be more acceptable than matched sentences with one or more low-frequency words, as in (17b).

(17)      a. The girl found the box.
          b. The seamstress found the satchel.

It also seems intuitively likely that such effects would only emerge with very extreme contrasts in frequency, as in the examples in (17). To my knowledge, however, intuitions like these have not been tested experimentally in a systematic way (but see Sag, Hofmeister, & Snider 2007). Since most acceptability experiments in syntax use lexically matched sets of stimuli, the issue of differences in lexical frequency does not typically arise.

Experimental studies of the effects of particular lexical items on the acceptability of syntactic structures do exist, of course (see, e.g., Fukuda 2012, 2017), though they are often based on the semantic properties of the lexical items in question, rather than their frequency. Frequency-based analyses also exist, however, such as in Bresnan and Ford (2010), where it is shown that speakers' acceptance of a given verb in one or another of the two patterns in the dative alternation (e.g. *gave the book to the girl* vs. *gave the girl the book*) correlates with the relative frequency of that pattern with the verb. With regard to the effect of the frequency of the structure, abstracting away from particular lexical items, and how this might affect acceptability, much less is known. On the face of it, however, it seems unlikely that frequency and acceptability will always correlate. Active clauses, for instance, are much more frequent than passive clauses in corpora, but it is not obvious that active clauses are more acceptable than passive clauses. Indeed, as discussed above for (13), there seems to be no significant difference between the two when this is tested experimentally. Frequency and acceptability thus seem to be largely independent measures. Some generalizations about the relationship between the two can be made, however, as Bermel and Knittl (2012) point out that if a structure is of high frequency, it will also be of high acceptability (but not vice versa), and that if a structure is of low acceptability, it will also be of low frequency (but not vice versa). Crucially, the reverse of each of these conditional statements is clearly not true. That is, if a structure is of high acceptability, we cannot conclude that it will also be of high frequency, and if a structure is of low frequency, we cannot conclude that it will also be of low acceptability.

## 1.4 Motivations for Doing Acceptability Experiments

In the previous sections, we have seen the many steps involved in creating a well-designed acceptability experiment and the reasons why the researcher should carry these steps out with appropriate care. We have also seen that sentence acceptability experiments are very sensitive not only to the grammaticality of the stimuli, as one would naturally assume, but also to factors that a syntactician might not initially feel the need to measure experimentally, such as the presence/absence of a dependency or the length of that dependency. Given all of this, one might reasonably conclude that doing acceptability experiments is a lot of trouble and that the payoff is not that great, in that the results are hard to interpret because of the uncertainty as to what is causing the level of acceptability that is measured.

In this section, we will see that this discouraging view of acceptability experiments, though based on fact, is not the whole story, and that there are a number of ways that researchers can use acceptability experiments to address important syntactic questions with a level of precision and insight that is not possible with other methods.

### 1.4.1 Testing Claims of (Un)acceptability

Perhaps the most obvious way that acceptability experiments can be useful is by adjudicating cases where more traditional methods of determining acceptability have yielded unclear or controversial results. One area where experimental work of this type has played an especially important role is in Superiority, the phenomenon in which an object *wh*-phrase may not be fronted when the subject is also a *wh*-phrase, as in (18) (see Chapter 5).

(18)    a. **Who** bought **what**?
        b. \***What** did **who** buy __ ?

It has sometimes been claimed that German does not show this effect (e.g. Grewendorf 1988), but Featherston (2005) uses the results of an acceptability experiment to argue that in fact it does, despite initial appearances. This is thus an instance where the experimental procedure is able to detect a contrast (i.e. between the equivalents of (18a) and (18b) in German) that more traditional methodologies had suggested might not exist.

There have also been examples going in the other direction, where traditional work claims that there is a contrast, but experimental work suggests that there is not. An example of this is Fedorenko and Gibson (2010), who examine the claim that Superiority violations like (18b) become more acceptable when a third *wh*-phrase is added, as in (19) (Bolinger 1978; Kayne 1984)

(19)   **What** did **who** buy __ **where**?

Fedorenko and Gibson present the results of an experiment suggesting that there is no difference in acceptability between (18b) and (19).

Another such example concerns the claim that *wh*-extraction from within an embedded subject, known to result in very low acceptability, shows significant amelioration when the containing subject is itself a *wh*-phrase that has been fronted within its clause (Torrego 1985; Lasnik & Saito 1992; Kayne 1984). For instance, (20c) is claimed to be more acceptable than (20a) or (20b).

(20)    a. [Which animal] will [several movies about __] be shown to the visitors?
        b. [Which animal] do you wonder whether [several movies about __] will be shown to the visitors?
        c. [Which animal] do you wonder [how many movies about __] will be shown to the visitors?

Some researchers have argued that this claim is not correct (e.g. Gallego 2009; Müller 2010), so I tested it by means of an acceptability experiment in which 48 participants saw four tokens of each of the conditions in (20), in addition to 9 other conditions and 57 filler items (Goodall 2015). Lists of stimuli were fully counterbalanced and pseudo-randomized. Participants rated each stimulus on a seven-point scale and the results (converted to *z*-scores) are presented in Figure 1.2.

The results show that the expected amelioration for extraction out of a fronted *wh*-subject, as in (20c), does not occur, suggesting that the initial claim about these structures was incorrect.

All of the above examples show that acceptability experiments can be an excellent supplement to (or even substitute for) acceptability judgments gathered in more traditional ways. None of this should suggest, however, that acceptability experiments are simply the handmaid of traditional methods, since even if the ultimate goal is merely to determine how

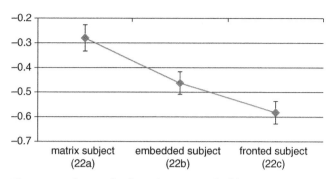

**Figure 1.2** *Wh*-extraction from three types of subjects

acceptable a given structure is, formal experiments can provide a type of evidence that more traditional methods are in principle incapable of doing.

One reason that experiments can do this is that they seem to be able to measure contrasts with equal precision in sentences of both high and low acceptability. A good example of this comes from an experimental study of the difference between bare *wh*-phrases (e.g. *who, what*, etc.) and more lexically elaborated *wh*-phrases (e.g. *what boy, which of the apples*, etc.), often referred to as D-linked *wh*-phrases (Goodall 2015). The experiment examines this difference in the case of extraction from embedded clauses, including both ordinary complement clauses, as in (21), and island clauses, as in (22) and (23).

(21)  a. **What** do you believe that he might buy __ ?
      b. **Which of the cars** do you believe that he might buy __ ?

(22)  a. **What** do you believe the claim that he might buy __ ?
      b. **Which of the cars** do you believe the claim that he might buy __ ?

(23)  a. **What** do you wonder who might buy __ ?
      b. **Which of the cars** do you wonder who might buy __ ?

It has long been noted that D-linking causes amelioration of island violations, so the (b) sentences in (22) and (23) are expected to be more acceptable than their counterparts in (a). The experimental results show this expected effect, but they also show an effect of approximately the same size in non-island stimuli such as (21). This is surprising because no such effect in non-islands had previously been noticed and it is not something that most standard accounts of D-linking would lead us to expect. This finding is thus of interest for our understanding of the larger phenomenon, but for present purposes, what matters more is the fact that this finding could probably not have been obtained by gathering acceptability judgments in the traditional way. For most speakers, the contrasts in (22) and (23) seem easy to articulate (e.g. "(a) sounds relatively bad and (b) sounds relatively good"), but this is much less true in (21), where both (a) and (b) sound good. Even if speakers could articulate the difference between (21a) and (21b), it is not clear that they could judge whether the amelioration there is of the same size as it is in (22) and (23), as the experimental results suggest.

The ability to measure "degrees of goodness," in addition to "degrees of badness," is thus one of the important attributes of acceptability experiments that is not shared by more traditional methods of ascertaining acceptability. Another concerns the fact that acceptability experiments typically make use of explicitly for-mulated factorial designs. Traditional work often uses minimal sets, which are created in a spirit very much in line with factorial designs, but they are usually less explicit, and the relative lack of precision in the measurements means that they can't be as informative as a factorial design. To see how useful factorial designs can be, con-sider the experimental study of the freezing effect in extraposition in Hofmeister, Culicover, and Winkler (2015). It has been known for many years that extraposed phrases become "frozen" to any subex-traction from within them (i.e. they become islands, in effect). Hofmeister et al. explore this by constructing stimuli with both Extraction (+ and –) and Extraposition (+ and –) as factors, as shown in (24).

(24)    a. Kenneth revealed that he overheard a nasty remark [about the President] earlier.
[–Extraction, –Extraposition]
       b. Kenneth revealed which President he overheard a nasty remark [about _] earlier.
[+Extraction, –Extraposition]
       c. Kenneth revealed that he overheard a nasty remark earlier [about the President].
[–Extraction, +Extraposition]
       d. Kenneth revealed which President he overheard a nasty remark earlier [about _].
[+Extraction, +Extraposition]

In many ways, the results obtained are what one would expect: there is a significant degradation associated with Extraction (e.g. (24b) is less acceptable than (24a)) and with Extraposition (e.g. (24c) is less acceptable than (24a)). Neither of these declines in acceptability is surprising given what we saw in Section 1.3.2 about the presence of dependencies. Also not surprising is the fact that condition (24d) is the least acceptable of all, since this is the "freezing" case. What is surprising is that condition (24d) does not show "superadditivity." That is, the level of unacceptability of (24d) can be accounted for by simply adding the degradation due to Extraction and the degradation to Extraposition, without the need for a separate freezing principle.[4] This study thus shows the utility of carefully setting up a factorial design and treating that design seriously. It is only by measuring the acceptability of each condition and examining the relationships among those four measurements that we can conclude that the low acceptability of (24d) falls out from the same factors that cause the degradation in (24b) and (24c).

There are many cases like (24d) in the syntax literature. That is, there are many cases where the low acceptability of a structure is noted, but a careful factorial design is not constructed and the possibility that the low acceptability might stem from the additive effect of other factors is not considered. To take just one example, consider the phenomenon of partial *wh*-movement ("simple partial *wh*-movement," in the terminology of Fanselow (2017)) found in a variety of languages around the world. In this phenomenon, *wh*-phrases may move to their scope position, move to a position lower than their scope position, or remain *in situ*. These possibilities are illustrated in (25) for Indonesian (Saddy 1991).

(25)    a.  **Siapa** yang Bill tahu    Tom cintai __ ?    (Full *wh*-movement)
          who   FOC  Bill knows  Tom loves

    b.  Bill tahu    **siapa** yang    Tom cintai __ ? (Partial *wh*-movement)
          Bill knows who  FOC    Tom loves

    c.  Bill tahu   Tom men-cintai **siapa**?        (*Wh-in situ*)
          Bill knows Tom loves     who
          'Who does Bill know that Tom loves?'

Full *wh*-movement in Indonesian obeys standard island constraints, as one might expect, and *wh-in situ* does not. Partial *wh*-movement also obeys island constraints, both with respect to the overt movement that occurs and with respect to the distance between the *wh*-phrase and its scope position (Saddy 1991; Cole & Hermon 1998, 2000). (26) shows representative sentences for the three types of *wh*-questions with a negative island.

(26)    a.  \***Apa**  yang  Tom tidak harap  Mary beli __? (Full *wh*-movement)
          what  FOC   Tom not   expect Mary bought

    b.  \*Tom tidak meng-harap **apa**  yang Mary beli __?
                                        (Partial *wh*-movement)
          Tom not  expect     what FOC  Mary bought

    c.  Tom tidak meng-harap Mary mem-beli  **apa**?      (*Wh-in situ*)
          Tom not  expect     Mary bought    what
          'What did Tom not expect that Mary would buy?'

---

[4] In fact, (24d) is slightly more acceptable than expected given this addition. See Hofmeister et al. (2015) for details.

Table 1.6 *A factorial design for measuring the island effect with partial* wh-*movement*

|  |  | Question type | |
| --- | --- | --- | --- |
|  |  | *in situ* | **partial movement** |
| Island structure | – | (25c) | (25b) |
| (negation) | + | (26c) | (26b) |

The crucial and perhaps most surprising fact here is the unacceptability of (26b), i.e. the sensitivity of the wh-phrase to an island structure through which it has not moved overtly. Viewing this data point in isolation, however, it is difficult to know whether there is truly an island effect here or whether the low acceptability of (26b) is due to the additive effect of the negative structure and the partial wh-movement. This issue could be addressed with a factorial design as in Table 1.6 (with items lexically matched appropriately).

If the unacceptability of (26b) can be reduced to the sum of the degradation induced by partial movement itself (seen by comparing (25c) and (25b)) and the degradation induced by the more complex island structure (seen by comparing (25c) and (26c)), then we could conclude that the island effect for partial movement is in a sense illusory; there is no separate island constraint. This is the type of conclusion, for instance, that Hofmeister et al. (2015) reach with respect to the freezing properties of extraposition. If, on the other hand, the unacceptability of (26b) is significantly greater than the sum of the partial movement effect and the island structure effect, then we could conclude that partial movement truly is sensitive to island constraints even when the wh-phrase has not moved overtly through the relevant structure. This is the type of conclusion, for instance, that Sprouse, Wagers, and Phillips (2012) reach with regard to a number of classical island effects in English (see Chapter 9). It is also the conclusion that has been adopted in the literature for partial wh-movement, but without an explicit design as in Table 1.6 and a precise means of measuring acceptability, it is hard to be sure that this conclusion is correct.

Determining the correct answer here and knowing whether the apparent island sensitivity of partial movement is truly due to an island constraint or is simply what happens when two relatively complex properties coexist in a single sentence is crucial to our understanding of extraction phenomena and locality in syntax, so a lot hinges on the outcome of an experiment such as that sketched in Table 1.6. The same can be said for many phenomena and issues in the syntax literature, and in this sense, formal acceptability experiments can provide important insights that more traditional techniques cannot.

### 1.4.2  Cross-linguistic Comparisons

Another important benefit of experimental approaches to acceptability comes from the ability to make precise and well-grounded cross-linguistic comparisons (see Chapter 7 for more extensive discussion of this point). Examples of a given structure being possible in one language but not in another are very common in the syntactic literature and uncovering and accounting for such cases is the syntactician's stock-in-trade. It is also common, however, to see claims that a given structure is possible (or impossible) in both languages under discussion, but that it is nonetheless more acceptable in one of the languages than in the other. Such observations have played an important role in the literature on phenomena such as parasitic gaps, weak islands, resumptive pronouns, and extraction from complement clauses, but it has sometimes been difficult to characterize these cross-linguistic differences, much less to account for them.

Acceptability experiments clearly have a lot to offer in this domain, because they allow us to quantify particular syntactic effects and then make comparisons across languages based on that. For example, if we were examining languages that seem to have the *that*-trace effect, we could conduct experiments along the lines of what was described in Section 1.2 above for each of the languages, calculate an effect size for each language based on the results (e.g. using DD-scores as in Sprouse, Wagers, and Phillips (2012)), and then compare these effect sizes across the languages. This kind of quantitative description is of course not an analysis, but it could plausibly be the first step toward one and to a deeper understanding of what lies behind this type of cross-linguistic variation. Alexopoulou and Keller (2007), Sprouse et al. (2011), Sprouse et al. (2016), and Chacón (2015) are all examples of this type of work.

### 1.4.3  Comparing Populations

Acceptability experiments can also be extremely useful when comparing groups of speakers, rather than individuals. Traditional fieldwork and similar techniques can only detect extremely robust between-group differences, but the fine-grained measurements, large participant pools, and statistical analyses of experiments make it possible to detect much more subtle differences that might otherwise go unnoticed. One traditional area where this is helpful is in looking for linguistic differences across regions. If one wants to know, for instance, whether the *that*-trace effect is valid and similarly robust across a wide geographical area, acceptability experiments offer a straightforward way to probe this, as Cowart (1997) and Chacón (2015) have in fact done (see Chapters 7 and 10). Conducting large-scale experiments across regions poses interesting challenges, such as the need to ensure that the experimental procedure is the same for all participants and that the lexical items used in the stimuli are equally comprehensible in all regions, but these challenges can be managed and the extra work is justified by the results, which typically cannot be obtained by other means. Guajardo and Goodall (2019) is an example of this type of work.

Another dimension along which groups of speakers are often compared concerns the speakers' acquisition history or general language background (see also Chapter 14). One might want to compare native speakers to non-native speakers, for instance, or those whose exposure to the language began at age 3 to those for whom it began at age 8. Here too, acceptability experiments allow the kind of fine-grained analysis in which subtle differences among such groups can be detected (or ruled out). Kim and Goodall (2016), for instance, perform a series of acceptability experiments testing island phenomena in Korean using two groups of participants: native speakers of Korean residing in Korea and heritage speakers of Korean who were born in the US (or moved to the US before age 7) and who reside in the US. The results showed an intricate pattern of behavior across different island types, but this pattern was remarkably similar across the two populations, despite the very different linguistic environments that the two groups were exposed to in childhood. Kim and Goodall use these results to argue that the island effects being examined are largely immune to environmental influences.

General cognitive measures have also been a common tool for comparing speakers in relation to their performance in acceptability experiments. In perhaps the most well-known example of this, Sprouse, Wagers, and Phillips (2012) conduct both an acceptability experiment and two measures of working memory capacity on a large group of participants. The acceptability experiment measures speakers' sensitivity to four types of island effects, but no correlation is found between speakers' island sensitivity and the measures of their working memory capacity. The authors use this lack of correlation to suggest that island effects are not ultimately due to limitations on processing capacity. Michel (2014) uses a wider battery of working memory measures but finds a similar lack of correlation with regard to acceptability. It would not be warranted to conclude that general cognitive measures are unrelated to acceptability, however, since Hofmeister, Staum Casasanto, and Sag (2014) find a clear correlation between reading span scores and acceptability, but only for sentences where low acceptability is attributable to processing costs (such as when arguments are relatively distant from their heads). There is little doubt that the relation between acceptability and other cognitive measures will remain a lively topic of research for many years (see Chapters 4, 9, and 24).

There are many other ways that one can distinguish among individuals or groups and that one can imagine might have an effect on their acceptability. Many traditional forms of categorization, for instance, such as gender or familial left-handedness (e.g. Bever et al. 1989), are known to have neurological correlates, and it is conceivable that these could affect one or more of the components that go into acceptability judgments (as described in Section 1.3). More broadly, known neuroanatomical differences across individuals or genetic markers of various types could also be examined for correlations with individuals' behavior in acceptability experiments. I am not aware of studies of this type, but given that acceptability experiments are relatively easy and quick to conduct, yet also yield very fine-grained results, it is probably only a matter of time before such work begins to be done.

## 1.5  Conclusion

Constructing, running, and analyzing a sentence acceptability experiment requires a number of techniques and concepts that are not traditionally part of most syntacticians' training, yet the benefits of learning how to do so make it worth the effort in many cases. As we have seen here, formal experiments allow us to measure acceptability with a degree of precision and confidence that is not possible with other methods, but they also give us a type of data that would not be accessible to us otherwise. They allow us to measure contrasts across the full range of acceptability, for instance, including among sentences that are presumably fully grammatical, and they allow us to determine whether a given effect might be the additive result of smaller effects or might require positing something additional. They also allow us to make well-defined comparisons across languages and across speaker populations that differ by region, age of acquisition, gender, or other factors.

Sentence acceptability experiments are often compared to more traditional methods of collecting acceptability judgments, such as fieldwork or reliance on one's own judgments. Much discussion in the literature has focused on the question of which is better, with some arguing that traditional methods are sufficient for most syntactic research and that experiments are only needed in exceptional cases, and others arguing that traditional methods should be abandoned and that experiments should be used in almost all cases (Phillips 2009; Culicover & Jackendoff 2010; Gibson & Fedorenko 2010, 2013; Gibson, Piantadosi, & Fedorenko 2013). Given what we know now about acceptability experiments, however, and especially what we know about the factors that these experiments are sensitive to (see Section 1.3) and the ways that these experiments can be put to use (see Section 1.4), this debate in the literature seems ill conceived. Traditional methods of measuring acceptability have been extraordinarily productive, both in documenting facts about understudied languages and uncovering new facts about languages that have already been studied extensively. It is not clear that experimental methods can take over all of these functions, but it is clear, as we have seen, that experimental methods can do many things that more traditional techniques cannot. Just as no one would argue that we need to choose between self-paced reading and ERP techniques for the study of syntax, similarly no one should argue that we need to choose between traditional methods and acceptability experiments. Each can do things that the other cannot and they both have important roles to play in syntactic research.

## References

Alexopoulou, T. & Keller, F. (2007). Locality, cyclicity, and resumption: At the interface between the grammar and the human sentence processor. *Language*, 83(1), 110–160.

Beltrama, A. & Xiang, M. (2016). Unacceptable but comprehensible: The facilitation effect of resumptive pronouns. *Glossa: A Journal of General Linguistics*, 1(1), 29. DOI:10.5334/gjgl.24

Bermel, N. & Knittl, L. (2012). Corpus frequency and acceptability judgments: A study of morphosyntactic variants in Czech. *Corpus Linguistics and Linguistic Theory*, 8(2), 241–275.

Bever, T. G., Carrithers, C., Cowart, W., & Townsend, D. J. (1989). Language processing and familial handedness. In A. M. Galaburda, ed., *From Reading to Neurons*. Cambridge, MA: MIT Press, pp. 331–360.

Bolinger, D. (1978). Asking more than one thing at a time. In H. Hiz, ed., *Questions*. Dordrecht: D. Reidel.

Bresnan, J. & Ford, M. (2010). Predicting syntax: Processing dative constructions in American and Australian varieties of English. *Language*, 86(1), 168–213.

Carlsson, A. M. (1983). Assessment of chronic pain. I. Aspects of the reliability and validity of the visual analogue scale. *Pain*, 16(1), 87–101.

Chacón, D. A. (2015). Comparative psychosyntax. Doctoral dissertation, University of Maryland.

Chomsky, N. (1957). *Syntactic Structures*. The Hague: Mouton.

Chomsky, N. (1965). *Aspects of the Theory of Syntax*. Cambridge, MA: MIT Press.

Chomsky, N. (1977). On *Wh*-movement. In P. Culicover, A. Akmajian, & T. Wasow, eds., *Formal Syntax*. New York: Academic Press, pp. 71–132.

Cole, P. & Hermon, G. (1998). The typology of *wh*-movement and *wh*-questions in Malay. *Syntax*, 1(3), 221–258.

Cole, P. & Hermon, G. (2000). Partial *Wh*-Movement: Evidence from Malay. In U. Lutz, G. Müller, & A. Von Stechow, eds., *Wh-scope Marking*. Amsterdam: John Benjamins, pp. 101–130.

Cowart, W. (1997). *Experimental Syntax*. New York: Sage.

Culicover, P. W. & Jackendoff, R. (2010). Quantitative methods alone are not enough: Response to Gibson and Fedorenko. *Trends in Cognitive Sciences*, 14(6), 234–235.

Davidson, R. J. (1992). Anterior cerebral asymmetry and the nature of emotion. *Brain and Cognition*, 20, 125–151.

Dehaene, S., Bossini, S., & Giraux, P. (1993). The mental representation of parity and number magnitude. *Journal of Experimental Psychology: General*, 122(3), 371.

Dworkin, R. H., Turk, D. C., Wyrwich, K. W., Beaton, D., Cleeland, C. S., Farrar, J. T., & Brandenburg, N. (2008). Interpreting the clinical importance of treatment outcomes in chronic pain clinical trials: IMMPACT recommendations. *Journal of Pain*, 9(2), 105–121.

Fanselow, G. (2017). Partial *wh*-movement. In M. Everaert & H. C. Van Riemsdijk, eds., *The Wiley Blackwell Companion to Syntax*, 2nd edn. New York: John Wiley & Sons.

Featherston, S. (2005). Universals and grammaticality: *Wh*-constraints in German and English. *Linguistics*, 43(4), 667–711.

Fedorenko, E. & Gibson, E. (2010). Adding a third *wh*-phrase does not increase the acceptability of object-initial multiple-*wh*-questions. *Syntax*, 13(3), 183–195.

Fiengo, R. & Higginbotham, J. (1981). Opacity in NP. *Linguistic Analysis*, 7, 347–373.

Fisher, R. A. (1935). The logic of inductive inference. *Journal of the Royal Statistical Society*, 98(1), 39–82.

Forouzanfar, T., Weber, W. E., Kemler, M., & van Kleef, M. (2003). What is a meaningful pain reduction in patients with complex regional pain syndrome type 1? *Clinical Journal of Pain*, 19(5), 281–285.

Fukuda, S. (2012). Aspectual verbs as functional heads: evidence from Japanese aspectual verbs. *Natural Language & Linguistic Theory*, 30(4), 965–1026.

Fukuda, S. (2017). Split intransitivity in Japanese is syntactic: Evidence for the Unaccusative Hypothesis from sentence acceptability and truth value judgment experiments. *Glossa: A Journal of General Linguistics*, 2(1), 28. DOI:10.5334/gjgl.268

Gallego, Á. (2009). On freezing effects. *Iberia: An International Journal of Theoretical Linguistics*, 1(1), 33–51.

Garrod, S. (2006). Psycholinguistic research methods. In K. Brown, ed., *Encyclopedia of Language and Linguistics*. Amsterdam: Elsevier, pp. 251–257.

Gibson, E. & Fedorenko, E. (2010). Weak quantitative standards in linguistics research. *Trends in Cognitive Sciences*, 14(6), 233.

Gibson, E. & Fedorenko, E. (2013). The need for quantitative methods in syntax and semantics research. *Language and Cognitive Processes*, 28(1–2), 88–124.

Gibson, E., Piantadosi, S. T., & Fedorenko, E. (2013). Quantitative methods in syntax/semantics research: A response to Sprouse and Almeida (2013). *Language and Cognitive Processes*, 28(3), 229–240.

Goodall, G. (2015). The D-linking effect on extraction from islands and non-islands. *Frontiers in Psychology: Language Sciences*, 5, 1493. DOI: 10.3389/fpsyg.2014.01493

Goodall, G. (2017). Referentiality and resumption in *wh*-dependencies. In J. Ostrove, R. Kramer, & J. Sabbagh, eds., *Asking the Right Questions: Essays in Honor of Sandra Chun*, pp. 65–80. eScholarship, University of California. http://escholarship.org/uc/item/8255v8sc

Grewendorf, G. (1988). *Aspekte der deutschen Syntax*. Tübingen: Narr.

Guajardo, G. & Goodall, G. (2019). On the status of Concordantia Temporum in Spanish: An experimental approach. *Glossa: A Journal of General Linguistics*, 4(1), 116. DOI:10.5334/gjgl.749

Harvey, B. M., Klein, B. P., Petridou, N., & Dumoulin, S. O. (2013) Topographic representation of numerosity in the human parietal cortex. *Science*, 341(6150), 1123–1126.

Hofmeister, P., Culicover, P., & Winkler, S. (2015). Effects of processing on the acceptability of "frozen" extraposed constituents. *Syntax*, 18(4), 464–483.

Hofmeister, P., Staum Casasanto, L., & Sag, I. A. (2014). Processing effects in linguistic judgment data: (Super-)additivity and reading span scores. *Language and Cognition*, 6(1), 111–145.

Householder, F. W. (1973). On arguments from asterisks. *Foundations of Language*, 10(3), 365–376.

Kayne, R. (1983). Connectedness. *Linguistic Inquiry*, 14, 223–249.

Kayne, R. S. (1984). *Connectedness and Binary Branching*. Dordrecht: Foris.

Keffala, B. (2011). Resumption and gaps in English relative clauses: Relative acceptability creates an illusion of "saving." In C. Cathcart et al., eds., *Proceedings of the 37th Annual Meeting of the Berkeley Linguistics Society*. Berkeley, CA: University of California, Berkeley Linguistics Society, pp. 140–154.

Keffala, B. & Goodall, G. (2011). Do resumptive pronouns ever rescue illicit gaps in English? Poster presented at the 24th Annual CUNY Conference on Human Sentence Processing, Stanford, California.

Keffala, B. & Goodall, G. (2013). On processing difficulty and the acceptability of resumptive pronouns. Paper presented at Linguistic Evidence – Berlin Special, Humboldt-Universität, Berlin.

Kim, B. & Goodall, G. (2016). Islands and non-islands in native and heritage Korean. *Frontiers in Psychology: Language Sciences*, 7. DOI:10.3389/fpsyg.2016.00134

Kim, D. & Goodall, G. (2018). Complexity effects in A- and A'-dependencies. Poster presented at 31st CUNY Conference on Human Sentence Processing, UC Davis.

Langsford, S., Perfors, A., Hendrickson, A. T., Kennedy, L. A., & Navarro, D. J. (2018). Quantifying sentence acceptability measures: Reliability, bias, and variability. *Glossa: A Journal of General Linguistics*, 3(1), 37. DOI: 10.5334/gjgl.396

Lasnik, H. & Saito, M. (1992). *Move Alpha: Conditions on Its Application and Output*. Cambridge, MA: MIT Press.

Lewis, S. & Phillips, C. (2015). Aligning grammatical theories and language processing models. *Journal of Psycholinguistic Research*, 44(1), 27–46.

Mahowald, K., Graff, P., Hartman, J., & Gibson, E. (2016). SNAP judgments: A small N acceptability paradigm (SNAP) for linguistic acceptability judgments. *Language*, 92(3), 619–635.

Michel, D. (2014). Individual cognitive measures and working memory accounts of syntactic island phenomena. Doctoral dissertation, University of Calfiornia, San Diego.

Müller, G. (2010). On deriving CED effects from the PIC. *Linguistic Inquiry*, 41 (1), 35–82.

Myers, J. (2009). Syntactic judgment experiments. *Language & Linguistics Compass*, 3(1), 406–423.

Myers, J. (2017). Acceptability judgments. In M. Aronoff, ed., *Oxford Research Encyclopedia of Linguistics*. Oxford: Oxford University Press. DOI: 10.1093/acrefore/9780199384655.013.333

Namboodiripad, S. (2017). An experimental approach to variation and variability in constituent order. Doctoral dissertation, University of Calfiornia, San Diego.

Natale, M., Gur, R. E., & Gur, R. C. (1983). Hemispheric asymmetries in processing emotional expressions. *Neuropsychologia*, 19, 609–613.

Omaki, A., Fukuda, S., Nakao, C., & Polinsky, M. (2020). Subextraction in Japanese and subject–object symmetry. *Natural Language & Linguistic Theory*, 38, 627–669.

Perlmutter, David M. (1971). *Deep and Surface Structure Constraints in Syntax*. New York: Holt, Rinehart, and Winston.

Pesetsky, D. (2017). Complementizer-trace effects. In M. Everaert & H. C. Van Riemsdijk, eds., *The Wiley Blackwell Companion to Syntax*. New York: John Wiley & Sons.

Phillips, C. (2009). Should we impeach armchair linguists? *Japanese/Korean Linguistics*, 17, 49–64.

Phillips, C. & Wagers, M. (2007). Relating structure and time in linguistics and psycholinguistics. In P. Levelt & A. Caramazza, eds., *The Oxford Handbook of Psycholinguistics*. Oxford: Oxford University Press, pp. 739–756.

Polinsky, M., Clemens, L. E., Morgan, A. M., Xiang, M., & Heestand, D. (2013). Resumption in English. In J. Sprouse & N. Hornstein, eds., *Experimental Syntax and Island Effects*. Cambridge: Cambridge University Press.

Ritchart, A., Goodall, G., & Garellek, M. (2016). Prosody and the *that*-trace effect: An experimental study. In K. Kim et al., eds., *Proceedings of the 33rd West Coast Conference on Formal Linguistics*. Somerville, MA: Cascadilla Proceedings Project, pp. 320–328.

Saddy, D. (1991). *Wh*-scope mechanisms in Bahasa Indonesia. *MIT Working Papers in Linguistics*, 15, 183–218.

Sag, I., Hofmeister, P., & Snider, N. (2007). Processing complexity in subjacency violations: the complex noun phrase constraint. In *Proceedings of the 43rd Annual Meeting of the Chicago Linguistic Society*. Chicago: Chicago Linguistic Society, pp. 215–229.

Schütze, C. T. (2016). *The Empirical Base of Linguistics: Grammaticality Judgments and Linguistic Methodology*. Berlin: Language Science Press.

Schütze, C. & J. Sprouse (2014). Judgment data. In R. Podesva & D. Sharma, eds., *Research Methods in Linguistics*. Cambridge: Cambridge University Press, pp. 27–51.

Sedarous, Y. & Namboodiripad, S. (2020). Using audio stimuli in acceptability judgment experiments. *Language and Linguistics Compass*, 14:e12377. DOI: 10.1111/lnc3.12377

Sprouse, J. & Almeida, D. (2012). Assessing the reliability of textbook data in syntax: Adger's Core Syntax. *Journal of Linguistics*, 48(3), 609–652.

Sprouse, J. & Almeida, D. (2017). Design sensitivity and statistical power in acceptability judgment experiments. *Glossa: A Journal of General Linguistics*, 2(1). DOI:10.5334/gjgl.236

Sprouse, J., Schütze, C. T., & Almeida, D. (2013). A comparison of informal and formal acceptability judgments using a random sample from Linguistic Inquiry 2001–2010. *Lingua*, 134, 219–248.

Sprouse, J., Wagers, M., & Phillips, C. (2012). A test of the relation between working-memory capacity and syntactic island effects. *Language*, 88(1), 82–123.

Sprouse, J., Caponigro, I., Greco, C., & Cecchetto, C. (2016). Experimental syntax and the variation of island effects in English and Italian. *Natural Language & Linguistic Theory*, 34(1), 307–344.

Sprouse, J., Fukuda, S., Ono, H., & Kluender, R. (2011). Reverse island effects and the backward search for a licensor in multiple *wh*-questions. *Syntax*, 14(2), 179–203.

Stevens, S. S. (1946). On the Theory of Scales of Measurement. *Science*, 103 (2684), 677–680.

Torrego, E. (1985). On empty categories in nominals. Unpublished manuscript, University of Massachusetts, Boston.

Zorzi, M., Priftis, K., & Umiltà, C. (2002). Brain damage: Neglect disrupts the mental number line. *Nature*, 417(6885), 138–139.

# 2

# Response Methods in Acceptability Experiments

Sam Featherston

## 2.1 Introduction

The range of questions about appropriate and effective response methods in acceptability elicitation experiments is large, but a number of these questions seem to have found fairly consensual answers for the present, while some others must still be regarded as controversial. In this chapter I will spend some time discussing the first group, since these are still important and relevant questions about methodology, even if experimental practice seems to show that preferred answers have been identified. I will spend much more time on the second group of questions, since practice among linguists still shows variation and there are multiple positions actively represented. Here I will sketch the methodological variants which are currently commonly used.

In the following I will first look at the nature of the stimulus to which we are eliciting a response, then move on to a discussion of what it is that we are expecting the informant's response to quantify. On the basis of these considerations, I will sketch out what methods people use and what factors we might take into account when deciding between these options. The chapter will finish with a discussion of what questions the field faces on the subject of response methods.

## 2.2 Stimulus

The central question addressed by this chapter is the choice of experimental task in acceptability studies. This means that we are focusing on what happens *after* the stimulus has been presented to the informant, but of

I worked on the topic of response methods in acceptability elicitation experiments in the projects *Suboptimal Syntactic Structures* of the SFB 441 *Linguistic Data Structures* and the project *Expressions of Extrapropositional Meaning: Synchrony and Diachrony* of the SFB 833 *Constructing Meaning*, both funded by the Deutsche Forschungsgemeinschaft – Project ID 75650358. Many thanks are due to the numerous excellent colleagues in Tübingen.

course the range of methodological options is not restricted to the procedure after this point. Above all, the stimulus can be presented in many different ways: presentation can be in visual or auditory modality, the stimulus can be a full sentence or a smaller chunk, there may be some discourse context or not, the stimulus can appear word-by-word, incrementally or simultaneously. These parameters affect what sort of responses can be elicited.

### 2.2.1 Presentation

Acceptability studies are generally intended to gather information on sentence-level samples, and crucially, the investigation usually concerns the status of the sample as a whole, so the normal case is for the stimulus to be a sentence-level language sample, presented all at once. Procedures where the informant is called upon to read segments until the input is perceived to become unacceptable (or in a popular formulation "stop making sense") can however also be seen as a form of incremental acceptability task, often embedded in a self-paced reading experiment (Tanenhaus et al. 1989; Boland et al. 1990), or more or less free-standing in the speed-accuracy trade-off task (McElree 1993).

Incremental presentation has the advantage that the point at which the stimulus is rejected gives information about what part of it causes unacceptability, much in the same way that a slowing of reading does in self-paced reading. This information is of course missing from standard "whole sentence" judgments, but the location of the unacceptability in the stimulus can usually be identified by testing minimal pairs, which isolate exactly the causal factor(s). Testing multiple minimal pairs is also desirable because it permits the amplitude of the violation costs of the contributory causal factors to be quantified.

An additional issue with incremental presentation is that the point at which unacceptability becomes apparent is not necessarily the point at which the causal factor is located. In the classic garden path example (1), for example, informants will only start to respond negatively at the word *fell*, but the critical issue is the interpretation of the word *raced*.

(1)     The horse raced past the barn fell.

Most studies therefore do not use an incremental procedure and we will not deal with them any further here.

There are acceptability experiments in which the stimulus is presented auditorily, but the most frequent case is for it to be presented visually in written form, unless the issue of interest is specific to the spoken form, such as phonetic variants or the effect of prosodic features. There are a number of reasons for this, which I shall briefly mention here. The first is that readers are thought to access the appropriate prosody for a text even in silent reading, the so-called *implicit prosody* (Chafe 1988, Fodor 2002).

This makes it plausible that effects associated with prosody are available automatically, even with a visually presented stimulus in written form, as long as there is a clear preferred reading.

A second reason is that auditory presentation adds an additional degree of variation compared to the written form, and this variation is difficult to control. Studies of prosody show that there are links between prosodic form and interpretation and thus acceptability, but that these are fairly loosely associative and not deterministic one-to-one mappings (Höhle 1982). Informants' perception and analysis of the prosodic features are thus difficult to pin down and predict, which is undesirable in an experimental design in which these factors are not essential components.

One more relevant factor is that the presentation of a speech stimulus is non-simultaneous, and it is generally slower than fast reading (e.g. Jones et al. 2005). A speech signal is also paced by the speaker (and experimenter) not the listener, which means that the focus of attention of the listener is monotonically progressive. This differs considerably from reading, which permits the signal recipient to deal with the stimulus as suits them best, with saccades and regressions as required. Auditory stimuli are thus ideal for the investigation of incremental parsing and interpretation, but less so for the investigation of the status of a whole sample. We shall thus generally assume simultaneous visual presentation of the whole stimulus here, and limit our discussion to possible responses to this type.

### 2.2.2 Interpretation

We should touch upon one other methodological issue related to the modality of stimulus presentation, namely the nature of the linguistic stimulus. It is essential that the stimulus be uniquely interpretable in order to produce usable data. For example, (2) would be ambiguous in written form, having both the meanings (3a) and (3b).

(2)     The ghost appears to Hamlet to avenge the regicide.

(3)     a. The ghost appears in front of Hamlet in order to avenge the regicide.
        b. It seems to Hamlet that the ghost avenges the regicide.

Simple judgments of (2) can thus tell us nothing useful about its structural acceptability, because we cannot know which of the two an informant adopts, or whether different informants adopt different interpretations and structures. Worse still, it is likely that this uncertainty will cause additional processing and thus distort our result. The generalization is thus that the object of a valid acceptability judgment must be a form/interpretation pair. We are therefore asking our informants: *How good is this form with this interpretation?*

Even though ambiguity in language is extremely common, the requirement for a unique analysis is not as problematic as it might seem, since informants seem to apply a sort of principle of 'charity' (Davidson 2011: 196–197) and consistently judge the best available reading of an example sentence, as long as it is clearly better than its next best competitor. This behavior is readily explicable as a result of the link between acceptability and processing ease: the most acceptable reading will also be the easiest to process, and thus also the first one to become available. When one reading is available, there is little reason for the reader to look for an additional less acceptable one, and so it is this first and best reading which is rated.

Examples with two roughly equally accessible readings will nevertheless require disambiguation. Auditory presentation is sometimes utilized as one means of disambiguation. Since such structural ambiguity is often resolved by prosodic features, an auditory presentation might be preferred for (2). The question would thus be: *How good is this example with an interpretation which is compatible with this prosodic form?*

However, disambiguation can also be achieved by adding linguistic context to prime the intended interpretation. So if we want the verb *appear* in (2) to have the meaning 'materialize,' we must provide a suitably priming context, as in (4).

(4)     What does the ghost of Hamlet's father do in Shakespeare's play?
        The ghost appears to Hamlet to avenge the regicide.

This is a very powerful tool to force the intended reading. Well-chosen contextual priming can also permit readings to be tested which would not otherwise be anything like the most accessible. Here is my attempt to make the classic *horse raced* garden path testable – (5).

(5)     The horse we raced behind the stables kept his feet in spite of the ice, but . . .
        the horse raced past the barn fell.

This requirement for unique interpretability also means that unnatural examples can only be tested to the extent that they are uniquely correctable to a particular form. I would suggest that (6a) is not uniquely correctable as it is not clear where the filler should find its gap, whereas (6b) can produce meaningful results, in spite of being unacceptable, because it is fairly clear that the filler should be associated with the resumptive pronoun *it* at the sentence end.

(6)     a. Which car did the police arrest the driver of the motorbike which skidded off the road?
        b. Which car did the police arrest the driver of the motorbike which skidded into it?

It is a moot point whether example sentences should always be presented with context, even if the intended reading is the most accessible. The argument in favor of this reduces to the idea that judging sentences in isolation is fundamentally unnatural and artificial, and thus provides a measure which does not resemble any part of normal language processing (see Schütze 1996). This idea is linked to the conception of judging as a separate metalinguistic skill or activity which was commonly held in the 1960s.

I suspect that this view is not current among linguists gathering experimental judgments today. I think it would be consensual that making judgments is not a separate skill or activity, but simply a conscious act of proprioception directed at the degree of effort involved in processing a language sample. We can readily tell whether for instance a mathematical calculation is easy or more difficult; judging a sentence would seem to be parallel to this. Mostly we do not pay attention to the degree of processing effort that language use entails, but we can if we choose to. This argument for using context in all studies seems weak.

There is also a fairly strong reason why we should not use context where it is not strictly required: every additional complexity in the stimulus dilutes the effect that we are actually interested in. We may instruct participants to read a context text for background information but base their rating on only the final sentence, but we cannot be sure that they will do exactly that. My own experience would suggest that this strict division is not adhered to; participants take factors such as the plausibility of the context text into account in their judgments. If there is context, the data we obtain is thus a response to the stimulus sentence plus some context-related factors, rather than just the intended stimulus sentence.

A final reason not to use context is that it potentially interferes with the effect of "charity." Given a sentence in a discourse vacuum, informants make the necessary assumptions in order to construct a scenario in which it is meaningful. Crucially, they seem to do this as economically as possible, so that each person makes the minimal assumptions necessary. Since each person will do it optimally, we obtain a high degree of control across informants: people may not make identical assumptions, but each person makes the assumptions most accessible to themselves. Adding context can interfere with this optimization, because it may conflict with the world views of some people and not with those of others. Less stimulus material may thus arguably offer a clearer picture, if the intended interpretation of the stimulus is clear. If it isn't, disambiguation is essential.

## 2.3 What Are We Testing?

Syntacticians carrying out acceptability studies are often adopting a theoretical and descriptive position that one might term *post-Chomskyan*, by which I mean that they wish to build upon the work done in the Chomskyan tradition of syntax, without necessarily subscribing to every feature of current Chomskyan models. This connection comes from Chomsky's insistence that acceptability judgments are the data type of choice for studying the grammar (Chomsky 1965: 19f.), which has been very broadly adopted in the field, so that we can think of grammars in the Chomskyan tradition as models of grammaticality as reflected in judgments. The underlying quantity that Chomsky (1965) specifies as criterial is grammaticality (or "grammaticalness"), but he himself admits that no known procedure is able to access this directly. He also states that he sees this quantity as being gradient, "Like acceptability, grammaticalness is, no doubt, a matter of degree" (Chomsky 1965: 11) and dependent upon complex interactions of causal factors: "a property that is attributable, not to a particular rule, but rather to the way in which the rules interrelate in a derivation" (Chomsky 1965: 12). I think most linguists would agree that judgments do not access any single homogeneous level of grammar representation but are responsive to a range of factors, including the ease of processing the input, the plausibility of the most accessible interpretation, perhaps some measure of the computational complexity of the structural representation, as well as the fundamental feasibility of the stimulus as a structure of the language. This view is represented in the psychophysics literature too; in fact there is a branch of psychophysics, *integration psychophysics*, which studies how the various aspects of a complex stimulus are reflected in an integrated response, typically additively (Anderson 1989; McBride 1993).

It follows that we have no simple answer to the question as to what we are measuring in acceptability studies, and consequently no single immediate answer to the question as to what instruction we should be giving to our informants, but insights from psychophysics suggest that this is not necessarily problematic. Linguistic judgments can function as a valid approach to examining linguistic structures, since we can assume that the full range of features in the stimulus example remain represented in the final single response.

Not knowing what we are measuring is not a good starting point for an experimental procedure, but although experimental syntacticians may not agree exactly on what they are measuring nor what to call it, there is a fair degree of consensus on what appropriate procedures for collection are, so that we can recognize the relevance and value of each other's findings, even if we don't necessarily agree on what to call the quantity measured or know how to describe its genesis in psycholinguistic terms. My own preferred name for the quantity is "perceived well-formedness," because this is descriptive and not theoretically laden, as "acceptability" and "grammaticality" are.

One important factor which permits the fairly wide agreement on the basic validity of the experimental approach is that most people thinking about language, whether they are linguists or stylists or teachers, begin with acceptability intuitions. Since experiments on judgments gather exactly these intuitions, there is a shared basis. Specifically for linguists, the approach can be directly motivated from Chomsky's writings. We have noted that he insists upon acceptability judgments as the ultimate criterion, but he mentions too that improved methods could gain us improved access to the core concept of grammaticality, furthermore, he even tells us what factors we should be excluding in order to filter out irrelevant influences:

> Linguistic theory is concerned primarily with an ideal speaker-listener, in a completely homogeneous speech-community, who knows its language perfectly and is unaffected by such grammatically irrelevant conditions as memory limitations, distractions, shifts of attention and interest, and errors (random or characteristic) in applying his knowledge of this language in actual performance. (Chomsky 1965: 1)

We might summarize that individual particularities, dialectal variants, and processing factors are to be excluded as far as possible. Crucially, this is more or less what an experimental approach, using groups of informants, and multiple lexical variants of the target structure, is designed to achieve. Experimental judgment studies thus arguably come as close as is currently possible to Chomsky's *competence*, whilst not, of course, accessing it without *performance* components.

Some experimental syntacticians, myself included, would assume that introspective judgments are just one more measure of processing complexity, parallel to the processing measure of reading times, but cumulated, and made up of a similar (but not identical) mix of lexical access time, integration effort, and storage costs. Notice that this position, while it does not have an explicit role for the effects of the grammar, also does not deny the existence of an autonomous grammar. Rather it takes the agnostic position that we cannot, and perhaps need not, know if there is an autonomous grammar and if so where its boundaries might lie. As long as we are gathering the same sort of data and attempting to minimize those effects which are agreed to be non-grammatical, we experimental syntacticians can talk to each other and progress can be made.

## 2.4 The Judgment Task

Informants seem to understand an instruction to judge whether a linguistic example is good or not, or how good it is, without too much explanation. In its simplest form, the task is simply to judge the stimulus sentence to be grammatical or ungrammatical, but very frequently a wider range of options are offered. Most commonly, ratings are given on a scale which is either overtly numerical or one whose non-numerical label values could assigned numbers with no radical change of concept. For example, a scale with the four labels "very acceptable," "quite acceptable," "quite unacceptable," "very unacceptable" could be understood as equivalent to a scale with points numbered 1–4.

The two main variants of the number assignment task are box ticking (or radio button clicking) and direct number input. The first type generally limits ratings to integers on a scale of fixed length, while the second more readily allows intermediate values and open-ended scales. Alternatives such as drawing lines to represent acceptability are occasionally employed but reduce to assigning numerical values (e.g. Aria 2004). While putting a numerical value on line lengths is frequently used as a practice exercise for informants who are to judge relative acceptability, it is not obvious that drawing lines of appropriate lengths is an easy or direct way for informants to express their perceptions of acceptability. In fact Adli (2004) writes that he asked his informants to initially mark the position on the scale where the line should end with X and only then draw the line up to it, since instinctive line-drawing can be quite wild. This would seem to reduce the line-drawing method to box ticking plus a post hoc join-the-dots exercise.

Our choice as experimenters thus chiefly relates to two questions: first, what criterion to give for the judgment; second, whether to give anchor points relative to which the ratings should be given. These issues have been investigated by considerable trial and error in the experimental syntax literature (for review, see Schütze 1996; Cowart 1997), and many lessons have been learned.

First, we should not ask informants about production, particularly their own production. Labov (1996) in particular has demonstrated that social and prestige factors hinder objective self-assessement, which is sufficient reason to avoid this approach, but there is a larger issue at stake: fundamentally, questions about production are not "intuitions" in the technical sense of propioceptive reports of the processing load due to language use. It is probably true that frequency of occurrence in the linguistic environment affects judgments, but it is also quite clear that the intuitions feeding judgments do not reduce to a reflexion of occurrence frequency. It is far better to ask informants about receptive processing, with a question such as "How natural does this sound?," because this excludes associations with status and prestige. The instantaneous intuition of well-formedness can be seen as deriving directly from the input processing of the stimulus.

My own preference is for the question "How natural does this sound?" rather than "How grammatical is it?" or "How acceptable?," because "natural" is an atheoretical but well-understood criterion, which does not run the risk of accessing notions of what *should* be or what "proper grammar" is, both of which risk introducing irrelevant normative valuations. Using the verb *sound* helps make it clear that we want informants to report their impressions of the degree of effort involved in the receptive processing of the stimulus, and not look for rationalizations or "right" answers.

Although it is not much discussed in the linguistic literature, I think that the issue of scale anchoring is a key one (we shall talk about scale type below). In the simplest of acceptability tasks, informants are instructed to give a binary judgment whether the stimulus example is acceptable (or natural ...) or not. This task implicitly assumes that informants have this category available to them and it is well defined. Other versions of the task give more options, for example, as well as some sort of "good" and "bad," they also offer "I don't know" or "unclear." Four and five scale points are fairly frequently used and here usually the scale points are labeled; for example, in Wasow (2002) the four labels were "fully accepta- ble," "probably acceptable, but awkward," "marginally acceptable, at best," and "completely unacceptable." Scales with more than four points usually just have the end points described with terms such as "fully acceptable" and "fully unacceptable." The main aim here is to ensure that people use the scale the right way round, rather than providing any clear indication of what point 1 or point 7 exactly represent.

All of these scales are only weakly anchored, because criteria such as "quite unacceptable" may be interpreted very differently by individuals. This is not surprising, because even we linguists do not have any specific definition. A much stronger anchoring is obtained with procedures which consist of comparing items with other items or with standard examples whose acceptability is consensually agreed. It is now fairly well established that our perception of the amplitude of a quantity is sharpened when there are multiple stimuli to be compared; that is, we are more sensitive to differences between stimuli than to the absolute values of individual stimuli (e.g. Laming 1997). Asked about the temperature of a cup of tea in degrees, people can only make rough guesses. Asked to judge which of two cups of tea is hotter, they can make fairly fine distinctions.

Linguists can make use of this by providing sets of examples which illustrate a contrast, rather than just providing single examples. For exam- ple, the difference between a clear *wh*-island violation (7a) and a long extraction over *whether* (7b) becomes apparent when we juxtapose the two.

(7)    a. Which king of Denmark did you wonder when was murdered by his brother?
       b. Which king of Denmark did you wonder whether was mur- dered by his brother?

Giving informants pairs of examples to be compared thus permits addi- tional detail to be accessed, but at the same time it grounds each judgment in relation to other judgments, which can make it more meaningful. It is thus more effective to anchor the points of the scale on which we instruct informants to give judgments with real examples, rather than to describe the points with abstract terms. Giving judgments on a scale anchored by example sentences avoids the interpersonal variance in the interpretation of the descriptive criteria and provides an (at least) intersubjective refer- ence point for judgments. I think this issue is more important than lin- guists realize; for example, Laming (1997) argues that we cannot speak of "measuring" something without some reference to a scale and the units in which the measurement takes place. Providing a sentence as a point of reference does not provide a true scale, but it goes some way toward ensuring that informants are using the same criterion for their judgments, rather than different criteria depending on their potentially very variant interpretations of a term such as "acceptable."

The Magnitude Estimation methodology makes use of this by providing an initial anchor item proportionate to which informants give all further ratings. The Speeded Judgments approach may achieve a similar sort of effect by presenting stimuli fast and for a binary judgment. The rapid presentation and simple task means that the perception of previous items and their judgments has not faded so much by the time the next one appears. Thermometer Judgments builds on this by having two standard items, which provide local comparison points but which also anchor the scale. I would argue that scale anchoring with example sentences is a step forward in methodology. We shall consider these alternatives in greater detail below.

## 2.5  Scale Type

We have mentioned some scales that have been used in the past but it is worth taking stock of the variables here. The nature of the scale depends partly on what the experimenter asks the informant to do, and partly on what range of options for responding the informant is given. Let us first distinguish ordinal, interval, and ratio scales (Stevens 1946). An ordinal scale consists of a sequence of points with monotonically changing values, but it does not require the distances between the points on the scale to be equidistant from one another or quantifiable in any way. A four-point scale with the values "fully acceptable," "quite acceptable," "quite unacceptable," "fully unacceptable" is an example of an ordinal scale. We can recognize this because we could easily insert an additional scale point such as "neither acceptable nor unacceptable" between the points "quite acceptable" and "quite unacceptable," making it a five-point scale, but with "quite acceptable" and "quite unacceptable" now two points apart instead of adjacent to each other. This shows that these labels give us an order, but not fixed spacing.

The issue of scale type is important because of what you can legitimately do with the data on the scale (see Chapter 3 for further discussion). An ordinal scale is not quantified, so you cannot add scores or calculate mean scores. To do these things we must use an interval scale, which is one which has equidistant points, like on a ruler. They can therefore be added and subtracted, mean values can be calculated, and common statistic tests can be applied. Since these are useful tools that linguists want to employ, this is an important reason not to use scales with merely descriptive labels.

But does this mean that we should only label our scale with numbers and nothing else? Try this thought experiment: visualize the four-point scale we mentioned above with the values "fully acceptable," "quite acceptable," "quite unacceptable," and "fully unacceptable." Now visualize the five-point scale we mentioned above with the additional point "neither acceptable nor unacceptable" in the middle. Now what most people see in their mind's eye in both cases are scales with equi-distant points, the only difference being that in the five-point scale there is one more point. We don't leave the gap between "quite acceptable" and "quite unacceptable" constant and just squeeze the additional point half way between them. As far as I can establish, everybody visualizes scales this way. This is interesting because it suggests that we actually see apparently ordinal scales as interval scales, so we probably apply them as interval scales when we use them. It is because of this effect that linguists often do carry out calculations on judgments on scales that do not really permit it, and little harm is probably done by the practice. Nevertheless, it is more satisfactory to use a real numerical and thus interval scale, as well as anchoring the values with example sentences (see below).

## 2.6 Current Methods

### 2.6.1 Classic Grammaticality Judgments
A linguist sits in their office, writing a paper. They need to illustrate a phenomenon associated with ill-formedness, so they wrack their brains for a moment and identify an example that has the relevant feature and sounds bad. They write it down in their paper, annotated with a star.

### 2.6.2 *n*-Point Scale
Acceptability judgments are often gathered on five-point and seven-point scales, labeled with numbers from 1 to 5 or 1 to 7. Informants are usually only allowed to give integers as judgments, and indeed this is often hard-wired into the response method, since the informants are to tick boxes on paper or click boxes on a screen; but in principle it would be possible to allow finer-grained input by using a response method where informants input a figure which could include fractions. The labeling of the points with numbers such as 1 to 7 implies that the scale is linear, and that the distances between the numerical points are equal, so that this scale type is an interval scale until the scale ends are reached. At least some of these points are usually given descriptive labels, such as "fully acceptable" at the top and "completely unacceptable" at the bottom. It is not usual to give example sentences to anchor the numerical scale values in acceptability values, but in theory nothing prevents this, and indeed it would be very desirable.

One problem with the anchoring of an $n$-point scale is that the most natural place to provide anchors is at the ends, but it is difficult or impossible to supply examples of these points. The upper end of a fixed-length scale must represent all the values from something like "very natural" all the way up to "infinitely natural"; the lower end must represent all possible stages between "very unnatural" down to "word salad or worse." Neither of these is easy to exemplify. Consider the examples of badness in (8a–e).

(8)     a. The woman has eating the cake.
        b. cake the eating the have woman
        c. the slithy toves did gyre in the wabe
        d. frig hana yoompy icle sofy vivs karo
        e. wghm gsbtlgn lcbtz ktj bsngr hc6jf

All of these values would have to be covered by an example sentence at the bottom end of a fixed-length scale, but they span an extremely wide range of well-formedness, so that no one example can illustrate them. An additional problem is found in examples such as (8a). This example is plainly not part of the English language and contains a clearly and uniquely identifiable error in the auxiliary verb, but such examples are often not perceived to be bad, either because speakers have an automatic unconscious error correction function or because we saccade from lexical word to lexical word when we read, skipping the function words.

A slightly different problem may be found at the top of the scale. While there are different degrees of naturalness, these seem to have a natural ceiling; while it is possible to descend through several grades of awfulness in (8a–e), there are fewer equivalent degrees of perfection at the top of the scale. There is still the complicating factor of length, however, since short examples are judged better than long ones, which would imply that the best possible example sentence would have length = 0.

Fortunately there is a solution to this anchoring problem: we do not anchor the scale end points, but rather the points one further in. On a five-point scale we would therefore anchor points 4 and 2, not 5 and 1. It is easier to identify examples which fit in the "quite good" and "quite bad" categories and which will be reliably perceived to be of this type. Additionally, anchoring these points provides closer comparison points toward the middle of the scale, where most judgments will be located. This is desirable, as the availability of local comparison points has been shown to increase judgment accuracy.

The $n$-point scale is a simple but nevertheless effective tool, which captures judgments in considerably more detail than either the binary distinction of "grammatical" or "ungrammatical" which is fundamental to a generative grammar, or else the three-way distinction of no symbol, question mark (?), and star (*), which is commonly used in the literature. While the $n$-point scale is a clear step up from the binary or ternary choice, it still has weaknesses. First of all, on a fixed scale, informants can only make the number of distinctions that the scale has points, which can mean that informants are unable to express distinctions that they perceive. Experience with freer scales shows that careful judgments can distinguish at least ten different levels of acceptability. This problem could in principle be addressed by permitting the use of non-integers, so that additional distinctions can always be made by those informants who wish to do so. However, in practice, informants tend to prefer to use integers over non-integers (and round numbers over other numbers), so this would require significant extra instructions and practice.

Second, informants can easily find themselves squeezed at one end of the scale or another, since they cannot know in advance how much better or worse later examples will be. This is particularly problematic since linguistic well-formedness does not have a clear distribution of values, nor can the informant know in advance what range of values will occur in the experiment. We can conclude that a five-point or seven-point scale will produce results of sufficient detail for most purposes, but is far from permitting the collection of the full range of acceptability impressions that speakers can access. To see why this is the case it is useful to look at the alternatives.

### 2.6.3 Magnitude Estimation

A approach that has been very influential is Magnitude Estimation (for an overview, see Stevens (1975), and for its use in linguistics, see Bard et al. (1996)), which was developed in work on psychophysics. The Magnitude Estimation procedure assumes that speakers perceive linguistic acceptability as magnitudes, not as a linear continuum. Informants first perform a practice stage to introduce the task. They are shown a reference line of a medium length and instructed to give its length a value, which they can choose freely. They are then presented other lines with varying lengths, some longer, some shorter. They are instructed to assign these subsequent lines values as fractions or multiples of the value that they chose for the first line, which remains on the screen. A second practice phase transfers this task to sentence acceptability. Again they see an initial reference item, this time an example sentence, and may freely choose a value to represent its acceptability. They are instructed to rate the acceptability of all subsequent example sentences as fractions or multiples of the value that they chose for the first example.

The method thus has advantages over the five-point or seven-point scale, since it has no scale ends and no minimum division. Informants can therefore always add a higher or lower score and they are always free to make all the distinctions that their perception of well-formedness requires. It also allows informants to choose their own reference value as the basis for subsequent judgments, so they can create for themselves the scale that they feel most comfortable with. The Magnitude Estimation method thus allows informants to express all and only the differences that they perceive with minimum interference from the scale. What is more, it provides a true interval scale, since there are no constraints on what values can be used. This additional finer-grained data has been very influential in making people think about the nature of grammatical well-formedness.

This methodology has been extensively used and works well, as it yields more finely differentiated patterns of judgment data than were previously available. We should note here that it is sometimes claimed that the difference between more informal judgments and some types of experimental judgments, particularly Magnitude Estimation, is less than experimenters might think (e.g. Weskott & Fanselow 2011; Fukuda et al. 2012; Sprouse et al. 2013). There is a lot to be said about this issue, but space does not permit it here.

As time has passed, however, more fundamental weaknesses have become apparent (e.g. Sprouse 2007; Featherston 2007). The first problem is that informants have a preference for integers, and a multiple scale consistently applied will often require non-integers among those judgments which are lower than the reference item. This is particularly acute for informants who choose a low value for the reference item, so that very many of their values would need to be expressed with non-integers. This effect can cause significant distortion and loss of differentiation, especially if judgments descend below the number 1.

A second problem concerns the pattern of the resulting data. Magnitude Estimation assumes that subjects give ratio judgments; thus if the reference item is assigned the value 10, an example twice as good will be 20, one half as good will be worth 5. Plotted on a simple graph with a linear $y$-axis scale, results for a random set of sentences should yield an upwardly concave pattern. But this pattern is not what we find in practice.

The reason is that informants do not in fact give ratio judgments even when instructed to do so; in fact, it is both theoretically and practically impossible for them to do so (Poulton 1989: xv). In order to calculate the multiple of a value, it is necessary to know the zero point. Linguistic well-formedness has no such zero point and so no statement that example A is twice as good as example B can be made. In this aspect, well-formedness is parallel to temperature. Is it true that a cup of tea at 80°C is twice as hot as a cup of tea at 40°C? While the idea initially seems appealing, it is in fact false, because 0°C is not a true zero point.

In fact it is not easy to determine exactly what scale informants use, because we have no objective measurement scale to compare it with. In the original psychophysics literature, the assumption was made that the perception of linguistic well-formedness and loudness were *additive* neural processes and thus obeyed a power law (Stevens & Gallanter 1957). This is now controversial even for loudness perception (e.g. Ellermeier &

Faulhammer 2000), where there are measures such as the sound pressure level which can function as an independent variable. Since there is no easy linguistic independent variable against which we compare well-formedness judgments, we cannot establish any fixed relation between stimulus and response (but cf. Keller (2000), who argues for the number of violations as an independent variable).

In practice, the most common assumption is that the data pattern is additive and linear, and this seems to be confirmed by the many published studies using Magnitude Estimation and linear scales. It would therefore appear that informants in Magnitude Estimation studies, not being able to produce judgments on a magnitude scale in spite of their instructions, simply produce data reflecting the amplitude of differences and thus produce something like a linear scale (e.g. Sprouse 2007; Featherston 2009). This conclusion is supported too in the psychophysical literature (e.g. Birnbaum 1980; Poulton 1989; Laming 1997).

## 2.6.4 Thermometer Judgments

Thermometer Judgments (Featherston 2009) is a methodology which is designed to retain the better features of the $n$-point scale and of Magnitude Estimation, but avoid the disadvantages of each. Like Magnitude Estimation, it utilizes an initial practice stage in which informants judge line lengths. Two lines are presented horizontally, one filling about 40 percent of the width of the screen or page, and the other about 60 percent of the page width. Informants are told that the first line has a length of 20 and the second a length of 30, without any unit being mentioned. Underneath these two reference lines, additional lines are then presented one at a time, and the informant is instructed to judge their lengths relative to the first two. The lines to be judged include some that are longer than both reference lines, some that are shorter than both, and some that lie between these values. This practice phase is intended to familiarize participants with the task of judging quantities relative to multiple reference examples.

Informants are next shown one fairly bad example sentence and one fairly good one. They are told that the first one is worth 20, and the second 30. Recent examples in English fulfilling this role have been:

(9)     *Example worth 20*
      The father fetches the wholemeal bread them.
      *Example worth 30*
      The father fetches the children the wholemeal bread.

These examples remain upon the screen with their valuations, but below them example sentences are presented one after another for judgment relative to the reference examples. Again, examples better, worse, and between the reference examples are included. After this second practice phase, the main part of the experiment begins, working just like the second practice phase and using the same reference examples.

This method avoids the distortion of the hard scale ends, since additional higher and lower scores can always be added. It avoids distortion near zero by locating even fairly bad examples around the 20 mark. The reference examples are chosen so that the vast majority of judgments lie between 15 and 35; ratings above 40 or below 10 have the quality of outliers. Between the values of 15 and 35 the scale thus resembles a 20-point version of the $n$-point scale described above, but without hard scale ends and with sufficient points so that even fine judgments can be given without resorting to non-integers.

The use of two anchor items provides fairly close comparison points – never more than five points away on the most used part of the scale from 15 to 35 – but it also defines both the location and spacing of the scale, which helps to reduce interjudger variability and thus makes the normalization of scores to informant-based $z$-scores less necessary.

This method thus has a number of positive features, but it is sometimes criticized as being too complex for informants. In fact I think that the chief problem is that it is unfamiliar rather than difficult, because it is at base just a more sophisticated version of the $n$-point scale. Additionally, I think many researchers regard an $n$-point scale as good enough for their purposes.

### 2.6.5 Speeded Judgments

This very different approach to gathering judgments utilizes the frequency of decisions as the primary dependent variable rather than the rating itself. Even though the task itself is just a binary choice of grammatical or ungrammatical, the distribution of these judgments provides a richly gradient pattern with fine distinctions. The method and the correspondence between this data type and the results of tasks which elicit gradient well-formedness values are discussed in Bader and Häussler (2010); for extensive discussion of results obtained with this approach see Bader and Bayer (2006). In their variant of the method, informants have sentences presented to them word-by-word on a computer screen at a fairly brisk pace. Each word is displayed for 300–400 ms, and when the last word has been presented, informants must quickly decide whether the sentence was grammatical or ungrammatical, with a time limit of about two seconds.

The method makes use of the fact that there is a degree of randomness in the attribution of a grammaticality status to an example. An ungrammatical example will more or less always be judged to be bad, and a fully grammatical example will more or less always be judged to be good, but between these two there are examples with intermediate statuses, which will receive both grammatical and ungrammatical judgments across the group of informants. These form a continuum from 100 percent ungrammatical judgments, via 50 percent good and 50 percent bad, to 100 percent grammatical judgments, as their status improves. The distribution of good and bad judgments thus reflects the naturalness of the examples in a gradient pattern.

This approach has the advantage that it measures a behavioral response to a degree of naturalness, which is a familiar and trusted model of psycholinguistic testing. In this it contrasts with the direct elicitation of intuitions of well-formedness, which still has an unscientific feel to it (e.g. Labov 1996). This method also produces a second dependent variable, that of the time taken to respond, the idea being that a more complex sentence will require a longer response time (e.g. Clifton et al. 1984; Frazier 1985). This factor is one of the reasons for the use of the word-by-word presentation method: the response latency requires a fixed point to start from. While this too is a behavioral variable, it can be doubted that the response time is a simple measure of the complexity of the stimulus. One might rather regard it as measuring the difficulty of the decision: the clear cases will be judged fast and the marginal cases more slowly. A prediction of this would be that examples with a 50–50 percent decision split will obtain the slowest judgments, while the clearer cases in either direction will be the fastest.

An interesting question about the speeded judgments method, which measures binary judgment frequencies, is how this data type relates to gradient acceptability judgments. In particular, we might wonder to what extent speeded judgments should be thought of as gathering data with a smaller "grammatical" component and larger processing component, because the judgments are given under time pressure. Recall our quote from Chomsky in Section 2.3 above about what linguistic theory is *not* concerned with: "such grammatically irrelevant conditions as memory limitations, distractions, shifts of attention and interest, and errors (random or characteristic) in applying his knowledge of this language ..." We may read this as suggesting that processing effects due to things like time pressure are not relevant to grammar, and in fact Bader and Bayer (2006) use precisely this data to model the syntactic parser, which would imply that they too see it as being relevant to processing. On the other hand, Bader and Häussler (2010) show that this data type is not so very different from judgments which are not gathered under speeded conditions. This leaves us with a choice: we can either conclude that the proportions of grammatical and processing information in speeded judgments are not that different to those in non-speeded task types or else – more radically – that there is no strict difference between grammatical effects and processing effects (e.g. Hofmeister et al. 2013). Space unfortunately prevents us from discussing this question further here.

One last question about this data type concerns the margins of its access to gradient data. We have noted that above some point of full naturalness,

sentences will be accepted more or less 100 percent of the time, and below
some threshold, bad sentences will more or less always be rejected. These
points are the limits beyond which this method cannot see, since it
depends upon the differential frequency of good and bad judgments.
As soon as an example is uncontroversially bad, so bad that even the
random error component in judgments never permits it to be judged
good, the ability of this methodology to perceive differences ends. This
approach therefore, like the *n*-point scale, fundamentally employs a scale
with hard ends, not an open-ended scale.

### 2.6.6  Pairwise Comparisons

The final method that we shall discuss makes use of the increased discrimination available when comparing closely related examples.
Informants are presented with pairs of examples and instructed to
choose the more acceptable of the pair (David 1988). Since our relative
discrimination is more sensitive than our absolute discrimination, this
approach may access more finely graded data than methods that require
the informant to place a rating on a scale. This approach therefore has
a degree of overlap with the previous one, in that the chief dependent
variable is the frequency of choice, not a well-formedness rating. It differs
from the previous one in that the comparison point is not stable: while
Speeded Judgments, like even the classic binary grammaticality
judgment, adopts the grammatical/ungrammatical borderline as its sole
criterion, Pairwise Comparisons has a varying reference point.
Potentially, this can lead to greater sensitivity, if the comparison point
is always chosen so that it is as close as possible to the item being judged
(Laming 1997). In practice, however, the two items to be compared are
usually chosen because they are minimal pairs which contrast some
linguistic feature (e.g. Sprouse, Schütze, & Almeida 2013). The items
may therefore be not very close in their well-formedness values, in
which case there may not be much additional discrimination.

The additional discriminatory power comes at a price, as paired comparisons yield results on an ordinal scale, not an interval scale: while our
informants have told us in what order they perceive our examples to be
well-formed, they have not told us how far apart any two items are. But this
information is inferable, to a degree. We will have multiple informants
and they will have judged multiple exemplars of each contrast, so that we
also have available the frequency with which one item of a comparison
pair was preferred to the other, and this allows us to draw conclusions
about their relative distance, just as the grammaticality judgment frequencies do in speeded judgments. This data could thus in principle be used to
develop an interval scale of well-formedness, with some reservations
(Saaty 2008). I am, however, not aware that this has been done for
acceptability.

## 2.7   Summary and Outlook

As will have become clear, the choice of a procedure for an acceptability study involves a number of trade-offs and compromises. One important issue is ease of use and accessibility, and it is here that the simple individual linguist's judgments score highly. As Phillips (2007) argues, linguists' judgments are good enough for many purposes, and we should not hesitate to use them and indeed trust them for straightforward questions.

But this should not be seen as carte blanche for non-experimental judgments, because there are a number of real problems. Traditional judgments given by a single linguist suffer from significant weaknesses that do not depend upon accuracy. First, there is the methodology issue of the independence of the data and subjective bias. This is so fundamental to good science that it requires us to gather judgments from a group of disinterested speakers. Second, there is the issue of generalization over the vocabulary of the language. As syntacticians, we know that lexical items can be associated with specific effects, so that we will normally only be interested in effects which can be shown to be a generalization over multiple lexical variants (e.g. Featherston 2007; Gibson & Federenko 2013).

A third issue is the random variation in individual judgments, which necessitates the use of some sort of scale which permits averaging over informants. A final point is less methodological and more linguistic: most things which are worth finding out are not simple contrasts of two items, because well-formedness is multifactorial and responds cumulatively to those factors, which may however interact. A full understanding of any phenomenon will require not just two conditions to be compared, but usually 2×2, or 2×2×2, or 2×2×4, or yet more. If we wish to find out how a grammar works, we need not only to identify the factors individually, but also learn how they interact. It is essential to know about an issue of *wh*-movement, for example, whether it applies equally to subjects and direct objects and indirect objects, and adjuncts, at very least. Does it work the same way in single-clause contexts and cyclically over multiple clauses? Does it pattern the same way for *wh*-questions and relative clauses (restrictive and non-restrictive), and topicalization? All of these questions must be answered in a full account of the phenomenon, and we need detailed multiple comparisons to capture the whole picture.

These four factors already show that our first methodology, classic grammaticality judgments, is useful for hypothesis generation, but it can only produce data – and therefore theory building – at a fairly coarse granularity. Sufficient studies have been done using experimental methods to show that this approach produces more detailed evidence which can support more detailed analyses. But the experimental methods have their advantages and disadvantages too, as we have noted above. My own opinion is that it does not much matter which of them we use: all of them are standardly employed together with multiple informants, multiple lexicalizations, and a scale which permits (ideally: encourages) informants to make as many distinctions in well-formedness as they perceive. While there may be differences in the strengths of the various methodologies, they are all so much better than the classic linguists' grammaticality judgments that much of our understanding of syntax is based upon, that these differences need not worry us unduly. The use of any of them will result in better data being collected, which will in turn permit better linguistic description and theory building.

It is nevertheless interesting to consider what method of judgment collection might constitute the next methodological step. Assuming that linguists require more detail and less distortion, the factors that can be optimized are as follows:

a. the scale should have no minimum division
b. the scale should have no restricting endpoints
c. the scale should avoid the distortion near zero
d. the scale points should be externally anchored
e. the task should involve pairwise comparisons to sharpen the accuracy

The trouble is that this final factor is not really compatible with the others, because pairwise comparisons do not involve reference to a scale, which the others do. And a scale is valuable, because it provides a basis for wider comparisons, not just binary comparisons. So what we want is a scale with anchored points to permit both finer relative judgments but also the ability to label judgments in a system of units.

To see how this could work, we return to our cup of tea analogy. We have said that people will not give very accurate judgments if asked to estimate the temperature of a cup of tea; but given two cups of tea, they will be able to say which of them is hotter. This is the differential sensitivity effect, which sharpens our perception of contrasts, but does not immediately yield a scale. We can, however, make use of this differential sensitivity by providing our tea tasters with multiple cups of tea at different temperatures as reference examples, for example at 30°, 45°, 60°, 75°, and 90°. To see how this helps, imagine judging the temperature of a new cup of tea relative to these reference cups of tea. You have the five cups of tea at known temperatures, you have to place the temperature of the new cup of tea relative to these reference cups.

What will happen? Well, since we have good differential sensitivity and plenty of local reference points, we will be able to say that the new experimental cup is, for instance, closer in temperature to the 60°Cup than the 75° Cup, quite a lot closer, so about 65°. Such accuracy would be quite impossible without the reference cups of tea with known temperatures. So the combination of a scale of numbers – in this case degrees Celsius – with reference items – here cups of tea – anchoring the scale in our direct perception will permit us to give fairly exact values on the temperature scale.

Phoneticians have applied this approach with their system of cardinal vowels. These are values anchored in the sensory world and thus intersubjectively identifiable: all phoneticians know their values. We have developed the equivalent for acceptability: a scale with a set of five points which are anchored with carefully selected examples which have independently established well-formedness values (for German, Featherston (2009); for English, Gerbrich et al. (2019)). Since there are five points which span the accessible range of linguistic well-formedness, there is always an example item close to the well-formedness value of the item to be judged, so that the additional sensitivity of local comparison is available. In addition, since the values of the standard items is known, the judgments given relative to the standard items are on a real scale.

Just as phoneticians would not dream of judging the place of articulation of a vowel without reference to the cardinal vowels, future syntacticians should refer every well-formedness judgment to these cardinal wellformedness examples in order to obtain more finely gradient data. At the same time, they provide an intersubjective anchored scale like the cardinal vowels, so that not only relative but also absolute statements can be made about the acceptability of examples.

This combination of local comparison points and judgments on an anchored scale would be my vision for the future of acceptability judgments. So here's the take-home message: it does not matter too much what judgment procedure you use. If you want the finest granularity, you'll choose the most sophisticated procedure; if you can make do with broader categories, you can use the simpler method. But all of them would benefit from being given relative to the cardinal well-formedness values.

# References

Adli, A. (2004). *Grammatische Variation und Sozialstruktur*. Berlin: Akademie Verlag.

Anderson, N. (1989). Integration psychophysics. *Behavioral Brain Science*, 12, 268–269.

Bader, M. & Bayer, J. (2006). *Case and Linking in Language Comprehension*. Dordrecht: Springer.

Bader, M. & Häussler, J. (2010). Toward a model of grammaticality judgments. *Journal of Linguistics*, 46(2), 273–330.

Bard, E., Robertson, D., & Sorace, A. (1996). Magnitude estimation of linguistic acceptability. *Language*, 72(1), 32–68.

Birnbaum, M. (1980). Comparison of two theories of 'difference' and 'ratio' judgements. *Journal of Experimental Psychology: General*, 109, 304–319.

Boland, J., Tanenhaus, M., & Garnsey, S. (1990). Lexical structure and parsing: Evidence for the immediate use of verbal argument and control information in parsing. *Journal of Memory and Language*, 29, 413–432.

Chafe, W. (1988). Punctuation and the prosody of written language. *Written Communication*, 5(4), 395–426.

Chomsky, N. (1965). *Aspects of the Theory of Syntax*. Cambridge, MA: MIT Press.

Clifton, C., Frazier, L., & Connine, C. (1984). Lexical expectations in sentence comprehension. *Journal of Verbal Learning and Verbal Behavior*, 23(6), 696–708.

Cowart, W. (1997). *Experimental Syntax: Applying Objective Methods to Sentence Judgements*. Thousand Oaks, CA: Sage.

David, H. (1988). *The Method of Paired Comparisons*. New York: Oxford University Press.

Davidson, D. (2011). *Inquiries into Truth and Interpretation*, 2nd ed. Oxford and New York: Clarendon Press.

Ellermeier, W. & Faulhammer, G. (2000). Empirical evaluation of axioms fundamental to Stevens's ratio-scaling approach: I. Loudness production. *Perception & Psychophysics*, 62, 1505–1511.

Featherston, S. (2007). Data in generative grammar: The stick and the carrot. *Theoretical Linguistics*, 33(3), 269–318.

Featherston, S. (2009). Why linguistics needs boiling and freezing points. In S. Featherston & S. Winkler, eds., *The Fruits of Empirical Linguistics*, vol. 1: *Process*. Berlin: De Gruyter, pp. 47–74.

Fodor, J. D. (2002). Prosodic disambiguation in silent reading. In M. Hirotani, ed., *Proceedings of NELS 32*. Amherst, MA: GLSA, pp. 113–132.

Frazier, L. (1985). Modularity and the representational hypothesis. *Proceedings of NELS 15*. Amherst, MA: GLSA, pp. 131–145.

Fukuda, S., Goodall, G., Michel, D., & Beecher, H. (2012). Is magnitude estimation worth the trouble? In J. Choi, E. A. Hogue, J. Punske, D. Tat, J. Schertz, & A. Trueman, eds., *Proceedings of the 29th West Coast Conference on Formal Linguistics*. Somerville, MA: Cascadilla Proceedings Project, pp. 328–336.

Gerbrich, H., Schreier, V., & Featherston, S. (2019). Standard items for English judgement studies: Syntax and semantics. In S. Featherston, R. Hörnig, S. von Wietersheim, & S. Winkler, eds., *Experiments in Focus: Information Structure and Semantic Processing*. Berlin: De Gruyter, pp. 305–327.

Gibson, E. & Fedorenko, E. (2013). The need for quantitative methods in syntax and semantics research. *Language and Cognitive Processes*, 28, 88–124.

Hofmeister, P., Jaeger, T. F., Sag, I., Arnon, I., & Snider, N. (2013). The source ambiguity problem: Distinguishing effects of grammar and processing on acceptability judgments. *Language and Cognitive Processes*, 28, 48–87.

Höhle, T. (1982). Markiertheit, Linking, Regelformat – Evidenz aus dem Deutschen. In T. Vennemann, ed., *Silben, Segmente, Akzente* (Linguistische Arbeiten 126). Tübingen: Niemeyer, pp. 99–139.

Jones, D., Shen, W., Shriberg, E., Stolcke, A., Kamm, T., & Reynolds, D. (2005). Two experiments comparing reading with listening for human processing of conversational telephone speech. *INTERSPEECH-2005*, 1145–1148.

Keller, F. (2000). Gradience in grammar: Experimental and computational aspects of degrees of grammaticality. Doctoral dissertation, University of Edinburgh.

Labov, W. (1996). When intuitions fail. In L. McNair, K. Singer, L. Dolbrin, & M. Aucon, eds., *Papers from the Parasession on Theory and Data in Linguistics* 32. Chicago: Chicago Linguistic Society, pp. 77–106.

Laming, D. (1997). *The Measurement of Sensation*. Oxford: Oxford University Press.

McBride, R. (1993). Integration psychophysicon as: The use of functional measurement in the study of mixtures. *Chemical Senses* 18, 83–92.

McElree, B. (1993). The locus of lexical preference effects in sentence comprehension. *Journal of Memory and Language*, 32, 536–571.

Phillips, C. (2007). Should we impeach armchair linguists? In S. Iwasaki, H. Hoji, P. M. Clancy, & S.-O. Sohn, eds., *Japanese/Korean Linguistics 17*. Stanford, CA: CSLI Publications, pp. 49–64.

Poulton, E. C. (1989). *Bias in Quantifying Judgments*. Hove and London: Lawrence Erlbaum.

Saaty, T. L. (2008). Relative measurement and its generalization in decision making: Why pairwise comparisons are central in mathematics for the measurement of intangible factors – the Analytic Hierarchy/Network Process. *Review of the Royal Academy of Exact, Physical and Natural Sciences, Series A: Mathematics (RACSAM)*, 102(2), 251–318.

Schütze, C. T. (1996). *The Empirical Base of Linguistics: Grammaticality Judgments and Linguistic Methodology: Grammaticality Judgements and Linguistic Methodology*. Chicago: University of Chicago Press.

Sprouse, J. (2007). A program for experimental syntax. Doctoral dissertation, University of Maryland.

Sprouse, J., Schütze, C. T., & Almeida, D. (2013). A comparison of informal and formal acceptability judgments using a random sample from *Linguistic Inquiry* 2001–2010. *Lingua*, 134, 219–248.

Stevens, S. (1946). On the theory of scales of measurement. *Science*, 103 (2684), 677–680.

Stevens, S. (1975). *Psychophysics: Introduction to Its Perceptual, Neural and Social Prospects*. New York: John Wiley.

Stevens, S. & Galanter, E. (1957). Ratio scales and category scale for a dozen perceptual continua. *Journal of Experimental Psychology*, 54, 377–411.

Tanenhaus, M., Boland, J., Garnsey, S., & Carlson, G. (1989). Lexical structure in parsing long-distance dependencies. *Journal of Psycholinguistic Research*, 18, 37–49.

Wasow, T. (2002). *Postverbal Behavior*. Stanford, CA: CSLI Publications.

Weskott, T. & Fanselow, G. (2011). On the informativity of different measures of linguistic acceptability. *Language*, 87(2), 249–273.

# 3

# Approaching Gradience in Acceptability with the Tools of Signal Detection Theory

Brian Dillon and Matthew W. Wagers

Intuitive judgments of sentence acceptability form the empirical basis of experimental syntax, and an important component of many psycholinguistic investigations (Schutze 1996; Cowart 1997). For this reason, one central methodological concern for experimental syntacticians is how best to collect and analyze acceptability judgment data. Experimental syntacticians continue to extend and refine the tools used to measure sentence acceptability. In this chapter we seek to contribute to this methodological expansion. We discuss the difficulties inherent in getting a quantitatively precise measurement of sentence acceptability. We suggest that the tools of signal detection theory can be applied to common acceptability judgment data. This analytical approach offers both an explicit theory of how speakers give acceptability judgments in the context of a rating task, and yields more precise measurements of sentence acceptability. The approach we outline builds on the work of previous researchers advocating similar approaches to acceptability data (e.g. Mauner 1995; Bader & Häussler 2010), as well as research on the magnitude estimation method for measuring acceptability judgments (Bard, Robertson, & Sorace 1996). The central goal of our chapter is to make the tools of Signal Detection Theory accessible to experimental syntacticians; to this end, we present a specimen experiment and a worked, tutorial-style analysis of acceptability judgment data using Signal Detection Theory.

## 3.1  Measuring Acceptability: A Brief Overview

There are a variety of methods for measuring sentence acceptability in experimental contexts. These methods differ both in the response options offered to participants and the task presented to participants. For measuring the acceptability of a single sentence in isolation, binary yes/no acceptability judgments, *n*-point Likert scales, and continuous "thermometer" ratings (Featherston 2008) are all widely used. Other techniques invite participants to compare one sentence against another. For example, in two alternative forced-choice tasks (2AFC), the participant chooses the more acceptable of two sentences presented. In magnitude estimation (ME) tasks, the participant is asked to rate a target sentence relative to a baseline (or *modulus*) sentence (Bard et al. 1996). For a detailed explanation of each type of experiment, we refer the reader to Chapter 2 and to Schütze and Sprouse (2014).

For all of these techniques, we might ask: how well can each acceptability measure recover true differences in acceptability between sentence tokens, or between classes of sentences? Head-to-head comparisons of the various acceptability measurements suggest that the different methods yield largely similar qualitative results for many sentence contrasts. In other words, if sentences of Type A are more acceptable than sentences of Type B as measured with one of the techniques above, other methods will generally recover this (ordinal) difference with high reliability (Bader & Häussler 2010; Sprouse & Almeida 2012, 2017; Weskott & Fanselow 2011). Commonly used methods in experimental syntax have a number of desirable properties: they generally have high test–retest reliability (Langsford et al. 2018), and in many cases yield results that are consistent with those achieved with informal methods of acceptability judgment collection (Sprouse & Almeida 2017). In short, if the experimental syntactician is interested in establishing that there exists a simple contrast between two classes of sentences, she has a number of reliable, powerful tools available at her disposal. It is fairly straightforward for a researcher to answer the binary question *is sentence type A better than, or worse than, sentence type B?*

However, it is less straightforward to answer the more gradient sister question: *to what extent is sentence type A better than, or worse than, sentence type B?* This is because this question implies that the researcher has a reliable quantitative measure of the acceptability differences between two classes of sentence, such that she can offer a meaningful, quantitatively precise answer to this gradient question.

For this reason, magnitude estimation has occupied a special role for researchers interested in asking questions about gradient acceptability. In their 1996 paper, Ellen Bard and colleagues argued that linguistic acceptability should be understood in terms similar to other psychophysical judgments. That is, acceptability constitutes psychological evidence in the same way that judgments of luminosity or loudness constitute psychological evidence that can be measured and modeled. The judgment of acceptability reflects a hidden, or latent, cognitive variable that can be reliably measured, one which is the truer guide in explaining the sources of gradience. From this perspective, acceptability judgments could be measured using some of the same tools that psychophysicists had developed to quantify latent psychological evidence in other domains. Magnitude estimation, one technique for doing this, was originally proposed by Stevens (1956) as a means of providing measurements of psychological evidence on a *ratio* scale; that is, a measurement scale with equal-sized units of measurement on which quantitative differences can be defined and directly interpreted, and for which there exists a true zero point. An example of a ratio-scale measurement is height, which has a clear zero point, licensing ratio comparisons among measurements (e.g. *Aunt Mary is twice as tall as Timmy*). A related type of measurement is that of an *interval*-scale measurement. Interval-scale measurements differ from ratio-scale measurements in not having a fixed zero point. An example is temperature measured in degrees Fahrenheit, which has no interpretable zero point, although it does offer equal-sized units of measurement.

The promise of a true ratio (or interval) measurement of acceptability set magnitude estimation apart from other techniques for measuring acceptability, which generally offered either *ordinal* measurements (Likert scales, yes/no ratings) or *categorical* measurements (2AFC). Ordinal measurements allow researchers to establish a rank ordering among sentence classes, but they do not allow more precise measurements of the quantitative differences between sentences. This is because the differences between points on a Likert rating scale need not be equal-sized units of "acceptability": there is no guarantee that the difference between 2 and 3 on the Likert scale is the same as the difference between 4 and 5 on the Likert scale. Thus, Likert ratings (and yes/no judgments) allow researchers to establish whether sentence type A is more acceptable than sentence type B with high fidelity, but they do not tell us by how much. Magnitude estimation seemed to correct that, and offer a true ratio scale judgment of acceptability. And since interval-scale or ratio-scale measurements of acceptability are required to provide a satisfactory answer to the gradient question, this methodological advance allowed the development and testing of theories that make fine-grained, quantitative predictions about acceptability (see, e.g., Keller 2000; Sorace & Keller 2005; Aarts 2007; Lau, Clark, & Lappin 2017).

Unfortunately, it has turned out to be less straightforward to apply ME to acceptability judgments than to other psychophysical judgments of stimulus quality. Unlike judgments of brightness or loudness, say, there is no objective physical stimulus against which acceptability judgments can be compared. The "physical axis" for brightness/loudness stimuli is important, because it allows researchers to validate the ME measurements by comparing the consistency of participant judgments against objective physical measurements of the stimulus. Since there is no physical axis for acceptability judgments, this is not possible. In its place, Bard and colleagues demonstrated that ME judgments of acceptability showed good cross-modal consistency: highly similar results were found when subjects estimated acceptability using a numerical value and when they estimated acceptability using line length. This cross-modal consistency is expected if there is a stable underlying acceptability percept that is "read out" in the various measurement contexts; the missing physical axis in ME judgments is implied by the cross-modal consistency (Stevens 1960; Bard et al. 1996). Despite this promising early result, several subsequent studies have raised questions about the utility of magnitude estimation as applied to acceptability judgments. In particular, Sprouse (2011) showed that some of the cognitive assumptions underlying magnitude estimation may not, in fact, hold. Langsford et al. (2018) showed that magnitude estimation has among the lowest test–retest reliability of the major experimental techniques for measuring acceptability reviewed here, although the absolute values of test–retest reliability were overall still quite high. Lastly, Weskott and Fanselow (2011) showed that magnitude estimation is not more informative than Likert or binary ratings, as indicated by the proportion of variance accounted for by experimental manipulations. In light of these results, it cannot be claimed that magnitude estimation provides a true, ratio-scale measurement of acceptability, and on a more practical level, it cannot be said that it more reliably recovers differences in acceptability between classes of sentences than other techniques of measuring acceptability.

## 3.2   We Really Do Want to Address the Gradient Question

One upshot of the preceding review is that if a researcher is interested only in establishing whether sentence class *A* is reliably more acceptable than sentence class *B*, then ordinal measurements of acceptability such as Likert scales or binary judgment measures serve the task very well. Similarly, if a researcher wishes to establish an acceptability ranking across a range of sentence classes, these same ordinal or categorical measures will suffice, and are quite easily deployed. In light of this, does experimental syntax really need to develop tools to answer the gradient question? Is there any value in getting a true ratio, or interval measure of acceptability? We believe there is value in this, for two reasons.

### 3.2.1   Reason 1: Disconnects between Statistical Hypotheses and Substantive Hypotheses

The first reason that interval scales of measurement are of broad importance is that even if a researcher's substantive hypotheses do not critically depend on obtaining a precise interval measurement of acceptability, this same researcher's *statistical* hypotheses almost always do. This disconnect between what is measured and what a statistical test assumes can lead to spurious conclusions. One very common situation where this arises is testing interaction effects in crossed factorial designs. For example, Sprouse, Wagers, and Phillips (2012) constructed a 2 × 2 factorial design to measure the presence of island effects. This experimental design crossed the site of extract for a *wh*-dependency (a matrix gap or embedded clause gap) with the type of embedded clause (an island environment or not). They reasoned that if the penalty for embedded *wh*-movement was greater when the embedded clause was an island than when it was not, then this would constitute evidence for some additional penalty levied on extractions from islands. In other words, they expected to see a superadditive interaction of gap position and embedded clause type. Statistically, this superadditivity is realized as an interaction in an ANOVA or similar. This statistical interaction corresponds to a *difference-of-differences* score (see Figure 3.1A). If the difference of differences is not zero, then the experimental factors in the 2×2 design interact, such that the effect of one factor depends on the level of the other. This use of this additive factors logic over *n*-point scale ratings is ubiquitous (indeed, we have routinely used this in our own work).

However, ANOVA-style interactions with Likert/*n*-point ratings – even *z*-transformed ratings – are potentially problematic. The reason is straightforward: the difference-of-differences logic, and the statistical tests used to evaluate the difference-of-differences score, critically relies on the assumption of an interval scale. That is, these tests assume that we can meaningfully compare the relative *magnitude* of the difference between pairs of conditions that sit at different points on the response scale. This assumption is not met in ordinal data, such as common Likert rating data or yes/no rating data. This opens up the possibility of misleading patterns in the data: differences in how a response scale is interpreted at the high and low end can create spurious interactions (for extensive discussion, see Loftus 1978; Heit & Rotello 2014; Rotello, Heit, & Dubé 2015). We suspect that most researchers using these techniques are implicitly aware of this possibility: we believe it to be widely recognized that so-called *floor* or *ceiling* effects can create spurious interactive patterns in bounded response scales (see also Liddell & Kurschke 2018). The point we raise here is that similarly spurious interactions may obtain, for essentially similar reasons, even in the absence of obvious floor or ceiling effects.

For example, consider Figure 3.1, Panel B. In this hypothetical example, there is compression in the response categories at the lower end of the response scale: the distance between the edges of the 2 category is smaller on the underlying acceptability dimension than it is for the 5 category, for example. This corresponds to an experimental context where a participant is overall less willing to assign lower values on the response scale. In Figure 3.1B, however, the underlying pattern of acceptability is one that is entirely additive between the four hypothetical conditions: the difference of differences in the means of the four Gaussian distributions represented

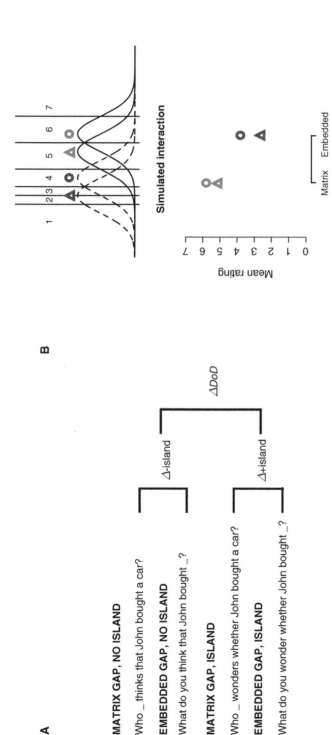

**A**

**MATRIX GAP, NO ISLAND**

Who _ thinks that John bought a car?

**EMBEDDED GAP, NO ISLAND**

What do you think that John bought _?

$\Delta$-island

**MATRIX GAP, ISLAND**

Who _ wonders whether John bought a car?

$\Delta$+island

**EMBEDDED GAP, ISLAND**

What do you wonder whether John bought _?

$\Delta DoD$

**B**

1  2|3  4  5  6  7

Simulated interaction

Mean rating

0  1  2  3  4  5  6  7

Matrix    Embedded

**Figure 3.1 A:** Sprouse et al.'s factorial design. In their design, they measured the difference in acceptability between the matrix and embedded gap conditions for non-islands ($\Delta_{-island}$), and the same acceptability difference for islands ($\Delta_{+island}$). The difference of these two differences ($\Delta_{DoD}$) measures the extent to which the difference in acceptability is greater for the island environments than non-island environments. **B:** A hypothetical illustration of how scale bias could create a spurious interaction in the difference of differences. The top figure shows four hypothetical distributions of acceptability for the four conditions in Panel A. These distributions are defined so that the difference of differences among them is zero. The vertical lines mark the demarcation of response boundaries on an *n*-point (Likert) scale; on the lower end of the scale, there is compression of the boundaries between rating categories. Because of this compression, averaged Likert ratings for these four conditions present a spurious superadditive interaction that is due to properties of the response scale, rather than the underlying acceptability distributions.

is zero. However, this underlying additive pattern interacts with the differences in the width of the category boundaries in the response task. As a result, we see an illusory interactive pattern in the ratings that mirrors a superadditive effect. Most importantly, if similar compression occurs across participants, then common methods of removing scale bias such as z-scoring will not remove it.

This simple example is intended to illustrate that in principle, properties of the response scale can interact with perfectly additive underlying patterns, and yield spurious interactive patterns when the resulting rating data are analyzed as if they were simple, interval measures of acceptability. This is only a hypothetical demonstration, however: It is not currently known whether this observation puts actual claims in the experimental syntax literature in peril,[1] and we do not wish to imply that any single interactive pattern is in fact an artifact of scale properties. However, it is a potential danger, and failure to recognize this has mislead researchers in related fields, for decades in some cases (see Rotello, Heit, & Dubé 2015). It suggests that at a minimum, researchers should adopt statistical practices for analyzing interactions in judgment experiments that do not implicitly assume an interval response scale.

### 3.2.2   Reason 2: We Can Get More out of Acceptability Judgment Measures

The second reason to seek an interval scale for measuring acceptability judgments is that establishing such a measurement for acceptability is a critical first step for asking more fine-grained questions about gradient effects on acceptability judgments. This arises when quantifying the relative impact various constraints have on acceptability cross-linguistically (Alexopoulou & Keller 2007; Almeida 2014; Häussler et al. 2015; Sprouse et al. 2016; Kush, Lohndal, & Sprouse 2018), as well as attempts to directly model the gradience in acceptability judgments (Lau, Clark, & Lappin 2017; Sprouse et al. 2018; Warstadt, Singh, & Bowman 2018).

To take one example of a research question that critically turns on having an interval measurement of acceptability: Dillon et al. (2017) were interested in measuring the acceptability of sentences like (2):

(2)    Which flowers is the gardener planting?

(2) is an object *wh*-question; the subject of the sentence is *the gardener*. Despite this, the sentence appears to be ill-formed. Dillon and colleagues proposed that the plural *wh*-phrase *which flowers* interferes with the processing of the agreement on the auxiliary that immediately follows (one

---

[1] In fact, we have reason to believe that the example chosen here is *not* a spurious interactive pattern: ROC Analysis of the original data in Sprouse, Wagers, and Phillips (2012) shows that the interactions reported in that paper are not due to scale compression.

particular example of an agreement attraction-like effect: for recent sum-maries of this large research area, please consult Bock & Middleton (2011) and Franck (2011)). One question that Dillon and colleagues asked of examples like (2) was whether the illusion of ungrammaticality was com-plete: when raters judged sentences like (2) to be unacceptable, were they treating them as fully ungrammatical sentences? In other words: is the illusion of unacceptability in (2) more akin to a bistable perception of ungrammatical/grammatical agreement (a linguistic version of the Necker cube, perhaps), or do sentences like (2) simply occupy an inter-mediate level of acceptability, perhaps because of interference or difficulty in processing the complex agreement relationships in these examples?

A visual inspection of their data suggested a bimodal distribution of ratings for examples like (2). This in turn suggests that the answer to this question was that the perception of these sentences was essentially bimo-dal, with participants variably treating them as fully acceptable or fully unacceptable sentences. However, Dillon et al. (2017) noted that a weakness of their approach was that it assumed that the ratings on the $n$-point scale constituted interval measurements. If this assumption is not met, then their conclusions may not hold. For example, spurious bimod-ality could arise in a distribution of ratings over $n$-point scales if partici-pants were for some reason unwilling or resistant to offer responses in the middle of an $n$-point scale (i.e. if there were scale compression in the middle of the scale). This kind of non-linearity in the mapping between underlying perception of acceptability and the response scale could create an illusion of bimodality in the responses, which in this hypothetical example would simply reflect a bias toward offering extreme responses on the response scale. If true, this would imperil these authors' conclusion about this particular linguistic illusion (we return to this effect later on in the chapter).

### 3.2.3  The Problem, the Solution

The reason that Likert and binary ratings do not yield interval scale mea-surements essentially boils down to what we will call *response bias*: what internal criterion do participants set on their internal perception of acceptability to render a "yes" judgment in a binary task? What internal criteria does a participant set to render a judgment of a 2 or a 3 on a Likert scale? This is known as a participant's *scale bias* in the experimental syntax literature. What makes a sentence a "5" on a seven-point Likert rating task is likely to vary from participant to participant in ways that are idiosyn-cratic and not of central interest to the experimental syntactician.

In the context of an $n$-point rating experiment, it is common to take a $z$-score transform of each participants' ratings to address this kind of scale bias. This normalizes ratings across participants, but it is not guar-anteed to result in a truly interval measure. However, an alternative approach is to attempt to directly model the underlying acceptability values and the response thresholds. From this perspective, we take seriously the claim that sentence acceptability derives from a latent, unobserved cognitive variable that is read out or reflected in different acceptability measures; it is this underlying variable that we wish to recover and measure. As a starting point, we might take this to be a scalar (unidimensional) real value. This underlying value is mapped onto response categories in the context of an experiment when participants set an internal criterion or criteria and compare their perception of acceptability for a given sentence token to their internally determined criteria. This sort of *latent variable model* seeks to recover the underlying acceptability values by jointly modeling the underlying latent acceptability variable and the response criteria (e.g. the response bias). In one study, Langsford et al. (2018) applied one widely studied latent variable model to binary judgment data: the Thurstone model. Applied to acceptability judgments, a Thurstone model seeks to recover the latent acceptability structure in a class of sentence comparisons through a series of pairwise comparisons among sentences (in this sense, it is formally similar to the Elo system for establishing chess rankings, which has also been applied to acceptability judgment data; Sprouse et al. 2018).

The Thurstone model is one example of a latent variable model for modeling judgment measures; other statistical approaches such as ordinal regression models may be interpreted in a similar fashion (Liddell & Kruschke 2018). The great strength of the latent variable approaches is that they offer an explicit theory of how numbers get placed on the response scale in the context of a judgment experiment, and in doing so, offer a framework for inferring the underlying acceptability values from readily available judgment measures such as Likert scales or binary judgment acceptability decisions. In the following section, we discuss how to apply one relatively well-understood type of latent variable approach, Signal Detection Theory, to acceptability judgment data.

### 3.2.4   Signal Detection Theory and Acceptability Judgments

One broad, widely used framework for modeling decision-making processes under uncertainty is Signal Detection Theory (SDT; Macmillan & Creelman 2005). This framework is commonly applied to an observer's judgments of whether some stimulus is present or absent. One very common example of this is a recognition memory task, where participants are asked to decide if a stimulus is one that they previously studied (*stimulus present*) or not (*stimulus absent*). The standard SDT analytical approach categorizes response behavior in an experiment like this into *hits* (e.g. *stimulus present* responses when it is the correct response) and *false alarms* (e.g. *stimulus present* responses when it is not). SDT describes how the distribution of hits and false alarms in a detection task can be used to recover different aspects of the stimulus detection process, such as how clearly the observer can discriminate signal from noise (e.g. their *sensitivity*) and what threshold they use in rendering their judgments (e.g. their *bias*). Although it is most commonly applied in detection tasks, the theoretical model of the decision process implied by SDT is very broad. According to SDT, the decision process is seen as a mapping from a noisy, continuous cognitive signal onto one or more discrete response options offered to a participant in an experimental setting.

This perspective on the decision-making process has value for the experimental syntactician, because a similar decision process is plausibly at work when speakers are asked to categorize linguistic stimuli into discrete categories in a judgment task. This hypothesized decision process for both binary rating tasks and *n*-point Likert tasks is presented in Figure 3.2. The strength of SDT is that it allows independent estimation of the underlying cognitive signal (in our case, the latent *Acceptability* values), as well as the likelihood that a participant will respond with one response category over another (that is, response bias or scale bias).

There have been several previous attempts to apply Signal Detection Theory to acceptability judgment tasks. Mauner (1995) was one early, important application of these tools. Mauner argued that SDT was critical for analyzing grammatical judgment data given by agrammatic aphasic patients. To our knowledge, the underlying SDT for acceptability judgments was most explicitly developed by Bader and Häussler (2010), who proposed a model of a binary acceptability judgment task grounded in SDT. On Bader and Häussler's analysis, the process of rendering an acceptability judgment could be logically decomposed into two distinct processes: the first is the computation of a continuous acceptability value for a given sentence, and the second is a mapping from that continuous acceptability value on one of two response options in a binary rating task. Their model explained how continuous acceptability can be converted to the probability of a response in one of two categories, which in turn gave insight into why Bader and Häussler found such a tight correlation between continuous (ME) and discrete (binary yes/no judgments) measurements of acceptability in their experiments (see also Weskott & Fanselow (2011) for a similar result). Moreover, Bader and Häussler showed that their simple two-stage decision model was able to achieve a close fit to their experimental data. That is, in their data, the proportion of "acceptable" responses was well modeled by a continuous distribution of acceptability and a single decision criterion that mapped that continuous value of acceptability into a binary yes/no decision. In short, SDT offers a theory of how categorical responses arise in acceptability judgment experiments while being based on a fundamentally continuous, noisy signal of acceptability.

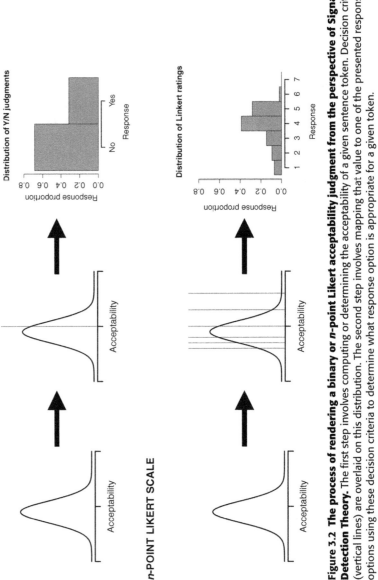

**Figure 3.2 The process of rendering a binary or *n*-point Likert acceptability judgment from the perspective of Signal Detection Theory.** The first step involves computing or determining the acceptability of a given sentence token. Decision criteria (vertical lines) are overlaid on this distribution. The second step involves mapping that value to one of the presented response options using these decision criteria to determine what response option is appropriate for a given token.

Dillon et al. (2019) further developed Bader and Häussler's Signal Detection Theoretic model of the acceptability judgment task. In their experiment, they measured speeded binary acceptability judgments, followed by a three-point confidence rating task. In their analysis, they combined the rapid acceptability judgment and the graded confidence ratings into a six-point scale, ranging from *very confident unacceptable* to *very confident acceptable,* and analyzed the resulting rating data using SDT. If raters use an *n*-point ordered response scale (as in a Likert task), then the SDT approach holds that the continuous acceptability value is mapped to one of the potential scale responses. More specifically, the rater would posit *n-1* decision criteria, which in turn partition the continuous acceptability signal into the *n* distinct, ordered response categories at the decision stage of the model (see Figure 3.2).

This model of an *n*-point rating task implies important new routes of analysis of acceptability data, which we will discuss in detail below. In broad strokes, these analytical approaches seek to deconfound *sensitivity* from *bias.* In the present context, *sensitivity* refers to the distance between two sentence types in the underlying perceptual space; the term *sensitivity* is borrowed from classical Signal Detection Theory, where it referred to an individual's ability to discriminate signal from noise (i.e. their *sensitivity* to whether a stimulus is present). Applied to acceptability judgments, the SDT-theoretic notion of sensitivity is the linguist's notion of *contrast* between a pair of sentences or sentence classes: SDT-theoretic measures of sensitivity quantify the degree of contrast between a minimal pair of sentence types, and so yield an answer to the gradient acceptability question *to what extent is sentence type A better than, or worse than, sentence type B?*

One familiar technique for computing independent measures of sensitivity and bias is simple $d'$ analysis. $d'$ measures the distance between the mean value of two distributions in standard deviation units. Strictly speaking, $d'$ is a measure of discriminability between two classes of stimuli in the decision space that supports judgments about the stimuli. Sensitivity in the context of acceptability judgment data is most appropriately understood as the distance between the two classes of sentence in the decision space that supports the acceptability judgment. At this early stage, we remain unclear what the underlying decision space that supports acceptability judgments is. On the plausible hypothesis that response behavior in an acceptability judgment task arises by mapping a unidimensional psychological value of *Acceptability* onto one of the response options (Bader & Häussler 2010), then the discriminability measure $d'$ can be considered a distance measure between the location of the acceptability distributions for two classes of stimuli. Furthermore, this interpretation of $d'$ only holds if the researcher is willing to adopt certain assumptions about the shape of the underlying distributions of acceptability judgments. For example, the $d'$ measure of discriminability assumes that the underlying distributions of acceptability are normal distributions, and that the two distributions compared have equal variance.

However, there are other techniques for identifying independent measures of sensitivity and bias that make fewer theoretical assumptions about the data. It is possible to relax the assumption of equal variance; in this case, an appropriate measure of discriminability is $d_a$, a measurement of the distance between the means of the two distributions expressed in units of their root mean squared standard deviation. Other techniques can be readily applied to common experimental data. In an experimental context where there are multiple, distinct response criteria (such as a Likert scale task, or a dual task that jointly measures acceptability and confidence), it is possible to construct an empirical *receiver operating characteristic* (ROC). An ROC curve can yield a measure of sensitivity as well. In our context, this sensitivity index is constructed between two conditions in an acceptability judgment experiment. We detail how to construct an ROC in the tutorial below, but at an intuitive level, it visualizes how the distribution of responses in two experimental conditions differ on a point-by-point basis across the response scale. This allows for a much more precise characterization of how two conditions may differ in acceptability that goes beyond the standard analyses of central tendency.

In sum, SDT-style analysis has much to offer experimental syntax, by allowing researchers to directly model the underlying cognitive variables that support acceptability judgments. The perspective developed here is a first, but critical, stepping stone. If the signal detection framework satisfactorily models acceptability judgments in $n$-point scale rating data, then SDT may offer a general framework for analyzing acceptability judgment data.

## 3.3  Tutorial: SDT and D-linking

In this section we will work an example with actual data, derived from an experiment designed to measure the acceptability of extraction dependencies and how that depends on D-linking (see Goodall 2015). Our goals are twofold. First, we seek to provide a simple proof-of-concept that the task model implied by SDT analysis provides a good approximation to response behavior in a real data set (see also Bader & Häussler 2010). Second, we aim to give a tutorial-style introduction to the application of these techniques to facilitate the wider application of these techniques.

First we spend a little time talking through the method and design considerations. While familiar, they are not identical to a "run of the mill" syntax experiment. The topics and methods discussed in this tutorial are familiar from other areas of psychology, engineering and even radiology – but they have not often been offered for an experimental syntax application. For reasons of space, we are unable to give a full treatment of all the various issues raised by this analysis. We recommend that the interested reader pair this section with the more complete and justified discussion of these issues in MacMillan and Creelman (1991/ 2005) and, in particular, their discussion of ratings experiments (in their Chapter 3).

### 3.3.1  Specimen Experiment

#### 3.3.1.1  Method

An ROC curve is revealing about the underlying distribution of Acceptability, the latent cognitive variable of interest, because it takes relative measurements of two Acceptability distributions at multiple criterion placements. There are a number of experimental design parameters that can be used to cause participants to adopt different biases (see MacMillan & Creelman 2005): for example, using payoffs to differentially reward correct "yes" responses and correct "no" responses; or using instructions that convey misleading estimates of the "true" rate of Grammatical and Ungrammatical stimuli. But the use of a ratings experiment is perhaps the simplest means for estimating an ROC curve, and, in our experience, a quite reliable means for doing so. In our specimen experiment, we explicitly asked people to first classify the stimuli and then rate their confidence on a three-point scale. As a consequence, they effectively gave a rating on an 1–6 scale.[2] We did not put them under time pressure to give either judgment. We implemented the experiment using Ibex on IbexFarm (Drummond 2013).

#### 3.3.1.2  Study Design Considerations

Our design must give participants a genuine opportunity to make a choice. And we need to compare the acceptability of classes of sentences that differ in a theoretically well-defined way. Therefore we must have a clear hypothesis about the mechanism that distinguishes two sentence classes. We adopt the hypothesis that D-linking improves the distinctiveness of *wh*-phrases – and thus their retrievability. Therefore we should compare sentences that differ not only in whether or not the *wh*-phrase is lexically restricted, but crucially also in whether or not retrieval is required to interpret the sentence grammatically.

Consider the following grammatical sentence:

(3)     Who do you think that the new professor is going to persuade?

---

[2] We suspect that much existing experimental syntax data, collected along an *n*-point Likert-style scale, could be profitably reanalyzed as a ROC curve – provided that the experiment was designed so that some conditions can be reasonably identified as sources of hits, and others as sources of false alarms. We have reanalyzed some of our own datasets, and find that the assumptions of an unequal variance normal–normal model are typically met (see Section 3.3.2.2). This is an obvious area for future research.

What would be an appropriate control for (3)? It should elicit an opposite response in the binary judgment task, i.e. "No," and differ minimally from (3) along almost every dimension, except the theoretically relevant ones.

To recognize (3) as grammatical, the perceiver must successively (i) encode the displaced *wh*-phrase, (ii) identify the contexts in which gaps could occur, and, when they do, (iii) retrieve the filler phrase (Wagers 2013). Therefore we constructed (4) as a control.

(4)     Who thinks that the new professor is going to persuade?

(4) has a short matrix subject extraction that imposes comparable demands for (i), but effectively blocks the processes associated with (ii)–(iii). At the same time, it uses nearly the same lexical items, the same biclausal structure, the same argument structure, etc. It necessarily contrasts in the matrix subject. Using the local person *you* in (3) enables a reasonable comparison, since pronominal subjects are known to engender minimal additional complexity and to effectively level subject/non-subject extraction differences (Gordon, Hendrick, & Johnson 2001).

The verb in (3)–(4) was selected to be obligatorily transitive: for example, practically all speakers of English require *persuade* to have a complement DP (Gahl, Jurafsky, & Roland 2004). This is important, because we want the acceptability in (3) to depend on the subprocesses of dependency comprehension succeeding. If the verb were optionally transitive (e.g. *attack*), the comprehender might assign (3) high Acceptability without engaging the processes of a theoretical interest, i.e. without finding a legitimate grammatical derivation. (5)–(6) are exactly the same as (3)–(4), but with a lexically restricted *wh*-phrase.

(5)     Which donor do you think that the new professor is going to persuade?

(6)     Which donor thinks that the new professor is going to persuade?

Finally, we must de-correlate grammaticality from whether or not there's a matrix subject ((4), (6)) or embedded object ((3), (5)) dependency. If participants implicitly learned this connection, then it would be possible to correctly classify the grammatical/ungrammatical stimuli without deeply parsing the sentences. It is in principle possible to do this by manipulating the filler sentences. We chose, instead, to do it as part of the experimental design by inserting an indefinite DP (*someone/anyone*) in the embedded object positions.

(7)     Who do you think that the new professor is going to persuade anyone?

(8)     Who thinks that the new professor is going to persuade anyone?

(9)     Which donor do you think that the new professor is going to per-
        suade anyone?

(10)    Which donor thinks that the new professor is going to persuade
        anyone?

This design thus realizes eight conditions: WhP (bare, or D-linked),
Embedded VP-type (gap, or filled gap), and Grammaticality (grammatical,
or ungrammatical). Table 3.1 repeats the full design with condition labels.


### 3.3.2   Analysis

#### 3.3.2.1   Simple Sensitivity and Bias

There are several possible ways to analyze the data that result from
a forced-choice experiment with confidence ratings. Let us start with the
simplest SDT analysis, based on *just* the binary judgment data. In Table 3.2,
we've summarized the response outcomes by condition. For each


Table 3.1 *Example item set*

| VP | WhP | Gram. | Sentence |
| --- | --- | --- | --- |
| 1  Gap | bare | Gram | Who do you think that the new professor is going to persuade? |
|  |  | Ungram | Who thinks that the new professor is going to persuade? |
| 2 | D-link | Gram | Which donor do you think that the new professor is going to persuade? |
|  |  | Ungram | Which donor thinks that the new professor is going to persuade? |
| 3  Filled Gap | bare | Gram | Who thinks that the new professor is going to persuade anyone? |
|  |  | Ungram | Who do you think that the new professor is going to persuade anyone? |
| 4 | D-link | Gram | Which donor thinks that the new professor is going to persuade anyone? |
|  |  | Ungram | Which donor do you think that the new professor is going to persuade anyone? |


Table 3.2 *Binary judgment results*

| VP | WhP | Grammaticality | correct | error | p.c | p.err | p.c_type | p.err_type |
| --- | --- | --- | --- | --- | --- | --- | --- | --- |
| 1 gap | bare | gram | 237 | 120 | **0.664** | 0.336 | Hit | Miss |
| 1 gap | bare | ungram | 236 | 118 | 0.667 | **0.333** | CR | FA |
| 2 gap | D-link | gram | 242 | 115 | **0.678** | 0.322 | Hit | Miss |
| 2 gap | D-link | ungram | 248 | 110 | 0.693 | **0.307** | CR | FA |
| 3 fld | bare | gram | 311 | 46 | **0.871** | 0.129 | Hit | Miss |
| 3 fld | bare | ungram | 293 | 66 | 0.816 | **0.184** | CR | FA |
| 4 fld | D-link | gram | 288 | 71 | **0.802** | 0.198 | Hit | Miss |
| 4 fld | D-link | ungram | 315 | 42 | 0.882 | **0.118** | CR | FA |

condition, the empirical proportion correct (p.c) and its complement proportion error (p.err) is reported. In the final columns, p.c and p.err are annotated with a traditional SDT label: Hit (Correct *yes*), False Alarm (FA; Incorrect *yes*), Miss (Incorrect *no*), Correct Rejection (CR; Correct *no*). Numbering of the table rows indicates condition pairs to be compared ("scaled against one another"), and within the p.c and p.err columns, the values to be scaled are placed in bold.

Based on the forced-choice responses alone, we can quantify participants' aggregate performance, factored into sensitivity and bias. Note that in this analysis, we are analyzing data aggregated across participants. In principle $d'$ could be calculated on an individual basis, however, and that clustered data further submitted to inferential tests. Bearing this in mind, we proceed with the aggregated approach, and return to the perils and pitfalls of this in Section 3.4.3.

The $d'$ measure of sensitivity, discussed above, is the distance between two Acceptability distributions expressed in standard deviation units. To compute $d'$, therefore, we must convert the probabilities in Table 3.2 into standard deviation units, or z-scores, using the inverse cumulative normal distribution function. This is $\Phi^{-1}(\bullet)$ in standard notation, and here we use the somewhat zippier notation $z(\bullet)$ for that function.

(11)     $d' = z(\text{Hits}) - z(\text{FA})$     NB:     $z(\text{Hits}) = -z(\text{Misses}); z(\text{FA}) = -z(\text{CR})$

In R this distribution is implemented by the function qnorm, which takes a probability as its argument and returns a z-score.[3] For the *Bare* WhP conditions, with a gapped VP, we calculate $d'$ as follows, with representative R code below:

(12)
```
# Write a function to implement d'=z(Hits)-z(FA)
sensitivity.ev <- function(Hits, FA) {
        dprime <- (qnorm(Hits) - qnorm(FA))
        return(dprime)
}
> sensitivity.ev(0.664, 0.333)
[1] 0.855049
```

Under the assumption of equal variance, this value implies a distribution of underlying acceptability as depicted in Figure 3.3: two standard normal distributions whose means are separated by 0.85 standard deviations.

---

[3] The Normal probability distribution is defined from $-\infty$ to $+\infty$, and even for very large z-scores, there is an infinitesimal non-zero density. Therefore, the inverse Normal will return $\pm\infty$ for either $z(0)$ or $z(1)$. In group data, and even in most experimental syntax applications, this will not often be a problem because it will be rare to have perfect performance. However in individual data, it is more likely a participant will respond entirely consistently in at least one condition. In those cases, a correction must be made so that $z(\bullet)$ is defined. The simplest option is to add a trial to the total count, and then split it evenly between "yes" and "no." Thus someone who gave 10 out of 10 (correct) "yes" responses, would be coded as having a corrected p.c of 10.5/11, or 0.955, and a correct p.err of 0.5/11, or 0.045. This is a form of "smoothing" that is used when estimating probabilities off empirical data; for a full discussion of the different approaches to correcting for extreme performance, see Hautus (1995).

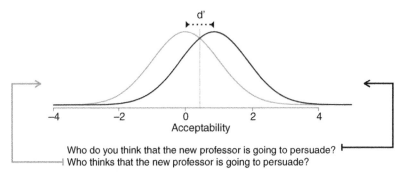

**Figure 3.3** Implied equal-variance signal/noise distributions in Bare/VP Gap conditions

Observe that these two distributions overlap substantially, and errorful performance is thus guaranteed. Participants will sometimes misidentify grammatical sentences as ungrammatical, and vice versa.

The optimal strategy to minimize errors is to set a response criterion halfway between the two peaks of the distributions – i.e. where the two density functions intersect (indicated by the dashed line; Theodoridis & Koutroumbas 2008). For any given value of acceptability the ratio of the heights of these two distributions (the black Grammatical distribution; the dark grey Ungrammatical distribution) define the odds that a given Acceptability value was drawn from that distribution. For higher values of acceptability, the odds in favor of the grammatical distribution grow. Where the two intersect, the odds are even – so values above that point on the *x*-axis should elicit a Grammatical/"yes" response and values below that point should elicit an Ungrammatical/"no" response. We can characterize *bias* in the experiment as how far away from this optimum the actual criterion was set. This value, *c*, can be calculated as follows:

(13)
```
# Write a function to implement c=-[z(Hits)+z(FA)]/2
bias.ev <- function(Hits, FA) {
  bias <- (qnorm(Hits)+qnorm(FA))*(-1/2)
  return(bias)
}
> bias.ev(0.664, 0.333)
[1] 0.004119758
```

In our dataset it is very close to 0, which suggests that overall bias is low in the experiment. The positive sign indicates a (slight) relative surplus of "no" responses; we will refer to positive values of *c* as "conservative" response strategies, and negative values of *c* as "liberal" response strategies. We can spot check this calculation by observing that Hits (0.664) in the Grammatical condition are nearly identical to Correct Rejections in the matched Ungrammatical condition (1–0.333=0.667; please see Table 3.2).

Table 3.3 *Summary of sensitivity and bias in the equal variance analysis*

|          | WhP    | $d'$  | $c$    |
|----------|--------|-------|--------|
| 1 gap    | Bare   | 0.855 | 0.004  |
| 2 gap    | D-link | 0.966 | 0.021  |
| 3 filled | Bare   | 2.031 | -0.115 |
| 4 filled | D-link | 2.034 | 0.168  |

A positive value for $c$ indicates that the empirical response criterion is somewhat higher (more conservative) than optimal: there are more "no" responses than optimal. Had there been more "yes" responses than optimal, we would have expected a greater Hit rate in grammatical conditions, but a lower Correct Rejection rate in ungrammatical conditions. And correspondingly we would have obtained a negative $c$. In Table 3.3, the values for $d'$/sensitivity and $c$/bias are given for pairs of conditions, grammatical and ungrammatical variants, within each level of VP-type and WhP-type. Impressionistically we can see that D-linked *wh*-phrases increase participants' sensitivity to conditions with a Gap in embedded object position, but not those with a Filled Gap (i.e. indefinite DP argument). There is bias shift in VP Filled Gap conditions, from more "yes" responses than optimal (negative $c$) when the WhP is bare to more "no" responses than optimal (positive $c$), when the WhP is D-linked. The bias measure $c$, in the context of our current experimental design, may be interpreted as a reflection of factors that influence the acceptability of a sentence class that are independent of the contrast of interest. For example, our observation that $c$ was greater for the filled D-link conditions means that there is some feature of the filled-gap D-linking stimuli that caused participants to reject them at higher rates than we would have expected: participants exhibited a tendency to reject these sentences. The fact that this effect was found in $c$, our bias measure, indicates that whatever the source of this effect, it is unrelated to the process of constructing a filler–gap dependency. It may be of independent interest in its own right, but in order to isolate and identify the source of this effect, we would need to find a plausible hypothesis about its source, and construct an experimental design that would allow us to isolate and test the factors that do create this effect. At present, this effect of D-linking appears to be a general effect on this class of sentences that is unrelated to the process of filler–gap dependency completion.

The foregoing analysis is a convenient representation of our forced-choice data – one which is arguably more digestible, as it transforms the dimensionality of the summary from 8 numbers to 4, setting bias aside. However, it makes a crucial assumption, one which we will usually find it necessary to relax. In Figure 3.3 the underlying Acceptability distributions have equal variance. But what if the Grammatical and Ungrammatical distributions over acceptability were not equal in variance? For the reasons explored in Section 3.4.2, knowing whether one class of sentences gives rise to a narrower or broader natural range of Acceptability values could be as theoretically revealing as knowing the centers of the distributions. To determine this, it will be necessary to construct a Receiver Operating Characteristic curve, or ROC curve.

### 3.3.2.2 Receiver Operating Characteristic Curve

An ROC curve describes Hits as a function of False Alarms across different degrees of bias. In our specimen experiment, we can construct this curve by grading our yes/no judgments using their confidence ratings. Consider the data just for the VP:Gap/WhP:Bare conditions, given in Table 3.4.

To construct the ROC, let us first reshape this table into a series of tables, as illustrated in Table 3.5. First, starting with "raw counts," we order the responses along a scale from "very confident" *yes* responses to "very confident" *no* responses.

While we analyze data from an experiment that combined a binary judgment of acceptability with a confidence rating, this is not necessary for the analysis that follows. In fact, the ROC analysis we pursue here is one that is in principle possible for any *n*-point Likert scale data. To highlight this equivalence, the columns in Table 3.5 are numbered from 6 to 1 descending. This numbering is both for convenience of reference but also to reinforce the mapping onto a common Likert response scale, and show how this analysis would be applied to similar data. While the analytical tools offered here may be applied to Likert scale data without loss of generality, it is not obvious that the quantitative results we report below would replicate with judgments collected in the Likert scale method (see Wagers & Dillon in prep).

Column 6 contains the most "very confident" *yes* responses to grammatical conditions. As a proportion (146/357), this represents 0.41 of all responses in that condition. Column 6 also contains the number of "very confident" *yes* responses to ungrammatical conditions; as a proportion (43/354), this represents 0.12 of all responses in that condition. We can think of this pair <0.12, 0.41> as a <FA, Hit> pair representing performance achieved with maximal *no* bias – only the highest Acceptability values would elicit a *yes* under that bias, and even then a few ungrammatical trials fall within that range. If we move to the next most stringent *no* bias, we would include the responses

Table 3.4 *Confidence ratings in VP:Gap/WhP:Bare conditions*

|   | VP WhP | Grammaticality | Answer.cr | No | Yes |
|---|---|---|---|---|---|
| 1 | gap bare | Gram | Not confident | 16 | 13 |
| 2 | gap bare | Gram | Somewhat confident | 53 | 78 |
| 3 | gap bare | Gram | Very confident | 51 | 146 |
| 4 | gap bare | Ungram | Not confident | 23 | 15 |
| 5 | gap bare | Ungram | Somewhat confident | 90 | 60 |
| 6 | gap bare | Ungram | Very confident | 123 | 43 |

Table 3.5 *Transforming confidence ratings to an ROC curve. Data shown are from the VP:Gap/WhP:Bare conditions*

**Raw counts**

| Grammatical? Confidence | YES | | | NO | | | |
|---|---|---|---|---|---|---|---|
| | Very | Smwhat | Not | Not | Smwhat | Very | Sum |
| | '6' | '5' | '4' | '3' | '2' | '1' | |
| GRAM | 146 | 78 | 13 | 16 | 53 | 51 | 357 |
| UNGRAM | 43 | 60 | 15 | 23 | 90 | 123 | 354 |

**Cumulative counts**

| Grammatical? Confidence | YES | | | NO | | | |
|---|---|---|---|---|---|---|---|
| | Very | Smwhat | Not | Not | Smwhat | Very | Sum |
| | '6' | '5' | '4' | '3' | '2' | '1' | |
| GRAM | 146 | 224 | 237 | 253 | 306 | 357 | 357 |
| UNGRAM | 43 | 103 | 118 | 141 | 231 | 354 | 354 |

**Cumulative proportions**

| Grammatical? Confidence | YES | | | NO | | | |
|---|---|---|---|---|---|---|---|
| | Very | Smwhat | Not | Not | Smwhat | Very | Sum |
| | '6' | '5' | '4' | '3' | '2' | '1' | |
| GRAM | 0.41 | 0.63 | 0.66 | 0.71 | 0.86 | 1 | 357 |
| UNGRAM | 0.12 | 0.29 | 0.33 | 0.40 | 0.65 | 1 | 354 |

under Column 5: 146+78 *Yes* responses to grammatical conditions (=224; =0.63) and 43+60 *yes* responses to ungrammatical conditions (=103; =0.29). Thus our next <FA, Hit> pair is <0.29, 0.63>. We continue doing this across the entire table – moving from conservative *no*-biased criteria to liberal *yes*-biased criteria. Ultimately, we will have generated a series of 6 pairs, culminating in <1, 1>. Intuitively, <1, 1> is what happens when we say *yes* to every trial: correctly capturing 100 percent of the grammatical conditions, but also trivially subsuming 100 percent of the ungrammatical conditions.

In Table 3.5, "Cumulative proportions," we've computed these pairs, and in Figure 3.4 (left column) we've plotted them, with False Alarms on the *x*-axis, and Hits on the *y*-axis. To complete these empirical ROCs, we added the point <0, 0>: what happens when we say *No* to every trial. Finally, we've gone ahead and – via the same method – computed the ROCs for all conditions in the experiment. In the right column, we've *z*-transformed each <FA, Hit> pair with the qnorm function. By inspecting the shape of these plots, we can already make a few first-pass conclusions about the underlying shape of the Acceptability distribution. Let us focus on the VP Gap conditions (in the top panels).

Firstly, in both the "raw" and *z*-transformed ROC curves, the dotted line indicates zero discrimination. But all curves representing our data, in blue, sit comfortably *above* that – our participants thus demonstrated the ability

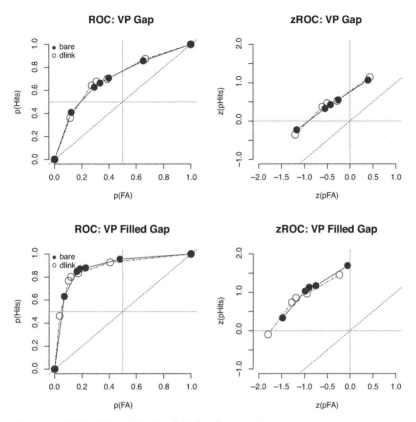

**Figure 3.4** ROCs, *left*, and zROCs, *right*, for all comparisons

to discriminate between the grammatical and ungrammatical conditions. This is akin to a positive $d'$ in the simple, equal variance calculation we performed in the previous section.

Secondly, notice that when we transformed the bowed ROC curve into $z$-coordinates, the resulting curve (for VP Gap) conditions is essentially a straight line. This is a good sign that the underlying distribution of acceptability is indeed normal (although this is in principle compatible with other distributions of acceptability). To a first approximation, this linear function seems consistent with the Gaussian observer model proposed by Bader and Häussler (2010). However, things look less clearly linear for the VP Filled Gap conditions, which still exhibit some curvilinearity in zROC space. As discussed below in Section 3.4.2, this is consistent with an underlying Acceptability distribution that is bimodal, or has some other kind of mixture distribution. The convex zROCs could also be attributed to other sources of noise in the data (Ratcliff, McKoon, & Tindall 1994).

Finally, you'll notice that the zROC line in VP Gap conditions is not quite parallel to the diagonal, and is somewhat shallow. In fact, its slope is less than 1. This is evidence that there is *more* variance in the Acceptability distribution for grammatical conditions than for ungrammatical conditions. Intuitively, the slope tells you the rate at which Hits accrue relative to False Alarms. A slope less than 1 means that Hits accrue relatively more slowly than False Alarms, a fact which implies greater variance in the signal (Grammatical) distribution. More precisely, the slope of the zROC is the ratio of the variance in the noise distribution to the variance in the signal distribution. For a slope of $s$, and a signal distribution whose variance is scaled to 1, then the variance of the noise distribution will be $s$; if instead the noise distribution's variance is scaled to 1, then the slope of the zROC is $1/s$, and $s$ is the variance in the signal distribution.

In (14) we make a simple estimate of $s$ by calling R's `lm` function, which returns the intercept and slope (in that order).[4] For WhP:Bare/VP:Gap conditions, $s$ is 0.8216.

(14)
```
> zFA <- qnorm(FA)
> zHits <- qnorm(Hits)
> lm(zHits~zFA)


Call:
lm(formula = zHits ~ zFA)


Coefficients:
(Intercept)  zFA
0.7609       0.8288
```

The fact that the variance of the underlying Acceptability distributions is unequal complicates the use of $d'$ as a simple measure of sensitivity because the obtained sensitivity will now vary with criterion. In geometric terms, $d'$ can be thought of as the distance between the zROC and the chance diagonal (zHits = zFA). When the slope of the zROC is 1, then this distance is constant across the range of zFA, and can be read directly off the intercept. But now distance to the zROC line varies along the range of zFA, and therefore $d'$ varies. If we want to express sensitivity by a single number, then we will have to take into account the fact that the underlying Acceptability distributions differ in their variance.

The measure $d_a$ makes a kind of compromise by scaling the difference in the means of the Acceptability distributions by the root-mean-square average of their variances. Algebraically, this comes to the expression in (15), and the R calculation illustrated in (16). The value $d'_2$ is the $y$-intercept of the empirical zROC.

---

[4] We offer estimate only as an example. It is not generally advisable to use linear regression to find the slope; this is because the $x$- and $y$-coordinates in the ROC both constitute dependent variables, and the estimate of each is subject to uncertainty. Getting a reliable estimate of $s$ involves fitting a full SDT model to the data, for example using Maximum Likelihood Estimation. To make a full UVSDT analysis accessible to researchers with a range of modeling backgrounds, Pazzaglia, Dubé, and Rotello (2013) published an implementation of this using Excel's SOLVER function.

(15)

$$d_a = \sqrt{\frac{2}{1+s^2}} \cdot d_{2'}$$

(16)
```
> emp.zROC <- lm(zHits~zFA)
> deetwo <- coef(emp.zROC)[1] # y-intercept
> s <- coef(emp.zROC)[2]      # slope
> da <- function(deetwo, s) sqrt(2/(1+s^2)) * deetwo
> da(deetwo, s)
[1] 0.8285487
```

The equation above may not be entirely intuitive at first. But it has another guise in a proportional measure of sensitivity that is perhaps more visually comprehensible: $A_z$.

$A_z$ is the area under the fitted normal ROC curve. Figure 3.5 demonstrates this graphically for the Bare/VP Gap conditions. The observed data points are given in blue, and the solid black line is the best-fitting curve to those points, constrained to describe the ratio between two normal distributions. The shaded area corresponds to all points <x,y> below the solid black line: here it covers 72.1 percent of the area, or $A_z = 0.721$. If there were no sensitivity in our experiment, such that Hits = FA, then $A_z$ would

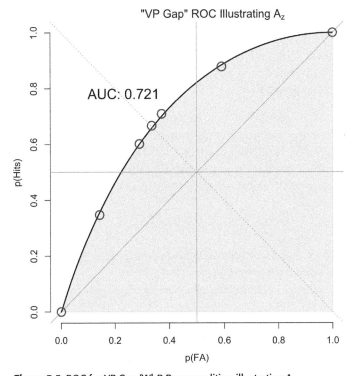

**Figure 3.5** ROC for VP Gap/WhP Bare condition illustrating $A_z$

be 0.5 – everything below the major diagonal. If there were perfect sensi-tivity, the shading would fill the entire plot, and $A_z$ would equal 1.

More generally, the area under the ROC curve is one important index of sensitivity. If one assumes that the underlying distributions that generate the ROC are normal, then $A_z$ equals the area under the curve (AUC). However, it is also possible to calculate the area under the ROC curve without making this assumption about the parametric shape of the under-lying distributions; in this case, the area under an empirical ROC can be calculated by simply using the "trapezoid" method, that is, successively summing the areas of trapezoids that connect the points in the empirical ROC (Melo 2013). It remains to be seen whether, in general, the assump-tion of normal acceptability distributions yields a good fit to acceptability judgment data. In our experience, however, fitted normal–normal ROCs often yield a very good fit to empirical ROCs (indeed; this can be seen in Figure 3.5: the empirical points lie quite close to the fitted curve).

$A_z$ can be converted to $d_a$ and vice-versa. The equation and code-snippet in (17) shows how to do this in both directions. We used the R library *pROC* (Robin et al. 2011) to fit the normal–normal ROC curve in Figure 3.5, to compute $A_z$ and to create the plot. In Section 3.4, we return to some recom-mendations about software and procedures.

(17)   a.      $d_a = \Phi^{-1}(A_z)\sqrt{2}$

```
> Az2 Da <- function (Az) qnorm (Az) * sqrt (2)
> Az2 Da (0.721)
[1] 0.8284672
```

   b.      $A_z = \Phi(d_a/\sqrt{2})$

```
> Da2Az <- function (Da) pnorm (Da/sqrt (2))
> Da2Az (0.8284672)
[1] 0.721
```

Table 3.6 summarizes the four crucial comparisons in our experiment, reporting both $d_a$ and $A_z$. Finally we report $s$, the ratio of the variance in the noise/ungrammatical distribution to the signal/grammatical distribution, as estimated from the zROC line. Figure 3.6 plots the implied Acceptability distributions.

Table 3.6 *Summary of sensitivity and variance in unequal variance analysis*

| VP | WhP | $d_a$ | $A_z$ | s |
|----|-----|-------|-------|---|
| 1 gap | bare | 0.83 | 0.72 | 0.83 |
| 2 gap | D-link | 0.86 | 0.73 | 0.89 |
| 3 filled | bare | 2.0 | 0.91 | 0.92 |
| 4 filled | D-link | 1.9 | 0.91 | 0.95 |

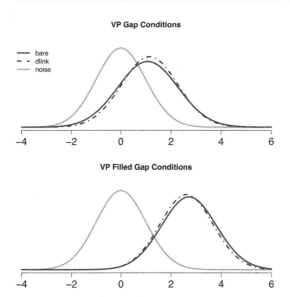

**Figure 3.6** Implied unequal-variance signal/noise distributions

### 3.3.3 Interpreting the Results

Constructing the ROC curve shows that, in our experiment, D-linking had, a best, a modest impact on sensitivity (and a non-significant one; see Section 3.4.1). It did not greatly shift the distribution of Acceptability. There was a modest effect on $s$, suggesting relatively less variance in the grammatical distribution when the WhP was D-linked compared to when it was bare.[5] Participants were considerably more sensitive in VP Filled Gap conditions. We hypothesize that this is because all of the information required to discriminate between grammatical and ungrammatical conditions accumulates before retrieval is ever necessary. The presence of the "filled gap" is enough to classify the ungrammatical sentences as ungrammatical. In other words, in these sentences, retrieval may never happen (cf. Wagers & Phillips 2014). Interestingly here D-linking modestly reduces sensitivity, which suggests that the distinctiveness, or goodness-of-fit, of the restricted *wh*-phrase makes it a tempting, if ungrammatical, lure to integrate into the filled gap site.

## 3.4 Discussion and Conclusions

In this chapter, we have pointed out that many standard methods of measuring acceptability judgments fall short as true interval

---

[5] Our results are not straightforwardly compatible with the finding of Goodall (2015) that D-linking improves acceptability even in non-island dependencies. That paper does note the existence of prior studies which also found limited effects of D-linking in non-island dependencies. But we do not read too much into this apparent non-replication, given the substantial differences between our two studies. We leave it as an area for future investigation.

measurements of acceptability, a situation that interferes with the statistical analysis of acceptability judgment data, and which presents a problem for researchers interested in drawing inferences from the distribution and gradience in their acceptability judgment data. Following Bader and Häussler (2010), we proposed that Signal Detection Theory offers a set of analytical tools that can resolve these issues. We presented a specimen experiment aimed at investigating the processing of filler–gap dependencies using acceptability judgment measurements, and a worked Signal Detection Theoretic analysis of these data. We discussed simple indices of sensitivity (such as $d'$) and ROC analysis as ways of quantifying the contrast in acceptability between two types of sentences.

For reasons of space, this is as far as this chapter can take us. However, there are many open, unresolved issues; researchers interested in applying SDT to their own judgment data will face these issues in practice. The most pressing of these issues is the issue of statistical inference with this type of analysis. For interested readers, we have made available an expanded pre-print of this chapter on the Open Scientific Framework at https://osf.io/wbd3v/. There, we take up these issues in more detail, including a tutorial on how to implement this analysis using a regression-based framework.

### 3.4.1 Why SDT?

We would like to close by reflecting on the question of why we think that the SDT approach pursued here should be pursued as an analytical approach to experimental syntax data. First, and perhaps foremost, is the simple observation that most work in experimental syntax implicitly, yet incorrectly, assumes that data from $n$-point ratings offers an interval scale measurement. This assumption underlies the simple tabulation of descriptive statistics like mean rating value and standard error, and the interval scale assumption is required for inferential statistical tests (most pressingly for those involving interactions). Despite this, it is widely recognized that ordinal Likert rating data does generally yield interval measurements of acceptability (cf. Cowart 1997). Interval-scale measurements are precisely what SDT's measures of discriminability and bias offer, making them more appropriate as scale-independent descriptive measures of effect size and (often) better dependent measures for the purposes of statistical inference.

Second, it seems to us that the theoretical perspective implied by the SDT model – an uncertain observer who maps a noisy, unidimensional acceptability value onto one of a handful of discrete response options – is a useful theoretical perspective on the acceptability judgment process. It offers a precise model for how acceptability judgment responses are given in the context of a judgment task, and it makes explicit the key parameters of the acceptability decision task (acceptability versus scale usage). Should it prove to be a valid model of the acceptability judgment task, this model will allow researchers to ask more precise questions about acceptability judgment data.

Last, there is a broader reason why we think the SDT perspective is useful for experimental syntax: it suggests a useful experimental design heuristic. In our specimen experiment, we expanded the experimental design of Goodall (2015) to include ungrammatical and grammatical variants of each condition. Part of this motivation was analytical: SDT analysis requires the analyst to sample both from the "signal" and the "noise" distributions, with the latter offering an unacceptable baseline that in turn allows the analyst to quantify response bias or scale usage for a given structural configuration. But these baselines also served to make a more diagnostic experimental design. Specifically, they allowed us to potentially distinguish the impact of D-linking on the retrieval of a filler phrase (i.e. the hypothesis we were testing) from other nuisance factors that might have contributed to differential ratings for D-linked and bare *wh*-phrases. In the context of our SDT analysis, these nuisance factors were captured in our "response bias" measures, which reflected baseline differences in the ratings between *d*-linked and bare *wh*-phrases. In this way, the SDT analysis and concomitant design heuristics may prove useful to experimental syntacticians in developing experimental designs that can help reduce some of this interpretive uncertainty.

### 3.4.2 Variance in Underlying Distributions

In this chapter we have focused on the role that ROC analysis can play in distinguishing sensitivity from bias in acceptability judgment experiments. But we also suggested at the outset that ROC analysis can help us ask more fine-grained distributional questions about acceptability judgment data. One way in which ROC analysis allows researchers to do this is by permitting some comparison of the relative variance in two stimulus categories: above, we did this by estimating the slope of the zROC. Recall that the slope of the zROC reflects the ratio of the variances of their Acceptability distributions. For this reason, the empirical (*z*)ROC can be informative about the relative variance in the stimulus categories. In other areas where ROC analysis is applied, a difference in slope has proven to be theoretically meaningful (Ratcliff, Sheu, & Gronlund 1992). The shape of the ROC can also in principle reflect more unusual distributions of acceptability. For example, if one underlying distribution is bimodal or other type of mixture distribution, then the resulting ROCs can exhibit curvilinearity (see de Carlo (2002) for extended discussion).

To illustrate this, let us return to the bimodal distribution of acceptability judgments in Dillon et al. (2017). (21a) is the critical configuration that Dillon and colleagues wanted to investigate; recall that the central empirical question was whether the distribution of ratings associated with these examples was bimodal or unimodal. (21b) is a matched ungrammatical control from Dillon et al.'s study that can be used for the purposes of SDT scaling.

(21)    a. Which flowers is the gardener planting?
        b. Which flowers is the gardeners planting?

The aggregated distribution of ratings is in the leftmost panel of Figure 3.7. It can be seen that there is a pronounced bimodality for (21a). Earlier, we raised the concern that the conclusions Dillon et al. drew on the basis of this could reflect a potential artifact of how the scale is used. However, in the middle and rightmost panels of Figure 3.7 we see a pronounced curvilinearity in the ROC, which is characteristic of a bimodal or mixture distribution (de Carlo 2002). The ROC analysis is consistent with the conclusion reached on the basis of reasoning about the distribution of raw Likert ratings: both suggest that the underlying acceptability distribution for sentences like *which flowers is the gardener planting* is bimodal.

Although in this instance, the conclusion licensed by the raw data and the ROC analysis align, this is not guaranteed. The broader point is that claims based on apparent distributions in Likert data are not watertight; ROC analysis can help secure empirical conclusions based on the distribution of rating data.

### 3.4.3    Conclusions

In this chapter, we have sketched how Signal Detection Theory can be applied to acceptability judgment data. We have argued that latent variable models such as SDT hold substantial promise for experimental syntacticians by offering a way of precisely answering the quantitative question in experimental syntax: *to what extent is sentence type A better than, or worse than, sentence type B?* We offered a worked, tutorial-style analysis of a sample dataset to show how ROC analysis can be applied to a dataset that has a similar structure to *n*-point rating tasks and binary forced-choice acceptability judgments in experimental syntax.

In closing, we noted several challenges that arise in the context of the analytical approach pursued here. In particular, there are unresolved issues concerning statistical inference using ROCs. A bit further afield, we note that the paradigm we used here – binary judgments with a secondary confidence rating – may yield results that are different from the Likert scale ratings that are more commonly deployed in the experimental syntax literature. Head-to-head comparisons of these methods of collecting judgment data would be valuable. Despite these challenges, we hope to have communicated our enthusiasm for this approach, and the promises we see for its application to acceptability judgment data.

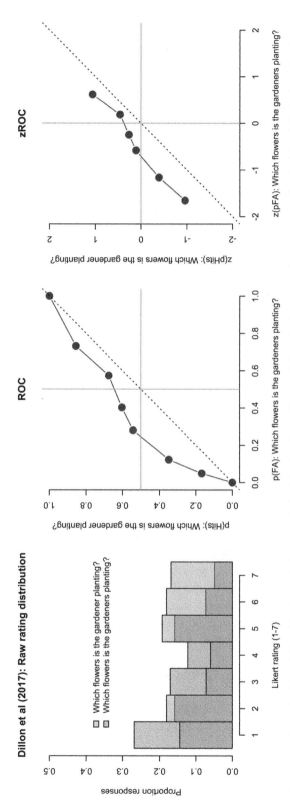

**Figure 3.7** Diagnosing bimodality with ROC analysis: a reanalysis of the data from Dillon et al. (2017). The ROC and zROC suggest that the bimodality in the rating data does not reflect a simple bias toward extreme responses in the task.

# References

Aarts, B. (2007). *Syntactic gradience: The nature of grammatical indeterminacy.* Oxford: Oxford University Press.

Alexopoulou, T. & Keller, F. (2007). Locality, cyclicity, and resumption: At the interface between the grammar and the human sentence processor. *Language*, 83(1), 110–160.

Almeida, D. (2014). Subliminal wh-islands in Brazilian Portuguese and the consequences for syntactic theory. *Revista da ABRALIN*, 13(2), 55–91.

Baayen, R. H., Davidson, D. J., & Bates, D. M. (2008). Mixed-effects modeling with crossed random effects for subjects and items. *Journal of Memory and Language*, 59(4), 390–412.

Bader, M. & Häussler, J. (2010). Toward a model of grammaticality judgments. *Journal of Linguistics*, 46(2), 273–330.

Bard, E. G., Robertson, D., & Sorace, A. (1996). Magnitude estimation of linguistic acceptability. *Language*, 71(2), 32–68.

Bock, K. & Middleton, E. L. (2011). Reaching agreement. *Natural Language & Linguistic Theory*, 29(4), 1033–1069.

Bürkner, P. C. & Vuorre, M. (2019). Ordinal regression models in psychology: A tutorial. *Advances in Methods and Practices in Psychological Science*, 2(1), 77–101.

Clark, H. H. (1973). The language-as-fixed-effect fallacy: A critique of language statistics in psychological research. *Journal of Verbal Learning and Verbal Behavior*, 12(4), 335–359.

Cowart, W. (1997). *Experimental Syntax*. Thousand Oaks, CA: Sage.

DeCarlo, L. T. (2002). Signal detection theory with finite mixture distributions: Theoretical developments with applications to recognition memory. *Psychological Review*, 109(4), 710.

DeLong, E. R., DeLong, D. M., & Clarke-Pearson, D. L. (1988). Comparing the areas under two or more correlated receiver operating characteristic curves: A nonparametric approach. *Biometrics*, 44(3), 837–845.

Dillon, B., Andrews, C., Rotello, C. M., & Wagers, M. (2019). A new argument for co-active parses during language comprehension. *Journal of Experimental Psychology: Learning, Memory, and Cognition*, 45(7), 1271.

Dillon, B., Staub, A., Levy, J., & Clifton Jr., C. (2017). Which noun phrases is the verb supposed to agree with? Object agreement in American English. *Language*, 93(1), 65–96.

Drummond, A. (2013). Ibex farm. Online server: http://spellout.net /ibexfarm.

Dube, C., Rotello, C. M., & Heit, E. (2010). Assessing the belief bias effect with ROCs: It's a response bias effect. *Psychological Review*, 117 (3), 831.

Efron, B. & Tibshirani, R. (1993). *An Introduction to the Bootstrap*. London: Chapman & Hall.

Featherston, S. (2008). Thermometer judgments as linguistic evidence. In C. M. Riehl & A. Rothe (eds.), *Was ist linguistische Evidenz?* Aachen: Shaker Verlag, pp. 69–90.

Featherston, S. (2009). Relax, lean back, and be a linguist. *Zeitschrift für Sprachwissenschaft*, 28(1), 127–32.

Franck, J. (2011). Reaching agreement as a core syntactic process. *Natural Language & Linguistic Theory*, 29(4), 1071–1086.

Fukuda, S., Goodall, G., Michel, D., & Beecher, H. (2012). Is Magnitude Estimation worth the trouble? In J. Choi, E. A. Hogue, J. Punske, D. Tat, J. Schertz, & A. Trueman, eds., *Proceedings of the 29th West Coast Conference on Formal Linguistics*. Somerville, MA: Cascadilla Proceedings Project, pp. 328–336.

Gahl, S., Jurafsky, D., & Roland, D. (2004). Verb subcategorization frequencies: American English corpus data, methodological studies, and cross-corpus comparisons. *Behavior Research Methods, Instruments, & Computers*, 36(3), 432–443.

Goodall, G. (2015). The D-linking effect on extraction from islands and non-islands. *Frontiers in Psychology*, 5, 1493.

Gordon, P. C., Hendrick, R., & Johnson, M. (2001). Memory interference during language processing. *Journal of Experimental Psychology: Learning, Memory, and Cognition*, 27(6), 1411.

Hanley, J. A. & McNeil, B. J. (1983). A method of comparing the areas under receiver operating characteristic curves derived from the same cases. *Radiology*, 148(3), 839–843.

Häussler, J., Grant, M., Fanselow, G., & Frazier, L. (2015). Superiority in English and German: Cross-language grammatical differences? *Syntax*, 18(3), 235–265.

Hautus, M. J. (1995). Corrections for extreme proportions and their biasing effects on estimated values of d′. *Behavior Research Methods, Instruments, & Computers*, 27(1), 46–51.

Hautus, M. J. (1997). Calculating estimates of sensitivity from group data: Pooled versus averaged estimators. *Behavior Research Methods, Instruments, & Computers*, 29(4), 556–562.

Heit, E. & Rotello, C. M. (2014). Traditional difference-score analyses of reasoning are flawed. *Cognition*, 131(1), 75–91.

Jaeger, T. F. (2008). Categorical data analysis: Away from ANOVAs (transformation or not) and towards logit mixed models. *Journal of Memory and Language*, 59(4), 434–446.

Keller, F. (2000). Gradience in grammar: Experimental and computational aspects of degrees of grammaticality. Doctoral dissertation, University of Edinburgh.

Kush, D., Lohndal, T., & Sprouse, J. (2018). Investigating variation in island effects. *Natural Language & Linguistic Theory*, 36(3), 743–779.

Langsford, S., Perfors, A., Hendrickson, A. T., Kennedy, L. A., & Navarro, D. J. (2018). Quantifying sentence acceptability measures: Reliability, bias, and variability. *Glossa: A Journal of General Linguistics*, 3(1). DOI: 10.5334/gjgl.396

Lau, J. H., Clark, A., & Lappin, S. (2017). Grammaticality, acceptability, and probability: A probabilistic view of linguistic knowledge. *Cognitive Science*, 41(5), 1202–1241.

Liddell, T. M. & Kruschke, J. K. (2018). Analyzing ordinal data with metric models: What could possibly go wrong? *Journal of Experimental Social Psychology*, 79, 328–348.

Liu, C. C. & Smith, P. L. (2009). Comparing time-accuracy curves: Beyond goodness-of-fit measures. *Psychonomic Bulletin & Review*, 16(1), 190–203.

Loftus, G. R. (1978). On interpretation of interactions. *Memory & Cognition*, 6 (3), 312–319.

Ma, H., Bandos, A. I., Rockette, H. E., & Gur, D. (2013). On use of partial area under the ROC curve for evaluation of diagnostic performance. *Statistics in Medicine*, 32(20), 3449–3458.

Macmillan, N. A. & Creelman, C. D. (2005). *Detection Theory: A User's Guide*. Mahwah, NJ: Lawrence Erlbaum.

Macmillan, N. A. & Kaplan, H. L. (1985). Detection theory analysis of group data: Estimating sensitivity from average hit and false-alarm rates. *Psychological Bulletin*, 98(1), 185.

Macmillan, N. A., Rotello, C. M., & Miller, J. O. (2004). The sampling distributions of Gaussian ROC statistics. *Perception & Psychophysics*, 66(3), 406–421.

Mauner, G. (1995). Examining the empirical and linguistic bases of current theories of agrammatism. *Brain and Language*, 50(3), 339–368.

McElree, B. (2000). Sentence comprehension is mediated by content-addressable memory structures. *Journal of Psycholinguistic Research*, 29(2), 111–123.

McElree, B., Foraker, S., & Dyer, L. (2003). Memory structures that subserve sentence comprehension. *Journal of Memory and Language*, 48(1), 67–91.

Melo, F. (2013). Area under the ROC curve. In W. Dubitzky, O. Wolkenhauer, K. H. Cho, & H. Yokota, eds., *Encyclopedia of Systems Biology*. New York: Springer New York, pp. 38–39.

Pazzaglia, A. M., Dube, C., & Rotello, C. M. (2013). A critical comparison of discrete-state and continuous models of recognition memory: Implications for recognition and beyond. *Psychological Bulletin*, 139(6), 1173.

Ratcliff, R., McKoon, G., & Tindall, M. (1994). Empirical generality of data from recognition memory receiver-operating characteristic functions and implications for the global memory models. *Journal of Experimental Psychology: Learning, Memory, and Cognition*, 20(4), 763.

Ratcliff, R., Sheu, C. F., & Gronlund, S. D. (1992). Testing global memory models using ROC curves. *Psychological Review*, 99(3), 518.

Robin, X., Turck, N., Hainard, A., Tiberti, N., Lisacek, F., Sanchez, J. C., & Müller, M. (2011). pROC: An open-source package for R and S+ to analyze and compare ROC curves. *BMC Bioinformatics*, 12(1), 77.

Rotello, C. M., Heit, E., & Dubé, C. (2015). When more data steer us wrong: Replications with the wrong dependent measure perpetuate erroneous conclusions. *Psychonomic Bulletin & Review*, 22(4), 944–954.

Schütze, C. T. (1996). *The Empirical Base of Linguistics: Grammaticality Judgments and Linguistic Methodology*. Chicago: University of Chicago Press.

Schütze, C. T. & Sprouse, J. (2014). Judgment data. In R. Podesva & D. Sharma, eds., *Research Methods in Linguistics*. Cambridge: Cambridge University Press, pp. 27–50.

Sorace, A. & Keller, F. (2005). Gradience in linguistic data. *Lingua*, 115(11), 1497–1524.

Sprouse, J. (2011). A test of the cognitive assumptions of magnitude estimation: Commutativity does not hold for acceptability judgments. *Language* 87(2), 274–288.

Sprouse, J. & Almeida, D. (2012). Assessing the reliability of textbook data in syntax: Adger's Core Syntax. *Journal of Linguistics*, 48, 609–652.

Sprouse, J. & Almeida, D. (2017). Design sensitivity and statistical power in acceptability judgment experiments. *Glossa: A Journal of General Linguistics*, 2(1), 1–32. DOI:10.5334/gjgl.236

Sprouse, J., Caponigro, I., Greco, C., & Cecchetto, C. (2016). Experimental syntax and the variation of island effects in English and Italian. *Natural Language & Linguistic Theory*, 34(1), 307–344.

Sprouse, J., Schütze, C. T., & Almeida, D. (2013). A comparison of informal and formal acceptability judgments using a random sample from *Linguistic Inquiry* 2001–2010. *Lingua*, 134, 219–248.

Sprouse, J., Wagers, M., & Phillips, C. (2012). A test of the relation between working-memory capacity and syntactic island effects. *Language*, 88, 82–123.

Sprouse, J., Yankama, B., Indurkhya, S., Fong, S., & Berwick, R. C. (2018). Colorless green ideas do sleep furiously: gradient acceptability and the nature of the grammar. *Linguistic Review*, 35(3), 575–599.

Stevens, S. S. (1956). The direct estimation of sensory magnitudes: Loudness. *American Journal of Psychology*, 69(1), 1–25.

Stevens, S. S. (1960). The psychophysics of sensory function. *American Scientist*, 48(2), 226–253.

Theodoridis, S. & Koutroumbas, K. (2008). *Pattern Recognition*. Burlington, MA: Academic Press.

Venkatraman, E. S. (2000). A permutation test to compare receiver operating characteristic curves. *Biometrics*, 56, 1134–1138.

Wagers, M. (2013). Memory mechanisms for wh-dependency formation and their implications for islandhood. In J. Sprouse & N. Hornstein (eds.), *Experimental Syntax and Island Effects*. Cambridge: Cambridge University Press, pp. 161–185.

Wagers, M. & Dillon, B. (in prep). Which sentences do speakers favor? ROC analysis of *d*-linking in filler–gap integration.

Wagers, M. W. & Phillips, C. (2014). Going the distance: memory and control processes in active dependency construction. *The Quarterly Journal of Experimental Psychology*, 67(7), 1274–1304.

Warstadt, A., Singh, A., & Bowman, S. R. (2018). Neural network acceptability judgments. arXiv preprint arXiv:1805.12471.

Weskott, T. & Fanselow, G. (2011). On the informativity of different measures of linguistic acceptability. *Language*, 87(2), 249–273.

# 4

# Variation in Participants and Stimuli in Acceptability Experiments

Jana Häussler and Tom S. Juzek

## 4.1 Introduction

Variation is an inherent feature of human language. Variation can be observed at all levels of language, both across speakers and within a single speaker. Different speakers use various ways to express the same meaning and a single speaker speaks differently, depending on the situation. The choices made by a speaker in a given situation are subject to several linguistic (linguistic context, communicative purpose, etc.) and non-linguistic factors (age, gender, social setting, etc.). Sociolinguists took an early interest in the variation between speakers in their usage of language (e.g. Labov 1966). Meanwhile, the study of linguistic variation is an integral and highly productive part of many fields of linguistic research, not only sociolinguistics or variationist linguistics.

At the same time, variability can be considered an obstacle for theory building, an epiphenomenon that is due to non-linguistic factors and that needs to be peeled off to see the core. Formal syntacticians idealize and abstract away from variation because they are interested in linguistic competence underlying the observed performance. Chomsky argues that any serious study will "abstract away from variation tentatively regarded as insignificant and from external interference dismissed as irrelevant at a given stage of inquiry" (Chomsky 1980). The idealization of homogeneity places variability outside the grammar. Variation occurs between grammars of different varieties. Intra-speaker variation may arise from the coexistence of separate grammars in the speaker (e.g. Kroch 1989). All other instances of variability are attributed to performance.

Experimental data can help to understand and abstract away from undesired variability, by distinguishing variation from noise. However, doing so can be difficult. In experimental data, and here we focus on data from sentence acceptability experiments, both variation and noise come in the form of variance. In fact, what distinguishes variation from noise is just a matter of definition. Variation is the variance that one is interested in, that is it is informative, and sometimes even desired. Such variation comes from linguistic sources (most notably from differing grammars) and often from extralinguistic variables that are speaker related (first language, dialect, age, gender, etc.). Noise, on the other hand, is the undesired and/or non-informative part of one's data. Such noise often comes from extralinguistic sources and includes lapses in attention or methodological artifacts.

The aim of this chapter is to discuss various sources of variation and noise, how to disentangle them, and how to interpret them. Arguably, all linguists view variation stemming from the grammar as informative. Such variation is discussed in Section 4.2. Section 4.3 discusses variation in the stimuli. Variation from social and demographic factors is also viewed as informative by most, if not all linguists, even by researchers who are not concerned with such factors. Those extragrammatical factors are discussed in Section 4.4.1. Other sources of variation, like memory limitations, are treated as confounds by some linguists, but are central for others, particularly psycholinguists and other linguists with an interest in cognitive processes. Such factors are discussed in Section 4.4.2 onwards. There are, however, some factors that most linguists view as noise, for example scale effects or the impact of non-cooperative behavior. Such methodological artifacts are discussed in Section 4.5. Section 4.6 provides a brief overview of statistical procedures.

## 4.2   Variation in the Grammar

For a long time, generative syntacticians pursued a strong idealization: speech communities are homogeneous, their native speakers converge on the same grammar. Under this view, individual differences, and most factors discussed in this chapter, are considered to be noise, from which linguistic theories have to abstract away when describing a grammar. However, even at strong levels of abstraction, variation occurs within what is often viewed as one speaker community, i.e. differences between closely related varieties, traditionally labeled as dialects. Such smaller differences within a speaker community are now discussed as microvariations (see Brandner (2012) for an overview).

### 4.2.1   Grammatical Microvariation

Participants in an acceptability judgment experiment (or any other kind of experiment) are not the ideal speaker–listeners Chomsky defined in *Aspects* (Chomsky 1965). In contrast to the ideal speaker–listener, real participants do not live in a homogeneous speech-community. Most speakers are bilingual under some definition, especially when we include active command of two closely related varieties (e.g. dialects of one language). Oftentimes, there are no sharp boundaries between dialects and it is virtually impossible to recruit homogeneous groups of speakers. As a result, speakers in the sample may base their decision on slightly different grammars. In this case, the variation would be informative about the different varieties and their respective grammars. Extracting this information, however, requires identifying groups of speakers, e.g. using cluster analysis (Gervain 2003). In practice, it is nearly impossible to establish dialectal differences post hoc in a single experiment, but explorative analyses can motivate further experiments which then include dialect or regional background as an independent variable. Several studies have shown that it is possible to identify dialectal differences by means of acceptability studies (e.g. Guajardo & Goodall (2019) for varieties of Spanish; Salzmann et al. (2013) for varieties of German).

The description and analysis of microvariation between closely related and in many respects similar varieties deepens our understanding of the language faculty and the ways languages may vary (cf. Brandner 2012). However, this kind of variation will always be there, including experiments that are not designed to examine microvariation. In this case, the variation is considered to be noise. Yet the variation affects the data and decreases the chance of finding an effect. In the worst case, two varieties that behave differently with respect to the factor under investigation are represented by an equal number of participants, such that they cancel each other out when averaging across all participants.

### Practical Recommendations

- Support the target variety by making appropriate lexical choices. This strategy is not perfect, but is the best practice so far. There is no guarantee that speakers can distinguish between two varieties at all in every single instance, especially when the two varieties are closely related and overlap to a great extent.
- Check for microvariation as a grouping factor: check for a multimodal distribution (e.g. through visual inspection by means of a histogram or a heat map) or apply cluster analysis (Gervain 2003).
- Use Linear Mixed Effects (LME) modeling to estimate the variation contributed by participants (see Baayen 2008; Winter 2019).
- If possible, include Group as a factor in the statistical analyses.

## 4.3   Variation across and within Items

Linguistic stimuli are intrinsically associated with a range of linguistic and extralinguistic factors which inevitably influence their acceptability. For this reason, experiments typically involve multiple items instantiating the same structure. In this way, unsystematic influences cancel each other out and judgments center around a "true" value for the corresponding structure (for a similar argument regarding random differences between participants see Featherston 2007). Ideally, items differ only in their lexical content but are identical in all other respects.[1] In reality, however, the variation in lexical content inevitably entails variation in other properties as well. Furthermore, items should not be too similar because otherwise participants might recognize the pattern and develop response strategies. The challenge is to find a good balance between similarity and variation. Appropriate fillers sharing some superficial features with the critical items but exhibiting other properties in terms of structure help as well.

To ensure that judgment differences between conditions are as much as possible due to the independent variables under investigation, items should differ between conditions as little as possible. In other words, a within-items design is preferable. Items are created as *paradigm-like token sets* (Cowart 1997: 13) and distributed across counterbalanced lists such that each list contains each item in only one of its versions and an equal number of items per condition. A token set consists of two or more versions (depending on the number of conditions) of an item (i.e. a lexicalization). Within each set, the versions should be identical as far as possible, differing only in the realization of the factor(s) under investigation. This is often hard to achieve. For instance, Clifton et al. (2006) examined the claim that a third *wh*-phrase amnesties a superiority violation in multiple *wh*-questions (Bolinger 1978; Kayne 1983). Their first experiment tested the obvious comparison between multiple questions violating superiority with and without a third *wh*-phrase.

(1)     a. What can who do about it?
        b. What can who do about it when?

The two versions of (1) are quite close to each other. Both are multiple questions in which the lower *wh*-phrase (the object *what*) is fronted while the higher *wh*-phrase (the subject *who*) stays in situ. Hence, both versions of (1) violate the superiority condition (Kuno & Robinson 1972; Chomsky 1973) which requires the higher of two *wh*-phrases to be fronted. The two versions of (1) differ in the presence of a third *wh*-phrase (*when* in (1b)), which is the factor under investigation. However, the presence of the third *wh*-phrase also changes the length of the sentence as well as its syntactic and semantic complexity. Since sentence length and complexity increase processing difficulty, which in turn is known to decrease acceptability (see Chapter 5 and Fanselow & Frisch (2006) for an overview), a potential mitigating effect of the third *wh*-phrase might be cancelled by the

---

[1] Accordingly, items are often called lexicalizations reflecting the idea that they represent the very same structure just with different lexical material.

increased difficulty. To examine this possibility, Clifton et al. (2006) included superiority obeying versions of (1) in a follow-up experiment.

(2)    a. What can who do about it?
    b. What can who do about it when?
    c. Who can do what about it?
    d. Who can do what about it when?

As expected, the versions obeying superiority, i.e. (2c) and (2d), received higher ratings than the versions violating superiority, i.e. (2a)/(2b). Crucially, however, mean ratings for (2a) and (2b) do not differ from each other (2.27 on a five-point scale) whereas mean ratings for (2c) are higher than for (2d) (3.73 vs. 3.02). The results show that length/complexity indeed does have an effect[2] and underline that including an appropriate control condition is vital (for further discussion on proper control conditions in this particular case see Gibson and Fedorenko (2010) and the response by Culicover and Jackendoff (2010), as well as Fedorenko and Gibson (2010)).

Pesetsky (1982) observed another factor that determines the strength of superiority: D(iscourse)-linking weakens or removes superiority effects (for experimental evidence see Hofmeister et al. 2007). A *wh*-phrase is D-linked when it triggers a choice from referents given in the discourse. A *wh*-phrase containing *which* calls for an answer identifying a referent out of a set already given in the discourse, e.g. *which book* asks for choosing a book or subset of books out of a pre-established set of books. Bare *wh*-pronouns like *what* typically do not refer to referents already part of discourse though they can. Discourse status correlates with accessibility and type of *wh*-expression (*which*-NP vs. bare *wh*-pronoun).

Speakers choose a referring expression according to the antecedent's degree of accessibility to the hearer (Givón 1983; Ariel 1990). If an antecedent is highly accessible, a pronoun is used; whereas for less accessible antecedents, non-pronominal expressions are used. Entities new to the discourse are typically introduced with an indefinite noun phrase (or a definite NP if the referent can be inferred from the given context; e.g. *the students* when talking about a lecture).

Accessibility is determined by the syntactic and discourse structure, including factors such as the topicality of the antecedent, the number and salience of competitors, the distance between the antecedent and the anaphoric noun phrase. At the same time, accessibility affects the ease of processing and also the acceptability of filler–gap dependencies. Object-extracted relative clauses are in general harder to process than subject-extracted relative clauses, but the effect decreases when the intervening subject is a pronoun (Warren & Gibson 2002). Likewise, accessibility has been shown to affect the processing and acceptability of cleft

---

[2] Note that nevertheless one cannot speak of an amnestying effect. Ratings for (2b) are clearly lower than for (2d).

sentences (Warren & Gibson 2005) and multiple *wh*-questions (Pesetsky 1982, 1987; Hofmeister et al. 2007).

Ease of retrieval is also relevant with respect to lexical retrieval. Lexical frequency is one of the factors determining the ease of lexical retrieval and it is also known to contribute to the acceptability of sentences containing the corresponding lexical item. Sentences containing more frequent words tend to be more acceptable than sentences with less frequent words (for an overview see Schütze (1996); for more recent evidence see Ambridge et al. (2008) and Divjak (2017)). Frequency effects are not restricted to the frequency of the lexical item itself but extend to subcategorization frames as in the dative alternation or the alternation between nominal and sentential complements (e.g. Seidenberg & MacDonald 1999; Wasow 2002; Bresnan & Ford 2010).

**Practical Recommendations**
- If possible, apply a within-items design and make sentences within each token set as identical as possible. This will allow observed differences between conditions to be attributed to the factor under investigation.
- When in doubt, create control conditions for factors that are inseparably tied to an experimental factor.
- In particular, maintain the length and complexity of sentences and accessibility of NP-antecedents. Avoid extremely infrequent lexical items.
- Try to keep items (lexicalizations) parallel as far as possible in terms of structure. This will reduce variation by items.

## 4.4  Extralinguistic Variation of Linguistic Relevance

Some non-linguistic factors are still relevant to linguists. Those factors vary, depending on the subarea. Sociolinguists, for example, systematically investigate social and demographic factors. Factors like memory load, satiation effects, and frequency effects, are particularly of interest to psycholinguists.

### 4.4.1  Individual Differences

#### 4.4.1.1  Social and Demographic Factors
An in-depth discussion of social (social status, social class, etc.) and demographic factors (age, gender, etc.) and their impact is beyond the scope of this chapter. Note, however, that such factors do affect acceptability

ratings, especially with marked constructions and constructions that are prescriptively stigmatized (e.g. Vogel 2019).

## Practical Recommendations

- In general, demographic factors will rarely influence common sentence acceptability experiments. The effects are too subtle to have a huge impact in most studies unless the sample is very unbalanced.
- If the relevant demographic factor is known, control for it by recruiting homogeneous or balanced groups of participants. If it is unknown, minimize systematic effects by recruiting a larger and heterogeneous sample.
- Include participants as a random factor in the statistical analyses.
- If applicable, include group as an independent factor in the statistical analyses.

Participants differ also in the way they process language. The factor which has received the most attention in this respect concerns readers' working memory capacity. We discuss this factor in turn.

### 4.4.1.2   Working Memory

The processing literature has accumulated evidence for the heterogeneity of neurological and cognitive mechanisms involved in language processing, even in healthy speakers (e.g. Just & Carpenter 1992; Pakulak & Neville 2010; Hancock & Bever 2013). Since any acceptability judgment requires that one first process the corresponding sentence, differences in the participants' processing may affect their judgments.

This is obvious for complex sentences challenging the comprehender's working memory, e.g. multiple center-embedding or long extractions. Performance-related variation is typically considered as noise. The challenge, however, is to disentangle performance effects from grammar-based effects, which makes the former relevant, even for those who are concerned with a highly abstract grammar. For instance, superiority effects and island constraints have been questioned to be genuine grammatical constraints. Processing accounts characterize island effects as epiphenomena of parsing difficulties. Arguments in favor of processing accounts relate to modulating effects of the type of *wh*-element(s) (D-linking) as well as correlation of acceptability ratings with processing data (e.g. reading times) and individual cognitive abilities (e.g. working memory span). The ongoing debate on island constraints is of particular interest here.

Island constraints were first proposed in Ross (1967). They block long extractions out of certain constructions. For instance, the Complex NP Constraint prevents extraction out of a clause that is part of a complex NP.[3] The complex NP is an island for extraction.

---

[3] Violations of the Complex NP Constraint are typically more severe with relative clauses than with complement clauses.

(3)      *[Which book]$_i$ did John meet [a child who read t$_i$]

Long-extractions as in (3) are no doubt difficult to parse. Reductionist accounts (e.g. Kluender 1998, 2004; Hofmeister & Sag 2010) attribute the degraded acceptability of island violations largely to limitations on the parsing mechanism and dispute a grammatical explanation. For instance, Hofmeister and Sag (2010) argue that the low acceptability of island violations is due to difficulties identifying the gap for the extracted filler – not because the gap is located in an illicit syntactic environment, but because the length of the dependency and the complexity of the structural representation burdens and sometimes exceeds memory resources. If so, participants with higher memory capacity should accept extractions out of an island more easily. Sprouse et al. (2012a) found no evidence for this claim (but see Hofmeister et al. (2012a) for arguments why the lack of a correlation between working-memory and acceptability rating does not undermine reductionist accounts as well as Sprouse et al. (2012b) for a reply). While the details of the processing-grammar debate go beyond the scope of the present chapter (but see Chapter 5 and Chapter 9 for further discussion), we note that memory load contributes to degradation in acceptability and that testing for correlations can help to disentangle the memory contribution and the contribution by grammatical factors.

**Practical Recommendations**
- Check your stimuli for potentially memory demanding items/conditions. If possible, keep the demands constant across conditions. If not possible, create a control condition that captures the memory effect.
- When memory effects are expected, include some kind of memory test. Conway et al. (2005) provide an overview of memory tests. Recently, Klaus and Schriefers (2016) developed a reading span test that can be used online for pre-screening of participants.[4]

### 4.4.2 Repeated Exposure

In a conversation or when reading a text, people quickly adapt to their interlocutor's accent, lexical choices, specific meanings of phrasal expressions, etc. Listeners and readers also adapt to syntactic structures though the evidence is less consistent (for reviews see Tooley & Traxler (2010); Kaan & Chun (2018)). Syntactic adaptation is discussed under various labels, which differ in their focus and scope. As far as we can see, *adaptation* is the term with the broadest scope though with a focus on dialogues. *Structural persistence* is used for the tendency to reuse structures heard or produced before. *Syntactic priming* is used for facilitation effects due to repeated exposure (both in production and comprehension; see Chapter

---

[4] www.socsci.ru.nl/memory/ (available for English, Dutch, and German)

26). *Syntactic satiation* refers to increased acceptability due to repetition (see Chapter 6 for detailed discussion).

Repeated exposure to a structure that is initially dispreferred or infrequent reduces processing difficulty and increases production of that structure. For instance, Fine et al. (2013) report that readers overcome the processing disadvantage of garden-path sentences when they encounter the dispreferred structure more often than the otherwise (outside the experiment) preferred structure (but see Harrington Stack et al. (2018) for failure to replicate these results). Fanselow et al. (2005) exposed speakers from northern areas of Germany to structures that are not used in their variety, namely long extractions out of finite complement clauses introduced by *dass* ('that').[5] After two sessions of exposure, the northern speakers produced long extractions out of finite complement clauses as often as the Bavarian (southern German) control group.

Fast adaptation can become evident in acceptability judgments as well, often termed syntactic satiation, as already mentioned. Adaptation in sentence comprehension results in easier processing. Since processing difficulty has an effect on perceived acceptability, this facilitation in processing may increase acceptability. Under the assumption that ungrammatical constructions lack a proper syntactic representation, only grammatical constructions can benefit from increased efficiency in generating syntactic representations. Hence, ungrammatical structures should resist adaptation. This expectation needs more empirical support. So far, existing evidence is mixed. Most studies investigating satiation effects examine different types of island violation, with no conclusive findings regarding the type of island violations that show satiation. *Whether*-islands tend to produce satiation (e.g. in Snyder (2000), Hiramatsu (2000), Francom (2009), Crawford (2012), but not in Sprouse (2009)), while adjunct islands never produce satiation (at least in the aforementioned studies). Subjects islands produce satiation in some studies (e.g. Hiramatsu 2000: Experiment 1; Francom 2009), but do not in others (Hiramatsu 2000: Experiment 2; Sprouse 2009; Crawford 2012). Given the controversial grammatical status of island violations and the methodological differences between the aforementioned studies, it is too early to draw definite conclusions.

At this point, there is no broad consensus as to what satiation really is and what satiation effects tell us about the grammatical status of the corresponding construction. If satiation is indeed restricted to grammatical structures, increased acceptability due to repeated exposure could be used for disentangling genuine grammatical effects from mere

---

[5] Speakers from northern and southern Germany differ in their production of long extractions. While speakers from the north basically don't extract out of finite verb-final clauses, speakers from the south are more liberal and produce long A'-movement, e.g. long *wh*-questions or long topicalization. For examples and discussion see Anderson and Kvam (1984); Bayer (1984); Lühr (1988).

performance effects. Under this view, syntactic satiation effects turn from an undesired confound into a valuable diagnostic.

**Practical Recommendations**

- In a binary judgment task, balance the number of grammatical and ungrammatical items. This will counter any equalization strategy which would produce satiation-like effects, i.e. an increase of acceptability during the course of an experiment (cf. Sprouse 2009).
- If applicable, present items with context. This will free participants from accommodating an appropriate context by themselves (though see Chapter 2 for a different view of this). With no need to learn to accommodate an appropriate context, potential learning effects by repetitive accommodation will not occur.
- If satiation is undesired, avoid lexical repetition across items. Lexical repetition has been shown to boost syntactic priming in production (Pickering & Branigan 1998; Traxler et al. 2014) and seems to be a prerequisite for syntactic priming in comprehension (Tooley & Bock 2014; but Traxler 2008).
- Pseudo-randomize the order of presentation such that no two items of the same condition follow each other. This will at least avoid immediate repetition priming, though structural priming has been shown to persist, at least in production (Hartsuiker et al. 2008)
- Check for satiation effects by comparing mean ratings in the first versus last third of the experiment or by including position in the list as a predictor in the statistical analyses (see Section 4.6, and for more details Chapter 3).

## 4.5   Variance from Other Sources

So far, we have discussed variation which is linguistically relevant but possibly creating a confound in a given experiment. In the current section, we turn to variation which is generally regarded as noise. Section 4.5.1 addresses scale effects, Section 4.5.2 discusses so-called non-cooperative behavior, i.e. not complying with the task.

### 4.5.1   Scale Effects

In the context of an acceptability judgment experiment, scale effects are an undesirable difference due to the choice of scale (see Chapter 2 for more details). The use of Magnitude Estimation and the Thermometer Method are typically motivated by the desire to reduce errors occurring when participants convert from their inherent, preferred scale to a pre-set scale (cf. e.g. Stevens (1946) and Bard et al.

(1996) in the context of Magnitude Estimation). Further, scales established by the Thermometer Method are considered to be self-anchoring, reducing anchoring effects (Kilpatrick & Cantril 1960; Featherston 2008). The direct outcomes of experiments using different scales can be hard to compare, though. This is one of the reasons why scores are often normalized.

On normalized data, researchers could not find any significant effects across various scales. Testing linguistic data, Weskott and Fanselow (2011) compared results obtained with a binary scale, a gradient seven-point scale and with Magnitude Estimation. Their data show high agreement between the three measures of sentence acceptability (for similar findings see Bader & Häussler (2010); Langsford et al. (2018)). Weskott and Fanselow (2011) also tested the claim that Magnitude Estimation yields richer data because participants are free to distinguish as many levels of acceptability as they wish, but their results indicate no difference in informativity. Langsford et al. (2018) examined test–retest reliability and found no general differences between data obtained with a five-point scale, Magnitude Estimation or two versions of a forced-choice task. Notably, Magnitude Estimation turned out to be less robust against variability by participants.

Other scale-related issues were mostly discussed in neighboring fields. Research in psychology has found that participants give higher ratings on a binary scale than on a gradient *n*-point-scale (Ghiselli 1939). For a gradient *n*-point-scale, the impact of offering a midpoint is unclear, especially with respect to linguistic data. While Mattel and Jacoby (1971) found that a midpoint had little effect, Garland (1991) argues that it is better to not offer a midpoint. Further, it has been shown that aggregated ratings given on a binary scale tend to cluster at the endpoints of the scale (Weijters et al. 2010). It is not clear, though, whether this is a true effect or an experimental artefact. Cox (1980) tends toward the latter, viewing this clustering as a potential loss of information. As to the optimal number of rating categories, five categories or more are typically regarded as reliable (for a review, see Cox 1980). Results in Preston and Colman (2000) indicate that seven- to eleven-point scales work well. It is likely that those findings also apply to linguistics, but this remains subject to validation.

The first few items affect a participant's interpretation of the scale. For instance, if a questionnaire begins with a series of highly degraded items and is then followed by an "in-between" item, then that mid-range item might receive unusually high ratings. This is another instantiation of the anchoring effect (cf. e.g. Tversky & Kahneman 1974) and it can be countered by including calibration items at the beginning of the questionnaire. Such items are used to familiarize participants with the task and the scale and should span the entire scale, including the mid-range.

An unbalanced set of stimuli can also lead to anchoring effects throughout a questionnaire, potentially distorting the results. There is a tendency toward higher ratings if one includes a lot of degraded items, and vice versa. A balanced set of filler items is advisable in any scenario, but especially if the set of critical items cannot be balanced, then a balanced set of filler items is a necessity. Gerbrich et al. (2019) give a suggestion for a balanced set of fillers.

## Practical Recommendations
- No matter which type of scale is used, it is highly likely that the results are interpretable and, if normalized, comparable.
- Arguably, a gradient $n$-point scale with four degrees or more is very easy to introduce and gives participants a sufficient degree of freedom to express finer distinctions without overwhelming them.
- Introduce the task with a few example items and start the experiment with a calibration phase. Calibration items are used to familiarize participants with the task and the scale. They should cover wide areas of the acceptability range; for $n$-point scales, calibration items should span the entire scale, including the mid-range.
- Calibration items also counter anchoring effects. Further, include a balanced set of filler items.

### 4.5.2   Non-cooperative Behavior
Participants for judgment tasks are increasingly recruited through crowdsourcing platforms like Amazon Mechanical Turk[6] and Prolific.[7] A potential downside seems to be that the number of participants who do not comply with the task but more or less blindly click their way through the experiment is higher than in lab or classroom environments. Kazai et al. (2011) argue that non-cooperative behavior can have a distorting effect on one's results. However, the exact extent and impact of non-cooperative behavior, particularly in linguistic studies, have yet to be quantified. In related fields, some studies observed that the rate of non-cooperative behavior is considerably higher in crowdsourced tasks than in tasks with "conventional" recruitment (e.g. Downs et al. 2010; Zhu & Carterette 2010; Kazai et al. 2011). Other studies report exclusion rates in crowdsourced tasks that are in line with rates in tasks with conventional recruitment (see e.g. Krantz & Dalal 2000; Dandurand et al. 2008; Paolacci et al. 2010; Mason & Suri 2012). Factors that increase the rate of non-cooperative

---

[6] www.mturk.com    [7] www.prolific.co

behavior are low payment (see Sorokin & Forsyth 2008; Kazai 2011) and task repetitiveness (Eickhoff & de Vries 2013). For linguistics tasks, reported rates of non-cooperative behavior vary between 11 and 25 percent (among others, Munro et al. 2010; Schnoebelen & Kuperman 2010; Sprouse 2011). Note that the numbers are not directly comparable across studies, because different rejection criteria are applied. Kazai et al. (2011) give an overview over the types of participants and types of non-cooperative behavior.

If one's study is conducted on a computer, one should consider recording response times, wherever possible. Response times can be used for further analyses, and crucially for detecting non-cooperative behavior. The responses of non-cooperative participants in comprehension questions are likely to be unusual. The response times of non-cooperative participants are also likely to stand out. Typically, non-cooperative participants are quick to finish the task. However, some non-cooperative participants switch back and forth between tasks (Buchholz & Latorre 2011), pause between items, and make their overall response times look normal.

## Practical Recommendations

- Adequate payment and non-repetitive tasks can reduce the amount of non-cooperative behavior.
- Further, one might even include a qualification task (cf. e.g. Soleymani & Larson 2010) and apply qualifying criteria, such as requiring task familiarity. One can also include yes/no comprehension questions, as advocated by Gibson et al. (2011). Such questions check whether a participant understood the meaning of a stimulus.
- Additionally, one could set clear expectations for which ratings count as a legitimate answer for certain items and exclude participants who do not fulfil one's expectations ("gotcha items"). For further details, see Häussler and Juzek (2017).
- If one is collecting response times, then they can also be used to detect non-cooperative behavior. It is advisable to check median response times instead of mean response times. A possible approach is to exclude outliers that are two or three standard deviations below the mean of median response times (e.g. Baayen & Milin 2010). However, once non-cooperative participants are in the majority, absolute values as cut-off points are a viable alternative. For instance, anything below 100 ms could be viewed as impossible (Luce 1986), as well as reading times below 200 ms per word (Jegerski 2014).
- Immediate warnings on repeatedly extremely short response times can prevent participants from quickly clicking through the experiment (Häussler & Juzek 2017).

## 4.6   Statistical Procedures

In an ideal world, the formal analysis is decided on prior to one's experiment. However, this is not always possible, especially if the data structure is not entirely clear prior to experimenting. So, prior to applying formal analyses, one should visually explore one's data and consider simple descriptives. This is then followed by a more formal analysis.

As a first explorative step, a visual inspection is advisable. The exact form, i.e. scatterplot, boxplot, etc., depends on one's data structure. A visualization helps to identify outliers. However, sometimes such outliers reflect real effects and ideally, exclusion criteria are specified prior to inspection. A visualization also helps to clarify the underlying distribution, e.g. to detect bimodal or multimodal distributions. For this purpose, histograms and heat maps are particularly useful. A basic summary, e.g. using the *summary* function in R, reports some basic descriptives like average, standard deviation, etc., and can give valuable insights. One might also check for clustering, using analyses such as k-means (Forgy 1965; Lloyd 1982) or k-nearest neighbors (Fix & Hodges 1989; Cover & Hart 1967).

Cohen's kappa can be used to test for inter-participant agreement (Cohen 1960). The kappa statistics measures agreement among participants against a random baseline, with 1 denoting perfect agreement, 0 denoting a result equal to chance, and an outcome below 0 denoting that the agreement is worse than random. The metric tests for general homogeneity. If homogeneity is not given, then it could be caused by any of the following: real linguistic differences among participants, considerable experimental artifacts, or even a considerable amount of non-cooperative behavior. If disagreement is given, then one needs to check what is causing it.[8]

Insights from the above will help in choosing the appropriate formal analysis. If an unsuitable analysis was chosen, then one should adjust the analysis, but state so explicitly. Note that often simple analyses like t-tests, ANOVAs, simple correlation measures, etc. will suffice. However, due to increasing complexity and the increasing importance of including random factors (e.g. the impact of concrete participants or concrete items), mixed-effect models are becoming more and more popular. Details on mixed-effect models are beyond the scope of this chapter, but see Baayen (2008) and Winter (2019). For statistical analyses for linguists in general, see also Gries (2013) and Levshina (2015).

---

[8] A practical note: the more points one's scale uses, the lower the chances that kappa will indicate high agreement. Two participants are more likely to choose the same category on a two-point scale than on a 100-point scale. To counter this, one could transform one's gradient data, which uses three or more categories, to binary data, "unacceptable" and "acceptable." Mid-values could be assigned randomly or be dropped entirely.

# References

Ambridge, B., Pine, J. M., Rowland, C. F., & Young, C. R. (2008). The effect of verb semantic class and verb frequency (entrenchment) on children's and adults' graded judgements of argument-structure overgeneralization errors. *Cognition*, 106, 87–129.

Andersson, S.-G. & Kvam, S. (1984). *Satzverschränkung im heutigen Deutsch. Eine syntaktische und funktionale Studie unter Berücksichtigung alternativer Konstruktionen*. Tübingen: Narr.

Ariel, M. (1990). *Accessing NP Antecedents*. Abingdon: Routledge.

Baayen, R. H. (2008). *Analyzing Linguistic Data: A Practical Introduction to Statistics Using R*. Cambridge: Cambridge University Press.

Baayen, R. H. & Milin, P. (2010). Analyzing reaction times. *International Journal of Psychological Research*, 3(2), 12–28.

Bader, M. & Häussler, J. (2010). Toward a model of grammaticality judgments. *Journal of Linguistics*, 46(2), 273–330.

Bard, E. G., Robertson, D., & Sorace, A. (1996). Magnitude Estimation of linguistic acceptability. *Language*, 72(1), 32–68.

Bayer, J. (1984). Comp in Bavarian syntax. *The Linguistic Review*, 3(3), 209–274.

Bolinger, D. (1978). Asking more than one thing at a time. In H. Hiz, eds., *Questions*. Dordrecht: Reidel, pp. 97–106.

Brandner, E. (2012). Syntactic microvariation. *Language and Linguistics Compass*, 6, 113–130.

Bresnan, J. & Ford, M. (2010). Predicting syntax: Processing dative constructions in American and Australian varieties of English. *Language*, 86 (1),168–213.

Buchholz, S. & Latorre, J. (2011). Crowdsourcing preference tests, and how to detect cheating. In P. Cosi, R. De Mori, G. Di Fabbrizio, & R. Pieraccini, eds., *INTERSPEECH 2011: 12th Annual Conference of the International Speech Communication Association*, pp. 3053–3056. ISCA Archive: www.isca-speech.org/archive/interspeech_2011

Chomsky, N. (1965). *Aspects of the Theory of Syntax*. Cambridge, MA: MIT Press.

Chomsky, N. (1973). Conditions on transformations. In S. Anderson & P. Kiparsky, eds., *A Festschrift for Morris Halle*. New York: Holt, Rinehart & Winston, pp. 232–286.

Chomsky, N. (1980). *Rules and Representations* (Woodbridge Lectures 11). New York: Columbia University Press.

Clifton, C., Jr., Fanselow, G., & Frazier, L. (2006). Amnestying superiority violations: Processing multiple questions. *Linguistic Inquiry*, 37, 51–68.

Clifton, C., Jr., Frazier, L., & Connine, C. (1984). Lexical expectations in sentence comprehension. *Journal of Verbal Learning and Verbal Behaviour*, 23, 696–708.

Cohen, J. (1960). A coefficient of agreement for nominal scales. *Educational and Psychological Measurement*, 20(1), 37–46.

Conway, A., Kane, M., Bunting, M., Hambrick, D. Z., Wilhelm, O., & Engle, R. (2005). Working memory span tasks: A methodological review and user's guide. *Psychonomic Bulletin and Review*, 12, 769–86.

Cover, T. M. & Hart, P. E. (1967). Nearest neighbor pattern classification. *IEEE Transactions on Information Theory*, 13(1), 1–27.

Cowart, W. (1997). *Experimental Syntax: Applying Objective Methods to Sentence Judgments*. Thousand Oaks, CA: Sage.

Cox, E. P (1980). The optimal number of response alternatives for a scale: A review. *Journal of Marketing Research*, 17(4), 407–422.

Crawford, J. (2012). Using syntactic satiation to investigate subject islands. In J. Choi, E. A. Hogue, J. Punske, D. Tat, J. Schertz, & A. Trueman, eds., *Proceedings of the 29th West Coast Conference on Formal Linguistics*. Somerville, MA: Cascadilla Proceedings Project, pp. 38–45.

Culicover, P. W. & Jackendoff, R. (2010). Quantitative methods alone are not enough: Response to Gibson and Fedorenko. *Trends Cognitive Science*, 14, 234–235.

Dandurand, F., Shultz, T. R., & Onishi, K. H. (2008). Comparing online and lab methods in a problem-solving experiment. *Behavior Research Methods*, 40(2), 428–434.

Divjak, D. (2017). The role of lexical frequency in the acceptability of syntactic variants: Evidence from *that*-clauses in Polish. *Cognitive Science*, 41(2), 354–382.

Downs, J. S., Holbrook, M. B., Sheng, S., & Cranor, L. F. (2010). Are your participants gaming the system? Screening Mechanical Turk workers. In E. Mynatt, ed., *CHI '10: Proceedings of the SIGCHI Conference on Human Factors in Computing Systems*. Atlanta, GA: Association for Computing Machinery, pp. 2399–2402.

Eickhoff, C. & de Vries, A. P. (2013). Increasing cheat robustness of crowd-sourcing tasks. *Information Retrieval*, 16(2), 121–137.

Fanselow, G. & Frisch, S. (2006). Effects of processing difficulty on judgments of acceptability. In G. Fanselow, C. Féry, M. Schlesewsky, & R. Vogel, eds., *Gradience in Grammar: Generative Perspectives*. Oxford: Oxford University Press, pp. 291–316.

Fanselow, G., Kliegl, R., & Schlesewsky, M. (2005). Syntactic variation in German *wh*-questions: Empirical investigations of weak crossover violations and long *wh*-movement. *Linguistic Variation Yearbook*, 5, 37–63.

Featherston, S. (2007). Data in generative grammar: The stick and the carrot. *Theoretical Linguistics*, 33, 269–318.

Featherston, S. (2008). Thermometer judgments as linguistic evidence. In C. M. Riehl & A. Rothe, eds., *Was ist linguistische Evidenz?* Aachen: Shaker Verlag, pp. 69–89.

Fedorenko, E. & Gibson, E. (2010). Adding a third *wh*-phrase does not increase the acceptability of object-initial multiple-*wh*-questions. *Syntax*, 13(3), 183–195.

Fine, A. B., Jaeger, T. F., Farmer, T. A., & Qian, T. (2013). Rapid expectation adaptation during syntactic comprehension. *PLoS ONE*, 8(10), e77661. DOI:10.1371/journal.pone.0077661

Fix, E. & Hodges, J. (1989). Discriminatory analysis. Nonparametric discrimination: Consistency properties. *International Statistical Review / Revue internationale de statistique*, 57(3), 238–247.

Forgy, E. W. (1965). Cluster analysis of multivariate data: Efficiency versus interpretability of classification. *Biometrics*, 21(3), 768–769.

Francom, J. (2009). Experimental syntax: Exploring the effect of repeated exposure to anomalous syntactic structure – evidence from rating and reading tasks. Doctoral dissertation, University of Arizona.

Garland, R. (1991). The mid-point on a rating scale: Is it desirable? *Marketing Bulletin*, 2, 66–70.

Gerbrich, H., Schreier, V., & Featherston, S. (2019). Standard items for English judgment studies: Syntax and semantics. In S. Featherston, R. Hörnig, S. von Wietersheim, & S. Winkler (eds.), *Experiments in Focus: Information Structure and Semantic Processing*. Berlin: De Gruyter, pp. 305–327.

Gervain, J. (2003). Syntactic microvariation and methodology: problems and perspectives. *Acta Linguistica Hungarica*, 50(3–4), 405–434.

Ghiselli, E. E. (1939). All or none versus graded response questionnaires. *Journal of Applied Psychology*, 23, 405–415.

Gibson E. & Fedorenko, E. (2010). Weak quantitative standards in linguistics research. *Trends Cognitive Science*, 14, 233–234.

Gibson, E., Piantadosi, S., & Fedorenko, K. (2011). Using Mechanical Turk to obtain and analyze English acceptability judgments. *Language and Linguistics Compass*, 5(8), 509–524.

Givón, T. (1983). *Topic Continuity in Discourse: A Quantitative Cross-Language Study*. Amsterdam: John Benjamins.

Gries, S. Th. (2013). *Statistics for Linguistics with R. A Practical Introduction*, 2nd, revised ed. Berlin and Boston, MA: De Gruyter Mouton.

Guajardo, G. & Goodall, G. (2019). On the status of Concordantia Temporum in Spanish: An experimental approach. *Glossa: A Journal of General Linguistics*, 4(1), 116. DOI: 10.5334/gjgl.749

Hancock, R. & Bever, T. G. (2013). Genetic factors and normal variation in the organization of language. *Biolinguistics*, 7, 75–95.

Harrington Stack, C. M., James, A. N., & Watson, D. G. (2018). A failure to replicate rapid syntactic adaptation in comprehension. *Memory & Cognition*, 46, 864–877.

Hartsuiker, R. J., Bernolet, S., Schoonbaert, S., Speybroeck, S., & Vanderelst, D. (2008). Syntactic priming persists while the lexical boost decays: Evidence from written and spoken dialogue. *Journal of Memory and Language*, 58, 214–238.

Häussler, J. & Juzek, T. S. (2017). Hot topics surrounding acceptability judgement tasks. In S. Featherston, R. Hörnig, R. Steinberg, B. Umbreit,

& J. Wallis, eds., *Proceedings of Linguistic Evidence 2016: Empirical, Theoretical, and Computational Perspectives*. University of Tübingen, http://dx.doi.org/10.15496/publikation-19039

Hiramatsu, K. (2000). Accessing linguistic competence: Evidence from children's and adults' acceptability judgments. Doctoral dissertation, University of Connecticut.

Hofmeister, P., Jaeger, T. F., Sag, I. A., Arnon, I., & Snider, N. (2007). Locality and accessibility in wh-questions. In S. Featherston & W. Sternefeld, eds., *Roots: Linguistics in Search of Its Evidential Base*. Berlin: Mouton de Gruyter, pp. 185–206.

Hofmeister, P. & Sag, I. A. (2010). Cognitive constraints and island effects. *Language*, 86, 366–415.

Hofmeister, P., Staum Casasanto, L., & Sag, I. A. (2012a). How do individual cognitive differences relate to acceptability judgments? A reply to Sprouse, Wagers, and Phillips. *Language*, 88, 390–400.

Hofmeister, P., Staum Casasanto, L., & Sag, I. A. (2012b). Misapplying working memory tests: A reductio ad absurdum. *Language*, 88(2), 408–409.

Jegerski, J. (2014). Self-paced reading. In J. Jegerski & B. VanPatten, eds., *Research Methods in Second Language Psycholinguistics*. New York: Routledge, pp. 20–49.

Just, M. A. & Carpenter, P. A. (1992). A capacity theory of comprehension: Individual differences in working memory. *Psychological Review*, 99(1), 122–149.

Kaan, E. & Chun, E. (2018). Priming and adaptation in native speakers and second-language learners. *Bilingualism: Language and Cognition*, 21, 228–242.

Kayne, R. (1983). Connectedness. *Linguistic Inquiry*, 14, 223–249.

Kazai, G. (2011). In search of quality in crowdsourcing for search engine evaluation. In P. Clough, C. Foley, C. Gurrin, G. Jones, W. Kraaij, H. Lee, & V. Murdock, eds., *Advances in Information Retrieval*. Heidelberg: Springer, pp. 165–176.

Kazai, G., Kamps, J., & Milic-Frayling, N. (2011). Worker types and personality traits in crowdsourcing relevance labels. In B. Berendt, A. de Vries, W. Fan, C. Macdonald, I. Ounis, & I. Ruthven, eds., *Proceedings of the 20th ACM International Conference on Information and Knowledge Management (CIKM'11)*. New York: ACM, pp. 1941–1944.

Kilpatrick, F. P. & Cantril, H. (1960). Self-anchoring scaling: A measure of individuals' unique reality worlds. *Journal of Individual Psychology*, 16, 158–173.

Klaus, J. & Schriefers, H. (2016). Measuring verbal working memory capacity: A reading span task for laboratory and web-based use. OSF Preprints. December 7. DOI:10.31219/osf.io/nj48x

Kluender, R. (1998). On the distinction between strong and weak islands: A processing perspective. In P. Culicover & L. McNally, eds., *The Limits of*

*Syntax* (Syntax and Semantics, 29). San Diego, CA: Academic Press, pp. 241–279.

Kluender, R. (2004). Are subject islands subject to a processing account? In V. Chand, A. Kelleher, A. J. Rodríguez, & B. Schmeiser, eds., *Proceedings of the 23rd West Coast Conference on Formal Linguistics*. Somerville, MA: Cascadilla Press, pp. 101–125.

Krantz, J. H. & Dalal, R. (2000). Validity of Web-based psychological research. In M. Birnbaum, ed., *Psychological Experiments on the Internet*. New York: Academic Press, pp. 35–60.

Kroch, A. (1989). Reflexes of grammar in patterns of language change. *Language Variation and Change*, 1, 199–244.

Kuno, S. & Robinson, J. (1972). Multiple *wh*-questions. *Linguistic Inquiry*, 3, 463–487.

Labov, W. (1966). *The Social Stratification of English in New York City*. Washington, DC: Center for Applied Linguistics.

Langsford, S., Perfors, A., Hendrickson, A. T., Kennedy, L. A., & Navarro, D. J. (2018). Quantifying sentence acceptability measures: Reliability, bias, and variability. *Glossa: A Journal of General Linguistics*, 3 (1), 37. DOI: 10.5334 /gjgl.396

Levshina, N. (2015). *How to Do Linguistics with R: Data Exploration and Statistical Analysis*. Amsterdam: John Benjamins.

Lloyd, S. P. (1982). Least squares quantization in pcm. *IEEE Transactions on Information Theory*, 28, 129–137.

Luce, R. D. (1986). *Response Times: Their Role in Inferring Elementary Mental Organization*. New York: Oxford University Press.

Lühr, R. (1988). Zur Satzverschränkung im heutigen Deutsch. *Groninger Arbeiten zur Germanistischen Linguistik*, 29, 74–87.

Mason, W. & Suri, S. (2012). Conducting behavioral research on Amazon's Mechanical Turk. *Behavior Research Methods*, 44(1), 1–23.

Mattel, M. & Jacoby, J. (1971). Is there an optimal number of alternatives for Likert scale items? Study I: Reliability and validity. *Journal of Applied Psychology*, 56(6), 506–509.

Munro, R., Bethard, S., Kuperman, V., Lai, V. T., Melnick, R., Potts, C., Schnoebelen, T., & Tily, H. (2010). Crowdsourcing and language studies: the new generation of linguistic data. In *NAACL HLT 2010 Workshop on Creating Speech and Language Data with Amazon's Mechanical Turk*, 122–130.

Pakulak, E. & Neville, H. J. (2010). Proficiency differences in syntactic processing of monolingual native speakers indexed by event-related potentials. *Journal of Cognitive Neuroscience*, 22(12), 2728–2744.

Paolacci, G., Chandler, J., & Ipeirotis, P. G. (2010). Running experiments on Amazon Mechanical Turk. *Judgment and Decision Making*, 5, 411–419.

Pesetsky, D. (1982). Paths and categories. Doctoral dissertation, Massachusetts Institute of Technology.

Pesetsky, D. (1987). Wh-in-Situ: Movement and unselective binding. In E. J. Reuland & A. G. B. ter Meulen, eds., *The Representation of (In)definitness.* Cambridge, MA: MIT Press, pp. 98–129.

Phillips, C. (2013). On the nature of island constraints. I: Language processing and reductionist accounts. In J. Sprouse & N. Hornstein, eds., *Experimental Syntax and Island Effects.* Cambridge: Cambridge University Press, pp. 64–108.

Pickering, M. J. & Branigan, H. P. (1998). The representation of verbs: Evidence from syntactic priming in language production. *Journal of Memory and Language*, 39, 633–651.

Preston, C. C. & Colman, A. M. (2000). Optimal number of response categories in rating scales: Reliability, validity, discriminating power, and respondent preferences. *Acta Psychologica*, 104(1), 1–15.

Rayner, K. & Duffy, S. A. (1986). Lexical complexity and fixation times in reading: Effects of word frequency, verb complexity, and lexical ambiguity. *Memory & Cognition*, 14, 191–201.

Ross, J. (1967). Constraints on variables in syntax. Doctoral dissertation, Massachusetts Institute of Technology.

Salzmann, M., Häussler, J., Bayer, J., & Bader, M. (2013). *That*-trace effects without traces. An experimental investigation. In S. Keine & S. Sloggett, eds., *Proceedings of the 42nd Annual Meeting of the North East Linguistic Society.* Amherst, MA: GLSA, vol. 2, pp. 149–162.

Schnoebelen, T. & Kuperman, V. (2010). Using Amazon Mechanical Turk for linguistic research. *Psihologija*, 43(4), 441–464.

Schütze, C. T. (1996). *The Empirical Base of Linguistics: Grammaticality Judgments and Linguistic Methodology.* Chicago: University of Chicago Press.

Seidenberg, M. S. & MacDonald, M. C. (1999). A probabilistic constraints approach to language acquisition and processing. *Cognitive Science*, 23(4), 569–588.

Snyder, W. (2000). An experimental investigation of syntactic satiation effects. *Linguistic Inquiry*, 31(3), 575–582.

Soleymani, M. & Larson, M. (2010). Crowdsourcing for affective annotation of video: development of a viewer-reported boredom corpus. In *ACM SIGIR 2010 Workshop on Crowdsourcing for Search Evaluation (CSE 2010)*, pp. 4–8.

Sorokin, A. & Forsyth, D. (2008). Utility data annotation with Amazon Mechanical Turk: Computer vision and pattern recognition workshops. In *IEEE Computer Society Conference on IEEE (CVPRW'08)*, pp. 1–8.

Sprouse, J. (2009). Revisiting satiation: Evidence for an equalization response strategy. *Linguistic Inquiry*, 40, 329–341.

Sprouse, J. (2011). A validation of Amazon Mechanical Turk for the collection of acceptability judgments in linguistic theory. *Behavior Research Methods*, 43(1), 155–167.

Sprouse, J., Wagers, M., & Phillips, C. (2012a). A test of the relation between working memory and syntactic island effects. *Language*, 88(1), 82–123.

Sprouse, J., Wagers, M., & Phillips, C. (2012b). Working-memory capacity and island effects: A reminder of the issues and the facts. *Language*, 88(2), 401–407.

Stevens, S. S (1946). On the theory of scales of measurement. *Science*, 103, 667–688.

Tooley, K. M. & Bock, K. (2014). On the parity of structural persistence in language production and comprehension. *Cognition*, 132(2), 101–136.

Tooley, K. M. & Traxler, M. J. (2010). Syntactic priming effects in comprehension: A critical review. *Language and Linguistics Compass*, 4(10), 925–937.

Traxler, M. J. (2008). Lexically independent syntactic priming of adjunct relations in on-line sentence comprehension. *Psychonomic Bulletin & Review*, 15, 149–155.

Traxler, M. J., Tooley, K. M., & Pickering, M. J. (2014). Syntactic priming during sentence comprehension: Evidence for the lexical boost. *Journal of Experimental Psychology: Learning, Memory and Cognition*, 40(4), 905–918.

Tversky, A. & Kahneman, D. (1974). Judgment under uncertainty: Heuristics and biases. *Science*, 185(4157), 1124–1131.

Vogel, R. (2019). Grammatical taboos: An investigation on the impact of prescription in acceptability judgement experiments. *Zeitschrift für Sprachwissenschaft*, 38(1), 37–79.

Warren, T. & Gibson, E. (2002). The influence of referential processing on sentence complexity. *Cognition*, 85, 79–112.

Warren, T. & Gibson, E. (2005). Effects of NP type in reading cleft sentences in English. *Language and Cognitive Processes*, 20, 751–767.

Wasow, T. (2002). *Postverbal Behavior*. Stanford: CSLI Publications.

Weijters, B., Cabooter, E., & Schillewaert, N. (2010). The effect of rating scale format on response styles: the number of response categories and response category labels. *International Journal of Research in Marketing*, 27, 236–247.

Weskott, T. & Fanselow, G. (2011). On the informativity of different measures of linguistic acceptability. *Language*, 87(2), 249–273.

Winter, B. (2019). *Statistics for Linguists: An Introduction Using R*. New York: Routledge.

Zhu, D. & Carterette, B. (2010). An analysis of assessor behavior in crowd-sourced preference judgments. In *SIGIR 2010 Workshop on Crowdsourcing for Search Evaluation (CSE 2010)*, pp. 17–20.

# 5

# Acceptability, Grammar, and Processing

Gisbert Fanselow

## 5.1 Introduction

Given that *acceptability judgments* are the primary data type in (generative) syntax research, it is somewhat disturbing that a consensus on a formal model of the formation of such judgments is still missing. However, there is at least widespread agreement that grammar figures prominently in the formation of acceptability judgments, while other factors contribute as well, including differences in the ease of processing. Thus, if some syntactic manipulation changes the acceptability of a structure, this need not imply that the rules of syntax are sensitive to the manipulation – the judgment effect could rather be due to changes of prosodic quality, sociolinguistic status, or ease of processing accompanying the syntactic manipulation. Acceptability differences do not necessarily indicate differences in grammatical well-formedness, in *grammaticality*. This insight has always guided the formulation of syntactic theories. For example, generative grammar disregards effects of constituent length and the degree of center-embedding on acceptability, by interpreting these as processing impacts. Sections 5.2 and 5.3 give an overview of effects on acceptability for which a processing origin is rather uncontroversial.

Processing accounts might replace grammar-based explanations in at least two domains: island and intervention constraints on movement. No consensus has been reached in this respect, as Section 5.4 will demonstrate. Section 5.5 is dedicated to a discussion of broader questions such as the role of individual differences and the possible shaping of grammar rules by processing needs.

For helpful comments, I am indebted to Grant Goodall, Shravan Vasishth, and the two reviewers. The work presented here was partially funded by the Deutsche Forschungsgemeinschaft, SFB 1287, Project Number C01.

## 5.2   Errors and Misapplications

The acceptability of a sentence can be at odds with its status in grammar whenever the parser fails to identify the grammatically correct analysis, or misapplies syntactic, semantic, and pragmatic heuristics in the computation of acceptability.

One of the first experiments on properties of acceptability, Marks (1967), already illustrated the implications of a failure of identifying the correct representation. He investigated whether the position of a syntactic violation (e.g. an inversion of the article and the noun) in a clause influences acceptability, and found that early incorrect inversions such as (1a) got a lower rating than late inversions such as (1b) (Marks 1967: 199).

(1)     a. *boy the hit the ball

        b. *the boy hit ball the

Since the strictness of grammatical rules does not decrease from left to right, the perception that (1a) is worse than (1b) cannot be attributed to grammar. Probably, a later violation is less prominent, hence more likely to be overlooked. One can hypothesize that the perceptual prominence of a grammatical violation correlates with the degree of unacceptability. Failure of detecting a violation with low prominence means that an ungrammatical sentence is judged as acceptable – an *illusion of grammaticality*.

### 5.2.1   Morphological Ambiguity

Morphological unambiguity contributes to the visibility of grammatical problems, with the unambiguous marking of number and case constituting a clear cue for identifying misanalyses, guiding reanalysis (e.g. Fodor & Inoue 2000; Bader & Bayer 2006), and acceptability judgments. In contrast, a morphological ambiguity may blur the status of a phrase, so that a problem can go unnoticed, possibly leading to an illusion of grammaticality.

Experimental data interpretable as an ambiguity driven illusion are reported in Fanselow and Frisch (2006). German split topicalization is fully acceptable only when the discontinuous NP is constructed with a plural or a mass noun (2a) (but there is some interspeaker variability), while structures such as (2b) involving a morphologically unambiguous singular count noun got a low rating. The reduction of acceptability for singular NPs was significantly smaller when the noun itself was number-ambiguous as in (2c),[1] with number being disambiguated later by the stranded numeral. In a sense, the participants of the experiment had a "grammaticality illusion" for (2c).

---

[1] Sentences with a non-uniform grammatical status are marked with "!".

(2)     a. Bücher    habe   ich   einige.
           book.PL   have   I     some
           'I have some books.'
        b. !Buch     habe   ich   nur   eines.
           book.SG   have   I     just  one
           'I just have one book.'
        c. !Koffer          habe   ich   nur   einen.
           suitcase.UNM    have   I     just  one
           'I just have one suitcase.'

The amelioration of (2c) can be attributed to *"shallow" processing* in the sense of Ferreira, Ferraro, and Bailey (2002) and Ferreira and Patson (2007) that does not compute a complete syntactic representation and relies in its decisions on heuristics related to syntax, semantics, and pragmatics. If the parser initially analyzes *Koffer* as a plural, the plurality restriction for discontinuous NPs is satisfied, and as long as no complete and consistent representation for the whole sentence is computed, the mismatch between singular *einen* and the plural postulated for *Koffer* will go unnoticed.

Morphological ambiguity does not always increase acceptability. For example, the fronting of a VP with an unambiguous accusative object (3a) is more acceptable in German than the fronting of a VP including an unambiguously marked nominative subject (3b). Fanselow and Frisch (2006) found no effect of case ambiguity in an offline rating experiment: Sentences in which the subject status of the NP in the fronted VP is expressed unambiguously (*ein Junge*, (3b)) were no worse than sentences in which the subject status of a case-ambiguous NP (*eine Frau*, (3d)) is only signaled indirectly by the case of a pronoun occurring later in the sentence.

(3)     a. (einen   Jungen    gelobt)   hatte   er    nicht
           a.ACC    boy.ACC   praised   had     he    not
           'Praised a boy, he had not.'
        b. !(ein    Junge     gelobt)   hatte   ihn   nicht
           the.NOM  boy.NOM   praised   had     him   not
           'A boy had not praised him.'
        c. (eine    Frau          gelobt)   hatte   er    nicht
           a.UNM    woman.UNM     praised   had     he    not
           'Praised a woman, he had not.'
        d. !(eine   Frau          gelobt)   hatte   ihn   nicht
           a.UNM    woman.UNM     praised   had     him   not
           'A woman had not praised him.'

However, in a speeded acceptability judgment experiment locally ambiguous (3d) was more readily accepted than (3b). In a fast processing mode, the parser seems more prone to commit errors, or to take decisions before the required syntactic analysis is complete, so that the judgment is based on more shallow heuristics.

The different susceptibility of (2c) and (3d) to a grammaticality illusion in normal judgments may stem from a difference in the relevance of morphology for interpretation. For identifying the left peripheral noun in (2) as a sentence topic, grammatical number is, essentially, unimportant, so that a shallow processing not resolving the number conflict in the discontinuous NP is semantically unproblematic. In contrast, an initial misanalysis of the NP in a fronted VP in (3d) as an accusative object will crash semantically even with shallow parsing once a "second" accusative NP is encountered.

In speeded rating, *morphological markedness* plays a role comparable to ambiguity in creating illusions of grammaticality (Bayer, Bader, & Meng 2001). The absence of any morphological cues for the assignment of grammatical roles may also *reduce* the acceptability of the marked interpretation of globally ambiguous sentences (as already noted by Chomsky (1965) for sentences that are globally ambiguous between a subject- and an object-initial analysis).

### 5.2.2 Temporary Attachment Ambiguity

Classical "garden-path sentences" such as (4) (Bever 1970) create an *illusion of ungrammaticality*. They involve a local attachment ambiguity, often between a main clause and an embedded/reduced relative clause attachment of a critical element (*floated*). A garden path arises when strong parsing heuristics (Frazier 1987) favor a resolution of the ambiguity (here: attachment of *floated* to the main clause) that later material renders incorrect. If attempts at reanalysis fail, and the correct parse is not identified, the sentence will be wrongly classified as ungrammatical by the parser. Cf., e.g., Waters and Caplan (1996) for experimental evidence for the reduced acceptability and greater processing difficulty of garden path sentences.

(4)    The boat floated down the river sank.

Many attachment ambiguities such as (5) are disambiguated prosodically (Kjelgaard & Speer 1999), so that a garden path effect arises in written language processing only. However, this may not characterize all garden path sentences (Wagner & Watson 2010, but also Grillo et al. 2018).

(5)    When Roger leaves the house is dark.

Ferreira and Henderson (1991) and Tabor and Hutchins (2004) show that the length of the misattached phrase (cf. the alternatives in (6)) is negatively correlated with acceptability, which supports a processing analysis of the garden-path phenomenon, because grammar is insensitive to the number of words in a phrase.

(6)    After the Martians invaded {the town / the town that the city bordered / the town the city bordered} was evacuated.

The heuristics favoring a subject + matrix verb analysis for the initial segment in (4) have an effect on acceptability even when the relevant substring is encountered *after* material that excludes such an analysis. Tabor, Galantucci, and Richardson (2004) found that whenever the segment set in italics in (7) locally allows a subject + predicate interpretation in terms of morphology (7a vs. b) and plausibility, the acceptability of the complete sentence is reduced, although the preceding words exclude the subject + verb analysis. The reduction of acceptability goes hand in hand with an increase in processing load. Apparently, the availability of a prominent alternative parse for a substring of the input disturbs processing even when that alternative analysis is incompatible with the word string computed so far. Cf. Frazier et al. (2014) for the role prosody plays for effects of analyses that are coherent only locally.

(7)    a. The coach smiled at *the player tossed* a frisbee by the opposing team.
       b. The coach smiled at *the player thrown* a frisbee by the opposing team.

The low acceptability of garden path sentences such as (4) is thus not merely caused by misanalysis, but also prices in distractions by the locally coherent subject–verb analysis which heuristic parsing suggests in the course of the analysis of a sentence.

Performance on garden path sentences involving attachment ambiguities improves with training for cognitive control (Novick et al. 2014), and there are age effects on performance (e.g. Christianson et al. 2006) – both facts corroborate a processing explanation of the acceptability decline in garden-path sentences.

### 5.2.3   Center Embedding

Sentences such as (8) involve multiple center embeddings of clauses: a relative clause containing a relative clause appears inside a matrix clause. Such sentences have figured as prime examples for a processing impact on acceptability since Yngve (1960), who attributed their low acceptability to working memory overload, cf. also Miller and Chomsky (1963) and Miller and Isard (1964). Apparently, the human parser is unable to identify the syntactic structure of (8), hence the illusion of ungrammaticality (De Vries et al. 2011).

(8)    The rat the cat the dog chased killed ate the malt. (Miller & Chomsky 1963: 286)

The memory overload during the parsing of (8) could stem from the number of syntactic predictions that must be kept in memory (Gibson & Thomas 1999), or the number of new discourse referents encountered after the formulation of such predictions (Gibson 2000). The processing difficulty could also result from interference (Lewis & Vasishth 2005, Häussler & Bader 2015).

Two factors modulate the acceptability of center embeddings. Bever (1976) noted an ameliorating effect of a pronominal realization of the most deeply embedded subject, compare (8) with (9), that is captured by models emphasizing the difficulties created by *new* discourse referents that must be memorized and integrated during processing (Gibson 2000).

(9)    The girl the man I scratched kicked died.

Center-embedded structures also pose a challenge at the prosody–syntax interface because the complex syntactic structure should be mapped onto a correspondingly rich prosodic grouping that is difficult to balance in terms of the weight of its prosodic constituents (Fodor, Nickels, & Schott 2017). Sentences constructed in such a way that prosodic phrases are balanced show increased acceptability; see (10) taken from Fodor et al. (2017):

(10)   The elegant woman // that the man Jill loves met // moved to Barcelona.
       3 + 6 + 3 words; 2 + 3 + 3 stressed syllables

An astonishing aspect of center-embedded structures is that the ungrammatical omission of the second of the three verbs (11) yields a structure that is at least as acceptable as the grammatically correct sentence, as first discussed by Frazier (1985), who attributes the observation to Janet Fodor.

(11)   *The patient the nurse the clinic had hired met Jack.

According to Frazier (1985), Gibson and Thomas (1999), and Vasishth et al. (2010), this missing-verb effect arises when syntactic nodes, or the predictions associated with these, are forgotten because of an overload of working memory. Häussler and Bader (2015) attribute the effect to a misalignment of the second verb to the highest NP.

Whether a missing verb effect can be detected in a language may depend on underlying head–complement order. Vasishth et al. (2010) failed to find an effect for speakers of Dutch and German in the processing of their languages, which was however present in their processing of English (Frank, Trompenaer, & Vasishth 2016). Frank et al. argue that there is a fine-tuning to structural frequencies: VVV sequences are frequent in

Dutch and German, but practically non-existent in English, so that the parser will have more problems when encountering such sequences in English than in Dutch and German. However, the status of missing-verb effects in German and Dutch has not yet been fully established; see Häussler and Bader (2015) and Frank and Ernst (2018).

Center-embedded structures can arise with complement clauses in SOV languages. It comes as little surprise that the addition of a third clausal layer in Hindi center-embedded infinitival constructions such as (12) increases processing time, and decreases acceptability (Vasishth 2002). The avoidance of center embedding by the extraposition of a clausal complement increases acceptability in German too (Bader, Häussler, & Schmid 2013; Bayer, Schmid, & Bader 2005).

(12)    Siitaa-ne (Hari-ko) Ravi-ko   kitaab khariid-neko (bol-neko) kahaa
        Sita-ERG  Hari-DAT Ravi-DAT book   buy-INF               tell-INF told
        'Sita told (Hari to tell) Ravi to buy a book.'

The processing difficulty of center-embedded sentences is not determined by the number of incomplete dependencies, because incomplete dependencies targeting an already postulated head do not increase difficulty. What is relevant is the number of postulated heads, as shown by Nakatani and Gibson (2010), with a self-paced reading experiment; see (13): after the processing of *tyuumonsyo-o,* there are four NPs with unresolved relations to verbs, yet the structure is easy to process, because three NPs relate to the same predicate, and the addition of *kokyaku-ni* even makes the structure easier to process (see also Konieczny 2000; Vasishth & Lewis 2006; Levy & Keller 2013). Bader (2016) established that the number of postulated heads is also the crucial factor for acceptability.

(13)    denwaban-ga                  sin'nyuusyain-ga   (kokyaku-ni)
        telephone receptionist-NOM   freshman-NOM       client-DAT
        tyuumonsyo-o   hassoosita  to    dentatusita   ato
        order sheet-ACC  sent       that  told          after
        'after the telephone receptionist told that the freshman had sent the order
        sheet to the client'

The claim that restrictions on center-embedded structures do not belong to grammar has not gone uncontested. Karlson (2007) lists further formal constraints on self-embedded relative clauses and argues that the confinement of embeddings to three clauses is a fact of grammar (but cf. Trotzke, Bader, & Frazier 2013). Connectionist models of language have been developed which imply the restrictions on self-embedding (and even the missing verb effect) without recourse to memory limitations (Christiansen & MacDonald 1998; Christiansen & Chater 1999).

### 5.2.4 Improper Antecedents

Several components of grammar require the licensing of an element by an antecedent. The agreement morphology of the verb is determined by the subject, negative polarity items need a c-commanding negation, etc. When the parser chooses a wrong antecedent, the acceptability of a sentence may be affected.

### 5.2.4.1 Agreement Attraction

Subject–verb agreement is quite vulnerable in language processing (see Chapters 22 and 26). For a subject with a singular head noun and an embedded PP with a plural head as in (14), there can be up to 13 percent agreement errors in production experiments (Eberhard et al. 2005), with participants going for a plural verb form instead of the correct singular.

(14)    the key to the cabinets is/*are on the table

This *agreement attraction* has been documented for many languages (see Acuña-Fariña 2012), with an emphasis on language production. Its strength and likelihood depends on the structural closeness of the attracting noun to the head of the subject, and not on the linear distance between the attracting noun and the verb (cf. Franck et al. 2002, but also Gillespie & Pearlmutter 2011). Agreement attraction is not confined to constellations such as (14). Relative pronouns can attract agreement as in (15) (Kimball & Aissen 1971), and so can objects of SOV clauses in German and Dutch (Hartsuiker et al. 2001; Kaan 2002; Hemforth & Konieczny 2003).

(15)    *the drivers who the runner wave to each morning honk back cheerfully

Agreement attraction also affects acceptability, with errors as in (14) being overlooked in a substantial number of cases (Clifton, Frazier, & Deevy 1999; Wagers, Lau, & Phillips 2009). As Wagers et al. point out, agreement attraction can be explained in, essentially, two ways. First, the number feature of the attracting noun in PP could incorrectly percolate up to the subject NP node during processing, so that agreement errors arise when the verb selects this incorrectly percolated feature for agreement. Alternatively, the number features of the two nouns may be confused in the agreement computation when activated simultaneously. At least in perception, the required additional activation of the plural feature in (14) results from the verbal number morphology. That agreement attraction depends on the activation of the attracting feature by (incorrect) verb morphology explains why grammatical structures are not rejected erroneously. The causes of attraction need not be the same for production and perception (Tanner, Nicol, & Brehm 2014).

In perception, attraction occurs in ungrammatical sentences only (Wagers et al. 2009; Dillon et al. 2013; Tanner et al. 2014), and is probably a result of confusion among simultaneously activated features. The relevant constellation also leads to a slowdown in processing. Vandierendonk et al. (2018) showed that there is a demand on executive control in the processing of (Dutch equivalents of) structures such as (14) only while the subject is processed, but not during the processing of the verb – the actual computation of the agreement relation appears to be a smooth automatic process. Comprehenders often misinterpret singular subjects as (semantic) plurals in the attraction triggering constellation (Patson & Husband 2016). These two observations are not fully compatible with the idea that attraction in comprehension involves a confusion of antecedents only when "plural" is activated by an overt feature of the verb.

### 5.2.4.2  Negative Polarity Items

Negative polarity items (NPI) such as *ever* can, in general, occur in a sentence only when licensed by a c-commanding negative element (Klima 1964), as seen in the contrast between (16a) and (16b). However, the set of licensing contexts is larger than just structures in the scope of negation; see Giannakidou (2011) for an overview.

In a speeded acceptability rating task (Drenhaus, Saddy, & Frisch 2005), participants did not always note the ungrammaticality of (16c), in which the negative NP *no beard* does not c-command the polarity element *ever*, and is, hence, not a possible licensor. The effect fails to arise, however, when judgments are made without time pressure (Xiang, Dillon, & Phillips 2006).

(16)    a. No man with a beard was ever thrifty.
        b. *A man with a beard was ever thrifty.
        c. *A man with no beard was ever thrifty.

There are a number of reasons to doubt that the NPI illusion is similar to agreement attraction (Parker & Phillips 2016). For example, the illusion disappears even in speeded rating when there is enough processing time between the possible licensor and the NPI because of an increase in the distance between the two elements. This time-dependency does not characterize agreement attraction, a fact from which Parker and Phillips (2016) conclude that agreement attraction and illusory NPI licensing are different phenomena.

Given that the illusion-prone element *ever* allows additional pragmatic licensing (Linebarger 1987), as illustrated by (17) taken from Xiang, Grove, and Giannakidou (2013), the proposal (Xiang et al. 2013) that the NPI illusion results from an overapplication of pragmatic licensing is plausible.

(17)   I am sorry that I ever met him.

Xiang, Grove, and Giannakidou (2013) show that participants with high pragmatic-inferential skills are more likely to show the NPI illusion than participants with low pragmatic skills. This corroborates the overapplication of pragmatic licensing analysis of NPI illusions.

### 5.2.4.3 Binding

An overapplication of pragmatic strategies may also affect the acceptability of reflexive pronouns (see Chapter 11 for general discussion of anaphora). When in object positions, reflexive pronouns must find a c-commanding antecedent within the same clause. However, for structurally higher positions in which a reflexive cannot be bound locally, there is an option of a logophoric interpretation (Pollard & Sag 1992; Reinhart & Reuland 1993; Charnavel & Sportiche 2016), in which the reflexive corefers with the logophoric or perspective center of the sentence. This pragmatic interpretation is grammatically blocked when binding by a local c-commanding antecedent is structurally possible.

Incorrect judgments of acceptability could arise when the parser chooses a wrong antecedent for a reflexive. For reading times, effects that can be traced back to an incorrect antecedent choice have not been found consistently (see Badecker & Straub (2002) and Patil et al. (2016) for positive results; Sturt (2003), Xiang, Dillon, & Phillips (2009), and Dillon et al. (2013) for negative ones; and Jäger et al. (2017) for a meta-analysis), which suggests that the processing of the structural binding of reflexive pronouns is relatively immune to interference or memory effects.

However, Sloggett (2017) found that reflexive pronouns can be incorrectly linked to the perspective center of a sentence in an overapplication of the logophoric strategy, leading to a grammaticality illusion. The target sentence in (18) is rated more acceptable when the gender of the matrix clause subject (= the perspective center) matches the gender of the reflexive pronoun, apparently because *the actress* (unlike *the actor*) can serve as an antecedent of *herself* in a grammatically illegal overapplication of the logophoric strategy (Experiment 2 of Sloggett 2017).

(18) (The salacious article was largely derided).
     The actor/actress said that it lied about herself.

The acceptabiliy of the binding of personal pronouns by quantifiers (Kush, Lidz, & Phillips 2015) and by *wh*-phrases (Kush, Lidz, & Phillips 2017) is only slightly affected by processing effects, if at all.

Let us add to the discussion of binding a brief remark on *wh*-phrases in situ. Such *wh*-phrases must link to another *wh*-phrase in the specifier of CP for scope taking (19), so they trigger a backwards search for an antecedent (comparable to the one for reflexives and NPIs), and the distance to the antecedent influences acceptability. As Sprouse et al. (2011) observe, sentences with *wh*-phrases inside *whether* islands are more acceptable than expected, and they explain this as an illusion of grammaticality arising when intervening *whether* is erroneously taken as the antecedent of *what* (implying shorter than necessary backward search).

(19)    a.   <u>Who</u> said that Mary brought <u>what</u>
        b.   Who wonders whether John did what

### 5.2.5   Improper Deletion/Reconstruction

That sentences such as (20) may appear acceptable (e.g. Montalbetti 1984; Myers 2009) has been termed the "comparative illusion." Relatively few studies have investigated the construction empirically. In controlled rating experiments, mean ratings of comparative illusions are much lower than those of normal comparatives, but higher than those of ungrammatical control sentences. The relatively low means of comparative illusions are due to a mixture of high and low ratings (Wellwood et al. 2018).

(20)   *More people have been to London than I have.

(20) is an instance of an illusion of *syntactic* well-formedness only to the extent that it arises by an improper application of the deletion processes that map full clausal comparatives to reduced ones in some models, as sketched in (21). However, as pointed out by Christensen (2016), it is unclear what the clausal source of the illusion underlying (20) could be like.

(21)   More people have been to London than to Rome.
       More people have been to London than people have been to Rome.

Processing data for corresponding Danish sentences presented in Christensen (2010) indicate that the increased brain activity arising in structures with elliptical reconstruction (21) is *absent* in (20): the sentence does not appear to be processed as a reduced comparative, but is assigned a simple syntactic representation lacking a coherent semantic interpretation. Wellwood et al. (2018) argue that (English) comparative illusions are interpreted as event comparisons ("people have been more often to London than I have") by semantic coercion. Christensen (2016) argues that there is a larger range of interpretations for the Danish counterpart of (20), but the difference may be due to the different languages investigated.

### 5.2.6   Summary

This section has discussed several constructions in which processing influences acceptability when the proper syntactic analysis is not identical with the output of the parse. If the parser fails to identify a syntactic analysis at all (as in center-embedded sentences and classical garden path sentences), very low acceptability results. The overapplication of pragmatic interpretation strategies may lead to illusions of grammaticality in domains such as negative polarity items, binding of reflexives, and comparatives. Morphological ambiguities may render grammatical errors invisible, and processing errors may lead to illusions of grammaticality in the domain of subject–verb agreement. Apart from these areas, the human processing system seems to operate with near perfection, so that processing errors distort grammaticality only to a small extent.

## 5.3 Processing Difficulty

The acceptability of a sentence can be lowered when the difficulty of processing it is factored into the judgment. This can be observed for constituent length (Section 5.3.1), dependency length (Section 5.3.2), and local ambiguity (Section 5.3.4), but also in the acceptability patterns found for VP-ellipsis (Section 5.3.3). When certain arguably ungrammatical aspects are introduced into a sentence in order to reduce its processing difficulty, the perception of unacceptability can be mitigated, as in the case of resumptive pronouns and doubled complementizers (Section 5.3.4).

The various factors reducing acceptability will mostly interact in an additive way. This was formulated as the *Linearity Hypothesis* by Keller (2000). When several factors interact in the determination of acceptability, the *gradient nature of judgments* is not unexpected. After all, the length of a dependency, the degree of similarity between two phrases, etc., come on a continuous scale (in a certain sense); they are not categorial. The gradience of such factors correlates with the gradience of the judgments (at least for constituent and dependency length). Whether the gradient nature of processing difficulty (and of the fit of a sentence into context) is the key factor that transforms categorial grammaticality into graded acceptability is an important issue that goes beyond the scope of the present chapter.

### 5.3.1 Constituent Length

That constituent length influences linearization was discovered quite some time ago (e.g. Behaghel 1909, 1932). There is a preference for shorter phrases preceding longer ones (at least in head initial structures) that also affects acceptability. Hawkins (1994) developed a processing model for the impact of length on serialization in which the number of words needed for the complete recognition of the constituent structure of some (head-initial) phrase plays the crucial role. Due to increased processing costs, structures in which longer constituents precede shorter ones can be less acceptable than their counterparts with reversed order.

The placement of relative clauses is influenced by their length (Francis & Michaelis 2016). The acceptability of English structures with relative clauses belonging to the subject decreases with an increasing length of the relative clause, while the acceptability of extraposed relative clauses was not much affected by their length (Francis 2010). The acceptability of the extraposition of relative clauses from direct objects in German verb-final structures increases with the length of the relative clause, but decreases with the distance between the direct object and the landing site of the extraposed relative clause (i.e. it decreases with dependency length; see next subsection) (Konieczny 2000). Surprisingly, the acceptability of a relative clause adjacent to the object is not only affected by its length, but it also increases with its distance from the potential attachment site at the right edge – as if the parser based its judgment on a comparison of the extraposed and the non-extraposed version of the sentences.

An inverse length effect arises for subject clauses and their extraposed counterparts (22). Erdmann (1988) reports a corpus study with the unspectacular result that rather long subject clauses are preferentially extraposed. A judgment study (Widmann 2005, cited in Davies & Dubinsky 2009) basically replicates this effect but revealed that the canonical position is optimal only for subject clauses of intermediate length. Davies and Dubinsky speculate that very short subject clauses may offer the parser "too little time" for recovering from an initial misanalysis of embedded clause material as main clause constituents (*did that players slipped annoy you?*).

(22)     a. That Sahra would replace Angie was obvious to everyone.
         b. It was obvious to everyone that Sahra would replace Angie.

Constituent length can be computed in different ways, but at least in corpora, these different measures are correlated to such an extent that their effects cannot be distinguished empirically (Wasow 1997). Length differences are correlated with differences in information structure, and it is difficult though not impossible to distinguish the effects of "short > long" and "given > new" (Thornton, MacDonald, & Arnold 2000; Arnold et al. 2000). Length differences also affect prosodic differences that may themselves influence acceptability.

Length must be distinguished from syntactic complexity. Longer constituents tend to be syntactically more complex. Following Chomsky (1955/75), Wasow and Arnold (2003) established the existence of an effect of syntactic complexity on acceptability independent of length. In experiments in which the length of the phrases was held constant while syntactic complexity was manipulated by the presence or absence of a sentential embedding, acceptability for a late placement of a long NP increased with its syntactic complexity in Heavy NP-Shift constructions, particle shift constellations and the dative alternation.

## 5.3.2 Dependency Length

As we have just mentioned, the acceptability of relative clause extra-position is negatively correlated with the distance between the relative clause and the NP it modifies, i.e. with the length of the dependency between the two elements (Konieczny 2000). This observation instantiates a general principle: increased dependency length reduces acceptability (see Chapters 1 and 9). Consequently, the longer *wh*-dependency makes (23b) less acceptable than (23a) (Sprouse 2007a: 157); cf. also Phillips, Kazaniona, and Abada (2005). Comparable results were found for German (Fanselow & Féry 2008; Häussler et al. 2019). The acceptability of sentences with in situ *wh*-phrases decreases with the distance between the in situ *wh*-phrase and the moved *wh*-phrase to which it is linked with respect to scope (24). The acceptability of quantificational binding in English (Sprouse et al. 2011) decreases for longer distances between quantifier and pronoun.

(23)     a. Who hoped that you knew **who** <u>the mayor would honor</u> **t**_

          b. Who knew **who** <u>you hoped that the mayor would honor</u> **t**

(24)     a. Who hoped that you knew **who** <u>would honor</u> *who*

          b. Who knew **who** <u>hoped that you would honor</u> *who*

Subjects are closer to the left periphery of a clause (Spec,CP) than objects, and the question arises whether that small length difference also affects the acceptability of *wh*-movement. Subject *wh*-questions *are* slightly more acceptable than their object-initial counterparts in English and German (Arnon et al. 2012; Häussler et al. 2015). This could be attributed to the different dependency length, but it might also just reflect the higher frequency of subject questions. Subject relative clause do not appear to be more acceptable than object relative clauses in English, despite the difference in processing difficulty (Staub 2010).

In German, object-initial declarative clauses are generally less acceptable than subject initial ones (cf. Krems (1984) and Hemforth (1993) for processing difficulty, and Weskott (2003) for acceptability judgments, among others), an effect for which dependency length was often made responsible (see also Chapter 12). However, object initiality signals distinctions of information structure, so that the drop in acceptability of object-initial sentences may also be related to pragmatic markedness. When the fronted object stands in a POSET-relation (Prince 1998) to the discourse topic, object-initial sentences even get a higher rating than their subject-initial counterparts (Weskott et al. 2011). Intervention effects contribute to the lowering of the acceptability of object-initial sentences; see Wierzba and Fanselow (2020). Taken together, there is no unequivocal support for the claim that acceptability differences between subject- and object-initial *wh*-questions and declaratives stem from a dependency length effect.

For OV order, "antilocality" comes in as a further factor: processing difficulty can decrease (and acceptability increase) when the distance between a direct object and a verb is enlarged by an inserted dative object (Konieczny & Döring 2003; Vasishth & Lewis 2006; Levy & Keller 2013), presumably because the processing of the dative object leads to a reactivation of frame predictions and makes them more precise.

### 5.3.3   VP-Ellipsis

Hankamer and Sag (1976) developed a model for so-called "surface anaphora" according to which the interpretation of the anaphoric element is determined by the syntactic structure of its antecedent. VP-ellipsis (25) is a surface anaphor – the elliptical VP must share the syntactic surface structure of its antecedent, which explains the contrast between (25) and (26) (ungrammatical because of a voice mismatch).

(25)   Someone had to take out the garbage, but Bill didn't ~~take out the garbage~~.

(26)   *The information was released, but Gorbachov didn't.

This original view on VP-ellipsis is not entirely correct, however, since there are attested examples (such as (27) taken from Arregui et al. 2006) that are acceptable, yet cannot be analyzed in terms of simple ellipsis because of a voice mismatch between the antecedent and the elided VP.

(27)   This information could have been released by Gorbachov, but he chose not to (release the information).

For VP-ellipsis constructions without surface identity between the overt and the elided VP, Arregui et al. (2006) identify a gradual decline in acceptability correlated with the degree of similarity between the elided VP and the overt antecedent. They argue that the correlation comes about by the degree to which "repair" operations must apply before antecedent and elided VP match. See Kim et al. (2011) for a different way of capturing the correlation between acceptability and the ease of reconstructing the elided VP.

### 5.3.4   Further Effects of Processing Difficulty

Hemforth et al. (2000) showed that attachment preferences for relative clauses lead to differences in acceptability: attaching a clause to a dispreferred site reduces acceptability. A preference study reported in Wasow and Arnold (2003) suggests that the avoidance of a local processing ambiguity by a change in constituent order increases acceptability.

The Active Filler Strategy (Frazier 1987) implies that the parser attempts to link a preposed *wh*-phrase to the first possible gap site. Whenever the first gap site is filled (compare (28b) with (28a)), processing is more difficult (Stowe 1986). Sprouse (2008) showed that this filled gap constellation implies a reduction of acceptability.

(28)   a My brother wanted to know *who* Ruth will bring __ home to Mom at Christmas.
       b. My brother wanted to know *who* Ruth will bring *us* home to __ at Christmas.

There is a discussion in the literature as to whether the unacceptability caused by island violations is mitigated by the replacement of the movement gap by a resumptive pronoun (29) (see Chapter 8).

(29)   This is the man who(m) you did not tell me when we should invite _ / him.

In English non-island contexts, the replacement of gaps by resumptive pronouns decreases acceptability. This acceptability difference is smaller in islands, but sentences with resumptive pronouns were never more acceptable than counterparts with gaps in the studies reported in Alexopoulou and Keller (2007). Only when participants rate comprehensibility rather than acceptability, resumptive pronouns are better than gaps in islands (Beltrama & Xiang 2016). An ameliorating effect of resumptive pronouns was argued for by McDaniel and Cowart (1999) for subject gaps in islands.

However, the idea that resumptive pronouns "mitigate" effects of constraint violations is not the only perspective. Kefalla (2011) and Kefalla and Goodall (2011) compared resumptive pronouns and gaps in various island and non-island contexts. These structural manipulations did not affect the acceptability of resumptive pronoun sentences very much, but had strong effects on extraction sentences, by which the acceptability of, e.g., a subject gap within a *wh*-island might end up below the acceptability rating of a resumptive structure. Thus, the use of resumptive pronoun may be more acceptable than extraction because the former is not affected by any of the constraints that hold for the latter.

Acceptability can sometimes even be raised by the addition of an ungrammatical feature such as a doubled complementizer (Staum Casasanto & Sag 2008) when the insertion of such elements improves processability.

## 5.4  Processing Accounts of Crossing Movement and Constraints on Extraction Domains?

With its seminal investigation of island effects on movement such as the ban on extractions from sentential subjects (30), Ross (1967) is one of the most influential works in syntax. Likewise, the discovery of the contrast in (30) showing that a wh-phrase (apparently) cannot cross another wh-phrase when it moves to the left periphery of the sentence (the superiority effect, Kuno and Robinson 1972) led to a general discussion of no-crossing constraints, such as the Minimal Link Condition (Chomsky 1995).

(30)     *Who is to listen to _ fun?

(31)     Who saw what
         *What did who see

Nevertheless, the status of the relevant constraints as part of syntax proper was already questioned very early; see, e.g., Erteshik-Shir (1973). A new dimension was added to this discussion by Kluender and Kutas (1993), by making the case for an analysis of island violations in terms of processing overload. A similar analysis was proposed for superiority effects by Arnon et al. (2012).

## 5.4.1  Superiority

The superiority effect looks like the streamlined outcome of a grammatical ban on crossing movement, as originally proposed by Kuno and Robinson (1972): a wh-phrase cannot move to the left of another wh-phrase. In processing accounts (Hofmeister et al. 2007; Arnon et al. 2012), however, there is nothing grammatically wrong with crossing movement. Rather, the crossing constellation is taken to be more difficult to process than its non-crossing alternative, so that the former is avoided and less acceptable. Crossing movement is more difficult because the movement path of the crossing phrase is longer than the path of the crossed-over phrase would be, because the grammatical function of a left-peripheral object may be hard to identify in languages with linear heuristics for recognizing grammatical functions, and because the parser must cope with the interference of the intervening wh-phrase on the link between the fronted wh-phrase and its trace.

   That superiority violations are indeed less acceptable in English than their non-crossing counterparts has been shown repeatedly (Featherston 2005; Clifton, Fanselow, & Frazier 2006; Hofmeister et al. 2007; Fedorenko & Gibson 2008; Arnon et al. 2012; Hofmeister et al. 2013; Häussler et al. 2015). The severity of the effect depends on the nature of the wh-phrases involved: the use of discourse-linked which-phrases (Pesetsky 2000) instead of wh-pronouns increases acceptability, with the amelioration being strongest for crossed-over discourse-linked phrases (Fedorenko & Gibson 2008; Hofmeister et al. 2013).

   Another modulating effect was found for animacy in German (Fanselow et al. 2011) and Czech (Meyer 2004): the superiority effect is larger when the two wh-phrases agree in animacy. When they agree, their featural composition is more similar, so that stronger interference from the in-situ phrase on the relation between the moved phrase and its trace is to be expected.

Effects of discourse linking and animacy on acceptability are not confined to superiority violations. They also show up in extractions out of English *wh*-islands (Atkinson et al. 2016): animacy differences lead to a very small increase of acceptability only, while the use of discourse linked phrases, in particular once again in the position crossed over, is much larger. Goodall (2015) found that extractions of *which*-phrases are more acceptable than extractions of *wh*-pronouns also for movement out of finite *that*-clauses and complex NPs. Since these constructions contain no second *wh*-phrase, the acceptability difference between *wh*-pronouns and discourse linked phrases cannot be a matter of interference. Because of their more detailed representations, *which*-phrases can perhaps be held in memory more easily than *wh*-pronouns, and yield more acceptable movement chains.

In languages in which case plays a crucial role for recognizing grammatical functions, the different case features of *wh*-subjects and *wh*-objects make them less similar than in English. Interference effects are thus expected to be smaller. This could account for the remarkable mitigation of the superiority effect in such languages (cf. Featherston (2005) and Häussler et al. (2015) for yoked studies of English and German, and Häussler et al. (2019) for further languages). The size of the crossing effect also decreases when a *wh*-adverb rather than a *wh*-DP crosses a *wh*-subject in German (Featherston 2005) and Dutch (Häussler et al. 2019), as one would expect if similarity-based interference matters. Nevertheless, a residual superiority effect remains visible in all languages studied, with the exception of Czech.

Hofmeister et al. (2013) report satiation effects for superiority violations: superiority violations were rated as more acceptable in the second half of an experiment than in the first one. Satiation was also observed by Hall (2018) for German, and in yet unpublished experiments of Jessica Brown, Gisbert Fanselow, and Reinhold Kliegl, for English. It is not obvious that the findings lend further support to a processing account of superiority effects, since the satiation effects were relatively small and not larger than the overall improvement found for structures of non-extreme acceptability.

Reductionist views would also have to be elaborated such that the interpretive differences between multiple questions with and without crossing movement (see, e.g., Pesetsky 2000) could be explained without recourse to grammar.

## 5.4.2  Subjacency

### 5.4.2.1  Narrowing Down the Issue: Superadditivity

The insights of Ross (1967) led to the conviction in generative grammar that grammatical constraints rule out extraction of elements that are embedded in *syntactic islands* such as adjunct clauses or indirect questions, as illustrated by the contrast in (32) (see also Chapter 9).

(32)     a. Who did she say that John had married _?
         b. *Who did she stay because/when John had married _ ?
         c. *Who do you wonder where she has met _ first?

Kluender and Kutas (1993) try to derive (certain) island restrictions from processing overload: extractions from complement questions (32c) and relative clauses do not only come with the memory costs of long movement, but also involve additional processing costs at the clause boundary where the processing of discourse referents is particularly demanding. Kluender and Kutas claim that these joint demands exceed the limits of working memory at the embedded *wh*-clause boundary (=*where* in (32c)) when the dependency of *who* linking from the matrix into the embedded clause must be kept in memory. Therefore, these structures are avoided and not processed by the parser, resulting in unacceptability. Hofmeister and Sag (2010) follow a similar line of reasoning, but assume that the island effect is caused by a multitude of processing difficulties at the clause edge, each of which reduces acceptability without leading individually to a breakdown of the parser.

One outcome of the discussion of the relation between processing and islands is the insight that postulating a constraint banning movement out of some island is warranted only if the acceptability decline of such structures exceeds the sum of the drop of acceptability caused individually by the factors that create an island (Kluender & Kutas 1993; Sprouse, Wagers, & Phillips 2012) – the so-called *factorial definition of island effects*. For example, a subject island constraint is justified only if the reduction of acceptability resulting from an extraction out of a sentential subject is larger than the sum of the decline in acceptability resulting from the addition of an subject clause, and the execution of long movement. The effect must be *superadditive* (Sprouse et al. 2012), because an additive effect will arise by the simple combination of two simple violations (*Linearity Hypothesis*, Keller 2000)

A superadditive effect can point to the existence of an additional grammatical constraint banning the combination of the two factors in question (Sprouse et al. 2012). When the factors reducing acceptability involve processing load, and tap into the same cognitive resource, their combination might also yield a superadditive effect whenever the combined demands exceed the capacity of the system, so that a breakdown results (Kluender & Kutas 1993). Superadditivity in contexts in which processing cannot have broken down because the structure is still moderately acceptable is thus difficult to reconcile with a non-grammatical account of the phenomenon. The island effects of Brazilian Portuguese and Hebrew discussed below could be a case in point.

Some experiments have shown superadditive interactions in the absence of a plausible candidate for an island constraint. Staum Casasanto, Hofmeister, and Sag (2010) found a strong superadditive interaction of the factors "presence or absence of a relative clause between the subject and the verb" and "inverting the order of subject and object by relativizing on the object." Individually, they only yield a small reduction of acceptability, but they interact superadditively. We can attribute the low acceptability of (33) to the high memory demands of the structure.

(33)    The administrator who the nurse who was from the clinic supervised scolded the medic while a patient was brought into the emergency room.

In their investigation of negative islands (Ross 1984), Gieselmann et al. (2013) found a superadditive interaction of the factor "positive vs. negative sentence" and the factor "referential and non-referential subject," as in (34). Note that the *wh*-phrase has not moved *across* the negation in such examples, so that the negative island condition (Ross 1984) cannot be invoked here. As Gieselmann et al. (2013) point out, one might understand the acceptability difference between referential and non-referential subjects in negative domains in semantic terms, yet both structures appear acceptable, so that memory overflow cannot account for the judgment differences.

(34)    {How many / which} interns (didn't) complete their projects during the internship?

### 5.4.2.2  Doubtful Island Status

At least two island types turn out to be problematic from the perspective of a factorial definition. Ross (1974) and Wexler and Culicover (1980) argue for a *freezing effect*: a phrase having undergone syntactic movement becomes an island for extraction; see (35) for movement from an NP that is in situ (35a) vs. from an NP that has moved to the right (35b) (Heavy NP-Shift). An independent *freezing constraint* could not be supported empirically, however: Hofmeister, Culicover, and Winkler (2015) and Konietzko, Winkler, and Culicover (2018) found that extractions from extraposed PPs and NPs having undergone Heavy NP-Shift come with low acceptability, but the acceptability decline is not larger than the summed effects of extraposing an NP or a PP, and extracting from NP or PP, i.e. there is no superadditivity.

(35)    a. Who$_i$ did you put [a picture of t$_i$] on the table?
        b. *Who$_i$ did you put t$_j$ on the table [a picture of t$_i$]$_j$?

*Subject Islands* (postulated as "Sentential Subject Constraint" by Ross (1967)) have yielded superadditive effects in several studies (Sprouse et al. 2011; Sprouse et al. 2016). Nevertheless, the island effect may result from an interaction of several independent grammatical factors from the perspective of generative syntax (cf. Greco, Marelli & Haegeman 2017). Furthermore, *wh*-movement and subject clauses do not go well together, even when the *wh*-phrase is not extracted *from* the subject but moved across it, with the acceptability of movement across a subject clause approaching the acceptability of extractions *from* subject clauses. Under certain semantic and pragmatic conditions, the acceptability difference between extractions from a complex subject and across one can even be eliminated (Clausen 2010, 2011; cf. also Abeillé et al. 2018). Chaves and Dery (2018) found a satiation effect (but see below for conflicting evidence), with ratings for subject island violations increasing up to the point where the acceptability difference between extractions from subject and object clauses was no longer significant. The status of the subject condition as an independent principle is thus somewhat undecided.

### 5.4.2.3  Clear Island Status: *Wh*-islands, Complex NPs, Adjuncts, and Negative Islands

Moving a *wh*-phrase out of an embedded question or relative clause leads to unacceptability, as shown in (36).

(36)    a. *What do you wonder who read _?
        b. *What did you meet a man who read _ ?

Because the *wh*-phrase *what* crosses a further phrase in Spec,CP (*who*), *wh*-islands lend themselves most easily to the idea of coming with unacceptably high processing costs, due to the combined cognitive demands of the clause boundary, the *wh*-chain targeting the main clause, and the *wh*-phrase sitting in the lower Spec,CP. The low acceptability of extractions from *wh*-islands could thus be interpreted as being due to these processing difficulties; cf., e.g., Kluender and Kutas (1993). Other kinds of island violations, e.g. extractions from complex NPs, and adjunct islands fit into such a reductionist account to the extent that high processing costs can be identified for them as well.

*Wh*-islands, complex noun phrases and adjunct islands show superadditive effects on the movement of question *wh*-phrases in English and Italian, but effects were much less clear for relative clauses (Sprouse et al. 2016). Superadditive response patterns for *wh*-islands (and others) were found in nearly all languages studied so far, but the island effect did not always render the structure unacceptable. In Norwegian, *whether*-islands are much weaker than in English, due to high variability among speakers (Kush, Lohndal, & Sprouse 2018). Sentences violating *wh*-islands received *intermediate* ratings, i.e. they were not judged as ungrammatical, in spite of superadditive *wh*-island response patterns in Danish (Christensen et al. 2013a, but see Christensen et al. 2013b), Brazilian Portuguese (Almeida 2014), and Hebrew (Keshev & Meltzer-Asscher 2019).

Thus, while extraction from *wh*-clauses (and similar islands) systematically lowers acceptability, this lowering need not imply unacceptability. Consequently, the processing difficulty of *wh*-island violations cannot be the *only* factor responsible for the unacceptability of (36), because it is difficult (though not impossible) to construct the processing model in such a way that the memory load would be different in different languages (Almeida 2014). However, additional factors may interact with the *wh*-island constraint in some languages, but not in others, and lead to different degrees of (un-)acceptability in different languages (Keshev & Meltzer-Asscher 2019).

For example, English *wh*-islands effects are modulated by the finiteness of the *wh*-clause (Ross 1967). This finiteness effect (see Michel & Goodall 2013 for experimental data from adjunct and Complex NP Constraint (CNPC) islands) does not show up for extractions from complement clauses, i.e. it is superadditive for the simple reason that it fails to exist outside islands. Whatever the exact nature of the constraint is, it is coupled to extractions from islands, and if its strength varies between languages, there is a possible way of understanding cross-linguistic differences in the severity of island violations.

The findings of Goodluck, Tsiwah, and Saah (2017) contribute to this picture. Questions in Akan asking for constituents of *wh*-islands, adjuncts, and complex noun phrases have reduced acceptability, but the absolute judgments were in the acceptable domain. Akan does not construct question by movement but with base-generated left-peripheral *wh*-phrases binding null and overt resumptive pronouns. The comparison of Akan and English suggests that there is a factor penalizing question dependencies into islands irrespective of their syntactic derivation, and a further factor additionally penalizing movement in such contexts, perhaps linked to the finiteness constraint uncovered by Michel and Goodall (2013).

Many East Asian languages do not need to front their question words, but if they do, they do not employ proper *wh*-movement but scrambling. Sprouse et al. (2011) found no island effects for Japanese *wh*-scrambling. The facts for Korean are less clear (Kim & Goodall 2016; Jung, Kim, & Kim 2017). In order to capture the difference between, say, English and Japanese, processing accounts of *wh*-islands would have to identify reasons for why *wh*-movement proper is more susceptible to memory constraints than *wh*-scrambling. There might indeed be different processing demands at the left periphery (embedded questions have no *wh*-phrase in Spec,CP in *wh*-scrambling languages). Acceptability differences might again be due to the finiteness factor (East Asian languages lack a finiteness distinction).

The generalizability of island constraints to further dependency types, in particular to the processing of cataphoric pronouns, has also been addressed by rating experiments. Yoshida et al. (2014) found no island effects on the processing of cataphoric dependencies, In contrast, Keshev and Meltzer-Asscher (2019) compared the acceptability of links of cataphoric pronouns to NPs embedded in *wh*-islands (as in (37)) to NPs embedded in *that*-clauses, using the factorial definition of islands, and found a superadditive *wh*-island effect on cataphoric pronouns. The authors explain their finding in terms of the burden of keeping two dependencies of referential items (the cataphoric pronoun seeking a coreferent NP, the *wh*-phrase seeking its trace) in memory at the same time. Given that cataphoric coreference is, syntactically, *not* subject to island constraints, Keshev and Meltzer-Asscher have thus identified a processing-triggered reduction of acceptability with *wh*-islands that cannot be understood in terms of a low *grammaticality* of the pertinent relation.

(37) axrey  še-ha-davarim  hicxiku  ota$_i$  ha-dayarot$_i$  ha-xadašot  sipru
     after  that-the-mailmen  made+laugh  her$_i$  the-tenants  the-new  told

     eifo  ha-šxenim  ya'asiku  et  ha-menaka  ha-yesodit.
     where  the-neighbors  will+employ  ACC  the-cleaner  the-thorough

     'After that the mailmen made her$_i$ laugh, the new tenants told where the neighbors will
     employ the thorough cleaner$_i$.'

If a structure's low acceptability comes from processing problems, acceptability may go up once repeated exposure to the structure has enabled the parser to learn how to cope with the difficulties (*satiation*). The literature on syntactic priming provides ample evidence that previous exposure affects the processing of a construction, and also its acceptability, as first shown by Nagata (1990): repeated exposure tends to make judgments more extreme (see Chapter 6).

Satiation effects would be a good way of addressing the nature of acceptability if, as Sprouse (2007b) argues, there can be satiation effects for grammatical structures only. However, Hofmeister, Staum Casanto, and Sag (2013) report that acceptability of clearly ungrammatical structures such as (38) improved after repeated exposure.

(38)   Iran has gun-control strict laws that bar private citizens carrying from firearms.

To the extent that satiation effects are indicative of a strong processing component in the acceptability profile of a construction, the CNPC appears to be affected most by processing difficulty, since satiation effects are regularly found for this island type (Snyder 2000; Goodall 2011; Do & Kaiser 2017, among many others). Satiation effects for adjunct islands have not been observed so far, while subject islands have produced a mixed picture (no satiation in Snyder (2000), Goodall (2011), and Do & Kaiser (2017), in contrast to the results of Crawford (2012) and Chaves & Dery (2014)), just as *whether*-islands (satiation found in Snyder (2000), Francom (2009), Crawford (2012), but not in Goodall (2011)). A strong processing contribution to unacceptability thus seems likely for CNPC and *whether*-islands.

Constructions of moderate (un-)acceptability in general have a chance of being perceived as more acceptable after repeated exposure (e.g. Luka & Barsalou 2005). The mechanisms by which repeated exposure affects acceptability have not really been clarified. Satiation effects might, e.g., simply reflect the development of semantic strategies for an increased fluency of comprehension (Zervakis & Mazuka 2013), and thus provide little evidence on how syntactic factors influence acceptability.

If islands are unacceptable because of a memory overload, individual variability in the acceptability of the islands might correlate with differences in working memory capacity. After all, individuals with a higher working memory capacity are less likely to run into memory problems when processing complex sentences, and should thus find them more acceptable. However, in a systematic study investigating syntactic judgments in combination with two working memory tests (serial recall task and n-back task), no correlation could be found between acceptability judgments for islands and working memory capacity (Sprouse et al. 2012), an observation replicated by Aldosari (2015), and by Michel (2014) with a larger cognitive test battery. While these results do not refute a processing account of *wh*-islands (see, e.g., Hofmeister, Staum Casasanto, & Sag 2012), they certainly to not lend additional support to the processing explanation.

This absence of a correlation between judgments for islands and memory capacity is all the more remarkable since Michel *did* find significant influences of individual differences in the memory lure tasks on the perception of long movement (speakers with a high performance score perceive a larger difference between short and long movement) and on the acceptability of the *presence* of an island (but not on extraction *from* the island). In particular, the differences between high- and low-span readers do not translate in a simple way into differences in the processing of islands: the processing pattern of the two groups may diverge at the left edge of the island, but converges at the gap position, so that, at the end of the sentences – when judgments are made – the previous differences no longer exist.

In general, the idea itself that high processing capacity makes it more likely that sentences are acceptable is too simple. High- and low-working-memory participants gave similar ratings for questions with D-linked expressions, but the two participant groups differed in their assessment of bare *wh*-questions (Michel 2014): for low-memory participants, bare questions got a rating *on par* with the D-linked questions, while high-memory participants gave a *lower* rating to bare questions as compared to D-linked ones. The judgments of high-memory participants may take more factors into account, so that ratings can be actually lower in the high-memory group. This was also found by Hofmeister et al. 2012 and by Sprouse (cited by Michel 2014: 132) for center-embedded structures. Finding out how differences in cognitive ability translate into differences in acceptability judgments is clearly an important task for future research.

## 5.5 Concluding Remarks

Constituent and dependency length, difficult attachment sites, and inter-ference among too similar phrases are among the factors that make sen-tence processing difficult, and lower the acceptability of sentences at the same time. A lot of evidence has been accumulated concerning such effects, but there are a few attempts only at models that make precise predictions for the acceptability of sentences as a function of the accumu-lated processing difficulty, such as the one formulated by Keller (2000). The identification of such a model, that should also allow the integration of prosodic, semantic, and pragmatic impacts and effects of frequency, is certainly a desideratum.

At the same time, it is obvious that "acceptability" is merely an ancillary concept. "Grammaticality" and "processing difficulty" are notions much closer to the core of syntax and psycholinguistics, respectively. Ideally, the field would be equipped with methods that address grammaticality in a more direct way than standard acceptability judgments. But hopefuls such as "repeated exposure" have so far not really delivered the expected benefits.

## References

Abeillé, A., Hemforth, B., Winckel, E., & Gibson, E. (2018). A construction-conflict explanation of the subject-island constraint. Poster presented at the 31st Annual CUNY Conference on Human Sentence Processing, University of California, Davis.

Acuña-Fariña, J. C. (2012). Agreement, attraction and architectural opportunism. *Journal of Linguistics*, 48, 257–295.

Aldosari, S. (2015). The role of individual differences in the acceptability of island violations in native and non-native speakers. Doctoral dissertation, University of Kansas.

Alexopoulou, T. & Keller, F. (2007). Locality, cyclicity, and resumption: At the interface between the grammar and the human sentence processor. *Language*, 83, 110–160.

Almeida, D. (2014). Subliminal *wh*-islands in Brazilian Portuguese and the consequences for syntactic theory. *Revista da ABRALIN*, 13(2), 55–93.

Arnold, J., Wasow, T., Losongo, A., & Ginstrom, R. (2000). Heavyness vs. newness: The effects of structural complexity and discourse status on constituent ordering. *Language* 76, 28–55.

Arnon, I., Snider, N., Hofmeister, P., Jaeger, T. F., & Sag, I. (2012). Cross-linguistic variation in a processing account: The case of multiple *wh*-questions. In M. J. Houser et al., eds., *Proceedings of the 32nd Annual Meeting of the Berkeley Linguistics Society*. Berkeley, CA: University of California, Berkeley Linguistics Society, pp. 23–36.

Arregui, A., Clifton, C., Frazier, L. & Moulton, K. (2006). Processing elided verb phrases with flawed antecedents: The recycling hypothesis. *Journal of Memory and Language* 55, 232–246.

Atkinson, E., Apple, A., Rawlins, K., & Omaki, A. (2016). Similarity of *wh*-phrases and acceptability variation in *wh*-islands. *Frontiers in Psychology*, 6, 2048.

Badecker, W. & Straub, K. (2002). The processing role of structural constraints on interpretation of pronouns and anaphors. *Journal of Experimental Psychology: Learning, Memory, and Cognition*, 28(4), 748–769.

Bader, M. (2016). The Limited Role of Number of Nested Syntactic Dependencies in Accounting for Processing Cost: Evidence from German Simplex and Complex Verbal Clusters. *Frontiers in Psychology*, 8, 2268.

Bader, M. & Bayer, J. (2006). *Case and Linking in Language Comprehension*. Berlin: Springer.

Bader, M., Häussler, J., & Schmid, T. (2013). Constraints on intra- and extraposition. In G. Webelhuth, M. Sailer, & H. Walker, eds., *Rightward Movement in a Comparative Perspective*. Amsterdam and Philadelphia: John Benjamins, pp. 1–60.

Bayer, J., Bader, M., & Meng, M. (2001). Morphological underspecification meets oblique case: syntactic and processing effects in German. *Lingua*, 111, 465–514.

Bayer, J., Schmid, T., & Bader, M. (2005). Clause union and clausal position. In M. Den Dikken, ed., *The Function of Function Words and Functional Categories*. Amsterdam and Philadelphia: John Benjamins, pp. 79–113.

Behaghel, O. (1909). Beziehungen zwischen Umfang und Reihenfolge von Satzgliedern. *Indogermanische Forschungen*, 25, 110–142.

Behaghel, O. (1932). *Deutsche Syntax*, vol. IV: *Wortstellung Periodenbau*. Heidelberg: Carl Winters.

Beltrama, A. & Xiang, M. (2016). Unacceptable but comprehensible: The facilitation effects of resumptive pronouns. *Glossa: A Journal of General Linguistics*, 1(1), 29. DOI:10.5334/gjgl.24

Bever, T. (1970). The cognitive basis for linguistic structures. In J. R. Hayes, ed., *Cognition and the Development of Language*. New York: John Wiley & Sons, pp. 279–362.

Bever, T. (1976). The influence of speech performance on linguistic structure. In T. Bever, J. Katz, & D. Langendoen, eds., *An Integrated Theory of Linguistic Ability*. New York: Crowell, pp. 65–88.

Charnavel, I. & Sportiche, D. (2016). Anaphor binding: What French inanimate anaphors show. *Linguistic Inquiry*, 47, 35–87.

Chaves, R. & Dery, J. (2014). Which subject islands will the acceptability of improve with repeated exposure? In R. Santana-La Barge, ed., *Proceedings of the 31st West Coast Conference on Formal Linguistics*. Somerville, MA: Cascadilla Proceedings Project, pp. 96–106.

Chaves, R. & Dery, J. (2018). Frequency effects in subject islands. *Journal of Linguistics*, 55, 1–47.

Chomsky, N. (1955/1975). *The Logical Structure of Linguistic Theory*. Chicago: University of Chicago Press.

Chomsky, N. (1965). *Aspects of the Theory of Syntax*. Cambridge, MA: MIT Press.

Chomsky, N. (1995). *The Minimalist Program*. Cambridge, MA: MIT Press.

Christensen, K. (2010). Syntactic reconstruction and reanalysis, semantic dead ends, and prefrontal cortex. *Brain and Cognition*, 73(1), 41–50.

Christensen, K. (2016). The dead ends of language: The (mis)interpretation of a grammatical illusion. In S. Vikner, H. Jørgensen, & E. van Gelderen, eds., *Let Us Have Articles Betwixt Us: Papers in Historical and Comparative Linguistics in Honour of Johanna L. Wood*. Aarhus: Dept. of English, School of Communication & Culture, Aarhus University, pp. 129–160.

Christensen, K., Kizach, J., & Nyvad, A. (2013a). Escape from the Island: Grammaticality and (reduced) acceptability of *wh*-island violations in Danish. *Journal of Psycholinguistic Research*, 42, 51–70.

Christensen, K., Kizach, J., & Nyvad, A. (2013b). The processing of syntactic islands: An fMRI study. *Journal of Neurolinguistics*, 26, 239–251.

Christiansen, M. & Chater, N. (1999). Toward a connectionist model of recursion in human linguistic performance. *Cognitive Science*, 23, 157–205.

Christiansen, M. & Macdonald, M. (1998). Processing of recursive sentence structure: Testing predictions from a connectionist model. *Cognition*, 45, 225–255.

Christianson, K., Williams, C., Zacks, R., & Ferreira, F. (2006). Younger and older adults' "good-enough" interpretations of garden-path sentences. *Discourse Processes*, 42(2), 205–238.

Clausen, D. (2010). Processing factors influencing acceptability in extractions from complex subjects. Unpublished manuscript, Stanford University.

Clausen, D. (2011). Informativity and acceptability of complex subject islands. Poster presented at the 24th Annual CUNY Sentence Processing Conference, Stanford.

Clifton, C., Fanselow, G., & Frazier, L. (2006). Amnestying superiority violations: Processing multiple questions. *Linguistic Inquiry*, 37, 51–68.

Clifton, C., Frazier, L., & Deevy, P. (1999). Feature manipulation in sentence comprehension. *Rivista di Linguistica*, 11(1), 11–39.

Crawford, J. (2012). Using Syntactic Satiation to Investigate Subject Islands. In J. Choi, E. A. Hogue, J. Punske, D. Tat, J. Schertz, & A. Trueman, eds., *Proceedings of the 29th West Coast Conference on Formal Linguistics*, Somerville, MA: Cascadilla Proceedings Project, pp. 38–45.

Davies, W. D. & Dubinsky S. (2009). On the existence (and distribution) of sentential subjects. In D. Gerdts, J. Moore, & M. Polinsky, eds., *Hypothesis A/Hypothesis B: Linguistic Explorations in Honor of David M. Perlmutter*. Cambridge, MA: MIT Press, pp. 111–128.

De Vries, M., Christiansen, M. H., & Petersson, K. M. (2011). Learning recursion: Multiple nested and crossed dependencies. *Biolinguistics*, 5, 010–035.

Dillon, B., Mishler, A., Sloggett, S., & Phillips, C. (2013). Contrasting intrusion profiles for agreement and anaphora: Experimental and modeling evidence. *Journal of Memory and Language*, 69, 85–103.

Do, M. & Kaiser, E. (2017). A closer look: Investigating the mechanisms of syntactic satiation. In A. Kaplan et al. eds., *Proceedings of the 34th West Coast Conference on Formal Linguistics*. Somerville, MA: Cascadilla Proceedings Project, pp. 187–194.

Drenhaus, H., Saddy, D., & Frisch, S. (2005). Processing negative polarity items: when negation comes through the backdoor. In S. Kepser & M. Reis, eds., *Linguistic Evidence – Empirical, Theoretical, and Computational Perspectives*. Berlin and New York: Mouton de Gruyter, pp. 145–165.

Eberhard, M. K., Cooper Cutting, J., & Bock, K. (2005). Making syntax of sense: Number agreement in sentence production. *Psychological Review*, 112(3), 531–559.

Erdmann, P. (1988). On the principle of "weight" in English. In C. Duncan-Rose & T. Vennemann, eds., *On Language*. Abingdon: Routledge, pp. 325–339.

Erteshik-Shir, N. (1973). On the nature of island constraints. Doctoral dissertation, Massachusetts Institute of Technology.

Fanselow, G. & Féry, C. (2008): Missing superiority effects: Long movement in German (and other languages). In J. Witkos & G. Fanselow, eds., *Elements of Slavic and Germanic Grammars: A Comparative View*. Frankfurt: Peter Lang, pp. 67–87.

Fanselow, G. & Frisch, S. (2006). Effects of processing difficulty on judgments of acceptability. In G. Fanselow, C. Féry, R. Vogel, & M. Schlesewsky, eds., *Gradience in Grammar*. Oxford: Oxford University Press, pp. 291–316.

Fanselow, G., Schlesewsky, M., Vogel, R., & Weskott, T. (2011). Animacy effects on crossing *wh*-movement in German. *Linguistics*, 49, 657–683.

Featherston, S. (2005). Universals and grammaticality: *Wh*-constraints in German and English. *Linguistics*, 43, 667–711.

Fedorenko, E. & Gibson, E. (2008). Syntactic parallelism as an account of superiority effects: Empirical investigations in English and Russian. Unpublished manuscript, MIT.

Ferreira, F., Ferraro, V., & Bailey, K. (2002). Good-enough representations in language comprehension. *Current Directions in Psychological Science*, 11, 11–15.

Ferreira, F. & Henderson, J. (1991). Recovery from misanalyses of garden-path sentences. *Journal of Memory and Language*, 30, 725–745.

Ferreira, F. & Patson, N. (2007). The "good enough" approach to language comprehension. *Language and Linguistics Compass*, 1, 71–83.

Fodor, J. D. & Inoue, A. (2000). Syntactic features in reanalysis: Positive and negative symptoms. *Journal of Psycholinguistic Research*, 29, 25–36.

Fodor, J. D., Nickels, S., & Schott, E. (2017). Center embedded sentences: What is pronounceable is comprehensible. In R. de Almeida & L. Gleitman, eds., *Minds on Language and Thought*. Oxford: Oxford University Press.

Francis, E. (2010). Grammatical weight and relative clause extraposition in English. *Cognitive Linguistics*, 21, 35–74.

Francis, E. & Michaelis, L. (2016). When relative clause extraposition is the right choice, it's easier. *Language and Cognition*, 9, 332–370.

Franck, J., Vigliocco, G., & Nicol, J. (2002). Subject–verb agreement errors in French and English: The role of syntactic hierarchy. *Language and Cognitive Processes*, 17(4), 371–404.

Francom, J. (2009). Experimental syntax: Exploring the effect of repeated exposure to anomalous syntactic structure evidence from rating and reading tasks. Doctoral dissertation, University of Arizona.

Frank, S. & Ernst, P. (2018). Judgements about double-embedded relative clauses differ between languages. *Psychological Research*, 83(7), 1–13.

Frank, S., Trompenaars, T., & Vasishth, S. (2016). Cross-linguistic differences in processing double-embedded relative clauses: Working-memory constraints or language statistics? *Cognitive Science*, 40(3), 554–578.

Frazier, L. (1985). Syntactic complexity. In D. Dowty, L. Karttunen, & A. Zwicky, eds., *Natural Language Processing: Psychological, Computational and Theoretical Perspectives*. Cambridge: Cambridge University Press, pp. 129–189.

Frazier, L. (1987). Sentence processing: A tutorial review. In M. Coltheart, ed., *Attention and Performance XII: The Psychology of Reading*. Hillsdale, NJ: Lawrence Earlbaum, pp. 559–586.

Frazier, L., Clifton, C., Carlson, K., & Harris, J. (2014). Standing alone with prosodic help. *Language, Cognition, and Neuroscience*, 29(4), 459–469.

Giannakidou, A. (2011). Negative and positive polarity items. In K. von Heusinger, C. Maienborn, & P. Portner, eds. *Semantics: An International Handbook of Natural Language Meaning*. Berlin: De Gruyter, pp. 1660–1712.

Gibson, E. (2000). The dependency locality theory: A distance-based theory of linguistic complexity. In Y. Miyashita, A. Marantz, & W. O'Neil, eds., *Image, Language, Brain*. Cambridge, MA: MIT Press, pp. 95–126.

Gibson, E. & Thomas, J. (1999). Memory limitations and structural forgetting: The perception of complex ungrammatical sentences as grammatical. *Language and Cognitive Processes*, 14(3), 225–248.

Gieselman, S, Kluender, R., & Caponigro, I. (2013). Isolating processing factors in negative island contexts. In Y. Fainleib, N. LaCara, & Y. Park, eds., *Proceedings of NELS 41*. Amherst, MA: GLSA, pp. 233–246.

Gillespie, M. & Pearlmutter, N. (2011). Hierarchy and scope of planning in subject–verb agreement production. *Cognition*, 118, 377–397.

Goodall, G. (2011). Syntactic satiation and the inversion effect in English and Spanish *wh*-questions. *Syntax*, 14, 29–47.

Goodall, G. (2015). The D-linking effect on extraction from islands and non-islands. *Frontiers in Psychology*, 5, 1493.

Goodluck, H., Tsiwah, F., & Saah, K. (2017). Island constraints are not the result of sentence processing. *Proceedings the Linguistic Society of America*, 2(15), 1–10.

Greco, C., Marelli, M., & Haegeman, L. (2017). External syntax and the cumulative effect in subject sub-extraction: An experimental evaluation. *The Linguistic Review*, 34, 479–531.

Grillo, N., Aguilar, A., Roberts, L., Santi, A., & Turco, G. (2018). Prosody of classic garden path sentences: The horse raced faster when embedded. https://ling.auf.net/lingbuzz/003868

Hall, R. (2018). Sättigungseffekte von multiplen W-Sätzen: Einfluss der Superiorität und Belebtheit. BSc thesis, Potsdam.

Hankamer, J. & Sag, I. (1976) Deep and surface anaphora. *Linguistic Inquiry*, 7, 391–426.

Hartsuiker, R., Anton-Mendez, I., & Van Zee, M. (2001). Object attraction in subject–verb agreement construction. *Journal of Memory and Language*, 45, 546–572.

Häussler, J. & Bader, M. (2015). An interference account of the missing VP effect. *Frontiers in Psychology*, 6, 766.

Häussler, J., Fanselow, G. Eythórsson, T., Šimik, R., & Vicente, L. (2019). Crossing movement paths: Multiple *wh*-questions in seven languages. Unpublished manuscript, University of Potsdam.

Häussler, J., Grant, M., Fanselow, G., & Frazier, L. (2015). Superiority in English and German: Cross-language grammatical differences? *Syntax*, 18, 235–265.

Hawkins, J. (1994). *A Performance Theory of Order and Constituency*. Cambridge: Cambridge University Press.

Hemforth, B. (1993). *Kognitives Parsing: Repräsentation und Verarbeitung sprachlichen Wissens*. Sankt Augustin: Infix.

Hemforth, B. & Konieczny, L. (2003). Proximity in agreement errors. In R. Alterman & D. Kirsh, eds., *The 25th Annual Conference of the Cognitive Science Society*. Boston, MA: Cognitive Science Society, pp. 557–562.

Hemforth, B., Konieczny, L., Seelig, H., & Walter, M. (2000). Case matching and relative clause attachment. *Journal of Psycholinguistic Research*, 29, 81–88.

Hofmeister, P., Culicover, P., & Winkler, S. (2015). Effects of processing on the acceptability of frozen extraposed constituents. *Syntax*, 184, 464–483.

Hofmeister, P, Jaeger, T. F., Sag, I., Arnon, I., & Snider, N. (2007). Locality and accessibility in *wh*-questions. In S. Featherston & S. Sternefeld, eds., *Roots: Linguistics in Search of its Evidential Base*. Berlin: Mouton de Gruyter, pp. 185–206.

Hofmeister, P., Jaeger, T. F., Sag, I., Arnon, I., & Snider, N. (2013). The source ambiguity problem: Distinguishing effects of grammar and processing on acceptability judgments. *Language and Cognitive Processes*, 28, 48–87.

Hofmeister, P. & Sag, I. (2010). Cognitive constraints and island effects. *Language*, 86, 366–415.

Hofmeister, P., Staum Casasanto, L., & Sag, I. (2012). How do individual cognitive differences relate to acceptability judgments? A reply to Sprouse, Wagers, and Phillips. *Language*, 88(2), 390–400.

Hofmeister, P, Staum Casasanto, L., & Sag, I. (2013). Islands in the grammar? Standards of evidence. In J. Sprouse & N. Hornstein, eds., *Experimental Syntax and Islands Effects*. Cambridge: Cambridge University Press, pp. 42–63.

Jäger, L. A., Engelmann, F., & Vasishth, S. (2017). Similarity-based interference in sentence comprehension: Literature review and bayesian meta-analysis. *Journal of Memory and Language*, 94, 316–339.

Jung, D.-H, Kim, Y., & Kim, J.-S. (2017). Island effects in Korean Scrambling: An experimental study. Unpublished manuscript, Korea University, www .researchgate.net/publication/311678736_Island_Effects_in_Korean_ Scrambling_An_Experimental_Study

Kaan, E. (2002). Investigating the effects of distance and number interference in processing subject–verb dependencies: An ERP study. *Journal of Psycholinguistic Research*, 31, 165–193.

Karlson, F. (2007). Constraints on multiple center-embedding of clauses. *Journal of Linguistics*, 43(2), 365–392.

Keffala, B. (2011). Resumption and gaps in English relative clauses: Relative acceptability creates an illusion of "saving." In C. Cathcart et al., eds., *Proceedings of the 37th Annual Meeting of the Berkeley Linguistics Society*. Berkeley, CA: University of California, Berkeley Linguistics Society, pp. 140–154.

Keffala, B. & Goodall, G. (2011). Do resumptive pronouns ever rescue illicit gaps in English? Poster presented at the CUNY 2011 Conference on Human Sentence Processing, Stanford University.

Keller, F, (2000). Gradience in grammar: Experimental and computational aspects of degrees of grammaticality. Doctoral dissertation, University of Edinburgh.

Keshev, M. & Meltzer-Asscher, A. (2019). A processing-based account of subliminal wh-island effects. *Natural Language and Linguistic Theory*, 37(2), 521–547.

Kim, B. & Goodall, G. (2016). Islands and non-islands in Native and Heritage Korean. *Frontiers in Psychology*, 7, 134.

Kim, C., Kobele, G., Runner, J., & Hale, J. (2011). The acceptability cline in VP ellipsis. *Syntax*, 14, 318–354.

Kimball, J. & Aissen, J. (1971). I think, you think, he think. *Linguistic Inquiry*, 2, 241–246.

Kjelgaard, M. & Speer, S. R. (1999). Prosodic facilitation and interference in the resolution of temporary syntactic closure ambiguity. *Journal of Memory and Language*, 40(2), 153–194.

Klima, E. (1964). Negation in English. In J. Fodor & J. Katz, eds., *The Structure of Language*. Englewood Cliffs, NJ: Prentice Hall, pp. 246–323.

Kluender, R. & Kutas, M. (1993). Subjacency as a processing phenomenon. *Language and Cognitive Processes*, 8, 573–633.

Konieczny, L. (2000). Locality and parsing complexity. *Journal of Psycholinguistic Research*, 29(6), 627–645.

Konieczny, L. & Döring, P. (2003). Anticipation of clause-final heads: Evidence from eye-tracking and SRNs. In *Proceedings of ICCS/ASCS*, pp. 13–17.

Konietzko, A., Winkler, S., & Culicover, P. (2018). Heavy NP Shift does not cause Freezing. *Canadian Journal of Linguistics/Revue Canadienne de Linguistique*, 63(3), 454–464.

Krems, J. (1984). *Erwartungsgeleitete Sprachverarbeitung*. Frankfurt/Main: Peter Lang.

Kuno, S. & J. Robinson. (1972). Multiple *wh*-questions. *Linguistic Inquiry*, 3, 463–87.

Kush, D., Lidz, J., & Phillips, C. (2015). Relation-sensitive retrieval: Evidence from bound variable pronouns. *Journal of Memory and Language*, 82, 18–40.

Kush, D., Lidz, J., & Phillips, C. (2017). Looking forwards and backwards: The real-time processing of Strong and Weak Crossover. *Glossa: A Journal of General Linguistics*, 2(1), 70. DOI:10.5334/gjgl.280

Kush, D., Lohndal, T., & Sprouse, J. (2018). Investigating variation in island effects. *Natural Language and Linguistic Theory*, 36, 743–779.

Levy, R. & Keller, F. (2013). Expectation and locality effects in German verb final structures. *Journal of Memory and Language*, 68, 199–222.

Lewis, R. & Vasishth, S. (2005). An activation based model of sentence processing as skilled memory retrieval. *Cognitive Science*, 29, 1–45.

Linebarger, M. (1987). Negative polarity and grammatical representation. *Linguistics and Philosophy*, 10, 325–387.

Luka, B. & Barsalou, L. (2005). Structural facilitation: Mere exposure effects for grammatical acceptability as evidence for syntactic priming in comprehension, *Journal of Memory and Language*, 52, 436–459.

Marks, L. (1967). Judgments of grammaticalness of some English sentences and semi-sentences. *American Journal of Psychology*, 80, 196–204.

McDaniel, D. & Wayne, C. (1999). Experimental evidence for a minimalist account of English resumptive pronouns. *Cognition*, 70, B15–B24.

Meyer, R. (2004). *Syntax der Ergänzungsfrage: Empirische Untersuchungen am Russischen, Polnischen und Tschechischen*. Munich: Sagner.

Michel, D. (2014). Individual cognitive measures and working memory accounts of syntactic island phenomena. Doctoral dissertation, University of Maryland.

Michel, D. & Goodall, G. (2013). Finiteness and the nature of island constraints In N. Goto, K. Otaki, A. Sato, & K. Takita, eds., *Proceedings of GLOW in Asia IX 2012: The Main Session*, pp. 187–197.

Miller, G. & Chomsky. N. (1963). Finitary models of language users. In D. Luce & B. Galanter, eds., *Handbook of Mathematical Psychology*, vol. II. New York: Wiley.

Miller, G. & Isard, S. (1964). Free recall of self embedded English sentences. *Information and Control*, 7, 292–303.

Montalbetti, M. (1984). After binding. Doctoral dissertation, Massachusetts Institute of Technology.

Myers, J. (2009). Syntactic judgment experiments. *Language and Linguistics Compass*, 3(1), 406–423.

Nagata, H. (1990). Speaker's sensitivity to rule violations in sentences. *Psychologia*, 33, 179–184.

Nakatani, K. & Gibson, E. (2010). An on-line study of Japanese nesting complexity. *Cognitive Science*, 34(1), 94–112.

Novick, J., Hussey, E., Teubner-Rhodes, S., Harbison, J. I., & Bunting, M. (2014). Clearing the garden-path: Improving sentence processing through cognitive control training. *Language, Cognition and Neuroscience*, 29(2), 186–217.

Parker, D. & Phillips, C. (2016). Negative polarity illusions and the format of hierarchical encodings in memory. *Cognition*, 157, 321–339.

Patil, U., Vasishth, S., & Lewis, R. (2016). Retrieval interference in syntactic processing: The case of reflexive binding in English. *Frontiers in Psychology*, 7, 329.

Patson, N. & Husband, E. M. (2016). Misinterpretations in agreement and agreement attraction. *Quarterly Journal of Experimental Psychology*, 69, 950–971.

Pesetsky, D. (2000). *Phrasal Movement and Its Kin*. Cambridge, MA: MIT Press.

Phillips, C., Kazanina, N., & Abada, S. (2005). ERP effects of the processing of syntactic long-distance dependencies. *Cognitive Brain Research*, 22, 407–428.

Pollard, C. & Sag, I. (1992). Anaphors in English and the scope of binding theory. *Linguistic Inquiry*, 23(2), 261–303.

Prince, E. (1998). On the limits of syntax, with reference to Left-Dislocation and Topicalization. In P. Culicover & L. McNally, eds., *The Limits of Syntax* (Syntax and Semantics, 29). New York: Academic Press, pp. 281–302.

Reinhart, T. & Reuland, E. (1993). Reflexivity. *Linguistic Inquiry*, 24(4), 657–720.

Ross, J. (1967). Constraints on variables in syntax. Doctoral dissertation, Massachusetts Institute of Technology.

Ross, J. (1974). Three batons for cognitive psychology. In W. Weimer & D. Palermo, eds., *Cognition and the Symbolic Processes*. Oxford: Lawrence Erlbaum.

Ross, J. (1984). Inner islands. In *Proceedings of the Tenth Annual Meeting of the Berkeley Linguistics Society*. Berkeley, CA: University of California, Berkeley Linguistics Society, pp. 258–265.

Sloggett, S. (2017). When errors aren't: How comprehenders selectively violate Binding theory. Doctoral dissertation, University of Amherst.

Snyder, W. (2000). An experimental investigation of syntactic satiation effects. *Linguistic Inquiry*, 31, 575–582.

Sprouse, J. (2007a). A program for experimental syntax: Finding the relationship between acceptability and grammatical knowledge. Doctoral dissertation, University of Maryland at College Park.

Sprouse, J. (2007b). Continuous acceptability, categorical grammaticality, and experimental syntax. *Biolinguistics*, 1, 118–129.

Sprouse, J. (2008). The differential sensitivity of acceptability judgments to processing effects. *Linguistic Inquiry*, 20, 686–694.

Sprouse, J., Caponigro, I., Greco, C., & Cecchetto, C. (2016). Experimental syntax and the variation of island effects in English and Italian. *Natural Language and Linguistic Theory*, 34, 307–344.

Sprouse, J., Fukuda, S., Ono, H., & Kluender, R. (2011). Reverse island effects and the backward search for a licensor in multiple *wh*-questions. *Syntax*, 14(2), 179–203.

Sprouse, J., Wagers, M., & Phillips, C. (2012). A test of the relation between working memory capacity and syntactic island effects. *Language*, 88(1), 82–123.

Staub, A. (2010). Eye movements and processing difficulty in object relative clauses. *Cognition*, 116, 71–86.

Staum Casasanto, L. & Sag, I. (2008). The advantage of the ungrammatical. In B. C. Love, K. McRae, & V. M. Sloutsky, eds., *Proceedings of the 30th Annual Meeting of the Cognitive Science Society*. Austin, TX: Cognitive Science Society.

Staum Casasanto, L., Hofmeister, P., & Sag, I. (2010). Understanding acceptability judgments: Additivity and working memory effects. In S. Ohlsson & R. Catrambone, eds., *Proceedings of the 32nd Annual Meeting of the Cognitive Science Society*. Austin, TX: Cognitive Science Society.

Stowe, L. (1986). Parsing *wh*-constructions: Evidence for online gap location. *Language and Cognitive Processes* 1(3), 227–245.

Sturt, P. (2003). The time-course of the application of binding constraints in reference resolution. *Journal of Memory and Language*, 48(3), 542–562.

Tabor, W., Galantucci, B., & Richardson, D. (2004). Effects of merely local syntactic coherence on sentence processing. *Journal of Memory and Language*, 50(4), 355–370.

Tabor, W. & Hutchins, S. (2004). Evidence for self-organized sentence processing: Digging-in effects. *Journal of Experimental Psychology: Learning, Memory, and Cognition*, 30, 431–450.

Tanner, D., Nicol, J., & Brehm, L. (2014). The time-course of feature interference in agreement comprehension: Multiple mechanisms and asymmetrical attraction. *Journal of Memory and Language*, 76, 195–215.

Thornton, R., MacDonald, M., & Arnold, J. (2000). The concomitant effects of phrase length and informational content in sentence comprehension. *Journal of Psycholinguistic Research*, 29(2), 195–203.

Trotzke, A., Bader, M., & Frazier, L. (2013). Third factors and the performance interface in language design. *Biolinguistics*, 7, 1–34.

Vandierendonck, A., Loncke, M., Hartsuiker, R., & Desmet, T. (2018). The role of executive control in resolving grammatical number conflict in sentence comprehension. *Quarterly Journal of Experimental Psychology*, 71, 759–778.

Vasishth, S. (2002). Working memory in sentence comprehension: Processing Hindi center embeddings. Doctoral dissertation, The Ohio State University.

Vasishth, S. & Lewis, R. (2006). Argument–head distance and processing complexity: Explaining both locality and anti-locality effects. *Language*, 82, 767–794.

Vasishth, S., Suckow, K., Lewis, R. L., & Kern, S. (2010). Short-term forgetting in sentence comprehension: Crosslinguistic evidence from verb-final structures. *Language and Cognitive Processes*, 25, 533–567.

Wagers, M., Lau, E., & Phillips, C. (2009). Agreement attraction in comprehension: Representations and processes. *Journal of Memory and Language*, 61, 206–237.

Wagner, M. & Watson, D. (2010). Experimental and theoretical advances in prosody: A review. *Language and Cognitive Processes*, 25, 905–945.

Wasow, T. (1997), Remarks on grammatical weight. *Language Variation and Change*, 9, 81–105.

Wasow, T. & Arnold, J. (2003). Post-verbal constituent ordering in English. In G. Rohdenburg & B. Mondorf, eds., *Determinants of Grammatical Variation in English*. Berlin: Mouton de Gruyter, pp. 119–154.

Waters, G. & Caplan. D. (1996). Processing resource capacity and the comprehension of garden path sentences. *Memory & Cognition*, 24, 342–355.

Wellwood, A., Pancheva, R., Hacquard, V., & Phillips, C. (2018). The anatomy of a comparative illusion. *Journal of Semantics*, 35(3), 543–583.

Weskott, T. (2003). Information structure as a processing guide. Doctoral dissertation, University of Leipzig.

Weskott, T., Hörnig, R., Fanselow, G., & Kliegl, R. (2011). Contextual licensing of marked OVS word order in German. *Linguistische Berichte*, 225, 3–18.

Wexler, K. & Culicover, P. (1980). *Formal Principles of Language Acquisition*. Cambridge, MA: MIT Press.

Widmann, C. (2005). Factors at play in determining the acceptability of sentential subjects in English: The role of constituent relative weight. Unpublished manuscript, University of South Carolina.

Wierzba, M. & Fanselow, G. (2020). Factors influencing the acceptability of object fronting in German. *Journal of Comparative Germanic Linguistics*, 23, 77–124.

Xiang, M., Dillon, B., & Phillips, C. (2006). Testing the strength of the spurious licensing effect for negative polarity items. Paper presented at the 19th Annual Meeting of the CUNY Conference on Human Sentence Processing (New York).

Xiang, M., Dillon, B., & Phillips, C. (2009). Illusory licensing effects across dependency types: Erp evidence. *Brain and Language*, 108(1), 40–55.

Xiang, M., Grove, J., & Giannakidou, A. (2013). Dependency–dependent interference: NPI interference, agreement attraction, and global pragmatic inferences. *Frontiers in Psychology*, 4, 708.

Yngve, H. T. (1960). A model and an hypothesis for language structure. *Proceedings of the American Philosophical Society*, 104, 444–466.

Yoshida, M., Kazanina, N., Pablos, L., & Sturt, P. (2014). On the origin of islands. *Language, Cognition and Neuroscience*, 29, 761–770.

Zervakis, J. & Mazuka, R. (2013). Effect of repeated evaluation and repeated exposure on acceptability ratings of sentences. *Journal of Psycholinguistic Research*, 42, 505–525.

# 6

# Satiation

William Snyder

## 6.1 Overview

"Syntactic satiation," or simply "satiation," refers to an occupational hazard in linguistics. There exist sentences, of several particular types, that initially sound starkly unacceptable – to linguists and non-linguists alike – but begin to sound better to the linguist as time goes by. The paradigm case in English is the sentence type in (1), where the *wh*-argument *who* has moved out of a *whether*-island.

(1)    Who does Mary wonder whether John likes?
       *[Answer: She wonders whether he likes Sam.]*

On first encounter, most native speakers of English reject (1) as impossible, and this is true of English-speaking linguists as well, hence the '*' on such examples in the syntax literature. Yet, by the time a linguist is presenting an example like (1) to the students in an introductory syntax course, the introspective perception of impossibility may have softened or even disappeared. If so, the linguist has "satiated" on this sentence type.

Fortunately for the field of linguistics, very few types of sentence give rise to satiation. As will be evident from the studies reviewed below, the usual pattern is for judgments of grammatical well-formedness to be stable. The big questions to be addressed in this chapter are (i) precisely which sentence types do give rise to satiation, (ii) under what conditions does it occur, and (iii) why does it happen?

### 6.1.1   Terminology: "Syntactic Satiation"
The usual assumption is that a linguist's introspective shift, for sentences of a "satiable" type, is somehow triggered by routine exposure to the sentences during day-to-day work in linguistics. The term "syntactic satiation" is based on a loose analogy to the phenomenon known as "semantic

satiation," discussed in the early 1960s by Leon Jakobovits. Semantic satiation has occurred, for example, when a native speaker of English repeats a common word (such as *father*) aloud for a period of 15 seconds and then, immediately afterward, judges it to sound "neutral or meaningless" (Jakobovits & Lambert 1961: 576).

Thus, *semantic* satiation involves a period of repeated exposure to a particular word, followed by a loss of confidence in one's native-speaker knowledge that it has the meaning that it does. For a linguist, the reasoning goes, *syntactic* satiation is a period of repeated exposure to a given sentence type, followed by a loss of confidence in one's expert knowledge that the sentence type is grammatically anomalous. On this view the linguist still recognizes (intellectually) that the sentence type "should" be unacceptable, but – truth be told – no longer has a strong native-speaker intuition to back that up.

## 6.1.2 The Early Days of Satiation Research (1985–2000)

The person who first had the idea of studying satiation experimentally was Karin Stromswold, who conducted pilot research in the 1980s as a graduate student at MIT, but never published her findings. It was Stromswold who named the phenomenon "syntactic satiation."[1] In the early 1990s, when Snyder began graduate studies at MIT, he learned about her work and, with her support, ran his own version of a satiation study. Snyder's interest had been triggered by class lectures of Noam Chomsky, who expressed the view that theoretical syntax stood to benefit if novel methods of data collection could be developed. Snyder wondered if the syntactic satiation experienced by linguists really did have a counterpart in non-linguists, as suggested by Stromswold's work. If so, would it be possible to induce satiation in non-linguists, under experimental conditions, as a new source of evidence for linguistic research?

In 1994 Snyder included his work on satiation as part of a poster presented at the CUNY Human Sentence Processing Conference. Afterwards, in an effort to bring his findings to the attention of a wider audience, he circulated a short manuscript, which was eventually published as a 2000 squib in *Linguistic Inquiry*. A pre-publication version inspired two of Snyder's students at the University of Connecticut, Kazuko Hiramatsu and David Braze, to begin follow-up studies. Their projects, which grew into dissertations (Hiramatsu 2000; Braze 2002), will be discussed below.

---

[1] Chaves and Dery (2018: 4 (n.5)) take exception to the term *(syntactic) satiation*, and prefer *amelioration*, because the resemblance to semantic satiation is limited. (See also Zervakis & Mazuka (2013: 507).) In the present work, however, the term *satiation* will be retained, on the grounds that Stromswold has "priority of discovery," and therefore owns the naming rights.

### 6.1.3   Characteristics of Satiation in Linguists

Based on informal surveys of colleagues, as well as his personal experience, Snyder found that satiation in linguists exhibits the characteristics in (2) (adapted from Snyder (2018: 2)).

(2)      a. *Lexical Generality:* Satiation operates at the level of a syntactic *structure.* It *generalizes* beyond the specific sentences that were judged in the past – at a minimum, to sentences with different open-class lexical items.

b. *Structural Specificity:* When satiation occurs, it affects only a limited number of sentence types. Sentence types violating different constraints are unaffected.

c. *Between-speaker Consistency:* At least across speakers of English, the *same* sentence types (notably sentences involving *wh*-extraction of an argument from a *Whether* Island, Complex NP, or Subject Island) are the ones for which satiation is likely to occur.

d. *Within-speaker Persistence:* Once an individual has experienced satiation on a given sentence type, it *persists* for a considerable period of time, even in the absence of routine exposure to sentences of that type.

In recent years there has arisen a small but growing body of work attempting to induce satiation experimentally. The characteristics in (2) can help us assess whether the effects obtained experimentally correspond to the effects reported by linguists.

### 6.1.4   Chapter Contents

The remainder of this chapter is divided into five parts. Sections 6.2 and 6.3 discuss methods for inducing, and measuring, satiation in the laboratory. Section 6.4 reviews selected studies from the satiation literature. Section 6.5 discusses findings on how long satiation persists after it is induced in the laboratory, and the "carryover" of satiation from one sentence type to another. Section 6.6 examines a number of possible explanations for satiation, and then touches on the potential for satiation experiments to inform (psycho)linguistic research.

## 6.2   Inducing Satiation in the Laboratory

The main finding in Snyder (2000) was that the satiation effects reported by linguists have a direct counterpart in non-linguists. According to the anecdotal reports Snyder had gathered from linguists (all of them native speakers of English), satiation sometimes occurs for *wh*-extraction of arguments from *Whether* Islands (3a) and/or certain types of complex NP (3b), but does not occur for *that*-trace (3c) or left-branch (3d) violations (for general discussion of island constraints, see Chapter 9, and for discussion of *that*-trace effects, see Chapter 10).[2,3]

(3)      a. *Whether*-Island violation:
            Who does John wonder whether Mary likes?
         b. Complex Noun Phrase Constraint (CNPC) violation:
            Who does Mary believe the claim that John likes?
         c. *That*-trace violation:
            Who does Mary think that likes John?
         d. Left-Branch Condition (LBC) violation:
            How many did John buy books?

The participants in Snyder's experiment were native English speakers who had never taken a course on linguistics. By the end of the session they showed increased acceptance of all, and only, the sentence types for which linguists had reported satiation: acceptance rose significantly for sentences like (3a–b), but remained very low for (3c–d). The findings thus supported the view that satiation of the kind found in linguists can be induced experimentally, and within a short period of time. Hence for present purposes, whether discussing linguists or non-linguists, an increase in perceived acceptability of specific, initially unacceptable sentence types will be termed *satiation*.[4]

In Snyder (2000), and the majority of studies that followed, the basic method of inducing satiation has been to require each participant to make acceptability judgments on a long series of sentences. Designing such an experiment requires a considerable number of decisions, on topics such as the instructions to the participant, the form of the participants' responses, the number of times a participant will be exposed to each sentence type, the number of distinct sentence types to be presented, the total number of items, and possibly (depending on the choice of response type) the number of items that are expected to elicit any given response (such as "Yes" versus "No").[5]

---

[2] Note that acceptability diacritics ("*," "?") are omitted in this chapter.

[3] Here and throughout, use of traditional syntactic terms ("*whether*-island," "CNPC") does not entail that these effects are necessarily due to grammar. Processing difficulty is also a live possibility.

[4] Note: the *selective* nature of satiation tends to distinguish it from *across-the-board* (ATB) effects, where participants become more accepting of sentences in general, regardless of grammatical structure. An ATB account of the Snyder (2000) findings, for example, would seem to require that satiable sentence types have the *highest* initial acceptability ratings, among the initially unacceptable types in the study. Only then could a change in the cutoff point move all, and only, the satiable types from "unacceptable" to "acceptable." Instead, as discussed by Snyder (2000), first-exposure numerical-scale judgments of the sentences in his study indicated there were non-satiating types with initial acceptability *higher than*, *lower than*, and *intermediate between* (3a) and (3b). Hence, an ATB change alone is insufficient to explain the data. Nonetheless, ATB effects can coexist with satiation, and have been reported by Luka and Barsalou (2005), among others.

[5] Note: none of the studies that are discussed in this chapter presented the exact *same* sentence repeatedly within a session. Such direct repetition has been examined by Nagata (1990, et seq.), who reports it does not yield satiation. Instead, participants seem to gain confidence in their initial judgment.

In this study, you are asked to provide a judgment of grammatical acceptability for each of 60 sentences. Every test sentence is in the form of a question. On each page of the experiment, you will see a declarative sentence (the "context" sentence), followed by a question based on the declarative sentence (the "test" sentence). We would like you to judge whether each test sentence is a "grammatically possible" sentence of English, given the meaning that fits the preceding context sentence.

By "grammatically possible" we mean possible for you as a native speaker of English. We are not concerned about whether the test sentence would be acceptable to a writing teacher – points of style and clarity are not the issue, and we are not concerned about "who" versus "whom," or ending a sentence in a preposition. Instead, we are interested in whether the test sentence could have the intended meaning and still be accepted as "English," in your opinion.

Some examples follow. We would expect most English speakers to answer "Yes" (grammatically possible) on the first example, and "No" on the second example. Many of the test sentences in this study are likely to fall between these two extremes. Even so, we would like you to give a yes/no judgment for each test sentence.

**Example I.**  [Context: Mary put a box on the table.]
Test sentence: "What did Mary put on the table?"
Judgment: _____ (Y/N)

**Example II.**  [Context: John wants very much for Mary to meet Bob.]
Test sentence: "Who does John want very much whether for who to meet Bob?"
Judgment: _____ (Y/N)

Please do not turn back to previous items. This is not a memory test. You are not required to remember the judgments that you gave for previous items. Many of the items will be quite similar to one another; to the best of your ability, you should simply ignore this fact and provide an "independent" judgment on each individual item. If you have any questions, especially questions about the intended meaning of a given sentence, PLEASE ASK.

**Figure 6.1** Participant instructions in Snyder (2000)

A first question is how to explain "acceptability" (or perhaps "grammaticality," "well-formedness," or "grammatical acceptability") to the participants. The approach of Snyder (2000) is shown in Figure 6.1. Note that the extremes of the judgment scale (in this case, "Yes" and "No") were established with examples. Note too that participants were told, in effect, that points of prescriptive grammar were not at issue; the question was instead whether they themselves would accept the test sentence as a "grammatically possible" sentence of English, "given the meaning that fits the preceding context sentence."

The view implicit in this last bit of the instructions ("given the meaning . . .") is that linguistic acceptability judgments should not, in the general case, concern a string of words in isolation. Rather, the native speaker should be asked whether the string of words is an acceptable way of expressing a specified meaning. (To take a simple example, the acceptability of "John likes him" depends critically on whether "him" is the same person as "John.") Indeed, one could argue that participants would ideally be given not only the intended meaning but also the intended pronunciation, and perhaps some information about the discourse context (or lack thereof). Yet several studies subsequent to Snyder (2000) have moved in the opposite direction and eliminated the context sentence altogether, so that participants are simply judging a string of printed words (see also Chapter 2 for further discussion of context in acceptability experiments). In Section 6.4 we will see that this change could perhaps account for some of the variability, across studies, in whether a satiation effect was obtained.[6]

Another point of variation in studies subsequent to Snyder (2000) has been the type of response elicited from the participant. The choice of a yes/no task in Snyder (2000) was based on a finding during pilot work, when a numerical scale was used: some of the participants appeared to have difficulty mapping linguistic acceptability onto a scale. (For example, one participant reported giving a score of 6 out of 7 to a *that*-trace violation, on the grounds that "*only one* of the words was wrong.") Hence, a dichotomous judgment task seemed more appropriate. Yet, as we will see in Section 6.4, several subsequent studies employed a numerical scale and obtained results comparable to those of Snyder (2000).[7]

One other response type, Magnitude Estimation (ME), has also been tried in a small number of studies. As will be seen in Section 6.4, in the few cases where one can do side-by-side comparisons of ME versus other response types for the same sentence type, the studies with ME appear less successful at inducing satiation. Yet a number of factors besides response type varied across those studies, and could have been responsible. Moreover, Hofmeister et al. (2013) have reported considerable success using ME to induce satiation on superiority violations. A general discussion of response methods in acceptability experiments is found in Chapter 2.

One further issue in the choice of response type is whether acceptability judgments are viewed as absolute or relative. From the perspective of the participant, judgments in yes/no tasks and numerical-scale tasks have generally been absolute, except insofar as the endpoints of the yes/no scale or the numerical scale were established with examples in the initial instructions to the participant. In contrast, the ME task explicitly requires the participant to judge each test sentence *relative* to a "modulus" sentence, which is normally held constant throughout the experiment.[8]

Other points of variation across satiation studies include (i) how many different types of grammatical violation are presented; (ii) how many exposures to a given sentence type the participant receives; and (iii) (in

---

[6] Without explicit guidance, different participants may imagine substantially different intonational patterns, and/or discourse contexts. These choices can affect whether a phrase is taken as "new" versus "given" information, and whether a *wh*-word is taken as discourse-linked. If these factors influence acceptability, it adds noise to the data.

[7] For in-depth discussion of issues surrounding the choice of response type, see Schütze (1996).

[8] Regardless of response type, however, if a study includes grammatical control items, the data analysis can compare responses on a given test item to responses on control items, ideally items that are similar in complexity and judged in the same block. The next section provides an example.

the case of a yes/no task) how many expected-*yes* versus expected-*no* items are presented. The question of how many distinct grammatical violations to include is related to the question of whether participants should be *aware* that they are repeatedly judging equivalent sentences. As will be seen in Section 6.4, there is evidence from Chaves and Dery (2014) suggesting that satiation can be obtained even when there is only a single type of grammatical violation presented; this in turn suggests that concealment is not essential. To anticipate some of the other findings described below, the *number of exposures* to a given sentence type appears to play a major role in whether satiation is obtained, at least in the case of Subject-Island violations (see especially Hiramatsu 2000); but in experiments using a yes/no task, the ratio of expected-*yes* to expected-*no* items does not appear to have much effect (see especially Snyder 2018: E3, in comparison with Snyder 2000; and Chaves & Dery 2014: 96).

## 6.3  Measuring Satiation

The first two characteristics of satiation presented in Section 6.1.3, Lexical Generality and Structural Specificity, suggest useful guidelines for analyzing data from a satiation experiment. When satiation of the kind found in linguists occurs, it is an increase in the acceptability of a particular syntactic *structure*. This increased acceptability should be relatively independent of the open-class lexical items that happen to instantiate the structure.[9]

From these considerations there follow three particular predictions that we can and should evaluate (both statistically and graphically). First, the degree (or frequency) of acceptance for a given sentence type should *reliably increase* by the end of the experiment, relative to the beginning, regardless of the order in which particular test items were presented. Second, when we examine data from participants who saw the same test items but in different orders of presentation, we should consistently see *similar levels* of acceptance after a given number of exposures. Third, if we examine the data for a *single test item* that was judged at different points in the experiment by different participants, we should consistently see a significantly higher level of acceptance among participants who saw it later in the experiment.

Increased acceptance at the end of the experiment can easily arise for at least two reasons other than satiation, and these need to be carefully excluded. First, examples of an ungrammatical sentence type that are presented later in the experiment might be intrinsically more acceptable than the items presented earlier, due to the particular open-class lexical

---

[9] "Open-class" refers to N, V, A, P. For extraction phenomena, however, lexical characteristics of an embedding V are important (independently of satiation). Hence, it may be more accurate to say satiation effects are independent of the choice among *equivalent* lexical items.

items that the various sentences happen to contain. Second, a particular item might be perceived as more (or less) acceptable than it would ordinarily, as a result of the specific item that was judged immediately prior (e.g. a severe grammatical violation versus a well-formed control item), in one particular ordering of the test items.

To illustrate these points, consider the findings from Snyder (2018: Experiment 3). This experiment was very similar to the one in Snyder (2000), again using a yes/no task, but it added a sufficient number of grammatically well-formed control items to obtain a perfect balance of expected-*yes* and expected-*no* items in every block of the experiment (cf. Sprouse 2009), and it included data from a total of 151 participants (as compared to 22, in Snyder 2000).

Much as in Snyder (2000), participants were randomly assigned to one of two orders of presentation. Aside from a small number of practice items at the beginning, and some post-test items at the end, there were 5 experimental blocks, each containing 7 test items and 7 control items, hence 70 test/control items in total. Each block contained a test item for *that*-trace, *wonder-whether*, CNPC, *want-for*, subject island, adjunct island, and left-branch extraction. Where Version A presented the (70) items in a "forward" order (1, 2, 3, ...), Version B presented the same items in reverse order (70, 69, 68, ...).

The resulting data were analyzed with Mixed-Effects (ME) Logistic Regression, in a "treatment-contrast" procedure that compared each participant's judgment on each ungrammatical item, to the same participant's judgments on the seven grammatically well-formed control items that were presented during the same block of the experiment. (These items were coded as belonging to type "Good," which was the designated baseline level for the factor "Type.") The Good items were designed to be similar in structural complexity to the Test items.

For any sentence type T that showed a satiation effect, there was expected to be a significant interaction: the effect of "changing" from judging a Good item to judging an item of type T should be *different* as a function of the block in which the judgments were made. Thus, even though the participants were not asked for judgments of relative acceptability (i.e. the acceptability of one sentence in relation to the acceptability of a specified comparison sentence), the analytic procedure evaluated their judgments of ungrammatical sentence types relative to their judgments of control items.

For a claim of satiation on sentence type T, a significant interaction between block and type=T was taken as necessary, but not sufficient. After a significant interaction was detected, the two versions (A and B) were examined separately. If the satiation was genuine, then it should be evident regardless of the sentences that were judged immediately prior to the critical test items, and regardless of the open-class lexical items used to instantiate the structure in those test items. Hence, if the significant interaction turned out to be attributable mainly to the results from one particular version of the materials, then the findings did not qualify as evidence of a satiation effect.

In addition, for any given type of test sentence, there were two exemplars that were presented in either the first or the final block, depending on the version. If there was satiation for a particular syntactic structure (i.e. independently of the open-class lexical items that instantiated it), then each of these individual test items ought to show a reliable increase in acceptance when judged at the end, as compared to the beginning. If there was not in fact a robust increase for each sentence when it was presented at the end, then the findings were not accepted as evidence of satiation.

Indeed, Experiment 3 yielded a significant block-by-typeT interaction for four values of T: whether-islands, CNPCs, that-trace, and subject islands. Yet only the first two satisfied the additional criteria. For example, in the case of CNPCs (which met the criteria), there was a small but highly consistent change in each of Versions A and B. In A, these items were accepted by an average of 5 percent of the participants in the first two blocks, and by an average of 13 percent in the last two blocks (Wilcoxon: $p < .05$); in B, the average acceptance rose from 4 to 11 percent ($p < .05$). For the two CNPC items that were presented in either the first or last block (depending on the version), both showed a clear increase in acceptance when judged at the end: from 4 to 14 percent on one item (Phi Coefficient=.19; Fisher Exact Test $p<.05$), and from 1 to 15 percent on the other ($\varphi$ =.24; $p<.005$).

In contrast when Snyder examined that-trace items, for example, there was an overall increase in acceptance from 25 percent in the first two blocks to 34 percent in the last two blocks, but this change was almost entirely driven by Version B, where acceptance rose from 25 to 43 percent (Wilcoxon: $p < .005$). In Version A, the change was from 25 to 27 percent ($p > .10$ NS). Also, examining the two items that appeared in the first or last block (depending on the version), the changes were (a bit) asymmetrical, and were not statistically reliable: one item rose in acceptance from 26 to 41 percent (FET: $p < .10$ MS), while the other rose from 24 to 34 percent ($p > .10$ NS). The conclusion was that the experiment had not yielded clear evidence of satiation on that-trace violations.

In sum, finding a statistically significant increase in acceptance, from the beginning to the end of the experiment, should be necessary but not sufficient for a claim that satiation has occurred. Before drawing that conclusion, one should confirm that the increase in acceptance is similar for each order of presentation, and that the increase is evident in the responses to individual test items, when they were judged later in the experiment. Evidence that does not meet these standards is likely to have resulted from accidental characteristics of the stimuli.

## 6.4    A Brief Review of the Literature

Since Snyder (2000) there has arisen a small but growing literature on the satiation phenomenon (e.g. Hiramatsu 2000; Braze 2002; Francom 2009; Sprouse 2009; Goodall 2011; Crawford 2012; Maia 2013; Christensen, Kizach, & Nyvad 2013; Hofmeister et al. 2013; Chaves & Dery 2014; Do & Kaiser 2017). In addition to efforts at inducing satiation experimentally, there have been works (e.g. Boeckx 2003: Ch. 3; Stepanov 2007) discussing possible implications of the phenomenon for syntactic theory. While most studies focus on English, there are also studies on Brazilian Portuguese (Maia 2013), Danish (Christensen et al. 2013), and Spanish (Goodall 2011). This section will review work on English (6.4.1) and other languages (6.4.2), but studies on persistence of satiation, and "carryover" to new sentence types, appear in Section 6.5.

### 6.4.1    English

In experimental studies of English, satiation effects have (sometimes) been reported for *wh*-extraction of an argument from a *whether*-island, from certain types of complex NP, and from certain types of subject island.[10] *Whether*-island studies are summarized in Table 6.1, where it can be seen that most investigators have found satiation effects for extraction of an argument from a *whether*-island, but Sprouse (2009) did not.[11,12] Strikingly, seven of the eight studies finding satiation provided participants with a *context sentence* to pin down the intended meaning of the test sentence, but the three experiments in Sprouse (2009) did not. Hence it appears likely that the use of a context sentence (or perhaps more generally, specification of the intended meaning of the test sentences) is playing an important role. Yet it will be best to reserve judgment until this hypothesis can be tested within a single *whether*-island study, holding all else constant.[13]

---

[10] Most studies subsequent to Snyder (2000) have tested for satiation in the same sentence types as Snyder, or slight variants thereof. The review in this section exploits this homogeneity to check for possible effects of methodological differences across these studies. Yet, as noted in Section 6.2, Hofmeister and colleagues have examined a new sentence type, superiority violations, and report satiation (Hofmeister et al. 2013). While this sentence type does not appear in the cross-study comparison tables of this section, it definitely merits further attention from satiation researchers.

[11] In the tables, "E1" refers to "Experiment 1" in the publication indicated. For (Sprouse 2009), Experiments 1–5 of section 3 have prefix A, and Experiments 1–2 of section 4 have B. Under "Task," "ME" is Magnitude Estimation; "Sc" refers to a numerical rating scale. "MS" is marginally significant ($.05 < p < .10$). (Tables 6.1–5 are expanded versions of Tables 1–2 in Snyder 2018.)

[12] Note: The studies listed in the tables are not exhaustive. Braze (2002) conducted both eye-tracker and judgment experiments, on different participants. Very interestingly, he found that "satiable" sentence types showed a distinctive pattern in the eye-tracker: reading time *increased* with repeated exposure. The data in this section, however, are from his judgment task. Francom (2009) includes five experiments, but E1–2 are the most relevant here. For Hiramatsu (2000), results reported here are from participants meeting her inclusionary criterion (answering at least 90 percent of filler/control items as expected).

[13] For one thing, lack of a context sentence seems *compatible* with satiation, for subject-island items (below).

Table 6.1 *Satiation experiments on argument/adjunct extraction from* whether-*islands*

| Sentence type | Wh-type | Satiation? | Study | Context sentence? | Number of participants | Number of exposures | Task |
|---|---|---|---|---|---|---|---|
| Whether-island | Argument | Yes | Braze 2002 | Yes | 35 | 9 | Y/N |
| | Argument | Yes | Crawford 2012 | Yes | 22 | 7 | Sc |
| | Argument | Yes | Francom 2009: E1 | No | 205 | 5 | Y/N |
| | Argument | Yes | Hiramatsu 2000: E1 | Yes | 33 | 7 | Y/N |
| | Argument | Yes | Hiramatsu 2000: E2 | Yes | 11 | 7 | Y/N |
| | Argument | Yes | Snyder 2000 | Yes | 22 | 5 | Y/N |
| | Argument | Yes | Snyder 2018: E1 | Yes | 20 | 5 | Y/N |
| | Argument | Yes | Snyder 2018: E3 | Yes | 151 | 5 | Y/N |
| | Argument | No | Sprouse 2009: A3 | No | 20 | 10 | ME |
| | Argument | No | Sprouse 2009: B1 | No | 25 | 5 | Y/N |
| | Argument | No | Sprouse 2009: B2 | No | 19 | 5 | Y/N |
| | *Adjunct* | No | Hiramatsu 2000: E2 | Yes | 11 | 7 | Y/N |

Also noteworthy in Table 6.1 is the fact that Hiramatsu (2000: E2) directly compared extraction of an argument *wh*-word (e.g. *what*, as in (4a)), versus an adjunct *wh*-word (e.g. *when*, as in (4b)) (Hiramatsu's examples 132 and 134, p. 122).

(4)  a. Context:   Yesterday, Kelly wondered whether Tina had read "Amistad."

  Question:   What did Kelly wonder whether Tina had read?

  b. Context:   Gary wondered whether, this year, Jordan would learn French.

  Question:   When did Gary wonder whether Jordan would learn French?

Linguists report satiation on argument extraction, but never adjunct extraction, from *whether*-islands, and Hiramatsu found the same pattern in her data.

Table 6.2 summarizes experiments on Complex Noun Phrase Constraint (CNPC) violations like (5) (cf. Snyder 2018: 5).[14,15]

(5)   *[Context: Mary believes the claim that John likes Susan.]*
  Who does Mary believe the claim that John likes?

Even among the six studies providing a context sentence, only three obtained a significant effect. One striking point of variation is number of participants: the studies *not* reporting satiation all had fewer than 40, while two of three studies reporting satiation had more than 40. Snyder

---

[14] CNPC violations like (5) must be distinguished from those with extraction from a relative clause, like (i).

  (i) *[Context: Mary likes the picture that John sent to Fred.]*
    Who does Mary like the picture that John sent to?

  The latter is structurally quite different. Here, "CNPC violation" will refer exclusively to items like (5).

[15] Francom (2009: E1, E2) are omitted from Table 6.2 because they used a much more diverse range of "CNPC" items.

Table 6.2 *Satiation experiments on CNPC violations*

| Sentence type | Satiation? | Study | Context sentence? | Number of participants | Number of exposures | Task |
|---|---|---|---|---|---|---|
| CNPC | Yes | Goodall 2011 | Yes | *45* | 5 | Y/N |
| | Yes | Snyder 2000 | Yes | *22* | 5 | Y/N |
| | Yes | Snyder 2018: E3 | Yes | *151* | 5 | Y/N |
| | No | Hiramatsu 2000: E1 | Yes | *33* | 7 | Y/N |
| | No | Snyder 2018: E1 | Yes | *20* | 5 | Y/N |
| | No | Sprouse 2009: A5 | Yes | *20* | 10 | ME |
| | No | Sprouse 2009: A4 | No | *17* | 10 | ME |
| | No | Sprouse 2009: B1 | No | *25* | 5 | Y/N |
| | No | Sprouse 2009: B2 | No | *19* | 5 | Y/N |

(2018) examined the effect size for satiation on CNPCs in E3 (N=151), and estimated his experimental design was unlikely to yield significance with fewer than about 76 participants. He proposed that satiation on different "satiable" sentence types can have different characteristics: the effect size appears to be substantially larger for *whether-* islands than CNPC violations. Moreover, the apparent absence of satiation, in the studies that did not detect it, may well be due to the smaller numbers of participants in those studies.

A third sentence type that sometimes shows satiation is *wh*-extraction of arguments from Subject Islands. Table 6.3 provides an overview; predicate types are shown in (6).[16]

(6)    a. What does Raymond believe that a pair of will be <u>visible</u> tonight? [A=Adjective]

       b. What does Marvin think that a picture of will <u>appeal</u> to Molly? [EO=Experiencer-Object]

       c. What does Edwin think that a whole stack of was accidentally <u>discarded</u>? [P=Passive]

       d. Which textbook did chapters of <u>seem</u> not well-organized? [RP=Raising-Predicate]

       e. What does Clinton worry that an ally of will <u>boycott</u> the airline? [T=Transitive]

       f. What does John know that a bottle of <u>fell</u> on the floor? [Ua=Unaccusative]

       g. What does Jack claim a crowd of <u>walked</u> into the store? [Ue=Unergative]

---

[16] Sprouse (2009) appears to have treated items like (i.a–b) (Sprouse 2009: 337, Table 5) as "subject islands":

   (i)     a. What will to admit in public be easier someday?

          b. What does that you bought anger the other students?

Yet these *clausal* subjects are substantially different from the subject DPs examined in other studies.

Table 6.3 *Satiation experiments on subject-island violations (for predicate types, see text)*

| Sentence type | Predicate type(s) | Satiation? | Study | Context sentence? | Number of participants | Number of exposures | Task |
|---|---|---|---|---|---|---|---|
| Subject-island | EO,P,RP,T,Ue,Ua | Yes | Chaves & Dery 2014: E1 | No | 60 | 20 | Sc |
| | A,P | Yes | Chaves & Dery 2014: E2 | No | 55 | 14 | Sc |
| | A,P,R,Ua | Yes | Francom 2009: E1 | No | 205 | 5 | Y/N |
| | P,R,T,Ua | Yes | Francom 2009: E2 | No | 22 | 8 | Y/N |
| | Ua | Yes | Hiramatsu 2000: E1 | Yes | 33 | 7 | Y/N |
| | T | No | Hiramatsu 2000: E2 | Yes | 11 | 7 | Y/N |
| | T/Ua/Ue | No | Crawford 2012 | Yes | 22 | 7 | Sc |
| | (Ua,*others?*) | No | Goodall 2011 | Yes | 45 | 5 | Y/N |
| | A,EO,P,Ua | No (MS) | Snyder 2000 | Yes | 22 | 5 | Y/N |
| | A,EO,P,Ua | No | Snyder 2018: E1 | Yes | 20 | 5 | Y/N |
| | A,EO,P,Ua | No | Snyder 2018: E3 | Yes | 151 | 5 | Y/N |
| | (unclear) | No | Sprouse 2009: A1 | No | 20 | 14 | ME |

For Hiramatsu (2000), the subject-island predicates in E1 were consistently unaccusatives, while those in E2 were consistently transitives; she obtained clear satiation in E1, but not E2.

In Table 6.3, one striking difference between the studies that did versus did not report satiation is the number of exposures to the sentence type. Of the six experiments where satiation was detected, five provided at least seven exposures. Indeed, Hiramatsu (2000) reported that in her data, the satiation evident after participants had received seven exposures was not yet evident at the point when they had received only five. Here too, Snyder (2018) proposes that the details of the satiation effect differ systematically as a function of the sentence type involved: much as satiation on CNPC violations is associated with a small effect size, and may be difficult to detect with a small number of participants, satiation on subject-island violations seems to begin more gradually, and require a greater number of exposures before it becomes readily detectable.[17]

Interestingly, the lack of a context sentence did not prevent the detection of satiation on subject islands in the experiments of Chaves and Dery or Francom, nor did the small numbersof participants in Francom (2009: E2) and Hiramatsu (2000: E2). At the same time, simply providing seven or more exposures did not guarantee satiation: two of the reported experiments (Sprouse 2009: A1; Crawford 2012) failed to detect a satiation effect with seven or even fourteen exposures.

English sentence types that have generally NOT shown a satiation effect include violations of the Left-Branch-Constraint (LBC) and violations of the adjunct-island, *that*-trace, and *want-for* constraints. Table 6.4 summarizes

---

[17] A similar idea arises in Do and Kaiser's (2017) syntactic-priming study, which finds very short-term priming (lasting across a single intervening sentence) for CNPC, but not subject islands. They propose (p. 193) that satiation on CNPCs (but not subject islands) may relate to a form of priming they term "lingering activation."

Table 6.4 *Satiation experiments on adjunct-island and LBC violations*

| Sentence type | Satiation? | Study | Context sentence? | Number of participants | Number of exposures | Task |
|---|---|---|---|---|---|---|
| Adjunct-island | No | Braze 2002 | Yes | 16 | 9 | Y/N |
| | No | Crawford 2012 | Yes | 22 | 7 | Sc |
| | No | Francom 2009: E1 | No | 205 | 5 | Y/N |
| | No | Francom 2009: E2 | No | 22 | 8 | Y/N |
| | No | Goodall 2011 | Yes | 45 | 5 | Y/N |
| | No | Hiramatsu 2000: E1 | Yes | 33 | 7 | Y/N |
| | No | Hiramatsu 2000: E2 | Yes | 11 | 7 | Y/N |
| | No | Snyder 2000 | Yes | 22 | 5 | Y/N |
| | No | Snyder 2018: E1 | Yes | 20 | 5 | Y/N |
| | No | Snyder 2018: E3 | Yes | 151 | 5 | Y/N |
| | No | Sprouse 2009: A2 | No | 24 | 14 | *ME* |
| | No | Sprouse 2009: B1 | No | 25 | 5 | Y/N |
| | No | Sprouse 2009: B2 | No | 19 | 5 | Y/N |
| Left branch | No | Francom 2009: E1 | No | 205 | 5 | Y/N |
| | No | Francom 2009: E2 | No | 22 | 8 | Y/N |
| | No | Goodall 2011 | Yes | 45 | 5 | Y/N |
| | No | Hiramatsu 2000: E1 | Yes | 33 | 7 | Y/N |
| | No | Hiramatsu 2000: E2 | Yes | 11 | 7 | Y/N |
| | No | Snyder 2000 | Yes | 22 | 5 | Y/N |
| | No | Snyder 2018: E1 | Yes | 20 | 5 | Y/N |
| | No | Snyder 2018: E3 | Yes | 151 | 5 | Y/N |
| | No | Sprouse 2009: B1 | No | 25 | 5 | Y/N |

studies of Adjunct Islands and LBC violations. For *that*-trace and *want-for* violations (Table 6.5), most studies report non-satiation, but two require some discussion. First, both Francom (2009) and Sprouse (2009) cite (Hiramatsu 2000:E1) as finding satiation on *that*-trace and *want-for*, but Hiramatsu describes things differently. She reports (p. 107) that multiple participants eventually began crossing out *that* or *for* on the test booklet, and marking "Yes." In fact, she seems concerned that other participants took a similar approach (without indicating it on the booklet), because on p. 111 she disavows the data for these sentences altogether: "As we saw in the previous section, we do not have a clear picture of the results for ... *That*-trace and *Want-for* sentences." Hence, the cautious approach is to set those findings aside.

For *want-for*, the one remaining study reporting satiation is Francom (2009: E1), which was modeled closely on Snyder (2000). Francom kindly allowed Snyder to check the data for consistency across versions and items. The increased acceptance was almost entirely confined to participants receiving the Version-B presentation order, and only one of the two test items in the first/last block (depending on version) increased when presented at the end. Hence, by the criteria in Section 6.3, the findings are not clear evidence of satiation.

Table 6.5 *Satiation experiments on* that-trace *and* want-for *violations*

| Sentence type | Satiation? | Study | Context sentence? | Number of participants | Number of exposures | Task |
|---|---|---|---|---|---|---|
| *That-trace* | *(See text)* | Hiramatsu 2000: *E1* | Yes | 33 | 7 | Y/N |
| | No | Francom 2009: E1 | No | 205 | 5 | Y/N |
| | No | Francom 2009: E2 | No | 22 | 8 | Y/N |
| | No | Goodall 2011 | Yes | 45 | 5 | Y/N |
| | No | Snyder 2000 | Yes | 22 | 5 | Y/N |
| | No | Snyder 2018: E1 | Yes | 20 | 5 | Y/N |
| | No | Snyder 2018: E3 | Yes | 151 | 5 | Y/N |
| *Want-for* | *(See text)* | (Hiramatsu 2000: *E1*) | Yes | 33 | 7 | Y/N |
| | *(See text)* | (Francom 2009: *E1*) | No | 205 | 5 | Y/N |
| | No | Snyder 2000 | Yes | 22 | 5 | Y/N |
| | No | Snyder 2018: E1 | Yes | 20 | 5 | Y/N |
| | No | Snyder 2018: E3 | Yes | 151 | 5 | Y/N |

## 6.4.2   Languages Other than English

Turning now to satiation studies in other languages, the first was a study by Grant Goodall, who tested for satiation on comparable sentences across English and Spanish. His findings for English were included in Tables 6.1–5 above, except for the sentence type in (7). Examples of his Spanish sentence types are shown in (8) (Goodall 2011: 37, examples 14a–f) (see also Chapter 17).

(7)      No inversion
        *What John will buy at the store?

(8)      a. No inversion
              *¿Qué   Juan compró en la   tienda?
                 what Juan bought  in  the store
              '*What Juan bought in the store?'
         b. Subject island
              *¿De qué  sabe   María que una botella se   cayó de   la   mesa?
                 of what know Maria that a    bottle refl fell  from the table
              '*Of what does Maria know that a bottle fell from the table?'
         c. CNPC
              *¿Qué   acepta Carmen la   idea de que Héctor venda?
                 what accept Carmen the idea of that Hector sells
              '*What does Carmen accept the idea that Héctor sells?'
         d. Adjunct island
              *¿A quién habló José con   Irma después de ver?
                 whom   spoke José with Irma after     of see
              '*Whom did José speak with Irma after seeing?'
         e. Left branch
              *¿Cuántos    compró Mario libros?
                 how-many bought  Mario books
              '*How many did Mario buy books?'

f. Double psych-fronting
   *A nadie   la   música le      gustó.
   to nobody the music   io.3sg pleased
   Intended: 'The music pleased nobody.'
   (= 'Nobody liked the music.')

Goodall employed a yes/no task. Materials were presented in a printed booklet, much as in Snyder (2000), with a context sentence before each test sentence. There were two versions, with "forward" or "reverse" order of presentation. The 59 Spanish-speaking participants had all grown up in Mexico and attended primary and secondary schools with Spanish as the language of instruction.

In 45 native English speakers, Goodall found no satiation on sentences like (7). Yet he found satiation on the Spanish counterpart to (7) in (8a). This supported his proposal that inversion requirements in English and Spanish have different sources. Interestingly, Goodall also found a strong satiation effect on extraction from CNPCs in English (as noted in Table 6.2), but not in Spanish; he tied this to the obligatory preposition (*de* 'of') in Spanish. Finally, he found satiation on "double psych-fronting" sentences like (8f).[18]

Satiation has also been examined in Brazilian Portuguese. Marcus Maia (2013: 21–25) reports on work with Wendy Barile. Their study examined *wh*-in-situ questions with the *wh*-expression inside an island, as in (9) (see Maia 2013: 22, glosses and translations by WS); all these sentences are normally considered unacceptable. The study also included fully acceptable control sentences, as in (10). Participants gave yes/no judgments on 16 test sentences and 16 control sentences.

(9)     a. Relative clause
           Você escreveu a    mensagem que dizia o    quê?
           you  wrote    the message   that said the what
           'You wrote the message that said what?'
        b. Factive island
           A   sua  filha    lamenta que você não trouxe   quem?
           the your daughter laments that you  not brought whom
           'Your daughter is sad that you didn't bring whom?'
        c. Adjunct island
           João chegou atrasado pedindo    os   formulários como?
           John arrived late     requesting the  forms       how
           'John came in late asking for the forms how?'
        d. Sentential subject
           É obrigatório que a    prova    seja entregue até    quando?
           is obligatory that the evidence be   delivered until when
           'It is obligatory that the evidence be delivered by when?'

---

[18] Do, Kaiser, and Zubizarreta (2016) build on Goodall's work to investigate adult-L2 acquisition of English by Spanish speakers. In contrast to L1 English speakers, the L2s satiate on English items like (7).

(10)  a. No    seu   último aniversário, você ganhou o    quê?
         on-the your  last   birthday     you received  the what
         'On your last birthday you received what?'

      b. Aquela encomenda está  sendo  enviada para  quem?
         that    order     is    being  sent    to    whom
         'That order is being sent to whom?'

      c. Ele  conseguiu uma bolsa de  estudos como?
         he   obtained   a   grant  of  studies how
         'He got a scholarship how?'

      d. Este  relatório deve   ser entregue até    quando?
         this  report    should be  delivered until when
         'This report should be delivered by when?'

Participants formed two groups. Group 1 were 24 university students who had
just completed a linguistics course on syntax, with several weeks of discussing
and analyzing sentences containing various types of syntactic islands. Group 2
were 24 students who had just finished courses in fields other than linguistics,
and who had never taken any course touching on syntactic islands.

The groups were similar on control items: Group 1 accepted nearly 100
percent, and Group 2 more than 80 percent. On test sentences, however,
Group 1 accepted almost 70 percent, while Group 2 fewer than 50 percent.[19]
(Maia does not break down the results by sentence type.) The researchers
also collected response times. Group 1 was significantly slower to reject test
items (on average, 1.776 ms) than Group 2 (1.331 ms).

Finally, satiation has been examined in Danish. Christensen, Kizach, and
Nyvad (2013) report on two experiments, both examining wh-island violations (see Chapter 18 for more detailed discussion of experimental work
on Germanic languages). E1 included the sentence types in (11) (from
Christensen et al. 2013: 55, Table 1), plus short- and long-distance wh-
movement of arguments and adjuncts without islands, and additional
controls (nine sentence types in total).

(11)  a. Argument extraction  from a Wh-Island:
         Hvad ved   hun godt  hvor  man kan leje?
         what knows she  well  where one  can rent
         'What does she know where you can rent?'
      b. Adjunct extraction from a Wh-Island:
         Hvor  ved    hun godt hvad man kan leje?
         where knows she  well what one  can rent
         'Where does she know what you can rent?'

Sixty students at Aarhus University judged 16 tokens of each type. A new
pseudo-random order was generated for each participant. Ratings were on
a five-point numerical scale. The authors report a significant (but weak)

---

[19] Maia takes average acceptance above 70 percent as genuine acceptance, and below 50 percent as non-acceptance.

positive correlation between ordinal position and acceptability for the *wh*-island items. (Results are not broken down by argument/adjunct.) The authors interpret these findings as a satiation (or "training") effect of the type in Snyder (2000).[20]

E2 was conducted later than E1, though the time-gap is not specified. Interestingly, the majority (23 out of 30) of the E2 participants had been in E1; the authors call these the "exp" group, versus "non-exp." Materials were similar to those of E1. Instead of simplex *wh*-words, E2 used D-linked *wh*-phrases (e.g. *hvilken båd* 'which boat'), and instead of holding the matrix verb constant (*ved* 'know(s)'), E2 used a range of verbs.

Acceptability was no longer significantly correlated with ordinal position, but there was a significant exp/non-exp contrast: the exp group gave significantly higher ratings than the non-exp group to *Wh*-Island extractions (and to long-distance movement without an island). The authors concluded satiation in the exp group had persisted from E1. The issue of how long experimentally induced satiation can persist between testing sessions is discussed next.

## 6.5  Persistence of Satiation, and Carryover Effects

One of the distinctive characteristics of satiation in linguists is Within-speaker Persistence: Once an individual satiates on a given sentence type, the effect persists for a considerable period of time. A natural question is whether satiation induced in the lab, in the space of 15–30 minutes, persists beyond the experimental session. To address this question, Snyder (2018) ran a pair of experiments: E1 was an almost exact replication of Snyder (2000). After completing E1, each of the 20 participants was invited to return for a second experiment (E2) one month later, and 15 did so. (The minimum gap between testing sessions was four weeks.) E2 was identical to E1 except for order of presentation.

Participants in E1 exhibited significant satiation on exactly one sentence type, *wh*-extraction of an argument from a *whether*-island. For the participants who completed both E1 and E2, the findings from E1 were as follows: in Blocks 1–2, the mean acceptance rate for *whether* was 26.7 percent; in Blocks 4–5, it was 66.7 percent. In E2 four weeks later, at the beginning of the session (Blocks 1–2), the same participants accepted *whether* at a mean rate of 73.3 percent.[21] Moreover, each individual's acceptance rate at the beginning of E2 was at least as high as it had been at the end of E1 (Blocks 4–5). Hence, this study provides striking evidence that experimentally induced satiation, like the satiation seen in linguists, can persist for a considerable period of time.

---

[20] Experiment 1 also yielded a weak but significant positive correlation between ordinal position and acceptability for long-distance *wh*-movement *without* an island.

[21] For all other sentence types, acceptance in E2:Blocks 1–2 resembled E1:Blocks 1–2 (NSD by Wilcoxon).

Another question is whether satiation "carries over" from the exact sentence type on which it was induced, to sentence types that are somewhat different on the surface, but closely related according to syntactic theory. So far this question has been examined in Snyder (2000) and Snyder (2018: E1,E3); the final block of each experiment was followed by a small number of post-test items. In Snyder (2000), satiation was induced with sentences like (12a–b), and the post-test included (13a–b).

(12)     a. Who does John <u>wonder whether</u> Mary likes?
         b. Who does Mary <u>believe the claim</u> that John likes?

(13)     a. What did Mildred <u>ask whether</u> Ted had visited?
         b. What did Madge <u>accept the idea</u> that Bob would do?

Although (12a) and (13a) are both *whether*-island violations, their only point of lexical overlap is the word *whether*. In the course of the experiment, participants judged five sentences like (12a), and then judged (13a) in the post-test. Similarly, while (12b) and (13b) are both CNPC violations, their only lexical overlap is the function words *the* and *that*. Participants judged five examples like (12b), and then judged (13b) in the post-test. If satiation operates at the level of abstract structures, not specific lexical items, the participants who satiate on items like (12a, b) should also become more accepting of (13a, b).

To evaluate this prediction, Snyder (2000) focused on participants who rejected a given sentence type in Blocks 1–2. All 22 participants rejected the CNPC violations (with *believe the claim*) in Blocks 1–2. Of these 22, 17 also rejected the CNPC violations in Blocks 3–5. Only four of these 17 "non-satiators" accepted (13b) in the post-test. In contrast, for the satiators (who had all accepted at least one of the two items in Blocks 4–5), four out of five accepted (12b) (binomial test: two-tailed $p<.05$). Similarly, for the 18 participants who initially rejected the *Whether* items, only three of the seven non-satiators accepted (13a), whereas 10 of the 11 satiators did ($p<.005$).

In Snyder (2018), E1 used the exact same materials (except for an increase in the number of control items). The experiment obtained significant satiation only for *whether*-island violations (not CNPC violations), but much as in Snyder (2000), there was significant carryover from *wonder whether* to *ask whether*.

In E3, the post-test was extended to include the items in (14) (and two more control items).

(14)     a. Who does Olga <u>wonder why</u> Sally likes?
         b. What does Sue <u>know how</u> Bill fixed?

In E3 there was significant satiation on CNPC violations (with *believe the claim*), and as in Snyder (2000) there was significant carryover to CNPC items with *accept the idea*. In E3 there was also significant satiation on *whether*-islands (with *wonder whether*), and this time the post-test was used to check for carryover to each of three sentence types: *ask whether, wonder why*, and *know how*. There was significant carryover from *wonder whether* to *wonder why*, although not to *ask whether* (in contrast to Snyder 2000 and Snyder 2018: E1) or *know how*.[22]

In sum, these three experiments provided evidence for carryover of satiation: from CNPC violations with *believe the claim*, to those with *accept the idea* (Snyder 2000, 2018: E3); from *whether*-island violations with *wonder whether*, to those with *ask whether* (Snyder 2000, 2018: E1); and from *whether*-island violations with *wonder whether*, to wh-island violations with *wonder why* (Snyder 2018: E3).

## 6.6 Explaining Satiation

To summarize Sections 6.4 and 6.5, a version of the satiation experienced by linguists can be induced in the laboratory, in non-linguists. The same sentence types satiate in both groups: for English, these include sentences with argument *wh*-extraction from a *whether*-island, a complex noun phrase, or a subject island. Where satiation in linguists may bring a lack of confidence in their expert knowledge that a sentence type is grammatically anomalous, the non-linguist simply judges the sentence type as more acceptable. Where satiation in linguists seems to be triggered by routine encounters with satiable sentence types during day-to-day work, satiation in the lab can be triggered by a long series of acceptability judgments, with periodic repetition of satiable sentence types. Much as satiation in linguists persists over time, the satiation induced in non-linguists is detectable in follow-up testing four weeks later.

The question now is why satiation exists. This section will examine possible contributions of grammar and sentence-processing. An overarching question will be whether satiation is a unitary phenomenon, with a single underlying cause for all the sentence types that exhibit it, or is better viewed as an "umbrella" concept for distinct effects, with different causes in different sentence types.

### 6.6.1 The Perspective from Grammar
One striking aspect of satiation is that it respects distinctions largely unknown outside generative linguistics. As noted in Section 6.4, Hiramatsu's (2000) participants satiated on *wh*-extraction of an argument, but not an adjunct, from a *whether*-island. Strikingly, the same pattern exists in the satiation reported by professional linguists. This degree of

---

[22] Snyder (2018: 31, n.22) suggests "non-satiators" in the comparison group might have been starting to satiate by the post-test; if so, they might not have differed sufficiently from the "satiators" to provide significant contrasts.

specificity is remarkable, and calls for an explanation that builds, in some way, on generative research.

Arguably, *Barriers* (Chomsky 1986) is the most recent work in generative syntax to address all the different island effects examined in the satiation literature. Thus, a natural question is whether the satiable sentence types in English constitute a natural class in *Barriers*, distinguishable from the non-satiable sentence types. The answer is yes and no: the satiable sentence types are similar to one another, in never violating the Empty Category Principle (ECP); but they vary in how many barriers are crossed. Moreover, among sentence types with movement across two barriers, satiability varies.

One major success of *Barriers*, when applied to the findings on satiation, is that it readily distinguishes between argument extraction (15a), and adjunct extraction (15b), from a *whether*-island. (The examples in (15) are based on (4), above.)

(15)    a. What$_1$ did Kelly wonder [$_{CP}$ whether [$_{IP}$ Tina had <u>read</u> t$_1$]]?
        b. When$_2$ did Gary wonder [$_{CP}$ whether [$_{IP}$ Jordan would learn French t$_2$]] ?

Suppressing many details, (15a) satisfies the ECP because *read* assigns a theta role to (or "L-marks") the trace, and thereby "properly governs" it. In (15b), the trace corresponding to the adjunct *when* does not receive a theta role and has to be "antecedent-governed" by *when*, either directly or through an intermediate trace. The CP node indicated in (15) is a barrier for t$_2$, and a single barrier is sufficient to block antecedent government. Hence (15b) violates the ECP, and (as expected) is severely degraded.[23] Moreover, the absence of satiation on (15b) is consistent with a (tentative) generalization that ECP violations never satiate.

In contrast to (15b), the trace in (15a) satisfies the ECP. Moreover, movement in (15a) crosses only one barrier (the CP node). Since Subjacency in *Barriers* prohibits movement across *two* barriers, (15a) (which satiates) violates neither the ECP nor Subjacency.

Indeed, one might speculate that by the time he was working on the *Barriers* system, Chomsky had himself experienced satiation on certain sentence types. In *Barriers*, *wh*-island and CNPC violations, which were treated as Subjacency violations in Chomsky (1977 and 1981), do not violate the new formulation of Subjacency. Consider the *wh*-island violation in (16), which was treated as a Subjacency violation prior to *Barriers*.

(16)    What$_1$ did Kelly wonder [$_{CP}$ how$_2$ [$_{IP}$ Tina had <u>repaired</u> t$_1$ t$_2$]]?

In (16) the *wh*-adjunct *how* moves into lower SPEC-CP, forcing the *wh*-argument *what* to cross a barrier on its way to matrix SPEC-CP. Yet there is only one barrier, not two, and the *Barriers* formulation of Subjacency is

---

[23] Note: in the relevant judgment, *when* concerns the time of learning, not wondering.

satisfied. If (16) is degraded, the problem lies outside the *Barriers* system, perhaps in the "weaker" Relativized-Minimality constraint of Rizzi (1990, et seq.).

Regardless, the fact that the *Barriers* system groups (15a) and (16) together, as argument extraction across a single barrier, invites the question of whether experimentally induced satiation on sentences like (15a) carries over to sentences like (16), even when participants have not seen the latter. This question is at least partially answered by a finding of Snyder (2018: E3) described above: participants who satiated on sentences like (12a) (repeated below), which is equivalent to (15a), were significantly more likely than non-satiators to accept (14a) on a post-test:

> (12) a. Who does John <u>wonder whether</u> Mary likes?
> (14) a. Who does Olga <u>wonder why</u> Sally likes?

In (14a), as in (16), an adjunct *wh*-word (here *why*) moves into the lower SPEC-CP, which forces the argument *wh*-word (*who*) to cross a barrier on its way to matrix SPEC-CP. Hence, at least in this case, satiation on one particular single-barrier sentence type (with *wh*-complementizer *whether*) does indeed carry over to another single-barrier type (with *wh*-adjunct *why*). An interesting question for future research will be whether this pattern holds up for additional types of *wh*-islands.

Up to this point, satiable sentences have been exactly the ones with argument-extraction across a single barrier, but the situation is more complicated. First, Section 6.4 presented evidence of satiation on argument extraction from a Complex NP. Yet, as shown in (17a) (repeating (3b)), extraction from a CNPC crosses *two* barriers. The N *claim* (arguably) does not assign any theta role to the lower CP; hence, both CP and NP are barriers to extraction of *Who*.

> (17)     a. Who$_1$ does Mary believe [$_{NP}$ the claim [$_{CP}$ t$_1$ that [John likes t$_1$]]]?
>          b. Mary met <u>Fred, a baker</u>.

Yet the analysis in (17a) takes the lower CP as an appositive, helping identify the claim under discussion, much as *a baker* in (16b) helps identify *Fred*. Kiss (1987: 218) proposes an alternative analysis in which CP is a thematic *complement* to N. If CP receives a theta role (and therefore is L-marked), neither CP nor NP is a barrier.[24]

Indeed, for CNPC violations the *mechanism* of satiation could be structural reanalysis: the CP in the complex NP originates as an appositive, but can (following multiple judgments) be reanalyzed as a complement. Note, however, that this would change a two-barrier extraction into a zero-barrier extraction (contrary to the suggestion linking satiation to one-barrier sentences); and the proposed mechanism (converting a CP-

---

[24] Note: the CP-appositive was a barrier because of no theta-role from *claim*, and the NP was a barrier *by inheritance*. L-marking the CP eliminates both instances of barrierhood.

appositive into a CP-complement) does not, in any obvious way, generalize to other satiable sentence types (e.g. the *whether*-island in (15a)).[25]

Finally, in terms of *Barriers*, the most challenging problem is the satiability of subject-island violations, and *not* adjunct-island violations. Both sentence types satisfy the ECP, and involve movement across *two* barriers. Hence, *Barriers* by itself may not provide the full range of distinctions needed to account for the satiation findings.[26]

### 6.6.2   The Perspective from Processing

Snyder (2000: 580) noted that satiability of a sentence type might indicate that its initial unacceptability is due to something outside the grammar, such as a difficulty in sentence processing (cf. Berwick & Weinberg (1984: 153–173), and Kluender & Kutas (1993), on classical – i.e. pre-*Barriers* – subjacency effects; and Chomsky (1965: 10–14) on center-embedding). Chaves and Dery (2014, 2018) take this approach to Subject Islands. Building on work of Hofmeister et al. (2013), they argue for a model with the following core tenets:

(i) "Subject Island effects are caused by the fact that subject-embedded gaps are pragmatically unusual – as the informational focus does not usually correspond to a dependent of the subject phrase – and therefore are highly contrary to comprehenders' expectations about the distribution of filler–gap dependencies." (Chaves & Dery 2018: 1)

(ii) *Satiation* on Subject-Island extraction can occur when "comprehenders have the chance to adjust to the unusual syntactic location of the gap by being exposed to multiple exemplars of such sentences. We argue that such amelioration is facilitated when the very mention of the subject-embedded referent is a highly felicitous discourse move to begin with." (Chaves & Dery 2018: 31)

In support of their model, Chaves and Dery note (for example) that structurally equivalent subject-island violations vary enormously in the acceptability judgments they elicit. In some cases – simply by virtue of open-class lexical choices, and without any form of satiation – the sentences are accepted as perfect (e.g. Chaves & Dery 2014: 97, (3a–c)). On their account it was simply an error when syntacticians sought to explain the unacceptability of (certain) "subject island" sentences in terms of a syntactic constraint. If this is correct, removing these sentences from the data to

---

[25] Nonetheless, this approach could account for non-satiation of the CNPC-items in note 15 (with extraction from a relative clause, RC). Since an RC is never N's argument, extraction crosses two barriers (CP,NP). If satiation is limited to sentences respecting ECP and crossing at most *one* barrier, RC-items should not satiate.

[26] *Barriers* could perhaps be modified to distinguish subjects, which (other than expletives) are theta-marked, from adjuncts (never theta-marked). A mechanism (cf. reanalysis of CP-appositives as CP-complements) *making* subject-DPs count as L-marked would permit alignment of subjects with Complex-NPs, for purposes of satiation. (Another option, discussed below: move restrictions on subject-extraction from the syntax into processing.)

be explained by syntactic theory should yield improvements both in syntactic theory, and in our understanding of *wh*-extraction from subjects.[27]

### 6.6.3   Is Satiation Unitary?

What about the other satiable sentence types, such as English CNPC violations and *whether*-island extractions? Does the Chaves–Dery account cover them too? Should it have to? These questions relate to a larger issue for research on satiation: is satiation a "unitary" phenomenon? This question has at least two senses, and both are relevant.

First there is the question of whether satiation is a single, unitary "change" in an individual. The idea would be that (at least in principle) a single change in a person's language capacities, broadly construed, might be directly responsible for that person's satiation (if any) on *all* the satiable sentence types. Under this scenario, a person would have a single "level" of satiation (not specific to any sentence type), which might or might not be sufficient to make a particular sentence type fall into the "acceptable" range. This scenario leads to strong testable predictions. For example, all individuals who have satiated to the point of accepting the more recalcitrant of the satiable sentence types in English (which, based on the evidence in Section 6.4, are CNPC and subject-island violations) should necessarily also accept *whether*-island violations, even if they have not been exposed to the latter violations. This prediction remains to be tested.

Alternatively, if the evidence points away from this first possibility, there is a second scenario to consider: is satiation fundamentally the same process, proceeding in *parallel* for different, satiable sentence types? Here we would not expect automatic carryover from one satiable type to all the others, but we would expect the separate processes of satiation for different sentence types to involve the same (or very similar) mechanisms, and to exhibit very similar characteristics.

For example, if the Chaves–Dery approach to satiation on Subject Islands wins out over competing accounts, the "parallel-mechanism" scenario would lead us to expect the same underlying mechanism to account for satiation on CNPC and *wh*-island violations: *low frequency* of gaps inside complex NPs and embedded *wh*-questions (rather than grammatical constraints) would account for the initial unacceptability of these sentence types; and acceptability would increase upon repeatedly parsing these sentences. An example of a consequent, testable prediction would be the following: given tenet (ii) of the Chaves–Dery approach, the degree to which acceptance of (say) CNPCs increases following repeated exposure

---

[27] Note: Chaves and Dery treat subject-island violations as severe garden-path (GP) effects; the parser prematurely rejects the correct parse (with subject-internal gap), and fails to recover. This fits neatly with (i) studies finding syntactic priming (e.g. Branigan 2007) for particular structures, in production and comprehension; and (ii) Zervakis and Mazuka's (2013) finding of a satiation-like effect (i.e. sustained, statistically reliable increase in acceptance) for certain (grammatical) GP sentences, following repeated acceptability judgments.

will be greatest when mention of the Complex-NP embedded referent is a highly *felicitous* discourse move.

In a third possible scenario, satiation is not unitary in either of the senses above. In this case, the mechanism of satiation on Subject Islands could turn out to be experience-based changes in parsing expectations (Chaves & Dery); the mechanism for CNPCs could be a general reanalysis operation on N+CP structures, as sketched above; and perhaps the mechanism of for *whether-* and other *wh*-islands will be something like the "dulling" of an introspective "error signal" that occurs whenever a syntactic structure requires extraction across a (single) barrier. Any of the various possibilities above leads to testable (and as-yet untested) predictions.

### 6.6.4   Satiation as a Diagnostic Method in Linguistics

Independently of whether satiation effects turn out to be better explained by grammar, sentence processing, or a combination, experimental induction of satiation is potentially a valuable investigational tool for linguistic research. Quite simply, evidence about satiation has a bearing on whether any two sentence types that are (initially) unacceptable owe their unacceptability to the *same* cause. Goodall (2011: 35) expresses it well:

> [I]f one unacceptable sentence type is satiation-inducing and another is not, it is unlikely that their unacceptability is attributable to the same underlying principle. This suggests, for instance, that violations of *whether* islands, which are susceptible to satiation, and *that*-trace violations, which are not, must be due to different underlying principles, in accord with the general consensus in the literature about these two phenomena.

## References

Berwick, R. C. & Weinberg, A. S. (1984). *The Grammatical Basis of Linguistic Performance: Language Use and Acquisition.* Cambridge, MA: MIT Press.

Boeckx, C. (2003). *Islands and Chains: Resumption as Stranding* (Linguistik Aktuell / Linguistics Today 63). Amsterdam: John Benjamins.

Branigan, H. (2007). Syntactic priming. *Language and Linguistics Compass*, 1 (1–2), 1–16. DOI: 10.1111/j.1749-818X.2006.00001.x

Braze, F. D. (2002). Grammaticality, acceptability, and sentence processing: A psycholinguistic study. Doctoral dissertation, University of Connecticut, Storrs.

Chaves, R. P. & Dery, J. E. (2014). Which subject islands will the acceptability of improve with repeated exposure? In R. E. Santana-LaBarge, ed., *Proceedings of the 31st West Coast Conference on Formal Linguistics.* Somerville, MA: Cascadilla Proceedings Project, pp. 96–106.

Chaves, R. P. & Dery, J. E. (2018). Frequency effects in Subject Islands. *Journal of Linguistics*, 1–47. DOI:10.1017/S0022226718000294

Chomsky, N. (1965). *Aspects of the Theory of Syntax*. Cambridge, MA: MIT Press.

Chomsky, N. (1977). On *wh*-movement. In P. Culicover, T. Wasow, & A. Akmanian, eds., *Formal Syntax*. New York: Academic Press, pp. 71–132.

Chomsky, N. (1981). *Lectures on Government and Binding*. Dordrecht: Foris.

Chomsky, N. (1986). *Barriers*. Cambridge, MA: MIT Press.

Christensen, K. R., Kizach, J., & Nyvad, A. M. (2013). Escape from the island: Grammaticality and (reduced) acceptability of *wh*-island violations in Danish. *Journal of Psycholinguistic Research*, 42, 51–70. DOI 10.1007/s10936-012-9210-x

Crawford, J. (2012). Using syntactic satiation effects to investigate subject islands. In J. Choi, E. A. Hogue, J. Punske, D. Tat, J. Schertz, & A. Trueman, eds., *Proceedings of the 29th West Coast Conference on Formal Linguistics*. Somerville, MA: Cascadilla Proceedings Project, pp. 38–45.

Do, M. & Kaiser, E. (2017). A closer look: Investigating the mechanisms of syntactic satiation. In A. Kaplan, A. Kaplan, M. K. McCarvel, & E. J. Rubin, eds., *Proceedings of the 34th West Coast Conference on Formal Linguistics*. Somerville, MA: Cascadilla Proceedings Project, pp. 187–194.

Do, M., Kaiser, E., & Zubizarreta, M. L. (2016). Spanish speakers' acquisition of English subject–verb inversion: Evidence from satiation. In D. Stringer, J. Garrett, B. Halloran, & S. Mossman, eds., *Proceedings of the 13th Generative Approaches to Second Language Acquisition Conference (GASLA 2015)*. Somerville, MA: Cascadilla Proceedings Project, pp. 45–59.

Francom, J. C. (2009). Experimental syntax: Exploring the effect of repeated exposure to anomalous syntactic structure – evidence from rating and reading tasks. Doctoral dissertation, University of Arizona, Tucson.

Goodall, G. (2004). On the syntax and processing of *wh*-questions in Spanish. In V. Chand, A. Kelleher, A. Rodríguez, & B. Schmeiser, eds., *Proceedings of the 23rd West Coast Conference on Formal Linguistics*. Somerville, MA: Cascadilla Press, pp. 237–250.

Goodall, G. (2011). Syntactic satiation and the inversion effect in English and Spanish *wh*-questions. *Syntax*, 14, 29–47.

Hiramatsu, K. (2000). Accessing linguistic competence: Evidence from children's and adults' acceptability judgments. Doctoral dissertation, University of Connecticut, Storrs.

Hofmeister, P., Jaeger, T. F., Arnon, I., Sag, I. A., & Snider, N. (2013). The source ambiguity problem: Distinguishing the effects of grammar and processing on acceptability judgments. *Language and Cognitive Processes*, 28(1–2), 48–87. DOI: 10.1080/01690965.2011.572401

Jakobovits, L. A. & Lambert, W. E. (1961). Semantic satiation among bilinguals. *Journal of Experimental Psychology*, 62(6), 576–582.

Kiss, K. É. (1987). Review of *Barriers* (Linguistic Inquiry Monograph 13) by Noam Chomsky. *Acta Linguistica Academiae Scientiarum Hungaricae*, 37(1), 213–221. www.jstor.org/stable/44362775

Kluender, R. & Kutas, M. (1993). Subjacency as a processing phenomenon. *Language and Cognitive Processes*, 8, 573–633.

Luka, B. J. & Barsalou, L. J. (2005). Structural facilitation: Mere exposure effects for grammatical acceptability as evidence for syntactic priming in comprehension. *Journal of Memory and Language*, 52, 436–459.

Maia, M. (2013). Linguística experimental: Aferindo o curso temporal e a profundidade do processamento. *Revista de Estudos da Linguagem*, 21, 9–42.

Nagata, H. (1990). Speaker's sensitivity to rule violations in sentences. *Psychologia*, 33, 179–184.

Rizzi, L. (1990). *Relativized Minimality*. Cambridge, MA: MIT Press.

Schütze, C. T. (1996). *The Empirical Base of Linguistics: Grammaticality Judgments and Linguistic Methodology*. Chicago: University of Chicago Press.

Snyder, W. (1994). A psycholinguistic investigation of weak crossover, islands, and syntactic satiation effects: Implications for distinguishing competence from performance. Poster presentation, CUNY Human Sentence Processing Conference, CUNY Graduate Center, New York. www.williamsnyder.org/papers/1994

Snyder, W. (2000). An experimental investigation of syntactic satiation effects. *Linguistic Inquiry*, 31, 575–582.

Snyder, W. (2018). On the nature of syntactic satiation. Manuscript, University of Connecticut, Storrs. www.williamsnyder.org/papers/2018

Sprouse, J. (2009). Revisiting satiation: Evidence for an equalization response strategy. *Linguistic Inquiry*, 40, 329–341.

Stepanov, A. (2007). The end of CED? Minimalism and extraction domains. *Syntax*, 10, 80–126.

Zervakis, J. & Mazuka, R. (2013). Effect of repeated evaluation and repeated exposure on acceptability ratings of sentences. *Journal of Psycholinguistic Research*, 42, 505–525. DOI: 10.1007/s10936-012-9233-3

# 7

# Acceptability (and Other) Experiments for Studying Comparative Syntax

Dustin A. Chacón

## 7.1 Introduction

Cross-language differences present a number of interesting challenges to linguistic theory. Theories of grammatical structure must be rigid enough to generate clear predictions about what a possible language may be, while maintaining enough flexibility to accommodate the attested variation in the world's languages. Similarly, because human languages are learnable, grammatical theories must interface with insights from language acquisition to explain how child learners correctly identify different features of their target languages given the statistics of their target language. Finally, theories of language comprehension and production must explain how presumably domain-general systems of memory and prediction are recruited to represent different kinds of grammatical structures. For these reasons, describing and explaining grammatical differences has been one of the primary goals of syntactic theory. However, despite the wide-ranging importance of comparative syntax, there has been less systematic application of experimental techniques in exploring grammatical differences.

Traditionally, research in syntax and semantics relies on consulting native speakers' intuitions about the well-formedness of sentences. As described by earlier chapters (see Chapters 1 and 2, in particular), quantitative and experimental methods may complement these traditional methods, and may be valuable for confirming intuitive judgments (Schütze 1996; Cowart 1997; Edelman & Christiansen 2003; Wasow & Arnold 2005; Gibson & Fedorenko 2010; Sprouse & Almeida 2012; Sprouse et al. 2013). Moreover, experimental methods have revealed judgment profiles that are subtler than those detected using traditional methods and that differ unexpectedly (Clifton et al. 2006; Alexopoulou & Keller 2007; Fedorenko & Gibson 2010; Hofmeister & Sag 2010; Beltrama & Xiang 2016; Ackerman et al. 2018). Additionally, experimental methods have been useful for examining how factors apart from grammatical well-formedness, such as limitations of the comprehension system, impact perception of acceptability (Chomsky & Miller 1963; Gibson & Thomas 1999; Vasishth et al. 2008; Wagers et al. 2009; Sprouse et al. 2012; Wellwood et al. 2018) (see Chapter 5).[1] Finally, because experimental methods typically rely on larger sample sizes, they may also be used for examining variation between participants in a systematic way (Cowart 2003; Han et al. 2007; Kush et al. 2018) (see Chapter 4).

The advantages of experimental methods are potentially greater in comparative syntax, which depends on a web of judgments across languages and native-speaker consultants for its evidential basis. In this chapter, I discuss ways in which experimental syntax has contributed to or called into question cross-language generalizations. I also highlight some successful strategies and challenges in conducting a research program in experimental syntax. In Section 7.2, I discuss cases in which experimental results appear to not reflect intuitive judgments reported in the comparative syntax literature. In this section, I argue that factorial designs and careful selection of control stimuli is crucial for establishing subtle judgments across languages. In Section 7.3, I discuss how applying experimental methods to well-established cross-language contrasts may be useful for informing representational theories. I also discuss some considerations of designing parallel experiments across languages. In Section 7.4, I discuss how quantifying individual variation between participants may further complement microcomparative syntax. Then, I conclude the chapter.

Much of this chapter focuses primarily on constraints on A′-movement (wh-movement; filler–gap dependencies). This reflects the fact that constraints on A′-movement are particularly well studied in both experimental syntax and comparative syntax. However, the general project of deploying experimental methods in studying cross-language phenomena is extendable to many other syntactic phenomena, such as binding, ellipsis, quantifier scope, and agreement phenomena (see Chapters 11 and 12). Theoretical concerns regarding the interpretation of these results are left aside here, but the reader is directed to Chapters 8, 9, and 10.

## 7.2  Mismatches Between Intuitive Judgments and Experimental Results between Languages

In this section, I review some critical cases where cross-language experimental results have yielded unexpected results. Comparative syntax

---

[1] Like experimental syntax, psycholinguistic research has largely focused on a small set of languages. Anand et al. (2010) found that the overwhelming majority of psycholinguistic experiments has focused on English or languages that are typologically similar to or genetically related to English. Thus, the nature and limits of cross-language variation in psycholinguistics is still not completely understood, with some results suggesting uniform processing strategies across languages and others suggesting differences (Cuetos & Mitchell 1988; Vasishth et al. 2010; Grillo & Costa 2014; Chacón et al. 2016; Lago et al. 2017; Keshev & Meltzer-Asscher 2018).

crucially depends on judgments collected from multiple languages, including languages that are understudied or poorly resourced. Furthermore, these judgments are collected in a variety of ways, e.g. some judgments are collected from native-speaking linguists, whereas some may come from elicitations in a fieldwork scenario. For these reasons, comparisons between intuitive judgments in different languages may be particularly susceptible to increased noise. Apparent conflicts between intuitive judgments and results from sentence acceptability judgments across languages demonstrate that this concern is well founded. Thus, applying experimental techniques to contrasts that are subtle and theoretically valuable may be useful to ensure reliability in comparative syntax. In this section, I also stress that factorial designs are useful for assessing subtle judgments in establishing cross-language generalizations.

### 7.2.1   Reliability of Judgments in Languages besides English

Many of the traditionally collected judgments in English are verifiable with formal experimental methods (Cowart 1997; Cowart 2003; Sprouse & Almeida 2012; Sprouse et al. 2013). In part, this may be due to a large community of English-speaking linguists capable of filtering out unreliable judgments during peer review or ignoring spurious judgments in theory-construction (Featherston 2009; Phillips 2009). However, these informal filters may be weaker in languages with smaller communities of linguists.

To test this, Linzen and Oseki (2018) conducted two sentence acceptability experiments in Japanese and Hebrew. For each language, they selected 14 acceptability contrasts that were reported in the theoretical syntax/semantics literature. They selected theoretically meaningful contrasts that they perceived to be subtle as native speakers, e.g. sentences demonstrating constraints on *wh*-movement or binding ("Class III judgments," Marantz 2005; "theoretically meaningful contrasts," Gibson et al. 2013). They found that approximately half of the judgments were not reliable when assessed this way. Moreover, three contrasts per language were rated in the opposite direction than reported, e.g. the unacceptable sentence was rated significantly higher than the acceptable sentence. For instance, (1b) and (2b) were reported to be less acceptable than their controls in (1a) and (2a), but Linzen and Oseki (2018) found that (1b) and (2b) were preferred.

(1)   Hebrew (Shlonsky 1992; Linzen & Oseki 2018: H2)
    a. Elu   ha-sfarim she-Dan tiyek otam bli     likro   otam.
       these the-books  that-Dan filed  them without to-read them.
       'These are the books that Dan filed without reading them.'
    b. *Elu   ha-sfarim she-Dan tiyek otam bli     likro.
       these the-books that-Dan filed  them without reading
       'These are the books that Dan filed without reading.'

(2)   Japanese (Sakai 1994; Linzen & Oseki 2018: J6)
    a.  Hanako-ga    Mary$_i$-no  kanazyo$_i$-ga  kii-tanokoto-nai  hihan-o    sita
        Hanako-NOM  Mary-GEN  she-NOM      hear-PRF-NEG      critic-ACC  did
        'Hanako made Mary's criticism that she has not heard.'
    b.  *Hanako-ga   Mary$_i$-no  kanazyo$_i$-no  kii-tanokoto-nai  hihan-o    sita
        Hanako-NOM  Mary-GEN  she-GEN      hear-PRF-NEG      critic-ACC  did
        'Hanako made Mary's criticism that she has not heard.'

Linzen and Oseki's (2018) study examined hand-picked "subtle" judgments. However, comparing their results to a similar study in English conducted by Sprouse et al. (2013), they suggested that there is a difference in reliability between reported English judgments and reported Hebrew and Japanese judgments. Although there are relatively large communities of Hebrew- and Japanese-speaking linguists, they may not be large enough to sufficiently filter out questionable judgments. Presumably, matters may be more concerning for less well-studied languages with smaller communities of native-speaking linguists, or for data that are collected primarily in fieldwork situations. For this reason, it is worthwhile to confirm reported judgments from other languages besides English that are crucial for theory construction, even in languages that appear to be well described. However, importantly, Linzen and Oseki's (2018) results also demonstrated that native-speaking linguists are capable of identifying contrasts that are subtle or questionable, and thus worth replicating experimentally, since the judgments that were not replicated were hand-picked for sounding questionable to the native-speaking authors.

### 7.2.2   Reliability of Cross-Language Comparisons

Experimental techniques allow the comparison of configurations between languages that may have divergent baselines. Acceptability judgments are defined relative to some standard. In sentence acceptability experiments, critical conditions are compared against some carefully selected control condition. Similarly, informal judgments are conducted by presenting native speakers with a carefully chosen minimal pair. In comparative syntax, researchers must assume that a reported contrast between a target sentence and its control is comparable to a similar contrast in another language. In other words, comparative syntacticians are interested in knowing whether a sentence assigned some acceptability judgment (acceptable, ?, ??, *, etc.) relative to some standard is (un)acceptable in the same way as a similar sentence compared to a similar standard in another language. In comparative syntax, there is a risk that the cross-language comparison is inappropriate (see Section 7.4.2). For instance, it is possible that processing factors, frequency, or differences in semantic/pragmatic plausibility may exaggerate or mitigate the perception of unacceptability in one language but not another, leading to the perception of a qualitative difference between the two languages. One solution to this challenge is to rely on factorial designs, where target sentences are compared against multiple control sentences with shared grammatical features in both languages (e.g. Cowart 1997).

This can be demonstrated with the phenomenon of "subliminal" islands (Almeida 2014). Sprouse et al. (2012) sought to examine the acceptability profile of syntactic island violations in English using a factorial design. They reasoned that acceptability ratings for sentences with longer dependencies were likely to be assigned lower ratings than shorter dependencies (Alexoupou & Keller 2007; Hofmeister & Sag 2010), and that the presence of complex syntactic island configurations may independently lower ratings (Kutas & Kluender 1993; Kluender 1998; Hofmeister & Sag 2010). Thus, lower acceptability was predicted for sentences like (3b) compared to (3a) due to the increased length of the A′-dependency, and lower acceptability was predicted for (3c) compared to (3a) due to the additional complexity of the *wh*-complement. They found that the ratings for (3d) were lower than the predicted value given the acceptability penalty observed for sentences like (3d) and (3c), e.g. there was a "superadditive" interaction effect. Thus, they proposed, there is a grammatical constraint specifically penalizing this combination of factors, i.e. long-distance extraction over the *wh*-island boundary (see Chapter 9 for discussion).

(3)     a. *Short, no island*
           **Who** ___ thinks that John bought a car?
        b. *Long, no island*
           **What** do you think that John bought ___ ?
        c. *Short, island*
           **Who** ___ wonders whether John bought a car?
        d. *Long, island*
           **What** do you wonder whether John bought ___ ?

Almeida (2014) used this approach to examine *whether*-islands in Brazilian Portuguese. Unlike English, Brazilian Portuguese is reported to not have the *whether*-island constraint (Mioto & Kato 2005), e.g. sentences like (4a) and (4b) are both reported to be acceptable in Brazilian Portuguese. However, Almeida (2014) found a similar superadditive interaction effect in Brazilian Portuguese to that found in English by Sprouse et al. (2012). Thus, Almeida proposed that both languages obeyed the *wh*-island constraint. To explain the mismatch between informal judgments and these experimental results, Almeida suggested that the syntactic island violation may be less severe in Brazilian Portuguese, rendering it harder to detect in intuitions (Featherston 2005b). In other words, in Brazilian Portuguese, *whether*-island violations only have a "murky" effect on intuitions, and thus may not be categorized as unacceptable. If this reasoning is correct, it suggests that some cross-language comparisons stated as a qualitative difference between grammars may in fact reflect quantitative differences in the "size" of a violation. Careful operationalization of an "effect" using a factorial design that controls for interfering factors may mitigate this concern.[2]

(4)  a. **O que** Pedro achou que a Maria comprou ___ ?
     what Pedro thought that Maria bought
     'What did Pedro think that Maria bought?'

  b. **O que** Pedro preguntou se a Maria comprou ___ ?
     what Pedro thought that Maria bought
     'What did Pedro think that Maria bought?'

Investigation into island phenomena for languages without overt *wh*-movement has similarly revealed informative mismatches between intuitive judgments and experimental results. Languages like Japanese or Mandarin Chinese do not exhibit overt A′-movement for *wh*-elements, shown in (5a). Reportedly, some island constraints apply, but only to adjunct *wh*-elements. For instance, in (5b), the in-situ argument *wh*-element *shéi* 'who' is reported to not incur a relative clause island violation, but the in-situ adjunct *wh*-element *wèishénme* 'why' in (5c) is reported to incur an adjunct island violation (Huang 1982; Lasnik & Saito 1984; see Bayer & Cheng 2017 for review).

(5)  Mandarin Chinese (Bayer & Cheng 2017)

  a. Bótōng xiǎng-zhīdào Húfēi mǎi-le shénme
     Botong want-know Hufei buy-PERF what
     'What does Botong want to know that Hufei bought?'

  b. Júdòu xǐhuān shéi xiě de shū
     Judou like who write de book
     'Who does Judou like the book that ___ wrote?'

  c. Qiáofēng xǐhuān Bótōng wèishénme xiě de shū?
     Qiaofeng like Botong why write de book
     'Why does Qiaofeng like the book that Botong wrote ___ ?'

Tanaka and Schwartz (2018) examined the status of the relative clause island in Japanese. Using a factorial design, they tested the acceptability of sentences with an argument *wh*-element *nani* 'what' embedded in a relative clause, (6d), by comparing it to sentences without a relative clause structure (6a, 6b) and without the *wh*-element (6a–c). They found an interaction, indicating lower ratings for a *wh*-element embedded in a relative clause.[3]

---

[2] Similar findings are reported by Sprouse et al. (2016) for Italian, Kush et al. (2018) for Norwegian, Stepanov et al. (2018) for Slovenian, and Keshev and Meltzer-Asscher (2019) for Hebrew. Like Brazilian Portuguese, these languages are reported to not have *whether*-island violations (Rizzi (1982) for Italian, Maling and Zaenen (1982) for Norwegian, Golden (1995) for Slovenian, Reinhart (1981) for Hebrew). However, these authors suggest alternative interpretations for these results. For instance, Keshev and Meltzer-Asscher (2019) suggested that the subliminal island arose due to processing factors. They suggested that the subliminal effect resulted from an increased cost of processing the A′-dependency while simultaneously processing the embedded *wh*-element (cf. Kluender & Kutas 1993).

[3] Despite this finding, Tanaka and Schwartz (2018) were hesitant to conclude that Japanese speakers obey the relative clause island constraint for argument *wh*-elements, because the ratings for these sentences had a higher magnitude than ungrammatical filler control sentences. However, this pattern is observed in other subliminal island cases, such as the Brazilian Portuguese study by Almeida (2014).

(6)     Japanese (Tanaka & Schwartz 2018)
    a. –RC, –Wh

        Momoko-wa [$_{CP}$ otoko no hito-ga kaban-o katta-to] iimashita-ka?
        Momoko-TOP    man-NOM       bag-ACC bought-C said-Q
        'Did Momoko say that the man bought a bag?'

    b. –RC, +Wh

        Momoko-wa [$_{CP}$ otoko no hito-ga nani-o    katta-to] iimashita-ka?
        Momoko-TOP    man-NOM       what-ACC bought-C said-Q
        'What did Momoko say that the man bought __ ?'

    c. +RC, –Wh

        Momoko-wa [$_{NP}$ [$_{RC}$ kaban-o katta] otoko no hito-o] mimashita-ka?
        Momoko-TOP      bag-ACC bought man-ACC       saw-Q
        'Did Momoko see the man that bought a bag?'

    d. +RC, +Wh

        Momoko-wa [$_{NP}$ [$_{RC}$ nani-o    katta] otoko no hito-o] mimashita-ka?
        Momoko-TOP      what-ACC bought man-ACC       saw-Q
        'What did Momoko see the man that bought __ ?'

Using a similar design, Lu et al. (2020) examined the reported difference between argument and adjunct *wh*-elements in Mandarin Chinese. They found a superadditive interaction effect for both arguments and adjunct *wh*-elements embedded in a relative clause, like Tanaka and Schwartz (2018). Importantly, however, even though sentences like (7a) and (7b) were assigned superadditively lower acceptability ratings, (7a) was rated significantly higher than (7b). This demonstrates that the reported asymmetry between in-situ argument *wh*-elements and adjunct *wh*-elements is reliable. Thus, Lu et al. (2020) reasoned that adjunct and argument *wh*-elements are sensitive to the *wh*-island constraint. However, the violation is subliminal for argument *wh*-elements.

(7)     Mandarin Chinese (Lu et al. 2020)
    a. Yuehan xiangzhidao Bier yudao-le chi shenme de nyuhai
       John    wonder      Bill meet-ASP eat what     de girl
       'John wondered what Bill met the girl that ate.'

    b. Yuehan xiangzhidao Bier jian-le     weishenme chi shousi de nyuhai
       John    wonder      Bill meet-ASP why       eat sushi  de girl
       'John wondered why Bill met the girl that ate sushi.'

The intuition that island constraints differentially apply to *wh*-in-situ phenomena and overt A′-dependencies is lent some support by Sprouse et al.'s (2011) study on *wh*-in-situ configurations in English and in Japanese. In their study, *wh*-elements were embedded in *whether*-islands, complex NP islands, subject islands, and adjunct islands in the two languages. In Japanese, there was no superadditive effect for in-situ *wh*-elements embedded in any of the four island configurations.[4] This finding is important because it confirmed the claim that island constraints apply differently to overt A′-dependencies and *wh*-in-situ phenomena. Taken together with the previous results, this finding further underscores that *wh*-in-situ configurations are island sensitive. However, judgment profiles are different between overt A′-dependencies, in-situ argument *wh*-elements, and in-situ adjunct *wh*-elements, which calls for careful theory construction.[5]

A similar unexpected cross-language similarity was discovered by Featherston (2005a) in a study examining the *that*-trace effect in German. The *that*-trace effect (see Chapter 10) is the reduced acceptability of an A′-dependency resolving with a gap immediately after a complementizer (Perlmutter 1971; Chomsky 1981; Rizzi 1982; see Pesetsky 2017 for review). The *that*-trace effect is theoretically significant, since it is a crucial subject–object asymmetry and appears to correlate with many other subject-related phenomena, such as *pro*-drop and rich subject–verb agreement. However, the *that*-trace effect is not reported in all languages (Rizzi 1982; Gilligan 1987; Pesetsky 2017). In English, using a factorial design, Cowart (1997, 2003) found that the acceptability for subject extraction over the complementizer *that*, as in (8d), was lower than would be expected from the presence of the complementizer and subject extraction alone, as measured by comparing (8d) to (8a–c) (see Chapter 10).

(8)    a. *Object extraction, no complementizer*
          **Who** does she think Johnson likes __ ?
       b. *Object extraction, complementizer*
          **Who** does she think that Johnson likes __?
       c. *Subject extraction, no complementizer*
          **Who** does she think __ likes Johnson?
       d. *Subject extraction, complementizer*
          \***Who** does she think that __ likes Johnson?

By contrast, German is reported to have no such effect (Haider 1983, 1993; Bayer 1990). To test this, Featherston (2005a) used a paradigm similar to the one used by Cowart (1997), exemplified in (9). Like Cowart, Featherston found that subject extraction over the complementizer *dass* 'that' (9d) was rated lower than expected. This superadditive effect suggests that German is sensitive to the *that*-trace effect, like English.

---

[4] Sprouse et al. (2011) found a superadditive effect for adjunct islands in Japanese. However, the directionality was unpredicted: sentences containing an adjunct *wh*-element embedded in an adjunct clause were rated higher than the controls.

[5] Like subliminal islands for overt *wh*-movement, the significance of these effects is subject to different interpretations. For instance, processing an in-situ *wh*-element may require retrieval of some structure to license it, such as a Spec,CP position (e.g. Sprouse et al. 2011; Xiang et al. 2014; Xiang et al. 2015). This retrieval may trigger processing difficulty depending on the structure of the sentence. For instance, Xiang et al. (2015) showed that the presence of multiple Spec,CP positions causes processing difficulty and lower acceptability ratings for *wh*-in-situ configurations in Mandarin Chinese outside island contexts, which they attribute to retrieval interference at the site of the *wh*-in-situ element.

(9) German (Featherston 2005a)

    a. **Wen** glaubst du [$_{CP}$ hat der Lehrer ausgeschimpft]?
       whom think you      has the teacher told off
       'Who do you think that the teacher told off?'

    b. **Wer** glaubst du [$_{CP}$ hat den Schüler ausgeschimpft]?
       whom think you      has the student told off
       'Who do you think told off the student?'

    c. **Wen** glaubst du [$_{CP}$ dass der Lehrer ausgeschimpft hat]?
       whom think you      that the teacher told off      has
       'Who do you think that the teacher has told off?'

    d. **Wer** glaubst du [$_{CP}$ dass den Schüler ausgeschimpft hat]?
       whom think you      that the teacher told off      has
       'Who do you think that told off the student?'

This finding is notable for two reasons. First, it demonstrates a subliminal effect for a grammatical phenomenon outside the typical island configurations discussed above. This shows that factorial definitions for subtle phenomena are portable. Secondly, the comparison between Cowart's (1997) and Featherston's (2005a) results demonstrates that it is possible to explore similar contrasts between languages using similar experimental designs (see Section 7.3). This makes it possible to control for language-specific properties. For instance, in the *that*-trace comparisons, the subject extraction/object extraction factor is instantiated in the items differently. In English, the grammatical function of the fronted *wh*-phrase is indicated by the position of the missing argument in the embedded clause. In German, the grammatical function of the fronted *wh*-element is reflected in its case, i.e. *wer* 'who-Nom' indicates subject extraction and *wen* 'who-Acc' indicates object extraction. Thus, the explanation for the *that*-trace phenomenon cannot reduce to any particular property that is not shared between English and German. Such insights are relevant for constraining theory building.

    In this section, I have surveyed a number of cases where experimental methods appear to contradict intuitive judgments. Following Linzen and Oseki (2018), I suggested that intuitive judgments in languages besides English are more likely to be unreliable. This is particularly concerning to comparative syntacticians, who depend on judgments collected from multiple languages. Moreover, I argued that carefully selecting control sentences and explicitly defining a grammatical "effect," e.g. factorial definition of islands, is a powerful tool for comparing grammatical phenomena between languages that may counteract the shortcomings of traditional methods. Given this survey of results, syntactic island phenomena and the *that*-trace effect seem more uniform across languages than previously described. If so, this has great consequences for syntactic theory, which has sought principled explanations for these reported differences. However, the presence of subliminal effects calls into question why certain grammatical violations should "register" more sharply than others, and what drives mismatches between intuitive judgments and formal acceptability studies.

## 7.3  Cross-Language Differences in Comparable Phenomena

In this section, I turn to cases where the cross-language comparisons appear to be robust and relatively well-understood.[6] In these cases, I also highlight some of the challenges and strategies for selecting comparable items in designing a cross-language acceptability judgment study, particularly relying on Alexopoulou and Keller's (2007) study of multiple embedding on long-distance A′-movement, and two studies from Chacón (2015).

One challenge in conducting research in comparative syntax is determining which configurations are comparable, given that orthogonal features between languages may conspire to conceal language similarities or produce superficial similarities. Many debates in comparative syntax concern whether the same syntactic analysis is appropriate for string-similar sentences with similar meanings, e.g. sluicing/ "sluicing-like" constructions (Merchant & Simpson 2012; Simpson et al. 2013), the internal structure of nominal expressions (Abney 1987; Cheng & Sybesma 1999; Bošković 2008), or verb-stranding ellipsis phenomena (Otani & Whitman 1991; Goldberg 2005; Landau 2018). Determining which comparisons are useful between languages is a process that is partly driven by top-down theory construction. Resolving such questions relies on comparisons of many grammatical properties both within and across languages, e.g. determining whether similar constructions pass the same set of syntactic/ semantic "diagnostics."

By contrast, in experimental syntax, researchers are typically interested in carefully isolating the effect of specific factors by comparing a small number of conditions. Additionally, it is relatively uncommon to conduct parallel studies in multiple languages. This makes it harder to use experimental results between languages to arbitrate between representational theories.

However, one notable case study of cross-language experimentation that makes representational claims is Alexopoulou and Keller (2007). These authors sought to examine the acceptability profile of resumption and its interaction with syntactic islands in English, German, and Greek. In each language, they examined the acceptability of an A′-dependency resolving with a gap or a resumptive pronoun in a non-island embedded clause, a *whether*-clause, and a relative clause. They also manipulated the

---

[6] For reasons of space, I focus on Alexopoulou and Keller's (2007) methodology. However, research on resumption generally has demonstrated the utility of combining acceptability judgments and reading time studies to explore the relationship between acceptability, grammaticality, and processing, both within and across languages (Farby et al. 2010; Francis et al. 2015; Hammerly 2018; Chacón 2019; Chen 2019; Tucker et al. 2019).

number of embeddings (0–2). A subset of their English items is shown in (10)–(12).

(10)   Non-island (*that*-clauses):
       a. Who will we fire __ / him?
       b. Who does Mary claim [we will fire __ / him]?
       c. Who does Jane think [that Mary claims [that we will fire __ / him]]?

(11)   *Whether*-islands:
       a. Who does Mary wonder [whether we will fire __ / him]?
       b. Who does Jane think [that Mary wonders [whether we will fire __ / him]]?

(12)   Relative clause islands:
       a. Who does Mary meet the people [that will fire __ / him]?
       b. Who does Jane think [that Mary meets the people [that will fire __ / him]]?

The English, Greek, and German items were closely matched, using similar lexical choices and similar constructions. This can be seen by comparing the English *whether*-island with two clausal embeddings in (11b) with its equivalent in Greek, (13a), and German, (13b). There are some superficial differences between these items, e.g. subjects followed the main verb in German and Greek, but not in English. However, the critical manipulations were identical in all three languages.

(13)   Greek and German (Alexopoulou & Keller 2007)
       a. Pion      nomizi o Petros oti  anarotiete i Maria an θa  __ / ton  apolisume?
          who-ACC thinks Peter  that wonder   Maria  if will __ / him fire?
       b. Wen       denkt Barbara, dass Petra überlegt, ob wir __ / ihn entlassen?
          who-ACC thinks Barbara that Petra wonders  if we __ / him fire
          'Who does Barbara/Peter think that Maria/Petra wonders if we will fire __ / him?'

Their results demonstrated a number of robust similarities. For instance, increased levels of embedding separating the head of the A′-dependency and its gap lowered ratings in all three languages. Additionally, "weak" *whether*-island violations were systematically rated higher than the "strong" relative clause island violations. Resumptive pronouns were never rated higher than gaps in any condition, and both gaps and resumptive pronouns were assigned the lowest ratings inside relative clauses. Because these findings were reliable across all three languages, this suggests that the cause of these effects may be language-independent. For instance, the increased judgment penalty associated with further embedding is presumably due to the increased cost of processing the A′-dependency (Frazier & Clifton 1989).

Alexopoulou and Keller (2007) also argued that some cross-languages differences that they discovered were indicative of different representational profiles. For instance, although resumption was not rated higher than gaps in any condition or language, the difference between resumption and gaps was different between the two languages. That is, the preference for gaps over resumption was significantly stronger in English compared to Greek in syntactic island contexts, and the ratings for resumption in Greek were stable across embedding levels. They interpreted the universal pattern to indicate that resumption was "intrusive" in all three languages (Chao & Sells 1983). To explain the difference in the contrast between gaps and resumption, they argued that resumptive dependencies were assigned a different analysis in Greek. Unlike English, Greek makes productive use of clitic left-dislocation dependencies (CLLD, (14)), in which a fronted NP is associated with a pronoun. In Greek, CLLD dependencies are not island-sensitive. Thus, it is possible to assign a CLLD analysis to sentences like (13a) that does not violate an island constraint, explaining the absence of embedding on resumption in Greek. However, Greek does not allow *wh*-elements to head a CLLD dependency. Thus, they reasoned that the unacceptability of sentences like (13a) reflects the unacceptability of a *wh*-element heading a CLLD dependency, instead of *wh*-dependency violating an island constraint. This analysis contrasts with previous analyses, which posited grammatical resumption in Greek (Tsimpli 1999).

(14)   To Jani   to          sinadisame   stin      aγora.
       John      him-ACC     met.1PL      at the    market
       ~'John, we met him at the market.'

This study demonstrates how parallel experiments conducted in multiple languages can benefit comparative syntax. First, parallel experiments conducted across languages can reveal universal properties, such as the judgment profiles for long-distance A′-dependencies and for intrusive resumption. Second, parallel experiments can inform representational theories. For instance, discovering quantitative differences like the resumption–gap contrast in Greek and English may motivate reconsideration of the representational analyses of these configurations.

Next, I turn to a case study examining the *that*-trace effect in English and Spanish. As discussed above, the *that*-trace effect has been explored in English and German (Cowart 1997, 2003; Featherston 2005a). However, the *that*-trace effect is not reported in a number of languages, such as Spanish and Italian (Rizzi 1982; Torrego 1984; Gilligan 1987). Theoretical analyses of why the *that*-trace effect is observed in some languages but not others vary (Pesetsky 2017), but many theories link the existence of the *that*-trace effect to some other grammatical property, such as the agreement system. However, as described in Section 7.2, the *that*-trace effect may be observable in languages where it is not reported (Featherston

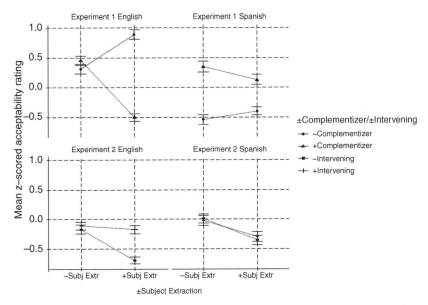

**Figure 7.1** Mean normalized ratings by condition and language for Experiments 1 and 2 (Chacón 2015). Error bars represent one standard error from the mean.

2005a). This raises the possibility that *that*-trace effects are under-reported cross-linguistically, and thus theories of the phenomenon may be misguided. Taken to the extreme, these results also raise the possibility that the *that*-trace effect is universal, and thus attempts to derive the cross-language differences may be unmotivated.

To test this, we conducted two parallel sentence acceptability experiments in English and Spanish, reported in Chacón (2015) and Chacón et al. (2019). The first study replicated Cowart's (1997, 2003) design in English and Spanish, with the factors ±Complementizer and ±Subject Extraction. The Spanish materials are exemplified in (15), and the glosses correspond to the English materials. Mean acceptability ratings for both studies are plotted in Figure 7.1.

(15)  a.  *–Subject Extraction, –Complementizer*

     (*)¿Con quién sugirió    Álvaro horneará    Lucía un pastel para la fiesta?

     with who   suggested Álvaro will bake    Lucy   a   cake   for   the party

     'Who did Allen suggest Lucy will bake a cake with __ for the party?'

  b.  *–Subject Extraction, +Complementizer*

     ¿Con quién sugirió    Álvaro que horneará    Lucía un pastel para la fiesta?

     with who   suggested Álvaro that will bake    Lucy   a   cake   for   the party

     'Who did Allen suggest that Lucy will bake a cake with __ for the party?'

  c.  *+Subject Extraction, –Complementizer*

     (*)¿Quién    sugirió     Álvaro horneará   con Lucía   un pastel    para   la fiesta?

     who     suggested   Álvaro will bake   with Lucy   a cake      for   the party

     'Who did Allen suggest __ will bake a cake with Lucy for the party?'

d. *+Subject Extraction, +Complementizer*

> ¿Quién    sugirió    Álvaro que  horneará con Lucía un pastel para la fiesta?
> who       suggested Álvaro that will bake with Lucy a   cake  for  the party
> **'*Who did Allen suggest __ will bake a cake with Lucy for the party?'

To briefly summarize the results, there was an interaction effect for English-speaking participants in the study, indicating lower judgments for (15d), indicating the *that*-trace effect. In Spanish, we unexpectedly also found an interaction effect, reflecting lower ratings for (15d). Instead of concluding that this indicates that Spanish has the *that*-trace effect, we interpreted this as an artifact of the experimental design. Unlike English, the complementizer *que* 'that' is obligatory for clausal embedding in Spanish, i.e. (15a) and (15c) are ungrammatical in Spanish. This was reflected in our acceptability ratings, since the –Complementizer sentences were rated at floor. We suggested that Spanish-speakers have some penalty associated with subject-extraction, but there is no specific penalty associated with subject extraction over *que* 'that.' Put differently, we reasoned that Cowart's (1997) design was inappropriate for testing the presence of the *that*-trace effect in Spanish, because it failed to test the effect of the factor ±Subject Extraction within each level of ±Complementizer, since ratings for the ungrammatical –Complementizer sentences were at floor.

We further clarified this point in Experiment 2. The *that*-trace effect is reported to be ameliorated if an adverb intervenes between the complementizer and the subject gap (Bresnan 1977; Culicover 1993), and has been verified experimentally in English (Sobin 2002). Thus, in Experiment 2, we manipulated ±Subject Extraction. In place of ±Complementizer, we manipulated whether an adverbial phrase (*every year*) intervened between the complementizer and the rest of the embedded clause (±Intervening). This design was more suitable for testing for the *that*-trace effect in both languages, because each manipulated factor was expected to be acceptable in both languages, and the only expected difference was the interaction between the two factors. Specifically, we expected to see an interaction effect indicating lowered ratings for +Subject Extraction, –Intervening in English, reflecting the lowered acceptability of *that* immediately adjacent to the subject gap. In Spanish, we expected no such interaction. Having improved on the design so that the control conditions were more stable, we found a much cleaner profile of the *that*-trace effect in English, replicating Sobin (2002). We also failed to find evidence for the *that*-trace effect in Spanish, as expected.

(16)   a. *–Subject Extraction, –Intervening*

> ¿Con quién remarca  Juana  cada año  que  va   Carmen de pesca?
> with who   remarked Joanna every year that goes Carmen fishing
> 'Who did Joanna remark every year that Carmen goes fishing with __?'

   b. *–Subject Extraction, +Intervening*

> ¿Con quién remarca  Juana  que  cada año  va   Carmen de pesca?
> with who   remarked Joanna that every year goes Carmen fishing
> 'Who did Joanna remark that every year Carmen goes fishing with __?'

c. *+Subject Extraction, –Intervening*

> ¿Quién  remarca  Juana  cada año  que va  con Carmen  de pesca?
>
> who  remarked Joanna every year that goes with Carmen fishing
>
> *'Who did Joanna remark every year that __ goes fishing with Carmen?'

d. *+Subject Extraction, +Intervening*

> ¿Quién  remarca  Juana  que cada año  va  con Carmen  de pesca?
>
> who  remarked Joanna that every year goes with Carmen fishing
>
> 'Who did Joanna remark that every year __ goes fishing with Carmen?'

Like the results reported in Alexopoulou and Keller (2007), these results largely confirmed previously reported judgments. More didactically, these studies demonstrate the importance of selecting appropriate designs. In the successful *that*-trace studies reported here and in Section 7.2, the critical condition was compared against 3 grammatical control conditions in a 2 × 2 design across languages. In Experiment 1 from Chacón (2015), the control conditions were not parallel in Spanish and English, i.e. 3 control conditions were grammatical in English, but 2 control conditions were ungrammatical in Spanish. Thus, Experiment 1 was not a well-controlled experiment. Fixing this issue in Experiment 2 more clearly revealed the difference in the effect that we sought. Thus, in cross-language experiments, it is critical to select a design where the target items are compared against controls that are thought to be approximately equally acceptable.

## 7.4 Exploring Individual Differences

Classically, comparative syntax has focused on identifying the range of possible grammatical variation across languages, e.g. identifying the differences between English and French (e.g. Chomsky 1981; Rizzi 1982; Huang 1982; Borer 1984; Rudin 1988). The goal of this endeavor was to seek compact characterizations of grammatical differences that could explain large clusters of grammatical properties. However, attention has shifted to explaining smaller differences between more closely related languages, dialects, and individual grammars, i.e. "microvariation" (Barbiers et al. 2001, Kayne 2005, *inter alia*). This has been due in large part to theoretical challenges (Uriagereka 2007; Boeckx 2014) and perceived failures in relating comparative syntax to typological findings (Newmeyer 2004, 2005; Haspelmath 2008) (but see Baker 2001, 2008, and Roberts & Holmberg 2005 for discussion). This newer strategy is valuable because comparison between closely related linguistic varieties minimizes the number of features that are uncontrolled in drawing comparisons. Moreover, this approach to comparative syntax also interfaces with sociolinguistic research on dialect variation, as demonstrated by projects like the Yale Grammatical Diversity Project (Zanuttini et al. 2018) (see also the discussion in Chapter 17).

Experimental methods can be valuable for the microvariation project (see Wood 2019). One possible contribution of experimental methods is exploratory analysis of individual differences and demographic effects in large-sample studies. Usually, hypotheses in experimental syntax are stated as binary contrasts between factors, e.g. one condition will have significantly higher or lower mean rating across participants than others. However, dividing participants into (theoretically motivated) subgroups can help test claims about dialect differences. Similarly, comparing variance in judgment patterns in one condition against another may help test hypotheses about systematic idiolectal differences. In this section, I demonstrate how experimental methods have been used to demonstrate uniformity across dialects of American English for the *that*-trace effect (Cowart 1997; Cowart 2003; Chacón 2015), and have been useful for demonstrating systematic individual differences in *whether*-islands in Norwegian (Kush et al. 2018) and scope and binding in Korean (Han et al. 2007; Han et al. 2016; Kim & Han 2016).

First, I discuss the case of the *that*-trace effect in American English. As discussed in Section 7.2, the status of the *that*-trace effect has been a cornerstone of syntactic theory. However, the evidential basis for the effect in English has been a matter of discussion (see Chapter 10). In a series of studies, Sobin argued that the effect is weak or absent for many English speakers (Sobin 1987, 2002, 2009). Most influentially, Sobin (1987) argued that the *that*-trace effect is absent in Midwestern American English.

To test the claim about dialectal variation, Cowart (1997, 2003) conducted a large-scale sentence acceptability experiment using the design in (8). Participants came from five different locations, including Midwestern locations. Across all participants, there was a superadditive effect yielding lower ratings for the *that*-trace configuration in (8d). Importantly, each individual population showed the same qualitative pattern of data, including Midwestern locations. In a follow-up study, Cowart (2003) used a test–retest paradigm, in which participants rated the same materials on two different trials one week apart. The majority (533 of 801 participants) systematically rejected the *that*-trace configuration in both phases, suggesting that most individual participants were self-consistent. In a replication of this finding using the Mechanical Turk platform to sample participants from many parts of the United States, I failed to find any consistent demographic variation between participants in an exploratory analysis (Chacón 2015). Additionally, following a suggestion from Cowart (2003), I compared the observed variance on the critical trials against the variance on control trials, and found no significant difference between these values. Thus, I proposed that the variability observed in these studies was likely reducible to experimental noise, and not idiosyncratic differences between grammars.

The strategy of examining variability in responses from individual participants has proven successful for discovering systematic individual differences. As discussed in footnote 2, Norwegian is reported to not exhibit many syntactic island effects, including *whether-*, relative clause, and complex NP islands (Maling & Zaenen 1982). In three large-scale experiments using Sprouse et al.'s (2012) design, Kush et al. (2018) found a superadditive interaction for *whether-*, complex NP, subject, relative clause, and adjunct islands. That is, for the sentences given in (17), they found that ratings for (17d) were significantly lower than expected across participants, given the ratings for (17a–c).

(17)    Norwegian, *whether*-island test materials (Kush et al. 2018)

     a.   *Short, no island*

       **Hvem** __ tror    [$_{CP}$ at    Hanne bakte kaken?]

       who       thinks     that Hanne baked   the cake?

       'Who __ thinks that Hanne baked the cake?'

     b.   *Long, no island*

       **Hva**    tror    gjesten    [$_{CP}$ at    Hanne bakte   __ ?]

       What   thinks   the guest      that Hanne baked

       'What does the guest think that Hanne baked __?'

     c.   *Short, island*

       **Hvem** __ lurer    på [$_{CP}$ om     Hanne bakte kaken?]

       who       wonders on    whether Hanne baked the cake?

       'Who __ wonders whether Hanne baked the cake?'

     d.   *Long, island*

       **Hva** lurer    gjesten   på [$_{CP}$ om     Hanne bakte __?]

       what wonders the guest on    whether Hanne baked

       'What does the guest wonder whether Hanne baked __ ?'

Importantly, Kush et al. (2018) then examined each participant's responses in each condition. They discovered that most Norwegian speakers rejected extraction from complex NP, subject, relative clause, and adjunct islands across trials. However, they discovered that ratings on extraction from *whether* clauses, such as (17d), did not show the same profile. In their three experiments, more than one-third of participants consistently accepted extraction over *whether*-clauses, but a significant proportion consistently rejected them. Thus, the mean acceptability ratings found for (17a–d) were misleading, since there is reliable by-participant variation with regard to the *whether*-island constraint. This suggests that there may be two distinct populations of Norwegian speakers, those who accept extraction over *whether*-clauses and those who do not, occluded by the mean acceptability ratings. Conversely, Norwegian speakers appeared to systematically reject other island violations.

Outside the domain of syntactic island phenomena, Han et al. (2007) examined the range of semantic interpretations available to Korean speakers for sentences containing an object quantifier and a "short" negation marker *an*, as in (18). In the Korean syntax literature, some authors report that an object quantifier scopes over negation (Suh 1989; Hagstrom 2000), whereas others report that the negation marker obligatorily scopes over the object (Baek 1998; Kim 2000). This data point is theoretically crucial, since it is argued to help adjudicate between analyses in which the V+Negation complex remains in VP, as in (18b), or raises to a higher projection T, as in (18c).

(18)   Korean (Han et al. 2007)
     a.   Khwukhi Monste-ka   motun  khwukhi-lul  an    mek-ess-ta
         Cookie Monster-NOM  every  cookie-ACC   NEG  eat-PST-DECL
         'Cookie Monster didn't eat every cookie'
     b.   Khwukhi Monste-ka [$_{TP}$ [$_{VP}$ motun khwukhi-lul an mek-ess-ta]]
         $\neg > \forall$
     c.   Khwukhi Monste-ka [$_{TP}$ [$_{VP}$ motun khwukhi-lul __] an mek-ess-ta]
         $\forall > \neg$

In a truth-value judgment study (Crain & Thornton 1998), Han et al. (2007) tested whether Korean-speaking adults and Korean-learning children would judge sentences like (18a) to be true in the critical context in which Cookie Monster ate some but not all of the cookies. This situation is compatible with the representation in (18b), but not the representation in (18c). For controls, they compared these items to sentences with the "long negation" marker *ani*, which obligatorily scopes over the entire proposition, and sentences with subject quantifiers, which obligatorily scope over *an*.

In the mean acceptance rates, Han et al. (2007) found that the sentence in (18) was judged to be true in 36 percent of the critical trials. Crucially, they found that the results were bimodally distributed, such that some participants consistently accepted (18) in the critical context, but the rest consistently rejected it. Furthermore, participants responded similarly in all other conditions. This comparison is crucial, because it underscores that the variability in interpretation of (18) was not likely attributable to normal experimental noise. From this, Han et al. (2007) concluded that Korean speakers form two distinct populations, one with a grammar that leaves the V+Neg complex in the VP as in (18b), and another that raises the V+Neg complex to T as in (18c) (see also Han et al. 2016).

A similar study by Kim and Han (2016) investigated bound-variable interpretation for the pronominal elements *ku* 'he' and *kunye* 'she.' As with the scope of short negation, Korean syntacticians disagree as to whether these pronouns may be bound by a quantifier. For instance, Suh (1990) and Koak (2008) report (19a) to be acceptable, but Hong (1985) and Kang (2000) report it as unacceptable.

(19)   Korean (Kim & Han 2016)
     a.   Motwu$_i$-ka       ku$_i$-uy   emeni-lul      salangha-n-ta
         everyone-NOM   he-GEN   mother-ACC   love-PRS-DECL
         'Everyone$_i$ loves his$_i$ mother.'

b. Motwu$_i$-ka     ku$_i$-ka     chwukkwu-lul cal ha-n-tako     sayngkakha-n-ta

   everyone$_i$-NOM he$_i$-Nom soccer-ACC     well do-PRS-COMP think-PRS-DECL

   'Everyone thinks that he is good at soccer.'

To test this, Kim and Han (2016) conducted two experiments in which participants were asked to rate whether a sentence correctly describes a situation. In the critical condition, participants were exposed to a context in which several people said something about themselves, (20a). They were then asked to decide whether a sentence like (20b) was true. If the comprehenders understood the pronoun *ku* 'he' to be bound by *motwu* 'everyone,' then they were predicted to judge (20b) true. By contrast, if the comprehenders could not understand *ku* 'he' as bound by *motwu* 'everyone,' then they were predicted to judge it false. Like Han et al. (2007), they compared sentences like (20b) with controls that were not predicted to yield significant variability. For instance, they compared (20b) with similar sentences in which the embedded subject was a null prominal (*pro*), which is unanimously reported to be bindable by a quantifier.

(20)     Sample context and item from Experiment 1 (Kim & Han 2016)
   a. Hanswu, Cinswu, and Minswu were playing basketball at a basketball court. Hanswu said that 'self' plays basketball well. Cinswu also said that 'self' plays basketball well. Minswu also said that 'self' plays basketball well.
   b. Motwu-ka     nongkwucang-eyse ku-ka     nongkwu-lul     cal     ha-n-tako

      everyone-NOM basketball court-at he-NOM basketball-ACC well do-PRS-COMP

      malha-yess-ta

      say-PST-DECL

      'Everyone said at the basketball court that he is good at basketball.'

They found that sentences like (20b) were accepted 54 percent of the time in this context, whereas the control sentences were accepted near ceiling. Similar to Han et al. (2007, 2016) and Kush et al. (2018), they then investigated individual participants' responses across trials, and found that participants either consistently accepted or rejected the critical condition in the critical context. As before, they interpreted this to suggest that there are two distinct populations of Korean speakers, those who allow *ku* 'he' to be bound by quantificational expressions, and those who do not.

Across these studies, the common key assumption is that individual participants' responses should be relatively consistent across all conditions, but that responses may vary between conditions by participant. Importantly, to ensure that the variance observed in the critical condition is not due to noise, the responses for the critical condition are compared to at least one other control condition. If the variance is not different (e.g. Cowart (2003), Chacón (2015) on the *that*-trace effect in English), then there is no evidence for variation. But, if there appears to be systematic variation on one condition, then it is more reasonable to infer that there are multiple grammars in the sample.

For microcomparative syntacticians, probing individual grammatical differences may be a useful exploratory technique for discovering relations between grammatical phenomena.[7] For instance, theories that tie grammatical phenomena $P$ and $Q$ together predict that responses to $P$ and $Q$ in a sentence acceptability experiment should be dependent, whereas theories that postulate that $P$ and $Q$ are independent do not. Similarly, claims about dialect differences can be more rigorously tested experimentally with larger sample sizes across populations, as demonstrated by Cowart (1997, 2003). In my view, this approach to experimental investigation of individual differences will most likely need to be further refined, specifically with regard to estimating and statistically evaluating variability in responses. However, this approach has the potential to be very powerful for delineating the space of possible languages and contributing to the program of comparative syntax in a novel way. Moreover, these findings demonstrate the utility of obtaining large sample sizes of native speakers when collecting judgment data, since discovering unexpected variability (as in Kush et al. 2018) may be informative for theory building.

## 7.5  Conclusion

One goal of syntactic theory is to explain universal patterns across languages while maintaining sufficient descriptive power to describe properties of specific languages. As syntactic theory increasingly incorporates experimental and other quantitative methods, comparative syntacticians will also need to incorporate and embrace more methodological techniques. Similarly, subfields of linguistics that traditionally rely on formal experimentation, such as psycholinguistics and language acquisition, are increasingly engaging with a greater breadth of languages. These subdisciplines are increasingly drawing on the wealth of knowledge and theory that has developed in comparative syntax. In this chapter, I discussed some of the prospects and challenges of incorporating these approaches, by focusing on some noteworthy studies that compared languages. Overall, I argued that experimental techniques are necessary for validating, elaborating, and exploring generalizations across languages, and that many of the advantages of deploying experimental techniques are magnified when comparing multiple languages simultaneously, as is typically done in experimental syntax.

---

[7] Han et al. (2007, 2016), Han and Kim (2016), and Chacón (2015) explicitly tie their findings on variability to considerations from language acquisition. For instance, Han et al. (2007, 2016) claim that children's linguistic input underdetermines the relative scope of an object NP relative to the V+Neg complex, and thus children arbitrarily choose one of two options. Conversely, I argued that the lack of variability regarding the *that*-trace effect in English speakers reflects that children's linguistic input must be relatively homogeneous in the relevant respects.

In Section 7.2, I discussed the possibility that reported judgments in the syntax literature may not be uniformly reliable across languages. Whereas many reported acceptability judgments in English are likely to be reliable, it is unclear that this generalizes to other languages (Linzen & Oseki 2018). If this is the case, this motivates the need to formally assess acceptability judgments reported in the comparative syntax literature, since theories in comparative syntax depend on many judgments collected from many languages. Additionally, well-defined factorial definitions of phenomena, such as Cowart's (1997) factorial definition of the *that*-trace effect and Sprouse et al.'s (2012) factorial definition of syntactic islands, have revealed surprising mismatches between experimental results and intuitive judgments. This suggests that it may be useful to re-evaluate the empirical basis of some claims of language similarities and differences.

In Section 7.3, I examined two cases in which experimental methods confirmed previously reported cross-language differences. In discussing Alexopoulou and Keller (2007), I described how comparing profiles of judgments across multiple conditions may inform representational theories. More didactically, I also discussed one successful and one failed experiment of my own that tested for the cross-language contrast in the *that*-trace effect. In discussing both studies, I suggested that carefully selected controls and maximizing similarity between items are crucial to avoiding spurious results.

Finally, in Section 7.4, I discussed the potential for using sentence acceptability experiments to examine individual differences. By examining variability between participants' responses, it is possible to discover (potential) microvariation. Similarly, claims about dialect differences can be tested by comparing performance between different samples. This is a potentially powerful tool for complementing microcomparative syntax and other approaches to variation.

# References

Abney, S. P. (1987). The English noun phrase in its sentential aspect. Doctoral dissertation, Massachusetts Institute of Technology.

Ackerman, L., Frazier, M., & Yoshida, M. (2018). Resumptive pronouns can ameliorate illicit island extractions. *Linguistic Inquiry*, 49(4), 847–859.

Alexopoulou, T. (1999). The syntax of discourse functions in Greek: A non-configurational approach. Doctoral dissertation, University of Edinburgh.

Alexopoulou, T. & Keller, F. (2007). Locality, cyclicity, and resumption: At the interface between the grammar and the human sentence processor. *Language*, 83(1), 110–160.

Almeida, D. (2014). Subliminal *wh*-islands in Brazilian Portuguese and the consequences for syntactic theory. *Revista da ABRALIN*, 13(2), 55–93.

Anand, P., Chung, S., & Wagers, M. W. (2010). Widening the net: challenges for gathering linguistic data in the digital age. http://people.ucsc.edu/schung/anandchungwagers.pdf

Baek, J. Y.-K. (1998). Negation and object shift in early child Korean. In U. Sauerland & O. Percus, eds., *The Interpretive Tract*. Cambridge, MA: MIT Department of Linguistics and Philosophy, pp. 73–86.

Baker, M. (2001). *The Atoms of Language*. New York: Basic Books.

Baker, M. (2008). The macroparameter in a microparametric world. In T. Bieberauer, ed., *The Limits of Syntactic Variation*. Amsterdam: John Benjamins.

Barbiers, S., Cornips, L., & van der Kleij, S. (2001). *Syntactic Microvariation*. Available at: www.meertens.knaw.nl/books/synmic/index.html

Bayer, J. (1990). Notes on the ECP in English and German. *Groninger Arbeiten zur Germanischen Linguistik*, 30, 1–55.

Bayer, J. & Cheng, L. L.-S. (2017). In M. Everaert & H. van Riemsdijk, eds., *The Blackwell Companion to Syntax*, 2nd ed. Hoboken, NJ: Wiley-Blackwell, 1–44.

Beltrama, A. & Xiang, M. (2016). Unacceptable but comprehensible: The facilitation effect of resumptive pronouns. *Glossa: A Journal of General Linguistics*, 1(1), 29. DOI:10.5334/gjgl.24

Bock, K. & Miller, C. A. (1991). Broken agreement. *Cognitive Psychology*, 23(1), 45–93.

Boeckx, C. (2014). What Principles and Parameters got wrong. In M. Carmen, ed., *Linguistic Variation in the Minimalist Framework*. Oxford: Oxford University Press.

Borer, H. (1984). *Parametric Syntax: Case Studies in Semitic and Romance Languages*. Dordrecht: Foris.

Bošković, Ž. (2008). What will you have, NP or DP? In E. Elfner & M. Walkow, eds., *Proceedings of the 37th North East Linguistic Society*. Amherst, MA: GLSA, pp. 101–114.

Bresnan, J. (1977). Variables in the theory of transformations. In P. W. Culicover, T. Wasow & A. Akmajian, eds., *Formal Syntax*. New York: Academic Press, pp. 157–196.

Chao, W. & Sells, P. (1983). On the interpretation of resumptive pronouns. In P. Sells & C. Jones, eds., *Proceedings of the 13th North East Linguistic Society*. Amherst, MA: GLSA.

Chacón, D. A. (2015). Comparative psychosyntax. Doctoral dissertation, University of Maryland.

Chacón, D. A. (2019). Minding the gap? Mechanisms underlying resumption in English. *Glossa: A Journal of General Linguistics*, 4(1), 68. DOI:10.5334/gjgl.839

Chacón, D. A., Fetters, M., Kandel, M., Pelz, E., & Phillips, C. (2019). Indirect learning and language variation: Reassessing the *that*-trace effect. Unpublished manuscript, New York University, Abu Dhabi.

Chacón, D. A., Imtiaz, M., Dasgupta, S., Murshed, S. M., Dan, M., & Phillips, C. (2016). Locality and word order in active dependency formation in Bangla. *Frontiers in Psychology*, 7(1235). DOI:10.3389/fpsyg.2016.01235

Chen, Y. (2019). The acquisition of Japanese relative clauses by L1 Chinese learners. Doctoral dissertation, University of Hawai'i at Mānoa.

Cheng, L. L.-S. & Sybesma, R. (1999). Bare and not-so-bare nouns and the structure of NP. *Lingusitic Inquiry*, 30, 509–542.

Chomsky, N. (1981). *Lectures in Government and Binding: The Pisa Lectures*. Berlin: Mouton de Gruyter.

Chomsky, N. & Miller, G. A. (1963). Introduction to the formal analysis of natural languages. In R. D. Luce, R. R. Bush, & E. Galanter, eds., *Handbook of Mathematical Psychology*, vol. 2. New York: Wiley, pp. 419–492.

Clifton, C., Fanselow, G., & Frazier, L. (2006). Amnestying superiority violations: Processing multiple questions. *Lingusitic Inquiry*, 37(1), 51–68.

Cowart, W. (1997). *Experimental Syntax: Applying Objective Methods to Sentence Judgments*. Thousand Oaks, CA: Sage.

Cowart, W. (2003). Detecting syntactic dialects: The *that*-trace phenomenon. Talk delivered at the 39th Regional Meeting of the Chicago Linguistics Society.

Crain, S. & Thornton, R. (1998). *Investigations in Universal Grammar: A Guide to Experiments on the Acquisition of Syntax and Semantics*. Cambridge, MA: MIT Press.

Cuetos, F. & Mitchell, D. C. (1988). Cross-linguistic differences in parsing: Restrictions on the use of the Late Closure strategy in Spanish. *Cognition*, 30(1), 73–105.

Culicover, P. W. (1993). Evidence against ECP accounts of the *that*-t effect. *Linguistic Inquiry*, 24, 557–561.

Edelman, S. & Christiansen, M. H. (2003). How seriously should we take Minimalist syntax? *Trends in Cognitive Sciences*, 7(2), 60–62.

Farby, S., Danon, G., Walters, J., & Ben-Shachar, M. (2010). The acceptability of resumptive pronouns in Hebrew. In Y. Falk, ed., *Proceedings of the Israel Association for Theoretical Linguistics 26*. Jerusalem: IATL.

Featherston, S. (2005a). *That*-trace in German. *Lingua*, 115(9), 1277–1302.

Featherston, S. (2005b). Magnitude estimation and what it can do for your syntax: Some wh-constraints in German. *Lingua*, 115(11), 1525–1550.

Featherston, S. (2009). Relax, lean back, and be a linguist. *Zeitschrift für Sprachwissenschaft*, 28(1), 127–132.

Fedorenko, E. & Gibson, E. (2010). Adding a third wh-phrase does not increase the acceptability of object-initial multiple-*wh*-questions. *Syntax*, 13(3), 183–195.

Francis, E., Lam, C., Zheng, C. C., Hitz, J., & Matthews, S. (2015). Resumptive pronouns, structural complexity, and the elusive distinction between grammar and performance: Evidence from Cantonese. *Lingua*, 162, 56–81.

Frazier, L. & Clifton, C. (1989). Successive cyclicity in the grammar and the parser. *Language and Cognitive Processes*, 4, 93–126.

Gibson, E. & Fedorenko, E. (2010). Weak quantitative standards in linguistics research. *Trends in Cognitive Sciences*, 14(6), 233–234.

Gibson, E. & Fedorenko, E. (2013). The need for quantitative methods in syntax and semantics research. *Language and Cognitive Processes*, 28(1–2), 88–124.

Gibson, E., Piantadosi, S. T., & Fedorenko, E. (2013). Quantitative methods in syntax/semantics research: A response to Sprouse and Almeida (2013). *Language and Cognitive Processes*, 28(3), 229–240.

Gibson, E. & Thomas, J. (1999). Memory limitations and structural forgetting: The perception of complex ungrammatical sentences as grammatical. *Language and Cognitive Processes*, 14(3), 225–248.

Gilligan, G. (1987). A cross-linguistic approach to the pro-drop parameter. Doctoral dissertation, University of Southern California.

Goldberg, L. M. (2005). Verb-stranding VP Ellipsis: A cross-linguistic study. Doctoral dissertation, McGill University.

Golden, M. (1995). Interrogative wh-movement in Slovene and English. *Acta Analytica*, 14, 145–187.

Gribanova, V. (2013). Verb-stranding verb phrase ellipsis and the structure of the Russian verbal complex. *Natural Language and Linguistic Theory*, 31, 91–136.

Grillo, N. & Costa, J. (2014). A novel argument for the Universality of Parsing principles. *Cognition*, 133(1), 156–187.

Hagstrom, P. (2000). Phrasal movement in Korean negation. In L. Vaselinova, S. Robinson, & L. Antieau, eds., *Proceedings of the 9th Student Conference in Linguistics (SCIL 9)*. Cambridge, MA: MIT Department of Linguistics and Philosophy, pp. 127–142.

Haider, H. (1983). Connectedness effects in German. *Groninger Arbeiten zur Germanischen Linguistik*, 23, 82–119.

Haider, H. (1993). *Deutsche Syntax – Generativ*. Tübingen: Narr.

Hammerly, C. (2018). Intrusive resumption can ameliorate island violations in real-time comprehension. Poster presented at the 31st CUNY Human Sentence Processing Conference.

Han, C.-H. (2013). On the syntax of relative clauses in Korean. *Canadian Journal of Linguistics*, 58(2), 319–347.

Han, C.-H., Lidz, J., & Musolino, J. (2007). V-raising and grammar competition in Korean: Evidence from negation and quantifier scope. *Linguistic Inquiry*, 38(1), 1–47.

Han, C.-H., Musolino, J., & Lidz, J. (2011). Endogenous sources of variation in language acquisition. *Proceedings of the National Academy of Sciences*, 113 (4), 942–947.

Haspelmath, M. (2008). Parametric versus functional explanations of syntactic universals. In T. Bieberauer, ed., *The Limits of Syntactic Variation*. Amsterdam: John Benjamins.

Hofmeister, P. & Norcliffe, E. (2013). Does resumption facilitate sentence comprehension? In P. Hofmeister & E. Norcliffe, eds., *The Core and the Periphery: Data-Driven Perspectives on Syntax Inspired by Ivan A. Sag*. Stanford, CA: CSLI Publications, pp. 225–246.

Hofmeister, P. & Sag, I. (2010). Cognitive constraints and island effects. *Language*, 86(2), 366–415.

Hong, S. (1985). A and A' binding in Korean and English: Government–Binding parameters. Doctoral dissertation, University of Connecticut.

Huang, C.-T. J. (1982). Logical relations in Chinese and the theory of grammar. Doctoral dissertation, Massachusetts Institute of Technology.

Kang, N.-K. (2000). Reflexives and the Linking Theory in Universal Grammar. Doctoral dissertation, University of Oxford.

Kayne, R. (2005). Some notes on comparative syntax, with special reference to English and French. In G. Cinque & R. Kayne, eds., *Handbook of Comparative Syntax*. Oxford and New York: Oxford University Press.

Keller, F. (1995). Towards an account of extraposition in HPSG. In S. Abney & E. W. Hinrichs, eds., *Proceedings of the 7th Conference of the European Chapter of the Association for Computational Linguistics*. Dublin: Association for Computational Linguistics, pp. 301–306.

Keshev, M. & Meltzer-Asscher, A. (2018). Active dependency formation in islands: How grammatical resumption affects sentence processing. *Language*, 93(3), 549–568.

Keshev, M. & Meltzer-Asscher, A. (2019). A processing-based account of subliminal *wh*-island effects. *Natural Language and Linguistic Theory*, 37(2), 621–657.

Kim, J.-B. (2000). *The Grammar of Negation: A Constraint-Based Approach*. Stanford, CA: CSLI Publications.

Kim, K.-B. & Han, C.-H. (2016). Inter-speaker variation in Korean pronouns. In P. Grosz & P. Patel-Grosz, eds., *The Impact of Pronominal Form on Interpretation*. Berlin: De Gruyter Mouton, pp. 347–372.

Kluender, R. (1998). On the distinction between strong and weak islands: A processing perspective. In P. Culicover & L. McNally, ed., *The Limits of Syntax* (Syntax and Semantics, 29). San Diego, CA: Academic Press, pp. 241–279.

Kluender, R. & Kutas, M. (1993). Subjacency as a processing phenomenon. *Language and Cognitive Processes*, 8(4), 573–633.

Koak, H. (2008). A morpho-syntactic approach to pronominal binding. *University of Pennsylvania Working Papers in Linguistics*, 14(1), 227–240.

Kush, D. W., Lohndal, T., & Sprouse, J. (2018). Investigating variation in island effects: A case study of Norwegian extraction. *Natural Language and Linguistic Theory*, 36(3), 743–779.

Lago, S., Sloggett, S., Schlueter, Z., Chow, W.Y., Williams, A., Lau, E., & Phillips, C. (2017). Coreference and antecedent representation across languages. *Journal of Experimental Psychology: Learning, Memory, and Cognition*, 43(5), 795–817.

Landau, I. (2018). Missing objects in Hebrew: Argument ellipsis, not VP ellipsis. *Glossa: A Journal of General Linguistics*, 3(1), 76. DOI:10.5334/gjgl.560

Lasnik, H. & Saito, M. (1984). On the nature of proper government. *Linguistic Inquiry*, 15, 235–289.

Linzen, T. & Oseki, Y. (2018). The reliability of acceptability judgments across languages. *Glossa: A Journal of General Linguistics*, 3(1), 100. DOI:10.5334/gjgl.528

Lu, J., Thompson, C. K., & Yoshida, M. (2020). Chinese wh-in-situ and islands: A formal judgment study. *Linguistic Inquiry*, 51(3), 611–623.

Maling, J. & Zaenen, A. (1982). A phrase structure account of Scandinavian extraction phenomena. In P. Jacobson & G. K. Pullum, eds., *The Nature of Syntactic Representation*. Dordrecht: Reidel, pp. 229–282.

Marantz, A. (2005). Generative linguistics within the cognitive neuroscience of language. *Linguistic Review* 22(2–4), 429–445.

Merchant, J. & Sipson, A. (2012). *Sluicing: Cross-Linguistic Perspectives*. Oxford: Oxford University Press.

Mioto, C. & Kato, M.A. (2005). As interrogativas-Q do português europeu e do português brasileiro atuais. *Revista da ABRALIN*, 4(1–2), 171–196.

Newmeyer, F. J. (2004). Against a parameter-setting approach to typological variation. *Linguistic Variation Yearbook*, 4(1), 181–234.

Newmeyer, F. J. (2005). *Possible and Probable Languages: A Generativist Perspective on Linguistic Typology*. Oxford: Oxford University Press.

Nishigauchi, T. (1990). *Quantification in the Theory of Grammar*. Dordrecht: Kluwer.

Otani, K. & Whitman, J. (1991). V-raising and VP-ellipsis. *Linguistic Inquiry*, 22, 345–358.

Perlmutter, D. (1971). *Deep and Surface Structure Constraints in Syntax*. New York: Holt, Rinehart, and Winston.

Pesetsky, D. (2017). Complementizer-trace effects. In M. Everaert & H. C. van Riemsdijk, eds., *The Blackwell Companion to Syntax*, 2nd ed. Hoboken, NJ: Wiley-Blackwell.

Phillips, C. (2009). Should we impeach armchair linguists? In S. Iwasaki, ed., *Japanese/Korean Linguistics*, vol. 17. Stanford: CSLI Publications, pp. 1–16.

Reinhart, T. (1981). A second COMP position. In A. Belletti, L. Brandi & L. Rizzi, eds., *Theory of Markedness in Generative Grammar*. Pisa: Scuole Normale Superiore, pp. 517–557.

Rizzi, L. (1982). Issues in Italian syntax. Doctoral dissertation, Massachusetts Institute of Technology.

Roberts, I. & Holmberg, A. (2005). On the role of parameters in Universal Grammar: A reply to Newmeyer. In H. Broekhuis, N. Corver, R. Huybregts, U. Kleinhanz, & J. Koster, eds., *Organizing Grammar: Linguistic Studies in honor of Henk van Riemsdijk*. Berlin: Mouton de Gruyter.

Ross, J. R. (1967). Constraints on variables in syntax. Doctoral dissertation, Massachusetts Institute of Technology.

Rudin, C. (1988). On multiple questions and multiple WH fronting. *Natural Language and Linguistic Theory*, 6(4), 445–501.

Sakai, H. (1994). Complex NP constraint and case conversion in Japanese. In M. Nakamura, ed., *Current Topics in English and Japanese*. Tokyo: Hitsuji Shobo, pp. 179–200.

Schütze, C. (1996). *The Emprical Base of Linguistics*. Chicago: Chicago University Press.

Shlonsky, U. (1992). Resumptive pronouns as a last resort. *Linguistic Inquiry*, 23(3), 443–468.

Simpson, A., Choudhury, A., & Menon, M. (2013). Argument ellipsis and the licensing of covert nominals in Bangla, Hindi, and Malayalam. *Lingua*, 134, 103–128.

Sobin, N. (1987). The variable status of COMP-trace phenomena. *Natural Language and Linguistic Theory*, 5, 33–60.

Sobin, N. (2002). The Comp-trace effect, the adverb effect and minimal CP. *Journal of Linguistics*, 38(3), 527–560.

Sobin, N. (2009). Prestige case forms and the comp-trace effect. *Syntax*, 12 (1), 32–59.

Sprouse, J. & Almeida, D. (2012). Assessing the reliability of textbook data in syntax: Adger's "Core Syntax." *Journal of Linguistics*, 48(3), 609–652.

Sprouse, J., Caponigro, I., Greco, C., & Cecchetto, C. (2016). Experiental syntax and the variation of island effects in English and Italian. *Natural Language and Linguistic Theory*, 34(1), 307–344.

Sprouse, J., Fukuda, S., Ono, H., & Kluender, R. (2011). Reverse island effects and the backward search for a licensor in multiple *wh*-questions. *Syntax*, 14(2), 179–203.

Sprouse, J., Schütze, C., & Almeida, D. (2013). A comparison of informal and formal acceptability judgments using a random sample from Linguistic Inquiry 2001–2010. *Lingua*, 134, 219–248.

Sprouse, J., Wagers, M. W., & Phillips, C. (2012). A test of the relation between working-memory capacity and syntactic island effects. *Language*, 88(1), 82–123.

Stepanov, A., Mušič, M., & Stateva, P. (2018). Two (non-) islands in Slovenian: A study in Experimental Syntax. *Linguistics*, 56(3), 435–476.

Suh, J.-H. (1989). Scope interaction in negation. In S. Kuno et al., eds., *Harvard Studies in Korean Linguistics III*. Cambridge, MA: Harvard University Department of Linguistics.

Suh, J.-H. (1990). Scope phenomena and aspects of Korean syntax. Doctoral dissertation, University of Southern California.

Tanaka, N. & Schwartz, B. (2018). Investigating relative clause island effects in native and nonnative adult speakers of Japanese. In A. B. Bertolini & M. J. Kaplan, eds., *Proceedings of the 42nd Annual Boston University Conference on Language Development.* Somerville, MA: Cascadilla Proceedings Project, pp. 750–763.

Torrego, E. (1984). On inversion in Spanish and some of its effects. *Linguistic Inquiry*, 15(1), 103–129.

Tsimpli, I. M. (1999). Null operators, clitics, and identification: A comparison between Greek and English. In A. Alexiadou, G. Horrocks, & M. Stavrou, eds., *Studies in Greek Syntax*. Dordrecht: Kluwer, pp. 241–262.

Tucker, M., Idrissi, A., Sprouse, J., & Almeida, D. (2019). Resumption ameliorates different islands differently: Acceptability data from Modern Standard Arabic. In A. Khalfaoui & M. A. Tucker, eds., *Perspectives on Arabic Linguistics, 30: Papers from the Annual Symposia on Arabic Linguistics, Stony Brook, New York, 2016 and Norman, Oklahoma, 2017*. Amsterdam: John Benjamins, pp. 159–193.

Uriagereka, J. (2007). Clarifying the notion "Parameter." *Biolinguistics*, 1, 99–113.

Vasishth, S., Brussow, S., Lewis, R., & Drenhaus, H. (2008). Processing polarity: How the ungrammatical intrudes on the grammatical. *Cognitive Science*, 32(4), 685–712.

Vasishth, S., Suckow, K., Lewis, R. L., & Kern, S. (2010). *Language and Cognitive Processes*, 25(4), 533–567.

Wagers, M., Lau, E., & Phillips, C. (2009). Agreement attraction in comprehension: Representations and processes. *Journal of Memory and Language*, 61(2), 206–237.

Wasow, T. & Arnold, J. (2005). Intuitions in linguistic argumentation. *Lingua*, 115, 1481–1496.

Wellwood, A., Pancheva, R., Hacquard, H., & Phillips, C. (2018). The anatomy of a comparative illusion. *Journal of Semantics*, 35(3), 543–583.

Wood, J. (2019). Quantifying geographical variation in acceptability judgments in regional American English dialect syntax. *Linguistics*, 57(6), 1367–1402.

Xiang, M., Dillon, B., Wagers, M. W., Liu, F. Q., & Guo, T. M. (2014). Processing covert dependencis: An SAT study on Mandarin *wh*-in-situ questions. *Journal of East Asian Linguistics*, 23(2), 207–232.

Xiang, M., Wang, S. P., & Cui, Y. L. (2015). Constructing covert dependencies: The case of wh-in-situ processing. *Journal of Memory and Language*, 84, 139–166.

Zanuttini, R., Wood, J., Zentz, J., & Horn, L. (2018). The Yale Grammatical Diversity Project: Morphosyntactic variation in North American English. *Linguistics Vanguard*, 4(1), 20160070.

# Part II

## Experimental Studies of Specific Phenomena

# 8

# Resumptive Pronouns in English

Chung-hye Han

## 8.1 Introduction

In many introspective judgment-based or corpus-based studies, resumptive pronouns (RPs) have been viewed as amnestying, ameliorating, or repairing island-violating wh-dependency structures in English, such as relative clauses or wh-questions (Ross 1967; Kayne 1981; Kroch 1981; Prince 1990; Erteschik-shir 1992; Cann et al. 2005). For example, for both (1a) and (1b), inserting an RP in place of the gap is said to improve the acceptability of otherwise unacceptable island-violating relative clauses (see Chapter 9 for general discussion of island phenomena).[1]

(1)      a. The manager fired a reporter who the editor speculated why ___ / he defamed the senator.
         b. The detective interrogated a man who the prosecutor knows why the officer arrested ___ / him.

A disagreement exists, however, as to why RPs have this ameliorating effect. Some take the position that the addition of an RP changes the structural analysis of island-violating wh-dependency structures making them grammatical (Ross 1967; Kayne 1981; Prince 1990; Cann et al. 2005). Others (Kroch 1981; Asudeh 2011, 2012, 2013) argue that resumption is not part of the grammar of English, but speakers produce RPs for extra-grammatical reasons. Kroch proposes that RPs are produced, especially with island-violating relative clauses, because of the performance pressure to maintain fluent speech in real-time sentence generation. Asudeh proposes that RPs are produced because in production, speakers prioritize local well-formedness over global well-formedness.

---

[1] While filler–gap structures are normally formed without a pronoun in the gap position in English, this is not the case cross-linguistically. Languages such as Irish and Hebrew can form filler–gap structures with or without a pronoun (McCloskey 1990; Shlonsky 1992).

More recently, a number of studies using both offline and online experimental methods have produced results that directly bear on the grammatical status of resumption in English. Section 8.2 presents several offline sentence acceptability studies on resumptive structures in English. These studies consistently found that native speakers of English do not judge island-violating dependency structures with resumptive pronouns to be more acceptable than the ones with gaps. Section 8.3 presents comprehensibility and reading studies that test comprehension benefits of resumption. These studies report that resumptive pronouns increase the comprehensibility of island-violating structures and facilitate processing of long dependencies. These results taken together suggest that although resumptive pronouns in islands do not have an ameliorating effect on grammaticality, they may confer a processing benefit, as they form an anaphoric dependency with the head noun.

## 8.2   Sentence Acceptability Experiments

In this section, I review several studies that elicited acceptability judgments on resumptive structures in English, employing various experimental methods, such as numerical scale and Magnitude Estimation.

Ferreira and Swets (2005) successfully elicited island-violating relative clauses with RPs in a laboratory setting (see Chapter 26 for general discussion of production studies). Participants were shown an array of three pictures with short descriptions of the pictures. For example, the first picture has a donkey with a description *lives in California*, the second one has a different donkey with a description *lives in Brazil* and the third one has yet another donkey with a description *I don't know* or *doesn't know*. Their task was to learn the pictures and the brief descriptions and then answer the question "What is this?" regarding each picture. This task structurally primed the participants to answer *This is a donkey that lives in California* and *This is a donkey that lives in Brazil* to the questions about the first and the second pictures. For the third picture, the participants produced (2a), which contains a relative clause with an RP in a *wh*-island, if the descriptor was *I don't know*, and (2b), which contains a relative clause with a subject gap in a non-island, if the descriptor was *doesn't know*.

(2)      a. This is a donkey that I don't know where it lives.
         b. This is a donkey that doesn't know where it lives.

But when participants were asked to provide acceptability judgments on resumptive structures as in (2a), and gapped structures as in (2b), which served as grammatical controls, by rating the sentences on a scale from 1 (perfect) to 5 (awful), the resumptive sentences were judged to be much more unacceptable (mean rating of 3.3) than the gapped structures (mean rating of 1.9).

Using a Magnitude Estimation Task, Alexopoulou and Keller (2007) investigated how embedding and island constraints interact with resumption in object *wh*-questions. Four different configurations were compared: complement clauses without *that* as in (4) (non-island bare clause), complement clauses with *that* as in (5) (non-island *that*-clause), complement clauses with *whether* as in (6) (weak island), and relative clauses as in (7) (strong island). Each configuration was instantiated with single or double levels of embedding, and with a gap or an RP. They also looked at sentences without embedding (zero embedding) as in (3), as a control condition.

(3)    Control condition
       Who will fire ___ / him?                                    (zero)

(4)    Non-island condition (bare clause)
       a. Who does Mary claim we will fire ___ / him?              (single)
       b. Who does Jane think Mary claims we will fire ___/him?   (double)

(5)    Non-island condition (*that*-clause)
       a. Who does Mary claim that we will fire ___ / him?        (single)
       b. Who does Jane think that Mary claims that we will       (double)
          fire ___ / him?

(6)    Weak-island condition (*whether*-clause)
       a. Who does Mary wonder whether we will fire ___ / him?   (single)
       b. Who does Jane think that Mary wonders whether we       (double)
          will fire ___ / him?

(7)    Strong-island condition (relative clause)
       a. Who does Mary meet the people that will fire ___ / him? (single)
       b. Who does Jane think that Mary meets the people that    (double)
          will fire ___ / him?

The results showed that gaps are significantly more acceptable than resumptives for bare clauses, *that*-clauses, and *whether*-clauses, but for relative clauses, no significant difference was found revealing low acceptability for both types. As for the effects of resumption on depth of embedding, although RPs were found to receive much lower acceptability ratings than gaps in *wh*-questions with no island violation, RPs in doubly embedded clauses (as in (4b)) were judged to be more acceptable than the ones in single embedded clauses (as in (4a)), which in turn were judged to be more acceptable than the ones in simple clauses (as in (3)). This finding confirms Erteschik-Shir's (1992) observation that resumption improves with multiple embedding. In island-violating *wh*-questions, however, acceptability of resumption remained low regardless of depth of embedding.

Heestand et al. (2011) also found that resumption does not improve acceptability for object gaps in declarative sentences with island-violating relative clauses. In three separate experiments, participants read declarative sentences containing relative clauses formed from complex NPs (8), relative clauses (9) or adjunct clauses (10), with or without an RP. Each experiment also tested grammatical controls that contained relative clauses without island violations, for a standard of comparison. Participants rated acceptability of these sentences on a scale from 1 (unacceptable) to 7 (perfectly acceptable).

(8)    Complex NP
       a. This is the man that the news that the police arrested ___ shocked the public.

(gap in an island)

       b. This is the man that the news that the police arrested him shocked the public.

(RP in an island)

       c. This is the man that Mary thought that the police arrested ___ to protect the president.

(grammatical control)

(9)    Relative clause
       a. This is the man that the policeman who arrested ___ saved the president's life.

(gap in an island)

       b. This is the man that the policeman who arrested him saved the president's life.

(RP in an island)

       c. This is the man that the policeman who arrested the thief saved ___.

(grammatical control)

(10)   Adjunct clause
       a. This is the dish that, although the chef overcooked ___, the guests were not upset.

(gap within an island)

       b. This is the dish that, although the chef overcooked it, the guests were not upset.

(RP within an island)

       c. This is the dish that, although the chef overcooked the sauce, the guests enjoyed ___.

(grammatical control)

The results showed that in all three experiments, the control conditions were rated higher than the conditions with island-violating relative clauses, and crucially the acceptability ratings for the resumptive structures were as low as the ratings for the corresponding gapped structures.

    McDaniel and Cowart (1999) compared acceptability ratings of subject and object resumption and the corresponding gapped structures in relative clauses formed from weak islands (*wh*-complement clauses). Participants rated sentences such as (11) using a ten-point scale, in comparison to a reference sentence that was assigned a value of 5. They were instructed to use the scale to indicate how much better or worse than the reference sentence each target sentence seemed.

(11)   a. That's the girl that I wonder when ___ met you.    (subject gap)
       b. That's the girl that I wonder when she met you.    (subject RP)
       c. That's the girl that I wonder when you met ___.    (object gap)
       d. That's the girl that I wonder when you met her.    (object RP)

McDaniel and Cowart (1999) found that while relative clauses with subject RPs were rated higher than the corresponding gapped relative clauses, no such difference was found in object resumption and the corresponding gapped structures.

Keffala and Goodall (2011) and Keffala (2013) also report findings similar to those of McDaniel and Cowart (1999), but at the same time, they found no difference in acceptability between relative clauses with subject resumption and object resumption. They examined relative clauses with no island violation (simple clause and *that*-clause), and island violating relative clauses formed from weak islands (*wh*-island) and strong islands (relative clause island), with or without an RP in subject or object position. Examples with a subject RP or gap are given in (12) and an object RP or gap in (13). Participants rated each target sentence on a scale from 1 to 11, where 1 represents lowest acceptability, and 11 represents highest acceptability.

(12)   Subject gap/RP
       a. This is the chef that ___ / she prepared the potatoes.    (simple clause)
       b. This is the chef that Ted realized that ___ / she prepared the potatoes.
                                                                    (*that*-clause)
       c. This is the chef that Ted inquired how ___ / she prepared the potatoes.
                                                                    (*wh*-island)
       d. This is the chef that Ted devoured the potatoes that ___ / she prepared.
                                                                    (relative clause island)

(13)   Object gap/RP
       a. These are the potatoes that Ted prepared ___ / them.    (simple clause)
       b. These are the potatoes that Ted realized that the chef prepared ___ / them.
                                                                    (*that*-clause)
       c. These are the potatoes that Ted inquired how the chef prepared ___ / them.
                                                                    (*wh*-island)
       d. These are the potatoes that Ted flirted with the chef that prepared ___ / them.
                                                                    (relative clause island)

Keffala and Goodall report uniformly low acceptability ratings for resumptive relative clauses regardless of the position of the RP in comparison to the gapped relative clauses formed from simple or *that*-clauses. They argue that the difference in the improvement of acceptability of subject and object resumptive relative clauses formed from *wh*-island or relative clause island in comparison to the corresponding gapped relative clauses is the result of the much less acceptable status of the island-violating subject gap relative clauses than the island-violating object gap relative clauses.

Han et al. (2012) tested relative clauses with indefinite heads. Their study was motivated by the fact that the materials used in most of the sentence acceptability experiments are relative clauses with definite heads, even though corpus studies (Prince 1990; Ariel 1999) report that RPs are found much more frequently in relative clauses with indefinite heads. In a Magnitude Estimation Task experiment, Han et al. tested sentences that contained an RP or a gap in a subject or an object position in relative clauses formed from non-islands or islands. Non-islands included simple clauses, one-level embedded clauses and two-level embedded clauses. Islands included both weak and strong islands: *wh*-complement clauses, adjunct clauses, and noun complement clauses. Examples of test sentences with a subject RP or gap are given in (14) and an object RP or gap are given in (15).

(14)    Subject gap/RP

    a.  The manager fired a reporter who ___/ he defamed the senator last year.

                (simple)

    b.  The manager fired a reporter who the editor thought ___ / he defamed the senator.

                (one-embedded)

    c.  The manager fired a reporter who Mary knew that John insisted ___ / he insulted Bob.

                (two-embedded)

    d.  The manager fired a reporter who the editor speculated why ___ / he defamed the senator.

                (*wh*-complement)

    e.  The manager fired a reporter who the editor was angry because ___ / he defamed the senator.

                (adjunct)

    f.  The manager fired a reporter who the fact that ___ / he blackmailed the senator was a secret.

                (noun complement)

(15)    Object gap/RP

    a.  The manager fired a reporter who the senator sued ___ / him last year for defamation.

                (simple)

b. The manager fired a reporter who the editor thought that the senator sued ___ / him for defamation.

(one-embedded)

c. The manager fired a reporter who Mary knew that John insisted Bob insulted ___ / him.

(two-embedded)

d. The manager fired a reporter who the editor wondered whether the senator sued ___ / him for defamation.

(*wh*-complement)

e. The manager fired a reporter who the editor was angry because the senator sued ___ / him for defamation.

(adjunct)

f. The manager fired a reporter who the fact that the senator sued ___ / him was a secret.

(noun complement)

Han et al. found that in island conditions, while subject resumptive relatives are rated significantly higher than subject gap relatives, the ratings of object resumptive relatives and object gap relatives are not different from each other. This subject–object asymmetry is consistent with the findings in McDaniel and Cowart (1999), Keffala and Goodall (2011), and Keffala (2013), and supports the idea that resumptive pronouns improve the acceptability of strong and weak island relatives with subject, but not with object gaps. However, they found a significant difference between subject gap relatives and object gap relatives in island conditions, while no difference was found between any of the resumptive pronoun conditions. That is, the acceptability of resumptive relative clauses is uniformly low across conditions, in comparison to the acceptability of gapped relative clauses which show variation between non-island and island conditions. Taken together, these results suggest that the subject–object asymmetry is not a function of resumption itself but is instead due to the fact that subject gap island relatives have a very low acceptability, as compared to object gap island relatives.

Studies using audio stimuli report similar findings. Ferreira and Swets (2005) asked participants to provide acceptability judgments on aurally presented island-violating relative clauses with RPs, which were elicited in a laboratory setting. Just as with visually presented resumptive structures, the aurally presented resumptive structures were given low acceptability ratings in comparison to the grammatical controls. Clemens et al. (2012) collected acceptability judgments on aurally presented island relative clauses with object resumption and definite head nouns and found that resumptive relative clauses did not improve acceptability in comparison to gapped relatives. Han et al. (2012) report the same findings for aurally presented indefinite relative clauses with subject resumption and object resumption.

Morgan and Wagers (2018) tested whether the tendency to produce an RP in a given structure depends on that structure's acceptability. To test this hypothesis, they elicited relative clauses with RPs using a Typed Elicited-Production Task. They presented participants with a base version of the target sentence (16a), followed by a prompt (16b), which included the beginning of a relative clause. Participants were asked to rephrase the original base sentence by completing the prompt. The target response was either a resumptive relative clause as in (17b) or a gapped relative clause as in (17b).

(16)    a. Base
            The news that the alien dissected the woman shocked Karl.
        b. Prompt
            I know the woman who the news that _____.

(17)    a. the alien dissected ___ shocked Karl.
        b. the alien dissected her shocked Karl.

Morgan and Wagers manipulated the base and the prompt sentences so that the extraction site of target relative clauses would be in non-islands (singly embedded clauses and doubly embedded clauses), and islands (wh-complements, complex subject NPs, complex object NPs, and adjuncts). Acceptability judgments on the target relative clauses, both with gaps and RPs, were independently collected on a 1–7 scale. They found that (a) the lower the acceptability of a given structure with a gap, the higher the occurrence of RPs in the same structure; and (b) relative clauses formed from islands had high occurrence of RPs, over and above the rate predicted by acceptability alone.

While all of the studies reviewed so far used rating tasks to collect acceptability judgments, Ackerman et al. (2018) used a Forced-Choice Task to test whether RP structures are more acceptable than the corresponding gapped structures. They presented the participants with a pair of wh-questions, where one contains a gap and the other an RP. The participants were asked to choose the sentence that was more acceptable out of the pair. These wh-questions had extraction sites from islands as in (18) or non-islands as in (19). The island types that were tested included relative clauses, adjunct clauses, and wh-clauses.

(18)    Island
        Which woman did Carlos report that [island the newscaster who exposed her /___] threatened the detective's case?

(19)    Non-island
        Which woman did Carlos report that [island the newscaster who exposed the criminal] threatened her / ___?

Ackerman et al. found that participants consistently preferred RPs over gaps across all island types, and gaps were preferred over RPs in non-islands.

They conclude that RPs thus do ameliorate island violations, the effect of which can be detected with a forced-choice task, and suggest that other rating task studies could not detect this effect possibly because the amelioration effect of RPs is weak.

Table 8.1 provides a brief summary of the studies reviewed in this section, listing the authors, the task, constructions tested, and the main finding for each study.

In sum, while a study based on a forced-choice task found a preference for RPs over gaps in islands, none of the sentence acceptability studies based on a rating task found resumption to increase the acceptability of island-violating *wh*-dependencies. Most researchers take these results to support the view that resumption is not part of the grammar of English. Nevertheless, the fact is that speakers do often produce structures with RPs (Prince 1990; Cann et al. 2005). As a way of reconciling the fact that speakers often produce resumptive structures while hearers judge them as unacceptable, Heestand et al. (2011) and Polinsky et al. (2013) argue that English RPs form anaphoric relations with the head noun, akin to cross-sentential anaphora (Sells 1984; Alexopoulou & Keller 2007; Asudeh 2011), and that they provide a coreferencing device that helps speakers keep track of coreference relations in production. Morgan and Wagers (2018) also take the position that RPs are ungrammatical, but their occurrence is epiphenomenal to the production system such that when in the process of producing a filler–gap structure, if a gap is not licensed, the production system abandons the filler–gap dependency, and instead realizes a pronoun in place of the gap to satisfy local subcategorization constraints, similarly to Asudeh's (2011, 2012, 2013) model of RP production.

On the other hand, Goodall (2017) takes the position that resumption is indeed part of the grammar of English, but the low acceptability ratings are due to the considerable processing costs RPs incur. Goodall argues that unlike gaps, pronouns are ambiguous between fillers and referring expressions and so when the processor encounters an RP, it might initially treat it as a referring expression, attempting to locate an entity in the discourse. And in a later stage of processing, in trying to resolve a *wh*-dependency, the processor must reanalyze the pronoun as a filler so that it is interpreted as resumptive. According to Goodall, such reanalysis would incur significant processing costs resulting in low acceptability judgments.

## 8.3  Comprehensibility and Self-Paced Reading Experiments

Regardless of the grammatical status of RPs in English, the question remains regarding the source of the intuition that resumption has an ameliorating effect in island-violating *wh*-dependency structures, given that the acceptability of such structures remains low, as shown by all the sentence acceptability studies reviewed in Section 8.2. In this section,

Table 8.1 *Summary of sentence acceptability studies on English resumption*

| Authors | Task | Construction | Main finding |
|---|---|---|---|
| Ferreira & Swets 2005 | Picture description, Numerical scale | relative clause | Island-violating structures with RPs were elicited. These resumptive structures were rated much lower than the grammatical controls, when presented visually or aurally. |
| Alexopoulou & Keller 2007 | Magnitude estimation | wh-question | Gaps in non-islands and weak islands were more acceptable than RPs. Gaps and RPs in strong islands showed low acceptability. Acceptability of RPs improved with multiple embedding. |
| Heestand et al. 2011 | Numerical scale | relative clause | Island-violating structures with RPs were rated as low as the corresponding gapped structures. |
| McDaniel & Cowart 1999 | Magnitude estimation | relative clause | Island-violating structures with subject RPs were rated higher than the corresponding gapped structures. Object resumption and gapped structures had similar ratings. |
| Keffala & Goodall 2011, Keffala 2013 | Numerical scale | relative clause | Resumptive structures formed from islands and non-islands showed uniformly low acceptability ratings regardless of the position of the RP, in comparison to the gapped non-island structures. |
| Han et al. 2012 | Magnitude estimation | relative clause | Resumptive structures were rated uniformly low across all conditions, in comparison to the gapped structures which showed variation between non-island and island conditions, for both visually and aurally presented stimuli. |
| Clemens et al. 2012 | Numerical scale | relative clauses | Island-violating structures with object RPs did not improve acceptability in comparison to the corresponding gapped structures for aurally presented stimuli. |
| Morgan & Wagers 2018 | Typed elicited- production, Numerical scale | relative clause | As the acceptability of a gapped structure decreases, the frequency of RPs in the same structure increases. Island-violating relative clauses showed very high occurrence of RPs. |
| Ackerman et al. 2018 | Forced-choice | wh-question | RPs were preferred over gaps in island-violating structures, but gaps were preferred over RPs in non-islands. |

I review studies that tested whether resumption enhances comprehensibility or processing of complex *wh*-dependency structures.

Beltrama and Xiang (2016) tested comprehensibility of resumption separately from acceptability. In one experiment, they presented test sentences with context sentences and asked the participants to rate the comprehensibility of the test sentences from 1 (the sentence is completely incomprehensible) to 7 (the sentence is perfectly comprehensible). The test sentences were declaratives containing gapped or resumptive relative clauses with or without an island violation formed with two-levels of embedding or three-levels of embedding. Example test materials in each condition are given in (20). In a separate experiment, using the same set of test materials as in the comprehensibility experiment, they asked the participants (who did not participate in the comprehensibility experiment) to rate the acceptability of the test sentences ranging from 1 (the sentence is completely unacceptable) to 7 (the sentence is perfectly acceptable).

(20)   Context:

Have you heard? Yesterday there were riots in the streets. Some people were wounded. Look here, they're talking about it in the paper.

Target sentence:

a.   This is the boy that the cop who was leading the operation beat up.

(Non-island, 2-level embedding, Gap)

b.   This is the boy that the cop who was leading the operation beat him up.

(Non-island, 2-level embedding, RP)

c.   This is the boy that the newspaper reports that the cop who was leading the operation beat up.

(Non-island, 3-level embedding, Gap)

d.   This is the boy that the newspaper reports that the cop who was leading the operation beat him up.

(Non-island, 3-level embedding, RP)

e.   This is the boy that the cop who beat up was leading the operation.

(Island, 2-level embedding, Gap)

f.   This is the boy that the cop who beat him up was leading the operation.

(Island, 2-level embedding, RP)

g.   This is the boy that the newspaper reports that the cop who beat up was leading the operation.

(Island, 3-level embedding, Gap)

h.   This is the boy that the newspaper reports that the cop who beat him up was leading the operation.

(Island, 3-level embedding, RP)

Beltrama and Xiang found that in non-islands, gaps were more comprehensible than RPs overall with a reduction of comprehensibility in longer embedded sentences. Crucially, in islands, RPs were more comprehensible than gaps in both two-level embedded and three-level embedded sentences. However, in the acceptability experiment, while in non-islands gaps were rated higher than RPs, in islands, RPs were no more rated higher than gaps. Acceptability of RPs was uniformly low across all test conditions, just as in all the sentence acceptability studies reviewed in Section 8.2. Beltrama and Xiang take these findings to suggest that while resumptive structures are unacceptable to native speakers of English, they nevertheless enhance the comprehensibility if used in island-violating environments.

Online studies such as Heestand et al. (2011) and Hofmeister and Norcliffe (2013) report findings that bear on the processing benefits of RPs. In addition to collecting acceptability ratings on resumptive structures in comparison to gapped structures in island-violating contexts, as in (8)–(10), Heestand et al. (2011) measured reaction times in rating these test sentences. They found that sentences with resumptive relative clauses had shorter mean reaction times than the sentences with gapped relative clauses. They conclude from this finding that RPs made it easier for participants to detect the ungrammaticality of the sentences, and thus judgments for sentences with RPs were given faster than judgments for sentences with illicit gaps.

Hofmeister and Norcliffe (2013) compared sentences with RPs and gaps, manipulating the dependency length between the gap/RP and the head noun, in a self-paced reading study. They wanted to test whether resumption facilitates processing of long dependencies that are otherwise difficult to process. Participants read, word-by-word, sentences containing an RP or a gap in a one-level embedded relative clause (long dependency condition), as in (21a, b), or a zero-level embedded relative clause (short dependency condition), as in (21c, d). The time each participant took to read each word was measured. The critical region was taken to be two words after either the RP or the gap. In a separate experiment, acceptability ratings of these sentences were also collected.

(21)    a. Mary confirmed that there was a prisoner who the prison officials had acknowledged that the guard helped ___ to make a daring escape.

(long-gap)

b. Mary confirmed that there was a prisoner who the prison officials had acknowledged that the guard helped him to make a daring escape.

(long-RP)

c. The prison officials had acknowledged that there was a prisoner that the guard helped ___ to make a daring escape.

(short-gap)

d. The prison officials had acknowledged that there was
   a prisoner that the guard helped him to make a daring escape.
   (short-RP)

Hofmeister and Norcliffe found that although resumptive structures were never given higher acceptability ratings than the corresponding gapped structures, which is consistent with the findings of previous sentence acceptability studies discussed in Section 8.2, reading times for resumptive structures were significantly shorter than the gapped structures in the long dependency condition. The reading times for resumptive and gapped structures in the short dependency condition showed no difference. Hofmeister and Norcliffe take these results to suggest that while RPs do not improve the acceptability of the structure, they do facilitate processing of long dependencies that are generally more difficult to process than short dependencies. Although Hofmeister and Norcliffe did not test island-violating resumptive structures, their findings imply that whatever mechanism allows RPs to reduce reading time in long dependencies should be active in island-violating dependencies as well.[2]

In sum, comprehensibility and online reading studies report enhanced comprehensibility and faster reading time for RPs than gaps in long dependency or island-violating structures. However, it is not clear from these studies whether the enhanced comprehensibility rating is actually due to the increased accuracy in interpreting the RPs. Further, while shorter reading time may be due to the reduced complexity of the RP structure, it could also be the result of shallow processing which could lead to inaccurate interpretation, as suggested by a reviewer. Studies reported in Morgan et al. (2018) address these questions. Morgan et al. (2018) found that in a self-paced reading study, RPs were read faster than gaps in islands. However, in a sentence-picture matching task study and a visual-world eye-tracking study, RPs resulted in more non-target-like interpretation than corresponding gaps, casting doubt on the idea that RPs support accurate anaphoric resolution in comprehension. The issue of the processing and comprehension benefit of RPs is clearly an unresolved question that opens an avenue for further research.

## 8.4  Conclusion

After reviewing a number of sentence acceptability studies and comprehensibility and processing studies on the resumptive structure in English, the picture that emerges is that although resumption does not enhance the acceptability of island-violating *wh*-dependencies, it may increase their

---

[2]  In a comprehension task study, Dickey (1996) also found that sentences with resumption in more deeply embedded positions exhibited shorter reaction times than the corresponding sentences with gaps.

comprehensibility and result in faster processing of long dependencies. These results suggest that the source of the ameliorating effect of resumption in English that linguists have observed is not grammar, but is a processing benefit, as RPs form appropriate anaphoric dependencies. However, there is also research that suggests that RPs may actually hinder accurate anaphoric resolution. Further research on processing of RPs and how they form anaphoric dependencies, and evaluating the experimental results on English against research on languages that have grammatical resumption such as Irish (McCloskey 2017) and Hebrew (Meltzer-Asscher et al. 2015; Fadlon et al. 2019) would enrich our understanding of English resumption.

## References

Ackerman, L., Frazier, M., & Yoshida, M. (2018). Resumptive pronouns can ameliorate illicit island extractions. *Linguistic Inquiry*, 49, 847–859.

Alexopoulou, T. & Keller, F. (2007). Locality, cyclicity, and resumption: At the interface between the grammar and the human sentence processor. *Language*, 83, 110–160.

Ariel, M. (1999). Cognitive universals and linguistic conventions: The case of resumptive pronouns. *Studies in Language*, 23, 217–269.

Asudeh, A. (2011). Local grammaticality in syntactic production. In E. M. Bender & J. E. Arnold, eds., *Language from a Cognitive Perspective*. Stanford, CA: CSLI Publications, pp. 51–79.

Asudeh, A. (2012). *The Logic of Pronominal Resumption*. Oxford: Oxford University Press.

Asudeh, A. (2013). Directionality and production of ungrammatical sentences. *Studies in Linguistics*, 6, 83–106.

Beltrama, A. & Xiang, M. (2016). Unacceptable but comprehensible: the facilitation effect of resumptive pronouns. *Glossa: A Journal of General Linguistics*, 1(1), 29. DOI:10.5334/gjgl.24

Cann, R., Kaplan, T., & Kempson, R. (2005). Data at the grammar-pragmatics interface: the case of resumptive pronouns in English. *Lingua*, 115, 1551–1577.

Clemens, L. E., Morgan, A., Polinsky, M., & Xiang, M. (2012). Listening to resumptives: An auditory experiment. A poster presented at CUNY 2012 Conference on Human Sentence Processing, March 14–16, 2012, CUNY.

Dickey, M. W. (1996). Constraints on the sentence processor and the distribution of resumptive pronouns. In M. W. Dickey & S. Tunstall, eds., *Linguistics in the Laboratory*. Amherst, MA: GLSA, pp. 157–192.

Erteschik-Shir, N. (1992). Resumptive pronouns in islands. In H. Goodluck & M. Rochemont, eds., *Island Constraints: Theory, Acquisition and Processing* (Studies in Theoretical Psycholinguistics 15). Dordrecht: Kluwer Academic Publishers, pp. 89–109.

Fadlon, J., Morgan, A. M., Meltzer-Asscher, A., & Ferreira, V. S. (2019). It depends: Optionality in the production of filler-gap dependencies. *Journal of Memory and Language*, 106, 40–76.

Ferreira, F. & Swets, B. (2005). The production and comprehension of resumptive pronouns in relative clause "island" contexts. In A. Cutler, ed., *Twenty-First Century Psycholinguistics: Four Cornerstones*. Mahwah, NJ: Lawrence Erlbaum, pp. 263–278.

Goodall, G. (2017). Referentiality and resumption in *wh*-dependencies. In J. Ostrove, R. Kramer, & J. Sabbagh, eds., *Asking the Right Questions: Essays in Honor of Sandra Chung*. eScholarship, University of California, pp. 65–80.

Han, C. Elouazizi, N., Galeano, C., Görgülü, E., Hedberg, N., Hinnell, J., Jeffrey, M., Kim, K., & Kirby, S. (2012). Processing strategies and resumptive pronouns in English. In N. Arnett & R. Bennett, eds., *Proceedings of the 30th West Coast Conference on Formal Linguistics*. Somerville, MA: Cascadilla Proceedings Project, pp. 153–161.

Heestand, D., Xiang, M. & Polinsky, M. (2011). Resumption still does not rescue islands. *Linguistic Inquiry*, 42, 138–152.

Hofmeister, P. & Norcliffe, E. (2013). Does resumption facilitate sentence comprehension? In P. Hofmeister & E. Norcliffe, eds., *The Core and the Periphery: Data-Driven Perspectives on Syntax Inspired by Ivan A. Sag.* Stanford, CA: CSLI Publications.

Kayne, R. (1981). "ECP" Extensions. *Linguistic Inquiry*, 12, 93–134.

Keffala, B. (2013). Resumption and gaps in English relative clauses: Relative acceptability creates an illusion of "saving." In C. Cathcart, I.-H. Chen, G. Finley, S. Kang, C. S. Sandy, & E. Stickles, eds., *Proceedings of the 37th Annual Meeting of the Berkeley Linguistics Society*. Berkeley, CA: University of California, Berkeley Linguistics Society, pp. 140–154.

Keffala, B. & Goodall, G. (2011). Do resumptive pronouns ever rescue illicit gaps in English? A poster presented at CUNY 2011 Conference on Human Sentence Processing, March 24–26, 2011, Stanford University.

Kroch, A. (1981). On the role of resumptive pronouns in amnestying island constraint violations. In R. A. Hendrick, C. S. Masek, & M. F. Miller, eds., *Papers from the 17th Regional Meeting, Chicago Linguistic Society*. Chicago: Chicago Linguistic Society, pp. 125–135.

McCloskey, J. (1990). Resumptive pronouns, A'-binding and levels of representation in Irish. In R. Hendrick, ed., *Syntax of the Modern Celtic Languages*. New York: Academic Press, pp. 199–248.

McCloskey, J. (2017). New thoughts on old questions: Resumption in Irish. In J. Ostrove, R. Kramer, & J. Sabbagh, eds., *Asking the Right Questions: Essays in Honor of Sandra Chung*. eScholarship, University of California, pp. 81–102.

McDaniel, D. & Cowart, W. (1999). Experimental evidence for a minimalist account of English resumptive pronouns. *Cognition*, 70, B15–B24.

Meltzer-Asscher, A., Fadlon, J., Goldstein, K., & Holan, A. (2015). Direct object resumption in Hebrew: How modality of presentation and relative clause position affect acceptability. *Lingua*, 166, 65–79.

Morgan, A. M., von der Malsburg, T., Ferreira, V. S., & Wittenberg, E. (2018). This is the structure that we wonder why anyone produces it: Resumptive pronouns in English hinder sentence comprehension. Presented at the 2018 CUNY Conference on Human Sentence Processing, MIT, Boston.

Morgan, A. M. & Wagers, M. W. (2018). English resumptive pronouns are more common where gaps are less acceptable. *Linguistic Inquiry*, 49, 861–876.

Polinsky, M., Clemens, L. E., Morgan, A. M., Xiang, M., & Heestand, D. (2013). Resumption in English. In J. Sprouse, ed., *Experimental Syntax and Island Effects*. Cambridge: Cambridge University Press, pp. 341–360.

Prince, E. (1990). Syntax and discourse: A look at resumptive pronouns. In K. Hall, J.-P. Koenig, M. Meacham, S. Reinman, & L. A. Sutton, eds., *Proceedings of the Sixteenth Annual Meeting of the Berkeley Linguistics Society: Parasession on the Legacy of Grice*. Berkeley, CA: University of California, Berkeley Linguistics Society, pp. 482–497.

Ross, J. R. (1967). Constraints on variables in syntax. Doctoral dissertation, Massachusetts Institute of Technology.

Sells, P. (1984). Syntax and semantics of resumptive pronouns. Doctoral dissertation, University of Massachusetts, Amherst.

Shlonsky, U. (1992). Resumptive pronouns as a last resort. *Linguistic Inquiry*, 23, 443–468.

# 9

# Island Effects

Jon Sprouse and Sandra Villata

## 9.1 Introduction

One of the defining characteristics of human languages is the existence of long-distance dependencies: dependencies that can exist between two elements with no apparent bound on the linear distance (as measured in words) or hierarchical distance (as measured in clauses) between them. The unboundedness of long-distance dependencies is illustrated in (1) using *wh*-dependencies in English. The head of the dependency is the *wh*-word *what*; the tail of the dependency is indicated with an underscore.

(1)     a. What did Lisa invent __?
        b. What did Dean think that Lisa invented __?
        c. What did Charlie say that Dean thinks that Lisa invented __?

Long-distance dependencies can involve a number of distinct items in the head position of the dependency, as illustrated in (2) for English, with the item in the head of the dependency in bold (this list is illustrative, not exhaustive, particularly for other languages).

(2)     a. **What** do you think that Lisa invented __?
        b. I do not understand **the algorithm** that you think that Lisa invented __.
        c. I do not care for Pepsi, but **Coke**, I think that I like __.
        d. **Complicated** though you think the algorithm is __, you can understand it.

Though long-distance dependencies are unbounded, they are constrained: when the tail of the dependency appears within certain structures, the sentence becomes unacceptable, as illustrated in (3) for several structures in English, with square brackets around the structures that appear to be responsible for the unacceptability.

(3)    a. What did you laugh [because Sam ate __ by accident]?       (adjunct island)
       b. What did you hear [the rumor that Jodie discovered __]? (complex NP island)
       c. What did [the story about __] impress Mary?              (subject island)
       d. What did you wonder [whether Lisa invented __]?          (*whether* island)

Ross (1967) metaphorically named these structures *islands*; with the effect that these structures have on the acceptability called *island effects*; and the grammatical constraints that are proposed to capture these effects called *island constraints*.

   Island effects are one of the most studied phenomena in experimental syntax. There are at least two reasons for this. First, at a theoretical level, island effects are a terrific case study for a number of important questions in linguistics (and cognitive science more generally): does the grammar require complex, abstract constraints, or can the phenomena we see be explained by appeal to independently motivated features of sentence processing? How do those constraints interact with real-time sentence processing mechanisms? Are there constraints on the patterns of cross-linguistic, or cross-dependency, variation? Does the acquisition of these constraints require innate, domain-specific mechanisms? (See Phillips (2013a) and (2013b) for extensive discussion of some of these issues.) Second, at a methodological level, island effects are a valuable case study for illustrating the three primary benefits of formal experiments:

   (i)  Formal experiments allow (and, in fact, force) researchers to explicitly define what it means to be an effect, often in the common terminology of factorial logic, thus allowing precise testing of different theories.
   (ii) Formal experiments allow (and, in fact, force) researchers to explicitly consider the source of the effect, thus allowing precise testing of different theories of the source.
   (iii) Formal experiments can often increase precision of the data, opening up new analysis possibilities, like correlating distinct data types, measuring effect sizes, and exploring variability across languages, constructions, participants, and items.

We will organize this chapter around these three potential benefits of formal experiments: Section 9.2 will focus on the definition of island effects, Section 9.3 will focus on the source of island effects, and Section 9.4 will focus on the benefits of increasing the precision of the data we have about island effects. Our goals are to (i) illustrate the benefits of formal experiments for island effects, (ii) review the major empirical contributions that formal experiments have made over the past two decades, and (iii) provide readers with a relatively comprehensive list of articles that used formal experiments to explore island effects. One limitation of this approach is that we will not provide a comprehensive review of specific theories of islands, though we will point out theoretical consequences of the experimental results that we review (for a theoretically oriented review, see Szabolcsi and Lohndal (2017)). Our hope is that this chapter will help researchers uncover trends in this research that will aid their own studies. To that end, Section 9.5 concludes with a brief discussion of some of the trends that we see in current investigations.

## 9.2   Defining Island Effects

The definition of an island effect in the syntax literature is something like this: low acceptability that (i) arises when the tail of a long-distance dependency is inside an island structure, and (ii) cannot be explained by any other property of the construction. All experiments in syntax, whether informal or formal, require the experimenter to explicitly define the effect of interest – to think through the syntactic property or properties that will be manipulated, and the effect that the manipulation will have on the response that will be measured. Formal experiments typically make this explicit by leveraging the terminology of factorial logic (see Chapter 1 for additional discussion of factorial design). The term *factor* means a property that can be manipulated, such as some dimension of the structure of a sentence; the term *level* is used to refer to the specific values that a factor can take. Factors can be continuous or categorical. The definition of island effects in the literature can be translated into factorial logic by using two categorical factors, each with two levels: the factor DEPENDENCY, with levels manipulating the clause containing the tail of the dependency, and the factor STRUCTURE, with levels manipulating the presence or absence of an island structure. We illustrate this design here using *whether*-islands (Sprouse 2007; Sprouse et al. 2011; Sprouse et al. 2012).

(4)     A 2×2 factorial design for *whether*-islands

|  |  | DEPENDENCY | STRUCTURE |
|---|---|---|---|
| a. | Who __ thinks [that Lisa invented the algorithm]? | matrix | non-island |
| b. | What do you think [that Lisa invented __]? | embedded | non-island |
| c. | Who __ wonders [whether Lisa invented the algorithm]? | matrix | island |
| d. | What do you wonder [whether Lisa invented __]? | embedded | island |

This is called a 2×2 design (read "two by two") – each digit in this name represents a factor in the design, and each value of the digits represents the number of levels. The goal of factorial logic is to isolate effects using subtraction. The difference (4a–b) isolates the effect of the length of the dependency (both structural and linear). The difference (4a–c) isolates the effect of the island structure. Recall that the definition of island effect says that something additional happens when the tail of the dependency is inside an island structure. In this factorial design, that means that the acceptability of (4d) is more than the linear sum of the effects of dependency length and structure. We can state this mathematically as: (4a–d) = (4a–b) + (4a–c) + X, where X is the additional effect that is not isolated by any of the factors, that is, X is the island effect. In statistical terms, this is a superadditive interaction, where the superadditive component isolates the island effect. It is sometimes useful to algebraically rearrange the equation to isolate X, such as (4b–d) – (4a–c) = X. The interaction term X in this equation is called a *differences-in-differences* score (Maxwell & Delaney 2003).

There are several advantages to using a factorial definition for island effects, at both the level of experimental design and the level of data analysis. At the level of experimental design, explicitly defining the factors in the design draws attention both to the effects that can be quantified (the length effect, the structure effect, and the island effect) and to the effects that are not being actively quantified (like the choice of *wh*-word). Experimenters can then easily evaluate the pros and cons of either adding additional factors for unquantified effects, holding them constant across all factors, or letting them vary freely. This plays out in a number of ways above. For example, we chose to define levels of the dependency factor as matrix-vs.-embedded instead of no-dependency-vs.-dependency (e.g. yes/no questions versus *wh*-questions) because the former allows us to isolate the effect of the length of the dependency, whereas the latter would yield a complex effect: it would capture both the effect of the presence and absence of a dependency, but also any other differences between yes/no and *wh*-questions. Ultimately, this would not impact the isolation of the island effect. One nice consequence of isolating the island effect in the interaction term is that the effects captured in the two factors should subtract out (unless they interact with the island effect). But the choice of the levels of the factors does influence which other properties we can quantify. In this case, we would like to explore a specific theory of island effects that posits a role for the length of the dependency (see Section 9.3.1 below), so this design is slightly more helpful. Similar considerations hold for the use of *who* in (4a) and (4c) versus *what* in (4b) and (4d). This difference will subtract out in the equations above as long as the choice of *wh*-word does not interact with island effects; but it does mean that the effect of dependency length will contain both the length manipulation and the *wh*-word manipulation. In short, factorial logic provides a framework for evaluating the properties of the conditions to determine precisely how they will impact the effects that can be quantified (the two main effects of the factors and the interaction).

The factorial definition of island effects also provides benefits at the level of data analysis. For one, the factorial definition provides a straightforward graphical prediction for the presence or absence of an island effect: when plotted in an interaction plot as in Figure 9.1, the absence of an island effect will appear as parallel lines (i.e. no interaction) as in the leftmost panel of Figure 9.1, and the presence of an island effect will appear as the "alligator mouth" pattern indicative of a monotonic superadditive interaction as in the center panel of Figure 9.1. The right-most panel of Figure 9.1 shows the results of an experiment from Sprouse and Messick (2015) using the factorial design for *whether*-islands, which show the characteristic superadditive interaction.

A closely related benefit is that the factorial definition provides a straightforward statistical definition for the presence or absence of an island effect: the presence or absence of a statistically significant interaction between the two factors in the design. Finally, the factorial definition provides a method for quantifying the size of the island effect: the size of the interaction term (or differences-in-differences score). Though effect sizes are rarely used in linguistic theory (or cognitive science more broadly), there are a number of questions about island effects for which effect sizes may yield relevant information; therefore effect sizes will arise throughout the discussions below.

Before leaving this section, there are three more advanced topics related to factorial designs that are worth mentioning. The first is that factorial logic is not just for island effects – factorial designs ultimately underlie all effects in the syntax literature (and cognitive science more generally). This means that all of the benefits that factorial designs provide for the investigation of island effects are in principle available for other phenomena. Our impression is that factorial designs have played a more explicit role in the island effects literature for the very same reasons that island effects have played such a large role in the experimental syntax literature – because island effects are an excellent case study for exploring questions about the source of effects, the complexity of the grammar, the interaction of the grammar and sentence processing, etc. We expect factorial designs to play a more central role as more phenomena are studied within the experimental syntax literature.

The second issue is that the benefits of isolating effects using super-additive monotonic interactions come with a minor methodological cost – superadditive monotonic interactions can be caused by non-linearity in the response scale (specifically, larger intervals at one end, and smaller intervals at the other). Unfortunately, for most cognitive measures, including acceptability judgments, there is no way to independently verify that the response scale is linear (see Chapter 1 for additional discussion of this issue). The explicitly linearly spaced numbers of the scale could map to a non-linear underlying scale in the minds of participants (that we therefore cannot observe). This means that superadditive monotonic interactions can arise even when there is no true interaction present. For this reason, such interactions are sometimes called *removable interactions* in the statistics literature (Loftus 1978; Wagenmakers et al. 2012). This is an issue that all users of factorial designs must keep in mind. We do not have space

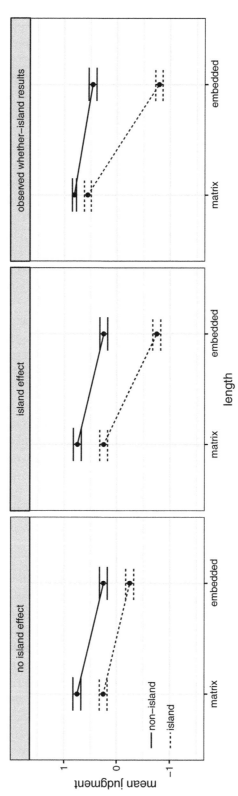

**Figure 9.1** The graphical predictions of the 2 x 2 design for *whether*-islands. The left panel is the prediction for the absence of an island effect (in the presence of two main effects of dependency length and structure); the center panel is the prediction for the presence of an island effect (a monotonic superadditive interaction); the right panel is what we observe for a real experiment in English. For the real data, judgments were z-score transformed prior to analysis, therefore the y-axis is the mean of z-scores.

here to review this issue in detail, but we would like to note that we do not believe that island effects are the result of an underlying non-linearity in the scale of acceptability. One piece of evidence for this is empirical: superadditive monotonic interactions do not appear to arise spuriously for phenomena that should not yield them, contrary to what we might expect if the underlying scale of acceptability were non-linear. Another piece of evidence is statistical: the interactions that indicate the presence of island effects survive even when researchers use statistical analysis techniques that are designed to circumvent the problem raised by removable interactions (such as signal detection theory, and cultural consensus theory).

The third issue is that factorial designs only instantiate one of the two components of the traditional definition of island effects – that the acceptability effect cannot be explained by other known factors. They do not enforce the second component – that the acceptability of the sentence containing the island effect is relatively low in the scale. Keller (2000) and Featherston (2005) both observed that acceptability judgment effects can be present in formal experiments without leading to low acceptability. Almeida (2014) was the first to observe this for island effects, demonstrating that *whether*-islands in Brazilian Portuguese show a small superadditive effect with all four conditions rated above the mid-point in the acceptability scale. Almeida calls this a *subliminal* island effect to reflect the fact that there is an acceptability effect (albeit a small one) that is unexplained in the factorial design, but that speakers may not report the critical sentence as unacceptable. As Almeida points out, subliminal island effects raise difficult questions about what it means to be an island effect, what the source of island effects are, and ultimately, what the overall architecture of the language faculty is. These questions were recently underscored by Keshev and Meltzer-Asscher (2019), who observe a subliminal island effect for *wh*-islands in Hebrew for both *wh*-dependencies, which is unexpected because Hebrew has been claimed to lack *wh*-islands (Reinhart 1981), and for backward binding dependencies, which is unexpected because binding dependencies are not typically claimed to show island effects. We will discuss research on the source of island effects in detail in the next section. The important point here is that formalizing the definition of island effects using a factorial design helps to bring these issues into sharp relief, thereby opening a number of new avenues of research.

## 9.3 The Source of Island Effects

One of the driving questions in linguistics is whether the grammar requires complex, abstract constraints, or whether the phenomena that we see in human languages can be explained by appealing to other, perhaps independently motivated, aspects of cognition. Island effects present a classic case study for this, as the components involved in island effects, such as long-distance dependencies and complex syntactic structures, raise the possibility that island effects could be reduced to an independently motivated consequence of sentence processing complexity (e.g. Kluender & Kutas 1993; Hofmeister & Sag 2010). In this section, we will primarily focus on the debate between approaches that postulate complex, abstract grammatical constraints to explain island effects, and approaches that seek to reduce island effects to independently motivated aspects of sentence processing. We see this as a first cut in the space of theories. After this cut, one could then explore different approaches within a tradition; for example, within the grammatical tradition, one could then explore the semantic approaches of Szabolcsi and Zwarts (1993) or Abrusán (2014), or the pragmatic approaches of Erteschik-Shir (1973) or Goldberg (2006). But for space reasons we will focus on the first cut in this chapter. We will review multiple strands of experimental research dedicated to this question, including studies on working memory capacity (Section 9.3.1), studies on the sentence processing dynamics of filler–gap dependencies (Section 9.3.2), studies on the sentence processing dynamics of binding dependencies (Section 9.3.3), and studies on judgment satiation (Section 9.3.4). Though the results of these studies do tend to support grammatical approaches to islands over sentence processing approaches, our focus will be on the way that formal experiments can be used to gather this kind of evidence.

### 9.3.1 Working Memory Capacity

Perhaps the most prominent sentence-processing-based theory of island effects is the working memory capacity theory proposed by Kluender and Kutas (1993) (recently advocated by Hofmeister and Sag (2010)). Kluender and Kutas observe that there are two sources of sentence processing complexity in the critical sentences of island effects (the (d) condition): the long-distance dependency, and the complex syntactic structure that we call an island. These sources of sentence processing complexity provide two potential explanations for the unacceptability that we see in island effects. One explanation could be called the *simple reductionist approach*. This approach argues that the long-distance dependency and the complex island structure each decrease acceptability (presumably due to their sentence processing costs), and that these decreases sum linearly as in the left panel of Figure 9.1. In this way, these two costs completely determine the acceptability of the critical sentence without any need for a grammatical constraint. The second type of explanation is a *complex reductionist approach*, in which independently motivated sentence processing factors lead to the superadditive interaction. Kluender and Kutas propose just such a theory. Under their theory, the processing of the long-distance dependency and the processing of the complex island structure each draw from the same limited pool of working memory resources. There are not enough resources in the pool to deploy both sets of processes simultaneously. This leads the parse to crash, yielding the perception of unacceptability. This working memory capacity theory can explain the superadditive pattern of acceptability in the center panel of Figure 9.1 (an interaction between dependency length and structure) without the need for a grammatical constraint. This means that, for the working memory capacity theory, the critical (d) sentences for island effects are grammatical, but are perceived as unacceptable because the parser does not have access to the working memory resources that it needs. These two approaches to reductionism lead to the following logic: the linearly additive pattern in the left panel of Figure 9.1 is unambiguously evidence of a simple reductionist theory of island effects, whereby the unacceptability is completely explained by the costs associated with the two factors of the factorial design; the superadditive pattern in the center panel is ambiguous – it shows that there is a mystery that needs to be explained, with the space of possible explanations including a grammatical constraint, the working memory capacity theory, or some other complex reductionist theory that has not yet been proposed.

Though the superadditive pattern is itself ambiguous, the factorial definition does allow us to potentially test unique predictions of the competing theories of the superadditive interaction. For example, Sprouse et al. (2012) argue that one potential prediction of the Kluender and Kutas (1993) working memory capacity theory is that variability in working memory capacity should lead to variability in the size of the island effect (based on discussion in Kluender and Kutas (1993) that the additional unacceptability may be driven by a mechanism in the memory system that penalizes the parse based on how much the processes exceed the pool of resources). Sprouse et al. then test this prediction by looking for correlations between the interaction term (the differences-in-differences score) from the factorial definition of island effects as a measure of the size of island effects, and both serial recall scores and performance in an *n*-back task as measures of working memory capacity. They find no evidence of a relationship between the two across two experiments, each testing four island types (*whether*, complex NP, subject, and adjunct islands), using both measures of working memory capacity, with relatively large samples sizes. These results were replicated in Michel (2014) using reading span tasks as the measure of working memory capacity. These results suggest that the most straightforward approach to working memory capacity is unlikely to be sufficient to explain island effects. However, these results do leave open the possibility of adopting more complex working memory capacity theories (e.g. Hofmeister et al. (2012) suggest that a step-like or sigmoidal relationship between working memory capacity and acceptability might account for these results). This kind of theory revision is the normal course for science. The primary point here is that formal experiments, and explicit factorial definitions of effects, can be leveraged to explore the source of island effects (and indeed all acceptability judgment effects), as long as the competing theories make unique, testable predictions. The ability of formal experiments to quantify effect sizes can be particularly useful if the predictions involve relationships with other types of measures, like working memory measures.

### 9.3.2   The Sentence Processing Dynamics of Long-Distance Dependencies

The sentence processing dynamics of long-distance dependencies is a complex topic in its own right; and, as such, we cannot hope to do it justice in one subsection (see Chapters 23 and 24 in this volume). Therefore here we will focus specifically on the ways in which this topic could potentially interact with the question of the source of island effects. The critical issue involves *gap-filling* – a cover term for the set of processes that the parser deploys to identify the tail of a long-distance dependency (the *gap*), retrieve the displaced element (the *filler*) from memory, and integrate it into the structure. One of the driving questions in the literature has been whether gap-filling is *passive*, such that the parser waits for unambiguous evidence for a gap (e.g. a sequence of words that could not appear together without a gap in between) to deploy gap-filling processes, or whether gap-filling is *active*, such that the parser attempts to deploy gap-filling processes before encountering unambiguous evidence for the gap. The consensus in the literature is that gap-filling is active: Crain and Fodor (1985) and Stowe (1986) first demonstrated this with an experimental diagnostic called the filled-gap effect, illustrated in (5) using examples from Stowe (1986).

(5)       a. My brother wanted to know **who** Ruth will bring <u>us</u> home to __
             at Christmas.
          b. My brother wanted to know **if** Ruth will bring <u>us</u> home to Mom
             at Christmas.

In a self-paced reading task, Stowe found that reading times at *us* are slower in a sentence with a long-distance dependency (5a) than in a sentence without a long-distance dependency (5b). This slow-down can be explained if the parser (actively) engages gap-filling processes prior to *us*, integrating the filler as the object of the verb, such that the parser must reanalyze the structure when it encounters the "filled-gap" represented by *us*. In addition to the filled-gap effect, Garnsey et al. (1989) demonstrated that active gap-filling can be revealed by manipulating the plausibility of a filler relative to the verb that potentially selects it, and later work, like Traxler and Pickering (1996) discussed below, showed that the plausibility manipulation also triggers a reading time slow-down at the verb. Building on results like these (and many others), Frazier and Flores d'Arcais (1989) formalized the idea of active gap-filling as the *Active Filler Strategy*, which states that the parser attempts to complete filler-gap dependencies at the first possible location. The "first possible location" has traditionally been taken to be the first gap-selecting category (such as a verb or preposition), but Omaki et al. (2015) have recently shown that gap-filling may in fact be *hyperactive*, such that the parser predicts the gap-selecting category (such as a transitive verb) before encountering it within sentences with filler–gap dependencies.

The active (or hyperactive) nature of gap-filling raises an interesting question for island effects – does the parser attempt to actively engage gap-filling inside islands? Stowe (1986) investigated this question in the second experiment of her seminal paper with the paradigm in (6):

(6)    a. The teacher asked **what** the team laughed about <u>Greg's</u> older brother fumbling __.
       b. The teacher asked **if** the team laughed about <u>Greg's</u> older brother fumbling the ball.
       c. The teacher asked **what** the silly story about <u>Greg's</u> older brother was supposed to mean __.
       d. The teacher asked **if** the silly story about <u>Greg's</u> older brother was supposed to mean anything.

She found the classic filled-gap effect in (6a) versus (6b) at *Greg's*, as expected. However, in (6c) and (6d), which contain a subject island structure, she found no filled-gap effect at *Greg's*, suggesting that active gap-filling is suppressed within subject islands. This close alignment between active gap-filling and island effects is tantalizing – it raises the possibility that active gap-filling may reveal information about island effects that we may not get from acceptability judgments alone. To be absolutely clear, as far as we can tell, the alignment of active gap-filling with island effects is logically independent of the source of island effects: active gap-filling could in principle align or not with island effects caused by grammatical constraint, and could in principle align or not with island effects caused by sentence-processing complexity. To our minds, the theoretical value of exploring the alignment of active gap-filling is that it can help to refine the space of possible theories of island effects for both types of sources.

Nearly all of the published studies on active gap-filling within islands using reading time measures are studies of English, and all test islands in subject position. The focus on subject position is methodological: investigating an island in subject position means that there is a potential acceptable continuation of the dependency after the island (typically in the form of a post-verbal gap). If there is no acceptable continuation of the sentence, it is possible that the parser might recognize the unacceptability of the sentence at the leading edge of the island, making it impossible to interpret reading time results within the island (see Phillips (2006) for a review of studies that find reading and ERP effects at the leading edge of islands). The focus on English is perhaps a consequence of the fact that English has subject island effects and is generally overrepresented in linguistics. What this means in practice is that there is quite a bit of information that we do not yet have – information on languages other than English, and on islands that cannot occur in subject position (like *wh*-islands and adjunct islands). What we do know is that subject islands in English appear to reliably suppress active gap-filling for *wh*-dependencies (Stowe 1986; Pickering et al. 1994), and that relative clauses in subject position (so, perhaps a type of double island effect) in English appear to reliably suppress active gap-filling for relative-clause dependencies (Traxler & Pickering 1996; Omaki et al. 2015). The one complication to this pattern was reported by Pickering et al. 1994 for *wh*-dependencies out of relative clauses in subject position, which did show evidence of active gap-filling (in contrast to the relative clause dependencies tested by Traxler and Pickering (1996). Setting aside the (still unexplained) results of Pickering et al. (1994), the general consensus in the literature is that subject islands suppress active gap-filling in English (see also Freedman and Forster (1985) for evidence using the sentence matching task, and Clifton and Frazier (1989) and Kurtzman and Crawford (1991) for evidence using speeded grammaticality).

Phillips (2006) investigated active gap-filling within subject islands that can host a parasitic gap. A parasitic gap is an acceptable gap that appears inside an island when there is a second gap outside the island; in other words, the gap inside the island is parasitic on the gap outside the island (Engdahl 1983; see Culicover and Postal (2001) for a review of the conditions on parasitic gaps). As a concrete example, (7a) is unacceptable in English, giving rise to a subject island effect. However, (7b) is acceptable, apparently because of the second gap added to the post-verbal object position. The ability of the subject in (7b) to host a parasitic gap appears to be tied to the finiteness of the relative clause; a finite relative clause is unacceptable regardless of the presence of the second gap (8a, b). All of these facts were corroborated by Phillips (2006) in a formal acceptability experiment.

(7)     a. *The outspoken environmentalist worked to investigate what the local campaign to preserve __ had harmed the annual migration.

        b. The outspoken environmentalist worked to investigate what the local campaign to preserve __ had harmed __.

(8)     a. *The outspoken environmentalist worked to investigate what the local campaign that preserved __ had harmed the annual migration.

     b. *The outspoken environmentalist worked to investigate what the local campaign that preserved __ had harmed __.

Phillips then used the plausibility mismatch paradigm in a self-paced reading study to show that non-finite subject relative clauses, like those in (7), show evidence of active gap-filling within the subject; whereas finite subject relative clauses, like those in (8), show no evidence of active gap-filling within the subject. The descriptive fact seems to be that active gap-filling is very tightly aligned with the ability to host an acceptable gap – subjects that can potentially host a parasitic gap (an acceptable gap) show evidence of active gap-filling, and subjects that cannot host a parasitic gap show no active gap-filling. The theoretical import of this is quite stunning. The critical fact is that the parser has no way of knowing whether the gap in the subject in (7) is licit or illicit at the time of active gap-filling. The parser simply deploys gap-filling because the subject could potentially host a gap if the right conditions hold later in the sentence. This means that the unacceptability that arises for sentences like (7a) cannot be caused by the inability of the parser to fill the gap in the subject. The parser can, and does, fill that gap during the first pass of the parse. The unacceptability in (7a) must occur later, after the parser has realized that there is no second gap to license the parasitic gap. The consequence of this is that any theory of the source of the island effect in (7a) must *not* prevent gap-filling wholesale. It must allow gap-filling, and then yield unacceptability later when the licensing condition is not met. As Phillips notes, a check of licensing is something that grammatical approaches to islands are well-equipped to handle; it is less clear how this can be achieved with the sentence processing approaches to island effects that are currently in the literature. (For additional evidence that the parser is aware of the licensing of parasitic gaps, see Wagers and Phillips (2009).)

    For completeness we should mention that there are a few electroencephalography (EEG) studies of island effects (see also Chapter 24). Neville et al. (1991) found a P600 response at the verb for subject islands (*What was a sketch of admired by the man). Kluender and Kutas (1993) found an N400 at the clause boundary for a *wh*-island (*What do you wonder who they caught at by accident?), as well as a LAN at the word after the gap. McKinnon and Osterhout (1996) found a positive component at the first word of an adjunct clause forming an adjunct island (*I wonder which of his staff members the candidate was annoyed when his son was questioned by?). These results all show that island effects are detected during online processing, but it is less clear how these results relate to the question of active gap-filling within islands. One problem that arises when trying to link these results to the active gap-filling literature is that there is no EEG response uniquely associated with active gap-filling. The two responses associated with gap-filling, a P600 at the verb (Kaan et al. 2000) and a LAN at the word after the gap (Kluender & Kutas 1993), are both later than the reading time effects that indicate active gap-filling. Another problem is that only subject islands allow an acceptable continuation, making it difficult to interpret effects that might arise inside other island types. Therefore, for now, we simply note that EEG can be used to detect island effects during real-time sentence processing, and that there is still quite a bit of potential to make advances in this literature.

### 9.3.3    The Sentence Processing Dynamics of Binding Dependencies

The binding dependencies that exist between the pronoun and the noun that it is coreferent with do not appear to give rise to island effects. Therefore it may seem odd to have a section dedicated to binding dependencies in a chapter about island effects. But this is in fact a strength. Binding dependencies share a number of sentence processing features with the long-distance dependencies that give rise to island effects: binding dependencies can be infinite in length; when the pronoun or anaphor appears before its coreferent noun in a configuration called *backward binding*, the parser engages in an *active* search for that noun (Van Gompel & Liversedge 2003) similar to active gap-filling; the active search for the coreferent noun is constrained by the licensing conditions on binding dependencies (Sturt 2003; Kazanina et al. 2007) similar to the way active gap-filling is constrained by island effects; and both long-distance dependencies and backward binding dependencies appear to increase activation in the left inferior frontal gyrus (Matchin et al. 2014). These similarities suggest that binding dependencies and long-distance dependencies may share substantially similar sentence-processing mechanisms. The fact that binding dependencies share these sentence-processing mechanisms but do not share island effects means that (backward) binding dependencies can serve as an interesting minimal pair with long-distance dependencies in studies designed to explore the role of sentence-processing mechanisms in island effects.

Yoshida et al. 2014 demonstrated that the active search for a coreferent noun in backward binding dependencies is not suppressed within relative clauses in subject position (a combination of a relative clause island and a subject island), but is suppressed by Binding Condition C. They did this using the *gender mismatch effect* – a slow-down in reading times that occurs when the gender of a pronoun and the gender of its potential coreferent NP do not match. A gender mismatch effect is typically interpreted as evidence that the parser has attempted to create a binding dependency between the pronoun and the NP. Yoshida et al. created two pairs of conditions, as in (9) and (10).

(9)    a. **His managers** revealed that the studio that notified <u>Jeffrey Stewart</u> about the new film selected a novel for the script, but Annie did not seem to be interested in this information.

b. **Her managers** revealed that the studio that notified <u>Jeffrey Stewart</u> about the new film selected a novel for the script, but Annie did not seem to be interested in this information.

(10)    a. **He** revealed that the studio that notified <u>Jeffrey Stewart</u> about the new film selected a novel for the script, but Annie did not seem to be interested in this information.

b. **She** revealed that the studio that notified <u>Jeffrey Stewart</u> about the new film selected a novel for the script, but Annie did not seem to be interested in this information.

The pair of conditions in (9) instantiates a gender mismatch paradigm between a possessive pronoun (*his/her managers*) and a proper noun inside of a relative clause (*Jeffrey Stewart*). This pair tests whether a binding dependency is actively constructed within relative clause islands in subject position. The pair in (10) is identical, except that the pronoun is no longer possessive (*he/she*). The pronouns in (10) now c-command the critical proper noun, violating Binding Condition C (crucially, the possessive pronouns in (9) do not c-command the critical proper noun, causing no Binding Condition C violation). In this way, (10) replicates the design of previous studies on backward binding and Binding Condition C (e.g. Kazanina et al. 2007). Yoshida et al. found a gender mismatch effect in (9), but not in (10). This suggests that the active search for a coreferent NP is not suppressed within islands, but is suppressed when Binding Condition C would be violated by a c-command relationship between the pronoun and its coreferent NP. Yoshida et al. interpret these results to indicate that island effects cannot be the result of sentence processing complexity driven by the sentence processing mechanisms that backward binding and long-distance dependencies share, otherwise we would expect islands to suppress binding dependencies, contrary to fact.

A recent sentence acceptability experiment by Keshev and Meltzer-Asscher (2019) raises a potential complication for the relationship between binding dependencies and island effects. Keshev and Meltzer-Asscher tested *wh*-islands in Hebrew using both *wh*-dependencies and backward binding dependencies. Hebrew is typically claimed to not have *wh*-island effects (Reinhart 1981). However, Keshev and Meltzer-Asscher find small superadditive interactions for both *wh*-dependencies and backward binding dependencies. Keshev and Meltzer-Asscher point out that the small superadditive effect for *wh*-dependencies looks like a subliminal island effect in the sense of Almeida (2014) (see Section 9.2). They further observe that the existence of a similar small interaction effect for backward binding dependencies could be taken to suggest that superadditive interactions can potentially be caused by something other than a grammatical island constraint, under the assumption that backward binding would not be subject to a grammatical island constraint. This means that it is possible that the superadditive interactions for both *wh*-dependencies and binding dependencies in Hebrew could be driven by a set of shared sentence-processing mechanisms (though the judgment experiments were not designed to isolate those mechanisms). No such interactions have been demonstrated in English (a language that has true *wh*-islands), so these results do not directly complicate the Yoshida et al. (2014) results. Nonetheless, these results add a layer of complication to the assumption that binding dependencies never give rise to effects that look like island effects. These results underscore the need for more research on subliminal island effects with both long-distance dependencies and binding dependencies across languages.

### 9.3.4   Satiation of Judgments

*Satiation* is the term that syntacticians tend to use to describe an increase in the perception of acceptability after repeated exposures to the same sentence or the same structure. As a phenomenon, satiation raises a number of interesting questions, such as whether it is related to the phenomenon of syntactic priming in production and reading time studies (see Do and Kaiser (2017)), and whether satiation as measured in the laboratory is the same phenomenon that professional linguists report after working on one phenomenon for an extended period of time (see Dabrowska (2010) for some investigations of potential differences between linguists and non-linguists). As such, satiation is the topic of its own chapter in this volume (Chapter 6). However, in this chapter, we would like to focus on the claim, to our knowledge first proposed by Snyder (2000), that satiation could be used to distinguish between unacceptability that arises due to the violation of a grammatical constraint and unacceptability that arises due to sentence processing issues, particularly with respect to island effects.

Table 9.1 presents our attempt to summarize the acceptability judgment satiation literature for four island types (we apologize for any studies that we inadvertently left out of this summary).

The first pattern that emerges is that there is no island that consistently shows satiation: adjunct islands do not show satiation in any of these studies, complex NP islands show satiation in 3 out of 10 studies, subject islands show satiation in 4 out of 13, and whether islands show satiation in 6 out of 10. The second pattern that emerges is that none of the obvious properties of these experiments can explain this variability: the results that show satiation span different tasks, different numbers of repetitions, and both the presence and absence of context sentences. The third pattern that emerges is that, for those studies that used a numerical scale and found a significant satiation effect, the size of the effect of satiation is very small: repetition increases the acceptability rating by between .02 and .12

Table 9.1 *A (potentially incomplete) summary of the acceptability judgment satiation literature for four island types. The first column identifies the study. The next four columns summarize information about the experiments: the experiment number, the task – yes/no (YN), magnitude estimation (ME), and five- and seven-point scales (5P and 7P), the number of repetitions of each condition, and whether the items were presented with context sentences. All tested English, except for Christensen et al. (2013), which tested Danish. A plus (+) indicates evidence of satiation according to some statistical test; a dash (–) indicates no evidence of satiation; and a blank cell indicates that the island was not tested. The size column reports the slope of the line of best fit for repetition for those studies that used linear regression as part of the analysis.*

| Study | Exp | Task | Reps | Context | Adjunct | Complex NP | Subject | *Whether* | Size |
|---|---|---|---|---|---|---|---|---|---|
| Snyder 2000 | 1 | YN | 5 | yes | – | + | – | + | |
| Hiramatsu 2000 | 1 | YN | 7 | yes | – | – | + | – | |
| Hiramatsu 2000 | 2 | YN | 7 | yes | – | – | – | + | |
| Sprouse 2009 | 1–3 | YN | 5 | yes | – | – | – | – | |
| Sprouse 2009 | 4–7 | ME | 14 | no | – | – | – | – | |
| Francom 2009 | 1 | YN | 5 | no | – | – | + | + | |
| Francom 2009 | 2 | YN | 5 | no | – | – | – | + | |
| Goodall 2011 | 1 | YN | 5 | yes | – | + | – | | |
| Crawford 2012 | 1 | 7P | 7 | no | – | | – | + | |
| Christensen et al. 2013 | 1 | 5P | 16 | no | | | | + | .12 |
| Christensen et al. 2013 | 2 | 5P | 12 | no | | | | – | |
| Chaves & Dery 2014 | 1 | 7P | 20 | no | | | + | | .02 |
| Chaves & Dery 2014 | 2 | 7P | 14 | no | | | + | | .10 |
| Do & Kaiser 2017 | 1 | 5P | 1 | no | | + | | – | .10 |
| Do & Kaiser 2017 | 2 | 5P | 1 | no | | – | | – | |

units on the scale (i.e. a five-point or seven-point scale) per repetition. For the largest effect, it would take eight repetitions to increase acceptability by approximately one point on the scale. (The reason that the YN tasks show satiation despite these small effects and the relatively low power of the YN task (Sprouse & Almeida 2017) is that the definition of satiation in these studies focuses on a comparison of first blocks to last blocks, and in some cases, ignores data from participants who show no changes in their judgments – two choices that likely increase the chances of detecting small effects.) Taken together, these three patterns suggest that, at a purely empirical level, satiation is unlikely to yield the kind of reliable results that we would need to make the strong claim that different island types should be divided into distinct classes.

We would also like to note that there is a deeper theoretical challenge facing satiation studies – there is no explicit theory of the mechanisms underlying satiation. To be clear, there are a number of phenomena in language studies that satiation could be related to, such as implicit learning (see Luka and Barsalou (2005) for a discussion) or syntactic priming (see

Do and Kaiser (2017) for a discussion). But these phenomena labels do not tell us what the underlying mechanisms are. Without a theory of those mechanisms, we cannot evaluate the proposal that satiation will affect constructions differently depending on the source of the violation (e.g. grammar versus sentence processing). It is clear that there is much work to be done to better understand satiation of island effects, but given that the effects appear to be very small and relatively fragile, we recommend caution to researchers deciding whether to invest significant time or resources in this topic.

## 9.4   Precision in the Data

The third major benefit of formal experimental work (for all phenomena) is that it allows us to increase the precision of our data, thereby potentially increasing the precision of our theories. In this section we will look at four topics in the islands literature for which experimental work is beginning to refine the dataset in potentially theoretically interesting ways: cross-linguistic variation, cross-dependency variation, the effect of complex wh-phrases, and the effect of resumptive pronouns.

### 9.4.1   Cross-Linguistic Variation

It is empirically valuable to establish the extent, and pattern, of cross-linguistic variation for any phenomenon because constraints on variation can help to refine the space of viable theories for that phenomenon (see Chapter 7). Island effects are no different. Much of the literature on island effects has sought to establish what, if any, constraints exist on their variation. When looking at the contribution of formal experimental studies, we think there are two questions that we can profitably ask. The first is whether the pattern that emerges using formal experiments differs in any meaningful way from the pattern that emerges using traditional informal experiments. Table 9.2 presents a list of formal experimental studies on island effects, organized first by language, then by dependency type. The data are reported by island: adjunct, complex NP, subject, relative clause, and wh-islands. For space reasons, we have collapsed all types of adjunct islands into one column, and have collapsed wh-islands and *whether* islands into one column. We restricted our attention to published studies using the (2×2) factorial definition of island effects discussed in Section 9.2 (we apologize for any studies that we have missed). If an island effect was found, we have listed the size of the island effect (the differences-in-differences score) in that cell. The scale column indicates the scale of the effect size – either a z-score scale or a raw judgment scale, with the number of points on the scale indicated in parentheses.

Table 9.2 *A (potentially incomplete) summary of formal experimental studies on island effects. The table is organized by language. The four island columns represent adjunct, complex NP, subject, relative clause, and wh-islands. For space reasons, we collapsed all adjuncts into one column, and both whether islands and wh-islands into one column. The numbers in the island columns indicate the size of the superadditive interaction as measured on the scale listed in the scale column (either a z-score scale or a raw judgment scale with the number of points in parentheses). Most of the effect sizes are reported directly in the articles, but some we estimated from plots (and rounded to two significant digits). A dash (–) indicates no evidence of an island effect; and a blank cell indicates that the island was not tested.*

| Study | Language | Dependency | Adj | NP | Sub | RC | Wh | Scale |
|---|---|---|---|---|---|---|---|---|
| Almeida 2014 | Br. Portuguese | bare *wh* | | | | | 0.6 | z-score |
| Almeida 2014 | Br. Portuguese | Topicalization | | | | | – | z-score |
| Lu et al. 2020 | Chinese | *wh*-arg-in-situ | | | | | 1.5 | raw (7) |
| Lu et al. 2020 | Chinese | *wh*-adj-in-situ | | | | | 1.6 | raw (7) |
| Christensen et al. 2013 | Danish | bare *wh* | | | | | 1.2 | raw (5) |
| Poulsen 2008 | Danish | Topicalization | 4.0 | | | | | raw (5) |
| Sprouse et al. 2016 | English | bare *wh* | 0.7 | 1.1 | 0.6 | | 1.2 | z-score |
| Sprouse et al. 2016 | English | complex *wh* | 0.8 | 0.5 | 0.5 | | 0.6 | z-score |
| Sprouse et al. 2016 | English | rel. clause | – | 0.5 | 0.5 | | 0.4 | z-score |
| Almeida 2014 | English | Topicalization | | | | | – | z-score |
| Sprouse et al. 2011 | English | *wh*-arg-in-situ | – | – | – | | – | z-score |
| Sprouse et al. 2016 | Italian | bare *wh* | 1.3 | 0.9 | 1.4 | | 1.7 | z-score |
| Sprouse et al. 2016 | Italian | rel. clause | 1.1 | 0.6 | – | | 0.7 | z-score |
| Omaki et al. 2019 | Japanese | NP scrambling | | | – | | | z-score |
| Sprouse et al. 2011 | Japanese | *wh*-arg-in-situ | – | – | – | | – | z-score |
| Kim & Goodall 2016 | Korean | *wh*-arg-in-situ | – | | | | 0.3 | z-score |
| Kim & Goodall 2016 | Korean | *wh*-arg-in-situ | – | | | | 0.7 | z-score |
| Ko et al. 2019 | Korean | NP scrambling | – | | | – | | z-score |
| Tucker et al. 2019 | MS Arabic | complex *wh* | 0.8 | 0.5 | | | 0.4 | z-score |
| Kush et al. 2018 | Norwegian | bare *wh* | 1.1 | 1.7 | 1.3 | 1.4 | 0.4 | z-score |
| Kush et al. 2018 | Norwegian | complex *wh* | 1.3 | 1.2 | 1.2 | 1.4 | 0.3 | z-score |
| Kush et al. 2019 | Norwegian | Topicalization | 0.2 | 0.5 | 1.7 | 0.7 | – | z-score |
| Stepanov et al. 2018 | Slovenian | bare *wh* | | | 0.6 | | – | z-score |

From Table 9.2, readers can evaluate any specific claims about cross-linguistic variation that they might have seen in the literature. For example, the Subjacency approach to island effects (explicit in Chomsky (1986), building on work by Rizzi (1982) and Torrego (1984)) makes the strong claim that subject islands and *wh*-islands will covary together (either both present or both absent). This is true for most of the languages in Table 9.2, but we also see that Italian provides evidence of a language with *wh*-islands but not subject islands, and Slovenian provides evidence of a language with subject islands but not *wh*-islands. The Subjacency versus ECP approach to *wh*-in-situ (building on work by Huang 1982) makes the strong claim that *wh*-arguments in situ will not show island effects, but *wh*-adjuncts in situ will. Again, this is true for Japanese, but we also see that

Korean shows *wh*-island effects with *wh*-arguments in situ, and that Chinese shows relative clause islands with *wh*-arguments in situ. The second question we can ask is whether there are any new patterns that emerge in these studies that could be used to constraint theories of island effects. A full evaluation of this question is beyond the scope of this chapter, but we can at least note that there are no obvious universal correlations: there are no two islands that are either always present together or always absent together. It is possible that more complex patterns may exist, or that there may be some sort of implicational hierarchy among island effects. It will take a larger sample of languages to explore these more complex hypotheses.

### 9.4.2   Cross-Dependency Variation and the Uniformity Hypothesis

Another dimension of variation in Table 9.2 above is cross-dependency variation: how island effects vary based on the type of long-distance dependency tested. At times there appears to be an unspoken assumption in the literature that all long-distance dependencies will behave the same with respect to island effects, at least within specific languages. This can be seen in any study that tests one specific kind of long-distance dependency but makes claims about island effects more generally in that language. We will call this assumption the *uniformity hypothesis* so that we can refer to it efficiently. The uniformity hypothesis likely has its roots in considerations of language acquisition – the acquisition process would be more complicated if children had to learn the constraints on each type of long-distance dependency separately. But the uniformity hypothesis appears to be false. Six of the languages in Table 9.2 show variation in island effects based on the dependency type tested. It is, of course, possible that future studies will find confounds in these studies that may explain the variability; but for now, both syntacticians and language acquisition researchers should consider the possibility that the uniformity hypothesis may be false.

### 9.4.3   Complex *Wh*-Phrases and Selective Islands

One proposal in the literature is that island types can be divided into two classes: *unselective islands*, which block extraction of all types of *wh*-items (and presumably all types of long-distance dependencies), and *selective islands*, which block certain types of *wh*-items, and allow others to pass. (Sometimes the terms *strong* and *weak* are used for *unselective* and *selective*, respectively; but these terms are also sometimes misinterpreted as labels for how large the island effect is, so we will use the terms *unselective* and *selective* in this chapter to avoid any ambiguity.) There is quite a bit of debate in the literature about (i) which islands constitute unselective and selective islands, and (ii) which *wh*-items, and heads of other long-distance dependencies, are blocked by selective islands. Despite these debates, there are some recurring claims in the literature. One recurring claim is that complex *wh*-phrases of the form *which* NP, *what* NP, or *which of the* NP are not blocked by selective islands. (Complex *wh*-phrases are also sometimes called d(iscourse)-linked *wh*-phrases in the literature, referring to a specific analysis of their properties (Pesetsky 1987). For this chapter, we prefer the theoretically neutral term *complex wh-phrase*.) Another recurring claim is that *wh*-islands and *whether* islands are selective islands. These two claims are easily characterized using the factorial definition of island effects: a selective island should either show no superadditive interaction for complex *wh*-phrases, or show a smaller superadditive interaction compared to bare *wh*-words. This is another example of formal experiments opening the door to productive investigations of some of the more enduring topics in the islands literature.

Two languages in Table 9.2 were tested using both complex *wh*-phrases and bare *wh*-words: English and Norwegian. In the Sprouse et al. (2016) experiments, English shows superadditive interactions for all four island types tested, with both complex *wh*-phrases and bare *wh*-words. This suggests that, if selectivity is defined as absolute elimination of island effects, there are no selective islands in this group of four island types in English. Though there were significant interactions for all four island types, *whether* islands and complex NP islands showed effect sizes with complex *wh*-phrases that are approximately one half of the size of the effect sizes with bare *wh*-words. This suggests that whether islands and complex NP islands could be considered selective islands in English, as long as selectivity is defined as smaller island effect sizes, and not complete elimination of the island effect. (We should note that Goodall (2015) found a main effect of complex *wh*-phrases that impacted both islands and non-island controls; this would imply that in a full factorial design, the size of the interaction would stay the same between bare *wh*-words and complex *wh*-phrases. The reason for this difference with the Sprouse et al. results remains a mystery.) In the Kush et al. (2018) experiments, Norwegian shows superadditive interactions for all five island types tested, with both complex *wh*-phrases and bare *wh*-words. Only complex NP islands show a reduced effect size with complex *wh*-phrases; however, the resulting effect size is still as large as or larger than effect sizes with bare *wh*-words in other languages. Therefore it is not clear whether complex NP islands should be considered selective islands in Norwegian. If we broaden the definition of selectivity to include other long-distance dependencies that involve NPs, such as relative clauses and topicalization, we see a number of additional effects. In English, *whether* islands and complex NP islands show reduced effect sizes with relative clauses; adjunct islands disappear completely with relative clauses (Sprouse et al. 2016). In both English and Brazilian Portuguese, *whether* islands disappear completely with topicalization (Almeida 2014). In Italian, relative clauses cause subject islands to disappear completely, *wh*-islands to be substantially smaller, and adjunct and complex NP islands to be a bit smaller (Sprouse et al. 2016). And, in Norwegian, topicalization causes whether islands to disappear completely, while adjunct, complex NP, and relative clause islands reduce substantially in size (Kush et al. 2019).

The broadened definition of selectivity entertained at the end of the preceding paragraph raises the question of whether selectivity in its classic, constrained form can be maintained or not. In its classic form, it refers to an invariable set of dependency types (e.g. complex *wh*-phrases), and is a binary phenomenon (an island is either selective or unselective). The broadened definition in the previous paragraph opens the door to considering different sets of dependencies for different islands, and consequently expanding beyond a binary classification (to different types of selective islands). This question interacts directly with the uniformity hypothesis discussed in the previous subsection. Selectivity is a departure from the uniformity hypothesis, as it means that two or more dependencies are behaving differently with respect to one island. Selectivity and the uniformity hypothesis can coexist if selectivity is constrained – for example, there is a long literature starting with Pesetsky (1987) that attempts to explain why it is that complex *wh*-phrases behave differently within selective islands. But once selectivity is no longer constrained, not only does the term selectivity lose meaning, but so too does the uniformity hypothesis.

Before leaving this section, it is important to note that there is a second strand of research on complex *wh*-phrases in the literature that explores their consequences for the *relativized minimality* approach to *wh*-islands (building on work beginning with Rizzi (1990)). Relativized minimality is a general configurational constraint that says no syntactic dependency can hold between two items if a third item of the same type intervenes between them, where *same type* is typically defined in terms of features, such as a *wh*-feature or noun-feature, and *intervenes* is typically defined in terms of c-command, such that the head of the dependency c-commands the intervener, and the intervener c-commands the tail of the dependency (see Rizzi (2013) for a review). Relativized minimality provides a potential analysis for *wh*-islands that does not rely on a specific island constraint: the *wh*-word at the edge of the island structure (the embedded *wh*-clause) intervenes between the *wh*-word at the head of the dependency and the tail of the dependency. Complex *wh*-phrases and bare *wh*-words potentially stand in a complex featural relationship with one another: they both involve a *wh*-feature, but complex *wh*-phrases likely involve an additional feature or features due to the extra specification of the noun. This raises the possibility that the size of the *wh*-island may vary based on the precise featural relationships between the head of the dependency and the intervener: the two can be identical, as in (*wh* ... *wh* ... __) or (*which* NP ... *which* NP ... __), and the two can partially match, as in (*wh* ... *which* NP ... __) or (*which* NP ... *wh* ... __). Atkinson et al. (2015) (English) and Villata et al.

(2016) (French) explore these featural relationships using formal judgment experiments. We do not attempt to summarize the results here because *relativized minimality* is only an analysis for *wh*-islands (not for other island types), and because the results are fairly complex (simultaneously confirming and falsifying various facets of the featural relativized minimality account). But we refer readers interested in relativized minimality and island effects to these articles for discussion of these issues.

### 9.4.4 Resumptive Pronouns

Resumptive pronouns have the formal shape of typical pronouns, but unlike typical pronouns, they appear in the tail position of long-distance dependencies, and are obligatorily coreferent with the item in the head of the long-distance dependency (see McCloskey (2006) for a review). Though there is quite a bit of debate surrounding the correct analysis of resumptive pronouns in the world's languages, many analyses divide languages into (at least) two types: those that allow resumptive pronouns as a completely grammatical option (e.g. Arabic, Hebrew, and Irish), and those that do not allow resumptive pronouns as a grammatical option (e.g. English; often called *intrusive resumption* following Sells (1984)). There are a number of interesting questions about resumptive pronouns, and their properties in different types of languages; as such, resumptive pronouns are the topic of their own chapter in this volume (Chapter 8). In this chapter, we would like to focus on the claim that resumptive pronouns can be used to eliminate island effects, both in languages that allow resumptive pronouns as a grammatical option, and in languages that do not allow resumptive pronouns as a grammatical option (Ross 1967; Kroch 1981; Sells 1984; Engdahl 1985, and much subsequent work).

The claim that resumptive pronouns eliminate or reduce island effects can be directly translated into the factorial definition of island effects: resumptive pronouns should either completely eliminate the superadditive interaction, or substantially decrease the size of the interaction relative to the size of the interaction with gaps. For languages that allow resumptive pronouns as a grammatical option, this would require a 2×2×2 design that uses the typical distance and structure factors, and adds a third factor with gap and resumption as levels (this design often devolves into a 2×2 because resumption languages typically do not allow resumptive pronouns in the matrix subject position, thus eliminating the short level from the distance factor). Tucker et al. (2019) used precisely such a design to study three island types (adjunct, complex NP, and *wh*-islands) with complex *wh*-phrases in Modern Standard Arabic. They found no reduction in the size of the superadditive interactions for resumptive pronouns versus gaps for any of the islands, contrary to the claim in the literature. For languages that do not allow resumptive pronouns as a grammatical option, the full factorial design cannot be used, because

Table 9.3 *A (potentially incomplete) summary of studies on resumptive pronouns using formal acceptability judgment methods. The scale column indicates the task: forced choice between two sentences (FC), comprehensibility (compr.) with the number of points on the scale indicated in parentheses, and acceptability (accept.) with the number of points on the scale indicated in parentheses. Most of the effect sizes are reported directly in the articles, but some we estimated from plots (and rounded to two significant digits). A dash (–) indicates no effect of resumption; and a blank cell indicates that the island was not tested.*

| Study | Language | Dependency | Adj | NP | Sub | RC | Wh | Scale |
|---|---|---|---|---|---|---|---|---|
| Alexopoulou & Keller 2007 | English | bare *wh* | | | | – | – | |
| Ackerman et al. 2018 | English | complex *wh* | 0.2 | | | 0.4 | 0.5 | FC |
| Omaki & Nakao 2010 | English | complex *wh* | – | | | | | |
| Beltrama & Xiang 2016 | English | rel. clause | | | | 0.4 | | compr. (7) |
| Beltrama & Xiang 2016 | English | rel. clause | | | | – | | accept. (7) |
| Heestand et al. 2011 | English | rel. clause | – | – | | – | | |
| Keffala 2013 | English | rel. clause | | | | 0.7 | 0.6 | accept. (11) |
| Morgan & Wagers 2018 | English | rel. clause | – | – | | – | | |
| Alexopoulou & Keller 2007 | German | bare *wh* | | | | – | – | |
| Alexopoulou & Keller 2007 | Greek | bare *wh* | | | | – | – | |
| Beltrama & Xiang 2016 | Italian | rel. clause | | | | 0.4 | | compr. (7) |
| Keshev & Meltzer-Asscher 2017 | Hebrew | rel. clause | | | 1.2 | | | accept. (7) |
| Tucker et al. 2019 | MS Arabic | bare *wh* | – | – | | | 0.1 | z-score |
| Tucker et al. 2019 | MS Arabic | complex *wh* | 0.5 | – | | | – | z-score |

resumptive pronouns cannot appear in non-island structures (so there would be a non-monotonic interaction). Therefore most studies in these languages focus on the relative difference between resumptive pronouns and gaps within islands (sometimes with additional conditions showing that resumptive pronouns are unacceptable in non-island structures). In Table 9.3, we list formal experimental studies on resumptive pronouns, organized first by language, and then by dependency type (and again we apologize for any studies that we inadvertently left off). This table includes both types of languages: languages without grammatical resumption (intrusive resumption) appear first, and languages with grammatical resumption appear second (below the solid horizontal line). For all languages without grammatical resumption and for the Keshev and Meltzer-Asscher (2017) Hebrew results, the data in the cells reports the relative difference between resumptive pronouns and gaps within island structures. For the Tucker et al. (2019) Modern Standard Arabic results, the cells report the change in the size of the differences-in-differences score in a factorial design.

Three patterns emerge in Table 9.3. The first is that resumption effects are not particularly reliable. There is no island that shows a resumption effect every time that it is tested. The second is that the effect appears to be difficult to detect with rating-scale acceptability judgment tasks. Only one rating-scale sentence acceptability study detected an effect in a language that does not allow grammatical resumption (Keffala 2013). The other positive results are either for languages that allow resumption as a grammatical option, or for other tasks, such as the forced-choice task of Ackerman et al. (2018) or the comprehensibility task of Beltrama and Xiang (2016). The difficulty of detecting an effect in judgments, coupled with the relative ease of eliciting resumptive pronouns in production tasks (Ferreira & Swets 2005; Morgan & Wagers 2018), could itself be a piece of evidence about the nature of resumptive pronouns in languages that do not allow resumption. The third pattern is that the resumption effect is very small in languages that do not allow resumption as a grammatical option. In the Beltrama and Xiang (2016) and Keffala (2013) results, the resumption effect is only about 6 percent of the size of the scale of the task. In languages that do allow resumption as a grammatical option, the effect is about twice as large (Keshev & Meltzer-Asscher 2017; Tucker et al. 2019). Taken together, these results suggest that, while there is certainly some empirical support for the claim that resumptive pronouns increase the acceptability of island effects, the effect is far less robust, and far smaller, than traditional studies had suggested. In many ways, resumption resembles satiation – the variability across studies suggests that more research is necessary to understand the phenomenon; but that variability also suggests that researchers should exercise caution in deciding to invest time and resources in this topic.

## 9.5 Moving Forward

In this chapter we focused on three benefits of formal experiments, and how they have helped to expand our knowledge of island effects, from exploring the definition of island effects, to probing the source of island effects, to increasing the precision of the data on the various properties of island effects. In this last section, we would like to briefly mention some of the patterns that are emerging in recent work on island effects in the hopes that it may help researchers formulate their own studies. One major pattern that is emerging is the role that differences in effect sizes may play in the theory. We see this both in fundamental questions such as whether subliminal island effects should be considered the same kind of effect as traditional island effects, and in higher-order questions such as whether the smaller effect sizes that we see with complex *wh*-phrases should be interpreted as selectivity or not. Exploring these questions will require both a concerted effort to quantify effect sizes in a comparable way across languages and dependency types, and a concerted effort to create a theory of the factors that can influence effect sizes. This is no small challenge – we know of no domain of cognitive science that has a substantive theory of effect sizes. Another major pattern that is emerging is that cross-linguistic and cross-dependency variation is similar to what has been reported using traditional informal experiments, but not quite identical. This suggests that there is real empirical value in systematically retesting languages for island effects, both to establish the range of variation across languages, and the range of variation within long-distance dependency types. Finally, it is apparent that much more work is needed to explore the space of possible sources of island effects, both within sentence processing and within the domains of grammatical theory. This work is likely to require creative thinking about the types of predictions that these theories make beyond basic acceptability judgment patterns, as all of these theories can typically explain these basic facts. The studies that push the field forward are likely to combine sentence acceptability studies with other data types, such as working memory measures, reading times, EEG, and semantic or pragmatic tasks.

## References

Abrusán, M. (2014). *Weak Island Semantics*. Oxford: Oxford University Press.

Ackerman, L., Frazier, M., & Yoshida, M. (2018). Resumptive pronouns can ameliorate illicit island extractions. *Linguistic Inquiry*, 49, 847–859.

Alexopoulou, T. & Keller, F. (2007). Locality, cyclicity, and resumption: At the interface between the grammar and the human sentence processor. *Language*, 83, 110–160.

Almeida, D. (2014). Subliminal *wh*-islands in Brazilian Portuguese and the consequences for syntactic theory. *Revista da ABRALIN*, 13.55–93. DOI: 10.5380/rabl.v13i2 .39611.

Atkinson, E., Apple, A. Rawlins, K., & Omaki, A. (2015). Similarity of *wh*-phrases and acceptability variation in *wh*-islands. *Frontiers in Psychology*, 6, 2048.

Beltrama, A. & Xiang, M. (2016). Unacceptable but comprehensible: the facilitation effect of resumptive pronouns. *Glossa: A Journal of General Linguistics*, 1(1), 29. DOI:10.5334/gjgl.24

Chaves, R. P. & Dery, J. E. (2014). Which subject islands will the acceptability of improve with repeated exposure? In R. E. Santana-La Barge, ed., *Proceedings of the 31st West Coast Conference on Formal Linguistics*. Somerville, MA: Cascadilla Proceedings Project, pp. 96–106.

Chomsky, N. (1986). *Barriers*. Cambridge, MA: MIT Press.

Christensen, K. R., Kizach, J., & Nyvad, A. M. (2013). Escape from the island: Grammaticality and (reduced) acceptability of *wh*-island violations in Danish. *Journal of Psycholinguistic Research*, 42, 51–70.

Clifton, C. & Frazier, L. (1989) Comprehending sentences with long-distance dependencies. In G. N. Carlson & M. K., Tanenhaus, eds., *Linguistic Structure in Language Processing* (Studies in Theoretical Psycholinguistics 7). Dordrecht: Springer, pp. 273–317.

Crain, S. & Fodor, J. D. (1985). How can grammars help parsers? In D. Dowty, L. Kartuunen, & A. Zwicky, eds., *Natural Language Parsing: Psychological, Computational, and Theoretical Perspectives*. Cambridge: Cambridge University Press.

Crawford, J. (2012). Using syntactic satiation to investigate subject islands. In J. Choi, E. A. Hogue, J. Punske, D. Tat, J. Schertz, & A. Trueman, eds., *Proceedings of the 29th West Coast Conference on Formal Linguistics*. Somerville, MA: Cascadilla Proceedings Project, pp. 38–45.

Culicover, P. W. & Postal, P. M. (eds.). (2001). *Parasitic Gaps*. Cambridge, MA: MIT Press.

Dąbrowska, E. (2010). Naive v. expert intuitions: An empirical study of acceptability judgments. *The Linguistic Review*, 27(1), 1–23.

Do, M. L. & Kaiser, E. (2017). The relationship between syntactic satiation and syntactic priming: A first look. *Frontiers in Psychology*, 8, 1851.

Engdahl, E. (1983). Parasitic gaps. *Linguistic Inquiry*, 6, 5–34.

Engdahl, E. (1985). Parasitic gaps, resumptive pronouns, and subject extractions. *Linguistics*, 23, 3–44.

Erteschik-Shir, N. (1973). On the nature of island constraints. Doctoral dissertation, Massachusetts Institute of Technology.

Featherston, S. (2005). Magnitude estimation and what it can do for your syntax: Some *wh* constraints in German. *Lingua*, 115, 1525–1550.

Ferreira, F. & Swets, B. (2005). The production and comprehension of resumptive pronouns in relative clause "island" contexts. In A. Cutler, ed., *Twenty-First Century Psycholinguistics: Four Cornerstones*. New York: Routledge, pp. 263–278.

Francom, J. C. (2009). Experimental syntax: Exploring the effect of repeated exposure to anomalous syntactic structure – evidence from rating and reading tasks. Doctoral dissertation, University of Arizona.

Frazier, L. & d'Arcais, G. B. F. (1989). Filler driven parsing: A study of gap filling in Dutch. *Journal of Memory and Language*, 28(3), 331–344.

Freedman, S. E. & Forster, K. I. (1985). The psychological status of over-generated sentences. *Cognition*, 19(2), 101–131.

Garnsey, S., Tanenhaus, M., & Chapman, R. (1989). Evoked potentials and the study of sentence comprehension. *Journal of Psycholinguistic Research*, 18, 51–60.

Goldberg, A. (2006). *Constructions at Work*. Oxford: Oxford University Press.

Goodall, G. (2011). Syntactic satiation and the inversion effect in English and Spanish *wh*-questions. *Syntax*, 14(1), 29–47.

Goodall, G. (2015). The D-linking effect on extraction from islands and non-islands. *Frontiers in Psychology*, 5, 1493.

Heestand, D., Xiang, M., & Polinsky, M. (2011). Resumption still does not rescue islands. *Linguistic Inquiry*, 42(1), 138–152.

Hiramatsu, K. (2000). Accessing linguistic competence: Evidence from children's and adults' acceptability judgments. Doctoral dissertation, University of Connecticut, Storrs.

Hofmeister, P. & Sag, I. A. (2010). Cognitive constraints and island effects. *Language*, 86: 366–415.

Hofmeister, P., Staum Casasanto, L., & Sag, I. A. (2012). How do individual cognitive differences relate to acceptability judgments? A reply to Sprouse, Wagers, and Phillips. *Language*, 88(2), 390–400.

Huang, C. T. J. (1982). Logical relations in Chinese and the theory of grammar. Doctoral dissertation, Massachusetts Institute of Technology.

Kaan, E., Harris, A., Gibson, E., & Holcomb, P. (2000). The P600 as an index of syntactic integration difficulty. *Language and Cognitive Processes*, 15, 159–201.

Kazanina, N., Lau, E. F., Lieberman, M., Yoshida, M., & Phillips, C. (2007). The effect of syntactic constraints on the processing of backwards anaphora. *Journal of Memory and Language*, 56, 384–409.

Keffala, B. (2013). Resumption and gaps in English relative clauses: Relative acceptability creates an illusion of 'saving.' In C. Cathchart, I.-H. Chen, G. Finley, S. Kang, C. S. Sandy, & E. Stickles, eds., *Proceedings of the 37th Annual Meeting of the Berkeley Linguistics Society*. Berkeley, CA: University of California, Berkeley Linguistics Society, pp. 140–154.

Keller, F. (2000). Gradience in grammar: experimental and computational aspects of degrees of grammaticality. Doctoral dissertation, University of Edinburgh.

Keshev, M. & Meltzer-Asscher, A. (2017). Active dependency formation in islands: How grammatical resumption affects sentence processing. *Language*, 93, 549–68.

Keshev, M. & Meltzer-Asscher, A. (2019). A processing-based account of subliminal *wh*-island effects. *Natural Language & Linguistic Theory*, 37(2), 621–657.

Kim, B. & Grant, G. (2016). Islands and non-islands in native and heritage Korean. *Frontiers in Psychology*, 7, 134.

Kluender, R. & Kutas, M. (1993). Subjacency as a processing phenomenon. *Language and Cognitive Processes*, 8, 573–633.

Ko, H., Chung, H.-B., Kim, K., & Sprouse, J. (2019). An experimental study on scrambling out of islands: To the left and to the right. *Language & Information Society*, 37.

Kroch, A. (1981). On the role of resumptive pronouns in amnestying island constraint violations. In R. Hendrick, C. Maseh, & M. Miller, eds., *Papers from the 17th Regional Meeting, Chicago Linguistic Society*. Chicago: Chicago Linguistic Society, pp. 125–135.

Kurtzman, H. S. & Crawford, L. F. (1991). Processing parasitic gaps. In T. Sherer, ed., *Proceedings of the 21st Annual Meeting of the North East Linguistic Society*. Amherst, MA: LSA Publications, pp. 217–231.

Kush, D., Lohndal, T., & Sprouse, J. (2018). Investigating variation in island effects: A case study of Norwegian *wh*-extraction. *Natural Language and Linguistic Theory*, 36, 743–779.

Kush, D., Lohndal, T., & Sprouse, J. (2019). On the island sensitivity of topicalization in Norwegian: An experimental investigation. *Language*, 95(3), 393–420.

Loftus, G. R. (1978). On interpretation of interactions. *Memory & Cognition*, 6, 312–319.

Lu, J., Thompson, C., & Yoshida, M. (2020). Chinese *wh*-in-situ and islands: A formal judgment study. *Linguistic Inquiry*, 51(3), 611–623.

Luka, B. J. & Barsalou, L. W. (2005). Structural facilitation: Mere exposure effects for grammatical acceptability as evidence for syntactic priming in comprehension. *Journal of Memory and Language*, 52, 436–459.

Matchin, W., Sprouse, J., & Hickok, G. (2014). A structural distance effect for backward anaphora in Broca's area: An fMRI study. *Brain and Language*, 138, 1–11.

Maxwell, S. E. & Delaney, H. D. (2003). *Designing Experiments and Analyzing Data: A Model Comparison Perspective*. Abingdon: Routledge.

Maxwell, S. E., Delaney, H. D., & Kelley, K. (2017). *Designing Experiments and Analyzing Data: A Model Comparison Perspective*, 2nd ed. Abingdon: Routledge.

McCloskey, J. (2006). Resumption. In M. Everaert & H. van Riemsdijk, eds., *The Blackwell Companion to Syntax*. Oxford: Blackwell, pp. 94–117.

McKinnon, R. & Osterhout, L. (1996). Event-related potentials and sentence processing: Evidence for the status of constraints on movement phenomena. *Language and Cognitive Processes*, 11, 495–523.

Michel, D. (2014). Individual cognitive measures and working memory accounts of syntactic island phenomena. Doctoral dissertation, University of California, San Diego.

Morgan, A. M. & Wagers, M. W. (2018). English resumptive pronouns are more common where gaps are less acceptable. *Linguistic Inquiry*, 49(4), 861–876.

Neville, H. J., Nicol, J., Barss, A., Forster, K. I., & Garrett, M. F. (1991). Syntactically based sentence processing classes: Evidence from event-related brain potentials. *Journal of Cognitive Neuroscience*, 3, 151–165.

Omaki, A., Fukuda, S., Nakao, C., & Polinsky, M. (2020). Subextraction in Japanese and subject–object symmetry. *Natural Language & Linguistic Theory*, **38**, 627–669.

Omaki, A., Lau, E. F., Davidson White, I., Dakan, M. L., Apple, A., & Phillips, C. (2015). Hyper-active gap filling. *Frontiers in Psychology*, 6, 384.

Omaki, A. & Nakao, C. (2010). Does English resumption really help to repair island violations? *Snippets*, 21, 11–12.

Pesetsky, D. (1987). *Wh*-in-situ: Movement and unselective binding. In E. Reuland & A. ter Meulen, eds., *The Representation of (In)definiteness*. Cambridge, MA: MIT Press, pp. 98–129.

Phillips, C. (2006). The real-time status of island constraints. *Language*, 82, 795–823.

Phillips, C. (2013a). On the nature of island constraints. I: Language processing and reductionist accounts. In J. Sprouse & N. Hornstein, eds., *Experimental Syntax and Island Effects*. Cambridge: Cambridge University Press, pp. 64–108.

Phillips, C. (2013b). On the nature of island constraints. II: Language learning and innateness. In J. Sprouse & N. Hornstein, eds., *Experimental Syntax and Island Effects*. Cambridge: Cambridge University Press, pp. 132–157.

Pickering, M. J., Barton, S., & Shillcock, R. (1994). Unbounded dependencies, island constraints, and processing complexity. In C. Clifton, Jr., L. Frazier, & K. Rayner, eds., *Perspectives on Sentence Processing*. London: Lawrence Erlbaum, pp. 199–224.

Poulsen, M. (2008). Acceptability and processing of long-distance dependencies in Danish. *Nordic Journal of Linguistics*, 31, 73–107.

Reinhart, T. (1981). A second COMP position. In A. Belletti, L. Brandi, & L. Rizzi, eds., *Theory of Markedness in Generative Grammar*. Pisa: Scuola Normale Superiore, pp. 517–557.

Rizzi, L. (1982). Violations of the *wh*-island constraint and the subjacency condition. In L. Rizzi, ed., *Issues in Italian Syntax*. Dordrecht: Foris, pp. 49–76.

Rizzi, L. (1990). *Relativized Minimality*. Cambridge, MA: MIT Press.

Rizzi, L. (2013). Locality. *Lingua*, 130, 169–186.

Ross, J. R. (1967). Constraints on variables in syntax. Doctoral dissertation, Massachusetts Institute of Technology. [Published as *Infinite Syntax!*, Norwood, NJ: Ablex, 1986.]

Sells, P. (1984). Syntax and semantics of resumptive pronouns. Doctoral dissertation, University of Massachusetts, Amherst.

Snyder, W. (2000). An experimental investigation of syntactic satiation effects. *Linguistic Inquiry*, 31, 575–582.

Sprouse, J. (2007). A program for experimental syntax. Doctoral dissertation, University of Maryland.

Sprouse, J. (2009). Revisiting satiation: Evidence for a response equalization strategy. *Linguistic Inquiry*, 40, 329–341.

Sprouse, J. & Almeida, D. (2017). Design sensitivity and statistical power in acceptability judgment experiments. *Glossa: A Journal of General Linguistics*, 2(1), 1–32. DOI:10.5334/gjgl.236

Sprouse, J., Caponigro, I., Greco, C., & Cecchetto, C. (2016). Experimental syntax and the variation of island effects in English and Italian. *Natural Language and Linguistic Theory*, 34, 307–344.

Sprouse, J., Fukuda, S., Ono, H., & Kluender, R. (2011). Reverse island effects and the backward search for a licensor in multiple *wh*-questions. *Syntax*, 14, 179–203.

Sprouse, J. & Messick, T. (2015). How gradient are island effects? Poster presented at NELS 46.

Sprouse, J., Wagers, M., & Phillips, C. (2012). A test of the relation between working memory capacity and syntactic island effects. *Language*, 88, 82–123.

Stepanov, A., Mušič, M., & Stateva, P. (2018). Two (non-)islands in Slovenian: A study in experimental syntax. *Linguistics*, 56(3), 435–476.

Stowe, L. A. (1986). Parsing *WH*-constructions: Evidence for on-line gap location. *Language and Cognitive Processes*, 3, 227–245.

Sturt, P. (2003). The time-course of the application of binding constraints in reference resolution. *Journal of Memory and Language*, 48(3), 542–562.

Szabolcsi, A. & Lohndal, T. (2017). Strong vs. weak islands. In M. Everaert & H. C. Riemsdijk, eds., *The Wiley Blackwell Companion to Syntax*, 2nd ed. New York: John Wiley & Sons.

Szabolcsi, A. & Zwarts, F. (1993). Weak islands and an algebraic semantics of scope taking. *Natural Language Semantics*, 1, 235–284.

Torrego, E. (1984). On inversion in Spanish and some of its effects. *Linguistic Inquiry*, 15, 103–129.

Traxler, M. J. & Pickering, M. J. (1996). Plausibility and the processing of unbounded dependencies: An eye-tracking study. *Journal of Memory and Language*, 35: 454–475.

Tucker, M. A., Idrissi, A., Sprouse, J., & Almeida, D. (2019). Resumption ameliorates different islands differentially: Acceptability data from Modern Standard Arabic. In A. Khalfaoui & M. A. Tucker, eds., *Perspectives on Arabic Linguistics, 30: Papers from the Annual Symposia on Arabic Linguistics, Stony Brook, New York, 2016 and Norman, Oklahoma, 2017.* Amsterdam: John Benjamins, pp. 159–193.

Van Gompel, R. P. & Liversedge, S. P. (2003). The influence of morphological information on cataphoric pronoun assignment. *Journal of Experimental Psychology: Learning, Memory, and Cognition*, 29(1), 128.

Villata, S., Rizzi, L., & Franck, J. (2016). Intervention effects and relativized minimality: New experimental evidence from graded judgments. *Lingua*, 179, 76–96.

Wagenmakers, E., Krypotos, A., Criss, A. H., & Iverson, G. (2012). On the interpretation of removable interactions: A survey of the field 33 years after Loftus. *Memory and Cognition*, 40, 145–160.

Wagers, M. W. & Phillips, C. (2009). Multiple dependencies and the role of the grammar in real-time comprehension. *Journal of Linguistics*, 45, 395–433.

Yoshida, M., Kazanina, N., Pablos, L., & Sturt, P. (2014). On the origin of islands. *Language, Cognition and Neuroscience*, 29, 761–770.

# 10

# The *That*-Trace Effect

Wayne Cowart and Dana McDaniel

## 10.1 Introduction

The *that*-trace effect (or COMP-trace effect) is one of the most discussed phenomena in generative syntax.[1] The effect was first described for French and English by David Perlmutter (1968, 1971) and is evident in cases such as these.

(1)    a. no-*that* object extraction
          Who did Sue think [Bill admired *t*]

       b. no-*that* subject extraction
          Who did Sue think [*t* admired Bill]

       c. *that* object extraction
          Who did Sue think [that Bill admired *t*]

       d. *that* object extraction
          * Who did Sue think [that *t* admired Bill]

Crucially, these cases involve a so-called "bridge verb" (*think* in this instance). Members of this small class of verbs tend to be relatively heavily used. They are unusual in that they allow a finite clause (CP) as their complement and provide a computational "bridge" (presumed to be the specifier of the CP node) whereby *wh*-elements originating inside the lower clause move across the clause boundary to surface as the specifier of CP in the higher clause; hence the structures are examples of "long-distance" (LD) extraction or movement. The element in the original position is a "trace" (*t* in the above examples).[2]

---

[1] Given that our primary concerns are methodological, here we offer only a brief sketch of the wide range of accounts that have been offered for *that*-trace phenomena. For a thorough review of this literature see Pesetsky (2017).

[2] There is a variety of accounts of movement structures, and different ways of analyzing the element termed "trace." Our use of the term is not meant to reflect any particular analysis.

Among the four examples here, (1a) and (1b) suggest that extraction of either subjects or non-subjects from the finite lower clause is acceptable, while (1a) and (1c) suggest that the overt complementizer *that* is optional in this environment, both properties being unremarkable in English. Nevertheless, in (1d) subject extraction seems to be blocked, at least superficially, by the fact that the complementizer *that* sits immediately left of a trace. Hence this is an instance of the *that*-trace effect, a conditional asymmetry where both subject and object extraction are allowed without *that*, but only object extraction is allowed with it.

Perlmutter's work included extensive consideration of languages that manifest the effect (French and English) and others that did not (Spanish and Serbo-Croatian). Subsequent work expanded both these lists. The effect appears in varieties of Arabic and some African languages (Nupe, Wolof), among others, but not in null subject languages.

From early on the *that*-trace effect was seen as a matter of considerable theoretical interest. Why there should be such an asymmetry between subject and non-subject extraction was, and remains, a mystery. Fundamental questions about the mind arise because the effect seems to manifest only in structures that may be so rare as to make the pattern unlearnable. If this is true, it suggests a Poverty of the Stimulus argument to the effect that innate properties of grammars – or the linguistic system as a whole – somehow determine features of sentences independently of their frequency of use (Phillips 2013).

This phenomenon is a challenge to theoretical syntax; the pattern of judgments that manifests the effect is easy to state, evident in a number of unrelated languages, absent from a definable class of others, and yet so far unexplained despite 50 years of investigation. A great many different approaches to the phenomenon have been explored, including those that focus on the linear structure of the surface string as well as those that look for an explanation based on hierarchical syntactic structure. Earlier approaches assumed that Universal Grammar (UG) provides a rich set of syntactic constraints whereas more recent approaches attempt to work within a much more spare conception of UG compatible with the Minimalist Program (Chomsky 1995). Somewhat further afield, there are accounts that place the phenomenon outside syntax proper, in domains such as prosody, information structure, or processing.

Another aspect of differing accounts is that they vary in the range of phenomena that are seen as analogous to the *that*-trace effect. An early example was Bresnan's (1977) generalization of the effect to all complementizers. Other examples of possibly analogous structures include adjunct extraction, agreeing complementizers, islands, and relative clauses.

The phenomenon is of particular interest in relation to the present volume because it has been approached experimentally by a number of investigators looking at a variety of languages, and those results have in some instances challenged the data on which syntactic analyses have generally relied, including the core contrasts in (1). The body of work on *that*-trace exemplifies both the need for and the benefits of experimental methods (see additional discussion in Chapters 1 and 7). Furthermore this body of research also provides a useful framework for considering questions about the relation between conventional judgment methods and experimental approaches.

## 10.2  Experimental Findings on the *That*-Trace Effect

Experimental work on the *that*-trace effect has contributed to our understanding of the phenomenon in two broad ways: (i) it has allowed us to test the validity of the core contrasts shown in (1) across languages/dialects, and (ii) it has been used to test accounts of the phenomenon. The bulk of this research has focused on Germanic languages/dialects, primarily English and German. We will survey some important findings, starting with those that concern the core contrasts in English (Section 10.2.1) and other Germanic languages (Section 10.2.2), and then giving some examples of those that test accounts (Section 10.2.3). We will limit our discussion to studies that report experimental data on judged acceptability. We will be looking at them in light of the distinction discussed above between taking the judgment of a single person confronting a single sentence as the object of inquiry and taking the average judgment of a linguistic community as the object of inquiry.

### 10.2.1   The Core Contrasts in English

As far as we know, Sobin (1987) was the first to explore the *that*-trace effect experimentally in a group of native speakers. He reports hearing from other linguists that they had encountered English speakers who accepted all four of the core *that*-trace sentence types, and cites White (1986: 13), who noted that a native-speaker control group in an L2 study had given the *that* subject extraction structure an unexpectedly high rating. Sobin conducted his experiment to investigate these reports systematically. His participants were native English-speaking undergraduates who were primarily from Iowa or Illinois. The sentence list included the four core types illustrated in (1), as well as extraction over *whether* (e.g. *Who do you wonder whether Tina saw?*), the core cases with an adverb at the front of the lower clause (e.g. *Who do you think that actually saw Tom?*) and various other structures. Three instances of each sentence type appeared on the list. Participants, who were seen individually, were given the list of sentences and were read each one and asked to repeat it, and then to place it in one of three categories: (i) a sentence they would say, (ii) a possible English sentence that they might hear or read, or (iii) an odd-sounding sentence that they wouldn't expect to encounter. The results indicated a higher than expected acceptance of the *that* subject extraction structure; in fact, there was no significant difference between those items and a structure that is taken to be grammatical (specifically, declaratives with *want* and the complementizer *for*, e.g. *I want for Mary to see Bill*). The *whether* subject extraction structures were also rejected significantly more than the *that* subject extraction structures. Interestingly, the adverbs appeared to have no effect, even though they are often considered to increase the acceptability of the *that* subject extraction structure. In light of his findings, Sobin proposed the existence of two versions of a *wh*/complementizer fusion rule licensing a subject trace, which accounted for the variation among English speakers, as well as for other reported cross-linguistic variation regarding the grammaticality of the *that* subject extraction structure.

Since Sobin conducted the study with participants from the US Midwest, the descriptive characterization of his findings was often put in terms of a regional dialect difference. In order to investigate the status of the core contrasts further, Cowart (1997, 2003) conducted a series of experiments on the phenomenon, including an initial study in a single localized population followed by two cross-regional investigations. The methodology was based on the approach to experimental syntax that he had proposed, which imported standard methods from psychology. The properties of these experiments are listed in (2).

(2)   Properties of Cowart's (1997, 2003) experiments

- Factorial design (e.g. the 2×2 structure of conditions represented in (1))
- Materials:
  - The materials were built as token sets, where each token set implemented all of the cells of the factorial design with four nearly identical sentences.
  - The materials were constructed with a view to minimizing effects attributable to frequency of lexical items, overall naturalness, sentence length, parsability, and ambiguity, both within and across token sets.
  - Applying the general notion of a Latin square, counterbalancing distributed each token set such that each participant saw exactly one version of every token set, and equal numbers of items representing each of the cells of the factorial design.
  - Filler items were included with a view to instantiating multiple levels of acceptability, including very low levels. The number of filler items exceeded the number of experimental items by a factor of at least two.
  - In order to suppress context effects, each questionnaire was matched to one or more other questionnaires that included exactly the same content. However, the materials were ordered differently on each member of a matched set of questionnaires.

- Measures: Various category scale techniques, as well as some aimed at getting ratio scale data, modeled on magnitude estimation techniques in psychophysics (Stevens 1975).
- Participants: The study sizes ranged from approximately three dozen total to more than 100 per demographic category.
- Instrument: Participants were given a written questionnaire.
- Analysis: Formal statistical tests were applied to all the factors (fixed and random) encoded in the design. Such techniques take account of two sources of variance intrinsic to almost any experiment on language: variance due to the participants and variance due to the specific materials presented to those participants.

Both an initial local study and two cross-regional ones found a robust *that*-trace effect. The results of the initial study are shown in Figure 10.1. (Note that the graph also shows a reliable difference between the two object extraction cases. We will return to this finding below.)

In the cross-regional studies, there was no evidence for regional variation, even though two of the regions (Iowa and Nebraska) were in the Midwest (see Chapter 7 for additional discussion). Figure 10.2 shows the results from one of these studies.

Cowart conducted a follow-up study with a local sample of 55 participants in order to investigate the possibility of individual (region-independent) dialect variation. Each participant judged twice as many sentences in each category of the design as in typical experiments of this type. Although there was individual variation, there was no evidence of clustering that would indicate stable dialectal groupings. This is shown in Figure 10.3, where the *x*-axis represents the difference between the no-*that* structures, and the *y*-axis represents the difference between the two *that* structures (subject minus object).

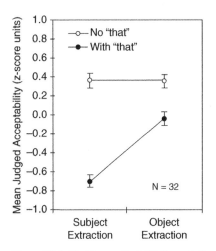

**Figure 10.1** *That*-trace effect (W. Cowart, *Experimental Syntax: Applying Objective Methods to Sentence Judgments*, Figure 4, p. 19, © 1997 by permission of Sage)

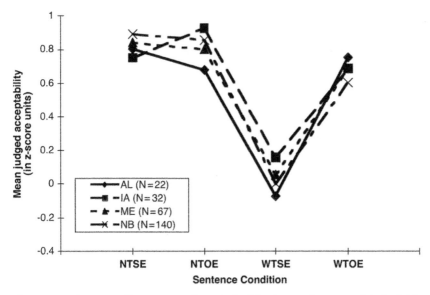

**Figure 10.2** *That*-trace effect across regions: Each of the four *x*-axis category labels of this graph corresponds to one of the four data points in Figure 10.1 (NTSE = No That/ Subject Extraction, NTOE = No That/Object Extraction, etc.; AL = Alabama, IA = Iowa, ME = Maine, NB = Nebraska) (Cowart 2003: Figure 3)

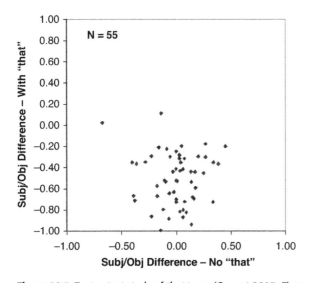

**Figure 10.3** Test, retest study of *that*-trace (Cowart 2003: Figure 1)

Almost all of the points are distributed in the same area, centered toward the lower end of the acceptability scale for cases with *that* but toward the middle of the scale for those without *that*, indicating a subject/object asymmetry for the *that* structures and no difference between the no-*that* structures. A population split between participants with the *that*-trace effect and those without an asymmetry in the *that* structures would show up on the graph as (at least) two distinct clusters. There may be a temptation to interpret the two uppermost data points as evidence of distinct dialects, but the variability of the dataset as a whole makes it highly unlikely that those differences are meaningful or replicable.

Furthermore, the same 55 participants were given the same experiment a second time. They were classified by *that*-trace dialect type on the basis of their responses separately for each round. If this procedure detects the dialect-specific properties of individual participants, classification on the first round should predict classification on the second round. But it did not. The reason why it did not may be that there are simply no dialect differences, or (more plausibly) that it takes a great deal more participant-specific data to detect reliable differences of this kind. The issue engaged here is about the contrast between strong population-specific behavioral tendencies and strong individual-specific differences. What the evidence discussed here suggests is that, as with many other domains, reliably detecting systematic differences across individuals calls for the collection of much more individual-specific evidence.

Up to this point, we have been focusing on questions of reliability across participants. Here we turn to the stability of the *that*-trace effect within each bridge verb. Figure 10.4 displays data collected in a large experiment with 332 participants distributed across three localities in the US (Nebraska: 192, Alabama: 33, Maine: 107). The data are organized into 20 cells by the verb on which each token set was based. Within each cell, there are three four-point lines, each representing the pattern of results for one of the three localities. In spite of the large overall number of participants, the number contributing to each data point in each cell is small, complicating statistical analysis. However, for each verb, the figure exhibits striking agreement across the three geographic cohorts on the pattern for that particular verb. The differences among the patterns across the verbs are noteworthy.

We now turn to another aspect of core *that*-trace contrasts that Cowart's experimental work uncovered, which we refer to as the "*that*-effect." The standard description of the *that*-trace effect in English is as a 3–1 contrast, with three grammatical structures and one ungrammatical. However, in Figure 10.1 above, the *that* object extraction structure, though significantly better than the *that* subject extraction structure, is reliably less acceptable than the no-*that* object extraction counterpart. This finding was replicated in all of the experiments discussed above, as well as others, totaling over 1,000 participants. The theoretical implications of this empirical result are largely unexplored.

Given the demonstrated variation in bridge verbs, it is possible that the *that*-effect, as manifest in the object extraction cases, is a consequence of a bias in particular verbs. In this case, the lower acceptability rating of the

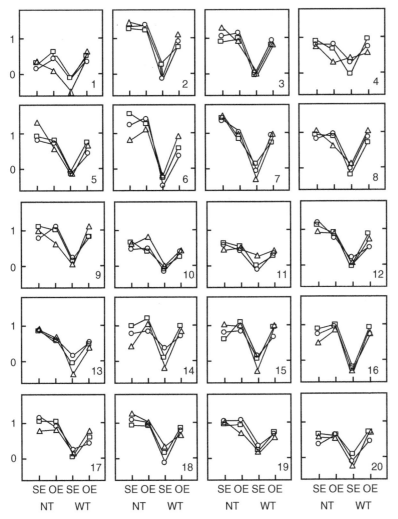

**Figure 10.4** *That*-trace effect across verbs. The verbs used (in the order presented above) are: *imagine, suppose, hope, announce, expect, think, feel, suspect, say, pretend, hear, assume, bet, insist, proclaim, wish, believe, presume, claim, dream* (W. Cowart, *Experimental Syntax: Applying Objective Methods to Sentence Judgments*, Figure 36, Appendix D, p. 164, © 1997 by permission of Sage)

*that* object extraction case would be due solely to verbs with a preference for a non-overt complementizer. In order to test for this possible confound, we recently conducted an experiment that included declaratives with and without *that* (e.g. *Sue thinks (that) Bill admired Fred*) in addition to the four core *wh*-question structures. Each token set consisted of the six structures (two declaratives and four *wh*-questions), so that the verb was consistent across structures. If the *that*-effect was due to a verb's preference for a non-overt complementizer, the effect should show up in the declaratives as well. With Amazon Mechanical Turk, we recruited 108 participants. The results are shown in Figure 10.5.

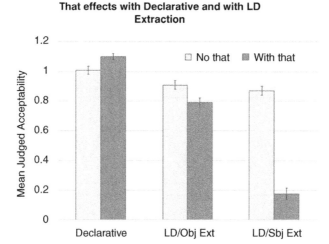

**Figure 10.5** *That*-trace effect relative to declarative controls

Figure 10.5 shows the usual *that*-trace effect and the *that*-effect in the four core *wh*-question structures. But the *that* effect does not manifest in declaratives. In fact, the declarative structure with *that* is actually preferred over its counterpart without *that*. Further analysis is required, but there is no evidence here for the *that*-effect being driven by any resistance to *that* arising from the verbs.

Schippers (2019) reports an online sentence acceptability experiment structured in the same way as the one we describe above, but using indirect question structures and three-clause declaratives. Her findings were statistically significant and parallel to those described for Figure 10.5 (though she did not find a difference between the two declarative conditions).

We hold that syntactic theory should take the *that*-effect into account. The evidence summarized above indicates that it is a reliable phenomenon in American English, and could also have some bearing on an adequate explanation of the *that*-trace effect. To our knowledge, the only accounts of the *that*-trace effect that address the *that*-effect are McDaniel et al. (2015) and Schippers (2019). Both accounts associate the *that* and *that*-trace effects with the general cross-linguistic resistance to LD extraction and with the accessibility hierarchy, indicating that subjects are the least extractible in such structures. Schippers analyzes (apparent) LD extraction structures in English as an indirect dependency between the *wh*-phrase and the embedded clause, where the embedded clause is formally a type of relative clause. She suggests that the preference for *that* deletion in these structures is due to ambiguity avoidance. McDaniel et al.'s account focuses on the sentence planning system. Their general approach is that the production system plays a role in shaping grammars. Their specific proposal to account for the resistance to LD extraction is that the clause is a major planning unit, which creates a planning challenge for a dependency that crosses a clause boundary. According to this account, the absence of *that* indicates joint planning of the clauses, making these structures preferable. The reason for the subject/object asymmetry with *that* is that subject extraction creates the additional challenge of beginning a new planning unit with a trace. (See also McDaniel (2018) for an extension of this account to similar structures.)

## 10.2.2 The Core Contrasts in Other Languages

We begin with experimental work on the core *that*-trace contrasts in German (see also Chapter 18; for a discussion of the facts in Spanish, see Chapter 7). The paradigm, given in (3), is more complicated than in English. (We label the structures using the German complementizer *dass*, but will continue to use the terms *that-trace effect* and *that-effect*.)[3]

(3)    a. No-*dass* object extraction

      Wen      meinst   du,    liebt    der    Junge?
      who(ACC)   think    you    loves   the    boy(NOM)
      'Who do you think the boy loves?'

   b. No-*dass* subject extraction

      Wer       meinst   du,    liebt    den    Jungen?
      who(NOM)   think    you    loves   the    boy(ACC)
      'Who do you think loves the boy?'

   c. *dass* object extraction

      Wen      meinst   du,    dass    der   Junge     liebt?
      who(ACC)   think    you    that    the   boy(NOM)   loves
      'Who do you think that the boy loves?'

   d. *dass* subject extraction

      Wer       meinst   du,    dass    den   Jungen   liebt?
      who(NOM)   think    you    that    the   boy(ACC)   loves
      'Who do you think that loves the boy?'

Two questions arise about German. One is a data question about whether the subject/object asymmetry exists, specifically whether (2c) and (2d) differ in grammaticality. The other question concerns the two no-*dass* cases (2a, b). Here the question is whether they belong in the paradigm; that is, are they actually parallel to the *dass* structures. Unlike in English, where the no-*that* and *that* structures differ from each other only in the presence or absence of *that*, the no-*dass* and *dass* structures in German also differ in word order. The answers to both of these questions

---

[3] German no-*dass* complement clauses have verb-second word order (with the verb as the first element in these examples due to *wh*-movement), and the *dass* complement clauses have verb-final order. The result is that the subject and object DPs in the complement clause of each pair (3a–b, 3c–d) occur in the same linear position. In these examples, the distinction is made by the case-marking on the *wh*-word and on the DP.

have fundamental consequences for analyses of the *that*-trace effect, as well as other aspects of German syntax. Both issues have been debated in the syntactic literature and, over the last two decades, both have been addressed experimentally, primarily by Featherston (2004, 2005) and Kiziak (2010). We will review their findings, starting with the question of the subject/object asymmetry and then turning to the status of the no-*dass* structures.

Prior to Featherston (2004, 2005), German, at least standard German, was often characterized as not having the *that*-trace effect. The general consensus was that both *dass* extraction structures are degraded, and the claim was that the *dass* subject extraction structure was no worse than the object one (see Featherston (2005) for discussion). Featherston (2004, 2005) conducted several experiments using magnitude estimation. The 2004 study, which focused on the properties of bridge verbs, included the four *that*-trace structures, as well as yes/no questions with and without the complementizer *dass*. The 2005 study investigated the *that*-trace effect in both *wh*-questions and topicalization. In both studies, he found the expected low acceptability ratings for the subject and the object *dass* structures, but also obtained a reliable subject/object asymmetry. Featherston (2008) illustrated the similarity between the English and German findings by placing the results from his 2004 study side-by-side with the graph from Cowart (1997) for English (Figure 10.1 of this chapter), as shown in Figure 10.6 (his Figure 5).

Featherston also categorized the participants of the 2004 experiment by region of origin in Germany (north: 7, south: 24, center: 11, none specified: 10), and found no regional differences, counter to claims in the literature that LD extraction is more acceptable in the south than in the north. In the topicalization experiment, he included adjunct extraction structures as well. The findings on adjuncts confirmed the intuition in the field that adjuncts are more extractable than subjects or objects.

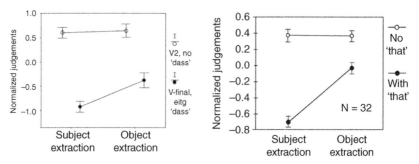

**Figure 10.6** *That*-trace effects in German (left) compared to English (right) (S. Featherston, "Thermometer judgements as linguistic evidence." In C. M. Riehl & A. Rothe, eds., *Was ist linguistische Evidenz?*, Figure 5, p. 86, © 2008 by permission of Shaker Verlag GmbH)

Kiziak (2010) conducted a series of 14 experiments on aspects of LD movement in German with online questionnaires using magnitude estimation and thermometer methods (the latter being a modification of the magnitude estimation task proposed by Featherston (2008); see Chapter 2). Her first three experiments, which included *dass wh*-question and topicalization structures, replicated Featherston's finding of a subject/object/ adjunct asymmetry. She also included extracted datives in different kinds of verbs, and determined that datives pattern like accusatives independently of verb class. Finally, she investigated extraction out of islands, finding the subject/object asymmetry in those structures as well (in addition to a lower rating for extraction out of islands than out of *dass* complements). Several of the other experiments in Kiziak's study were designed to investigate accounts of the subject/object asymmetry, which we discuss below. For now, we emphasize that all of her experiments that included *dass* subject and object extraction structures found the asymmetry. This project therefore has made an extremely important data contribution to the field of German syntax, where the lack of a subject/object asymmetry has often been claimed.

We now turn to the second question about German that relates to the core *that*-trace contrasts, namely the status of the no-*dass* structures. The controversy in the literature regarding these structures is whether the second clause is truly a complement of the first, as in the English equivalent, or whether the upper clause is parenthetical. Generative syntacticians have tended to assume the non-parenthetical analysis. (See Kiziak (2010) for extensive discussion.) In order to illustrate the parenthetical analysis, we repeat (3a, b) in (4), with brackets indicating the material that would be parenthetical, in the German sentence, as well as the English translation.

(4)  a. No-*dass* object extraction
Wen       [meinst  du]   liebt   der   Junge?
who(ACC)  [think    you]  loves   the   boy(NOM)
'Who [do you think] the boy loves?'

b. No-*dass* subject extraction
Wer       [meinst  du]   liebt   den   Jungen?
who(NOM)  [think    you]  loves   the   boy(ACC)
'Who [do you think] loves the boy?'

Note that the English translation of (4a) demonstrates that the parenthetical analysis would not work for English (at least not for object extraction), since the structure without the bracketed material is missing I-to-C movement (*do*-insertion here). In the case of German, though, the structures with the bracketed parts removed correspond to the word order of a standard short-distance question. If these structures indeed involve parentheticals, then they aren't part of the *that*-trace paradigm in German.

Putting aside parentheticals, then, the overt complementizer would be obligatory in German. This effectively would remove the *that* (*dass*) part of the characterization of the *that*-trace effect. Though evidence might still be found to support an account in terms of the complementizer, the basic data would only indicate a subject/object asymmetry in LD extraction, a structure which is overall dispreferred.

Featherston's (2004) study on bridge verbs provided some support for the non-parenthetical analysis, in that the degree to which a verb allowed a complementizer-less complement clause was significantly related to the degree to which it allowed extraction from a *dass* complement. Whereas Featherston did not discuss his findings in terms of the parenthetical account, Kiziak (2010) conducted four experiments specifically designed to address this question. The logic behind the design was that the patterns of ratings for the questionable structures should align with those of structures of the same type. She therefore tested them against a variety of structures that clearly did or did not involve parentheticals. Overall, the findings supported the parenthetical account.

We now turn to Dutch, which is interestingly different from English and German, in that the overt complementizer (*dat*) is obligatory in finite complement clauses in non-extraction structures. Perlmutter (1971) and others have also characterized Dutch as allowing both subject and object extraction out of *dat* clauses, though the literature is inconsistent on whether there is a subject/object asymmetry and suggests variation in the subject extraction structure that depends on dialect and on other aspects of the structure (e.g. Bennis 1986). So far, there is very little experimental research investigating these structures in Dutch. Strik (2008) included a sentence acceptability experiment on Dutch-speaking adults as part of a larger study investigating child Dutch and French. The focus was on alternatives to LD extraction (partial *wh*-movement and *wh*-copying structures). The materials included these structures as well as long-distance structures with *dat*, all with both subject and object extraction. The sentences to judge were given in token sets following a short story that provided a context. The contexts and sentences were presented aurally. Participants were asked to judge whether each sentence was acceptable or not, and to rate the acceptable ones on a five-point scale. The experiment was taken online by 649 Dutch speakers. The results showed a high acceptance rate for both subject and object extraction out of *dat* clauses. In addition, subject extraction was rated significantly lower than object extraction. However, this finding cannot necessarily be attributed to a *dat*-trace effect, since the same subject/object asymmetry occurred in the alternative structures without *dat*.

We conclude this subsection with Bentzen (2014), a study that explored the *that*-trace effect in Scandinavian varieties. This study differs from the ones discussed up to this point in that the judgment data do not come from a specific experiment conducted by the researcher, but rather from a database, the Nordic Dialect Corpus and Syntax Database (NSD; Lindstad et al. 2009). In addition to a corpus of spontaneous speech data from northern Germanic languages, it has a database of judgments, which is described on the website as consisting of "judgments by 924 Nordic dialect speakers from 207 places to a list of sentences that illustrate various syntactic phenomena." The questionnaire consists of approximately 140 sentences presented aurally by a prerecorded local/regional voice, and participants judge the sentences on a five-point scale (Westergaard et al. 2017). Bentzen (2014) reported data on the four core *that*-trace structures, as well as their equivalents with the complementizer *som* (used with relative clauses) in place of *at* (used with complement clauses) in Norway, Sweden, Finland (Fenno-Swedish), and the Faroe Islands. The non-overt complementizer structures were widely accepted across the region. Object extraction with the complementizer *at* was also widely accepted, though there were some medium and low scores in parts of Norway. Object extraction with the complementizer *som* was widely rejected. Variation was found in the subject extraction structures with an overt complementizer. While these structures were rejected in most regions, subject extraction with *at* was accepted in Finland and parts of Eastern Norway, and subject extraction with *som* was accepted in other parts of Norway. These results, based on the NSD, are notable for the amount of data collected, the range of communities represented, the use of auditory presentation of target sentences, and the use of a speaker of each local dialect to produce the stimuli. As with any effort aimed at creating such a large dataset, methodological compromises are inevitable. Getting reliable evidence of differences in degree of acceptability across different communities is likely to require a closer approach to the standards enumerated in (2) above. Nevertheless, the NSD project provides interesting evidence of where potentially important syntactic dialect differences may exist. As these are more narrowly defined, they can be pursued with more rigorous (hence, more costly and time-consuming) methods.

### 10.2.3   Testing Accounts of the *That*-Trace Effect

Of course, the findings on the core *that*-trace contrasts have implications for the analysis of the phenomenon, and much of the work reviewed above includes suggestions for how to handle the data. But in this subsection our focus is on experiments that are designed to test specific accounts of the *that*-trace phenomenon that make predictions about other structures. We review four examples here, the first two of which are further experiments conducted by Kiziak (2010).

As discussed above, Kiziak's initial set of experiments found a robust subject/object asymmetry for German *dass* extraction and supported a parenthetical account of the no-*dass* structures. The subject/object asymmetry is therefore in need of an explanation, which doesn't necessarily have to do with the complementizer. Kiziak proposes three factors, summarized in (5), one or more of which might be responsible for the asymmetry.

(5)    Factors potentially responsible for subject/object asymmetry tested by Kiziak (2010)

   A. The subject extraction structures are degraded due to the nominative case on the fronted *wh*-word appearing to clash with the upper verb, which has a different subject (a processing-based account).
   B. The complementizer *dass* cannot be followed by the subject trace. (In other words, the *that*-trace effect is responsible for the asymmetry even though the no-*dass* equivalents don't exist.)
   C. Some property of external arguments (which are typically subjects) prevents them from moving over a clause boundary.

Kiziak tested factor A by manipulating the morphological case-marking on the *wh*-phrases, comparing ambiguously and non-ambiguously case-marked DPs. She tested factor B by manipulating the morphological case-marking on the non-subject DP following *dass*, which could then be temporarily misanalyzed as the subject, circumventing a *dass*-trace sequence. Finally, she tested factor C with structures in which the extracted element is nominative but is the internal argument of the lower verb, such as passives. The results of these experiments were inconclusive, but provided some support for each of the three factors. Though inconclusive, they model an experimental approach to the questions and set the stage for further research.

One of Kiziak's (2010) experiments tested an information-structural account of the *that*-trace effect (Bayer 2005). This account is based on the fact that subjects are generally topics. The proposal is that a topic cannot extract out of a finite clause. Kiziak constructed materials that included scrambling in the embedded clause, such that the extracted subject was not the topic. The subject/object asymmetry persisted, counter to the predictions of the account.

Salzmann et al. (2013) proposed an account of the *that*-trace effect in German (which they suggest could extend to English) that attributes the unacceptability of the subject *dass* extraction structure to the complementizer–verb (finite) sequence rather than to the complementizer–trace sequence. They propose a phonological EPP, a requirement that a functional projection between C and vP needs to be overtly filled at PF. Their account predicts that, if overt material is in that position, the subject *dass* extraction structure will improve, and furthermore, that the same improvement will occur in structures with a C–V(finite) sequence that don't involve LD extraction. They report an experiment using a magnitude estimation task. Participants in the first experiment were standard German speakers from two regions of Germany (south: 35, north: 28) and speakers of Swiss German (77). The materials included six conditions: the subject *dass* extraction structure, a non-LD extraction verb-raising structure with the C–V(finite) sequence, and a similar verb-raising structure without the C–V(finite) sequence; and each of the preceding three with material moved to a position between the complementizer and the verb. Their predictions were borne out for each participant group; the moved material improved acceptability ratings for the two structures with the C–V(finite) sequence and not for the third structure.

Next we turn to Ritchart et al. (2016), who tested prosodic accounts of the *that*-trace effect (e.g. Kandybowicz 2006). Such accounts attribute the unacceptability of the *that* subject extraction structure to a prosodic filter that disallows adjacency between a complementizer and a trace within the same prosodic phrase when the complementizer is at the left edge of the phrase. Kandybowicz (2006) cites the structures illustrated in (6) as evidence in support of this account.[4] The bracket and subscript *intP* indicates an intonation phrase boundary.

(6)     a. ? Who do you think that [$_{intP}$ WROTE Barriers?
        b. ? [$_{intP}$ Who do you suppose that'll leave early?

Ritchart et al. conducted two experiments, one to test each of these claims. The stimuli were prerecorded by a phonetician (Ritchart). Participants heard each item once and rated each on a seven-point scale. The first experiment included six LD subject extraction conditions: *that* and no-*that*, each with focus on the matrix verb, focus on the embedded verb, and no focus. There were also six parallel LD object extraction conditions. Each sentence was preceded by a context to make the contrastive focus felicitous. The second experiment included three LD subject extraction conditions: with *that* and a non-contracted auxiliary (e.g. *that will*), with *that* and a contracted auxiliary (*that'll*), and without *that*. There were also three parallel conditions with the *wh*-word originating as the subject of the matrix clause and a relative clause modifying the object (e.g. *Who talked to the man that'll irritate the judge?*). The findings from Experiment 1 showed that the focus on the embedded verb did improve acceptability in the subject extraction condition. However, the improvement also occurred in the no-*that* condition and with focus on the matrix verb, indicating that the improvement couldn't be attributed to the prosodic phrase with *that*. The results of Experiment 2 showed the usual *that*-trace effect, but no effect of contraction. This study therefore failed to support the predictions of the account.

---

[4] Example (6a) is Kandybowicz's (9b), and Ritchart et al.'s (4); and example (6b) is Kandybowicz's (10a), and Ritchart et al.'s (5).

## 10.3 Conclusion

In (7) we list the *that*-trace-related findings discussed in this chapter. A review of the list reveals a lack of a coherent theme in the experimental approach to the phenomenon. Some of the studies are the products of long-running, focused efforts with a consistent theme, whereas others are relatively isolated projects. We believe that this circumstance reflects primarily the immaturity of this line of research. In comparison to the broader body of research on the *that*-trace effect, the subset of issues that have been approached experimentally constitute a relatively arbitrary selection from the range of possibilities that could, and probably should, be studied using experimental methods.

(7)    The *that*-trace-related experimental findings include:

- Evidence for the *that*-trace effect in English across regions of the US
- Evidence for a *that* effect in English
- Evidence for a subject/object asymmetry in LD *dass* extraction in German
- Support for a parenthetical account of no-*dass* extraction structures in German
- Acceptance of the *dat*-trace structure in Dutch, though also some indication of a general subject/object asymmetry
- Support for the *at*-trace effect in most Norwegian, Swedish, and Faroese varieties, but also indications that some varieties accept subject extraction with *at* and others with *som*
- Some support for the role of certain factors in the subject/object asymmetry in German: case clash, complementizer, extraction of internal vs. external argument
- Evidence against an information-structural account of the *that*-trace effect
- Evidence for an account that attributes the *that*-trace effect in German to a prohibition on the sequence C–V(finite)
- Evidence against a prosodic account of the *that*-trace effect

Despite the unsystematic nature of the set of studies considered above, we believe that the data can be handled by a uniform account. Several of the findings suggest that the phenomenon is more general than the *that*-trace effect descriptively implies, but also that language/dialect variation has to do with properties of the complementizer. The accounts proposed by McDaniel et al. (2015) and Schippers (2019), discussed in Section 10.2.1, address both of these points, attributing the *that*-trace effect – as well as the *that* effect – to a general dispreference for LD movement that interacts with the status of the complementizer. Needless to say, data from non-Germanic languages, and more and better data in general, should be valuable for further explorations along these lines (see Chapter 7 for additional discussion).

The philosophical conjecture that lies at the foundation of generative linguistics is that there is a computational system underpinning sentence syntax and interpretation. This is not seen as a computational system that is merely involved in some way, as in processing, but one that defines what a sentence is, that determines or constrains what that sentence may mean, and that consists in a system of recursive rules projecting an infinite space of possible sentences.

A notable methodological conjecture, central to this volume, that arose with generative theory is that judgments of acceptability (often termed "grammaticality") can serve well as the principal source of empirical evidence for syntactic theory. On the strength of this conjecture, generative linguistics has been widely seen by its practitioners as an incipient special science in the sense of Fodor (1974), a discipline whose theoretical proposals are subject to empirical tests. The body of work reviewed above suggests that this methodological conjecture is sound. Whatever difficulties may attach to the informal methods syntactic researchers often use, the work reviewed here shows that those methods have succeeded in detecting genuinely interesting phenomena, ones that continue to bear on important questions in generative theory. They also show, however, that sentence acceptability can exhibit subtle, but stable, systematic patterns that are not easily captured by traditional methods.

# References

Bayer, J. (2005). Was beschränkt die Extraktion? Subjekt–Objekt vs. Topik–Fokus. In F.-J. D'Avis, ed., *Deutsche Syntax: Empirie und Theorie*. Gothenburg: Acta Universitatis Gothoburgensis, pp. 233–257.

Bennis, H. (1986). *Gaps and Dummies*. Dordrecht: Foris.

Bentzen, K. (2014). Subject and object extraction from embedded clauses. *Nordic Atlas of Language Structures*, 1, 435–446.

Bresnan, J. (1977). Variables in the theory of transformations. In P. W. Culicover, T. Wasow, & A. Akmajian, eds., *Formal Syntax*. New York: Academic Press, pp. 157–196.

Chomsky, N. (1995). *The Minimalist Program*. Cambridge, MA: MIT Press.

Cowart, W. (1997). *Experimental Syntax: Applying Objective Methods to Sentence Judgments*. Thousand Oaks, CA: Sage.

Cowart, W. (2003). Detecting syntactic dialects: the that-trace phenomenon. Presentation at the 39th Meeting of the Chicago Linguistic Society, April, University of Chicago.

Featherston, S. (2004). Bridge verbs and V2 verbs – the same thing in spades? *Zeitschrift für Sprachwissenschaft*, 23(2), 181–209.

Featherston, S. (2005). *That*-trace in German. *Lingua*, 115(9), 1277–1302.

Featherston, S. (2008). Thermometer judgements as linguistic evidence. In C. M. Riehl & A. Rothe, eds., *Was ist linguistische Evidenz?* Aachen: Shaker Verlag, pp. 69–90.

Fodor, J. A. (1974). Special sciences (or: The disunity of science as a working hypothesis). *Synthese*, 28(2), 97–115.

Kandybowicz, J. (2006). Comp-trace effects explained away. In D. Baumer, D. Montero, & M. Scanlon, eds., *Proceedings of the 25th West Coast Conference on Formal Linguistics*. Somerville, MA: Cascadilla Proceedings Project, pp. 220–228.

Kiziak, T. (2010). *Extraction Asymmetries: Experimental Evidence from German*. Amsterdam: John Benjamins.

Lindstad, A., M., Nøklestad, A., Johannessen, J. B., & Vangsnes, Ø. A. (2009). The Nordic Dialect Database: Mapping microsyntactic variation in the Scandinavian languages. In K. Jokinen & E. Bick, eds., *Proceedings of the 17th Nordic Conference of Computational Linguistics (NoDaLiDa)* (NEALT Proceedings Series, 4). Helsinki: Northern European Association for Language Technology, pp. 283–286.

McDaniel, D. (2018). Long-distance extraction attraction: A production-based account of an unexpected cross-linguistic structure. *Glossa: A Journal of General Linguistics*, 3(1), 95.

McDaniel, D., McKee, C., Cowart, W., & Garrett, M. F. (2015). The role of the language production system in shaping grammars. *Language*, 91(2), 415–41.

Perlmutter, D. M. (1968). Deep and surface structure constraints in syntax. Doctoral dissertation, Massachusetts Institute of Technology.

Perlmutter, D. M. (1971) *Deep and Surface Structure Constraints in Generative Grammar*. New York: Holt, Rinehart, and Winston.

Pesetsky, D. (2017) Complementizer-trace effects. In M. Everaert & H. C. van Riemsdijk, eds., *The Wiley Blackwell Companion to Syntax*, 2nd ed. New York: John Wiley & Sons, pp. 1–34.

Phillips, C. (2013). On the nature of island constraints. II: Language learning and innateness. In J. Sprouse & N. Hornstein, eds., *Experimental Syntax and Island Effects*. Cambridge: Cambridge University Press, pp. 132–157.

Ritchart, A., Goodall, G., & Garellek, M. (2016). Prosody and the *that*-trace effect: An experimental study. In K.-m. Kim, P. Umbal, T. Block, Q. Chan, T. Cheng, K. Finney, M. Katz, S. Nickel-Thompson, & L. Shorten, eds., *Proceedings of the 33rd West Coast Conference on Formal Linguistics*. Somerville, MA: Cascadilla Proceedings Project, pp. 320–328.

Salzmann, M., Häussler, J., Bader, M., & Bayer, J. (2013). *That*-trace effects without traces: An experimental investigation. Presented at the NELS 42.

Schippers, A. (2019). COMP-trace revisited: An indirect dependency analysis. Unpublished manuscript.

Sobin, N. (1987). The variable status of comp-trace phenomena. *Natural Language & Linguistic Theory*, 5(1), 33–60.

Stevens, S. S. (1975). *Psychophysics: Introduction to its Perceptual, Neural, and Social Prospects*. New York: Wiley.

Strik, N. (2008). Syntaxe et acquisition des phrases interrogatives en français et en néerlandais: une étude contrastive. Doctoral dissertation, University of Paris VIII.

Westergaard, M., Vangsnes, Ø. A., & Lohndal, T. (2017). Variation and change in Norwegian *wh*-questions: The role of the complementizer *som*. *Linguistic Variation*, 17(1), 8–43.

White, L. (1986). Island effects in second language acquisition. *Montreal Working Papers in Linguistics*, 3, 1–27.

# 11

# Anaphora: Experimental Methods for Investigating Coreference

Elsi Kaiser

## 11.1 Introduction[1]

The topic of anaphora has played an important role in the development of syntactic theories. For example, reflexive binding is widely used as a diagnostic for c-command, the distribution of reflexives and pronouns has played a central role in theories of predicate-argument structure, and phi-feature (mis)matches between antecedents and anaphora inform investigations of feature checking. Binding Theory – which aims to characterize the distribution and interpretation of anaphora – is a central component of syntactic theorizing, and experimental syntacticians have investigated the predictions of Binding Theory in different syntactic configurations[2] and in various languages. At the same time, the processing of anaphora is of central interest for psycholinguistic work on the representations and mechanisms involved in the processing of anaphoric dependencies.

Methodologically, anaphora has been investigated using a variety of methods, with the choice of method often shaped by the empirical and

[1] In this chapter, I use the term "coreference" fairly broadly to mean situations when two linguistic expressions refer to the same entity and when one linguistic expression provides an antecedent for another linguistic expression. Under this usage, a reflexive and its antecedent are "coreferential," and a personal pronoun and its antecedent are also "coreferential," even if they cross a clause boundary. I do not intend the word "coreference" to be construed as excluding "binding" (see e.g. Bach & Partee (1980), Reinhart (1982, 1983a, 1983b) and others for an important semantic distinction that is often reflected in the terms *coreference* vs. *binding*). In this chapter, I intentionally use the term "coreference" in a broader way, but this terminological choice is not intended to detract from the existence of a semantic distinction between coreference and variable binding. See Frazier and Clifton (2000) and Carminati et al. (2002) for experimental work on this distinction. Most online psycholinguistic studies on anaphora have tended to focus on coreference relations, but see work by Frazier and colleagues, Kush, Lidz, and Phillips (2015) and Cunnings, Patterson, and Felser (2015) on variable binding.

[2] This chapter focuses mainly on reflexive and personal pronouns with sentence-internal antecedents – i.e. contexts where the distribution of pronouns and reflexives is (expected to be) governed by syntactic principles (e.g. Binding Theory). For work on cross-sentential (discourse-level) reference resolution, see e.g. Garnham (2001).

theoretical goals of a particular investigation. Acceptability judgments (also called grammaticality judgments; more on this distinction below) are one of the traditional tools of experimental syntax, and have been fruitfully used to investigate which antecedents are judged acceptable for a given anaphoric expression (e.g. to better understand the principles that constitute Binding Theory). However, as I discuss below, investigating coreference by means of acceptability judgments poses some very specific challenges that demand adjustments to the traditional acceptability judgment methods in order to avoid potentially uninterpretable results. I provide a detailed methodological discussion of how to make the necessary adjustments, caveats to watch out for, as well as related methods that can be used to complement acceptability judgment tasks.

Research using acceptability judgments and other *offline methods* (such as questions probing antecedent-choice) can be complemented by *online methods* such as self-paced reading, eye-tracking during reading and visual world eye-tracking. These methods allow researchers to tap into online processes that occur before comprehenders reach their final interpretation of the anaphoric expression, to detect fluctuations in processing load and potentially transient consideration (or lack thereof) of competing antecedents.

Ultimately, the choice of method depends largely on the research aims. Offline acceptability judgments can be used, for example, to assess whether a specific syntactically defined coreference configuration is judged acceptable by native speakers. But online methods are needed to assess questions such as whether processing an anaphoric expression only triggers activation of the Binding-Theory licensed antecedent, or whether syntactically inaccessible but featurally compatible referents are also activated. In this chapter, I mostly focus on acceptability-based methods, but I also include some comparative discussion on the merits of different methods such as eye-tracking.

Before continuing, let us acknowledge one of the hotly debated issues in experimental syntax in recent years, namely whether experimental methods are needed when investigating syntactic acceptability judgments. While some researchers argue that data from linguists' intuitions closely replicate data from psycholinguistic experiments, suggesting that experiments are not needed (e.g. Phillips & Lasnik 2003; Bornkessel-Schlesewsky & Schlesewsky 2007; Sprouse et al. 2013), others claim that psycholinguistic experiments either help or are necessary for obtaining reliable data (e.g. Gibson & Fedorenko 2013; Häussler & Juzek 2017) and that linguists' judgments differ from those of naïve native speakers (e.g. Dabrowska 2010). The present chapter will not address this debate and presupposes that readers are interested in an experimental approach to syntax in general and anaphora in particular (see Chapters 1 and 22 for further discussion).

Another broad, ongoing debate concerns the question of whether grammaticality itself is binary or continuous (and whether this is even a well-formed question). Researchers largely agree that, empirically, acceptability judgments are continuous (see e.g. Bader & Häussler 2010 for recent discussion): when participants are asked to judge the acceptability of sentences, their responses yield gradient data (see Chapter 3 for detailed discussion of gradience). However, as noted by Bader and Häussler (2010), "it is one thing to accept the gradience of grammaticality judgments but quite another thing to accept the notion of gradient grammaticality" (p. 276).

Before going further, it's worth noting that I follow Cowart (1997), Schütze and Sprouse (2013) and many others in talking about "acceptability judgments" rather than "grammaticality judgments." In generative grammar, the grammar is traditionally regarded as a mental construct that we cannot directly consciously access. When people report whether a given sentence is a possible sentence in their language (i.e. whether it is "acceptable"), their response is influenced not only by the grammar but also by factors such as real-world plausibility, frequency and ease of processing; see e.g. Schütze (1996) for discussion of these issues, which go back to the original competence–performance distinction. Furthermore, we cannot measure *directly* whether a given sentence is perceived to be acceptable by a participant: instead, we ask people to report their perception – more specifically, to report how acceptable they perceive that sentence to be – using various methods such as binary yes/no questions, multiple-point scales and so on (see also Bard et al. 1996; Schütze 1996). In this chapter, then, we are talking about acceptability judgments, known to be gradient (for further discussion of these issues, see Chapters 1–5).

The structure of this chapter is as follows. I first consider a fundamental issue that researchers conducting experimental work on anaphora need to address, especially if they are using acceptability judgment tasks: given that use of subscripts with naïve participants is typically avoided, how can researchers indicate the intended antecedent for an anaphor? If a researcher is interested in whether a particular coindexation relation is acceptable, how can this information be conveyed to naïve participants? Ignoring this important issue can yield uninterpretable data. I provide an in-depth discussion of different methodological approaches that can be used to indicate coreference when researchers want to elicit acceptability judgments, and compare these methods to other approaches that do not measure acceptability directly but rather ask participants to identify the preferred antecedents for anaphors.

The focus of this chapter is largely methodological. For an overview of some of the central theoretical issues regarding the processing of coreference (in particular reflexive pronouns), the reader is referred to Dillon (2014). For a typological overview of anaphora, see e.g. Huang (2000).

### 11.1.1　Using Acceptability Judgments to Investigate Coreference

Acceptability judgment tasks investigating syntactic issues outside the realm of anaphora typically involve participants rating the acceptability of individual sentences or the relative acceptability of sentence pairs. However, once we turn to the domain of anaphora, we need to distinguish two situations: does the researcher want to test (i) whether a given sentence is acceptable (assessing *sentence acceptability*) or (ii) whether a given anaphoric coindexation configuration is acceptable (assessing *coindexation acceptability*).

In many domains of experimental syntax, judgments of *sentence acceptability* provide the relevant data. However, in the domain of anaphora, the situation is slightly different: if a native speaker is asked about the acceptability of a sentence like (1a), she will presumably respond that (1a) is an acceptable sentence of English. Furthermore, when comprehending the sentence, she will presumably assign to the sentence the interpretation that *himself* is coreferential with Bob. However, the participant's response that "yes, this sentence is acceptable" does not provide a direct measure of what coreferential interpretation she gave to the reflexive pronoun. Thus, if a researcher wants to find out whether *himself* could also be coindexed with the matrix subject Alexander – a question that becomes especially relevant in languages with long-distance reflexives (e.g. Mandarin Chinese) – then simply asking a participant about the acceptability of the sentence as a whole fails to answer this question.

(1)　　a. Alexander said that Bob congratulated himself.

For a trained linguist, this situation has a straightforward answer: the use of subscripts (indices). In linguistic work, the intended coreferential interpretation – coindexation – is indicated by subscripted letters or numbers. Asterisks on the subscripts can be used to signal unacceptability of coindexation, as illustrated in (1b). Although theoretical linguists are familiar with these notational conventions, they may not be transparent for non-specialists. Thus, when conducting experiments with naïve, non-linguist participants, researchers typically opt not to use subscripts and signal the intended coreferential relation by other means (see Section 11.2).

(1)　　b. Alexander$_i$ said that Bob$_j$ congratulated himself$_{*i/j}$.

However, lack of any overt indication of coindexation patterns is not always a problem. For example, if a researcher is investigating reflexive pronouns in contexts where only one possible antecedent is present (and in a language where reflexives are known to not allow clause-external antecedents), then we can infer that if a participant judges the sentence to be acceptable, they also judge the one possible coindexing relation to be acceptable. This is the case for sentences like (2b): If a participant reports that this is an acceptable sentence of English, we can infer that they accept the coindexation configuration where *herself* refers to Joan. In this case, assessing sentence acceptability allows us to assess coindexation acceptability.

(2)    a. Joan respects her.
       b. Joan respects herself.
       c. She respects Joan.

But caution is called for, even in sentences that only contain one candidate antecedent, if the anaphoric form being tested is a personal pronoun – due to the possibility of a sentence-external antecedent. Consider (2a) and (2c), from Gordon and Hendrick (1997). Both of these sentences are unacceptable if the name and pronoun are coindexed, but fully acceptable if we assume that the pronoun is not coindexed with Joan – i.e. if a sentence-external referent is assumed for the pronoun.[3] Thus, simply asking participants about the acceptability of sentences like (2a, c) – without any coindexation information – will not allow a researcher to conclude that coreference between *Joan* and *her* in (2a) and *She* and *Joan* in (2c) is unacceptable. Thus, if our aim is to use acceptability judgments to investigate which coreferential relations are acceptable, we need to pin down what the intended coreferential relations are.

One solution is to explicitly tell participants to not consider any sentence-external referents. This was the tack taken by Lago et al. (2018) in recent work on possessive pronouns in German. Lago et al. used sentences with only one mentioned character and – to prevent participants from considering sentence-external referents – they explicitly instructed people to "provide their judgments only based on the current sentence context." In a speeded-acceptability task, the responses of native German speakers patterned as expected (i.e. they accepted sentences where the possessive pronoun gender-matched the mentioned referent more than sentences where the possessive pronoun did not gender-match the mentioned referent, 96% vs. 21%). The finding that participants largely reject sentences that would have been acceptable if a sentence-external referent had been considered indicates that the participants did indeed follow the instructions of only using/considering the sentence provided in the experiment.

[3] The challenges raised by the possibility of sentence-external antecedents can also occur with reflexives, see example (i). Pollard and Sag (1992) note that here, *John* can be coindexed with *himself*, despite being in a different sentence. Reflexives in certain syntactic environments (such as picture-NPs) are known to allow sentence-external referents. Thus, even with reflexives, absence of coindexation can result in data that is hard to interpret. The extent to which this complicates judgment tasks with reflexives depends on how widespread long-distance reflexives and "exempt" reflexives are in a given language. In English, we know from a large body of prior work that the distribution of so-called exempt reflexives is restricted to certain syntactic contexts.

(i) John$_i$ was furious. The picture of himself$_i$ in the museum had been mutilated. (from Pollard & Sag 1992)

## 11.2 Acceptability Judgments: How to Indicate Coreference without Subscripts

What about acceptability judgments of sentence containing more than one candidate antecedent – a configuration that is often a key test case for adjudicating between different theories (see Section 11.6)? In such a situation, if we cannot use subscripts to convey the intended coreference relation, how can participants be told what kind of referential dependency they are being asked to evaluate?

### 11.2.1 Enforcing Coreference by Means of Gender, Number or Person Cues

One means of spelling out the coreference relation that the researcher wants participants to assess is by using sentences where only one of the nouns featurally matches the anaphor. In this section, I discuss possible ways of enforcing coreference by means of (i) gender, (ii) number, or (iii) person cues – in essence, making sure that the anaphor only has one potential antecedent with matching phi-features.[4]

In English, where reflexives are marked for person, number, and gender, all of these features can be used to indicate the intended coindexation configuration. First, let's consider gender. (3a) allows us to test the acceptability of a local binder for the reflexive and (3b) allows us to test the acceptability of a non-local binder, by means of gendered names. In addition to names, nouns with definitional gender (*aunt, uncle, king, queen*), as in (3c, d), and professional roles with stereotypical gender (as determined by norming studies) have also been used (3e, f). There exists a lot of online processing work in English that has used gender features to investigate the processes involved in the real-time processing of reflexives.

Interestingly, processing work on English suggests that nouns with definitional gender and stereotypical gender pattern alike during real-time processing of anaphoric configurations but not in cataphoric configurations (e.g. Kreiner et al. 2008) – in essence, stereotypes can be overcome. Thus, for offline acceptability tasks, if one's aim is to pin down a certain interpretation by means of gender features, names and roles with definitional gender may provide clearer results than roles with stereotypical gender.[5]

---

[4] Another feature that could be used to constrain antecedent availability is animacy (specifically, use of inanimates), but creating minimal pairs of the type discussed below is often virtually impossible with inanimates.

[5] In some situations, however, researchers may want to use roles with stereotypical gender (as in (3e, f)) if they do not want to present participants with potentially ungrammatical sentences (compare (3d), which is ungrammatical, and (3f), which may be hard to process due to the stereotype violation but is not, strictly speaking, ungrammatical).

(3)    a. *[names]*          Alexandra said that *Bob* congratulated *himself/him.*

       b.                    *Alexander* said that Barbara congratulated *himself/him.*

       c. *[definitional gender]*    The aunt said that the *uncle* congratulated *himself/him.*

       d.                    The *uncle* said that the aunt congratulated *himself/him.*

       e. *[stereotypical gender]*    The beautician said that the *firefighter* congratulated *himself/him.*

       f.                    The *firefighter* said that the beautician congratulated *himself/him.*

However, it is worth noting that, typologically speaking, reflexive pronouns with *gender marking* (like English *himself/herself*) are quite rare. Thus, for many languages, using *person or number cues* instead of gender may be helpful when designing sentences for acceptability studies involving coreference. This is demonstrated in (4a, b) for person cues (first-person "I" vs. a third-person name) and in (5a, b) for number cues.

(4)    a. *[person cues]*    I said that *Bob* congratulated *himself/him.*
       b.                    *Bob* said that I congratulated *himself/him.*
       c. *[number cues]*    The children said that *Bob* congratulated *himself/him.*
       d.                    *Bob* said that the children congratulated *himself/him.*

Thus, rather than subscripts, we are using person, number, and gender features to pin down the intended coreference relations between a reflexive and its antecedent. With this set-up, we can ask a participant to assess the acceptability of a particular coindexation relation.

It is important to acknowledge that the logic of this approach treats morphosemantic cues like gender as "hard-and-fast" cues that cannot be violated and thus provide an inviolable mean of pinning down the intended interpretation we want the participant to consider. However, one might wonder whether, during online processing, comprehenders ever "overlook" featural information and perhaps consider featurally mismatching antecedents to some extent.

So far, a considerable body of prior work seems to suggest that this is unlikely. There is some evidence that comprehenders may temporarily ignore structural constraints on anaphor resolution (Binding Theory) but there does not appear to be clear evidence that comprehenders would overlook phi-features such as gender, person, or number if those features are marked on the relevant anaphors in their language. (In fact, the "gender mismatch paradigm" hinges on the idea that presence of a gender-matching but structurally inaccessible referent improves the acceptability of sentences that otherwise *lack* a gender-matching antecedent – suggesting that comprehenders pay attention to gender cues. The picture is somewhat less clear for cross-clausal /cross-sentential pronouns; see e.g. Rigalleau, Caplan, and Baudiffier (2004) for a review; see also Fukumura, Hyönä, and Scholfield (2013).)

However, there also exists processing work – building on typological and theoretical work on the Feature Hierarchy – suggesting that *number features* are privileged over gender features during reference resolution (see Carminati 2005).

Thus, while gender, number, and person features can be useful in many languages for indicating the intended coreference relation, the question of how "hard-and-fast" these kinds of cues are in guiding comprehenders' reference resolution processes is not yet fully settled.

So far, we have considered how phi-features can be used to "pin down" the intended coreference relation for reflexives. What about personal pronouns? The approach of using gender, number, and person cues to preclude certain referents from consideration does not work as well with personal pronouns due to the possibility of a sentence-external referent. For example, under a sentence-external interpretation of *him*, all the examples in (4) are acceptable. Given that, for many theoretical issues, we want to be able to investigate and compare *both* pronouns and reflexives, this is a potential limitation of the "features-as-signalers-of-coreference" approaches. However, based on Lago et al. (2018), as discussed above, it may be possible to simply instruct participants to only consider referents mentioned in the provided sentences.

An example of an offline acceptability task using gender to disambiguate the referent comes from Foraker (2003), who investigated reflexives and pronouns in sentences like (5). Here, only *Megan* matches in gender with *her/herself*. Because the anaphoric form is part of a coordination, it is widely viewed as not being subject to Binding Theory – thereby raising the question of what are the interpretation preferences for pronouns and reflexives these configurations, and whether they differ from each other. Foraker manipulated the locality of the gender-matching antecedent (e.g. *Megan*) relative to the pronoun and reflexive:

(5)    a. *Megan* wondered if Isaac had found out that Rick wanted to invite Sally and {*herself/her*} to the birthday party.

       b. Isaac wondered if *Megan* had found out that Rick wanted to invite Sally and {*herself/her*} to the birthday party.

       c. Rick wondered if Isaac had found out that *Megan* wanted to invite Sally and {*herself/her*} to the birthday party.

Participants rated the acceptability of sentences on a seven-point scale (1 = "nonsense/unacceptable," 7 = "makes perfect sense/fully acceptable"). Reflexives were rated more acceptable with local antecedents in the same finite clause (5c) than with antecedents in non-local positions (5a, b). Conversely, pronouns were rated more acceptable with non-local antecedents (5a, b) than local antecedents (5c). These results suggest that reflexives and pronouns inside coordination are not as fully "exempt" from Binding Theory as is often assumed, since they still exhibit the standard locality effects even when inside coordination structures.

In closing, we need to acknowledge that, in some languages, disambiguation by means of person, number, or gender may not be easily achievable. For example, Chinese *ziji* 'self' does not mark gender, number, or person. In the next section, I discuss alternative ways of indicating the intended coreference relation when asking participants to assess sentence acceptability.

Before continuing, a word of warning: on a conceptual level, we need to keep in mind that participants are, in essence, often faced with two kinds of information when considering the kinds of sentences discussed in this section: (i) is the sentence acceptable under *some* syntactically licensed coindexation option and (ii) is the sentence acceptable under *the particular (experimenter-specified)* coindexation option? If the answer to (i) is "yes" but the answer to (ii) is "no" (e.g. consider example (1b)), one may wonder whether participants will be able to fully dissociate these two answers when rating the acceptability of the sentence.[6] Is there a risk of interference effects? In other words, is there a danger that participants will perceive a sentence as more acceptable due to the existence of a potential grammatically licensed antecedent (even if the one indicated by the experimenter is not actually an acceptable antecedent), and thus report artificially high acceptability scores? This appears to still be an open question.

## 11.2.2   Signaling Coreference by Typographic Means: Bold Font, Capitalization, Color, Boxed Font

The coreferential interpretation whose acceptability participants are asked to assess can also be indicated metalinguistically using means other than subscripts. A number of prior studies have used typographical means as a metalinguistic signal for coreference, rather than excluding certain coreferential options by means of gender, number, or person features.

In this section we consider four different typographic means of indicating the intended coreference relations: (i) bold font, (ii) all-caps, (iii) colored font, and (iv) use of a box around the anaphoric expression. These methods work well for materials presented in writing to literate participants, but (i) do not allow effects of prosody/intonation to be assessed,[7] (ii) are not suitable for investigating non-literate or pre-literate

---

[6] Note that studies investigating the Gender Mismatch Effect (GMME) typically use sentences where the answer to (i) is "no," i.e. where there exists *no grammatically licensed* antecedent that matches the anaphor in gender features (hence the term mismatch).

[7] Thus, they differ from the featural-disambiguation approach described in the preceding section, which allows for auditory presentation of the stimuli.

populations (e.g. young children), and (iii) may pose challenges for populations unfamiliar with thinking about language in metalinguistic terms.

The earliest work in this tradition, by Gordon and Hendrick (1997), used bold font to indicate the nouns whose coreferential relations were being investigated, as in (6). Among other things, Gordon and Hendrick set out to investigate how the core claims of Chomskyan Binding Theory correspond to the judgments of naïve participants.

(6)     a. **Joan** respects **her.**
        b. **Joan** respects **herself.**

In some of their studies, participants were instructed to simply indicate (in a binary manner) whether or not each sentence was acceptable if the two boldfaced elements corefer: Gordon and Hendrick state that "each sentence was accompanied by a check-off to indicate whether it would be acceptable if the boldfaced NPs it contained were coreferential" (Gordon & Hendrick 1997: 337). In addition, some studies used a six-point rating scale, labeled as follows: 1 *Completely Unacceptable*, 2 *Unacceptable*, 3 *Just Barely Unacceptable*, 4 *Just Barely Acceptable*, 5 *Acceptable*, 6 *Completely Acceptable*. Participants used the scale to indicate the acceptability of the two bolded NPs being coreferential. (By labeling all points on the scale, Gordon and Hendrick depart from Cowart (1997: 71), who recommends only identifying the endpoints of the scale and leaving the points in the middle unlabeled. One of the reasons to only label the endpoints is that this can help yield interval (as opposed to ordinal) data; see Chapters 1 and 2 and Cowart (1997) for further discussion.)

A second typographic means of indicating coreference is capitalization. For example, Keller and Asudeh (2001) used a Magnitude Estimation task (see Section 11.3.3) to investigate the coreferential possibilities for pronouns and reflexives in a variety of syntactic positions, and used capitalization to indicate which elements should be interpreted as coreferential. Their instructions were: "Your task is to judge how acceptable each sentence is by assigning a number to it. By acceptability we mean the following: Every sentence will contain two expressions in ALL CAPITALS. A sentence is acceptable if these two expressions can refer to the same person." As a whole, Keller and Asudeh's work builds on Gordon and Hendrick (1997) but also investigated configurations traditionally viewed as being outside the purview of Binding Theory ("exempt from" BT), in particular picture-NP constructions (*picture of herself/her*). The coreference possibilities of pronouns and reflexives in picture-NPs have been the subject of much debate over the years, and by adopting an experimental approach, Keller and Asudeh show that while structural factors play a larger role than often assumed, the structural effects at play are not the ones that traditional Binding Theory leads us to expect.

In subsequent work, Kaiser, Nichols, and Wang (2018) used both bold font and underlining in a study investigating what kinds of anaphoric expressions can be used to refer to "imposters" such as *Mommy* and *Daddy* when used by parents to refer to themselves, as in (7). Imposters are expressions which are syntactically third person but semantically refer to the first-person speaker or the second-person addressee, e.g. *the present authors* when used by the authors to refer to themselves, *Mommy/Daddy* when used by parents to refer to themselves. We wanted to investigate the featural properties of pronouns (first- vs. third-person) that are coreferential with imposters and whether the acceptability of such coreference relations is influenced by the singular/plural distinction. We opted to use both underlining and bold font to ensure that the critical words would be clearly marked when displayed on different internet browsers.

(7)  a.  *Father says to child*: **Daddy and Mommy** have to finish {**their/ our**} coffees.
     b.  *Father says to child*: **Daddy** has to finish {**his/my**} coffee.

A third typographic convention, namely colored font, was used by Temme and Verhoeven (2017) and by Moulton et al (2018), who color-coded the two elements whose availability for coreference was being tested. Temme and Verhoeven investigated cataphoric configurations like (8), where the pronoun precedes its (quantified) referent. They investigated German, with a focus on investigating what factors influence whether syntactic objects that are experiencers can bound by a preceding pronoun (8b, c). (I use bold font here for ease of exposition, but they used color to mark the relevant words.) They tested a variety of verb classes and case-marking configurations (e.g. accusative and dative shown in (8b, c)).

(8)  a.  **His** health worried **every patient**. (Reinhart 2002: 271)
     b.  Neulich haben die Meinungen **seiner** Schwester **jeden** verwundert.
         'Recently the opinions of **his** sister astonished **everyone**.' (my translation)
     c.  Letztens haben die Träume **seiner** Kinder **jedem** gefallen.
         'Lately **his** children's dreams pleased **everyone**.'

The question that Temme and Verhoeven (2017) posed to their participants was "Do you find the sentence acceptable under the condition that the highlighted words relate to the same person?" (their translation of the German original: "Finden Sie den Satz akzeptabel unter der Bedingung, dass sich die beiden markierten Wörter auf dieselbe Person beziehen?"). Participants were instructed to provide a binary "acceptable/not acceptable" response. The results show both syntactic and semantic considerations are relevant for cataphora. Both verb class (experiencer vs. agentive verbs) and case-marking (accusative vs. dative) modulate acceptability: backwards binding is more acceptable with datives and with experiencer verbs.

In related work, Moulton et al. (2018) presented the critical words in green in their investigation of cataphora in sentences like (9).

(9)     Question: Who did John's wife hug? (object focus) OR Who hugged John? (subject focus)
        Target sentence: **His** wife hugged **John** OR **His** wife hugged **him**.

(I again use bold font here for ease of exposition; they used color.) Moulton et al. were interested to see whether coreference between the possessive pronoun and the subsequent R-expression or pronoun was more acceptable when the R-expression/pronoun was focused or unfocused. The critical sentences were presented in writing (with two words in green) and were preceded by an auditorily-presented *wh*-question which focused the subject or object of the critical sentence. Participants gave a binary yes/no response to the question "Can the two parts in green refer to the same person?" The results suggest that being unfocused boosts the likelihood of coreference with the preceding possessive pronoun, which they link to QUD-related effects.

Finally, a fourth typographical option is to put a box around the anaphor, as done by Cunnings and Sturt (2014, 2018) in their investigation of pronouns and reflexives in co-argument positions and in non-co-argument positions (specifically, picture-NPs). It is important to point out that Cunnings and Sturt did not ask their participants to rate acceptability and thus their task differs from the others reviewed in this section: Their participants saw sentences like (10), and "were instructed to choose who they thought the boxed pronoun most likely referred to, and were given the options to choose person (A), person (B) or either of them" (Cunnings & Sturt 2018: 1246). This task asks participants to select an antecedent for the pronoun, an approach I discuss more in Section 11.4.

(10)    a.  The surgeon remembered that Jonathan had noticed $\boxed{\text{him}}$ near the back of the lunch queue.
        b.  The surgeon remembered about Jonathan's picture of $\boxed{\text{him}}$ near the back of the lunch queue.

This method could easily be adapted to fit an acceptability judgment task, by putting a box around the anaphor and another box around the antecedent being tested – thus paralleling the other typographical, metalinguistic approaches described in this section. This approach can also avoid concerns regarding color blindness or differences in how colors are displayed on different screens.

In sum, a variety of typographical means have been used to circumvent the need for subscripts while still indicating that two elements are to be construed as referring to the same person. However, like subscripts, these typographical means are inherently *metalinguistic*, and participants (a) need to be told that their task is to assess whether the two typographically marked elements can "refer" to the same person and (b) presumably may also need some examples or additional explanation about what it means to "refer." Thus, the instructions for this kind of task are not as intuitive as for some other methods.

A possible concern with some of the typographical methods is the risk of participants perceiving the marked words as being emphasized in some way. This can introduce a confound: if typographic emphasis renders the referent more salient/prominent/accessible – or indicates that it is contrastively emphasized – this could (i) render the referent more available as an antecedent for a reflexive or pronoun than might otherwise be the case or (ii) evoke other potential antecedents as part of the alternative set evoked by contrastive focus. Indeed, recent work by Fraundorf et al. (2013) and Maia and Morris (2019) suggests that words presented in all-capitals evoke alternatives, indicating that they are interpreted as being contrastively focused. These studies, however, did not look at reflexives, and it is unclear whether these kinds of contrast effects have arisen in the prior anaphor-resolution studies. Nevertheless, the risk of "boosting" or otherwise affecting the representation of the typographically marked referent is a potential complication associated with those typographical formats that are conventionally used to indicate emphasis in text (such as all caps, italics, bold font, and underlining). However, this is probably less of a concern with color coding and boxes, as those are not conventionally used for marking emphasis or contrast in text.

### 11.2.3  Signaling Coreference by Other Means: Linguistic and Visual Context

Researchers have also used non-typographic means to indicate the intended coreference relation that they want participants to evaluate. In this section I review two options: (i) providing additional linguistic context and (ii) providing a visual context. An example of specifying the intended coreference relation by means of linguistic context comes from Featherston's (2002) investigation of German object-position pronouns, reflexives, as well as reflexives modified by the intensifier *selbst* ('self'). He used a preceding context as well as an explicit paraphrase at the end of the sentence to clarify the intended meaning. This is exemplified in (11), where both the story context and the addition of the "i.e." clause (in German *d.h.*, short for 'das heisst') indicate that Martin saw Martin, and not someone else. Participants were instructed to judge whether each sentence sounded natural, and indicated their naturalness ratings using the Magnitude Estimation method, discussed in Section 11.3.3.

(11)    Martins neuer Bundeswehrhaarschnitt gibt ihm den Anschein
        eines Sträflings. Manche finden es jedoch gemein von mir, dass
        ich Martin sich im Spiegel gezeigt habe. (*d.h. Martin sah Martin*)
        'Martin's new army haircut made him look like a convict. But
        some people thought it was mean of me that I showed Martin
        himself in the mirror. (*i.e. Martin saw Martin*).'

Another non-typographic approach uses the picture-verification task:
Participants are presented with a pictorial depiction of the intended anaphoric relation, and indicate whether (or not) the sentence and the picture
match (see also Chapter 13). For example, Kaiser et al. (2009) investigated
the interpretation of reflexives and pronouns in picture-NPs with and
without possessors (e.g. *picture of him/himself, Mary's picture of her/herself*).
One of the questions we tested was which anaphoric relations are acceptable for pronouns and reflexives in sentences like (12), which have two
potential antecedent candidates.

(12)    John {told/heard from} Peter about the picture of {him/himself}.

We asked whether pronouns can refer to subject antecedents and reflexives to non-subject antecedents (contrary to what is typically assumed) and
whether this is modulated by the discourse/semantic properties of that
referent (source or perceiver of information), modulated by the verb. In
a picture-verification task, participants were shown images with, for
example, John and Peter and a framed picture of either John (subject
antecedent) *or* Peter (object antecedent). Participants indicated (yes/no)
whether the sentence matches the image. If participants respond that
yes, the sentence matches the picture, this indicates that the anaphoric
relation represented in the picture (subject or object antecedent) is acceptable for the pronoun or reflexive in the sentence. Our results show that
a purely syntactic account is not sufficient: while pronouns elicit more
"yes" responses for object antecedents and reflexives for subject antecedents, the proportion of "yes" responses for both is also modulated by
referent's thematic role: reflexives exhibit a preference for sources of
information, while pronouns prefer perceivers of information.

This method does not ask people to categorize sentences or anaphoric
dependencies as "acceptable" or "unacceptable." Providing instructions to
participants is thus relatively straightforward, as the metalinguistic notion
of acceptability does not need to be mentioned. This method does not
provide a *direct* measure of how unacceptable a certain anaphoric dependency is, but the proportion of "yes, sentence matches image" vs. "no,
sentence does not match image" provides a measure of how willing participants are to accept different anaphoric dependencies.

Given its intuitiveness, it is not surprising that the picture-verification
task originated in language acquisition research. For example, in their
influential work on the acquisition of Binding Theory, Chien and Wexler

(1990) presented children with sentences like "Is Mama Bear touching her/
herself?" and showed them images with Mama Bear and Goldilocks where
Mama Bear was touching herself (subject antecedent) or was touching
Goldilocks (sentence-external antecedent). The task was to answer "yes"
or "no." This picture-verification method has been widely used in acquisition work, and has the advantage of not requiring metalinguistic explanation or reasoning about acceptability or notions like "refer."

## 11.3   How Do Participants Give Their Responses to Acceptability Tasks?

The preceding section reviewed different means of indicating the intended
coreference relation to naïve participants, without using subscripts. In this
section, we consider the nature of the dependent variable – how do participants indicate whether they judge the sentence to be acceptable? In
addition to allowing participants to make distinctions at different grain
sizes, the nature of the dependent variable (e.g. binary responses, $n$-point
scales, continuous scales) also has important implications for the suitability of different statistical analyses (see e.g. Cowart 1997; Bard et al. 1996).
Research on acceptability in general has used a wider range of dependent
variables than research specifically on coreference. This section assumes
that the broader methodological points are also relevant for coreference,
although this is ultimately an empirical question.

### 11.3.1   Binary Responses

The simplest acceptability judgment tasks ask participants to provide
a binary response, in line with the traditional categorical distinction of
grammatical vs. ungrammatical. For example, Gordon and Hendrick
(1997) asked participants to indicate by checking a box whether
a sentence "would be acceptable if the boldfaced NPs it contained were
coreferential" (Gordon & Hendrick 1997: 337; see also Section 11.2).
A binary yes/no response can also be elicited by means of a picture-
verification task, as described above.

A variant of the yes/no binary acceptability task is a speeded acceptability judgment task: participants see sentences word-by-word, with
each word displayed for approx. 300–400 ms, and then provide a binary
yes/no acceptability as fast as possible, with fast responses enforced by
a response deadline of approx. 2 seconds (e.g. Bader & Häussler 2010;
Wagers, Lau, & Phillips 2009). Lago et al. (2018) used speeded acceptability judgments to test processing of possessive pronouns in German by
native speakers of English and Spanish. Lago et al.'s participants showed
similar patterns in their response times to the speeded acceptability task
and in a self-paced reading study, though the proportion of acceptances

("yes" responses) in the speeded acceptability task yielded somewhat different results. Thus, the reaction time component of speeded acceptability judgment tasks provides a sensitive means of tapping into processing.

## 11.3.2  Scales

Intuitively, people often feel that a binary yes/no response is not sufficient to express finer nuances of acceptability (which relates to the still-debated question of whether grammaticality is underlyingly continuous or inherently categorical, with variance attributed to performance factors; see Section 11.1). One alternative is to use *n*-point scales, where participants have the choice between more options than simply "acceptable" and "unacceptable." Empirically, researchers are still debating how the data obtained by means of binary responses compares to data obtained from *n*-point scales (see Chapter 2, as well as Weskott & Fanselow (2011), Sprouse & Almeida (2017), and Langsford et al. (2018), for different perspectives).

When using scales, one challenge to keep in mind has to do with how to interpret responses at the middle of the scale. Consider the five-point scale in (13). If a participant is *uncertain* about whether *him* and *John* can corefer, they would presumably choose 3. However, if a participant is very *certain* that this coreference relation has an *intermediate acceptability status*, they would presumably also choose 3. Thus, there are concerns about conflating certainty with acceptability (see also Ionin & Zyzyk 2014).

While it has been suggested that this challenge could be mitigated by using a scale with an even number of points (e.g. 1 to 6, as also shown in (13)),[8] it is not clear that an even-point scale fully solves the problem: Participants who are uncertain could still chose a number near the middle of the scale (3–4) and participants who are certain about a middling level of acceptability could also still choose a number near the middle of the scale. ((13) uses the metalinguistic labels "Unacceptable" and "Acceptable," which would need to be explained to participants beforehand.) Arguably, though, a clear midpoint (on an odd-numbered scale) is probably more likely to be construed as a means of responding "I don't know" (low certainty) than the middle of the scale on an even-numbered scale.

(13)  **John** heard from Peter about the picture of **him**.
      Unacceptable 1 2 3 4 5 Acceptable     (odd number of points)
      Unacceptable 1 2 3 4 5 6 Acceptable   (even number of points)

---

[8] Gerken and Bever (1986)'s early work on pronouns used a four-point acceptability scale. Gordon and Hendrick (1997) used a six-point rating scale (see Section 11.2). It is worth noting that neither four- nor six-point scales have a midpoint, and thus participants are forced to make a decision about whether a sentence is more acceptable or unacceptable. (Five- and seven-point scales – also commonly used in linguistic experiments – offer a midpoint.)

As an alternative (or a supplement) to using an even-point scale, the experimenter could provide a separate "I don't know" answer choice that is distinct from the scale, or include an additional scale that asks participants to indicate their certainty/confidence in their answer (see Chapter 3, and also Rebuschat (2013), Ionin & Zyzyk (2014), Montrul, Dias & Santos (2011)). It is worth keeping in mind that use of a binary yes/no (acceptable/unacceptable) response avoids this scale midpoint complication. Thus, each method has its pros and cons.

In addition to considering scales anchored between acceptable and unacceptable, rating scales used to investigate coreference could also be constructed to be between two antecedent choices, as in (14). Such scales do not provide information about acceptability but rather about which referent is preferred as the antecedent (see e.g. Kaiser 2015).

(14)    Lisa heard from Kate about the picture of herself on the wall.

Who is shown in the picture?

Lisa  1   2   3   4   5   6   Kate

Let us briefly consider another manipulation done by Gordon and Hendrick (1997) – namely the use of two kinds of instructions: what they term "reflective instruction" (which encouraged participants to reflect on the sentences before responding) and "immediate instructions" (which encouraged participants to respond immediately without reflecting). Although they found no main effects of instruction type, a closer look at the different conditions they tested suggests that in some conditions, the reflective instructions elicited stronger effects of c-command than the immediate instructions. (See also Cowart (1997: 57) for findings showing no effect of instruction type.)

## 11.3.3   Magnitude Estimation

In the 1990s a new method gained popularity which essentially offers participants an unlimited number of response options, namely Magnitude Estimation (ME) – a method that is widely used in psychophysics research (see Stevens 1975), and was introduced to linguistics by Bard et al. (1996) (see Chapter 2 for discussion). In this method, participants evaluate stimuli relative to a "reference stimulus," often a sentence of intermediate acceptability. Participants are instructed to judge the acceptability of the experimental stimuli relative to the acceptability of the reference stimulus. Crucially, participants can make as many distinctions as they perceive to be necessary.[9]

Keller (2000) and Keller and Asudeh (2001) were the first to systematically use Magnitude Estimation to probe coreference judgments.

---

[9] A related method is the thermometer task pioneered by Featherston. This method, however, differs in some important ways from Magnitude Estimation (see e.g. Featherston 2008 for more discussion).

Experiment 1 in Keller and Asudeh (2001) tested standard Binding Theory configurations using Magnitude Estimation methodology; Experiment 2 turned to a more contentious domain, namely picture-NPs (e.g. *the picture of her/herself*). Keller and Asudeh indicated coreference by means of capitalization. Their reference sentence was "Jill told the people HE trusts all about SAM" (see Keller 2000).

Experiment 1 in Keller and Asudeh (2001) replicates Experiment 3 of Gordon and Hendrick (1997), and shows that with uncontroversial Binding configurations (where Chomskyan Binding Theory makes clear claims about what coreference relations are grammatical for pronouns and reflexives), binary responses and Magnitude Estimation yield comparable acceptability rating data. Keller and Asudeh also investigated picture-NPs, and found that Magnitude Estimation can yield fine-grained information about coreference in this construction as well.

However, given the relative complexity of the method, one may wonder whether, in the words of Fukuda et al. (2012), this method is "worth the trouble." Indeed, a growing body of work suggests that Magnitude Estimation may not be "worth the trouble," in the sense of not yielding data that is more informative or stable than data obtained by means of a seven-point or a five-point scale (e.g. Bader & Häussler 2010; Weskott & Fanselow 2011; see also Langsford et al. (2018), who also tested Thurstonian methods from psychophysics; Thurstone 1927; Roberts et al. 1999; Fabrigar & Paik 2007). Although these methodological comparisons did not investigate coreference judgments, it seems reasonable to assume that their conclusions would also extend to the reference resolution domain.

## 11.4  Offline Methods Used in Work on Anaphors that Do Not Measure Acceptability

So far, we have focused on situations where the aim is to test whether a particular coreferential configuration – specified by the experimenter – is judged to be acceptable. However, there are also situations where the researcher wants to test which of two (or more) coindexation configurations is preferred. In this section, I consider methods that allow researchers to identify which is the "winning" antecedent for a particular anaphor in a particular syntactic or semantic configuration. Consider examples such as *John told Peter about the picture of him* or *Mary told Kate about the fountain near her* – who does the pronoun refer to? Crucially, one should not infer that a dispreferred interpretation is unacceptable/unavailable. It may be entirely acceptable but less preferred.

Prior work on coreference has used different means to convey the interpretations that participants have to choose between, including (i) asking participants to answer multiple-choice questions that present different interpretation options, (ii) asking participants to choose between two pictures that depict two different antecedent choices, and (iii) asking participants to act out the meaning of the sentence using dolls (and thus indicating antecedent choice).

Let us first consider studies where participants answer multiple-choice questions, where the choices represent different interpretation options. One example comes from Kaiser and Runner's (2008) work on pronouns, reflexives, and emphatic forms in picture-NP constructions in German and Dutch, where participants read sentences like (15) (in Dutch) and answered a question about who is shown in the picture.

(15)  a. Arne {vertelde/hoorde van} Hans over de foto van {hem/zichzelf/ hemzelf}.
    Arne {told/heard from} Hans about the picture of {pronoun/ reflexive/emphatic pronoun}

The answer choices for (15) were (i) Arne (coded as subject), (ii) Hans (object), (iii) it could be either Arne or Hans, or (iv) someone else. Inclusions of the two final options allowed us to probe for level of ambiguity as well as potential configurations where sentence-external referents are strongly preferred. Our question wording allowed us to avoid metalinguistic notions like "refer to." Building on Kaiser et al. (2009), the verb type was manipulated (tell/hear from) as was the anaphoric form (pronoun/reflexive) in order to investigate how the distinction between sources (subject of tell, object of hear from) and perceivers (object of tell, subject of hear from) influences the interpretation of pronouns and reflexives.

In earlier work, Sturt (2003) also used multiple-choice questions but with only two answer choices, as illustrated in (15b). (These questions were part of a follow-up self-paced reading study.)

(15)  b. Jonathan was pretty worried at the City Hospital. He remembered that the surgeon had pricked himself with a used syringe needle.
    *Who had been pricked with a used needle? Jonathan | the surgeon*

Multiple-choice questions, but with more metalinguistic wording, were also used by Cunnings and Sturt (2014, 2018). They compared co-argument and non-co-argument configurations, as exemplified in (16a, b): In (16a), *him* is in a coargument configuration with *John*, but in the picture-NP structure in (16b), *him* is not a coargument of *John*. Cunnings and Sturt put a box around the anaphor in each sentence and asked people to "choose who they thought the boxed reflexive or pronoun most likely referred to" (Cunnings & Sturt 2014: 313). A multiple-choice format was used: in example (16), the choices were *Jonathan, the surgeon* or "either." (Cunnings and Sturt did not give their participants the option of selecting "someone else.")

(16)    a. The surgeon remembered that Jonathan had noticed $\boxed{\text{him}}$ near the back of the lunch queue.

       b. The surgeon remembered about Jonathan's picture of $\boxed{\text{him}}$ near the back of the lunch queue.

The "boxed pronoun" approach of Cunnings and Sturt (2014, 2018) is reminiscent of the earlier "circled pronoun" approach of Carden and Dieterich (1981): they investigated cataphora using sentences like (17a, b).

(17)    a. The directors discussed the situation with Smith all afternoon. They finally decided that they would have to put (him) under the new Vice President, whether McIntosh liked it or not.

       b. The directors discussed the situation with Smith all afternoon. They finally decided that (he) would have to report to the new Vice President, whether McIntosh liked it or not.

Here, an anaphoric candidate antecedent is available (*Smith*), but Carden and Dieterich note that real-world plausibility should bias *McIntosh*. One of the key research questions was how people interpret the object position pronoun *him* in (17a), given that a subject-position pronoun (in (17b), *he*) is more clearly judged to *not* be able to corefer with a subsequent name that it c-commands (Binding Principle C) – this question bears on different definitions of "command" (C-command vs. S-Command).

What is of interest to us, from a methodological perspective, is that Carden and Dieterich did not provide a list of answers to choose from, but instead instructed their participants to underline "the word to which the circled pronoun refers" (1981: 592). Thus, like Cunnings and Sturt (2014, 2018), they ask a metalinguistic question about reference, but did not provide people with a pre-existing set of answers to choose from. This can be advantageous, as it has been suggested that providing participants with specific lists of referents to choose from may artificially boost the salience of referents that would otherwise (normally) not be considered. (Underlining may have other drawbacks, e.g. unclear marks and manual data entry.)

Carden and Dieterich found that participants tend to interpret both subject and object pronouns as referring to *Smith* (anaphora) and not *McIntosh* (cataphora) – even though in other cataphoric conditions without any kind c-command participants were willing to interpret pronouns cataphorically – suggesting that the kind of structural superiority at play includes objects as well as subjects.

Another example of metalinguistic questions being used to probe referential interpretation comes from Patterson et al. (2014). In their study on native and non-native speakers' use of Binding Principle B, they used structures like (18) and asked participants to "read each sentence carefully and decide who the pronoun probably referred to" (2014: 4). Patterson et al. used the word "probably" to signal that another interpretation (a sentence-external referent) is also possible, but was not given as one of the multiple-choice options. After each sentence, participants saw the meta-linguistic question "Who does [pronoun] refer to?" (see (18)) and had three options to choose from, as shown in (18).

(18)     The boy remembered that Matthew had bought him a new computer game.
          *Who does "him" refer to?*
          The boy
          Matthew
          Either

So far, we have considered methodologies where the competing ante-cedent choices were presented linguistically/in writing. There are also studies where participants are asked to choose between two pictures depicting two different antecedent choices. One example is Sekerina et al.'s (2004) work on reflexives and short-distance pronouns (e.g. in locative constructions such as *behind herself/her*). This work relates to the broader question of whether pronouns and reflexives in locative preposi-tional phrases are in complementary distribution in terms of their ante-cedent choices. In one of their studies participants read preamble-question sequences like (19) and were presented with two pictures for each item: one with a sentence-internal referent for the anaphor (e.g. the box is behind the boy, and a man is standing nearby) and one with a sentence-external referent for the anaphor (e.g. the box is behind the man, and the boy is standing nearby).

(19)     *Preamble:* In these pictures, you see a boy, a man, and a box. The boy has placed the box on the ground.
          *Question:* Which picture shows that the boy has placed the box behind {himself/him}?
          (a) the left picture
          (b) the right picture
          (c) both pictures

In another version, participants were presented with sentences like (20) and two images (one on the left and one on the right), and pressed a button to indicate their choice of the left or the right image (while their reaction times were recorded and eye movements tracked).

(20)     Which picture shows that the boy has placed the box behind himself/him?

The results of both experiments reveal a non-complementarity in how pronouns and reflexives are interpreted: In their final responses, partici-pants mostly choose sentence-internal referents for both reflexives and pronouns, but pronouns are more ambiguous than reflexives in also allowing sentence-external referents in approx. 20 percent of the cases. This pattern is also reflected in eye movements. Reaction times were also longer for those pronouns trials where participants chose sentence-external referents. Sekerina et al. conclude that pronouns inside locative PPs are indeed ambiguous between a subject antecedent and a sentence-external antecedent.

In addition to methods where the antecedent possibilities that participants had to choose between were presented either linguistically or depicted visually, some researchers have opted for a combination of linguistic and visual presentation. An example of using both images and linguistic choices comes from Moulton et al. (2018). They investigated effects of focus on (potentially) cataphoric pronouns using sentences such as *His mother greeted Benny*, preceded by question contexts which either put the R-expression in focus (e.g. *His mother greeted which guy?*) or rendered it discourse-old and unfocused (e.g. "Who greeted him?") After hearing the question-answer sequence and seeing an image depicting four labeled characters (e.g. Benny, Benny's mother, Larry, Larry's mother), participants saw the question "The question you just heard was about Benny and WHO?" accompanied by images of Benny's mother and Larry's mother (labeled as such, so there was no memory burden). The task was to click with the mouse on the answer, which provides a measure of whether participants interpret the genitive *his/her* in the critical sentence as cataphoric (referring to *Benny*) or not. Thus, similar to Kaiser et al. (2009) and Kaiser and Runner (2008), this set-up allows the researchers to get a measure of participants' anaphor resolution without using metalinguistic terms such as "refer to."

It is also worth considering potential differences in short-term memory load induced by these methods. If the critical sentence is still visible when the question is presented, participants do not need to rely on a memory representation when answering the question. This is the case with Cunnings and Sturt (2014, Experiment 4) and Kaiser and Runner (2008), for example. If, however, the question is presented *after* the sentence has disappeared – as was the case in Sturt's (2003) follow-up study (as in (15b)), participants are answering based on their memory of the critical sentence. In this case, one may wonder if Binding-incompatible responses could be (partially) due to participants having to rely on a potentially "noisy" memory representation of the sentence.

In addition to these kinds of multiple-choice questions (where participants choose between written or visually presented options), some researchers have asked participants to act out the meaning of the critical sentence, thereby indicating how they interpret the anaphor. For example, Runner et al. (2003) researched the interpretation of pronouns and reflexives in possessed picture NPs (e.g. *Harry's picture of him/himself*). In possessed PNPs, according to standard Binding Theory, the reflexive must be, and the pronoun cannot be, coreferential with the possessor. To test participants' interpretations of the anaphor inside the possessed PNP, Runner et al. used sequences like (21). Participants heard these while seated in front of a board with three male dolls seated in front of it (each doll was seated below three photographs, each showing one of the three dolls). The task was to act out the instruction provided in the second sentence. Participants' eye movements as well as their offline responses were recorded. Although harder to implement than some of the other methods, and not suitable for all linguistic configurations, the act-out task is very intuitive, has simple instructions (participants can simply be instructed to "do what they are told"), and does not involve any explicitly metalinguistic components.

(21)    Look at Ken. Have Joe touch Harry's picture of himself.

Runner et al. found that contrary what traditional Binding Theory leads us to expect, (i) reflexives can be interpreted as coreferential with referents other than the possessor, and (ii) reflexives and pronouns are not in complementary distribution.

In sum, experimental work on coreference has also used a range of methods to probe choice of antecedent (Section 11.4) – differing in how the answer choices are presented and how metalinguistic the questions are – in addition to methods assessing acceptability of pre-specified coreference configurations (Section 11.2). The next section discusses the benefits of using both approaches in tandem.

### 11.4.1 Complementary Benefits of Acceptability Tasks and Antecedent-Choice Tasks

The methods described in the preceding section do not ask participants to assess the acceptability of a pre-specified coreference relation, but they can nevertheless provide useful complementary data for research that uses acceptability judgment tasks. This holds especially for non-co-argument contexts where reflexives and pronouns are not in fully complementary distribution, such as picture-NP contexts (e.g. *a picture of her/herself, a joke about him/himself*), locative structures (e.g. *near him/himself*) and other structures such as coordinations and comparatives (e.g. *linguists like her/herself*). Consider a situation where an anaphor can be coreferential with either of two possible antecedents, i.e. both coreference configurations are rated highly acceptable. Crucially, the antecedent-choice tasks described above could still reveal that one of the two candidate antecedents is preferred over the other, even though both are acceptable. Considering only the results of the acceptability judgment task would lead a researcher to overlook this difference.

Conversely, using only an antecedent-choice task could lead a researcher to observe that one of the candidate antecedents always wins over the other – which could lead a researcher to incorrectly conclude that the other candidate antecedent is unavailable and/or unacceptable. However, this conclusion may also be incorrect, as it could simply be that the other candidate antecedent is dispreferred (i.e. it "loses out" to the other competitor) even if it is fully acceptable.

In sum, the antecedent-choice tasks and acceptability rating tasks are best used in tandem and viewed as complementary approaches. Which is most suited depends on the hypothesis being tested, and often using both can yield valuable information.

## 11.5  Real-time Methods Used in Experiments on Anaphora

The offline methods we have discussed so far provide information about participants' final interpretation or assessment of a coreference relation. They do not provide direct information about the time-course of people's decision-making, about the load that the response placed on the processing system, or possible transient processing effects that occurred before people reached their final decision. This kind of information can be obtained by means of online methods, including (i) eye-tracking during reading, (ii) visual-world eye-tracking, and (iii) self-paced reading. Neurolinguistic methods such as ERP have also been used (see e.g. Harris et al. (2000), Xiang et al. (2009) on neurolinguistic investigations of coreference). These online methods allow researchers to obtain information about processing that occurs before a comprehender reaches their "final decision" about what an anaphor refers to (see Chapters 22–24 for further discussion).

To see how the three most widely used methods can provide information about real-time processing, I review an example of each. In self-paced reading, participants read sentences word-by-word (or chunk-by-chunk) and the reading time for each word is measured. In the "moving window" variant of self-paced reading, preceding and upcoming words are masked. Using this method, Badecker and Straub (2002) investigated sentences like (22) to see whether, when participants encounter the reflexive *himself* or the pronoun *him*, they only consider the structurally licensed antecedent (the local subject *Bill* in the case of *himself*, and the non-local subject *John* in the case of *him*) or whether people's reading times are sensitive to the presence of a gender-matching but structurally inaccessible candidate referent. If Binding constraints "kick in" right away, the presence/absence of a gender-matching, structurally inaccessible referent should have no effect:

(22)     a. {Jane/John} thought that Bill owed himself another opportunity
             to solve the problem.
         b. John thought that {Bill/Beth} owed him another opportunity to
             solve the problem.

With reflexives (22a), the presence of a gender-matching matrix subject
should not, according to Binding Theory, influence the processing of the
reflexive because the matrix subject is structurally inaccessible. Similarly,
with pronouns (22b), the presence of a gender-matching embedded subject
should not influence processing of the pronoun, because the local subject
is not, according to Binding Theory, a potential antecedent for the
pronoun.

However, Badecker and Straub (2002) found that both pronouns and
reflexives in sentences with two gender-matching "candidate antecedents" were read slower than sentences with no gender-matching inaccessible antecedent – suggesting competition from the supposedly
inaccessible candidate. Badecker and Straub conclude that during real-
time processing, comprehenders initially consider all sufficiently salient
referents, regardless of whether they meet the structural requirements for
coreference. These slowdowns are an example of online methods being
able to pick up on transient processes that can inform theories of reference
resolution. However, there is an ongoing debate about who exactly gets to
compete in the processing of anaphoric dependencies.

Eye-tracking during reading offers a more fine-grained way of measuring
reading time, because in this paradigm, readers can freely move through
the text, including back-tracking and rereading. Thus, instead of a single
reaction time per word, as is the case with self-paced reading, self-paced
reading allows researchers to obtain multiple measures, such as (i) first-
fixation duration (the duration of the first fixation on a particular region),
(ii) first-pass reading time (the sum of all the fixation durations in a region
from when a reader first enters it to when they first leave the region), and
(iii) second-pass reading time (the sum of all fixation durations on a region
after that region has already been exited once). Sturt (2003) used eye-
tracking during reading to investigate the same question as Badecker
and Straub (2002), using sentences involving stereotypically gendered
nouns (e.g. *surgeon*), as shown in (23):

(23)     Jonathan/Jennifer was pretty worried at the City Hospital. He/She
         remembered that the surgeon had pricked himself/herself with
         a used syringe needle. There should be an investigation soon.

Sturt found no effects of the structurally inaccessible character on first-
fixation times, but he did find effects of the inaccessible character
on second-pass reading times. This led him to conclude that although the
structurally inaccessible referent has an effect during the later stages of
processing, Binding Theory constraints nevertheless kick in very early on,

contrary to the conclusions of Badecker and Straub. The availability of both early and late reading time measures means that eye-tracking during reading can provide a more detailed look at online processing than self-paced reading. Relatedly, work on the processing of cataphora (e.g. Drummer & Felser (2018) with eye-tracking during reading, Kazanina et al. (2007) with self-paced reading) has led to divergent results, which Drummer and Felser (2018) suggest may be due to the less fine-grained timing information available from self-paced reading.

In addition to methods that measure *processing time* (e.g. self-paced reading and eye-tracking during reading), other online methods such as visual-world eye-tracking offer a means of probing *antecedent activation* over time. For example, in Runner et al.'s (2003) study, described above, participants heard sentences like "Pick up Joe. Look at Ken. Have Joe touch Harry's picture of himself/him." Runner et al. tested picture-NPs with possessors – a structure where, according to Binding Theory, reflexives should always be interpreted as coreferential with the possessor and pronouns should never receive this interpretation. Participants were seated at a board with three male dolls (Ken, Joe, Harry) sitting in front of it, and each doll was seated below three photographs (one of each of the dolls). The participants acted out the instruction, thereby indicating their offline response, while their eye movements to the different dolls and pictures were recorded, thereby providing a measure of what participants are considering as potential antecedents (and not a measure of processing slowdowns or processing load).

Crucially, the eye movements in the reflexive conditions show no evidence that people are looking at the possessor doll (e.g. Harry) earlier than the subject doll (e.g. Joe) – in other words, Runner et al. find no evidence of looks to "structurally accessible" (Binding-Theory-compatible) referents preceding looks to "structurally inaccessible" (Binding-Theory-incompatible) referents. The information about what potential antecedents participants consider at different points in time is crucial for Runner et al. to argue against a view of Binding Theory as an "initial filter" that constrains the earliest moments of processing (e.g. Nicol & Swinney 1989). Offline data about the proportion of antecedent choices could not be used to shed light on claims regarding the timing of when Binding principles kick in. That being said, it is important in this paradigm to collect *both* offline and online data. Because Runner et al. also had data about offline choices, they were able to conduct a follow-up analysis looking at eye movements in only those trials where participants chose the possessor as the antecedent of the reflexive (i.e. made the doll touch the picture of Harry) – and they find that even on these trials, where participants' offline responses are in line with standard Binding Theory, there is no sign of people looking at the Binding-Theory-compatible possessor earlier than the non-Binding-Theory-compatible subject referent. In this way, online and offline data can be used to complement each other.

The modality of stimulus presentation is different in visual-world eye-tracking and eye-tracking during reading: auditory vs. written. Thus, visual-world eye-tracking can be used to investigate anaphora processing in preliterate children, and can also be used to investigate prosodic effects. (Conversely, when recording stimuli for visual-world experiments, it is important to control the prosodic properties of the stimuli to avoid inadvertent confounds such as certain pitch accent patterns present in some conditions but not in others.)

It is worth noting that the three online methods discussed here typically do not require a metalinguistic task – i.e. participants are typically not asked to judge whether a sentence is acceptable or whether a certain word can refer to the same entity as another word – in contrast to many of the acceptability methods described earlier in this chapter.

## 11.6 Empirical and Theoretical Results

A full discussion of the empirical and theoretical results of experimental work on coreference is beyond the scope of this chapter. However, in this section I will briefly review some of the key contributions and ongoing debates that have come out of experimental work on coreference.

As has already become clear over the course of this chapter, experimental approaches using offline methods have contributed significantly especially in areas where intuitions tend to be murky. We have already mentioned experimental work using acceptability-judgment tasks and related methods that investigated structures such as picture-NPs (e.g. Keller & Asudeh 2001; Kaiser & Runner 2009), locative PPs (e.g. Sekerina et al. 2004), anaphora inside coordinations (Foraker 2003), as well as cataphoric configurations (e.g. Moulton et al. 2018; Temme & Verhoeven 2017). The results of these studies help to clarify the empirical landscape, thereby strengthening syntactic theorizing and our understanding of the relation between syntactic, semantic, and pragmatic information.

In addition to helping to clarify theoretically significant judgments, experimental work on coreference contributes to our understanding of the memory representations and processes involved in the interpretation of dependencies. Traditionally, the question of whether comprehenders only consider structurally licensed, Binding-Theory-compatible antecedents during online processing of anaphora, or whether feature-matching but structurally inaccessible referents are also temporarily activated as possible antecedents emerged as one of the key questions in the late 1980s. Independently of how exactly the principles of Binding Theory are formulated in different syntactic frameworks, a key question is whether or not these principles fully constrain language processing from the earliest moments onwards.

Before getting into the processing details of this question, it is worth emphasizing that one first needs to reliably establish what are the structural constraints that guide comprehenders' ultimate choices about anaphoric coreference. In order to see when and to what extent real-time processing is guided by structural considerations, we need to know what the relevant structural factors are. This is relatively well researched for languages like English: Linguists' intuitions about core Binding Theory configurations have been (largely) confirmed by experimental work such as Gordon and Hendrick (1997). There also exists some foundational experimental work in areas where the complementarity of pronouns and reflexives is less clear, such as picture-NPs (*picture of her/herself*) and locative PPS (*behind her/herself*). However, if one wants to investigate the time course of Binding constraints in a less well-researched language, then offline, acceptability-based investigations would presumably be conducted beforehand or simultaneously with online processing studies. Even if one's ultimate aim is an investigation of real-time anaphoric processing, the offline methodologies described in the earlier parts of this chapter can be used to provide the backdrop that is needed for interpreting the online data.

The online status of Binding Theory has far-reaching consequences for our understanding of the mechanisms involved in anaphor resolution and the construction of linguistic dependencies more generally. If we regard anaphor resolution as a memory search problem, the question becomes: When faced with an anaphoric element, comprehenders have to search through memory to find its antecedent. Is this memory search/ retrieval process subject to interference from structurally inaccessible referents that match the phi-features of the anaphoric expression? Or is it purely structurally guided and insensitive to non-structural cues such as gender, person, and number? (See e.g. Dillon (2014) for a recent overview.) Furthermore, given that language involves many other kinds of dependencies as well (e.g. subject–verb agreement, licensing of negative polarity items, etc.), one would like to know whether the retrieval process involved with anaphora is similar to the retrieval processes involved in these other kinds of dependencies. To be able to answer these questions, we need to be able to tap into the incremental, moment-by-moment processes that comprehenders engage in after encountering an anaphoric expression.

Early work by Nicol and Swinney (1989) argued in favor of an initial-filter approach, according to which Binding Theory constrains processing immediately and successfully. According to this kind of view, reflexive dependencies are not subject to interference from structurally inaccessible elements. However, Badecker and Straub (2002) – discussed above – found evidence that the processing of both pronouns and reflexives involved competition between structurally accessible and inaccessible referents. But this finding has not been consistently replicated for object-position reflexives: subsequent findings are mixed (e.g. Sturt 2003; Cunnings & Felser 2013; Dillon et al. 2013; Cunnings & Sturt 2014, 2018; Patil et al., 2016). Looking at non-object-position reflexives, Runner et al.'s (2003) and Kaiser et al.'s (2009) work on possessed picture-NPs found no evidence for early effects of Binding Theory.

Further complicating the picture,[10] in recent work, Parker et al. (2015) tested null subject anaphora (in configurations where they are often analyzed as PRO by syntacticians) and found that while overt reflexive pronouns seem impervious to interference effects, the resolution of null PRO subjects is susceptible to interference (thereby resembling other kinds of dependency formation processes such as subject–verb agreement and the licensing of negative polarity items; see e.g. Pearlmutter et al. 1999; Vasishth et al. 2008; Xiang et al. 2009; Wagers et al. 2009). This finding leads Parker et al. to conclude that different kinds of anaphora may differ in their susceptibility to interference (see also Parker & Phillips 2017). This is an active area for future work.

## 11.7    Open Questions and Future Directions

Recent years have seen an increase in experimental work related to anaphor resolution that had generated fruitful empirical and theoretical insights. Nevertheless, many questions are still open and many phenomena and languages remain under-investigated.

In terms of cross-linguistic research, prior experimental work on anaphora in languages including Mandarin, Korean, German, and Dutch (e.g. Kaiser & Runner 2008; Schumacher et al. 2011; Dillon et al. 2014; Han et al. 2015; Dillon et al. 2016; He & Kaiser 2016) has already significantly broadened our understanding of how anaphora resolutions work in morphologically diverse systems. However, further broadening the empirical domain of investigation beyond commonly researched (and often typologically similar) languages is important, if our aim is to gain an understanding of human language (see also Chapter 7). It's also worth noting that phenomena that may at first appear to be limited in scope may be present in other languages as well, once we know how to look for them (see e.g. Sloggett & Dillon's (2018) finding that English long-distance reflexives exhibit person blocking effects similar to Mandarin). Thus, increased research on less-researched languages also has the potential to improve our understanding of more commonly researched languages. In general, working on under-researched languages is a domain where one can clearly see the utility of simple, offline methods that can be utilized in settings outside of the typical university laboratories but that nevertheless allow us to get a sense of the amount of variability vs. stability in the data.

---

[10] See also Nicenboim et al. (2018) on the small magnitude of interference effects the domain of agreement, which hints at the possibility that lack of power may be preventing the detecting of interference effects.

In terms of linguistic phenomena, there exist various phenomena having to do with reference that are known in theoretical linguistics but have received little or no attention in experimental work. Consider, for example, the pronouns in examples (24a–c) below (from Büring 2011). These are all pronouns that *cannot* be interpreted as "pointing to" a specific previously mentioned (or upcoming) entity. Thus, they differ from the majority of the cases that are typically investigated in psycholinguistic work and raise intriguing questions for current psycholinguistic models of anaphora.

(24)　　a. This year the president is a Republican, but one fine day, <u>he</u> will be a member of the Green Party.

　　　　b. Mary, who deposited her paycheck at the ATM, was smarter than any woman who kept <u>it</u> in her purse.

　　　　c. Every farmer who owned a donkey had Lucy vaccinate <u>it</u>.

In (24a) the pronoun *he* does *not* refer to the actual referent of the noun *the president* in the preceding clause. In other words, (24a) does not mean that the person who is the current president will one day become a member of the Green Party. Instead, *he* denotes a function that picks out the individual who is the president at the relevant time in the relevant world (see e.g. Büring (2011) for an overview). This means that the pronoun in (24a) cannot be interpreted as being straightforwardly coreferential with what might at first blush appear to be its antecedent, i.e. the referent of *the president* in the preceding clause. These kinds of pronouns are called *pronouns of laziness* (Geach 1962). A related challenge is posed by examples like (24b). Here, the pronoun *it* does not refer to Mary's paycheck. Instead it can be thought of as meaning 'her paycheck' where *her* is a bound pronoun bound by *any woman*. Thus, similar to (24a), the relation between the pronoun *it* and its antecedent is more complex than with regular referential pronouns. Pronouns like *it* in (24b) are called *paycheck pronouns* (Karttunen 1969). A third class are *donkey pronouns or E-type pronouns* (Evans 1977), illustrated in (24c). In (24c), *it* does not point to a specific donkey – instead, the sentence means something like 'Every farmer who owned a donkey had Lucy vaccinate the donkey owned by *him*'. So the pronoun *it* acts like a definite description containing a pronoun (*him*) that is bound by *every farmer*.

All of these examples are grammatical and comprehensible, but they involve pronouns that are not simply pointers to an already mentioned or upcoming referent. Thus, they differ from sentences like *Lisa was tired. Joan helped her* or *Joan helped herself*, where we can think of the anaphoric expression as pointing to a specific antecedent (*Lisa* or *Joan*). There exists extensive theoretical literature one each of these three pronoun types, but their consequences for psycholinguistic models of reference remain largely underexplored (but see e.g. Grosz et al. (2015), Kush & Eik (2019) for experimental work on donkey anaphora). Other reference-related topics, such as reciprocal pronouns (*each other*, *one another*) and locative constructions (e.g.

*behind her/herself,* also known as "snake sentences") are known to exhibit some unusual binding properties in English as well as considerable cross-linguistic variation, but have received relatively little attention in the experimental literature.

Broadly speaking, using experimental methods to investigate reference-related phenomena that have not previously been approached from a psycholinguistic perspective can have at least two advantages (depending on the topic): first, in some cases the judgments can be murky, so experimental methods would allow researchers to obtain additional data and to assess the extent of inter- and intraspeaker variance. From this point of view, experimental syntax can help clarify the empirical bases of formal linguistic theories on anaphora.

Second, many of these phenomena can potentially help contribute to central debates in psycholinguistics, such as the questions regarding the kinds of retrieval mechanisms that are involved in interpreting anaphoric dependencies.

In conclusion, although the experimental investigation of coreference – in particular the use of acceptability judgments without recourse to subscripts – requires one to tread carefully when implementing one's experiment, the resulting insights can contribute to work in both theoretical and experimental syntax.

# References

Bach, E. & Partee, B. H. (1980). Anaphora and semantic structure. In J. Kreiman & A. E. Ojeda, eds., *Papers from the Parasession on Pronouns and Anaphora.* Chicago: Chicago Linguistic Society, pp. 1–28. [Reprinted in Partee, B. H. 2004. *Compositionality in Formal Semantics: Selected Papers by Barbara H. Partee.* Oxford: Blackwell, 122–152.]

Badecker, W. & Straub, K. (2002). The processing role of structural constraints on interpretation of pronouns and anaphors. *Journal of Experimental Psychology: Learning, Memory, and Cognition,* 28(4), 748–769.

Bader, M. & Häussler, J. (2010). Toward a model of grammaticality judgments. *Journal of Linguistics,* 46, 273–330.

Bard, E. G., Robertson, D., & Sorace, A. (1996). Magnitude estimation of linguistic acceptability. *Language,* 72, 32–68.

Bornkessel-Schlesewsky, I. & Schlesewsky, M. (2007). The wolf in sheep's clothing: against a new judgment-driven imperialism. *Theoretical Linguistics,* 33, 319–333.

Büring, D. (2011). Pronouns. In K. von Heusinger, C. Maienborn, & P. Portner, eds., *Semantics: An International Handbook of Natural Language Meaning* (Handbücher zur Sprach- und Kommunikationswissenschaft / Handbooks of Linguistics and Communication Science 33/2). Berlin: De Gruyter Mouton, pp. 971–996.

Carden, G. & Dieterich, T. (1981). Introspection, observation, and experiment: An example where experiments pay off. In *PSA: Proceedings of the Biennial Meeting of the Philosophy of Science Association, 1980.* Chicago: University of Chicago Press, pp. 583–597.

Carminati, M.-N. (2005). Processing reflexes of the Feature Hierarchy (Person > Number > Gender) and implications for linguistic theory. *Lingua*, 115, 259–285.

Carminati, M.-N., Frazier, L., & Rayner, K. (2002). Bound variables and c-command. *Journal of Semantics*, 19, 1–34.

Chien, Y.-C. & Wexler, K. (1990). Children's knowledge of locality conditions in binding as evidence for the modularity of syntax and pragmatics. *Language Acquisition*, 1, 225–295.

Cowart, W. (1997). *Experimental Syntax: Applying Objective Methods to Sentence Judgments.* Thousand Oaks, CA: Sage.

Culbertson, J. & Gross, S. (2009). Are linguists better subjects? *British Journal for the Philosophy of Science*, 60, 721–736.

Cunnings, I. & Felser, C. (2013). The role of working memory in the processing of reflexives. *Language and Cognitive Processes*, 28, 188–219.

Cunnings, I., Patterson, C., & Felser C. (2015) Structural constraints on pronoun binding and coreference: Evidence from eye movements during reading. *Frontiers in Psychology*, 6, 840.

Cunnings, I. & Sturt, P. (2014). Coargumenthood and the processing of reflexives. *Journal of Memory and Language* 75, 117–139.

Cunnings, I. & Sturt, P. (2018). Coargumenthood and the processing of pronouns. *Language, Cognition and Neuroscience*, 33(10), 1235–1251.

Dąbrowska, E. (2010). Naïve v. expert intuitions: An empirical study of acceptability judgments. *The Linguistic Review*, 27, 1–23.

Dillon, B. (2014). Syntactic memory in the comprehension of reflexive dependencies: An overview. *Language and Linguistics Compass*, 8(5), 171–187.

Dillon, B., Chow W.-Y., Wagers, M., Guo, T., Liu, F., & Phillips, C. (2014). The structure-sensitivity of memory access: Evidence from Mandarin Chinese. *Frontiers in Psychology*, 5, 1025.

Dillon, B., Chow, W.-Y., & Xiang, M. (2016). The relationship between anaphor features and antecedent retrieval: Comparing Mandarin *ziji* and *ta-ziji*. *Frontiers in Psychology*, 6, 1966.

Dillon, B., Mishler, A., Sloggett, S., & Phillips, C. (2013). Contrasting intrusion profiles for agreement and anaphora: Experimental and modeling evidence. *Journal of Memory and Language*, 69, 85–103.

Drummer, J.-D. & Felser, C. (2018). Cataphoric pronoun resolution in native and non-native sentence comprehension. *Journal of Memory and Language*, 101, 97–113.

Evans, G. (1977). Pronouns, quantifiers, and relative clauses. *The Canadian Journal of Philosophy*, 7(3), 467–536.

Fabrigar, L. R. & Paik, J.-E. S. (2007). Thurstone scales. In N. Salkind, ed., *Encyclopedia of Measurement and Statistics*. Thousand Oaks, CA: Sage, pp. 1003–1005.

Featherston, S. (2002). Coreferential objects in German: Experimental evidence on reflexivity. *Linguistische Berichte*, 192, 457–484.

Featherston, S. (2008). Thermometer judgments as linguistic evidence. In C. M. Riehl & A. Rothe, eds., *Was ist linguistische Evidenz?* Aachen: Shaker, pp. 69–90.

Foraker, S. (2003). The processing of logophoric reflexives shows discourse and locality constraints. Paper presented at the 38th Annual Meeting of the Chicago Linguistic Society.

Fraundorf, S. H., Benjamin, A. S., & Watson, D. G. (2013). What happened (and what didn't): Discourse constraints on encoding of plausible alternatives. *Journal of Memory and Language*, 69, 196–227.

Frazier, L. & Clifton, C. (2000). On bound variable interpretations: The LF-Only Hypothesis. *Journal of Psycholinguistic Research*, 29, 125–139.

Fukuda, S., Goodall, G., Michel, D., & Beecher, H. (2012). Is Magnitude Estimation worth the trouble? In J. Choi, E. A. Hogue, J. Punske, D. Tat, J. Schertz, & A. Trueman, eds., *Proceedings of the 29th West Coast Conference on Formal Linguistics*. Somerville, MA: Cascadilla Proceedings Project, pp. 328–336.

Fukumura K., Hyönä, J., & Scholfield, M. (2013). Gender affects semantic competition: The effect of gender in a non-gender-marking language. *Journal of Experimental Psychology: Learning, Memory, and Cognition*, 39(4), pp. 1012–1021.

Garnham, A. (2001). *Mental Models and the Interpretation of Anaphora*. Hove: Psychology Press.

Geach, P. (1962). *Reference and Generality*. Ithaca, NY: Cornell University Press.

Gerken, L.-A. & Bever, T. (1986). Linguistic intuitions are the result of interactions between perceptual processes and linguistic universals. *Cognitive Science*, 10, 457–476.

Gibson, E. & Fedorenko, E. (2013). The need for quantitative methods in syntax and semantics research. *Language and Cognitive Processes*, 28(1–2), 88–124.

Gordon, P. C. & Hendrick, R. (1997). Intuitive knowledge of linguistic co-reference. *Cognition*, 62, 325–370.

Grosz, P. G., Patel-Grosz, P., Fedorenko, E., & Gibson, E. (2015). Constraints on donkey pronouns. *Journal of Semantics*, 32(4), 619–648.

Han, C.-h., Storoshenko, D., Leung, B., & Kim, K. (2015). The time course of long distance anaphor processing in Korean. *Korean Linguistics*, 17 (1), 1–32.

Harris, T., Wexler, K., & Holcomb, P. (2000). An ERP investigation of binding and coreference. *Brain and Language*, 75, 313–346.

Häussler, J. & Juzek, T. S. (2017). Hot topics surrounding acceptability judgement tasks. In S. Featherston, R. Hörnig, R. Steinberg, B. Umbreit,

& J. Wallis, eds., *Proceedings of Linguistic Evidence 2016: Empirical, Theoretical, and Computational Perspectives*. University of Tübingen. http://dx.doi.org /10.15496/publikation-19039

He, X. & Kaiser, E. (2016). Processing the Chinese reflexive "ziji": Effects of featural constraints on anaphor resolution. *Frontiers in Psychology*, 7, 284.

Huang Y. (2000). *Anaphora: A Cross-Linguistic Approach*. Oxford: Oxford University Press.

Ionin, T. & Zyzik, E. (2014). Judgment and interpretation tasks in second language research. Review article for *Annual Review of Applied Linguistics*. *Annual Review of Applied Linguistics*, 34, 1–28.

Kaiser, E. (2015). Perspective-shifting and free indirect discourse: Experimental investigations. In S. D'Antonio, M. Moroney, & C. R. Little, eds, *Proceedings of Semantics and Linguistic Theory 25 (SALT 25)*, pp. 346–372.

Kaiser, E., Nichols, J., & Wang, C. (2018). Experimenting with imposters: What modulates choice of person agreement in pronouns? *Proceedings of Sinn und Bedeutung*, 22(1), 505–521.

Kaiser, E. & Runner, J. T. (2008). Intensifiers in German and Dutch Anaphor Resolution. In N. Abner & J. Bishop, eds., *Proceedings of the 27th West Coast Conference on Formal Linguistics*. Somerville, MA: Cascadilla Proceedings Project, pp. 265–273.

Kaiser, E., Runner, J., Sussman, R., & Tanenhaus, M. (2009). Structural and semantic constraints on the resolution of pronouns and reflexives. *Cognition*, 112, 55–80.

Karttunen, L. (1969). Pronouns and variables. In R. I. Binnick, A. Davidson, G. M. Green, & J. L. Morgan, eds., *Proceedings of the Fifth Regional Meeting of the Chicago Linguistic Society*. Chicago: Chicago Linguistic Society, pp. 108–116.

Kazanina, N., Lau, E. F., Lieberman, M., Yoshida, M., & Philips, C. (2007). The effect of syntactic constraints on the processing of backwards anaphora. *Journal of Memory and Language*, 56, 384–409.

Keller, F. & Asudeh, A. (2001). Constraints on linguistic coreference: Structural vs. pragmatic factors. In J. Moore & K. Stenning (eds.), *Proceedings of the 23rd Annual Conference of the Cognitive Science Society*. Mahwah, NJ: Lawrence Erlbaum, pp. 483–488.

Keller, F. (2000). Gradience in grammar: Experimental and computational aspects of degrees of grammaticality. Doctoral dissertation, University of Edinburgh.

Kreiner, H., Sturt, P., & Garrod, S. (2008). Processing definitional and stereotypical gender in reference resolution: Evidence from eye-movements. *Journal of Memory and Language*, 58(2), 239–261.

Kush, D. & Eik, R. (2019). Antecedent accessibility and exceptional covariation: Evidence from Norwegian Donkey Pronouns. *Glossa: A Journal of General Linguistics*, 4(1), 96. DOI:10.5334/gjgl.930

Kush, D., Lidz, J., & Phillips, C. (2015). Relation-sensitive retrieval: Evidence from bound variable pronouns. *Journal of Memory and Language*, 82, 18–40.

Labov, W. (1972). *Sociolinguistic Patterns*. Philadelphia: University of Pennsylvania.

Lago, S., Stutter Garcia, A., & Felser, C. (2018). The role of native and non-native grammars in the comprehension of possessive pronouns. *Second Language Research*, 35(3), 319–349.

Langsford, S. et al. (2018). Quantifying sentence acceptability measures: Reliability, bias, and variability. *Glossa: A Journal of General Linguistics*, 3(1), 37. DOI:10.5334/gjgl.396

Maia, J. & Morris, R. (2019). The semantics–pragmatics of typographic emphasis in discourse. Poster presented at the 32nd Annual CUNY Conference on Human Sentence Processing.

Montrul, S., Dias, R., & Santos, H. (2011). Clitics and object expression in the L3 acquisition of Brazilian Portuguese: Structural similarity matters for transfer. *Second Language Research*, 27, 21–58.

Moulton, K., Chan, Q., Cheng, T., Han, C.-h., Kim, K., & Nickel-Thompson, S. (2018). Focus on cataphora: Experiments in context. *Linguistic Inquiry* 49 (1) 151–168.

Myers, J. (2009). Syntactic judgment experiments. *Language and Linguistics Compass*, 3, 406–423.

Nicenboim, B., Vasishth, S., Engelmann, F., & Suckow, K. (2018). Exploratory and confirmatory analyses in sentence processing: A case study of number interference in German. *Cognitive Science*, 42, 4, 1075–1100.

Nicol, J. & Swinney, D. (1989). The role of structure in coreference assignment during sentence comprehension. *Journal of Psycholinguistic Research*, 18, 5–20.

Parker, D. & Phillips, C. (2017). Reflexive attraction in comprehension is selective. *Journal of Memory and Language*, 94, 272–290.

Parker, D., Lago, S., & Phillips, C. (2015). Interference in the processing of adjunct control. *Frontiers in Psychology*, 6, 1–13.

Patil, U., Vasishth, S., & Lewis, R. L. (2016). Retrieval interference in syntactic processing: The case of reflexive binding in English. *Frontiers in Psychology*, 7, 1–18.

Patterson C., Trompelt, H., & Felser, C. (2014). The online application of binding condition B in native and non-native pronoun resolution. *Frontiers in Psychology*, 5, 147.

Pearlmutter, N., Garnsey, S., & Bock, K. (1999). Agreement processes in sentence comprehension. *Journal of Memory and Language*, 41, 427–456.

Phillips, C. & Lasnik, H. (2003). Linguistics and empirical evidence: Reply to Edelman and Christiansen. *Trends in Cognitive Sciences*, 7, 61–62.

Pollard, C. & Sag, I. (1992). The processing of logophoric reflexives shows discourse and locality constraints. *Linguistic Inquiry*, 23(2), 261–303.

Rebuschat, P. (2013). Measuring implicit and explicit knowledge in second language research. *Language Learning*, 63, 595–626.

Reinhart, T. (1982). Pragmatics and linguistics: An analysis of sentence topics. *Philosophica*, 27, 53–94.

Reinhart, T. (1983a). *Anaphora and Semantic Interpretation*. London: Croom Helm.

Reinhart, T. (1983b). Coreference and bound anaphora: A restatement of the anaphora question. *Linguistics and Philosophy*, 6, 47–88.

Reinhart, T. (2002). The theta system: An overview. *Theoretical Linguistics*, 28, 229–290.

Rigalleau, F., Caplan, D., & Baudiffier, V. (2004). New arguments in favour of an automatic gender pronominal process. *Quarterly Journal of Experimental Psychology A: Human Experimental Psychology*, 57A(5), 893–933.

Roberts, J., Laughlin, J., & Wedel, D. (1999). Validity issues in the Likert and Thurstone approaches to attitude measurement. *Educational and Psychological Measurement*, 59(2), 211–233.

Runner, J. T., Sussman, R. S., & Tanenhaus, M. K. (2003). Assignment of reference to reflexives and pronouns in picture noun phrases: Evidence from eye movements. *Cognition*, 89, B1–B13.

Schumacher, P. B., Bisang, W., & Sun, L. (2011). Perspective in the processing of the Chinese reflexive *ziji*: ERP evidence. *Lecture Notes in Computer Science*, 7009, 119–131.

Schütze, C. (1996). *The Empirical Base of Linguistics*. Chicago: University of Chicago Press.

Schütze, C. & Sprouse, J. (2013). Judgment data. In R. J. Podesva & D. Sharma, eds., *Research Methods in Linguistics*. Cambridge: Cambridge University Press, pp. 27–50.

Sekerina, I., Stromswold, K., & Hestvik, A. (2004). How adults and children process referentially ambiguous pronouns. *Journal of Child Language*, 31, 123–152.

Sloggett, S. & Dillon, B. (2018). Person blocking in reflexive processing: When "I" matter more than "them." Talk given at CUNY 2018, UC Davis.

Sprouse, J. (2007). Continuous acceptability, categorical grammaticality, and experimental syntax. *Biolinguistics*, 1, 123–134.

Sprouse, J. & Almeida, D. (2017). Design sensitivity and statistical power in acceptability judgment experiments. *Glossa: A Journal of General Linguistics*, 2(1), 14.1–32. DOI:10.5334/gjgl.236

Sprouse, J., Schütze, C. T., & Almeida, D. (2013). A comparison of informal and formal acceptability judgments using a random sample from *Linguistic Inquiry* 2001–2010. *Lingua*, 134, 219–248.

Stevens, S. (1975). *Psychophysics: Introduction to Its Perceptual, Neural, and Social Prospects*. New York: John Wiley.

Sturt, P. (2003). The time-course of the application of binding constraints in reference resolution. *Journal of Memory and Language*, 48, 542–562.

Temme, A. & Verhoeven, E. (2017). Backward binding as a psych effect: A binding illusion? *Zeitschrift für Sprachwissenschaft*, 36(2), 279–308.

Thurstone, L. (1927). A law of comparative judgment. *Psychological Review*, 34(4), 273.

Vasishth, S., Brüssow, S., Lewis, R. L., & Drenhaus, H. (2008). Processing polarity: How the ungrammatical intrudes on the grammatical. *Cognitive Science*, 32(4), 685–712.

Wagers, M. W., Lau, E. F., & Phillips, C. (2009). Agreement attraction in comprehension: Representations and processes. *Journal of Memory and Language*, 61(2), 206–237.

Weskott, T. & Fanselow, G. (2011). On the informativity of different measures of linguistic acceptability. *Language*, 87(2), 249–273.

Xiang, M., Dillon, B., & Phillips, C. (2009). Illusory licensing effects across dependency types: ERP evidence. *Brain and Language*, 108, 1, 40–55.

# 12

# Constituent Order and Acceptability

Thomas Weskott

## 12.1 Overview

According to a very basic conception, the task of syntax in a grammar of a given language is to specify which orders of words that the lexicon of that language provides constitute a sentence, and which ones do not. In somewhat more technical terms: the syntax of a language has to (i) determine how constituents are built up from words, and (ii) decide which serializations of constituents are admissible structures in the language. Thus, to repeat a notorious example from Noam Chomsky's *Syntactic Stuctures* (1957), while (1) and (2) are equally nonsensical, only the former conforms to the criteria (i) and (ii) above, while the latter does not.

(1)     Colorless green ideas sleep furiously.

(2)     Furiously sleep ideas green colorless.

Here, we will be concerned only with violations of the second criterion and will not go into the internal syntax of constituents. Rather, this contribution will be concerned with the effects of different serializations of the constituents of a given sentence on the acceptability of that sentence, that is, with non-canonical constituent orders that are derived from canonical constituent orders by a dislocation of one or more syntactic constituents. The two central notions, *Constituent Order* and *Acceptability*, are both multifactorial phenomena. The surface constituent order of a given sentence is subject to a multitude of factors from all levels of grammar, and, perhaps even more dramatically, to influences from outside of grammar, mainly from pragmatics. In a similar fashion, the acceptability value that a given sentence gets is the outcome of a cognitive process which is also influenced by a variety of factors. The goal of this contribution, then, is to review the literature for experimental studies that have investigated the effects of some of the multiple possible interactions of the factors behind constituent order on the one hand, and some of the factors that drive acceptability on the other. Hopefully, this will allow me to chart at least parts of this territory, and to call attention to some of the white spots on the map as we pass them.

The plan for the chapter is the following: after a short methodological note, Section 12.3 provides a roundup of the main conceptual background connected to the notions of acceptability and constituent order. The bulk of the chapter is then laid out in Section 12.4, which tries to give an overview of the experimental studies that have addressed particular interactions between factors driving word order[1] and acceptability. Section 12.5 concludes the chapter by giving an outlook on topics for further research.

## 12.2 A Note on Methodology

Since the effect of a given non-canonical constituent order always has to be established vis-à-vis its canonical counterpart, the natural way to exemplify effects of constituent order variation are minimal pairs, or pairs of minimal pairs. It probably goes without saying that within these minimal pairs, unless indicated otherwise, all other things – the prosody of the sentence, its interpretation etc. – have to be kept constant (wherever possible); i.e. the relative acceptability within such pairs is always assessed *ceteris paribus*. In what follows, I will assume that this *ceteris paribus* assumption holds, and alert the reader to cases where it does not.

Apart from being a matter of convenience in presenting these pairs, the representation of constituent order variants as pairs of minimal pairs is rooted in the methodological necessity to keep confounds to a minimum. While this is a methodological imperative in experimental syntax in general, it is of particular importance in the case of experimental investigations of constituent order variation: as mentioned above, and as we are about to develop in more detail below, constituent order is related to and correlated with countless properties of sentences, both grammatical and pragmatic. All of these properties pose a challenge to the interpretability of results if not controlled for properly.

These methodological problems besetting the experimental study of non-canonical constituent orders have prompted some researchers to take a rather skeptical position on the enterprise of disentangling the factors involved in constituent order variation. For example, Gärtner and Steinbach (2003) note that the combinatorics of different factors entering into the study of Scrambling in German yields the forbidding number of 10,368 sentence types one may have to take into account when studying the relative order of three arguments in the German *Mittelfeld* (more on

---

[1] In order to not have to use the somewhat cumbersome term *constituent order* over and over again, I will replace it with *word order* from time to time. Although not every word is a constituent in the sense relevant here, I will use the two terms interchangeably, and hope that the reader bears with me.

that below). While this estimate is probably a bit too high, since not all combinations of properties (for example, definiteness, accentuation, pronominalization) are actually compatible, it points to the necessity to apply a strategy of *divide and conquer*: it is only by taking into account the full complexity of factors, and by exerting meticulous control over all possible confounds that the data from experiments on word order variation can actually be interpreted, and thus add to our understanding of how syntax interfaces with other grammatical and extragrammatical modules.[2]

A further methodological question which has also been brought up by a reviewer is related to the pragmatic nature of the factors influencing word order. Given that some word orders are less acceptable not due to syntactic, but mostly due to pragmatic reasons, shouldn't the property that researchers ask participants to judge in experiments on constituent orders, rather than well-formedness, or acceptability, be something like felicity, or naturalness? Although it is hard to answer such practical questions definitively, experience tells us that whatever factors are employed in the materials of the experiment will lead participants, if correctly instructed, to employ the relevant categories, be they syntactic, phonological, semantic, or pragmatic, and will drive their judgments accordingly. If I understand him correctly, this is also the stance that Wayne Cowart takes in his (1997) book (see in particular his Chapter 9). This is to say that if the linguistic properties manipulated are sufficiently homogeneous throughout the materials, it is of minor importance how the actual scale presented to the participants is labeled. This of course implies that a given experiment should not mix categorical manipulations with huge effect sizes like, e.g., subject–verb agreement violations, with rather subtle and possibly even continuous predictors like the distance of a definite NP to its antecedent, measured in number of intervening discourse referents. With this methodological aside, we now turn to the bulk of conceptual properties involved in the study of non-canonical constituent orders.

## 12.3  Acceptability and Constituent Order: A Bit of Conceptual Background

Constituent order is a phenomenon at the core of grammar: the grammar of a given language should allow us to tell the admissible constituent orders from those that are not part of the grammar of that language. Thus, we could expect there to be a rather straightforward connection between constituent order variation of sentence types on the one hand, and acceptability on the other. However, this expectation is bound to be disappointed: there is more to constituent order than the syntax of a language can tell us; and there is, needless to say, more to acceptability

---

[2] Frank Keller's (2000) dissertation is a prime example of how to execute this research strategy.

than mere grammaticality (see Chapters 4 and 5, for example). While this chapter cannot provide a detailed account of how the notions in question should be analyzed, it seems worthwhile to at least enumerate those correlations between the two notions that are pertinent to this chapter.

The term *constituent order* in the sense relevant here describes the serial ordering of the major components of a given clause: the verb, its subject, the verbal complements, and possibly some adverbial material. For languages that allow different serializations of the same lexical material, one can ask the question whether there is a basic constituent order; and if there is, whether the other orderings can be derived from that basic order – the term *derivation* being used in a pre-theoretic way here. For example, Czech allows all six possible permutations of the three major constituents of a sentence with a transitive verb:[3]

(3)     a. Pepík vypil       tři    piva.
             Pepík PERF-drank   three  beers
             'Pepík drank three beers.'
       b. Pepík tři piva vypil.
       c. Vypil Pepík tři piva.
       d. Vypil tři piva Pepík.
       e. Tři piva Pepík vypil.
       f. Tři piva vypil Pepík.

For the sentences in (3), we can ask which of them represents the basic constituent order, and how the other serializations are derived from it. Though this is a point of contention, most linguists working in experimental syntax would probably agree that this derivation can be described in terms of a dislocation of one or more phrases from its position in the basic ordering. This dislocation in turn can be described as a movement or copying of this phrase from one position to another one, or as structure sharing between these two positions.[4] Similarly for the parallel sentences in English:

(4)      a. John drank three beers.
       b. *John three beers drank.
       c. *Drank John three beers.
       d. *Drank three beers John.
       e. Three beers John drank.
       f. *Three beers drank John.

---

[3] Czech is kind of a random pick here; there are numerous other languages with a similarly liberal constituent order, among them Finnish (see Vilkuna 1989; Kaiser & Trueswell 2004; Nikanne 2017); Swedish (Hörberg 2016); and Malayalam (Namboodiripad 2017), to name just a few. For Czech, there is, to my knowledge, only one experimental investigation of non-canonical constituent orders, in Bojar et al. (2004).

[4] Thus, the term *dislocation* is used here in the sense of a cover term for all instances of a constituent appearing in a sentence position different from its position in the basic, unmarked ordering. Moreover, it is not used in the more specific sense of the terms *left* or *right dislocation*, which describe more specific types of non-canonical positioning of constituents. Thanks to an anonymous reviewer for pointing this out.

The comparison of (3) to (4) shows that the grammar of English is much more restrictive with respect to constituent order than Czech: the former allows only the topicalized order in (4e) in addition to the basic ordering in (4a). But even though the grammar of Czech declares all six variants of the sentence as licit structures, there are differences in distribution, and, as a consequence, also in acceptability: the orders in (3c) and (3d) can only be used as polarity questions, and the subject-last orders in (3d) and (3f) will be perceived as rather strange by non-linguists, and be termed highly marked by linguists. The same holds for (4e) – all these would receive degraded acceptability judgments in comparison to their base ordering counterparts.

What these examples show us is that the dislocation of constituents affects acceptability differently in different languages. (This is just a clumsy way of stating that languages differ with respect to constituent orders.) What they also show is that we cannot rely on grammaticality to tell the acceptability status of the examples in (3) apart: other properties of these sentences must be responsible for the degraded acceptability. We will look into these properties in more detail in the section after the next. But first, let us establish a few basic facts about the syntactic properties that are affected by constituent order variation, and how this in turn affects acceptability.

### 12.3.1   How Is Acceptability Affected by Dislocation?

#### 12.3.1.1   Syntax and Processing of Dislocation

Formally, we can conceive of acceptability as a two-place function from (pairs of) sentence tokens and individuals into some measurement space (nominal or numeric; see Chapter 2). From this, it follows that both properties of the stimulus (the sentence) and the judging individual will run into the acceptability value. Intra-individual components of acceptability are working memory capacity, reading span (see Chapters 4 and 5), dialect/sociolect,[5] language proficiency and literacy, and world knowledge. Properties of the stimulus sentence that enter into the outcome of the judgment process are grammaticality, syntactic and lexical ambiguity, plausibility and truth, register and style, information structure and frequency, and, possibly, modality (written vs. spoken vs. signed; see Chapter 21).

---

[5] For attempts at bringing dialect as a factor to bear on constituent order, see Fanselow et al. (2005), and Fanselow and Weskott (2010). Since we mention dialect as a factor here, it should be noted that there is a factor affecting acceptability that cannot be captured on the individual level: normativity. Normativity is a factor that is governed by a (more or less) institutionalized notion of what is grammatical in a language. Sentences exhibiting marked word orders are sometimes perceived as being outright deviant by participants, as witnessed by comments like "One doesn't/shouldn't speak that way." What participant reactions like these suggest is that they seem to assume that non-canonical word orders violate some normative rules of language. We have nothing to say on these matters, but point the interested reader to Vogel (2018).

But only some of these properties are relevant for constituent orderings. Let us begin with what probably is the only intra-individual property that might be suspected to influence acceptability of constituent orders. If we conceive of a non-canonical word order as being the result of a dislocation, then it will involve a syntactic dependency. The first way in which such dependencies might affect acceptability is that the position in the structure where the constituent was dislocated from is a position from which such dislocation is not allowed in the language under consideration; syntactic islands of all sorts, and locality constraints more generally are examples of these types of constraints, the violation of which will lead to degraded acceptability; see (5) for an example and Chapter 9 for more detail.

(5)      a. Peter asked [whether John will come to the party.]
         b. *Who did Peter ask [whether_____ will come to the party?]

The second way in which dependencies can affect acceptability is that, according to most contemporary sentence processing models, non-canonical constituent orders will tax working memory, since a representation of the dislocated constituent will have to be held in memory in order to be connected to the position it was dislocated from.[6] This taxation on working memory resources, illustrated in (6), is dependent on two further factors: firstly, the length of the dependency path (as measured in terms of embedded clauses, bounding nodes/barriers/phases in the generative literature, or in terms of (immediate) constituents (as, for example, in Hawkins (1994)) or discourse referents, or some other measure of dependency length).

(6)      a. Who did you invite_____to the party?
         b. Who did Peter say Mary thought you did invite___to the party?

Another way in which dislocated constituents can affect working memory is constituted by cases where two constituents have been dislocated: their dependency paths can either be nested within each other as in (7a), or they can cross as in (7b).

(7)      a. Which violin$_i$ is this sonata$_j$ easy to play_____$_j$ on_____$_i$ ?
         b. Which sonata$_i$ is this violin$_j$ easy to play_____$_i$ on_____$_j$ ?

Fodor (1978), from where these examples are taken,[7] has shown that the human sentence processing mechanism strongly prefers dependencies of the former kind to those of the latter, and it is this parsing preference that drives the acceptability pattern in favor of nesting dependencies over crossing ones (see Clifton & Frazier (1986), Experiment 2, and much

---

[6] The somewhat vague terminology here is intentional and should be understood as an attempt to avoid too much theoretical commitment. What I am thinking of are of course filler–gap dependencies in the sense of Fodor (1978).
[7] The original observation being due to Ross (1967: 418f.).

subsequent evidence). There are further ways in which dislocation of
a constituent can affect acceptability: if the dependency created by the
dislocation crosses an element that is scope-bearing (either semantically or
syntactically; see Chapters 5 and 13), the non-canonical structure resulting
from the dislocation in most cases will be less acceptable (under the
intended interpretation) than the canonical one, or it will receive
a different interpretation:

(8)     a. Jeder        Linguist  verehrt  einen  Philosophen.
           every-NOM  linguist   idolizes  a-ACC  philosopher-ACC
           'Every linguist idolizes one philosopher.'
        b. Einen   Philosophen       verehrt  jeder       Linguist.
           a-ACC   philosopher-ACC  idolizes  every-NOM  linguist
           'A/one philosopher is idolized by every linguist.'

While (8a) is compatible with both the specific and the unspecific reading of the indefinite NP *einen Philosophen* (i.e. is true both in a scenario
where every linguist idolizes a different philosopher, and the scenario
where they all idolize just one and the same), in (8b) there is a strong
preference to interpret the topicalized indefinite NP as specific, thus
inducing only the latter reading; see Frey (1993) and Ebert (2009). Note
that this interpretation is dependent on a specific intonational contour,
the so-called "hat contour" or "bridge accent"; see Jacobs (1997) and Steube
(2001) for the relevant details. In Section 12.4, we will see how different
constituent orders (e.g. Scrambling) can affect the interpretive potential of
a sentence. Similarly, if two constituents in the canonical order exhibit
a syntactic binding relation, then the resulting non-canonical order will
incur an acceptability penalty if it changes the order of the two elements in
the relation; again, only if the interpretation of the sentence (in the sense
of coindexations of NPs) is held constant:

(9)     a. [This syntactician]$_i$ is very fond of himself$_i$.
        b. *Himself$_i$, [this syntactician]$_i$ is very fond of.

These effects of dislocation have been well known at least since Ross's
(1967) original formulation of the Crossover Condition. Apart from binding relations, there are a few other relational properties of constituents
that can be said to piggyback on canonical orders (although some researchers would describe this relation inversely): subjects tend to precede objects
in most languages; agents and experiencers precede themes and goals;
definite and nominal expressions are preferably serialized before indefinite ones, pronominals before full NPs, and animates before inanimates
(see Chafe 1976). At least some of these constraints on serialization may
have to do with contextual properties (definiteness and pronominalization
may be related to discourse givenness), while others do not (animacy).
What they have in common – apart from being notoriously difficult to

incorporate into purely syntactic accounts of dislocation[8] – is that whenever relative order of the constituents that are the bearers of these properties is changed, acceptability is affected negatively; see Aissen (1999), Müller (1999), and Keller (2000) on how these correlations can be accounted for in terms of alignment principles cast in different versions of Optimality Theory. Thus, even if a language allows for all permutations of a subject, a direct object, and a verb, it will have one unmarked, canonical constituent order (e.g. SVO), which may be explained in terms of prototypical properties of the syntactic functions performed by the arguments: subjects, prototypically, are carriers of a higher thematic role in the argument hierarchy than objects; they tend to be definite, animate, topical, and discourse-given, while objects tend toward indefiniteness, inanimacy, and being focal (and hence discourse-new). These correlations can be the source of unacceptability if a given order violates them. Keller (2000) and Sorace and Keller (2005) have argued that violations against these kinds of alignment patterns constitute cases of *weak* constraint violations in terms of non-classical Optimality Theory.

So far, we have seen that the sheer fact that non-canonical constituent orders create dependencies which incur processing costs may explain their degraded acceptability in comparison to their respective canonical counterparts. Note that we have only looked at *negative* effects on acceptability exerted by dislocation: whenever dislocation takes place, the acceptability of the resulting sentence will be degraded. This raises the question of why certain languages – indeed, most of them – should indulge in the luxury of non-canonical word orders in the first place. There must be some factors that cash in on the processing costs, to which we will turn now.

### 12.3.1.2  Markedness: Dislocation and Context Restriction

To illustrate the problem raised above, take an English sentence with a topicalized object (example taken from Ward & Birner 2004: 159):

(10)    ?A bran muffin I can give you_____.

Here, the theme argument of the verb *to give* has been dislocated from its sentence-final position to the sentence-initial position, creating a dependency that we can hold responsible for the degraded acceptability of (10). In addition, the serialization violates the constraints that inanimates follow animates, and that indefinites follow definites, which may add to the distinct feeling of oddness the sentence instills, and which is represented by the question mark annotated to the example. Again, one

---

[8] The problem here being that any account that tries to incorporate the contextual properties of constituents into syntax (e.g. in terms of features/functional projections that represent them) will have to say something on why dislocation, despite being driven by syntactic features, appears to be truly optional. Since the topic of this contribution lies in experimental, not in theoretical syntax, I can only wave my hands at this problem, and point the interested reader to Müller (2001).

may ask why a language, in this case, English, should choose to express a content in such a dispreferred manner. Part of the answer to this question comes with the addition of a suitable context (again taken from Ward & Birner 2004: 159):

(11)    A:    Can I get a bagel?
         B:    Sorry – all out.
         A:    How about a bran muffin?
         B:    A bran muffin I can give you.

Apparently, embedding the sentence into a context seems to soothe the feeling of oddness that the sentence creates when presented out of context. (Accordingly, the question mark annotated to (10) was deleted.) What has changed by providing the context is the information packaging in the sentence: the topicalized expression *a bran muffin* is rendered *discourse-given* by the context, and it is *contrasted* with the expression *a bagel* from the first turn of the dialogue. It appears that these properties are effectual in ameliorating the unacceptability of (10). Ward and Birner (2004), following Prince (1999), argue convincingly that the decreased acceptability of topicalized structures like the one in (10)/(11)[9] is due to its syntactic markedness, and that the function of these marked forms is to facilitate discourse processing (Ward & Birner 2004: 153f.). More specifically, they argue that preposing an NP is dependent on the discourse referent corresponding to the NP has to stand in a *Poset*-relation[10] to a discourse referent in the preceding context – only then is the preposing exempt from the decrease in acceptability. What this means in terms of acceptability is that the decrease in acceptability due to the processing costs and constraint violations incurred by the dislocation must be balanced or even outweighed by the advantage in discourse processing that this information packaging brings about, and that seems to boost acceptability. The notion of markedness can be taken quite literally and in Jakobson's sense here: the deviation from a syntactic default *marks* a specific way in which the content of the sentence is to be related to the context. This idea of relating a marked constituent order to a type of context was originally formulated by Tilman N. Höhle (1982), in an article on "normal" word order and "normal" intonation. Normality in this sense is related to minimal contextual restriction: a canonical sentence, one that is unmarked with respect to constituent order, is unrestricted (or, perhaps more accurately: minimally restricted) with respect to the number and type of contexts it can appear in. A non-canonical sentence – one with, say, a preposed direct object – is comparatively more restricted: it imposes onto its context the restriction that that context provides a discourse referent to which the discourse

---

[9] "Preposing" in their terminology. They extend their account of non-canonical word orders to a number of other constructions like left-disclocation, postposing, passives, etc.

[10] "Poset relation" stands for *partially ordered set relation*. Poset relations are either asymmetric, irreflexive, and transitive, or symmetric, reflexive, and transitive, and thus include identity in the latter case.

referent of the direct object stands in a Poset relation. If that restriction on the discourse, or the common ground (in the technical sense of Stalnaker (1973)) is met, the sentence will not be perceived as unacceptable, or as having degraded acceptability. Note that, trivially, a null context cannot but fail to meet the contextual restriction a sentence with non-canonical constituent order induces.

Yet another way of putting this is in terms of *contextual licensing* (on which see Weskott et al. (2011)): a context with a certain information profile over discourse referents, i.e. their order of mention, and the relations they enter into, can then be said to *license* a certain non-canonical constituent order of a sentence that is uttered in that context. The canonical order is then licensed by all contexts (or, more correctly: by the maximal number of contexts).[11] This way of putting it allows us to relate a further property that is correlated with canonicality of constituent order: frequency. If we conceive of a given non-canonical order as restricting the set of context types it can appear in relative to some canonical order to which it is related by dislocation, then the lower frequency of the non-canonical variant as compared to that of its canonical counterpart is predicted. Moreover, it is predicted as what it is: a mere correlate of the interaction of discourse-level and sentence-level constraints, and not as a theoretical property in its own right.

To sum up this section: we have argued that the costs that the dislocation of a constituent incurs can be cashed in by an advantage in discourse processing, and that the connection between these two levels – information structure on the discourse level and on the sentence level – is moderated by markedness. A non-canonical word order restricts the number of context types it can felicitously appear in. The dislocation can be said to mark (or *signal* in the game-theoretic sense) this special relation between sentence-level and discourse-level information. The lower frequency of marked constituent orders then falls out as a mere correlate of contextual restriction. We will discuss some specific examples of contextual restriction in connection with the review of the experimental literature to be given in Section 12.4.

### 12.3.1.3 Limits of Contextual Licensing

While the notion of contextual restriction plays a central role in developing an explanatory account of the relation between acceptability and constituent order, there are a few properties that it cannot account for. Firstly, the notion of context restriction puts a lot of weight on the relation between syntax and pragmatics/information structure, while it has little or nothing to say on the relation between syntax and phonology/prosody. The fact – also noted by Höhle (1982) – that marked word order and marked prosody often go hand in

[11] Note that what we are counting here are not context *tokens*, but rather context *types*: these context types are individuated by their information profiles.

hand has no natural explanation in this account. Why should a non-canonical structure that is marked in syntax be additionally marked by prosodic means, or, for that matter, by morphological and/or lexical elements in languages that mark information structure by those means?

In a similar vein, the context restriction story fails to provide an explanation for the relation between dislocation and length/weight (see Wasow (2002), among others), since the relation between the weight of a phrase and its discourse status is largely unclear. It seems that the most plausible explanation of how constituent order is affected by length is the processing-related one put forward by Behaghel (1909): processing mechanisms both on the production and the comprehension side prefer to delay the processing of larger chunks until the processing of smaller chunks is accomplished. More recent accounts of production macro- and micro-planning (Levelt (1981, 1989), and much work following it) also provides possible explanations for certain ordering preferences: since given information can be more easily accessed in and retrieved from memory, it may also be serialized earlier in production (see Clark & Haviland (1977), and subsequent work).

Furthermore, the relation between dislocation, ambiguity, and acceptability so far remains unexplained by the account presented in this section. While dislocation can create ambiguity, it can also help disambiguate; and local ambiguity and acceptability entertain a rather complicated relation, as documented by Fanselow and Frisch (2006). Similarly, on the production side the relation between non-canonical structures and their disambiguating potential is somewhat less straightforward than one would expect (see Haywood, Pickering, & Branigan (2005), for some interesting data), and hence not easily to account for by contextual licensing.

One last fact that awaits further elucidation is that certain stylistic, genre-related constituent order patterns seem hard to explain with the notion of a Poset relation licensing dislocation: in German newspaper texts, one can observe a certain tendency to dislocate constituents that carry high informational load in the discourse into the *Vorfeld* position, especially in discourse-initial environments (Anita Steube, p.c.):

(12)  Einen   grausigen   Fund      machte  in den   frühen
      a             ghastly        discovery made    in the   early
      Morgenstunden   des       Dienstags    der    Hundebesitzer    Gunter G.
      morning-hours    of-the   Tuesday     the    dog-owner        Gunter G.
      im       Grunewalder Forst.
      in-the   Grunewald   Forest
      'A ghastly discovery was made by the dog owner Gunter G. in the early morning
      hours on Tuesday in the Grunewald Forest.'

It remains to be seen whether this constituent order pattern (a specific indefinite preceding all other arguments and adjuncts, all of them definite) is best captured by an extension of the context restriction account to genres with explicit constituent order rules (e.g. "Place the important information in discourse- and sentence-initial position!"), or whether such patterns fall outside the realm of linguistics proper, and should rather be dealt with by stylistics, or rhetoric.

## 12.4   Acceptability Studies of Constituent Order Variation

In this section, we will review some paradigmatic experimental studies of constituent order variation. Needless to say, there can be no claim to exhaustivity here, neither with respect to the languages, nor the constructions covered. What I hope to show is how different studies have operationalized the idea that we can use factorial designs in acceptability studies to disentangle the complex interactions between dislocation and the factors behind it on the one hand, and the multifactorial dependent variable acceptability on the other.

Since the bulk of this section will be devoted to studies that try to account for the complex interaction between marked constituent orders on the one hand, and one or more information structure and discourse-related factors on the other, we will first go through a number of phenomena that have been studied which most probably have no relation to information structure and/or discourse.

### 12.4.1   Syntactic Properties of Non-canonical Constituent Orders Producing a Decrease in Acceptability

There are some kinds of dislocation which are "triggered" by factors that, although possibly discourse-related, cannot easily be explained in information-structural terms. For example, the dislocation of the verbal head from the clause-final to a position following the first constituent in German and related languages (the so-called "verb-second property") marks embedding, and possibly some other factors, but the information-packaging it results in is probably not the driving force behind the dislocation itself. This is not meant to say that the two types of clauses in these languages – verb-second and verb-final – do not have distinct information-packaging potential (see Section 12.4.3 on topicalization and scrambling below). Similarly, the dislocation of a *wh*-pronoun to the sentence-initial position in English and numerous other languages is itself driven by sentence type, marking interrogativity of the utterance; but in and of itself, it does not perform an information-packaging function in the same way that, for example, topicalization of a constituent does. Still, the constraints that apply to *wh*-movement are mostly due to syntactic factors, to which we will turn now.

### 12.4.1.1  Islands

We have already mentioned the scenario in which the dislocation of a constituent leads to a decrease in acceptability due to properties of the dislocation site: island phenomena. These probably constitute the best-studied constituent-order phenomena in experimental syntax. Thus, if a *wh*-pronoun is dislocated ("extracted" being the preferred term in the literature) from a constituent with island status (e.g. a clause headed by *whether* as in (13b) below), the resulting sentence is unacceptable:

(13)    a. Mary wonders [whether John comes to the party].
        b. *Who does Jane wonder [whether_____ comes to the party].

For an overview of the factors involved in island phenomena and the experimental literature, we refer the reader to Chapter 9 of this book.

### 12.4.1.2  Subextraction and Freezing

It has been hypothesized that once a constituent has been subject to dislocation, its parts cannot be dislocated in a further step from the landing site of the first dislocation step. This has sometimes been termed a *ban on subextraction*, but sometimes also *freezing*.

(14)    a. Jane said that [a picture of John], Mary will never pin on the wall.
        b. *Who did Jane say that [a picture of_____], Mary will never pin on the wall.

Although originally conceived of as a "hard" constraint, the conditions on subextraction seem themselves to be subject to a number of factors, information structure and length being but two of them (see Konietzko (2018) for a prime example of how to experimentally tease apart the factors at work in subextraction from (un)shifted heavy-NPs), producing a much more complex acceptability profile than would be expected if only grammaticality were at issue. For an excellent recent overview of both the theoretical, as well as the experimental approaches to subextraction and freezing we refer the reader to Hartmann et al. (2018).

### 12.4.1.3  Dislocation and Ambiguity

We have already noted that, although some languages like, e.g. Czech, exhibit a relatively free constituent order, there still are, even in these languages, strong defaults that make one order the unmarked and, hence, most frequent one. These defaults are governed by the alignment principles alluded to earlier in Section 12.3.1.1. In languages in which a dislocation cannot be reliably read off the properties of the dislocated constituent (in terms of case, or some other morphological marking), dislocation can create ambiguities. Given the alignment principles, these ambiguities are then especially interesting for experimental syntacticians since they allow one to draw inferences with respect to the way in which the human sentence processing mechanism makes use of the correlations that these alignment principles supervene on. A prime example of how acceptability studies, alone and backed-up by processing data, can allow us to draw inferences about the processes underlying sentences with constituent order variation resulting in ambiguities is the dissertation by Meng (1999). Meng shows how the locus of disambiguation (on argument NPs or on the finite verb)[12] and the case of the dislocated constituent (dislocated accusatives incurring a stronger acceptability penalty than datives) modulate processing difficulty, and how the latter relates to acceptability. Meng's results are complemented by findings by Fanselow and Frisch (2006), who show that the overall acceptability of sentences containing local ambiguities depends not only on the processing difficulty induced by the ambiguity, but also on the preferred interpretation initially assigned to the ambiguous string; see also Chapter 5 of this volume.

To conclude this section: there seems to be sufficient experimental evidence to maintain that there are indeed purely syntactic effects of constituent order variation. Whenever dislocation violates hard syntactic constraints (like "strong" islands; on the terminology of "strong" vs. "weak" islands, see Chapter 9 of this volume) or creates local or global ambiguities, acceptability is immediately affected. Syntactic processing thus shows a sensitivity to non-canonical orderings which can be seen as the form-related side of the markedness relation that these sentences exploit, the function-related side being the integration of the sentence content into the common ground, or the larger discourse model. These are the information and discourse structural effects of marked word order construction to which I shall turn now.

### 12.4.2    Discourse-Level Effects of Non-Canonical Constituent Orders

For this section, I have selected a few marked constituent order constructions for which there exist experimental data which have been carried out in order to help us answer the question as to where exactly the discourse-level pay-off of the marked syntactic structure lies. Again, there can be no claim to exhaustivity; the studies referred to in what follows have been picked for their paradigmatic use of factorial designs to disentangle the complex syntax–discourse interaction of non-canonical structures.

---

[12] Kaan (1996) provides similar data for Dutch subject vs. object relative clauses.

### 12.4.2.1 Dative Alternation

A prime example of how experimental syntax can deepen our understanding of constituent order patterns is the dative alternation in English:[13]

(15)      a. He sent a letter to a colleague.
           b. He sent a colleague a letter.

(16)      a. He sent the letter to a colleague.
           b. He sent a colleague the letter.

The (a) variants exhibit the so-called PP-construction (where the goal argument of the transfer verb is expressed as a prepositional object); this is arguably the unmarked variant. The (b) variants show the double object construction, which supposedly is the marked variant. How can the relative markedness status be assessed? One way would be to claim that the PP-construction is more frequent, and thus less marked, than the double object construction. Note, however, that this would not be entirely satisfactory: markedness would be defined in terms of frequency, and frequency (as measured, e.g., in a sufficiently large corpus) could be driven by just any factor, be it linguistic, or non-linguistic. It seems more promising to relate markedness to the notion of context restriction: while the (a) variants do not show a huge difference in acceptability between the indefinite-definite ((15)) and the definite-indefinite order ((16)), the (b) variants show a sensitivity to the definiteness manipulation: in the double-NP construction, the indefinite-definite order is strongly dispreferred as compared to the definite-indefinite order. This has been found to hold in a series of acceptability judgment experiments by Clifton and Frazier (2004) in which the various other factors (animacy, argument structure, proximity to the verb) were carefully controlled for. Indeed, Clifton and Frazier showed that it is not the relative definiteness, but rather the relative discourse givenness that drives the acceptability data: while there is neither a given-new, nor a new-given preference for the PP-construction, new-given is strongly dispreferred for the double-NP construction, once again showing that the more marked form exhibits a higher sensitivity to contextual factors. The findings by Clifton and Frazier were corroborated by acceptability and corpus data in Bresnan et al. (2007), and by online processing data by Brown, Savova, and Gibson (2012).

## 12.4.3 Topicalization and Scrambling

As mentioned above in Section 12.3.1.2, the notion of contextual licensing has been proposed by Weskott et al. (2011), to account for certain acceptability patterns in German topicalization. In particular, the authors predict

---

[13] See Kizach (2015), for similar data in Danish.

that *strong contextual licensing* of marked word order should be found in cases where the marked form is perceived as more acceptable than its unmarked counterpart. (This pattern would instantiate what has been called "markedness reversal" in phonology; see Battistella (1996), for more details.) The dislocation that reorders argument order in the German *Mittelfeld* – the region in the sentence between the verb-second position which root sentences show, and the verb-final position typical of embedded sentences – is called *Scrambling*, following Ross (1967). The ordering where a constituent is dislocated to the position in front of the verb-second posititon, the *Vorfeld*, is called *Topicalization*. Both Scrambling and Topicalization have been the subject of numerous theoretical analyses, starting with Lenerz (1977) on Scrambling, and Altmann (1981) on Topicalization. While Topicalization has often been linked to the encoding of givenness or contrastiveness (marking a contrastive relation between the topicalized constituent and a referent in the preceding discourse), the moving force behind Scrambling has been less clear. Scrambled OSV structures have been shown experimentally to exhibit a weaker acceptability penalty when the scrambled order complies to ordering constraints mentioned in Section 12.3.1.1: definiteness, pronominalization, animacy, etc. (see Pechmann et al. (1994) and Keller (2000) for details). A further factor ameliorating the penalty incurred for scrambling an object across a subject is the case of the scrambled object: structures in which a dative was scrambled across a subject receive higher mean acceptability values than those in which an accusative was scrambled; see Bader and Häussler (2010), for the relevant data.

One of the first studies to investigate German Topicalization experimentally is Hemforth (1993), who showed that even in unambiguous structures, OVS structures are harder to process and receive degraded judgments in comparison to the unmarked SVO counterpart. Similar results were obtained by Bayer and Marslen-Wilson (1992). In the years following these pioneering works, several authors attempted to show that there are *weak licensing* contexts. By this, we mean contexts in which the marked word order, with a direct object either moved across the subject in the *Mittelfeld*, resulting in OSV order, or to the *Vorfeld* position (resulting OVS) in German receives acceptability ratings that are not significantly different from those for the unmarked SOV, or SVO, respectively. For example, Bader (1999) found that the acceptability of a scrambled OSV order is not significantly different from that of SOV in contexts where the discourse referent of the scrambled object was inquired after in a preceding question. Similar results were reported by Keller (2000), and Fanselow, Lenertová, and Weskott (2008). Bornkessel and Schlesewsky (2006) report on an acceptability experiment where they found OSV to be more acceptable than SOV; their contexts employed both contrastivity and a parallel structure effect (only if a sentence preceding the critical one had the same structure as the target sentence would the ameliorating effect of the contrast factor show; see Weskott (2003) for similar results for OVS structures). The first evidence for strong licensing in an acceptability study was reported by Weskott et al., (2011) who found that the topicalization of objects was licensed by contexts that featured a Poset-related discourse referent. In these contexts, marked OVS constituent structures received higher ratings than the unmarked SVO, while reverse pattern held for the no-context condition, where sentences were presented in isolation. The authors employed *whole–part* contexts of the following type; the whole–part relation holds between the constituents printed in **boldtype**:

(17)    Peter   hat   **den**       **Wagen**   gewaschen.
        Peter   has   the-ACC   car         washed
        'Peter has cleaned the car.'

   a. Er   hat   **den**       **Außenspiegel**   ausgelassen.
      He   has   **the-ACC**   **outside-mirror**   left-out.
      'He left out the rear-view mirror.'

   b. **Den Außenspiegel** hat er ausgelassen.

Weskott et al. (2011) showed that strong licensing is indeed possible, even for highly marked OVS structures where the direct object is dislocated to the sentence-initial position. In a follow-up experiment, they further investigated the nature of the licensing effect. In (17b) the object referent may be construed as standing in a contrastive relation to the referent of the noun phrase *den Wagen* (the latter, but not the former, being cleaned). However, Weskott et al. (2011) found the same licensing effect – the OVS variant is judged as more acceptable than the SVO variant in the licensing context, while the opposite is true in the null context – in a context that is much less susceptible to a contrastive construal:

(18)    Peter   hat   **den**       **Wagen**   gewaschen.
        Peter   has   the-ACC   car         washed.
        'Peter has cleaned the car.'

   a. Er   hat   **den**       **Außenspiegel**       besonders   gründlich
      he   has   **the-ACC**   **outside-mirror**   particularly diligently
      gewienert.
      polished
         'He polished the rear-view mirror with particular diligence.'

   b. **Den Außenspiegel** hat er besonders gründlich gewienert.

The acceptability data for strong licensing are backed up by processing evidence coming from two self-paced reading studies. Furthermore, Bader and Portele (2018) provided additional evidence for strong licensing in contexts that render the object referent discourse-given, and in which the object takes on the form of a so-called strong pronoun. As in the materials of Weskott et al. (2011), those of Bader and Portele had pronominal subjects. As of now, it is unclear why strong licensing of OVS has so far only been found in contexts with pronominal subjects.

Why do we report these findings in such detail? Because the fact that strong contextual licensing can be obtained shows that the idea that the markedness of a non-canonical word order pattern like OVS indeed has two sides to it: on the one hand, it is costly on the level of the individual sentence exhibiting the non-canonical syntactic pattern. On the other hand, these costs can be outweighed by the benefits that the OVS has by signaling the way in which the information that the sentence conveys has to be integrated into the discourse context. In relation to the examples above, this means that the discourse relation by which the context sentence and the critical sentence have to be related is signaled by the marked constituent order, and discourse integration can thus proceed faster; whereas, if it is not marked, discourse integration is more costly. This is exactly the constellation of factors that predicts a strong licensing pattern in acceptability. And the fact that predicting and finding this pattern repeatedly and in a number of languages (see Hörberg (2016) on Swedish; and Weskott et al. (2019) on English) tells us that the function of these information-structurally marked forms may indeed consist in packaging the sentence-level content in a way that facilitates its integration into the common ground. It has to be noted, though, that there is also evidence *against* this account (see Vasishth (2004) on the failure to license non-canonical orders by discourse factors in Hindi), and that no similar account of the function of Scrambling seems to be in the offing; see Section 12.5 below for further discussion.

### 12.4.4  Dislocation in Object Experiencer Verb Constructions

It has been noted early on that certain verbs seem to have a weaker asymmetry between subject and object as far as serial order is concerned. Postal (1971) already showed that object-experiencer psych verbs are exempt from Ross's (1967) Crossover Condition (on which see above Section 12.3.1.1). In addition, the asymmetries usually found with subject and object in cases of "regular," i.e. agent–theme subcategorization frames, are weakened or non-existent in the case of psych verbs whose argument structure consists of an experiencer and a stimulus argument. In particular, object-experiencer verbs like *frighten* or *annoy* show almost no order preference in languages allowing topicalization and/or scrambling of the experiencer object:

(19)   a. Das      Geräusch   nervt    den        Nachbarn.
          the NOM   noise      annoys   the ACC    neighbor.
       b. Den      Nachbarn   nervt    das        Geräusch.
          the ACC   neighbor   annoys   the NOM    noise.
          'The noise annoys the neighbor.'

Most speakers of German would probably have a hard time to say which of these constituent orders they prefer over the other; and even if they do have a preference for (19a) over (19b), it is probably much weaker than in cases of word order variations involving subjects and objects of causative verbs. Temme and Verhoeven (2016) report on an extensive study of word order variation in four languages (German, Greek, Hungarian, and Korean). They employed a forced-choice decision design in which participants had to choose between two argument orders for each sentence presented to them. The authors carefully controlled for the possible confounds (definiteness, animacy, agentivity, control, etc.) and compared the psych verb constructions to non-psych verb constructions which were otherwise kept as similar as possible. Two further factors were manipulated: object case (accusative vs. dative), and licensing by an aboutness relation. Temme and Verhoeven's results show that (i) languages differ considerably with respect to the extent to which they allow the experiencer object to precede the stimulus object; (ii) non-canonical constituent orders with dative experiencer objects are preferred when compared to those with accusative experiencers; (iii) non-canonical constituent orders with dative experiencer objects are more susceptible to contextual licensing by an aboutness relation than those with accusative experiencer objects; and, finally, (iv) contextual licensing is more effective for experiencer objects than non-experiencer objects. Although the method employed – two-alternative forced choice with only $n=8$ items per verb class – calls for a replication of the effects in the single languages using a somewhat subtler task, and, possibly, higher statistical power, these results show that despite the large number of factors involved, a carefully designed experiment can teach us something about the interaction of these factors, and even do so in a typologically informed setting.

### 12.4.5 Clefts

Cleft structures constitute a rather crass case of how information packaging requirements can change the syntax of a canonical sentence. This, of course, presupposes that (20b) is in some way derived from the underlying (20a).

(20)     a. Peter ate the cookies.
        b. It was Peter who ate the cookies.

The information packaging function of *it*-clefts and similar biclausal constructions like pseudo-clefts has been recognized early on (see, e.g., Chomsky 1971). The clefted part has been analyzed as providing the assertion (in the case of (20b): it was Peter who did $\varphi$) to the presupposition (there is a unique individual $x$ such that $x$ ate the cookies) that the quasi-relative adds. Although there is still little experimental evidence on the contextual restrictions of cleft constructions, work by DeVeaugh et al.

(2018) shows that the clefted constituent, or rather the NP part thereof, constitutes the exhaustive true answer to a question that is raised by the preceding discourse and which can be formed by binding the variable in the presupposition by a question operator, yielding the *question-under-discussion* (QUD; see Roberts (1996)) of the discourse at the point where the cleft sentence is uttered. It is exactly in contextual circumstances such as these that a cleft sentence, despite its dramatic deviation from canonical constituent order, may be judged as more acceptable than its non-clefted counterpart.

### 12.4.6  Inversion

Another rather extreme form of non-canonical word order is instantiated by different forms of inversion phenomena; see Birner (1996), and Bresnan (1994), for an overview of the facts. While there is online evidence that locative inversion in both German and English can speed up premise integration in three-term series reasoning tasks (see Hörnig, Oberauer, & Weidenfeld 2005; Hörnig et al. 2006), there is, to our knowledge, no evidence so far indicating that there are contexts in which the inverted word order is equally acceptable as the canonical one, or even preferred over the latter. This comes as rather a surprise given that locative inversion constitutes a case of information packaging whose contextual requirements have been described in quite some detail in the literature. This brings us to the section on further research.

## 12.5  Topics for Further Research

By way of concluding this contribution, let us look at a (non-exhaustive) collection of the topics that, to the best of our knowledge, have so far either been ignored by experimental syntax research, or – which is also not unlikely – have produced data too inconclusive to draw safe inferences from them.

One such topic that we have mentioned in passing and that possibly belongs to the latter category is the question of which factors – information-structural, discourse-related, or of whatever kind – may be responsible for non-canonical orders derived by scrambling. There are numerous conjectures around about the "triggers" for scrambling – altruistic scrambling (Haider & Rosengren 1998, 2003), egoistic scrambling (Neeleman 1994), both of which have to do with certain focus-background structures; contrastive scrambling; scrambling as a scope-widening operation (Haider 1993) – there seem to be no reliable experimental data on any of these licensing factors. One of the reasons for this might be the fact that scrambling affects both the semantic–pragmatic as well as the prosodic properties of sentences, which necessitates acoustic presentation, and meticulous control of the relevant semantic and contextual factors. As far as the semantics is concerned, it still seems to be a matter of debate whether a scrambled object reconstructs to its base position, and, if so, whether this reconstruction is syntactic or semantic; on which see Sternefeld (2000). While dislocation operations in which constituents appear to the left of their position in the canonical order, extraposition, i.e. dislocation "to the right," has received far less attention, with the exception of Averintseva-Klisch (2009), and the papers collected in Vinckel-Roisin (2015), most notably Kleemann-Krämer et al. (2015), who identify information-structural and prosodic factors governing extraposition to the German *Nachfeld*. Again, there seem to be no controlled acceptability studies testing these factors in a systematic fashion.

Further research topics that, to my knowledge, have not received wider attention from the experimental syntax community are stylistic influences on constituent order variation: there is early work on word order variation in poetry contexts in German by Christoph Scheepers and Ralf Rummer (1999), testing for the influence of stress patterns and rhyme on the acceptability and processing of non-canonical constituent orders, and there is a recent paper by Häussler et al. (2019) which expands on this. Given that poetry contexts have a strong potential to license marked structures, and even ungrammatical and semantically anomalous ones, the lack of experimental evidence is somewhat surprising.

Finally, there is the role of meta- and paralinguistic factors that seems to be understudied experimentally. For example, one may ask whether there is a decrease in acceptability if the truth of the sentence, due to its self-referential nature, interacts with its word order (here presented in German):

(21) Der Linguist behauptete,
the linguist claimed

    a. dass        das Subjekt        dem Objekt        vorangeht.   (CCO,TRUE)
        that        the subject$_{NOM}$    the object$_{DAT}$    precedes

    b. dass        das Subjekt        dem Objekt        folgt.       (CCO,FALSE)
        that        the subject$_{NOM}$    the object$_{DAT}$    follows

    c. dass dem   Objekt   das      Subjekt   folgt        (NCCO,TRUE)
        that the$_{DAT}$ object  the$_{NOM}$  subject  follows

    d. dass dem   Objekt   das      Subjekt   vorangeht.   (NCCO,FALSE)
        that the$_{DAT}$ object  the$_{NOM}$  subject  precedes

To check for possible intrusions from metalinguistic knowledge, further complications could be induced by manipulating the descriptions of the phrases (by, e.g., declaring a dative object an accusative object, etc.). Research topics such as these, although they might seem to verge on the silly, show that experimental studies of constituent order have not exhausted the space of possible questions, and, given the affordability and easy access to acceptability data, answers are relatively easy to get.

# References

Aissen, J. (1999). Markedness and subject choice in Optimality Theory. *Natural Language and Linguistic Theory*, 17(4), 673–711.

Altmann, H. (1981). *Formen der "Herausstellung" im Deutschen: Rechtsversetzung, Linksversetzung, Freies Thema und verwandte Konstruktionen*. Tübingen: Niemeyer.

Averintseva-Klisch, M. (2009). *Rechte Satzperipherie im Diskurs: NP-Rechtsversetzung im Deutschen*. Tübingen: Stauffenberg.

Bader, M. (1999). Die Verarbeitung von Subjekt-Objekt-Ambiguitäten im Kontext. In *Proceedings der 4. Fachtagung der Gesellschaft für Kognitionswissenschaft*. St. Augustin: Infix.

Bader, M. & Häussler, J. (2010). Toward a model of grammaticality judgments. *Journal of Linguistics*, 46, 273–330.

Bader, M. & Portele, Y. (2018). Givenness licenses object-first order in German. Talk presented at CGSW 2018 Göttingen.

Battistella, E. (1996). *The Logic of Markedness*. Oxford: Oxford University Press.

Bayer, J. & Marslen-Wilson, W. (1992). Configurationality in the light of language comprehension: The order of arguments in German. Manuscript, University of Konstanz.

Behaghel, O. (1909). Beziehungen zwischen Umfang und Reihenfolge von Satzgliedern. *Indogermanische Forschungen*, 25, 110–142.

Birner, B. J. (1996). *The Discourse Function of Inversion in English*. Abingdon: Routledge.

Bojar, O., Semecky, J., Vasishth, S., & Kruijff-Korbayova, I. (2004). Processing noncanonical word order in Czech. Poster presented at conference on Architectures and Mechanisms for Language Processing, September 2004, Aix-en-Provence, France (AM-LaP 2004).

Bornkessel, I. & Schlesewsky, M. (2006). The role of contrast in the local licensing of Scrambling in German: Evidence from online comprehension. *Journal of Germanic Linguistics*, 18(1), 1–43.

Bresnan, J. (1994). Locative inversion and the architecture of Universal Grammar. *Language*, 70(1), 72–131.

Bresnan, J., Cueni, A., Nikitina, T., & Baayen, R. H. (2007). Predicting the dative alternation. In G. Bouma, I. Krämer, & J. Zwarts, eds., *Cognitive Foundations of Interpretation*. Amsterdam: Royal Netherlands Academy of Science, pp. 69–94.

Brown, M., Savova, V., & Gibson, E. (2012). Syntax encodes information structure: Evidence from on-line reading comprehension. *Journal of Memory and Language*, 66(1), 194–209.

Chafe, W. L. (1976). Givenness, contrastiveness, definiteness, subjects, topics, and point of view. In C. N. Li, ed., *Subject and Topic*. New York: Academic Press, pp. 25–55.

Chomsky, N. (1957). *Syntactic Structures*. The Hague: Mouton.

Chomsky, N. (1971). Deep structure, surface structure and semantic interpretation. In D. Steinberg & L. Jakobovits, eds., *Semantics*. Cambridge: Cambridge University Press.

Clark, H. H. & Haviland, S. (1977). Comprehension and the given-new contract. In R. Freedle, ed., *Disourse Production and Comprehension*. Hillsdale, NJ: Lawrence Erlbaum, pp. 1–40.

Clifton, C. J. & Frazier, L. (1986). The use of syntactic information in filling gaps. *Journal of Psycholinguistic Research*, 15(3), 209–224.

Clifton, C. J. & Frazier, L. (2004). Should given information come before new? Yes and no. *Memory & Cognition*, 32(6), 886–895.

Cowart, W. (1997). *Experimental Syntax*. Thousand Oaks, CA: Sage.

DeVeaugh-Geiss, J., Tönnis, S., Onea, E., & Zimmermann, M. (2018). That's not quite it: An experimental investigation of (non-)exhaustivity in clefts. *Semantics & Pragmatics*, 11(3). DOI:10.3765/sp.11.3

Ebert, C. (2009). *Quantificational Topics: A Scopal Treatment of Exceptional Wide Scope Phenomena* (Studies in Linguistics and Philosophy, 86). Heidelberg: Springer.

Fanselow, G. & Frisch, S. (2006). Effects of processing difficulty on judgments of acceptability. In G. Fanselow, C. Féry, R. Vogel, & M., Schlesewsky, eds., *Gradience in Grammar*. Oxford: Oxford University Press, pp. 291–316.

Fanselow, G., Lenertová, D., & Weskott, T. (2008). Studies on the acceptability of object movement to Spec,CP. In A. Steube, ed., *The Discourse Potential of Underspecified Structures*. Berlin: Walter de Gruyter, pp. 413–438.

Fanselow, G. & Weskott, T. (2010). A short note on long movement in German. *Linguistische Berichte*, 222, 129–140.

Fodor, J. D. (1978). Parsing strategies and constraints on transformations. *Linguistic Inquiry*, 9, 427–473.

Frey, W. (1993). *Syntaktische Bedingungen für die semantische Interpretation: über Bindung, implizite Argumente, und Skopus* (Studia Grammatica, 35). Berlin: Akademie Verlag.

Gärtner, H.-M. & Steinbach, M. (2003). What do reduced pronomnals reveal about the syntax of Dutch and German? Part I: Clause-internal positions. *Linguistische Berichte*, 195, 257–294.

Gibson, E. (1998). Linguistic complexity: Locality of syntactic dependencies. *Cognition*, 68(1), 1–76.

Haider, H. (1993). *Deutsche Syntax – generativ*. Tübingen: Narr.

Haider, H. & Rosengren, I. (1998). *Scrambling* (Sprache and Pragmatik, 49). Lund: Lund University.

Haider, H. & Rosengren, I. (2003). Scrambling: Nontriggered chain formation in OV languages. *Journal of Germanic Linguistics*, 15(3), 203–267.

Hartmann, J., Jäger, M., Kehl, A., Konietzko, A., & Winkler, S., eds. (2018). *Freezing: Theoretical Approaches and Empirical Domains*. Berlin: De Gruyter Mouton, pp. 387–402.

Häussler, J., Mucha, A., Schmidt, A., Weskott, T., & Wierzba, M. (2019). Experimenting with Lurchi: V2 and agreement violations in poetic contexts. In J. M. M. Brown, M. Wierzba, & A. Schmidt, eds., *Of Trees and Birds: A Festschrift for Gisbert Fanselow*. Potsdam: Potsdam University Press, pp. 307–321.

Hawkins, J. A. (1994). *A Performance Theory of Order and Constituency*. Cambridge: Cambridge University Press.

Haywood, S. L., Pickering, M. J., & Branigan, H. P. (2005). Do speakers avoid ambiguities during dialogue? *Psychological Science*, 16(5), 362–366.

Hemforth, B. (1993). *Kognitives Parsing–Repräsentation und Verarbeitung sprachlichen Wissens*. St. Augustin:Infix.

Höhle, T. N. (1982). Explikationen für "normale Betonung" und "normale Wortstellung." In W. Abraham, ed., *Satzglieder im Deutschen*. Tübingen: Narr, pp. 75–153.

Hörberg, T. (2016). Probabilistic and prominence-driven incremental argument interpretation in Swedish. Doctoral dissertation, Stockholm University.

Hörnig, R., Oberauer, K., & Weidenfeld, A. (2005). Two principles of premise integration in spatial reasoning. *Memory & Cognition*, 33(1), 131–139.

Hörnig, R., Weskott, T., Kliegl, R., & Fanselow, G. (2006). Word order variation in spatial descriptions with adverbs. *Memory & Cognition*, 34 (5), 1183–1192.

Jacobs, J. (1997). I-Topikalisierung. *Linguistische Berichte*, 168, 91–133.

Kaan, E. (1996). *Processing Subject–Object-Ambiguities in Dutch*. Groningen Dissertations in Linguistics, 20, Rijksuniversiteit Groningen.

Kaiser, E. & Trueswell, J. (2004). The role of discourse context in the processing of a flexible word-order language. *Cognition*, 94(2), 113–147.

Keller, F. (2000). Gradience in grammar: Experimental and computational aspects of degrees of grammaticality. Doctoral dissertation, University of Edinburgh.

Kizach, J. (2015). Animacy and the ordering of postverbal prepositional phrases in Danish. *Acta Linguistica Hafniensia*, 47(2), 1–21.

Kleemann-Krämer, A., Kügler, F., & Pötzl, S. (2015). Zur Anbindung extraponierter PPen an ihre Bezugsstruktur. In H. Vinckel-Roisin, ed., *Das Nachfeld im Deutschen: Theorie und Empirie*. Berlin: De Gruyter, pp. 299–318.

Konietzko, A. (2018). Heavy NP shift in context: On the interaction of information structure and subextraction from shifted constituents. In J. Hartmann, M. Jäger, A. Kehl, A. Konietzko, & S. Winkler, eds., *Freezing: Theoretical Approaches and Empirical Domains*. Berlin and Boston, MA: De Gruyter, pp. 387–402.

Lenerz, J. (1977). *Zur Abfolge nominaler Satzglieder im Deutschen*. Tübingen: Narr.

Levelt, W. J. M. (1981). The speaker's linearization problem. *Philosophical Transactions of the Royal Society*, B 295, 305–315.

Levelt, W. J. M. (1989). *Speaking: From Intention to Articulation*. Cambridge, MA: MIT Press.

Meng, M. (1998). *Kognitive Sprachverarbeitung: Rekonstruktion syntaktischer Strukturen beim Lesen*. Wiesbaden: Deutscher Universitätsverlag.

Müller, G. (1999). Optimality, markedness, and word order in German. *Linguistics*, 37, 777–818.

Müller, G. (2001). Optionality in Optimality-Theoretic syntax. In L. Cheng & R. Sybesma, eds., *The Second Glot International State-of-the-Article Book*. Berlin: Mouton, pp. 289–312.

Namboodiripad, S. (2017). An experimental approach to variation and variability in constituent order. Doctoral dissertation, University of California, San Diego.

Neeleman, A. (1994). *Complex Predicates*. Utrecht: Led.

Nikanne, U. (2017). Finite sentences in Finnish: Word order, morphol- ogy, and information structure. In L. R. Bailey & M. Sheehan, eds., *Order and Structure in Syntax I: Word Order and Syntactic Structure*. Berlin: Language Science Press, pp. 69–97.

Pechmann, T., Uszkoreit, H., Engelkamp, J., & Zerbst, D. (1994). Word order in the German Middlefield. *Computerlinguistik an der Univerität des Saarlandes*, 43.

Postal, P. M. (1971). *Cross-over Phenomena*. New York: Holt, Rinehart, and Winston.

Prince, E. F. (1999). How not to mark topics: "Topicalization" in English and Yiddish. *Texas Linguistics Forum*. Austin: University of Texas, Ch. 8.

Roberts, C. (1996). Information structure: Towards an integrated theory of pragmatics. In J. H. Yoon & A. Kathol, eds., *Papers in Semantics* (OSU Working Papers in Linguistics, 49). Columbus, OH: The Ohio State University.

Ross, J. R. (1967). Constraints on variables in syntax. Doctoral dissertation, Massachusetts Institute of Technology.

Sorace, A. & Keller, F. (2005). Gradience in linguistic data. *Lingua*, 115, 1497–1524.

Scheepers, C. & Rummer, R. (1999). Genre-specific parsing: Non-additive influences of metrical stress pattern on sentence processing. Talk held at KogWis (Fachtagung der Gesellschaft für Kognitionswissenschaft) in Leipzig.

Stalnaker, R. C. (1973). Presuppositions. *Journal of Philosophical Logic*, 2, 447–457.

Sternefeld, W. (2000). Semantic vs. syntactic reconstruction. Unpublished manuscript, University of Tübingen.

Steube, A. (2001). Grammatik und Pragmatik von Hutkonturen. *Linguistische Arbeitsberichte*, 77, 7–29. Leipzig University.

Temme, A. & Verhoeven, E. (2016). Verb class, case, and order: A crosslinguistic experiment on non-nominative experiencers. *Linguistics*, 54(4), 769–813.

Vasishth, S. (2004). Discourse context and word order preferences in Hindi. *Yearbook of South Asian Languages*. New Delhi and Thousand Oaks, CA: Sage, pp. 113–128.

Vilkuna, M. (1989). *Free Word Order in Finnish: Its Syntax and Discourse Functions*. Helsinki: Finnish Literature Society.

Vinckel-Roisin, H., ed. (2015). *Das Nachfeld im Deutschen: Theorie und Empirie*. Berlin: De Gruyter.

Vogel, R. (2018). Sociocultural determinants of grammatical taboos in German. In L. Liashchova, ed., *The Explicit and the Implicit in Language and Speech*. Newcastle upon Tyne: Cambridge Scholars Publishing, pp. 116–153.

Ward, G. & Birner, B. (2004). Information structure and non-canonical syntax. In L. R. Horn & G. Ward, eds., *The Handbook of Pragmatics*. Malden, MA: Blackwell, pp. 153–174.

Wasow, T. (2002). *Postverbal Behavior*. Stanford, CA: CSLI Publications.

Weskott, T. (2003). Information structure as a processing guide: The left periphery of German verb-second sentences an its interpretation in context. Doctoral dissertation, University of Leipzig.

Weskott, T., Hörnig, R., Fanselow, G., & Kliegl, R. (2011). Contextual licensing of marked OVS word order in German. *Linguistische Berichte*, 225, 3–18.

Weskott, T., Hörnig, R., & Webelhuth, G. (2019). On the contextual licensing of English locative inversion and topicalization. In S. Featherston, R. Hörnig, S. von Wietersheim, & S. Winkler, eds., *Experiments in Focus: Information Structure and Semantic Processing*. New York: De Gruyter, pp. 153–182.

# 13

# Acceptability Judgments at the Syntax–Semantics Interface

Jesse Harris

## 13.1  Introduction

This chapter reviews the theoretical and conceptual issues central to acceptability judgment tasks, and related paradigms, at the syntax–semantics interface, and provides a broad overview of core results obtained from research in this domain. Challenges faced by studies in experimental semantics are distinct from those in experimental syntax, which at times require different linking hypotheses, research questions, or experimental paradigms. However, the current state of affairs suggests that acceptability and other offline judgments will continute to contribute highly informative and profitable tools for the exploration of phenomena at the syntax–semantics interface. For comparison, we start with the role of syntactic acceptability judgments in establishing the shape of tacit grammatical knowledge.

Within the generative linguistics tradition, there is an explicit and long-standing endorsement of a *mental grammar*, i.e. a grammatical device that generates strings of the language, to which native speakers are assumed to have implicit access. An important methodological question is how we, as theorists, are to access this implicit knowledge to characterize key properties of the grammar from native speakers of a language. In other words, *how can the empirical foundations of linguistic theory be best established*?

There are, naturally, a wide spectrum of answers to this question, although it is doubtful that any approach could avoid consulting native-speaker judgments. While some approaches question the usefulness of introspection from the syntactician (Gibson & Fedorenko 2010; Gibson, Piantadosi, & Fedorenko 2013), others have argued either that

Many thanks to Grant Goodall and two anonymous reviewers for comments on this chapter. Thanks also to Jessica Rett for comments on an early draft. Any mistakes or misrepresentations are my own.

introspection is enough in principle, given the robust nature of syntactic judgments (Newmeyer 1983), or that theoretically naive native speakers' judgments of core syntactic data reliably conform to the intuitions of syntacticians (Culicover & Jackendoff 2010; Sprouse & Almeida 2013, 2017, among others). In any event, interest in establishing methodological best practices is rapidly increasing, as is controlled experimental research in large-scale language judgment experiments, thanks, in part, to easier access to subject populations afforded by online crowdsourcing platforms. The increased interest has yielded an expanding array of tasks used in language research – e.g. magnitude estimation (Bard, Robertson, & Sorace 1996; Featherston 2005) or thermometer tasks (Featherston 2008), among others. These developments have been reviewed in much greater depth elsewhere than will be mentioned here, for instance, in Part I of this handbook or in Schütze (2011).

The great majority of these studies concentrate on questions related to syntactic well-formedness (whether a sentence expression is syntactically generated by the grammar of the language). In this chapter, we address the role of acceptability judgments (and other experimental paradigms) in investigating the link between syntactic structures and linguistic meanings. Of course, this project presupposes a systematic, welldefined relation between syntactic and semantic representations. Though there are many conceivable relations that one might pursue, we will follow a fairly standard view of the syntax–semantics interface here, briefly reviewed in Section 13.2.1. Furthermore, studies in syntax and semantics raise similar methodological and conceptual issues, including a need for explicit *linking hypotheses*: assumptions about how observed behavior or action is related to underlying, unobservable cognitive processes and mental states, introduced in Section 13.2.2. Methods for investigating the syntax–semantics interface are briefly discussed in Section 13.2.3, and case studies concentrating predominantly on the interpretation of quantified sentences are discussed in Section 13.3. The chapter concludes with some speculations on prospects and challenges faced in future studies.

## 13.2    Acceptability at the Syntax–Semantics Interface

### 13.2.1    The Relation between Syntax and Semantics

A fairly innocuous assumption is that a sentence of a language represents a pairing between a valid linguistic form (composed of sounds or signs) and a meaning. At its most abstract, then, a language L can be characterized as the rules governing how the set of forms $F$ are paired with a set of meanings $M$. Generative syntax traditionally seeks to characterize the syntactic devices that yield structures in $F$, i.e. the sentences of L. The empirical questions around $F$ are relatively straightforward: what are the sentences that comprise $F$, and what theories of syntax make the correct predictions?

Thus, common goals of a syntactic acceptability judgment experiment include (i) determining whether native speakers agree on the status of a sentence, and, to a lesser extent, (ii) providing evidence for a syntactic operation or constraint implicated in forming a structure. The many successes, and persistent challenges, of this enterprise have been thoroughly documented in this handbook.

In addition to a set of devices responsible for generating syntactic strings, we can posit a corresponding *semantic engine*, responsible for composing sentential meanings from the meanings of its subconstituents. Until recently, the empirical foundation of semantic theory and the syntax–semantics interface has received far less attention, though it is growing rapidly on many fronts (see Pylkkänen & McElree 2006; Bott et al. 2011 for review). While there are no inherent barriers to using judgment data in exploring the syntax–semantic interface, there are somewhat unique challenges faced by researchers in this area. The case studies reviewed below should reveal cause for cautious optimism, as such challenges are offset by the rich theoretical and empirical gains to be made in the study of the native speaker's knowledge of linguistic meaning.

What is knowledge of meaning? Intuitive answers are surprisingly illusive. A common starting place within semantic theory is to associate knowledge of meaning with knowledge of *truth conditions*: to understand the meaning of a sentence S is to understand the conditions under which S is true. For example, understanding the meaning of the sentence *Every cat has a black tail* (1a) amounts to understanding that the sentence is true just in case for any entity (within some contextually salient set of entities) that is a cat, that cat has a tail which is black (e.g. Larson 1995 for introduction).[1] Semantic competence requires that speakers be able to identify the situation or situations that make any given sentence true, and to correctly reject those that make it false. Semantic competence also requires that speakers understand how words and sentences are related to each other, as in entailment, synonymy, or antonymy. For example, the truth of sentences (1a) and (1b) together entail the truth of (1c).

(1)     a. Every cat has a black tail.
        b. Mikey is a cat.
        c. Therefore, Mikey has a black tail.

Experimentalists frequently capitalize on knowledge of truth conditions in exploring how comprehenders calculate the meaning of a sentence. In the truth-value judgment task, for example, subjects are asked to judge whether the sentence is true in a depiction of a situation (usually pictures or scenes acted out by an actor or puppet). Although the task was developed for studies of child language development (Abrams et al. 1978; Crain

---

[1] Although the role of truth-conditions in semantics is not without its critics (e.g. Dummett 2006; Schiffer 2015; Soames 1992), discussion of these criticisms here would take us too far afield for present purposes.

1991; Gordon 1998), variants have been adapted for use with adult populations, typically to test how sentences with quantifiers are verified for truth
or falsity (e.g. Lidz et al. 2011).

Another cornerstone of semantic theory is that meaning is *compositional*,
as formulated by Partee (1995):

(2)    **Principle of Compositionality:** The meaning of an expression
       is a function of the meanings of its parts and of the way those parts
       are syntactically combined.

A natural consequence of compositionality is that subexpressions of sentences themselves have meanings, which compose with the meanings of
other expressions in the sentence. This meaning is standardly represented
as a form of (higher-order) predicate logic, a kind of *logical form* consisting
of logical operators, functions, and their arguments. The meaning of an
expression, e.g. $\alpha$, is conventionally represented by double square brackets
$[\![\alpha]\!]$. For two expressions $\alpha$, $\beta$ whose mother node is $\gamma$, their meanings, $[\![\alpha]\!]$
and $[\![\beta]\!]$, may be combined together via a compositional operation $\circ$ to
produce a composite meaning for $\gamma$: $([\![\alpha]\!]\circ[\![\beta]\!]) \Rightarrow [\![\gamma]\!]$.

(3)    *A transparent syntax-to-meaning mapping:*

Compositionality comes in two basic variants (e.g. Janssen 1997; Pagin &
Westerståhl 2010). On a strongly compositional view, every semantic element and operation corresponds to a unique element in the syntax. In
other words, there is a one-to-one match between semantic representations and syntactic structures – every *syntactic* element $\gamma$ has a corresponding *semantic* element $[\![\gamma]\!]$, and vice versa. In case a semantic operator lacks
an overt syntactic analogue, a silent, unpronounced operator is realized
within the phrase structure tree, to preserve the one-to-one mapping
between syntactic and semantic elements. On a weakly compositional
view, in contrast, some semantic operations may have no syntactic analogue, so that there is a many-to-one relation between semantic and syntactic structures. On this view, meanings may be transformed through
nonsyntactic operations that change the semantic type or category of the
element, in operations known as type-shifting (e.g. Partee & Rooth 1983).
Although the two views of compositionality cover much of the same
empirical ground, they may do so with somewhat different mechanisms,
and predict divergent mappings between syntactic and semantic
representations.

What is the precise relation between a linguistic form and its meaning?
Clearly, form and meaning are highly correlated: syntactic units typically form
coherent units of interpretation. Most current models of the syntax–semantics

interface assume that forms and meanings are mediated by a syntactic level of representation, which feeds the compositional engine underlying interpretation. This level of *Logical Form* or LF is distinguished from a *logical form* in that LF is not yet semantically interpreted, and is still fundamentally syntactic nature (as discussed in May 1977, 1985).

The basic idea is that the syntax of an expression constrains how its subconstituents combine, by determining the order in which compositional operations may apply. Crucially, however, the location where an element is interpreted may diverge from where it is pronounced. Assuming that LF representations are generated by the same (or very similar) kinds of displacement operations as operate in syntax, the syntax yields a covertly expressed LF, which determines the way in which meanings may be composed: *Syntax* ⇒ *Logical Form* ⇒ *Semantic representations*.

Logical Form was motivated in large part by May's (1977, 1985) influential solution to a problem posed by the compositional interpretation of quantifiers in different syntactic positions. Semantically, a quantifier encodes a relation between two sets (Generalized Quantifier Theory: Barwise & Cooper 1981; Keenan & Stavi 1986), which are sometimes called the *restrictor* (the domain to which the quantifier applies) and the *nuclear scope* (a condition predicated of the domain). Furthermore, quantificational phrases like *every student* must bind a variable $x$ within its scope. It is straightfoward to give a compositional first-order logic representation for quantifiers in subject position; for example, *every* in (4b) translates into the logical quantifier ∀, where it takes scope over the variables it binds.

(4)     a. Every [Restrictor student] (Nuclear scope laughed)
        b. $\forall x: [student(x) \rightarrow laughed(x)]$
            For every $x$: if $x$ is a student, then $x$ laughed.

Problems arise when interpreting quantifiers in object position (5), as the denotation of the object (*every student*) cannot be directly composed with the verb without changing its meaning (Heim & Kratzer 1998, for discussion). May proposed the operation of *Quantifier Raising* (QR), in which a quantificational phrase like *every student* covertly adjoins above the sentence to [Spec, CP] where it can bind the variable $x$ associated with the trace left by the movement operation (May 1977, 1985).

(5)     *Example of quantifier raising*
        a.  *Syntax:* John greeted every student.
        b.  *Logical Form:* [Spec, CP every student ]$_1$ [ TP John greeted $t_1$ ]
        c.  *Semantics:* $\forall x [student(x) \rightarrow greet(j, x)]$
                For every $x$: if $x$ is a student, then John greeted $x$

Compelling evidence for QR initially came from the fact that covert quantifier movement appeared to parallel overt forms of movement, in particular *wh*-movement, as in *Who$_1$ did John greet t$_1$*, which was also argued to apply covertly in *wh-in-situ* languages like Chinese (Huang 1982). Though not identical, both forms of movement trigger crossover effects and show similar locality restrictions governing movement. Importantly for the discussion below, a QR account also provided an appealing treatment of quantifier scope ambiguity, in which one syntactic string permits multiple construals of quantificational scope, the surface and the inverse scope interpretations:

(6)     Every student speaks two languages.

     a.   *Surface scope: The universal takes wide scope*

[$_{Spec, CP}$ every student ]$_1$ [$_{Spec, CP}$ two languages ]$_2$ [$_{TP}$ t$_1$ speaks t$_2$ ]      ($\forall > 2$)

*Every student speaks two (possibly different) languages.*

     b.   *Inverse scope: The numeral takes wide scope*

[$_{Spec, CP}$ two languages ]$_2$ [$_{Spec, CP}$ every student ]$_1$ [$_{TP}$ t$_1$ speaks t$_2$ ]      ($2 > \forall$)

*There are two languages that every student speaks.*

However, a host of empirical and theoretical challenges to QR were soon uncovered. Among the more major concerns were (i) that it is hard to reconcile differences between *wh*-movement and QR, (ii) the fact that different quantifiers permit different scope-taking possibilities, and (iii) the observation that indefinites are seemingly unaffected by constraints on movement. Nonetheless, many theorists assume that LF mediates the syntax–semantics interface, primarily to account for cases in which overt constituent order fails to map onto a compositional semantic derivation (notable exceptions include directly compositional approaches to scope and compositionality, e.g. Jacobson 1999 or Barker 2002, 2012).

The relationship between structure and meaning can take many forms, and the interface between them can be more or less direct. A good deal of experimental research has addressed properties of the syntax–semantics interface via studies on quantifier scope ambiguity, some of which is reviewed in Section 13.3.1.1 below. However, experimental research requires making key "linking hypotheses," i.e. theories that explain the relationship between processes responsible for language interpretation, on the one hand, and behavioral responses, on the other. These issues are discussed in the next section.

## 13.2.2   Linking Hypotheses

Although they are rarely formalized explicitly, linking hypotheses play a crucial role in establishing arguments for mental representations from observable responses or behaviors, such as performance on a questionnaire or the pattern of eye movements while reading. As a single action or behavior may be associated with any number of causes, linking hypotheses are needed for any area within the psychological sciences. To take a common sense example, a diner might compliment a chef's cooking because he truly enjoyed the meal, or because he did not wish to offend. Similarly, a participant's behavior on an acceptability judgment task might transparently reflect the state of her internal grammar, or it might instead reflect an application of prescriptive rules or how plausible she thinks the sentence is. Without direct access to mental states, the best we can do is infer representations indirectly on the basis of theory and behavior.

A case in point is the distinction between the twin concepts of grammaticality and acceptability. The *grammaticality* of a structure is a theory-internal construct, which is not directly accessible to native speakers (Chomsky 1969). Instead, language judgments ultimately require trading in the related notion of *acceptability*, which reflects the feelings or responses that native speakers have about sentences in their native language (see in particular Schütze 1996). Linking hypotheses assumed in most syntactic acceptability studies are relatively straightforward: performance on, for example, a sentence rating task is the product of the percept of acceptability, which itself is influenced not only by the subject's grammatical knowledge, but also by a host of unrelated factors (as reviewed in Sprouse 2018), such as those influencing the processing of the sentence (e.g. complexity, plausibility, frequency, etc.) or the task (e.g. comparison with other items in the experiment, saturation, habituation, etc.). By collecting judgments on various sentences from many subjects, a properly designed acceptability judgment study will expose the underlying factors of interest, typically the tacit grammatical knowledge shared by members of a linguistic community. Syntactic acceptability studies are thus usually designed to reduce the effect of non-grammatical factors on acceptability judgments.

Linking hypotheses in experimental semantics and pragmatics are currently in need of development. Progress in this area demands a clear articulation of what a theory of interpretation entails, and researchers are faced with numerous, seemingly daunting questions not only about the *object*, but also about the *method*, of study. In terms of the object of study, experimentalists are confronted with a set of related questions: What are the mental representations that correspond to (sentence) meanings, and what are the mechanisms that yield those mental representations? How are those meanings formed compositionally? Are there distinct mental percepts for interpretation, similar to those posited for acceptability?

An equally thorny set of questions arise around the method of study. What are the methods that best identify the meaning or meanings that speakers access when performing the task? Are acceptability judgments an appropriate methodology for probing meaning? What is the semantic analogue to "How acceptable is this sentence?" It is certainly not "How meaningful is this sentence?" because meaning is not, at least *prima facie*, a gradable concept. Rather, experimentalists are usually more concerned with what meaning or meanings are (first) available to participants, and the extent to which those meanings are affected by structural considerations and contextual bias.

The primary domain of study within experimental semantics is the interpretation of ambiguous strings. How should a comprehender interpret a sentence string with multiple meanings? For example, does she compute all possible interpretations, or just the salient ones? Of the many possible answers, just two are mentioned here for illustration.

According to Grice's (1975) cooperative principle, typical speakers and comprehenders are engaged in a rational exchange of information. Comprehenders should assume that speakers intend to convey relevant information accurately, and may accordingly adopt the *Principle of Charity*, by which a sentence is disambiguated according to *the context of utterance*.

(7)    **Principle of Charity:** Whenever possible, assume that the speaker speaks truthfully, and select whatever interpretation makes the sentence true.

(Davidson 1974; Gualmini et al. 2008)

Alternatively, comprehenders may resolve ambiguity according to whatever interpretation is most accessible or salient, independent of the speaker's likely intentions. Of course, what determines accessibility itself requires a separate account, and may involve constraints on grammatical computations, discourse and performance factors, or some combination of the two.

(8)    **Truth Dominance:** Whenever an ambiguous sentence S is true in a situation on its most accessible reading, we must judge sentence S to be true in that situation.

(Meyer & Sauerland 2009)

In some respects, linking hypotheses in experimental semantics parallel those raised in experimental syntax. However, the range of possible solutions diverge in important ways, especially as the notion of *acceptability* in syntax lacks an obvious analogue in current semantic theory. While syntactic acceptability judgment studies address whether (or to what extent) a sentence could have been generated by the grammar, there is less agreement on what mental representations are investigated in studies of sentence meaning. Possibilities include the existence of a semantic representation (a possible interpretation for a sentence), the existence of derivational mechanism (a syntactic or semantic operation) that yields a meaning, or a preference for a particular meaning in a context. The case studies reviewed below do not necessarily investigate the same issues, though all are valid approaches to the empirical study of interpretation.

### 13.2.3  Ways to Study Meanings: Acceptability and Beyond

Linguistic meaning depends on a complex interaction between linguistic form and context. Experimental studies tend to investigate meaning in one of two ways (Bott et al. 2011). First, one can manipulate one or more factors from context or form, in order to determine the effect on meaning. Conversely, one can manipulate the meaning to determine which contexts or linguistic forms are felicitous. Manipulating meaning requires that it be conveyed in another, non-linguistic fashion, so as not to confound form and meaning. As Bott et al. (2011) observed, the dependence of meaning on form is one of the reasons why experimental studies in meaning are often more complex than studies in syntax, which are designed to study form independently of its meaning.

Various methods are standardly employed in the empirical study of meaning, some of which are enumerated in 1–3 below. As with any experimental question, there is no single method or paradigm that is uniformly suited for all manipulations or is entirely free of confounds or alternative interpretations. However, tasks used in experimental syntax do not always translate to experimental semantics well, and often adjustments must be made. For example, studies that use fixed-point scales (e.g. the standard Likert rating) usually ask participants to judge not acceptability, but *naturalness* or *appropriateness* within a context. Another possibility is the extent to which a paraphrase that disambiguates a sentence is acceptable, with or without a context. Other offline tasks include asking subjects to paraphrase the meaning of a sentence, to select a paraphrase, or to complete a sentence whose completion will disambiguate the interpretation. Some of the major kinds of tasks are summarized below, though the list is certainly not exhaustive:

1. Target sentence in context

    i. *Continuation acceptable in context:* Judge whether a target is an *acceptable* continuation of the context or not (e.g. Kurtzman & MacDonald 1993).
    ii. *Verification in context:* Judge whether the target sentence is *true* in a context or not (e.g. Ionin 2010; Brasoveanu & Dotlačil 2012).
    iii. *Ratings in context:* Rate *how acceptable* a target sentence follows from a context (e.g. Harris, Clifton, & Frazier 2013).
    iv. *Forced choice interpretation:* Select which paraphrase best corresponds to the interpretation (e.g. Frazier et al. 2005; Harris & Potts 2009; Amaral 2010).

2. *Picture matching:* Select which picture, scene, video, etc. best corresponds to the situation described by the target sentence (e.g. Lidz et al. 2011; Radó & Bott 2012).
3. *Diagrams:* Complete or draw a diagram that best conveys the (first, most natural, etc.) interpretation of the target sentence (e.g. Gillen 1991; Bott & Radó 2007; Gyuris & Jackson 2018).

These tasks primarily address which meaning M is appropriate given a form from F (and some context of utterance), and therefore the mapping between a form and a meaning. They are less well suited, however, to investigating the semantic engine that drives the computation of meanings *within the set M itself.* With some exceptions, the question of *how* a meaning is computed is better addressed with online measures, which can capture delays in performance that are associated with recruiting additional linguistic operations or other cognitive resources needed to generate a meaning. The relation between offline and online measures is discussed briefly in connection with complement coercion in Section 13.3.3 below.

## 13.3  Case Studies

I now review studies that highlight major themes in the syntax–semantics interface: the interpretation of quantified sentences, evidence for incremental interpretation, and resolving semantic mismatch with complement coercion.

### 13.3.1  Interpreting Quantification

#### 13.3.1.1  Quantifier Scope Ambiguity
One of the better-studied areas in the syntax–semantics interface is the interpretation of expressions with multiple quantifiers (e.g. Dayal 2013, for review). For example, a sentence like *Every kid climbed a tree* (9) is ambiguous with respect to the relative order of its quantified phrases: the universal DP *every kid* and the existential DP *a tree*. On one construal, the universal DP takes scope over existential (9a); on another, it is the existential that takes wide scope over the universal (9b).

(9)     Every kid climbed a tree.
     a. $\forall x\ [kid(x) \rightarrow \exists y[tree(y) \wedge climb(x)(y)]]$             ($\forall > \exists$)
        For any $x$: if $x$ is a kid, then there is some tree $y$ such
        that $x$ climbed $y$.
     b. $\exists y\ [tree(y) \wedge \forall x[kid(x) \rightarrow climb(x)(y)]]$            ($\exists > \forall$)
        For some $y$: $y$ is a tree, and for all $x$, if $x$ is a kid, then $x$
        climbed $y$.

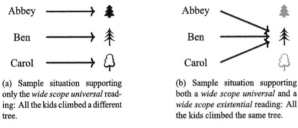

(a) Sample situation supporting only the *wide scope universal* reading: All the kids climbed a different tree.

(b) Sample situation supporting both a *wide scope universal* and a *wide scope existential* reading: All the kids climbed the same tree.

**Figure 13.1** Pictorial representations of scope interpretations

For simplicity, suppose that the contextually salient domain of kids consists of *Abbey*, *Ben*, and *Carol*, and the domain of trees consists of three individual trees (🌲, 🌲, 🌳). A *wide-scope universal construal* (9a) is true in a situation where all the contextually salient kids climbed some tree or other, and so a universal wide scope interpretation is validated if Abbey, Ben, and Carol all climbed one of the trees in the domain. However, the truth conditions of (9a) are satisfied whether one tree or multiple trees were climbed. The tree can be the same tree for all three kids, or possibly distinct trees, as shown in Figure 13.1a. In contrast, a *wide-scope existential construal* (9b) is true in a situation where just one tree was climbed by all the contextually salient kids – in our example, just in case Abbey, Ben, and Carol all climbed the same tree, as shown in Figure 13.1b. Therefore, the wide-scope universal construal (9a) entails the wide-scope existential (9b) construal, but not vice versa.

Linguists have long been interested in scope ambiguity for many reasons. As discussed above, a prominent strand of research addresses the relation between the grammar and the interpretive system, particularly whether interpretations are constrained by syntactic operations at LF. At minimum, this requires understanding which readings are grammatically permissible. A correspondence between the availability of an interpretation and the availability of its associated syntactic representation would lend strong support for the idea that similar (or even identical) operations are involved in producing overt syntactic structures and covert LF structures that are interpreted by the semantics.

Although the ambiguity of doubly quantified sentences like (9) is widely recognized, judgments about which interpretations are available for related sentences have varied widely in the literature. A sentence containing *n* number of quantifiers has, in principle, *n*! logically possible scope construals. Yet the sentence below (10) contains three quantifiers, and has been argued to have fewer than the predicted six scope configurations: five by Hobbs and Shieber's (1987) count, and four by Park's (1995).

(10)  Every representative of a company saw most samples.

What is the correct answer? How many interpretations *does* such a sentence have? One might be tempted to simply poll linguistically naïve subjects to settle the issue. But several of the possible readings are difficult to articulate or distinguish without training in logic or semantics. If experts cannot agree, where does that leave our participants? In addition, simply because an interpretation is not accessible to a particular participant does not mean that it is not a valid interpretation, as a particular meaning may be avoided because it is hard to compute, is implausible without proper context, or is simply not necessary for a shallow or incomplete parse of the sentence that may be sufficient for the task (e.g. Bott et al. 2011). What, then, can experiments tell the theorist when semantic intuitions are so variable?

Ioup (1975) and others have addressed this issue head on, by constructing accounts not of which readings are *available* to the grammar, but of which readings are *most accessible*, and which gradient discourse factors (topicality, specificity, discourse-linking, etc.) contribute to the prominence of a scope construal. In a series of speeded naturalness experiments, Kurtzman and MacDonald (1993) explored which scope construals are preferred in doubly quantified sentences. They adopted a constraint-based approach in which multiple interpretations are initially available, but the comprehender must ultimately choose the one that best satisfies the most relevant constraints. Several different constraint types were considered; some were based on syntactic or string order preferences, whereas others referenced the semantic or information structure properties of the language. Examples of the former include the *external subject preference* (assign wide scope to the subject) and the *linear order preference* (preserve surface order of quantificational elements), each of which predicts that the subject in canonical SVO word order would favor wide scope of the subject. However, the preferences make distinct predictions for non-canonical word orders, like the passive: a principle favoring wide scope for the external subject would yield different interpretations than one favoring wide scope of the first quantifier. In addition, discourse-based preferences, like the *topic principle*, can be defined to favor a wide scope construal for the topic (roughly, what the sentence is about). It should be clear that no single one of these principles can, nor was intended to, capture all interpretations – for example, in sentences with three quantifiers, the topic principle would have nothing to say about the relative order of any non-topic constituents. Instead, the interpretation that satisfies the most important relevant principles or constraints is selected.

In Kurtzman and MacDonald's (1993) study, participants rated two-sentence discourses in which a doubly quantified sentence was followed by a continuation that was assumed to disambiguate toward a particular scope construal. The singular continuation (11a) disambiguated the previous sentence (11) to the wide scope existential interpretation, in that it strongly implies that one tree was climbed by all the kids. In contrast, the plural version (11b) supports the wide scope universal interpretation, in that multiple trees are made salient. Both orders of the quantifiers were tested (12).

(11)    Every kid climbed a tree.
        a. The <u>tree was</u> full of apples.    (*Bias to inverse scope / existential wide scope*)
        b. The <u>trees were</u> full of apples.  (*Bias to surface scope / universal wide scope*)

(12)    A kid climbed every tree.
        a. The <u>kid was</u> full of energy.    (*Bias to surface scope / existential wide scope*)
        b. The <u>kids were</u> full of energy.  (*Bias to inverse scope / universal wide scope*)

A surface preference was observed for both quantifier types (11b, 12a), but was stronger for the existential than the universal (which was interpreted in terms of a single reference principle). However, when the quantified sentence was presented in the passive voice (e.g. *A tree was climbed by every kid*), there was no consistent preference for one interpretation over another. Kurtzman and MacDonald proposed that the null effect resulted from a conflict between constraints favoring wide scope of the first DP (constraints favoring scope setting by linear order, surface subject, or topic preferences) and those favoring wide scope of the second DP (constraints favoring wide scope of the external argument or the thematically most salient constituent).

There were, as many others have noted, problems with the study (e.g. Tunstall 1998; Bott & Radó 2009, among others). Most crucially, the continuations do not fully disambiguate the scope construals. As discussed in connection with Figure 13.1, the truth conditions of a wide scope universal construal entail the truth conditions of a narrow scope reading, and a situation where all the kids climb a single tree supports either scope configuration, and so the singular continuation in (11a) does not fully exclude the wide scope universal construal. Other studies have confronted this issue by employing alternative methods for disambiguation (Gillen 1991; Bott & Radó 2007; Gyuris & Jackson 2018). For instance, in some of Gillen's (1991) studies, participants were asked to draw or choose between diagrams representing their preferred interpretation of doubly quantified sentences, not unlike Figure 13.1 above. In others, participants rated how well the diagrams cohered with their interpretation of the sentence. Her results paralleled judgments observed in the literature, as well as those observed in corpus studies. Bott and Radó (2007) explicitly compared language judgments in response to (i) disambiguating linguistic contexts (question–answer pairs) and (ii) two kinds of diagrams (depicting abstract vs. concrete scenarios). Linguistic contexts and abstract diagrams elicited scope judgments similar to those observed in previous studies. In contrast, diagrams depicting more concrete scenarios displayed an across-the-board universal wide scope preference, which they attributed to the interference of extralinguistic verification strategies, which favor the observed interpretation.

Diagram methods have several advantages over disambiguation by rating sentence completions or by asking for a linguistic paraphrase, both of which require the comprehender to calculate and retain one or more meaning, while simultaneously judging the sentence for contextual felicity. Diagram methods avoid ambiguity left open by context sentences and paraphrases, and may also offload some of the cognitive difficulty that may be associated with calculating and remembering interpretations. This last point is especially important, as difficulty imagining a situation that would support a particular scope construal might make the reading less accessible, but not necessarily unavailable as a possible meaning for the sentence. Thus, a result favoring situations that are easier to imagine might not reveal much about what interpretations are available for the sentence, although it would be all too easy to conflate the two. This again highlights how the challenges that studies on the syntax–semantics interface must contend with are somewhat distinct from the challenges of syntactic acceptability judgment studies.

Another issue is that not all quantifiers pattern alike with respect to scope-taking possibilities, in contrast to May's (1977) early QR approach, in which QR can apply to quantifiers in any sequence. For instance, Beghelli and Stowell (1997) organize quantifiers into distinct semantic classes, and propose that quantifier types are located in different structural positions at LF (along the lines of the series of functional projections advocated by Cinque 1999 and others). The structural position of the functional projection determines the scope construal possibilities: a quantificational element Q1 will scope above another quantificational element Q2 if (a) the functional position of Q1 structurally dominates the functional position of Q2, and (b) Q1 can move to its functional position (e.g. is not contained with an island, etc.) at LF. This account was motivated by several intriguing empirical gaps left open by an unconstrained QR approach. For instance, Beghelli and Stowell (1997) observed that group-denoting quantifiers (those that denote groups of individuals, like *some* and numerals) must take wide scope over sentence negation in (13b), even though both scope construals seem to be possible in (13a). They account for the asymmetrical scope relations by positing that group-denoting subjects must move to a position above the negation at LF and cannot reconstruct into their θ-marked position (where the thematic relation is assigned).

(13)     a. No student read two books.                    (*No* > *two*; *Two* > *no*)
          b. Two students read no books.                   (*Two* > *no*; * *No* > *two*)

The strong predictions of configurational accounts are still in need of exploration. However, a few studies concentrating on distributivity suggest that configurational restrictions alone are not sufficient to explain preferential scope construals (Bott & Radó 2009; Brasoveanu & Dotlačil 2012).

### 13.3.1.2 Indefinites

It is not clear that all determiners behave uniformly as quantifiers. Indefinites like *a professor* in (15) pose a particularly complex problem for the theory of scope construal; they can be interpreted in positions where quantifiers cannot, and are said to take "exceptional wide scope" (Fodor & Sag 1982; Ruys 1992, among others). Positions allowing a wide scope construal of indefinites crucially include syntactic islands, from which movement is normally prohibited (Ross 1967), such as the relative clause island below (14), or the antecedent of a conditional (see Ionin (2010) or Schwarz (2011) for review).

(14)   *Relative clause islands:*

   a. John read every article [$_{RC}$ that Mary assigned ].

   b. * Who$_1$ did John read every article [$_{RC}$ that $t_1$ assigned ] ?

(15)   *Exceptional wide scope of indefinite:*
   John read every article [$_{RC}$ that a professor assigned].
   i.   *Wide scope for indefinite:* There is a (particular) professor, such that John read every one of the articles that professor assigned.         (*A professor > every article*)
   ii.  *Narrow scope for indefinite:* For every article that was assigned by John's professor, John read it.
                                                    (*Every article > a professor*)

The ambiguity of the indefinite *a professor* in the relative clause contrasts with sentences in which a universally quantified phrase *every professor* can only be interpreted within the relative clause (16.ii).

(16)   *No wide scope construal of universal in relative clause:*
   John read an article [$_{RC}$ that every professor assigned].
   i. * *No wide scope for universal:* Every professor assigned some (possibly distinct) article, which John read.
                                    (**Every professor > an article*)
   ii. *Narrow scope for universal:* There was an article that every professor assigned, and John read that article.
                                    (*An article > every professor*)

Many approaches to the exceptional nature of indefinites have been pursued, starting with Fodor and Sag's (1982) *referential account*, in which an indefinite is directly interpreted as an individual the speaker has in mind, not as a quantifier. However, problems with interpreting the indefinite as a particular individual arise when the speaker does not (or cannot) have a particular referent when uttering the sentence (Ludlow & Neale 1991). Several current approaches now adopt a variant of the *choice function* analysis (Reinhart 1997; Winter 1997; Kratzer 1998; cf. Geurts 2000). Informally, a function $f_{CF}$ is a choice function if it selects some non-empty member of a set and applies it to its domain. For example, a choice function $f_{CF}$ with a domain of professors $f_{CF}$ (professor) would select some non-empty member from the set of professors, e.g. Dr. Jones. The choice function effectively mimics the existential by picking out at least one individual that makes the sentence true, without necessarily contributing quantificational force to the expression. A variant of the choice function account employs a mixed approach, where an indefinite can be interpreted as a quantifier in some environments and a choice function in others (e.g. Winter 1997; Schwarz 2001; Ionin 2010). These approaches are motivated, in part, by the fact that when indefinites are modified by *a certain*, they permit very different scope construals (Hintikka 1986).

In a series of questionnaire studies, Ionin (2010) tested the predictions for scopal interpretations of *single* (only quantificational or only choice function) versus *mixed* (both quantificational and choice function) mechanism accounts of indefinites. She compared bare *a* indefinites with *a-certain* indefinites in contexts biasing toward wide, intermediate, and narrow scope construals. Target sentences, e.g. *Every coach thinks that a (certain) player is missing*, were judged as appropriate or not given their preceding contexts, biased toward widest scope, intermediate, or narrow scope construal of the indefinite.

Whereas *a* indefinites showed high acceptance rates in all contexts in simple matrix clauses, *a-certain* indefinites were more often rejected, showing that they are incompatible with narrow scope interpretations. However, *a-certain* indefinites were accepted more often when they were to be interpreted outside the scope of a relative clause or the antecedent of a conditional island. The results lend initial support to accounts that posit different mechanisms for deriving bare *a* and *a-certain* indefinites (e.g. Schwarz, 2001), suggesting that at least some kinds of indefinites may be interpreted as non-quantificational. Given the great deal of cross-linguistic variation between indefinites, particularly for those that appear to lexically encode an element of speaker-ignorance (e.g. Kratzer & Shimoyama 2002; Alonso-Ovalle & Menéndez-Benito 2013, among many others), the issue of just how indefinites get their scope continues to be an active area of research.

### 13.3.1.3 Quantification and Anaphora

Sentences with a single quantifier can also be ambiguous. In the second sentence of (17), the quantificational phrase *three ships* and its bare quantifier variant (*three*) can be interpreted anaphorically with respect to a previously mentioned group of ships (*the five ships*). This is the *subset* or *presuppositional* interpretation. An alternate, and intuitively less preferred, interpretation is the *new set* or *existential* reading, in which the quantifier refers to another three ships, in addition to the five mentioned in the preceding sentence.

(17)   Five ships appeared on the horizon. Three (ships) sank.

Frazier's Minimal Lowering account explains the preference for subset interpretations by a general injunction against unmotivated movement at LF (Frazier 1999, 2000; Frazier et al. 2005). For illustration, assume that subjects are generated within the Specifier of VP/vP and move to subject position [Spec, TP] for independent reasons (e.g. McCloskey 1997, among others), and need not adjoin above the sentence via Quantifier Raising (May 1985) or to a dedicated quantifier position (Beghelli & Stowell 1997) at LF. Sentential subjects (*a dog* in (18)) could then be interpreted in two positions at LF: either at a surface subject position (18a), or a "lowered" position within the VP, where they are reconstructed for interpretation (18b).

(18)   A dog was in the garden.

a. $[_{\text{Spec, TP}}$ A dog$_i$ $[_{\text{TP}}$ was $[_{\text{VP}} t_i t_v$ $[_{\text{PP}}$ in the garden $]]]]$       (*Subject position*)

b. $[_{\text{Spec, TP}}$ DP$_i$ $[_{\text{TP}}$ was $[_{\text{VP}}$ a dog$_i$ $t_v$ $[_{\text{PP}}$ in the garden $]]]]$       (*Lowered into VP*)

The position of the subject was hypothesized to have consequences for interpretation. According to Diesing's (1992) *Mapping Hypothesis*, the interpretation of a subject DP (including quantifiers) depends on its position at LF. DPs interpreted outside the VP at LF (18a) are understood as presupposed or quantificational (yielding the subset reading). In contrast, those interpreted inside the VP at LF (18b) are interpreted as existential, and contribute a new (non-presupposed) referent to the discourse. Minimal Lowering proposes that DPs are preferentially interpreted at LF in their surface positions, in order to avoid potentially unnecessary operations (19). Subset interpretations are thus preferred because the interpretive system avoids generating LF structures that would yield the new set interpretation, i.e. a structure with a lowered subject.

(19)   **Minimal Lowering:** "Lower" only when necessary, e.g. interpret a DP in its surface position if possible.                    (Frazier 2000)

When Frazier et al. (2005) tested how subjects interpreted sentences with ambiguous quantifiers (17) using simple yes/no questions, e.g. "Were the three ships that sank among the five ships that appeared on the horizon?", subset interpretations were selected about 60 percent of the time. Similar results were obtained with questions probing cardinality, e.g.

"How many ships appeared on the horizon? Five or two." Eye-tracking results revealed that the subset interpretation was also preferred during real-time processing, as readers slowed down when they were forced to adopt a new set interpretation later in the text. The general findings appear to hold across multiple languages (German and Korean: Frazier et al. 2005; Dutch: Wijnen & Kaan 2006 and Kaan, Dallas, & Barkley 2007).

Minimal Lowering makes crucial reference to constraints governing the preferred syntactic configuration of elements at LF, which in turn yield distinct discourse interpretations for quantifiers. As a consequence, it is a relatively indirect explanation of the subset preference. More direct alternatives have also been proposed, which attribute the subset preference to discourse biases that avoid introducing new referents into the discourse (e.g. Gordon & Hendrick 1998). Paterson, Filik, and Liversedge (2008) found reading penalties for quantifiers that introduce a new discourse referent, regardless of whether the quantifier was structurally ambiguous (Kaan et al. 2007; see also Paterson, Filik, & Moxey 2009 for review). Although the two approaches are not mutually exclusive, they do presuppose potentially different linking hypotheses, differentiated by whether LF structures or discourse representations are most relevant.

### 13.3.1.4  Quantificational Domain Resolution

Harris, Clifton, and Frazier (2013) addressed yet another aspect of quantification. In addition to interacting with other linguistic elements, quantifiers rely on context to determine the domain of objects in their range that is relevant to its evaluation (e.g. Bach et al. 1995). In (20), for example, quantifiers like *every* are typically restricted by an overt noun phrase *kid*, which limits what kinds of elements the quantifier ranges over.

(20)    Every kid laughed.

Adverbs of quantification typically lack an explicit domain restriction, leaving open the kinds of elements they range over (Lewis 1975; Berman 1987; Hinterwimmer 2008). For example, *mostly* in (21) is ambiguous between a reading in which the adverb ranges over subsets of a contextually salient group of students (21a), and one in which it ranges over times or events of walking (21b).

(21)    Students mostly walk to school.
        a. On occasions when they go to school,    (*Quantification over times*)
           most often they walk.
        b. Most students walk to school.    (*Quantification over individuals*)

Harris et al. (2013) adopted Majewski's (2014) *No Extra Times* principle, which states that sentences are preferentially interpreted as describing a single event when possible (22), as a general conceptual economy principle. Assuming that sentences referencing multiple occasions also require multiple mental representations of those situations, comprehenders should avoid postulating complex representations unless necessary.[2]

(22)    **No Extra Times:** A sentence describes a single occasion (unless there is evidence to the contrary).            (Majewski 2014)

Pairs of sentences were constructed with one of three quantified sentences as the first sentence: an ambiguous adverb of quantification (23a), a quantifier with the domain explicitly quantifying over individuals (23b), or a quantifier with the domain explicitly quantifying over times (23c). The second sentence disambiguated to an interpretation consistent with multiple individuals (24.i) or multiple times (24.ii). For example, an item with an ambiguous quantificational adverb disambiguated toward a multiple times interpretation would be *The students were mostly here. Some of the time they weren't however.*

(23)    *Quantified sentence*
        a. The students were mostly here.            (*Ambiguous*)
        b. Most of the students were here.    (*Quantification over individuals*)
        c. Most of the time the students were here.    (*Quantification over times*)

(24)    *Disambiguation sentence*
        i. Some of them weren't however.    (*Disambiguation to individuals*)
        ii. Some of the time they weren't however.    (*Disambiguation to times*)

Ambiguous sentences (23a) patterned with unambiguous quantification over individuals sentences (23b), as both elicited a ratings penalty when followed by a sentence disambiguating to times (24.ii) compared to sentences disambiguating to individuals (24.i). Sentences that quantified over times showed the opposite pattern: a penalty for disambiguation to individuals. The results suggest that readers were not simply leaving the domain of quantification vague or underspecified, at least by the end of the sentence, nor were they picking an interpretation at random.

Harris et al. (2013) provide additional evidence that readers selected a domain for the quantifier that respected the No Extra Times principle was observed in an eye-tracking study. Reading was disrupted when subjects were presented with a sentence for which a single event interpretation was implausible (e.g. *The inspector was mostly in the capital*), which suggests that the inspector was located in the capital on many occasions, not that parts of the inspector were mainly distributed in the capital, compared to sentences that permit or are biased toward a multiple times interpretation (e.g. *The army/attack was mostly in the capital*). In all, these findings support

---

[2] Evidence for such a a single event preference has been observed in areas as diverse as collective/distributive ambiguities (Clifton & Frazier 2013), coordination (Clifton & Frazier 2012), reciprocals (Majewski 2014), and serial verb constructions in Russian (Harris & Korotkova 2019). Space constraints prohibit a detailed discussion here.

the idea that a domain of quantification is selected incrementally during sentence processing.

### 13.3.2  Incremental Interpretation

Most research in online (real-time) sentence processing assumes that sentences are interpreted incrementally, word by word (Just, Carpenter, & Woolley 1982). In general, offline methods lack the proper sensitivity to capture the more temporarily subtle factors in structure building, and such questions are usually explored with online measures, such as self-paced reading, eye-tracking, electrophysiological measures, and so on (reviewed in Part IV of this handbook). However, particularly robust incremental processes have been shown to appear in end-of-sentence judgments – for example, when a structure violates a very strong preference for parsing *wh*-movement (Fanselow & Frisch 2006; Hofmeister et al. 2007; Sprouse 2008). Far less research has addressed the extent to which incremental semantic processes can be detected with offline methods.

One example involves the licensing of Negative Polarity Items (NPIs), which appear only in particular semantic contexts (Fauconnier 1975; Ladusaw 1979).[3] In a downward-entailing (DE) environment like negation, one can infer the truth of a sentence *The teacher didn't drink red wine* from another *The teacher didn't drink wine*, when the situation described by the first sentence is entailed by the situation described in the second. The NPI construal of *ever* is licensed in DE environments, such as negation (25a) or relative clauses (25b), but not positive counterparts (25c).

(25)     a. The teacher didn't **ever** drink wine in class.
         b. A teacher who **ever** drinks wine in class will be fired.
         c. * The teacher **ever** drank wine in class.

Clifton and Frazier (2010) used the licensing properties of *ever* to investigate whether the language processing system identifies DE environments incrementally (*local computation*) or only after the entire sentence has been processed (*global computation*). If computed locally, *ever* should appear to be unlicensed when the syntactic analysis is not locally compatible with a DE environment, e.g. when it is temporarily tempted to parse the sentence incorrectly as a non-DE environment. In contrast, global computation would predict that a temporarily unlicensed *ever* would fail to affect sentence processing, as the local ambiguity has been resolved by the end of the sentence.

Clifton and Frazier tested these predictions in an acceptability rating task, using reduced-clause garden-path sentences (26), in which a verb

---

[3] The work on NPIs is expansive and suggests that the licensing of NPIs is more complicated than presented here (e.g. Giannakidou 1998). Proposals include syntactic, semantic, and pragmatic conditions on licensing, or that NPIs may be (spuriously) licensed in other environments (Saddy, Drenhaus, & Frisch 2004; Xiang, Grove, & Giannakidou 2016).

(*arrested*) in a reduced relative clause structure is preferentially interpreted as the main clause verb (Bever 1970; Frazier 1979, among many others). Sentences with reduced relative clauses are known to disrupt online processing, and may require reinterpretation of the structure (e.g. Ferreira & Clifton 1986). Assuming that readers take *arrested* as the main verb in (26a) on first encounter, *ever* should be initially interpreted as appearing in a main clause environment and would therefore appear to be unlicensed, along the lines of (25c).

(26)    a. A man (**ever**) arrested in this country won't break the law here again.
        b. A man who was (**ever**) arrested in this country won't break the law here again.

The crucial finding was an interaction in acceptability between the two conditions, so that the acceptability penalty for *ever* was increased when it appeared inside a reduced relative clause – i.e. just when *ever* would have been temporarily unlicensed by the structure, compared to a full relative clause control (26b). In a second experiment, the penalty for *ever* was eliminated when a negative quantifier created a licit downward-entailing environment. The results are highly compatible with recent findings that pragmatic implicatures are computed incrementally during online sentence processing. They also offer evidence that the online computation of semantic context may, in some cases, be detectable with offline acceptability measures. It should be noted, however, that the correct licensing conditions in this experiment also depended on the proper identification of the correct structural analysis of the reduced relative clause. As syntactic and semantic properties traveled together in this design, it is hard to know whether the semantic anomaly would have been detected in offline measures without a corresponding syntactic misanalysis. Our final case study is one in which a semantic operation arguably has no direct correlate in the syntax, as a more transparent illustration of semantic composition.

### 13.3.3 Semantic Mismatch

Thus far, this chapter has concentrated on the mapping between form and meaning $\langle F, M \rangle$, and the ways in which comprehenders prefer to resolve ambiguous structures, without having devoted much discussion to the generation of semantic representations within $M$ itself. One particularly interesting question in this area is the resolution of semantic mismatch, in which two elements combine even though they cannot be (transparently) combined compositionally. These mismatches between form and meaning pose an apparent challenge to the strongest forms of compositionality (Pylkkänen & McElree 2006). One such example is *complement coercion*, in which the selectional requirements of an event-selecting verb (*start* or *begin*) clashes with its entity-denoting object (*the book*).

(27)    a. The author read the book.
        b. The author started the book.
        c. The author started (writing/reading/copying) the book.

Though uncommon, a syntactic account might assert that a covert verb form is introduced into the structure, so that any cost associated with interpreting the selectional mismatch would be attributed to recovering this missing, essentially elliptical, structure (see Pylkkänen & McElree (2006) for arguments against this brand of approach). On a semantic coercion account, event-selecting verbs "coerce" entity-denoting complements into an event by enriching their semantic representation. Such accounts propose that the enrichment occurs only at the level of interpretation, i.e. is a non-syntactic operation, in which the ontological type of the noun is shifted into a salient event. The precise mechanisms vary between approaches, and include type coercion (Pustejovsky 1991, 1995) and underspecification (Egg 2005) of the event, as well as richer aspectual dimensions encoded within the lexicon (Piñango & Deo 2015).

Penalties for complement coercion structures have been observed in many online processing studies employing a diverse range of methods, including self-paced reading (e.g. McElree et al. 2001; Traxler, Pickering, & McElree 2002), eye-tracking (e.g. Pickering et al. 2004; Pickering, McElree, & Traxler 2005; McElree, Frisson, & Pickering 2006), and neuroimaging techniques (e.g. Pylkkänen & McElree 2007; Pylkkänen et al. 2009; Baggio et al. 2010; Kuperberg et al. 2010; Husband, Kelly, & Zhu 2011). Online studies tend to use plausibility ratings to control differences between items, in order to remove the possibility that disruptions in online measures could reflect overall differences in acceptability. The materials in these studies are therefore designed specifically to avoid offline differences in acceptability. In addition, comprehenders may lack the motivation to commit to a specific interpretation in offline tasks, if they can recover enough of the message to form a basic judgment about its felicity. Nonetheless, some studies have observed both offline and online processing costs for coerced complements: for example, sentences with complement coercion have been found to elicit offline naturalness ratings penalties, as well as disruptions during reading (Frisson & McElree 2008; Kuperberg et al. 2010). These findings indicate that readers are sensitive to at least some kinds of local selectional mismatches that are resolved with non-syntactic mechanisms, though a fuller range of non-syntactic operations must be explored to determine precisely how sensitive subjects are to semantic processes. This project is just one of many in need of further exploration.

## 13.4   Future Directions

This chapter introduced some of the core themes behind language and acceptability judgments at the syntax–semantics interface. We noted that studies that focus on meaning must confront a different set of methodological and theoretical issues than studies that address form. As sentence meaning depends on its structure, experimental research in semantics inherits a great deal of the concerns that arise in experimental syntax. However, as the percept of acceptability is likewise influenced by meaning as well as form, studies of syntactic phenomena must also ultimately contend with semantic factors as well.

This review has concentrated primarily on quantification, in which a rich array of theoretically important issues can be investigated. In particular, we highlighted studies that addressed quantifier scope ambiguity, the interpretation of quantificational anaphora, and the selection of a quantificational domain. Of course, an introductory chapter of this size cannot do justice to the field, and a great many issues were omitted by necessity.

Although the empirical coverage of the syntax–semantics interface is rapidly growing, the theory of semantic judgments is still in its relative infancy. Currently, there is very little theory detailing which classes of semantic phenomena will be observable in different kinds of measures, even at the coarse-grained level of comparing offline and online measures. Although different measures are likely to reflect distinct cognitive processes, some degree of overlap between methodologies is expected. As a starting place, a theory of semantic judgments should reference the relevant percept that gives rise to judgments of infelicity. As with native-speaker judgments about syntactic acceptability, semantic judgments might be heavily influenced by the detection of an error signal and/or processes recruited to resolve semantic conflict. The perception of an error may originate from many potential sources, including violating preferred interpretations of the discourse, goodness of fit with previous context, or some syntactic constraint needed to produce a particular meaning. In general, it is possible that such errors would be detected, thereby requiring resolution, when they have been calculated and the comprender has committed to the interpretation to some extent. Even if the interpretation is discarded or suppressed by the time of the language judgment, the resources needed to resolve the conflict may contribute to the percept of semantic well-formedness used in making the judgment.

In all, the empirical base of semantic theory is well positioned to develop the necessary set of robust results, methodologies, and linking hypotheses to make major advances in the future. Although there are a great many remaining challenges, the current state of affairs promises to lead to ever more informative findings and predictive theories.

# References

Abrams, K., Chiarello, C., Cress, K., Green, S., & Ellelt, N. (1978). The relation between mother-to-child speech and word-order comprehension strategies in children. In R. N. Campbell, & P. T. Smith, eds., *Recent Advances in the Psychology of Language*. New York: Plenum Press, vol. 4, pp. 337–347.

Alonso-Ovalle, L. & Menéndez-Benito, P. (2013). Two views on epistemic indefinites. *Language and Linguistics Compass*, 7(2), 105–122.

Amaral, P. (2010). Entailment, assertion, and textual coherence: The case of *almost* and *barely*. *Linguistics*, 48(3), 525–545.

Bach, E., Jelinek, E., Kratzer, A., & Partee, B. H. (1995). *Quantification in Natural Languages*. Dordrecht: Kluwer Academic Publishers.

Baggio, G., Choma, T., Van Lambalgen, M., & Hagoort, P. (2010). Coercion and compositionality. *Journal of Cognitive Neuroscience*, 22(9), 2131–2140.

Bard, E. G., Robertson, D., & Sorace, A. (1996). Magnitude estimation of linguistic acceptability. *Language*, 72(1), 32–68.

Barker, C. (2002). Continuations and the nature of quantification. *Natural Language Semantics*, 10(3), 211–242.

Barker, C. (2012). Quantificational binding does not require c-command. *Linguistic Inquiry*, 43(4), 614–633.

Barwise, J. & Cooper, R. (1981). Generalized quantifiers and natural language. *Linguistics and Philosophy*, 4(2), 159–219.

Beghelli, F. & Stowell, T. (1997). Distributivity and negation: The syntax of *each* and *every*. In A. Szabolcsi, ed., *Ways of Scope Taking*. New York: Springer, pp. 71–107.

Berman, S. (1987). Situation-based semantics for adverbs of quantification. In J. Blevins & A. Vainikka, eds., *University of Massachusetts Occasional Papers in Linguistics*. Amherst, MA: GLSA Publishing, vol. 12, pp. 45–68.

Bever, T. G. (1970). The cognitive basis for linguistic structures. *Cognition and the Development of Language*, 279(362), 1–61.

Bott, O., Featherston, S., Radó, J., & Stolterfoht, B. (2011). The application of experimental methods in semantics. In C. Maienborn, K. von Heusinger, & P. Portner, eds., *Semantics: An International Handbook of Natural Language Meaning*, vol. 1. Berlin: De Gruyter Mouton, pp. 305–321.

Bott, O. & Radó, J. (2007). Quantifying quantifier scope: a cross-methodological comparison. In S. Featherston & W. Sternefeld, eds., *Roots: Linguistics in Search of Its Evidential Base*. Berlin: Walter de Gruyter, pp. 53–74.

Bott, O. & Radó, J. (2009). How to provide exactly one interpretation for every sentence, or what eye movements reveal about quantifier scope. In S. Featherston & S. Winkler, eds., *Fruits of Empirical Linguistics*, vol.1: *Processes* (Studies in Generative Grammar, 101). Berlin: De Gruyter Mouton, pp. 25–46.

Brasoveanu, A. & Dotlačil, J. (2012). Licensing sentence-internal readings in English. In M. Aloni, V. Kimmelman, F. Roelofsen, G. W. Sassoon, K. Schulz,

& M. Westera, eds., *Logic, Language and Meaning*. Berlin: Springer-Verlag, pp. 122–132.

Chomsky, N. (1969). *Aspects of the Theory of Syntax*. Cambridge, MA: MIT Press.

Cinque, G. (1999). *Adverbs and Functional Heads: A Cross-Linguistic Perspective*. Oxford: Oxford University Press.

Clifton, Jr., C. & Frazier, L. (2010). When are downward-entailing contexts identified? The case of the domain widener *ever*. *Linguistic Inquiry*, 41(4), 681–689.

Clifton, Jr., C. & Frazier, L. (2012). Interpreting conjoined noun phrases and conjoined clauses: Collective versus distributive preferences. *Quarterly Journal of Experimental Psychology*, 65(9), 1760–1776.

Clifton, Jr., C. & Frazier, L. (2013). Partition if you must: Evidence for a No Extra Times principle. *Discourse Processes*, 50(8), 616–630.

Crain, S. (1991). Language acquisition in the absence of experience. *Behavioral and Brain Sciences*, 14(4), 597–612.

Culicover, P. W. & Jackendoff, R. (2010). Quantitative methods alone are not enough: Response to Gibson and Fedorenko. *Trends in Cognitive Sciences*, 14(6), 234–235.

Davidson, D. (1974). On the very idea of a conceptual scheme. *Proceedings and Addresses of the American Philosophical Association*, 47, 5–20. Reprinted in D. Davidson (1984). *Inquiries into Truth and Interpretation: Philosophical Essays*. Oxford: Clarendon Press.

Dayal, V. (2013). The syntax of scope and quantification. In M. den Dikken, ed., *The Cambridge Handbook of Generative Syntax*. Cambridge: Cambridge University Press.

Diesing, M. (1992). *Indefinites*. Cambridge, MA: MIT Press.

Dummett, M. (2006). *Thought and Reality*. Oxford: Oxford University Press.

Egg, M. (2005). *Flexible Semantics for Reinterpretation Phenomena*. Palo Alto, CA: CSLI Publications.

Fanselow, G. & Frisch, S. (2006). Effects of processing difficulty on judgments of acceptability. In G. Fanselow, C. Féry, M. Schlesewsky, & R. Vogel, eds., *Gradience in Grammar: Generative Perspectives*. Oxford: Oxford University Press, pp. 291–316.

Fauconnier, G. (1975). Pragmatic scales and logical structure. *Linguistic Inquiry*, 6(3), 353–375.

Featherston, S. (2005). Magnitude estimation and what it can do for your syntax: Some *wh-* constraints in German. *Lingua*, 115(11), 1525–1550.

Featherston, S. (2008). Thermometer judgments as linguistic evidence. In C. M. Riehl & A. Rothe, eds., *Was ist linguistische Evidenz?* Aachen: Shaker Verlag, pp. 69–89.

Ferreira, F. & Clifton, Jr., C. (1986). The independence of syntactic processing. *Journal of Memory and Language*, 25(3), 348–368.

Fodor, J. D. & Sag, I. A. (1982). Referential and quantificational indefinites. *Linguistics and Philosophy*, 5(3), 355–398.

Frazier, L. (1979). On comprehending sentences: Syntactic parsing strategies. Doctoral dissertation, University of Connecticut, Storrs.

Frazier, L. (1999). *On Sentence Interpretation*. Dordrecht: Kluwer Academic Publishers.

Frazier, L. (2000). On interpretation: Minimal "lowering." In M. W. Crocker, M. Pickering & C. Clifton Jr., eds., *Architectures and Mechanisms for Language Processing*. Cambridge: Cambridge University Press, pp. 303–323.

Frazier, L., Clifton, Jr., C., Rayner, K., Deevy, P., Koh, S., & Bader, M. (2005). Interface problems: Structural constraints on interpretation? *Journal of Psycholinguistic Research*, 34 (3), 201–231.

Frisson, S. & McElree, B. (2008). Complement coercion is not modulated by competition: Evidence from eye movements. *Journal of Experimental Psychology: Learning, Memory, and Cognition*, 34(1), 1–11.

Geurts, B. (2000). Indefinites and choice functions. *Linguistic Inquiry*, 31(4), 731–738.

Giannakidou, A. (1998). *Polarity Sensitivity as (Non) Veridical Dependency*. Amsterdam and Philadelphia: John Benjamins.

Gibson, E. & Fedorenko, E. (2010). Weak quantitative standards in linguistics research. *Trends in Cognitive Sciences*, 14(6), 233–234.

Gibson, E., Piantadosi, S. T., & Fedorenko, E. (2013). Quantitative methods in syntax/semantics research: A response to Sprouse and Almeida (2013). *Language and Cognitive Processes*, 28(3), 229–240.

Gillen, K. (1991). The comprehension of doubly quantified sentences. Doctoral dissertation, Durham University.

Gordon, P. (1998). The truth-value judgment task. In D. McDaniel, H. Smith Cairns, & C. McKee, eds., *Methods for Assessing Children's Syntax*. Cambridge, MA: MIT Press, pp. 211–232.

Gordon, P. C. & Hendrick, R. (1998). The representation and processing of coreference in discourse. *Cognitive Science*, 22(4), 389–424.

Grice, H. P. (1975). Logic and conversation. In P. Cole & J. Morgan, eds., *Syntax and Semantics*, vol. 3. New York: Academic Press.

Gualmini, A., Hulsey, S., Hacquard, V., & Fox, D. (2008). The question–answer requirement for scope assignment. *Natural Language Semantics*, 16(3), 205–237.

Gyuris, B. & Jackson, S. R. (2018). Scope marking and prosody in Hungarian. *Glossa: A Journal of General Linguistics*, 3(1), 83. DOI:10.5334/gjgl.311

Harris, J. A., Clifton, Jr., C., & Frazier, L. (2013). Processing and domain selection: Quantificational variability effects. *Language and Cognitive Processes*, 28(10), 1519–1544.

Harris, J. A. & Korotkova, N. (2019). Preference for single events guides perception in Russian: A phoneme restoration study. In E. Ronai, L. Stigliano, & Y. Sun, eds., *Proceedings of the 54th Annual Meeting of the Chicago Linguistic Society*. Chicago: Chicago Linguistic Society, pp. 149–163.

Harris, J. A. & Potts, C. (2009). Perspective-shifting with appositives and expressives. *Linguistics and Philosophy*, 32(6), 523–552.

Heim, I. & Kratzer, A. (1998). *Semantics in Generative Grammar*. Oxford: Blackwell.

Hinterwimmer, S. (2008). *Q-Adverbs as Selective Binders: The Quantificational Variability of Free Relatives and Definite DPs*. Berlin and New York: Walter de Gruyter.

Hintikka, J. (1986). The semantics of *a certain*. *Linguistic Inquiry*, 17(2), 331–336.

Hobbs, J. R. & Shieber, S. M. (1987). An algorithm for generating quantifier scopings. *Computational Linguistics*, 13(1–2), 47–63.

Hofmeister, P., Jaeger, T. F., Sag, I. A., Arnon, I., & Snider, N. (2007). Locality and accessibility in *wh*-questions. In W. Sternefeld & S. Featherston, eds., *Roots: Linguistics in Search of Its Evidential Base*. Berlin: Mouton de Gruyter, pp. 185–206.

Huang, C. T. J. (1982). Move WH in a language without *wh*-movement. *The Linguistic Review*, 1(4), 369–416.

Husband, E. M., Kelly, L. A., & Zhu, D. C. (2011). Using complement coercion to understand the neural basis of semantic composition: Evidence from an fMRI study. *Journal of Cognitive Neuroscience*, 23(11), 3254–3266.

Ionin, T. (2010). The scope of indefinites: An experimental investigation. *Natural Language Semantics*, 18(3), pp. 295–350.

Ioup, G. (1975). The treatment of quantifier scope in a transformational grammar. Doctoral dissertation, City University of New York.

Jacobson, P. (1999). Towards a variable-free semantics. *Linguistics and Philosophy*, 22(2), 117–185.

Janssen, T. M. V. (1997). Compositionality. In J. van Bentham & A. ter Meulen, eds., *Handbook of Logic and Language*. Amsterdam: Elsevier, pp. 417–474.

Just, M. A., Carpenter, P. A., & Woolley, J. D. (1982). Paradigms and processes in reading comprehension. *Journal of Experimental Psychology: General*, 111(2), 228–238.

Kaan, E., Dallas, A. C., & Barkley, C. M. (2007). Processing bare quantifiers in discourse. *Brain Research*, 1146, 199–209.

Keenan, E. L. & Stavi, J. (1986). A semantic characterization of natural language determiners. *Linguistics and Philosophy*, 9(3), 253–326.

Kratzer, A. (1998). Scope or pseudoscope? Are there wide-scope indefinites? In S. Rothstein, ed., *Events and Grammar*. Dordrecht: Kluwer Academic Publishers, pp. 163–196.

Kratzer, A. & Shimoyama, J. (2002). Indeterminate pronouns: The view from Japanese. In Y. Otsu, ed., *Papers Presented at the 3rd Tokyo Conference on Psycholinguistics*. Tokyo: Hituzi Syobo, pp. 1–25.

Kuperberg, G. R., Choi, A., Cohn, N., Paczynski, M., & Jackendoff, R. (2010). Electrophysiological correlates of complement coercion. *Journal of Cognitive Neuroscience*, 22(12), 2685–2701.

Kurtzman, H. S. & MacDonald, M. C. (1993). Resolution of quantifier scope ambiguities. *Cognition*, 48(3), 243–279.

Ladusaw, W. A. (1979). Polarity sensitivity as inherent scope relations. Doctoral dissertation, University of Texas, Austin.

Larson, R. (1995). Semantics. In L. R. Gleitman & M. Liberman, eds., *An Invitation to Cognitive Science*, vol. 1: *Language*. Cambridge, MA: MIT Press, pp. 361–380.

Lewis, D. (1975). Adverbs of quantification. In E. Keenan, ed., *Formal Semantics of Natural Language*. Cambridge: Cambridge University Press, pp. 3–15.

Lidz, J., Pietroski, P., Halberda, J., & Hunter, T. (2011). Interface transparency and the psychosemantics of most. *Natural Language Semantics*, 19(3), 227–256.

Ludlow, P. & Neale, S. (1991). Indefinite descriptions: In defense of Russell. *Linguistics and Philosophy*, 14(2), 171–202.

Majewski, H. (2014). Comprehending each other: weak reciprocity and processing. Doctoral dissertation, University of Massachusetts, Amherst.

May, R. (1977). The grammar of quantification. Doctoral dissertation, Massachusetts Institute of Technology.

May, R. (1985). *Logical Form: Its Structure and Derivation*. Cambridge, MA: MIT Press.

McCloskey, J. (1997). Subjecthood and subject positions. In L. M. V. Haegeman, ed., *Elements of Grammar*. Dordrecht: Kluwer Academic Publishers, pp. 197–235.

McElree, B., Frisson, S., & Pickering, M. J. (2006). Deferred interpretations: Why starting Dickens is taxing but reading Dickens isn't. *Cognitive Science*, 30(1), 181–192.

McElree, B., Traxler, M. J., Pickering, M. J., Jackendoff, R. S., & Seely, R. E. (2001). Coercion in on-line semantic processing. *Cognition*, 78, B17–B25.

Meyer, M.-C. & Sauerland, U. (2009). A pragmatic constraint on ambiguity detection. *Natural Language & Linguistic Theory*, 27(1), 139–150.

Newmeyer, F. J. (1983). *Grammatical Theory: Its Limits and its Possibilities*. Chicago: University of Chicago Press.

Pagin, P. & Westerståhl, D. (2010). Compositionality I: Definitions and variants. *Philosophy Compass*, 5(3), 250–264.

Park, J. C. (1995). Quantifier scope and constituency. In *Proceedings of the 33rd Annual Meeting on Association for Computational Linguistics*. Stroudsburg, PA: Association for Computational Linguistics, pp. 205–212.

Partee, B. (1995). Lexical semantics and compositionality. In L. R. Gleitman & M. Liberman, eds., *An Invitation to Cognitive Science*, vol. 1: *Language*. Cambridge, MA: MIT Press, pp. 311–360.

Partee, B. & Rooth, M. (1983). Generalized conjunction and type ambiguity. In P. Portner & B. Partee, eds., *Formal Semantics: The Essential Readings*. Oxford: Blackwell, pp. 334–356. Originally published in R. Bäuerle, C. Schwarze, & A. von Stechow, eds., (1983). *Meaning, Use and the Interpretation of Language*. Berlin: Walter de Gruyter, pp. 361–393.

Paterson, K. B., Filik, R., & Liversedge, S. P. (2008). Competition during the processing of quantifier scope ambiguities: Evidence from eye movements during reading. *Quarterly Journal of Experimental Psychology*, 61 (3), 459–473.

Paterson, K. B., Filik, R., & Moxey, L. M. (2009). Quantifiers and discourse processing. *Language and Linguistics Compass*, 3(6), 1390–1402.

Pickering, M. J., Frisson, S., McElree, B., & Traxler, M. J. (2004). Eye movements and semantic composition. In M. Carreiras & C. Clifton, Jr., eds., *The On-line Study of Sentence Comprehension: Eyetracking, ERPs, and Beyond*. New York:Psychology Press, pp. 33–50.

Pickering, M. J., McElree, B., & Traxler, M. J. (2005). The difficulty of coercion: A response to de Almeida. *Brain and Language*, 93(1), 1–9.

Piñango, M. M. & Deo, A. (2015). Reanalyzing the complement coercion effect through a generalized lexical semantics for aspectual verbs. *Journal of Semantics*, 33(2), 359–408.

Pustejovsky, J. (1991). The generative lexicon. *Computational Linguistics*, 17 (4), 409–41.

Pustejovsky, J. (1995). *The Generative Lexicon*. Cambridge, MA: MIT Press.

Pylkkänen, L., Martin, A. E., McElree, B., & Smart, A. (2009). The anterior midline field: Coercion or decision making? *Brain and Language*, 108(3), 184–190.

Pylkkänen, L. & McElree, B. (2006). The syntax-semantics interface: On-line composition of sentence meaning. In M. Traxler & M. A. Gernsbacher, eds., *Handbook of Psycholinguistics*, 2nd ed. Amsterdam: Elsevier, pp. 539–579.

Pylkkänen, L. & McElree, B. (2007). An MEG study of silent meaning. *Journal of Cognitive Neuroscience*, 19(11), 1905–1921.

Radó, J. & Bott, O. (2012). Underspecified representations of scope ambiguity? In M. Aloni, V. Kimmelman, F. Roelofsen, G. W. Sassoon, K. Schulz, & M. Westera, eds., *Logic, Language and Meaning*. Berlin: Springer-Verlag, pp. 180–189.

Reinhart, T. (1997). Quantifier scope: How labor is divided between QR and choice functions. *Linguistics and Philosophy*, 20(4), 335–397.

Ross, J. R. (1967). Constraints on variables in syntax. Doctoral dissertation, Massachusetts Institute of Technology. Published as *Infinite Syntax* (1986). Norwood, NJ: Ablex.

Ruys, E. G. (1992). The scope of indefinites. Doctoral dissertation, Utrecht University.

Saddy, D., Drenhaus, H., & Frisch, S. (2004). Processing polarity items: Contrastive licensing costs. *Brain and Language*, 90(1–3), 495–502.

Schiffer, S. (2015). Meaning and formal semantics in generative grammar. *Erkenntnis*, 80(1), 61–87.

Schütze, C. T. (1996). *The Empirical Base of Linguistics: Grammaticality Judgments and Linguistic Methodology*. Chicago: University of Chicago Press.

Schütze, C. T. (2011). Linguistic evidence and grammatical theory. *Wiley Interdisciplinary Reviews: Cognitive Science*, 2(2), 206–221.

Schwarz, B. (2001). Two kinds of long-distance indefinites. In R. van Rooy & M. Stokhof, eds., *Proceedings of the 13th Amsterdam Colloquium*. Amsterdam, pp. 192–197.

Schwarz, B. (2011). Long distance indefinites and choice functions. *Language and Linguistics Compass*, 5(12), 880–897.

Soames, S. (1992). Truth, meaning, and understanding. *Philosophical Studies*, 65(1–2), 17–35.

Sprouse, J. (2008). The differential sensitivity of acceptability judgments to processing effects. *Linguistic Inquiry*, 39(4), 686–894.

Sprouse, J. (2018). Acceptability judgments and grammaticality, prospects and challenges. In N. Hornstein, C. Yang, & P. Patel-Grosz, eds., *Syntactic Structures after 60 Years: The Impact of the Chomskyan Revolution in Linguistics*. Berlin: De Gruyter Mouton, pp. 195–224.

Sprouse, J. & Almeida, D. (2013). The empirical status of data in syntax: A reply to Gibson and Fedorenko. *Language and Cognitive Processes*, 28(3), 222–228.

Sprouse, J. & Almeida, D. (2017). Setting the empirical record straight: Acceptability judgments appear to be reliable, robust, and replicable. *Behavioral and Brain Sciences*, 40, e311.

Traxler, M. J., Pickering, M. J., & McElree, B. (2002). Coercion in sentence processing: Evidence from eye-movements and self-paced reading. *Journal of Memory and Language*, 47(4), 530–547.

Tunstall, S. (1998). The interpretation of quantifiers: semantics and processing. Doctoral dissertation, University of Massachusetts, Amherst.

Wijnen, F. & Kaan, E. (2006). Dynamics of semantic processing: The interpretation of bare quantifiers. *Language and Cognitive Processes*, 21(6), 684–720.

Winter, Y. (1997). Choice functions and the scopal semantics of indefinites. *Linguistics and Philosophy*, 20(4), 399–467.

Xiang, M., Grove, J., & Giannakidou, A. (2016). Semantic and pragmatic processes in the comprehension of negation: An event related potential study of negative polarity sensitivity. *Journal of Neurolinguistics*, 38, 71–88.

# Part III

## Experimental Studies of Specific Populations and Language Families

# 14

# Acceptability Studies in L2 Populations

Tania Ionin

## 14.1 Introduction

The use of sentence acceptability experiments with learners or speakers of a second language (L2) goes back to the earliest experimental research with this population. Acceptability studies with L2 populations (and bilingual populations more generally) have been used to examine a variety of issues, including age effects on acquisition, the role of cross-linguistic influence, and the involvement of explicit vs. implicit knowledge, among others. While no counts are available, it is likely that acceptability judgment tasks, in their various forms, are among the most common data collection methodologies used in studies with non-native speakers. The goal of this chapter is to examine the issues that arise with regard to the use of sentence acceptability experiments with L2 populations, including both decisions that researchers have to make when designing an acceptability experiment, and questions about what acceptability tasks used with non-native speakers tell us about these speakers' underlying grammars. This chapter is not intended as an overview of L2 studies that use the acceptability judgment task methodology (see Ionin & Zyzik (2014) for one such overview).

Before going any further, it is important to address the issue of terminology. Literature on experimental syntax consistently uses the term acceptability judgment task (AJT) rather than grammaticality judgment task (GJT). Cowart (1997) makes the case that a task can measure acceptability but not grammaticality, since the latter is an abstract concept that is not directly measurable. According to Cowart, each sentence is either grammatical or ungrammatical in a given speaker's mental grammar. In contrast, sentences can have different degrees of (un)acceptability, depending on whether they violate grammatical constraints, are difficult to process, etc. (see Chapter 5 on the relationship between acceptability, grammar, and processing). Experimental tasks, then, measure only acceptability, but the results can lead researchers to make inferences about grammaticality.

On the other hand, literature on judgment tasks in L2 research often uses the term GJT rather than AJT. This goes both for older studies (e.g. Johnson & Newport 1989; White & Genesee 1996) and more recent ones (e.g. Bruhn de Garavito 2011), while other studies use the term AJT rather than GJT (e.g. Montrul, Dias, & Santos 2011). This seems to be an issue of terminology rather than content, with the terms GJT and AJT both used to describe a task in which participants judge sentences with regard to how grammatically (un)acceptable they are; the term AJT is perhaps more commonly used if the study uses a numerical scale of acceptability ratings (see also Section 14.3.5), while the term GJT is often used for tasks with a binary yes/no scale. For the purposes of the current chapter, no distinction will be made between studies that use the term GJT and those that use the term AJT; the term "sentence acceptability experiments" is taken to cover both.

## 14.2   Common Uses of Sentence Acceptability Experiments in L2 Research

Sentence acceptability experiments in L2 research can be divided into two broad types: those with a broad focus on linguistic knowledge as a whole, and those with a specific focus on a particular linguistic structure (see Ionin & Zyzik (2014) for more on this divide). We discuss each one in turn.

### 14.2.1   Sentence Acceptability Experiments with a Broad Focus

On the one hand are studies that use acceptability tasks (typically termed GJTs; see above) in order to obtain a fairly global measure of learners' linguistic knowledge. Many such studies have the goal of correlating this measure with such variables as age of acquisition, aptitude, motivation, etc. (for sample studies, see, e.g., Johnson & Newport (1989), DeKeyser (2000), Birdsong & Molis (2001), Abrahamsson & Hyltenstam (2008), among many others). In some of these studies (e.g. Johnson & Newport 1989) the acceptability experiment is the only measure of L2 speakers' linguistic knowledge, while in others (e.g. Abrahamsson & Hyltenstam 2008, 2009), it is one among a battery of tests. Other studies with a broad focus (e.g. Ellis 2005; Loewen 2009) use the (untimed) acceptability experiment as a measure of participants' explicit knowledge, and compare performance to that on other tasks that are argued to target more implicit knowledge (see Section 14.4.1 for more discussion).

The judgment tasks used in these studies ask learners to judge sentences representing quite a wide variety of morphosyntactic structures; the challenge is to determine the choice of structures to test. Some studies, e.g.

Johnson and Newport (1989) and its many replications, as well as Ellis (2005) and other studies that use the AJT as a measure of explicit knowledge, select a variety of sentence structures that represent the basic properties of the language, including word order, tense/agreement marking, etc.: e.g. (1) presents five of the ungrammatical sentence types from Johnson and Newport (1989), which include errors of morphology as well as syntax, omission as well as misuse (the task also included the corresponding grammatical counterparts of each ungrammatical sentence).

(1)    a. A shoe salesman sees many foots throughout the day.
        b. A bat flewed into our attic last night.
        c. Tom is reading book in the bathtub.
        d. Susan is making some cookies for we.
        e. Kevin called Nancy for a date up.

In contrast, studies with advanced and near-native L2 speakers, such as Coppieters (1987), Birdsong (1992), and Abrahamsson and Hyltenstam (2008), make a point of selecting particularly complex structures, ones that are likely to be challenging even to very proficient L2 speakers. These studies aim to determine whether adult L2 learners can perform in a fully native-like manner on even the most challenging and subtle aspects of the L2 (the conclusions on this point differ).

## 14.2.2 Sentence Acceptability Experiments in the Generative Framework

A different use of acceptability tasks in L2 research is to examine, in detail, what L2 speakers know about a particular structure or structures. Many such studies are conducted from the generative perspective, and use judgment tasks in order to investigate whether adult L2 learners have access to Universal Grammar (UG). L2 studies conducted within the Principles and Parameters framework often use judgment tasks to examine whether adult L2 learners are sensitive to UG principles such as Subjacency (e.g. Johnson & Newport 1991; White & Genesee 1996), or to examine whether learners are capable of acquiring new parameter settings not instantiated in their L1 (e.g. Slabakova 1999). Example ungrammatical sentences from White and Genesee (1996), which include Subjacency violations (see Chapter 9), are given in (2).

(2)    a. What did you hear the announcement that Ann had received?
                                              [complex NP]
        b. Who did you meet Tom after you saw?      [adjunct island]

Other studies focus more on the nature of the L2 acquisition process, and the degree to which it is affected by cross-linguistic influence (transfer) from the learners' L1; such studies test specific structures that are differently instantiated in the L1 and the L2 (see, e.g., Montrul (2005); Whong-Barr & Schwartz (2002)). For example, the sentences in (3), from Whong-Barr and Schwartz (2002), were used to examine whether L1-Japanese and L1-Korean L2-English child learners have acquired the dative alternation in English, given that double object constructions work quite differently in those two languages relative to English (and relative to each other as well).

(3)      a. The giraffe made the pig a cup of tea.
         b. The giraffe made a cup of tea for the pig.

The underlying assumption of all such studies is that acceptability tasks are a direct window into the learners' underlying linguistic competence.[1] However, this assumption has been challenged, as will be discussed in Section 14.4. Before addressing the issue of what acceptability tasks measure, however, we discuss some issues that arise in the construction of sentence acceptability experiments in L2 research (see also Ionin (2012)).

## 14.3  Issues in the Design of Sentence Acceptability Experiments in L2 Research

Researchers conducting sentence acceptability experiments with L2 speakers must make a number of decisions about the task format. Some of these decisions – for example, what type of scale to use – also arise for sentence acceptability experiments with native speakers. However, many other decisions, such as timing, modality, and the need for corrections, are largely specific to research with L2 speakers and other non-monolingual populations.

### 14.3.1  Modality
While sentence acceptability experiments with native speakers are typically in written format, this is not always the case for studies with non-native or non-monolingual populations. For example, Johnson and Newport (1989) used aural presentation for their judgment task with L2 speakers, while White and Genesee (1996) used visual presentation on a computer screen. Many studies choose one modality over another with no particular motivation, yet the choice of modality does influence performance, as shown by Murphy (1997). In Murphy's study, L2-English learners as well as L2-French learners were more accurate (and faster)

---

[1]  A different use of the AJT can be found in intervention studies, where it is used to measure learners' performance on a particular linguistic structure or structures before and after a particular instructional treatment (see Gass & Alvarez Torres (2005) for an example). This chapter leaves such uses aside.

when tested on the visual version of an acceptability experiment than when tested on the aural version.

Recent research has found that different populations have advantages in different modalities: while adult L2 learners may have an advantage in the written domain, heritage speakers may have an advantage in the oral/aural domain, perhaps due to lower literacy skills (see e.g. Montrul 2008; Montrul, Foote, & Perpiñán 2008). Use of written vs. aural format for an acceptability experiment can thus potentially influence performance; one solution is to use bimodal presentation, as Montrul, Bhatt, and Girju (2015) do in their study of heritage speakers. And of course the aural format is a must when the study is conducted with young children, as in Whong-Barr and Schwartz (2002).

### 14.3.2  Timed vs. Untimed Tasks

The question of whether acceptability judgment tasks should be timed or untimed is relevant for native as well as non-native speakers. Schütze (1996) points out that adding time pressure makes participants less likely to be influenced by prescriptive norms, or to think about what structures are being tested. Tremblay (2005) adds that since timed tasks are usually administered via a computer, they can be set up so that participants are unable to go back and change their earlier answers. By forcing participants to respond with their first intuitive response, not giving them a chance to think of rules or to revisit their earlier answers, timed tasks make it more likely that participants access their implicit rather than their explicit knowledge (Ellis 2005), a point to which we will return in Section 14.4.1.

### 14.3.3  Reasons for Accepting or Rejecting Sentences

An issue that arises with L2 and other non-native populations is whether participants reject ungrammatical sentences for the "right" reason: for example, a learner might reject a sentence with a missing article because she does not think that the verb is in the right aspectual form, rather than because she noticed the missing article. Some studies have addressed this issue through asking learners to correct the sentences that they judge as ungrammatical, either immediately (e.g. Falk & Bardel 2011) or after they have recorded their judgments (e.g. Gass & Alvarez Torres 2005). As discussed in Ionin and Zyzik (2014), the first method has two possible downsides: it may bias the learners toward accepting sentences in order to avoid the work of error correction, and it makes the task considerably more explicit and metalinguistic; the second option (correcting the errors only after all the judgments have been provided) avoids these problems, but depends on the learners remembering exactly why they rejected the sentence as ungrammatical the first time around. An alternative way of ensuring that sentences are rejected for the right reason is to use a Latin

Square design, with counterbalancing across participants: if ungrammatical sentences are rejected, but their minimally different grammatical
counterparts are accepted, this is a strong indication that the ungrammatical sentences are rejected for the right reason. Use of the Latin Square
design, with multiple lists counterbalanced across participants, has long
been a hallmark of research in experimental syntax (see Chapter 1 and
Cowart 1997) and is becoming more and more common in research with L2
populations (see e.g. Kim 2015). There are other reasons besides the one
discussed above for the Latin Square design to become a must in research
with L2 populations: this design controls for potential effects of other
extragrammatical factors, such as plausibility or learners' (lack of) familiarity with individual lexical items.

Just as one cannot be certain that learners reject sentences for the right
reason, one cannot be certain that learners accept sentences for the right
reason, i.e. because they consider them to be grammatical. Many studies
note that learners are more accurate at accepting grammatical sentences
than at rejecting ungrammatical ones (see Orfitelli & Polinsky (2017) and
the references cited therein). One way to address this in analysis is to use
measures that correct for response bias, such as the A' statistic (Grier 1971;
Pollack & Norman 1964).[2] A' corrects for response bias in a task with
a binary scale (such as grammatical/ungrammatical), by taking into
account both the rate of hits and the rate of false alarms (in the case of
acceptability experiments, these would correspond, respectively, to the
rate of correct rejections of ungrammatical sentences, and the rate of
incorrect rejections of grammatical sentences). For a sample acceptability
experiment that uses A', see Blackwell, Bates, and Fisher (1996).

### 14.3.4 Sentence Acceptability Experiments that Involve Context
While traditional AJTs present sentences in isolation, a variation presents
sentences in context; the context can be anything from one sentence to
a paragraph, and/or a picture. There is no agreed-upon name for tasks that
ask for judgments of acceptability in context; as shown by the examples
below, different studies use different terms for this type of task.

Contexts are a must for studies of phenomena at the syntax/semantics or
syntax/pragmatics interface, where the question is not simply whether the
sentence is acceptable, but whether it is acceptable with a particular
interpretation (the one made salient by the context) (see Chapters 2 and
13 for further discussion). As one example, consider the interpretation of
NPs with and without articles, from Ionin, Montrul, and Crivos (2013). This
was a bidirectional study which examined what interpretation L1-Spanish
L2-English learners as well as L1-English L2-Spanish learners assign to
plural NPs with and without a definite article. Study 2 in Ionin et al.

[2] Thank you to an anonymous reviewer for pointing this out.

(2013) used an AJT with contexts, as in (4); the context was followed by multiple target sentences, two of which are discussed in the paper: a variant with a bare (article-less) plural NP in subject position, as in (4a), and a variant with a definite plural NP in subject position, as in (4b). Participants rated sentences on a scale from 1 (unacceptable) to 4 (acceptable).

(4)    It's my niece's birthday this Saturday – she is going to be three years old. I'm not sure what to get her. Maybe I'll just get her some toy, like a stuffed dog or bear. I can't go wrong with that. We all know that …

    a. Toy animals are good children's gifts.
    b. The toy animals are good children's gifts.    (Ionin et al. 2013: 24)

Both variants are grammatical in English, but only (4a) matches the context, since it expresses a generic interpretation (toy animals generally make good gifts); in contrast, (4b) is not a good match for the context, since no specific toys are mentioned in the context, hence the use of the definite NP in (4b) is infelicitous. On the other hand, in Spanish, the equivalent of (4a) is ungrammatical (since bare plurals are, with some exceptions, disallowed preverbally), while the equivalent of (4b) allows both definite and generic interpretations, and is thus fully acceptable.

A different use of context can be found in Montrul and Slabakova (2003), who used a sentence-conjunction judgment task in which participants were presented with sentences containing coordinated clauses, as in (5). Here, the choice of grammatical aspect (imperfect, as in (5a), vs. preterite, as in (5b)) makes the sentences either logical or contradictory. The participants were instructed to rate the sentences on a scale from -2 to +2 based on how well the two clauses went together.

(5)    a. La clase era a las 10 pero empezó a las 10:30. (logical)
      'The class was-IMPF at 10 but started at 10:30.'
    b. La clase fue a las 10 pero empezó a las 10:30. (contradictory)
    c. 'The class was-PRET at 10 but started at 10:30.'
                             (Montrul & Slabakova 2003: 369)

Note that even though Montrul and Slabakova (2003) presented the sentences in isolation, the sentences formed their own context: the target form was in the second clause, while the first clause provided the context which established the second clause as either acceptable (logical) or unacceptable (contradictory).

Yet another variation on the use of context is found in Gabriele (2009), a bidirectional study about aspect in English and Japanese. In a story compatibility task, participants were presented digitally recorded stories accompanied by pictures, and had to judge sentences presented with those stories. The stories established an event as either complete or incomplete. As an example, consider (6), from the English version of the task; the story involved either Picture 1 followed by Picture 2a, or else Picture 1 followed by Picture 2b, while the target sentence was either (6a) or (6b).

(6)   Picture 1:  This is the plane to Tokyo. At 4:00 the plane is near the airport.
      Picture 2a: At 5:00 the passengers are at the airport.
      Picture 2b: There is a lot of wind. At 4:30 the plane is still in the air.
      a. The plane arrived at the airport.
      b. The plane is arriving at the airport.    (based on Gabriele 2009: 384)

In English, (6b) is acceptable with Picture 2b but not with Picture 2a, while the opposite is the case for (6a). In contrast, the Japanese version of (6b) is acceptable with Picture 2a but *not* with Picture 2b, since imperfective morphology with achievement verbs in Japanese results in a reading akin to the present perfect in English, *The plane has arrived at the airport*. Thus, the sentence type in (6b), presented with the two different types of context, allowed for the testing of L1 transfer from Japanese to English (and vice versa, in the Japanese version of the study).

In all of the above examples, the phenomena being tested fall at the interface between syntax and semantics, and hence require context. Context is not required for studies that test narrow syntactic or morpho-syntactic phenomena, but some researchers choose to use contexts in such cases as well. For example, the study by Whong-Barr and Schwartz (2002), discussed in Section 14.2.2, presented target sentences such as (3) in context (in this case, the context, established by a preceding dialogue, of a giraffe making tea for a pig). The context was used to ensure that the child participants did not assign some other, irrelevant, interpretation to the target sentences.

## 14.3.5  Type of Scale

In addition to the decisions concerning modality and the use (and type) of context, another decision that must be made in a sentence acceptability experiment with any type of population is what type of scale to use (see Chapter 2; see also Cowart (1997: Ch. 6), for discussion of different response scale types). Common options include a binary option (yes/no, grammatical/ungrammatical, good/bad, etc.), a numerical scale (with or without a midpoint), or a ratio scale, as used in the Magnitude Estimation method (Bard, Robertson, & Sorace 1996, Sorace 2010). Older acceptability studies with L2 populations (e.g. White & Genesee 1996) typically used the binary option, while more recent studies are more likely to use a numerical scale with, typically, anywhere between four and seven points. Binary scales are sufficient for contrasts that are very clear and straightforward: for example, if a study tests learners' understanding of English word order, SOV is clearly ungrammatical while SVO is grammatical, and it is not clear what would be gained by having more than two options on the scale. However, when more subtle contrasts are being tested, and when multiple factors are expected to influence (un)acceptability (see e.g. Chapters 1 and 9, as well as Sprouse, Wagers, & Phillips (2012), on the use of factorial design in sentence acceptability experiments), a numerical scale with multiple points is to be preferred.

Some studies use a scale with both negative and positive integers (e.g. -3 through +3), while others use exclusively positive integers (e.g. 1 through 5). Ionin and Zyzik (2014) argue against the use of a zero midpoint, or, ideally, any midpoint at all (i.e. they recommend the use of a scale with an even number of points), since L2 learners may treat the midpoint as meaning "I don't know" rather than "neither grammatical nor ungrammatical." Indeed, some studies have explicitly defined the zero midpoint as meaning "I don't know" or "not sure." In that case, (un)grammaticality becomes confounded by (un)certainty, a situation which can potentially be remedied if all zero responses are discarded from analyses. Other studies (e.g. Montrul et al. 2011) address this issue by having "I don't know" as a separate option that is not part of the scale, and subsequently discarding all "I don't know" responses from analyses.

Finally, some L2 studies have used the Magnitude Estimation technique, in which participants rank sentences relative to one another, rather than using absolute values of (un)acceptability (see Chapter 2 for more detailed discussion of this). Sorace (2010) argues that Magnitude Estimation has a number of advantages over the numerical scale method. However, several studies with native speakers, including Sprouse (2011) and Westcott and Fanselow (2011), have shed doubt on this claim, by showing that Magnitude Estimation does not yield more information than binary or scale data, and that acceptability tasks do not meet the assumptions of the Magnitude Estimation method. While no corresponding study has been done with non-native speakers, there is no reason to expect that Magnitude Estimation works better for this population than for native speakers.

Even as sentence acceptability experiments with L2 speakers most typically use a numerical scale, there is still variation in exactly how the points on the scale are defined. First of all, studies differ in whether they ask participants to judge acceptability, grammaticality, logic, etc. Second, studies differ in whether they label only the endpoints of the scale, or each individual point. For example, the story compatibility task in Gabriele (2009), described in Section 14.3.4 above, used a scale from 1 to 5, in which each point received a particular label. For example, 1 was defined as "I definitely cannot say this sentence in the context of the story," while 3 corresponded to "I might be able to say this sentence in the context of the story," and 5 indicated that "I definitely can say this sentence in the context of the story" (2009: 382).

According to Cowart (1997: Ch. 6), labeling each point on the scale is undesirable because participants may not consider intervals between adjacent points to be equal (e.g. the labels for 1 and 2 may cause them to be perceived as being closer together than the labels for 2 and 3). However, this issue arises even when only the endpoints are labeled: there is no way to ensure that participants consider the interval between 1 and 2 to be equal to that between 2 and 3, or between 3 and 4, etc. The reason why this matters is that parametric statistical tests such as t-tests and ANOVAs (the most commonly used tests in experimental linguistic research at the time of Cowart's writing) assume that the data are interval data, whereas numerical scales (whether with midpoints labeled or not) result in ordinal rather than interval data. However, as researchers in both experimental syntax and second language acquisition move away from ANOVAs and toward mixed-effects modeling (see, e.g., Baayen, Davidson, & Bates 2008), this is no longer an issue, given the existence of statistical tools specifically designed to work with ordinal data (e.g. Christensen 2018) (see also Chapters 1–3 for discussion of this issue).

To sum up, L2 researchers designing sentence acceptability experiments must determine the modality, presentation type (with or without context), timing, and response scale for their study. Beyond these decisions, L2 researchers must give some thought to whether the task is valid: whether it measures what the researchers think it measures. We turn to this next.

## 14.4  What Do Sentence Acceptability Experiments Measure?

A question that has been much discussed in the L2 literature is what exactly sentence acceptability experiments measure. In experimental syntax research with native speakers, the assumption is that sentence acceptability experiments provide a direct window into speakers' linguistic competence (but see Chapters 4 and 5 and Schütze (1996) on ruling out extralinguistic factors). This was the assumption in early L2 research with sentence acceptability experiments as well, where the focus was on determining whether the mental grammars of adult L2 learners is UG-constrained. For example, some of the earliest studies that used sentence acceptability experiments, such as Johnson and Newport (1991) and White and Genesee (1996), had the goal of examining whether adult L2 learners' grammars are constrained by Universal Grammar, the principle of Subjacency in particular. The implicit assumption of these studies is that results of a sentence acceptability experiment can inform us about the learners' linguistic competence. This assumption was made both by studies that ultimately concluded that adult L2 learners do not have access to

UG (e.g. Johnson & Newport 1991), because their performance differed from that of native speakers; and by studies that ultimately concluded that adult L2 learners *do* have access to UG (e.g. White & Genesee 1996), because, at the highest levels of proficiency, their performance did not differ from that of native speakers.

The assumption that sentence acceptability experiments inform us about linguistic competence is quite reasonable: unlike production studies, where participants may not produce a target structure despite having it in their grammar, sentence acceptability experiments ask participants to share their linguistic intuitions of the structure in question. The concern in L2 studies, however, is that when learners provide a judgment, they are basing it on something other than intuition; for example, instructed learners may base their judgments on rules that they learned in the classroom, rather on their own intuitions. This relates closely to the distinction made in the literature between explicit and implicit knowledge, discussed below.

### 14.4.1 Measuring Explicit vs. Implicit Knowledge in L2 Populations

Linguistic competence is what governs speakers' *implicit knowledge*, or "knowledge how," but adult speakers of a language – both native and non-native – are generally assumed to also have *explicit knowledge*, or "knowledge that" (see, e.g., Hulstijn & Ellis (2005); Ellis et al. (2009) for an overview of the issues). Native speakers are assumed to draw upon their implicit knowledge when giving linguistic judgments. The question for L2 researchers is whether a learner's performance on a given task is reflecting the learner's implicit knowledge or her explicit knowledge; if a learner's judgment is based primarily on her explicit knowledge, then it is not reflecting her implicit knowledge, or her linguistic competence.

The main way in which researchers have addressed the question of learners' level of knowledge is by comparing how learners perform on a variety of tasks, and how performance across tasks differs or correlates. With regard to sentence acceptability experiments, the two factors that have been argued to play a role in whether explicit or implicit knowledge is being targeted are time pressure and item grammaticality, as described below.

A seminal study on this topic, Ellis (2005), tested a large sample of L2-English learners (70.5 percent of whom had Chinese as their L1) on a variety of linguistic structures, using a battery of tasks. The criteria for determining whether a given task was more likely to target explicit or implicit knowledge included degree of awareness, time available, focus of attention, and metalinguistic knowledge. Two of the tasks were judgment tasks: one timed and one untimed. Both tasks were classified as involving awareness "by rule" (as opposed to "by feel," as in the case of an oral narration task), and as focusing attention on form (rather than meaning).

The untimed experiment was furthermore classified as not involving time pressure, and as involving metalinguistic knowledge (since participants would have time to think about what they'd learned in the classroom). In contrast, the timed experiment was classified as involving time pressure, and not involving metalinguistic knowledge (the rationale being that participants would not have time to think about what they'd learned in the classroom; however, the involvement of metalinguistic knowledge cannot be definitively excluded in any task that requires metalinguistic judgments of acceptability). Thus, the timed task was predicted to target implicit knowledge to a greater extent than the untimed one, yet both were predicted to target explicit knowledge more than the two meaning-based tasks (imitation and oral narration). The results largely bore out this prediction: a principal component factor analysis with two factors showed that the timed task loaded on the same underlying factor as the two oral tasks, while the untimed task loaded more strongly on the second factor. This was interpreted as the timed experiment targeting implicit knowledge more than the untimed experiment, and the opposite for explicit knowledge. A number of studies since Ellis (2005) have similarly found that time pressure influences task performance (e.g. Bowles 2011; Ellis & Loewen 2007). Godfroid et al. (2015) replicated this finding in an eye-tracking study.

The learners in the Ellis (2005) study were also considerably more accurate on the untimed than the timed experiment, at 82 vs. 54 percent correct; this result suggests that, if the timed experiment provides a better estimate of what learners know at an implicit level, relying on untimed experiment results (as many L2 studies do) overestimates their underlying knowledge. Interestingly, however, the native-speaker controls in the study were also more accurate on the untimed experiment compared to the timed one, at 96 vs. 80 percent correct; given that native speakers by definition have full implicit knowledge of their language, this result suggests that a timed task may in fact underestimate participants' implicit knowledge. Putting native speakers under various stressors (including, but not limited to, time pressure) has in fact been argued to impair performance, a point that we will be returning to in Section 14.4.3 below.

Thus, there is suggestive evidence that putting learners under time pressure leads to a greater reliance on implicit knowledge, and makes it more likely that learners' performance is indicative of their underlying linguistic competence. At the same time, it is worth pointing out that the grammatical phenomena examined in studies of explicit/implicit knowledge tend to be fairly basic syntactic and morphological phenomena (e.g. verbal inflectional morphology, question formation, articles, etc. – see e.g. Ellis (2005: Table 3)) which are likely to be subject to explicit classroom instruction. Furthermore, such studies often do not control for the learners' L1, or consider predictions based on cross-linguistic influence. In contrast, L2 studies conducted from the generative perspective pay much attention to what knowledge learners can transfer from their L1, as well as whether or not learners are instructed on the target linguistic phenomena. Studies that argue that adult L2 acquisition is UG-constrained strive to show that the target phenomena cannot be learned on the basis of classroom instruction, or frequent occurrences in the input, or transfer from the learners' L1. When such criteria are met, the phenomenon qualifies as a *Poverty of the Stimulus (PoS)* phenomenon, and acquisition of PoS phenomena is taken as evidence for UG (see Schwartz & Sprouse (2000), and much work by Dekydtspotter and colleagues, e.g. Dekydtspotter & Hathorn (2005)). For example, if particular constraints on long-distance movement are neither present in the L1 nor taught in the classroom, and given that long-distance *wh*-questions are highly infrequent in the input, then learners' sensitivity to such constraints, even in a fairly explicit task like an untimed acceptability experiment, can be argued to provide evidence of UG constraining the learners' underlying linguistic competence. To the best of my knowledge, there has not been a direct comparison of how learners perform on timed vs. untimed tasks specifically with regard to linguistic constructions that qualify as PoS phenomena.

### 14.4.2   Judgments of Grammatical vs. Ungrammatical Items

A very common finding of sentence acceptability experiments conducted with L2 populations is that learners perform worse on ungrammatical than on grammatical items (see, among many others, Murphy 1997; Flege, Yeni-Komshian, & Liu 1999): i.e. learners are mainly non-targetlike in accepting ungrammatical items, rather than in rejecting grammatical ones, a finding often attributed to a yes-bias (but see also Orfitelli & Polinsky 2017).

Studies on explicit vs. implicit knowledge furthermore argue that performance on grammatical vs. ungrammatical items reflects different types of knowledge. For example, Ellis (2005) found that, in the case of the untimed task, performance on the grammatical sentences correlated most strongly with performance on the oral tasks and the timed task, while performance on the ungrammatical sentences correlated most strongly with performance on a test of metalinguistic knowledge. Ellis suggested that learners drew on their implicit knowledge (their intuitions) when judging grammatical sentences, but on their explicit knowledge (what they had explicitly learned) when judging ungrammatical sentences. The same conclusion was reached by Gutiérrez (2013), who found that item grammaticality was a more crucial factor than time pressure in the factor analysis.

Godfroid et al. (2015), in an eye-tracking study of acceptability judgments, found that item grammaticality had an effect only in the untimed acceptability task, not the timed one. Godfroid et al. (2015) suggest that grammatical sentences in a timed task actually draw on explicit knowledge the most, because learners reread the sentence in order to ensure that they did not miss an error; in contrast, for ungrammatical sentences, they have evidence of ungrammaticality as soon as they come across an error, and have no need for rereading. Thus, the conclusion of Godfroid et al. (2015) is quite different from that of Ellis (2005), for whom it was the ungrammatical sentences that drew on explicit knowledge the most. At present, there is no definitive consensus in the literature with regard to what item (un)grammaticality means for the type of knowledge tested.[3]

### 14.4.3   Sentence Acceptability Experiments and Processing Limitations

The literature on explicit vs. implicit knowledge, discussed above, suggests that judgment tasks (at least untimed ones), by targeting primarily explicit knowledge, may overestimate what learners know at an implicit, underlying level. The opposite argument is made in a recent paper by Orfitelli and Polinsky (2017), who argue that judgment tasks *underestimate* learners' knowledge. Orfitelli and Polinsky (2017) discuss findings from both L2 learners and heritage speakers, and argue that processing limitations may cause learners to perform poorly in sentence acceptability experiments even when they have the relevant underlying knowledge.

One piece of evidence in favor of this argument is the finding of an ERP study by Tokowicz and MacWhinney (2005): in this study, classroom L2-Spanish learners who performed at-chance in a sentence acceptability experiment on Spanish morphosyntax nevertheless showed robust effects of sensitivity to ungrammaticality in their ERP waveforms. If brain responses are taken as indicative of underlying implicit knowledge, then this finding suggests that behavioral tasks such as an acceptability experiment may underestimate what learners know.

The second part of Orfitelli and Polinsky's argument has to do with the findings that even native speakers show degraded performance in sentence acceptability experiments when placed under memory strain (e.g. Blackwell & Bates 1995), and that there are parallels between the structures on which learners make errors, and the structures on which native speakers make errors when placed under pressure (McDonald 2000, 2006). In particular, McDonald (2006) tested adult L2-English learners from a variety of L1s on a subset of the sentence types from Johnson and Newport (1989). In the first experiment, McDonald (2006) found that L2 learners performed worse than native speakers on both grammaticality judgments and a variety of processing measures. Some of the processing

---

[3] An anonymous reviewer observes that since a learner must make a decision about whether a sentence is grammatical or ungrammatical, it is not clear how the learner can draw on two different types of knowledge for grammatical vs. ungrammatical items. This point is not clearly explained in the studies that discuss effects of item grammaticality.

measures (specifically, measures of working memory and decoding ability) correlated with performance on the judgment task. In the second experiment, native English speakers were placed under a variety of processing and memory stressors, and performed considerably worse than unstressed native speakers. Some grammatical phenomena (e.g. regular inflectional morphology) were more vulnerable to disruption under the various stressors than others (e.g. word order was quite robust). The patterns of performance in the native-speaker group that was placed under the stressor of noise were especially similar to the patterns exhibited by the L2 learners: e.g. both groups performed particularly well on word order and particularly poorly on articles (see in McDonald (2006: Table 8) for performance across all ten constructions tested). Based on these findings, McDonald (2006) argues that the fact that adult L2 learners differ from unstressed native speakers should not be taken as indicating lack of grammatical knowledge on the part of the L2 learners; rather, their performance is argued to be indicative of processing difficulties.

In light of these findings, Orfitelli and Polinsky (2017) argue that the existence of extragrammatical (e.g. processing) factors makes it very difficult to draw conclusions about learners' underlying grammar on the basis of judgment task results. Orfitelli and Polinsky suggest using comprehension tasks instead, as these do not draw as much on metalinguistic knowledge, and, in prior studies cited by Orfitelli and Polinsky (Waters, Caplan, & Rochon 1995; Dick et al. 2001; Waters, Caplan, & Yampolsky 2003) have been found not to cause impaired performance in native speakers placed under a stressor; this in turn suggests that comprehension tasks are less subject than judgment tasks to processing and other extragrammatical factors. Orfitelli and Polinsky (2017) provide an example of a study with L2 learners, by Orfitelli and Grüter (2014), in which L1-Spanish L2-English learners performed in a more target-like manner with regard to null subjects on a truth-value judgment task (TVJT) than on an acceptability task.

A word of caution is needed with regard to this conclusion, however, or rather, two words of caution. First, it is not clear that enough research with native speakers has been done to determine that the comprehension tasks commonly used in research with L2 learners are not vulnerable to disruption under stressors (e.g. none of the studies cited with regard to this point in Orfitelli & Polinsky (2017), see above, used the TVJT). Thus, we cannot be certain that processing and memory limitations do not affect (some) comprehension tasks just as they do acceptability tasks. Second, the finding of Orfitelli and Grüter (2014) that learners do better on a comprehension task than on a judgment task does not necessarily generalize across studies. For example, Ionin et al. (2013) report on two separate studies on the interpretation of definite plurals and bare plurals with both L1-English L2-Spanish learners and L1-Spanish L2-English learners. The first study used a TVJT, in which generic and specific readings of definite plurals were juxtaposed. The second study used a context-based acceptability task, discussed in Section 14.3.4. The acceptability task, while context-based and hence not a traditional AJT, clearly placed a greater metalinguistic burden on learners, since it required judging sentences as (un)acceptable on a scale, whereas the TVJT was entirely meaning-focused. However, learners performed in a more target-like manner on the acceptability task than on the TVJT, the opposite of what Orfitelli and Grüter (2014) found in their study. The differences with regard to task advantages were most likely due to the specifics of the tasks within each study.

## 14.5    Conclusion: What Do Sentence Acceptability Experiments with L2 Populations Show?

In light of the discussion in the previous section, we are left with a conundrum. On the one hand, studies that focus on explicit vs. implicit knowledge suggest that untimed judgment tasks may overestimate learners' knowledge, testing their explicit, metalinguistic knowledge rather than their underlying linguistic competence. On the other hand, studies that focus on the role of processing suggest that judgment tasks (untimed as well as timed ones) may underestimate learners' knowledge, with the non-target patterns due to processing limitations rather than lack of grammatical knowledge.

While explicit knowledge and/or processing limitations may potentially be at work in any given study of acceptability judgments, it is also possible to find studies that are arguably not affected by either. A recent example is the dissertation by Kim (2015), which used an acceptability experiment on island phenomena with Korean/English bilinguals; the participants were English-dominant heritage speakers of Korean with different ages of exposure to English. Kim found that the bilinguals exhibited fairly target-like knowledge of island phenomena in both English and Korean, including in those places (notably, adjunct islands) where the two languages behave very differently. Since island phenomena are not subject to classroom instruction and are not something that non-linguists are consciously aware of, it is very unlikely that the learners could have achieved target-like performance through explicit knowledge alone. At the same time, the fact that the bilinguals performed in a target-like manner in both of their languages suggests that they were not impaired by processing limitations in this domain.

At the same time, the fact that participants in one study were not affected by processing limitations does not mean that this holds for all studies. Notably, as discussed above, L2 studies which use a variety of tasks tend to find somewhat different performance across task types. At present, there is no consensus as to whether learners are always more accurate on one type of task over another (e.g. judgment vs. comprehension), though some trends do emerge, such as generally better performance on untimed and written tasks relative to timed and oral ones, in the case of adult L2 learners (but not necessarily in the case of heritage speakers – see Section 14.3.1). The take-home message is that researchers working with L2 populations probably should not rely on the results of any one task in order to reach conclusions about non-native competence. On the one hand, convergent findings from multiple tasks provide particularly convincing evidence about what learners know or don't know. On the other hand, different findings from different tasks that test the same linguistic phenomena need to be explained; such explanations may make reference to the degree to which a given task targets explicit vs. implicit knowledge, as well as to the degree to which the task places processing and memory demands on the participants.

Ultimately, acceptability judgment tasks are not by default either better or worse than other tasks available to researchers working with L2 populations. On the one hand, acceptability tasks can provide information that other tasks cannot: first, they can ask learners about phenomena that do not show up in production; and second, they are particularly appropriate to narrow syntactic and morphological phenomena that may not naturally lend themselves to comprehension tasks. At the same time, researchers conducting sentence acceptability experiments with non-native populations need to be aware that the findings may not always be indicative of learners' underlying competence. However, the same holds for other tasks as well, including production, reaction-time, and comprehension tasks. Processing limitations may cause learners to fail to retrieve a morphological element from memory in production (this is in fact the basis of the Missing Surface Inflection Hypothesis of Prévost and White (2000)), or to slow down in a reaction-time task. Adult learners may draw on explicit knowledge even while completing a comprehension task. And so on.

Today, researchers working with L2 populations have a great variety of tasks at their disposal, including online tasks such as self-paced reading and eye-tracking, as well as brain measures such as ERPs (see, e.g., Roberts 2012; Steinhauer 2014; see also Chapters 23 and 24). Such tasks arguably target more implicit knowledge than acceptability tasks do, since they typically focus on meaning rather than form, and use measures that are outside learners' conscious control, such as reading times and brainwave patterns. At the same time, acceptability tasks arguably provide a more direct window into learners' linguistic competence (as long as the roles of explicit knowledge as well as processing limitations are taken into consideration), while psycholinguistic tasks require us to posit a link between an entirely non-linguistic measure (such as reaction time or increased positivity) and linguistic competence (see Chapter 22 for further discussion of this point). Crucially, the different task types are not mutually exclusive, but instead complement each other, and both have their place in research with L2 and bilingual populations. For more discussion of the place of sentence acceptability experiments in SLA, the interested reader is directed to the recent volume by Spinner and Gass (2019).

# References

Abrahamsson, N. & Hyltenstam, K. (2008). The robustness of aptitude effects in near-native second language acquisition. *Studies in Second Language Acquisition*, 30, 481–509.

Abrahamsson, N. & Hyltenstam, K. (2009). Age of onset and nativelikeness in a second language: Listener perception versus linguistic scrutiny. *Language Learning*, 59(2), 249–306.

Baayen, R. H., Davidson, D. J., & Bates, D. M. (2008). Mixed-effects modeling with crossed random effects for subjects and items. *Journal of Memory and Language*, 59(4), 390–412.

Bard, E. G., Robertson, D., & Sorace, A. (1996). Magnitude estimation of linguistic acceptability. *Language*, 72, 32–68.

Birdsong, D. (1992). Ultimate attainment in second language acquisition. *Language*, 68, 706–755.

Birdsong, D. & Molis, M. (2001). On the evidence for maturational constraints in second-language acquisition. *Journal of Memory and Language*, 44(2), 235–249.

Blackwell, A. & Bates, E. (1995). Inducing agrammatic profiles in normals: Evidence for the selective vulnerability of morphology under cognitive resource limitation. *Journal of Cognitive Neuroscience*, 7(2), 228–257.

Blackwell, A., Bates, E., & Fisher, D. (1996). The time course of grammaticality judgment. *Language and Cognitive Processes*, 11, 337–406.

Bowles, M. A. (2011). Measuring implicit and explicit linguistic knowledge. *Studies in Second Language Acquisition*, 33, 247–271.

Bruhn de Garavito, J. (2011). Subject/object asymmetries in the grammar of bilingual and monolingual Spanish speakers: Evidence against connectionism. *Linguistic Approaches to Bilingualism*, 1, 111–148.

Christensen, R. H. B. (2018). *ordinal – Regression Models for Ordinal Data*. R package version 2018.4–19. www.cran.r-project.org/package=ordinal/

Coppieters, R. (1987). Competence differences between native and near-native speakers. *Language*, 63, 544–573.

Cowart, W. (1997). *Experimental Syntax*. Thousand Oaks, CA: Sage.

DeKeyser, R. (2000). The robustness of critical period effects in second language acquisition. *Studies in Second Language Acquisition*, 22, 499–533.

Dekydtspotter, L. & Hathorn, J. (2005). Quelque chose … de remarquable in English–French acquisition: Mandatory, informationally encapsulated computations in second language interpretation. *Second Language Research*, 21, 291–323.

Dick, F., Bates, E., Wulfeck, B., Utman, J. A., Dronkers, N., & Gernsbacher, M. A. (2001). Language deficits, localization, and grammar: Evidence for a distributive model of language breakdown in aphasic patients and neurologically intact individuals. *Psychological Review*, 108 (4), 759–788.

Ellis, R. (2005). Measuring implicit and explicit knowledge of a second language: A psychometric study. *Studies in Second Language Acquisition*, 27(2), 141–172.

Ellis, R. & Loewen, S. (2007). Confirming the operational definitions of explicit and implicit knowledge in Ellis (2005): Responding to Isemonger. *Second Language Research*, 29, 119–126.

Ellis, R., Loewen, S., Elder, C., Erlam, R., Philip, J., & Reinders, H. (2009). *Implicit and Explicit Knowledge in Second Language Learning, Testing, and Teaching*. Bristol: Multilingual Matters.

Falk, Y. & Bardel, C. (2011). Object pronouns in German L3 syntax: Evidence for the L2 status factor. *Second Language Research*, 27, 59–82.

Flege, J. E., Yeni-Komshian, G. H., & Liu, S. (1999). Age constraints on second-language acquisition. *Journal of Memory and Language*, 41(1), 78–104.

Gabriele, A. (2009). Transfer and transition in the SLA of aspect: A bidirectional study of learners of English and Japanese. *Studies in Second Language Acquisition*, 31, 371–402.

Gass, S. M. & Alvarez Torres, M. J. (2005). Attention when? An investigation of the ordering effect of input and interaction. *Studies in Second Language Acquisition*, 27(1), 1–31.

Godfroid, A., Loewen, S., Jung, S., Park, J.-H., Gass, S., & Ellis, R. (2015). Timed and untimed grammaticality judgments measure distinct types of knowledge: Evidence from eye-movement patterns. *Studies in Second Language Acquisition*, 37(2), 269–297.

Grier, J. B. (1971). Non-parametric indexes for sensitivity and bias: Computing formulas. *Psychological Bulletin*, 75(6), 424–429.

Gutiérrez, X. (2013). The construct validity of grammaticality judgment tests as measures of implicit and explicit knowledge. *Studies in Second Language Acquisition*, 35, 423–449.

Hulstijn, J. & Ellis, R., eds. (2005). *Implicit and Explicit Second-Language Learning (Studies in Second Language Acquisition*, 27(2) (special issue)).

Ionin, T. (2012). Formal theory-based methodologies. In A. Mackey & S. Gass, eds., *Research Methods in Second Language Acquisition: A Practical Guide*. Oxford: Wiley-Blackwell, pp. 30–52.

Ionin, T., Montrul, S., & Crivos, M. (2013). A bidirectional study on the acquisition of plural noun phrase interpretation in English and Spanish. *Applied Psycholinguistics*, 34, 483–518.

Ionin, T. & Zyzik, E. (2014). Judgment and interpretation tasks in second language research. *Annual Review of Applied Linguistics*, 34, 1–28. DOI:10.1017/S0267190514000026

Johnson, J. & Newport, E. (1989). Critical period effects in second language learning: The influence of maturational state on the acquisition of English as a second language. *Cognitive Psychology*, 21, 60–99.

Johnson, J. & Newport, E. (1991). Critical period effects on universal properties of languages: The status of subjacency in the acquisition of a second language. *Cognition*, 39, 215–258.

Kim, B. (2015). Sensitivity to islands in Korean-English bilinguals. Doctoral dissertation, University of California, San Diego,

Loewen, S. (2009). Grammaticality judgment tests and the measurement of implicit and explicit L2 knowledge. In R. Ellis, S. Loewen, C. Elder, R. Erlam, J. Philip, & H. Reinders, eds., *Implicit and Explicit Knowledge in Second Language Learning, Testing, and Teaching*. Bristol: Multilingual Matters, pp. 65–93.

McDonald, J. L. (2000). Grammaticality judgments in a second language: Influences of age of acquisition and native language. *Applied Psycholinguistics*, 21(3), 395–423.

McDonald, J. L. (2006). Beyond the critical period: Processing-based explanations for poor grammaticality judgment performance by late second language learners. *Journal of Memory and Language*, 55(3), 381–401.

Montrul, S. A. (2005). On knowledge and development of unaccusativity in Spanish L2-acquisition. *Linguistics*, 43(6), 1153–1190.

Montrul, S. A. (2008). *Incomplete Acquisition in Bilingualism: Re-examining the Age Factor*. Amsterdam: John Benjamins.

Montrul, S. A., Bhatt, R., & Girju, R. (2015). Differential object marking in Spanish, Hindi, and Romanian as heritage languages. *Language*, 91(3), 564–610.

Montrul, S. A., Dias, R., & Santos, H. (2011). Clitics and object expression in the L3 acquisition of Brazilian Portuguese: Structural similarity matters for transfer. *Second Language Research*, 27, 21–58.

Montrul, S. A., Foote, R., & Perpiñán, S. (2008). Gender agreement in adult second language learners and Spanish heritage speakers: The effects of age and context of acquisition. *Language Learning*, 58, 503–553.

Montrul, S. A. & Slabakova, R. (2003). Competence similarities between native and near-native speakers: An investigation of the preterite-imperfect contrast in Spanish. *Studies in Second Language Acquisition*, 25, 351–398.

Murphy, V. A. (1997). The effect of modality on a grammaticality judgement task. *Second Language Research*, 13(1), 34–65.

Orfitelli, R. & Grüter, T. (2014). Do null subjects really transfer? In J. Cabrelli-Amaro, T. Judy, & D. Pascual y Cabo, eds., *Proceedings of the 12th Generative Approaches to Second Language Acquisition Conference*. Somerville, MA: Cascadilla Press.

Orfitelli, R. & Polinsky, M. (2017). When performance masquerades as comprehension: Grammaticality judgments in non-native speakers. In M. Kopotev, O. Lyashevskaya, & A. Mustajoki, eds., *Quantitative Approaches to the Russian Language*. Abingdon: Routledge, pp. 197–214.

Pollack, I. & Norman, D. A. (1964). A nonparametric analysis of signal detection experiments. *Psychonomic Science*, 1, 125–126.

Prévost, P. & White, L. (2000). Missing surface inflection or impairment in second language acquisition? Evidence from tense and agreement. *Second Language Research*, 16, 103–133.

Roberts, L. (2012). Review article: Psycholinguistic techniques and resources in second language acquisition research. *Second Language Research*, 28, 113–127.

Schütze, C. (1996). *The Empirical Base of Linguistics: Grammaticality Judgments and Linguistic Methodology*. Chicago: University of Chicago Press

Schwartz, B. D. & Sprouse, R. A. (2000). When syntactic theories evolve: Consequences for L2 acquisition research. In J. Archibald, ed., *Second Language Acquisition and Linguistic Theory*. Oxford: Blackwell, pp. 156–186.

Slabakova, R. (1999). The parameter of aspect in second language acquisition. *Second Language Research*, 15(3), 283–317.

Sorace, A. (2010). Using Magnitude Estimation in developmental linguistic research. In E. Blom & S. Unsworth, eds., *Experimental Methods in Language Acquisition Research*. Amsterdam: John Benjamins, pp. 57–72.

Spinner, P. & Gass, S. M. (2019). *Using Judgments In Second Language Acquisition Research*. Boca Raton, FL: CRC Press.

Sprouse, J. (2011). A test of the cognitive assumptions of magnitude estimation: Commutativity does not hold for acceptability judgments. *Language*, 87, 274–288.

Sprouse, J., Wagers, M., & Phillips, C. (2012). A test of the relation between working-memory capacity and syntactic island effects. *Language*, 88, 82–123.

Steinhauer, K. (2014). Event-related potentials (ERPs) in second language research: A brief introduction to the technique, a selected review, and an invitation to reconsider critical periods in L2. *Applied Linguistics*, 35(4), 393–417.

Tokowicz, N. & MacWhinney, B. (2005). Implicit and explicit measures of sensitivity to violations in second language grammar: An event-related potential investigation. *Studies in Second Language Acquisition*, 27(2), 173–204.

Tremblay, A. (2005). Theoretical and methodological perspectives on the use of grammaticality judgment tasks in linguistic theory. *Second Language Studies*, 24, 129–167.

Waters, G., Caplan, D., & Rochon, E. (1995). Processing capacity and sentence comprehension in patients with Alzheimer's disease. *Cognitive Neuropsychology*, 12(1), 1–30. DOI:10.1080/02643299508251990

Waters, G., Caplan, D., & Yampolsky, S. (2003). On-line syntactic processing under concurrent memory load. *Psychonomic Bulletin & Review*, 10(1), 88–95.

Westcott, T. & Fanselow, G. (2011). On the informativity of different measures of linguistic acceptability. *Language*, 87(2), 249–273.

White, L. & Genesee, F. (1996). How native is near-native? The issue of ultimate attainment in adult second language acquisition. *Second Language Research*, 12, 233–265.

Whong-Barr, M. & Schwartz, B. D. (2002). Morphological and syntactic transfer in child L2 acquisition of the English dative alternation. *Studies in Second Language Acquisition*, 24(4), 579–616.

# 15

# Judgments of Acceptability, Truth, and Felicity in Child Language

Rosalind Thornton

## 15.1 Introduction

Since the early 1970s, researchers have made numerous attempts to elicit acceptability judgments from young children. Such experiments have been termed grammaticality judgment tasks in much of the acquisition literature. In this chapter, we will refer to them as sentence acceptability experiments. In the first studies using these tasks, it made sense to address questions about children's emerging linguistic competence using the same kinds of experimental methods that were used to assess linguistic knowledge in adults. It soon became apparent, however, that sentence acceptability experiments present significant challenges for children younger than about 6 or 7 years of age. The inherent difficulties children experience in making judgments about sentence acceptability led researchers to adapt the tasks to make them more accessible for children. There are now a number of research methods that are custom designed for child participants, and which can be used successfully to elicit judgments of various kinds from young children. This chapter offers a historical overview of the basic literature on sentence acceptability experiments with child participants, with special attention to the new research methods that have emerged over the last 50 years, and are in current use.

At the broadest cut, according to Fukuda et al. (2012), sentence acceptability experiments can be partitioned into two classes of forced choice tasks. One class invites participants to make a binary decision. The other class invites participants to make gradient responses, based on a gradient scale with three or more options (see Chapter 2 for detailed discussion of response methods). Most research in child language has employed a variety of two-option forced choice tasks, but there is a growing literature using finer-grained judgments.[1] Like their predecessors, however, tasks of both kinds have proved to be challenging for school-age children (at ages 5 or 6), and many tasks have proven to be beyond the cognitive capabilities of the majority of preschool children. It turns out, however, that sentence acceptability tasks can be made accessible to children as young as 3 or 4 if they are augmented with information about the meanings of the sentences. The development of sentence acceptability tasks that young children can successfully perform has enabled researchers to address questions about various aspects of children's linguistic knowledge, including linguistic principles that were developed over the years. In addition to sentence acceptability experiments, other new research methods have been devised which have enabled researchers to probe different aspects of children's linguistic knowledge, including children's judgments about the truth or falsity of sentences, and about pragmatic inferences. One of the virtues of these new tasks is that they can also be used successfully to probe the linguistic knowledge of children as young as age 3 or 4.

The present chapter reviews both past and recent research using sentence acceptability experiments, and other judgment tasks, as research tools for investigating children's linguistic knowledge. We begin by describing early experimental studies that probed children's knowledge of constraints on word order. Then we review studies that used sentence acceptability tasks to assess children's knowledge of complex sentence structures, including sentences with parasitic gaps, passives, and argument structure. The second section discusses research methods that were developed later, in response to advances in linguistic theory, most notably the advent of the Principles and Parameters framework. The new tasks that emerged were designed to reveal children's knowledge of constraints on the meanings that children can assign to sentences. The final section discusses tasks that have been employed to investigate children's pragmatic inferences. For example, recent studies have assessed the inferences that children license in their understanding of sentences with disjunction words (e.g. English *or*). For adults, sentences with disjunction typically license a "not both" inference, and sentences that contain both disjunction and a modal verb (e.g. *is allowed to*) license what are called free choice (conjunctive) inferences. Although children's semantic/pragmatic inferences have been of general interest for over 20 years, this research area has witnessed increased attention recently, largely due to advances in semantic/pragmatic theory.

In describing how children's linguistic knowledge is assessed, several practical questions assume center stage. One practical question is the age at which child participants can successfully perform a given task. A second question is whether a given task is useful in bringing out differences

---

[1] A third kind of task is Magnitude Estimation. We will not discuss this task, as it has been used sparingly in experimental research on child language.

between the linguistic behavior of children and adults. Young children rapidly converge on a grammar that is sufficiently equivalent to that of adult speakers to foster successful communication. Until child language learners have attained the "final state," however, their judgments about sentence forms and meanings do not necessarily match those of adults. Several of the observed mismatches have provided valuable insights into children's developing grammatical knowledge as well as critical evidence in adjudicating between competing accounts of child language. A final practical question is the extent to which a given task reveals the nature of children's grammars, rather than other aspects of children's cognitive apparatus. To ensure that grammatical knowledge underpins children's behavior, care must be taken to control for cognitive factors extraneous to grammar. Tasks for assessing children's grammatical knowledge incorporate certain design features that enable researchers to be confident that the source of children's judgments is their grammatical knowledge. We will describe these design features as we proceed.

## 15.2   Excursions into Sentence Acceptability

### 15.2.1   Early Investigations

At the inception of the generative enterprise, it was not clear that it would be possible to reliably assess children's developing knowledge of linguistic structure using the kinds of tasks that were used to assess the linguistic knowledge of adult speakers (see, e.g., Lenneberg 1967; Pinker 1984). The earliest evidence of young children's emerging linguistic competence came from their spontaneous productions. Production data are a valuable tool for addressing many questions about children's linguistic knowledge. After all, if children are able to produce the same sequences of words as adults do, in the same contexts, this is compelling evidence of their underlying linguistic knowledge of the syntactic and semantic principles of the adult grammar. In fact, it is highly unlikely that a child could "accidentally" produce a single adult-like utterance in the same context as adults do without the requisite knowledge. However, production data have more limited value in addressing certain questions. For example, children's spontaneous production data do not provide information about children's knowledge that certain sequences of words are ill-formed in the target language. It soon became apparent in the 1970s that experimental paradigms were needed to probe when children have internalized the rules that determine possible word orders in the target language.

Early attempts to investigate the time frame of children's language development examined very young children's sensitivity to word order violations. By compressing the time frame required for language learning, early emergence has long been considered to be a benchmark for nativist accounts of language acquisition. That is, early emergence is one source of presumptive evidence for innate knowledge, especially in the absence of decisive and abundant evidence in the primary linguistic data (Crain 1991). The initial study of children's knowledge of word order was by Brown, Fraser, and Bellugi (1964). The Brown et al. study investigated this topic by asking children to judge the "silliness" of sentences that violated English word order. According to de Villiers and de Villiers (1974), the Brown et al. use of this methodology to investigate knowledge of word order rules seemed to be "doomed to failure" (de Villiers & de Villiers 1974: 16). A subsequent attempt by Gleitman, Gleitman, and Shipley (1972) that was reported in the first volume of *Cognition* was slightly more successful. Children's improved performance was probably due to the fact that children made their acceptability judgments when immersed in a role-playing activity. Gleitman et al. tested the sensitivity of three children, each roughly 30 months old, to violations of word order in imperative sentences. The children participated in a game with the experimenter and the child's mother. Each of them took turns at being the "teacher." To begin, the experimenter played the teacher role, and asked the mother to judge whether a succession of sentences were "good" or "silly". The student's task (the mother, in this condition) was to repeat the good sentences, and repair the silly ones to make them sound "good." In the critical condition, the mother was the teacher and the child was the student. Again, the child was to repeat the "good" imperatives and fix up the silly ones. The sentences included both grammatical and ungrammatical sequences of words (e.g. *Bring me the ball*; *Ball me the bring*; *Bring ball*; *Ball bring*) which were assigned the intonation contour of either an imperative or a telegraphic sentence. Children's responses were reported to be "not random," and the authors credited them with being able to view language "as an object." Nevertheless, these children's judgments of sentence acceptability were also described as "feeble" (Gleitman et al. 1972: 144), and only two of the three children were prepared to repair the ill-formed sentences. Furthermore, the corrections made by these two children tended to correct meaning, not form.

As De Villiers and de Villiers (1974) point out, the correction component of the Gleitman et al. (1972) sentence acceptability task was critical. Without the correction component of the task, it would not have been possible to tell from children's judgments how they interpreted the sentences – this was evident from the revisions they introduced when they judged sentences to be "silly." In a follow-up experiment, de Villiers and de Villiers interviewed eight slightly older children (MLU > 5, 3.5+ years old). This study asked children to tell a puppet if the sentences it produced were "right" or "wrong." When a child judged the puppet's sentence to be wrong, the child was asked to tell the puppet the "right way to say it." Again, this "correction" component of the task was critical for assessing the interpretations that children assigned to the test sentences.

In the first session, the child participants judged imperative sentences with correct word order (e.g. *Pat the dog*) and reversed word order (*Cake the eat*). In a second session, the sentence acceptability judgment hinged on meaning, rather than form (e.g. *Drink the chair*). De Villiers and de Villiers found a trend between children's MLU and their ability to produce judgments. Basically, the youngest children failed to perform the task. The more linguistically advanced children, as assessed by MLU, could perform the task, but their sentence corrections were mainly based on meaning, such that only the most advanced children were able to correct word order violations. These findings led de Villiers and de Villiers (1974) to conclude that children are not able to provide appropriate judgments of word order until they are 4 or 5 years old.

When children have reached the "final state" of grammar formation, they have converged on a system of principles that is remarkably similar to that of other members of the same linguistic community. Children converge on many of these principles by age 3 or 4, despite a considerable latitude in experience (see Crain, Koring, & Thornton 2017). At this same stage, however, most children are not able to correct unacceptable sentences, or judge that some sentences are ambiguous and so on. These abilities are generally classified as metalinguistic knowledge. The child's grammar enables her to produce and understand sentences, but it is not the source of this metalinguistic knowledge. Presumably, children's metalinguistic abilities emerge once their grammars are more or less fully formed. When children and adults differ in performance on a task, therefore, researchers must try to rule out such performance factors as the source of the difference, before drawing the conclusion that children's grammars differ from those of adult speakers.

The problems for researchers do not end, moreover, with a competence/performance dichotomy. As de Villiers and de Villiers (1974) point out, the syntactic and semantic knowledge of children can easily be masked by subtle features of experimental tasks that have little consequence for adults. In addition to their syntactic and semantic structures, for example, many lexical items and sentence structures carry presuppositions. For example, ordinary pronouns and definite descriptions refer to individuals that should have been previously introduced into the conversational context, and sentences with relative clauses and sentences with temporal terms often express information that should have been previously established in the conversational context. It was recognized early in the study of child language that adults readily accommodate unsatisfied presuppositions. By contrast, the failure to satisfy presuppositions in an experimental task with young child participants has been shown to seriously impede their performance, exacerbating differences between children and adults (e.g. Hamburger & Crain 1982; Crain 1982). Such investigations suggest that children's non-adult responses should not be credited to a lack of linguistic knowledge unless steps are taken to ensure that the source of the child's response can be identified.

## 15.2.2 Complex Syntax

Researchers have introduced several design features in an attempt to certify that children's non-adult responses are based on their linguistic knowledge, and not extraneous factors. One of the first steps in this direction was taken by McDaniel and Cairns, who developed a sentence acceptability method that included contextual support for the judgment (see McDaniel & Cairns 1990, 1996; McDaniel, Cairns, & Hsu 1990, 1990/ 1991; McDaniel & Maxfield 1992). Rather than asking for a direct sentence acceptability judgment, a modified task was developed, illustrated in (1) (from McDaniel & Cairns 1996: 235) and in (2), to include referents for the pronouns and referring expressions that are mentioned in the test sentences (McDaniel & Cairns 1996: 244):

(1)  *Experimenter:*  If there are two boys and Grover is talking to this one [points to a boy], does it sound right or wrong to say, "This [holds up the boy Grover talked to] is the boy what Grover talked to"?

     *Participant:*  Wrong

(2)  *Experimenter:*  Suppose we have Grover and Bert, and Grover is doing some patting, like this [makes Grover pat Bert] Does this sound right or wrong?: "Grover is patting him."

     *Participant*  Right

     *Experimenter:*  How about if Grover's doing this? [makes Grover pat himself] Does it sound right or wrong now to say, "Grover is patting him."

In their study McDaniel and Cairns included a training and a pre-test session for each child participant which they contend were critical for the success of the task. To ensure that the child attended to form rather than meaning, they first engaged each child participant in a conversation about language, such as the fact that both the child and experimenter spoke English, that babies are learning to use English, that linguists are scientists who study language, and so forth. The training session included practice in making judgments with sequences of words that violated rules of word order, gender agreement, or had omissions of function words. The pre-test session followed, and the results from this session were used to exclude children who failed to understand the aims of task. The pre-test was composed of 3 ungrammatical word sequences and 3 grammatical ones. To be included in the main session of the experiment, a child participant must have rejected all three of the ungrammatical sentences and accepted at least 2 out of 3 of the grammatical ones. McDaniel and Cairns suggest that between 10 and 25 percent of the children they initially interviewed were not able to successfully pass the pre-test (McDaniel & Cairns 1996). Put differently, the suggestion is that between 75 and 90 percent of 3- and 4-year-old children can be trained to serve as reliable informants about the acceptability of word order sequences.

The sentence acceptability task developed by McDaniel and Cairns was subsequently used with child participants to address fine-grained questions about linguistic theory. For example, McDaniel and Maxfield (1992) used the task to investigate the source of the anti-c-command requirement in sentences containing parasitic gaps. The theoretical literature offered two possibilities as the source, Principle C and Subjacency. To resolve the issue, the McDaniel and Maxfield study included sentences with parasitic gaps, sentences governed by Principle C, and sentences that violated Subjacency. For each, there was one acceptable test sentence and one unacceptable test sentence. Example (3a) is the acceptable parasitic gap test sentence. Example (3b) is the unacceptable version, which violates the anti-c-command requirement. We omit the acceptable sentences related to Principle C and Subjacency, and just present the unacceptable versions. Example (3c) is the test sentence that violated Principle C, and example (3d) is the test sentence that violated Subjacency. Unacceptability is indicated by an asterisk in front of a sentence, and the indices indicate the reference of an expression, such that NPs with the same index refer to the same individual. So, coreference (as indicated by coindexation) is prohibited by Principle C in example (3c) and it is prohibited by Subjacency in example (3d).

(3)  a. That's the girl $[_{CP}$ $O_i$ [that [Grover kissed $t_i$ before $[_{CP}$ $O_i$ [Cookie Monster patted $e_i$ ]]]]]
    b. *That's the girl $[_{CP}$ $O_i$ [that [$t_i$ hugged the zebra before $[_{CP}$ $O_i$ [Cookie Monster talked to $e_i$]]]]]
    c. *He$_i$ said that Grover$_i$ is hungry.
    d. *Who$_i$ did you hug Bert before $[_{CP}$ [you patted $t_i$]]

The aim of the McDaniel and Maxfield study was to see whether those children who accepted the anti-c-command sentence (3b) also accepted the example sentence that violated Principle C (3 c) or, instead, accepted the example sentence that violated Subjacency (3d). The pattern of children's linguistic behavior was to be taken as relevant evidence about the source of the anti-c-command requirement in children's grammars. Children's knowledge of c-command had been established earlier in the study, using other materials.

The McDaniel and Maxfield study interviewed 13 children, who ranged in age from 3;4 to 5;11, with an average age of 4;9. All of the child participants completed the training session, and had passed the pre-test. Here are the findings of the main experimental session. One of the child participants rejected the grammatical parasitic gap sentence (3a) and was excluded from further analysis. Of the remaining 12 child participants, 7 rejected both sentences (3b) and (3c), and 6 of these 7 also rejected (3d). The 6 child participants who rejected all three test sentences exhibited adult-like behavior, so their data could not be used to determine whether Principle C or Subjacency is the source of the constraint on sentences with parasitic gaps. The judgments of the remaining 5 children were used to address the aims of the study. Four of these 5 child participants accepted (3b), the sentence that violated the constraint on parasitic gaps, and they accepted (3d), the sentence that violated Principle C. These 4 children also rejected the sentence that violated Subjacency (3d).[2] For these 4 children, then, the acceptability of parasitic gaps was on a par with Principle C, and so Principle C was potentially the source of the anti-c-command requirement. However, the conclusion that the Principle C is the source of the anti-c-command requirement for sentences with parasitic gaps receives only circumstantial support, based on the pattern of response by just 4 child participants. As the authors acknowledge, a much larger sample of participants and experimental items is needed to determine if the pattern of responses by these children represents a stage of language acquisition at which children respond in the same way to sentences governed by Principle C and ones governed by the constraint on parasitic gaps.

There is another reason for exercising caution in interpreting the findings of the experiment. As we saw, there were 4 child participants whose responses were critical to the conclusion that Principle C underpins the constraint on parasitic gaps. These 4 children accepted the sentence that violated Principle C. But this finding does not align with that of other studies, where early adherence to Principle C has been reported.[3] To deal with this discrepancy across studies, McDaniel and Maxfield (1992) concede that, in all likelihood, the grammars of these child participants adhered to Principle C. Rather, McDaniel and Maxfield propose that the acceptances by these children to both the illicit parasitic gap sentence and the sentence that violated Principle C were due to some factor extraneous to grammar. If Principle C is the source of the unacceptability of sentences with parasitic gaps, it makes sense, in their view, that whatever factors prevented children from rejecting the illicit sentence governed by Principle C should also have prevented them from rejecting the illicit sentence with a parasitic gap (McDaniel & Maxfield 1992: 668). What is

---

[2] The fifth child accepted violations of all three kinds.
[3] For studies illustrating robust knowledge of Principle C see Crain and Thornton (1998), and references therein.

not explained, however, is why such "extraneous" factors were operative in this task, but not in previous studies of children's adherence to Principle C. It is noteworthy nonetheless that the task developed by McDaniel and Maxfield was able to probe sentence acceptability judgments from 4- to 5-year-old child participants using some extremely complex sentences.

A recent experiment by Crawford (2012) used a sentence acceptability task to probe children's representations of passive structures. The Crawford study was designed to address an ongoing debate over whether young children's grammars generate an adult-like representation for verbal passives or whether children default to a representation for adjectival passives which does not require movement. The innovation of the Crawford study was to see whether or not children judged a purpose clause to be an acceptable addition to the test sentences (cf. Borer & Wexler 1987). For adults, both verbal passives and their active counterparts permit the addition of a purpose clause, as illustrated by the acceptability of (4) and (5). By contrast, adjectival passives and inchoatives do not allow an implicit agent and therefore do not permit the addition of a purpose clause, as indicated by the unacceptability of (6) and (7) (Crawford 2012: 171).

(4)      The candy bar is being broken PRO to share with friends. (verbal passive)

(5)      John is breaking the candy bar PRO to share with friends.          (active)

(6)      *The candy bar is unbroken to share with friends.      (adjectival resultative)

(7)      *The candy bar breaks/is breaking to share with friends.      (inchoative)

Crawford devised an ingenious and novel way of addressing the debate about the presence or absence of verbal passives in young children's grammars. The experiment asked the child participants to judge the acceptability of inchoatives with purpose clauses, and passives with purpose clauses. If children's grammars generated a verbal passive, then they would be expected to accept passive sentences with a purpose clause, as in (4), but they would be expected to reject inchoative sentences with a purpose clause, as in (5). On the other hand, if children judged both inchoative sentences with purpose phrases and passive sentences with purpose clauses as unacceptable, then this would be presumptive evidence that the grammars of children and adults differ in their analysis of passive sentences; children presumably would be analyzing the passives as adjectival passives.

Adopting procedures used by McDaniel and Cairns (1996), the experiment was comprised of three phases: a training session, a pre-test, and the main experiment which together took about 45 minutes. Children first received training in performing acceptability judgments. Then, they proceeded to the pre-test, which assessed how each child judged inchoatives with a purpose clause. The pre-test contained 6 items, including 3 actives and 3 inchoatives, both with purpose clauses. Children who rejected all three of the inchoatives with a purpose clause proceeded to the main experimental session, which addressed the issue of children's grammatical knowledge of the structure of the passive. Those children who failed to reject all three ungrammatical inchoatives were excluded from the main session. In the main session, all of the experimental items contained purpose clauses. These included active sentences, passive sentences, and two kinds of inchoative sentences, ones combined with a progressive aspectual marker and ones combined with a verb in the simple present tense. The two groups of inchoatives were included to ensure there were enough potential "no" responses. Children judged the sentences alongside pictures that supported the intended meaning.

The data from 21 children were used to address the research question. These children were between 4;0 and 7;0 years-old, with a mean age of 5;4. Ten children were excluded from the analysis, five of these children were excluded because of their performance on the pre-test. The main finding was a significant difference in acceptability between the passives and the inchoative sentences. Children judged the passives to be acceptable about 70 percent of the time, the inchoatives in the progressive acceptable about 45 percent of the time, and the inchoatives in the simple present about 38 percent of the time (see Crawford 2012: 192, Figure 18). The significant difference between the acceptability of the passives and inchoatives with purpose clauses was taken as evidence that children's grammars assign the structure associated with the verbal passive in adult grammars. Despite the significant difference in children's acceptance of the passives and the inchoatives, as Crawford notes, the responses by the child participants differed from those of adults. The child participants accepted (unacceptable) inchoatives with a purpose clause roughly 40 percent of the time. This rate of acceptance is high, considering that these children had all rejected all three of these items in the pre-test. Crawford suggests that the child participants may have become fatigued by the length of the experiment, accepting more items as the experiment progressed. A follow-up analysis of the data from individual subjects revealed two groups of children. One group of 8 children rejected the inchoatives more than 80 percent of the time. A second group rejected these sentences at chance. One might conclude that the grammars of only 8 of the 21 children were, in fact, equivalent to that of adult speakers. But even the data from these 8 children raise some questions. Although these children rejected the inchoatives with purpose clauses, they only judged the well-formed passive sentences to be acceptable about 55 percent of the time. This is puzzling. It would have been useful to compare children's performance with that of adults. Although adults' acceptability judgments for similar sentences were tested in a separate experiment, one would like to know how adults would perform in the same experiment. In the experiment presented to children, how often would an adult accept passives with a purpose clause as opposed to inchoatives with a purpose clause? Without these data, it is difficult to know how to interpret the child data, even of the "successful" group of 8 children. In summary, the question addressed in the Crawford study certainly lent itself to an acceptability judgment task, but the findings once again highlight some of the difficulties involved in using this task with children.

### 15.2.3  Argument Structure

The investigation of argument structure was a major focus of research in child language in the 1980s. These investigations initially centered on young children's non-adult productions from their spontaneous speech (Bowerman 1982: 8). An early observation was that young children sometimes used intransitive verbs in sentences that require transitive verbs for adults; *Mommy can you stay this open?* and *He deaded the cat* are examples. It was also observed that children sometimes used transitive verbs where adults require intransitive verbs. An example of this non-adult utterance type is *My clothes are putting on*. Children's non-adult utterances of both types flagged questions of language learnability. One study that investigated the source of children's non-adult utterances was Hochberg (1986). This was a sentence acceptability task with 3- and 4-year-old children that comprised several kinds of children's non-adult sentences reported in the previous literature. More specifically, the child participants judged sentences with transitive verbs that elicit a periphrastic causative from adults, as in (4), and sentences with transitive verbs for which there is no periphrastic causative counterpart, as in (5). Children also judged unacceptable sentences in which intransitive verbs are used transitively, as in (6). Three additional sentence-pairs served as controls.

(4)     a. I'm gonna make the frog jump.    Adult periphrastic causative
        b. I'm gonna jump the frog.         Transitive error

(5)     a. I'm gonna drop the rock.          Adult transitive
        b. I'm gonna fall the rock.          Transitive error[4]

(6)     a. I'm putting on my clothes.        Adult transitive
        b. My clothes are putting on.        Intransitive error

The task took the form of a game that involved two puppets. Each puppet produced a different version of one of the sentence types; one was acceptable for adult speakers, and one was not. On each trial, the child participant was asked to indicate which of two puppets produced an "okay" sentence

---

[4] This example uses an unaccusative verb *fall* but the items in this category are not all unaccusative verbs. Hochberg names them "suppletive." What is clear is that the adult counterpart is the use of a completely different verb rather than a periphrastic causative.

and which one produced a "silly" sentence. On each trial, the child participant rewarded the puppet that produced the "okay" sentence with a sticker.
For sentence pairs like (4), one of the puppets acted-out the sentence with
toys. This task is what is often termed a felicity judgment task.

This young cohort of children yielded a high rate of attrition. Only 20 of the
49 3- and 4-year-old children who were recruited produced analyzable data:
10 failed to understand the task, 11 lost interest mid-way through the testing
session, and 8 rewarded their favorite puppet, rather than basing their
decisions on the utterances the puppets produced. The analysis divided the
20 children into a younger group of 3-year-olds and an older group of 4-year-
olds (and one 5-year-old). The findings revealed that children made more
errors in judging transitive sentence pairs (4) and (5) than intransitive pairs
like (6). Children exhibited the poorest performance, however, judging sentences like (4) which adults would express using a periphrastic causative. The
proportion of non-adult judgments by age and by sentence type are shown in
the Table 15.1 (adapted from Hochberg 1986: 323, Table 1).

The child participants in both age groups were reported as able to perform the sentence acceptability task. Moreover, the trend in the pattern of
responses by the 3-year-old child participants was similar to that of the
4-year-old children, although younger children made more errors. Taking
into consideration the rates of performance by 3-year-olds to sentence
types (5) and (6), even the "chance level" performance in response to the
transitive sentences in (4) could, potentially, represent a non-adult stage of
grammar, but without a design feature that provides independent evidence about the source of children's judgments, we have no way to tell.

Child language researchers who adopt the constructivist framework
have tested the predictions of a process known as "entrenchment" by
examining children's acquisition of argument structure (e.g. Theakston
2004; Ambridge et al. 2008). In the constructivist framework, entrenchment is a learning mechanism that is proposed to "protect" children from
making errors. The idea is that argument structure patterns that are
frequent in the input become entrenched and are therefore more easily
accessed by a child as compared to ones that are less frequent, such as the
ones that are the product of children's mistaken generalizations. As
Ambridge et al. state, the frequent use of a verb in the input will cause
the child to form "a probabilistic inference state that adult speakers do not
use that particular verb in non-attested constructions" (Ambridge et al.

Table 15.1 *Percentage of non-adult judgments by group*

| Structure | Transitives like (4) (%) | Transitives like (5) (%) | Intransitives like (6) (%) |
|---|---|---|---|
| 3-year-old group (mean = 3;7) | 52 | 22 | 16 |
| 4-year-old group (mean = 4;8) | 32 | 8 | 0 |

2008: 97). A similar line of argument holds for children's argument structure violations. Constructivists predict that argument structure violations for high-frequency verbs will be easier for children (and adults) to detect than those for low-frequency verbs, which may not be entrenched in the child's grammar.

Ambridge et al. (2008) tested the entrenchment hypothesis using a task that judged sentence acceptability on a five-point scale. The study included adult controls, as well as children. While numerical scales are commonly used with children in some cognitive domains, they have not generally been used to test sentence acceptability in the domain of language. The Ambridge et al. experiment tested two groups of child participants, a younger group that consisted of 5- to 6-year-olds, and an older group of 9- to 10-year-olds. The experiment elicited the participants' judgments of both grammatical intransitive sentences and their ungrammatical transitive counterparts. In the ungrammatical sentences, the intransitive verb was used as a causative transitive (e.g. *Bart disappeared* vs. *The magician disappeared Bart*). Intransitives were included to establish a baseline of acceptability ratings for each individual verb. The test sentences used verbs from three semantic classes, and included both high-frequency and low-frequency verbs. To avoid frequency effects altogether, a condition with novel verbs was included. The novel verbs were created for each semantic class, and their meanings were taught to the child participants. The entrenchment hypothesis yielded three predictions. First, it was predicted that children would reject argument structure violations that are associated with high-frequency verbs, since these should be entrenched in children's grammars. The second prediction was children would reject violations associated with lower-frequency verbs less often. Third, children were expected to rarely, if ever, reject violations of sentences with novel verbs, given that they had no prior experience with their use. These predictions motivated the use of a gradient sentence acceptability task.

The rating scale was composed of five emoji faces. There was a neutral face in the middle, half red and half green. On one side of the neutral face were two green smiley faces – one with a small smile and one with a big smile. On the other side of the neutral face were two red sad faces – one a small frown and one with a big frown. As in the study by McDaniel and Cairns (1996), children judged sentences with contextual support. Preceding each test sentence, children watched a computer animation of the action denoted by the verb that was contained in the test sentence. In a training session, the children learned the novel verb meanings and practised rating sentences. In the practice session, there were seven sentences. The first two test sentences were judged by the experimenter. For the next two sentences, the child was asked to produce a simple yes or no judgment. Finally, the experimenter explained how to use the scale for the final three test items. No children were excluded from the experiment. The experimental test sentences were judged the day following the training.

Table 15.2 *The difference in ratings between ungrammatical intransitive verbs and ungrammatical transitive causative verbs for different frequency verbs by age*

| Raw ratings collapsed across semantic class of verbs | 5–6-year old children | 9–10-year-old children | Adults |
|---|---|---|---|
| High-frequency verbs | 1.72 | 2.78 | 2.81 |
| Low-frequency verbs | 0.81 | 2.04 | 2.17 |
| Novel verbs | 0.33 | 1.49 | 1.19 |

The analysis of the experimental hypothesis was based on the difference in ratings between the grammatical intransitive (the baseline) and the ungrammatical transitive causative. The difference between the two ratings was expected to be greatest for high-frequency verbs, where intransitives should be rated high on the scale and ungrammatical transitive causatives should be rated low on the scale. The findings are summarized in Table 15.2 (adapted from Ambridge et al. 2008: Appendix D).

For both older and younger groups of children, the findings showed the greatest difference in the ratings for high-frequency verbs, followed by low-frequency verbs, with the novel verbs showing the smallest difference. These findings were as expected by the entrenchment hypothesis and suggested that even children in the 5- to 6-year-old range are capable of rating sentences in a gradient sentence acceptability task. However, one aspect of the findings did not align well with the experimental hypotheses, based on entrenchment, and they cast doubt on the general utility of the gradient judgment task using a numerical (or smiley face) scale. By its very nature, entrenchment is expected to increase by age, with age equating to language exposure. If entrenchment is operative, then there should be a steady increase by age in the observed differences between the ratings by participants for intransitive and transitive verbs. However, this increase was not observed. Although there was a difference in the younger and older groups of children, there was no significant difference between the older group of children and adults. Ambridge et al. suggest this may be due to the training procedure for the task in which 2 of the 7 practice sentences were word order violations (e.g. *His teeth man the brushed*). This might have led older children and adults to reserve the lowest score ("1") on the scale for word order violations, which are "worse than" argument structure violations. If this is the case, though, then different age groups of participants were using the scale differently. This finding raises questions about how younger children should be trained to do acceptability judgments. If they are trained on sentences with serious word order violations in order to illustrate what is meant by an unacceptable sentence, but this then interferes with adult ratings, we have to question whether or not the same acceptability judgment gradient rating scheme can be used to compare children and adults.

Wrapping up this section, although there are questions that are best answered with an acceptability judgment task, it is clear that they present many challenges if they are to be used with child populations. It remains unclear, whether sentence acceptability tasks can be used successfully with children younger than age 5 or 6. Many younger children are not able to do this kind of metalinguistic judgment, which leads to considerable attrition in participants. Even where child participants can successfully perform the task, there are often considerable individual differences. Finally, these tasks do not always lead to clear indications about the source of children's non-adult performance.

## 15.3  Ambiguity and Constraints

As noted earlier, it took some time for researchers in child language to develop methodological tools that could be used with confidence to address questions about children's grammars. Having established these tools, child language researchers were able to address a number of different questions over the years. With the introduction of the "Principles and Parameters" model in the 1980s (Chomsky 1981), child language researchers embarked on assessments of children's knowledge of the recently devised principles and parameters of Universal Grammar. This came to be known as the biolinguistic approach to language.

One area of interest within the Principles and Parameters framework was children's adherence to the principles of Binding Theory (see Chapter 11 for detailed discussion of studies of Binding Theory in the context of adults). This inquiry led researchers to develop new methodological tools, ones that could demonstrate when children found sentences to be ambiguous or unambiguous. Such tools were required to determine whether children knew that certain principles eliminate sentence interpretations that would otherwise be expected. Prior to this point, researchers had come to reply on figure manipulation (act-out, do-what-I-say) tasks to investigate the meanings that children assign to sentences. In the act-out task, the experimenter gives the child a set of toys, presents the child with the target sentence, and instructs the child to "make it happen." Whatever the child does with toys is taken to indicating the meaning they assign to the experimenter's sentence. As Lasnik and Crain (1985) pointed out, however, act-out tasks only show the interpretations that children can assign to sentences. These tasks do not indicate the interpretations that children cannot assign.[5] A different kind of task was clearly needed for this purpose.

---

[5]  Act-out tasks can be argued to impose other non-linguistic demands on the child. The child needs to hold the experimenter's test sentence in verbal working memory while devising a plan for acting out the sentence, and then the child has to execute the plan. This process could be taxing for children (Crain & Thornton 1998).

The question as to which sentences are ambiguous, and which are unambiguous was addressed with the kind of sentence acceptability task conducted by McDaniel, Cairns, and colleagues already reviewed above. This inquiry into ambiguity was possible since their acceptability judgment task incorporated an accompanying act-out of the intended meaning, although the act-out was minimal. This was illustrated for Binding Theory in (2) above. (See also McDaniel, Cairns, & Hsu (1990) for an acceptability judgment experiment investigating binding principles.) A new task, expressly designed to study ambiguity and lack of ambiguity due to a constraint of Universal Grammar was devised by Crain and McKee (1985). This task is now known as the truth-value judgment task in the child language acquisition literature (see also Crain & Thornton 1998; Thornton 2017). The task moved away from asking whether a particular sentence was acceptable in a particular context to whether a given sentence was true or false in a particular context. Although the data gathered from children in this task are truth-values of sentence/meaning pairs, these data are, nevertheless, informative about the child's underlying syntactic knowledge, which is what sentence acceptability judgment tasks aim to tap (see Chapter 14 for discussion of this task in adult L2 populations).

The truth-value judgment task was introduced in a study by Crain and McKee (1985). In the Crain and McKee task events were acted-out in front of the child participants in real time, using toys and props. For this reason it is sometimes referred to as the dynamic truth-value judgment task (which is not the case if judging whether pictures match a sentence, for example). Some of the events that transpired corresponded to an interpretation that was possible for adults, and other events corresponded to an interpretation that was not possible for adults, due to Principle C. So, the test sentences were unambiguous for adults, due to this linguistic principle. If children lacked Principle C, they were expected to license an interpretation that was not tolerated by adults.

A dynamic truth-value judgment task requires two experimenters, so the task is more labor intensive than tasks that can be administered by one person, such as ones with pictures. However, the dynamic nature of the task permits the experimenter to implement several design features that cannot easily be implemented in other versions of truth-value judgment tasks. One experimenter acts out "stories" with toys and props. The second experimenter plays the role of a puppet who watches the events unfold, along with the child. At the end of the story, the puppet says what it thought happened in the story, using a test sentence. The child's task is to tell the puppet if the puppet's description of the story was right or wrong (that is, true or false). In warm-up stories, it is made clear to the child that the puppet sometimes pays attention to the stories, but sometimes the puppet does not pay attention. Whenever the puppet fails to pay attention, and describes the story incorrectly, the child is asked to explain "what really happened?" so that the puppet can pay closer attention to the next story. If the child judges the puppet to be right, the child rewards the puppet, perhaps with a bite of his favorite food. On the other hand, if the child judges the puppet to be wrong, he is given a lesser reward, perhaps a less-favored food. Children enjoy judging the puppet's performance, unaware that, in fact, their own linguistic knowledge is being assessed, using their judgments about what the puppet said, and their corrections when the puppet says the wrong thing.

Crain and McKee (1985) devised the task to assess children's knowledge of Principle C. Recall that Principle C prevents coreference between NPs in sentences in which a name (that is, a referring expression such as *John* or *the Queen*) is c-commanded by a pronoun that could potentially refer to the individual that is named. Compare examples (7) and (8). In example (7), the pronoun *he* does not c-command the name, *the lion*. Therefore, *the lion* and the pronoun can refer to the same individual. Since, the pronoun comes first, this kind of anaphoric reference is known as "backwards anaphora." In addition, to the backwards anaphora interpretation of (7), the pronoun can also refer to some male not mentioned in the sentence. This is called the "extrasentential," "deictic," or "direct reference" interpretation of the pronoun. The ambiguity in example (7) is not replicated in example (8). In (8), the backwards anaphora interpretation is ruled out, due to Principle C. Here, the only permissible interpretation is the extrasentential interpretation of the pronoun, at least for adults. So, example (8) can only mean that some salient male, denoted by the pronoun *he*, ate the hamburger when the Smurf was in the box.

(7)    When *he* stole the chickens, *the lion* was in the box.

(8)    *He* ate the hamburger when *the Smurf* was in the box.

The study by Crain and McKee was designed to test children's access to the two alternative interpretations of (7). Crain and McKee hypothesized that children, like adults, would judge example (7) to be ambiguous. The experimental question was whether or not children, like adults, judged (8) to be unambiguous, due to Principle C. In order to compare the backwards anaphora interpretation and the extrasentential interpretation, the two interpretations were presented in the same way to the child participants, on different trials. Each trial consisted of a story that was acted out by one of the two experimenters. To give the two alternative interpretations an equal chance, on one type of trial, the backwards anaphora interpretation was a true description of the events that took place in the story, and the extrasentential reading was a false description. Other trials had the extrasentential reading as the true description, and the backward anaphora interpretation as the false one. The two interpretations were both compared in true contexts for a reason. According to the Principle of

Charity (Davidson 1984), hearers will assume that a speaker is telling the truth, when they can, and so hearers will try to assign a "Yes" response where possible. By comparing the interpretations in a context in which they were both true, a fair comparison could be made. To illustrate with an example, on the trial testing children's access to the backwards anaphora reading of (7), the story was about a lion who was in the box when he stole some chickens. On another trial, the lion was in the box when someone else stole the chickens.

For sentences like (8), which are subject to Principle C and therefore *unambiguous*, the meaning ruled out by the constraint was designed to be a true description of the events that unfolded in the story acted out for children. By making the meaning prohibited by the constraint true, the task favored the null hypothesis that children's grammars initially lack Principle C. By making the prohibited meaning true, the experimental design thus guarded against a Type 1 error. In the story context for (8), then, the Smurf did eat a hamburger while he was inside the box. Thus, if children's grammars lacked Principle C, they would be expected to judge sentences governed by Principle C for adults, but not for children, to be ambiguous. If so, then children should accept sentence (8) on the interpretation on which the pronoun, *he*, refers to the Smurf. On the other hand, if children's grammars contain Principle C, then they should only have access to the adult interpretation, where the pronoun *he* refers to a salient male character that is not mentioned in the sentence. To make this interpretation available in the story context, a salient male character (Gargamel, the Smurfs' nemesis) did not eat the hamburger when the Smurf was in the box. If the pronoun was interpreted as referring to this male character (Gargamel), then children should judge the sentence to be a false description of the events that took place in the story. This research strategy of making the sentence false on the adult interpretation is termed the *Condition of Falsification* in Crain and Thornton (1998). The two potential meanings for (8) are presented in (9), where the asterisk indicates the illicit meaning, which children are expected to access if their grammars lack Principle C.

(9)    *Meaning 1, True: The Smurf ate the hamburger while he (the Smurf) was in the box.
       Meaning 2, False: He (Gargamel) ate the hamburger while the Smurf was in the box.

The alternative hypotheses are recapped in (10).

(10)    $H_0$: Children lack Principle C, and permit Meaning 1 and Meaning 2.
        $H_1$: Children engage Principle C, and permit only Meaning 2.

For the task to be successful, the contexts introduced in the truth-value judgment task must be designed to match both a (potentially) true interpretation of the test sentence, as well as the interpretation of the sentence that is false for adults. As we have seen, children are expected to adopt the Principle of Charity. It follows that children should inform the puppet that his statement is correct (true) if their grammars allow the sentence meaning that is ruled out by Principle C. This bias to say "Yes" is further augmented by the general bias that people have when they fail to understand something, or are unsure about a decision. It is important, therefore, to ensure that the events corresponding to the false interpretation are highlighted in the story context. This is achieved by satisfying the *Condition of Plausible Dissent* (Crain & Thornton 1998). The condition of plausible dissent requires the assertion of the test sentence (which is ultimately false) to be under consideration as a likely outcome at some point in the story. This is why the toy characters in the story discuss the pros and cons of their actions. As the events of the story unfold, it gradually becomes clear that the meaning of the test sentence is false. In (8), then, it should appear as though Gargamel is going to eat the hamburger while the Smurf is in the box, although events take a different turn at a later point in the story, and this does not eventuate, for some reason. For example, it could be the case that Gargamel thought about eating the hamburger while the Smurf was in the box, but there was also a delicious-looking cupcake available, and so he decided to eat the cupcake instead of the hamburger. Notice that by implementing the condition of plausible dissent, the task makes available for children a salient reason for the sentence to be false. If the puppet is deemed to be wrong, the child can explain the actual outcome – what really happened in the story, e.g. "Gargamel ate the cupcake not the hamburger." The child's justification for rejecting the puppet's statements is critical data, ensuring that they understood the story, and rejected the test sentences as descriptions of the stories for the right reason.

Using this dynamic truth-value judgment task, Crain and McKee tested 62 2- to 6-year-old children. The main finding was that children could access both the backwards anaphora and extrasentential interpretations of ambiguous sentences like (7). They accepted the backwards anaphora reading 73 percent of the time when it was presented in a true context, and they accepted the extrasentential interpretation even more often, 81 percent of the time, when it was a true description of the story events. On the other hand, children rejected sentences like (8) on 88 percent of the trials. This finding was taken as evidence that the only interpretation available to children for sentences like (8) was one that made the sentence false. Children were unable to assign a backwards anaphora reading to such sentences, even though it was true in the context presented to children. This experimental finding suggested that children's grammars incorporate Principle C.

The truth-value judgment task has been found to access much more secure and reliable judgments from children than sentence acceptability tasks. First, design features of the task ensure that the two possible judgments (on the scale), true or false, are both accessible to children. Second, it solves the all-important "checks and balances" problem that arises with many sentence acceptability tasks. The truth-value judgment task asks children to explain their judgment when it is false, which gives important insight into why children are rejecting the sentence. If an adult rejects the sentence for the same reason, then it can be inferred that the child's grammar is the same as the adult's in this respect. Thus, children's understanding of the task can be assessed. Third, in contrast to sentence acceptability tasks, the truth-value judgment task can reliably be used with children as young as 3 years (and sometimes younger). It does not give rise to the attrition levels seen in the sentence acceptability task when used with young children, partly because the truth-value judgment is embedded in a game that children enjoy, partly due to design features of the task, and partly because it does not seem to require children to access the metalinguistic knowledge necessary for sentence acceptability judgment tasks. Having pointed out some advantageous design features of the truth-value judgment task, it is nevertheless important to remember that there are certain questions that cannot be answered by a truth-value judgment task and which are better answered by a sentence acceptability task.

In addition to the Binding principles, the truth-value judgment task has been used to test many issues, including children's interpretation of quantification, constraints on quantification in discourse, scope, control, disjunction, interpretations of passive sentences, among other topics.

## 15.4  Pragmatic inferences

In the last decade, another field of inquiry has received considerable attention in the experimental literature, namely children's semantic and pragmatic knowledge. Of particular importance is experimental work on children's sensitivity to what are called scalar inferences.

A distinction must be drawn between the literal meaning of a sentence, and the inferences that speakers make when they produce certain sentences. Inferences are components of meanings that are not simply based on the words that make up a sentence. Inferences depend on the speaker's use of a particular expression, rather than another expression that the speaker might have opted to use instead. For example, inferences are licensed when speakers produce sentences that contain the existential expression *some*, and when they produce sentences that contain the disjunction word *or*. These inferences arise because the expressions *some* and *or* are scalar terms. *Some* resides on a scale with several "stronger" words: *many, most,* and *all*. So, the scale, from weaker to stronger, is: <some, many, most, all>. The disjunction word *or* is the weaker term on a scale with the stronger term *and*, i.e. <or, and>. To say that one term is stronger than another just means that sentences with the stronger terms are true in a narrower range of circumstances, as compared to the corresponding sentences with the weaker term. So, sentences with *and* (*Tommy ate ice cream and cake*) are stronger (true in a narrower range of circumstances) than sentences with *or* (*Tommy ate ice cream or cake*). The scalar inference that arises with *some* can be illustrated using example (11). Adults typically reject (11), on the grounds that the speaker should have used *all*, instead of *some*. The use of *some* licenses the (false) inference that *not all* giraffes have long necks (see Noveck 2001).

(11)    Some giraffes have long necks.

One of the most interesting discoveries in the past two decades is that children younger than 5- or 6-years old are far less sensitive to scalar inferences than adults are. Unlike adults, young children typically accept sentence (11), despite knowing that all giraffes have long necks. Moreover, younger children accept a sentence with disjunction, such as *Tommy ate ice cream or cake*, as a true description of a circumstance in which Tommy ate both desserts. Unlike adults, younger children do not find sentences with the weaker term, *or*, to be pragmatically odd in circumstances in which a sentence with the stronger term, *and*, could have been used.[6] Numerous investigations have attempted to identify the source of the difference in behavior between children and adults. This section reviews some of the ways researchers have employed different experimental methods to figure out why younger children lack sensitivity to scalar inferences.

Two seminal studies, by Smith (1980) and Noveck (2001), investigated children's interpretation of sentences with the existential expression *some*, as in (11), but in the absence of any accompanying pictures or story contexts. The 8- to 10-year-old French-speaking children interviewed by Noveck (2001) accepted sentences with the French equivalent to *some*, '*certains.*' The 8-year-old child participants accepted such sentences 89 percent of the time and the 10-year-olds accepted them 85 percent of the time. However, it turned out that even adults accepted the test sentences 41 percent of the time, which clearly suggests that real world knowledge in the absence of contextual support may not suffice to reliably evoke scalar inferences, even from adults.

Children's scalar inference corresponding to (11) was investigated in Italian, by Foppolo, Guasti, and Chierchia (2012). These researchers used a truth-value judgment task, with children at different ages: 4-, 5–6-, and 7-year-olds. In the experiment, the stories were about five characters. In the story context, all five characters performed the action mentioned in the test sentence. An English example is (12).[7]

---

[6] The finding that children accept sentences with *or* in circumstances in which both disjuncts are true indicates that they understand *or* to be an inclusive disjunction, as in classical logic. This is an important finding in its own right.

[7] In some experiments, only three characters were included in the stories, but this could be argued to be infelicitous if the test sentence contains the quantifier *all*, which arguably presupposes that at least three characters are under consideration.

(12)   Some Smurfs went on a boat.

The story that preceded the puppet's target sentence in (12) was about some Smurfs who had the option of traveling down a river by boat or going to a forest by car. At one point in the story, it appeared that some of the Smurfs would go to the forest by car. In the end, however, all of the Smurfs decided to travel down the river by boat. Both the children at age 4 and those at age 5 accepted (12) as a description of what happened in the story, over 40 percent of the time. By contrast, the 6- and 7-year-old children, and adults, rejected the test sentences over 80 percent of the time. The findings suggest a developmental turning point for scalar inferences at roughly 6 years of age.

Another refinement to judgment tasks was implemented by Chierchia et al. (2001) to enhance their suitability for investigating children's knowledge of pragmatic inferences. In the Chierchia et al. study, the child participants were asked to judge the "felicity" of pairs of sentences, rather than the truth or falsity of individual sentences. The tasks involved two puppets. Each puppet produced a different description of the events that had transpired in a story. The child's task was to reward the puppet who provided the better description of the story. The change in task was designed to alleviate the processing cost associated with simultaneously maintaining two alternative representations of a sentence in verbal working memory. Each of the puppets' descriptions contained one of the terms on a scale. In one experiment, children were asked to decide between *or* and *and* when these terms were used in the predicate phrase of sentences with *every*, as illustrated in examples (13) and (14). In the relevant story, some farmers were deciding which animals to bathe. In the end, each farmer decided to clean both a horse and a rabbit.

(13)   Every farmer cleaned a horse or a rabbit.

(14)   Every farmer cleaned a horse and a rabbit.

After the puppets produced (13) and (14), children made their judgment about which sentence was a better description of the story. The child participants ranged in age from 3;5 to 6;2 with a mean age of 5;2. The child participants rewarded the puppet whose sentence contained *and* 93 percent of the time. In another experiment using the truth-value judgment task, children witnessed similar stories but were presented with sentences with just the weaker scalar term, *or*, as in (13). In that condition, children only accepted the test sentences 50 percent of the time.

Using a felicity judgment task, Foppolo et al. (2012) investigated whether a similar change in children's behavior would be forthcoming in sentences with *some*, as in (12). Like Chierchia et al. (2001), Foppolo et al. (2012) found that children's performance improved dramatically, as compared to a truth-value judgment task, when both terms on the scale <some, all> were made explicit. In the felicity judgment task, children selected the puppet who used *all* 95 percent of the time, as compared to the puppet who used *some*. Further confirmation that children perform better on tasks which make lexical alternatives explicit have been revealed in studies by Barner et al. (2011) and by Skordos and Papafragou (2016).

When both scalar terms were made explicit to children, children evinced adult-like performance, in preferring the stronger scalar term. This finding suggests that the source of children's inability to compute scalar inferences resides in the performance system. Presumably children are not able to compute scalar inferences online, due to a limitation in accessing the lexical alternatives that form the relevant scale. When these alternatives are made explicit, however, children indicate knowledge that the sentence with the stronger scalar term is more informative than the sentence with the weaker term. The relative informativeness of different sentences is not revealed using the truth-value judgment task, because the child participants are not presented with the scalar alternatives. Without explicit alternatives, children are apparently unable to mentally compute scalar inferences. What the truth-value judgment task does reveal, however, is children's knowledge of the basic meanings of scalar terms. That is, the task reveals children's knowledge that sentences with *some* are true in circumstances in which all of the characters have performed a designated action, and they know that sentences with *or* are true when both of the events designated by the disjuncts have taken place.

A different way of demonstrating children's knowledge that sentences with weaker scalar terms are underinformative was devised by Katsos and Bishop (2011). As in the studies with the felicity judgment task, Katsos and Bishop (2011) conducted two experiments. One experiment was a (binary choice) truth-value judgment task. In that experiment, the 5- to 6-year-old child participants only rejected underinformative sentences with *some* 26 percent of the time. The second experiment was a ternary judgment task. In that experiment, the "stories" consisted of characters moving on a computer screen. After the animation, the experimenter posed a question to a character situated at the bottom of the screen, "Mr. Caveman." Mr Caveman produced either an underinformative sentence (with *some*), or an informative sentence (with *all*), or a false sentence. The child participants' task was to reward Mr. Caveman, according to his answer, by pointing to one of three strawberries – a "small" strawberry, a "big" strawberry, or a "huge" strawberry. Children were not given any special instructions about how to use the scale, and no children were excluded from the task. When the Caveman produced an informative sentence, children pointed to the huge strawberry 85 percent of the time. When Mr. Caveman produced a false sentence, children pointed to the small strawberry 95 percent of the time. Crucially, when the sentence was underinformative, children pointed to the middle-sized strawberry 89 percent of the time. The pattern of responses by children was similar to that of adults. Like the felicity judgment task, the findings of the ternary judgment task revealed children's knowledge that sentences with *some* are underinformative. This aspect of children's linguistic competence is not evident from the truth-value judgment task. As Katsos and Bishop put it, children appear to be "tolerant of pragmatic infelicity" when asked to judge the truth or falsity of sentences. One of the drawbacks to the ternary judgment task, however, is that there is no indication of why children judged sentences with *some* to be underinformative. The felicity judgment task is more insightful in this regard. Because the weaker and stronger alternatives are made explicit in this task, the basis for the child's decision is clear.

The reliability of ternary judgment tasks is also a concern. A ternary judgment task was used by Renans et al. (2018) to compare children's responses to different kinds of pragmatic inferences. For our purposes, the critical inferences were the same as those investigated by Katsos and Bishop (2011) – scalar inferences that arise in sentences with *some*. The child participants were 4- to 7-year-old children. The ternary judgment was among sets consisting of one, two, or three strawberries (rather than different sized strawberries), and the child participants were given instructions on the use of the ternary scale. The experimental findings reported in the Renans et al. study (2018: Figure 5) differ, however, from those reported by Katsos and Bishop (2011). In response to underinformative sentences with *some*, the child participants in the Renans et al. study selected the optimal reward (the set of three strawberries) 60 percent of the time. The child participants selected the middle-sized set (with two strawberries) only 33 percent of the time, as compared to 89 percent of the time in the Katsos and Bishop study. The difference between these two studies suggests that it is premature, therefore, to reach any firm conclusions at this point about the utility of ternary judgment tasks to investigate children's knowledge of pragmatic inferences.

## 15.5  Summary

Researchers who study child language have a range of tasks available to them for assessing children's linguistic knowledge, and to address important questions about the course of language development. Different tasks have been devised over the last 50 years to address different aspects of children's knowledge of different aspects of language. Whereas a sentence acceptability experiment would be the ideal task to address questions about children's knowledge of the forms sentences can and cannot take, a truth-value judgment task would be more appropriate for addressing questions about the meanings children can and cannot assign to sentences. As we have discussed, there is no magic bullet that can be used to assess children's linguistic knowledge of all kinds. A review of research using sentence acceptability judgment experiments has shown that using this task is extremely challenging for children younger than about 6 years of age. Only "metalinguistically aware" pre-school children can succeed in this task, without the addition of contextual support that reveals the intended meaning of the test sentences. It is also difficult to determine why children judge sentences to be acceptable or unacceptable. This makes it difficult to reach conclusions about the source of children's responses, whether children's non-adult responses are based on their grammars or on some limitation in processing. Children older than about 6 years are clearly better able to participate in sentence acceptability judgment experiments. Nevertheless, when a numerical scale is employed, questions remain about whether children are using the scale in the same way as adults.

By contrast to sentence acceptability experiments, experiments using truth-value judgment tasks have been successfully used with children as young as 3 years old. This task works well, however, only if care is taken to make both the true and false interpretations of the sentences correspond to events that are acted-out in the stories. When the right steps are taken, the truth-value judgment task is an enjoyable experience for children, so there is rarely any attrition. This task also naturally incorporates a check on children's interpretation by asking them to answer the question "What really happened?" when they judge the puppet's statement to be false. A truth-value judgment task has not proven useful in assessing children's knowledge of pragmatic inferences, however. Two new tasks have evolved recently for this purpose: the felicity judgment task and the ternary judgment task. In light of different findings across experiments, the jury is still out concerning the usefulness of the ternary judgment task. The felicity judgment task has been used reliably in several recent studies, and has the additional potential advantage of revealing the source of children's decisions, by presenting explicit alternatives as the basis of the child's decision.

## References

Ambridge, B., Pine, J., Rowland, C., & Young, C. R. (2008). The effect of verb semantic class and verb frequency (entrenchment) on children's and adults' graded judgments of argument structure overgeneralization errors. *Cognition*, 106, 87–129.

Barner, D., Brooks, N., & Bale, A. (2011). Accessing the unsaid: The role of scalar alternatives in children's pragmatic inference. *Cognition*, 118, 84–93.

Borer, H. & Wexler, K. (1987). The maturation of syntax. In T. Roeper & E. Williams, eds., *Parameter Setting*. Dordrecht: Reidel, pp. 123–172.

Bowerman, M. (1982). Evaluating competing linguistic models with language acquisition data: Implications of developmental errors with causative verbs. *Quaderni di Semantica*, 3, 5–66.

Brown, R., Fraser, C., & Bellugi, U. (1964). Explorations in grammar evaluation. In. U. Bellugi & R. Brown, eds., *The Acquisition of Language* (Monograph of the Society of Research in Child Development, 29). Lafayette, IN: Society for Research in Child Development, pp. 79–92.

Chierchia, G., Crain, S., Guasti, M. T., Gualmini, A., & Meroni, L. (2001). The acquisition of disjunction: Evidence for a grammatical view of scalar implicatures. In A. H.-J. Do, L. Domínguez, & A. Johansen, eds., *Proceedings of the 25th Boston University Conference on Child Language Development.* Somerville, MA: Cascadilla Press, pp. 157–168.

Chomsky, N. (1981). *Lectures on Government and Binding: The Pisa Lectures.* Dordrecht: Foris.

Crain, S. (1982). Temporal terms: Mastery by age five. *Papers and Reports on Child Language Development,* 21, 33–38.

Crain, S. (1991). Language acquisition in the absence of experience. *Behavioral and Brain Sciences,* 14, 597–612.

Crain, S., Koring, L., & Thornton, R. (2017). Language acquisition from a biolinguistic perspective. *Neuroscience and Biobehavioral Reviews,* 81, 120–149.

Crain, S. & McKee, C. (1985). Acquisition of structural restrictions on anaphora. In S. Berman, J. McDonough, & J.-W. Choe, eds., *Proceedings of the 16th North East Linguistic Society.* Amherst, MA: GLSA, pp. 94–110.

Crain, S. & Thornton, R. (1998). *Investigations in Universal Grammar: A Guide to Experiments on the Acquisition of Syntax and Semantics.* Cambridge, MA: MIT Press.

Crawford, J. (2012). Developmental perspectives on the acquisition of the passive. Doctoral dissertation, University of Connecticut.

Davidson, D. (1984). Radical translation. In D. Davidson, ed., *Inquiries into Truth and Interpretation.* Oxford: Clarendon Press, pp. 125–139.

De Villiers, J. & de Villiers, P. (1974). Competence and performance in child language: Are children really competent to judge? *Journal of Child Language,* 1, 11–22.

Foppolo, F., Guasti, M. T., & Chierchia, G. (2012). Scalar implicatures in child language: Give children a chance. *Language Learning and Development,* 8, 365–394.

Fukuda, S., Goodall, G., Michel, D., & Beecher, H. (2012). Is magnitude estimation worth the trouble? In J. Choi, E. A. Hogue, J. Punske, D. Tat, J. Schertz, & A. Trueman, eds., *Proceedings of the 29th West Coast Conference on Formal Linguistics.* Somerville, MA: Cascadilla Proceedings Project, pp. 328–336.

Gleitman, L. R., Gleitman, H., & Shipley, E. (1972). The emergence of the child as grammarian. *Cognition,* 1, 137–164.

Hamburger, H. & Crain, S. (1982). Relative acquisition. In Stan A. Kuczaj II, ed., *Language Development, Syntax and Semantics,* vol. 1. Hillsdale, NJ: Lawrence Erlbaum, pp. 245–274.

Hochberg, J. (1986). Children's judgements of transitivity errors. *Journal of Child Language,* 13, 317–334.

Katsos, N. & Bishop, D. V. M. (2011). Pragmatic tolerance: Implications for the acquisition of informativeness and implicature. *Cognition,* 120, 67–81.

Lasnik, H. & Crain, S. (1985). On the acquisition of pronominal reference. *Lingua,* 65, 135–154.

Lenneberg, E. (1967). *Biological Foundations of Language*. New York: John Wiley & Sons.

McDaniel, D. & Cairns, H. S. (1990). The child as informant: Eliciting linguistic intuitions from young children. *Journal of Psycholinguistic Research*, 19, 331–344.

McDaniel, D. & Cairns, H. S. (1996). Eliciting judgments of grammaticality and reference. In D. McDaniel, C. McKee, & H. S. Cairns, eds., *Methods for Assessing Children's Syntax*. Cambridge, MA: MIT Press, pp. 233–254.

McDaniel, D., Cairns, H. S., & Hsu, J. R. (1990). Binding principles in the grammars of young children. *Language Acquisition*, 1, 121–139.

McDaniel, D., Cairns, H. S., & Hsu, J. R. (1990/1991). Control principles in the grammars of young children. *Language Acquisition*, 1, 297–335.

McDaniel, D. & Maxfield, T. (1992). The nature of the anti-c-command requirement: Evidence from young children. *Linguistic Inquiry*, 23, 667–671.

Noveck, I. A. (2001). When children are more logical than adults: Experimental investigations of scalar implicature. *Cognition*, 78, 165–188.

Pinker, S. (1984). *Language Learnability and Language Development*. Cambridge, MA: Harvard University Press.

Renans, A., Romoli, J., Makri, M. M., Tieu, L., de Vries, H., Folli, R., & Tsoulas, G. (2018). The abundance inference of pluralised mass nouns is an implicature: Evidence from Greek. *Glossa: A Journal of General Linguistics*, 3(1), 103. DOI:10.5334/gjgl.531

Skordos, D. & Pappafragou, A. (2016). Children's derivation of scalar implicatures: Alternatives and relevance. *Cognition*, 153, 6–18.

Smith, C. L. (1980). Quantifiers and question answering in young children. *Journal of Experimental Child Psychology*, 30, 191–205.

Theakston, A. (2004). The role of entrenchment in children's and adults' performance on grammaticality judgment tasks. *Cognitive Development*, 19, 15–34.

Thornton, R. (2017). The truth value judgment task: An update. In M. Nakayama, Y. C. Su, & A. Huang, eds., *Studies in Chinese and Japanese Language Acquisition: In Honor of Stephen Crain*. Amsterdam: John Benjamins, pp. 13–39.

# 16

# Acceptability and Truth-Value Judgment Studies in East Asian Languages

Shin Fukuda

## 16.1 Introduction

Since the early development of modern syntactic theory, empirical data from three major East Asian languages, Chinese, Japanese, and Korean, have often challenged empirical generalizations and theoretical proposals based on data from the better-studied Indo-European languages, especially English (e.g. Kuroda 1965; Kuno 1973; Huang 1982). Experimental syntax also began with studies of phenomena in English and other major Indo-European languages (e.g. Sorace 1993, 1995; Bard et al. 1996; Schütze 1996; Cowart 1997; Keller 2000; Keller & Sorace 2003; Featherston 2005a, 2005b; Sprouse 2007). More recently, however, a growing number of experimental syntactic studies have focused on East Asian languages, especially in the past decade. This chapter highlights three phenomena explored in the rapidly growing body of experimental syntactic research with Chinese, Japanese, and Korean: (i) *split intransitivity* (Section 16.2), (ii) *quantifier scope* (Section 16.3), and (iii) *wh-in-situ* (Section 16.4). The goal of the chapter is to show that, while the literature on East Asian experimental syntax is still at an early stage, it has already accumulated interesting experimental data on syntactic phenomena with important theoretical implications.

## 16.2 Split Intransitivity

Split intransitivity (SI) refers to the generalization that intransitive verbs across languages divide into two subgroups with respect to certain linguistic phenomena. The most influential hypothesis concerning SI has been the *Unaccusative Hypothesis* (UH; Perlmutter 1978; Burzio 1981, 1986). The UH accounts for SI by postulating two distinct underlying structures for intransitive verbs. The *unergative* structure involves an external argument base-generated outside VP as its sole nominal argument, while the *unaccusative* structure involves an internal argument base-generated inside VP as its sole nominal argument.

SI is one of the first syntactic phenomena for which sentence acceptability judgment experiments were employed (Sorace 1993, 1995; Bard et al. 1996), and the resultant findings played an important role in the development of another influential approach to SI. Based on acceptability judgment data, Sorace (1993, 1995, 2000) argued that the mapping of intransitive verbs onto unaccusative/unergative structures is mediated by a hierarchical organization of the intransitive verbs based on their lexical semantic features, such as the Auxiliary Selection Hierarchy (ASH) in (1).

(1)     The ASH (Sorace 2000)
        CHANGE OF LOCATION ('come,' 'fall,' 'drop,' etc.)   (CORE UNACCUSATIVE)
        CHANGE OF STATE ('die,' 'be born,' 'appear,' etc.)
        CONTINUATION OF A PRE-EXISTING STATE ('remain,' 'stay,' 'survive,' etc.)
        EXISTENCE OF STATE ('be,' 'exist,' 'belong,' etc.).
        UNCONTROLLED PROCESS ('tremble,' 'sweat,' 'shiver,' etc.)
        CONTROLLED MOTIONAL PROCESS ('walk,' 'swim,' 'dance,' etc.)
        CONTROLLED NON-MOTIONAL PROCESS ('talk,' 'work,' 'play,' etc.)
                                                            (CORE UNERGATIVE)

The ASH is based on auxiliary selection phenomena in West European languages. According to the ASH, intransitive verbs that belong to core unaccusative classes exhibit clear and stable unaccusative behavior (e.g. categorically selecting the BE auxiliary) while intransitive verbs that belong to core unergative classes in the hierarchy show clear and stable unergative behavior (e.g. categorically selecting the HAVE auxiliary), both cross-linguistically and language-internally. In contrast, verbs in the mid-range of the ASH show indeterminate behaviors and more cross-linguistic and language-internal variability (e.g. alternating between the BE and the HAVE auxiliaries).

Both the UH and the ASH have inspired many experimental syntactic studies in Chinese, Japanese, and Korean. This section reviews some of those studies, focusing on two diagnostics: the selection of aspect markers in Chinese (Section 16.2.1) and (ii) the licensing of floating numeral quantifiers in Japanese (Section 16.2.2).

### 16.2.1   Aspect Marker Selection in Chinese
One commonly discussed SI diagnostic in Chinese is the locative inversion (LI) construction (e.g. Huang 1987; Pan 1996; Yuan 1999; Liu 2007). LI in Chinese involves a pre-verbal locative phrase and a post-verbal subject NP that must be indefinite. Intransitive verbs in LI are usually required to co-occur with an aspect marker, either perfective *le*

or durative *zhe*. Importantly, the selection of aspect markers (henceforth Aspect Marker Selection, AMS) appears to be determined by the lexical semantics of intransitive verbs, and it has also been linked to the unaccusative/unergative distinction among Chinese intransitive verbs (e.g. Liu 2007).

Laws and Yuan (2010) ran an acceptability judgment experiment to examine AMS with Chinese intransitive verbs in the context of the ASH. Twenty-three Chinese intransitive verbs in nine lexical semantic classes, ranging from core to peripheral unaccusative verbs (2), were presented (i) in two constructions (LI and a post-verbal subject without a pre-verbal locative phrase) and (ii) with two aspect markers (*le* and *zhe*). Their acceptability was judged on a five-point scale (-2 to +2). No (potential) unergative verbs were tested.

(2)     a. change of location: *dào* 'arrive,' *lái* 'come,' *táo* 'escape,' *diē-dǎo* 'fall,' *dǎo* 'fall'
        b. inherently telic change of state: *chū-shēng* 'be born,' *sǐ* 'die'
        c. appearance: *chūxiàn* 'appear,' *fāshēng* 'happen'
        d. internally caused change: *làn* 'rot,' *zhǎng* 'grow,' *kūwěi* 'wither'
        e. directed motion: *luò-xià* 'descend,' *shēng-qǐ* 'rise'
        f. continuation of condition with inanimate subjects: *jìxù* 'continue,' *chí-xù* 'persist,' *tíng-liú* 'remain'
        g. continuation of condition with animate subjects: *dāi* 'remain,' *xìng-cún* 'survive'
        h. verbs of posture with inanimate subjects: *zuòluò* 'sit,' *chùlì* 'stand'
        i. verbs of posture with animate subjects: *zuò* 'sit,' *zhàn* 'stand'

The results largely confirmed the prediction of the ASH, as the perfective marker *le* was clearly preferred with the intransitive verbs in the first five classes, (a–e). In the other four categories, either the difference between the two aspect markers is not significant (g), or the durative marker *zhe* is preferred (f, h–i). However, several findings were inconsistent with the ASH. First, the ASH predicts that the mean acceptability judgments for core unaccusative verbs like verbs of change of location (a) and inherently telic change (b) with *zhe* should be close to -2, as they are expected to show a categorical preference for *le*. Yet mean acceptability judgments of these verbs with *zhe* were unexpectedly high (change of location verbs: -0.53; inherently telic change verbs: -0.89). Second, the ASH predicts a clear difference between the acceptability of core unaccusative verbs with *le* and *zhe* and the acceptability of peripheral unaccusative verbs with *le* and *zhe*. Countering this prediction, the study found the mean acceptability judgments for the verbs of change of location (a) with *le* (1.40) and *zhe* (-0.53) to be similar to those for the verbs of directed motion (e) with *le* (1.58) and *zhe* (-0.63). Based on these findings and others, Laws and Yuan

(2010) proposed that core unaccusative verbs in Chinese consist of the following individual verbs: three verbs of change of location (*dào* 'arrive,' *lái* 'come,' *táo* 'escape'), three verbs of change of state (*sǐ* 'die,' *chū-shēng* 'be born,' *chūxiàn* 'appear') and one directed motion verb (*luò-xià* 'descend'). Thus, while the findings from Law and Yuan's study seem broadly consistent with the ASH, the core versus peripheral distinction among Chinese unaccusative verbs that the authors proposed categorizes some change of location verbs, arguably core unaccusative verbs, as peripheral unaccusative verbs. As such, the lexical semantic classes seem to have less predictive power for the AMS behavior of Chinese intransitive verbs than for the auxiliary selection behavior of intransitive verbs in West European languages.

### 16.2.2  Licensing of Floating Quantifiers in Japanese

Sorace and Shomura (2001) conducted one of the first acceptability judgment studies in Japanese, examining whether acceptability judgments provided by Japanese native and L2 speakers concerning SI diagnostics in the language show their sensitivity to the ASH.[1] One of the diagnostics the study examined is the licensing of floating numeral quantifiers (FNQs). Numeral quantifiers (NQs) are combinations of a numeral like *san* 'three' and a classifier like *-nin*, which agrees with a semantic feature of the modified NP (its *associate*; e.g. [+human] with *-nin*). Miyagawa (1989) observed that subjects of some intransitive verbs such as *ku-ru* 'come' readily license an NQ that is separated from its associate, that is, an FNQ, as in (3a), while subjects of other intransitive verbs such as *wara-u* 'laugh' do not (3b). A similar contrast has been attested in Korean (e.g. Gerdts 1987; Lee 1989; Ahn 1990; O'Grady 1991; Kang 2002; Miyagawa 2006; Ko 2005, 2007).[2]

(3)  a. **Gakusee-ga**  (✓**san-nin**) ofisu-ni  (✓**san-nin**)  ki-ta.
     student-NOM  (three-CL)  office-LOC (three-CL)  come-PST
     'Three students came to the office.'
   b. **Gakusee-ga**  (✓**san-nin**) geragera-to  (#**san-nin**) warat-ta.
     student-NOM  (three-CL)  loudly  (three-CL)  laugh-PST
     'Three students laughed loudly.'

Miyagawa (1989) argued that the ability of Japanese intransitive subjects to license FNQs is sensitive to SI. According to Miyagawa, an NQ and its associate must be in a syntactically local configuration in their base-

---

[1]  To the best of my knowledge, Hirakawa's (1999, 2001) experimental studies, using a picture selection task with L2 learners, were the first on split intransitivity in Japanese.
[2]  One important difference between Japanese and Korean with respect to the licensing of FNQs is that FNQs can be case-marked only in Korean. It has been claimed that the contrast shown in (3) is observed in Korean only with case-less NQs (e.g. Ahn 1990; Ko & Oh 2010, 2012). For experimental studies on FNQs in Korean (including case-marked FNQs) and their interaction with SI, see Ko and Oh (2010, 2012) and Lee (2011).

generated positions, but the associate can "strand" the NQ by undergoing syntactic movement. Under this analysis, the FNQ in (3a) is licensed despite the presence of the intervening PP, because *ku-ru* 'come' is an unaccusative verb and its subject is base-generated as an internal argument inside VP, where it was in the required local configuration with the FNQ (4a). In contrast, (3b) with the FNQ is degraded because *wara-u* 'laugh' is an unergative verb and its subject is an external argument base-generated outside VP (e.g. Spec, VoiceP; Kratzer 1994, 1996). Thus, it was never in the required local configuration with the FNQ (4b).

(4)  a.

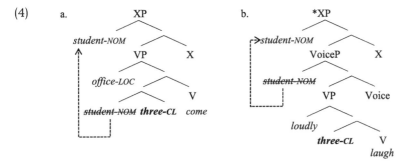

Miyagawa's proposal predicts that Japanese (and Korean) intransitive verbs would split into two groups with respect to FNQ-licensing. However, if the ASH in (1) applies to FNQ-licensing by intransitive subjects, there should be a gradient change in the contrast between intransitive sentences with the NQ adjacent to the associate (henceforth [–FNQ]) and those with an FNQ (henceforth [+FNQ]), from core unergative verbs to core unaccusative verbs. Sentences with core unergative verbs should exhibit a clear contrast while sentences with core unaccusative verbs should not, while the contrasts with intransitive verbs in the middle of the hierarchy should be weaker than those with core unergative verbs but stronger than those with core unaccusative verbs.

Sorace and Shomura (2001) selected three verbs from 13 classes (39 in total) of Japanese intransitive verbs, ranging from core unergatives to core unaccusatives, and created experimental sentences with these verbs in [–FNQ] and [+FNQ] conditions. Acceptability judgments were collected from native Japanese speakers and L2 Japanese learners using magnitude estimation as the task (see Chapter 2 for a discussion of magnitude estimation tasks). The predictions of the ASH were nicely borne out with the native speakers' judgments on the unergative verbs. Core unergative verbs such as controlled non-motional process verbs (e.g. *uta-u* 'sing') and relatively highly ranked peripheral unergative verbs such as controlled motional process verbs (e.g. *oyog-u* 'swim') showed clearer contrasts between the [–FNQ] and [+FNQ] conditions, while lower-ranked peripheral unergative verbs such as uncontrolled process verbs (e.g. *hikar-u* 'flash') showed less pronounced contrasts. However, the results with unaccusative verbs were less clear. In particular, the native speakers judged sentences with change of location verbs such as *tsuk-u* 'arrive,' in the core unaccusative class in the ASH, as if they were unergative verbs, with a significant difference between the [−FNQ] and [+FNQ] conditions.

Fukuda (2017) followed the basic design of Sorace and Shomura (2001), examining 10 Japanese intransitive verbs in five different lexical semantic classes, shown in (5), all of which had been discussed in previous studies with various SI diagnostics in Japanese.

(5)     a. Class 1 (change of location): *hair-u* 'enter,' *ochi-ru* 'fall'
        b. Class 2 (change of state): *araware-ru* 'appear,' *kie-ru* 'disappear'
        c. Class 3 (stative): *i-ru* 'be,' *nokor-u* 'remain'[3]
        d. Class 4 (controlled motional process): *odor-u* 'dance,' *oyog-u* 'swim'
        e. Class 5 (controlled non-motional process): *asob-u* 'play,' *hatarak-u* 'work'

The study conducted an acceptability judgment experiment with a 2 × 5 design crossing FNQ ([−FNQ] vs. [+FNQ]) and VERB CLASS (Classes 1, 2, 3, 4, and 5), with a seven-point scale. The interaction between FNQ and VERB CLASS was significant only with Classes 4 and 5. These results suggest that FNQ-licensing divides the 10 Japanese intransitive verbs in these five lexical semantic classes into two subgroups, providing support for the UH. At the same time, the same results fail to support the ASH for Japanese intransitive verbs and FNQ-licensing, as the ASH would predict gradual differences in the acceptability of the [−FNQ] and [+FNQ] conditions across the five verb classes. Specifically, it predicts that the difference in mean acceptability judgments between [FNQ] and [+FNQ] conditions would be smallest with Class 1 and largest with Class 5, with Class 3 somewhere in between. Instead, the study found the differences between the two conditions to be smallest with Classes 2 and 3, only slightly larger with Class 1, and largest with Classes 4 and 5.

## 16.2.3  Summary

This section reviewed acceptability judgment studies on split intransitivity (SI) in East Asian languages, focusing on two SI diagnostics: the selection of aspect markers (AMS) and the licensing of floating numeral quantifiers (FNQ-licensing). Although the findings from these studies give us good starting points for discussion, they are far from conclusive. First, while Laws and Yuen's (2010) findings with AMS provide partial support for the ASH, Fukuda's (2017) findings with FNQ-licensing contradict it. Second,

---

[3] Fukuda (2017) treated the two subclasses of stative verbs, continuation of a pre-existing state and existence of state, as a single class, stative verbs, because (i) the number of stative verbs is small in Japanese and (ii) the results reported by Sorace and Shomura (2001) showed no difference between these two classes in terms of sensitivity to FNQ-licensing.

although Fukuda's findings suggest that intransitive verbs split into two groups, providing support for the UH, the study's finding of a lack of gradient judgments could be due to insufficient sensitivity of the methods used. As this review demonstrates, we need more experimental syntactic studies on this topic.

## 16.3  Quantifier Scope

Chinese, Japanese, and Korean are considered "scopally rigid" languages (see Chapter 13 for detailed discussion of scope interactions in general). This means that doubly quantified sentences in these languages often have only the surface scope reading, unless there are reasons to believe that the quantifiers have been displaced through some syntactic operation (e.g. Kuroda 1970; Kuno 1973; Huang 1982; Hoji 1985; Lee 1986; Ahn 1990; Aoun & Li 1993; Sohn 1995). Thus, with a doubly quantified Japanese transitive sentence in canonical SOV order like (6a), the only available reading of the two quantifiers is the surface scope reading, in which the existential quantifier subject *dareka* 'someone' takes scope over the universal quantifier object *subete* 'all.' However, in (6b), with the universal quantifier object scrambled to sentence-initial position, the sentence is ambiguous between the surface and inverse scopes of the quantifiers.

(6)     a. Dareka-ga     kono heya-no  subete-no  hon-o     yon-da.
           someone-NOM  this room-GEN  all-GEN      book-ACC  read-PST
           'Someone read all the books in this room.' $\{\exists > \forall; {}^*\forall > \exists\}$
      b. [Kono heya-no   subete-no hon-o]$_i$     dareka-ga      t$_i$ yon-da.
          [this   room-GEN all-GEN      book-ACC]$_i$ someone-NOM t$_i$ read-PST
          'Someone read all the books in this room.' $\{\exists > \forall, \forall > \exists\}$

Section 16.3.1 reviews several experimental studies that probe scope rigidity with doubly quantified sentences in Chinese. They reveal two factors that must be considered when quantifier scope in doubly quantified sentences is examined: (i) the scope of quantifiers is not always predictable from their structural positions and (ii) individual quantifiers may have different distributional and interpretational restrictions. Section 16.3.2 discusses studies that exploit the scopally rigid property of Korean (and Japanese) to investigate a different syntactic phenomenon: verb-raising.

### 16.3.1  Scope Rigidity in Chinese
Zhou and Gao (2009) and Han et al. (2009a) are some of the first experimental studies that probed whether doubly quantified sentences in Chinese and Japanese exhibit the alleged scope rigidity. Zhou and Gao examined the availability of the inverse scope reading in doubly quantified sentences in Chinese with a sentence acceptability experiment and a reading time experiment. The study presented examples like (7), with a

universal quantifier in the subject position and a numeral in a non-subject position, in two contexts: one compatible only with the surface scope and one compatible only with the inverse scope of the two quantifiers.

(7)    Mei-ge     ren      dou   qu-le   yi-jia   gongchang.
       every-CL   person   all   go-ASP  one-CL   factory
       'Everyone went to a factory.'

Participants judged whether the meaning of each sentence matched the corresponding context, with a five-point scale. The mean acceptability judgments of the inverse scope reading of sentences like (7) were above 3.0. Based on this finding, the authors concluded that the inverse interpretation is indeed available with doubly quantified sentences in Chinese.

Scontras et al. (2014, 2017) also examined scope rigidity in Chinese, coming to the opposite conclusion. The study first provides two arguments that the inverse scope reading of (7) is available not because Chinese lacks scope rigidity, but because the second quantifier in the example is a numeral, *yi-jia* 'one-CL.' First, numerals, and indefinites in general, are known to take wide scope over another quantifier in the same sentence regardless of their structural positions (e.g. Fodor & Sag 1982; Reinhart 1997; Kratzer 1998; on the scope of numerals and other quantifiers in Chinese: Liu 1997; Jiang 2012). Second, the inverse scope reading of (7) (one > ∀) and its surface scope reading counterpart (∀ > one) are not logically independent of each other, as the truth of the former entails the truth of the latter (e.g. Reinhart 1976, 1997; Cooper 1979; Ruys 1992). That is, if it is true that there was a specific factory to which everyone went, then it must also be true that everyone went to a factory. Thus, (7) under the inverse scope scenario could be judged as a true statement with the surface scope interpretation. Scontras et al. (2014, 2017) also argued that these two confounding factors can be avoided if the order of the two quantifiers is reversed. If the numeral *yi-jia* 'one-CL' is the subject and the universal quantifier *mei* 'every' is the object, then their scope would be determined by their respective structural positions, because (i) universal quantifiers such as *mei* 'every' cannot take scope over another quantifier that c-commands them, and (ii) the inverse scope of a doubly quantified sentence with a numeral (or existential) subject and a universal object is independent of the surface scope interpretation. That is, every factory being visited by one person (∀ > one) does not entail that the same person visited each factory (one > ∀). Thus, such a sentence with an inverse scope scenario would not be judged as a true statement unless the inverse scope is available. With this background, Scontras et al.'s (2014) experiment examined the availability of inverse scope in doubly quantified Chinese sentences with a universal quantifier and an existential quantifier in two different orders: the universal quantifier preceding the existential quantifier (8a) and the existential quantifier preceding the universal quantifier (8b).

(8)  a. Mei   yi   tiao shayu dou gongji le   yi   ge haidao.
   every one  CL   shark  DOU attack PERF one  CL pirate
   'Every shark attacked a pirate.'

  b. You  yi   tiao shayu gongji le   mei  yi   ge haidao.
   have one  CL   shark attack PERF every one  CL pirate
   'A shark attacked every pirate.'

Sixteen sentences like (8a–b) were pre-recorded, and each was presented with two pictures. For (8a), the surface scope picture shows many sharks, each attacking one of many pirates (on separate boats), while the inverse scope picture shows many sharks attacking a single pirate. For (8b), the surface scope picture shows a single shark attacking many pirates (on a single boat), while the inverse scope picture shows many sharks, each attacking one of many pirates (on separate boats). Participants judged whether the sentence was a true statement with respect to the picture they saw. Sentences like (8a) with surface scope pictures were judged true 100 percent of the time, while sentences like (8b) with surface scope pictures were judged true 76 percent of the time. In contrast, sentences like (8b) were never judged true with inverse scope pictures (0 percent), while sentences like (8a) with inverse scope pictures were judged true 25 percent of the time. The complete rejection of the inverse scope reading with the crucial condition with the existential quantifier preceding the universal quantifier (8b) seems to provide support for the claim that Chinese is scopally rigid.

However, as the astute reader might have already noticed, the experimental sentences in (8) contain at least two potential confounds, as Scontras et al. (2014) themselves point out. First, the quantifier *yi* 'one' can be interpreted as the numeral *one* or the indefinite article *a*, which are two different items in English. Second, the critical condition in (8b), with the existential quantifier preceding the universal quantifier, is a presentational construction with *you* 'have,' which could have a biclausal structure. These two factors could be responsible for the complete rejection of the inverse scope reading for (8b). Hence, it is possible that in addressing two potential confounding issues – types of quantifier and their structural positions in doubly quantified sentences – Scontras et al. might have introduced a new set of confounding factors.[4]

---

[4] In an attempt to address these two issues, Scontras et al. (2017) ran a similar experiment with doubly quantified English sentences (i) with the universal quantifier *every* and either the numeral *one* or the indefinite *a* as the other quantifier, and (ii) in the plain transitive structure (e.g. *A shark attacked every pirate.*) or the presentation construction (e.g. *There is a shark that attacked every pirate.*). The results show that the numeral *one* (as opposed to the indefinite *a*) and the existential construction (as opposed to the plain transitive structure) do suppress the availability of inverse scope. However, the mean acceptability judgments of these English sentences were still significantly higher than zero, the mean for the inverse scope for Chinese sentences like (8b). The authors argued that (i) neither the possibility of the numeral interpretation of *yi* nor the possible biclausal structure of the presentational constructions can account for the "floor-level" acceptability of the inverse scope reading of Chinese sentences like (8b) and, therefore, (ii) their results conclusively show that Chinese is a scopally rigid language.

The studies reviewed in this subsection highlight the importance of using the right quantifiers in the right positions in order to probe the availability of inverse scope in doubly quantified sentences. Even when the right quantifiers are situated in the right hierarchical relations, language/item-specific distributional and interpretational restrictions with quantifiers can prevent experimental sentences from being ideal minimal pairs.[5] Thus, future studies on scope rigidity in East Asian languages should aim to develop experimental and material designs that circumvent the complications deriving from language/item-specific distributional and interpretational restrictions with individual quantifiers in these languages.

## 16.3.2 Scope Rigidity and Verb-Raising in Korean (and Japanese)

While Section 16.3.1 highlighted the challenges of experimental research on scope rigidity in Chinese, the previous studies' findings do suggest that Chinese is more scopally rigid than scopally flexible languages like English. As mentioned, Scontras et al. (2014) found 0 percent acceptance of the inverse scope reading for doubly quantified sentences in Chinese. In contrast, Anderson (2004) reported that the inverse scope interpretation of English doubly quantified sentences like *An experienced climber scaled every cliff* (one > ∀) was available for about half of the English speakers she tested (53 percent). Thus, it seems safe to conclude that inverse scope readings of doubly quantified sentences are significantly harder to obtain in Chinese than in English.

If, in East Asian languages, scope ambiguity obtains between two quantifiers only when one of them undergoes syntactic movement, the absence/presence of scope ambiguity may be used as a diagnostic for the presence/absence of syntactic movement. This is what the studies of Han et al. (2007) and Han et al. (2009b) did. These studies took advantage of the assumed scopally rigid property of Korean and Japanese to examine whether a verb raises to a higher functional head position in these languages, a highly contested issue (e.g. Otani & Whitman 1991; Park 1992; Yoon 1994; Park 1998; Koizumi 2000; Fukushima 2003). It is widely assumed that a verb overtly raises in some languages (e.g. French) but not in others (e.g. English), based on a well-known contrast in possible positions of certain adverbs (e.g. Emonds 1978; Pollock 1989). But in head-final languages like Korean and Japanese, the effects of verb-raising, if present, are not as readily detectable, and previous studies on the existence of verb-raising

---

[5] When Han et al. (2009a) examined the availability of the inverse scope reading of doubly quantified sentences in Japanese, they faced similar problems to those encountered by Zhou and Gao (2009) and Scontras et al. (2014, 2017). Namely, some of the quantifiers they tested are interpreted as having wide scope over another quantifier that c-commands them, and some of them have idiosyncratic distributional and interpretational restrictions that prevented them from appearing in the same syntactic positions. The latter situation resulted in non-trivial differences in terms of the position of the second quantifiers in the doubly quantified sentences used by Han et al.

in Korean and Japanese present conflicting observations. Han et al. (2007) designed experiments to test this issue based on three assumptions: (i) Korean is scopally rigid, (ii) the object of transitive verbs raises to a position outside VP but still lower than I in Korean, and (iii) one of the negative markers in Korean cliticizes to the verb. These assumptions together with the presence/absence of verb-raising make the following predictions about the scope of negation and a quantifier object in sentences like (9). If there is no verb-raising, then the quantifier object should take scope over the negation, as the verb and the cliticized negative marker remain inside VP (10a). If the verb raises to I, on the other hand, the negation should take scope over the object (10b).

(9)   Khwukhi  Monste-ka     motun   khwukhi-lul   an-mek-ess-ta.
      Cookie    Monster-NOM   every   cookie-ACC    NEG-eat-PST-DECL
      'Cookie Monster didn't eat every cookie.'

(10)   a.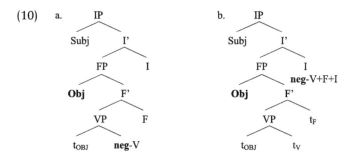

These predictions were tested with a truth-value judgment experiment that was part of a larger study.[6] Participants were divided into two groups and asked to judge whether sentences like (9) are true under two different conditions. The first group was assigned to the NEG > ∀ condition. Continuing to use (9) as our example, for the NEG > ∀ condition, participants watched a video clip in which Cookie Monster is given three cookies but only eats two of them, and a puppet describes the situation with (9). The second group was assigned to the ∀ > NEG condition. These participants watched a clip in which Cookie Monster eats none of the cookies, and again a puppet describes the situation with (9).

The mean percentage of "true" answers with the NEG > ∀ condition was 37 percent, while the mean percentage of "true" answers for the ∀ > NEG condition was 98 percent.[7] Because the truth of the ∀ > NEG condition entails the truth of the NEG > ∀ condition (e.g. if all cookies are such that they have not been eaten, then it is necessarily true that it is not the case

---

[6] The larger experiment reported by Han et al. (2007) involved two other conditions that manipulated (i) position of the quantifier (subject, object) and (ii) type of negation ("high" negation requiring a light verb, "low" negation that is cliticized to the verb). Here, we only discuss the combination of the object quantifier and low negation.

[7] Lee (2009) examined the same paradigm and reported slightly different results, which, however, are still consistent with Han et al.'s (2007) results. The percentages of "true" answers were 65.99 percent with the ∀ > NEG condition and 34.01 percent with the NEG > ∀ scope condition.

Table 16.1 *Numbers of participants who accepted* NEG >∀ *scope*

|                        | 0 out 4 | 1 out of 4 | 2 out of 4 | 3 out of 4 | 4 out of 4 |
|------------------------|---------|------------|------------|------------|------------|
| Number of participants | 10      | 2          | 2          | 0          | 6          |

that all cookies were eaten), only the results with the NEG >∀ condition are informative in terms of the presence/absence of verb-raising, as this condition can be judged as true only if the intended NEG >∀ scope is available. Under the three assumptions described above, the fact that sentences like (9) with the NEG >∀ scenario were judged to be true 37 percent of the time suggests that the verb is raised in these cases. Thus, these findings provide novel experimental evidence for the existence of verb-raising in Korean. Han et al. (2007) further claimed that the participants who judged sentences like (9) to be true with a NEG >∀ condition scenario fell into two groups: those who always accepted the NEG >∀ scope and those who always rejected it. Table 16.1 summarizes how many times out of four test trials each participant accepted the NEG >∀ scope.

Given the distribution of "true" answers in Table 16.1, the authors make an intriguing claim that their participants were split between two grammars: a grammar that does not allow verb-raising and an alternative grammar that does. The former generates only the ∀ > NEG scope, because the negation is c-commanded by the universal quantifier object that moves out of VP (10a). Thus, speakers with this grammar are expected to always reject the NEG >∀ scope, just like the 10 participants who never accepted the NEG >∀ scope in the study. The alternative grammar with verb-raising allows the NEG >∀ scope, because negation ends up c-commanding the universal quantifier object after it is raised to I (10b). Thus, speakers with this grammar are expected to always accept the NEG >∀ scope, just like the six participants who did so in all trials in the study. Han et al. (2009b) conducted a similar study with Japanese and obtained similar results.[8]

### 16.3.3  Summary

Section 16.3.1's review shows that experimentally probing scope rigidity in East Asian languages can be difficult because of idiosyncratic differences among quantifiers. Nevertheless, previous experimental studies' results suggest that the inverse scope of doubly quantified sentences is significantly more difficult to obtain with Chinese than with scopally flexible languages

---

[8] Han et al. (2007) treated scope as a between-subject condition, not a within-subject condition, because "once participants become aware of one of the possible interpretations for these statements, they may later find it difficult to assign a similar statement a different interpretation" (p. 27). This hypothesized initial scope bias is a viable alternative account for the findings of Han et al. (2007) and Han et al. (2009b).

like English. The studies reviewed in Section 16.3.2 assumed the same for Korean and Japanese, and used it to examine the existence of verb-raising in these languages. Their findings not only provide novel evidence for the existence of verb-raising in these languages, but raise the interesting possibility that speakers of these languages split into two groups with respect to the availability of verb-raising. These studies are great examples of how acceptability judgment experiments can lead to discoveries that would have been difficult to make without them.

## 16.4  *Wh*-in-situ and Islands in Chinese, Japanese, and Korean

Chinese, Japanese, and Korean are all *wh*-in-situ languages, where *wh*-phrases typically stay in their thematically licensed positions.

(11)  Zhangsan  kandao  *shenme?*
      Zhangsan  saw  *what*
      'What did Zhangsan see?'

These languages are also known to be insensitive to some of the *island constraints* (Ross 1967, 1987). The island constraints are descriptive generalizations that a filler–gap dependency – a relationship between a displaced element and its assumed "original" position, as in *wh*-questions, scrambling, relativization, and topicalization – should not involve a set of syntactic environments known as "islands." The crossing of an island by a long-distance dependency significantly degrades the acceptability of the sentence. Such effects are called "island effects."

Island effects have been the most intensively studied, most productive research topic in the experimental syntactic literature (see Chapter 9 and Sprouse & Hornstein 2013 for overviews). One of the most important outcomes of this research has been the establishment of a factorial definition that isolates island effects with two binary factors (Sprouse et al. 2011, 2012): (i) the length of dependency, i.e. whether it is between two positions in the matrix clause (short) or between a matrix position and an embedded position (long), and (ii) the structure of the embedded clause, i.e. whether it is a potential island or not (island vs. non-island). These two factors create the following four types of experimental sentences.

(12)  a. sentences with a short dependency with a non-island embedded clause
      b. sentences with a long dependency with a non-island embedded clause
      c. sentences with a short dependency with a potential island embedded clause
      d. sentences with a long dependency with a potential island embedded clause

If a longer dependency has significant effects on the acceptability of these sentences, the acceptability of types (12a) and (12c), with a short dependency, would be significantly better than that of types (12b) and (12d), with a long dependency. If the mere presence of a potential island structure has significant effects on the acceptability of these sentences, the acceptability of types (12a) and (12b), with a non-island embedded clause, would be significantly better than those of types (12c) and (12d), with a potential island embedded clause. Importantly, if there is nothing else, i.e. if there is no island effect, then we expect these factors' effects to be additive. In terms of statistical analysis, this would result in no interaction between the two factors. However, if there are island effects, i.e. if there are penalties of having a long dependency with a potential island embedded clause, as in (12d), such penalties would cause additional degradation of the acceptability of (12d), beyond what we would expect from the effects of the two factors. In terms of statistical analysis, the presence of island effects would result in a significant interaction between the dependency length and the embedded clause structure (see Chapter 9 for a more complete discussion of the factorial definition of island effects).

The factorial definition of island effects established a standard measurement for examining potential island constructions across languages and inspired a good number of experimental studies investigating cross-linguistic variation in island effects, including in East Asian languages. This section reviews several acceptability judgment studies that investigated potential island effects with *wh*-in-situ in East Asian languages.[9] The studies' findings show that island effects can indeed be found with *wh*-in-situ in East Asian languages.

### 16.4.1  *Wh*-in-situ and Islands in Japanese

Sprouse et al. (2011) were the first to experimentally examine whether island effects can be observed with *wh*-in-situ inside different potential island structures. The study used a 2 × 2 design with DEPENDENCY LENGTH (matrix *wh*-in-situ vs. embedded *wh*-in-situ) and EMBEDDED STRUCTURE (CP vs. a potential island) to examine if these two factors show an interaction. (13) shows schematic examples from the study with complex NP (CNP) as an example of a potential island structure.

(13)    a. Matrix *wh* with CP
          **Who**-NOM [CP  NP-NOM  NP-ACC    Verb-COMP]          Verb-Q
        b. Matrix *wh* with CNP
          **Who**-NOM [CNP [NP-NOM  NP-ACC    Verb-COMP] N]-ACC Verb-Q

---

[9] Experimental studies have also examined scrambling in Japanese (Jurka 2010; Jurka et al. 2011; Fukuda et al. 2016; Omaki et al. 2020), relativization in Korean (Han 2013) and topicalization in Chinese (Myers 2012; Zenker & Schwartz 2017).

c. Embedded *wh* with CP

    NP-NOM    [CP  NP-NOM  **what**-ACC Verb-COMP]        Verb-Q

d. Embedded *wh* with CNP

    NP-NOM    [CNP [NP-NOM  **what**-ACC Verb-COMP] N]-ACC Verb-Q

Among the four potential island structures they tested, *whether*-clauses, CNPs, subjects, and adjuncts, they found a significant interaction between DEPENDENCY LENGTH and EMBEDDED STRUCTURE only with adjuncts. However, this significant interaction turns out to be for the wrong reasons, with the means for the adjunct conditions numerically higher than the means for the CP conditions. Thus, none of the four structures appears to be an island with respect to *wh*-in-situ in Japanese.

More recently, however, Tanaka and Schwarz (2018) examined the acceptability of *wh*-in-situ inside embedded CPs and relative clauses (RCs) in the context of second language acquisition of Japanese. The study aimed to examine whether L1 English learners of Japanese can learn that *wh*-in-situ inside an RC like (14) is acceptable despite the fact that *wh*-extraction out of RCs in English is unacceptable (e.g. Huang 1982; Choe 1987; Nishigauchi 1990; Richards 2008).

(14)    Taro-wa [RC [ec$_i$ ***nani*-o**    kat-ta] onnanoko$_i$]-o mi-mashi-ta-ka?

          T-TOP    [RC [ec ***what*-ACC** buy-PST] girl]-ACC      see-POL-PST-Q

          'What did Taro see the girl who bought?'

Their experiment had a 2 × 2 design with QUESTION TYPE (yes/no vs. *wh*-in-situ) and EMBEDDED STRUCTURE (CP vs. RC). Schematic examples of their experimental sentences are given in (15).

(15)    a. Yes/no question with CP

        NP-TOP  [NP-NOM  NP-ACC    Verb]-COMP  Verb-Q

    b. Yes/no question with RC

        NP-TOP  [RC [ec$_i$  NP-ACC    Verb] NP$_i$]-ACC Verb-Q

    c. *Wh*-in-situ with CP

        NP-TOP  [NP-NOM  **what**-ACC    Verb]-COMP  Verb-Q

    d. *Wh*-in-situ with RC

        NP-TOP  [RC [ec$_i$  **what**-ACC    Verb] NP$_i$]-ACC Verb-Q

Participants were asked to judge the acceptability of the experimental sentences on a four-point scale with "I don't know" as an out-of-scale option. Interestingly, the results with their 16 native speakers showed a significant interaction between QUESTION TYPE and STRUCTURE, with the mean for the sentences with *wh*-in-situ inside an RC (15d) showing additional degradation of acceptability, i.e. island effects.

It is important to note that Tanaka and Schwartz (2018) also examined the acceptability of the adjunct *wh*-in-situ, *naze* 'why,' inside RCs, as adjunct *wh*-phrases that mean 'why' in Chinese, Japanese and Korean are known to incur island violations (e.g. Huang 1982; Fukui 1988; Lasnik & Saito 1992;

Aoun & Li 1993; Tsai 1994, 1997, 1999; Kishimoto 2005; Ko 2005). When they compared the means for sentences with *naze* 'why' inside RCs and sentences with *nani* 'what' inside RCs (15d), the means for the latter were significantly higher than those for the former. In addition, while the mean acceptability for *naze* 'why' inside RCs was below the overall mean, the mean acceptability for (15d) was above it. These observations suggest that what Tanaka and Schwartz discovered with *wh*-in-situ inside RCs in Japanese is an instance of "subliminal island effects," where there is a significant interaction between the dependency length and the embedded structure, suggesting the presence of island effects, although the mean acceptability judgments of all four conditions are relatively high (e.g. Almeida 2014; Kush et al. 2018; Keshev & Meltzer-Asscher 2019). The question is where the subliminal island effects that Tanaka and Schwartz discovered come from. Are they reflections of a grammatical violation or influences of extragrammatical factors?

### 16.4.2  *Wh*-in-situ and Islands in Korean

Kim (2015) and Kim and Goodall (2016) examined whether *wh*-in-situ inside an interrogative embedded clause in Korean can take the matrix scope, i.e. whether it can "escape" the interrogative embedded clause. In Korean, as in many other languages, *wh*-phrases involve "indeterminate pronouns" licensed by an interrogative marker. For instance, the indeterminate pronoun *nwukwu* is interpreted as a *wh*-expression *who* when it is in a particular structural relationship with an interrogative marker such as *ni* in (16). When *nwukwu* is not licensed by an interrogative marker, it is interpreted as an existential pronoun (i.e. 'someone'). Thus, questions like (16) are potentially ambiguous between *wh*-questions and yes/no questions, as indicated below.[10]

(16)    Mary-nun [Obama-ka **nwukwu**-ul manna-ss-ta-**ko**] tul-ess-**ni**?
        M-TOP    O-NOM    **who**-ACC    meet-PST-DECL-C hear-PST-Q
        *Wh*-question reading: 'Who did Mary hear that Obama met?'
        Yes/no question reading: 'Did Mary hear that Obama met somebody?'

In a 2 × 2 experiment, Kim and Goodall (2016) manipulated the embedded structure (declarative embedded clauses vs. interrogative embedded clauses) and the position of indeterminate pronouns (matrix vs. embedded), as schematically represented in the (a) examples (17a–20a) below. The resulting four conditions were paired with two different answers. One type of answer provided an identity of an individual (e.g.

---

[10] Japanese *wh*-phrases also involve indeterminate pronouns (e.g. Kuroda 1965; Nishigauchi 1990). However, the indeterminate pronouns in Japanese do not exhibit the same kind of ambiguity, as they must be adjacent to the interrogative marker in order to be interpreted as existential pronouns, as in *dare-ka* 'someone.'

*Hillary-nun* 'Hillary-NOM'), as in the (b) examples in (17b–20b), which is felicitous only as an answer to a *wh*-question. The other type of answer provided an affirmative answer to the question (*Ney, Verb-ess-eyo* 'Yes, Verb-PST-DECL'), as in the (c) examples in (17c–20c), which is felicitous only as an answer to a yes/no question.

(17)    Declarative/matrix indeterminate pronoun
        a. Q: **Who**-NOM  [NP-NOM  NP-ACC  Verb-c]  Verb-Q
        b. A: NP-NOM. (*wh*-question answer)
        c. A: Yes, Verb. (yes/no question answer)

(18)    Interrogative/matrix indeterminate pronoun
        a. Q: **Who**-NOM  [NP-NOM  NP-ACC  Verb-Q]  Verb-Q
        b. A: NP-NOM. (*wh*-question answer)
        c. A: Yes, Verb. (yes/no question answer)

(19)    Declarative/embedded indeterminate pronoun
        a. Q: NP-NOM  [NP-NOM  **who**-ACC  Verb-c]  Verb-Q
        b. A: NP-ACC. (*wh*-question answer)
        c. A: Yes, Verb. (yes/no question answer)

(20)    Interrogative/embedded indeterminate pronoun
        a. Q: NP-NOM  [NP-NOM  **who**-ACC  Verb-Q]  Verb-Q
        b. A: NP-ACC. (*wh*-question answer)
        c. A: Yes, Verb. (yes/no question answer)

Each question–answer pair was preceded by a context that provided the location and a list of people involved. Participants read the questions and the paired answers and judged the acceptability of the answers with respect to the paired questions on a seven-point scale.

The study found a significant interaction between the two factors, the embedded structure and the position of indeterminate pronouns. Sentences with an interrogative embedded clause and an embedded indeterminate pronoun like (20a) with the *wh*-question answer (20b) were rated significantly lower than sentences with a declarative embedded clause with an embedded indeterminate pronoun like (19a) with the *wh*-question answer (19b). The authors argued that their findings show that indeterminate pronouns inside an interrogative embedded clause cannot take the matrix scope, unlike ones inside a declarative embedded clause, even though there is an interrogative particle in the matrix domain in both cases. In other words, interrogative embedded clauses are islands with *wh*-in-situ in Korean. The study also examined potential island effects of adjuncts with *wh*-in-situ, with a similar 2 × 2 factorial experiment with the embedded structure (declarative vs. adjunct clause headed by *ttay* 'when') and the position of the *wh*-in-situ (matrix vs. embedded). The results showed no significant interaction between these two factors.

Kim and Goodall (2016) further argued that the island effects observed with indeterminate pronouns inside interrogative embedded clauses in Korean are expected, under the assumption that there is a dependency between an indeterminate pronoun and an interrogative marker. If this dependency determines the scope of indeterminate pronouns, in terms of processing, it follows that the scope of indeterminate pronouns inside interrogative embedded clauses will always be limited to the embedded clause, because the search for an interrogative marker will always be satisfied within the embedded clause. A similar conclusion can be drawn if the grammar dictates that the dependency between an indeterminate pronoun and an interrogative marker must be local.

### 16.4.3  *Wh*-in-situ and Islands in Chinese

To the best of my knowledge, only one experimental study has examined *wh*-in-situ and its potential interaction with islands in Chinese, that of Lu et al. (2020). The study examined the following well-known contrast between argument *wh*-in-situ and adjunct *wh*-in-situ inside an island such as an RC.

(21)    a. Akiu  kan-bu-qi        [$_{RC}$ [$ec_i$        zuo **shenme**]        de ren$_i$]

          Akiu  look-not up        [$_{RC}$ [ec        do  **what**]        DE person]

          'What is the thing/job x such that Akiu despises people who do x?'

       b. *Akiu xihuan        [$_{RC}$ [Luxun        **weishenme** xie  $ec_i$ de        shu$_i$]

          Akiu  like        [$_{RC}$ [Luxun        **why**        write ec] de]        book]

          'What is the reason x such that Akiu likes books that Luxun wrote for x?'

          (Tsai 1999: 42–43, (6a), (6b))

As mentioned in Section 16.4.2, adjunct *wh*-phrases that mean 'why' in Chinese, Japanese, and Korean have been claimed to be island-sensitive, unlike argument *wh*-phrases e.g. (Huang 1982; Fukui 1988; Lasnik & Saito 1992; Aoun & Li 1993; Tsai 1994, 1999; Kishimoto 2005; Ko 2005). Lu et al. experimentally tested this claim with Chinese with a 2 × 2 × 2 design acceptability judgment experiment that manipulated three binary factors: (i) DEPENDENCY LENGTH (short vs. long), (ii) EMBEDDED STRUCTURE (CP vs. RC) and (iii) WH-PHRASE (who/what vs. why), which resulted in the following eight conditions.

(22)    a. Short dependency & CP & argument *wh*-phrase

          NP Verb [**who** Verb [$_{CP}$ NP        Verb        NP]]

       b. Short dependency & CP & adjunct *wh*-phrase

          NP Verb [NP  **why** Verb        [$_{CP}$ NP        Verb  NP]]

       c. Short dependency & RC & argument *wh*-phrase

          NP Verb [**who** Verb [$_{RC}$ [$ec_i$ Verb    NP]        de        NP$_i$]]

       d. Short dependency & RC & adjunct *wh*-phrase

          NP Verb [NP  **why** Verb        [$_{RC}$ [$ec_i$ Verb    NP]  de  NP$_i$]]

e. Long dependency & CP & argument *wh*-phrase
   NP Verb [NP   Verb [CP NP           Verb           ***what***]]
f. Long dependency & CP & adjunct *wh*-phrase
   NP Verb [NP   Verb [CP NP           ***why***           Verb   NP]]
g. Long dependency & RC & argument *wh*-phrase
   NP Verb [NP   Verb [RC [eci Verb   ***what***]           de       NPi]]
h. Long dependency & RC & adjunct *wh*-phrase
   NP Verb [NP   Verb [RC [eci ***why***   Verb           NP]   de   NPi]]

The study found a significant interaction between DEPENDENCY LENGTH and EMBEDDED STRUCTURE, but not between EMBEDDED STRUCTURE and WH-PHRASE or DEPENDENCY LENGTH and WH-PHRASE. While the mean for the sentences with an argument *wh*-phrase inside RCs was numerically higher than the mean for the sentences with an adjunct *wh*-phrase (*why*) inside RCs, the difference is not significant. Importantly, the island effects were found in both the argument *wh*-phrase and the adjunct (*why*) *wh*-phrase conditions, contradicting the well-accepted claim that the contrast in (21) exists.

### 16.4.4  Section Summary

There are several interesting findings from the recent experimental studies on *wh*-in-situ in East Asian languages. First, *wh*-in-situ is sensitive to some island structures possibly for different reasons. Second, RC emerges as a clear case of an island with respect to *wh*-in-situ.[11] Third, there may be non-trivial differences among *wh*-in-situ in these languages. In Japanese, an argument *wh*-in-situ inside RC shows what appear to be subliminal island effects, with its mean acceptability clearly higher than that of an adjunct (*why*) *wh*-in-situ inside RC.[12] In contrast, a *wh*-in-situ inside RC seems to show real island effects in Chinese, regardless of the argument/adjunct status of the *wh*-phrase. These findings raise a new set of questions about *wh*-in-situ in East Asian languages.

## 16.5  Concluding Remarks

This chapter surveyed recent acceptability and truth-value judgment studies in Chinese, Japanese, and Korean that investigated three syntactic phenomena: split intransitivity (Section 16.2), quantifier scope

---

[11] Findings from an experimental study reported by Fukuda and Sprouse (2019) suggest that RCs are islands with respect to scrambling in Japanese as well, while complex NPs headed by *to yuu* 'that say' are not islands.

[12] Omaki et al. (2020) also found a significant difference in the acceptability of an argument *wh*-in-situ and an adjunct (*why*) *wh*-in-situ inside complex NP subjects and objects.

(Section 16.3), and *wh*-in-situ (Section 16.4). There are many other syntactic phenomena in East Asian languages that have also been experimentally investigated. Studies on pronouns and anaphors are good examples. There have been a number of studies that experimentally examined possible interpretations of morphologically simple and complex anaphors in Chinese, Japanese, and Korean (Lee 1990; Kim et al. 2009; Kim & Yoon 2009; Han et al. 2010; Joo 2014; Chen 2019). The question of whether or not null and overt pronouns in Japanese and Korean can be interpreted as bound-variables has also motivated many experimental syntactic studies (Kanno 1997; Kim & Han 2016; Hong & Nakayama 2017; Kim 2019).

The fact that some of the experimental studies reviewed in this chapter provided novel empirical observations that conflict with the relevant observations in previous studies (e.g. *wh*-in-situ inside RCs in Japanese and Chinese) might raise a question about the replicability of informal acceptability judgments in previous theoretical studies that focused on East Asian languages. Myers (2009) examined the informal judgments presented in a single journal article on a topic in Chinese syntax (Li 1998) and showed that only four out of six acceptability contrasts discussed were replicated in his acceptability judgment experiment ($\approx$ 67 percent). More recently, Linzen and Oseki (2018) examined 14 potentially controversial acceptability contrasts taken from 14 different theoretical syntax studies on Japanese (as well as 14 acceptability contrasts in Hebrew) and showed that only 10 of them replicated with a significant difference in the expected direction ($\approx$ 71 percent). Now, there is a substantial body of literature on replicability of informal acceptability judgments in the theoretical literature with English data (e.g. Sprouse & Almeida 2012, 2013; Gibson & Fedorenko 2013; Gibson et al. 2013; Sprouse et al. 2013), and a consensus among these studies appears to be that the replication rates are generally high, at 80 to 90 percent. Setting aside the question of whether these numbers are high enough, they are higher than the replication rates found by Myers (2009) and Linzen and Oseki (2018), which are around 70 percent. Furthermore, Linzen and Oseki noted that, out of 148 contrasts that Sprouse et al. (2013) examined, 13 of them were originally question-marked, suggesting that they involve subtler judgments. Out of those 13 subtle contrasts, only one failed to replicate in the original study. In contrast, as mentioned above, four out of the 14 potentially controversial contrasts with Japanese sentences that Linzen and Oseki examined failed to replicate.

Do the lower replication rates with the informal judgments with Chinese and Japanese sentences mean that the informal judgments in these languages are less reliable than the informal judgments in English? Linzen and Oseki (2018) made another observation that suggests that the picture is more complicated than these numbers suggest. They pointed out that 20 of the 148 contrasts that Sprouse et al. (2013) examined involve less than "medium" effect sizes, and of those, five showed a numerical tendency opposite to the claims of the original observations (i.e. the ones that are supposed to be less acceptable were rated better than the ones that are supposed to be more acceptable). As for the results of the Japanese study by Linzen and Oseki, among the four out of 14 contrasts that did not reach significance, three of them showed the opposite numerical tendency to the claimed contrast. These numbers – five out of 20 (Sprouse et al. 2013) and three out of 14 (Linzen & Oseki 2018) – are comparable. Given these conflicting findings, Linzen and Oseki suggested that studies that involve more direct comparisons between languages in terms of replicability of informal judgments would be informative.

# References

Ahn, S.-H. (1990). Korean quantification and Universal Grammar. Doctoral dissertation, University of Connecticut.

Almeida, D. (2014). Subliminal *wh*-islands in Brazilian Portuguese and the consequences for syntactic theory. *Revista da ABRALIN*, 13, 55–93.

Anderson, C. (2004). The structure and real-time comprehension of quantifier scope ambiguity. Doctoral dissertation, Northwestern University.

Aoun, J. & Li, Y.-H. A. (1993). *Syntax of Scope*. Cambridge, MA: MIT Press.

Bard, E. G., Robertson, D., & Sorace, A. (1996). Magnitude estimation of linguistic acceptability. *Language*, 72, 32–68.

Burzio, L. (1981). Intransitive verbs and Italian auxiliaries. Doctoral dissertation, Massachusetts Institute of Technology.

Burzio, L. (1986). *Italian Syntax: A Government and Binding Approach*. Dordrecht: Reidel.

Chen, Y. (2019). The acquisition of Japanese relative clauses by L1 Chinese learners. Doctoral dissertation, University of Hawai'i at Mānoa.

Choe, J. W. (1987). LF movement and pied-piping. *Linguistic Inquiry*, 18, 348–353.

Cooper, R. (1979). Variable binding and relative clauses. In F. Guenthner & S. J. Schmidt, eds., *Formal Semantics and Pragmatics for Natural Languages*. Dordrecht: Reidel, pp. 131–169.

Cowart, W. (1997). *Experimental Syntax: Applying Objective Methods to Sentence Judgments*. Thousand Oaks, CA: Sage.

Emonds, J. (1978). The verbal complex V'-V in French. *Linguistic Inquiry*, 9, 151–175.

Featherston, S. (2005a). *That*-trace in German. *Lingua*, 115, 1277–1302.

Featherston, S. (2005b). Magnitude estimation and what it can do for your syntax: Some *wh*-constraints in German. *Lingua*, 115, 1525–1550.

Fodor, J. & Sag, I. (1982). Referential and quantificational indefinites. *Linguistics and Philosophy*, 5, 355–398.

Fukuda, S. (2017). Split intransitivity in Japanese is syntactic: Evidence for the Unaccusative Hypothesis from sentence acceptability and truth value judgment experiments. *Glossa: A Journal of General Linguistics*, 2(1), 83. DOI: 10.5334/gjgl.268

Fukuda, S, Nakao, C., Omaki, A., & M. Polinsky. (2016). Japanese subjects and objects are equally open to subextraction. Why? In A. Sugawara, S. Hayashi, & S. Ito, eds., *Proceedings of the Eighth Formal Approaches to Japanese Linguistics* (FAJL8). Cambridge, MA: MIT Working Papers in Linguistics, pp. 13–29.

Fukuda, S. & Sprouse, J. (2019). Islandhood of Japanese complex NPs and the factorial definition of island effects. Manuscript, University of Hawai'i at Mānoa and University of Connecticut.

Fukui, N. (1988). LF extraction of *naze*: Some theoretical implications. *Natural Language and Linguistic Theory*, 6, 503–526.

Fukushima, K. (2003). Verb-raising and numeral classifiers in Japanese: Incompatible bedfellows. *Journal of East Asian Linguistics*, 12, 313–347.

Gerdts, D. (1987). Surface case and grammatical relations in Korean: The evidence from quantifier float. *Studies in Language*, 11, 181–197.

Gibson, E. & Fedorenko, E. (2013). The need for quantitative methods in syntax and semantics research. *Language and Cognitive Processes*, 28, 88–124.

Gibson, E., Piantadosi, S. T., & Fedorenko, E. (2013). Quantitative methods in syntax/semantics research: A response to Sprouse and Almeida (2013). *Language and Cognitive Processes*, 28, 229–240.

Han, C.-H. (2013). On the syntax of relative clauses in Korean. *Canadian Journal of Linguistics*, 58, 319–347.

Han, C.-H., Lidz, J., & Musolino, J. (2007). Verb-raising and grammar competition in Korean: Evidence from negation and quantifier scope. *Linguistic Inquiry*, 38, 1–47.

Han, C.-H., Storoshenko, D. R., & Sakurai, Y. (2009a). An experimental investigation into scope rigidity in Japanese. *Current Issues in Unity and Diversity of Languages: Collection of the Papers Selected from the 18th International Congress of Linguistics*. Seoul: The Linguistic Society of Korea.

Han, C.-H., Storoshenko, D. R., & Sakurai, Y. (2009b). An experimental investigation into the placement of the verb in the clause structure of Japanese. *Proceedings of the 2007 International Conference on Linguistics in Korea* (ICLK-2007). Seoul: The Linguistic Society of Korea.

Han, C.-H., Storoshenko, D. R., & Walshe, R. C. (2010). An experimental study of the grammatical status of *caki* in Korean. *Japanese/Korean Linguistics*, 19, 81–94.

Hirakawa, M. (1999). L2 acquisition of Japanese unaccusative verbs by speakers of English and Chinese. In K. Kanno, ed., *The Acquisition of Japanese as a Second Language*. Amsterdam: John Benjamins, pp. 89–113.

Hirakawa, M. (2001). L2 acquisition of Japanese unaccusative verbs. *Studies in Second Language Acquisition*, 23, 221–245.

Hoji, H. (1985). Logical Form constraints and configurational structures in Japanese. Doctoral dissertation, University of Washington.

Hong, S. & Nakayama, N. (2017). *Kare* and the acquisition of bound variable interpretations by Korean speaking learners of Japanese. In M. Nakayama, Y.-C. Su, & A. Huang, eds., *Studies in Chinese and Japanese Language Acquisition: In Honor of Stephen Crain*. Amsterdam: John Benjamins, pp. 85–106.

Huang, C.-T. J. (1982). Logical relations in Chinese and the theory of grammar. Doctoral dissertation, Massachusetts Institute of Technology.

Huang, C.-T. J. (1987). Existential sentences in Chinese and (in)definiteness. In E. J. Reuland & A. G. B. ter Meulen, eds., *The Representation of (In)definiteness*. Cambridge, MA: MIT Press, pp. 226–253.

Jiang, L. (2012). Nominal arguments and language variation. Doctoral dissertation, Harvard University.

Joo, K.-J. (2014). Children's interpretation of the Korean reflexive pronouns *caki* and *caki-casin*. Doctoral dissertation, University of Hawai'i at Mānoa.

Jurka, J. (2010). The importance of being a complement: the CED effects revisited. Doctoral dissertation, University of Maryland, College Park.

Jurka, J., Nakao, C., & Omaki, A. (2011). It's not the end of the CED as we know it: Revisiting German and Japanese subject islands. In M. B. Washburn, K. McKinney-Bock, E. Varis, A. Sawyer, & B. Tomaszewicz, eds., *Proceedings of the 28th West Coast Conference on Formal Linguistics*. Somerville, MA: Cascadilla Proceedings Project, pp. 124–132.

Kang, B.-M. (2002). Categories and meanings of Korean floating quantifiers: With some reference to Japanese. *Journal of East Asian Linguistics*, 1, 375–398.

Kanno, K. (1997). The acquisition of null and overt pronominals in Japanese by English speakers. *Second Language Research*, 13(3), 265–287.

Keller, F. (2000). Gradience in grammar: Experimental and computational aspects of degrees of grammaticality. Doctoral dissertation, University of Edinburgh.

Keller, F. & Sorace, A. (2003). Gradient auxiliary selection and impersonal passivization in German: An experimental investigation. *Journal of Linguistics*, 39, 57–108.

Keshev, K. & Meltzer-Asscher, A. (2019). A processing-based account of subliminal *wh*-island effects. *Natural Language and Linguistic Theory*, 37, 621–57.

Kim, B. (2015). Sensitivity to islands in Korean–English bilinguals. Doctoral dissertation, University of California, San Diego.

Kim, B. & Goodall, G. (2016). Islands and non-islands in native and heritage Korean. *Frontiers in Psychology*, 7, 134. DOI: 10.3389/fpsyg.2016.00134

Kim, J.-H., Montrul, S., & Yoon, J.-H. (2009). Binding interpretations of anaphors by Korean heritage speakers. *Language Acquisition*, 16, 3–35.

Kim, J.-H. & Yoon, J.-H. (2009). Long-distance bound local anaphors in Korean: An empirical study of the Korean anaphor *caki-casin*. *Lingua*, 119, 733–755.

Kim, K.-M. (2019). The syntax of Korean anaphora: An experimental investigation. Doctoral dissertation, Simon Frazer University.

Kim, K.-M. & Han, C.-H. (2016). Inter-speaker variation in Korean pronouns. In P. Grosz & P. Patel-Grosz, eds., *The Impact of Pronominal Form on Interpretation*. Berlin: De Gruyter Mouton, pp. 347–372.

Kishimoto, H. (2005). Wh-in-situ and movement in Sinhala questions. *Natural Language and Linguistic Theory*, 23, 1–51.

Ko, H. (2005). Syntax of *why*-in-situ: Merge into [Spec, CP] in the overt syntax. *Natural Language and Linguistic Theory*, 23, 867–916.

Ko, H. (2007). Asymmetries in scrambling and cyclic linearization. *Linguistic Inquiry*, 38, 49–83.

Ko, H. & Oh, E. (2010). A hybrid approach to floating quantifiers: Experimental evidence. *Japanese/Korean Linguistics*, 19, 171–184.

Ko, H. & Oh, E. (2012). A hybrid approach to floating quantifiers: Some experimental evidence. *Linguistic Research*, 29, 69–106.

Koizumi, M. (2000). String vacuous overt verb-raising. *Journal of East Asian Linguistics*, 9, 227–285.

Kratzer, A. (1994). On external arguments. In E. Benedicto & J. Runner, eds., *Functional Projections: University of Massachusetts Occasional Papers 17*, Amherst, MA: University of Massachusetts, GLSA, pp.103–130.

Kratzer, A. (1996). Severing the external argument from the verb. In J. Rooryck & L. Zariing, eds., *Phrase Structure and the Lexicon*. Dordrecht: Kluwer, pp. 109–137.

Kratzer, A. (1998). Scope or pseudoscope? Are there wide scope indefinites? In S. Rothstein, ed., *Events and Grammar*. Dordrecht: Kluwer, pp. 163–196.

Kuno, S. (1973). *The Structure of the Japanese Language*. Cambridge, MA: MIT Press.

Kuroda, S.-Y. (1965). Generative grammatical studies in the Japanese language. Doctoral dissertation, Massachusetts Institute of Technology. Reprinted, New York: Garland, 1979.

Kuroda, S.-Y. (1970). Remarks on the notion of subject with reference to words like *also, even*, or *only*, part 2. *Annual Bulletin – Research Institute of Logopedics and Phoniatrics, Tokyo University*. Tokyo: Tokyo University, vol. 4, pp. 127–152.

Kush, D., Lohndal, T., & Sprouse, J. (2018). Investigating variation in island effects: A case study of Norwegian *wh*-extraction. *Natural Language and Linguistic Theory*, 36, 743–779.

Lasnik, H. & Saito, M. (1992). *Move α: Conditions on Its Application and Output*. Cambridge, MA: MIT Press.

Laws, J. & Yuen, B. (2010). Is the core-peripheral distinction for unaccusative verbs cross-linguistically consistent? Empirical evidence from Mandarin. *Chinese Language and Discourse*, 1, 220–263.

Lee, C.-M. (1989). (In-)definites, case-markers, classifiers and quantifiers in Korean. In S. Kuno, I.-H. Lee, J. Whitman, S.-Y. Bak, Y.-S. Kang & Y.-J. Kim, eds., *Harvard Studies in Korean Linguistics*, 3, 469–487.

Lee, H. (1990). Logical relations in the child's grammar: Relative scope, bound variables, and long-distance binding in Korean. Doctoral dissertation, University of California, Irvine.

Lee, S. (2009). Interpreting scope ambiguity in first and second language processing: Universal quantifier and negation. Doctoral dissertation, University of Hawai'i at Mānoa.

Lee, T. (2011). Grammatical knowledge of Korean heritage speakers. *Linguistic Approaches to Bilingualism*, 1, 149–174.

Lee, T. H.-T. (1986). Studies on quantification in Chinese. Doctoral dissertation, University of California, Los Angeles.

Li, Y.-H. A. (1998). Argument determiner phrases and number phrases. *Linguistic Inquiry*, 29(4), 693–702.

Linzen, T. & Oseki, Y. (2018). The reliability of acceptability judgments across languages. *Glossa: A Journal of General Linguistics*, 3(1), 100. DOI:10.5334/gjgl.528

Liu, F.-H. (1997). *Scope and Specificity*. Amsterdam: John Benjamins.

Liu, F.-H. (2007). Auxiliary selection in Chinese. In R. Aranovich, ed., *Split Auxiliary Systems*. Amsterdam: John Benjamins, pp. 181–205.

Lu, J., Thompson, C. K., & Yoshida, M. (2020). Chinese *wh*-in-situ and islands: A formal judgment study. *Linguistic Inquiry*, 51(3), 611–623.

Miyagawa, S. (1989). *Structure and Case Marking in Japanese*. San Diego, CA: Academic Press.

Miyagawa, S. (2006). Locality in syntax and floated numeral quantifiers in Japanese and Korean. *Japanese/Korean Linguistics*, 14, 270–282.

Myers, J. (2009). The design and analysis of small-scale syntactic judgment experiments. *Lingua*, 119, 425–444.

Myers, J. (2012). Testing adjunct and conjunct island constraints in Chinese. *Language and Linguistics*, 13, 437–470.

Nishigauchi, T. (1990). *Quantification in the Theory of Grammar*. Dordrecht: Kluwer.

O'Grady, W. (1991). *Categories and Case: The Sentence Structure of Korean*. Amsterdam: John Benjamins.

Omaki, A., Fukuda, S., Nakao, C., & Polinsky, M. (2020). Subextraction in Japanese and subject–object symmetry. *Natural Language and Linguistic Theory*, 38, 627–669.

Otani, K. & Whitman, J. (1991). V-raising and VP-ellipsis. *Linguistic Inquiry*, 22, 345–358.

Pan, H. (1996). Imperfective aspect *zhe*, agent deletion, and locative inversion in Mandarin Chinese. *Natural Language and Linguistic Theory*, 14, 409–432.

Park, K. (1992). Light verb constructions in Korean and Japanese. Doctoral dissertation, University of North Carolina, Chapel Hill.

Park, M.-K. (1998). Negation and the placement of verb in Korean. *Language Research*, 34, 709–736.

Perlmutter, D. M. (1978). Impersonal passives and the unaccusative hypothesis. In *Proceedings of the 4th Annual Meeting of the Berkeley Linguistics Society*. Berkeley, CA: University of California, Berkeley Linguistics Society, pp. 157–185.

Pollock, J.-Y. (1989). Verb movement, Universal Grammar, and the structure of IP. *Linguistic Inquiry*, 20, 365–424.

Reinhart, T. (1976). The syntactic domain of anaphora. Doctoral dissertation, Massachusetts Institute of Technology.

Reinhart, T. (1997). Quantifier scope: How labor is divided between QR and choice functions. *Linguistics and Philosophy*, 20, 335–397.

Richards, N. (2008). *Wh*-questions. In S. Miyagawa & M. Saito, eds., *The Oxford Handbook of Japanese Linguistics*. Oxford: Oxford University Press, pp. 348–371.

Ross, J. R. (1967). Constraints on variables in syntax. Doctoral dissertation, Massachusetts Institute of Technology.

Ross, J. R. (1987). *Infinite Syntax!* Norwood, NJ: Ablex.

Ruys, E. G. (1992). The scope of indefinites. Doctoral dissertation, Utrecht University.

Schütze, C. T. (1996). *The Empirical Base of Linguistics: Grammaticality Judgments and Linguistic Methodology*. Chicago: University of Chicago Press.

Scontras, G., Polinsky, M., Tsai, C.-Y. E., & Mai, K. (2017). Cross-linguistic scope ambiguity: When two systems meet. *Glossa: A Journal of General Linguistics*, 2 (1), 36. DOI: 10.5334/gjgl.198

Scontras, G., Tsai, C.-Y. E., Mai, K., & Polinsky, M. (2014). Chinese scope: An experimental investigation. *Proceedings of Sinn und Bedeutung*, 18, 396–414.

Sohn, K.-W. (1995). Negative polarity items, scope and economy. Doctoral dissertation, University of Connecticut.

Sorace, A. (1993). Incomplete vs. divergent representation of unaccusativity in non-native grammars of Italian. *Second Language Research*, 9, 22–47.

Sorace, A. (1995). Acquiring linking rules and argument structures in a second language: The unaccusative/unergative distinction. In L. Eubank, L. Selinker, & M. Sharwood Smith, eds., *The Current State of Interlanguage: Studies in Honor of William E. Rutherford*. Amsterdam and Philadelphia: John Benjamins, pp. 153–175.

Sorace, A. (2000). Gradients in auxiliary selection with intransitive verbs. *Language*, 76, 859–890.

Sorace, A. & Shomura, Y. (2001). Lexical constraints on the acquisition of split intransitivity. *Studies in Second Language Acquisition*, 23, 247–278.

Sprouse, J. (2007). A program for experimental syntax. Doctoral dissertation, University of Maryland, College Park.

Sprouse, J. & Almeida, D. (2012). Assessing the reliability of textbook data in syntax: Adger's core syntax. *Journal of Linguistics*, 48, 609–652.

Sprouse, J. & Almeida, D. (2013). The empirical status of data in syntax: A reply to Gibson and Fedorenko. *Language and Cognitive Processes*, 28, 222–228.

Sprouse, J., Fukuda, S., Ono, H., & Kluender, R. (2011). Reverse island effects and the backward search for a licensor in multiple *wh*-questions. *Syntax*, 14, 179–203.

Sprouse, J. & Hornstein, N. (2013). *Experimental Syntax and Island Effects*. Cambridge: Cambridge University Press.

Sprouse, J., Schütze, C. T., & Almeida, D. (2013). A comparison of informal and formal acceptability judgments using a random sample from *Linguistic Inquiry* 2001–2010. *Lingua*, 134, 219–248.

Sprouse, J., Wagers, M., & Phillips, C. (2012). A test of the relation between working memory capacity and syntactic island effects. *Language*, 88, 82–123.

Tanaka, N. & Schwartz, B. D. (2018). Investigating relative clause island effects in native and nonnative adult speakers of Japanese. In A. B. Bertolini & M. J. Kaplan, eds., *Proceedings of the 42nd Annual Boston University Conference on Language Development*. Somerville, MA: Cascadilla Proceedings Project, pp. 750–763.

Tsai, W.-T. D. (1994). On nominal islands and LE extraction in Chinese. *Natural Language and Linguistic Theory*, 12, 121–175.

Tsai, W.-T. D. (1997). On the absence of island effects. *Tsing Hua Journal of Chinese Studies, New Series*, 27, 125–149.

Tsai, W.-T. D. (1999). On lexical courtesy. *Journal of East Asian Linguistics*, 8, 39–73.

Yoon, J.-H. (1994). Korean verbal inflection and Checking Theory. In H. Harley & C. Phillips, eds., *MIT Working Papers in Linguistics 22: Morphology–Syntax Connection*. Cambridge, MA: MIT Press, pp. 251–270.

Yuan, B. (1999). Acquiring the unaccusative/unergative distinction in a second language: Evidence from English-speaking learners of L2 Chinese. *Linguistics*, 37, 275–296.

Zenker, F. & Schwartz, B. D. (2017). Topicalization from adjuncts in English vs. Chinese vs. Chinese–English interlanguage. In M. LaMendola & J. Scott, eds., *Proceedings of the 41st Annual Boston University Conference on Language Development*. Somerville, MA: Cascadilla Proceedings Project, pp. 806–819.

Zhou, P. & Gao, L. (2009). Scope processing in Chinese. *Journal of Psycholinguistic Research*, 38, 11–24.

# 17

# Acceptability Experiments in Romance Languages

Tania Leal and Timothy Gupton

## 17.1 Introduction: The Empirical and Methodological Landscape

Generative linguistics proposes a theory which, based on the features of human language, attempts to account for linguistic phenomena across languages (Chomsky 1975). To achieve this goal, some of the earliest tests of generative theory applied theoretical models to cross-linguistic data from (informal) acceptability judgments, where speakers provide their spontaneous impressions (intuitions) on whether or not a particular sentence string is possible in their language (Schütze & Sprouse 2014). For instance, Perlmutter (1971) provided intuitions regarding referential null subjects in Romance languages that provided ground-breaking insight leading later to the formulation of the Null-Subject Parameter and Standard Parameter Theory (Chomsky 1981). Since then, data-gathering methods have been recognized as a vital tool in linguistic research, with acceptability judgments being particularly useful to generative researchers. Acceptability judgment *experiments* – formal experiments that systematically elicit speaker intuitions – move beyond informal acceptability judgment elicitation and can range from yes/no tasks to magnitude estimation tasks that can be time-sensitive and involve reaction times. Because of their importance, our main goal here is to highlight the vital role that acceptability experiments have played in the generative study of Romance languages.

Acceptability experiments have been central to generative linguistics in part because the framework has historically prioritized linguistic *competence* (the abstract linguistic knowledge of a form) over *performance* (the use of a form in real time), which may be particularly vulnerable to extralinguistic factors. The value of acceptability experiments resides in the fact that these are sophisticated tools attempting to factor out the performance-level variability that has been shown to affect speaker data. For instance, when speakers do not produce a given structure, we cannot conclude that the structure is impossible or absent from their grammar. Acceptability experiments, on the other hand, can elicit judgments on sequences that might occur infrequently or be absent in corpora or spontaneous production (see Chapter 25 for more detailed discussion of corpus studies). Therefore, such data hold the potential to provide the linguistic researcher with a vital window on what is possible as well as impossible in language. Researchers such as Schütze and Sprouse (2014) have argued that for these, and other, reasons, acceptability experiments are vital to the field's progress.

Any attempt to investigate the ways in which acceptability experiments have contributed to the study of Romance languages must necessarily constitute a selective overview. Our goal is to present examples of research in which acceptability experiments have played a distinct role in advancing our knowledge of the grammars of particular varieties and, in turn, linguistic theory. The first section focuses on the experimental results from acceptability experiments in the study of Romance languages. First, we focus on word order in *wh*-questions as an example where acceptability experiments have been used to build the theory. This research, which has been dependent on acceptability experiments, shows that our cross-linguistic knowledge of word order in *wh*-questions has increased in sophistication, ultimately revealing a hierarchy of gradient acceptability. Next, we show how acceptability experiments are flexible tools that can be modified (e.g. adding a modality or including a discourse context) to study infrequent structures, such as Clitic left dislocation (CLLD) and Fronted Focus, which involve multiple interfaces.

Building on the notion of data triangulation, we then discuss informational focus in Spanish, where data from acceptability experiments has allowed researchers a more nuanced view of the results gathered from elicited production. In particular, we concentrate on Zubizarreta's (1998) proposal of prosodically motivated movement, exploring how methodological choices can impact results. Finally, we survey the research on the area of control and raising, where the data stemming from acceptability experiments has helped to identify areas of debate and disagreement, highlighting the need for further research with alternative methodologies.

A secondary goal of our chapter is to outline future directions in the research of Romance languages using acceptability experiments. First, we consider some pros and cons of using acceptability experiments in the study of less-studied Romance languages. Next, we discuss the importance of data from acceptability experiments working in consort with data from other theoretical paradigms in order to provide a more complete view of the grammar. Although we believe that multiple paradigms can benefit from using acceptability experiments for the purposes of data triangulation, we concentrate on instruments typically used by variationist linguists in particular. Finally, we offer concluding remarks.

## 17.2 Empirical Results from Romance Employing Acceptability Experiments

Our point of departure is the notion that a theory of language should account for evidence from different sources, including judgment, production, and processing data. These different tasks yield data that might be more or less affected by extralinguistic factors (considering, for example, the myriad factors that can affect real-time speech), because, in essence, these are all performances. As such, acceptability experiments must be carefully constructed to avoid bias. Sprouse (2018) notes that both processing factors (e.g. complexity, frequency, ambiguity, plausibility) and factors inherent to a given experiment (length-induced fatigue, repetition effects, comparison effects, etc.) can impact judgments. While we do not explore these factors in any detail, we refer interested readers to Chapters 4 and 5 for further discussion. Overall, however, we aim to highlight the fact that acceptability experiments can be useful for providing complementary data to production and processing tasks and for improving on traditional informal judgments with increased methodological rigor.

In this section, we focus on cases where acceptability experiments have provided data that has been used to refine our knowledge of the syntax of *wh*-dependencies in Romance languages.

### 17.2.1 Word Order in Questions

Researchers working on word order in *wh*-questions in Spanish have shown that although many Romance languages are characterized by flexible word order, some display obligatory subject–verb inversion effects in *wh*-questions (1a–e; verbs in **bold**):[1]

(1)  a. [Che cosa] **ha**     **detto**   Maria [*t*]?            (Italian)
        what thing AUX.3SG say.PTCP Maria

      b. [Qu'] **a**       **dit**       Marie [*t*]?           (French)
        what AUX.3SG say.PTCP Marie

      c. [Que] **disse**      a   Maria [*t*]?    (European Portuguese)
        what say.PST.3SG   the Maria

      d. [Què] **ha**      **dit**      Maria [*t*]?          (Catalan)
        what AUX.3SG say.PTCP Maria

      e. [Qué] **dijo /**     **ha**     **dicho**   María [*t*]?      (Spanish)
        what say.PST.3SG AUX.3SG say.PTCP María
        'What **did** Maria say?'

---

[1] We use the trace (*t*) convention here to indicate the initial merge position of the direct object. In early generative work, thematic roles (e.g. Jackendoff 1972, 1974) are assigned to arguments in the Deep Structure, followed by transformational rules (Chomsky 1977, 1981) that net the order evidenced in questions. While nothing hinges on these theoretical assumptions, they are implicitly assumed by Goodall (2010) in the subsequent discussion.

Torrego (1984) shows that subject–verb inversion is obligatory in Spanish *wh*-questions (2).

(2)  \*Qué María **dijo** /     **ha**     **dicho** [*t*]?          (Spanish)
   what Maria say.PST.3SG / AUX.3SG say.PTCP
   'What **did** Maria say?'

Comparing examples (1a–e) with their English glosses, one might suspect that these subject–verb inversion processes are similar. Goodall (2011: 30–31) notes, however, that English non-subject *wh*-phrases do not behave like subject *wh*- in matrix clauses (3). Additionally, embedded *wh*-phrases (4a) do not trigger the same inversion effects found in languages like Spanish (4b, c).

(3)    \*Who does go to school? (\*non-emphatic *do*)

(4)    a. \*I wonder [what will Mary say.]
     b. \*No  sé          [qué  Juan  compra]
        not  know.PRS.1SG  what  Juan  buy.PRS.3SG
     c. No  sé          [qué  compra      Juan.]
        not  know.PRS.1SG  what  buy.PRS.3SG  Juan
        'I don't know what Juan buys.'

Goodall (2011) refined our cross-linguistic knowledge of *wh*-questions by examining syntactic satiation effects as reported in Snyder (2000). Satiation effects are evinced when repeated exposure to a typically unacceptable structure (e.g. (3), (4a, b)) improves its acceptability in a speaker's judgment (see Chapter 6 for detailed discussion). Snyder found that not all sentence types are subject to satiation. Goodall (2011) examined satiation effects among English and Spanish native speakers to determine which structures were susceptible to judgment satiation effects. Participants were exposed to six structures typically found to be unacceptable and four structures typically found to be grammatical in their respective native languages. Five tokens of each of the ten structures were presented, followed by the question "Does this sound good?", to which participants had a forced-choice yes/no response option. Results revealed differential satiation patterns: structures violating the Complex NP Constraint (5) triggered a significant effect in English, while No-Inversion structures (6) triggered a significant effect in Spanish.

(5)    \*What does Brenda accept the idea that Tom should sell? (Complex NP)

(6)    \*Qué  Juan  compró      en  la  tienda? (No inversion)
     what  Juan  buy.PST.3SG  in  the  store
     'What did Juan buy in the store?'

Based on these results, Goodall argues that analyses suggesting that a lack of inversion effects violates the same syntactic principle in both languages (e.g. Rizzi's 1996 *Wh*-Criterion) are not sustainable because English questions with intervening subjects never netted satiation effects.[2] Instead, Goodall suggests that processing differences play a role in cross-linguistic subject–verb inversion judgment asymmetries.

Although the preceding studies represent important evidence for word-order restrictions for non-Caribbean varieties of Spanish, researchers have noted that Caribbean varieties – in particular Dominican Spanish (see e.g. Henríquez Ureña 1940) – allow suppression of this inversion effect with subject pronouns (from Toribio 1993: 52, ex. 37a).

(7)   Qué    yo    voy          a    mandar [t]   a    esos    muchachos?
      what   I     go.PRS.1sg   to   send.INF     to   those   boys
      'What am I going to send to those boys?'

Ordóñez and Olarrea (2006) conducted an experimental acceptability judgment study among Dominican Spanish speakers from Santo Domingo. The authors examined the acceptability of intervening (i.e. non-inverted) subjects in Dominican Spanish questions and, based on accept-ability proportions, proposed the following acceptability hierarchy (8) according to subject type.[3]

(8)    2p pronoun > 3p pronoun > lexical > complex lexical

Goodall (2010) observed that lack of inversion effects had already been noted in non-Caribbean varieties with adjunct *wh*-phrases (Torrego 1984: 106):

(9)   a. Cuándo Juan consiguió          por fin   abrir       la  puerta ayer [t]?
         when   Juan achieve.PST.3SG   for end   open.INF    the door   yesterday
         'When did Juan finally manage to open the door yesterday?'
      b. Cómo Juan ha                   conseguido   meter allí   a   su hijo [t]?
         how  Juan has AUX.PRS.3SG      achieve.PTCP put.INF there to  his son
         'How did Juan finally manage to get his son in there?'

Comparing the data in (9a, b) with ungrammatical (2), which has an argument (direct object) *wh*-phrase, an adjunct–argument asymmetry emerges for non-Caribbean Spanish.[4] However, this distinction provides little insight into these effects with argument *wh*-phrases in Caribbean varieties. Goodall (2010: 233–234) thus suggested that experimental evidence could yield

---

[2] The types of structures that exhibit satiation effects in the literature vary. Therefore, evidence of satiation effects should be treated with caution. We refer the interested reader to Chapter 6 and to Hofmeister et al. (2013). We are grateful to an anonymous reviewer for this suggestion.

[3] Ordóñez and Olarrea (2006) report approximate acceptability rates rather than *n*-point scale acceptability ratings, a methodological difference that complicates comparison to numerical scale means. Nevertheless, what we seek to highlight is the acceptability hierarchy that emerges.

[4] See Rizzi (1991, 2001) for a discussion of similar facts in Italian.

additional insight into the nature of the filler–gap dependency created between the gap (trace) and the filler (*wh*-phrase) by providing "more precision in dealing with subtle contrasts" related to subject–verb inversion phenomena in *wh*-questions. Goodall noted that although the preceding facts for Spanish varieties were well documented, there existed no evidence about the role of the intervening (i.e. non-inverted) subject. To investigate question formation in Mexican and Caribbean Spanish, Goodall (2010) conducted a study gathering acceptability data from native speakers employing a five-point scale. His results showed that while the absence of an intervening subject elicited near-ceiling ratings, responses revealed a pattern of *gradient* acceptability according to subject type. Among overt subjects, second-person pronouns were rated highest, followed by third-person pronouns and lexical DPs, which were rated lowest, netting the hierarchy in (10).

(10)   2p pronoun   >   3p pronoun   >   lexical

Goodall used the rating differences among subject types to examine whether these were more easily processed, following Warren and Gibson's (2002) proposal that lexical DPs (followed by third-person pronouns and second-person pronouns) require more processing resources – the exact hierarchy in (10). Following Gibson (2000), a *wh*-movement dependency creates processing demands because speakers must keep the filler in working memory until they have processed the predicate that creates the gap dependency, thus allowing the link to the filler. Goodall followed Warren and Gibson's (2002) suggestion that processing gap dependencies utilizes the same pool of resources as processing the reference of an intervening (non-inverted) subject, leading him to predict that the type of intervening subject should affect processing of *wh*-dependencies.

Furthermore, assuming that complex *wh*-elements are less taxing on working memory than simple(r) *wh*-elements (i.e. *cuáles de estos libros* 'which of these books' vs. *qué libros* 'what books' or *qué* 'what'), Goodall predicts that questions with complex *wh*-elements should receive higher acceptability ratings when an intervening subject is present.[5] Two additional predictions follow: (i) that *wh*-elements that do not create a filler–gap dependency (e.g.

---

[5] Goodall (2010: 235) states that "complex *wh*-elements are believed to be able to survive in working memory at a higher activation level than bare *wh*-words," citing Hofmeister (2007) and Kluender (1998). However, an examination of the source materials reveals some disagreement in the literature. Kluender (1998: 252) cites DeVicenzi (1996): "*which* N-phrases in Italian cause a heavier processing load … than interrogative pronouns [i.e. bare *wh*-elements], in that they are less easily integrated into the overall sentence representation." Hofmeister (2007: 24) cites Bard, Robertson, and Sorace (1996), who found that more complex *which*-N phrases make processing easier, thus improving judgments and acceptability. He also cites Hofmeister et al. (2007), who found that complex *wh*-phrases significantly improve acceptability over bare *wh*-phrases, as well as Frazier and Clifton (2002), who found that complex *wh*-phrases result in faster reading times over bare *wh*-phrases, thus claiming that the former make better antecedents. In Hofmeister's conclusion, he notes that complex *wh*-phrases are syntactically and semantically more informative, which helps to elevate their activation level. This is discursively necessary when the activation level of a particular referent is low; when the activation level is high, however, less informative forms (i.e. bare *wh*-forms) are necessary.

*por qué* 'why') should receive higher acceptability ratings with an intervening subject, and (ii) adverbials like *cuándo* 'when' and *dónde* 'where,' which are categorially different from subjects, should be rated higher than *wh*-expressions like *qué* 'what' and *a quién* 'who/(to) who(m),' because these are categorially more similar to subjects. These predictions are borne out in Goodall (2010). Complex *wh-* phrases received ratings that were significantly higher than those assigned to bare *wh*-elements in comparable contexts. Additionally, the interrogative *por qué* received near-ceiling mean ratings with intervening subjects – significantly higher than *dónde* and *cuándo,* as well as *qué* and *a quién,* revealing the hierarchy in (11).

(11)    why  >  complex *wh-*  >  how  >  where/when  >  what/who

Goodall (2010) shows the importance of acceptability experiments as experimental tools because they can capture ease of processing in terms of a hierarchy – a finding that refines the original claim on the argument/adjunct asymmetry (e.g. Torrego 1984; Suñer 1994). Goodall also notes that, despite important differences between mainland and Caribbean Spanish, the hierarchy in (6) is virtually identical to Ordóñez and Olarrea's (2006).

Based on these results, Goodall speculates that referent accessibility is related to overt pronoun rates such that geographic areas with higher rates of overt pronoun production should exhibit greater acceptability rates for non-inversion in *wh*-questions.[6] These predictions are ripe for experimental investigation not only among Spanish varieties, but in other Romance languages. The benefits of methodological triangulation are evident here: although forced-choice judgments were revealing, data from a numerical scale provided additional insight, thus revealing the finer-grained hierarchies in (10) and ( 11), an important step in further understanding filler–gap dependencies and constraints on intervening constituents in Spanish.

### 17.2.2   The Study of Infrequent Structures Using Acceptability Experiments

We have seen that acceptability experiments have not only prompted important hierarchical differences regarding question formation, but also highlighted important differences between Romance languages and English that inform our theoretical models of these languages. The experimental study of discourse-dependent structures constitutes another example of how methodological choices can affect advancement of the theory. In this section, we review research focusing on structures at the syntax–discourse interface. Some accounts have suggested that, compared to internal interfaces such as syntax–morphology, syntax–discourse mappings lead to higher processing loads, particularly when said mappings

---

[6] See e.g. Otheguy, Zentella, and Livert (2007) for a summary of overt pronoun rates.

occur in real time (Sorace 2011). In this section, we review research on Clitic-left dislocation, Fronted Focus, and information focus in Romance.

### 17.2.2.1 Examples of the Study of Infrequent Structures: Clitic-Left Dislocation (CLLD), Fronted Focus (FF), and Information Focus Marking

We have seen that generative theory accounts for linguistic phenomena by proposing a model of a speaker's abstract linguistic system. In practical terms, the construct "abstract linguistic system" implies that linguists can only access this system indirectly – often by proving the system's limits using methods such as acceptability experiments. Within generativism, the centrality of acceptability experiments to the study of speakers' grammars is easily explained: we are not only interested in what is possible in a given system (that which can be confirmed in production) but also what is *not* possible: a sequence that cannot be interpreted, meaning that the speaker's system cannot generate an appropriate structure for it (Kempchinsky 2018: 18). Because acceptability experiments are flexible tools, their use can circumvent some of the difficulties associated with the study of discourse-dependent structures (e.g. avoidance of the structure under study) and reliably prove knowledge not only of (un)grammaticality, but also (in)felicity of infrequent structures.

In fact, when we investigate syntax–discourse structures, the central issue is typically not whether structures can or cannot be generated by the system (i.e. (un)grammaticality) but rather whether grammatical sequences are felicitous under a specific discourse context (see Chapter 12 for more detailed discussion). In Spanish, two discourse-dependent structures that exemplify this state of affairs are Clitic Left Dislocation (CLLD) and Fronted Focus (FF). These structures, which share some surface-level commonalities (e.g. both involve dislocations to the left periphery), differ in their encoding of information structure. CLLD, which connects a dislocated phrase to its antecedent via a doubling clitic, constitutes a *topicalization* realization, whereas FF, wherein the dislocated phrase need not have an antecedent in the discourse, exemplifies *focus realization*. Examples (12) (Davies 2016) and (13) exemplify the two structures.

**CLLD**

(12)    A    los americanos los           conozco,     señor, como a  mis manos.
             DOM the Americans CL.ACC.M.PL  know.PRS.1SG sir     like   to my hands
             'Sir, I know the Americans like I know my own hands.'

**FF**

(13)    A     PEDRO    ascendieron,    no    a       Román.
             DOM   Pedro     raise.PST.3PL   NEG  DOM  Roman
             'They gave a raise to Pedro, not to Román.'

Example (12) shows that the left-dislocation of the DP *los americanos*, which must be either explicitly mentioned in the previous discourse or else be easily retrievable based on the discourse context, is doubled by the accusative clitic (*los*). The left-dislocated phrase *Pedro* in (13), on the other hand, does not require that this phrase be previously mentioned, given that FF opens and closes a variable simultaneously. Additionally, as noted by the caps in (13), FF is marked with a special intonation.

Because of the multiple interfaces involved (syntax, discourse, phonology, morphology), investigating structures such as FF and CLLD is methodologically challenging. One reason is that these structures represent only one of many possible ways of encoding topicalization or focalization in Spanish. This means that corpus data, as well as data from any experiment that offers latitude in terms of responses such as an oral elicitation task, might result in speakers avoiding the structures under study. Designing an experiment wherein speakers produce complex structures in a natural way, while encoding the expected information structure, has been considered a significant methodological challenge (Katz & Selkirk 2011).[7] This state of affairs is further complicated because these structures are often less frequent in naturally occurring discourse. While CLLD is thought to be relatively frequent in Spanish (Slabakova 2015; Leal & Slabakova 2019), some studies estimate that it occurs in about 1 percent of spoken sentences (Leal & Slabakova 2019). In the case of FF, the estimates are even lower: Leal and Slabakova (2019) found a single exemplar of FF in a small corpus including 2,924 T-units, where a T-unit was operationalized as a clause along with its subordinate clauses (following Young 1995).

Meticulously designed acceptability experiments have been reliably used to elicit judgments on infrequent structures to counteract some of these challenges (Slabakova, Rothman, & Kempchinsky 2011; Leal, Slabakova, & Rothman 2014; Leal Méndez, Slabakova, & Rothman 2015). These studies have used contextualized, bimodal (audio + text) acceptability experiments because discourse-dependent structures such as CLLD and FF typically have distinct intonational patterns. For instance, CLLD is typically accented and has both left and right boundaries, ending with a high-edge tone (see Feldhausen 2016), while lacking the emphatic stress associated on the fronted constituent in FF. Including a discourse context is equally crucial because the felicity of the structures depends on the appropriate discourse context. In most experiments testing these structures, it is precisely the discourse context that triggers (in)felicity, given that structures would be grammatical if presented in isolation.

Overall, the existing experimental research has found that speakers of Spanish (native, heritage, and advanced L2) can reliably judge the felicity of CLLD and FF in context, as outlined by syntactic theory (Slabakova,

---

[7] Other possibilities include production tasks that limit the choices of speakers (e.g. by offering a sentence frame; see Valenzuela (2005)), although these tasks are not representative of naturally occurring discourse.

Rothman, & Kempchinsky 2011; Leal, Slabakova, & Rothman 2015; Leal 2016). Without the use of contextualized, bimodal acceptability experiments, however, the investigation of these structures would have been severely hindered.

As we have seen, researchers have used evidence from acceptability experiments to refine theoretical claims that were originally based on intuition or production data (see Goodall's work above). In the following, we will focus on a range of discourse-dependent structures used to realize information focus in Spanish. Unlike Fronted (contrastive) Focus, which both opens and closes a variable in the discourse, information focus simply resolves it. An example of information focus in Spanish is found in (14).

(14)　So, who found the piñata in the end?

　　　a. Tras　　mucho　buscar,　　#los niños　　encontraron
　　　　behind　much　　search.inf　the children　find.pst.3pl
　　　　la　piñata　　　　　　　　　　　　#SVO (in-situ)
　　　　the piñata.

　　　b. Tras　　mucho　　buscar,　　encontraron　la　piñata
　　　　behind　much　　search.INF　find.PST.3PL　the piñata
　　　　los niños.　　　　　　　　　　　　VOS (movement)
　　　　the children

　　　'After much searching, the children found the piñata.'

The leading syntactic analysis proposes that Spanish exploits its word order to realize information structure such that information focus is realized via movement to rightmost position (e.g. Zubizarreta 1998; Büring & Gutiérrez-Bravo 2001; Casielles-Suárez 2004). In terms of the proposed derivation, Zubizarreta (1998) offers one of the most detailed (and accepted) syntactic accounts, proposing that rightmost movement is driven by prosody. She proposes that movement results from the interaction of two stress-placement rules: The Focus Prominence Rule (FPR) and the Nuclear Stress Rule (NSR). The FPR stipulates that focus must receive main stress, while the NSR requires that stress should fall on the lowest constituent under asymmetrical c-command. In an example such as (14a) above, these rules clash because the focused constituent (*los niños* 'the children') does not appear rightmost. In order to reconcile these two rules, Zubizarreta proposes that the object moves over the subject due to prosodically motivated movement (p-movement) so that the focus constituent receives stress according to both the FPR and the NSR (as in (14b)).

Within the last decade, however, the facts of Spanish information focus have been debated after a series of experimental investigations using production and judgment data found that speakers of multiple dialects not only accepted in-situ subject focus marking (e.g. Hoot 2012; Gupton & Leal Méndez 2013; Muntendam 2013), but also produced subject focus in situ almost exclusively (Gabriel 2010; Jiménez-Fernández 2015; Hoot 2016; Leal, Destruel, & Hoot 2018). Collectively, these studies show that, while various focus realization strategies are possible, p-movement does not feature prominently in the speakers' responses or judgments.

Nevertheless, as noted by Hoot and Leal (2020), a complicating factor in this context is that in-situ subject focus results in SVO, which also happens to be the canonical order in Spanish. Canonical orders, typically the most frequent, have been argued to fit any information structure context (Bader & Meng 1999); even more, some researchers argue that preferences for canonical orders cannot be "overridden" by information structure configurations (Hopp 2009). Therefore, the possibility exists that results obtained from production tasks (where SVO is always an option in the minds of speakers) and from judgment tasks (which contrast canonical SVO with non-canonical orders) can obscure some important evidence for theory-building purposes.

Hoot and Leal (2020) used a variant of an acceptability task, a forced-choice task, to investigate subject presentational focus in a group of native Spanish speakers (N=76) from two different dialects (Mérida, Mexico, and Barcelona, Spain).[8] In order to avoid potential biases toward the canonical SVO order, the two alternatives in the forced choice task only included verb-initial orders: VOS (felicitous under subject focus, given that focus would be rightmost) and VSO (infelicitous under subject focus). The results showed that the native speakers from both regions accepted VOS at significantly higher rates than VSO, as expected in the theoretical literature but in contrast with the results obtained both in production tasks or in tasks where SVO was one of the available options. These results echo findings from other investigations using *n*-point scale tasks to investigate presentational focus (Gupton (2017) for peninsular Spanish; Leal Méndez and Slabakova (2011) for Mexican Spanish).

So what do acceptability experiments add to the landscape of information focus research? Although the production data has rightly called into question the descriptive and explanatory adequacy of a hard version of the p-movement proposal, it is important to note that production tasks can be affected by extragrammatical factors such as conceptual availability or frequency, which can shape the form of a sentence beyond syntactic and discourse questions alone (Cowles 2012). While acceptability experiments are also affected by linguistic and extralinguistic factors, using the data from production and judgments in tandem shows that, while speakers do prefer rightmost focus in some contexts, orders encoding sentence-final focus are not preferred when canonical orders are among the choices. Although, going forward, more research on information focus and word order is needed, we recommend that it be examined in light of the competence/performance distinction to determine how methodological

---

[8] Speakers also completed a self-paced reading task. Although this task is not discussed here, the results were comparable to those obtained using the forced-choice task.

choices affect research outcomes. Thus, while a strong version of Zubizarreta's proposal appears to be in question, results from acceptability experiments with V-initial options show that speakers can indeed note a difference between final and non-final focus as long as the canonical option is absent – a result that lends support to a weaker version of Zubizarreta's hypothesis.

### 17.2.3   Control and Raising in Brazilian Portuguese

Occasionally, alternative methods can provide additional insights in the face of conflicting findings. In this section, we review the findings in the area of control and raising.

Early accounts of control in English (e.g. Williams 1980; Chomsky 1981) indicated that, despite ostensible similarities, sentences like (15a) and (15b) received different syntactic analyses.

(15)     a. Doug is likely to leave Athens.
         b. Doug is reluctant to leave Athens.

Differing analyses for these sentences are based on the fact that the predicate *is likely* in (15a) takes as its only argument the proposition [that Doug will leave Athens], as in (16a, b). In (16a), the clausal proposition [that Doug will leave Athens] checks an edge/EPP feature in Spec,TP, while the expletive *it* is proposed to do the same in (16b).

(16)     a. [That Doug will leave Athens] is likely.
         b. It is likely [that Doug will leave Athens].

The predicate *is reluctant* in (15b), however, does not behave the same way in (17a, b) because the proposition [that Doug will leave Athens] is unable to saturate this predicate.

(17)     a. *It is reluctant [that Doug will leave Athens].
         b. *[That Doug will leave Athens] is reluctant.

Instead, the predicate [is reluctant] requires two arguments: an experiencer [Doug] and a proposition [to leave Athens]. Additionally, *Doug* appears to be assigned theta-roles by the predicate [is reluctant] and by the proposition [to leave Athens] – a clear violation of the theta-criterion (Chomsky 1981). Thus, (18a) has been traditionally analyzed as an instance of raising (18a), while (16b) has been analyzed as an instance of (subject) control (18b).

(18)     a. Doug$_i$ is likely [t$_i$ to leave Athens]
         b. Doug is reluctant [PRO to leave Athens]

In (18a), [Doug to leave Athens] is theta-marked as a theme by the predicate [is likely], while [Doug] is proposed to raise out of this small-

clause-like structure to Spec,TP, where it checks an [EPP] feature and
Nominative Case is checked.[9] In (18b), the phonologically null (and case-
less) pronoun PRO is proposed to absorb the surplus theta-role from the
infinitive.

Examining raising and control in Spanish, Bosque and Gutiérrez-Rexach
(2009: 385–392) note that control predicates typically express volition,
influence, and other behaviors normally attributed to humans and animals. Therefore, subjects in control structures are typically restricted to
animate DPs (19a), despite some exceptional examples with inanimate
entities, such as in (19b).

(19) a. El  leopardo  desea          [PRO atrapar  a    la    cebra.]
        the leopard   want.PRS.3SG        trap.INF DOM the zebra
        'The leopard wants to trap the zebra.'
     b. La  ropa      se     arruga              después de [PRO secarse.]
        the clothes  cl.SE  wrinkle.PRS.3SG after  of      dry.INF-CL.SE
        'Clothes wrinkle after drying.'

Different semantic restrictions associate with each predicate type: while
inanimate subjects such as *la mesa* 'the table' (20a) and *la lluvia* 'the rain' in
(20b) can appear with raising predicates like *parecer* 'to seem' and *resultar*
'to turn out,' they may not appear with classic volitional predicates like
*intentar* 'to try' (21a) and *obligar* 'to oblige' (21b).

(20)    a. La  lluvia parece          haber     llegado      tarde.
           the rain   seem.PRS.3SG  have.INF  arrive.PTCP late
           'The rain seems to have arrived late.'
        b. La  mesa   resultó          estar    desnivelada.
           the table  result.PRS.3sg  be.INF   wonky
           'The table turned out to be wonky.'

(21)    a. #La  lluvia  intentó          llegar     tarde.
           the rain    try.PRS.3SG    arrive.INF late
           'The rain tried to arrive late.'
        b. #La  mesa obligó          a   Pedro a   desnivelarla.
           the table oblige.PST.3SG to Pedro to make-wonky.INF-CL.F.ACC.SG
           'The table obliged Pedro to make it wonky.'

Bosque and Gutiérrez-Rexach argue that there are three crucial
differences between control and raising. The first is the lack of thematic
relation between the subjects *the rain* and *the table* and the raising predicate
in (21a, b), arguing that subjects should be analyzed instead as arguments
of the subordinate-clause infinitive forms.

---

[9] That Nominative Case is assigned in this position is demonstrated by substitution of a pronoun in the same position (i).

(i) He/*Him is likely to leave Athens.

The second difference relates to the semantic results of passivization for the two predicate types (see also Davies & Dubinsky (2004) and Rosenbaum (1967)).

(22)  a. Lola   parece        haber      recompensado  a      Marcos.
          Lola   seem.PRS.3SG  have.INF   repay.PTCP     DOM   Marcos
          'Lola seems to have repaid Marcos.'
      b. Marcos parece        haber    sido      recompensado por Lola.
          Marcos seem.PRS.3SG  have.INF be.PTCP  repay.PTCP      by Lola
          'Marcos seems to have been repaid by Lola.'

(23)  a. Lola   intentará     recompensar  a    Marcos.
          Lola   try.FUT.3SG   repay.INF     to   Marcos
          'Lola will try to repay Marcos.'
      b. Marcos intentará     ser      recompensado por  Lola.
          Marcos try.FUT.3SG   be.INF   repay.PTCP      by   Lola
          'Marcos will try to be repaid by Lola.'

While in (22a, b) *Lola* remains the agent in the presence of a raising predicate, a thematic asymmetry results with a control predicate, suggesting that the agentive *Marcos* in (23b) is not the product of passivization movement in (23a).

The third difference between raising and control predicates in Spanish involves the ability of raising verbs to take impersonal or meteorological predicates as complements (24a, b), while volitional predicates may not (25a, b).

(24)  a. Parece        haber     nevado      mucho    últimamente.
          seem.PRS.3SG  have.INF  snow.PTCP   a.lot     lately
          'It seems to have snowed a lot lately.'
      b. Parece        ser       necesario  que     vengas.
          seem.PRS.3SG  be.INF    necessary   that   come.SBJ.PRS.2SG
          'It seems to be necessary that you come.'

(25)  a. #Intentó       nevar     mucho.
             try.PST.3SG   snow.INF  a.lot
          'It tried to snow a lot.'
      b. *Obligó        a   ser      necesario que vengas.
             oblige.PST.3SG  to  be.INF  necessary que come.SBJ.PRS.2SG
          *'It obliged to be necessary for you to come.'

Boeckx and Hornstein (2006) propose the Movement Theory of Control (MTC) in which instances of apparent control are analyzed as movement. This development is partly based on Brazilian Portuguese (BP) data from Rodrigues (2004) showing an agreement asymmetry between obligatory control (26a) and non-obligatory control (26b) structures.

(26)  a. A vítima₍ᵢ₎ tentou     ser    transferida₍ᵢ₎   / ??transferido₍ᵢ₎  para a
         the victim try.PST.3SG be.INF transfer.PTCP.F / transfer.PTCP.M for   the
         delegacia de    polícia   de    College Park.
         station     of   police    of    College Park
         'The victim tried to be transferred to the police station at College Park.'

      b. A vítima₍ᵢ₎ disse      que    ser    ??levada₍ᵢ₎  / levado₍ᵢ₎    para a
         the victim say.PST.3SG that   be.INF take.PTCP.F / take.PTCP.M for   the
         delegacia de         polícia não   é              uma          boa idéia.
         station     of        police not    be.PRS.3SG a               good idea
         'The victim said that being taken to the police station is not a good idea.'

In (26a), with obligatory control, the grammatically feminine *vítima*
'victim' agrees with the passive participle, regardless of whether the victim is male or female. In (26b), however, with non-obligatory control, the
passive participle agrees with the gender of the victim in question instead
of the grammatical gender of the word. For Rodrigues, agreement between
PRO and its antecedent [*a vítima*] in these examples should be either
transparent or blocked, but no asymmetry should be expected. For
Boeckx and Hornstein, these facts are straightforwardly explained if,
instead of PRO, we assume that agreement reflexes in (26) are the result
of movement-related agreement processes. In (26a) a copy of [*a vítima*]
appears in Spec, TP, while in (26b) *pro* appears in this same position,
receiving an arbitrary reading based on context.

Modesto (2010), however, provided experimental acceptability data
from inflected infinitives in Brazilian Portuguese (BP) as evidence against
the MTC account. Modesto used Landau's (2000, 2004) distinction between
*Partial Control*, selected by a desiderative, factive, or propositional predicate, and *Exhaustive Control*, selected by an implicative, aspectual, or modal
predicate. While inflected infinitives may appear with Partial Control
structures (27), which have an obligatory control reference that includes
the matrix subject with the embedded clause subject, the same reading is
impossible with Exhaustive Control structures (28).

(27)   O presidente₁ preferiu/odiou/afirmou PRO₁₊      se reunirem    às    6.
       the chair       prefer/hate/agree.PST.3SG       SE meet.INF.3PL at-the 6
       'The chair preferred/hated/agreed to gather at 6.'

(28)   *O presidente₁ conseguiu/começou/precisou PRO₁₊ se reunirem    às    6.
       the chair       manage/start/need.PST.3SG        SE meet.INF.3PL at-the 6
       'The chair managed/started/needed to gather at 6.'

Modesto argues that one cannot appeal to a notion of semantic plurality
to explain the asymmetry above, as Landau does for English, because of the
existence of syntactic agreement in Partial Control infinitives. The problem for the MTC account, then, is how to explain that the copy of
a singular syntactic object should participate in plural agreement in
a Partial Control structure (as in e.g. (27)).

Modesto also notes that the MTC account makes erroneous predictions in Exhaustive Control structures. Under the MTC, a plural controller should trigger plural agreement in the infinitive as a reflex of its movement copy. However, this is not the case in BP (29).

(29)    Os meninos  conseguiram       vender(*em)  a     casa.
        the boys     manage.PST.3PL    sell.INF(*3PL)  the   house
        'The boys managed to sell the house.'

In view of disagreements regarding the data, Rodrigues and Hornstein (2013) collected acceptability and truth-value judgment data focusing on inflected infinitives with Brazilian undergraduate students. Although space constraints preclude a full review of this research, we focus on the truth-value judgment results related to a Partial Control sentence (30).

(30)    O  director  preferia        nos    reunirmos    na     quinta-feira.
        the director  prefer.IMPFV.3SG CL.1PL meet.INF.1PL on-the Thursday
        'The director preferred us to meet on Thursday.'

Against the predictions of Modesto's (2010) claim regarding (30), 22/26 (84.6 percent) of the participants judged the sentence as true (however, see Sheehan (2012) for the claim that PC readings do not require matching number or person). In light of these results, Rodrigues and Hornstein also point to the findings of a series of studies examining the L1 acquisition of inflected infinitives in European and Brazilian Portuguese suggesting that inflected infinitives do not form part of the core grammar of BP (Rothman 2007; Pires & Rothman 2009; Pires & Rothman 2010; Pires, Rothman, & Santos 2011). Rodrigues and Hornstein therefore reject the notion that evidence involving inflected infinitives should be used to inform theoretical debate. Admittedly, the conclusions of this experimental study will take many readers by surprise, since the conclusion seeks to invalidate intuitions related to acceptability judgments of inflected infinitives.

This state of affairs highlights some of the limitations of the acceptability findings described above. Thus, future studies of EP should seek to replicate the findings employing acceptability experiments supplemented with additional experimental measures (e.g. eye-tracking in Modesto & Maia (2017); see also Chapter 23) and production data (e.g. Martins 2011; Gonçalves, Santos, & Duarte 2014; see also Chapter 26) to assist in data triangulation.

## 17.3 Further Directions for Acceptability Experiments in Romance

Having viewed some of the contributions of acceptability experiments to the study of Romance languages, we consider future directions for the use of this methodology. We first consider some advantages and disadvantages of acceptability experiments in the study of minority and less-commonly studied Romance languages. Then, we discuss the potential advantages of incorporating methodologies from other theoretical perspectives.

## 17.3.1  Acceptability Experiments in the Study of Minority and Less-Studied Romance Languages

Studies on minority languages in the theoretical generative literature have offered important insight for the analysis of majority Romance languages. For example, research on the Northern Italian Dialects (NID) Fiorentino (31a) and Trentino (31b) in Brandi and Cordin (1989: 111–112) display subtle differences in comparison with standard Italian (32a), while appearing to behave more like standard French (32b).

(31)    a. *(Tu)  parli.         (Fiorentino)
          you    speak.PRS.2SG
       b. *(Te)  parli.         (Trentino)
          you    speak.PRS.2SG
          'You speak.'

(32)    a. (Tu)  parli.          (Standard Italian)
          you    speak.PRS.2SG
       b. *(Tu)  parles.        (French)
          you    speak.PRS.2SG
          'You speak.'

In French, all forms of the verbal paradigm require a subject pronoun, yet in a number of Italian dialects, including Fiorentino and Trentino, only certain forms in the paradigm require it.[10] A robust debate has followed, with some researchers proposing that French subject clitics are argumental elements that appear in a subject position within the syntax but cliticize onto the verb at the phonological level. Others have argued that they are agreement-marking affixes. Culbertson (2010) presents prosodic and corpus data as well as speaker judgments to inform debate and argue in favor of the latter.[11] Culbertson and Legendre (2014) gathered acceptability ratings of informal French sentences from speakers of Continental French using a seven-point scale with contextualized question–answer pairs presented in Amazon Mechanical Turk. To verify their linguistic profile, participants completed a sociolinguistic questionnaire and a fluency test task, in addition to having their location verified via IP address. The authors examined ratings of non-referential *il*-drop (indicated with [Ø] in examples (33a–d)) with four verb classes that require the expletive

---

[10] See Poletto and Tortora (2016) for an overview, Cardinaletti and Repetti (2004, 2010) on other NIDs. See Poletto (2000) for the relevance of clitics for the left periphery, Poletto and Pollock (2005) on *wh*-clitics.
[11] See also Roberge (1990) and Auger (1994) for arguments in favor of this analysis.

pronoun *il* in standard French: weather expressions (33a), non-modal constructions (33b), presentational contexts (33c), and modal constructions (33d).

(33)    a. Oui,  mais [Ø]  neige         tout  le    temps.
            yes   but         snow.PRS.3SG  all   the  time
            'Yes, but (it) snows all the time.'

           b. Oh [Ø]   m'arrive                  de faire    des
            oh         CL.DAT.1SG-happen.PRS.3SG  of make.INF  of.the
            erreurs  parfois.
            mistakes  sometimes
            'Oh, (it) happens that I make mistakes sometimes.'

           c. Non, [Ø]  reste             deux  heures.
            no         remain.PRS.3SG  two   hours
            'No, (there) are two hours left.'

           d. Ouais, [Ø]  vaux            y       aller    en plein jour
            yeah     be.worth.PRS. 3SG  cl.LOC  go.INF  in plain  day
            avec      plusiers    potes.
            with      several     friends
            'Yeah, it is better to go there in the daytime with a bunch of friends.'

The authors correctly hypothesized that verbs with higher frequency would lead to greater rates of *il*-drop, and that quasi-argumental uses (e.g. weather predicates) would result in lower rates. In general, the expressions with higher frequency (*il faut (que)* …, *il y a* …, *il parâit que*) resulted in the greatest rates of *il*-drop, a result supporting a frequency-based account of morphosyntactic language change (as in Bybee & Hopper 2001). However, this explanation does not account for all of the data; among the remaining constructions was *il*-drop with weather expressions, which was rated lowest while *il*-drop with modal expressions was rated highest. The other two constructions (non-modals and presentational constructions) were rated in the middle. The authors conclude that these correspond with non-argumental null pronouns in Rizzi's (1986) typology of *pro* (34).

(34)    Typology of null pronominals in Rizzi (1986)

          a.  $pro_{expl\ +A}$  quasi-argumental
          b.  $pro_{expl-A}$  non-argumental
          c.  $pro_{+ref}$  argumental/referential

By the classification in (34), the authors reason that the set of phi-features in the null pronominal regulate the triggering of agreement and the presence of the subject clitic, thus explaining the low ratings of meteorological expressions with *il*-drop. Referential/argumental $pro_{+ref}$ has an identifiable complete set of phi-features, while the quasi-argumental $pro_{expl+A}$ found in weather predicates has just enough phi-features (i.e. number) to trigger agreement. Non-argumental $pro_{expl-A}$ that occurs in non-modals and presentational constructions, however, lacks a set of identifiable phi-features and therefore may not trigger agreement or permit a null pronominal in spoken French. Studies in this vein, combining cross-linguistic comparison and analysis with experimental methodology, further inform parametric inquiry, leading to proposals in macroparameters, mesoparameters, microparameters, and nanoparameters that are charting new directions in investigations of diachrony (see also, e.g., Biberauer & Roberts 2012; Roberts 2014; Ledgeway 2015).

An experimental study by Vermès, Collet, and Huet (1999) on the syntactic acceptability of a variety of sentences in Réunion Island (réunionnais) Creole and hexagonal (Continental) French found that Creole speakers (N=18) correctly accepted grammatical French sentences (91.25 percent) and ungrammatical French sentences (2.33 percent) at rates similar to non-Creole speakers (N=16, 95.91 percent grammatical, 4.09 percent ungrammatical). However, with respect to the Creole L1, they found that participants' ratings and judgments were unstable. The authors attribute this asymmetric metalinguistic knowledge to the absence of Creole instruction in the educational system. While the education system may be to blame at least in part, apparent instability in Réunionnais French speakers may be an artifact of the yes/no acceptability scale employed by the authors, and for this reason, we endorse the use of $n$-point scales for acceptability studies (see Chapter 2 for more detailed discussion of response methods in acceptability experiments).

As important as such data is, it brings to light an important consideration that must be taken into account when researching minority varieties. For many minority languages, domestic and institutional support may be lacking – a standardized orthography and/or a standardizing academy may not exist. Even when one or both of the preceding exist, speakers may be unfamiliar with a standard language form if the language has not been normalized and incorporated into the public education system. This may pose a confound leading to functional illiteracy and perhaps even indeterminate linguistic intuitions (see, e.g., Labov 1996). The former may result in an inability to read experimental prompts and stimuli, necessitating the use of aural equivalents. Even among otherwise literate participants, there may be competing standard forms, as is the case of Galician/Galegan. When orthographic norms are in competition, the choice of one standard over the other is a political one, which may have the unfortunate consequence of difficult exchanges for the linguistic researcher. Despite the challenges, recent research on minority languages like Asturian (Fernández-Rubiera 2009) and Galician (Gupton 2014) has made important contributions to studies of the syntax of cliticization and information structure. In the case of Gupton (2014), semi-spontaneous production data that is more typically associated with ethnographic and sociolinguistic studies was also gathered in order to confirm experimental findings. Given the case of languages lacking an orthographic standard as mentioned previously, field interviews can be used to supplement and confirm oral acceptability consultations.

## 17.3.2 Acceptability Experiments Beyond Generativism: The Potential of Data Triangulation

We have highlighted the importance of experimental methods in generative linguistics while advocating the use of various methodologies in tandem to study the same linguistic phenomena, a practice known as methodological triangulation (Boyd 2001). Methodologists in language research have argued that triangulation increases validity while decreasing method and investigator bias (e.g. Mackey & Gass 2015). More generally, the literature on triangulation notes that in addition to curbing bias, other goals of the practice include data confirmation and obtaining a more complete (or authentic) dataset (Denzin 1978, 1989; Jick 1979; Knafl & Breitmayer 1991; Redfern & Norman 1994; Halcomb & Andrew 2005; Casey & Murphy 2009).

We have suggested that generative researchers should aim to account for data stemming from different instruments and modalities. Here, we propose that the data stemming from acceptability judgments can also be productively used by linguists in other research traditions. Although we consider that this argument should ring true across many different frameworks, we limit ourselves here to discussing the generative and variationist frameworks, given that both have contributed substantially to our understanding of well-studied phenomena such as subject pronoun expression in Spanish.[12]

As mentioned earlier, generative linguistics concerns itself with proposing a theory of language to account for a range of linguistic phenomena using language features (Chomsky 1975). The study of language variation, on the other hand, focuses on investigating the relationships between linguistic forms (as used in a certain context) and a variety of linguistic and non-linguistic factors. These linguistic factors may include tense, aspect, mood, person, number, specificity of the referent, or the presence/absence of a pronominal subject, among others. Non-linguistic factors may include discourse-related factors (e.g. discourse type, subject matter, information status) but also social factors such as age, gender, income level, or social status. The inclusion of social factors, notably, stands in sharp distinction to how data is gathered in generative research, where these factors have been mostly relegated to the background (but see

---

[12] An external reviewer makes the case, based on Gilquin and Gries (2009), that non-generative linguists already use these instruments more than generative researchers use non-acceptability methods. While we believe that generative linguists – especially those working in acquisition – do use a plethora of methods beyond acceptability experiments (as evidenced by the multiple volumes focusing on methodology, e.g. Blom & Unsworth (2010), our point here is to highlight potential benefits of methodological cross-pollination.

Miller's work (e.g. Miller & Schmitt 2010) on the effects of variable input in the acquisition of Spanish plural of Spanish, which examines both the effects of geographical differences and differences in socio-economic status).

These theoretical and methodological differences have resulted in these traditions, especially working largely in isolation. Although both generative and variationist researchers have focused on the same linguistic structures (e.g. null vs. overt subject pronoun expression in Spanish), and have found comparable results (e.g. pragmatic features such as switch reference affect subject pronoun expression), more work that systematically explores how the data produced in one tradition can work in a complementary fashion to the other is needed (see, e.g., Yang 2002; Adger 2006)).

While this lack of connection is unsurprising if one takes into consideration that the goals of generative and variationist research are distinct (or, some may argue, incompatible, owing to how the interaction between competence and performance is viewed), this lack of cross-pollination may represent a missed opportunity. Despite using different methodologies, research on subject pronoun expression in Spanish from the generative (e.g. Montrul & Rodríguez Louro 2006; Rothman 2009) and variationist traditions (e.g. Travis 2007; de Prada Pérez 2009; Ortiz López 2011) converges in concluding that pronoun expression is affected by linguistic factors such as *switch-reference* (topic-shift), where overt pronouns are typically associated with a change in referent. However, whereas generative research focuses on linguistic representations (e.g. the acquisition of the uninterpretable features associated with the morphology and the acquisition of the pragmatic features that constrain the distribution of overt subjects), variationist researchers typically focus on understanding the factors determining a form's use.

## 17.4   Conclusions and Future Directions

One of our driving goals has been to show how acceptability experiments have contributed to the linguistic study of Romance languages, where examining judgments has gone beyond simple documentation. The examination of this language family serves to test current linguistic theory, motivating a model of the internal grammar of speakers. The sum of these models, in turn, informs our knowledge of human language.

In the experimental studies of *wh*-questions in Spanish that we surveyed, the use of acceptability experiments has informed a gradient scale of acceptability for subject types, improving upon previous findings and hypothetical constructs across varieties. An examination of *wh*-questions in multiple varieties, particularly Dominican Spanish, has had important implications for theory-building and for future studies of nominal constructions.

Through studies of clitic-left dislocation (CLLD) and Fronted Focus (FF) in Spanish, we examined the importance of methodological decisions when eliciting judgments of infrequent structures. These enhanced acceptability experiments have also deepened our understanding of how focus and prosody affect word order; moreover, the examination of multiple varieties of Spanish over the past ten years has led to important discoveries and challenges to extant theoretical accounts.

Our examination of control in Brazilian Portuguese has shown how conflicting results, especially when judgments are unstable and based on structures largely absent from the primary linguistic data, have required an examination of additional linguistic factors with alternative methodologies.

A common thread throughout these studies is the importance of data triangulation to adequately examine the structures under study. We strongly advocate rigorous hypothesis testing to stimulate theoretical advances, as well as transparency in reporting the methodologies employed so that experimental results may be replicable and falsifiable.

We have seen that minority languages may provide novel insight beyond the five hegemonic Romance languages (French, Italian, Portuguese, Romanian, and Spanish) – an important issue because not all languages are covered equitably in the theoretical and experimental literature. Nevertheless, it is important to acknowledge the potential limitations of such languages with respect to acceptability experiments and other methodologies that require pre-existing levels of standardization, normalization, and literacy in order to be able to effectively implement them. Additionally, corpus creation is crucial to documentation, especially with minority languages, many of which are currently endangered. Sociolinguistic interviews can work in tandem with acceptability experiments, as these may serve an important role regardless of language vitality/morbidity because these could confirm the productivity of linguistic structures and capture variation. In studies of majority as well as minority languages, we advocate collaborative pursuits and methodologies that seek to capture competence as well as performance in order to provide a more complete vision of speaker grammars and human language in general. The more we know about processing, production, interpretation, and speaker judgments, the better able we will be to explore beyond descriptive and explanatory adequacy.

# References

Adger, D. (2006). Combinatorial variability. *Journal of Linguistics*, 42, 503–530.

Auger, J. (1994). Pronominal clitic in Québec colloquial French: A morphological analysis. Doctoral dissertation, University of Pennsylvania.

Bader, M. & Meng, M. (1999). Subject–object ambiguities in German embedded clauses: An across-the-board comparison. *Journal of Psycholinguistic Research*, 28(2), 121–143.

Bard, E., Robertson, D., & Sorace, A. (1996). Magnitude estimation of linguistic acceptability. *Language*, 72(1), 32–68.

Biberauer, T. & Roberts, I. (2012). Towards a parameter hierarchy for auxiliaries: Diachronic considerations. *Cambridge Occasional Papers in Linguistics*, 6, 267–294.

Blom, E. & Unsworth, S., eds. (2010). *Experimental Methods in Language Acquisition Research*. Amsterdam: John Benjamins.

Boeckx, C. & Hornstein, N. (2006). The virtues of control as movement. *Syntax*, 9, 118–130.

Boeckx, C. & Hornstein, N. (2007). On (non-)obligatory control. In W. D. Davies & S. Dubinsky, eds., *New Horizons in the Analysis of Control and Raising*. Dordrecht: Springer, pp. 251–262.

Bosque, I. & Gutiérrez-Rexach, J. (2009). *Fundamentos de sintaxis formal*. Madrid: Ediciones Akal.

Boyd, C. O. (2001). Combining qualitative and quantitative approaches. In P. L. Munhall, ed., *Nursing Research: A Qualitative Perspective*. Sudbury, MA: Jones & Bartlett, pp. 579–598.

Brandi, L. & Cordin, P. (1989). Two Italian dialects and the Null Subject Parameter. In O. Jaeggli & K. Safir, eds., *The Null Subject Parameter*. Dordrecht: Springer, pp. 111–142.

Büring, D. & Gutiérrez-Bravo, R. (2001.) Focus-related constituent order variation without the NSR: A prosody-based crosslinguistic analysis. In S. MacBhloscaidh, ed., *Syntax at Santa Cruz*, vol. 3. University of California, Santa Cruz, pp. 41–58.

Bybee, J. & Hopper, P. (2001). *Frequency and the Emergence of Language Structure*. Amsterdam: John Benjamins.

Cardinaletti, A. & Repetti, L. (2004). Clitics in Northern Italian dialects: Phonology, syntax and microvariation. *University of Venice Working Papers in Linguistics*, 14, 7–106.

Cardinaletti, A. & Repetti, L. (2010). Proclitic vs enclitic pronouns in northern Italian dialects and the null-subject parameter. In R. D'Alessandro, A. Ledgeway, & I. Roberts, eds., *Syntactic Variation: The Dialects of Italy*. Cambridge: Cambridge University Press, pp. 119–134.

Casey, D. & Murphy, K. (2009). Issues in using methodological triangulation in research. *Nurse Researcher*, 16(4), 40–55.

Casielles-Suárez, E. (2004). *The Syntax–Information Structure Interface: Evidence from Spanish and English*. New York: Routledge.

Chomsky, N. (1975). *Reflections on Language*. New York: Pantheon.

Chomsky, N. (1977). On WH-movement. In P. Culicover, T. Wasow, & A. Akmajian, eds., *Formal Syntax*. New York: Academic Press, pp. 71–132.

Chomsky, N. (1981). *Lectures on Government and Binding: The Pisa Lectures*. Dordrecht: Foris.

Cowles, H. W. (2012.) The psychology of information structure. In M. Krifka & R. Musan, eds., *The Expression of Information Structure*. Berlin and Boston: De Gruyter, pp. 287–318.

Culbertson, J. (2010). Convergent evidence for categorical change in French: From subject clitic to agreement marker. *Language*, 86(1) 85–132.

Culbertson, J. & Legendre, G. (2014). Prefixal agreement and impersonal 'il' in Spoken French: Experimental evidence. *French Language Studies*, 24, 83–105.

Davies, W. D. & Dubinsky, S., eds. (2004). *The Grammar of Raising and Control: A Course in Syntactic Argumentation*. Oxford: Blackwell.

Davies, M. (2016–). *Corpus del Español: Two Billion Words, 21 Countries*. Available online at www.corpusdelespanol.org/web-dial/

Denzin, N. (1978). *The Research Act*. New York: McGraw-Hill.

Denzin, N. (1989). *The Research Act: A Theoretical Introduction to Sociological Methods*. Englewood Cliffs, NJ: Prentice Hall.

DeVicenzi, M. (1996). Syntactic analysis in sentence comprehension: Effects of dependency types and grammatical constraints. *Journal of Psycholinguistic Research*, 25(1), 117–133.

Feldhausen, I. (2016). Inter-speaker variation, Optimality theory, and the prosody of clitic left-dislocations in Spanish. *Probus*, 28(2), 293–333.

Fernández-Rubiera, F. (2009). Clitics at the edge: clitic placement in Western Iberian Romance languages. Doctoral dissertation, Georgetown University.

Frazier, L. & Clifton, C. (2002). Processing 'd-linked' phrases. *Journal of Psycholinguistics*, 31(6), 633–659.

Gabriel, C. (2010). On focus, prosody, and word order in Argentinean Spanish: A Minimalist OT account. *Revista Virtual de Estudos da Linguagem*, 4, 183–222.

Gibson, E. (2000). The dependency locality theory: a distance-based theory of linguistic complexity. In Y. Miyashita, A. Marantz, & W. O'Neil, eds., *Image, Language, Brain*. Cambridge, MA: MIT Press, pp. 95–126.

Gilquin, G. & Gries, S. T. (2009). Corpora and experimental methods: A state-of-the-art review. *Corpus Linguistics and Linguistic Theory*, 5(1), 1–26.

Gonçalves, A., Santos, A. L., & Duarte, I. (2014). (Pseudo-)Inflected infinitives and control as *Agree*. In K. Lahousse & S. Marzo, eds., *Selected Papers from "Going Romance" Leuven 2012*. Amsterdam: John Benjamins, pp. 161–180.

Goodall, G. (2010). Experimenting with *wh*-movement in Spanish. In K. Arregi, Z. Fagyal, S. Montrul, & A. Tremblay, eds., *Romance Linguistics 2008: Interactions in Romance. Selected Papers from the 38th Linguistic Symposium on Romance Languages (LSRL), Urbana-Champaign, April 2008*. Amsterdam: John Benjamins, pp. 233–248.

Goodall, G. (2011). Syntactic satiation and the inversion effect in English and Spanish *wh*-questions. *Syntax*, 14, 29–47.

Grosjean, F. (2001). The bilingual's language modes. In J. Nicol, ed., *One Mind Two Languages*. Oxford: Blackwell, pp. 1–22.

Gupton, T. (2014). *The Syntax–Information Structure Interface: Clausal Word Order and the Left Periphery in Galician*. Boston: De Gruyter Mouton.

Gupton, T. (2017). Early minority language acquirers of Spanish exhibit focus-related interface asymmetries: Word order alternation and optionality in Spanish–Catalan, Spanish–Galician, and Spanish–English bilinguals. In F. Lauchlan & M. C. Parafita-Couto, eds., *Bilingualism and Minority Languages in Europe*. Newcastle upon Tyne: Cambridge Scholars, pp. 214–241.

Gupton, T. & Leal-Méndez, T. (2013). Experimental methodologies: Two case studies investigating the syntax–discourse interface. *Studies in Hispanic & Lusophone Linguistics*, 6(1), 139–164.

Halcomb, E. & Andrew, S. (2005). Triangulation as a method for contemporary nursing research. *Nurse Researcher*, 13(2), 71–82.

Henríquez Ureña, P. (1940). *El español en Santo Domingo*. Buenos Aires: Coni.

Henry, A. (2005). Non-standard dialects and linguistic data. *Lingua*, 115(11), 1599–1617.

Hofmeister, P. (2007). Representational complexity and memory retrieval in language comprehension. Doctoral dissertation, Stanford University.

Hofmeister, P., Jaeger, T., Sag, I., Arnon, I., & Snider, I. (2007). Locality and accessibility in *wh*-questions. In S. Featherston & W. Sternefeld, eds., *Island Constraints: Theory, Acquisition and Processing*. Dordrecht: Kluwer, pp. 195–222.

Hofmeister, P., Jaeger, T., Arnon, I., Sag, I., & Snider, I. (2013). The source ambiguity problem: Distinguishing the effects of grammar and processing on acceptability judgments. *Language and Cognitive Processes*, 28(1), 48–87.

Hoot, B. (2012). Presentational focus in heritage and monolingual Spanish. Doctoral dissertation, University of Illinois.

Hoot, B. (2016). Narrow presentational focus in Mexican Spanish: Experimental evidence. *Probus*, 28(2), 335–365.

Hoot, B. & Leal, T. (2020). Native speaker processing of narrow focus in Spanish. *Probus: International Journal of Romance Linguistics*, 32(1), 93–127.

Hopp, H. (2009). The syntax–discourse interface in near-native L2 acquisition: Off-line and on-line performance. *Bilingualism: Language and Cognition*, 12(4), 463–483.

Jackendoff, R. (1972). *Semantic Interpretation in Generative Grammar*. Cambridge, MA: MIT Press.

Jackendoff, R. (1974). A deep structure projection rule. *Linguistic Inquiry*, 5(4), 481–505.

Jick, T. D. (1979). Mixing qualitative and quantitative methods: Triangulation in action. *Administrative Science Quarterly*, 24(4), 603–611.

Jiménez-Fernández, A. L. (2015). Towards a typology of focus: Subject position and microvariation at the discourse–syntax interface. *Ampersand*, 2, 49–60.

Katz, J. & Selkirk, E. (2011). Contrastive focus vs. discourse-new: Evidence from phonetic prominence in English. *Language*, 87(4), 771–816.

Kempchinsky, P. (2018). Generative linguistics: Syntax. In K. Geeslin, ed., *The Cambridge Handbook of Hispanic Linguistics*. Cambridge: Cambridge University Press, pp. 9–30.

Kluender, R. (1998). On the distinction between strong and weak islands: A processing perspective. P. Culicover & L. McNally, eds.,*The Limits of Syntax* (Syntax and Semantics, 29). San Diego, CA: Academic Press, pp. 241–279.

Knafl, K. A. & Breitmayer, B. J. (1991). Triangulation in qualitative research: Issues of conceptual clarity and purpose. In J. M. Morse, ed., *Qualitative Nursing Research: A Contemporary Dialogue*. Newbury Park, CA: Sage, pp. 226–239.

Labov, W. (1996). When intuitions fail. In L. McNair, K. Singer, L. Dolbrin, & M. Aucon, eds., *Papers from the Parasession on Theory and Data in Linguistics*. Chicago: Chicago Linguistic Society, pp. 77–106.

Landau, I. (2000). *Elements of Control: Structure and Meaning in Infinitival Constructions*. Dordrecht: Kluwer.

Landau, I. (2004). The scale of finiteness and the calculus of control. *Natural Language & Linguistic Theory*, 22, 811–877.

Leal, T. (2016). Look before you move: Clitic left dislocation in combination with other elements at the Spanish left periphery. *Spanish Review of Applied Linguistics*, 29(2), 396–428.

Leal, T., Destruel, E., & Hoot, B. (2018). The realization of information focus in monolingual and bilingual native Spanish. *Linguistic Approaches to Bilingualism*, 8(2), 217–251.

Leal, T. & Slabakova, R. (2019). The relationship between L2 instruction, exposure, and the acquisition of a syntax–discourse property in L2 Spanish. *Language Teaching Research*, 23(2), 237–258.

Leal, T., Slabakova, R., & Rothman, J. (2014). A rare structure at the syntax–discourse interface: Heritage and Spanish-dominant native speakers weigh in. *Language Acquisition*, 21(4), 411–429.

Leal Méndez, T. & Slabakova, R. (2011). Pragmatic consequences of P-movement and focus fronting in L2 Spanish: Unraveling the syntax-discourse interface. In J. Herschensohn & D. Tanner, eds., *Proceedings of the 11th Generative Approaches to Second Language Acquisition Conference (GASLA 2011)*. Somerville, MA: Cascadilla Proceedings Project, pp. 63–75.

Leal Méndez, T., Slabakova, R., & Rothman, J. (2015). Discourse-sensitive clitic-doubled dislocations in heritage Spanish. *Lingua*, 155, 85–97.

Ledgeway, A. (2015). Parallels in Romance nominal and clausal microvariation. *Revue Roumaine de Linguistique*, 60 (2–3) 105–127.

Mackey, A. & Gass, S. M. (2015). *Second Language Research: Methodology and Design*, 2nd ed. Abingdon: Routledge.

Martins, A. M. (2011). Coordination, gapping, and the Portuguese inflected infinitive: The role of structural ambiguity in syntactic change. In

D. Jones, J. Whitman, & A. Garrett, eds., *Grammatical Change: Origins, Nature, Outcomes*. Oxford: Oxford University Press, pp. 275–292.

Mayol, L. (2010). Refining salience and the position of antecedent hypothesis: A study of Catalan pronouns. *University of Pennsylvania Working Papers in Linguistics*, 16(1), 127–136.

Miller, K. & Schmitt, C. (2010). Effects of variable input in the acquisition of plural in two dialects of Spanish. *Lingua*, 120(5), 1178–1193.

Modesto, M. (2010). What Brazilian Portuguese says about control: Remarks on Boeckx & Hornstein. *Syntax*, 13(1), 78–96.

Modesto, M. & Maia, M. (2017). Representation and processing of the inflected infinitive in Brazilian Portuguese: An eye-tracking study. *Revista de Estudos da Linguagem*, 25(3), 1183–1224.

Molsing, K. (2010). On the L2 Acquisition of the Overt Pronoun Constraint in Brazilian Portuguese. In P. Guijarro-Fuentes & L. Domínguez, eds., *New Directions in Language Acquisition: Romance Languages in the Generative Perspective*. Newcastle Upon Tyne: Cambridge Scholars, pp. 267–298.

Montrul, S. & Rodríguez Louro, C. (2006). Beyond the syntax of the Null Subject Parameter: A look at the discourse-pragmatic distribution of null and overt subjects by L2 learners of Spanish. In V. Torrens & L. Escobar, eds., *The Acquisition of Syntax in Romance Language*. Amsterdam: John Benjamins, pp. 401–418.

Muntendam, A. G. (2013). On the nature of cross-linguistic transfer: A case study of Andean Spanish. *Bilingualism: Language and Cognition*, 16(1), 111–131.

Ordóñez, F. & Olarrea, A. (2006). Microvariation in Caribbean/non Caribbean Spanish interrogatives. *Probus*, 18, 59–96.

Orozco, R. & Guy, G. (2008). El uso variable de los pronombres sujetos: ¿Qué pasa en la costa Caribe colombiana? In M. Westmoreland & J. A. Thomas, eds., *Selected Proceedings of the Fourth Workshop on Spanish Sociolinguistics*. Somerville, MA: Cascadilla Proceedings Project, pp. 70–80.

Ortiz López, L. A. (2011). Spanish in contact with Haitian Creole. In M. Díaz-Campos, ed., *The Handbook of Hispanic Sociolinguistics*. Malden, MA, and Oxford: Blackwell, pp. 418–445.

Otheguy, R. & Zentella, A. C. (2012). *Spanish in New York*. Oxford: Oxford University Press.

Otheguy, R., Zentella, A. C., & Livert, D. (2007). Language and dialect contact in Spanish in New York: Toward the formation of a speech community. *Language*, 83, 770–802.

Perlmutter, D. (1971). *Deep and Surface Constraints in Syntax*. New York: Holt, Rinehart & Winston.

Pires, A. & Rothman, J. (2009). Disentangling sources of incomplete acquisition: An explanation for competence divergence across heritage grammars. *International Journal of Bilingualism*, 13(2), 211–238.

Pires, A. & Rothman, J. (2010). Building bridges: Experimental L1 acquisition meets diachronic linguistics. In P. Guijarro-Fuentes & L. Domínguez, eds., *New Directions in Language Acquisition: Romance Languages in the Generative Perspective*. Newcastle upon Tyne: Cambridge Scholars, pp. 357–385.

Pires, A., Rothman, J., & Santos, A.L. (2011). L1 acquisition across Portuguese dialects: Modular and interdisciplinary interfaces as sources of explanation. *Lingua*, 121, 605–622.

Poletto, C. (2000). *The Higher Functional Field. Evidence from Northern Italian Dialects*. Oxford: Oxford University Press.

Poletto, C. & Pollock, J.-Y. (2005). On wh-clitics, *wh*-doubling and apparent *wh*-in-situ in French and some North Eastern Italian dialects. *Recherches linguistiques de Vincennes*, 33, 135–156.

Poletto, C. & Tortora, C. (2016). Subject clitics: Syntax. In A. Ledgeway & M. Maiden, eds., *The Oxford Guide to the Romance Languages*. Oxford: Oxford University Press, pp. 772–785.

de Prada Pérez, A. (2009). Subject expression in Minorcan Spanish: Consequences of contact with Catalan. Doctoral dissertation, Penn State University.

Redfern S. J. & Norman, I. J. (1994). Validity through triangulation. *Nurse Researcher*, 2, 41–56.

Rizzi, L. (1986). Null objects in Italian and the theory of pro. *Linguistic Inquiry*, 17, 501–57.

Rizzi, L. (1991). *Residual Verb Second and the Wh- Criterion*. Geneva: University of Geneva.

Rizzi, L. (1996). Residual verb second and the Wh-Criterion. In A. Belletti & L. Rizzi, eds., *Parameters and Functional Heads: Essays in Comparative Syntax*. Oxford: Oxford University Press, pp. 63–90.

Rizzi, L. (2001). On the position "Int(errogative)" in the left periphery of the clause." In G. Cinque & G. Salvi, eds., *Current Studies in Italian Syntax*. Amsterdam: Elsevier, pp. 287–296.

Roberge, Y. (1990). *The Syntactic Recoverability of Null Arguments*. Montreal: McGill-Queen's University Press.

Roberts, I. (2014). Syntactic change. In A. Carnie, D. Siddiqi, & Y. Sato, eds., *The Routledge Handbook of Syntax*. Abingdon: Routledge, pp. 391–408.

Rodrigues, C. A. N. (2004). Impoverished morphology and A-movement out of Case domains. Doctoral dissertation, University of Maryland.

Rodrigues, C. & Hornstein, N. (2013). Epicene agreement and Inflected Infinitives when the data is "under control": A reply to Modesto (2010). *Syntax*, 16(3), 217–309.

Rosenbaum, P. (1967). *The Grammar of English Predicate Complement Constructions*. Cambridge, MA: MIT Press.

Rothman, J. (2007). Heritage speaker competence differences, language change, and input type: Inflected infinitives in Heritage Brazilian Portuguese. *International Journal of Bilingualism*, 11(4), 359–389.

Rothman, J. (2009). Pragmatic deficits with syntactic consequences? L2 pronominal subjects and the syntax–pragmatics interface. *Journal of Pragmatics*, 41(5) 951–973.

Schütze, C. & Sprouse, J. (2014). Judgment data. In D. Sharma & R. Podesva, eds., *Research Methods in Linguistics*. Cambridge: Cambridge University Press, pp. 27-50.

Sheehan, M. (2012). A new take on partial control: Defective thematic intervention. *Occasional Papers in Linguistics*, 6, 1–47.

Slabakova, R. (2015). The effect of construction frequency and native transfer on second language knowledge of the syntax–discourse interface. *Applied Psycholinguistics*, 36(3), 671–699.

Slabakova, R., Rothman, J., & Kempchinsky, P. (2011). Gradient competence and the syntax–discourse interface. *EUROSLA Yearbook*, 11, 218–243.

Snyder, W. (2000). An experimental investigation of syntactic satiation effects. *Linguistic Inquiry*, 31(3), 575–582.

Sorace, A. (2011). Pinning down the concept of "interface" in bilingualism. *Linguistic Approaches to Bilingualism*, 1(1), 1–33.

Sprouse, J. (2018). Acceptability judgments and grammaticality, prospects and challenges. In N. Hornstein, C. Yang, & P. Patel-Grosz, eds., *Syntactic Structures after 60 Years: The Impact of the Chomskyan Revolution in Linguistics*. Berlin: De Gruyter Mouton, pp. 195–224.

Suñer, M. (1994). V-movement and the licensing of argumental *wh*-phrases in Spanish. *Natural Language and Linguistic Theory*, 12, 335–372.

Toribio, A. J. (1993). Parametric variation in the licensing of nominals. Doctoral dissertation, Cornell University.

Torrego. E. (1984). On inversion in Spanish and some of its effects. *Linguistic Inquiry*, 15, 103–129.

Travis, C. E. (2007). Genre effects on subject expression in Spanish: Priming in narrative and conversation. *Language Variation and Change*, 19(2), 101–135.

Valenzuela, E. (2005). L2 ultimate attainment and the syntax–discourse interface: The acquisition of topic constructions in non-native Spanish and English. Doctoral dissertation, McGill University.

Vermès, G., Collet, S.-M., & Huet, E. (1999). Réflexion métalinguistique en langue minorisée: Le cas du créole pour les enfants réunionnais en France. *Bulletin suisse de linguistique appliquée*, 69(2), 73–86.

Warren, T. & Gibson, E. (2002). The influence of referential processing on sentence complexity. *Cognition*, 85, 79–112.

Williams, E. (1980). Predication. *Linguistic Inquiry*, 11, 203–238.

Yang, C. (2002). *Knowledge and Learning in Natural Language*. Oxford: Oxford University Press.

Young, R. (1995). Conversational styles in language proficiency interviews. *Language Learning*, 45(1), 3–42.

Zubizarreta, M. L. (1998). *Prosody, Focus, and Word Order*. Cambridge, MA: MIT Press.

# 18

# Acceptability Studies in (Non-English) Germanic Languages

Markus Bader

## 18.1 Introduction

With the adaptation of magnitude estimation for the purposes of theoretical linguistics by Bard, Robertson, and Sorace (1996) and Cowart (1997), experimental investigations of syntactic issues started to come into widespread use. The first studies applying magnitude estimation were dedicated to issues of English and Italian syntax (see Sorace (1992) for the latter), but it did not take long for other languages to come into focus too. This chapter surveys experimental studies of Germanic languages other than English, including the Scandinavian languages, Dutch, and German. Experimental investigations of the syntax of these languages are mainly of two types. The first type concerns syntactic phenomena that are found in both English and the other Germanic languages. Many important syntactic constraints that have been claimed to be part of Universal Grammar and thus to hold for languages in general have been first postulated on the basis of investigations of English. Given the historical and typological relatedness of the Germanic languages, one should expect that purportedly universal constraints have similar effects in these languages. Cases for which this expectation does not seem to be borne out have been discussed long before the advent of experimental syntax. An important subpart of experimental studies on the Germanic languages other than English has taken a new look at these cases in order to determine on a broader empirical basis whether the same or different patterns of acceptability are found. Research of this type has been concerned mainly with various constraints on extraction. This strand of research is discussed in Section 18.2.

English and the other Germanic languages share many properties, but they are not identical. There is accordingly a second strand of experimental syntactic research focusing on syntactic phenomena that are only found in (a subset of) the non-English Germanic languages. These include word-order alternations related to the verb-second property of the non-English Germanic languages, to the less rigid word order observed in a subset of the Germanic languages, and to the syntax of verbs. Experimental studies concerned with word order are reviewed in Section 18.3.

Due to space limitations, this chapter must necessarily be selective. The selection of syntactic phenomena followed several guidelines. First, the phenomenon should have attracted a fair amount of attention in the syntactic literature already before experimental investigations began to flourish. Second, the phenomenon should have been the subject of several published experimental studies, preferentially in more than a single language. This latter requirement could only partially be met, however, in particular because the number of experimental studies varies widely across the different non-English Germanic languages. For that reason, not all languages are represented to an equal degree. A list of phenomena that could not be discussed is given in the final summary in Section 18.4. A further restriction was that only experimental studies with a focus on syntactic theorizing were included. This excludes the rather vast experimental literature concerned with issues of applying syntax during language comprehension or language production; pointers to the relevant literature are given when appropriate. Note finally that all effects and differences that are reported when summarizing experimental studies were significant unless explicitly stated otherwise.

## 18.2   Constraints on Movement

The movement of phrases away from their canonical position has played a major role in the development of generative syntax. A prime example of movement is seen in *wh*-questions. For example, the object NP *what* in (1) has been moved away from its canonical position immediately after the verb (indicated by __) to the clause-initial position.

(1)     What$_i$ did Mary read __$_i$?

One of the interesting features of movement is that it is not clause-bounded. Sometimes, a constituent can be moved across a clause boundary into a higher clause, a process which can be applied repeatedly, thereby increasing the distance between the moved element (also called the filler) and its canonical position (also called the gap) further and further. This is illustrated in (2).

(2)     a. What$_i$ did Paul claim [$_S$ that Mary read __$_i$]?
        b. What$_i$ do you think [$_S$ that Paul claimed [$_S$ that Mary read __$_i$]]?

In principle, long extraction as in (2) is unbounded in the sense that the gap can be arbitrarily far away from the filler. Although unbounded, long extraction is not unconstrained. Ever since Ross (1967), constraints on extraction took a central place within syntactic theory (see Boeckx (2007) for a short overview). For example, *wh*-phrases can be moved out of a complement clause that is the object of a verb, as in (2), but they cannot be moved out of an embedded *wh*-clause or a clause that is the complement of a noun (see (3b)) or a relative clause (see (3c)). *Wh*-clauses and complex NPs are thus *extraction islands*, a term coined by Ross (1967) (see Chapter 9 and Sprouse & Hornstein (2013) for an overview of experimental work on island constraints).

(3)    a. *Wh*-island
          What$_i$ did you wonder [$_S$ who bought ___$_i$]]?
       b. Complex NP island
          What$_i$ did you make [$_{NP}$ the claim [$_S$ that Sigrid bought ___$_i$]?
       c. Relative clause island
          What$_i$ did you meet [$_{NP}$ the woman [$_S$ who bought ___$_i$]]?

An influential syntactic account of island constraints was proposed by Chomsky (1973). According to the *Subjacency Condition* of Chomsky (1973), long extraction may cross one bounding node, but not more, where S and NP count as bounding nodes (IP and DP in more recent syntactic theory). In island configurations, long extraction crosses several bounding nodes whereas in licit cases, only one bounding node is crossed under the assumption of cyclic movement. Thus, what looks like a very long extraction in (2b) is in fact a series of short movements, as indicated in (4).

(4)    What$_i$ do you think [$_{S'}$ ___$_i$ [$_S$ that Paul claimed [$_{S'}$ ___ $_i$ [$_S$ that Mary read ___$_i$]]]]?

NPs do not have an "escape hatch" allowing cyclic movement, and in *wh*-clauses the escape hatch is already filled, preventing the *wh*-word to land there. Long extraction can therefore not proceed cyclically in island configurations.

An alternative to grammatical accounts of island constraints are processing accounts that try to reduce the unacceptability of sentences containing island violations to independently motivated properties of the human parsing routines. Such accounts are therefore also known as *reductionist accounts* (see Phillips (2013) for a discussion of this issue in a wider context). Prominent reductionist accounts of island constraints have been proposed by Kluender and Kutas (1993) (see also Kluender (1998)), and Hofmeister and Sag (2010). Common to reductionist accounts is the assumption that language-independent, cognitive constraints on working memory are crucially involved in explaining island constraints. Long extractions in general are assumed to be cognitively complex because the clause-initial *wh*-phrase must be held active in working memory for quite a while until the extraction site is encountered. According to Kluender and Kutas (1993), storage of the filler in working memory may be disrupted when complex computations are required before the gap is reached. The computations necessary to process sentences with acceptable long-distance extractions as in (2) are assumed to be relatively easy, in particular because the clause-initial complementizer *that* is just a grammatical marker that does not cause any semantic processing costs. Sentences with unacceptable extractions from islands as in (3), in contrast, involve complex computations when encountering the complex clause. In (3), for example, additional computations become necessary because the clause containing the extraction site is embedded within an additional NP layer.

Although reductionist accounts of island constraints differ sharply from grammatical accounts that postulate universal, innate grammatical constraints on extraction from islands, the two kinds of accounts nevertheless share an important property. Both accounts explain the reduced acceptability of extraction from islands in terms of properties that are independent from the grammar of particular languages. All else being equal, both accounts therefore predict that island constraints should apply in the same way to all languages. This prediction is not always borne out, however. How to account for seemingly language-particular variation has accordingly been a major question discussed in research on island constraints. The mainland Scandinavian languages have played a major part in this discussion. In the last ten years, a growing number of experimental studies have investigated to which degree island violations are indeed acceptable in the mainland Scandinavian languages. These studies are reviewed in Section 18.2.1. Two further constraints on extraction – the *comp-trace effect* and the *superiority effect* – are discussed in Sections 18.2.2 and 18.2.3, respectively.

### 18.2.1   Island Constraints

As early as 1973, Nomi Erteschik-Shir pointed out that the Mainland Scandinavian languages – Danish, Norwegian, and Swedish – provide certain systematic exceptions to the island constraints formulated by Ross (1967) (Erteschik-Shir 1973; see also Engdahl (1982) and references below). For example, the following Swedish sentence discussed by Engdahl (1982) violates the relative-clause island constraint but the sentence is nevertheless considered grammatical.

(5)   Den teorin$_i$   känner   jeg   [$_{DP}$ ingan   [$_{CP}$ som   tror      på__$_i$]].
      that   theory   know      I            no.one   who   believe   in
      'That theory$_i$ I know no one who believes in __$_i$.'

A Danish example that is judged as grammatical despite violating the *wh*-island constraint is shown in (6) (from Nyvad, Christensen, & Vikner 2017).

(6) 　Hvilken 　film₁ 　var 　det 　du 　gerne 　ville 　vide
　　　　which 　　film 　was 　it 　you 　like 　would 　know
　　　　[CP hvem₂ 　der__₂ havde instrueret __₁]?
　　　　　who 　　that 　had 　directed
　　　　'Which film₁ would you like to know who directed __₁?'

Although certain islands can be violated in the Mainland Scandinavian languages, this seems to be possible only under certain pragmatic and semantic conditions (e.g. Erteschik-Shir & Lappin 1979; Engdahl 1997). Several of these conditions have been the subject of experimental investigations, but the presumed differences were not confirmed. Most research in this regard has been done for Danish. Poulsen (2008) tested extraction from adverbial clauses (adjunct islands) and found no difference depending on the degree of cohesion between main and adverbial clause. Christensen, Kizach, and Nyvad (2013) did not find an adjunct/argument asymmetry in extraction from *wh*-islands. In an investigation of relative clause islands, Christensen and Nyvad (2014) failed to find a purported difference between true relative clauses and relative clauses that have been claimed to be small clauses instead. From a reading time study investigating relative clause islands in Swedish, Tutunjian et al. (2017) conclude that such islands are islands in Swedish too, but weak islands and not strong islands as in English. Finally, a recurrent finding of the experiments on extraction islands in the Scandinavian languages has been that sentences with island violations often received astonishingly low ratings given that they have been claimed to be exceptions to the island constraints.

The most comprehensive experimental investigation of island constraints in Scandinavian so far is presented in Kush, Lohndal, and Sprouse (2018). This study tested a range of island constraints in Norwegian, using an experimental design that was used before in studies of English (Sprouse, Wagers, & Phillips 2012) and other languages as well, e.g. Italian (Sprouse et al. 2016). The experiments of Kush et al. (2018) therefore allow a direct comparison of the acceptability of island violations in English and island violations in Norwegian.

Following Sprouse et al. (2012), Kush et al. (2018) tested each island type using an experimental design that was intended to reveal island effects independently of the absolute acceptability of a sentence with an island violation. The design for *whether*-islands is illustrated by the sentence pairs in (7) and (8). In both pairs, the first sentence involves short extraction internal to the matrix clause, whereas the second clause involves long movement from the embedded into the matrix clause.

(7) 　　Control sentences for *whether*-island
　　　　a. Hvem/Hvilken gjest __ᵢ tror 　　[at 　Hanne bakte kaken?]
　　　　　　who/which 　　guest 　thinks 　that Hanne baked cake.DEF
　　　　　'Who/Which guest thinks that Hanne baked the cake?'

    b. Hva/Hvilken    kake  tror    gjes       [at   Hanne  bakte ___$_i$?]
        what/which    cake  thinks  guest.DEF  that Hanne  baked
        'What/Which cake does the guest think that Hanne baked?'

(8)     *Whether*-island
    a. Hvem/Hvilken    gjest lurer    på  [om        Hanne  bakte kaken?]
        who/which     guest wonders on  if/whether  Hanne  baked cake.DEF
        'Who/which guest wonders whether Hanne baked the cake?'
    b. Hva/Hvilken  kake lurer    gjesten   på  [om      Hanne  bakte ___$_i$?]
        what/which  cake wonders guest.DEF on  if/whether  Hanne  baked
        'What/which cake does the guest wonder whether Hanne baked?'

Independent of whether an island is involved or not, long extraction is predicted to be more complex than short extraction because of the longer dependency between filler and gap (Gibson 2000). The purpose of including the two control sentences was to measure the complexity of long extraction. Assuming that long extraction causes some decrease in acceptability for the control sentences, the question is then whether long extraction from an island leads to an even larger drop in acceptability. If so, the additional decrease can be attributed to the island status of the clause from which extraction took place.

    In addition to *whether*-islands, Kush et al. (2018) tested complex-NP islands, subject islands, adjunct islands (*if*-clause), and relative-clause islands, using the experimental design explained above. An example for each island type is given below (control sentences are not shown for reasons of space). As indicated in the following examples, Kush et al. (2018) included sentences with bare *wh*-phrases and with *which*-phrases in their study (see Goodall (2015) for this distinction in relation to island constraints).

(9)   Subject island
    Hvem/Hvilken millionær    tror    journalisten    [at    møtet       med ___$_i$
    who/which    millionaire thinks journalist.DEF   that  meeting.DEF with
    forsinket    den   politiske  enigheten?
    destroyed   the   political  union?
    'Who/Which millionaire does the journalist think that the meeting with destroyed the political union?'

(10)  Complex NP island
    Hva/Hvilken  medalje rapporterte dommeren nyheten  om    at   Anders vant ___$_i$?
    what/which  medal   reported   judge.DEF  news.DEF about that Anders won
    'What/Which medal did the judge report the news that Anders won?'

(11)  Adjunct island (*if*-clause)
    Hva/Hvilken mappe blir    du  glad   om advokaten glemte ___$_i$ på kontoret?
    what/which folder  become you happy if   lawyer.DEF forgot    at office.DEF
    'What/Which folder are you happy if the lawyer forgot at the office?'

(12)     Relative-clause island

     Hva/Hvilken     film snakket    regissøren    med et par

     what/which     film spoke     director.DEF   with a   few

     kritikere    som  hadde stemt     på __$_i$?

     critics      that  had    voted     for

     'What/Which film did the director speak with a few critics that had
     voted for?'

The major results of the three experiments presented in Kush et al. (2018) can be summarized as follows. First, with the exception of *whether*-islands, sentences containing an island violation showed a decrease in acceptability that was much larger than the decrease for the control sentences with long extractions. In fact, the pattern was not different from the one formerly found for English. Second, sentences with *whether*-island violations also showed a larger acceptability decrease than corresponding control sentences, but the decrease was much smaller than for the other island violations, and also much smaller than the decrease caused by *whether*-island violations in English. Third, a large amount of interindividual variation was found for *whether*-islands. Across the three experiments, between a third and a half of the participants did not show any *whether*-island effect at all. Fourth, the same pattern showed up for bare *wh*-words and for *which*-phrases.

In summary, experimental investigations of island effects in the Mainland Scandinavian languages have mainly found rather low acceptability ratings for sentences with island violations, with *whether*-islands being the major exception, although even they show a decrease in acceptability. How the results obtained so far fit prior claims that the Mainland Scandinavian languages are exceptions to certain island constraints is an open question (see Nyvad et al. (2017) for a recent syntactic analysis taking experimental evidence into account), particularly because linguists' intuitions do not seem to be unreliable in general (Sprouse, Schütze, & Almeida 2013). Furthermore, theoretical discussions of island constraints being violable in the Scandinavian languages have regularly been backed up by authentic examples (Erteschik-Shir & Lappin 1979; Engdahl 1997).

## 18.2.2 *That*-Trace Effect

Declarative complement clauses are not islands, as discussed in the preceding section. Extraction from such clauses is nevertheless constrained in some languages. In English, and other languages too, long extraction can apply both to the subject and the object of a declarative complement clause when the clause is not introduced by the complementizer *that* (see (13)). When the complementizer is present, however, only movement of the object leads to a grammatical sentence whereas movement of the subject results in ungrammaticality (see (14)).

(13)     a. Who do you think __ᵢ met the teacher?
         b. Who do you think the teacher met __ᵢ?

(14)     a. *Who do you think that __ᵢ met the teacher?
         b. Who do you think that the teacher met __ᵢ?

The difference between (13) and (14), which is known as *complementizer-trace* or *that-trace effect*, seems like a rather inconspicuous asymmetry between subject and object, which nevertheless has spurred a large body of syntactic research (see Pesetsky (2017) for a general review and Chapter 10 for a review of the experimental literature).

The robustness of the *that*-trace effect was already confirmed in Cowart's (1997) large-scale study of English. An additional finding of Cowart (1997) has been that even for object extraction, extraction is somewhat less acceptable when *that* is present than when it is not. The decrease in acceptability when the object is moved across *that* was small, however, in comparison to the decrease brought about by moving the subject across *that*. The finding that even the extraction of an object out of a *that* clause reduces acceptability to some degree has been confirmed in later research (e.g. Sprouse et al. 2012) (see Chapter 10 for extensive discussion).

Chomsky and Lasnik (1977) proposed a universal filter banning the *that*-trace configuration in all languages except those that allow the dropping of subject pronouns (pro-drop languages). Based on data from Dutch and Icelandic, Maling and Zaenen (1978) argued against the universality of this filter, because neither language is a pro-drop language. Overall, the non-English Germanic languages show a diverse pattern with regard to the *that*-trace effect (for Dutch, see Bennis (1986); for the Scandinavian languages, see Lohndal (2007)). Experimental studies, however, seem to exist only for German. A German example with either subject or object extraction is provided in (15).

(15)     a. Wer          denkst du,    dass __ᵢ den       Lehrer  getroffen hat?
            who.NOM   think  you    that     the.ACC teacher met      has
            'Who do you think that __ᵢ met the teacher?'
         b. Wen         glaubst du,   dass der       Lehrer  getroffen hat?
            Who. ACC  think you    that the.NOM  teacher met      has
            'Who do you think that the teacher met __ᵢ?'

In the syntactic literature on German, the existence of a *that*-trace effect has been a controversial issue. A subject–object asymmetry has been claimed to be absent in Southern varieties of German (e.g. Fanselow 1987). A *that*-trace effect has sometimes been claimed to hold in Standard German and Northern varieties, but it is not even clear whether long extraction from *that*-clauses is possible there at all (see Fanselow & Weskott (2010) for experimental evidence).

Long extraction in general and the *that*-trace effect in particular were already the topic of an early experimental study by Andersson and Kvam (1984). Using the method of magnitude estimation, Featherston (2005b) reopened the experimental approach to *that*-trace effects in German. Featherston (2005b) investigated sentences like those in (15), using sentences with embedded V2-clauses as controls. For the controls, there was no difference between subject and object extraction.[1] For sentences with extraction out of embedded *that*-clauses, the results showed a clear decrease in acceptability in comparison to the control sentences. This decrease was substantially stronger for sentences with subject extraction than for sentences with object extraction. The pattern found by Featherston (2005b) for German was similar to the pattern found by Cowart (1997) for English, the difference being that extraction across a complementizer is generally less acceptable in German than in English. From his findings, Featherston (2005b) concludes that, as far as long extraction is concerned, German is subject to the same constraints as English, but that these constraints are less visible, or have a lower violation cost, in German than in English. As pointed out in Featherston (2005b), notions like "less visible" or "lower violation costs" are descriptive terms in need of further explication. Featherston considers several ways how to flesh out these notions. For example, the *that*-trace effect may have a stronger effect on acceptability in English than on German because due to the rather rigid word order of English, native speakers of English have much stronger expectations of finding the subject directly following the complementizer than German speakers, whose expectations are less strong due to the flexible word order of German.

A book-length investigation of extraction phenomena in German is provided by Kiziak (2010). With regard to the *that*-trace effect, Kiziak (2010) by and large confirmed Featherston's (2005b) finding that subject extraction is less acceptable in German than object extraction. In only one out of over ten experiments were sentences with subject extraction judged as acceptable as sentences with object extraction. This experiment tested sentences such as those in (16).

(16)   a. Welcher  Anwalt   meinst  du,   dass __$_i$  den
          which    lawyer   think   you   that      the
          Richter   angerufen  hat.
          judge    called    has
          'Which lawyer do you think called the judge?'

       b. Welchen  Richter  meinst  du,   dass  der  Anwalt
          which    judge    think   you   that  the  lawyer
          __$_i$   angerufen  hat.
                  called    has
          Which judge do you think that the lawyer called?'

[1] Sentences with seeming extraction out of embedded V2 clauses are nowadays often analyzed as parenthetical constructions (e.g. Reis 1995). Acceptability experiments on this issue are found in Kiziak (2010).

     c. Welcher Anwalt meinst du, dass __ᵢ angerufen wurde.
       which   lawyer think  you that    called     was
       'Which lawyer do you think was called?'

The two sentences (16a) and (16b) are instances of subject and object extraction from a *that*-clause with a standard transitive verb. For sentences of this type, Kiziak (2010) found the expected acceptability decrease for sentences with subject extraction in comparison to sentences with object extraction. Sentence (16c) is again a sentence with subject extraction, but this time of the subject of a verb in the passive voice. Note that sentence (16c) contains the same verb in the embedded clause as the other two sentences in (16), but the subject is identical to the subject of the active clause. For sentences with the subject of a passive verb extracted, acceptability was as high as for sentences with object extraction. As pointed out above, this was the only case without an acceptability penalty for subject extraction. In particular, other types of nonstandard subjects, like the subjects of unaccusative verbs, still induced an acceptability decrease in comparison to objects when extracted across a complementizer. Although this does not exclude the possibility that the derived status of a passive subject contributed to the relatively high acceptability of sentences like (16c), Kiziak (2010) points out that this finding may also be due to the fact that sentences like (16c) contain only a single argument, in contrast to all other sentences investigated by her which always had at least two arguments (a subject and an object). A similar proposal was already made by Andersson and Kvam (1984).

    Experimental research of the *that*-trace effect in German is still ongoing. For example, Bayer and Salzmann (2013) and Salzmann et al. (2013) have run experiments investigating syntactic configuration that in English are exceptions to the *that*-trace effect (e.g. Culicover 1993).

### 18.2.3  Superiority

The sentence pair in (17) illustrates a further subject–object asymmetry that has been observed in English. In a multiple *wh*-question, the subject has to precede the object. If the object is moved across the subject, an ungrammatical sentence results (see Chapter 5 for additional discussion of this phenomenon).

(17)    a. Who __ᵢ read what?
        b. *Whatᵢ did who read __ᵢ?

    As with the *that*-trace effect, the superiority effect does not hold without exceptions in English. As originally discussed by Pesetsky (1987), the superiority effect disappears when *which*-phrases are used instead of bare *wh*-phrases, as in (18) (from Pesetsky 1987: 106).

(18)    a. Mary asked which man __ᵢ read which book?

       b. Mary asked which book which man read __ᵢ?

Pesetsky (1987) coined the term *d(iscourse)-linking* for *which*-phrases in order to express that such phrases presuppose that the set induced by the noun is already given in the prior discourse. According to Pesetsky (1987), in situ bare *wh*-phrases, but not in situ *which*-phrases, are subject to movement at LF (Logical Form) and thus to constraints on movement.

For German, both orders of the *wh*-phrases have been considered as grammatical, even in the case of two bare *wh*-phrases, as in (19) (e.g. Grewendorf 1988; Haider 1993). This has been taken as evidence that German lacks the kind of subject–object asymmetry that is found in English.

(19)    a. Wer          hat    was        gelesen?

          who.NOM   has    what.ACC   read

          'Who read what?'

       b. Was          hat    wer        gelesen?

          what.ACC   has    who.NOM   read

          'What did who read?'

Featherston (2005a) was the first to investigate the superiority effect in German by experimental means. He tested ditransitive sentences containing a large variety of pairs of *wh*-phrases appearing in both possible orders. An example in which the subject and the direct object are *wh*-phrases is shown in (20).

(20)    a. Wer          hat    dem        Patienten   was      empfohlen?

          who.NOM   has    the.DAT    patient     what     recommended

          'Who has recommended what to the patient?'

       b. Was    hat    wer        dem        Patienten   empfohlen?

          what    has    who.NOM   the.DAT    patient     recommended

          'Who has recommended what to the patient?'

Two experiments using magnitude estimation as experimental procedure yielded the following results. First, sentences in which a bare *wh*-subject stayed in situ and another bare *wh*-phrase moved over it received substantially lower ratings than sentences in which a bare *wh*-subject occupied the sentence-initial position. Second, when the subject was a *which*-phrase, acceptability was equally high whether the subject came first or second. Taken together, this acceptability pattern is nothing else than the pattern known from English – a superiority effect for bare *wh*-phrases but not for *which*-phrases. The similarity to English was further confirmed by Featherston (2005a) in a third experiment testing equivalent English sentences. This experiment yielded the acceptability pattern expected from the theoretical literature on the superiority effect in English – a pattern closely resembling the one Featherston found for German.

Given the common opinion that German lacks superiority effects, Featherston's results came as a surprise.[2] His conclusion that German shows a superiority effect similar to English, reflecting violations of grammatical constraints in both languages, has accordingly not gone unchallenged. In a series of experimental investigations, Fanselow and colleagues refuted Featherston's conclusion, although not his results (see, among others, Fanselow et al. (2011); Häussler et al. (2015)).

The major result yielded by the experiments of Fanselow et al. (2011) is that the observation of a superiority effect in German depends on the animacy of the wh-phrases. For example, in Experiment 4 of Fanselow et al. (2011), participants heard recorded sentences such as those in (21) and had to decide quickly whether the sentences are grammatical or not. In contrast to the sentence materials of Featherston (2005a), the sentences in (21) contain simple transitive verbs instead of ditransitive verbs. The subject was always an animate wh-phrase whereas the object was either an animate or an inanimate wh-phrase.

(21)    a. Wer     hat  wen    im     Garten  besucht?
          who.NOM  has  who.ACC  in-the  garden  visited
          'Who visited who in the garden?'

       b. Wen    hat  wer     im     Garten  besucht?
          who.ACC  has  who.NOM  in-the  garden  visited

       c. Wer     hat  was     im     Keller     gesucht?
          who.NOM  has  what.ACC  in-the  basement  searched
          'Who looked for what in the basement?'

       d. Was     hat  wer     im     Keller     gesucht?
          what.ACC  has  who.NOM  in-the  basement  searched

When the object wh-phrase was inanimate, sentences were judged as grammatical in about 98 percent of all cases, whether the subject or the object wh-phrase came first. When the object was animate, in contrast, subject initial sentences were again judged as grammatical at a high value of 98 percent, but for object-initial sentences, the grammaticality rate fell to a substantially lower value of 70 percent.

Taken together, the experimental results presented in Fanselow et al. (2011) allow the conclusion that in sentences with simple transitive verbs, a superiority effect occurs when the two wh-phrases are of equal animacy but not when the two wh-phrases differ in animacy. This is in agreement with the prior syntactic literature insofar as the examples used to demonstrate that German differs from English in not showing a superiority effect typically had an animate subject and an inanimate object (see (19) above). Fanselow et al. (2011) attribute the observation

---

[2] Wiltschko (1997) in fact already proposed that superiority effects are absent in German only for D-linked wh-phrases. For her, however, even bare wh-phrases can be D-linked under certain conditions, thus accounting for the reported absence of superiority effects in sentences like (19).

of a superiority effect with two *wh*-phrases of equal animacy to increased processing load. Interestingly, in their last experiment Fanselow et al. tested sentences with ditransitive verbs like those tested by Featherston (2005a). For such sentences, they replicated Featherston's finding of a superiority effect, despite the fact that the subject *wh*-phrase was animate and the object *wh*-phrase inanimate. Why ditransitive verbs differ from simple transitive verbs in this way remains a puzzle that is left by Fanselow et al. (2011) as a task for future research. So far, this puzzle does not seem to have been solved.

Häussler et al. (2015) present several follow-up experiments directly comparing superiority violations in English and German. These experiments were run to show that superiority effects in English reflect the violation of some grammatical constraint(s) whereas superiority effects in German are the result of parsing difficulties. In their first experiment, native speakers of English had to rate sentences such as those in (22) and native speakers of German had to rate corresponding German sentences (not shown here for reasons of space).

(22)    a. The employees knew exactly who __ᵢ criticized who at the office.
        b. The employees knew exactly who who criticized __ᵢ at the office.
        c. The employees knew exactly who __ᵢ criticized what at the office.
        d. The employees knew exactly what __ᵢ who criticized at the office.

The English speakers gave the sentences with a superiority violation rather low ratings, with no difference depending on the animacy of the object *wh*-phrase. The results of the German speakers differ from those of the English speakers, but they are also somewhat different from the results reported in Fanselow et al. (2011). First of all, sentences with a superiority violation were rated as less acceptable than sentences without such a violation, independent of the animacy of the *wh*-phrases. In contrast to English, the decrease in acceptability was only moderate. Furthermore, sentences with two animate *wh*-phrases showed a larger difference between SO and OS order than sentences with *wh*-phrases of different animacy. In comparison to Fanselow et al. (2011), the effect of animacy was small, however. Thus, whereas the results of Fanselow et al. (2011) indicated that there is no superiority effect at all for sentences with unlike animacy, the results of Häussler et al. (2015) point more to a general, although weak superiority effect that is somewhat diminished when the two *wh*-phrases differ in animacy.

The experiment just described included control sentences containing a relative-clause island violation. These sentences received equally low ratings in English and in German. This rules out the possibility that the differences between English and German for the superiority sentences in (22) reflect a general difference between English and German native speakers' sensitivity to violations of constraints on extraction. Two further experiments showed an independence of the superiority effect in English from pragmatic influences and no difference between English and German with regard to the distance between *wh*-phrase and gap; in both languages, distance did not affect acceptability. Taken together, Häussler et al. (2015) argue that their results suggest a grammatical account of the superiority effect in English but a processing account for those cases where German shows degraded acceptability in superiority configurations. However, neither the grammatical account for English nor the processing account for German is spelled out in Häussler et al. (2015).

In summary, experimental studies of superiority effects in German have led to a differentiated picture. Given the results of Fanselow et al. (2011) and Häussler et al. (2015), it seems fair to conclude that German differs from English, but questions regarding the nature of the differences remain, in particular because the results for German also differ across the two studies. In addition, the original findings of Featherston (2005a), later replicated by Fanselow et al. (2011), are still in need of explanation.

### 18.2.4   Summary: Extraction

Already before the advent of experimental syntax, it has been discussed whether constraints on extraction apply in the same way in English, for which these constraints were first postulated, and the other Germanic languages. With the growing interest in experimental investigations of syntactic issues, the various *island constraints*, the *that-trace effect*, and the *superiority effect* have become a thriving area of research. A repeated finding of this research has been that categorical differences between English and one or more other Germanic languages turned out to be less categorical than formerly thought. All constraints on movement have been shown to be active in the other Germanic languages as well. This does not mean that there are no differences. Some constraints have been shown to have weaker effects (e.g. *whether*-islands in Norwegian in the study by Kush et al. (2018)) or effects only under certain conditions (e.g. the animacy sensitivity of the superiority effect in German in the study of Fanselow et al. (2011)). Accounting for the intricate pattern of commonalities and differences is an important task for future research that is closely tied to more general questions, in particular concerning the nature of gradient acceptability (see Chapter 3 for further discussion of gradience in acceptability).

## 18.3   Word-Order Alternations

With regard to word order, a major difference between English and the other Germanic languages concerns the verb-second property. With the exception of English, the Germanic languages are generally verb-second languages, meaning that the finite verb in a main clause must occur immediately after the first phrase. According to a common analysis of verb-second, the finite verb first moves up to C° and then a phrase from the domain below CP is moved to SpecCP. English still shows a residual form of verb-second for question formation, but setting a few exceptions aside, declarative clauses in English are exempt from the verb-second requirement. Experimental investigations concerned with the word-order options that result from the general verb-second property of the non-English Germanic languages are the topic of Section 18.3.1.

Below the level of CP, several differences exist between English and various subsets of the other Germanic languages. One striking difference concerns the headedness of VP. Dutch and German are considered OV languages, while English as well as the Scandinavian languages are VO languages. In contrast to the relatively rigid word order of the Germanic VO languages, the order of arguments and adverbials is relatively free below CP in German and – to a lesser extent – Dutch. Experimental studies investigating this aspect of word order freedom are discussed in Section 18.3.2.

### 18.3.1   Filling the Clause-Initial Position

The verb-second property of the non-English Germanic languages allows a phrase of basically any category to be moved to SpecCP, thereby making word order in declarative main clauses quite flexible. However, the various word-order alternatives do not all have the same status. A few high-frequency orders can be used in a broad set of contexts. These orders are considered canonical. In all Germanic languages, subject-initial clauses have canonical word order. Sentences starting with the object, in contrast, are a prototypical case of non-canonical word order (see Chapter 12 for further discussion of non-canonical word order). The question of how speakers decide which phrase to move to SpecCP has been investigated intensively within psycholinguistics research on language production (Skopeteas & Fanselow 2009; Bader et al. 2017) and within corpus linguistics (e.g. Bouma 2008; Speyer 2008; Bader & Häussler 2010).

An even larger set of psycholinguistic experiments has investigated the comprehension of sentences with canonical and non-canonical word order (see Bornkessel & Schlesewsky (2009) for an overview). As a concrete example, consider Kristensen, Engberg-Pedersen, and Poulsen's (2014) study of subject- and object-initial sentences in Danish. In one condition, a supportive two-sentence context preceded the target sentence, which could either have SO word order (23) or OS word order (24).

(23)     a. Context sentences:
             Denne historie handler om *Peter. De andre drenge brød sig ikke om Anne.*
             'This story is about Peter. The other boys did not like Anne.'
         b. Target sentence:
             Peter ville dog invitere Anne til festen.
             'Peter would, however, invite Anne for the party.'

(24)     a. Context sentences:
             Denne historie handler om *Anne. Peter brød sig ikke om de andre piger.*
             'This story is about Anne. Peter did not like the other girls.'
         b. Target sentence:
             Anne ville Peter dog invitere til festen.
             'Anne, Peter would, however, invite for the party.'

Unsupportive contexts were derived from supportive contexts by replacing each word that is printed in italics in (23) and (24) with "XXX." Participants had to read the context and the target sentence and then had to answer a yes/no question like *Ville Peter invitere Anne?* ('Would Peter invite Anne?'). The most striking results are provided by the response accuracy for the yes/no questions. For SO sentences, the questions were answered with an accuracy of about 90 percent, whether the context was supportive or not. For OS sentences, response accuracy was as low as 51 percent, which is chance level, when the context was unsupportive. When the context was supportive, accuracy for OS sentences rose to 75 percent, which is much better than with an unsupportive context but still substantially lower than for SO sentences.

The finding that sentences with non-canonical word order – which means OS order in the present context – are more difficult to process during language comprehension has been obtained for several languages using a diverse set of experimental procedures. A supportive context typically reduces the disadvantage found for OS sentences, but does not eliminate it, as in Kristensen, Engberg-Pedersen, and Poulsen's (2014) experiment discussed above. Of course, the contexts might simply not have been of the right sort. Thus, an important question is whether contextual conditions exist in which object-initial sentences are as acceptable, or even more acceptable, than subject-initial sentences. Only a few studies have addressed this question.

Fanselow, Lenertova, and Weskott (2008) investigated this question using *wh*-questions to control the information structure of the following answer. In their first experiment, the object NP was established as focus in the answer. As illustrated in (25), the answer appeared either with SO or with OS order and the subject was either a definite NP or a pronoun.

(25)  Wen        wollte die         Krankenschwester wegen      Rick verlassen?
      who.ACC    wanted the.NOM     nurse                because-of  Rick leave
      'Who did the nurse want to leave because of Rick?'

    a. Sie/Die   Krankenschwester wollte den       Medizinstudenten
       she/the     nurse                    wanted the.ACC  student-of-medicine
       wegen       Rick    verlassen
       because-of  Rick    leave
       'The nurse/she wanted to leave the student of medicine because
       of Rick.'

    b. Den       Medizinstudenten  wollte sie/die    Krankenschwester
       the.ACC     student-of-medicine wanted she/the     nurse
       wegen       Rick      verlassen.
       because-of  Rick      leave

All four sentence types illustrated in (25) received mean ratings of about 6.2 on a seven-point scale, with no difference depending on word order or referential form of the subject. This result was corroborated in a second experiment, which in addition showed that the animacy of the object has no effect on the acceptability of object-initial sentences and that incongruent question–answer pairs lead to reduced acceptability. The latter finding is important because all findings concerning word order are null-effects, that is, sentences with SO order did not differ in acceptability from sentences with OS order. Null-effects can be caused by a lack of sensitivity of the experimental task, so showing that incongruent sentence pairs indeed reduce acceptability argues against this possibility. In a third experiment, Fanselow et al. (2008) found that object preposing is equally acceptable when the object is the focus as when the object is the accented part of a focused VP.

In a follow-up study, Weskott et al. (2011) extended the findings of Fanselow et al. (2008) to short discourses as shown in (26).

(26)  Peter  hat   den       Wagen   gewaschen.
      Peter  has   the.ACC   car     washed
      'Peter has washed the car.'

    a. Er        hat  den       Außenspiegel  ausgelassen.
       he.NOM     has  the. ACC  side-mirror   left-out
       'He left the side mirror out.'

    b. Den       Außenspiegel  hat  er        ausgelassen.
       the.ACC     side-mirror   has  he.NOM    left-out

The first sentence introduces two referents. The referent of the subject NP serves as topic in the next sentence, where it is taken up by a subject pronoun. The referent of the object NP of the second sentence is a part of the referent of the object NP in the first sentence. The part-of relation that connects the two referents in (26) is an instance of a partially ordered set

relation (poset relation) that has figured prominently in research on preposing in English (e.g. Prince 1981; Birner & Ward 1998). The two sentences in (26) stand in an adversative relation because the second clause
mentions an exception to the claim made by the first sentence. Weskott et
al.'s experiment included a second condition in which the second clause
stood in an elaboration relation to the first sentence (*besonders gründlich
gewienert* 'particularly diligently polished' instead of *ausgelassen* 'left out').
The third condition was whether participants saw the initial context
sentence shown in (26) or not.

In all conditions, Weskott et al. (2011) found relatively high ratings
(> 5.6 on a seven-point scale), showing that all sentences and all
context-sentence pairings are grammatical. There were a range of
fine-grained distinctions, however. First, whereas the presence or
absence of the context sentence had no effect on the acceptability
of SO sentences, the acceptability of OS sentences improved when
the context sentence was added. Second, with the whole–part context
sentence, OS sentences were judged as more acceptable than SO sentences. This is thus a rare case where OS order is not only highly
acceptable but even more acceptable than SO order. It remains to be
seen whether other cases of this sort – which is called *strong licensing of
the OS order* by Weskott et al. (2011) – exist.

For the other Germanic V2-languages, the issue of subject- versus
object-initial main clauses does not seem to have been investigated by
means of acceptability studies. There is, however, a growing number
of corpus studies (see, among others, Bouma (2008) for Dutch, and
Hörberg (2018) for Swedish) as well as psycho- and neurolinguistic
studies (see, among others, Kristensen, Engberg-Pedersen, & Poulsen
(2014) and Kristensen, Engberg-Pedersen, & Wallentin (2014) for
Danish, and Hörberg, Koptjevskaja-Tamm, & Kallioinen (2013) for
Swedish).

### 18.3.2   Phrase Order below the CP Level

Among the Germanic languages, German is the one with the highest
degree of word order freedom below the CP level. For example, in a
sentence like (27) with a ditransitive verb, the three arguments can be
ordered in six ways. All are considered as grammatical by syntacticians of
German (see Haider (2010) for a review of the syntactic literature).

(27)    ...dass  der Sänger  dem Produzenten  die Gitarre  geschenkt  hat.
        ...that  the singer  the producer     the guitar   given      has
        '...that the singer gave the guitar to the producer.'

Even if grammatical, the six possible orders are not all of equal acceptability. The order subject before dative object before accusative object is

usually considered the canonical order for a sentence like (27). Just as for the sentences discussed in the preceding section, in which either the subject or the object occupied the initial position of a main clause, psycholinguistic research on language comprehension has revealed a disadvantage for OS sentences even when presented within a supportive context (e.g. Meng, Bader, & Bayer 1999). The question therefore arises again whether there are contextual conditions under which OS sentences are as acceptable as corresponding SO sentences.

This question was addressed by Keller (2000b) in an early application of magnitude estimation to issues of German grammar (see also Keller 2000a). In Experiment 10 of Keller (2000b), participants saw sentences with either SO or OS order as in (29) in one of four contexts, two of which are shown in (28) (not shown are a null context and an all focus context).

(28)     a. Subject Focus: Wer kauft den Wagen? 'Who will buy the car?'
         b. Object Focus: Was kauft der Vater? 'What will the father buy?'

(29)     a. Maria glaubt,  dass der      Vater den      Wagen kauft.
            Maria believes that the.NOM father the.ACC car      buys
            'Maria believes that the father will buy the car.'
         b. Maria glaubt,  dass den      Wagen der      Vater kauft.
            Maria believes that the.ACC  car      the.NOM father buys

At least since the seminal work of Lenerz (1977), it has been a common assumption among syntacticians of German that SO order can be used independently of whether the subject or the object is questioned. OS order, in contrast, is considered felicitous only when the subject is focused. In a nutshell, the reason for this restriction is that moving the object in front of the subject below the CP level (so-called "scrambling") is only licit if scrambling has the result that the sentence focus is in its preferred position directly in front of the verb. Note that this is different from movement to SpecCP, which, as discussed above, can also apply to focused objects.

The main finding of Keller (2000b) was that OS sentences like (29b) receive much lower acceptability ratings than corresponding SO sentences even when preceded by a supportive context. This finding is not only unexpected given that such question–answer pairs are considered as fully acceptable in the syntactic literature, it also stands in striking contrast to the results of Fanselow et al. (2008), who found that with a supporting *wh*-question, object-initial main clauses are as acceptable as subject-initial main clauses. A short discussion of the theoretical implications of this difference can be found in Fanselow (2006). Why moving the object to SpecCP and moving the object in front of the subject below the level of CP affect acceptability in such different ways is a question that awaits further experimental investigations.

In addition to contextual licensing conditions, a range of word-order constraints have been identified in typological research, including principles like "animate before inanimate" or "pronoun before non-pronoun" (see Croft 2003). Keller (2000b) contains a second experiment on word order below the CP level that tests the validity of a subset of these word-order principles. The main purpose of this experiment was to investigate how different constraints jointly affect acceptability. For example, when a sentence violates several constraints, does acceptability decrease by an amount that is the sum of the decrease observed for each constraint violation in isolation? The results of this and related experiments have led to the development of *Linear Optimality Theory* (Keller 2000b, 2006), a variant of Optimality Theory with weighted constraints. A more comprehensive investigation of word-order constraints and of *Linear Optimality Theory* was provided by Ellsiepen and Bader (2018). Among other constraints, Ellsiepen and Bader (2018) investigated the interaction between the animacy constraint (animate before inanimate) and the agent constraint (agent before non-agent).

It has been known for a long time that OS order is often unmarked for sentences with an animate object, an inanimate subject, and a verb assigning the semantic role of theme to its subject (see Lenerz (1977) and much subsequent work), as in the example in (30).

(30)    Hoffentlich  ist  dem  Erfinder  eine  Lösung    eingefallen.
        hopefully    is   the  inventor  a     solution  occurred
        'Hopefully, a solution occurred to the inventor.'

Furthermore, corpus studies of German (e.g. Kempen & Harbusch 2004; Bader & Häussler 2010) have shown that animacy is the best predictor of word order below the CP level in German. What had not been considered in these corpus studies, probably because such examples are too rare, are sentences with an inanimate subject, an animate object and a causative verb, as illustrated in (31).

(31)    a. Mir   ist   erzählt   worden,  dass das       Feuer den
           me    is    told      was      that the.NOM   fire  the.ACC
           Winzer            ruiniert hat.
           wine-grower      ruined   has
           'I was told that the fire ruined the wine grower.'
        b. Mir   ist  erzählt  worden,  dass den       Winzer       das
           me    is   told     was      that the.ACC   wine-grower  the.NOM
           Feuer ruiniert hat.
           fire  ruined   has

For sentences such as those in (31), Ellsiepen and Bader (2018) found that the SO variant was rated as highly acceptable whereas the OS variant received substantially lower ratings. This contrasts with findings for sentences with a non-agentive subject, as in (30). For sentences similar to (30), Ellsiepen and Bader (2018) found higher ratings for OS than for SO order, confirming the importance of the animacy constraint for German word order. The agent constraint, however, is even more important, as witnessed by the results for sentences such as those in (31). Given this finding, Ellsiepen and Bader (2018) also searched for corresponding corpus examples. Although such examples are relatively rare in comparison to (30), they still occur with some regularity and almost always show up with SO order. This study thus shows how corpus linguistics can benefit from research in experimental syntax (see Chapter 25 for a detailed exploration of corpus studies in syntax).

The studies reviewed so far have been concerned with the empirical question of what factors determine the acceptability of the order of subject and object, and with the theoretical question of how graded acceptability can be modeled within syntactic theory. Other studies have taken up more specific questions related to particular syntactic analysis. One question that has already led to several experimental investigations is whether there is a designated topic position within the German clause structure. In the wake of Rizzi's (1997) seminal work on the cartography of the left periphery, Frey (2004) postulated a topic phrase between CP and IP for German. The boundary between IP and TopicP can be overtly marked by a sentence adverbial. All experiments that took Frey's claim to an empirical test made use of this possibility.

Fanselow (2006) had participants rate sentences such as (32) on a 1–7 scale. All sentences contained two cataphoric pronouns in a preposed adverbial clause. According to Frey (2004), such a cataphoric relationship is only possible if the antecedent is a topic.

(32)    a. Obwohl    er$_i$   sie$_j$   liebt, hat   gestern $\Delta_1$ der Hans$_i$ $\Delta_2$
          although   he   her   loves has   yesterday the Hans
          seine   Freundin$_j$ $\Delta_3$   verlassen.
          his     girlfriend     left
          'Although he loves her, Hans surprisingly left his girlfriend yesterday.'
    b. $\Delta$ = überraschenderweise 'surprisingly'

The main clause always contained a sentence adverbial; what was varied was the position of the subject and the object relative to this sentence adverbial. According to Frey (2004), cataphoric binding is only possible when the adverbial occurs at position $\Delta_3$ and the two potential antecedents thus occupy the presumed topic position. In an additional condition not shown here, cataphoric binding was prevented by morphosyntactic means. This resulted in strongly reduced acceptability. For sentences such as (32), however, acceptability was generally high. In accordance with Frey (2004), sentences with both antecedents preceding the sentence adverbial received a significantly higher mean acceptability value than sentences in which the adverbial preceded one or both antecedents, but the magnitude of the difference was small, suggesting that cataphoric binding is possible for all three positions of the sentence adverbial. As pointed out in Fanselow (2006), this finding does not rule out the existence of a designated topic position in German, but it undermines some of the evidence for it.

The opposite conclusion was reached by Störzer and Stolterfoht (2018), who probed the existence of a designated topic position as hypothesized by Frey (2004) by investigating NPs with different referential properties. An example stimulus from their first experiment is shown in (33).

(33)  a.  Der Nachbar erwahnte, dass SUBJ vielleicht SUBJ das Auto gewaschen hat.
          the neighbor mentioned that        maybe        the car   washed    has
          'The neighbor mentioned that maybe SUBJECT washed the car.'

      b.  SUBJ(ECT) = $\begin{cases} \text{der Junge 'the boy'} \\ \text{zwei Jungen 'two boys'} \\ \text{kein Junge 'no boy'} \end{cases}$

The subject of the embedded clause could appear either in front of or behind the sentence adverbial *vielleicht* ('perhaps') and it could be of one of three types. It was either a referential NP (definite NP), or a possibly referential NP (a numerically quantified NP), or a non-referential NP (a negatively quantified NP). Participants had to rate sentence acceptability on a scale from 1 to 5. The results show that referential NPs are preferred in front of the sentence adverbial, non-referential NPs are preferred behind the sentence adverbial, and possibly referential NPs show no preference. Störzer and Stolterfoht (2018) take this pattern of acceptability as evidence for Frey's hypothesized sentence structure because referential NPs are preferentially topics whereas non-referential NPs are banned from the topic position.

## 18.4  Summary

This chapter has reviewed research that has applied the tools of experimental syntax to the non-English Germanic languages. The chapter focused on two broad classes of syntactic phenomena: constraints on movement – island constraints, the *that*-trace effect, and superiority effects – and word-order alternations, including alternations involving SpecCP and alternations below the CP level. These phenomena were selected for review because they represent central issues of syntactic research and because they have been subject to a large number of experimental studies. A range of further syntactic phenomena for which experimental evidence exists but which could not be included in the current chapter are listed in Table 18.1.

Table 18.1 *Overview of additional syntactic phenomena that have been the subject of acceptability studies but are not discussed in this chapter*

| Phenomenon | Language | Literature |
|---|---|---|
| Verb movement (V → I and I → C) | Danish, Icelandic, Faroese | Heycock et al. (2010) |
| Verb clusters | Dutch, German | Bader & Schmid (2009), Barbiers, Bennis, & Dros-Hendriks (2018) |
| Auxiliary selection in the perfect tense (choice between a form of 'to be' or 'to have') | German | Keller & Sorace (2003) |
| Extraposition of relative clauses | German | Uszkoreit et al. (1998), Konieczny (2000) |
| Dative alternation | Danish | Kizach & Balling (2013) |
| Discourse particles | German | Bayer et al. (2016) |

So far, the experimental study of the non-English Germanic languages has already led to a wealth of empirical data. Yet it seems premature to draw firm conclusions of a general nature. A pattern that has been revealed recurrently in the studies reviewed above is that purported differences between English and the other Germanic languages turned out to be less striking than one would have expected from the prior syntactic literature. This is not to say that there are no differences at all, but they are often not so sharp that one can easily determine what the locus of the differences is. For example, is an observed difference due to different grammars per se, or due to processing differences that depend only indirectly on properties of the grammar? For English, the issue of separating grammar and processing in determining sentence acceptability has become one of the most active areas of research. Further advances in this regard are to be expected by extending this kind of research to experimental cross-linguistic studies of the Germanic languages. Furthermore, combining experiments with corpus data can be highly informative when interpreting acceptability data, as in the case of relative clause island violations in the Scandinavian languages.

## References

Andersson, S.-G. & Kvam, S. (1984). *Satzverschränkung im heutigen Deutsch.* Tübingen: Narr.

Bader, M., Ellsiepen, E., Koukoulioti, V., & Portele, Y. (2017). Filling the prefield: Findings and challenges. In C. Freitag, O. Bott, & F. Schlotterbeck, eds., *Two Perspectives on V2: The Invited Talks of the DGfS 2016 Workshop "V2 in Grammar and Processing: Its Causes and Its Consequences."* Konstanz: University of Konstanz, pp. 27–49.

Bader, M. & Häussler, J. (2010). Word order in German: A corpus study. *Lingua*, 120(3), 717–762.

Bader, M. & Schmid, T. (2009). Verb clusters in Colloquial German. *Journal of Comparative Germanic Linguistics*, 12(3), 175–228.

Barbiers, S., Bennis, H., & Dros-Hendriks, L. (2018). Merging verb cluster variation. *Linguistic Variation*, 18(1), 144–196.

Bard, E. G., Robertson, D., & Sorace, A. (1996). Magnitude estimation of linguistic acceptability. *Language*, 72(1), 32–68.

Bayer, J., Häussler, J., & Bader, M. (2016). A new diagnostic for cyclic Wh-movement: Discourse particles in German questions. *Linguistic Inquiry*, 47(4), 591–629.

Bayer, J. & Salzmann, M. (2013). That-trace effects and resumption: How improper movement can be repaired. In P. Brandt & E. Fuß, eds., *Repairs: The Added Value of Being Wrong*. Berlin: De Gruyter, pp. 275–333.

Bennis, H. (1986). *Gaps and Dummies*. Dordrecht: Foris.

Birner, B. J. & Ward, G. (1998). *Information Status and Noncanonical Word Order in English*. Amsterdam and Philadelphia: John Benjamins.

Boeckx, C. (2007). Islands. *Language and Linguistics Compass*, 2(1), 151–167.

Bornkessel, I. & Schlesewsky, M. (2009). *Processing Syntax and Morphology: A Neurocognitive Perspective*. Oxford: Oxford University Press.

Bouma, G. J. (2008). Starting a sentence in Dutch: A corpus study of subject- and object- fronting. Doctoral dissertation, University of Groningen.

Chomsky, N. (1973). Conditions on transformations. In S. R. Anderson & P. Kiparsky, eds., *A Festschrift for Morris Halle*. New York: Holt, Rinehart & Winston, pp. 232–286.

Chomsky, N. & Lasnik, H. (1977). Filters and control. *Linguistic Inquiry*, 8, 425–504.

Christensen, K. R., Kizach, J., & Nyvad, A. M. (2013). Escape from the island: Grammaticality and (reduced) acceptability of *wh*-island violations in Danish. *Journal of Psycholinguistic Research*, 42, 51–70.

Christensen, K. R. & Nyvad, A. M. (2014). On the nature of escapable relative islands. *Nordic Journal of Linguistics*, 48(1), 37–65.

Cowart, W. (1997). *Experimental Syntax: Applying Objective Methods to Sentence Judgments*. Thousand Oaks, CA: Sage.

Croft, W. (2003). *Typology and Universals*. Cambridge: Cambridge University Press.

Culicover, P. W. (1993). Evidence against ECP accounts of the *that*-t effect. *Linguistic Inquiry*, 24(3), 557–561.

Ellsiepen, E. & Bader, M. (2018). Constraints on argument linearization in German. *Glossa: a Journal of General Linguistics*, 3(1), 1–36. DOI:10.5334/gjgl.258

Engdahl, E. (1982). Restrictions on unbounded dependencies in Swedish. In E. Engdahl & E. Ejerhed, eds., *Readings on Unbounded Dependencies in Scandinavian Languages*. Stockholm: Almqvist & Wiksell, pp. 151–174.

Engdahl, E. (1997). Relative clause extractions in context. *Working Papers in Scandinavian Syntax*, 60, 51–79.

Erteschik-Shir, N. (1973). On the nature of island constraints. Doctoral dissertation, Massachusetts Institute of Technology.

Erteschik-Shir, N. & Lappin, S. (1979). Dominance and the functional explanation of island phenomena. *Theoretical Linguistics*, 6(1–3), 41–86.

Fanselow, G. (1987). *Konfigurationalität: Untersuchungen zur Universalgrammatik am Beispiel des Deutschen*. Tübingen: Narr.

Fanselow, G. (2006). On pure syntax (uncontaminated by information structure). In P. Brandt & E. Fuss, eds., *Form, Structure and Grammar*. Berlin: Akademie Verlag, pp. 137–158.

Fanselow, G., Lenertova, D., & Weskott, T. (2008). Studies on the acceptability of object movement to Spec, CP. In A. Steube, ed., *The Discourse Potential of Underspecified Structures*, vol. 8. Berlin: De Gruyter, pp. 413–438.

Fanselow, G., Schlesewsky, M., Vogel, R., & Weskott, T. (2011). Animacy effects on crossing *wh*-movement in German. *Linguistics*, 49(4), 657–683.

Fanselow, G. & Weskott, T. (2010). A short note on long movement in German. *Linguistische Berichte*, 222, 129–140.

Featherston, S. (2005a). Magnitude estimation and what it can do for your syntax: Some *wh*-constraints in German. *Lingua*, 115(11), 1525–1550.

Featherston, S. (2005b). *That*-trace in German. *Lingua*, 115(9), 1277–1302.

Frey, W. (2004). A medial topic position for German. *Linguistische Berichte*, 198, 153–190.

Gibson, E. (2000). The dependency locality theory: A distance-based theory of linguistic complexity. In A. Marantz, Y. Miyashita, & W. O'Neil, eds., *Image, Language, Brain. Papers from the First Mind Articulation Project Symposium*, Cambridge, MA: MIT Press, pp. 95–126.

Goodall, G. (2015). The D-linking effect on extraction from islands and non-islands. *Frontiers in Psychology*, 5, 1–11.

Grewendorf, G. (1988). *Aspekte der deutschen Syntax: Eine Rektions-Bindungs-Analyse*. Tübingen: Narr.

Haider, H. (1993). *Deutsche Syntax – generativ. Vorstudien zu einer projektiven Theorie der Grammatik*. Tübingen: Narr.

Haider, H. (2010). *The Syntax of German*. Cambridge: Cambridge University Press.

Häussler, J., Grant, M., Fanselow, G. & Frazier, L. (2015). Superiority in English and German: Cross-language grammatical differences? *Syntax*, 18(3), 235–265.

Heycock, C., Sorace, A., & Hansen, Z. S. (2010). V-to-I and V2 in subordinate clauses: An investigation of Faroese in relation to Icelandic and Danish. *Journal of Comparative Germanic Linguistics*, 13(1), 61–97.

Hofmeister, P. & Sag, I. A. (2010). Cognitive constraints and island effects. *Language*, 86(2), 366–415.

Hörberg, T. (2018). Functional motivations behind direct object fronting in written Swedish: A corpus-distributional account. *Glossa: A Journal of General Linguistics*, 3(1), 81. DOI:10.5334/gjgl.502

Hörberg, T., Koptjevskaja-Tamm, M., & Kallioinen, P. (2013). The neuro-physiological correlate to grammatical function reanalysis in Swedish. *Language and Cognitive Processes*, 28(3), 388–416.

Keller, F. (2000a). Evaluating competition-based models of word order. In L. R. Gleitman & A. K. Joshi, eds., *Proceedings of the 22nd Annual Conference of the Cognitive Science Society*. Mahwah, NJ: Lawrence Erlbaum, pp. 747–752.

Keller, F. (2000b). Gradience in grammar: Experimental and computational aspects of degrees of grammaticality. Doctoral dissertation, University of Edinburgh.

Keller, F. (2006). Linear optimality theory as a model of gradience in grammar. In G. Fanselow, C. Féry, R. Vogel, & M. Schlesewsky, eds., *Gradience in Grammar: Generative Perspectives*. New York: Oxford University Press, pp. 270–287.

Keller, F. & Sorace, A. (2003). Gradient auxiliary selection and impersonal passivization in German: An experimental investigation. *Journal of Linguistics*, 39, 57–108.

Kempen, G. & Harbusch, K. (2004). Generating natural word orders in a semi-free word order language: Treebank-based linearization preferences for German. In A. Gelbukh, ed., *Fifth International Conference on Intelligent Text Processing and Computational Linguistics (CICLing2004), Seoul, South Korea* (Lecture Notes in Computer Science, 2945). Berlin: Springer, pp. 350–354.

Kizach, J. & Balling, L. W. (2013). Givenness, complexity, and the Danish dative alternation. *Memory & Cognition*, 41(8), 1159–1171.

Kiziak, T. (2010). *Extraction Asymmetries: Experimental Evidence from German*. Amsterdam and Philadelphia: John Benjamins.

Kluender, R. (1998). On the distinction between strong and weak islands: A processing perspective. In P. W. Culicover & L. McNally, eds., *The Limits of Syntax* (Syntax and Semantics, 29). San Diego, CA: Academic Press, pp. 241–279.

Kluender, R. & Kutas, M. (1993). Subjacency as a processing phenomenon. *Language and Cognitive Processes*, 8, 573–633.

Konieczny, L. (2000). Locality and parsing complexity. *Journal of Psycholinguistic Research*, 29, 627–645.

Kristensen, L. B., Engberg-Pedersen, E., & Poulsen, M. (2014). Context improves comprehension of fronted objects. *Journal of Psycholinguistic Research*, 43(2), 125–140.

Kristensen, L. B., Engberg-Pedersen, E., & Wallentin, M. (2014). Context predicts word order processing in Broca's region. *Journal of Cognitive Neuroscience*, 26(12), 2762–2777.

Kush, D., Lohndal, T., & Sprouse, J. (2018). Investigating variation in island effects. *Natural Language & Linguistic Theory*, 36, 743–779.

Lenerz, J. (1977). *Zur Abfolge nominaler Satzglieder im Deutschen*. Tübingen: Narr.

Lohndal, T. (2007). That-t in Scandinavian and elsewhere: Variation in the position of C. *Working Papers in Scandinavian Syntax*, 79, 47–73.

Maling, J. & Zaenen, A. (1978). The nonuniversality of a surface filter. *Linguistic Inquiry*, 9(3), 475–497.

Meng, M., Bader, M., & Bayer, J. (1999). Die Verarbeitung von Subjekt-Objekt-Ambiguitäten im Kontext. In I. Wachsmuth & B. Jung, eds., *KogWiss99. Proceedings der 4. Fachtagung der Gesellschaft für Kognitionswissenschaft.* St. Augustin: Infix Verlag, pp. 244–249.

Nyvad, A. M., Christensen, K. R., & Vikner, S. (2017). CP-recursion in Danish: A cP/Cpanalysis. *The Linguistic Review*, 34(3), 449–477.

Pesetsky, D. (1987). Wh-in-situ: Movement and unselective binding. In E. J. Reuland & A. G. B. ter Meulen, eds., *The Representation of (In)definiteness*, Cambridge, MA: MIT Press, pp. 98–129.

Pesetsky, D. (2017). Complementizer-trace effects. In M. Everaert & H. van Riemsdijk, eds., *The Wiley Blackwell Companion to Syntax*, 2nd ed. New York: John Wiley & Sons, pp. 1–34.

Phillips, C. (2013). Some arguments and nonarguments for reductionist accounts of syntactic phenomena. *Language and Cognitive Processes*, 28(1–2), 156–187.

Poulsen, M. (2008). Acceptability and processing of long-distance dependencies in Danish. *Nordic Journal of Linguistics*, 31(1), 73–107.

Prince, E. F. (1981). Toward a taxonomy of given-new information. In P. Cole, ed., *Radical Pragmatic*. New York: Academic Press, pp. 223–255.

Reis, M. (1995). Extractions from verb-second clauses in German? In U. Lutz & J. Pafel, eds., *On Extraction and Extraposition in German*. Amsterdam: John Benjamins, pp. 45–88.

Rizzi, L. (1997). The fine structure of the left periphery. In L. Haegeman, ed., *Elements of Grammar*. Dordrecht: Kluwer, pp. 281–337.

Ross, J. R. (1967). Constraints on variables in syntax. Doctoral dissertation, Massachusetts Institute of Technology.

Salzmann, M., Häussler, J., Bader, M., & Bayer, J. (2013). *That*-trace effects without traces: An experimental investigation. In S. Kleine & S. Sloggett, eds., *NELS 42: Proceedings of the 42nd Meeting of the North East Linguistic Society*, vol. 2. CreateSpace Independent Publishing Platform, pp. 149–162.

Skopeteas, S. & Fanselow, G. (2009). Effects of givenness and constraints on free word order. In M. Zimmermann & C. Féry, eds., *Information Structure: Theoretical, Typological, and Experimental Perspectives*. Oxford: Oxford University Press, pp. 307–331.

Sorace, A. (1992). Conditions on syntactic knowledge: Auxiliary selection in native and non-native grammars of Italian. Doctoral dissertation, University of Edinburgh.

Speyer, A. (2008). German Vorfeld-filling as constraint interaction. In A. Benz & P. Kühnlein, eds., *Constraints in Discourse*. Amsterdam and Philadelphia: John Benjamins, pp. 267–290.

Sprouse, J., Caponigro, I., Greco, C., & Cecchetto, C. (2016). Experimental syntax and the variation of island effects in English and Italian. *Natural Language & Linguistic Theory*, 34(1), 307–344.

Sprouse, J. & Hornstein, N., eds. (2013). *Experimental Syntax and Island Effects*. Cambridge: Cambridge University Press.

Sprouse, J., Schütze, C., & Almeida, D. (2013). A comparison of informal and formal acceptability judgments using a random sample from *Linguistic Inquiry* 2001–2010. *Lingua*, 134, 219–248.

Sprouse, J., Wagers, M., & Phillips, C. (2012). A test of the relation between working-memory capacity and syntactic island effects. *Language*, 88(1), 82–123.

Störzer, M. & Stolterfoht, B. (2018). Is German discourse-configurational? Experimental evidence for a topic position. *Glossa: A Journal of General Linguistics*, 3(1), 1–24.

Tutunjian, D., Heinat, F., Klingvall, E., & Wiklund, A.-L. (2017). Processing relative clause extractions in Swedish. *Frontiers in Psychology*, 8, 2118.

Uszkoreit, H., Brants, T., Duchier, D., Krenn, B., Konieczny, L., Oepen, S., & Skut, W. (1998). Studien zur performanzorientierten Linguistik Aspekte der Relativsatzextraposition im Deutschen. *Kognitionswissenschaft*, 7, 129–133.

Weskott, T., Hörnig, R., Fanselow, G., & Kliegl, R. (2011). Contextual licensing of marked OVS word order in German. *Linguistische Berichte*, 225, 3–18.

Wiltschko, M. (1997). D-Linking, scrambling und superiority in German. *GAGL: Groninger Arbeiten zur germanistischen Linguistik*, 41, 107–142.

# 19

# Acceptability Studies in Semitic Languages

Aya Meltzer-Asscher

## 19.1   Introduction

The Semitic language family is a branch of the Afroasiatic language family, spoken mostly in Western Asia and North Africa. There are about 330 million speakers of Semitic languages in the world today; the most widely spoken language in this family is Arabic, in its various vernaculars (300 million speakers), followed by Amharic (20 million), Hebrew (9 million), Tigrinya (7 million), Tigre (1 million), Aramaic (0.5–1 million), and Maltese (0.5 million).

Most Semitic languages do not have a large number of speakers; however, for geographical, historical, and sociological reasons, some of them have sizeable linguistics communities, and have played an important role in modern theoretical linguistics. The investigation of Semitic languages has shed light on issues such as derivational and inflectional morphology, clause structure and word-order variations, the syntax of noun phrases, the syntax of *wh*-dependencies, the null subject parameter, and more.

Traditionally, theoretical linguists investigating these and other topics have relied on their own intuitions (or those of a handful of informants) for determining the (un)grammaticality of structures, as a basis for developing syntactic theories. In recent years, however, the theoretical linguist's toolbox has been expanded to include formal sentence acceptability experiments. While, ultimately, the goal of these experiments if often to determine the grammaticality status of a sentence, this is not achieved by an introspective decision as to whether the structure belongs to the grammar of the language or not; rather, participants are asked to rate the acceptability of the structure on a scale. Such acceptability ratings reflect, to a large degree, the grammatical status of the sentence. However, they also reflect any number of other factors: the sentence's plausibility, its structure's frequency and complexity; the processing difficulty associated with it, etc. (see Chapters 1–4 and Cowart 1997; Sprouse 2007

Almeida 2014; Schütze 2016). The mapping between acceptability and grammaticality is thus not always straightforward. However, as exemplified below, with careful design eliminating confounding factors, acceptability ratings can offer extremely valuable insights about the grammar of a language, while additionally providing us with other types of information, e.g. regarding processing costs (see Chapter 5 for further discussion of acceptability and grammaticality). Thus, this type of research can contribute to both grammatical (in particular syntactic) theory and psycholinguistic theory.

The need for conducting formal sentence acceptability experiments is under ongoing debate. While some authors have argued that linguists should not rely solely on their own informal judgments (e.g. Ferreira 2005; Wasow & Arnold 2005; Gibson et al. 2013), others maintain that individual judgments can in most cases be trusted (Phillips 2010). In support of the latter claim, several studies have shown that data collected in formal sentence acceptability studies overwhelmingly replicate informal judgments from the linguistic literature (see Chapter 1 for further discussion, and Sprouse et al. 2013).

Importantly, however, a recent paper by Linzen and Oseki (2018) highlights the need for formal acceptability studies for languages with smaller communities of linguists. Linzen and Oseki collected formal acceptability ratings from a large sample of speakers for Hebrew and Japanese sentence pairs which were argued in the theoretical literature to contrast in grammaticality. They found that only about half of the reported contrasts replicated, whereas the others failed to replicate (and in certain cases even showed a contrast in the opposite direction). It should be noted that the authors purposefully chose contrasts which they considered questionable to begin with. However, the conclusion still stands that idiosyncratic judgments of individual authors can make their way into the literature. Linzen and Oseki argue that this possibility is especially real in the case of smaller language (or linguistics) communities. The reason for this is that in these instances, idiosyncratic judgments can "slip through the cracks" more easily, since there are not a lot of native-speaking linguists available to identify or correct them in the various stages of the peer-review process. The authors emphasize that not every claim about (un)grammaticality needs to be backed up by experimentation. There is a large number of structures that are very obviously grammatical or ungrammatical (e.g. 'the boys sings'). However, for subtler intuitions, Linzen and Oseki's findings underline the importance of appealing to a larger set of speakers (and of sentences) to verify authors' intuitions.

Indeed, as in the syntactic research community in general, the last decade has seen more experimental studies of sentence acceptability in Semitic languages, compared to previous years. Nevertheless, such studies are still very rare, and to our knowledge, all the published results are either from Arabic or Hebrew.[1] Notably, the only field where systematic research using acceptability studies was carried out is that of *wh*-dependencies. This research is presented in Section 19.2. Other phenomena, in particular Semitic agreement patterns and dative constructions, were the subject of sporadic research, which is summarized in Section 19.3, along with some underexplored topics in Semitic grammars which could benefit from future studies.[2] Section 19.4 discusses some of the challenges that face researchers carrying out acceptability studies (and other types of experimental work) in Semitic languages, as well as some possible ways to address them.

## 19.2 Contributions from Acceptability Studies to Understanding Semitic *Wh*-Dependencies

In this section, I will present results from sentence acceptability studies in Semitic languages, designed to address questions relating to *wh*-dependencies. *Wh*-dependencies (also termed A′-dependencies or filler–gap dependencies) are structures in which an antecedent, which appears in the periphery of the clause, is interpreted in a thematic position (the trace/gap position) inside the clause, as exemplified in (1) (in the examples, the antecedent, also termed filler, is underlined; the thematic position is marked by a trace, t). These structures are used cross-linguistically to create constituent questions, relative clauses (RCs) and clefts, among other constructions.

(1)     a. Iraqi     Arabic *wh*-question          (Wahba 1992):
            <u>meno$_i$</u>     Mona   šaafa t$_i$?
            who       Mona   saw
            'Who did Mona see?'
        b. Tigrinya RC   (Overfelt 2009):
            ʔita   ʔiti   səbʔaj sənuj     t$_i$ tsiħifuwa zinəbərə          <u>dəbdabe$_i$</u>
            that   that   man    Monday    wrote    REL-AUX-3M.SG letter
            'The letter that the man wrote on Monday'

   Languages vary in the ways they form *wh*-dependencies and in the constraints posed on the formation of these structures. Two such dimensions of variation have received considerable attention in the theoretical literature: adherence to island constraints and use of resumptive pronouns

---

[1] Other types of experimental work on Semitic languages are also relatively scarce. While there has been experimental work on language acquisition and language disorders, psycholinguistic research on online processing in typical adult speakers is still rather scant. Within research of online processing, relatively much work was done on word-level processing, with fewer studies examining sentence processing.

[2] There have also been acceptability studies in Semitic languages which addressed lexical questions (e.g. Ibrahim 2016), morphological issues, particularly the (non)existence of the Semitic root (see review in Prunet 2006), or semantic topics (Fadlon, Sassoon, & Schumacher 2018). These will not be discussed in this chapter.

(RPs). Since Ross (1967), it has been known that there are certain domains, called islands, from which a *wh*-element cannot be extracted (see Chapter 9 for extended discussion of this topic). For example, the ungrammaticality of (2) in Hebrew (and in its English translation) shows that noun phrases (NPs) containing relative clauses are islands, and cannot accommodate traces.

(2)    *ʔeize  sefer$_i$   pagašta      ʔet   ha-sofer      še-katav  t$_i$?
       Which  book    met-2M.SG   ACC   the-author   that-wrote
       *'Which book did you meet the author who wrote?'

Although island constraints are relatively consistent cross-linguistically, certain languages have been argued to not obey (or partially obey) various islands (e.g. Scandinavian languages, Erteschik-Shir 1973; Engdahl 1997). The cross-linguistic status of island constraints potentially carries far-reaching implications. As noted by Phillips (2013), islands are often considered to be a prime example of a subtle, arbitrary syntactic phenomenon which is not learnable from the input to which the child is exposed, and therefore must be universal and innate. Thus, any difference between languages with regard to island sensitivity requires close attention (see Sprouse et al. 2016). The facts from Semitic bearing on this issue are presented in Section 19.2.1.

Another dimension of *wh*-dependency formation on which languages differ is the nature of the tail of the dependency, namely the element in the thematic position. Traditionally (see e.g. Sells 1984), languages were classified into "intrusive resumption" languages (e.g. English), in which dependencies are resolved with traces/gaps, versus "grammaticized resumption" ones (e.g. Celtic) which allow, and in some cases obligate, dependencies to be resolved with a resumptive pronoun. In this early literature, traces were often analyzed as the result of A´-movement, whereas RPs were analyzed as pronouns bound in situ by an A´-operator, with no movement operation involved (see Chapters 7 and 8 for additional discussion of resumptive pronouns).

Semitic languages are generally categorized as grammaticized resumption languages. However, these languages vary in the precise distribution of RPs, e.g. whether they appear in relative clauses only or also in *wh*-questions, and in what sentential positions they can or must appear. For example, in Lebanese Arabic, a gap is excluded and an RP is mandatory in object positions of restrictive RCs (3); in Moroccan Arabic, gaps and RPs freely alternate in this position (4) (examples from Choueiri (2017), which offers a review of resumption in Arabic).

(3)    l-mmasil$_i$         lli    (šifti-i$_i$          / *šifte t$_i$)
       the-actor-M.SG   that  saw-2F.SG-him     saw-2F.SG
       b-l-matʕam        miš   mašhuur.
       in-the-restaurant   NEG   famous-M.SG
       'The actor that you saw in the restaurant is not famous.'

(4)  žbar-t      l-ktab$_i$    lli    nsiti      (-h$_i$ / t$_i$)  f-l-qism.
     found-1.SG  the-book    that   forgot-2.SG  it        in-the-class
     'I found the book that you forgot in the classroom.'

In recent years it has become apparent that even in "grammaticized resumption" languages, the picture is more complex than it originally appeared to be. Much research, focusing mainly on Semitic languages (Aoun, Choueiri, & Hornstein (2001) and Aoun, Benmamoun, & Choueiri (2010) on Lebanese Arabic; Malkawi & Guilliot (2007) on Jordanian Arabic; Sichel (2014) on Hebrew) has revealed that even within a language, resumption is not a unified phenomenon. Rather, it was argued (based mostly on reconstruction facts) that certain RPs are "real" resumptives, bound in situ, whereas others are pronounced copies of a trace of a moved element. In addition, there is evidence that RPs are not always completely acceptable in presumably grammaticized resumption languages. Section 19.2.2 presents the results from acceptability studies bearing on the status of resumption in Semitic.

Another area where the facts turned out to be more complex than originally thought is the interaction of resumption with islands. An early observation maintained that RPs "salvage" islands; islands with RPs in place of gaps were claimed to be grammatical, presumably since in these cases binding, rather than movement, was involved (e.g. Erteschik-Shir 1992, Ross 1967). However, a number of recent studies failed to show that the acceptability of island violations is improved with resumption (e.g. Alexopoulou & Keller 2007; Heestand, Xiang, & Polinsky 2011; though see Ackerman, Frazier, & Yoshida 2018; for review see Meltzer-Asscher 2021). Section 19.2.3 details the relevant results from Semitic languages. The following subsections thus discuss island constraints, resumption outside of islands, and resumption inside islands, respectively. It is important to note, however, that these topics are inherently intertwined, so the division into subsections is to some degree arbitrary.

### 19.2.1 Cross-Linguistic Variation in Island Constraints

As explained above, there have been claims that different languages do not obey certain island constraints. One island whose cross-linguistic status has received much attention is the *wh*-island, where *wh*-movement occurs from within an embedded *wh*-clause, as in (5). A similar configuration is the *whether*-island, in which the embedded clause is a yes/no question (6). This latter configuration is sometimes judged as a "weaker" island, not resulting in stark ungrammaticality (see e.g. Kluender 1998).

(5)  *This is the woman$_i$ that John asked [who$_j$ t$_j$ saw t$_i$].

(6)  ?This is the woman$_i$ that John asked [whether Pete saw t$_i$].

Over the years, it was observed in the theoretical literature that *wh*-island structures are grammatical in Hebrew (Reinhart 1981; Preminger 2010). Keshev and Meltzer-Asscher (2019) set out to test this claim experimentally, using the superadditivity paradigm, developed by Sprouse et al. (2011, 2013, 2016); for an explanation of the paradigm and its rationale, see Chapter 9. Their first experiment manipulated the length of the dependency (gap in matrix clause/embedded clause) and the complexity of the embedded clause (*that*-clause/*wh*-question), as exemplified in (7). Condition (7d), with an extraction out of an embedded *wh*-question, is the *wh*-island condition. If the acceptability penalty for this structure is larger than the sum of the independent penalties for length and complexity, this would suggest a grammatical island constraint, reducing acceptability over and above the decrease expected due to these reasons.

(7)     a. Matrix resolution | Embedded *that*-clause:

| ha-safranit | makira | ?et | ha-profesor |
|---|---|---|---|
| the-librarian | knows | ACC | the-professor |
| ha-kašuax$_i$ | še-t$_i$ | hisik | še-ha-metargelet |
| the-strict | that | understood | that-the-assistant |
| telamed | ?et | ha-student | ha-mitkaše. |
| will+teach | ACC | the-student | the-weak |

'The librarian knows the strict professor$_i$ who t$_i$ understood that the assistant will teach the weak student.'

b. Embedded resolution | Embedded *that*-clause:

| ha-safranit | makira | ?et | ha-student |
|---|---|---|---|
| the-librarian | knows | ACC | the-student |
| ha-mitkaše$_i$ | še-ha-profesor | | ha-kašuax |
| the-weak | that-the-professor | | the-strict |
| hisik | še-ha-metargelet | telamed | t$_i$. |
| understood | that-the-assistant | will+teach | |

'The librarian knows the weak student$_i$ that the strict professor understood that the assistant will teach t$_i$.'

c. Matrix resolution | Embedded *wh*-question:

| ha-safranit | makira | ?et | ha-profesor |
|---|---|---|---|
| the-librarian | knows | ACC | the-professor |
| ha-kašuax$_i$ | še-t$_i$ | hisik | matay |
| the-strict | that | understood | when |
| ha-metargelet | telamed | ?et | ha-student |
| the-assistant | will+teach | ACC | the-student |
| ha-mitkaše. | | | |
| the-weak | | | |

'The librarian knows the strict professor$_i$ who t$_i$ understood when the assistant will teach the weak student.'

d. Embedded resolution | Embedded *wh*-question:

| ha-safranit | makira | ʔet | ha-student | ha-mitkaše$_i$ |
|---|---|---|---|---|
| the-librarian | knows | ACC | the-student | the-weak |
| še-ha-profesor | ha-kašuax | hisik | matay | |
| that-the-professor | the-strict | understood | when | |
| ha-metargelet | telamed | t$_i$. | | |
| the-TA | will+teach | | | |

'The librarian knows the weak student$_i$ that the strict professor understood when the TA will teach t$_i$.'

The authors found that the *wh*-island sentences did not receive low ratings characteristic of ungrammatical sentences. Nevertheless, there was a significant interaction between dependency length and structure complexity, namely a superadditive effect. On the face of it, this seems to provide evidence for the existence of a grammatical *wh*-island constraint in Hebrew, contra the claims in the theoretical literature. However, the authors propose that the observed superadditivity can be attributed to additional processing costs unique to *wh*-island structures, specifically to the cost of maintaining two fillers in working memory. To test this, the authors ran an additional experiment, examining backward-anaphora (cataphora) structures (e.g. "After the mailman made her$_i$ laugh, the tenants asked when the neighbors will employ the cleaning-lady$_i$") in Hebrew. The processing of cataphora sentences was argued to involve active maintenance of the pronoun (Yoshida et al. 2014), but these structures are not assumed to be grammatically constrained by islands. Similar to the *wh*-island experiment, the sentences manipulated dependency length and structure complexity, as schematized in (8).

(8)  a. Matrix resolution | Embedded *that*-clause: [[before … pronoun$_i$] NP$_i$ … [that …]]

b. Embedded resolution | Embedded *that*-clause: [[before … pronoun$_i$] … [that … NP$_i$]]

c. Matrix resolution | Embedded *wh*-question: [[before … pronoun$_i$] NP$_i$ … [when …]]

d. Embedded resolution | Embedded *wh*-question: [[before … pronoun$_i$] … [when … NP$_i$]]

This experiment yielded a superadditive effect similar in size to the one found in the first experiment. This suggests that maintenance costs can lead to an acceptability penalty, even in the absence of a grammatical island constraint. In their final experiment, the authors directly compared cataphora and *wh*-dependency sentences in Hebrew. In addition, in this experiment both types of dependencies were resolved in the embedded subject, rather than object, position, in order to minimize the cost of maintaining two elements in working memory throughout the processing of the embedded clause. The results revealed that under these conditions, there were no superadditive effects in either dependency type (cataphora or *wh*-dependency). This provides strong evidence that the source of the super-additive effect observed in the first experiment was increased maintenance costs, rather than a grammatical constraint applying uniquely to *wh*-dependency structures.

The conclusion from this set of experiments is that, in line with the intuition expressed in the theoretical literature, the *wh*-island constraint seems not to be operative in Hebrew, suggesting cross-linguistic variation in the application of this constraint.

### 19.2.2 Acceptability of Resumptive Pronouns outside Islands

As explained above, Semitic languages are often characterized as "grammaticized resumption" languages, allowing or even requiring RPs to appear in certain positions in RCs and/or *wh*-questions. However, recent studies have suggested that even in these languages, resumption might not necessarily be the preferred mechanism for dependency resolution (see McCloskey (2017) for a similar claim on Irish). Much of the recent experimental research on resumption in these languages has focused on direct object RPs in Hebrew, traditionally claimed to alternate freely with gaps (e.g. Borer 1984; Shlonsky 1992; but see Ariel 1999).

Farby et al. (2010, Experiment 2) compared the acceptability of direct object RPs and gaps in short (one-clause) and long (two-clause) Hebrew RCs. Seventy-two participants rated the acceptability of the sentences on a 1–5 scale. Sentences with RPs were judged as slightly (~0.5 point) but significantly less acceptable than their gapped counterparts, in both short and long dependencies, with no interaction between occurrence of RP and dependency length.

Meltzer-Asscher et al. (2015) also compared sentences with direct object RPs and gaps in Hebrew RCs. In this experiment, the position of the NP containing the RC was also manipulated (it was either in the subject, direct object, or indirect object position of the matrix sentence). In addition, presentation of the sentences was manipulated between participants, with one group judging written sentences and the other group auditory sentences. One hundred and eight participants rated the sentences on a 1–7 scale. Similar to Farby et al. (2010), a small but reliable main effect of resumption was found, such that RPs rendered sentences less acceptable. The effect did not interact with NP position. However, it interacted with modality of presentation; whereas resumption significantly decreased the acceptability of written sentences, it did so only marginally for sentences presented auditorily.

Finally, in an unreported study, Dan Glasserman and the current author also investigated the acceptability of Hebrew direct object RPs. In particular, our experiment tested the hypothesis that RPs might be more acceptable as complements of object-Experiencer verbs (such as *surprise*, *annoy*), with the materials crossing RP occurrence (RP/gap) with verb type (object-Experiencer/non-object-Experiencer), as in (9):[3]

(9)  ʔinbal niška ʔet ha-noseʔaᵢ      še-ha-dayelet                 hošiva / hilxica (tᵢ / ʔotoᵢ).
     Inbal kissed ᴀᴄᴄ the-passenger that-the-flight attendant seated stressed  him
     'Inbal kissed the passenger that the flight attendant seated/stressed.'

The results showed again a main effect of resumption, such that RPs had a detrimental effect on the acceptability of the sentence. Resumption interacted with verb type, leading to a larger decrease in acceptability in non-object-Experiencer verbs compared to object-Experiencer ones. However, the decrease was significant in both verb types.

Summarizing these results, we observe two generalizations: (i) Direct object RPs are consistently judged as less acceptable than gaps in Hebrew RCs. The effect is small, but reliable. (ii) This decrease in acceptability is diminished under certain conditions, i.e. when sentences were auditorily presented or when they included an object-Experiencer verb.

What can be made of these patterns? First, the fact that the decrease in acceptability is overall small strongly suggests that direct object resumption is not ungrammatical in Hebrew. It rather seems to constitute a grammatical option which is nevertheless dispreferred. As suggested in Meltzer-Asscher et al. (2015), the slight decrease in acceptability may reflect a minor processing difficulty which is caused by optional RPs. It is well known that during the processing of *wh*-dependencies, comprehenders attempt to posit a gap and resolve the dependency as soon as possible, typically at the verb (e.g. Stowe 1986; see review in Phillips & Wagers 2007). If upon encountering the relative clause verb, Hebrew comprehenders resolve the dependency by predicting a subsequent gap, then the occurrence of an RP necessitates some form of reanalysis. Indeed, recent experimental evidence shows the online costs of this revision process (Fadlon et al. 2018). Presumably, this processing cost is also reflected by a slight decrease in acceptability.

Why is the decrease in acceptability induced by RPs mitigated with auditory presentation and in sentences with object-Experiencer verbs? Arguably, these conditions are somewhat more challenging in terms of processing. In auditory presentation, the filler has to be remembered, and cannot be retrieved by reading back to the RC head. Clauses with object-Experiencer verbs require non-canonical mapping of arguments to syntactic positions, since an animate argument is mapped to object,

---

[3] Landau (2010) claimed that in Hebrew RCs, resumption is necessary in the complement position of object-Experiencer verbs, when the subject of the verb is inanimate, e.g. *ha-muamadim še-ha-toca'ot hifti'u *(otam)* 'The candidates that the results surprised *(them)'. The reported experiment did not test this claim, as the RC subject in all the experimental sentences was animate.

rather than subject, position, which was argued to elicit increased pro-cessing costs (e.g. Bornkessel, Schlesewsky, & Friederici 2002). It is thus conceivable that under these challenging conditions, resolution of the dependency by the comprehender at the verb by positing a direct object gap is harder, and may not happen in every instance. Thus, RPs in these cases are less redundant, and necessitate a reanalysis only in a portion of the trials, leading to the observed reduction in the acceptability cost they induce.

Interestingly, however, this proposal may not hold cross-linguistically. As part of a larger experiment investigating islands and resumption (dis-cussed further in the next section), Tucker et al. (2019) compared the acceptability of long *wh*-questions with gaps versus RPs in Modern Standard Arabic (MSA), as in (10):

(10)   ?ajja   miħfaðˤaᵢ   jaˤtaqidu   ?aš-šurtˤii       ?anna   maħmood   saraqa(tᵢ / -huᵢ)?
        which   wallet     thinks       the-policeman that   Mahmoud   stole      it
        'Which walletᵢ does the policeman think that Mahmoud stole (tᵢ / itᵢ)?'

Their results showed that for these long dependencies, resumption is preferred over use of a gap. This is in line with the classification of Arabic as a grammaticized resumption language, but contrasts with the Hebrew results (specifically from Farby et al. (2010), which also included depen-dencies with an embedded clause). As Tucker et al. note, it is not the case that resumption is always preferred to gaps in MSA, or that the ratings of sentences with gaps signal clear ungrammaticality. As in Hebrew, other factors, perhaps related to processing, seem to be at play here and affect ratings for certain structures. Undoubtedly, the discrepancy between MSA and Hebrew calls for further research. As noted by Tucker et al., one obvious direction is examining MSA RCs, rather than *wh*-questions, since it was research on RCs that led to theoretical generalizations about resumption in Arabic. This will also allow a more direct comparison with Hebrew, where RCs, rather than *wh*-questions, were experimentally tested.

### 19.2.3   Acceptability of Resumption inside Islands

Experimental investigation of the interaction between islandhood and resumption has also focused on Hebrew and MSA. This section presents the relevant results organized by island type: *wh/whether*-island, complex NP island, and adjunct island.

### 19.2.3.1   *Wh/whether*-Islands

Tucker et al. (2019) used the superadditivity paradigm with *wh*-questions to diagnose the existence of islands, as well as the possible effect of resump-tion on islandhood, in MSA. To test *whether*-islands, their materials crossed dependency length (matrix resolution/embedded resolution) and structure complexity (embedded *that*-clause/embedded *whether*-clause).[4] The design also included a resumption factor (dependency resolved by RP/gap). This factor, however, was not fully crossed with the others, as RPs in MSA are banned from the highest subject position, and are therefore ungrammatical in the short dependency experimental sentences. The design thus only included resumptives in long dependencies, for a total of six conditions (2×2+2), as exemplified in (11).

(11)    a. Matrix resolution (no resumption) / Embedded *that*-clause:

        man$_i$    jaʕtaqidu t$_i$    ʔanna    maḥmood saraqa ʔal-miḥfaðˤa?

        who    thinks    that    Mahmoud stole the-wallet

        'Who$_i$ t$_i$ thinks that Mahmoud stole the wallet?'

    b. Embedded resolution (with/without resumption) / Embedded *that*-clause:

        ʔajja    miḥfaðˤa$_i$  jaʕtaqidu ʔaš-šurtˤii    ʔanna mahmood

        which    wallet    thinks    the-policeman that    Mahmoud

        saraqa    (t$_i$/-hu$_i$)?

        stole    it

        'Which wallet$_i$ does the policeman think that Mahmoud stole (t$_i$/it$_i$)?'

    c. Matrix resolution (no resumption) / Embedded *whether*-clause:

        man$_i$ jatasaaʔalu t$_i$ maa ʔiðaa  kaana  maḥmood saraqa    al-mifaða?

        who    wonders    whether  had    Mahmoud stole    the-wallet

        'Who$_i$ t$_i$ wonders whether Mahmoud stole the wallet?'

    d. Embedded resolution (with/without resumption) / Embedded *whether*-clause:

        ajja    mifaða$_i$ jatasaaalu aš-šurtii    maa iðaa kaana  mamood

        which    wallet    wonders    the-policeman whether had    Mahmoud

        saraqa (t$_i$/-hu$_i$)?

        stole    it

        'Which wallet$_i$ does the policeman wonder whether Mahmoud stole (t$_i$ / it$_i$)?'

Results of the gap and RP conditions were analyzed separately. A marginal superadditive effect was found with gaps, and a significant effect was found with RPs. Namely, in both cases, the island structures received ratings which were lower than what would be predicted based solely on the length of the dependency and the existence of a *whether*-clause in the sentence. This is evidence that *whether*-islands exist in MSA, on a par with other languages. The size of the superadditive effect was relatively small, which dovetails with the generalization that *whether*-islands are weak islands. The fact that an island effect was observed for the RP conditions suggests that resumption does not ameliorate *whether*-islands in MSA. This conclusion is supported by the pairwise comparison between the two island conditions in (10d), namely with and without an RP, which did not reveal a significant difference in ratings.

---

[4] The results reported here are from Experiment 2 in Tucker et al. (2019). Experiment 1 was very similar, but included 'what' instead of 'which NP' questions. As noted by the authors, RPs in MSA are judged not to be acceptable with 'what' antecedents, which may have confounded the results of that experiment.

The lack of amelioration by resumption is similar to the case of *wh*-islands in Hebrew. Keshev and Meltzer-Asscher (2019) ran an experiment identical to the one described in Section 19.2.1. above (see (7)), with RPs instead of gaps. This resulted in a smaller, non-significant superadditive effect, suggesting, on the face of it, an ameliorating effect of resumption. However, upon closer inspection, it was observed that the interaction was non-significant in the RP sentences not due to higher ratings of the island condition, but due to lower ratings of long, non-island sentences (namely, a dispreference for RPs outside of islands, as discussed above). Supporting this conclusion was the comparison between the acceptability of the island condition with and without an RP, which was not significant, similar to the MSA results. Thus, resumption does not seem to affect the grammaticality of *wh/whether*-island structures, neither in MSA nor in Hebrew.

### 19.2.3.2 Complex NP (CNP) Islands

In contrast to *wh*-islands, complex NP islands (with extraction from within an RC embedded inside a noun phrase) consistently show amelioration by resumption in Hebrew. Farby et al. (2010: Experiment 1) compared gaps and RPs in CNP island sentences as in (12):

(12)  Dina     maskima    lifgoš       ʔet      ha-calement$_i$
      Dina     agrees     to-meet      ACC      the-photographer-F
      še-ha-xaver          še-pagaš    (t$_i$/ʔota$_i$)   be-xeyfa
      that-the-friend     that-met     her      in-Haifa
      nasa    le-šam       be-mikre.
      went    there        by-chance
      'Dina agrees to meet the photographer$_i$ that the friend who met (t$_i$/her$_i$) in Haifa went there by chance.'

The authors found a highly significant difference between the ratings of the two sentence types, with gapped versions receiving lower ratings than their RP counterparts. A very similar result is reported in Keshev and Meltzer-Asscher (2017: Experiment 1). It is interesting to note that in both studies the ratings of sentences with RPs in CNP structures, despite being significantly higher than those of sentences with gaps, were still low (average ~2.3 on a five-point scale in Farby et al.; average ~2.8 on a seven-point scale in Keshev & Meltzer-Asscher). This highlights the difficulty in straightforwardly mapping acceptability ratings to grammaticality status. Keshev and Meltzer-Asscher (2017) proposed that resumption in CNP islands is a grammatical option in Hebrew, and that the low acceptability of these structures reflects their complexity, rather than their ungrammaticality.

Results from MSA seem to present a different picture with regard to resumption in CNP islands. Tucker et al. (2019) investigated CNP islands with extraction out of a sentential complement of a noun (rather than an RC), as exemplified in (13).

(13) ʔajja  laħm;  ʔankarta        [ʔal-ħaqiiqa  ʔanna  ʔaaħmed  ʔakala(-t;/hu;)]?
     which  bread  denied-2 M.S  the-fact        that    Ahmed    ate        it
     'Which bread; did you deny the fact that Ahmed ate (t; / it;)?'

The materials were designed in the super-additive paradigm as explained in Section 19.2.3.1, namely in a 2×2+2 design. Looking separately at the gap and RP sentences, Tucker et al. found a superadditive effect, signifying the existence of a grammatical island constraint, in the gap conditions, but not in the resumption conditions. This may seem to suggest that RPs ameliorate CNP violations in MSA. However, in this case too, closer inspection showed that the lack of island effect in the RP conditions stemmed from lower ratings of non-island sentences with RPs, rather than from higher ratings of island sentences with RPs. This was also evidenced by the lack of difference between the ratings of the island sentences with gaps and RPs.

These results therefore suggest that unlike the situation in Hebrew, resumption does not "salvage" CNP violations in MSA. More research is needed in order to understand whether there is a real, grammatical difference between Arabic and Hebrew, or whether this discrepancy is an artefact of the difference in the structures investigated (*wh*-questions vs. RCs, extraction out of sentential complements vs. relative clauses), the experimental designs, the populations tested, or some other factor.

### 19.2.3.3  Adjunct Islands

Finally, Tucker et al. (2019) also investigated, using the superadditivity paradigm, adjunct islands with *if*-clauses, as exemplified in (14):

(14)    ʔajja            ħaqiiba;      taqlaqu        ʔiðaa nasiija(t;/-hu;)
        which            briefcase     worry-2 M.S  [if    forgot    it
        ʔal-muħaamii fii-l-maktab?
        the-lawyer     in-the-office
        'Which briefcase; did you worry if the lawyer forgot (t; / it;) in the office?'

The results showed a superadditive effect of dependency length and island structure, namely an island effect, in both the gap conditions and the RP conditions. The adjunct island showed the largest superadditive effect compared to the other islands investigated in the study. Despite the superadditivity in the RP conditions, a pairwise comparison of the ratings for the island structure with a gap and an RP showed that RPs significantly increased the acceptability of this structure. These results suggest that RPs somewhat ameliorate adjunct islands in MSA.

Amelioration by RPs in adjunct islands was found also in Hebrew. Keshev (2016) tested three types of adjunct structures, with and without RPs: finite clause adjuncts, non-finite clause adjuncts, and PP-adjuncts, as exemplified in (15):

(15)    a. Finite clause adjuncts:

| ha-mazkirot | raʔu | ʔet | ha-naʔar$_i$ | še-ha-psixologit |
|---|---|---|---|---|
| the-secretaries | saw | ACC | the-boy | that-the-psychologist |
| pagša | ʔet | ha-horim | ʔaxrey | še-hi |
| met | ACC | the-parents | after | that-she |
| ʔivxena | (t$_i$/ʔoto$_i$). | | | |
| diagnosed | him | | | |

'The secretaries saw the boy$_i$ that the psychologist met the parents after she diagnosed (t$_i$/him$_i$).'

b. Non-finite clause adjuncts:

| ha-mazkirot | raʔu | ʔet | ha-naʔar$_i$ | še-ha-psixologit |
|---|---|---|---|---|
| the-secretaries | saw | ACC | the-boy | that-the-psychologist |
| pagša | ʔet | ha-horim | kedey | le-ʔaxven | (t$_i$/ʔoto$_i$). |
| met | ACC | the-parents | in-order | to-diagnose | him |

'The secretaries saw the boy$_i$ that the psychologist met the parents in order to diagnose (t$_i$/him$_i$).'

c. PP adjuncts:

| ha-mazkirot | raʔu | ʔet | ha-naʔar$_i$ | še-ha-psixologit | | pagša |
|---|---|---|---|---|---|---|
| the-secretaries | saw | ACC | the-boy | that-the-psychologist | | met |
| ʔet | ha-horim | bimkom | (t$_i$/ ʔoto$_i$). | | | |
| ACC | the-parents | instead | him | | | |

'The secretaries saw the boy$_i$ that the psychologist met the parents instead (t$_i$/of him$_i$).'

The results showed a main effect of resumption, such that sentences with RPs were rated as more acceptable than those with gaps. The effect of resumption interacted with adjunct type; the amelioration by RPs was more pronounced for PP adjuncts than for the two types of clausal adjuncts, which did not differ from one another. It is worth mentioning that similarly to the results concerning CNP islands, all ratings in this study were relatively low. As mentioned above, this underscores once more the elusive mapping from acceptability to grammaticality, in particular when superadditivity is not employed. Does resumption render these islands grammatical, with low ratings arising from other factors, namely complexity? Or are these structures ungrammatical, on a par with their gapped versions, but easier to process? Other types of evidence are needed to adjudicate this issue (for an argument that resumption does not make the processing of island structures easier, see discussion in Keshev & Meltzer-Asscher (2017)).

To conclude this section, results from Semitic seem to generally show that islands are relatively stable cross-linguistically (with the exception of the *wh*-island in Hebrew, as also claimed in the theoretical literature). In addition, the results show that the simple claim that resumption salvages islands cannot be maintained, not even for grammaticized resumption languages. Rather, a more nuanced view on resumption needs to be articulated, and specific languages and island types, as well as processing considerations, should be taken into account. As described above, current syntactic theory allows different types of RPs, some argued to be copies of moved elements, and some bound in situ with no movement involved. Data of the types reported here may help us refine our understanding of the different types of resumption instantiated in different languages and different structures. It is also important to note that there are many facets of the syntax of A′-dependencies in Semitic languages that have not yet been experimentally investigated, and stand to benefit from data collected in sentence acceptability studies. These include the distribution of *wh*-in-situ in certain dialects of Arabic (see e.g. Wahba 1992; Lassadi 2003), the lack of intervention effects in Amharic (Eilam 2008), and the existence of null RPs in Tigrinya (Overfelt 2009), among others.

## 19.3  Underexplored and Unexplored Topics in Semitic Experimental Syntax

As mentioned above, sentence acceptability studies have been scarce in areas of Semitic syntax other than A′-dependencies. In this section I briefly discuss agreement phenomena (Section 19.3.1) and ditransitivity (Section 19.3.2), where very preliminary work is available. In Section 19.3.3 I point out some unexplored domains where no experimental work has been carried out to date.

### 19.3.1  Agreement

Many of the world's languages, Semitic languages included, display agreement relations between the verb and its arguments. A very simple case is presented by English, in which a verb agrees with its subject in number. The questions of how agreement is represented, and how it is computed in real time (in production as well as comprehension), have drawn a lot of attention in recent years, with much of the research taking advantage of so-called "agreement attraction" errors, namely cases where the verb agrees with a structurally illicit distractor (e.g. *The key to the cabinets are lost* (Bock & Miller 1991)). Despite being ungrammatical, such sentences are produced quite commonly, and their ungrammaticality often goes unnoticed by comprehenders. Investigation of the patterns of attraction errors has helped shed light on the mechanisms of agreement. For example, it was found that attraction is asymmetric – plural distractors are more effective as attractors than singular ones (e.g. Wagers, Lau, & Phillips, 2009). This suggests a markedness hierarchy between singular and plural forms, which has processing consequences.

Most of the work on agreement and agreement attraction was carried out in Germanic and Romance languages. However, as noted by Gollan and Frost (2001), Deutsch and Dank (2011), and Tucker, Idrissi, and Almeida (2015), Semitic languages can contribute substantially to this line of research. As noted by these authors, one crucial aspect of Arabic and Hebrew agreement systems is that they include gender agreement, in addition to number agreement.[5] Unlike number marking, gender marking for inanimate nouns is arbitrary. And although this marking is systematic to a large degree, it shows, at least in Hebrew, many irregularities. This opens the possibility to investigate numerous crucial questions with regard to agreement, e.g. are agreement representations and processes governed by semantic properties or by grammatical features? And are these grammatical features abstract features associated with the lemma, or morphological features associated with specific morphemes? Work by the authors mentioned above has begun exploring these questions using production as well as online measures of comprehension (i.e. reading times). While this research is beyond the scope of this chapter, it is important to note that agreement attraction effects may also be detected offline, using acceptability experiments. For example, in a recent study in our lab (unpublished results), we found that RPs that did not agree in gender with the relative head were judged as more acceptable in the presence of a matching attractor earlier in the sentence.

One acceptability study looking at agreement in Hebrew is Danon (2013a), which discusses the very intriguing case of agreement with quantified nouns phrases (QNP), such as *xeci me-ha-kita* 'half of the class.' In Hebrew, sentences with QNP subjects can be observed in which the verb agrees with the quantifier (Q-agr, (16a)) or with the noun (N-agr, (16b)), or where it displays "semantic agreement," namely agreement with the QNP's denotation (S-agr, (16c)).

(16)      Xeci         me-ha-kita ...
          half-M.SG    of-the-class-F.SG

    a. ... hevin
       understood-M.SG
    b. ... hevina
       understood-F.SG
    c. ... hevinu
       understood-PL

[5] There have been studies on agreement in Slavic languages, which likewise exhibit gender agreement (e.g. Badecker & Kuminiak 2007). However, in these languages Case marking is obligatory, and constitutes a strong cue as to the identity of the controller of agreement (i.e. the subject).

Danon reports preliminary findings from a binary grammaticality judgment experiment. These results show that when the head noun is plural, speakers overwhelmingly prefer N-agr (or S-agr, as they are identical in this case) to Q-agr. However, for singular head nouns, as in (16), Q-agr seems to be tolerable to a much larger degree. These results are argued by Danon to support an analysis which postulates abstract agreement features, rather than morphologically marked ones (see also Danon 2013b). This study exemplifies the potential of using acceptability studies to advance our understanding of the representations and mechanisms involved in agreement processes.

### 19.3.2   Ditransitive Structures

The study of dative and other ditransitive constructions lies at the interface between lexical semantics, argument structure and Case theory, and has drawn much attention, including in Semitic languages, and in particular in the various Arabic vernaculars (see e.g. Wilmsen 2010, 2012; Ryding 2011;Camilleri, Elsadek, & Sadler 2014). However, to my knowledge, Gafter (2014), described below, is the only acceptability study carried out to date to characterize properties of dative constructions in Semitic languages.

In Hebrew, a DP following the dative preposition *le-* ('to') can be interpreted as the possessor of another argument, as in (17). This possibility is limited, however. For example, in (18) the dative-marked DP cannot have a possessive reading.

(17)    ha-ʔiparon   nafal   le-dan.
        the-pencil   fell    to-Dan
        'Dan's pencil fell.'

(18)    ha-poʔalim       ʔavdu       li.
        the-workers      worked      to+me
        intended meaning: 'My workers worked.'

Borer and Grodzinsky (1986) propose that in order for the possessive reading to be possible, the possessor (namely the dative PP) must c-command the possessee or its trace. From this generalization, they derive a diagnostic to distinguish unaccusative from unergative verbs in Hebrew. As first argued by Perlmutter (1978), the subject of unaccusative verbs, unlike that of unergative ones, is generated in complement position, and moved to subject position. The contrast between (17) and (18) then becomes clear: *nafal* 'fell,' in (17), is an unaccusative verb; its subject is generated in object position; and the dative PP c-commands its trace. In contrast, *ʔavad* 'worked' is unergative, with the subject base-generated in spec,TP. In no stage of the derivation does the dative PP c-command it.

Borer and Grodzinsky's diagnostic for unaccusativity in Hebrew became a standard tool in studies of argument structure (e.g. Landau 1999; Meltzer-Asscher & Siloni 2013). However, Gafter (2014) notes that the judgments leading to Borer and Grodzinsky's generalization might have been confounded. Specifically, the sentences giving rise to the generalization were similar to (17)–(18), in that those sentences with unaccusative verbs also included inanimate subjects, whereas those with unergative verbs had animate subjects. To tease these two factors apart, Gafter conducted a sentence acceptability experiment with sentences similar to those in (17)–(18), but in which verb type (unergative/unaccuative) was crossed with the animacy of the possessor as well as the possessee. The results showed that acceptability was highest for sentences in which the possessor was animate and the possessee inanimate; in contrast to Borer and Grodzinsky's hypothesis, verb type (unaccusative vs. unergative) did not predict acceptability. Gafter proposes that for a possessive interpretation to be possible, the possessor needs to be more prominent than the possessee; syntactic prominence (c-command) is one way to achieve this; but other dimensions of prominence, such as animacy (as well as grammatical function, definiteness, and others) are also relevant.

Gafter (2014) is a good example for the importance of formal sentence acceptability studies; in this case, informal judgments collected over the years used sentences which routinely confounded verb type with animacy. Gafter's study is a first experimental step toward disentangling the factors affecting the acceptability of the possessive dative structure in Hebrew. Of course, many questions still remain, both with regard to this structure (for example, what is the relative weight of different prominence scales in determining acceptability) and with regard to characteristics of other dative structures in the language (e.g. the ethical dative or the reflexive dative, see Borer & Grodzinsky 1986).

### 19.3.3   Some Unexplored Topics in Semitic Syntax

Having presented the extant literature on Semitic experimental syntax, it is obvious that there are many structures still awaiting empirical work. Almost every phenomenon that was described in the theoretical literature, as well as those that have not yet been studied theoretically, can benefit from formal acceptability experiments. In this section, I very briefly mention three syntactic phenomena typical of Semitic languages, which constitute obvious targets for future work.

### 19.3.3.1   Free Word Order

The basic, canonical word order in a sentence is different from one Semitic language to the next; in MSA, it is VSO (Bakir 1979); in many spoken Arabic dialects and in Hebrew it is SVO (e.g. El-Yasin 1985; Shlonsky 1997); in

Amharic and Tigrinya, it is SOV (Kramer & Eilam 2012). However, most Semitic languages do not display a rigid word order. The relatively rich systems of agreement and Case marking allow arguments, as well as modifiers, to shift rather freely around the clause (see e.g. Shlonksy (1997) for Hebrew; Ford (2009) for Arabic; Fabri & Borg (2002) for Maltese). Despite this relative flexibility, it can be intuitively observed that (i) not all word orders are acceptable to the same degree, even in those languages with "free" word order; (ii) the acceptability of specific word orders depends to a large degree upon information structure considerations, i.e. the role of the different arguments in the discourse. These complex and subtle interactions between word-order patterns and pragmatic factors are an extremely fertile ground for future empirical work (see Chapter 12 for discussion of research on this topic in other languages).

### 19.3.3.2 *Verbless Sentences*

Another syntactic property which is typical of Semitic languages is the existence of verbless (sometimes referred to as nominal or copular) clauses, i.e. clauses whose main predicate is a noun, an adjective, or a preposition phrase. These clauses can include no copula, or may include a copula which is not verbal. In Hebrew, for example, verbless clauses can include a bare predicate (19a), a copula identical to the third-person pronoun (19b), or a copula identical to the demonstrative/impersonal pronoun (19c). Similar examples can be found in Arabic and in Maltese (Fassi Fehri 1993; Benmamoun 2000, 2008; Falk 2004).

(19)    a. ʔugat   gezer   tova   la-briʔut.
           cake    carrot  good   for+the-health
      b. ʔugat   gezer   hi   briʔa.
           cake    carrot  she  healthy
      c. ʔugat   gezer   ze   bari.
           cake    carrot  it/this  healthy
      'Carrot cake is healthy.'

Verbless clauses exhibit unique patterns of (non-)agreement, Case marking and definiteness. For example, in MSA, when the predicate is a definite noun or adjective, the clause must include the third-person copula; also in MSA, if the verbless clause is embedded, both subject and predicate must be assigned accusative Case (Al-Horais 2006). In addition, specific structural choices in these clauses are accompanied by subtle shifts in interpretation. For example, non-agreeing Hebrew verbless clauses with the demonstrative copula (e.g. (19c)) were argued to undergo "denotation widening," with the predicate applying to some eventuality related to the subject noun, rather than to the actual denotation of the subject (Heller 1999; Greenberg 2008; Danon 2012). Empirical investigations of the acceptability of different variants of nominal clauses is certain to further our understanding of their structural properties and the constraints they obey.

### 19.3.3.3  *Nominal Syntax and Construct States*

Semitic noun phrases can appear in two so-called "states": the free state (20a) or the construct state (20b), as in the following examples in Moroccan Arabic (from Shlonsky & Ouhalla 2002).

(20)     a. d-dar              dyal l-wazir
              the-apartment of   the-minister
              'The apartment of the minister'

         b. dar               l-wazir
              apartment    the-minister
              'The minister's apartment'

Importantly, in the construct state, the two nouns must be adjacent; no modifiers can appear following the head noun. In addition, the head noun cannot be preceded by a determiner, but is interpreted as definite if its complement is definite (as in (20b)). Because of these and other unique constraints obeyed by construct states, they have attracted a lot of attention in theoretical syntax, and different analyses were proposed for their representation (Mohammed 1988; Hazout 1990; Ouhalla 1991; Ritter 1991; Fassi Fehri 1993; Borer 1999; Benmamoun 2000; Siloni 2001; Shlonsky 2004). Obviously, the correct analysis hinges on a precise identification of the range of possible structures involving construct states. However, there seems to be a lot of disagreement on the relevant facts. Taking, for example, Siloni (2001), the paper notes at least three cases for which there is no clear agreement on judgments: the status of quantified noun phrases as non-head elements in construct states in Hebrew; the status of Arabic constructs with a parenthetical intervening between the two nouns; and the status of definite constructs modified by weak determiners. Clearly, there is a wealth of phenomena in the field of construct states awaiting future research.

## 19.4  Special Issues in Semitic Experimental Syntax

This section briefly discusses some of the challenges facing researchers conducting experimental studies in Semitic languages. Some of these are unique to certain languages, and others apply to all Semitic languages, or indeed to all "smaller," less-studied languages.

### 19.4.1  Issues of Diglossia

#### 19.4.1.1  Arabic

Arabic presents one of the most widespread cases of diglossia in the world. Essentially, all speakers of Arabic are exposed to two variants of the language: MSA, the formal language (used in schools, in the media, and in formal functions) and a spoken vernacular, which varies regionally. While these two languages share some core characteristics, they differ widely in all aspects of the lexicon and the grammar – including different phonetic inventories, different morphological systems, and different syntactic rules and generalizations. Naturally, the spoken dialect is acquired first; exposure to the standard language becomes significant later in life, particularly during school years. Another difference between the two languages is that while MSA has a writing system, the spoken vernaculars do not. Traditionally, these languages were only spoken, never written. Interestingly, this state of affairs has very recently started to change. With the rising prominence of texting and social media, young Arabic speakers have sought ways to write their spoken dialects. One of the most common techniques is so-called "3arabizi," an informal alphabet popular among younger Arabic speakers for use in texting, chatting, and social media. This variant is basically Arabic (in any of its dialects) transliterated with Latin script, with the use of Roman numerals for Arabic sounds that have no phonetic equivalent in English, e.g. 3 for the voiced pharyngeal fricative and 5 for the voiceless pharyngeal fricative.

The diglossic nature of Arabic poses numerous challenges to researchers studying this language, of which I will mention here only a few.

- Since there is no standardization of the spoken languages, these tend to vary considerably even within the same country, and sometimes even within the same region. Thus, it can be challenging to recruit a large enough homogeneous sample of speakers for a study of a specific spoken dialect, particularly if there are other constraints on the participants (e.g. their age, proficiency in other languages, etc.).
- Also relevant for studies investigating the spoken dialects, since these have no standard writing system, studies should be carried out using auditory, rather than written, stimuli. Granted, carrying out auditory experiments is not impossible, and in many cases has advantages over written questionnaires. However, it is generally more time-consuming, both in terms of stimuli preparation and data collection. As "3arabizi" use becomes more widespread, it may be possible to conduct experiments using this script (for younger participants).
- For studies investigating MSA, it should be taken into consideration that this language resembles a second language in the way it is acquired and used. Thus, data on proficiency levels should be collected and taken into account in the analysis.
- More generally, no matter what variant is investigated, the researcher should bear in mind that data are collected from diglossic participants. It is always advisable to pay attention to specific linguistic aspects relevant to the experiment which are similar or different when comparing the standard and spoken language.

A study which shows the relevance of some of these points is Khamis-Dakwar, Froud, and Gordon (2012). The authors conducted a grammaticality judgment experiment in MSA and Palestinian Colloquial Arabic (PCA) with children aged 6–11. The experiment included ten structures. In four of these, MSA and PCA behave on a par ("match" structures, e.g. in both languages the noun agrees in definiteness with its modifying adjective). In the other six, the two languages behave differently ("mismatch" structures, e.g. in PCA the subject always agrees in number with the verb, whereas in MSA, plural subjects appear with verbs marked in the singular in VSO sentences). The results showed overall lower accuracy in MSA compared to PCA, as expected based on the lower proficiency of the children in this language. This effect was qualified by an interaction with the "match/mismatch" factor, such that the decreased accuracy in MSA was primarily driven by the structures that mismatched PCA. This suggests some type of interference from PCA in the acquisition of MSA. The authors note that the accuracy of a group of adult controls was at ceiling for all structures in both PCA and MSA, showing that the cross-variety effects seen in childhood are short-lived. Nonetheless, this study underscores the complexity of running sentence acceptability studies in diglossic populations.

### 19.4.1.2  Maltese

Malta is also often thought of as a diglossic society. Although Maltese is the dominant language and is spoken at home by the vast majority of the population, English also has an official status in the country. A large portion of the population is bilingual, often from childhood, and code-switching is common. There are radio and television channels and programs in both languages, and the print media is dominated by English (Vella 2013). There are even claims that a new dialect is emerging in Malta, Mixed Maltese English (Borg 1986). This complex linguistic situation calls for particular care when conducting acceptability experiments on Maltese.

### 19.4.2  Technical Challenges

Here, I point out some other challenges which are common to experimental research of many lesser-studied languages. First and foremost, Semitic languages suffer from a paucity of linguistic corpora, databases, and norms. Several publicly available corpora of certain Semitic languages do exist (e.g. Sketch Engine; for additional resources on Arabic see https://corplinguistics.wordpress.com/2012/02/06/arabic-corpora/; on Hebrew see e.g. http://mila.cs.technion.ac.il/resources_corpora.html; on Amharic see Rychlý & Suchomel 2016; Gezmu et al. 2018), but other languages, in particular some of the spoken Arabic dialects, lack such resources. In addition, most existing corpora are currently inaccurate or lacking, compared to e.g. English or German corpora, in terms of parsing or part-of-speech tagging. One reason for this is that several Semitic languages (including Hebrew and Arabic) do not necessarily represent vowels orthographically, resulting in a large proportion of homophones, many of which are between-category (e.g. the Hebrew word ספר 'spr' can be read as *sefer* 'book' – a noun, or as *safar* 'counted' – a verb). The lack of comprehensive, annotated corpora makes controlling for the frequency of words or structures when constructing materials for an experiment challenging. One solution is to replace frequency measures with so-called "subjective frequency" or familiarity ratings, collected in a pre-test.

Databases or norms for other properties of words, which are often needed for building experimental stimuli (e.g. age of acquisition, argument structure information, imageability, neighborhood size, semantic relatedness, valence, etc.) are likewise very scarce and fragmentary across Semitic. The upshot of this is that extensive norming is required before every experiment. With more experimental work carried out, it would be extremely beneficial if researchers routinely shared the results of norming studies and pre-tests with the relevant linguistic communities via institutional websites, designated archives or even published papers.

A second set of challenges pertains to data collection. A first, relatively minor obstacle is posed by experimental software. For stimuli in Semitic, this needs to support Unicode, and in some cases right-to-left presentation. This is not the case for some commercial software, and additional programming is sometimes required. A more substantial problem is the issue of participant recruitment. In recent years, many sentence acceptability studies in major languages are conducted using massive crowd-sourcing platforms (such as Mechanical Turk). In general, the availability of such platforms outside the US is limited. Similar platforms may exist in several countries, but they are more expensive and do not provide the same response rate. Thus, recruitment for acceptability studies is often done using social media, by word of mouth, or on campus, resulting in longer times for data collection, lower numbers of participants, and in some cases increased costs. The fact that the pool of participants is limited can also lead to participants taking part in multiple similar experiments, leading to risks of satiation or the development of strategies (see Chapter 6 for further discussion of the satiation phenomenon). Care must be taken to avoid "returning participants" in those cases where answering a previous questionnaire can bias or contaminate the results of the next one.

## 19.5  Conclusion

Semitic languages present an interesting and unique case; they are not among the most well-studied languages in linguistics, but their social position makes them accessible to large research communities. Arabic and Hebrew in particular were central to the progress of linguistic theory.

Despite this, experimentation remains relatively rare in these languages. Acceptability work is particularly alluring as an entry point into more experimental work, due to its low cost and relative simplicity. This type of research is also especially important for these less-studied languages, as argued by Linzen and Oseki (2018). In addition, Semitic languages exhibit a number of interesting linguistic and sociolinguistic characteristics (e.g. Arabic diglossia), offering a fertile ground for exciting future research. Hopefully, the coming years will see a surge in this type of work, leading to new generalizations and theoretical advancement.

# References

Ackerman, L., Frazier, M., & Yoshida, M. (2018). Resumptive pronouns can ameliorate illicit island extractions. *Linguistic Inquiry*, 49, 847–859.

Alexopoulou, T. & Keller, F. (2007). Locality, cyclicity, and resumption: At the interface between the grammar and the human sentence processor. *Language*, 83, 110–160.

Al-Horais, N. (2006). Arabic verbless sentences: Is there a null VP? *Pragmalinguistica*, 14, 101–116.

Almeida, D. (2014). Subliminal *wh*-islands in Brazilian Portuguese and the consequences for syntactic theory. *Revista da ABRALIN*, 13, 55–93.

Aoun, J. E., Benmamoun, E., & Choueiri, L. (2010). *The Syntax of Arabic* (Cambridge Syntax Guides). Cambridge: Cambridge University Press.

Aoun, J., Choueiri, L., & Hornstein, N. (2001). Resumption, movement, and derivational economy. *Linguistic Inquiry*, 32, 371–403.

Ariel, M. (1999). Cognitive universals and linguistic conventions: The case of resumptive pronouns. *Studies in Language*, 23, 217–269.

Badecker, W. & Kuminiak, F. (2007). Morphology, agreement and working memory retrieval in sentence production: Evidence from gender and case in Slovak. *Journal of Memory and Language*, 56, 65–85.

Bakir, M. (1979). Aspects of clause structure in Arabic. Doctoral dissertation. Indiana University, Bloomington.

Benmamoun, E. (2000). *The Feature Structure of Functional Categories: A Comparative Study of Arabic Dialects*. Oxford: Oxford University Press.

Benmamoun, E. (2008). Clause structure and the syntax of verbless sentences. In R. Freidin, C. P. Otero, & M. L. Zubizarreta, eds., *Foundational Issues in Linguistic Theory*. Cambridge, MA: MIT Press, pp. 105–131.

Bock, K. & Miller, C. A. (1991). Broken agreement. *Cognitive Psychology*, 23, 45–93.

Borer, H. (1984). Restrictive relatives in modern Hebrew. *Natural Language & Linguistic Theory*, 2, 219–260.

Borer, H. (1999). Deconstructing the construct. In K. Johnson & I. G. Roberts, eds., *Beyond Principles and Parameters*. Dordrecht: Kluwer, pp. 43–89.

Borer, H. & Grodzinsky, Y. (1986). Syntactic cliticization and lexical cliticization: The case of Hebrew dative clitics. In H. Borer, ed., *The Syntax of Pronominal Clitics* (Syntax and Semantics, 19). New York: Academic Press, pp. 175–217.

Borg, A. (1986). *The Maintenance of Maltese as a Language: What Chances?* Strasbourg: Council of Europe.

Bornkessel, I., Schlesewsky, M., & Friederici, A. D. (2002). Beyond syntax: Language-related positivities reflect the revision of hierarchies. *NeuroReport*, 13, 361–364.

Camilleri, M., ElSadek, S., & Sadler, L. (2014). A cross dialectal view of the Arabic dative alternation. *Acta Linguistica Hungarica*, 61, 3–44.

Choueiri, L. (2017). Resumption in varieties of Arabic. In E. Benmamoun & R. Bassiouney, eds., *The Routledge Handbook of Arabic Linguistics*. Abingdon: Routledge, pp. 131–154.

Cowart, W. (1997). *Experimental Syntax: Applying Objective Methods to Sentence Judgments*. Thousand Oaks, CA: Sage.

Danon, G. (2012). Nothing to agree on: Non-agreeing subjects of copular clauses in Hebrew. *Acta Linguistica Hungarica*, 59, 85–108.

Danon, G. (2013a). Hebrew QNP agreement: Towards an empirically based analysis. *Bucharest Working Papers in Linguistics*, 15, 5–23.

Danon, G. (2013b). Agreement alternations with quantified nominals in Modern Hebrew. *Journal of Linguistics*, 49, 55–92.

Deutsch, A. & Dank, M. (2011). Symmetric and asymmetric patterns of attraction errors in producing subject–predicate agreement in Hebrew: An issue of morphological structure. *Language and Cognitive Processes*, 26, 24–46.

Eilam, A. (2008). Intervention effects: Why Amharic patterns differently. In N. Abner & J. Bishop, eds., *Proceedings of the 27th West Coast Conference on Formal Linguistics*. Somerville, MA: Cascadilla Proceedings Project, pp. 141–149.

El-Yasin, M. K. (1985). Basic word order in classical Arabic and Jordanian Arabic. *Lingua*, 65, 107–122.

Engdahl, E. (1997). Relative clause extractions in context. *Working Papers in Scandinavian Syntax*, 60, 51–79.

Erteschik-Shir, N. (1973). On the nature of island constraints. Doctoral dissertation, Massachusetts Institute of Technology.

Erteschik-Shir, N. (1992). Resumptive pronouns in islands. In H. Goodluck & M. Rochemont, eds., *Island Constraints*. Dordrecht: Springer, pp. 89–108.

Fabri, R. & Borg, A. (2002). Topic, focus and word order in Maltese. In Y. Abderrahim, F. Benjelloun, M. Dahbi, & Z. Iraqui-Sinaceur, eds., *Aspects of the Dialects of Arabic Today. Proceedings of the 4th Conference of the International Arabic Dialectology Association (AIDA)*. Rabat: Amapatril, pp. 354–363.

Fadlon, J., Keshev, M., & Meltzer-Asscher, A. (2018). A shift in gap manifestation incurs processing costs: Evidence from Hebrew. Poster presented at the 31st CUNY Conference on Human Sentence Processing, Davis, CA.

Fadlon, J., Sassoon, G. W., & Schumacher, P. B. (2018). Discrete dimension accessibility in multidimensional concepts. *The Mental Lexicon*, 13, 105–142.

Falk, Y. N. (2004). The Hebrew present-tense copula as a mixed category. In *Proceedings of the Lexical Functional Grammar 04 Conference*. Stanford, CA: CSLI.

Farby, S., Danon, G., Walters, J., & Ben-Shachar, M. (2010). The acceptability of resumptive pronouns in Hebrew. In Y. Falk, ed., *Proceedings of the Israeli Association for Theoretical Linguistics 26*. Jerusalem: IATL.

Fassi-Fehri, A. (1993). *Issues in the Structure of Arabic Clauses and Word Order*. London: Kluwer Academic.

Ferreira, F. (2005). Psycholinguistics, formal grammars, and cognitive science. *The Linguistic Review*, 22, 365–380.

Ford, D. (2009). The influence of word order on Modern Standard Arabic information structure. *GIALens (Special Electronic Publication of the Graduate Institute of Applied Linguistics)*, 3(2). www.gial.edu

Gafter, R. J. (2014). The distribution of the Hebrew Possessive Dative construction: Guided by unaccusativity or prominence?. *Linguistic Inquiry*, 45, 482–500.

Gezmu, A. M., Seyoum, B. E., Gasser, M., & Nürnberger, A. (2018). Contemporary Amharic Corpus: Automatically morpho-syntactically tagged Amharic corpus. In *Proceedings of the First Workshop on Linguistic Resources for Natural Language Processing*, 65–70.

Gibson, E., Piantadosi, S. T., & Fedorenko, E. (2013). Quantitative methods in syntax/semantics research: A response to Sprouse and Almeida (2013). *Language and Cognitive Processes*, 28, 229–240.

Gollan, T. H., & Frost, R. (2001). Two routes to grammatical gender: Evidence from Hebrew. *Journal of Psycholinguistic Research*, 30, 627–651.

Greenberg, Y. (2008). Predication and equation in Hebrew (nonpseudocleft) copular sentences. *Current Issues in Generative Hebrew Linguistics*, 1, 161–196.

Hazout, I. (1990). Verbal nouns: Theta-theoretical studies in Hebrew and Arabic. Doctoral dissertation, University of Massachusetts, Amherst.

Heestand, D., Xiang, M., & Polinsky, M. (2011). Resumption still does not rescue islands. *Linguistic Inquiry*, 42, 138–152.

Heller, D. (1999). The syntax and semantics of specificational pseudoclefts in Hebrew. MA thesis, Tel Aviv University.

Ibrahim, I. I. (2016). Gender assignment to lexical borrowings by heritage speakers of Arabic. *Western Papers in Linguistics/Cahiers linguistiques de Western*, 1, article 1.

Keshev, M. (2016). Active dependency formation in syntactic islands: Evidence from Hebrew sentence processing. MA thesis, Tel Aviv University.

Keshev, M. & Meltzer-Asscher, A. (2017). Active dependency formation in islands: How grammatical resumption affects sentence processing. *Language*, 93, 549–568.

Keshev, M. & Meltzer-Asscher. A. (2019). A processing-based account of subliminal *wh*-island effects. *Natural Language & Linguistic Theory*, 37, 621–657.

Khamis-Dakwar, R., Froud, K., & Gordon, P. (2012). Acquiring diglossia: Mutual influences of formal and colloquial Arabic on children's grammaticality judgments. *Journal of Child Language*, 39, 61–89.

Kluender, R. (1998). On the distinction between strong and weak islands: A processing perspective. In P. W. Culicover & L. McNally, eds., *The Limits of Syntax* (Syntax and Semantics, 29). San Diego, CA: Academic Press, pp. 241–280.

Kramer, R. & Eilam, A. (2012). Verb-medial word orders in Amharic. *Journal of Afroasiatic Languages*, 5, 75–104.

Landau, I. (1999). Possessor raising and the structure of VP. *Lingua*, 107, 1–37.

Landau, I. (2010). *The Locative Syntax of Experiencers* (Linguistic Inquiry Monograph, 53). Cambridge, MA: MIT Press.

Lassadi B. (2003). Optional *wh*-movement in French and Egyptian Arabic. *Cahiers linguistiques d'Ottawa*, 31, 67–93.

Linzen, T. & Oseki, Y. (2018). The reliability of acceptability judgments across languages. *Glossa: A Journal of General Linguistics*, 3(1), 100. DOI:10.5334/gjgl.528

Malkawi, N. & Guilliot, N. (2007). Reconstruction & Islandhood in Jordanian Arabic. In M. A. Mughazy, ed., *Perspectives on Arabic Linguistics*, vol. XX. Amsterdam: John Benjamins, pp. 87–104.

McCloskey, J. (2017). Resumption. In M. Everaert & H. C. Van Riemsdijk, eds., *The Wiley Blackwell Companion to Syntax*, 2nd ed. New York: John Wiley & Sons, pp. 1–30.

Meltzer-Asscher, A. (2021). Resumptive pronouns in language comprehension and production. *Annual Review of Linguistics*, 7, 1.1–1.18.

Meltzer-Asscher, A., Fadlon, J., Goldstein, K., & Holan, A. (2015). Direct object resumption in Hebrew: How modality of presentation and relative clause position affect acceptability. *Lingua*, 166, 65–79.

Meltzer-Asscher, A. & Siloni, T. (2013). Unaccusative. In *The Encyclopedia of Hebrew Language and Linguistics*. Leiden: Brill.

Mohammad, M. (1988). On the parallelism between IP and DP. In H. Borer, ed., *Proceedings of the 7th West Coast Conference on Formal Linguistics (WCCFL 7)*. Stanford, CA: CSLI, pp. 241–254.

Ouhalla, J. (1991). *Functional Categories and Parametric Variation*. New York: Routledge.

Overfelt, J. D. (2009). The syntax of relative clause constructions in Tigrinya. Doctoral dissertation, Purdue University.

Perlmutter, D. M. (1978). Impersonal passives and the unaccusative hypothesis. In *Proceedings of the 4th Annual Meeting of the Berkeley Linguistics Society*. Berkeley, CA: University of California, Berkeley Linguistics Society, pp. 157–190.

Phillips, C. (2010). Should we impeach armchair linguists? *Japanese/Korean Linguistics*, 17, 49–64.

Phillips, C. (2013). On the nature of island constraints. I: Language processing and reductionist accounts. In J. Sprouse & N. Hornstein, eds., *Experimental Syntax and Island Effects*. Cambridge: Cambridge University Press, pp. 64–108.

Phillips, C. & Wagers, M. (2007). Relating structure and time in linguistics and psycholinguistics. In M. G. Gaskel, ed., *Oxford Handbook of Psycholinguistics*. Oxford: Oxford University Press, pp. 739–756.

Preminger, O. (2010). Nested interrogatives and the locus of *wh*. In E. Phoevos Panagiotidis, ed., *The Complementizer Phase: Subjects and Operators*. Oxford: Oxford University Press, pp. 200–235.

Prunet, J. F. (2006). External evidence and the Semitic root. *Morphology*, 16, 41–67.

Reinhart, T. (1981). A second COMP position. In A. Belletti, L. Brandi, & L. Rizzi, eds., *Theory of Markedness in Generative Grammar*. Pisa: Scuola Normale Superiore, pp. 517–557.

Ritter, E. (1991). Two functional categories in noun phrases. S. Rothstein, ed., *Perspectives on Phrase Structure* (Syntax and Semantics, 25). New York: Academic Press, pp. 37–62.

Ross, J. R. (1967). Constraints on variables in syntax. Doctoral dissertation, Massachusetts Institute of Technology.

Rychlý, P. & Suchomel, V. (2016). Annotated Amharic Corpora. In P. Sojka, A. Horak, I. Kopachek, & K. Pala, eds., *Proceedings of the 19th International Conference on Text, Speech, and Dialogue*. New York: Springer, pp. 295–302.

Ryding, K. C. (2011). Arabic datives, ditransitives, and the preposition li. In B. Orfali, ed., *The Shadow of Arabic: The Centrality of Language to Arabic Culture*. Leiden: Brill, pp. 283–299.

Schütze, C. (2016). *The Empirical Base of Linguistics: Grammaticality Judgments and Linguistic Methodology*. Berlin: Language Science Press.

Sells, P. (1984). Syntax and semantics of resumptive pronouns. *Linguistic Review*, 4, 261–267.

Shlonsky, U. (1992). Resumptive pronouns as a last resort. *Linguistic Inquiry*, 23, 443–468.

Shlonsky, U. (1997). *Clause Structure and Word Order in Hebrew and Arabic: An Essay in Comparative Semitic Syntax*. New York: Oxford University Press.

Shlonsky, U. (2004). The form of Semitic noun phrases. *Lingua*, 114, 1465–1526.

Shlonsky, U. & Ouhalla, J. (2002). *Themes in Arabic and Hebrew Syntax*. Dordrecht: Springer.

Sichel, I. (2014). Resumptive pronouns and competition. *Linguistic Inquiry*, 45, 655–693.

Siloni, T. (2001). Construct states at the PF interface. *Linguistic Variation Yearbook*, 1, 229–266.

Sprouse, J. (2007). Continuous Acceptability, categorical grammaticality, and experimental syntax. *Biolinguistics*, 1, 118–129.

Sprouse, J., Caponigro, I., Greco, C., & Cecchetto, C. (2016). Experimental syntax and the variation of island effects in English and Italian. *Natural Language and Linguistic Theory*, 34, 307–444.

Sprouse, J., Fukuda, S., Ono, H., & Kluender, R. (2011). Reverse island effects and the backward search for a licensor in multiple *wh*-questions. *Syntax*, 14, 179–203.

Sprouse, J., Schütze, C., & Almeida, D. (2013). A comparison of informal and formal acceptability judgments using a random sample from *Linguistic Inquiry* 2001–2010. *Lingua*, 134, 219–248.

Stowe, L. (1986). Parsing *wh*-constructions: Evidence for on-line gap location. *Language and Cognitive Processes*, 1, 227–245.

Tucker, M., Idrissi, A., & Almeida, D. (2015). Representing number in the real-time processing of agreement: self-paced reading evidence from Arabic. *Frontiers in Psychology*, 6, 347.

Tucker, M., Idrissi, A., Sprouse, J., & Almeida, D. (2019). Resumption ameliorates different islands differentially: Acceptability data from Modern Standard Arabic. In A. Khalfaoui & M. Tucker, eds., *Perspectives on Arabic Linguistics, 30: Papers from the Annual Symposia on Arabic Linguistics, Stony Brook, New York, 2016, and Norman, Oklahoma, 2017*. Amsterdam: John Benjamins, pp. 159–193.

Vella, A. (2013). Languages and language varieties in Malta. *International Journal of Bilingual Education and Bilingualism*, 16, 532–552.

Wagers, M. W., Lau, E. F., & Phillips, C. (2009). Agreement attraction in comprehension: Representations and processes. *Journal of Memory and Language*, 61(2), 206–237.

Wahba, W. A. (1992). LF movement in Iraqi Arabic. In J. Huang & R. May, eds., *Logical Structure and Linguistic Structure*. Dordrecht: Springer, pp. 253–276.

Wasow, T. & Arnold, J. (2005). Intuitions in linguistic argumentation. *Lingua*, 115, 1481–1496.

Wilmsen, D. (2010). Dialects of written Arabic: Syntactic differences in the treatment of object pronouns in Egyptian and Levantine newspapers. *Arabica*, 57, 99–128.

Wilmsen, D. (2012). The ditransitive dative divide in Arabic: Grammaticality assessments and actuality. In R. Bassiouney & E. G. Katz, eds., *Arabic Language and Linguistics*. Washington, DC: Georgetown University Press, pp. 215–232.

Yoshida, M., Kazanina, N., Pablos, L., & Sturt, P. (2014). On the origin of islands. *Language, Cognition and Neuroscience*, 29, 761–770.

# 20

# Experimental Syntax and Slavic Languages

Arthur Stepanov

## 20.1 Introductory Remarks

Slavic formal syntax benefits from the experimental perspective in at least four different, though interrelated, aspects. One aspect has to do with clarifying and/or streamlining the acceptability status of some syntactic constructions that, for one reason or another, receive diverging and/or inconclusive judgments among speakers. Pertinent constructions and phenomena include, but are not limited to, the following:

- island constructions (Section 20.2.1)
- multiple *wh*-questions, including Superiority effects and availability of particular interpretations (Section 20.2.2)
- flexible word order and scrambling (Section 20.2.4)
- quantifier scope and interaction, availability of surface vs. inverse scope readings (Section 20.3.4)

Another aspect bears on the source of apparent unacceptability of a particular construction. A case in point is island configurations, often thought to arise from an interaction of grammatical and processing factors, the former including factors like the structural type of the embedding verb, and the latter factors like length or structural complexity (Section 20.2.1; see also Chapter 9; Phillips 2006; Sprouse et al. 2012). By carefully decomposing potential factors that influence acceptability, an experimental framework allows a statistically robust evaluation of the role of each of these factors and their contribution to the observed acceptability status.

The third kind of benefit concerns teasing apart concurrent theoretical accounts or explanations of a specific construction or phenomenon. One example is the issue as to which order of indirect and direct object in Slavic double object constructions should be regarded as basic, which, in light of the circumstantial evidence, is difficult to reconcile in one or another direction (Section 20.3.3). A focus on large-scale data collection in relevant cases like this allows a sharper and more fine-grained differentiation of the observed patterns and determining clear trends, which helps one choose eventually in favor of a more descriptively adequate account.

Last, but not least, there is a benefit in enlarging the cross-linguistic database of phenomena established on a unified, statistically robust, and methodologically consistent empirical basis. A single, unified design of experiments intended to study a particular syntactic construction, e.g. subject islands, may be applied across different Slavic languages to track and map the distribution and acceptability status of this construction along the typological scale.

The following overview surveys a selective range of topics in Slavic generative syntax explored from the experimental perspective in the form of large-scale sentence acceptability studies and related methodology (e.g. elicited production), insofar as the latter addresses pertinent issues in syntactic theory. The topics covered below represent only a subset of the themes actively explored over the last decade or so and range from issues in syntax proper (e.g. word order, agreement) through topics at the interfaces with morphology, semantics, and pragmatics. This chapter's main purpose is to offer the reader a bird's-eye view of this dynamically growing and productive subfield of Slavic linguistics.

## 20.2 Sentence Acceptability Studies

### 20.2.1 Islands and Locality

Studies in locality of syntactic dependencies has dominated generative syntax since its earliest stages (Chomsky 1964; Ross 1967), and this interest naturally carried over to Slavic linguistics, especially as concerns *wh*-movement dependencies and (un)acceptability of various island configurations in the Slavic languages (see Chapter 9 for a detailed discussion of island phenomena in general). At present, there are at least two trends of research in this area of Slavic syntax that received an articulated experimental dimension. We consider these in turn.

One trend has to do with evaluating different theories of syntactic locality and islands. One class of these theories, falling under the rubric of Condition on Extraction Domains (CED, Huang 1982), considers subject islands and adjunct islands as conforming to the same set of structural constraints. At the same time, it is becoming increasingly clear that subject islands appear cross-linguistically more variable in acceptability than adjunct islands, the latter being uniformly "strong" islands (Uriagereka 1988; Stepanov 2007). In addition, language-internal factors like structural properties of the main predicate, in particular, the unaccusative–unergative distinction, may affect acceptability of a subject island construction (cf. Chomsky 2008). Against this backdrop, Sturgeon et al. (2010) and

Polinsky et al. (2013) experimentally investigated acceptability of subject island sentences in Czech and Russian, in comparison with English. According to the authors, these Slavic languages offer particularly convenient testing grounds for testing lexically driven variation in acceptability of subject islands, due to availability of transparent diagnostic tests for unaccusativity as well as the dedicated A-bar topic position (Czech) and regular *wh*-movement to the left periphery (Russian). Potential influence of the subject position, preverbally or postverbally, was also taken into account. The researchers experimentally compared acceptability ratings and reading performance in sentences involving *wh*-extraction out of subjects with unaccusative, unergative, and transitive verbs, compared with *wh*-extraction out of objects, as illustrated in (1) for Russian:

(1)    a. Kakie         ty   mečtaeš́  [čtoby _ aktjory okazaliś  na scene]?
          what-kind-of  you dream        COMP  actors  appeared on stage
          'What kind of actors do you hope to appear on the stage?'      /unacc./
       b. Kakie         ty   mečtaeš́  [čtoby _ gruppy tancevali na scene]?
          what-kind-of  you dream        COMP  groups danced  on stage
          'What kind of groups do you hope to dance on the stage?'       /unerg./
       c. Kakie         on prosil [čtoby _ sotrudniki blagodarili direktora]?
          what-kind-of  he asked  COMP  employees  thanked     director
          'What kind of staff members did he ask to thank the director?' /trans./
       d. Kakie         ty   xočeš́ [čtoby _ otmetki ob"javil    professor]?
          what-kind-of you want  COMP  grades announced professor
          'What kind of grades do you want the professor to announce?'   /obj./

(Russian, adapted from Polinsky et al. 2013: (18)–(21))

In these studies, sentences involving *wh*-extraction from subjects with unaccusative verbs were rated higher than sentences involving the other two verb types. The critical regions in these sentences also tended to be read faster than in the other two sentence types when the subject was postverbal. This kind of rating and reading advantage is consistent with the unaccusative hypothesis according to which the base position of unaccusative subjects is comparable to that of transitive objects, namely, an internal argument, as opposed to transitive subjects. In addition, preverbal subject sentences tended to be read slower than postverbal ones, for all predicate types, an asymmetry that the authors attribute to the special status of the topic position which may add complexity to the online process of dependency formation in these languages. Finally, extraction from subjects of the transitive verbs seems to be most difficult out of the three verbal types, extraction from unergative subjects being the second in difficulty. The results of these studies support the class of theories of islands and *wh*-extraction based on the CED and also underscore the importance of the base position for extraction. At the same time, the authors argue that their results do not support the "freezing" accounts of subject islands whereby further extraction is not possible out of a previously moved constituent (e.g. Takahashi 1994; Rizzi 2007; Stepanov 2007). The progressive scale of acceptability and reading times across the different verb types involved in subject island sentences thus offers a powerful means for evaluating different theories of extractability on a sound and fine-grained empirical basis.

The second identifiable trend driving experimental investigations of island phenomena in Slavic has to do with the long-standing question whether and to what extent the intuitively felt deviance in acceptability associated with island phenomena may be due to processing-related factors such as length of the dependency (the linear or structural distance between the head and tail of the dependency) and complexity of an island-inducing structure, e.g. a complex NP. This issue has been taken up recently from a new and interesting experimental perspective, utilizing a factorial definition of island whereby an island effect can be deduced from a statistical interaction of factors *length* and *structure* in the above sense. By hypothesis, each of these factors contributes to the degraded status of an island sentence, but only an additive effect would indicate an effect over and above their respective contribution (see Chapter 9 for extensive discussion of this point, as well as Sprouse et al (2012) and Sprouse et al. (2016)).

Stepanov et al. (2018) experimentally investigated *wh*-island and subject island effects in Slovenian. Primary empirical reports indicated that this language may not observe a *wh*-island and a subject-island constraint, while observing the adjunct, Complex NP, and Coordinate Structure constraint in *wh*-questions (Golden 1995, 1996, 1997). The following examples, adapted from Golden (1995), exemplify the *wh*-island, subject island and adjunct island sentences along with the judgments reported in that work:

(2)    a. Kaj   se   je   Peter spraševal, kako je   Špela popravila __?
          what REFL AUX Peter wondered how AUX Špela fixed
          "What did Peter wonder how Špela fixed?'

       b. Čigavim   predlogom   se   mu je   [ugovarjati _ na oddelčnih
          Whose      proposals    REFL him AUX discuss-INF  at departmental
          sestankih]  Zdelo    nesmiselno?
          meetings    seemed pointless
          "Whose proposals did to discuss at the departmental meetings
          seem pointless to him?'

       c. *Kaj   se   oglasi      pri nas,  preden kupiš _ ?
          what REFL drop-by   at us    before buy-2SG.
          "What do you drop by before you buy?'

(Slovenian, Golden 1995)

The observed diverging pattern of acceptability of different island configurations presents an a priori challenge for the existing theories of syntactic locality (see above). The primary goal of Stepanov et al.'s study was to validate these empirical patterns and assess their robustness. The authors used the method of magnitude estimations (Bard et al. 1996) in a sentence acceptability task, in an experimental design crossing the factors length and structure.

The results of this study indicated that *wh*-island sentences are indeed degraded, but the observed degradation was not an additive effect or interaction of the two factors; each factor contributed to the degradation separately. In other words, assuming that interaction of length and structure is indicative of a true island effect, such an effect was not found. With respect to the subject island sentences, the authors reported a clear island effect that emerged as a result of interaction of the two factors. The subject island effect was replicated in Stepanov et al. (2016), a similarly designed study that used a slightly different shape of the target sentences to control for a potential confound (the latter study involved a PP extraction out of subject, whereas the former involved the so-called "left branch" extraction typical for many Slavic languages). The primary reports on Slovenian were thus only partially confirmed, and a larger-scale approach then allowed for more fine-grained and stable generalizations. Another interesting finding that emerged as a result of the latter study was a possible latent Comp-trace effect in Slovenian, which is also a *pro*-drop language (see Chapters 7 and 10 for further discussion of the Comp-trace effect from a cross-linguistic perspective). This effect is not typically reported in the theoretical syntactic literature on this language, but is apparently detectable in a larger-scale study. A similar situation was attested earlier in German, a non-*pro*-drop language (Featherston 2005; see also Chapter 18). Revealing latent intuitions such as this is yet another benefit of using an experimental approach in this domain.

## 20.2.2  Multiple *Wh*-Questions and Superiority Effects

The structure and the interpretation of multiple *wh*-questions have undoubtedly become one of the most prominent themes in Slavic syntax and the syntax–semantics interface (cf. Rudin 1988). In contrast to languages like English in which only one *wh*-phrase is fronted, all *wh*-phrases undergo fronting in a typical Slavic multiple *wh*-question. Multiple *wh*-questions attract the researchers' attention as a window to numerous theoretical issues including the fine structure of the left periphery, contrastive focus, triggers and driving force(s) of syntactic movement, mechanisms of licensing and interaction of interpretable and uninterpretable features, the conceptual status of the Superiority condition, and much more, thus providing rich sources of insight in these domains (cf. e.g. Bošković 2002; see Chapter 5 for discussion of Superiority and related issues). There is also a significant degree of variability among speakers concerning acceptability of sentences with particular sequences of *wh*-phrases in contrast to others, sometimes also within a single Slavic language.

Factors that play a role here include linear precedence, animacy, type of *wh*-phrase (argument or adjunct), grammatical function, thematic structure, and D-linking, among others.

Meyer (2004) reports the results of an experimental investigation of different orderings of *wh*-words in multiple *wh*-questions in Czech, Polish, and Russian. The order of *wh*-phrases in questions like *Who bought what?* in these languages is typically rather free (e.g. Bošković 2002). (3) exemplifies this for Russian:

(3)    a.  Kto   kogo   videl?  b.  Kogo   kto   videl?
           who   whom  saw       whom  who  saw
           'Who saw whom?'      'Who saw whom?'    (Russian)

The study used the method of magnitude estimations in an acceptability rating task. In one part of this study, the order of *wh*-subject and *wh*-object, animacy of the object *wh*-phrase, and the level of embedding (matrix or embedded clause) were manipulated. The results generally suggested no preference for a particular order of *wh*-arguments, in accord with the expectations, unless both *wh*-phrases referred to animate entities, in which case the preferred order was *wh*-subject ≫ *wh*-object in all three languages. In another part of this study, the order of an *wh*-argument (subject and object) and a *wh*-adjunct was tested. There was generally no preference for a particular order of *wh*-arguments and *wh*-adjunct in Czech and Polish, and a weak preference for *wh*-subjects to precede *wh*-adjuncts. D-linking *wh*-phrases was shown to result in a greater flexibility of the *wh*-word orders, consistent with the previous theoretical literature (Pesetsky 1987). In addition, embedding had no significant effect on the observed pattern of results. A very similar pattern of results was reported for Slovenian in Mišmaš (2015), which included an important modification to Meyer's (2004) design: a preceding context was added on the basis of which an "appropriate sounding" order of the two *wh*-phrase had to be chosen. On a comparative note, a similar issue was also experimentally explored in German in which the order *wh*-object ≫ *wh*-subject was found to be acceptable only if the animacy specification of the two differs (cf. Fanselow et al. 2011; see also Chapter 18).

These and related studies raise an interesting question as to why the ordering preference among animate *wh*-arguments observed in an experimental study shows up, often in contrast to the individual judgments predominant in the literature. A more pertinent theoretical question is how this can be incorporated into the existing theories of multiple *wh*-movement in Slavic languages. Perhaps this is another point where purely syntactic and processing factors entangle in an intricate way. Regardless of its actual nature, it appears that involving a larger sample of datapoints helps bring out a hidden or less pronounced empirical effect (similar to the latent *that*-trace effect in Slovenian; see Section 20.2.1). This situation also underscores the need for special care in utilizing the experimental techniques for data collection when investigating syntactic constructions of increased complexity.

### 20.2.3 Case Matters

The majority of the modern Slavic languages are characterized by rich Case morphology. The morphological visibility of Case allows for investigation of empirical patterns pertaining to Case theory with greater precision and reliability, using the experimental approach, leading to solidifying important empirical generalizations and theoretical insights.

Łęska (2016) experimentally validates peculiar subject–verb agreement restrictions in Polish relative clauses that bear on a featural distinction between virile and non-virile forms. Relative clauses in Polish can be introduced either by a morphologically invariant complementizer *co* or by the relative pronoun *który* that inflects for number, gender, and Case, and, in addition in the plural form, it distinguishes virile (human male) and non-virile forms (see also Section 20.2.5). Clausal subjects in the form of numerically quantified QPs with either virile or non-virile nouns trigger default subject–verb agreement, as shown in (4) and (5). Interestingly, when such a QP serves as a controller for a respective relative clause introduced by complementizer *który*, only full subject–verb agreement inside the relative clause is possible with virile QPs (6), while non-virile heads may trigger either full or default (third-person singular neuter) agreement, as shown in (7). Note that the Case of the external head (genitive) does not match the case of the relativizer. In contrast, in relative clauses introduced by (Case-invariant) *co*, both default and full clause-internal agreement are equally possible.

(4)  Siedmiu   mężczyzn   weszło /   *weszli        do domu ...
     seven-ACC men-GEN.VIR. entered-3SG./entered-3PL.VIR. into house
     'Seven men entered the house ...'

(5)  Siedmiu  kobiet        weszło /   *weszły       do domu ...
     seven-ACC women-GEN.NVIR. entered-3SG./entered-3PL.NVIR. into house
     'Seven women entered the house ...'

(6)  Siedmiu  mężczyzn,   którzy   weszli /       *weszło
     seven-ACC men-GEN.VIR. who-NOM entered-3PL.VIR/ entered-3SG.N
     do         domu ...
     into       house
     'Seven men who entered the house ...'

(7)  Siedem    kobiet,       które      weszli /
     seven-ACC women.GEN.NVIR. who-NOM/ACC entered.3PL.NVIR/
     weszło       do    domu ...
     entered.3SG.N into   house
     'Seven women who entered the house ...'

(Polish, adapted from Łęska 2016: (12)–(14))

The author considers the observed contrasts as instances of the Case matching phenomenon whereby the syncretic Accusative of the non-virile relativizer, but not the Nominative of the virile one, is matched with the external numeral (assumed to be inherently Accusative as well). Subtle preferences in choosing the default vs. full agreement options with matching and non-matching heads are also reliably identified in this study. These experimentally validated results offer new interesting grounds for evaluating theoretical accounts such as Case attraction and Case stacking previously proposed in the literature to tackle the Case matching phenomenon in other languages, such as German (Bader & Bayer 2006). According to these accounts, the Case feature of the relativized head may optionally be transmitted to the relative pronoun and morphologically surface instead of the Case licensed within the relative clause (e.g. Nominative). The experimental approach here helps uncover and explore the morphological component of the Case matching process, and pinpoint specific structural conditions for its realization.

The Person-Case Constraint (PCC) is another widely discussed and important topic in the generative syntactic literature (Perlmutter 1971; Bonet 1991; Nevins 2007, among others). The PCC is relevant when the dative and accusative arguments of a ditransitive verb are phonologically weak elements or clitics; in that case, roughly, the PCC disallows a dative≫accusative combination involving an accusative object with a first- or second-person feature value. Sturgeon et al. (2012) performed a large-scale acceptability judgment experiment of Case patterns in Czech ditransitive verbs to investigate the status of the PCC in this language (also accompanied by a corpus study). The results of this study confirm that Czech speakers rate dative≫accusative significantly lower if the second argument has a first- or second-person specification. But there is an important exception: Czech appears to allow reverse accusative≫dative combinations as a way to obviate a potential PCC effect, as some sort of a saving strategy. The authors propose an Optimality Theoretic treatment whereby the exceptional pattern emerges as a result of interaction of two general constraints on linearization of complex heads: one determining a particular order of precedence of the clitic arguments according to the hierarchy of person features (1 > 2 > 3), and the other determining the order of precedence in accord with the preference hierarchy of Case (Dative > Accusative). An important implication of this proposal is that Czech may not be subject to PCC after all. PCC-like effects were also reported in Runić (2013) who used an acceptability judgment task to test speakers of clitic-second languages Croatian/Serbian, Slovenian, Czech, and Slovak. This study, too, argues that PCC effects or lack thereof emerge as a result of interaction of independent (person and thematic role) hierarchy-based constraints, in the form of "filters" that may be activated or deactivated in individual grammars depending on the positive evidence.

### 20.2.4  Word Order and Information Structure

The relative freedom of word orders and their derivations is a staple in Slavic syntactic research. This flexibility of word orders has also been tested and verified experimentally (see e.g. Kallestinova (2007) for Russian). A major issue here is the extent to which this flexibility can be accounted for given the tools and mechanisms of modern syntactic theory, teasing apart possible post-syntactic effects. As far as the latter is concerned, a major role is attributed to information structure, whose exploration has a long tradition (cf. Mathesius 1947; Hajičová 1993; Kiss 1995; Vallduví & Engdahl 1996; Rizzi 1997; Hajičová et al. 1998; Schwarzchild 1999, among others): topics precede foci; old, or given information precedes new. Sentence constituents can be realigned in accord with the information-structural demands. The relevance of an experimental perspective to this topic lies in its capability to elucidate syntactic aspects of these discourse-oriented factors (see Chapter 12 for a detailed discussion of these issues). Here the majority of present-day experimental work has concentrated on (i) exploration of the role of prosody in choosing a particular word order over others; (ii) uncovering the topic-focus structure as a close correlate of respective syntactic rela-tionships; (iii) understanding the nature of scrambling and its relation to both structure types; and (iv) clarifying the role of context in positioning constituents according to the given-new scheme.

A recent experimental study in Šimik and Wierzba (2017) reevaluates different word-order rearrangements reflecting particular information-structural demands in three West Slavic languages, namely, Czech, Polish, and Slovak, in terms of prosodic requirements in these languages (see also Šimík, Wierzba, & Kamali (2014) and Šimík & Wierzba (2015)). These authors compare the word-order hypothesis encoded in statements like "foci are sentence-final" and the prosodic hypothesis encoded in generalizations like "given expressions cannot bear sentence stress," which, together with the general rules on stress assignment (e.g. "sentence stress is sentence final"), derive particular word orders with respect to the given-new or topic-focus scheme. The authors also consider a combined hypothesis containing both the prosodic and word-order statements. The key assumption is that sentences that will violate one or the other type of generalization will be con-sistently perceived as degraded to a similar degree, taken as an indica-tion that the respective generalization is descriptively adequate. The target sentences included, among others, the "given object" paradigm illustrated in (8):

(8)          Context 1: 'Do you have an idea why Marta made          S new
             a phone call?'
             Context 2: 'Do you have an idea why Marta called          S given
             the aunt?'

a. Protože pry      teta      poveze do nemocnice **Martu**.   SVPPO
   because allegedly  aunt.NOM take   to hospital   Marta.ACC

b. Protože pry teta poveze Martu do **nemocnice**.          SVOPP

c. Protože pry teta Martu poveze do **nemocnice**.          SOVPP

d. Protože pry Martu teta poveze do **nemocnice**.          OSVPP
   'Because allegedly the aunt will take Marta to hospital.'

(Czech, adapted from Šimik & Wierzba 2017: (29))

According to the authors, reduced acceptability on answers (a), (b), and (c) (the latter in Context 1) is consistent with the word-order hypothesis, while reduced acceptability only on (a) is consistent with the prosodic as well as the combined hypotheses. This design is contrasted with similar word-order possibilities in the context "all new" ("what happened"), used as a baseline. Yet another manipulation crossed word-order possibilities (SVO vs. SOV) and the position of sentence stress (on O vs. on V). The results of the acceptability task were interpreted via multiple regression modeling taking acceptability scores to be a function of the weights of the violated constraints (cf. examples of generalizations above). Under these assumptions, the authors conclude that the combined hypothesis provides the best fit for the data. The authors argue, contrary to common accounts, that the prosodic approach to information structure is to be preferred over the word-order approach because of a consistent and robust interaction between prosodic factors (e.g. prohibition of stressing the given item) and information structure compared to a somewhat less robust interaction between the latter and word order.

### 20.2.5  Resumption in Relative Clauses

In some languages, a resumptive pronoun within the relative clause co-refers with the relative operator or pronoun (e.g. Shlonsky 1992; McCloskey 2005). A resumptive pronoun may only occur in island-violating contexts, thus serving as a kind of a repair device. Alternatively, resumption may not be restricted to island contexts (see Chapters 7, 8, and 19 for further discussion of resumptive pronouns). These resumptive strategies are also present in the Slavic languages, and often correlate with the use of morphologically invariant complementizer vs. a morphologically rich relative pronoun (see Section 20.2.3). Hladnik (2015) adopts the theoretical view that resumption serves to ensure recoverability of feature representation: phi-features and Case must be morphologically visible, either via a relativizer or via a resumptive pronoun. This accounts for both patterns of relativization in Slovenian, illustrated in (9a) and (9b), but presents a puzzle for the third type of resumption identified in this work, whereby a relative pronoun appears together with the resumptive pronoun, cf. (9c).

(9)   a.   To   je   človek,   ki      *(ga)        iščejo.
           this  is  man    <rel>  him.ACC   search.3PL
           'This is the man they look for.'

      b.   To   je   človek,   katerega  (*ga)       isčejo.
           this  is  man     which     him.ACC  search.3PL
           'This is the man which they look for.'

      c.   Poznam       človeka,     katerega    mislim,    da
           know.1SG     man.ACC     which.ACC  think.1SG  that
           ga          iščejo.
           him.ACC      search.3PL
           'I know the man who I think they are looking for.'

                 (Slovenian, adapted from Hladnik 2015: 26 (34) and 163, (6))

Hladnik hypothesizes that the availability of (9c) may be due to processing considerations and working memory load, rather than syntax itself.
To test the hypothesis, an acceptability judgment task was conducted with
speakers of Bosnian/Croatian/Serbian, Polish, and Slovenian, in which the
third resumption type has been attested. The experiment revealed that
acceptability of "feature doubling"constructions varies depending on the
distance between the relative pronoun and the resumptive pronoun, measured in the number of embedded clauses. Based on these results,
a processing factor is likely to play a key role in this type of resumption.
In this case, again, the experimental approach leads to sharpening the
division of labor between the competence and performance systems.

### 20.2.6   Verb Movement

Pollock (1989) suggested that adverb placement can be used as a diagnostic
for verb movement in a particular language. The underlying intuition is
based on the fact that in English, a VP-modifying adverb cannot intervene
between a transitive verb and its object, whereas in French, such adverbs
must follow the verb. The latter is taken to indicate *verb raising* whereby the
verb moves outside the projection in which it is generated (e.g. *v*P). Because
of the flexible word order and other intervening factors, it is not easy to
determine whether the verb raises out of *v*P in Russian on the basis of other
diagnostic tests for raising including coordination, distribution of negation, pronoun fronting etc. as such tests often yield controversial results
(cf. Bailyn 1995; King 1995). Kallestinova and Slabakova (2008) report an
acceptability judgment experiment in Russian manipulating word order
(SVO vs. OVS), position of the adverb (preverbally, postverbally), adverb
type (manner, frequency), verb perfectivity, and focus scope (over VO vs.
over O). A parallel version of the task was conducted in English in which
adverb type was manipulated. The results showed a main effect of adverb
placement in Russian, with preverbal adverbs strongly preferred over
postverbal ones. On the basis of these results the authors suggest that

there is no syntactic verb raising out of *v*P in Russian. At the same time, postverbal adverbs were still not rated as low as in English, a typical non-raising language. This is taken to reflect a stronger influence of the pragmatic component in Russian than in English.

## 20.2.7　The Structure of Comparatives

English sentences like *John ate more than five sandwiches* are ambiguous between the *many*-reading (e.g. John ate ten sandwiches) or the so called *much*-reading (e.g. John ate a three-course meal). Ionin and Matushansky (2013) observe that in Russian, these readings correspond to different grammatical sources: both readings are available in clausal comparatives as in (10a), whereas only a *many*-reading is available in phrasal comparatives as in (10b):

(10)　　a.　Ja　s'jela　bol'še,　čem　pjat'　　buterbrodov.
　　　　　　I　　ate　　more　　than　five.ACC　sandwiches.
　　　　　　'I ate more than five sandwiches.'　[OK '*many* reading,'
　　　　　　　　　　　　　　　　　　　　　　　　OK '*much* reading']
　　　　　b.　Ja　s'jela　bol'še　pjati　　　buterbrodov.
　　　　　　I　　ate　　more　five.GEN　sandwiches
　　　　　　'I ate more than five sandwiches.'　[OK '*many* reading,'
　　　　　　　　　　　　　　　　　　　　　　　　# ' *much* reading']

(Russian, adapted from Ionin & Matushansky 2013: (2))

Three different syntactic analyses for *than*-comparatives were proposed in the syntactic literature: that of a reduced *wh*-clause, a small clause, and a measure degree phrase (cf. Pancheva 2006). Ionin and Matushansky (2013) ask, among other things, which of these structures can be assigned to each type of the comparative construction in (10) in English, Bulgarian, Czech, Polish, and Russian. To this end, the authors collected speakers' acceptability data, while testing for availability of *many*-reading vs. *additive much* reading (e.g. 'five sandwiches and a soup') vs. *replacement much*-reading (e.g. 'a three-course meal'). The results revealed a complex pattern of judgments which indicated some preferences of one structural analysis over others. For instance, a reduced *wh*-clause may be unlikely to underlie amount comparatives, whereas small clause and measure degree analyses are available. The authors argue, in particular, for the degree analysis of examples like (10b), and for the small clause analysis of sentences like (10a) in Russian and a subset of the other tested languages. A certain degree of cross-linguistic variation was also attested which called for further investigations in this intricate net of distributional patterns. Studies like this contribute directly to a more enhanced vision and a choice between several syntactic analyses that, on the surface, account for the same data equally well.

### 20.2.8  Sentential Prosody

Zybatow and Mehlhorn (2000) identified the focus structure of a typical Russian declarative sentence via tracking prosodic markers of topicalization and focus when applied to different structural chunks or constituents of the sentence in the analysis of natural speech (for similar studies in other Slavic languages, see e.g. Oliver and Andreeva (2004) on Bulgarian and Polish, Smiljanić (2006) on Serbian/Croatian, Stopar (2017) on Slovenian, and Antonyuk-Yudina and Mykhaylyk (2013) on Ukrainian). Specific combinations of tested prosodic parameters include placement and prosodic characteristics of pitch accents, rise and/or fall of the fundamental frequency, and/or lengthening of the accented syllable (focus exponent) at prosodic boundaries. Taking this line of investigation further, Meyer and Mleinek (2006) identified pertinent prosodic markers in Russian yes/no questions. These authors investigated potential interactions of prosodic factors characterizing yes/no questions, on the one hand, and contrastive focus on different sentence components such as verb and/or object, on the other. To this end, the authors conducted a perception and categorization study among native speakers of Russian asking them to differentiate between declaratives, exclamatives, and yes/no questions on the basis of various combinations of prosodic markers as mentioned above. In this study, distinctive prosodic markers facilitated recognition of the respective sentence types, while similar prosodic signatures (e.g. pitch accents) in yes/no questions and declaratives with focused elements led to perception difficulties. These results bear potentially important repercussions for syntactic theories, in particular, underscoring the need to formally distinguish different kinds of focus and interaction of focus features with other sentence-level properties (e.g. the Q-operator), but also theories of object scrambling, definiteness, and syntax–phonology interface at large.

## 20.3  Syntactic Constructions Investigated with Other Experimental Methods

As noted in Section 20.1, the experimental approach proves particularly useful for investigating syntactic phenomena in which individual acceptability judgments appear to be subject to greater interspeaker or cross-linguistic variation and/or instability. In situations like this, methods like elicited production and sentence-picture verification often complement the acceptability judgment task as efficient and reliable experimental tools for testing speakers' syntactic intuitions. As such, these other methods gain increasing popularity in modern Slavic syntax, on a par with acceptability studies. Below we consider some representative examples.

## 20.3.1  Numeral-Based Quantifier Phrases

The structure of numeral-based quantifier phrases (QPs) involving adjectival modification such as *five (very) old chairs,* in which the numeral and the noun is separated by any amount of intervening material such as adjectives and/or adverbs, is an important and actively explored topic in Slavic morphosyntax (e.g. Franks 1995; Ionin & Matushansky 2006, 2018). This is an area in which one can observe an intricate interplay of distinct syntactic mechanisms licensing agreement and Case, as well as their interaction with morphology and semantics. The experimental approach in this area is likely to shed light on these important syntactic and interface issues, as well as on those that have to do with encoding relevant semantic concepts such as atomicity and countability.

One long-standing and intriguing syntactic phenomenon explored in the theoretical literature on this topic concerns a heterogeneous pattern of adjective–noun agreement observed in Russian QPs associated with "lower" numerals from 1 to 4, whereby the adjective receives genitive plural, whereas the noun takes what is traditionally seen as genitive singular. With "higher" numerals, greater than 4, the agreement pattern is homogeneous: the noun and adjective both receive genitive plural. This is exemplified in (11):

(11)  a. tri  (varenyx)  jajca        b. vosem' (dlinnyx)  linij
         three boiled-GEN.PL.egg-GEN.SG.N.    eight  long- GEN.PL. line-GEN.PL.F.
         'three (boiled) eggs'              'eight (long) lines'

                                                         (Russian)

The origins of the heterogeneous pattern of agreement is a non-trivial syntactic issue that has generated a great deal of debate in the theoretical syntactic literature, leading to proposals that have substantial repercussions for syntactic theory in general (e.g. Babby 1987; Pesetsky 2013). One recent proposal, developed in detail in Stepanov and Stateva (2018), maintains that what looks like an agreement discrepancy in (11a) is essentially a result of mislabeling: the alleged Genitive singular is, rather, a marker of atomicity and/or countability akin to numerical classifiers in some East Asian languages, whose morphological shape coincides with Genitive singular for historical reasons. To support their conclusions, the authors conducted an experimental study in the form of a cloze-like production task in which participants read, in the auto-paced reading mode, sentential preambles containing a numeral-based QP with a missing final noun. A lemma for that noun was provided afterwards. The participants' task was to supply the correct form of the noun based on the remaining part of the QP (and the sentence).

(12)    V   koridore  stojali  pjatj  starinnyx  lakirovannyx
        in  corridor  stood    five   old.GEN.PL  lackered.GEN.PL
        'In the corridor there were five old lackered ...'
        Lemma:  [stul]
               chair

                    (Russian, adapted from Stepanov & Stateva 2018: (34))

The type of the numeral (lower, higher), the number of intervening adjectives and the gender of the noun were manipulated. The prediction was that, if two theoretically possible endings on the noun (genitive plural and the alleged genitive singular) are treated on an equal basis in the grammar (e.g. as values of the same functional head), then, under memory-taxing conditions imposed by the auto-paced reading mode, the participants may make errors in supplying the relevant form of the noun in a more or less equal proportion, suggesting a chance performance. If, on the other hand, the two seemingly similar values are operated by different syntactic mechanisms, then the ratio of such production errors will be affected systematically. The participants in this study indeed made errors in providing the required noun forms, supplying Genitive singular when the Genitive plural was required, and vice versa. Furthermore, the ratio of observed errors in both directions was 1:4 with a strong bias toward a false "genitive singular." The number of intervening adjectives did not play a significant role in the error ratio. According to the authors, this is consistent with the view that "genitive singular" is licensed by a different mechanism from the one licensing genitive plural.

### 20.3.2   Conjunct Agreement Phenomena

The syntactic research on Slovenian has recently focused on the phenomenon of last conjunct agreement whereby, in preverbal contexts, the predicate (a verbal participle in a composite tense) agrees in gender with the last conjunct of a coordinated subject such as *the cows and the calves*, as illustrated in (13a). Alternatively, the agreement may default to masculine plural, as shown in (13b).

(13)   a.   [Teleta   in   krave]   so   odšle /   *odšla   na pašo.
            calf.N.PL.  and  cow.F.PL.  AUX  went.F.PL.  went.N.PL.  on grazing
            'Calves and cows went grazing.'

       b.   [Teleta   in   krave]   so   se   prodali   včeraj.
            calf.N.PL.  and  cow.F.PL.  AUX  REFL  sold.M.PL.  yesterday
            'Calves and cows were sold yesterday.'

(Slovenian, Marušič, Nevins, & Saksida 2007: (10), (11))

The phenomenon is also documented in Bosnian/Croatian/Serbian (Bošković 2009) and Polish (Bogucka 2012, cited in Marušič, Nevins, & Badecker 2015). It contrasts with the other well-known phenomenon, that of first conjunct agreement in postverbal (VS) contexts documented in other Slavic and non-Slavic languages (see the above sources for references).

Several issues of considerable interest to syntactic theory are at play here, including mechanisms of valuation of agreement features, their transmission to the root NP label and sharing with the verbal projection, and especially the role of linear contiguity in computing agreement as opposed to c-command and structural hierarchy (coordination NPs are commonly viewed as hierarchical configurations in the literature). Exploring these and related issues, Marušič, Nevins, and Badecker (2015) conducted a series of experiments based on written and spoken elicitation tasks. The written elicitation task involved a fill-in-the-blank style of questionnaire with target sentences that included conjoined NPs in preverbal and postverbal positions, with blanks in place of auxiliary and morphological ending on the participle. In the spoken elicitation task, participants saw a model sentence on the computer screen, with a non-conjoined (singular) subject, along with a target NP, and were asked to produce an utterance in which the model subject is replaced with the target NP.

(14)  Model sentence: caj  mu  je  olajšal  bolečine.

  tea  him  AUX.SG  milded.M.SG.  pains

  'Tea made his pains milder.'

  Target coordination: tablete,  injekcije  in  zdravila ...

  pills.F.PL.  injections.F.PL. and  medications.N.PL.

(Slovenian, Marušič, Nevins, & Badecker 2015: (31))

The authors pinpointed and identified three different strategies for computing gender agreement with mixed-gender conjunctions: (default) agreement with the entire Boolean Phrase, highest conjunct or structural agreement, and closest-conjunct or linear agreement. Other potential strategies, such as medial conjunct agreement (in case of three conjuncts), were not attested. The authors argue that speakers manifest a true syntactic optionality in choosing among the set of attested agreement strategies. This kind of optionality, in particular, the choice between the closest-conjunct and the highest conjunct agreement, is not always sustained with number agreement which seems to be more restricted. The authors place these strategies in the context of the minimalist agreement mechanisms and discuss important theoretical repercussions (cf. also Benmamoun, Bhatia, & Polinsky 2010; Bhatt & Walkow 2013).

Building on these and related studies, the large-scale research project "Coordinated research in the Experimental Morphosyntax of South Slavic languages" (funding source: Leverhulme Trust (UK); duration: 2014–2018; Research Head: Andrew Nevins) had further exploration of the patterns of conjunct agreement among its main foci, along with theoretical and experimental investigations of other aspects of agreement in these languages. The framework of the project enabled a coordinated collection of acceptability judgment and elicited production data on conjunct agreement across six different locations in Bosnia and Herzegovina, Croatia, Serbia, and Slovenia while controlling for language variety, data collection location as well as structural placement of the conjunction within a sentence (preverbally vs. postverbally). These studies further scrutinized various patterns of conjunct agreement in the South Slavic languages while exploring the linear, as opposed to hierarchical structure-based, agreement as a viable speaker strategy. In addition, other interesting tendencies were established and/or replicated, for instance, (i) a reduced ratio of default masculine gender agreement with the feminine+neuter or neuter+feminine combinations occurring postverbally, compared to pre-verbal contexts; (ii) the relative prominence of neuter gender controllers eliciting a greater ratio of respective (non-default) agreement as compared to feminine gender controllers, among other findings. Pertinent results are reported and discussed, in particular, in Willer-Gold et al. (2016) and Willer-Gold et al. (2018). Experimental investigations exploring patterns of conjunct agreement are currently becoming a lively and fruitful research area supplementing traditional theoretical studies in this subdomain of Slavic syntax (see also the collection of experimental reports in the Journal of Slavic Linguistics (2016), Arsenjević & Mitić (2019), among others). These explorations strengthen the empirical basis of the conjunct agreement phenomenon and lead to new theoretical insights and proposals concerning agreement mechanisms, markedness and other important constructs.

### 20.3.3 Double Object Constructions

The flexibility of word order in Slavic extends to internal arguments of ditransitive constructions: in many Slavic languages the orders indirect object–direct object (IO–DO) and direct object–indirect object (DO–IO) are equally possible (cf. English *John gave Bill a book* vs. *John gave the book to Bill*). In Slavic ditransitive constructions, different structural tests often appear to provide conflicting evidence, and individual judgments are not always conclusive. Consequently, some authors in the theoretical syntactic litera-ture defend the IO–DO order as basic, while others argue for DO–IO as the basic order (cf. Bailyn 1995; Dyakonova 2007 for Russian) or that both underlying orders are available in the grammar (e.g. Marvin & Stegovec (2012) for Slovenian; Dvořák (2010) for Czech). The issue is further com-plicated by information-structural demands that were shown to play an important role in this construction. The experimental approach offers a fresh perspective on this matter.

Using an elicited production task, Kallestinova (2007) and Mykhaylyk, Rodina, and Anderssen (2013) investigate the structure of double object constructions in Russian and (the latter work) Ukrainian, focusing on the of information structure/givenness in the ordering of indirect and direct objects, as illustrated in (15) and (16):

(15)   a.  Petja    dal    devočke   knigu.                          (Russian)
       b.  Petryk  dav   divčynci  knyhu.                          (Ukrainian)
           Peter gave girl.DAT book.ACC
           'Peter gave the girl a book.'

(16)   a.   Petja   dal    knigu     devočke.              (Russian)
       b.   Petryk  dav    knyhu     divčynci.             (Ukrainian)
            Peter   gave   book.ACC  girl.DAT
            'Peter gave the book to a girl.'

                                          (Mykhaylyk et al. 2013: (1)–(2))

The above studies corroborate the view that, while in discourse-neutral circumstances both word-order possibilities are produced, the new information status of one of the objects strongly correlates with placing the latter second in the sequence: thus the IO–DO order is strongly preferred if the direct object, or theme, is new and the indirect object, or recipient, is given, while the DO–IO order is preferred if the recipient is new and the theme is given. This highlights the need to take information structure into consideration in syntactic accounts of the underlying word order in these languages.

### 20.3.4   Scope Phenomena

Another domain witnessing extensive theoretical discussion in the Slavic syntactic literature concerns the scope of quantifiers (see Chapter 13 for general discussion of this topic from an experimental perspective). It is commonly recognized that quantifier scope in sentences involving two quantifiers (usually an existential and a universal: e.g. *One boy saw every girl*) in many Slavic languages tends to be more "surface-oriented" or "frozen" than in English, but the extent to which this is the case remains under debate (e.g. Ionin 2003; Antonyuk 2015). Part of the reason for the lack of strict consensus here could be the attested individual variation in speakers' judgments due to factors potentially complicating the judgments. One potential group of intervening factors includes information structure, topic/focus and given/new dichotomies substantially affecting word order in quantifier sentences. The experimental perspective helps straighten out the relevant empirical patterns here and formulate better empirical generalizations.

A sentence with a quantified subject and object in Russian can appear with an SVO or OVS word order, as illustrated in (17a) and (17b), respectively:

(17)   a. Odin      mal'chik  poceloval  kazhduju  devochku.
          one.NOM   boy.NOM   kissed     every.ACC  girl.ACC
          'One boy kissed every girl'

       b. Kazhduju  devochku  poceloval  odin      mal'chik.
          every.ACC girl.ACC  kissed     one.NOM   boy.NOM
          'One boy kissed every girl.'                  (Russian)

Stoops and Ionin (2013) used a truth-value judgment task in the context of preceding stories and found a preference for surface scope which was, however, stronger in the SVO order than in the OVS order. Exploring this issue from the prosodic perspective, Luchkina and Ionin (2015) establish a prosodic signature of indefinite quantifiers in scope interaction sentences using a sentence–picture verification task whereby participants listened to target sentences with a variable intonational contour and decided whether they properly correspond to associated pictures. The authors found that the inverse scope reading is reliably associated with a number of prosodic markers of prominence pitch accent, vowel segment intensity and duration, among others, and that these markers signal an information-structural configuration in which a preverbal object is interpreted as contrastively focused. Furthermore, Ionin and Luchkina (2015, 2018) find that in non-emotive sentences (with neutral prosody) the surface scope is preferred both in SVO and OVS word orders, but the contrastive prosody effectively facilitates an inverse scope reading in OVS sentences, but not in SVO sentences. The authors also find that providing a background context for the task does not substantially affect the pattern of results: speakers draw information-structural cues mostly from prosody. These studies emphasize the important role of prosodic factors as part of information-structural properties that enter into the computation of quantifier scope, also in line with current trends in the semantics and pragmatics literature (e.g. Schwarzchild 1999; Büring 2008; Wagner 2012).

## 20.4   Future Directions

The studies surveyed in this chapter serve to illustrate the four types of benefit of the experimental approach as outlined in Section 20.1. In addition, we may pinpoint some general conceptual issues in syntactic theory, where we believe Slavic experimental syntax has a potential to make a particularly strong contribution:

**- Optionality of syntactic movement**
Optionality is a non-trivial issue in modern generative syntax in which operations are, by hypothesis, triggered. Because of the flexible word order in Slavic languages, many constituent displacements seem optional, and their triggers are often difficult to identify. By using experimental methods, we may either explain it away by testing potential sources for the seemingly optional behavior, or confirm it using the statistical power of the method (e.g. whether the difference in the distribution of two optional patterns is or is not statistically significant).

## - Preferences

Another intricate issue concerns speakers' preferences in choosing a particular construction or interpretation, in the absence of sufficient intuitive grounds for excluding others as unacceptable. This is often the case, in particular, in sentences involving scope interaction in Slavic (see Section 20.3.4). Experimental techniques help establish these preferences on a much finer-grained scale than at the level of individual judgments, and enable one to estimate their effect size. This, in turn, leads to a better prediction as to whether these preferences arise as part of some processing routine that intervenes during accessing a particular reading, or, possibly, as noise in the data. Alternatively, the observed superficial preferences may even prove non-existent when estimated over a larger pool of participants (cf. e.g. Anderson 2004).

## - Division of labor

We have seen that the experimental approach is effective in delineating core syntactic phenomena from potential processing effects involving working memory, length of a dependency or complexity of a particular structure. This is particularly valuable in light of the view that sees potential sources of syntactic complexity in various aspects of the "third factor," some general computational capacity not directly related to the syntactic module but affecting its output in a way typical for language use (cf. Chomsky 2005). By identifying these non-syntactic effects, one is able to delineate the set of core phenomena that reflects the workings of the language faculty, and better estimate its properties and function.

The survey above demonstrates that the experimental approach is used in a wide variety of topics in Slavic syntax. Research areas in which experimental studies are still relatively sparse at this time include "genitive of negation," secondary predication, null subject phenomena, NPI licensing, and ellipsis, although there are indications that things are changing in those domains as well (see e.g. Vakareliyska 1996; Dočekal & Dotlačil 2016; Murphy et al. 2018; Vaiksnoraite 2019). These topics are expected to benefit from the experimental approach along the four dimensions outlined in Section 20.1, and fruitfully complement the existing theoretical studies.

As the experimental framework is gaining more momentum among researchers in Slavic syntax, it seems safe to say that the spectrum and diversity of experimentally covered topics in this field of study will only continue to increase. Another factor that directly contributes to the growing popularity of the experimental approach is the increasing availability of and access to online web-based platforms for conducting surveys and online questionnaires on sentence acceptability that allow the researcher to reach much wider pools of participants than was possible before, which comes in handy particularly given the vast geographic distribution of the Slavic languages and their speakers. An increasing number of experimental acceptability studies are reported at the two prominent conferences in Slavic linguistics, the Formal Approaches to Slavic Linguistics (FASL) and Formal Description of Slavic Languages (FDSL), organized in the US and Europe, respectively. An informal look at the language distribution in the focus of acceptability and related studies within the Slavic family suggests that Russian is currently in the lead, although this situation may soon change in light of the steadily growing amount of quality experimental studies on South Slavic (Slovenian, Bosnian/Croatian/Serbian) and West Slavic (Czech, Polish and Slovak) languages as well as Ukrainian, somewhat less so on Belarusian, Bulgarian, and Macedonian, the latter obviously signaling promising venues for experimental explorations.

The studies in Slavic experimental syntax have overlapping aims and foci with Slavic psycholinguistics (see Sekerina (2017) for a recent review of the latter). Insofar as the studies of linguistic performance revolve around or otherwise shed light on syntactic theory, the research agendas of the two subfields are likely to see an increasing convergence, a welcome result that fits well with the aims of the early psycholinguistic research agenda (see e.g. Fodor 1974). Despite the notable difference in the type of dependent variables employed (e.g. global acceptability measures vs. online performance markers), both types of studies, nevertheless, show a promising potential to contribute to the same goal, that of uncovering deeper aspects of syntactic structure and mental representation of syntactic, or grammatical, competence in the mind of an actual speaker/comprehender. More generally, an optimal synergy will be achieved when theoretical explorations in the diverse aspects of the grammars of the Slavic languages are informed and strengthened by the solid empirical base furnished by the experimental approach.

## References

Anderson, C. (2004). The structure and real-time comprehension of quantifier scope ambiguity. Doctoral dissertation, Northwestern University.

Antonyuk, S. (2015). Quantifier scope and scope freezing in Russian. Doctoral dissertation, Stony Brook University.

Antonyuk-Yudina, S. & Mykhaylyk, R. (2013). Prosody of scrambling. In S. Kan, C. Moore-Cantwell, & R. Staubs, eds., *Proceedings of NELS 40*. Amherst, MA: GLSA Publications, pp. 31–44.

Babby, L. (1987). Case, prequantifiers, and discontinous agreement in Russian. *Natural Language and Linguistic Theory*, 5, 91–138.

Bader, M. & Bayer, J. (2006). *Case and Linking in Language Comprehension: Evidence from German.* Dordrecht: Springer.

Bailyn, J. F. (1995). A configurational approach to Russian "free" word order. Doctoral dissertation, Cornell University.

Bard, E. G., Robertson, D., & Sorace, A. (1996). Magnitude estimation of linguistic acceptability. *Language*, 72, 32–68.

Benmamoun, E., Bhatia, A., & Polinsky, M. (2010). Closest conjunct agreement in head final languages. *Linguistic Variation Yearbook*, 9, 67–88.

Bhatt, R. & Walkow, M. (2013). Locating agreement in grammar: An argument from agreement in conjunctions. *Natural Language and Linguistic Theory*, 31, 951–1013.

Bonet, E. (1991). Morphology after syntax: Pronominal clitics in Romance. Doctoral dissertation, Massachusetts Institute of Technology.

Bogucka, J. (2012). Single conjunct agreement with coordinated subjects in Polish. Talk given at Young Linguists' Meeting in Poznan.

Bošković, Ž. (2002). On multiple *wh*-fronting. *Linguistic Inquiry*, 33, 351–383.

Bošković, Ž. (2009). Unifying first and last conjunct agreement. *Natural Language & Linguistic Theory*, 27, 455–496.

Büring, D. (2008). What's new (and what's given) in the theory of focus? In *Proceedings of the 34th Annual Meeting of the Berkeley Linguistics Society.* Berkeley, CA: Berkeley Linguistics Society, pp. 403–424.

Chomsky, N. (1964). *Current Issues in Linguistic Theory.* The Hague: Mouton.

Chomsky, N. (2005). Three factors in language design. *Linguistic Inquiry*, 36, 1–22.

Chomsky, N. (2008). On phases. In R. Freidin, C. P. Otero, & M.-L. Zubizarreta, eds., *Foundational Issues in Linguistics.* Cambridge, MA: MIT Press, pp. 133–166.

Dočekal, M. & Dotlačil, J. (2016). Experimental evidence for Neg-raising in Slavic. *Linguistica*, 56(1), 93–109.

Dvořák, V. (2010). On the syntax of ditransitive verbs in Czech. In *Proceedings of Formal Approaches to Slavic Linguistics 18.* Ann Arbor, MI: Michigan Slavic Publications, pp. 161–177.

Dyakonova, M. (2007). Russian double object constructions. *ACLC Working Papers*, 2, 3–30. Available at http://home.hum.uva.nl/oz/hengeveldp/pub lications/2007_hengeveld.pdf#page=3

Fanselow, G., Schlesewsky, M., Vogel, R., & Weskott, T. (2011). Animacy effects on crossing *wh*-movement in German. *Linguistics*, 49(4), 657–683.

Featherston, S. (2005). *That*-trace in German. *Lingua*, 115(9), 1277–1302.

Fodor, J. (1974) *The Psychology of Language.* New York: McGraw-Hill.

Franks, S. (1995). *Parameters of Slavic Morphosyntax.* New York: Oxford University Press.

Golden, M. (1995). Interrogative *wh*-movement in Slovene and English. *Acta Analytica*, 14, 145–187.

Golden, M. (1996). K-premik in skladenjski otoki v slovenski skladnji. *Razprave SAZU, Razred II*, vol. 15. Ljubljana: SAZU, pp. 237–253.

Golden, M. (1997). *O jeziku in jezikoslovju*. Ljubljana: Filozofska fakulteta.

Hajičová, E. (1993). *Issues of Sentence Structure and Discourse Patterns*. Prague: Charles University Press.

Hajičová, E., Partee, B. H., & Sgall, P. (1998). *Topic-Focus Articulation, Tripartite Structures, and Semantic Content*. Dordrecht: Kluwer.

Hladnik, M. (2015). Mind the gap: resumption in Slavic relative clauses. Doctoral dissertation, Utrecht University.

Huang, C.-T. J. (1982). Logical relations in Chinese and the theory of grammar. Doctoral dissertation, Massachusetts Institute of Technology.

Ionin, T. (2003). The one girl who was kissed by every boy: Scope, scrambling and discourse function in Russian. In M. van Koppen et al., eds., *Proceedings of ConSole X*. Student Organization of Linguistics in Europe, pp. 65–80.

Ionin, T. & Luchkina, T. (2015). One reading for every word order: Revisiting Russian scope. In U. Steindl et al., eds., *Proceedings of the 32nd West Coast Conference on Formal Linguistics*. Somerville, MA: Cascadilla Proceedings Project, pp. 21–30.

Ionin, T. & Luchkina, T. (2018). Focus on Russian scope: An experimental investigation of the relationship between quantifier scope, prosody, and information structure. *Linguistic Inquiry*, 49 (4), 741–779.

Ionin, T. & Matushansky, O. (2006). The composition of complex cardinals. *Journal of Semantics*, 23, 315–360.

Ionin, T. & Matushansky, O. (2013). More than one comparative in more than one Slavic language: An experimental investigation. In *Proceedings of Formal Approaches to Slavic Linguistics 21: The Third Indiana Meeting*. Ann Arbor, MI: Michigan Slavic Publications, pp. 91–107.

Ionin, T. & Matushansky, O. (2018). Cardinals: The syntax and semantics of cardinal-containing expressions. Cambridge, MA: MIT Press.

*Journal of Slavic Linguistics*, 24(1) (2016).

Kallestinova, E. (2007). Aspects of word order in Russian. Doctoral dissertation, University of Iowa.

Kallestinova, E. & Slabakova, R. (2008). Does the verb move in Russian? In A. Antonenko, J. Bailyn, & C. Bethin, eds., *Proceedings of Formal Approaches to Slavic Linguistics 16: The Stony Brook Meeting*. Ann Arbor, MI: Michigan Slavic Publications, pp. 199–214.

King, T. (1995). *Configuring Topic and Focus in Russian*. Stanford: CSLI Publications.

Kiss, K., ed. (1995). *Discourse Configurational Languages*. Oxford: Oxford University Press.

Łęska, P. (2016). Agreement under Case Matching in Polish *co* and *który* relative clauses headed by numerically quantified nouns. *Journal of Slavic Linguistics*, 24(1), 113–136.

Luchkina, T. & Ionin, T. (2015). The effect of prosody on availability of inverse scope in Russian. In *Proceedings of Formal Approaches to Slavic Linguistics 23: The Berkeley Meeting*. Ann Arbor, MI: Michigan Slavic Publications, pp. 418–437.

Marušič, F., Nevins, A., & Saksida, A. (2007). Last-conjunct agreement in Slovenian. In R. Compton, M. Goledzinowska, & U. Savchenko, eds., *Proceedings of Formal Approaches to Slavic Linguistics 15: The Toronto Meeting*. Ann Arbor, MI: Michigan Slavic Publications, pp. 210–227.

Marušič, F., A. Nevins, & Badecker, W. (2015). The Grammars of conjunction agreement in Slovenian. *Syntax*, 18(1), 39–77.

Marvin, T. & Stegovec, A. (2012). On the syntax of ditransitive sentences in Slovenian. *Acta Linguistica Hungarica*, 59 (1–2), 177–203.

Mathesius, V. (1947). *Čeština a obecný jazykozpyt ('Czech language and general linguistics')*. Prague: Melantrich.

McCloskey, J. (2005). Resumption. In M. Everaert & H. van Riemsdijk, eds., *The Blackwell Companion to Syntax*, vol. 4. Oxford: Blackwell, pp. 94–117.

Meyer, R. (2004). Superiority effects in Russian, Polish and Czech: Judgments and grammar. *Cahiers linguistiques d'Ottawa*, 32, 44–65.

Meyer, R. & Mleinek, I. (2006). How prosody signals force and focus a study of pitch accents in Russian yes-no questions. *Journal of Pragmatics*, 38 (10), 1615–1635.

Mišmaš, P. (2015). On the optionality of *wh*-fronting in a multiple *wh*-fronting language. Doctoral dissertation, University of Nova Gorica.

Mitić, I. & Arsenijević, B. (2019). Plural conjuncts and syncretism facilitate gender agreement in Serbo-Croatian: Experimental evidence. *Frontiers in Psychology*, 10, 942. DOI: 10.3389/fpsyg.2019.00942

Murphy, A., Puškar, Z., & Naranjo, M. G. (2018). Gender encoding on hybrid nouns in Bosnian/Croatian/Serbian: Experimental evidence from ellipsis. In D. Lenertová, R. Meyer, R. Šimík, & L. Szucsich, eds., *Advances in Formal Slavic Linguistics 2016*. Berlin: Language Science Press, pp. 313–336.

Mykhaylyk, R., Rodina, Y., & Anderssen, M. (2013). Ditransitive constructions in Russian and Ukrainian: Effect of givenness on word order. *Lingua*, 137, 271–289.

Nevins, A. (2007). The representation of third person and its consequences for person–case effects. *Natural Language and Linguistic Theory*, 25, 273–313.

Oliver, D. & Andreeva, B. (2004). Peak alignment in broad and narrow focus in Polish and Bulgarian: A cross-language study. In G. Zybatow, L. Szucsich, U. Junghanns, & R. Meyer, eds., *Proceedings of Formal Description of Slavic Languages V*. Berlin: Peter Lang, pp. 26–29.

Pancheva, R. (2006). Phrasal and clausal comparatives in Slavic. In J. Lavine, S. Franks, M. Tasseva-Kurktchieva, & H. Filip, eds., *Proceedings of Formal Approaches to Slavic Linguistics 14: The Princeton Meeting*. Ann Arbor, MI: Michigan Slavic Publications, pp. 236–257.

Perlmutter, D. (1971). *Deep and Surface Structure Constraints in Syntax.* New York: Holt, Rinehart and Winston.

Pesetsky, D. (1987). *Wh*-in situ: Movement and unselective binding. In E. J. Reuland & A. G. B. ter Meulen, eds., *The Representation of (In)definiteness.* Cambridge, MA: MIT Press, pp. 98–129.

Pesetsky, D. (2013). *Russian Case Morphology and the Syntactic Categories.* Cambridge, MA: MIT Press.

Phillips, C. (2006). The real-time status of island phenomena. *Language*, 82 (4), 795–823.

Polinsky, M., Gallo, C. G., Graff, P., Kravtchenko, E., Morgan, A. M., & Sturgeon, A. (2013). Subject islands are different. In J. Sprouse, ed., *Experimental Syntax and Island Effects.* Cambridge: Cambridge University Press, pp. 286–309.

Pollock, J.-Y. (1989). Verb movement, Universal Grammar, and the structure of IP. *Linguistic Inquiry*, 20, 365–424.

Rizzi, L. (1997). The fine structure of the left periphery. In L. Haegeman, ed., *Elements of Grammar: Handbook in Generative Syntax.* Dordrecht: Kluwer, pp. 281–337.

Rizzi, L. (2007). On some properties of criterial freezing. In V. Moscati, ed., *CISCL Working Papers on Language and Cognition, 1: StiL Studies in Linguistics.* University of Siena, pp. 145–158.

Ross, J. R. (1967). Constraints on variables in syntax. Doctoral dissertation, Massachusetts Institute of Technology.

Rudin, C. (1988). On multiple questions and multiple *wh*-fronting. *Natural Language and Linguistic Theory*, 6, 445–501.

Runić, J. (2013). The Person–Case Constraint: A morphological consensus. *Linguistics Society of America Annual Meeting Extended Abstracts 2013*, 37, 1–5. Available at: https://journals.linguisticsociety.org/proceedings/index.php/ExtendedAbs/issue/view/23

Schwarzschild, R. (1999). GIVENness, AvoidF, and other constraints on the placement of accent. *Natural Language Semantics*, 7(2), 141–177.

Sekerina, I. (1997). The syntax and processing of scrambling constructions in Russian. Doctoral dissertation, City University of New York.

Sekerina, I. (2017). Slavic psycholinguistics in the 21st century. *Journal of Slavic Linguistics*, 25(2), 465–489.

Shlonsky, U. (1992). Resumptive pronouns as a last resort. *Linguistic Inquiry*, 23, 443–468.

Šimík, R. & Wierzba, M. (2015). The role of givenness, presupposition, and prosody in Czech word order: An experimental study. *Semantics and Pragmatics*, 8(3), 1–103. DOI: 10.3765/sp.8.3

Šimík, R. & Wierzba, M. (2017). Expression of information structure in West Slavic: Modeling the impact of prosodic and word-order factors. *Language*, 93(3), 671–709.

Šimík, R., Wierzba, M., & Kamali, B. (2014). Givenness and the position of the direct object in the Czech clause. In C. Chapman, O. Kit, & I. Kučerová, eds., *Proceedings of Formal Approaches to Slavic Linguistics 22: The McMaster Meeting 2013*. Ann Arbor, MI: Michigan Slavic Publications, pp. 302–318.

Smiljanić, R. (2006). Early vs. late focus: Pitch-peak alignment in two dialects of Serbian and Croatian. In L. Goldstein, D. H. Whalen, & C. T. Best, eds., *Laboratory Phonology 8*. Berlin: Mouton de Gruyter, pp. 495–518.

Sprouse, J., Caponigro, I., Greco, C., & Cecchetto, C. (2016). Experimental syntax and the variation of island effects in English and Italian. *Natural Language and Linguistic Theory*, 34, 307–344.

Sprouse, J., Wagers, M., & Phillips, C. (2012). A test of the relation between working-memory capacity and syntactic island effects. *Language*, 88(1), 82–123.

Stepanov, A. (2007). The end of CED? Minimalism and extraction domains. *Syntax*, 10, 80–126.

Stepanov, A., Mušič, M., & Stateva, P. (2016). Asymmetries in sub-extraction out of NP in Slovenian: A magnitude estimation study. *Linguistica*, 56 (1), 253–271.

Stepanov, A., Mušič, M., & Stateva, P. (2018). Two (non-)islands in Slovenian: A study in experimental syntax. *Linguistics*, 56(3), 435–476.

Stepanov, A. & Stateva, P. (2018). Countability, agreement and the loss of the dual in Russian. *Journal of Linguistics*, 54(4), 779–821.

Stoops, A. & Ionin, T. (2013). Quantifier scope and scrambling in Russian: An experimental study. In *Proceedings of the Annual Workshop on Formal Approaches to Slavic Linguistics: The Bloomington Meeting*. Ann Arbor, MI: Michigan Slavic Publications, pp. 344–358.

Stopar, A. (2017). The prosody of focus: Non-contrastive, contrastive and verum focus in Slovenian, English and Russian. *Linguistica*, 57(1), 293–312.

Sturgeon, A., Harizanov, B., Polinsky, M., Kravtchenko, E., Gallo, C. G., Medová, L., & Koula, V. (2012). Revisiting the Person Case Constraint in Czech. In *Proceedings of Formal Approaches to Slavic Linguistics 19*. Ann Arbor, MI: Michigan Slavic Publications, pp. 116–130.

Sturgeon, A., Polinsky, M., G., Kravtchenko, Gallo, C. E., Medová, L., & Koula, V. (2010). Subject islands in Slavic: The syntactic position matters! Paper presented at Formal Approaches to Slavic Linguistics 19, University of Maryland.

Takahashi, D. (1994). Minimality of movement. Doctoral dissertation, University of Connecticut.

Uriagereka, J. (1988). On government. Doctoral dissertation, University of Connecticut.

Vaiksnoraite, E. (2019). Russian is the new Czech? An experimental investigation of Genitive of Negation in Russian. Poster at Formal Approaches to Slavic Linguistics 28, May 3–5, 2019, Stony Brook University.

Vakareliyska, C. M. (1996). Subject/topic slots in Bulgarian: Evidence from aphasia. In J. Toman, ed., *Papers from the Third Annual Workshop on Formal Approaches to Slavic Linguistics*. Ann Arbor, MI: Michigan Slavic Publications, pp. 273–290.

Vallduví, E. & Engdahl, E. (1996). The linguistic realization of information packaging. *Linguistics* 34(3), 459–519.

Wagner, M. (2012). Focus and givenness: A unified approach. In I. Kučerová & A. Neeleman, eds., *Contrasts and Positions in Information Structure*. Cambridge: Cambridge University Press, pp. 102–148.

Willer-Gold, J., Arsenijević, B., Batinić, M., Čordalija, N., Kresić, M., Leko, N., Marušič, F. L., Milićev, T., Milićević, N., Mitić, I., Nevins, A., Peti-Stantić, A., Stanković, B., Šuligoj, T., & Tušek, J. (2016). Conjunct agreement and gender in South Slavic: From theory to experiments to theory. *Journal of Slavic Linguistics*, 24(1), 187–224.

Willer-Gold, J., Arsenijević, B., Batinić, M., Becker, M., Čordalija, N., Kresić, M., Leko, N., Marušič, F. L., Milićev, T., Milićević, N., Mitić, I., Peti-Stantić, A., Stanković, B., Šuligoj, T., Tušek. J., & Nevins, A. (2018). When linearity prevails over hierarchy in syntax. *Proceedings of the National Academy of Sciences*, 115(3), 495–500.

Zybatow, G. & Mehlhorn, G. (2000). Experimental evidence for focus structure in Russian. In T. H. King & I. A. Sekerina, eds., *Proceedings of the Annual Workshop on Formal Approaches to Slavic Linguistics 8*. Ann Arbor, MI: Michigan Slavic Publications, pp. 414–434.

# 21

# Acceptability Judgments in Sign Linguistics

Vadim Kimmelman

## 21.1 Introduction

Sign languages are natural languages existing in the visual modality and used primarily by deaf people (Pfau et al. 2012). Over the past 50 years, much research on sign languages from all around the world has demonstrated fundamental commonalities between signed and spoken languages, such as comparable or identical phonological, morphological, syntactic, semantic, and pragmatic processes and structures, leading to the claim that generally, grammatical concepts and models are modality independent, that is, they can be applied to all natural languages, no matter whether they are spoken or signed. However, the research has also discovered important differences known as *modality effects* (Sandler & Lillo-Martin 2006; Meier 2012). Investigating sign languages and uncovering such modality effects are crucial for our understanding of linguistic universals and the human linguistic capacity.

In order to frame the following discussion, I need to introduce some of the crucial differences between signed and spoken languages (see Meier (2012) for an extensive discussion, including other modality effects that I will not address). First, sign languages are highly iconic on many levels. Many individual lexical signs are iconic: the signs resemble their referents (Taub 2012). But, more importantly, many grammatical features, such as marking of number and aspect, verbal agreement, and verbal expression of motion and location, among others, are also iconic (Liddell 2003; Wilbur 2008; Davidson 2015). For instance, the verb $_1$CL(ROUND)-GIVE$_a$ in example (1)[1] and Figure 21.1, from Russian Sign Language (RSL), has several iconic components: the handshape reflects the fact that the given object (the ball) is round, and the movement and orientation of the sign depict the fact that the ball is transferred from the signer to a person to the right of the signer;

---

[1] See Appendix A for the glossing conventions.

(a)                              (b)

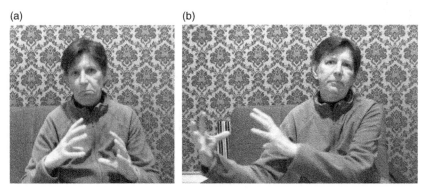

**Figure 21.1** RSL sign ₁CL(ROUND)-GIVE_a (first and last frames)

in addition, the fact that the movement occurs only once reflects that the event occurred only once.

(1)     INDEX₁ BALL ₁CL(ROUND)-GIVE_a                              (RSL)
        'I gave him a ball.'

Second, sign languages exhibit much simultaneity at all levels of the grammar and some serious restrictions on sequential structures. For instance, within signs, the handshape, the movement, and the location all occur simultaneously, and so several morphemes, as in example (1), can be expressed in parallel to each other, although some sequential phonological structure can also be present. At the same time, sequential morphology is almost absent in sign languages (Aronoff et al. 2005). It has been shown experimentally that people can store fewer signs than words in short-term memory, which can probably be attributed to the large amount of simultaneous information encoded in the visual channel (Boutla et al. 2004; Geraci et al. 2008).

In addition, signers use non-manual markers, that is, facial expressions and movements of the head and body, to encode grammatical information. For instance, in many sign languages, negation can be expressed by means of headshake and furrowed eyebrows alone without an overt manual marker of negation, as in example (2) from Sign Language of the Netherlands (Nederlandse Gebarentaal, NGT). This further increases the amount of simultaneous information conveyed in signed utterances, and makes it necessary for the addressee to divide attention between the hands and the face of the signer.

(2)                           _headshake_
        INDEX₁   KNOW INDEX TRUE                                    (NGT)
        'I don't know whether that's true.' (Oomen & Pfau 2017: 23)

Sign languages are different from spoken languages not only due to modality differences, but also sociolinguistically. It has been estimated that, in Western countries, less than 5 percent of deaf children have deaf parents (Mitchell & Karchmer 2004). This means that a large majority of signers acquire sign languages late (mostly at school) and from peers, not parents. In addition, in Western countries, all signers are taught a spoken language (at least in the written form), which makes them bilingual (Quadros et al. 2016). Moreover, in most countries, in addition to the natural sign language, manual communication systems exist, which use signs from the natural sign language but grammatical rules and elements from the spoken language (Adam 2012). Due to bilingualism and the existence of manual communication systems, various types of cross-language effects (code-switching, code-mixing, and borrowing) can occur (Woodward 1994).

Despite these differences between signed and spoken languages, the study of both types of languages belongs to general linguistics, and common methodology is used for both types. Similar to spoken languages, one of the main methods used by sign linguists is *acceptability judgments by native signers*. However, in contrast to spoken languages, very little research has been done on validity or reliability of this method. Given that modality effects and socioinguistic differences exist, it is reasonable to expect to find some differences between modalities when it comes to the suitability of specific methods.

In this chapter, I first present an overview of the current practice in using acceptability judgments in the field of sign linguistics (Section 21.2). While little to no methodological research exists, researchers use various approaches, and sometimes favor the use of a particular method. I argue that there are clear indications that methodological research is necessary, as often contradictory descriptions of the same phenomena can be found in the literature (Section 21.3). Given modality-related and sociolinguistic peculiarities of sign languages, I propose which questions should be addressed in future methodological studies (Section 21.4). Finally, I provide some recommendations for using acceptability judgments as a tool in sign linguistics at the moment – until further methodological research delivers new insights (Section 21.5).[2]

## 21.2   Current Practice in the Field

Browsing the literature in the field of sign linguistics, it is quite easy to see that acceptability judgments by native signers of various types are commonly used. Specifically, researchers have used:

---

[2] This chapter is only devoted to the use of acceptability judgments. Going beyond eliciting judgments, eliciting data by means of visual stimuli is preferred in order to avoid influence from spoken language – but this method has limitations as not all phenomena are easily elicited with pictures, and no negative data can be elicited. Corpus data are often considered ideal/most natural, but many structures are not or scarcely attested in corpora, and again no negative data are directly available. I discuss the use of corpora in comparison to eliciting judgments later in the chapter. For general recommendations on methodology in sign linguistics, see e.g. Orfanidou et al. (2015).

- phonological judgments (well-formedness of phonologically modified signs (Arendsen et al. 2010) or determining where stress falls (Wilbur & Schick 1987));
- morphological judgments (well-formedness of morphologically modified signs (e.g. Krebs, Wilbur, & Roehm 2017));
- syntactic judgments (well-formedness of sentences: many examples, see below);
- semantic and pragmatic judgments (e.g. whether a certain utterance can be used to express a certain meaning in a given context (e.g. Davidson 2013)).

Given the scope of this handbook, in the rest of the chapter, I mostly focus on syntactic acceptability judgments, which are incidentally also the most common type.

Despite the fact that acceptability judgments are often used, close to no methodological research discussing them and/or comparing them to other methods exists.[3] A rare exception is Neidle et al. (2000: Ch. 2), where the authors discuss the methodology they used to describe the syntax of American Sign Language (mostly syntactic acceptability judgments) and provide insightful instructions on how to use this method. Note, however, that these recommendations are based purely on the authors' experience and observations and not on any systematic quantitative analysis.

It is instructive to investigate how the collection of judgments is commonly handled. To determine the recent common practice in theoretical sign linguistics, I have skimmed through all the research papers published in the journal *Sign Language & Linguistics* in the years 2010–2017. It turned out that 9 out of the 28 papers used acceptability judgments, and only 3 of those 9 applied experimental methods and statistics. Thus using judgments is a common method, but the most common approach to collecting judgment data is informal (as opposed to experimental), which goes against the current recommendations for conducting judgment elicitation (Schütze & Sprouse 2014). Given the recent findings that informally collected judgments are highly correlated with judgments collected using experimental methods (Sprouse et al. 2013), this might not be a serious shortcoming. However, whether this can also be generalized to using judgments in sign language research is questionable, as will be discussed in the following sections.

Note that this sample of articles from *Sign Language & Linguistics* is very small and hardly representative of the field of theoretical sign linguistics. Upon further inspection of the publications in the field, it appears that more recent research tends to use experimental methods more often. Several recent studies used an experimental setup to elicit

---

[3] Note that I am not claiming that no methodological research on sign languages exists: see, for instance, van Herreweghe and Vermeerbergen (2012) and Orfanidou et al. (2015). However, for some reason, existing methodological studies hardly ever discuss acceptability judgments, focusing instead on other methods of data collection, ethical issues, etc.

judgments and applied statistical analysis to interpret the findings (Gökgöz 2013; Davidson 2014; Börstell 2017; Loos 2017; Kimmelman 2018).

Recently, a group led by Philippe Schlenker has been using a new method of collecting syntactic and semantic judgments, which they call the "playback method" (e.g. Schlenker 2014, 2017). In this method, a native signer is asked to sign a paradigm of sentences (minimal pairs or sets of sentences different in the aspect relevant to the research question, including some which are expected to be ill-formed); these sentences are recorded on video. The resulting videos are later shown to the same signer who is asked to rate the sentences on a seven-point scale; multiple judgments on the same sentences are collected on multiple occasions. It seems useful to conduct methodological research to establish validity and reliability of this method, as I discuss in Section 21.4.

Moving from theoretical sign linguistics to other topics, in psycholinguistic research, acceptability judgments are commonly used, and in an experimental setup accompanied by statistical analysis. Specifically, acquisition of sign languages and comparison of early vs. late learners are topics which have been extensively studied using syntactic judgments (Boudreault & Mayberry 2006; Cormier et al. 2012; Henner et al. 2016; Novogrodsky et al. 2017). Note that in these studies, the judgment task is used as a tool to assess the level of competence in a sign language rather than to gain insight into the structure of the language.

In most studies that use either informal or experimental collection of acceptability judgments, no space is devoted to discussing methodological issues connected to this method or to comparing judgments with other methods such as corpus research (some exceptions are discussed in the next section). One of the questions that has been widely discussed for spoken languages is whether experimental methods are necessary when collecting judgments; there are researchers arguing both for and against the reliability of using informal methods (Featherston 2007; Sprouse et al. 2013). For sign languages, no such research has been conducted. However, as I show in the next section, there are indications that current practices of collecting judgment data are not completely reliable and thus should be evaluated by conducting methodological studies.

## 21.3 Why Methodological Studies Are Needed

It is trivial that theoretical research must be based on a good empirical fundament. If the primary data on which a theory is based is faulty, it might completely undermine the validity of that theory. However, in the field of sign linguistics, it is not difficult to find examples of elaborate theories, e.g. formal analyses with important general implications, based on contested data. Let's consider two examples.

One important domain in which sign languages are different from spoken languages is the structure of *wh*-questions. While in spoken languages *wh*-words either move to the left periphery of the sentence or stay in situ, in many sign languages *wh*-signs have been shown to either occupy a clause-final position or occur twice (Cecchetto 2012). Somewhat simplifying, in generative approaches, the spoken language data are explained by postulating that *wh*-movement targets the specifier of the CP layer, that this specifier can only be on the left, and that therefore only leftward *wh*-movement exists (Kayne 1994). If sign languages in fact have the specifier of the CP layer on the right and allow rightward *wh*-movement, the general theory of *wh*-movement has to be revised, and the peculiar behavior of sign languages must be explained. In addition, the possibility to double the *wh*-sign has to be explained as well. However, the relevant data from at least some sign languages are contested.

For instance, two different analyses of *wh*-questions in American Sign Language (ASL) exist.[4] Neidle et al. (1997, 1998) argue that the specifier of CP is on the right and that *wh*-signs in ASL indeed move to the right. This implies the necessity to revise the theory of *wh*-movement in general. In contrast, Petronio and Lillo-Martin (1997) argue that the specifier of CP is on the left and that *wh*-signs in ASL move to the left. They claim that when a *wh*-sign occurs in the right periphery of a sentence, it is a double of the original *wh*-sign base-generated in the C head (which is on the right). Given this line of reasoning, the theory of movement developed for spoken languages also applies to sign languages.

Clearly the two analyses make different predictions. Specifically, there are three crucial test cases: an object *wh*-sign in the left periphery of the sentence (3a), a subject *wh*-sign in the right periphery of the sentence (3b), and a phrasal *wh*-constituent in the right periphery of the sentence (3c). Neidle et al. (1997, 1998) predict that (3a) is ungrammatical, while (3b) and (3c) are grammatical; Petronio and Lillo-Martin (1997) make the exact opposite predictions.[5] Intriguingly, their findings are in agreement with their own predictions, but in disagreement with each other.[6]

(3)    a. WHO JOHN HATE?                                                              (ASL)
         'Who does John hate?'
         Neidle et al. (1998: 822): *; Petronio and Lillo-Martin
         (1997: 50): OK

---

[4] For reasons of space, my recap of the debate on *wh*-questions in ASL is unavoidably an oversimplification. For instance, I do not discuss and do not gloss non-manual marking. Please consult the original articles and references therein for all the details.

[5] (3c) should be ungrammatical according to Petronio and Lillo-Martin (1997) because the phrasal *wh*-constituent cannot occur in the C head; (3b) is ungrammatical for a subtler reason: while the sign WHO can occur in the C head, the ungrammaticality is caused by the absence of the original WHO in situ or in the left periphery.

[6] The two sources do not always discuss the exact same sentences, but they discuss structurally identical ones. For instance, (3a) is an example from Neidle et al. (1998: 822), and Petronio and Lillo-Martin (1997: 50) include a structurally identical example WHO YOU LIKE? 'Who do you like?' as grammatical.

b. HATE JOHN WHO?
   'Who hates John?'
   Neidle et al. (1998: 822): OK; Petronio and Lillo-Martin
   (1997: 36): judgments vary
c. JOHN BUY YESTERDAY WHICH COMPUTER?
   'Which computer did John buy yesterday?'
   Neidle et al. (1998: 827): OK; Petronio and Lillo-Martin
   (1997: 38): *

Both groups of researchers used acceptability judgments provided by multiple native signers administered informally. The differences in their findings indicate that the reliability of this method must be questioned. Furthermore, both groups discuss far-reaching theoretical implications of their findings, which makes the necessity for reliable data ever more obvious.

As mentioned above, another common pattern in *wh*-questions (also attested in ASL) is that the *wh*-sign is doubled (i.e. occurs twice in a sentence, usually clause-initially and clause-finally). Interestingly, for Italian Sign Language (Lingua dei Segni Italiana, LIS), using informal elicitation of judgments, Cecchetto et al. (2009) found that such doubling of *wh*-signs is not possible. A follow-up corpus study conducted by some of the same researchers, however, uncovered that naturalistic data contain multiple clear examples of this construction, as in (4) (Branchini et al. 2013). Branchini et al. (2013) also collected acceptability judgments for such sentences from two native signers, who this time found them to be acceptable.

(4)    WHAT INDEX$_1$ DO WHAT?                                    (LIS)
       'What shall I do?' (Branchini et al. 2013: 168), compare to Cecchetto
       et al. (2009: 285)

In addition to, once again, casting doubts on the informal elicitation of judgments, the LIS case also points to the phenomenon of possible discrepancies between judgments and corpus data. With the recent emergence of annotated corpora of several sign languages, it becomes possible (and necessary) to further investigate the relation between judgments and naturally produced data, as will be discussed in Section 21.4.

More examples of contradictory descriptions based on (informally elicited) acceptability judgments, leading to contradictory theories, can be found in the literature – compare, for instance, Wilbur (1996) to Hoza et al. (1997) and Caponigro and Davidson (2011) on the status of pseudo-cleft-like constructions in ASL, or Neidle et al. (2000) to Abner (2013) on possessive constructions in ASL. Most of these examples concern ASL, but this is due to the fact that this sign language is by far the best studied. For many sign languages, only single descriptions of most phenomena exist, and in the absence of methodological research or replication studies, there is no way to determine whether these descriptions are trustworthy.

Since I only discuss a few isolated examples of contradictory judgments reported in the literature, I can by no means draw the conclusion that informal syntactic judgments in sign linguistics are unreliable in general. It might very well be the case that, similar to what has been found for spoken languages (Sprouse et al. 2013), once we experimentally test a large sample of informally collected judgments reported in the literature, we will find them to be reliable. What I argue instead is that the contradictory judgments observed in the literature provide enough motivation to conduct such a methodological study for sign languages.

## 21.4　Future Research Directions

Given the lack of methodological research, in the remainder of the chapter, instead of summarizing the literature, I will propose possible research topics that should be investigated and provide some arguments for the need to investigate them. I start from the general methodological questions and then turn to sign-language-specific issues in need of further study.

### 21.4.1　General Methodological Studies

As discussed in the previous section, a general quantitative research on the reliability of acceptability judgments in sign linguistics is necessary. This could be a replication of the study by Sprouse et al. (2013): one can take a sample of reportedly grammatical and ungrammatical sentences from theoretically oriented sign linguistics papers and test their acceptability using a large sample of signers and proper experimental design. This type of research almost necessarily must use data from ASL, as for other sign languages either not enough published research exists, or it would be difficult to find a sufficiently large sample of native signers (see also the discussion in Section 21.4.3 below).

An alternative approach to testing reliability of acceptability judgments is not to use judgments from the literature, but (1) to collect judgments both experimentally and informally in a single study[7] or (2) for experimentally collected data, to investigate within and between participant reliability, as for instance in Langsford et al. (2018). The advantage of this approach is that it can be applied to any sign language – even a relatively poorly studied one.

As discussed in the previous section, some researchers have used the "playback" method (Schlenker 2014), where a paradigm of potentially grammatical and ungrammatical sentences is signed by a native signer

---

[7] This might prove difficult as in collecting judgments informally the researcher has many choices, each of which can potentially influence the outcome. Judgments reported in the literature come from different authors using different methodological decisions, and thus they are a better representation of using informal collection methods in general.

and later assessed by the same signer. It is clear that the generalizability of the findings gathered by using this method is questionable. Even if the purpose of the researcher is not to generalize beyond the single signer, the method's reliability within participant should be investigated (note that inconsistent judgments of a single sentence at different time points are sometimes reported). On the other hand, the method is attractive as it is relatively simple to use and also transparent: the sentences and the judgments are recorded and available for inspection. A potential extension of this method is to use a small number of signers (e.g. five) instead of just one, who do not only assess their own production (Myers 2009). Therefore, it would surely be beneficial to conduct a methodological study of this method and to compare it to other informal and formal methods of collecting acceptability judgments.

Finally, it would be very instructive to conduct studies comparing judgments and corpus data (see also Chapter 25 in this volume). Research on spoken languages has demonstrated that judgments are not always consistent with actual language production as reflected by corpora (see e.g. Divjak (2017) and references therein).

Recently, relatively large annotated corpora of several sign languages have become available: NGT: www.ru.nl/corpusngtuk/introduction/wel come/ (Crasborn et al. 2008); Australian Sign Language: www .auslan.org.au/about/corpus/; British Sign Language (BSL): http://bslcorpu sproject.org/data/; LIS (Geraci et al. 2011); a large corpus of German Sign Language is presently being created: www.sign-lang.uni-hamburg.de/dgs-korpus/index.php/welcome.html. Smaller corpora are also available for other sign languages, including RSL: http://rsl.nstu.ru/ (Burkova 2015).

Importantly, several corpus-based studies report two types of findings: (i) structures which were previously reported to be ungrammatical are found to be present in the corpus, and (ii) much more variation is attested in the corpus than would be expected based on published findings. One such study on *wh*-doubling in LIS was discussed above in Section 21.3 (Branchini et al. 2013). Another clear example comes from NGT. Oomen and Pfau (2017) study negation based on the corpus of NGT and find that, contrary to previous claims in the literature based on judgments (Van Gijn 2004), a manual negative sign is often present in negative sentences, and also that there is more variation in word order and the scope of non-manuals than has been reported. More examples of corpus data contradicting previous findings and demonstrating much variation can be found in recent publications (de Beuzeville et al. 2009; Couvee & Pfau 2018; Fenlon et al. 2018).

Corpora are generally considered a very reliable data source in spoken language research, as they reflect real language use well. However, due to the extremely time-consuming process of annotating sign language data leading to much smaller corpora than available for many spoken languages, and also due to sociolinguistic factors discussed in Section 21.4.3 below, the data in sign language corpora might not be as representative. Furthermore, small corpora especially cannot be used to provide negative data. It is therefore clear that a careful study of the differences between data obtained via acceptability judgments and data present in corpora of sign languages, as well as of the causes of these differences, is necessary (see also Kimmelman et al. (2018) for some discussion).

### 21.4.2   Studies of Possible Modality Effects

As discussed in Section 21.1, sign languages are to some extent shaped by the visual modality and are thus in some respects different from spoken languages. The two modality effects that might influence acceptability judgments are iconicity and simultaneity.

### 21.4.2.1   Iconicity

One important modality effect is the abundance of iconicity (Taub 2012). Extensive research on the role of iconicity at the lexical level for sign language acquisition and processing exists (Perniss et al. 2010). In second language acquisition, lexical iconicity unsurprisingly facilitates learning; and, despite some controversy, there is also some evidence that it plays a role in first language acquisition (Thompson et al. 2012). Furthermore, it has been shown that lexical iconicity plays a role in various processing tasks (Perniss et al. 2010).

More relevant for the possible effects of iconicity on syntactic/semantic acceptability judgments is existing research on effects of grammatical iconicity on perception. Recall example (1), repeated here as (5), see also Figure 21.1. The predicate $_1$CL(ROUND)-GIVE$_a$ in this example is a so-called classifier predicate (Zwitserlood 2012). It has been shown that all phonological components of such signs (handshape, location, and movement) are iconic. For instance, the handshape iconically depicts the round shape of the object BALL in (5).

(5)     INDEX$_1$ BALL $_1$CL(ROUND)-GIVE$_a$                                   (RSL)
        'I gave him a ball.'

Crucially, the iconic components have the potential of being gradually modified. For instance, the handshape and the distance between the hands depicted in Figure 21.1 suggest a certain size of the moved object, and a slightly smaller handshape and distance might refer to a slightly smaller size, and a slightly larger handshape and distance to a slightly larger size, etc. The same is true for location and movement: minute changes can be meaningful. Interestingly, some research in the categorical perception paradigm shows that in ASL, at least, iconic handshapes, despite being potentially gradual, are perceived categorically by native signers (Emmorey & Herzig 2003). Other research on BSL, however, finds evidence of both categorical and gradual perception of such handshapes (Sehyr & Cormier 2015).

The main question that needs investigation is how iconicity influences acceptability judgments. More specifically, it would be useful to study how iconicity violations are judged by native signers. For instance, we can modify the verb in example (5) in two ways, as shown in (6). In (6a), the first location is incorrect: the verbal sign could be interpreted as 'person B is giving a round object to person A,' but not as 'I give a round object to person A.' This can be analyzed as a grammatical violation of verbal agreement with the first-person subject, and an iconicity violation: the first location and the movement of the sign do not correctly depict the movement of the ball. In (6b), the handshape is incorrect: it refers to a square object, while the theme object is in fact round. This can be analyzed as a grammatical violation of verbal agreement with the object, and an iconicity violation: the handshape does not resemble the object it refers to.

(6)  a. INDEX$_1$ BALL $_b$CL(ROUND)-GIVE$_a$  (RSL)
     b. INDEX$_1$ BALL $_1$CL(**SQUARE**)-GIVE$_a$

Consequently, the examples in (6) involve a combination of a grammatical and an iconic violation. It is also possible to imagine cases of iconicity violations without a grammatical violation. For instance, in (7a) the verb moves not from location *a* but from the neutral space. Grammatically, this is not a mistake, because subject agreement in sign languages is almost always optional (Lillo-Martin & Meier 2011). However, this is less iconic than the alternative in (7b) and thus constitutes an iconicity violation.

(7)  a. INDEX$_a$ BALL CL(ROUND)-GIVE$_b$  (RSL)
     b. INDEX$_a$ BALL $_a$CL(ROUND)-GIVE$_b$  (RSL)
     'She/he gave her/him a ball.'

Modifications of iconic components can also be made subtler: instead of the location or handshape clearly not matching the relevant subjects or objects, a small gradual modification of the sign might be applied. Again, this might lead to an iconicity violation without necessarily making the sentence ungrammatical. Note that some research indeed reports semantic and syntactic effects of gradual modifications of iconic components of signs (Schlenker 2014; Kuhn & Aristodemo 2017).

At the moment, it is not clear to me what to expect with respect to judgments on such iconicity violations in comparison to grammatical violations in non-iconic structures. On the one hand, iconic violations might be easier to spot and thus easier to judge as unacceptable. On the other hand, if gradual perception is at play for such constructions, subtle violations of iconicity might not be perceived as problematic as clear violations of grammaticality in non-iconic structures. Finally, it is not clear whether acceptability of iconicity violations can or should be elicited using the same task formulations as grammaticality violations. Given that many grammatical structures in sign languages also have an iconic component, this might call for special attention to be paid to the creation of acceptability judgment experiments. I thus conclude that there is a need for research that specifically addresses acceptability judgments for iconic structures.

### 21.4.2.2  Simultaneity

Another important modality effect is the amount of simultaneity in sign languages. Components of signs are combined (mostly) simultaneously; morphemes are almost always combined simultaneously; finally, a lot of grammatical information is expressed via non-manual markers occurring in parallel with manual signs (Pfau & Quer 2010). I argue that it is reasonable to expect at least two types of effects of simultaneity on acceptability judgments. First, it might be the case that judgments on longer sentences might be more challenging and consequently less consistent than would be the case for spoken languages. Second, judgments on word/sign order in general might be less reliable.

The motivation for these possible effects comes from psycholinguistic research. Several studies have shown that working memory capacity for signs is smaller than for words in sequential recall tasks (Wilson & Emmorey 1997; Boutla et al. 2004; Geraci et al. 2008).[8] This is most likely explained by the amount of simultaneous information in signs, and by the less important role serial order plays in the visual modality (ibid.). If working memory capacity for signs is smaller, it is natural to expect that longer sentences – which are more difficult to process even in spoken language – would be even more challenging in an acceptability judgment task. Moreover, it is reasonable to hypothesize that all sign order judgments might be less stable. In fact, some researchers have proposed that sign order in general plays a lesser role in sign languages (Bouchard & Dubuisson 1995). However, a common acceptability judgment task used in psycholinguistic research is fully based on sign order violations (Boudreault & Mayberry 2006; Novogrodsky et al. 2017).

I thus suggest that it would be useful to test reliability and variation in acceptability judgments concerning word order and longer sentences. Judgments on structures concerning seriality should be compared to judgments on other grammatical aspects where order of elements is not important.

Furthermore, it might be the case that judgments concerning grammatical non-manuals are less reliable than or at least different from judgments concerning manual signs. The motivation for this hypothesis comes from numerous psychological and neurological studies showing that dividing attention is costly (Styles 2008). A signer has to perceive both

---

[8] Note that these studies show that the difference in memory capacity is not connected to deafness. Crucially, hearing native signers (hearing children of deaf parents who have acquired a sign language from birth) have a larger working memory for words than for signs (Boutla et al. 2004).

manual signs and non-manual markers; note that the two are actually in separate parts of the visual field. While non-manuals are clearly linguistically relevant in many cases (recall the discussion of expression of negation), manual signs are indispensable as they contain both lexical and grammatical information. It is thus reasonable to hypothesize that more attention will be allocated to the manual signs, and thus perception of non-manuals will be less focused, leading to less clear acceptability judgments.[9]

In fact, there is some evidence of differences between manual signs and non-manuals in judgment experiments. Davidson (2013) studied scalar implicatures in ASL in two different constructions in a felicity judgment experiment. One condition involved manual signs with quantificational meaning, such as SOME and ALL. It is well known that in spoken languages, quantifiers like *some* create scalar implicatures: a sentence like *Some of the cans are red* would not be used to describe a situation where all the cans are red – even though semantically this sentence is true – due to the presence of a stronger alternative (*All of the cans are red*). Davidson has demonstrated that ASL signers also compute such implicatures and reject a description containing SOME in contexts where ALL could be used, so at least for some manual signs scalar implicatures in signed languages work as expected. However, a situation is different when we turn to non-manual markers.

Another example of a scale which produces scalar implicatures in spoken languages is the scale consisting of conjunctions *or* and *and*. While semantically *A or B* is true when both A and B are true, if a speaker of English says *A spoon is in the mug or a spoon is in the bowl*, it implies that it's not true that there is a spoon in the mug and in the bowl (by the same mechanism as with quantifiers). Interestingly, ASL expresses the meanings of 'and' and 'or' by two similar non-manual strategies. The signer leans to one side over the first conjunct, and to the other side over the second conjunct in both contexts; the difference between 'and' and 'or' is expressed by the position of eyebrows. Crucially, it turns out that signers, when seeing a sentence accompanied by disjunctive non-manuals (meaning 'or') in a situation where a conjunctive interpretation is compatible with the context, are much more accepting than with mismatched implicatures of quantifiers. Davidson demonstrates that it is not the case that non-manuals are completely ignored in the judgment: descriptions of disjunctive situations by conjunctive non-manual markers are in fact correctly rejected. Davidson concludes that signers are less likely to compute scalar implicatures for this non-manual marker of coordination, and that the two versions of the marker do not form a scale. This experiment shows that while non-manual marking is used in ASL to disambiguate the

---

[9] It has been shown that signers in fact have enhanced visual attention to the periphery in comparison to non-signers (Bavelier et al. 2000); however, this still does not mean that processing both manuals and non-manuals in signed communication is not resource-intensive. It has also been shown that the visual attention is centered mostly on the face of the interlocutor, not on the hands (Neville & Lawson 1987).

two types of conjunction, it does not seem to produce the same semantic/pragmatic effects as manual signs.

I argue that it is thus useful to conduct further investigation on acceptability judgments concerning non-manual markers. Judgments on ungrammatical non-manual markers should be compared to judgments in grammaticality violations purely in the manual channel.

### 21.4.3  Sociolinguistic Issues

Sign languages are sociolinguistically different from many spoken languages because most signers in the population are non-native (late learners) and bilingual. These facts might influence acceptability judgment experiments in a variety of ways.

Existing research shows that non-native signers are different from native signers in a syntactic acceptability judgment experiment (Boudreault & Mayberry 2006; Cormier et al. 2012; Novogrodsky et al. 2017). Importantly, the differences are not always trivial: it is not the case that non-native or late learners are always significantly worse in judging all types of structures (Cormier et al. 2012) although mostly they do show a non-native level of correct answers; see also Chapter 14 of this volume for a discussion of using judgments in L2 speakers.

Most crucially, these studies compared native and non-native signers in only two sign languages (ASL and BSL), with six structures (simple sentences, sentences with negation, sentences with agreeing verbs, *wh*-questions, relative clauses, and sentences with classifier predicates) all of which were made ungrammatical by changing sign order (recall also the discussion in Section 21.4.2.2). It might be helpful to conduct more research on judgments in native vs. non-native signers on a larger number of structures and on different types of grammatical violations. The main reason to do such research is practical: if non-native signers turn out to be not different from native signers for at least some types of tasks, it would make conducting experimental elicitation much easier by making the population of potential participants larger. This would matter most for research on sign languages with a small number of signers (e.g. NGT has 7,500 deaf signers including late learners (Wheatley & Pabsch 2012)) for which it is often not realistic to get a sufficiently large sample of native signers.

The fact that most signers are bilingual need not necessarily have an effect on acceptability judgment experiments. For instance, bilingual speakers of spoken languages do not seem to differ in such tasks from monolinguals (Johnson & Newport 1989): speakers are able to suppress one language when they have to make judgments about another one. However, there are reasons to believe that the situation with sign–spoken language bilingualism (often called bimodal bilingualism (Quadros et al. 2016)) is different – at least in some countries.

The main reason that I think spoken language might interfere more with sign language judgment experiments is the existence of manual communication systems. For instance, RSL coexists with the system which can be called Signed Russian; this system uses signs from RSL but also a large number of artificial signs: for instance, signs for Russian prepositions or even case endings. This system is mostly used in parallel with spoken language and the sign order follows the word order of the spoken utterance. It is often used by hearing people interacting with deaf signers, including sign language interpreters and teachers, but deaf signers also use it among themselves.

Such a situation of coexistence of two means of manual communication – a natural sign language and a partially artificial spoken-language-based system – is common to most countries with organized deaf education and interpreting services. For historical reasons (see e.g. Rietveld-van Wingerden 2003), natural sign languages often have a lower status than a spoken language and even the manual communication system. For instance, in Russia, some members of the deaf community assume that more educated deaf people would and should use Signed Russian rather than RSL. This preference for the manual communication system might result in signers accepting spoken-language-based structures in an acceptability judgment experiment.

In addition to the issue of lower status of the natural sign language, it is also often difficult to clearly differentiate between the natural sign language and the manual communication system. Signers often switch between the two systems in natural communication. Some signers are not aware of the existence of the two systems, and even among those who are aware, not all are comfortable providing metalinguistic judgments on what belongs to sign language proper and what does not.

Delineation is further complicated by the fact that borrowing of lexical and grammatical elements from the spoken language is a common phenomenon (Adam 2012). For instance, if we find a structure in a corpus of a sign language that looks like a structure from the corresponding spoken language, it might result either from borrowing or from code-switching to the manual communication system, and there is no way to distinguish the two by looking at isolated cases.

All of this implies that, in acceptability judgment experiments, it is not clear whether and how signers would judge structures that result from code-switching or from borrowing. Two undesirable effects can occur: first, signers might accept structures that are grammatical in the spoken language but do not in fact belong to the natural sign language, and second, signers might reject structures that are grammatical in the spoken language and have in fact been borrowed by the sign language or are accidentally similar in the sign language. The former mistake would be caused by the failure to distinguish the sign language from the manual communication system or by a preference for the manual communication system. The latter mistake would be due to hypercorrection: trying too hard to distinguish the natural sign language from the spoken language. It is likely that the formulation of the judgment task might play a role: whether the signers are instructed to distinguish the natural sign language from spoken language or not; however, given that mistakes can go in both directions, it is not a priori clear how to formulate the instructions properly.

It is thus necessary to empirically test whether judgments on structures which overlap with similar structures in a spoken language are different from judgments on structures which are unique to the sign language. Effects of the formulation of the task should also be studied.

There are some other sociolinguistic factors that should also be taken into account when designing acceptability experiments, such as age, regional variation, and other sociolinguistic variables that are also relevant for spoken languages.[10]

Considering age differences, sign languages are comparatively young; some sign languages, such as Nicaraguan Sign Language and Al-Sayyid Bedouin Sign Language, have emerged within recent decades (Senghas et al. 2004; Sandler et al. 2005). Research has shown that sign languages change extremely rapidly in the first decades after their emergence, so signers from different generations in fact have very different grammars (ibid.). More established sign languages, such as ASL or BSL, have also been shown to change relatively rapidly (Stamp et al. 2015), which means that generational differences can be visible in acceptability experiments.[11] While I do not think that it is necessary to conduct acceptability experiments to directly study age effects, such effects need to be taken into account when designing experiments (see also the next section).

Another factor is possible regional variation (see also Chapter 4 for a discussion of this issue in spoken language experiments). Comparatively little research has been done on regional variation in grammar of sign languages, but it is obvious that such variation exists, and for some sign languages, one can speak of the existence of dialects (Schembri & Johnston 2012). Again, this should be taken into account when designing experiments, either by focusing on one regional variant, or by including region as a variable deliberately.

## 21.5  Practical Recommendations

While in the previous section I have argued that much methodological research is needed before we gain a good understanding of the validity and reliability of acceptability judgment experiments in sign linguistics, some general practical recommendations for researchers using such tasks

---

[10]  I thank William Matchin (p.c.) for bringing this to my attention.

[11]  Note that most existing research on age differences in established sign languages concerns lexical or phonological variation, so there is no solid basis to argue that grammar also varies across age groups. However, informal impressions of researchers working in the field suggest that grammatical variation is present.

at the moment can be formulated based on spoken language research and past experiences of sign linguists. I briefly summarize them here.

First, the general methodological recommendations that apply to spoken languages can also be used in creating judgments experiments for sign languages (see Chapters 1–4 and Schütze & Sprouse (2014)). It is important to collect data from multiple signers, to use multiple lexicalizations of the same phenomenon, to pseudorandomize the order of items, to use fillers, and to formulate instructions carefully (see below). The data should be analyzed statistically. Some sociolinguistic factors can influence experiments in both spoken and signed languages, so possible regional and age variation should be taken into account.

Second, it is important to use the appropriate medium of presentation. Sentences which are to be assessed have to be presented as videos, and so should the instructions. To minimize possible interference of spoken language, ideally, no spoken language (also in a written form) should be used at any point during the experiment. In addition, it is well known that mere presence of a hearing researcher might increase the influence of a spoken language (Van Herreweghe & Vermeerbergen 2012), so the task should be either administered by a deaf native signer, or be fully computerized so that no communication with the researcher is necessary. Moreover, including deaf signers as collaborators and not only as participants addresses important ethical issues of Deaf identity and language ownership (see in Orfanidou et al. 2015: Chs. 1–3).

Third, it is very important to formulate instructions in a judgment task appropriately. The instruction for a syntactic task should make it clear that the researchers are not interested in semantic plausibility. A common method in spoken linguistics, which will probably work for sign languages as well, is to ask the participant the following: "If someone signs this sentence, would they look like a native signer?" Although no research on this issue exists yet, it seems reasonable to ask signers to also pay attention to non-manuals if non-manuals are relevant for the phenomenon under investigation.

Neidle et al. (2000) also argue that signers should always be asked to repeat the sentence themselves before judging its acceptability. They claim that signers are often too accepting when they simply view the item and that this effect can be mitigated by asking them to repeat it. While this issue has not been formally investigated, this advice seems reasonable and easy to apply, at least if elicitation is conducted by a researcher and not via the Internet.

As an illustration, I briefly sketch a hypothetical experiment to study the effect of verb class on word order in RSL.[12] In many sign languages, plain

---

[12] This is a toy example, so only one factor influencing word order is considered, while in reality there are multiple factors that can influence it, and they should be studied together. Furthermore, this example does not address any of the modality-specific or sociolinguistic issues discussed in Section 21.4.

(non-agreeing) verbs favor the SVO order, while agreeing verbs favor the SOV order (Napoli & Sutton-Spence 2014). Kimmelman (2012) argued that RSL does not conform to this pattern, as both plain and agreeing verbs favor the SVO order. However, this study was based on a very small-scale dataset of narratives and picture descriptions, so it might be reasonable to revisit this issue.

Following the general methodological considerations, 12 plain verbs and 12 agreeing verbs are selected to avoid the individual effects of specific lexemes.[13] For each verb, two stimuli are created: one with the SVO order and one with the SOV order, illustrated by (8).

(8)       a. BOY INDEX$_a$ $_a$SEE$_b$ GIRL INDEX$_b$ → agreeing verb, SVO
          b. BOY INDEX$_a$ GIRL INDEX$_b$ $_a$SEE$_b$ → agreeing verb, SOV
          c. BOY INDEX$_a$ LOVE GIRL INDEX$_b$ → plain verb, SVO
          d. BOY INDEX$_a$ GIRL INDEX$_b$ LOVE → plain verb, SOV

The acceptability task will contain 12 test items (6 with plain verbs – 3 with each word order, 6 with agreeing verbs – 3 with each word order, such that one participant never sees the same verb twice). Several versions of the task are created: two versions are necessary to include all the verbs in both word orders, and each of these versions should be presented in at least two different item orders. In addition to the test items, the task should contain at least 12 filler items, and 6 training items to be placed at the beginning of the task to get the participant familiar with the procedure. The fillers and the training items target a phenomenon not related to word order.

The test items, the filler items, and the instruction are signed by a native signer of RSL and recorded as video files. The instruction is roughly as follows: "You will now watch 30 short clips of phrases in RSL. Please see whether they look correct or not. To make your assessment, imagine this: if someone signs this sentence, do you think this person is a native signer? Please give each sentence a grade from 0 to 5, where 0 means the signer is clearly not native, and 5 means that the signer is clearly native." Alternatively, if the experiment will not be conducted via the Internet but by a researcher in person, the instruction can also contain the following: "When you see the sentence, please repeat it first, and then give your grade."

Next, 12 signers of RSL are recruited as participants. Given that the research question does not concern sociolinguistic variables, only native signers from the same region and from roughly the same age group are selected. Different versions of the task are distributed evenly across participants. The task is presented on a laptop/desktop so that the participants

---

[13] The numbers of items and signers given here are mere suggestions; to determine the real number of items and signers necessary, potential effect sizes should be estimated and a power study should be conducted first (Schütze & Sprouse 2014).

can watch the videos of the instruction and the test items and click on buttons to grade the videos.

The resulting dataset is analyzed using a mixed-effects model (Baayen et al. 2008) so that individual effects of participants and lexical items could be taken into account. If we find a significant difference in acceptability of the SVO vs. SOV word order for plain vs. agreeing verbs, we have found evidence against Kimmelman's (2012) claim. If no significant difference is found, the experiment is not informative.

## Appendix A: Glossing Conventions

**Glossing conventions:** Signs are glossed with approximate translations in SMALL CAPS. INDEX stands for a pointing sign; subscripts represent a person (1) or a location in space (a, b): pointing signs and verbs can be modified to agree with arguments this way; CL stands for a classifier handshape followed by the form it refers to. Non-manual markers are placed above the glosses, and the underscore reflects the scope of the non-manual.

**Abbreviations:** ASL – American Sign Language; BSL – British Sign Language; LIS – Italian Sign Language; NGT – Sign Language of the Netherlands; RSL – Russian Sign Language.

## References

Abner, N. (2013). Gettin' together a posse: The primacy of predication in ASL possessives. *Sign Language & Linguistics*, 16(2), 125–156.

Adam, R. (2012). Language contact and borrowing. In R. Pfau, M. Steinbach, & B. Woll, eds., *Sign Language: An International Handbook*. Berlin: De Gruyter Mouton, pp. 841–862.

Arendsen, J., Doorn, A. J. van, & Ridder, H. de. (2010). Acceptability of sign manipulations. *Sign Language & Linguistics*, 13(2), 101–155.

Aronoff, M., Meir, I., & Sandler, W. (2005). The paradox of sign language morphology. *Language*, 81(2), 301–344.

Baayen, R. H., Davidson, D. J., & Bates, D. M. (2008). Mixed-effects modeling with crossed random effects for subjects and items. *Journal of Memory and Language*, 59(4), 390–412.

Bavelier, D., Tomann, A., Hutton, C., … & Neville, H. (2000). Visual attention to the periphery is enhanced in congenitally deaf individuals. *Journal of Neuroscience*, 20(17), RC93–RC93.

Börstell, C. (2017). Object marking in the signed modality: Verbal and nominal strategies in Swedish Sign Language and other sign languages. Doctoral dissertation, Stockholm University.

Bouchard, D. & Dubuisson, C. (1995). Grammar, order & position of *wh*-signs in Quebec Sign Language. *Sign Language Studies*, 1087(1), 99–139.

Boudreault, P. & Mayberry, R. I. (2006). Grammatical processing in American Sign Language: Age of first-language acquisition effects in relation to syntactic structure. *Language and Cognitive Processes*, 21(5), 608–635.

Boutla, M., Supalla, T., Newport, E. L., & Bavelier, D. (2004). Short-term memory span: Insights from sign language. *Nature Neuroscience*, 7(9), 997–1002.

Branchini, C., Cardinaletti, A., Cecchetto, C., Donati, C., & Geraci, C. (2013). *Wh*-duplication In Italian Sign Language (LIS). *Sign Language & Linguistics*, 16(2), 157–188.

Burkova, S. (2015). *Russian Sign Language Corpus*. Retrieved April 1, 2018, from http://rsl.nstu.ru/

Caponigro, I. & Davidson, K. (2011). Ask, and tell as well: Question–answer clauses in American Sign Language. *Natural Language Semantics*, 19(4), 323–371.

Cecchetto, C. (2012). Sentence types. In R. Pfau, M. Steinbach, & B. Woll, eds., *Sign Language: An International Handbook*. Berlin: De Gruyter Mouton, pp. 292–315.

Cecchetto, C., Geraci, C., & Zucchi, S. (2009). Another way to mark syntactic dependencies: The case for right-peripheral specifiers in sign languages. *Language*, 85(2), 278–320.

Cormier, K., Schembri, A., Vinson, D., & Orfanidou, E. (2012). First language acquisition differs from second language acquisition in prelingually deaf signers: Evidence from sensitivity to grammaticality judgement in British Sign Language. *Cognition*, 124(1), 50–65.

Couvee, S. & Pfau, R. (2018). Structure and grammaticalization of serial verb constructions in Sign Language of the Netherlands: A corpus-based study. *Frontiers in Psychology*, 9. DOI:10.3389/fpsyg.2018.00993

Crasborn, O., Zwitserlood, I., & Ros, J. (2008). *Corpus NGT: An Open Access Digital Corpus of Movies with Annotations of Sign Language of the Netherlands*. Retrieved from www.ru.nl/corpusngtuk/introduction/welcome/

Davidson, K. (2013). "And" or "or": General use coordination in ASL. *Semantics and Pragmatics*, 6. DOI: 10.3765/sp.6.4

Davidson, K. (2014). Scalar implicatures in a signed language. *Sign Language & Linguistics*, 17(1), 1–19.

Davidson, K. (2015). Quotation, demonstration, and iconicity. *Linguistics and Philosophy*, 38(6), 477–520.

de Beuzeville, L., Johnston, T., & Schembri, A. C. (2009). The use of space with indicating verbs in Auslan: A corpus-based investigation. *Sign Language & Linguistics*, 12(1), 53–82.

Divjak, D. (2017). The role of lexical frequency in the acceptability of syntactic variants: Evidence from *that*-clauses in Polish. *Cognitive Science*, 41(2), 354–382.

Emmorey, K. & Herzig, M. (2003). Categorical versus gradient properties of classifier constructions in ASL. In K. Emmorey, ed., *Perspectives on Classifier Constructions in Signed Languages*. Mahwah, NJ: Lawrence Erlbaum, pp. 222–246.

Featherston, S. (2007). Data in generative grammar: The stick and the carrot. *Theoretical Linguistics*, 33(3). DOI: 10.1515/TL.2007.020

Fenlon, J., Schembri, A., & Cormier, K. (2018). Modification of indicating verbs in British Sign Language: A corpus-based study. *Language*, 94(1), 84–118.

Geraci, C., Battaglia, K., Cardinaletti, A., … & Mereghetti, E. (2011). The LIS Corpus project: A discussion of sociolinguistic variation in the lexicon. *Sign Language Studies*, 11(4), 528–574.

Geraci, C., Gozzi, M., Papagno, C., & Cecchetto, C. (2008). How grammar can cope with limited short-term memory: Simultaneity and seriality in sign languages. *Cognition*, 106(2), 780–804.

Gökgöz, K. (2013). The nature of object marking in American Sign Language. Doctoral dissertation, Purdue University, West Lafayette.

Henner, J., Caldwell-Harris, C. L., Novogrodsky, R., & Hoffmeister, R. (2016). American Sign Language syntax and analogical reasoning skills are influenced by early acquisition and age of entry to signing schools for the deaf. *Frontiers in Psychology*, 07. DOI: 10.3389/fpsyg.2016.01982

Hoza, J., Neidle, C., MacLaughlin, D., Kegl, J., & Bahan, B. (1997). A unified syntactic account of rhetorical questions in American Sign Language. In C. Neidle, D. MacLaughlin, & R. G. Lee, eds., *Syntactic Structure and Discourse Function: An Examination of Two Constructions in American Sign Language*. Boston, MA: ASLLRP Publications, pp. 1–23.

Johnson, J. S. & Newport, E. L. (1989). Critical period effects in second language learning: The influence of maturational state on the acquisition of English as a second language. *Cognitive Psychology*, 21(1), 60–99.

Kayne, R. S. (1994). *The Antisymmetry of Syntax*, Cambridge, MA: MIT Press.

Kimmelman, V. (2012). Word order in Russian Sign Language. *Sign Language Studies*, 12(3), 414–445.

Kimmelman, V. (2018). Impersonal reference in Russian Sign Language. *Sign Language & Linguistics*, 21(2), 204–231.

Kimmelman, V., Klomp, U., & Oomen, M. (2018). Where methods meet: Combining corpus data and elicitation in sign language research. In *Proceedings of 8th Workshop on the Representation and Processing of Sign Languages: Involving the Linguistic Community*. Paris: ELRA, pp. 95–100.

Krebs, J., Wilbur, R. B., & Roehm, D. (2017). Two agreement markers in Austrian Sign Language (ÖGS). *Sign Language & Linguistics*, 20(1), 27–54.

Kuhn, J. & Aristodemo, V. (2017). Pluractionality, iconicity, and scope in French Sign Language. *Semantics and Pragmatics*, 10(6). DOI: 10.3765/sp.10.6

Langsford, S., Perfors, A., Hendrickson, A. T., Kennedy, L. A., & Navarro, D. J. (2018). Quantifying sentence acceptability measures: Reliability, bias, and variability. *Glossa: A Journal of General Linguistics*, 3(1), 37. DOI:10.5334 /gjgl.396

Liddell, S. K. (2003). *Grammar, Gesture, and Meaning in American Sign Language*. Cambridge: Cambridge University Press.

Lillo-Martin, D., & Meier, R. P. (2011). On the linguistic status of "agreement" in sign languages. *Theoretical Linguistics*, 37(3–4). DOI: 10.1515/ thli.2011.009

Loos, C. (2017). The syntax and semantics of resultative constructions in Deutsche Gebärdensprache (DGS) and American Sign Language (ASL). Doctoral dissertation, University of Texas at Austin.

Meier, R. P. (2012). Language and modality. In R. Pfau, M. Steinbach, & B. Woll, eds., *Sign Language: An International Handbook*. Berlin: De Gruyter Mouton, pp. 77–112.

Mitchell, R. E. & Karchmer, M. A. (2004). Chasing the mythical ten percent: Parental hearing status of deaf and hard of hearing students in the United States. *Sign Language Studies*, 4(2), 138–163.

Myers, J. (2009). The design and analysis of small-scale syntactic judgment experiments. *Lingua*, 119(3), 425–444.

Napoli, D. J. & Sutton-Spence, R. (2014). Order of the major constituents in sign languages: Implications for all language. *Frontiers in Psychology*, 5. DOI: 10.3389/fpsyg.2014.00376

Neidle, C., Kegl, J., Bahan, B., Aarons, D., & MacLaughlin, D. (1997). Rightward *wh*-movement in American Sign Language. In D. Beerman, D. LeBlanc, & H. Van Riemsdijk, eds., *Rightward Movement*. Amsterdam and Philadelphia: John Benjamins, pp. 247–278.

Neidle, C., Kegl, J., MacLaughlin, D., Bahan, B., & Lee, R. G. (2000). *The Syntax of American Sign Language: Functional Categories and Hierarchical Structure*. Cambridge, MA: MIT Press.

Neidle, C., MacLaughlin, D., Lee, R. G., Bahan, B., & Kegl, J. (1998). The rightward analysis of *wh*-movement in ASL: A reply to Petronio and Lillo-Martin. *Language*, 74(4), 819–831.

Neville, H. & Lawson, D. S. (1987). Attention to central and peripheral visual space in a movement detection task: An event-related potential and behavioral study (Parts I, II, III). *Brain Research*, 405, 253–294.

Novogrodsky, R., Henner, J., Caldwell-Harris, C., & Hoffmeister, R. (2017). The development of sensitivity to grammatical violations in American Sign Language: Native versus nonnative signers: Sensitivity to grammatical violations in ASL. *Language Learning*, 67(4), 791–818.

Oomen, M. & Pfau, R. (2017). Signing not (or not): A typological perspective on standard negation in Sign Language of the Netherlands. *Linguistic Typology*, 21(1), 1–51.

Orfanidou, E., Woll, B., & Morgan, G., eds. (2015). *Research Methods in Sign Language Studies: A Practical Guide*. Hoboken, NJ: Wiley-Blackwell.

Perniss, P., Thompson, R. L., & Vigliocco, G. (2010). Iconicity as a general property of language: Evidence from spoken and signed languages. *Frontiers in Psychology*, 1. DOI:10.3389/fpsyg.2010.00227

Petronio, K. & Lillo-Martin, D. (1997). *WH*-movement and the position of Spec-CP: Evidence from American Sign Language. *Language*, 73(1), 18–57.

Pfau, R. & Quer, J. (2010). Nonmanuals: their prosodic and grammatical roles. In D. Brentari, ed., *Sign Languages*. Cambridge: Cambridge University Press, pp. 381–402.

Pfau, R., Steinbach, M., & Woll, B., eds. (2012). *Sign Language: An International Handbook*. Berlin: De Gruyter Mouton.

Quadros, R. M. de, Lillo-Martin, D., & Chen Pichler, D. (2016). Bimodal bilingualism: Sign language and spoken language. In M. Marschark & P. E. Spencer, eds., *The Oxford Handbook of Deaf Studies in Language*. Oxford: Oxford University Press, pp. 181–196.

Rietveld-van Wingerden, M. (2003). Educating the deaf in The Netherlands: A methodological controversy in historical perspective. *History of Education*, 32(4), 401–416.

Sandler, W. & Lillo-Martin, D. C. (2006). *Sign Language and Linguistic Universals*. Cambridge: Cambridge University Press.

Sandler, W., Meir, I., Padden, C., & Aronoff, M. (2005). The emergence of grammar: Systematic structure in a new language. *Proceedings of the National Academy of Sciences*, 102(7), 2661–2665.

Schembri, A. & Johnston, T. (2012). Sociolinguistic aspects of variation and change. In R. Pfau, M. Steinbach, & B. Woll, eds., *Sign Language: An International Handbook*. Berlin: De Gruyter Mouton, pp. 788–816.

Schlenker, P. (2014). Iconic features. *Natural Language Semantics*, 22(4), 299–356.

Schlenker, P. (2017). Super monsters I: Attitude and Action Role Shift in sign language. *Semantics and Pragmatics*, 10(9). DOI: 10.3765/sp.10.9

Schütze, C. T. & Sprouse, J. (2014). Judgment data. In D. Sharma & R. Podesva, eds., *Research Methods in Linguistics*. Cambridge: Cambridge University Press, pp. 27–50.

Sehyr, Z. S. & Cormier, K. (2015). Perceptual categorization of handling handshapes in British Sign Language. *Language and Cognition*, 8(4), 501–532.

Senghas, A., Kita, S., & Özyürek, A. (2004). Children creating core properties of language: Evidence from an emerging sign language in Nicaragua. *Science*, 305(5691), 1779–1782.

Sprouse, J., Schütze, C. T., & Almeida, D. (2013). A comparison of informal and formal acceptability judgments using a random sample from *Linguistic Inquiry* 2001–2010. *Lingua*, 134, 219–248.

Stamp, R., Schembri, A., Fenlon, J., & Rentelis, R. (2015). Sociolinguistic variation and change in British Sign Language number signs: Evidence of leveling? *Sign Language Studies*, 15(2), 151–181.

Styles, E. A. (2008). *The Psychology of Attention*. Hove: Psychology Press.

Taub, S. F. (2012). Iconicity and metaphor. In R. Pfau, M. Steinbach, & B. Woll, eds., *Sign Language: An International Handbook*, Berlin: De Gruyter Mouton, pp. 388–412.

Thompson, R. L., Vinson, D. P., Woll, B., & Vigliocco, G. (2012). The road to language learning is iconic: Evidence from British Sign Language. *Psychological Science*, 23(12), 1443–1448.

Van Gijn, I. (2004). The quest for sytactic dependency: Sentential complementation in Sign Language of the Netherlands. Doctoral dissertation, University of Amsterdam.

Van Herreweghe, M. & Vermeerbergen, M. (2012). Handling sign language data. In R. Pfau, M. Steinbach, & B. Woll, eds., *Sign Language: An International Handbook*. Berlin: De Gruyter Mouton, pp. 1023–1045.

Wheatley, M. & Pabsch, A. (2012). *Sign Language Legislation in the European Union*, 2nd ed. Brussels: European Union of the Deaf.

Wilbur, R. (1996). Evidence for function and structure of *wh*-clefts in American Sign Language. In W. H. Edmondson & R. Wilbur, eds., *International Review of Sign Linguistics*. Mahwah, NJ: Lawrence Erlbaum, pp. 209–256.

Wilbur, R. B. (2008). Complex predicates involving events, time, and aspect: Is this why sign languages look so similar? In J. Quer, ed., *Signs of the Time: Selected Papers from TISLR 2004*. Hamburg: Signum, pp. 217–250.

Wilbur, R. B. & Schick, B. S. (1987). The effects of linguistic stress on ASL signs. *Language and Speech*, 30(4), 301–323.

Wilson, M. & Emmorey, K. (1997). A visuospatial "phonological loop" in working memory: Evidence from American Sign Language. *Memory & Cognition*, 25(3), 313–320.

Woodward, J. (1994). *Describing Variation in American Sign Language: Implicational Lects on the Deaf Diglossic Continuum*. Burtonsville, MD: Linstok Press.

Zwitserlood, I. (2012). Classifiers. In R. Pfau, M. Steinbach, & B. Woll, eds., *Sign Language: An International Handbook*. Berlin: De Gruyter Mouton, pp. 158–186.

# Part IV

# Experimental Syntax beyond Acceptability

# 22

# Theories All the Way Down

## Remarks on "Theoretical" and "Experimental" Linguistics

Colin Phillips, Phoebe Gaston, Nick Huang,
and Hanna Muller

## 22.1 Introduction

We expect both too much and too little from experiments in linguistics, including the recent wave of interest in "experimental syntax." We often encounter the hope that experiments will give us more precise data that will allow us to settle difficult theoretical questions, but such hopes are rarely realized. We believe that this is because we have unrealistic expectations about the ability of experiments to answer questions that syntacticians already had. Meanwhile, researchers have underappreciated the value of experiments for allowing us to address new questions that were not even on our radar previously.

Linguistic theories that are constructed based on traditional data collection methods, i.e. yes/no acceptability judgments, unsurprisingly make claims that are well suited to those methods. For example, they make claims about sentences that are well-formed and ill-formed, based on properties of their structural organization, typically with no reference to how those mental representations are constructed. This does not mean that only those claims count as "theories." Nor does it mean that other data collection methods are of "theoretical" interest only if they address those existing claims. In order for linguistic theories to most benefit from experimental research, it is important to take an inclusive approach to what counts as a linguistic theory and what counts as a theoretically interesting contribution.

We have had a similar experience, repeatedly, in multiple projects, spanning many years. We have been attracted to explore a topic because

This research was supported in part by NSF training grant DGE-1449615 to the University of Maryland (Phillips, PI), and by University of Maryland Flagship Fellowship awards to Phoebe Gaston and Hanna Muller. We are grateful to many people for helpful discussions of the issues addressed here, and especially to Ellen Lau and Iria de Dios Flores for pushing us to tackle the main challenge addressed here.

of its purported impact for "theoretical" linguistics, typically because some experimental finding bears on a generalization or claim that we are fond of. This could be a specific generalization about how constraints on anaphora are represented, or a broad generalization about syntax–semantics relations.

When we start to explore, we find that the experiment that initially drew our interest does not wear its interpretation on its sleeve. This is because understanding the conclusions of the study depends on a "linking hypothesis." A linking hypothesis is a theory of the experimental task that connects mental linguistic operations, i.e. the things that we really care about, to observed experimental measures such as button presses, eye movements, scalp voltages, etc. Once we better understand the linking hypothesis, we often realize that the theoretical consequences are not as decisive as we first thought, because of additional assumptions that we had been unaware of. Armed with a clearer linking hypothesis, we often also realize that there were confounds in the experimental set-up. Once those confounds are addressed, we then often find that the theoretical conclusions are different than where we started.

Importantly, once we articulate a clearer linking hypothesis we often find that it includes interesting claims about linguistic computations, often at a more fine-grained level of analysis than we are used to thinking about. And those computations often become fruitful research themes in their own right.

Some of our previous work has, perhaps correctly, been seen as painting a negative picture of the contributions that experiments can make to questions about grammatical theory, including debates about the representation of filler–gap dependencies (Phillips & Wagers 2007) or disputes over the licensing of ellipsis (Phillips & Parker 2014). In these and other cases we have argued, for example, that timing data is of limited use for deciding among theories that make no clear timing predictions.

But the negative stance in those cases was because the focus was on how experiments bear on the traditional questions asked by theoretical syntax. We can assure the reader that we do not spend our time feeling miserable about the theoretical irrelevance of our research. On the contrary, we enjoy discovering many new theoretical questions that we weren't previously aware of, and these then become research focus topics in their own right.

The situation is reminiscent of a famous anecdote, attributed to different philosophers and scientists over the years. The main protagonist gives a public lecture on the structure of the earth and the universe, and is then approached by an old lady who offers an alternative: the earth is flat, and it is supported on the back of a large turtle. The scientist tries to politely point to the flaw in the old lady's argument, by asking what is supporting the large turtle. The old lady replies that the first turtle is sitting on the back of a second one, and so on – "It's turtles all the way down!"

And so it is with linguistic theories. The questions posed by standard linguistic theory are interesting and important, but they abstract away from a great amount of detail at lower levels of analysis. Once we dig deeply into those levels, we uncover many new questions that we were unaware of previously. These are theoretically interesting. They are just not the theoretical questions that we started with.

This scenario has played out repeatedly in our work, and we describe a few examples here. We start with cases involving linking hypotheses that are close to standard linking hypotheses in syntax, and we then move to cases that are further afield theoretically.

## 22.2 Acceptability and Well-formedness

Although we most often think about linking hypotheses in the context of sophisticated experimental methods, they are just as relevant for the simplest kinds of linguistic data, i.e. acceptability judgments. Already in this domain we have found that by looking closely at challenges to standard assumptions we have uncovered interesting new questions.

Standard practice in linguistics combines one very simple linking hypothesis with one more opaque linking hypothesis. We all know that acceptability judgments are not a transparent reflection of grammatical well-formedness – the unacceptability of double center-embeddings is a parade case. But most of the time we assume a simple link from acceptability to well-formedness: if a sentence sounds fine, then it corresponds to a well-formed representation. However, acceptability judgments are necessarily filtered through the language comprehension system, and most syntacticians are adamant that the structure-building mechanisms that they describe are different than the structure-building mechanisms that are invoked in language comprehension. This means that there must be a relatively complex link between real-time comprehension processes and acceptability judgments, one that is almost never spelled out in detail.

A starting point for some of our group's work was an attempt to question the standard disconnect between comprehension processes and acceptability judgments. The link would be simpler if grammatical derivations and the operations of the comprehension system were the same, aside from the uncertainty that is specific to the comprehension task, i.e. the fact that comprehenders have to figure out what the speaker is trying to convey.

We reasoned that a transparent link between structure-building processes in comprehension and grammatical derivations should predict a straightforward alignment between the representations that are entertained during comprehension and the representations that are judged acceptable in offline judgment tasks. This motivated a research program looking at the real-time status of various well-known grammatical constraints. Many studies did indeed reveal a close alignment between what speakers find acceptable in untimed judgment tasks and the possibilities that they entertain in real-time processes (e.g. Stowe 1986; Sturt 2003; Phillips 2006; Kazanina et al. 2007). But many other studies did not, and those mismatches turned out to be rather more interesting (Lewis & Phillips 2015).

### 22.2.1  Grammatical Illusions

Standard syntactic reasoning relies on contrasts in acceptability in minimal pairs – we conclude that a difference in acceptability arises due to a difference in grammaticality, unless other explanations for unacceptability can be identified. With this simple linking hypothesis, we can observe that some speakers find (2) intuitively more acceptable than (1) (from Bock & Miller 1991), suggesting a contrast in the grammatical status of the two (see Chapter 5 for further discussion of this phenomenon).

(1)      * The key to the cabinet are rusty.

(2)      * The key to the cabinets are rusty.

Accordingly, we find claims in the formal syntax literature that (some) sentences that show subject–verb mismatches are in fact grammatical for certain dialects of American English (e.g. Kimball & Aissen 1971; Baker 2008). If this contrast truly is a grammatical contrast, this would have important implications for subject–verb agreement more generally, since c-command appears to be irrelevant to the dependency.

However, the judgment that (2) is more acceptable than (1) is somewhat fragile. Measures that tap into earlier representations, such as reading times and speeded judgments, reveal a greater contrast than slower measures that require more careful judgment. In other words, the more you think about it, the worse (2) sounds. The discovery that this pattern of acceptability is in fact geographically widespread (i.e. not dialect-dependent), and that it aligns closely with well-documented production errors, led to reconceptualizing these sentences as a parser–grammar mismatch, rather than a grammatical phenomenon (Wagers et al. 2009). That is, the grammar rules out both sentences, but a contrast arises because of an illusion of acceptability. This kind of mismatch has since been documented in many different areas – negative polarity item (NPI) licensing, comparatives, argument roles (Vasishth et al. 2008; Wagers et al. 2009; Chow et al. 2016; Parker & Phillips 2016; Wellwood et al. 2018, among others) – and the study of the specific types of dependencies that give rise to illusions, compared to the many dependencies that the parser computes accurately, has become a fruitful line of research (Phillips et al. 2011; Dillon et al. 2013).

Once we think of these sentences as a parser–grammar mismatch, the question becomes not what the grammatical representation of the sentence is, but what mechanisms are used to generate and access that representation. These are important linking assumptions for all of syntax, but also interesting questions in their own right.

Turning our attention to the online generation and access of syntactic structures calls for measurements that tap into online processes. In the case of agreement attraction and other illusions, self-paced reading and speeded acceptability are often useful tools, since they allow us to infer representations and processes that are entertained before a final, careful acceptability judgment. Note, however, that both of these measurements require a series of linking hypotheses of their own. In self-paced reading, the progression from one word to the next is mediated not only by the linguistic representations of interest but also by visual processing of the stimulus, decision-making, and motor planning to execute a keypress (see Chapter 23 for a broader discussion of self-paced reading).

While we do not intend to advocate any particular account of agreement attraction phenomena, we find this area to be a useful example of how probing the "linking hypotheses" of theoretical syntax can open up interesting new questions. The various explanations for illusions essentially differ in where in the process of detecting ungrammaticality the blame lies. One class of hypotheses posits that the representation of linguistic information *prior to* the verb is defective in some way, such as in the way that features are represented on nodes of the tree. If the plural feature on *cabinets* is occasionally permitted to spread to the entire DP *the key to the cabinets*, and if we accept the linking assumption that detecting grammaticality is essentially a feature-matching process, then consulting this defective representation should sometimes yield the incorrect decision that the sentence is grammatical, leading to faster reading times (Pearlmutter et al. 1999; Eberhard et al. 2005; Hammerly et al. 2019). The details of this feature spreading could be spelled out in various ways.

Other work has led to the suggestion that the representations generated are in fact perfectly accurate, and the problem arises with the processes by which the representations are accessed in memory (Wagers et al. 2009). Importantly, the feature spreading account also assumes a memory retrieval process, but the consistent success of that process is an unspecified linking assumption for this theory.

The memory retrieval account points to independent research suggesting that retrieval relies on parallel cue-based activation of nodes in memory (McElree 2006; Jonides et al. 2008). This mechanism could lead to retrieval of the wrong part of the representation (i.e. *cabinets* instead of *key*) on some proportion of trials because of a partial match in retrieval cues. That is, if the retrieval cues are [subject] and [plural], then *cabinets* and *key* should each match exactly one cue. If the wrong node is accessed, this could also lead to the incorrect decision regarding the grammaticality of *are* in this position, and this incorrect decision leads to faster reading times. This explanation is motivated by the grammatical asymmetry that is often observed in agreement attraction studies: an illusion of grammaticality arises for (3), but no illusion of ungrammaticality arises for (4).

(3)     * The key to the cabinets are rusty.

(4)     The key to the cabinets is rusty.

The memory retrieval account naturally accounts for this contrast because a search initiated by *is* in (4) should match *key* on all features and it should match *cabinets* on none.

However, recent work has suggested that the grammatical asymmetry can be better accounted for by properties of the decision-making process itself, rather than by retrieval errors. Both the feature spreading account and the memory retrieval account typically leave unspecified this part of the linking hypothesis, and assume a trivial decision procedure. Hammerly et al. (2019) argue that response bias toward acceptance might be responsible for the observed grammatical asymmetry in speeded acceptability tasks. When they created scenarios where participants expected to see a high proportion of ungrammatical sentences, illusions of ungrammaticality were observed.

Similar insights have come from research on other grammatical illusions. An influential early proposal was that a number of different types of illusion could be subsumed under the same memory retrieval framework, with illusions understood as instances of mis-retrieval due to partially matching retrieval cues (Lewis et al. 2006; Phillips et al. 2011). For example, illusory licensing of negative polarity items could be understood as mis-retrieval of an inappropriate negative element in the same way that agreement attraction can be understood as mis-retrieval of an inappropriate number-marked noun (Vasishth et al. 2008). However, subsequent research has revealed that NPI illusions have a different temporal profile than agreement attraction (Parker & Phillips 2016) and that they have rather specific triggers (Muller et al. 2019). This has led to a new set of hypotheses and questions about the time course of semantic interpretation.

Thus, illusions have prompted investigation into several components of the linking hypothesis that underlies the use of acceptability judgments in syntax, including the nature of stored representations of linguistic input, the retrieval process by which they are accessed, and the process by which a decision regarding acceptability is reached. These processes are important as linking hypotheses, but they have also led to productive new avenues for research.

## 22.2.2 Resumptive Pronouns

Research on resumptive pronouns (RPs) is another area where the consistency of acceptability judgments has come under close scrutiny (see Chapters 7, 8, 9, and 19 for extensive discussion of resumptive pronouns). As in the case of linguistic illusions, the focus is on sentences that are judged as surprisingly acceptable. But whereas the illusions literature treats those surprising acceptances as errors caused by lower-level mechanisms, in the RPs literature a key question is how to classify cases of surprising acceptability. Experimental studies on RPs have deepened the puzzle by showing that judgments that linguists have taken for granted for decades are more elusive than expected.

A conventional claim found in generative syntax since Ross (1967) is that *wh*-movement out of an island is ungrammatical, but the representation can be "repaired," with a resumptive pronoun (RP) in the place of the gap. This claim was founded on informal introspection. In English, for example, sentences like (6) are reported to be more acceptable than (5). Similar dependencies with RPs are attested in naturally occurring contexts across many languages. In languages like Hebrew and Irish, RPs can even occur in non-island contexts.

(5) *The detective interrogated a man who the prosecutor knows why the officer arrested ___.

(gap in embedded *wh*-island)

(6) The detective interrogated a man who$_1$ the prosecutor knows why the officer arrested him$_1$.

(resumptive pronoun) (from Han et al. 2012, ex. 1)

Recent research has challenged the standard view of RPs. In a number of languages, behavioral measures have not consistently reproduced the contrast in pairs like (5) and (6). This is surprising, since informal linguistic judgments reported by linguists typically converge with ratings given by naive participants in large-scale acceptability judgment studies (Phillips 2010; Sprouse & Almeida 2012; Sprouse et al. 2013).

Efforts to reconcile this difference between received wisdom and the experimental record have led to a debate about the syntactic status of RPs in island configurations. A popular interpretation of the discrepant acceptability ratings holds that RPs are actually ill-formed. However, because RPs explicitly indicate where the dependency ends and what morphosyntactic features their antecedents have, they provide a production or comprehension advantage, which is responsible for the perception of acceptability in informal introspection (Alexopoulou & Keller 2007; Heestand et al. 2011; Beltrama & Xiang 2016; Chacón 2015, among others).

We consider it unlikely that this proposal is correct. It implies that linguists are bad at distinguishing percepts of well-formedness from

plausibility and comprehensibility, and that typical experimental participants are better at this. Most other evidence suggests the opposite. Also, we
consider it unlikely that linguists have been fooling themselves for decades over the intuition that RPs improve acceptability for island-crossing
dependencies.

A review of a broader set of studies suggests that typical acceptability
rating measures might not be the best way to tap into the percept of
improvement that linguists report. Ackerman et al. (2018) argue that the
choice of task affects judgments of sentences with RPs. Studies that do
not consistently find a contrast between RPs and their gapped counterparts tend to be those that use standard acceptability ratings, while
studies that do find a contrast tend to be those where participants
make an explicit choice between ending an island-violating *wh*-
dependency with a gap or an RP. In this setting, participants prefer
island-violating *wh*-dependencies that end with an RP (e.g. Zukowski &
Larsen 2004; Ferreira & Swets 2005; Ackerman et al. 2018). Acceptability
ratings may be a blunt tool, especially when a rating for an entire
sentence is used as a proxy for the status of one specific piece of that
sentence, such as an RP. Forced choice tasks may yield greater sensitivity
in this case because they direct speakers' attention to the one part of the
sentence that differs between the alternatives.

The question of how to reconcile linguists' intuitions with findings from
large-scale judgment studies is at most an intermediate question. And it is
probably an over-simplification to regard the question as figuring out
whether unbounded dependencies with RPs are genuinely well-formed
or genuinely ill-formed. Discrete notions of well-formedness applied to
entire sentences are probably no more than a useful simplification that
helps us to build generalizations at a high level of description. What is
really at stake is more likely the question of what are the representations
and processes that are involved in RP dependencies, and what is it specifically about the insertion of an RP that (sometimes) leads speakers to be
happier with those dependencies. The underlying mental representations
and computations are what we most care about. How those are mapped
onto quantifiable behavioral responses as percepts of (un)acceptability is
an important linking question, but its interest is justified mostly by how it
leads us to a clearer understanding of the representations and
computations.

There is also a useful methodological lesson here. It is sometimes presumed that "experimental syntax" will deliver clarity to linguistics simply
by gathering large quantities of scalar acceptability judgments (Ferreira
2005; Gibson & Fedorenko 2013). This should overcome the biases that
surely plague decades of informal introspection by linguists. But in the
case of RPs we now know that different quantitative measures point to
different conclusions about the status of RPs. Simply asking lots of people
does not help in this case.

A good example of a subliterature where these issues are worked out in more detail is the literature on voice mismatches in ellipsis, where there are competing detailed hypotheses about the computations that are responsible for gradient judgments (Arregui et al. 2006; Kim et al. 2011).

## 22.3    Clarifying Linking Hypotheses

In this section we describe case studies involving methods that are further from standard acceptability judgments, and that require linking hypotheses in additional domains. These are scenarios in which care must be taken to rule out any confounds in the many steps between the question and the experimental data. Often we start with a question that is guided by debates in standard (high-level) linguistic theory, but once we spell out the linking hypotheses we find that we are led to different conclusions, and discover interesting new theoretical questions that we have been unaware of previously.

### 22.3.1    Children's Interpretation of Pronouns

One of the experimental findings that has most captured the imagination of researchers in (traditional) linguistic theory involves preschoolers' mastery of Principle B of Binding Theory (see Chapter 11 for an overview of experimental approaches to Binding Theory and Chapter 15 for further discussion of child language). Our group's original interest in this topic was motivated by the claim that developmental dissociations can help to decide among competing high-level theories. But as we looked more closely, new theoretical questions began to emerge at a finer grain of detail that we had not been aware of previously.

Classic versions of the Binding Theory due to Chomsky (e.g. Chomsky 1981) treated instances of coreference and bound variable anaphora equivalently, whereas Reinhart (1983) and others argued that binding constraints apply to bound variable relations but not to coreference. So, if we focus on binding Principle B, which blocks a pronoun from being bound by a co-argument, Chomsky's account treats (7)–(8) as equivalent. The subject NP cannot bind the object pronoun in either case, and for the same reason. Reinhart's account regards quantificational (8) as straightforwardly excluded by Principle B, because it clearly involves bound variable anaphora. But additional machinery is needed to capture (7). If (7) is treated as an instance of coreference, then it should not be subject to Principle B. Yet speakers of English clearly perceive that *Mama Bear* and *her* cannot be the same individual. So Reinhart needed to invoke an additional pragmatic constraint that forces instances of possible coreference to be treated as bound variable anaphora, all other things being equal.

(7)    Mama Bear washed her.

(8)    Every bear washed her.

Reinhart's theory received a significant boost from the finding that pre-schoolers appear to treat (7) and (8) differently. Chien and Wexler (1990) replicated earlier findings that preschoolers often entertain interpreta-tions of (7) in which *her* refers to Mama Bear. But they found that the same group of children did not allow *her* in (8) to be bound by *every bear*. Children of this age are independently known to have difficulty in some areas of pragmatics, so the results fit remarkably well with the idea that these children are following Reinhart's Principle B. Further studies pro-vided further evidence for the so-called *quantificational asymmetry* (McDaniel et al. 1990; Philip & Coopmans 1996; Thornton & Wexler 1999).

The key linking assumption behind these studies was that children consider sentence interpretations that are allowed by their grammar, and that they do not consider sentence interpretations that their grammar disallows. This seems like a reasonable starting assumption, but it pre-sumes a tight and effective link between grammar and interpretation (Crain & Thornton 1998).

One of us swooned when, as a graduate student in the 1990s, he learned of this developmental dissociation. Experimental data could turn up sur-prising evidence that cut through difficult theoretical disputes. So the appearance of Elbourne (2005), which argued that the quantificational asymmetry reflected an experimental confound, was not welcomed. He recruited some students to help try to respond to Elbourne's concerns, fully expecting to show that the concerns were unfounded. The upshot of this was the finding that Elbourne was at least partly correct (Conroy et al. 2009).

In a series of truth-value judgment tasks Conroy et al. (2009) went to great lengths to provide a matched test of children's interpretation of pronouns with quantificational and referential antecedents. When they did this, two key findings emerged. First, as Elbourne had predicted, the quantificational asymmetry disappeared. Second, children performed rather well across-the-board, giving 85–90 percent adultlike judgments. Set against the many studies that have documented children's non-adultlike interpretations for sentences like (7) this seemed puzzling, but further investigation revealed a more interesting picture.

A review of over 30 prior studies with children revealed that the findings of Conroy et al. were not unprecedented. In particular, they were rather similar to Kaufman (1988), a largely forgotten contemporary of the famous Chien and Wexler (1990) study. But they lay at one end of a wide range of performance by the children in different studies. Some studies showed a quantificational asymmetry, but just as many did not (Lombardi & Sarma 1989; Avrutin & Wexler 1992; Hestvik & Philip 1999/2000; Grolla 2005).

Some studies showed very high rates of interpretations that violate Principle B, while other studies showed quite low rates of violation. The spread in findings was more than would be expected by chance. Furthermore, a closer look at the experimental designs revealed that the varying outcomes were somewhat predictable based on the scenarios that were used to test the children. When the grammatical interpretation of the pronoun, i.e. disjoint from the subject NP, was supported by a prominent referent ("availability") and an at-issue proposition ("disputability") children were good at selecting that interpretation over an illicit bound interpretation of the pronoun.

So the empirical conclusion is that preschoolers have the linguistic knowledge needed to successfully apply Principle B. But they are very fragile. When experimental conditions are not set up just right, they can easily be pushed to entertain interpretations that violate Principle B. Moreover, there is a strikingly close alignment between children and adults. The cases where children appear to get stuck on non-adultlike interpretations in their offline interpretations align closely with cases where adults fleetingly consider illicit interpretations in their online interpretations. And cases where children's interpretations are more robustly adultlike correspond to cases where adults' online interpretations are relatively impervious to illicit lures (Phillips & Ehrenhofer 2015).

These findings lead to new theoretical questions: why are some illicit interpretations considered fleetingly in the course of parsing while others are not? This aligns closely with questions raised by linguistic illusions. Relatedly, how are (combinatorial) interpretations generated, using a combination of grammatical and situational knowledge? These are rather different than the questions that first led us to study children's pronoun interpretations, but they are at least as interesting, and they bear on theories of human linguistic interpretation at least as much as the questions that we first started with.

### 22.3.2 Lexical Activation and Response Probability

A similar story plays out in the study of the role of linguistic context in language understanding. We started with simple high-level generalizations and some apparently anomalous findings, but we were led to discover new theoretical questions that we were not even aware of when we started.

There is much recent interest in the role of context in linguistic and psycholinguistic theory. In psycholinguistics the focus has been on how comprehenders use contextual constraints to constrain the parsing and interpretation of upcoming input. At a high level, much of this work can be understood as an investigation of cross-talk between different parts of the language system: can information in one level of representation be used to constrain operations in another level of representation (e.g. Fodor 1983).

Our starting point was one of the simplest contextual constraints that we can find. When a sentence context strongly predicts the syntactic category of the next word, how does that constraint affect the process of recognizing the next word? For example, the word onset *br* ... could turn out to be either a noun (e.g. *brownie*) or a verb (e.g. *browse*). If the context strongly predicts a verb (e.g. *She wanted to br* ...) is the phonological input matched against all compatible words in the mental lexicon, or only those that are verbs? This is a long-standing question, and studies using different experimental measures have reached different conclusions. Some have concluded that syntactic category does not limit lexical access (Tanenhaus et al. 1979; Tyler 1984), whereas others have concluded that it does (Magnuson et al. 2008; Strand 2018). We wanted to better understand these conflicts.

In this case, computational modeling provided crucial clarification of the questions. The TRACE model (McClelland & Elman 1986) treats auditory word recognition as a process of activating feature, phoneme, and then word-level representations in a connectionist network. So, continuously varying activation levels are the key currency of lexical computation in this model. In behavioral studies of word recognition, lexical activation levels are, of course, not directly observable. Instead, researchers have used accuracy, reaction time, eye movements, and neural activity as proxies for lexical activation levels.

Although TRACE is not designed to directly model context effects, it is informative to translate context effects into the lexical activation currency of the model. In discussions of syntactic category constraints that we are aware of, it is generally assumed that if syntactic category constrains word recognition, this would mean that only words that match the expected category are considered. This amounts to a strong inhibitory constraint, one that in a verb context would effectively turn off the link between *br* ... and *brownie*. It would mean that upon encountering a syntactic context that predicts a verb, the abstract expectation for a verb would need to be translated into an instruction that inhibits links between sounds and lexical entries for all items that are not a verb. This kind of inhibitory mechanism is potentially difficult to implement, and it could be problematic in that a word might become unrecognizable if the context is misheard and the word is then mistakenly ruled out as a candidate. A promising alternative is for links from syntactic category to lexical entries to be facilitatory, such that a verb context boosts the activation of all verbs, while leaving other categories unaffected. The theoretical contrast between inhibitory and facilitatory context effects makes a big difference to the empirical consequences of context effects. And yet the contrast had eluded us until we tried to capture context effects in terms of an explicit model. As we then discovered, the empirical record fits well with a facilitatory effect of context.

Explicit modeling also proved invaluable for understanding the link between lexical activation, i.e. what we really care about, and the various behavioral and neural measures that we use to try to infer lexical activation. In some paradigms the dependent measure can be thought of as a response probability: how likely is a participant to choose, fixate, or produce one lexical candidate rather than another? It is tempting to think of response probabilities as direct reflections of changes in activation, just as acceptability judgments are often treated as transparent reflections of grammatical well-formedness. But an important idea that models like TRACE make clear is that lexical activation and response probability are not the same thing. The transformations that map activations to response probabilities are affected by the details of task and response candidate set.

For example, the visual world paradigm typically tracks visual fixations to a small set of pictured items while participants listen to auditory input. In this paradigm a participant can only fixate on one item at any moment in time. Fixation probabilities on a picture are dependent on the lexical activation of the picture's name. A straightforward mapping is to assume that fixation probability is computed by dividing lexical activation for a given candidate by the sum of the activation values for all response candidates. This means that shifts in fixations to one picture could reflect a shift in activation of that picture's name. Or it could reflect a shift in activation of other pictures' names. A change in activation of the item we care about will only lead to a change in fixation probability if it changes more or less than the rest of the set. This principle turns out to be crucial in interpreting behavioral results, but it is lost without a transparent linking hypothesis between activation and response probability. Insights of this nature certainly do not necessarily require computational modeling techniques. They are in the category of insights that make sense with the benefit of hindsight, but that are easily missed without the aid of modeling.

Lexical competition in the visual world paradigm is indexed by an increase in fixations to a cohort competitor of the auditory target, relative to an unrelated distractor. Such competition is well-established when the competitor is of the same syntactic category as the target. Two studies have shown that lexical competition does not occur when the cohort competitor is of a different syntactic category from the target, suggesting that syntactic context can prevent the activation of syntactically incompatible lexical candidates (Magnuson, Tanenhaus, & Aslin 2008; Strand et al. 2018).

However, we found that when we further controlled the visual world design such that the syntactically inappropriate cohort competitor is the only candidate in the response candidate set whose activation can be expected to change in response to the auditory input, lexical competition is indeed detectable (Gaston et al. 2019). For example, in a context like *She wanted to browse* we found increased fixations to a picture of a broom, just as in a context like *She chose the brownie*. In neither case was a broom mentioned in the utterance, but the phonological onset *br* ... led to increased looks in either case.

Our visual world study showed that incoming sounds can activate any compatible words in the mental lexicon, even when this conflicts with a syntactic constraint. This could mean that the syntactic constraint is simply ineffective. Or it could reflect that the effect of the syntactic constraint is a facilitatory one. Our visual world results do not distinguish those possibilities, but results from other studies lend support to the facilitatory mechanism. For example, a meta-analysis of classic cross-modal priming studies on homophone processing (Lucas 1999) showed that both meanings of a homophone are activated, even when one meaning conflicts with the context. Lucas found that across the literature (though this effect is very subtle in individual studies) there is more priming for the meaning that is consistent with the context. Most of the studies in this meta-analysis are concerned with semantic context, but the study on syntactic context that is included (Tanenhaus et al. 1979) also fits this pattern. For example, this would mean more priming for the word *look* after hearing *I began to watch* (same category) than after hearing *I bought the watch* (different category).

Furthermore, the facilitatory mechanism makes sense of otherwise puzzling findings from a magnetoencephalography (MEG) study of contextual constraints. Earlier studies had discovered that MEG activity patterns correlate with properties of the set of words that are under consideration during auditory word recognition (Gagnepain, Henson, & Davis 2012; Ettinger, Linzen, & Marantz 2014; Gwilliams & Marantz 2015). Gaston and Marantz (2018) built on this finding by testing whether activity elicited in a syntactically constraining context correlates with a syntactically constrained set of words, e.g. only verbs, or with a syntactically unconstrained set of words, i.e. all words compatible with the phonological onset of the word. Gaston and colleagues found that the MEG activity correlated with both the constrained and the unconstrained word sets. This seemed oddly contradictory at first, but in retrospect it is just as predicted by a facilitatory effect of syntactic context on lexical activations.

This example resembles the other examples, in the respect that the starting point was high-level generalizations that we regarded as straightforward, but that led us to new theoretical questions that we had not been aware of. What is notable in this case is the role of (relatively simple) computational modeling in helping us to recognize the new questions, and the role of diverse experimental methods in revealing the difference between surface measures and underlying mental processes.

### 22.3.3   Role Reversals and the Semantic P600

Sometimes our starting point has been a theoretical controversy in the linguistics literature. In other cases the starting point is a claim that is largely uncontroversial, but that is challenged by a psycholinguistic finding. As elsewhere, what we initially regard as important is often not what turned out to be most important.

One of the most influential event-related potential (ERP) findings on language comprehension in the past 15 years comes from a study by Kim and Osterhout (2005) on sentences with "thematic role reversals" (see Chapter 24 for a more extended discussion of ERP). This study appeared to show that comprehenders build interpretations that are inconsistent with the syntactic structure of the sentence. This finding drew our group's attention because it challenged the largely uncontroversial assumption that syntactic and semantic combinatorics are tightly coupled, i.e. the syntactic structure of a sentence guides how the meanings of words are combined to form larger meanings. However, as we dug deeper our original motivation faded, and we discovered new theoretical questions that we had not been aware of previously, involving the use of linguistic information to access non-linguistic information in memory.

Kim and Osterhout (2005) compared ERPs to sentences like (9)–(10), where (9) is a grammatically appropriate and plausible passive sentence and (10) contains the same open-class words but is a grammatically well-formed but implausible active sentence. The verb *devouring* in (10) elicited the P600 effect commonly seen in response to syntactic anomalies, despite the fact that the sentence is syntactically well-formed. It did not elicit the N400 effect typically associated with semantic anomalies, despite being highly semantically anomalous.

(9)     The hearty meal was devoured . . .

(10)    The hearty meal was devouring . . .

Kim and Osterhout proposed that this pattern arose because comprehenders perceived (10) as syntactically anomalous, despite the fact that it is syntactically well-formed. Under this account, comprehenders recognize that *meal* is an attractive theme of *devour* and they construct a corresponding interpretation, ignoring the fact that the sentence is active rather than passive. As a result, the sentence is initially perceived as plausible and no N400 effect is elicited. Subsequently they notice that the syntactic form of the sentence mismatched the interpretation, and hence a P600 effect is elicited.

Kim and Osterhout's finding was not the first of its kind, and many others have reported similar ERP effects in response to role reversals and similar anomalies (Kuperberg et al. 2003; Kolk et al. 2003; Hoeks et al. 2004; Ye & Zhou 2008). One of the most distinctive contributions of Kim and Osterhout's study is that they present evidence that the effect specifically depends on the presence of "semantic attraction" between the verb and the arguments. In a second experiment they compared *hearty meal* with *dusty tabletop* in sentences like (10). Both are poor agents of *devour*, but only *hearty meal* is an attractive theme. They found that *dusty tabletop* elicited a more typical pattern of an N400 effect and no P600 effect. So they concluded that their initial effect was specifically due to interpretations that are semantically attractive but syntactically unsupported. This is a strong experimental argument.

The key linking assumptions for Kim and Osterhout's argument were the long-standing view that N400 effects reflect (combinatorial) semantic processing and that P600 effects reflect syntactic processing. Combining Kim and Osterhout's data with these assumptions leads to the conclusion that semantic interpretation can proceed independent of syntax. This challenges such a basic theoretical assumption that our group began to examine the processing of role reversals in more detail. As in many other cases, this led us somewhere very different from where we had started. Summarizing a number of years of research by our group and many others, we learned the following.

First, some of the empirical generalizations offered by Kim and Osterhout (2005) are robust, but others are not. Role reversal sentences do consistently elicit P600 effects, despite the fact that they are syntactically well-formed. This is compatible with Kim and Osterhout's claims. However, the P600 effect is not limited to cases of semantic attraction. Relatively few studies have manipulated the presence of attraction as Kim and Osterhout did, but those that have done so have generally found that the P600 is elicited even in the absence of semantic attraction (e.g. Van Herten et al. 2006; Kuperberg et al. 2006; Stroud 2008; Paczynski & Kuperberg 2011; Stroud & Phillips 2012; Chow & Phillips 2013).

Kim and Osterhout's N400 findings are generally robust, but they appear to reflect a broader generalization: N400 effects reflect the degree to which an incoming word is expected in context, and this in turn is influenced by lexical associations between the incoming word and prior words in the context. So, in Kim and Osterhout's key second experiment *meal . . . devour* elicits a smaller N400 than *tabletop . . . devour* because *meal* is more closely associated with *devour*. A widespread current view is that the N400 reflects lexical processes, rather than combinatorial semantic processes, and that those processes are modulated by earlier processes that make a word more or less expected. Evidence for this view of the N400 comes from lexical priming effects, neuroanatomical evidence, predictive grammatical agreement, and phonological effects, among others (Kutas & Federmeier 2000; van Berkum et al. 2005; Lau et al. 2008; Mantegna et al. 2019).

Furthermore, our group has found that the "blindness" of the N400 to thematic role reversals can be cured if there is more time between the predictive cues and the target verb. For example, Chow et al. (2018) replicated in Mandarin the standard finding that a verb with role-reversed arguments fails to elicit an N400 effect. This is the same as Kim and Osterhout (2005). But they also found that when the verb is presented at a greater delay after the same arguments then the N400 effect reappears. So, timing matters. They also found that this reappearance occurs only when the arguments strongly predict the verb. So, timing matters specifically for prediction. We see similar effects in role-reversed sentences in Japanese, and in speeded cloze tasks in English (Chow et al. 2015; Momma et al. 2016; Burnsky et al. 2019).

Based on these findings, we argued that comprehenders accurately parse and interpret incoming sentences, and that they use all available information to make predictions about upcoming words. However, not all information is used equally quickly. Early predictions are based primarily on lexical associations. Further refinement of those predictions based on thematic roles does occur, but it takes more time. This is why canonical and role-reversed sentences elicit identical N400s at short latencies, because the sentence types are matched in terms of lexical associations. But when more time elapses between the arguments and the verb the N400 to canonical and role-reversed sentences differs, reflecting the emergence of more specific predictions based on thematic roles.

Why should it take time for predictions based on thematic roles to impact lexical expectations? We have suggested that this may be because lexical prediction is the result of a memory access process, that is slower when the memory access cues mismatch the format of semantic memory. We suggest that our long-term knowledge of events is not encoded in terms of abstract thematic roles like "agent" and "patient," and so a multistep process is needed to map from linguistic argument role cues to event memory (Chow et al. 2016).

So, what began as an investigation into long-standing claims about syntax–semantics relations in a standard linguistic architecture turned into new questions about the relationship between grammatical information and world knowledge. Still theoretical, certainly interesting, but not the question that we started with.

## 22.4  In Search of Linking Hypotheses

In the examples described in Sections 22.2 and 22.3 we highlighted the interest of theoretical questions at finer grains of analysis than traditional linguistic theories. But one could object that this side steps the question of what experiments can contribute to theoretical questions at the traditional higher level. Wouldn't it be good if we could experimentally target the higher level without needing to get tied down in lower-level questions? A number of recent lines of work claim to do that using ingenious experimental arguments. Our impression is that the experimental arguments are only ever as good as the linking hypotheses.

## 22.4.1   Neurosyntax

A growing body of work uses computational models to predict neural activity during naturalistic reading or listening (see Chapter 27 for general discussion of the neural representation of syntax). For example, a study might model brain activity while participants listen to passages from stories like *Alice in Wonderland* or *The Little Prince*. This is a radically different approach than traditional experiments that use tightly controlled materials that are manipulated to isolate an effect of interest. In naturalistic reading or listening studies the choice of linguistic material is relatively arbitrary, and instead all the action is in the analysis of the linguistic material that is used to model the neural activity.

To take an oversimplified toy example, neural recordings taken during listening to a story could be modeled using a super-simple analysis that consists only of a sequence of words, and a slightly more complicated analysis that distinguishes lexical categories. Each model is then fit to the neural data, and the analyst can ask whether the model that includes lexical category distinctions better explains the variability in the data.

Neurocomputational models of this sort generally have multiple components: a grammar, an algorithm, an oracle, a complexity metric, and a response function. As described in Brennan's review of the approach (Brennan 2016), a grammar (sequence-based, context-free, Minimalist, etc.) defines well-formed syntactic representations for the linguistic input, and a parsing algorithm (top-down, left-corner, bottom-up, etc.) determines how to apply the grammar to incrementally presented input. An *oracle* is used to make decisions in the case of, for example, syntactic ambiguities, and the oracle can vary in the information it has access to. The grammar, algorithm, and oracle together make up the syntactic parser, which takes in words and returns mental states. Mental states can be, for example, syntactic trees. A complexity metric is then used to describe or quantify those mental states, in terms of such dimensions as the number of nodes added to the tree, the reduction in entropy over possible syntactic trees (if the oracle is not choosing a single tree at each step), the surprisal of the syntactic category of the incoming word, or the number of open dependencies, among many other possibilities. Complexity metrics are combined with response functions that try to take into account the relationship between hypothesized neural states and the neural signals measurable in methods like functional magnetic resonance imaging (fMRI), electroencephalography (EEG), magnetoencephalography (MEG), or electrocorticography (ECoG). This final step is what allows us to compare predicted neural signal and actual neural signal, in response to specific input.

"L-studies," as Brennan (2016) terms them, test the predictions of different versions of the model against the neural signal from a constrained set of brain areas. This approach has been used in order to ask, for example, whether sequence-based grammars or grammars allowing abstract hierarchical structure better predict neural activity in areas known to be associated with syntactic processing. "N-studies," in contrast, take a given parametrization of the model and then ask about the location or timing of correlations between its predictions and actual neural activity in all areas of the brain.

A number of interesting findings have emerged from this approach. Brennan et al. (2016) report that node counts from an audiobook story's proposed syntactic structure predict the time-course of participants' fMRI BOLD signal while they listen to that story. Brennan and Pylkkänen (2017) show that the number of left-corner parse steps associated with visually presented sentences predicts MEG activity in the anterior temporal lobe. Similarly, Nelson et al. (2017) describe neural evidence for a merge operation (among other claims), in ECoG, and Hale et al. (2018) argue for RNN grammars with beam search on the basis of their findings in EEG.

However, the conclusions that can be drawn from this approach are only ever as good as the hypotheses (models) that are used to model the naturalistic input. Typically, the models of parsing operations that are used specify limited detail, and there is a high degree of correlation between competing grammatical and parsing models. This is evident in the sheer number of different grammars, parsing algorithms, and complexity metrics that have found support in recent work. It can easily be the case that different hypotheses for the grammar or parser yield similar outcomes with respect to their complexity metrics, which means that predicted neural signals from many different model parameterizations can be highly correlated with each other.

To take one example, an experiment that compares sequence-based grammars with grammars with hierarchical syntactic structure might find that the hierarchical grammar better captures the observed neural recordings. This supports claims of a hierarchical grammar, or any other linguistic system that better correlates with the hierarchical grammar than the sequential grammar. Since the existence of hierarchical structure in meanings is fairly obvious – in *two dogs barked*, the expression *two dogs* is a unit to the exclusion of *barked* – that could capture the advantage of a model with hierarchical structure, regardless of the form of the grammar.

We do not claim that modeling neural responses to naturalistic language input is a fruitless activity. It is a rapidly developing area and it holds much promise. We merely caution that there is no magic solution to isolating the processes or level of analysis that we want to know about. In traditional experimental designs our arguments are only as good as our experimental materials and our (all too often vague) linking hypotheses. We obsess about identifying and removing confounds from our experimental materials. We work hard to ensure that our experimental conditions are represented by diverse items that are representative of the more abstract category that we are interested in. Naturalistic studies abandon the focus on the design of materials, but this does not remove the need to obsess about materials and linking hypotheses. The linking hypotheses are made explicit in the models that are used to describe the language materials. Anything that is not included in the model is not controlled, and hence a potential confound. And the question of whether the abstract categories in the model are associated with diverse examples – e.g. are the nouns in the materials a diverse and representative sample? – is often overlooked.

### 22.4.2   Structural Priming

Syntactic priming is an experimental technique that has been put forward as a measure that might offer a privileged view into abstract structural properties of sentences, independent of questions about how they are constructed and how they are encoded at more fine-grained levels of analysis. Branigan and Pickering (2017) argue that this allows structural priming to arbitrate some long-standing debates in traditional syntactic theories.

Syntactic priming is the name for the facilitation observed when a recently used structure is reused, even when there is no lexical overlap between the initial use (prime) and the reuse (target). For example, a passive is more easy to produce when another passive sentence has been recently encountered, even if the two passive sentences have no words in common, aside from closed-class morphology (Bock 1989; Bock et al. 1992). Abstract syntactic priming effects have mostly been observed in measures of production probability, e.g. how often speakers describe a given picture prompt with a passive rather than an active. But syntactic priming effects have also been observed in comprehension and production timing measures (Traxler et al. 2014; Momma et al. 2017; see also Chapter 26).

Branigan and Pickering (2017) argue that syntactic priming can be used to arbitrate between transformational and non-transformational grammatical theories. Since this dispute has attracted so much attention over the past few decades, the evidence deserves attention.

Transformational theories of grammar have always maintained that there are several levels of syntactic representation; a standard view is that there are at least three within syntax: one level that has consequences for both semantics and phonology (roughly S-structure in government-binding theory, "narrow syntax" in some more recent minimalist work), one level that specifically impacts semantics ("LF"/"Logical Form"), and another level that specifically impacts morphophonology ("PF"/"Phonetic Form").

All grammatical theories assume that sentences somehow simultaneously encode multiple different syntactic, semantic, and phonological properties (e.g. thematic structure, scope relations, linear order). Many theories assume that at least some of these properties are encoded in distinct structural representations (e.g. *Lexical–Functional Grammar,*

Bresnan et al. 2015; *Categorial Grammar*, Steedman 2000). The distinctive claim of transformational theories has always been that the multiple representations are related by means of transformational operations that move items between different positions in a phrase marker, e.g. moving a noun phrase from a position that encodes its thematic status to a higher position that encodes its scope. Traditionally, evidence for the different levels of representation in transformational theories, especially LF, comes from informal acceptability judgments (e.g. Huang 1982; May 1985).

Branigan and Pickering (2017) argue for a single level ("monostratral") syntax without transformations, based on evidence for priming between sentences that are surface identical but that are argued to be structurally different in transformational theories.

For example, English and other languages distinguish two types of intransitive verbs. *Unergative* verbs have a single argument that bears an agent role, whereas *unaccusative* verbs have a single argument that bears a theme or patient role (Levin & Rappaport Hovav 1995). Unaccusatives and unergatives differ in many ways across languages, but they appear in very similar surface forms in English. Transformational theories claim that the surface subject of an unaccusative verb is derived by moving the single argument from an underlying direct object position to the surface subject position.

Branigan and Pickering point to evidence that English unaccusative sentences like *The snow melted* are primed to the same degree by other unaccusative sentences, such as *The water froze* and by unergative sentences like *The children sang*. They reason that the syntactic representation of unaccusatives must therefore be identical to that of unergatives. More specifically, they argue that this shows that there is no representation where the argument of an unaccusative verb is found in an object position before moving to a subject position, as suggested by transformational or Relational Grammar theories. Rather, the argument of unaccusative and unergative verbs only ever occupies the same structural position, the standard subject position. This, together with a number of similar cases, is used to argue that syntax is monostratal, in the sense that there are no distinct levels of representation connected by movement/transformation operations.

The arguments against transformational theories are only as good as the linking hypothesis that connects structural similarity to syntactic priming effects. These linking hypotheses are underdeveloped, despite the large amount of empirical research on structural priming. All grammatical theories agree that there is some degree of shared structure between English unaccusatives and unergatives. And all also agree that there is some difference between unaccusatives and unergatives, in order to capture their semantic differences, which also impact various structural diagnostics (Levin & Rappaport Hovav 1995) and give rise to differences in production planning (Momma et al. 2018). The similarities between

unaccusatives and unergatives that everybody agrees upon could be sufficient to drive syntactic priming effects. Branigan and Pickering would like
to use syntactic priming as evidence for a lack of differences between a pair
of structures. But there is little evidence that syntactic priming is an
effective tool for such arguments.

Structural priming is a potentially powerful way of diagnosing the
structural content of sentences, but this will only be possible once
a more articulated theory of priming is available, and there is little reason
to regard it as somehow more reliable or privileged as a diagnostic of
syntactic structure. For further discussion see Gaston et al. (2018).

### 22.4.3  Memory Access Diagnostics

A different experimental approach to diagnosing transformations is pursued by Xiang and colleagues using evidence from speed-accuracy tradeoff
(SAT) and memory interference paradigms in studies on Mandarin Chinese
(Xiang et al. 2014; Xiang et al. 2015). A strength of these studies is that they
rely on explicit and independently motivated linking hypotheses.

Mandarin differs from English in the surface form of wh-questions.
Whereas English fronts wh-phrases to a position that indicates the scope
of the question as a direct or indirect question, leaving the thematic position of the wh-phrase empty, Mandarin adopts a wh-in-situ strategy, where
the wh-phrase occupies the thematic position and the scope of the question
must be recovered from other cues (see Chapter 16 for further discussion of
this property of Mandarin and other languages of East Asia).

Transformational analyses since at least Huang (1982) have argued that
English and Mandarin wh-questions are more structurally similar than they
appear on the surface. Under these accounts, Mandarin wh-questions
involve a structural dependency between the thematic position and the
scope position, just as in English. The only difference between the languages lies in which piece of this structural dependency is signaled overtly.

Xiang and colleagues apply to Mandarin two paradigms that have been
used to diagnose memory access processes in sentence comprehension.
They argue that the processing of Mandarin wh-in-situ constructions is
sensitive to the length of the dependency between the thematic position
and the scope position of the wh-phrase, thus indirectly providing evidence
for the online construction of (invisible) wh-dependencies. To probe this
question experimentally, they assume that covert wh-movement involves
the retrieval of previously encountered syntactic structures, specifically,
a clause-edge position that marks the scope position of the wh-phrase.

By assuming that wh-dependency formation involves memory retrieval,
Xiang and colleagues (2014) justify their use of SAT, a paradigm where
there is a relatively clear consensus on how to analyze and interpret the
data. For example, it is standard practice to convert responses into d-prime
measures and to model d-primes as a function of time and three

parameters: asymptote, rate, and intercept. There are also generally accepted interpretations of these parameters. Distance manipulations that give rise to rate differences implicate a serial search and retrieval process. Distance manipulations that lead to asymptote differences implicate parallel access in content-addressable memory (CAM). See McElree (2006) for more extensive discussion. Xiang and colleagues find that the distance between scope and thematic positions in Mandarin is associated with asymptote differences, motivating the claim that invisible *wh*-dependencies are formed via a parallel access process. Similarly, the assumption of a memory retrieval process justifies the use of a memory interference logic in self-paced reading paradigms, leading to a similar conclusion (Xiang et al. 2015).

The conclusions from these studies on Mandarin *wh*-dependencies are open to question, as always. But the linking hypotheses are sufficiently explicit that it is clear what is at stake.

## 22.5 Conclusion: Theories All the Way Down

Standard linguistic theory is a cognitive theory at a rather high level of analysis, one that abstracts away from many important properties of neurocognitive systems. It typically makes a series of assumptions about the discreteness of representations, and it abstracts away from issues of the real-time order and timing of cognitive processes, or how linguistic representations are encoded in memory or in neural circuitry. This high level of analysis sets aside a lot of detail, and in so doing it allows for rapid progress and broad coverage. But this is not to say that there is a shortage of interesting theories and theoretical questions at finer-grained levels of analysis. In fact, many of these questions are amenable to experimental investigation and have led us to new insights.

If one is interested only in the theoretical questions that already came from traditional linguistic theory, then one could be forgiven for concluding that the advent of experimental approaches has brought limited theoretical insight. But once we allow that new empirical approaches reveal questions that we were not able to address or that we were not even aware of previously, then the outlook becomes a great deal more promising.

## References

Ackerman, L., Frazier, M., & Yoshida, M. (2018). Resumptive pronouns can ameliorate illicit island extractions. *Linguistic Inquiry*, 49, 847–859.

Alexopoulou, T. & Keller, F. (2007). Locality, cyclicity, and resumption: At the interface between the grammar and the human sentence processor. *Language*, 83, 110–160.

Arregui, A., Clifton, C. Jr., Frazier, L., & Moulton, K. (2006). Processing verb phrases with flawed antecedents: The recycling hypothesis. *Journal of Memory and Language*, 55, 232–246.

Avrutin, S. & Wexler, K. (1992). Development of Principle B in Russian: Coindexation at LF and coreference. *Language Acquisition*, 2, 259–306.

Baker, M. C. (2008). *The Syntax of Agreement and Concord*. Cambridge: Cambridge University Press.

Beltrama, A. & Xiang, M. (2016). Unacceptable but comprehensible: The facilitation effect of resumptive pronouns. *Glossa A Journal of General Linguistics,* 1(1), 29. DOI:10.5334/gjgl.24

Bock, K. (1989). Closed-class immanence in sentence production. *Cognition*, 31, 163–186.

Bock, K., Loebell, H., & Morey, R. (1992). From conceptual roles to structural relations: Bridging the syntactic cleft. *Psychological Review*, 99, 150–171.

Bock, K. & Miller, C. A. (1991). Broken agreement. *Cognitive Psychology*, 23, 45–93.

Boster, C. (1991). Children's failure to obey Principle B: Syntactic problem or lexical error? Unpublished MS, University of Connecticut, Storrs.

Branigan, H. P. & Pickering, M. J. (2017). An experimental approach to linguistic representation. *Behavioral and Brain Sciences*, 40, E282.

Brennan, J. (2016). Naturalistic sentence comprehension in the brain. *Language and Linguistics Compass*, 10, 299–313.

Brennan, J. R. & Pylkkänen, L. (2017). MEG evidence for incremental sentence composition in the anterior temporal lobe. *Cognitive Science*, 41, 1515–1531.

Brennan, J. R., Stabler, E. P., Van Wagenen, S. E., Luh, W., & Hale, J. (2016). Abstract linguistic structure correlates with temporal activity during naturalistic comprehension. *Brain and Language*, 157, 81–94.

Bresnan, J., Asudeh, A., Toivonen, I., & Wechsler, S. (2015). *Lexical Functional Syntax*, 2nd ed. Malden, MA, and Oxford: Wiley Blackwell.

Burnsky, J. & Staub, A. (2019). Completion tasks reveal misinterpretations of noncanonical sentences. Talk at Psycholinguistics in Iceland – Parsing and Prediction. Reykjavik, Iceland.

Chacón, D. A. (2015). Comparative psychosyntax. Doctoral dissertation, University of Maryland.

Chien, Y. C. & Wexler, K. (1990). Children's knowledge of locality conditions in binding as evidence for the modularity of syntax and pragmatics. *Language Acquisition*, 1, 225–295.

Chomsky, N. (1981). *Lectures on Government and Binding: The Pisa Lectures*. Dordrecht: Foris.

Chow, W.-Y., Kurenkov, I., Buffinton, J., Kraut, R., & Phillips, C. (2015). How predictions change over time: Evidence from an online cloze paradigm. Poster presented at the 28th annual CUNY Sentence Processing Conference. Los Angeles, California.

Chow, W.-Y., Lau, E., Wang, S., & Phillips, C. (2018). Wait a second! Delayed impact of argument roles on on-line verb prediction. *Language, Cognition and Neuroscience*, 33, 803–828.

Chow, W.-Y., Momma, S., Smith, C., Lau, E. F., & Phillips, C. (2016). Prediction as memory retrieval: Timing and mechanisms. *Language, Cognition and Neuroscience*, 31, 617–627.

Chow, W.-Y. & Phillips, C. (2013). No semantic illusion in the semantic P600 phenomenon: ERP evidence from Mandarin Chinese. *Brain Research*, 1506, 76–93.

Chow, W.-Y., Smith, C., Lau, E., & Phillips, C. (2016). A "bag-of-arguments" mechanism for initial verb predictions. *Language, Cognition and Neuroscience*, 31, 577–596.

Conroy, A., Takahashi, E., Lidz, J., & Phillips, C. (2009). Equal treatment for all antecedents: How children succeed with Principle B. *Linguistic Inquiry*, 40, 446–486.

Crain, S. & Thornton, R. (1998). *Investigations in Universal Grammar*. Cambridge, MA: MIT Press.

Dillon, B., Mishler, A., Sloggett, S., & Phillips, C. (2013). Contrasting interference profiles for agreement and anaphora: Experimental and modeling evidence. *Journal of Memory and Language*, 69, 85–103.

Eberhard, K. M., Cutting, J. C., & Bock, J. K. (2005). Making syntax of sense: Number agreement in sentence production. *Psychological Review*, 112, 531–559.

Elbourne, P. (2005). On the acquisition of Principle B. *Linguistic Inquiry*, 36, 333–365.

Ettinger, A., Linzen, T., & Marantz, A. (2014). The role of morphology in phoneme prediction: Evidence from MEG. *Brain and Language*, 129, 14–23.

Ferreira, F. (2005). Psycholinguistics, formal grammars, and cognitive science. *The Linguistic Review*, 22, 365–380.

Ferreira, F. & Swets, B. (2005). The production and comprehension of resumptive pronouns in relative clause "island" contexts. In A. Cutler, ed., *Twenty-First Century Psycholinguistics: Four Cornerstones*. Mahwah, NJ: Lawrence Erlbaum, pp. 263–278.

Fodor, J. A. (1983). *The Modularity of Mind*. Cambridge, MA: MIT Press.

Gagnepain, P., Henson, R. N., & Davis, M. H. (2012). Temporal predictive codes for spoken words in auditory cortex. *Current Biology*, 22(7), 615–621.

Gaston, P., Huang, N., & Phillips, C. (2017). The logic of syntactic priming and acceptability judgments. *Behavioral and Brain Sciences*, 40, e289.

Gaston, P., Lau, E., & Phillips, C. (2019). Syntactic category does not inhibit lexical competition. In *Proceedings of the 11th International Conference on the Mental Lexicon* (Mental Lexicon 2018). Edmonton: University of Alberta. DOI: 10.7939/r3-1t0d-5833

Gaston, P. & Marantz, A. (2018). The time course of contextual cohort effects in auditory processing of category-ambiguous words: MEG evidence for a single "clash" as noun or verb. *Language, Cognition and Neuroscience*, 33, 402–423.

Gibson, E. & Fedorenko, E. (2013). The need for quantitative methods in syntax and semantics research. *Language and Cognitive Processes*, 28, 88–124.

Grodzinsky, Y. & Reinhart, T. (1993). The innateness of binding and coreference. *Linguistic Inquiry*, 24, 69–101.

Grolla, E. (2005). Pronouns as elsewhere elements: Implications for language acquisition. Doctoral dissertation, University of Connecticut, Storrs.

Gwilliams, L. & Marantz, A. (2015). Non-linear processing of a linear speech stream: The influence of morphological structure on the recognition of spoken Arabic words. *Brain and Language*, 147, 1–13.

Hale, J., Dyer, C., Kuncoro, A., & Brennan, J. R. (2018). Finding syntax in human encephalography with beam search. *arXiv*, preprint arXiv:1806.04127

Hammerly, C., Staub, A., & Dillon, B. (2019). The grammaticality asymmetry in agreement attraction reflects response bias: Experimental and modeling evidence. *Cognitive Psychology*, 110, 70–104.

Han, C., Elouazizi, N., Galeano, C., Görgülü, E., Hedberg, N., Hinnell, J., Jeffrey, M., Kim, K., & Kirby, S. (2012). Processing strategies and resumptive pronouns in English. In N. Arnett & R. Bennett, eds., *Proceedings of the 30th West Coast Conference on Formal Linguistics*. Somerville, MA: Cascadilla Proceedings Project, pp. 153–161.

Heestand, D., Xiang, M., & Polinsky, M. (2011). Resumption still does not rescue islands. *Linguistic Inquiry*, 42, 138–152.

Hestvik, A. & Philip, W. (1999/2000). Binding and coreference in Norwegian child language. *Language Acquisition*, 8, 171–235.

Hoeks, J. C. J., Stowe, L. A., & Doedens, G. (2004). Seeing words in context: The interaction of lexical and sentence level information during reading. *Cognitive Brain Research*, 19, 59–73.

Huang, C. T. J. (1982). Logical relations in Chinese and the theory of grammar. Doctoral dissertation, Massachusetts Institute of Technology.

Jonides, J., Lewis, R. L., Nee, D. E., Lustig, C. A., Berman, M. G., & Moore, K. S. (2008). The mind and brain of short-term memory. *Annual Reviews in Psychology*, 59, 193–224.

Kaufman, D. (1988). Grammatical and cognitive interactions in the study of children's knowledge of binding theory and reference relations. Doctoral dissertation, Temple University, Philadelphia, PA.

Kazanina, N., Lau, E. F., Lieberman, M., Yoshida, M., & Phillips, C. (2007). The effect of syntactic constraints on the processing of backwards anaphora. *Journal of Memory and Language*, 56, 384–409.

Kim, A. & Osterhout, L. (2005). The independence of combinatory semantic processing: Evidence from event-related potentials. *Journal of Memory and Language*, 52, 205–225.

Kim, C., Kobele, G. M., Runner, J. T., & Hale, J. T. (2011). The acceptability cline in VP-ellipsis. *Syntax*, 14, 318–354.

Kimball, J. & Aissen, J. (1971). I think, you think, he think. *Linguistic Inquiry*, 2, 241–246.

Kolk, H. H. J., Chwilla, D. J., van Herten, M., & Oor, P. (2003). Structure and limited capacity in verbal working memory: A study with event-related potentials. *Brain and Language*, 85, 1–36.

Kuperberg, G. R., Caplan, D., Sitnikova, T., Eddy, M., & Holcomb, P. J. (2006). Neural correlates of processing syntactic, semantic, and thematic relationships in sentences. *Language and Cognitive Processes*, 21, 489–530.

Kuperberg, G. R., Sitnikova, T., Caplan, D., & Holcomb, P. J. (2003). Electrophysiological distinctions in processing conceptual relationships within simple sentences. *Cognitive Brain Research*, 217, 117–129.

Kutas, M. & Federmeier, K. D. (2000). Electrophysiology reveals semantic memory use in language comprehension. *Trends in Cognitive Sciences*, 4, 463–470.

Lau, E. F., Phillips, C., & Poeppel, D. (2008). A cortical network for semantics: (De)constructing the N400. *Nature Reviews Neuroscience*, 9, 920–933.

Levin, B. & Rappaport Hovav, M. (1995). *Unaccusativity: At the Syntax – Lexical Semantics Interface*. Cambridge, MA: MIT Press.

Lewis, R. L., Vasishth, S., & Van Dyke, J. (2006). Computational principles of working memory in sentence comprehension. *Trends in Cognitive Sciences*, 10, 447–454.

Lewis, S. & Phillips, C. (2015). Aligning grammatical theories and language processing models. *Journal of Psycholinguistic Research*, 44, 27–46.

Lombardi, L. & Sarma, J. (1989). Against the bound variable hypothesis of the acquisition of Condition B. Paper presented at the annual meeting of the Linguistic Society of America, Washington, DC.

Lucas, M. (1999). Context effects in lexical access: A meta-analysis. *Memory & Cognition*, 27(3), 385–398.

May, R. (1985). *Logical Form: Its Structure and Derivation*. Cambridge, MA: MIT Press.

Magnuson, J. S., Tanenhaus, M. K., & Aslin, R. N. (2008). Immediate effects of form-class constraints on spoken word recognition. *Cognition*, 108(3), 866–873.

Mantegna, F., Hintz, F., Ostarek, M., Alday, P. M., & Huettig, F. (2019). Distinguishing integration and prediction accounts of ERP N400 modulation in language processing through experimental design. *Neuropsychologia*, 134: 107199. DOI: 10.1016/j.neuropsychologia.2019.107199

McClelland, J. L. & Elman, J. L. (1986). The TRACE model of speech perception. *Cognitive Psychology*, 18(1), 1–86.

McDaniel, D., Cairns, H., & Hsu, J. (1990). Binding principles in the grammars of young children. *Language Acquisition*, 1, 121–139.

McElree, B. (2006). Accessing recent events. *Psychology of Learning and Motivation*, 46, 155–200.

Momma, S., Kraut, R., Slevc, L. R., & Phillips, C. (2017). Timing of syntactic and lexical priming reveals structure building mechanisms in production. Talk at the 30th annual CUNY Conference on Human Sentence Processing. Cambridge, MA.

Momma, S., Luo, Y., Sakai, H., Lau, E., & Phillips, C. (2016). Lexical predictions and the structure of semantic memory: EEG evidence from case changes. Talk at the 29th annual CUNY Conference on Human Sentence Processing. Gainesville, FL.

Momma, S., Slevc, L. R., & Phillips, C. (2018). Unaccusativity in sentence production. *Linguistic Inquiry*, 49, 181–194.

Muller, H., de Dios Flores, I., & Phillips, C. (2019). Not (just) any licensors cause negative polarity illusions. Talk at Psycholinguistics in Iceland – Parsing and Prediction. Reykjavik, Iceland.

Nelson, M. J., El Karoui, I., Giber, K., Yang, X., Cohen, L., Koopman, H., Cash, S. S., Naccache, L., Hale, J. T., Pallier, C., & Dehaene, S. (2017). Neurophysiological dynamics of phrase-structure building during sentence processing. *Proceedings of the National Academy of Sciences*, 114, E3669-E3678.

Paczynski, M. & Kuperberg, G. R. (2011). Electrophysiological evidence for the use of the animacy hierarchy, but not thematic role assignment, during verb argument processing. *Language and Cognitive Processes*, 26(9), 1402–1456.

Parker, D. & Phillips, C. (2016). Negative polarity illusions and the format of hierarchical encodings in memory. *Cognition*, 157, 321–339.

Pearlmutter, N. K., Garnsey, S. M., & Bock, J. K. (1999). Agreement processes in sentence comprehension. *Journal of Memory and Language*, 41, 427–456.

Philip, W. & Coopmans, P. (1996). The double Dutch delay of Principle B effect. In A. Stringfellow, D. Cahana-Amitay, E. Hughes, & A. Zukowski, eds., *Proceedings of the 20th Annual Boston University Conference on Language Development*. Somerville, MA: Cascadilla Press, pp. 576–587.

Phillips, C. (2006). The real-time status of island phenomena. *Language*, 82, 795–803.

Phillips, C. (2010). Should we impeach armchair linguists? In S. Iwasaki, H. Hoji, P. Clancy, & S.-O. Sohn (eds.), *Japanese–Korean Linguistics 17*. Stanford, CA: CSLI Publications, pp. 49–64.

Phillips, C. & Ehrenhofer, L. (2015). The role of language processing in language acquisition. *Linguistic Approaches to Bilingualism*, 5, 409–453.

Phillips, C. & Parker, D. (2014). The psycholinguistics of ellipsis. *Lingua*, 151, 78–95.

Phillips, C. & Wagers, M. (2007). Relating structure and time in linguistics and psycholinguistics. In G. Gaskell, ed., *The Oxford Handbook of Psycholinguistics*. Oxford: Oxford University Press, pp. 739–756.

Phillips, C., Wagers, M. W., & Lau, E. F. (2011). Grammatical illusions and selective fallibility in real-time language comprehension. *Experiments at the Interfaces*, 37, 147–180.

Reinhart, T. (1983). Coreference and bound anaphora: A restatement of the anaphora questions. *Linguistics and Philosophy*, 6, 47–88.

Ross, J. R. (1967). Constraints on variables in syntax. Doctoral dissertation, Massachusetts Institute of Technology.

Sprouse, J. & Almeida, D. (2012). Assessing the reliability of textbook data in syntax: Adger's *Core Syntax*. *Journal of Linguistics*, 48, 609–652.

Sprouse, J., Schütze, C. T., & Almeida, D. (2013). A comparison of informal and formal acceptability judgments using a random sample from *Linguistic Inquiry* 2001–2010. *Lingua*, 134, 219–248.

Steedman, M. (2000). *The Syntactic Process*. Cambridge, MA: MIT Press.

Stowe, L. A. (1986). Evidence for on-line gap location. *Language and Cognitive Processes*, 1, 227–245.

Strand, J. F., Brown, V. A., Brown, H. E., & Berg, J. J. (2018). Keep listening: Grammatical context reduces but does not eliminate activation of unexpected words. *Journal of Experimental Psychology: Learning, Memory, and Cognition*, 44, 962–973.

Strauss, T. J., Harris, H. D., & Magnuson, J. S. (2007). jTRACE: A reimplementation and extension of the TRACE model of speech perception and spoken word recognition. *Behavior Research Methods*, 39, 19–30.

Stroud, C. (2008). Structural and semantic selectivity in the electrophysiology of sentence comprehension. Doctoral dissertation, University of Maryland.

Stroud, C. & Phillips, C. (2012). Examining the evidence for an independent semantic analyzer: An ERP study in Spanish. *Brain and Language*, 120, 107–126.

Sturt, P. (2003). The time course of the application of binding constraints in reference resolution. *Journal of Memory and Language*, 48, 542–562.

Tanenhaus, M. K., Leiman, J. M., & Seidenberg, M. S. (1979). Evidence for multiple stages in the processing of ambiguous words in syntactic contexts. *Journal of Verbal Learning and Verbal Behavior*, 18, 427–440.

Thornton, R. & Wexler, K. (1999). *Principle B, VP Ellipsis, and Interpretation in Child Grammar*. Cambridge, MA: MIT Press.

Traxler, M. J., Tooley, K. M., & Pickering, M. J. (2014). Syntactic priming during sentence comprehension: Evidence for the lexical boost. *Journal of Experimental Psychology: Learning, Memory, and Cognition*, 40, 905–918.

Tyler, L. K. (1984). The structure of the initial cohort: Evidence from gating. *Perception and Psychophysics*, 36, 417–427.

Van Berkum, J. J. A., Brown, C., Zwitserlood, P., Kooijman, V., & Hagoort, P. (2005). Anticipating upcoming words in discourse: Evidence from ERPs and reading times. *Journal of Experimental Psychology: Learning, Memory and Cognition*, 31, 443–467.

Van Herten, M., Chwilla, D. J., & Kolk, H. H. J. (2006). When heuristics clash with parsing routines: ERP evidence for conflict monitoring in sentence perception. *Journal of Cognitive Neuroscience*, 18, 1181–1197.

Vasishth, S., Brüssow, S., Lewis, R. L, & Drenhaus, H. (2008). Processing polarity: How the ungrammatical intrudes on the grammatical. *Cognitive Science*, 32, 685–712.

Wagers, M., Lau, E. F., & Phillips, C. (2009). Agreement attraction in comprehension: representations and processes. *Journal of Memory and Language*, 61, 206–237.

Wellwood, A., Pancheva, R., Hacquard, V., & Phillips, C. (2018). The anatomy of a comparative illusion. *Journal of Semantics*, 35, 543–583.

Xiang, M., Dillon, B., Wagers, M., Liu, F., & Guo, T. (2014). Processing covert dependencies: An SAT study on Mandarin *wh*-in-situ questions. *Journal of East Asian Linguistics*, 23, 207–232.

Xiang, M., Wang, S., & Cui, Y. (2015). Constructing covert dependencies: The case of Mandarin *wh*-in-situ dependency. *Journal of Memory and Language*, 84, 139–166.

Ye, Z. & Zhou, X. (2008). Involvement of cognitive control in sentence comprehension: evidence from ERPs. *Brain Research*, 1203, 103–115.

Zukowski, A. & Larsen, J. (2004). The production of sentences that we fill their gaps. Poster presented at the 17th annual CUNY Sentence Processing Conference, University of Maryland.

# 23

# Eye-Tracking and Self-Paced Reading

Claudia Felser

## 23.1 Introduction

Unlike end-of-sentence judgment tasks, self-paced reading and eye-tracking can provide windows into syntactic computation as it occurs. Even though formal linguistics does not traditionally view the computation of syntactic representations as reflecting processes that occur over time, using experimental methods that allow us to chart the time course of sentence processing can provide valuable insights into the nature of syntactic derivations and representations.

For one thing, data from real-time reading or listening – in the absence of any metalinguistic task – can provide more implicit measures of grammatical sensitivity compared to metalinguistic judgment tasks. Secondly, methods that tap into real-time processing can help reveal the sources of unacceptability, which cannot always be reliably determined from judgment data. Measuring processing difficulty at individual words or phrases allows us to identify the precise point during reading or listening at which a grammatical anomaly is detected. Observing how sentence representations are built in real time moreover allows us to test sentence complexity metrics (e.g. Gibson 2000) and to evaluate theoretical claims to the effect that grammatical constraints might reflect, or were shaped by, processing constraints (Berwick & Weinberg 1984; Kluender & Kutas 1993; Hawkins 2004; Kluender 2004, among many others). Carefully designed processing experiments can also provide evidence for the mental reality of grammatical distinctions, operations, and constraints by examining their processing reflexes (e.g. Traxler & Pickering 1996; Sturt 2003; Gibson & Warren 2004; Phillips 2006; Kazanina et al. 2007; Tutunjian & Boland 2008). Last but not least, data from online reading or listening tasks can inform linguistic theory-building by helping ensure that models of grammar are psychologically plausible.

In real-time language production and comprehension, grammatical representations are assembled incrementally in left-to-right order, which seems to be at odds with formal linguistic models according to which derivations are built from right to left in a strictly bottom-up fashion. In the generative-transformational tradition, successive-cyclic movement, for example, is assumed to proceed from right to left, and from bottom to top, in a series of local steps (Chomsky 1973), or from phase to phase (Chomsky 2000). However, the presumed atemporal nature of syntactic derivations makes it possible for "[d]erivations that move elements from one phase to the next [to] be readily translated from a bottom-to-top order into other orders," as Phillips and Lewis (2013: 28) note. In fact, viewing grammatical phenomena and constraints from the perspective of left-to-right processing can offer novel insights into their nature (compare e.g. Shan & Barker 2006; Chesi 2007; Zwart 2009; Hofmeister & Sag 2010; Phillips & Lewis 2013).

Assuming that the parser is guided by the constraints of the mental grammar (see Lewis & Phillips (2015) for arguments that the two may in fact be one and the same system), we might expect real-time processing data to generally align with offline (e.g. judgment) data. Although parsing is highly sensitive to grammatical constraints and to configurational information such as c-command relations (e.g. Cunnings, Patterson, & Felser 2015; Kush, Lidz, & Phillips 2015), cases of misalignment between online and offline data are also well documented. Grammatical violations may go unnoticed during real-time processing, notably in sentences that contain so-called "grammatical illusions" (Phillips, Wagers, & Lau 2011), or a given constraint may be violated during processing even though it is respected in participants' offline judgments (e.g. Felser & Cunnings 2012; Boxell & Felser 2017; Drummer & Felser 2018). As Lewis and Phillips (2015) point out, cases of misalignment can usually be explained by the way grammatical constraints are implemented locally by the parser during the time course of processing, or can be attributed to memory retrieval errors or computational resource limitations.

In the following, I will focus on experimental psycholinguistic techniques that allow us to chart comprehenders' reading or listening profiles over time, discussing how linguists may benefit from including these techniques in their methodological repertoire. I first take a look at self-paced reading, a technique that is inexpensive and much easier to use than eye-tracking, and which can also be used for collecting data via the World Wide Web. I then consider eye-movement monitoring during reading, followed by a brief discussion of the eye-tracking-during-listening technique.

## 23.2  Self-Paced Reading

### 23.2.1  Method Overview
Self-paced reading (SPR) is an experimental psycholinguistic technique that involves measuring word-by-word (or phrase-by-phrase) reading

times, with participants being allowed to move from one sentence segment to the next at their own pace (Just, Carpenter, & Woolley 1982). The
rationale underlying the SPR technique is known as the "eye–mind
assumption" (Just & Carpenter 1980), the idea that reading time reflects
processing time. Elevated reading times at a given sentence segment
(relative to a control condition) are thought to signal processing difficulty
at or around this sentence region. Processing difficulty may be caused, for
example, by the detection of a grammatical or semantic anomaly, or by an
unexpected sentence continuation such as the appearance of the disambiguating word *sank* in classical "garden-path" (GP) sentences such as *The
log floated down the river sank.*

In SPR tasks, stimulus sentences are displayed on a computer monitor
either cumulatively, with each subsequent word added to the previous
ones until the entire sentence is visible, or non-cumulatively. Here the
previous word disappears every time the participant brings up a new one
via a button press, so that only one word or phrase is visible at any time.
Sentence segments may either be displayed at the center of the screen or
linearly. The most commonly used variant of the SPR technique involves
a linear word-by-word display, where the number of words in a sentence is
indicated visually (e.g. by using dashes separated by spaces) but only one
word is visible at a time, as illustrated in example (1). This variant is also
known as the "moving-window procedure."

(1)    The – – – – – – .
          – cat – – – – – .
          – – fell – – – .
          – – – off – – .
          – – – – the – .
          – – – – – tree .

Usually participants are given a secondary task such as responding to an
end-of-sentence comprehension question, whose main purpose is to help
ensure that the stimulus items are attended to properly. Comprehension
accuracy scores may also be analyzed as an additional dependent variable.
End-of-sentence acceptability judgments are also sometimes used, which
then turns the SPR task into a metalinguistic one (e.g. Blackwell, Bates, &
Fisher 1996). Another SPR judgment variant is the "stop-making-sense"
task (Boland, Tanenhaus, & Garnsey 1990), where participants are
instructed to terminate the presentation of a stimulus sentence as soon
as they think they have detected an anomaly. In all variants of the SPR task,
the computer records the times between individual button-presses, thus
creating a segment-by-segment reading-time profile for each type of stimulus sentence or experimental condition.

SPR is a low-cost, easy-to-use technique that taps into real-time syntactic
computation. SPR is able to provide implicit measures of grammatical
sensitivity which can complement, or serve as an alternative to, data

from metalinguistic judgments; or metalinguistic judgment tasks can be augmented by using self-paced stimulus presentation. SPR experiments can be run on standard desktop or laptop computers, which makes this a suitable method for collecting data outside the laboratory or in the field. SPR data can also be collected via the World Wide Web (see e.g. Keller et al. 2009; Enochson & Culbertson 2015; Kush, Lidz, & Phillips 2017).

The technique's main drawback is the fact that due to the need for the researcher to predetermine how the stimulus sentences are divided into presentation segments, participants are forced to read in a potentially unnatural way. Non-cumulative stimulus presentation does not allow for the rereading of previous segments, which may put an unusually heavy burden on participants' working memory. The SPR technique also requires participants to be fluent readers. This makes the technique unsuitable for some populations, including young children, speakers of languages that lack a writing system, or bilinguals who are non-literate in the language under investigation. For these populations a less widely known variant of the SPR technique, the self-paced listening technique, could possibly be used instead (e.g. Booth, MacWhinney, & Harasaki 2000; Felser, Marinis, & Clahsen 2003).

### 23.2.2   SPR Studies of Grammatical Phenomena

The SPR technique has been used to investigate a wide range of grammatical phenomena, and processing difficulty as measured by an SPR task often aligns closely with acceptability judgments (Phillips 2006; Hofmeister & Sag 2010; but cf. e.g. Parker & Phillips 2016). Unlike judgment data, data from SPR tasks can also be used to identify the point at which an anomaly is detected, uncover the mechanisms that give rise to grammatical illusions, trace a displaced constituent's derivational history, or observe reflexes of covert properties of grammatical representations. Below I will provide a selective review of findings from SPR tasks to illustrate the method's potential usefulness for experimental syntacticians.

### 23.2.2.1   Detecting Grammatical Anomalies

An SPR incremental judgment task carried out by Blackwell et al. (1996: exp. 2) revealed that grammatical ill-formedness is not necessarily recognized at a specific "decision point" during the sentence, but that judgment formation may be protracted across a "decision region" instead. Blackwell et al.'s stimulus materials included a variety of ungrammatical sentences which contained either agreement (2a), omission (2b), or transposition errors (2c), as well as grammatical controls.

(2)     a. *The writer were holding a very big party.
        b. *Mrs. Brown working quietly in the church kitchen.
        c. *Miss Hope sending was several green dresses that Lisa had ordered.

While agreement violations as in (2a) were detected immediately, both omission and transposition errors tended to trigger uncertainty, with participants sometimes not making up their minds regarding a sentence's grammaticality until they reached the end of the sentence. Blackwell et al. (1996) concluded that the point at which a judgment is made is not necessarily identical to the point at which a violation becomes noticeable, and that some types of violation are easier to identify and more quickly identified than others.

Certain types of grammatical anomaly may even remain undetected in processing tasks, which can be informative about how grammatical dependencies are computed in real time. The disruption of subject–verb agreement in the presence of a number-mismatching non-subject in sentences such as *The key to the cabinets were rusty* is a well-known example of a grammatical illusion (Bock & Miller 1991). Agreement attraction has also been observed in comprehension tasks (e.g. Nicol, Forster, & Veres 1997; Pearlmutter, Garnsey, & Bock 1999; Wagers, Lau, & Phillips 2009). Wagers et al., for example, report that not only nouns within prepositional modifiers (such as *cells* in (3a)) that intervene between the subject head and the verb give rise to attraction effects in an SPR task, but also non-intervening heads of relative clauses (RCs) such as the noun *musician* in (3b).

(3)  a. The key to the cells unsurprisingly {was/*were} rusty from many years of disuse.
  b. The musicians who the reviewer {praises/*praise} so highly will probably win a Grammy.

Attraction effects were reflected in the lack of (un)grammaticality effects around the manipulated verb region in sentences such as (3a, b), that is, in the absence of the slowdown in reading times for ungrammatical relative to grammatical sentences that is typically observed for grammatical/ungrammatical sentence pairs that do not contain an attractor. Wagers et al. (2009) argue that together with their finding that attraction effects were limited to ungrammatical sentences, the fact that even RC heads can trigger agreement attraction argues against accounts of attraction in terms of faulty representations of the subject noun phrase ("feature percolation"; see e.g. Nicol et al. 1997). The authors note that the structural distance between the RC head and the embedded verb should have made feature percolation unlikely, and argue instead for an account of agreement attraction in terms of the erroneous retrieval of a non-subject from memory in the face of a subject–verb mismatch (see also Tanner, Nicol, & Brehm (2014) for supporting evidence from ERPs).

Agreement attraction effects have also been observed in both speeded (e.g. Wagers et al. 2009: exp. 7) and offline acceptability judgment tasks (Dillon et al. 2017), which indicates that whichever processing mechanisms give rise to grammatical illusions of this type can also affect participants' metalinguistic judgment ability.

The SPR technique can also measure readers' reaction to perceived local anomalies in globally grammatical sentences. Psycholinguists use locally ambiguous GP sentences such as *The log floated down the river sank* primarily to gauge which of two possible structural analyses is initially preferred at some choice point, in order to uncover the linguistic or processing constraints that favor one analysis over the other. Knowing what kind of structures reliably elicit GP effects (that is, longer reading times around the word or phrase that disambiguates the sentence toward the dispreferred analysis) can also help us examine other properties of syntactic representations that are not open to direct observation.

Czypionka, Dörre, and Bayer (2018), for example, carried out a set of SPR experiments using GP sentences to examine the phenomenon of inverse case attraction in German. Case attraction involves the case feature of an RC head noun overwriting the relative pronoun's case feature (e.g. Pittner 1995). The reverse process – a relative pronoun's case feature being transferred to the RC head noun – has been claimed to be no longer licensed in Modern Standard German. Czypionka et al. (2018) used stimulus sentences that contained either canonically (SO, as in (4)) or non-canonically (OS, as in (5)) ordered complement clauses whose subject was modified by a relative clause.

(4)      SO-DAT: subject–object, dative
         Ich     glaube,  dass     Klaus,       dem
         I       believe  that     Klaus.(NOM)  who.DAT
         die Leute             gerne zuhören,   Ida und Paul
         the people.(NOM)      gladly listen.to.pl [Ida and Paul].(DAT)
         gefolgt   ist,    als     er    spazieren   war.
         followed  AUX.SG  when    he    walking     was
         'I believe that Klaus – who people like to listen to – followed Ida and Paul when he went for a walk.'

(5)      OS-DAT: object–subject, dative
         Ich              glaube,      dass Klaus,        dem
         I                believe      that Klaus.(DAT)   who.DAT
         die Leute            gerne        zuhören,    Ida und Paul
         the people.(NOM)     gladly       listen.to.PL [Ida and Paul].(DAT)

         gefolgt   sind,   als     sie   spazieren   waren.
         followed  AUX.PL  when    they  walking     were.
         'I believe that Ida and Paul followed Klaus – who people like to listen to – when they went for a walk.'

                                            (Czypionka et al. 2018: 152)

The RC head noun was a proper name (*Klaus* in the examples above) which itself was always case-ambiguous, and the RC pronoun following it was either marked for dative (as in examples (4) and (5) above) or for accusative case. Whether the RC head noun carries nominative or non-nominative case – and therefore, its grammatical function – is only revealed later on by number marking on the clause-final auxiliary (singular *ist* in (4) vs. plural *sind* in (5)). Given the RC head noun's temporary ambiguity and the fact that SO word order is strongly preferred over OS order in Modern Standard German, a strong GP effect would normally be expected for sentences with OS order, due to readers' initially assuming that *Klaus* is the RC subject and thus carries nominative case.

Czypionka et al. (2018) found that the expected GP effects, reflected in longer reading times after the disambiguating auxiliary was processed in OS compared to SO sentences, were attenuated if the RC pronoun was dative-marked but not if it was accusative marked. The authors interpret this ameliorated GP effect as evidence for inverse case attraction, with the RC pronoun's dative feature reducing the likelihood of the RC head noun in OS sentences being mistaken for a nominative noun phrase (NP) initially. The observed dative–accusative asymmetry furthermore supports the theoretical distinction between structural and lexical/inherent case, with only inherent case features able to transfer to the preceding RC head noun. Note that the observed case attraction effect was only seen in the SPR data but was not visible in the data from a complementary offline judgment task.

### 23.2.2.2 Tracing Derivational Steps
The SPR technique can provide evidence for the mental reality of covert ingredients of linguistic representations such as intermediate traces (or copies) of fronted elements (Gibson & Warren 2004; Lee 2004). Gibson and Warren (2004), for example, measured English speakers' word-by-word reading times as they read through *wh*-movement sentences such as (6a, b).

(6)    a. The manager who$_i$ the consultant claimed [$_{CP}$ __ $_{i'}$ that the new proposal had pleased __ $_i$] will hire five workers tomorrow.
        b. The manager who$_i$ the consultant's claim [$_{PP}$ about the new proposal] had pleased __ $_i$ will hire five workers tomorrow.

Only (6a), but not (6b), allows for *wh*-movement to take place successive-cyclically by providing an intermediate (Spec,CP) position as a non-terminal "landing site." Sentence processing research has shown that when encountering a fronted constituent or "filler" (such as the *wh*-pronoun *who* in (6)), comprehenders start actively searching for associated "gaps," that is, for structural positions that could possibly host a representation of the filler (Clifton & Frazier 1989; Omaki et al. 2015, among others). If processing *wh*-movement sentences such as (6a, b) involves retracing the derivational steps that resulted in a *wh*-constituent appearing at the left clausal periphery, then we might expect *wh*-gaps to be included in the mental sentence representations built during left-to-right comprehension. From a processing perspective, intermediate *wh*-gaps as in (6a) should help reduce the computational burden associated with keeping a filler active in working memory until a suitable lexical licenser (subcategorizer) can be identified. Thus, if comprehenders mentally reconstruct or reactivate the filler *who*, which refers to *the manager*, at the intermediate gap site in (6a) – a possibility that is not available in (6b) – then they should find it easier to integrate the filler with its subcategorizer (the verb *please*) further downstream in (6a) than in (6b). Gibson and Warren (2004) found indirect evidence that readers did indeed make use of this intermediate position when processing sentences like (6a), in the shape of shorter reading times at the subcategorizing verb region (*had pleased*) for (6a) compared to (6b).

Evidence for structural gaps also comes from so-called "filled-gap" effects (Stowe 1986). Using a filled-gap paradigm, Lee (2004) found evidence for the active postulation of subject gaps in sentences such as (7a). In the filled-gap paradigm, a potential gap position (indicated through parentheses in (7a)) turns out to be occupied by another constituent. An increase in reading times when encountering a filled gap, relative to a control condition, reveals that gap creation was initially attempted. Note that from a left-to-right processing perspective, the first grammatically possible gap to link the relative pronoun *which* to in (7a) is the RC's subject position.

(7)  a.  That is the school which$_i$, during the summer holiday, (__ $_i$) Julie appointed an architect to design a new building for __ $_i$ .
     b.  That is the school [for which]$_i$, during the summer holiday, Julie appointed an architect to design a new building __ $_i$ .

Comparing sentences that contained the ambiguous *wh*-pronoun *which* to sentences that contained an unambiguous prepositional *wh*-phrase such as *for which* in (7b), Lee reports that finding the subject position already occupied by a proper name (e.g. *Julie*) triggered elevated reading times at the name for (7a) in comparison to (7b). This suggests that readers initially tried to construe *which* in (7a) as a subject, an analysis that needed to be revised when the real subject *Julie* was encountered.

The SPR technique has also been used to examine intervention effects triggered by object gaps (Franck, Colonna, & Rizzi 2015) and to investigate possible processing reflexes of quantifier raising during the comprehension of antecedent-contained deletion structures (Hackl, Koster-Hale, &

Varvoutis 2012; but cf. Gibson et al. (2015) and Gibson, Piantadosi, & Levy (2017) for critical discussion of the findings reported). Several SPR studies have examined the processing of scope ambiguities (e.g. Anderson 2004; Bott & Schlotterbeck 2015; Dwivedi 2013; Brasoveanu & Dotlačil 2015; Lee & O'Grady 2016). Their results indicate that computing inverse scope readings requires more processing resources than computing surface scope readings. This has been argued to support theoretical claims to the effect that computing inverse scope readings involves additional derivational steps (Anderson 2004; but cf. Brasoveanu & Dotlačil 2015).

## 23.3   Eye-Movement Monitoring During Reading

### 23.3.1   Method Overview

Eye-movement monitoring during reading (henceforth, EMM) is similar to SPR in that successive reading times are recorded for individual words or other sentence regions of interest, and in that both techniques rely on the eye–mind assumption. The main differences to SPR concern the way the stimuli are presented and the nature and number of reading-time measures that can be obtained. See Clifton and Staub (2011) and Clifton, Staub, and Rayner (2007) for more extensive discussion of how the EMM method can be applied to the study of language processing.

Regarding stimulus presentation, sentences (or short text paragraphs) are normally presented in their entirety on a single screen, and participants are instructed to read through them as they normally would at their own pace. As participants are not forced to read in a strictly serial manner, they may occasionally skip some words or return to earlier sentence regions for rereading. As with SPR, participants usually have to answer end-of-trial comprehension questions as a secondary task.

Miniature infrared cameras record participants' eye movements as they read through the stimulus items. These cameras capture large amounts of data, which the eye-tracking software translates into several distinct eye-movement measures, resulting in much more detailed time-course information compared to SPR. Sensitivity to experimental manipulations in the stimulus items may be reflected, for example, in the duration of readers' initial fixations on a critical word or sentence region, or it may only become evident during their rereading of this region. A distinction is often made between "early" processing measures such as first fixation durations or first-pass reading times, and "late" measures such as rereading times, but researchers should be aware of some caveats regarding the functional interpretation of eye-movement data (see e.g. Vasishth, von der Malsburg, & Engelmann 2013). Total reading time for a given sentence region of interest is a cumulative eye-movement measure which sums the durations of both initial and all subsequent fixations on that region. Eye movements between individual fixations from one sentence region to another are called saccades. The likelihood of a given word to trigger regressive saccades may be another indicator of processing difficulty, which is why proportions of regressions in or out of a given interest region are also often analyzed. A less frequently used physiological measure is the dilation of readers' pupils, which is also thought to index processing difficulty (Demberg & Sayeed 2016).

EMM is superior to SPR in terms of its time-course sensitivity and the level of detail of the reading profiles that it can provide. One disadvantage of eye-tracking (in comparison to both SPR and offline tasks) is the fact that it is rather expensive. Using eye-tracking equipment correctly also requires some training. Even though portable eye-tracking systems are available, these tend to be rather heavy and awkward to move around, so that most researchers prefer to collect eye-tracking data in a dedicated laboratory room. Besides the obvious requirement that participants need to be able to read, testing may sometimes be difficult or impossible if a participant wears glasses or contact lenses. Analyzing eye-tracking data is more complicated than analyzing SPR data, due mainly to the availability of multiple eye-movement measures, as well as the fact that these measures are less independent from one other than other behavioral measures (von der Malsburg & Angele 2016).

### 23.3.2   EMM Studies of Syntactic Phenomena

Like SPR, the EMM technique has proven useful for investigating a variety of grammatical phenomena. Given that eye-tracking is normally used to examine comprehension under fairly naturalistic input conditions, presenting globally ungrammatical sentences has traditionally been avoided (but cf. e.g. Braze et al. 2002). The method has been used successfully to study grammatical illusions, however (e.g. Pearlmutter et al. 1999). Due to its high time-course sensitivity EMM has also often been used to pinpoint the exact point during processing at which structure-sensitive constraints are applied, and to examine the conditions under which these can (temporarily) be violated. Whilst the more user-friendly SPR method may be sufficient for many purposes, using EMM yields a more fine-grained record of structure-building or dependency formation than the former method. Eye-tracking may, for example, reveal delays in the application of structure-sensitive constraints that are missed in corresponding SPR studies (e.g. Patterson & Felser 2019).

### 23.3.2.1   Real-time Computation of Binding and Coreference

Both SPR and EMM have frequently been used to investigate anaphor resolution, including the application of binding constraints (Chomsky 1981) during real-time processing (see Sturt (2013) for review and discussion, as well as Chapter 11 for an overview of experimental studies of anaphora). While many of these studies have examined anaphor resolution from the perspective of psycholinguistic models of memory search and retrieval (see Jäger, Engelmann, & Vasishth (2017) for a review), other studies have used the EMM method to put specific theoretical linguistic claims and hypotheses to the test. One such hypothesis is the "binding preference hypothesis" (BPH), which claims that binding relationships are easier to compute than coreference relationships, leading to binding being preferred over coreference assignment if both options are available (Reinhart 1983). The BPH forms part of the Primitives of Binding (POB) model (Reuland 2001, 2011), which combines a modular view of the language system with the assumption of an economy hierarchy guiding the formation of referential dependencies. The BPH is based on the assumption that establishing binding relationships can be accomplished at the semantic level of representation whereas establishing coreference relationships additionally requires accessing discourse-level representations, thus making coreference interpretations more laborious to compute. This theoretical claim has more recently been recast as a processing hypothesis, supported by the results from several EMM studies (Koornneef 2008, 2010; Koornneef et al. 2011).

To test the BPH in a more direct way than was done in previous studies, Cunnings, Patterson, and Felser (2014) carried out an EMM study whose materials included sentences such as (8) which offered two potential antecedents for an ambiguous pronoun: a quantified NP (*every soldier*) that c-commanded the pronoun and a proper name (*James* or *Helen*) that did not.

(8)     The squadron paraded through town. Every soldier who knew that {James/Helen} was watching was convinced that {he/she} should wave as the parade passed.

Assuming that binding requires the binder to c-command the bindee, the non c-commanding named antecedent in (8) can only be linked to the embedded subject pronoun *(s)he* via discourse-based coreference assignment. The quantified NP *every soldier*, on the other hand, can only be linked to the pronoun via binding.

As is very common in reading-time studies examining anaphor resolution, Cunnings et al. used a gender-mismatch paradigm for diagnosing referential dependency formation (compare e.g. Sturt 2003). A real or perceived gender mismatch between an anaphor and a potential antecedent NP (e.g. *James . . . he* vs. *James . . . she*) is expected to give rise to elevated reading times at the anaphor region if readers try to establish a dependency between the anaphor and the NP.

For sentences such as (8), the BPH predicts that the subject pronoun *(s)he* should preferentially be linked to the binding antecedent *every soldier*, reflected in a stereotypical gender-mismatch effect for feminine pronouns. This prediction was not confirmed, however. Instead, the eye-movement data from Cunnings et al.'s first experiment revealed that participants tried to link the pronoun to the coreference antecedent *James* immediately after reading the pronoun and did not consider the binding antecedent at all during processing. This suggests that discourse-based coreference assignment is not necessarily harder than establishing a binding relationship, and that coreference relationships are not only construed as a "last resort" where binding fails (cf. Reinhart 1983). A second EMM experiment revealed that binding antecedents were considered only if they appeared linearly closer to the pronoun than a competing coreference antecedent. Together, these findings illustrate that, when reinterpreting theoretical linguistic hypotheses as processing hypotheses, relevant processing factors and mechanisms also need to be taken into account. In Cunnings et al.'s (2014) study, effects of antecedent proximity were also observed in a complementary offline task.

Data from reading-time studies can also be informative about how constraints on reference resolution interact with other syntactic operations. Felser and Drummer (2017) carried out an EMM study to examine native and non-native readers' sensitivity to crossover configurations (Postal 1971) in German. Their materials included sentences such as those in (9) which contained a pronoun in either a strong (9a) or a weak crossover (9b) configuration.

(9) a. Von      welchem  Spieler  aus      Frankreich  er   noch  lernen
       from     which    player   from     France      he   still learn
       konnte,  das      sah      Fabian   schnell.
       could    this     saw      F.       quickly
       'From which player from France he could still learn Fabian saw quickly.'

   b. Von      welchem Spieler aus      Frankreich  sein  Teamkollege    noch lernen
      from     which   player  from     France      his   team.colleague still learn
      konnte, das      sah     Fabian schnell.
      could   this     saw     F.     quickly
      'From which player from France his team colleague could still learn Fabian saw quickly.'

In strong crossover (SCO) configurations as in (9a), *wh*-movement of *von welchem Spieler* ('from which player') has crossed the subject pronoun *er* ('he'), a configuration in which coreference between *Spieler* ('player') and *er* ('he') should be ruled out by Condition C (but cf. e.g. Shan & Barker (2006) for an alternative proposal). On the assumption that (a portion of) the fronted *wh*-phase is reconstructed at LF (e.g. Fox 1999), as indicated in (10) below, the pronoun c-commands the material that is reconstructed at the *wh*-movement gap, including the NP headed by *Spieler*. Since Condition C demands that referring expressions remain unbound, a reading according to which the pronoun and the NP headed by *Spieler* refer to the same individual should be ruled out for sentences such as (9a).

(10)      [~~von welchem Spieler aus Frankreich~~] er noch [von welchem
          Spieler aus Frankreich] lernen konnte, das sah Fabian schnell.

In corresponding weak crossover (WCO) configurations as in (9b),
the pronoun *sein* 'his' functions as a prenominal possessive modifier
and thus does not c-command the *wh*-gap, so that Condition C cannot
be invoked as a possible explanation for WCO effects. Acceptability
ratings often show that WCO violations are perceived as less severe
than SCO violations, and WCO effects have been claimed to be altogether absent in some languages (Bresnan 1998). Felser and Drummer
(2017) found that both native and non-native readers respect the SCO
but not the WCO constraint during processing. Their reading-time data
showed that participants tried to link the pronoun to *Spieler* ('player')
only in WCO sentences (9b) but not in corresponding SCO sentences
(9a). A parallel difference was seen in the data from a complementary
offline task, with participants allowing a coreference interpretation
significantly more often for WCO than for SCO sentences. Together,
these results not only reveal clear differences between the strength of
SCO and WCO constraints in German, but also show that WCO "violations" already occur during the earliest measurable processing stages.
Kush, Lidz, and Phillips (2017) report similar findings for English
native speakers using the SPR method.

### 23.3.2.2   The Real-time Status of Island Constraints

A number of reading-time studies have investigated whether online sentence processing is sensitive to restrictions on unbounded movement
collectively known as "island constraints" (Ross 1967; see Chapter 9 for
an overview of experimental studies of island phenomena). Using EMM,
Traxler and Pickering (1996) were among the first to demonstrate that
readers respect RC islands in sentences such as (11) in that they did not
attempt to link the RC head *book* to the embedded verb *wrote* if the verb was
within a syntactic island, whilst attempting to do so if the verb was not in
an island region.

(11)      We like the {book/city} that the author who wrote (___) unceas-
          ingly and with great dedication saw ___ while waiting for
          a contract.

To avoid presenting ungrammatical sentences, Traxler and Pickering
used sentences that contained a "false" gap (indicated again through
parentheses), that is, a putative gap position whose presence is disproved
by subsequent sentence material. A plausibility manipulation was used as
a diagnostic for dependency formation here. If readers try to link the RC
head noun *(book/city)* to the optionally transitive embedded verb *wrote*, then
an implausible direct object analysis (*#wrote the city*) should trigger longer
reading times around the verb region compared to a plausible one (*wrote*

*the book*). In Traxler and Pickering's study, island sensitivity was reflected in the absence of plausibility effects at the verb *wrote* in sentences such as (11). For corresponding non-island sentences, on the other hand, nouns that were implausible direct objects of the embedded verb gave rise to significantly longer reading times at the verb region in comparison to plausible direct objects.

The results from other EMM studies have shown that at least some island types are violable during processing, however (e.g. Pickering, Barton, & Shillcock 1994; Boxell 2014). Pickering et al. (1994), for example, found evidence of gaps being postulated inside RCs that modified a subject in sentences such as (12).

(12)  I realise what$_i$ the artist who painted (__ $_i$) the large mural ate __ $_i$ today.

Examining sentences that contained complex "double" islands such as (13), Boxell (2014) found that readers would attempt to link the fronted *wh*-phrase to the most deeply embedded verb *built*, albeit only if the *wh*-phase was lexically specified (*which stage*) but not if it was a *wh*-pronoun (*what*).

(13)  The fans discussed {which stage/what} the host [who wondered [whether the unreliable contractors built (__) the correct stand]] stood by __ during the show at Wembley.

This confirms and extends earlier findings from SPR and judgment tasks showing that lexically specified ("d-linked") *wh*-phrases can reduce processing difficulty and improve the acceptability of island sentences (Frazier & Clifton 2002; Hofmeister & Sag 2010; Goodall 2015, among others).

Comparing the processing of restrictive and non-restrictive RC islands in Swedish, Tutunjian et al. (2017) found evidence that readers postulated gaps inside restrictive but not in non-restrictive RCs, supporting earlier claims to the effect that restrictive RCs are weak islands in Swedish. The results from a second EMM experiment indicated that gaps may also be postulated in complex subject NPs, even though these are normally assumed to be strong islands in Swedish. Complex subject islands were also found to be violated during processing by proficient non-native speakers of English who had demonstrated native-like knowledge of the relevant constraint in an offline task (Boxell & Felser 2017). The effect indicative of this violation was only fleeting, however, in that it was restricted to first-pass reading times.

Taken together, the above studies on the processing of syntactic islands illustrate how reading-time data can usefully complement data from offline methods. The EMM technique is sensitive to constraint violations that are corrected at later processing stages and thus may not necessarily be reflected in end-of-sentence judgments.

## 23.4 Eye-Tracking During Listening

### 23.4.1 Method Overview

The eye-tracking methodology can also be used to monitor changes over time in participants' gaze direction during listening (Cooper 1974). This normally involves participants' viewing a visual scene or an array of pictures or objects whilst listening to pre-recorded linguistic stimuli. Also known as the "visual-world paradigm" (VWP), this technique is based on the assumption that visual and language processing are closely linked, and that listeners tend to look at objects as these are mentioned (see e.g. Altmann (2011); Huettig, Rommers, & Meyer (2011) for review and discussion). Both the likelihood of participants' gaze being directed at a specific object and the time it takes for eye movements to that object to be launched may be informative. Saccades are sometimes launched even before a critical word or phrase has become available in the input, which makes this method particularly suitable for measuring anticipatory processing (Altmann & Kamide 1999). Other studies have investigated competition effects, including the question of when a correct referent is identified in the presence of one or more distractors. Participants may be instructed to listen to the stimulus items passively, in which case they may later be prompted to respond to some end-of-trial questions, or to perform some action such as clicking on or manipulating a particular object. The VWP is rarely used to assess participants' sensitivity to ungrammatical stimuli, however.

The main advantage of the VWP over reading-based methods is that it is also suitable for non-standard populations such as young children, non-fluent readers, and individuals with aphasia. Similar to eye-movement monitoring during reading, the VWP allows for sentence stimuli to be presented in a fairly natural, uninterrupted way, and the relevant online measurements are not contaminated by the requirement that participants press a button or perform some other secondary task. Disadvantages include the relatively high cost and the need for training, as well as some experimental design challenges. Materials creation is restricted by the need for critical words or phrases to be depictable, and controlling for potential effects of sentence prosody may require the spoken materials to be carefully spliced or computer-generated, which may however compromise their perceived naturalness. Selecting visual materials also requires a lot of care: if, for example, one picture or object in a display is perceived as being inherently more interesting than another, it may attract disproportionally more looks, interfering with the above-mentioned linking assumption.

Experiment programming, data extraction, and data analysis all provide further challenges. The presentation of the visual and auditory stimuli must be coordinated and the critical parts of the auditory stimuli need to be time-locked to participants' gaze behavior. Depending on the eye-tracker's sampling rate huge amounts of eye-movement data may be generated, and there are currently no clear standards regarding the analysis of visual-world eye-tracking data. Carrying out analyses of the fixation data with a fine-grained time-course resolution requires considerable statistical expertise (see e.g. Mirman, Dixon, & Magnuson 2008).

### 23.4.2   Visual-World Eye-Tracking Studies of Syntactic Phenomena

The VWP is often used to investigate grammatical abilities in non-standard populations, for example by studying heritage bilingual listeners' sensitivity to grammatical distinctions (e.g. Arslan, Bastiaanse, & Felser 2015) or the ability of people with aphasia to interpret non-canonically ordered sentences (e.g. Dickey, Choy, & Thompson 2007). The VWP is also suitable for studying online reference resolution (e.g. Clackson, Felser, & Clahsen 2011; Runner & Head 2014; Runner, Sussman, & Tanenhaus 2003, 2005, 2006; Sekerina, Stromswold, & Hestvik 2004). A series of studies by Runner and colleagues used the VWP to investigate the online application of binding constraints. Runner et al. (2003, 2005, 2006), for example, showed that reflexives in so-called "picture" noun phrases with possessors (such as *John's picture of himself*) violate Binding Condition A, which demands that reflexive anaphors are locally bound, in that they readily take antecedents outside their local binding domain. This finding confirms and extends earlier claims to the effect that reflexives in picture noun phrases are logophors (e.g. Pollard & Sag 1992).

In another study, Runner and Head (2014) observed that during the processing of both reflexives and pronouns in sentences such as (14a, b), a binding-theoretically illicit competitor antecedent was also considered.

(14)     a. The pharmacist(f) that Molly met drove herself to the party.
         b. The pharmacist(f) that Molly met drove her to the party.

Note that Binding Condition A identifies *the pharmacist* as the only licit antecedent for the reflexive *herself* in (14a), whilst Condition B rules out *the pharmacist* as a possible antecedent for the pronoun *her* in (14b). VWP studies on anaphor resolution rely on the assumption that the proportion of fixations on a potential referent reflects the likelihood of this referent being considered as the intended target of a spoken stimulus (Allopenna, Magnuson, & Tanenhaus 1998). In Runner and Head's (2014) study, the illicit competitor antecedent was represented by a picture of a female character called "Molly" in (14a), and by a picture of a female pharmacist in (14b). The authors report that even though participants mostly chose the binding-compatible referent in their end-of-trial click responses, their eye-gaze data revealed effects of the presence of a gender-matching but illicit competitor antecedent. That is, the likelihood of the correct referent being fixated was reduced if a gender-matching competitor (e.g. a female pharmacist in (14b)) was present in the visual array, in comparison to visual arrays that contained gender-mismatching competitors (such as a male pharmacist). The finding that binding-incompatible referents are considered during processing is problematic for the "binding-as-initial-filter" hypothesis, which states that the parser does not consider structurally inappropriate antecedents (e.g. Nicol & Swinney 1989).

Runner and Head (2014) further report that the illicit competitor antecedent was considered for longer for pronouns (14b) than for reflexives (14a). This finding is consistent with the POB framework (Reuland 2001, 2011), according to which Conditions A and B apply at different levels of representation and interpreting non-reflexive pronouns is computationally more complex than interpreting reflexives. Runner and Head's (2014) findings on reflexives are surprising, however, given that violations of Condition A have rarely been observed in reading-time tasks (except in non-native readers; see Felser & Cunnings 2012).

## 23.5  Concluding Remarks

Besides providing brief methodological overviews of self-paced reading and eye-tracking, the current chapter's main aim was to illustrate how data from online reading or listening experiments can provide insights into the nature of syntactic derivations and representations. Some of the phenomena considered above would have been difficult or impossible to investigate using offline judgments. Space limitations only allowed me to highlight a small selection of studies and grammatical phenomena, and many theoretically relevant findings could not even be touched upon. For further discussion of how real-time processing data may bear on theoretical linguistic issues and hypotheses, see e.g. Felser (2015), Pablos, Doetjes, and Cheng (2018), and Phillips and Wagers (2007). Real-time sentence processing data should not be expected to be able to adjudicate between different syntactic models or formalisms, however (see Chapter 22 for extended discussion of this point). What I hope to have shown here is how data from online reading or listening tasks can usefully complement judgment data, or, depending on the research question or phenomenon under investigation, could be used in place of the latter. Although most of the studies reviewed above report findings from adult native speakers, reading-time techniques (Jegerski 2014; Keating 2014) and the VWP (Dussias, Valdés Kroff, & Gerfen 2014) are also frequently used to probe the implicit grammatical abilities of non-native speakers, whose offline judgments may be particularly prone to being affected by prescriptive norms imposed on them through instruction.

# References

Allopenna, P. D., Magnuson, J. S., & Tanenhaus, M. K. (1998). Tracking the time course of spoken word recognition using eye movements: Evidence for continuous mapping models. *Journal of Memory and Language*, 38(4), 419–439.

Altmann, G. T. M. (2011). The mediation of eye movements by spoken language. In S. P. Liversedge, I. D. Gilchrist, & S. Everling, eds., *The Oxford Handbook of Eye Movements*. Oxford: Oxford University Press, pp. 979–1004.

Altmann, G. T. M. & Kamide, Y. (1999). Incremental interpretation at verbs: Restricting the domain of subsequent reference. *Cognition*, 73(3), 247–264.

Anderson, C. (2004). The structure and real-time comprehension of quantifier scope ambiguity. Doctoral dissertation, Northwestern University.

Arslan, S., Bastiaanse, R., & Felser, C. (2015). Looking at the evidence in visual world: Eye-movements reveal how bilingual and monolingual Turkish speakers process grammatical evidentiality. *Frontiers in Psychology*, 6, 1387. DOI: 10.3389/fpsyg.2015.01387

Berwick, R. & Weinberg, A. (1984). *The Grammatical Basis of Linguistic Performance*. Cambridge, MA: MIT Press.

Blackwell, A., Bates, E., & Fisher, D. (1996). The time course of grammaticality judgment. *Language and Cognitive Processes*, 11, 337–406.

Bock, J. K. & Miller, C. A. (1991). Broken agreement. *Cognitive Psychology*, 23, 45–93.

Boland, J. E., Tanenhaus, M. K., & Garnsey, S. M. (1990). Evidence for immediate use of verb-based "control" information in sentence processing. *Journal of Memory and Language*, 29, 413–432.

Booth, J., MacWhinney, B., & Harasaki, Y. (2000). Developmental differences in visual and auditory processing of complex sentences. *Child Development*, 71, 981–1003.

Bott, O. & Schlotterbeck, F. (2015). The processing domain of scope interaction. *Journal of Semantics*, 32, 39–92.

Boxell, O. (2014). Lexical fillers permit real-time gap-search in island domains. *Journal of Cognitive Science*, 15, 97–135.

Boxell, O. & Felser, C. (2017). Sensitivity to parasitic gaps inside subject islands in native and non-native sentence processing. *Bilingualism: Language and Cognition*, 20, 494–511.

Braze, D., Shankweiler, D., Ni, W., & Palumbo, L. C. (2002). Readers' eye movements distinguish anomalies of form and content. *Journal of Psycholinguistic Research*, 31, 25–45.

Brasoveanu, A. & Dotlačil, J. (2015). Sentence-internal same and its quantificational licensors: A new window into the processing of inverse scope. *Semantics and Pragmatics*, 8, 1–52.

Bresnan, J. (1998). Morphology competes with syntax: Explaining typological variation in weak crossover effects. In P. Barbosa, D. Fox, P. Hagstrom, M. McGinnis, & D. Pesetsky, eds., *Is the Best Good Enough? Optimality and Competition in Syntax*. Cambridge, MA: MIT Press, pp. 59–92.

Chesi, C. (2007). Five reasons for building phrase structures top-down from left to right. *Nanzan Linguistics: Special Issue*, 3(1), 71–105.

Chomsky, N. (1973). Conditions on transformations. In S. Anderson & P. Kiparsky, eds., *A Festschrift for Morris Halle*. New York: Holt, Rinehart & Winston, pp. 232–286.

Chomsky, N. (1981). *Lectures on Government and Binding*. Dordrecht: Foris.

Chomsky, N. (2000). Minimalist Inquiries: The framework. In R. Martin, D. Michaels, J. Uriagereka, & S. J. Keyser., eds., *Step by Step: Essays on Minimalist Syntax in Honor of Howard Lasnik*. Cambridge, MA: MIT Press, pp. 89–155.

Clackson, K., Felser, C., & Clahsen, H. (2011). Children's processing of reflexives and pronouns in English: Evidence from eye movements during listening. *Journal of Memory and Language*, 65, 128–144.

Clifton, C. & Frazier, L. (1989). Comprehending sentences with long-distance dependencies. In G. M. Carlson & M. K. Tanenhaus, eds., *Linguistic Structure in Language Processing*. Dordrecht: Kluwer Academic Publishers, pp. 273–317.

Clifton, C. & Staub, A. (2011). Syntactic influences on eye movements in reading. In S. P. Liversedge, I. D. Gilchrist, & S. Everling, eds., *The Oxford Handbook of Eye Movements*. Oxford: Oxford University Press, pp. 895–909.

Clifton, C., Staub, A., & Rayner, K. (2007). Eye movements in reading words and sentences. In R. P. G. van Gompel, M. H. Fischer, W. S. Murray, & R. L. Hill, eds., *Eye Movements: A Window on Mind and Brain*. Amsterdam: Elsevier, pp. 341–372.

Cooper, R. M. (1974). The control of eye fixation by the meaning of spoken language: A new methodology for the real-time investigation of speech perception, memory, and language processing. *Cognitive Psychology*, 6, 84–107.

Cunnings, I., Patterson, C., & Felser, C. (2014). Variable binding and coreference in sentence comprehension: Evidence from eye movements. *Journal of Memory and Language*, 71, 39–56.

Cunnings, I., Patterson, C., & Felser, C. (2015). Structural constraints on pronoun binding and coreference: Evidence from eye movements during reading. *Frontiers in Psychology*, 6, 840. DOI: 10.3389/fpsyg.2015.00840

Czypionka, A., Dörre, L., & Bayer, J. (2018). Inverse Case attraction: Experimental evidence for a syntactically guided process. *Journal of Comparative Germanic Linguistics*, 21(7), 135–188.

Demberg, V. & Sayeed, A. (2016). The frequency of rapid pupil dilations as a measure of linguistic processing difficulty. *PLOS One*, 11(1). DOI: 10.1371/journal.pone.0146194

Dickey, M. W., Choy, J. J., & Thompson, C. K. (2007). Real-time comprehension of *wh*-movement in aphasia: Evidence from eyetracking while listening. *Brain and Language*, 100, 1–22.

Dillon, B., Staub, A., Levy, J., & Clifton, C. (2017). Which noun phrases is this verb supposed to agree with? Object agreement in American English. *Language*, 93(1), 65–96.

Drummer, J.-D. & Felser, C. (2018). Cataphoric pronoun resolution in native and non-native sentence comprehension. *Journal of Memory and Language*, 101, 97–113.

Dussias, P. E., Valdés Kroff, J. R., & Gerfen, C. (2014). Using the visual world to study spoken language processing. In J. Jegerski & B. VanPatten, eds., *Research Methods in Second Language Psycholinguistics*. New York: Routledge, pp. 93–126.

Dwivedi, V. D. (2013). Interpreting quantifier scope ambiguity: Evidence of heuristic first, algorithmic second processing. *PLOS One*, 8(11), e81461. DOI: 10.1371/journal.pone.0081461

Enochson, K. & Culbertson, J. (2015). Collecting psycholinguistic response time data using Amazon Mechanical Turk. *PLOS One*, 10(3), 1–17. DOI: 10.1371/journal.pone.0116946

Felser, C. (2015). Syntax and language processing. In T. Kiss & A. Alexiadou, eds., *Syntax – Theory and Analysis: An International Handbook*. Berlin: De Gruyter Mouton, pp. 1875–1911.

Felser, C. & Cunnings, I. (2012). Processing reflexives in English as a second language: The role of structural and discourse-level constraints. *Applied Psycholinguistics*, 33, 571–603.

Felser, C. & Drummer, J.-D. (2017). Sensitivity to crossover constraints during native and non-native pronoun resolution. *Journal of Psycholinguistic Research*, 46, 771–789.

Felser, C. , Marinis, T., & Clahsen, H. (2003). Children's processing of ambiguous sentences: A study of relative clause attachment. *Language Acquisition*, 11, 127–163.

Fox, D. (1999). Reconstruction, binding theory, and the interpretation of chains. *Linguistic Inquiry*, 30, 157–196.

Franck, J., Colonna, S., & Rizzi, L. (2015). Task-dependency and structure-dependency in number interference effects in sentence comprehension. *Frontiers in Psychology*, 6, 349. DOI: 10.3389/fpsyg.2015.00349

Frazier, L. & Clifton, C. (2002). Processing "d-linked" phrases. *Journal of Psycholinguistic Research*, 31, 633–660.

Gibson, E. (2000). The dependency-locality theory: A distance-based theory of linguistic complexity. In Y. Miyashita, A. P. Marantz, & W. O'Neill, eds., *Image, Language, Brain*. Cambridge, MA: MIT Press, pp. 95–126.

Gibson, E. & Warren, T. (2004). Reading-time evidence for intermediate linguistic structure in long-distance dependencies. *Syntax*, 7, 55–78.

Gibson, E., Jacobson, P., Graff, P., Mahowald, K., Fedorenko, E., & Piantadosi, S. T. (2015). A pragmatic account of complexity in definite Antecedent-Contained-Deletion relative clauses. *Journal of Semantics*, 32 (4), 579–618

Gibson, E., Piantadosi, S. T., & Levy, R. (2017). Post-hoc analysis decisions drive the reported reading time effects in Hackl, Koster-Hale & Varvoutis (2012). *Journal of Semantics*, 34, 539–546.

Goodall, G. (2015). The D-linking effect on extraction from islands and non-islands. *Frontiers in Psychology*, 5, 1493. DOI: 10.3389/fpsyg.2014.01493

Hackl, M., Koster-Hale, J., & Varvoutis, J. (2012). Quantification and ACD: Evidence from real-time sentence processing. *Journal of Semantics*, 29(2), 145–206.

Hawkins, J. A. (2004). *Efficiency and Complexity in Grammars*. Oxford: Oxford University Press.

Hofmeister, P. & Sag, I. A. (2010). Cognitive constraints and island effects. *Language*, 86, 366–415.

Huettig, F., Rommers, J., & Meyer, A. S. (2011). Using the visual world paradigm to study language processing: A review and critical evaluation. *Acta Psychologica*, 137, 151–171.

Jäger, L. A., Engelmann, F., & Vasishth, S. (2017). Similarity-based interference in sentence comprehension: Literature review and Bayesian meta-analysis. *Journal of Memory and Language*, 94, 316–339.

Jegerski, J. (2014). Self-paced reading. In J. Jegerski & B. VanPatten, eds., *Research Methods in Second Language Psycholinguistics*. New York: Routledge, pp. 20–49.

Just, M. A. & Carpenter, P. A. (1980). A theory of reading: From eye fixations to comprehension. *Psychological Review*, 85, 109–130.

Just, M. A., Carpenter, P. A., & Woolley, J. D. (1982). Paradigms and processes in reading comprehension. *Journal of Experimental Psychology*, 3, 228–238.

Kazanina, N., Lau, E. F., Lieberman, M., Yoshida, M., & Philips, C. (2007). The effect of syntactic constraints on the processing of backwards anaphora. *Journal of Memory and Language*, 56, 384–409.

Keating, G. (2014). Eye-tracking with text. In J. Jegerski & B. VanPatten, eds., *Research Methods in Second Language Psycholinguistics*. New York: Routledge, pp. 69–92.

Keller, F., Gunasekharan, S., Mayo, N., & Corley, M. (2009). Timing accuracy of Web experiments: A case study using the WebExp software package. *Behavior Research Methods*, 41, 1–12.

Kluender, R. (2004). Are subject islands subject to a processing account? In B. Schmeiser, V. Chand, A. Kelleher, & A. Rodriguez, eds., *Proceedings of the 23rd West Coast Conference on Formal Linguistics (WCCFL 23)*. Somerville, MA: Cascadilla Press, pp. 101–125.

Kluender, R. & Kutas, M. (1993). Subjacency as processing phenomenon. *Language and Cognitive Processes*, 8, 573–633.

Koornneef, A. W. (2008). Eye-catching anaphora. Doctoral dissertation, Utrecht University (LOT Dissertation Series, 90). Utrecht, NL: Netherlands Graduate School of Linguistics (LOT).

Koornneef, A. W. (2010). Looking at anaphora: The psychological reality of the primitives of binding model. In M. B. H. Everaert, T. Lentz, H. De Mulder, Ø. Nilsen, & A. Zondervan, eds., *The Linguistics Enterprise: From Knowledge of Language to Knowledge In Linguistics*. Amsterdam and Philadelphia: John Benjamins, pp. 141–166.

Koornneef, A. W., Avrutin, S., Wijnen, F., & Reuland, E. (2011). Tracking the preference for bound-variable dependencies in ambiguous ellipses and only-structures. In J. Runner, ed., *Experiments at the Interfaces* (Syntax and Semantics, 37). Leiden: Brill, pp. 69–100.

Kush, D., Lidz, J., & Phillips, C. (2015). Relation-sensitive retrieval: evidence from bound variable pronouns. *Journal of Memory and Language*, 82, 18–40.

Kush, D., Lidz, J., & Phillips, C. (2017). Looking forwards and backwards: the real-time processing of strong and weak crossover. *Glossa: A Journal of General Linguistics*, 2(70). DOI: 10.5334/gjgl.280

Lee, M.-W. (2004). Another look at the role of empty categories in sentence processing (and grammar). *Journal of Psycholinguistic Research*, 33, 51–73.

Lee, S. & O'Grady, W. (2016). Psycholinguistic evidence for inverse scope in Korean. *Journal of Psycholinguistic Research*, 45, 871–882.

Lewis, S. & Phillips, C. (2015). Aligning grammatical theories and language processing models. *Journal of Psycholinguistic Research*, 44(1), 27–46.

Mirman, D., Dixon, J. A., & Magnuson, J. S. (2008). Statistical and computational models of the visual world paradigm: Growth curves and individual differences. *Journal of Memory and Language*, 59(4), 475–494.

Nicol, J. L., Forster, K. I., & Veres, C. (1997). Subject–verb agreement processes in comprehension. *Journal of Memory and Language*, 36(4), 569–587.

Nicol, J., & Swinney, D. (1989). The role of structure in coreference assignment during sentence comprehension. *Journal of Psycholinguistic Research*, 18, 5–20.

Pablos Robles L., Doetjes J., & Cheng, L.-S. (2018). Backward dependencies and in-situ wh-questions as test cases on how to approach experimental linguistics research that pursues theoretical linguistics questions. *Frontiers in Psychology*, 8, 2237. DOI: 10.3389/fpsyg.2017.02237

Parker, D. & Phillips, C. (2016). Negative polarity illusions and the format of hierarchical encodings in memory. *Cognition*, 157, 321–339.

Patterson, C. & Felser, C. (2019). Delayed application of binding condition C during cataphoric pronoun resolution. *Journal of Psycholinguistic Research*, 48(2), 453–475.

Pearlmutter, N. J., Garnsey, S. M., & Bock, K. (1999). Agreement processes in sentence comprehension. *Journal of Memory and Language*, 41, 427–456.

Phillips, C. (2006). The real-time status of island phenomena. *Language*, 82, 795–823.

Phillips, C. & Lewis, S. (2013). Derivational order in syntax: Evidence and architectural consequences. *Studies in Linguistics*, 6, 11–47.

Phillips, C. & Wagers, M. (2007). Relating structure and time in linguistics and psycholinguistics. In G. Gaskell, ed., *The Oxford Handbook of Psycholinguistics*. Oxford: Oxford University Press, pp. 739–756.

Phillips, C., Wagers, M., & Lau, E. F. (2011). Grammatical illusions and selective fallibility in real-time language comprehension. In J. Runner, ed., *Experiments at the Interfaces* (Syntax and Semantics, 37). Leiden: Brill, pp. 147–180.

Pickering, M., Barton, S. B., & Shillcock, R. (1994). Unbounded dependencies, island constraints and processing complexity. In C. Clifton, L. Frazier, & K. Rayner, eds., *Perspectives on Sentence Processing*. Hillsdale, NJ: Lawrence Erlbaum, pp. 199–224.

Pittner, K. (1995). The case of German relatives. *The Linguistic Review*, 12, 197–231.

Pollard, C. & Sag, I. A. (1992). Anaphors in English and the scope of Binding Theory. *Linguistic Inquiry*, 23, 261–303.

Postal, P. (1971). *Crossover Phenomena*. New York: Holt, Rinehart, & Winston.

Omaki, A., Lau, E., White, I. D., Dakan, M., Apple, A., & Phillips, C. (2015). Hyper-active gap filling. *Frontiers in Psychology*, 6, 384. DOI: 10.3389/fpsyg.2015.00384

Reinhart, T. (1983). *Anaphora and Semantic Interpretation*. Chicago: University of Chicago Press.

Reuland, E. (2001). Primitives of binding. *Linguistic Inquiry*, 32, 439–492.

Reuland, E. (2011). *Anaphora and Language Design*. Cambridge, MA: MIT Press.

Ross, J. R. (1967). Constraints on variables in syntax. Doctoral dissertation, Massachusetts Institute of Technology.

Runner, J. T. & Head, K. D. L. (2014). What can visual world eye-tracking tell us about the binding theory? In C. Piñón, ed., *Empirical Issues in Syntax and Semantics*, vol. 10. Paris: Colloque de Syntaxe et Sémantique à Paris (CSSP), pp. 269–286.

Runner, J. T., Sussman, R. S., & Tanenhaus, M. K. (2003). Assignment of reference to reflexives and pronouns in picture noun phrases: Evidence from eye movements. *Cognition*, 89, B1–B13.

Runner, J. T., Sussman, R. S., & Tanenhaus, M. K. (2005). Reflexives and pronouns in picture noun phrases: Using eye movements as a source of linguistic evidence. In S. Kepser & M. Reis, eds., *Linguistic Evidence: Empirical, Theoretical and Computational Perspectives*. New York: Mouton de Gruyter, pp. 393–412.

Runner, J. T., Sussman, R. S., & Tanenhaus, M. K. (2006). Processing reflexives and pronouns in picture noun phrases. *Cognitive Science*, 30, 193–241.

Sag, I. A. (1976). Deletion and Logical Form. Doctoral dissertation, Massachusetts Institute of Technology.

Sekerina, I. A., Stromswold, K., & Hestvik, A. (2004). How do adults and children process referentially ambiguous pronouns? *Journal of Child Language*, 31(1), 123–152.

Shan, C.-C. & Barker, C. (2006). Explaining crossover and superiority as left-to-right evaluation. *Linguistics and Philosophy*, 29, 91–134.

Stowe, L. A. (1986). Parsing wh-constructions: evidence for on-line gap location. *Language and Cognitive Processes*, 1, 227–245.

Sturt, P. (2003). The time-course of the application of binding constraints in reference resolution. *Journal of Memory and Language*, 48, 542–562.

Sturt, P. (2013). Syntactic constraints on referential processing. In R. P. G. van Gompel, ed., *Sentence Processing*. Hove: Psychology Press, pp. 136–159.

Tanner, D., Nicol, J., & Brehm, L. (2014). The time-course of feature interference in agreement comprehension: Multiple mechanisms and asymmetrical attraction. *Journal of Memory and Language*, 76, 195–215.

Traxler, M. J. & Pickering, M. J. (1996). Plausibility and the processing of unbounded dependencies: An eye-tracking study. *Journal of Memory and Language*, 40, 542–562.

Tutunjian, D. & Boland, J. E. (2008). Do we need a distinction between arguments and adjuncts? Evidence from psycholinguistic studies of comprehension. *Language and Linguistic Compass*, 2, 631–646.

Tutunjian, D., Heinat, F., Klingvall, E., & Wiklund, A.-L. (2017). Processing relative clause extractions in Swedish. *Frontiers in Psychology*, 8, 2118. DOI: 10.3389/fpsyg.2017.02118

Vasishth, S., von der Malsburg, T., & Engelmann, F. (2013). What eye movements can tell us about sentence comprehension. *Wiley Interdisciplinary Reviews: Cognitive Science*, 125–134.

von der Malsburg, T. & Angele, B. (2016). False positives and other statistical errors in standard analyses of eye movements in reading. *Journal of Memory and Language*, 94, 119–133.

Wagers, M., Lau, E., & Phillips, C. (2009). Attraction in comprehension: Representation and processes. *Journal of Memory and Language*, 61, 206–237.

Zwart, J.-W. (2009) Prospects for top-down derivation. *Catalan Journal of Linguistics*, 8, 161–187.

# 24

# Nothing Entirely New under the Sun: ERP Responses to Manipulations of Syntax

Robert Kluender

At the end of 1999 – 20 years ago from the time of this writing – a symposium was held at UC San Diego on "The Nature of Explanation in Linguistic Theory," the proceedings of which were later edited and published (Moore & Polinsky 2003). At the time, received wisdom in theoretical linguistics was that the direction of explanation should proceed from functionalist[1] theories of the mind/brain relation to biological (neuroanatomical and neurophysiological) implementations and confirmations thereof (Chomsky 1986, 1993 *inter alia*). I took exception to this expressed view and made the following argument in the proceedings:

> ... a new generation of scholars is currently being trained who at least have passing familiarity with, and in some cases are well versed in, both sides of the mind/brain slash as far as language is concerned. This can only augur well for the field, which stands to gain great benefits from such a joint endeavor. In the meantime, if the rest of us can just hold off making premature pronouncements on the utility of adhering to either a functionalist (computational) or reductionist (eliminative) approach, as if one had to choose between them, things can simply proceed as history does generally, namely inexorably. That is, the conditions have already been set for a merger of these two strands of research, and so it remains to the rest of us to simply sit back (and sit tight) and wait for the results, which should speak for themselves.               (Kluender 2003: 200)

So was I right? On one count, I think history has indeed borne me out: psycho- and neurolinguistic methods are by now well accepted within the

---

[1] This is not a reference to functional linguistics, but to a particular view of the mind/body problem from the philosophy of mind (Fodor 1981; Churchland 1984: 36–42), tacitly assumed but only rarely explicitly stated or acknowledged in generative linguistics (see Chomsky 1980: 11, 1993: 42–43). For more details, the reader is referred to Kluender (2003), where this issue is discussed at length.

field and have become almost *de rigueur* for most graduate students in linguistics. But what about the results (based on these methods) "which should speak for themselves"? Have they lived up to expectations? That's the question that this chapter aims to address.

One point of clarification: when I refer to "linguistic ERP components" in the ensuing discussion, by no means do I mean to imply that any ERP component is specific to language or entirely linguistic in nature – in fact, as will become clear, I suspect that no known ERP response is purely linguistic. Instead, "linguistic ERP component" should be read quite literally as "linguistic-event-related (brain) potential component" – in other words, an ERP component merely elicited in the context of a linguistic event. This is a widely held view within the linguistic ERP community, and hence, I presume, should not be controversial in our discussion here.

## 24.2 Setting the Stage

### 24.2.1 Basic Methodological Issues

Let's first set the stage methodologically. Event-related brain potentials (ERPs) are derived from the electroencephalogram (EEG), a continuous record of the electrical activity coming off the head. Unfortunately for our purposes, not all of this activity is generated by the brain: muscles and even skin give off electric potentials as well. Moreover, bone is a very bad conductant, so what we see in the way of electrical activity outside the skull is much attenuated relative to what's going on inside it. For these reasons, ERP methodology relies on averaging across many trials in order to improve the signal to noise ratio, filtering out extraneous, random background electrical activity that has nothing to do with the signal, and accentuating that which is consistent across trials. This procedure rests on the assumption that participants are responding in the same way, i.e. with the same brain responses, to the same type of stimulus. As discussed in Section 24.3.4 on individual differences in response to morphosyntactic stimuli, this is unfortunately not always the case across participants. But this can be determined by examining individual within-participant averages of all relevant trials before averaging all of these together into the so-called grand average across participants.

A common misconception is that EEG and the ERPs derived from it reflect the firing of neurons in so-called action potentials. Instead, ERPs reflect what are known as postsynaptic potentials, the aggregate effect of all the inputs that a neuron gets from other neurons on its membrane potential, the difference in voltage across its membrane from inside to outside, which determines whether it will fire or not. The reason this can be recorded from outside the head is that assemblies of neurons known as pyramidal cells – so called because they are shaped roughly like pyramids – tend to act in concert, receiving similar inputs and subsequently firing synchronously. This similarity in behavior amplifies the electrical signal such that it can be picked up outside the head. Because of the nature of electrical dipoles, EEG picks up the voltage fluctuations of pyramidal cells arrayed perpendicular to the scalp, while the magnetoencephalogram or MEG picks up the activity of the rest of them due to the nature of magnetic relative to electrical fields.

Even though we know how EEG is generated in the brain, we typically don't know where. The scalp topography of ERPs (where the response appears largest or most reliably over the head) is a very unreliable indicator of its source. It's impossible to infer from the distribution of an ERP component over the scalp where it's being generated. A good example of this is the N400, which is often larger over the right side of the head than over the left, but has nonetheless been determined via other means to be coming primarily from the left hemisphere. There are technical procedures for estimating where an ERP response is coming from, but if that's what an investigator really needs to know, she is better off running an MEG experiment. Functional magnetic resonance imaging (fMRI) is actually the best imaging technique for localizing responses in the brain, short of the electrocorticogram (ECoG), which involves recording from the cortical surface of (generally epileptic) patients undergoing brain surgery (see Chapter 27 for an introduction to imaging techniques in the study of syntax).

While scalp distribution is not a good indicator of where a particular type of response is being generated, it is nonetheless one of the parameters that can help to distinguish between types of ERP responses.[2] If two ERP responses show different scalp topographies, this is an indication that the underlying neural source generators differ in some combination of location, polarity, or relative strength (Urbach & Kutas 2002). Distribution over the scalp thus constitutes what is called a qualitative difference between ERPs, indicating that they are not the same response. Other qualitative differences are polarity (positive vs. negative voltage) and less commonly, morphology, or the general shape of the ERP. For example, the N400 reliably shows a negative voltage peak in amplitude somewhere around 400 ms (hence its name), whereas other linguistic ERPs do not exhibit such reliable peaks. Differences in latency (the time window in which the response is statistically significant) and amplitude (the size of the response) are considered quantitative in nature and insufficient for distinguishing between types of ERP responses. For example, the P300, one of the first cognitive ERP components discovered, as discussed below, exhibits a wide range of onset latencies. Another example closer to the concerns of this chapter is a study by Featherston et al. (2000), a well-conceived and -executed attempt to distinguish the brain responses to raising and

---

[2] As discussed in Section 24.3.3, this has become more of a problem in linguistic ERP research in recent years than was originally anticipated.

subject control constructions in German. But the late positivity (P600 effect; see Section 24.3.2) elicited relative to transitive sentence controls was merely larger in amplitude in the raising condition than in the subject control condition, and a quantitative difference in amplitude by itself cannot justify a qualitative distinction.

## 24.2.2  Early Foundational Studies of Syntactic Processing

Kutas and Hillyard's (1980a) *Science* study constituted the first report in the literature of an N400 effect in response to semantic anomaly (*He spread the warm bread with **socks***). Although there was a visible late positivity following the N400 effect at the parietal midline electrode in their grand averages (1980a: 203, Figure 1), as well as in most of their individual subject averages (1980a: 204, Figure 2 – Pz), this late positive difference turned out not to be significant when measured between 600 and 900 ms (i.e. immediately following the latency window of 300 to 600 ms used to measure the N400 in this study). This was important because at the time, the authors were at pains to dissociate the N400 from other established cognitive ERP responses in the literature, especially the general cognitive, modality-independent P300 (Sutton et al. 1965) and the modality-dependent (i.e. auditory or visual) N200 related to stimulus discrimination that often precedes it (Courchesne et al. 1975; Simson et al. 1977). Kutas and Hillyard argued that since the late positivity following the N400 component in response to semantic anomaly was not significant, the N400 could not be related to either the N200 or the P300 elicited in response to sudden changes in the font size of their visually presented language stimuli used as a control condition (see also Kutas & Hillyard 1980b). In their discussion they went on to point out that "It remains to be seen whether N400 is specific to semantically inappropriate words or whether it accompanies the violation of other linguistic or nonlinguistic expectancies as well. However, N400 is not a general response to all linguistic or meaningful stimuli because *judgments* [emphasis mine] about such stimuli have been specifically associated with the P300 wave" (Kutas & Hillyard 1980b: 204).

Kutas and Hillyard (1983) first attempted to answer this question by comparing the brain responses to semantic anomalies in English vs. (mostly) morphosyntactic anomalies in connected narrative prose: violations of subject–verb number agreement (*Then she **dig** a hole with her feet*), noun phrase number, including concord (*All turtles have four **leg** and a tail*) and count/mass noun errors (*Some storms have **thunders** and lightning*), and verb finiteness (i.e. finite verb forms substituted for non-finite forms and vice versa: *Air does not always **had** the same humidity*). While neither the morphosyntactic anomalies themselves nor the words to which they were compared were perfectly controlled, divergent ERP patterns nevertheless emerged that are clearly recognizable with hindsight: a negativity that was significant for all three morphosyntactic violation types between 300 and 400 ms, and that appeared to have an anterior scalp distribution over lateral electrodes, and a late positivity visible starting at 600 ms at several electrodes (Kutas & Hillyard 1983: 544) but never measured because at the time it was assumed to be a response to the following word. These two responses represent what came to be called "left anterior negativity" or "LAN," and the "P600" a decade later. Kutas and Hillyard (1983: 546) were well aware of the implication of these results for issues of modularity, noting that "grammatical aberrations are processed in a different fashion (either qualitatively or quantitatively) from . . . semantic deviations." They go on to note that "These results bear on the question of the separability of semantic and syntactic processing levels and their respective roles in comprehension," and that "The finding of an N400 component associated with semantic, but not with grammatical, anomalies is consistent with the hypothesis of separate modes of processing."

These initial results lay fallow for almost ten years, until the beginning of the 1990s, when a number of researchers began to take an interest in ERP techniques and applied them to questions of theoretical syntactic and psycholinguistic work. This was the period of great (re)discovery of the hints that Kutas and Hillyard had provided in their early work. At around the same time in the early 1990s, a handful of studies aspired to investigate brain responses to syntactic or morphosyntactic violations from a variety of angles.

Neville et al. (1991) was a clever and admirable attempt to differentiate not only between semantic and syntactic processing, but also between competing syntactic theories of how the brain responds to well- vs. ill-formed long-distance dependencies. At issue was how such dependencies are best captured by the grammar. Generalized Phrase Structure Grammar (GPSG) and its descendant Head-driven Phrase Structure Grammar (HPSG) to this day make the strong claim that long-distance dependencies can be accommodated by phrase structure rules alone, making for a more parsimonious grammar and a better fit with the parser (J. D. Fodor 1983). Chomskyan grammar (at the time) relied on additional external constraints superimposed on the output of the phrase structure rules to weed out ill-formed dependencies (Chomsky 1981). To this end, in addition to standard semantic anomalies (*The scientist criticized Max's **event** of the theorem*), Neville et al. (1991) tested three types of syntactic violation: phrase structure violations created by permuting words in the linear string (*The scientist criticized Max's **of** proof the theorem*), specificity condition violations created by extracting out of a complex noun phrase object with a specifier (*\*What did the scientist criticize [Max's **proof** of __]?*), and subjacency violations created by extracting out of a complex noun phrase in subject position (*\*What was [a proof of __] **criticized** by the scientist?*).

The results were mixed. Phrase structure violations elicited a larger N125 (essentially a slightly delayed N100) over the left side of the head, a subsequent left anterior negativity or LAN between 300 and 500 ms, and a following widespread late positivity starting around 500 ms. Specificity condition violations elicited both a larger N125 and greater LAN, but no late positivity; however, the early negative differences began too early at 0 ms and were thus unreliable. Subjacency violations elicited only a late positivity beginning at 500 ms with no preceding negativities. So in the end it was hard to ascertain what exactly the brain had been responding to in each individual instance, and therefore unfortunately impossible to distinguish between theoretical accounts. What was clear however was that, as in Kutas and Hillyard (1983), while semantic violations elicited a standard N400 effect, syntactic violations did not.

Kluender and Kutas (1993a, b) likewise investigated long-distance dependencies in the interest of isolating the brain responses to subjacency violations, this time in the form of *wh*-islands. The hope was to relate these findings to an emerging, more general processing account of islands (Kluender 1992, 1998). Hence this was another valiant early attempt at using ERP data to decide between theoretical proposals. However, the brain turned out to be most concerned about something entirely different: namely, how to process all the grammatical (*Who isn't he sure [that **the** TA explained it to __ **in** lab]?*), marginal (*?\*Who isn't he sure [if **the** TA explained it to __ **in** lab]?*), and ungrammatical (*\*Who_a isn't he sure [what_b **the** TA explained __a to __b **in** lab]?*) long-distance dependencies thrown at it.

The upshot of the study was that whenever a long-distance *wh*-question was compared to a corresponding yes/no question, the encoding of the *wh*-filler into working memory elicited a LAN effect. Thus when compared to grammatical *wh*-questions (containing embedded *that* complementizers) or marginal *wh*-questions (containing embedded *if* complementizers), the second, embedded *wh*-phrase in an ungrammatical *wh*-island (*what* in the preceding example) also elicited a LAN effect as soon as it became clear that it was not the subject of the embedded clause (i.e. at *the*), but rather had been displaced from an object position internal to it. In other words, this *wh*-phrase was also going to need to be encoded in working memory pending identification of an appropriate gap position for it downstream. The brain seemed to care more about this than the fact that it was confronted with an ungrammatical structure: there was no obvious response related to ill-formedness upon encountering the second *wh*-phrase at the left edge boundary of the island. Following prepositional object gap positions (associated with the matrix *wh*-filler) in the embedded clause (at *in*), *wh*-questions again elicited LAN effects when compared to corresponding yes/no questions. When this same post-gap position (at *in*) was then compared across all *wh*-question conditions, including *wh*-islands, the only difference was in the amplitude of the LAN response to gap filling: larger in ungrammatical *wh*-islands and marginal *if*-clauses than in grammatical *that*-clauses.[3]

---

[3]  End-of-sentence effects in this study will be discussed in the next section of this chapter.

Osterhout and Holcomb (1992) took a different tack, using subject vs. object control sentences (*The broker hoped **to** sell the stock* vs. *\*The broker persuaded **to** sell the stock*) to contrast the brain responses to unsalvageable subcategorization – and therefore also phrase structure – violations vs. temporary processing garden paths involving reduced relative clauses that either did (*[The broker [persuaded **to** sell the stock]] **was** sent to jail*) or did not (*\*[The broker [hoped **to** sell the stock]] **was** sent to jail*) end up being well-formed. This was simultaneously a test of Frazier's (1978) minimal attachment parsing principle: if minimal attachment holds, the parser should prefer the simpler object control parse over the possible but unlikely passive reduced relative clause parse (we now know of course that constructional frequency also plays a role here as well). The object control sentences elicited an effect of late positivity in response to **to** in both of these contexts, namely the point at which it becomes clear that the subcategorized object is missing. This is consistent with both minimal attachment and constructional frequency considerations. Subject control sentences on the other hand elicited both LAN and late positive effects in response to **was** following the reduced passive relative clause attempting to be formed on an intransitive verb. It was difficult at the time to figure out why there was also a LAN effect only in response to **was**. But again with hindsight it is possible to speculate that the parser was at this point frantically trying to find a legitimate subject for this verb, and therefore retrieving previously parsed material from working memory to evaluate for its appropriateness; see Section 24.3.5. Like Neville et al. (1991), Osterhout and Holcomb concluded that the brain responses to syntactic violations differed in kind from those to semantic violations. However, they also reported larger N400 responses to the final words of ungrammatical sentences (*\*The broker persuaded to sell the **stock***), as well as larger N400-like responses to the final words of unsalvageable parses (*\*[The broker [hoped to sell the stock]] was sent to **jail***) that persisted beyond 600 ms through to the end of the epoch. These responses were interpreted as indexing the impairment of "message-level" interpretation caused by violations of syntax.

Hagoort, Brown, and Groothusen (1993) compared the brain responses to semantic anomalies with those to three types of grammatical violation in their ERP study of Dutch: errors of subject–verb number agreement, subcategorization (in this case, assigning direct objects to intransitive verbs), and phrase structure (created by switching the adverb and adjective in modified DPs: *the rather emotional response* vs. *\*the emotional rather response*). Semantic violations predictably elicited standard N400 effects. While the subcategorization errors elicited uninterpretable ERPs, the agreement and phrase structure violations both elicited broad late positivity similar to the responses in Osterhout and Holcomb (1992) and Neville et al. (1991). Hagoort et al. likewise interpreted these late positive effects as specific to syntactic processing. Also, like Osterhout and Holcomb (1992), Hagoort et al. reported end-of-sentence N400-like effects that appeared to be sustained rather than transient in nature. These were presumed to be an index of semantic integration difficulty.

Finally, Friederici, Pfeifer, and Hahne (1993) contrasted a variety of violations in simple German passive sentences presented auditorily. In addition to selectional restriction violations (*Die Wolke wurde* **begraben** 'The cloud was buried'), essentially semantic anomalies, the morphosyntactic violations consisted of substituting a present tense indicative verb form inflected for first-person singular ('[I] polish') instead of the expected sentence-final passive participle ('polished'): *Das Parkett wurde* **bohnere** 'The floor was polish-1S'). The phrase structure violations were created by substituting passive participle verb forms for the expected DP objects of prepositions. This was accomplished by eliminating the DP object altogether. These violations are somewhat difficult to capture in English because of the differences in word order: the German sentences (e.g. *Der Freund wurde im* **besucht**) translate into English word order as 'The (boy)friend was visited in the,' but the word-by-word gloss in German word order is 'The friend was in the visited.' The morphosyntactic violations elicited a broad negativity – possibly a combination in the same time window of a LAN effect over the front of the head and an N400 effect over the back of the head – followed by a late positivity at posterior electrodes (see Section 24.3.5). The responses to the phrase structure violations, on the other hand, consisted of a broad frontal negativity that began earlier (around 50 ms) and peaked around 180 ms at the left anterior electrode. Friederici et al. interpreted these early findings conservatively, allowing that the early negativity may have been influenced by prosodic factors, and that the late positivity in response to the morphosyntactic violations could be a P300 response. They also made the following conjecture, however:

> Once these effects observed in correlation with syntactic processing, i.e. the early negativities and the late positivity, are validated by further experiments, they may be taken to support a two-stage module of syntactic parsing, with a first stage during which a structure-driven parser assigns an initial structure to the input based on major category information, and a second stage during which structural and semantic aspects are made available before final interpretation takes place. (Friederici et al. 1993: 191)

In the interest of fast forwarding to studies of specifically syntactic processing, I will next give a summary overview of collective wisdom about these components at the time of this writing. It may well soon change, as this still constitutes a moving research target, but it is important to point out that I have outlined what was initially reported in these early studies of syntactic processing in some detail precisely because they laid all the relevant cards out on the table. Specifically, the inventory of syntactically related brain responses has not substantially changed since that time, with some minor possible exceptions. While the following summary will invariably reveal my own biases and predilections, I will at the same time do my best to identify them as such, and also to highlight the differing views of other researchers.

## 24.3 Taking Stock: The Current State of Knowledge

### 24.3.1 N400

The N400 enjoys something of a privileged status among linguistic ERP components, both in terms of its familiarity and the success with which its functional significance has been narrowed down over the years. In part this is because it has (arguably) been around a good decade longer than the other linguistic ERP components that succeeded it temporally, but more importantly, also because its functional significance has been relentlessly and doggedly pursued. This research agenda has thus had the added advantage of liberating the N400 from the confines of anomaly. Kutas and Hillyard (1984) and Kutas, Lindamood, and Hillyard (1984) established two crucial facts about the N400 early on in its history. First, the amplitude of the N400 is inversely correlated with cloze probability – that is, the degree to which a particular word is expected to occur within a particular linguistic context: the lower the cloze probability, the larger the N400 response. This effect is independent of actual incongruity. A word can be of low cloze probability and still yield a coherent and well-formed, if somewhat less likely, sentence interpretation, and elicit a larger N400 response (*The bill was due at the end of the* **hour** > **month**). The second important finding was that a low cloze probability word, even a semantic anomaly, elicits a relatively smaller amplitude N400 if it is semantically related to the expected word in that particular context (*She put on her high-heeled* **bricks** > **boots** > **shoes**). This led to the important insight that the N400 can be used as a tool to probe the inner architecture of the lexicon, and the manner in which the long-term memory representations it contains are activated in online sentence processing.

In line with this, much attention has been devoted over the past 20 years to the degree to which the N400 indexes not only integration of a word into its sentence context, but also its pre-activation in the lexicon based on preceding sentence context. A string of studies has shown across a variety of languages that an article or prenominal modifying adjective that does not match the expected head noun of the phrase in gender (Spanish: Wicha, Moreno, & Kutas 2003; Wicha, Bates, Moreno, & Kutas 2003), phonological (English: DeLong, Urbach, & Kutas 2005), or animacy features (Polish: Szewczyk & Schriefers 2013) elicits an N400 effect all its own, i.e. before the expected head noun is even encountered.[4] Kwon et al. (2017)

---

[4] Two studies have reported positivities in response to such experimental manipulations: a further study of Spanish article gender mismatches (Wicha, Moreno, & Kutas 2004), and a study of Dutch prenominal modifying adjectives mismatching in gender with the expected head noun of the phrase (Van Berkum et al. 2005). The reasons for this discrepancy across studies are not entirely clear, but may be related to the individual differences in response type across participants discussed in Section 24.3.4.

reported similar N400 effects for mismatching classifiers in Chinese. In this case, the prenominal N400 effect was moreover inversely correlated with the degree of semantic overlap between the classifier and head noun: the closer the semantic overlap between the mismatching classifier and the head noun, the smaller the N400 effect. Altogether, these studies suggest that context serves to pre-activate specific lexical representations in long-term working memory during sentence processing.[5]

Recall from our discussion of early ERP studies of syntax in the preceding section that N400-like effects – often more sustained than transient in nature – are commonly elicited at or near the end of syntactically ill-formed sentences. We will return to this issue in the discussion of individual differences in Section 24.3.4. A number of studies have also reported immediate (rather than sentence-end) N400 effects preceding P600 effects in response to subject–verb agreement errors of various types across languages: English number (Kutas & Bates, unpublished data), Hebrew gender (Deutsch & Bentin 2001), Dutch number (Severens, Jansma, & Hartsuiker 2008),[6] Spanish person (Mancini et al. 2011a) and arguably Spanish number (Mancini et al. 2011b). These studies will also become relevant below in Section 24.3.4.

### 24.3.2    P600/SPS/LPC/Late Positivity

The various alternative names assigned to this component in the section heading above reflect its rather contentious nomenclatural and ideological history. Let's start with its most uncontentious manifestation. Sutton and colleagues (1965, 1967) first introduced the P300 component, a modality-independent general cognitive response time-locked to the resolution of uncertainty, largest over centro-parietal regions of scalp with a peak amplitude latency of 300 ms. Sutton and colleagues never actually referred to this response as a P300, but rather as a "late positive component" or "positive(-going) process." This was perhaps both a fortuitous and foresightful choice, as the specific latency of P300 responses can vary widely, dependent on how long it takes to evaluate and categorize the stimulus (Sutton et al. 1967). From the beginning, Sutton et al. (1965) demonstrated the sensitivity of the P300 to the objective probability of occurrence of a particular stimulus (namely, the less likely the occurrence, the larger the response), as well as to participants' subjective expectations for a particular stimulus to occur (i.e. incorrect guesses elicited larger responses). Squires, Squires, and Hillyard (1975) also demonstrated that what is known as the P3b portion of the P300 – for all practical purposes,

---

[5] This entire line of research, and the phonological mismatch results of DeLong, Urbach, and Kutas (2005) in particular, have in recent years been reported not to replicate in studies by Ito, Martin, and Nieuwland (2017a), as well as in a large-scale, multi-lab study by Nieuwland et al. (2018). See DeLong, Urbach, and Kutas (2017) for a reply to the Ito, Martin, and Nieuwland (2017a) study, and Ito, Martin, and Nieuwland (2017b) for a response to the reply.

[6] This study elicited only N400 effects, with no subsequent P600 effect.

the classic P300 – is dependent on the task relevance of the stimulus, that is, the evaluation of the stimulus must be of consequence for the task at hand. For example, during a standard categorical perception task, participants actively monitoring for a phoneme on one voicing continuum show no noticeable P300 response to voicing distinctions on a simultaneously presented orthogonal continuum containing other phoneme pairs (Toscano et al. 2010). Models of the P300 (or more exactly, the P3b) characterize it alternatively as an index of the match between a mental representation of a target stimulus and the actual target itself, or more generally, the updating of a mental model based on current context (Donchin 1981).

This simple picture became more complicated in the early 1990s when, as discussed above, Neville et al. (1991), Osterhout and Holcomb (1992), and Hagoort et al. (1993) all reported late positive responses to (morpho)syntactic violations. Osterhout and Holcomb (1992: 791) labeled this response, measured between 500 and 800 ms, the P600 because "[a]lthough the component did not have a clearly defined peak, its midpoint rested around 600 ms poststimulus." Yet they also entertained the possibility that it "might be a member of the family of late positive components (P300 and related components)" (1992: 798). Neville et al. (1991: 160) noted the similarity of the late positivity elicited in their study to that of Osterhout and Holcomb (1992), but expressed doubt that it could be a general response to syntactic ill-formedness, as their specificity constraint violation condition did not elicit a late positive response. Hagoort et al. (1993) on the other hand committed explicitly to the functional specificity of the late positive component elicited by their stimuli by labeling it the "syntactic positive shift" (or "SPS"). Their justification for dissociating the SPS from the more general P300 family was that, while Neville et al. (1991) and Osterhout and Holcomb (1992) had used an acceptability judgment task (more generally a stimulus categorization task, known to elicit P300 responses) simultaneously with presentation of the stimuli in their studies, Hagoort et al. (1993) had not. Their argument was that the morphosyntactic errors in their stimuli were therefore not task-relevant (i.e. there was no subsidiary task aside from reading in this experiment), but had still elicited the late positive response. Their participants were, however, informed before the experiment began that the sentences they would see would contain grammatical errors, setting the expectation for implicit categorization of the stimuli. And while there were equivalent numbers of grammatically correct and incorrect sentences, each type of violation (subject–verb agreement, word order, and subcategorization) constituted one-sixth of the total stimulus set. The significance of this fact will become apparent at the close of this section.

To cut to the twenty-first-century chase, most linguistic event-related potential researchers now agree that the P600 is not syntax-specific, and many believe that it is not even language-specific, but rather a member of the more general P300 family of responses. However, this issue is still contentious at the time of this writing, and opinions differ. What follows is a very brief, logical rather than chronological history of how we arrived at this point of consensus or disagreement, as the case may be.

Over the past 20 years it has become increasingly clear that what can plausibly be considered semantic and/or pragmatic violations will under certain circumstances also elicit late positive responses. Earlier isolated studies had foreshadowed this finding. In an unpublished study of Spanish modeled after the grammatical violation study of Kutas and Hillyard (1983; see Section 24.2), Kutas and Bates observed that in a connected prose narrative text, Spanish verb forms marked correctly for person and number agreement morphology but placed in the wrong tense elicited a late positive component from native Spanish speakers. This arguably created more of a semantic/pragmatic than a morphosyntactic problem for readers (*Los dinosaurios ponían huevos pero los mamíferos **traerán** al mundo una descendencia viviente* 'Dinosaurs laid eggs but mammals will leave a living legacy on earth'). Shao and Neville (1998) reported late positivity in response to hyponomy violations (*Jane does not eat any meat at all, and instead she eats lots of **beef** and vegetables*) that was accompanied by a preceding LAN effect (the significance of which will become clear further on below in the discussion of probability manipulations). Then in the early 2000s, a number of independently but simultaneously conducted studies in both English and Dutch reported late positive responses to the verb in the following thematic (agent–patient) violations: Kuperberg et al. (2003: *For breakfast the eggs would only **eat** toast and jam*), Kolk et al. (2003: *De vos die op de stroopers* [pl.] ***joeg*** [sing.] ... 'The fox that hunted the poachers ... '), Hoeks, Stowe, and Doedens (2004: *De speer heft de atleten **geworpen*** 'The javelin threw the athletes'). Kim and Osterhout (2005) proposed that such errors are underlyingly morphosyntactic: patient-first word order leads the parser to interpret the morphological marking on the verb as incorrect (i.e. singular instead of plural, active instead of passive, etc., as the case may be). However, even when eliminating this confound in Dutch, van Herten, Kolk, and Chwilla (2005: *De vos die op de strooper* [sing.] ***joeg*** [sing.] ... 'The fox that hunted the poacher ... ') reported the same late positive response with the same scalp distribution as elicited by true subject–verb agreement errors. They concluded that what is at issue in these cases is pragmatic plausibility. A number of useful review papers appeared around the same time addressing this conceptual conundrum (Kolk & Chwilla 2007; Kuperberg 2007; Bornkessel-Schlesewsky & Schlesewsky 2008; Kos et al. 2010), to which the reader is referred for extensive discussion of this still unresolved problem. We will return to this issue of the so-called "semantic P600" in the next section. In the meantime, the point for now is that late positivity can be elicited not only in response to (morpho)syntactic errors, but also in response to semantic/pragmatic anomalies of a certain type. This suggests that the P600 is not syntax-specific.

Second, Münte et al. (1998) compared semantic, morphosyntactic, and orthographic anomalies in German (*Die Hexe benutzte ihren **Besen** /**Traum** /*

*Besens* /*Behsen*, um *zum Wald zu fliegen* 'The witch used her **broom** / **dream** / **broom's** / **brume** to fly to the forest'[7]) inserted in connected prose stories. All three types of anomalies elicited late positive responses (following an N400 effect in the case of the semantic anomalies). The scalp distributions of the P600 responses to morphosyntactic and orthographic violations were notably indistinguishable. The orthographic violation P600 results were later replicated by Vissers, Chwilla, and Kolk (2006). Taken together, these studies suggested that the P600 is not specific to traditional levels of linguistic analysis, since the orthographic "errors" in Münte et al. (1998) neither altered the phonology of the target word nor flouted German orthographic conventions.

Third, a number of studies all using similar designs reported late positive responses to violations in cognitive domains other than language that closely resembled the P600 in both physical parameters and function. Besson and Macar (1987) and Verleger (1990) both reported large P300 responses to melodic violations in familiar tunes and scales, while Janata (1995) reported P300 (specifically, P3b) responses to harmonic violations that reflected the degree of violation: dissonant chords terminating major chord progressions elicited larger P300 responses than minor chords. Patel et al. (1998) took this paradigm one step further by comparing degrees of harmonic violation with degrees of syntactic violation, comparing both garden path sentences with reduced passive relative clauses (*Some of the senators endorsed promoted **an old idea** of justice*) and completely unsalvageable, ungrammatical sentences (*Some of the senators endorsed the promoted **an old idea** of justice*) to well-formed sentences. Relative to these controls, both sets of stimuli elicited late positive components with similar scalp distributions whose amplitude reflected the degree of violation. Nuñez-Peña and Honrubia-Serrano (2004) applied this same degree-of-violation paradigm to ascending and descending series of numbers that ended with the predicted number (7 10 13 16 19 22 **25**), one digit off from the predicted number (7 10 13 16 19 22 **24**), or with a number far off from the target (7 10 13 16 19 22 **50**). Again, these stimuli elicited large late positivities whose amplitude reflected the degree of violation. Taken together, these studies suggested that the P600 may not even be language-specific.

Finally, a number of studies manipulated typical morphosyntactic violation paradigms using variables that the P300 is known to be sensitive to, most consistently probability of occurrence. Osterhout et al. (1996) was a systematic manipulation not only of probability, but also of task relevance. Their first experiment compared the brain responses to font size

---

[7] The orthographic violation in German (*Behsen*) obeys the rules of German orthography and is pronounced exactly the same as the target word (*Besen*), but is a non-existent form. Nor does it suggest an alternative low-frequency word, as does *brume* ('mist') in English. Likewise, the use of genitive case-marking (*Besens*) on the accusative object in the German example does not allow a parse in which the genitive-marked possessor can be followed by a head noun – as *broom's* does in English, e.g. *the broom's handle* – because the preceding possessive adjective (*ihren* 'her-ACC') is also marked accusative and thus blocks a possessive interpretation.

changes (known to elicit P300 responses:[8] *The doctors* **BELIEVE** *the patient will recover*) and subject–verb agreement errors (known to elicit P600 responses: *The doctors* **believes** *the patient will recover*) in both an end-of-sentence acceptability judgment condition (in which the errors were task-relevant) and a passive reading condition (in which they were less so). The difference in amplitude of the late positive response between the passive reading and the acceptability judgment conditions was significant for font size changes but not for subject–verb agreement errors (though the amplitude increased numerically in this comparison as well), suggesting that task relevance influences the amplitude of P300 but not of P600 responses. In a second experiment,[9] Osterhout et al. (1996) manipulated the probability of occurrence of oddball sentences: the control condition (*The doctors* **believe** *the patient will recover*) comprised 20% of the stimulus set, while the font size and agreement errors comprised either 20% or 60% of alternative versions of the stimulus set. While font size changes and agreement violations both elicited larger amplitude late positivity when they comprised 20% of the stimulus than when they comprised 60%, this difference was significant only for the font size changes. Osterhout et al. therefore concluded that because the response to font size changes exhibited the expected sensitivity to probability, it was a member of the P300 family, whereas the response to agreement violations was not.[10]

The probability experiment in Osterhout et al. (1996) was quickly followed by a number of disconfirming replications (the task relevance and additivity – see footnote 9 – experiments, however, were never directly challenged). Gunter, Stowe, and Mulder (1997) varied 25% vs. 75% inflectional violations in Dutch (*De vuile matten werden door de hulp* **geklopt**/*\*kloppen* 'The dirty doormats were beaten/\*beat [infinitive] by the housekeeper') in alternative stimulus sets and found that the amplitude of the late positive response to the inflectional violations was significantly reduced when they made up 75% of the stimulus set, while, notably, an earlier LAN response to the inflectional violations around 300–400 ms was unaffected by the same probability manipulation. Gunter et al. (1997) reported a somewhat smaller probability effect for the grammatical stimuli as well: the late positive response to the grammatical stimuli was larger at three left posterior electrodes in the 25% vs. 75% grammatical

---

[8]  See Kutas and Hillyard (1980a, b).

[9]  In a third experiment, Osterhout et al. (1996) included a fourth condition containing a double violation (*The doctors* BELIEVES *the patient will recover*) in order to see if the late positive responses to font changes and morphosyntactic errors were additive in nature, and therefore plausibly independent of each other. The results of this experiment were largely equivocal; see Osterhout et al. (1996) for details.

[10]  In Experiment 1, Osterhout et al. reported slightly different scalp distributions of the late positive response to the two types of violation (left-lateralized for agreement errors and right-lateralized for font size changes) when they were followed by an acceptability judgment task, but not under passive reading. In Experiment 2, which again used an acceptability judgment task, these same topographical differences emerged, but this time did not survive statistical correction for number of comparisons. While these data can be taken to suggest that the source generators of the two responses might not have been exactly the same, given the tenuousness of the finding, they do not provide conclusive evidence for the claim.

stimulus set. They attributed the robust effects of probability on the font size but not the morphosyntactic manipulation in Osterhout et al. (1996) to the salience of the former stimuli compared to the latter (third-person singular present tense indicative agreement errors being common in both non-native speech and non-standard dialects of English), as salience is known also to affect P300 amplitude.

Coulson, King, and Kutas (1998) also used 20% vs. 80% violations, but of two different types: subject–verb agreement errors, as in Osterhout et al. (1996), and pronominal case errors (*The plane took **us**/*we to paradise and back* and *He fell down and skinned **his**/*he knee*) in order to test this effect of salience: the prediction was that the more egregious nature of pronoun case errors would elicit larger late positive effects. This turned out to be the case. Pronoun case violations also elicited a reliable LAN effect that, in contrast to Gunter et al. (1997), showed sensitivity to the probability manipulation, i.e. was larger in amplitude in the 20% than in the 80% violation stimulus set. With regard to the late positive response, the main effects of grammaticality and probability showed strikingly similar scalp distributions, suggesting that they had similar source generators. Like Gunter et al. (1997), Coulson et al. reported that late positive responses to both grammatical and ungrammatical sentences were smaller when either one constituted 80% of the stimulus set – in order words, there were effects of probability for both grammatical and ungrammatical sentences. This likewise suggested common neural generators for effects of probability and grammaticality. Coulson et al. attributed the differences in their findings from those of Osterhout et al. (1996) to (a) the inconsequential nature of subject–verb agreement errors in English, as alluded to above, and (b) the differences in probability between the two studies. They argued that since natural language stimuli bring with them a rich set of expectations for native speakers, experimental manipulations of objective probability need to be more highly contrastive in order to counteract and compensate for participants' subjective assessments of probability based on a lifetime of experience with the language under study.

Hahne and Friederici (1999) reported largely similar results in German using 20% vs. 80% phrase structure violations from the original Friederici, Pfeifer, and Hahne (1993) stimulus paradigm (for example, *Die Kuh wurde im **gefüttert*** 'The cow was fed in the'). The late positive response to these errors essentially disappeared in the 80% violations stimulus set (in fact, it was numerically but not significantly smaller, i.e. more negative, than the response to 20% grammatical sentences in the same stimulus set), while an earlier eLAN response to the violations between 100 and 300 ms post stimulus onset was unperturbed by the same manipulation. Hahne and Friederici interpreted this difference as consistent with their hypothesis that the eLAN indexes an automatic, modular first-pass parsing process (see Section 24.2) while the P600 indexes a controlled, post-modular process of integration and reanalysis. They found no effect of probability on their grammatical sentences, however.

Taken together, probability studies of the P600 suggest that it shares properties of the more general P300 response. It is this fact, in conjunction with the apparent lack of domain specificity in the nature of P600 responses as demonstrated in the other studies discussed above, that has led many researchers to conclude that the P600 is a member of the P300 family.[11] But as pointed out at the outset of this section, this conclusion still remains controversial. For this reason, I will continue to use the terms P600, late positive response/component, and late positivity interchangeably throughout the rest of this chapter.

### 24.3.3  N400 and P600 Interactions

Recall from Section 24.2 that in their first reports, Kutas and Hillyard (1980a, b) were at pains to dissociate the N400 from the more general P300 response, and the N200 component that typically precedes it. Nevertheless, late positive effects following the N400 effect were visible right off the bat in Figure 1 of each of Kutas and Hillyard's (1980a, 1983, 1984) studies. Recall further from Section 24.3.2 that Münte et al. (1998) reported effects of late positivity in response to violations of morphosyntax, orthography, and semantics in their German prose stories – in the latter case, following the N400. It turns out that this is a fairly common though not predominant pattern in the literature. Van Petten and Luka (2012) conducted a literature search of ERP studies using sentence-final semantic anomalies in the absence of an explicit judgment or acceptability task, which independently tends to elicit late positive responses. Out of 45 such studies including 64 relevant comparisons that they identified, about one-third included a late positivity following the N400 response, even without an acceptability judgment task. The remainder yielded only an N400 effect.

All this in and of itself is not that disturbing, particularly at sentence end, which commonly elicits a very large positivity anyway as participants realize that the sentence they are reading is over. What complicates matters is that an N400 + P600 complex has also been elicited by other types of anomalies. In Section 24.3.2 we discussed early studies reporting a so-called "semantic P600." Subsequent research showed that in many if not most of these studies, violations of this type actually elicit N400 + P600 complexes. Paczynski and Kuperberg (2011, 2012) demonstrated that the N400 + P600 complex elicited in response to animacy violations was impervious to the type of thematic role involved (*At headquarters the manager interviewed/surprised the **application** for/after ten minutes*) and the

---

[11]  See Sassenhagen and Bornkessel-Schlesewsky (2015) for a novel approach to the same question that nonetheless again reaches the same conclusion, namely that the P600 is a member of the P300 family.

relatedness of the inanimate anomaly to the expected animate noun (*The pianist played his music while the bass was strummed by the **drum/coffin** during the song*). Chow and Phillips (2013) further demonstrated that in Chinese, the P600 part of the N400 + P600 complex appears to be a response to the actual animacy violation (*gaocaisheng ba shuxueti **nandao-le/kunzhu-le** 'The student **baffled/restrained** the math problem'*) while the N400 is a response to the inability to form any kind of plausible semantic relationship between the preposed direct object and the final verb (*gaocaisheng ba shuxueti **guaqi-le/kunzhu-le** 'The student **hung/restrained** the math problem'*). However, they also confirmed that the "semantic P600" response was not uniquely tied to animacy violations, as originally suggested by the data in Kolk et al. (2003) and van Herten, Chwilla, and Kolk (2005): sentences with reversed arguments ('Inspector Chen arrested the suspect/The suspect arrested Inspector Chen') still elicited a P600 effect in Chinese when the two arguments of the verb were controlled for equivalent animacy (a visible N400 difference at the midline was not significant; see Frenzel et al. (2011) for related findings in English). This latter finding was later replicated in English (Chow et al. 2015). Finally, Chow et al. (2018) showed that while the N400 part of the N400 + P600 complex was sensitive to the distance of the verb from its arguments, the P600 was not.

A third context in which N400 + P600 complexes have been elicited is sometimes collapsed with the argument reversal findings described above. While the two datasets are related in that with both types it is difficult to ascertain who is doing what to whom, they are slightly different in character, as in this instance the ambiguity is created by manipulating both case-marking and word order. In one paradigm, when both the subject and the direct object of transitive German verbs were marked nominative (Frisch & Schlesewsky 2001), dative, or accusative (Frisch & Schlesewsky 2005), the second case-marked argument elicited an N400 + P600 complex. Roehm et al. (2004) showed that the N400 + P600 complex can be elicited regardless of animacy, though the N400 responses were reported to evoke power in different frequency bands, and thus claimed to be different in nature.

In the other paradigm, when the two arguments of transitive German verbs – one a singular proper name unmarked for case, the other a plural bare noun ambiguously marked for case – were followed by either a singular or plural verb form that disambiguated which was subject and which was object, the less frequent and unexpected OSV word order again elicited an N400 + P600 complex (Bornkessel et al. 2004; Haupt et al. 2008; see also Chapters 12 and 18 for discussion of acceptability studies of word order in German).

These various datasets, regardless of eliciting condition, have led to a greater discussion in the literature of what is referred to as component overlap. Since the N400 is usually measured somewhere between 300 and 500–600 ms poststimulus onset, and the P600 between 500–600 and

900 ms, the amplitude of one affects the amplitude of the other. In other words, if the N400 is large, it can "pull up" the P600 and make it appear smaller, and therefore non-different from a control condition, while the P600 when of large amplitude can likewise "pull down" the N400 to minimize the N400 effect. This presents something of a methodological conundrum. In one proposal addressing the problem, Brouwer and Crocker (2017) suggested that ERP experiments focusing on the P600 should include judgment tasks in order to induce late positivities triggered by stimulus categorization, i.e. P300 effects, in order to provide some kind of constant baseline against which to evaluate N400 effects and/or lack of same. On the other hand, many researchers contend that doing so vitiates the great advantage of linguistic ERP research, namely that it provides an excellent window into online language processing without requiring extraneous responses in subsidiary tasks that will almost invariably elicit irrelevant P300 effects.

### 24.3.4 N400 and P600 Individual Differences

From the very beginning of ERP research into syntactic anomalies, individual differences in response have been apparent. In Section 24.3.1 we noted that Osterhout and Holcomb (1992) and Hagoort et al. (1993) both reported N400-like responses to the final words of sentences that contained (morpho)syntactic anomalies. Kluender and Kutas (1993b) reported that while half their participants likewise produced N400-like effects at the end of sentences containing *wh*-island violations, the other half produced either late positive effects or showed no discernible difference between conditions. This split in type of effect correlated imperfectly with family history of handedness: right-handed individuals with only right-handed family members (henceforth RRs) were responsible for two-thirds of the N400-like effects but only one-third of the late positive effects; those right-handers with left-handed immediate family members (henceforth RLs) showed the opposite pattern. Osterhout (1997) subsequently reported a similar end-of-sentence split between participants who produced N400 effects and those who produced P600 effects in response to reduced relative garden path sentences (*The boat sailed down the river **sank***). Osterhout speculated that those participants producing a P600 effect might still be attempting syntactic reanalysis of the garden path, while N400 participants may have abandoned syntactic reanalysis and simply treated the garden path as semantically anomalous.

This line of reasoning was followed up in studies of second language processing which reported that subject–verb agreement errors in German (Tanner et al. 2013) and English (Tanner, Inoue, & Osterhout 2014) elicited an N400 + P600 complex in adult second language learners directly, i.e. not just at sentence end. However, when learners' responses were examined individually, it turned out that some participants produced primarily an N400 response to the agreement violations, some primarily a P600 response, and some a biphasic N400 + P600 complex. P600 effects correlated with good and N400 effects with poor performance on an accompanying acceptability judgment task in Tanner et al. (2013), but P600 effects instead correlated with age of arrival and with motivation level in Tanner et al. (2014).

Immediately divergent responses to critical morphosyntactically anomalous words have been documented in native speakers as well. Tanner and van Hell (2014) reported N400 effects in roughly one-third to one half of their participants in response to verb agreement (*The clerk at the clothing boutique* **were** *severely underpaid and unhappy*) and other verbal complex errors (*The crime rate was* **increase** *despite the growing police force*); the remaining participants showed P600 effects. Only family history of handedness correlated weakly with this difference (accounting for 19% of the variance), reminiscent of the pattern of end-of-sentence N400 vs. P600 effects in Kluender and Kutas (1993b). Grey, Tanner, and van Hell (2017) followed up on this finding by using the same materials with strictly left-handed individuals and comparing their responses to those of the two right-handed groups (i.e. those with and without familial sinistrality) in Tanner and van Hell (2014). Whereas RRs as a group showed only P600 effects in response to both types of verbal error, left-handers patterned with RLs in showing N400 + P600 complex effects, independent of performance on the accompanying acceptability judgment task. Once again, this biphasic response pattern was found to result from N400 effects in roughly half the left-handers/RLs and P600 effects in the other half, while nearly all RRs showed only P600 effects. The authors attributed these brain differences to differences in greater reliance on lexical/semantic processing (N400 effects) in left-handers and RLs vs. morphosyntactic processing (P600 effects) in RRs, consistent with greater variability in hemispheric dominance in left-handers and RLs (Caplan 1987; Kutas & Hillyard 1980b).

### 24.3.5  LAN

Left anterior negativity (LAN) is perhaps the least well understood of the linguistic ERP components, because from the outset it has been elicited under seemingly orthogonal circumstances: in response to morphosyntactic violations (Neville et al. 1991; Osterhout & Holcomb 1992; Friederici et al. 1993[12]) and to long-distance dependencies, both grammatical (Kluender & Kutas 1993a) and ungrammatical (Neville et al. 1991; Osterhout & Holcomb 1992;[13] Kluender & Kutas 1993b).

---

[12] See Section 24.2.    [13] See Section 24.2.

The latter type of LAN, tied to working memory, will be discussed at length in Section 24.4. Here we will focus on the morphosyntactic LAN.

Based on the individual differences they found in N400 vs. P600 native-speaker responses to morphosyntactic violations, Tanner and Hell (2014) suggested that the morphosyntactic LAN may simply be an artifact of component overlap between the N400 and P600 (see Section 24.3.3). They showed how the presence of a P600 effect with a central-posterior scalp distribution elicited in response to a morphosyntactic error could "pull down" a simultaneous N400 effect, which likewise usually exhibits a (right) central-posterior maximum, when the two effects are averaged together, both across and within individuals. This then leaves only the smaller left anterior portion of a broad N400 effect visible in the grand average (Tanner & Hell 2014: 207, Figure 5). In support of this account, Tanner and van Hell cited some of the studies mentioned at the end of Section 24.3.1 that reported N400 + P600 complex effects in response to morphosyntactic violations. If their account is accurate, it would solve a long standing problem of interpretation in the literature.

### 24.3.6   eLAN

It is at this point probably safe to say that most (but again, not all) linguistic ERP researchers consider the early left anterior negativity (eLAN) response to be artifactual in nature. Recall from the end of Section 24.2 how Friederici et al. (1993) speculated that the eLAN might be indexing an automatic first-pass stage of syntactic parsing in which sentence structure is initially deter-mined solely by grammatical category, while the later LAN-like effect and late positivity are instead reflective of other semantic and syntactic processes that play a role in final sentence interpretation. Over subsequent years, this view became received wisdom. More specifically, the latency window of the N400 and LAN (300–500 ms) was interpreted as indexing semantic and morpho-syntactic processes, and the late positivity around 600 ms as indexing pro-cesses of syntactic reanalysis and repair (Friederici 2002).

This view of early negative responses was subsequently challenged both empirically and methodologically. On the empirical side, a number of inconsistent findings were reported. Federmeier et al. (2000) reported only N400 + P600 complex effects in response to substituting nouns for verbs (*John wanted to **beer***) and vice versa (*John wanted the **eat***), with no preceding early negative difference. Lau et al. (2006) showed that preced-ing structural context influenced the amplitude of the eLAN, inconsistent with its proposed role of indexing only the identification of the gramma-tical category of the next word in the input string in an informationally encapsulated way. Roll, Horne, and Lindgren (2007) and Zhang and Zhang (2008) reported effects of early negativity even when the unexpected word was of the same grammatical category as the expected word. Dikker et al. (2010) elicited early negativity in response to mismatches between the expected physical form of an upcoming noun and the form of the actual noun presented, i.e. within the same lexical category, while Dikker and Pylkkänen (2011) elicited early negativity in simple picture/word mismatches. This is actually consistent with an early study by Besson and Macar (1987) that reported N100 differences preceding the N400 effect in French sentences ending in a semantic anomaly (*Il porte sa fille dans ses* **narines** 'He carries his daughter in his nostrils').

Steinhauer and Drury (2012) presented a thoroughgoing analysis of the entire eLAN paradigm and noted further empirical problems, but their most damaging critiques concerned the methodology employed in eLAN studies. The same basic experimental stimulus paradigm outlined in Section 24.2 was used without significant modification for the entire series. The first problem with this is that the verbal prefixes used to signal grammatical category information in experiments using auditory presentation were not in fact specific to verbs. Second, all the studies held the target word constant and manipulated the surrounding context, rather than holding the context constant and manipulating the form of the target word. This caused the target word to be preceded frequently by different word types, namely open- vs. closed-class words (*Die Kuh wurde im [Stall]* **gefüttert** 'The cow was **fed** in the [stall]'), known to elicit vastly different ERP responses (Kutas & Hillyard 1983; Kutas, Van Petten, & Besson 1988; Van Petten & Kutas 1991). This in turn affects the baseline of the target word, which assumes as a methodological convenience that no voltage differences exist before word onset. If this assumption is not met, spurious differences can and often do appear in the ERP to the target word – especially those starting at 0 ms, as in Neville et al. (1991; specificity condition violations) and Friederici et al. (1993; syntax violations). Steinhauer and Drury (2012: 142, Figure 2) demonstrated how such spill-over effects from the previous word could easily account for the early negative differences reported to the next (target) word, ostensibly because it belongs to the wrong grammatical category. The interested reader is referred to Steinhauer and Drury (2012) for more illuminating and insightful details on this topic.

## 24.4 Prospects Going Forward

As may have been apparent thus far, much of the research on ERP responses to syntactic manipulations has focused primarily on morphosyntax. Since current generative theories of syntax place heavy emphasis on agreement relations in the phrase structure tree, this emphasis is perhaps not out of place, though it leaves out much of what interests syntacticians at the sentence level. The other disadvantage of this focus has been that it is tightly bound to violation paradigms, which tell us a lot about how the brain responds when sentence processing is disrupted, but not necessarily very much about what the brain is doing when it processes unremarkable language. In this section I will therefore focus primarily on those ERP studies that have investigated grammatical sentence processing. It seems, on reflection, that this line of research has had a fair amount of success in establishing basic knowledge about how the brain handles language, which has been built upon, amplified, and refined over the past three decades without the constant need for backtracking and fundamental re-evaluation that was part of the intended takeaway message of Section 24.3.

### 24.4.1  Quantification

The surprisingly consistent finding over decades of study using ERPs thus far is that adult native speakers have a fair amount of difficulty computing the use of quantification in online sentence processing without adequate contextual support (see Chapter 13 for more discussion of quantification).[14] This was first shown by Fischler et al. (1983), who investigated whether the N400 was sensitive to propositional as well as lexical semantic content. Participants were presented with statements, either affirmative or negative (*A robin is [not] a **bird**/**tree***), and asked to rate them true or false. The upshot was that the brain simply ignored the negation and relied on simple lexical association, yielding an N400 effect whenever *robin* co-occurred in the same sentence as *tree*, regardless of whether the sentence was true or false, and despite the possible semantic association of robins inhabiting trees. Fischler et al. (1983) used these data to argue for the delayed processing of negation, claiming that the proposition embedded under negation is processed first and the negation operation itself only secondarily.

   This claim received pushback from a number of researchers at the same time. Staab (2007) used paradigms with the following inferential contexts (in order to avoid generic contexts) to force a truth-value judgment:

*During his long flight Joe needed a snack. The flight attendant could only offer him pretzels and cookies.*

(1)   *Joe wanted something salty/sweet.*
(2)   *Joe didn't want anything salty/sweet.*

*So he bought/didn't buy the **pretzels**/**cookies**.*

The results were somewhat mixed. Following positive context (*Joe wanted something salty*), only false affirmative target sentences (*So he bought the **cookies***) elicited a reliable N400 effect of truth value in an

---

[14] Ivano Caponigro (p.c.) points out that this could be due to the fact that ERP studies of quantification have thus far been restricted to generic contexts. To my knowledge, no ERP study has yet looked at universal quantification or its scope interaction with other quantifiers – probably due to the apparent difficulty researchers have had in finding reliable evidence for online computation of quantificational elements.

early time window of 200–400 ms. Following negative context (*Joe didn't want anything sweet*), both false affirmative (*So he bought the **cookies***) and false negative target sentences (*So he didn't buy the **pretzels***) elicited N400 effects reflecting truth value. Yet the N400 effect was reduced in false negative sentences, underscoring persistent difficulty with processing negation. Nieuwland and Kuperberg (2008) took a similar approach, contrasting the effects of pragmatically licensed negation in restrictive contexts (*With proper equipment, scuba diving is/ isn't very **safe**/**dangerous***) vs. pragmatically unlicensed negation in generic contexts (*Bulletproof vests are/aren't very **safe**/**dangerous***). Crucially, however, they employed a reading comprehension task rather than a truth-value judgment task in their experiment. They reported equivalent N400 effects of truth value in response to both false affirmative (*With proper equipment, scuba diving is very **dangerous***) and false negative target sentences (*With proper equipment, scuba diving isn't very **safe***) when negation was pragmatically licensed, but only to false affirmative sentences (*Bullet proof vests are **dangerous***) when it was not.

Similar to the Fischler et al. (1983) study of negation, Kounios and Holcomb (1992) reported only lexical association N400 effects and insensitivity to truth value in experiments using universal and existential quantifiers (*All/Some/No gems are **rubies**/**spruces***). Urbach and Kutas (2010) revisited the issue, using generic contexts – avoiding universal quantifiers (*Most/Few farmers grow **crops**/**worms** as their primary source of income*) – and replicated N400 effects of lexical association and insensitivity to the plausibility of the statements. However, when providing contrastive contexts (*Alex was an unusual toddler in that he favored broccoli and peas over cookies and candy. Most/few kids prefer **sweets**/**vegetables** to other foods.*), Urbach, DeLong, and Kutas (2015) were able to elicit N400 effects of typicality in response to both types of false statement (*Most kids prefer **vegetables** . . . /Few kids prefer **sweets** . . .*). Interestingly, however, and similar to Nieuwland and Kuperberg (2008), this was the case only when (a) pragmatic licensing context was provided and (b) participants were reading for comprehension and not rating the sentences on a five-point scale for plausibility.[15]

The takeaway message here is that while online processing of quantification seems to be a delicate affair, when quantification is used in contexts that approximate the conditions of normal language use (i.e. with adequate context and without extraneous task demands of categorization), the brain seems perfectly capable of handling it on the fly.

---

[15] To be clear, *most*-type sentences showed N400 effects of typicality (i.e. larger N400 responses to *Most kids prefer vegetables* than to *Most kids prefer sweets*) regardless of whether context was provided or not, and independent of task. *Few*-type sentences on the other hand only showed such effects when context was provided with the subsidiary reading comprehension task.

### 24.4.2 Long-Distance Dependencies

Although the following statement reveals my own personal biases, I don't think it's unfair to claim that perhaps the most consistent and therefore successful linguistic ERP results – across experimental designs, linguistic structures, languages, labs, and time – have come from research on long-distance dependencies. Cumulative results and collective wisdom in this domain have yielded important insights – which have thus far not required extensive revision – into how the brain processes discontinuous but linked syntactic positions. I will also assert that this progress is due in large part to the fact that most of the research on long-distance dependencies has eschewed the use of violation paradigms. For the immediate purposes of this section, long-distance dependencies can be taken to be synonymous with Ā-dependencies; this will be the focus of our discussion. The cross-linguistic studies to be reviewed include *wh*-questions, relative clauses, topicalization structures to a more limited degree, and long-distance scrambling (see Chapters 7, 9, 10, and 12 for discussion of acceptability studies of some of these phenomena).

In Section 24.2.2 it was pointed out that the very first ERP studies of syntactic processing included comparisons of both grammatical and ungrammatical *wh*-questions (Neville et al. 1991; Kluender & Kutas 1993) as well as reduced relative clauses (Osterhout & Holcomb 1992). Before that, however, Garnsey, Tanenhaus, and Chapman (1989) had published a study which has long been taken as a prime example of how ERPs can be used to answer questions of theoretical interest. At the time there was a debate in the literature as to whether the parser would use non-syntactic (e.g. lexical semantic) information in order to avoid filling semantically implausible gaps. To test this, Garnsey et al. (1989) compared embedded questions of the following type: *The businessman knew which* **customer/article** *the secretary called __ at home*. In the spirit of predictive parsing, note that it would be perfectly reasonable for the parser to project a different syntactic structure that would accommodate the *wh*-filler more readily (Fodor 1978), e.g. "The businessman knew which article the secretary called the news-paper up about __ ." However, what Garnsey et al. (1989) instead found was that *called* elicited an N400 effect when preceded by the filler *article* – a clear indication that the parser was not hedging its bets and waiting for a more conducive gap site to appear downstream, but rather attempting to assign the filler *article* to the direct object position, even though this filler–gap association is semantically implausible. Frazier and Clifton (1989) independently proposed the so-called "active filler strategy" of gap filling the same year; this study provided a nice confirmation of the proposal (see Chapters 5 and 23 for further discussion of the active filler strategy). This is really an example of linguistic ERP research at its best.

As also pointed out in Section 24.2.2, Kluender and Kutas (1993a) reported localized LAN effects in response to words intervening between filler and gap in *wh*-questions whenever one condition containing a long-distance *wh*-dependency was compared to another lacking the same dependency. This was interpreted as an index of the working memory costs associated with processing discontinuous sentence positions mutually dependent on each other for their interpretation. In large part, this interpretation was based on Ruchkin et al. (1992), who reported slow left-lateralized anterior negative potentials indexing extrinsic verbal working memory load in a monotonic fashion (i.e. the greater the number of nonsense syllables to be retained in the experimental task, the greater the negative amplitude of the slow potential response). However, because Kluender and Kutas (1993a) did not control their stimuli for sentence length, it was impossible to track the processing of the dependency across its entire length in order to see if these local LAN effects were in fact mere snapshots of a longer-lasting left-lateralized negativity over the front of the head.

This problem was addressed and solved by King and Kutas (1995), who were the first to report bilateral slow anterior negative potentials following both introduction of the relative pronoun, a *wh*-filler, and the location of its gap at the main clause verb in response to object relative clauses (*The reporter* [*who* **the senator** *harshly attacked* ___] **admitted** *the error*) vs. subject relative clauses (*The reporter* [*who* {___} **harshly attacked** *the senator*] **admitted** *the error*) in English. In other words, the response was again tied to the presence of a long-distance dependency in object relatives that was missing in subject relatives. This was especially the case for those participants who showed good comprehension of the stimulus sentences, as determined by an end-of-sentence true/false test, taken as a proxy for superior working memory capacity in the absence of reliable reading span differences across the participants.

Moreover, by comparing the responses to the matrix verb (*admitted*) in the relative clause sentences to the second verb appearing in coordinate or subordinate clauses of filler sentences, King and Kutas (1995) were also able to show that the local ERP response to the matrix verb was likely sensitive to intrinsic verbal working memory load: the local LAN effect was larger in response to subject relative clauses – in which retrieval of the matrix subject (*the reporter*) is required at the matrix verb following the intervening relative clause – than in filler sentences, and larger again for object relative clauses – in which the matrix subject needs to be associated both with the matrix verb and with the embedded direct object position inside the relative clause – than in subject relative clauses.

One final finding of King and Kutas (1995) again demonstrates how ERPs can help to distinguish between theoretical accounts. Gibson's (1998, 2000) model of verbal working memory suggested that every word intervening between a filler and its gap would add to the cost of maintaining the dependency in purely incremental fashion.[16] In addition to across-

---

[16] This claim is also implicit in Kluender (1992).

sentence averages, King and Kutas (1995) also performed individual averages of every word in the sentence. Somewhat surprisingly, under rebaselining at the beginning of every word, the sustained anterior negative differences in the across-sentence averages largely disappeared, except for local LAN effects in object relative sentences elicited by the word immediately following the object *wh*-filler (i.e. *the senator*) and the words immediately preceding (the relative clause verb *attacked*) and following (the matrix verb *admitted*) the actual gap position. This suggests that the main costs incurred in processing a long-distance dependency occur at its beginning and its end, and that computing the words intervening between a filler and its gap do not seem to add to the overall costs of processing the dependency in the way predicted by Gibson's model. In retrospect, this finding could be taken as evidence for more recent models of verbal working memory that emphasize the costs of encoding and retrieval over those of maintenance. In any case, there is no ERP evidence that each word intervening between a filler and its gap adds to the processing costs of computing the dependency.

One additional finding relevant to long-distance dependencies was reported by Kaan et al. (2000) in their study of embedded *wh*-questions in English. They pursued the hypothesis that gap location (i.e. at the pre-gap position) in a filler–gap dependency elicits late positivity,[17] and that this late positivity indexes neither reanalysis (Friederici 1995; Münte, Matzke, & Johannes 1997) nor reprocessing (Osterhout, Holcomb, & Swinney 1994), but rather syntactic integration processes (Gibson 1998). This turned out to be a reliable effect. However, the interpretation of this finding has always been somewhat problematic. In a second experiment, Kaan et al. (2000) included both simple subject–verb agreement violations and gap-filling in the same design (*Emily wonders {whether/who} the performers in the concert* **imitate** */*imitates {a pop star/__} for the audience's amusement*) in an attempt to investigate the relationship between the late positivity elicited by both. If the amplitude of the late positivity in response to ungrammaticality alone or to gap-location alone summates when they are combined, this is an indication that they are independent of each other and that there are differences in their source generators. If on the other hand the two effects interact with each other in any way, this is an indication that they have the same source (see also footnote 9). In the analysis, the two factors did not interact in the omnibus ANOVA, but were found to interact marginally at two electrodes out of 29, in only one of two time windows measured. Kaan et al. (2000: 185) nevertheless concluded, based on the size in microvolts of the interaction effect at these two electrodes, that the two factors could not be entirely additive and that they therefore "may involve dependent [i.e. overlapping – RK] generators," and that "the processing of a 'who'-

---

[17] Originally, Edith Kaan (p.c.) spied a late positivity at a gap position in my dissertation data that had entirely escaped my notice, and she pursued that idea in this study.

phrase at the verb can be said to be related to the positivity generated by syntactic violations" (p. 187). This was in turn taken as supporting evidence for interpreting the late positivity in response to gap-location and syntactic violations as an index of general syntactic integration processes, and this has more or less become received wisdom. We will return to this issue in the next section.

Both of these findings have been replicated cross-linguistically across many labs and multiple types of Ā-dependency.[18] Kluender et al. (1998) replicated both the slow anterior negative potential effects and local LAN effects between filler and gap in German object wh-questions, as well as local LAN effects in English object wh-questions. Felser, Clahsen, and Münte (2003) replicated slow anterior negative potentials and local LAN effects in German object wh-questions and topicalization structures, which – reminiscent of King and Kutas (1995) – were significantly different from control sentences earlier but not later in the dependency. They also replicated late positive effects at gap location, but only in object wh-questions (i.e. not in topicalization structures), which they attributed to the quantificational nature of a wh-dependency. Fiebach, Schlesewsky, and Friederici (2001, 2002) likewise replicated slow anterior negative potential effects in embedded German object vs. subject wh-questions, but only in longer dependencies in which there were six (vs. two words) intervening between filler and gap. This effect was larger in low-span than in high-span participants (Fiebach et al. 2002: 262). They also replicated effects of greater late positivity at gap location in object vs. subject wh-questions, which was significant in both long and short object wh-questions, in contrast to the slow negative anterior effect, which was significant only in long object wh-questions. Phillips, Kazanina, and Abada (2005) replicated the slow anterior negative potential effects in response to embedded object wh-questions vs. declarative that-clauses in English. Like Fiebach et al. (2001, 2002), Phillips et al. (2005) reported greater amplitude effects in response to longer dependencies (in this case, the object filler and gap were either in the same clause or separated by a clause boundary). However, in contrast to Fiebach et al. (2001, 2002), Phillips et al. (2005) reported that the amplitude of late positive effects at gap location was not sensitive to dependency length: instead, they found that the effect onset was slightly delayed in longer dependencies. They likewise replicated the King and Kutas (1995) finding that rebaselining every word within the dependency suggests that the main processing cost is at the start of the dependency (i.e. at encoding), and that subsequent words intervening between filler and gap do not make independent contributions to the overall cost.[19]

---

[18] However, it is also important to point out that both McKinnon and Osterhout (1996) and Kaan et al. (2000) were unable to replicate slow anterior negative potential effects in response to embedded wh-questions in English, for reasons that are still unclear.

[19] Phillips et al. (2005) regrettably did not analyze the responses to words following the gap position in their stimulus sentences.

Vos et al. (2001: 53, Figure 2) elicited larger amplitude slow anterior negative potentials in response to Dutch sentences containing subject relative clauses (intervening between matrix subject and verb) compared to conjoined clauses (cf. King & Kutas 1995). An extrinsic working memory task that had participants monitor the stimulus sentences for the occurrence of one vs. three nouns showed that the higher working memory load condition elicited a larger slow anterior negative potential as well. As in Fiebach et al. (2001, 2002), this effect was larger in their low-working-memory-span participants (Vos et al. 2001: 58, Figure 5). Vos et al. (2001) also reported late positive effects in response to subject–verb agreement violations (i.e. standard ungrammaticality rather than gap location effects) that were delayed in the high extrinsic working memory load condition, as well as in low-working-memory-span participants. This is perhaps related to the delay of the late positivity in response to gap filling in longer (and therefore more difficult) dependencies reported by Phillips et al. (2005).

All the long-distance dependency effects discussed thus far have been in (largely) head-initial West Germanic languages. There was therefore a subsequent push to see if similar effects could be found in non-Indo-European, and particularly in head-final languages. Researchers therefore turned their attention to the main East Asian languages, especially Japanese and Korean.[20] Here the results have been surprisingly consistent: long-distance dependencies elicit equivalent ERP effects in these languages even though typological and constructional details differ (see Chapter 16 for further discussion of long-distance dependencies in East Asian languages). For example, leftward scrambling in Japanese elicits the same ERP responses as *wh*-movement processes in West Germanic languages: slow anterior negative potentials between the leftward scrambled element and its gap (presumed as in West Germanic languages to be attributable to working memory demands), effects of late positivity (and LAN effects as well in Ueno & Kluender 2003) at pre-gap positions, and effects of anterior negativity at post-gap positions (Ueno & Kluender 2003; Hagiwara et al. 2007).[21] Ueno and Kluender (2009) also reported slow anterior negative potentials between in situ *wh*-phrases and associated clause-final *wh*-scope-marking question particles in Japanese. Somewhat surprisingly, these *wh*-scope-marking question particles did not elicit

---

[20] There have also been ERP studies of head-final relative clauses in Chinese, but due to the language's mixed headedness, the question of whether subject or object relatives are more difficult to process has been plagued among other things by the fact that pre-nominal object relative clauses in an SVO language emulate basic SVO word order (Kanno 2007): [S V __] O

[21] Wolff et al. (2008) also investigated short-distance scrambling of objects (both accusative and dative) before subjects using visual presentation in Japanese, but did not compute multi-word averages between the displaced object and its canonical sentence position, making it difficult to compare results in this respect. However, they did report similar effects of anterior negativity at the sentence-final verb position. In a companion auditory experiment, this study demonstrated that insertion of a prosodic boundary after the scrambled object eliminated what the authors refer to as a scrambling negativity elicited when no prosodic boundary was present. See Wolff et al. (2008) for details.

effects of late positivity, even at sentence end, as one might reasonably expect in response to unambiguous determination of *wh*-scope.

In these studies, the lexical item in the dependency occurred earlier in the string and the functional dependent element later, as in the West Germanic languages. What happens when this relationship is reversed, and the dependent functional element appears first in the string and the lexical element comes later? This is the situation in head-final relative clauses: on the assumption that there is in fact a gap internal to a head-final relative clause (see Comrie 1996), it precedes the relative clause head. Gibson's (1998, 2000) model of verbal working memory, which is based on linear distance in the surface string, predicts that subject relative clauses should be more difficult to process than object relative clauses in strictly head-final languages (i.e. with SOV word order and final head nouns), because the subject gap position is farther away from the head noun in the linear string. Based on prior ERP research, the prediction would then be that this processing difficulty should manifest as larger anterior negativity in response to head-final subject relative clauses. However, in a study of Japanese relative clauses, Ueno and Garnsey (2008) instead reported slower reading times at the head noun position as well as larger slow anterior negative responses to the relative clause verb (that persisted at the subsequent head noun position) in object vs. subject relative clauses. Similarly, in a study of Korean relative clauses, Kwon et al. (2013) reported larger left-lateralized anterior negativity in response to the head noun position in object relative clauses.[22] There are two takeaways from these studies: the subject processing advantage holds in strictly head-final languages, and linear distance is not the determining factor.[23]

Thus far we have discussed only nominative–accusative languages. What about the processing of relative clauses in ergative languages? Does the subject advantage hold there as well? In a study of Basque relative clauses, Carreiras et al. (2010) reported that subject relative clauses elicited slower reading times and a greater left anterior positivity compared to object relative clauses. Despite the fact that this left anterior positivity had the same scalp distribution and morphology as the LAN effects we have been discussing in other studies, Carreiras et al. used the latency of their response to argue that it could not be a LAN response to object relative clauses, as it had a slightly delayed onset for a LAN (400 vs. 300 ms), and

---

[22] Previous reading time (Kwon, Polinsky, & Kluender 2006) and eye-tracking studies (Kwon et al. 2010) had provided additional evidence for greater processing difficulty at the head noun position of Korean object vs. subject relative clauses.

[23] The subject advantage in these studies has two different possible explanations that may be notational variants of each other. First, objects are more deeply embedded in the phrase structure tree than subjects, and therefore more difficult to access at the head noun position (O'Grady 1997). Alternatively, in head-final subject relative clauses, the verb phrase of the relative clause is already compiled during processing of the relative clause, and the head noun merely supplies the subject of predication. In head-final object relative clauses, on the other hand, the verb phrase cannot be compiled until the head noun position is reached, and only after that operation is completed can the relative clause subject predicate over it. See Kwon et al. (2013) for further discussion.

persisted beyond the critical word that acted as a point of comparison across conditions. However, as pointed out in Section 24.2.1, quantitative differences like latency alone are not sufficient to distinguish between components, and moreover many LAN effects do persist beyond the critical word. Recent studies of relative clauses in another ergative language, Georgian, suggest that this may in fact be a LAN effect after all: Georgian object relative clauses were read more slowly (Foley & Wagers 2017) and elicited familiar patterns of increased anterior negativity (Lau et al. 2019) compared to subject relative clauses. While these findings are not conclusive and are in need of further replication, it nonetheless seems simultaneously both astonishing and satisfying that brain responses could be conserved across diverse Ā-dependency types and typologically diverse languages in this way.

### 24.4.3   Referential Processing

Using both visual (van Berkum, Brown, & Hagoort 1999) and auditory presentation (van Berkum, Brown, & Hagoort 2003), van Berkum and colleagues elicited anterior negative brain responses to temporarily ambiguous DP anaphors (e.g. reference to 'the girl' following a discourse paragraph involving two girls as opposed to one involving a girl and a boy). Van Berkum et al. (2004) extended this paradigm to include pronouns in sentence contexts (*David shot at Linda/John as **he** jumped over the fence*) and reported similar results of anterior negativity in response to pronouns with two possible referents. As had been the case with regard to anterior negative brain responses to syntactic long-distance dependencies, these results were initially interpreted as indexing effects of verbal working memory (i.e. more difficulty in retrieving the relevant referent as antecedent). And indeed, Nieuwland and van Berkum (2006) showed that the amplitude of the response correlated with reading span scores: high-working-memory-span participants drove the effect in this instance. Nieuwland, Otten, and van Berkum (2007) replicated the originally reported anterior negative responses to DP anaphors with two possible referents, but demonstrated that the effect could be eliminated by removing one of these referents at the contextualizing discourse level (e.g. via departure or death in the narrative context). The results were again interpreted as a burden on verbal working memory imposed by (truly) ambiguous anaphors.

Subsequently, these anterior negative responses began to be interpreted as a specific index of referential ambiguity, which was then lent a functional label: the referentially induced frontal negativity, or "Nref." The implication was that this response is induced only in contexts of referential ambiguity, and this functional name has consequently stuck in the literature (see Barkley & Kluender (2018) for further discussion).

However, a number of studies in recent years have called this repurposing of the response into question, suggesting that the original interpretation may have been the correct one all along: namely, this is merely another example of verbal working memory-related LAN effects in syntactic processing. Barkley, Kluender, and Kutas (2015) compared the responses to object relative clauses (*The soldier [who the sailor roughly pushed ___] smashed a bottle against the bar* vs. *The soldier roughly pushed the sailor and smashed a bottle against the bar*) and to unambiguous pronouns preceded by clear antecedents (*After a covert mission that deployed Will/required deployment for nine terrible months, he longed for home*). While the scalp topography of the two responses differed slightly,[24] the responses to unambiguous pronouns had virtually the exact same scalp distribution as classic Nref responses, despite the fact that no referential ambiguity was involved. This result was interpreted as indexing the operations involved in retrieving the antecedent for a pronoun from working memory, just as fillers need to be retrieved from working memory for assignment to their gaps. Recall from Sections 24.2.2 and 24.4.2 that LAN effects can differ in amplitude in a way that reflects the difficulty of retrieval (Kluender & Kutas 1993b; King & Kutas 1995).[25] This provides an economical way of characterizing the amplitude difference between Nref effects in response to a pronoun or DP anaphor with two vs. one potential referents.

Consistent with this interpretation, Karimi, Ferreira, and Swaab (2018) showed that facilitating the retrieval of antecedents from working memory by anchoring their representations within the discourse model with elaborated referential expressions (*The actor /[who was visibly upset]/ walked away from the cameraman /[who was critical of the show]/; after a while, he realized it was getting late and took a taxi home.*) substantially attenuates the Nref effect attributed to ambiguity. More strikingly, facilitating retrieval from working memory in this way has the same attenuating effect even when the antecedent is unambiguous (*The actor /[who was visibly upset]/ walked away from the actress /[who was critical of the show]/; after a while, he realized it was getting late and took a taxi home*). Fiorentino, Covey, and Gabriele (2018) also replicated the Nieuwland and van Berkum (2006) finding that larger Nref responses to ambiguous pronouns were elicited from participants with higher count (as opposed to reading) span scores.

This issue is not resolved, however, and further investigation is necessary. But if the Nref can be subsumed under the larger family of effects of anterior negativity in language processing, it could offer an elegant,

---

[24] In a subsequent experiment with a different set of participants, the exact same stimulus materials using object relative clauses and their conjoined controls elicited a left anterior negative response with a scalp distribution virtually identical to that of the unambiguous pronouns in Barkley, Kluender, and Kutas (2015), and to that of typical Nref effects.

[25] It is sometimes argued that because the Nref is nowadays often measured between 400 ms and 1100 ms post-stimulus onset, its latency distinguishes it from a typical LAN response. But as pointed out with regard to Basque object relative clauses (Carreiras et al. 2010) in Section 24.4.2, latency differences alone cannot distinguish between components, and in any case LAN effects also often persist beyond the critical word.

perhaps universal account of how the brain handles long-distance relationships of all types in language processing. While this would not be entirely
consistent with decades of syntactic theoretical work dissociating Ā-
dependencies from other types of syntactic dependencies, it would nevertheless provide an interesting window into how our brains cope with the
otherwise bewildering array of discontinuous but related syntactic elements across the world's languages.

### 24.4.4  Syntactic Islands

While we have emphasized studies with stimulus designs that avoid violation paradigms thus far in this section, there is one violation paradigm that
is worth revisiting as an example of how ERP evidence can not only help
adjudicate between competing syntactic processing proposals, but can
also lead us to rethink our assumptions about fundamental theoretical
syntactic processing issues. As pointed out in Section 24.2.2, a number of
early ERP studies of syntactic processing focused on syntactic islands –
perhaps somewhat overambitiously, as one can now venture from the
perspective of 30 years' worth of research (see Chapter 9 for general
discussion of islands from an experimental perspective). The reader is
therefore referred back to the discussion in Section 24.2.2 of Neville et al.
(1991), in which extractions out of subject islands elicited effects of late
positivity after the gap position (*What was [a proof of __] **criticized** by the
scientist?). Kluender and Kutas (1993b), a study of wh-islands (*Who$_a$ isn't he
sure [that/if/what$_b$ the TA explained it/[__ $_b$] to __$_a$ **in** lab]?), instead reported
differential amplitude of a LAN response following gap positions in
ungrammatical wh-islands, marginal if-clauses, and grammatical that-
clauses (reflecting the degree of grammatical well-formedness), which
can be interpreted as indexing the difficulty of retrieval of the filler across
the three conditions. There was no noticeable effect at the left edge of the
wh-island itself in this study, but another early ERP study, McKinnon and
Osterhout (1996), reported late positive effects at the left edge of an
adjunct island (I wonder which of his staff members/whether the candidate was
annoyed [**when** his son was questioned by [__]/his staff member]). Note however
that this late positive response could also have been triggered by the
absence of a licensing preposition in the main clause (I wonder which of his
staff members the candidate was annoyed <u>by</u> when ...).
    To further investigate these issues, Michel (2014) revisited the proces-
sing of wh-islands (Who __ had the sailor assumed that/inquired whether the
captain **befriended** __ **openly before** the final mutiny hearing?). Although
there was a slowdown at whether in the reading time study, there was –
just as in Kluender and Kutas (1993b) – no concomitant ERP effect at the
clause boundary in the wh-island condition. Therefore, whether entering
an island environment immediately shuts off filler–gap processing
remains unclear and seems thus far to depend on the measure employed.

At *befriended*, the pre-gap position, there was a broad effect of late positivity between 600 and 900 ms. Such effects of late positivity are common at the sentence position immediately preceding a gap in English. As discussed in Section 24.4.2, positivity of this kind has often been characterized as an index of syntactic integration. However, this interpretation may have been influenced originally by the fact that the sentence element eliciting this response is almost invariably also the subcategorizer in SVO languages, while it is usually a co-argument of the filler in SOV languages (with the exception of Felser, Clahsen, & Münte 2003).

The brain response to *before*, two words downstream from *befriended*, and following the gap position, was a classic LAN effect of equal amplitude in both the grammatical and ungrammatical object *wh*-question conditions, when compared to the response to the same word in grammatical subject *wh*-questions used as controls (*Who __ had openly assumed that/inquired whether the captain befriended the sailor **before** the final mutiny hearing?*). This LAN effect persisted past the critical word. On the assumption, consistent with studies of filler–gap dependencies discussed in Sections 24.2.2 and 24.4.2, that post-gap LAN effects index retrieval of a filler for purposes of gap assignment,[26] one would be forced to conclude from these data that fillers are assigned to their gaps in both grammatical and ungrammatical embedded clauses. In other words, an island environment does not prevent gap assignment.

Moreover, if gap assignment operations are active at post-gap positions, it becomes difficult to claim that effects of late positivity at pre-gap positions index syntactic integration, i.e. before filler–gap assignment has even occurred. A much more parsimonious interpretation, based on the studies reviewed in Section 24.3.2, would be that pre-gap late positivity is actually just a P300 response indexing gap identification. This would be totally in keeping with the monitoring function that has been ascribed to the P300 since its discovery (see Section 24.3.2 for details).

Given the design of these stimuli, it was also possible to investigate the gap position itself, simultaneous with presentation of *openly* in the embedded clause. This made it possible to test whether the expectation for a gap is effectively shut off within an island environment (Stowe 1986; Phillips 2006). While there were large N400 responses to *openly* (the gap position) in both conditions, there was in fact a small but significant N400 effect when *openly* in the *wh*-island condition was compared to the same position in an embedded *that*-clause, suggesting that it was somewhat less expected in a *wh*-island.

However, this N400 effect was significant only in high-reading-span participants. Low-span participants showed equivalent N400 responses to gap positions in both grammatical and ungrammatical environments. Thus,

---

[26] Or, as we saw in the preceding section, in response to a head noun filler following a gap in a prenominal object relative clause in Japanese and Korean.

while the N400 response interacted with working memory capacity, it suggested that high-span participants exhibit greater sensitivity to fine distinctions of grammaticality, whereas low-span participants simply have trouble filling gaps of any type. Similarly, as measured by reading times, low-span participants had equal difficulty processing *whether* as a complementizer whether it marked a clause boundary over which a dependency ranged or not. High-span participants, on the other hand, only showed increased reading times when entering a *wh*-island environment marked by *whether*. So, once again, working memory interacted in this case with processing of the clause boundary, but in ways that suggested greater sensitivity to grammatical distinctions among those with greater working memory capacity.

In sum, these results were (in)consistent with both grammatical and processing accounts of islands. Reading time and offline acceptability judgments – as in previous studies – were consistent with the view that entering a syntactic island environment shuts off the process of gap-filling, while the ERP results produced no such evidence: based on the brain responses, the parser seemed perfectly willing to enter an island environment and fill gaps inside it. Similarly, there was a small but significant N400 effect in response to filling ungrammatical vs. grammatical gaps, which can be construed as consistent with the grammatical account claim that gaps are unexpected in island environments. On the other hand, there were large N400 responses to both grammatical and ungrammatical gaps, and only high-span participants showed this small N400 expectancy-related difference. This suggests, in line with previous research (King & Just 1991), that high-verbal-working-memory participants exhibit greater sensitivity to the differences in processing difficulty between dependency types, while low-working-memory individuals appear to be at capacity processing even easy, straightforward long-distance dependencies. This, along with ERP results we have reviewed reporting larger effects of sustained anterior negativity in both low (Vos et al. 2001; Fiebach, Schlesewsky, & Friderici 2002) and high-working-memory-capacity individuals (King & Kutas 1995; Münte, Schiltz, & Kutas 1998; Nieuwland & Van Berkum 2006; Fiorentino, Covey, & Gabriele 2018), suggests that a closer examination of the relationship between verbal working memory capacity and gap-filling is in order. Moreover, our assumptions about the processing of islands may have up to now been too simplistically black and white (i.e. in terms of grammatical vs. processing accounts) and may need to be rethought.

## 24.5   Conclusion

This brings me back to the questions I started out with at the beginning of this chapter: was I right? Do syntactic ERP processing results of the past 20 years actually speak for themselves? Have they lived up to expectations? I have three basic takes on this issue. As indicated already at the outset of this chapter, the use of electrophysiological measures has become relatively common practice in linguistic research over the past 20 years, and that is a welcome result. That said, a crucial linchpin in making further progress lies in careful interpretation of results, as I hope this review has made clear: there have been several conceptual starts and stops along the way, with periodic need for re-evaluation. This is not necessarily anything to be ashamed of: that's simply how experimental and theoretical science proceed when they work hand in hand. But for better or worse, we cannot safely assume that the brain is necessarily going to respond in ways determined by our theoretical preconceptions; sometimes the brain responds to something entirely different from what we think we are manipulating. And this is not a problem or a critique specific to linguistically inspired research: Steve Luck makes exactly the same point in Chapter 2 of his (2005) general guide to ERP methodology. Thus the takeaway message here is that we are well advised to proceed with caution and circumspection, and with a look to the long view.

And that is the second point: over time, multiple studies of multiple languages across multiple laboratories have allowed an increasingly clear picture of what the brain is doing when it processes linguistic stimuli to emerge. We now have a much better sense of the functional significance of the various linguistic ERP components than we did 20 or 30 years ago, even though there are still many unanswered questions. One point of emerging clarity, I have argued, is the realization that linguistic ERP components are not tied to specific types of linguistic phenomena, but rather a reflection of more general cognitive processes operating within the language domain. The other assertion I would make – and again, one that I freely admit reveals my own prejudices – is that we are likely to make more progress and learn far more interesting things when we don't force the brain to process violations of the language system, but rather simply observe how it deals with the garden variety syntactic phenomena that decades of linguistic research have unearthed. As we have seen, we do not have a very reliable handle on what exactly the brain is reacting to when it is unable to compute a linguistic stimulus.

All of this is not to say that we should approach our research atheoretically, however – far from it. There are plenty of syntactic phenomena that localize to specific junctures of sentence processing that would lend themselves nicely to the precise time-locking required in order to compute a usable grand average across participants. While a claim that linguistic ERP studies have thus far had a huge impact on linguistic theorizing is unwarranted, it's also not the case that they have been without theoretical merit. N400 studies have played a crucial role in influencing our views of predictive processing, and ERP studies of long-distance dependencies have decided a number of important theoretical questions on the processing of discontinuous constituents. I for one am optimistic that, proceeding with sobriety, caution, and care, we can expect more such results in the future. It's simply a matter of recognizing that the brain is a pretty miraculous instrument that in some ways has a life all its own, and if we are lucky enough, and treat it with enough respect, it may continue to reveal its secrets to us.

# References

Barkley, C. & Kluender, R. (2018). Processing anaphoric relations: An electrophysiological perspective. In J. Gundel & B. Abbott, eds., *The Oxford Handbook of Reference*. Oxford: Oxford University Press, pp. 384–410.

Barkley, C., Kluender, R., & Kutas, M. (2015). Referential processing in the human brain: An event-related potential (ERP) study. *Brain Research*, 1629, 143–159.

Besson, M. & Macar, F. (1987). An event-related potential analysis of incongruity in music and other non-linguistic contexts. *Psychophysiology*, 24(1), 14–25.

Bornkessel, I., McElree, B., Schlesewsky, M., & Friederici, A. D. (2004). Multidimensional contributions to garden path strength: Dissociating phrase structure from case marking. *Journal of Memory and Language*, 51 (4), 495–522.

Bornkessel-Schlesewsky, I. & Schlesewsky, M. (2008). An alternative perspective on "semantic P600" effects in language comprehension. *Brain Research Reviews*, 59(1), 55–73.

Brouwer, H. & Crocker, M. W. (2017). On the proper treatment of the N400 and P600 in language comprehension. *Frontiers in Psychology*, 2. DOI: 10.3389/fpsyg.2017.01327

Brouwer, H., Fitz, H., & Hoeks, J. (2012). Getting real about semantic illusions: Rethinking the functional role of the P600 in language comprehension. *Brain Research*, 1446, 127–143.

Caplan, D. (1987). *Neurolinguistics and Linguistic Aphasiology: An Introduction*. Cambridge: Cambridge University Press.

Carreiras, M., Duñabeitia, J. A., Vergara, M., De La Cruz-Pavía, I., & Laka, I. (2010). Subject relative clauses are not universally easier to process: Evidence from Basque. *Cognition*, 115(1), 79–92.

Chomsky, N. (1980). Rules and representations. *Behavioral and Brain Sciences*, 3(1), 1–15.

Chomsky, N. (1981). *Lectures on Government and Binding*. Cambridge, MA: MIT Press.

Chomsky, N. (1986). *Knowledge of Language: Its Nature, Origin, and Use*. Westport, CT: Praeger.

Chomsky, N. (1993). *Language and Thought*. Wakefield, RI: Moyer Bell.

Chow, W.-Y., Lau, E., Wang, S., & Phillips, C. (2018). Wait a second! Delayed impact of argument roles on on-line verb prediction. *Language, Cognition and Neuroscience*, 33(7). DOI:10.1080/23273798.2018.1427878

Chow, W.-Y. & Phillips, C. (2013). No semantic illusions in the "Semantic P600" phenomenon: ERP evidence from Mandarin Chinese. *Brain Research*, 1506, 76–93.

Chow, W.-Y., Smith, C., Lau, E., & Phillips, C. (2015). A "bag-of-arguments" mechanism for initial verb predictions. *Language, Cognition and Neuroscience*, 31(5), 577–596.

Churchland, P. M. (1984). *Matter and Consciousness*. Cambridge, MA: MIT Press.

Comrie, B. (1996). The unity of noun-modifying clauses in Asian languages. In *Pan-Asiatic Linguistics: Proceedings of the Fourth International Symposium on Languages and Linguistics*, 3. Salaya, Thailand: Institute of Language and Culture for Rural Development, Mahidol University at Salaya, pp. 1077–88.

Coulson, S., King, J. W., & Kutas, M. (1998). Expect the unexpected: Event-related brain response to morphosyntactic violations. *Language and Cognitive Processes*, 13(1), 21–58.

Courchesne, E., Hillyard, S. A., & Galambos, R. (1975). Stimulus novelty, task relevance and the visual evoked potential in man. *Electroencephalography and Clinical Neurophysiology*, 39(2), 131–143.

Delong, K. A., Urbach, T. P., & Kutas, M. (2005). Probabilistic word pre-activation during language comprehension inferred from electrical brain activity. *Nature Neuroscience*, 8(6), 1117–1121.

Delong, K. A., Urbach, T. P., & Kutas, M. (2017). Is there a replication crisis? Perhaps. Is this an example? No: A commentary on Ito, Martin, and Nieuwland (2016). *Language, Cognition and Neuroscience*, 32(8), 966–973.

Deutsch, A. & Bentin, S. (2001). Syntactic and semantic factors in processing gender agreement in Hebrew: Evidence from ERPs and eye movements. *Journal of Memory and Language*, 45(2), 200–224.

Dikker, S. & Pylkkänen, L. (2011). Before the N400: Effects of lexical–semantic violations in visual cortex. *Brain and Language*, 118(1–2), 23–28.

Dikker, S., Rabagliati, H., Farmer, T., & Pylkkänen, L. (2010). Early occipital sensitivity to syntactic category is based on form typicality. *Psychological Science*, 21(5), 629–634.

Donchin, E. (1981). "Surprise! . . . Surprise?" *Psychophysiology*, 18(5), 493–513.

Featherston, S., Gross, M., Clahsen, H., & Münte, T. (2000). Brain potentials in the processing of complex sentences: An ERP study of control and raising constructions. *Journal of Psycholinguistic Research*, 29(2), 141–154.

Federmeier, K. D., Segal, J. B., Lombrozo, T., & Kutas, M. (2000). Brain responses to nouns, verbs and class-ambiguous words in context. *Brain*, 123(12), 2552–2566.

Felser, C., Clahsen, H., & Münte, T. F. (2003). Storage and integration in the processing of filler–gap dependencies: An ERP study of topicalization and *wh*-movement in German. *Brain and Language*, 87(3), 345–354.

Fiebach, C. J., Schlesewsky, M., & Friederici, A. D. (2001). Syntactic working memory and the establishment of filler–gap dependencies: Insights from ERPs and fMRI. *Journal of Psycholinguistic Research*, 30(3), 321–338.

Fiebach, C. J., Schlesewsky, M., & Friederici, A. D. (2002). Separating syntactic working memory costs and syntactic integration costs during parsing: The processing of German WH-questions. *Journal of Memory and Language*, 47(2), 250–272.

Fiorentino, R., Covey, L., & Gabriele, A. (2018). Individual differences in the processing of referential dependencies: Evidence from event-related potentials. *Neuroscience Letters*, 673, 79–84.

Fischler, I., Bloom, P. A., Childers, D. G., Roucos, S. E., & Perry Jr., N. W. (1983). Brain potentials related to stages of sentence verification. *Psychophysiology*, 20(4), 400–409.

Fodor, J. A. (1981). The mind–body problem. *Scientific American*, 244(1), 114–123.

Fodor, J. D. (1978). Parsing strategies and constraints on transformations. *Linguistic Inquiry*, 9(3), 427–473.

Fodor, J. D. (1983). Phrase structure parsing and the island constraints. *Linguistics and Philosophy*, 6(2), 163–223.

Foley, S. & Wagers, M. (2017). The Subject Gap Preference in a split-ergative language: Reading time evidence from Georgian. Paper presented at the 48th Annual Meeting of the North East Linguistics Society, University of Iceland, Reykjavik, Iceland.

Frazier, L. (1978). On comprehending sentences: Syntactic parsing strategies. Doctoral dissertation, University of Connecticut.

Frazier, L. & Clifton Jr., C. (1989). Successive cyclicity in the grammar and the parser. *Language and Cognitive Processes*, 4(2), 93–126.

Frenzel, S., Schlesewsky, M., & Bornkessel-Schlesewsky, I. (2011). Conflicts in language processing: A new perspective on the N400–P600 distinction. *Neuropsychologia*, 49(3), 574–579.

Friederici, A. D. (1995). The time course of syntactic activation during language processing: A model based on neuropsychological and neurophysiological data. *Brain and Language*, 50(3), 259–281.

Friederici, A. D. (2002). Towards a neural basis of auditory sentence processing. *Trends in Cognitive Sciences*, 6(2), 78–84.

Friederici, A. D., Pfeifer, E., & Hahne, A. (1993). Event-related brain potentials during natural speech processing: Effects of semantic, morphological and syntactic violations. *Cognitive Brain Research* 1(3), 183–192.

Frisch, S. & Schlesewsky, M. (2001). The N400 reflects problems of thematic hierarchizing. *NeuroReport*, 12(15), 3391–3394.

Frisch, S. & Schlesewsky, M. (2005). The resolution of case conflicts from a neurophysiological perspective. *Cognitive Brain Research*, 25(2), 484–498.

Garnsey, S. M., Tanenhaus, M. K., & Chapman, R. M. (1989). Evoked potentials and the study of sentence comprehension. *Journal of Psycholinguistic Research*, 18(1), 51–60.

Gibson, E. (1998). Linguistic complexity: Locality of syntactic dependencies. *Cognition*, 68(1), 1–76.

Gibson, E. (2000). The dependency locality theory: A distance-based theory of linguistic complexity. In A. Marantz, Y. Miyashita, & W. O'Neil, eds., *Image, Language, Brain*. Cambridge, MA: MIT Press, pp. 95–126.

Grey, S., Tanner, D., & van Hell, J.G. (2017). How right is left? Handedness modulates neural responses during morphosyntactic processing. *Brain Research*, 1669, 27–43.

Gunter, T. C., Stowe, L. A., & Mulder, G. (1997). When syntax meets semantics. *Psychophysiology*, 34, 660–676.

Hagiwara, H., Soshi, T., Ishihara, M., & Imanaka, K. (2007). A topographical study on the event-related potential correlates of scrambled word order in Japanese complex sentences. *Journal of Cognitive Neuroscience*, 19(2), 175–193.

Hagoort, P., Brown, C., & Groothusen, J. (1993). The syntactic positive shift (SPS) as an ERP-measure of syntactic processing. *Language and Cognitive Processes*, 8(4), 439–483.

Hahne, A. & Friederici, A. D. (1999). Electrophysiological evidence for two steps in syntactic analysis: Early automatic and late controlled processes. *Journal of Cognitive Neuroscience*, 11(2), 194–205.

Haupt, F. S., Schlesewsky, M., Roehm, D., Friederici, A. D., & Bornkessel-Schlesewsky, I. (2008). The status of subject–object reanalyses in the language comprehension literature. *Journal of Memory and Language*, 59 (1), 54–96.

Hoeks, J. C. J., Stowe, L. A., & Doedens, G. (2004). Seeing words in context: The interaction of lexical and sentence level information during reading. *Cognitive Brain Research*, 19(1), 59–73.

Ito, A., Martin, A. E., & Nieuwland, M. S. (2017a). How robust are prediction effects in language comprehension? Failure to replicate article-elicited N400 effects. *Language, Cognition and Neuroscience*, 32(8), 954–965.

Ito, A., Martin, A. E., & Nieuwland, M. S. (2017b). Why the A/AN prediction effect may be hard to replicate: A rebuttal to Delong, Urbach, and Kutas (2017). *Language, Cognition and Neuroscience*, 32(8), 974–983.

Janata, P. (1995). ERP measures assay the degree of expectancy violation of harmonic contexts in music. *Journal of Cognitive Neuroscience* 7(2), 153–164.

Kaan, E., Harris, A., Gibson, E., & Holcomb, P. (2000). The P600 as an index of syntactic integration difficulty. *Language and Cognitive Processes*, 15(2), 159–201.

Kanno, K. (2007). Factors affecting the processing of Japanese relative clauses by L2 learners. *Studies in Second Language Acquisition*, 29(2), 197–218.

Karimi, H., Swaab, T. Y., & Ferreira, F. (2018). Electrophysiological evidence for an independent effect of memory retrieval on referential processing. *Journal of Memory and Language*, 102, 68–82.

Kim, A. & Osterhout, L. (2005). The independence of combinatory semantic processing: Evidence from event-related potentials. *Journal of Memory and Language*, 52(2), 205–222.

King, J. W. & Just, M. A. (1991). Individual differences in syntactic processing: The role of working memory. *Journal of Memory and Language*, 30(5), 580–602.

King, J. W. & Kutas, M. A. (1995). Who did what and when: Using word- and clause-level ERPs to monitor working memory usage in reading. *Journal of Cognitive Neuroscience*, 7(3), 376–395.

Kluender, R. (1992). Deriving island constraints from principles of predication. In H. Goodluck & M. Rochemont, eds., *Island Constraints: Theory, Acquisition, and Processing*. Dordrecht: Kluwer Academic Publishers, pp. 223–258.

Kluender, R. (1998). On the distinction between strong and weak islands: A processing perspective. In P. W. Culicover & L. McNally, eds., *The Limits of Syntax* (Syntax and Semantics, 29). San Diego, CA: Academic Press, pp. 241–279.

Kluender, R. (2003). In search of the golden slash: Prospecting for biological explanations of language. In J. Moore & M. Polinsky, eds., *The Nature of Explanation in Linguistic Theory*. Stanford, CA: CSLI Publications, pp. 191–212.

Kluender, R. & Kutas, M. (1993a). Bridging the gap: Evidence from ERPs on the processing of unbounded dependencies. *Journal of Cognitive Neuroscience*, 5(2), 196–214.

Kluender, R. & Kutas, M. (1993b). Subjacency as a processing phenomenon. *Language and Cognitive Processes*, 8(4), 573–633.

Kluender, R., Münte, T., Cowles, H. W., Szentkuti, A., Walenski, M., & Wieringa, B. (1998). Brain potentials to English and German questions. Poster presented at the Annual Meeting of the Cognitive Neuroscience Society.

Kolk, H. & Chwilla, D. (2007). Late positivities in unusual situations. *Brain and Language*, 100, 257–261.

Kolk, H. H. J., Chwilla, D. J., van Herten, M., & Oor, P. J. W. (2003). Structure and limited capacity in verbal working memory: A study with event-related potentials. *Brain and Language*, 85(1), 1–36.

Kos, M., Vosse, T., van den Brink, D., & Hagoort, P. (2010). About edible restaurants: Conflicts between syntax and semantics as revealed by ERPs. *Frontiers in Psychology*, 1. DOI: 10.3389/fpsyg.2010.00222

Kounios, J. & Holcomb, P. J. (1992). Structure and process in semantic memory: Evidence from event-related brain potentials and reaction times. *Journal of Experimental Psychology: General*, 121(4), 459–479.

Kuperberg, G. R. (2007). Neural mechanisms of language comprehension: Challenges to syntax. *Brain Research*, 1146, 23–49.

Kuperberg, G. R., Sitnikova, T., Caplan, D., & Holcomb, P. J. (2003). Electrophysiological distinctions in processing conceptual relationships within simple sentences. *Cognitive Brain Research*, 17(1), 117–129.

Kutas, M. & Hillyard, S. A. (1980a). Reading senseless sentences: Brain potentials reflect semantic incongruity. *Science*, 207(4427), 203–205.

Kutas, M. & Hillyard, S. A. (1980b). Event-related brain potentials to semantically inappropriate and surprisingly large words. *Biological Psychology*, 11(2), 99–116.

Kutas, M. & Hillyard, S. (1983). Event-related brain potentials to grammatical errors and semantic anomalies. *Memory and Cognition*, 11(5), 539–550.

Kutas, M. & Hillyard, S. (1984). Brain potentials during reading reflect word expectancy and semantic association. *Nature*, 307(5947), 161–163.

Kutas, M., Lindamood, T., & Hillyard, S. (1984). Word expectancy and event-related brain potentials during sentence processing. In S. Kornblum & J. Requin, eds., *Preparatory States and Processes*. Hillsdale, NJ: Lawrence Erlbaum, pp. 217–237.

Kutas, M., Van Petten, C., & Besson, M. (1988). Event-related potential asymmetries during the reading of sentences. *Electroencephalography and Clinical Neurophysiology*, 69(3), 218–233.

Kwon, N., Kluender, R., Kutas, M., & Polinsky, M. (2013). Subject/object processing asymmetries in Korean relative clauses: Evidence from ERP data. *Language*, 8(3), 537–585.

Kwon, N., Lee, Y., Gordon, P.C., Kluender, R., & Polinsky, M. (2010). Cognitive and linguistic factors affecting subject/object asymmetry: An eye-tracking study of prenominal relative clauses in Korean. *Language*, 86 (3), 546–582.

Kwon, N., Polinsky, M., & Kluender, R. (2006). Subject preference in Korean. In D. Baumer, D. Montero, & M. Scanlon, eds., *Proceedings of the 25th West Coast Conference on Formal Linguistics*. Somerville, MA: Cascadilla Proceedings Project, pp. 1–14.

Kwon, N., Sturt, P., & Liu, P. (2017). Predicting semantic features in Chinese: Evidence from ERPs. *Cognition*, 166, 433–446.

Lau, E., Clarke, N., Socolof, M., Asatiani, R., & Polinsky, M. (2019). A subject relative clause preference in a split-ergative language: ERP evidence from Georgian. Unpublished manuscript, University of Maryland.

Lau, E. & Liao, C.-H. (2017). Linguistic structure across time: ERP responses to coordinated and uncoordinated noun phrases. *Language, Cognition and Neuroscience* 33(5), pp. 633–647.

Lau, E., Stroud, C., Plesch, S., & Phillips, C. (2006). The role of structural prediction in rapid syntactic analysis. *Brain and Language*, 98(1), 74–88.

Luck, S. J. (2005). *An Introduction to the Event-Related Potential Technique.* Cambridge, MA: MIT Press.

Mancini, S., Molinaro, N., Rizzi, L., & Carreiras, M. (2011a). When persons disagree: An ERP study of Unagreement in Spanish. *Psychophysiology*, 48, 1361–1371.

Mancini, S., Molinaro, N., Rizzi, L., & Carreiras, M. (2011b). A person is not a number: Discourse involvement in subject–verb agreement computation. *Brain Research*, 1410, 64–76.

McKinnon, R. & Osterhout, L. (1996). Constraints on movement phenomena in sentence processing: Evidence from event-related brain potentials. *Language and Cognitive Processes*, 11(5), 495–524.

Michel, D. (2014). Individual cognitive measures and working memory accounts of syntactic island phenomena. Doctoral dissertation, University of California, San Diego.

Moore, J. & Polinsky, M., eds.. (2003). *The Nature of Explanation in Linguistic Theory.* Stanford, CA: CSLI Publications.

Münte, T. F., Heinze, H.-J., Matzke, M., Wieringa, B. M., & Johannes, S. (1998). Brain potentials and syntactic violations revisited: No evidence for specificity of the syntactic positive shift. *Neuropsychologia*, 36(3), 217–226.

Münte, T. F., Matzke, M., & Johannes, S. (1997). Brain activity associated with syntactic incongruencies in words and pseudo-words. *Journal of Cognitive Neuroscience*, 9(3), 318–329.

Münte, T. F., Schiltz, K., & Kutas, M. (1998). When temporal terms belie conceptual order. *Nature*, 395(6697), 71–73.

Neville, H., Nicol, J., Barss, A., Forster, K., & Garrett, M. (1991). Syntactically based sentence processing classes: Evidence from event-related brain potentials. *Journal of Cognitive Neuroscience* 3(2), 151–165.

Nieuwland, M. S. & Kuperberg, G. (2008). When the truth is not too hard to handle: An event-related potential study on the pragmatics of negation. *Psychological Science*, 19(12), 1213–1218.

Nieuwland, M. S., Otten, M., & van Berkum, J. J. A. (2007). Who are you talking about? Tracking discourse level referential processing with event-related brain potentials. *Journal of Cognitive Neuroscience*, 19(2), 228–236.

Nieuwland, M. S., Politzer-Ahles, S., Heyselaar, E., Segaert, K., Darley, E., Kazanina, N., von Grebmer zu Wolfsthurn, S., Bartolozzi, F., Kogan, V., Ito, A., Mézière, D., Barr, D. J., Rousselet, G. A., Ferguson, H. J., Busch-Moreno, S., Fu, X., Tuomainen, J., Kulakova, E., Husband, E. M., Donaldson, D. I., Kohút, Z., Rueschemeyer, S.-A., & Huettig, F. (2018). Large-scale replication study reveals a limit on probabilistic prediction in language comprehension. *eLIFE*. DOI: 10.7554/eLife.33468.001

Nieuwland, M. S. & van Berkum, J. J. A. (2006). Individual differences and contextual bias in pronoun resolution. *Brain Research*, 1118(1), 155–167.

Núñez-Peña, M.I. & Honrubia-Serrano, M.L. (2004). P600 related to rule violation in an arithmetic task. *Cognitive Brain Research*, 18(2), 130–141.

O'Grady, W. (1997). *Syntactic Development*. Chicago: Chicago University Press.

Osterhout, L. (1997). On the brain response to syntactic anomalies: Manipulations of word position and word class reveal individual differences. *Brain and Language*, 59(3), 494–522.

Osterhout, L. & Holcomb, P. (1992). Event-related brain potentials elicited by syntactic anomaly. *Journal of Memory and Language*, 31(6), 785–806.

Osterhout, L., Holcomb, P. J., & Swinney, D. A. (1994). Brain potentials elicited by garden-path sentences: Evidence of the application of verb information during parsing. *Journal of Experimental Psychology: Learning, Memory, and Cognition*, 20(4), 786.

Osterhout, L., McKinnon, R., Bersick, M., & Corey, V. (1996). On the language specificity of the brain response to syntactic anomalies: Is the syntactic positive shift a member of the P300 family? *Journal of Cognitive Neuroscience*, 8(6), 507–526.

Paczynski, M. & Kuperberg, G. R. (2011). Electrophysiological evidence for use of the animacy hierarchy, but not thematic role assignment, during verb-argument processing. *Language and Cognitive Processes*, 26(9), 1402–1456.

Paczynski, M. & Kuperberg, G. R. (2012). Multiple influences of semantic memory on sentence processing: Distinct effects of semantic relatedness on violations of real-world event/state knowledge and animacy selection restrictions. *Journal of Memory and Language*, 67(4), 426–488.

Patel, A. D., Gibson, E., Ratner, J., Besson, M., & Holcomb, P. J. (1998). Processing syntactic relations in language and music: An event-related potential study. *Journal of Cognitive Neuroscience*, 10(6), 717–733.

Phillips, C. (2006). The real-time status of island phenomena. *Language*, 82 (4), 795–823.

Phillips, C., Kazanina, N., & Abada, S. H. (2005). ERP effects of the processing of syntactic long-distance dependencies. *Cognitive Brain Research*, 22 (3), 407–428.

Roehm, D., Schlesewsky, M., Bornkessel, I., Frisch, S., & Haider, H. (2004). Fractionating language comprehension via frequency characteristics of the human EEG. *Cognitive Neuroscience and Neuropsychology*, 15(3), 409–412.

Roll, M., Horne, M., & Lindgren, M. (2007). Object shift and event-related brain potentials. *Journal of Neurolinguistics*, 20(6), 462–481.

Ruchkin, D. S., Johnson Jr., R., Grafman, J., Canoune, H., & Ritter, W. (1992). Distinctions and similarities among working memory processes: An event-related potential study. *Cognitive Brain Research*, 1(1), 53–66.

Sassenhagen, J. & Bornkessel-Schlesewsky, I. (2015). The P600 as a correlate of ventral attention network reorientation. *Cortex*, 66, A3–A20.

Severens, E., Jansma, B. M., & Hartsuiker, R. J. (2008). Morphophonological influences on the comprehension of subject–verb agreement: An ERP study. *Brain Research*, 1228, 135–144.

Shao, J. & Neville, H. (1998). Analyzing semantic processing using event-related brain potentials. *Newsletter of the Center for Research in Language*, 11(5), 3–20.

Simson, R., Vaughan, H. G., & Ritter, W. (1977). The scalp topography of potentials in auditory and visual discrimination tasks. *Electroencephalography and Clinical Neurophysiology*, 42(4), 528–535.

Squires, N. K., Squires, K. C., & Hillyard, S. A. (1975). Two varieties of long-latency positive waves evoked by unpredictable auditory stimuli in man. *Electroencephalography and Clinical Neurophysiology*, 38(4), 387–401.

Staab, J. (2007). Negation in context: Electrophysiological and behavioral investigations of negation effects in discourse processing. Doctoral dissertation, University of California, San Diego.

Steinhauer, K. & Drury, J. E. (2012). On the early left-anterior negativity (ELAN) in syntax studies. *Brain and Language*, 120(2), 135–162.

Stowe, L. A. (1986). Parsing WH-constructions: Evidence for on-line gap location. *Language and Cognitive Processes*, 1(3), 227–245.

Sutton, S., Braren, M., Zubin, J., & John, F. R. (1965). Evoked potential correlates of stimulus uncertainty. *Science*, 150(3700), 1187–1188.

Sutton, S., Tueting, P., Zubin, J., & John, E. R. (1967). Information delivery and the sensory evoked potential. *Science*, 155(3768), 1436–1439.

Szewczyk, J. M. & Schriefers, H. (2013). Prediction in language comprehension beyond specific words: An ERP study on sentence comprehension in Polish. *Journal of Memory and Language*, 68(4), 297–324.

Tanner, D., Inoue, K., & Osterhout, L. (2014). Brain-based individual differences in online L2 grammatical comprehension. *Bilingualism: Language and Cognition*, 17(2), 277–293.

Tanner, D., McLaughlin, J., Herschensohn, J., & Osterhout, L. (2013). Individual differences reveal stages of L2 grammatical acquisition: ERP evidence. *Bilingualism: Language and Cognition*, 16(2), 367–382.

Tanner, D. & Van Hell, J. G. (2014). ERPs reveal individual differences in morphosyntactic processing. *Neuropsychologia*, 56, 289–301.

Toscano, J. C., McMurray, B., Dennhardt, J., & Luck, S. A. (2010). Continuous perception and graded categorization: Electrophysiological evidence for a linear relationship between the acoustic signal and perceptual encoding of speech. *Psychological Science*, 2(10), 1532–1540.

Ueno, M. & Garnsey, S. M. (2008). An ERP study of the processing of subject and object relative clauses in Japanese. *Language and Cognitive Processes*, 23(5), 646–688.

Ueno, M. & Kluender, R. (2003). Event-related brain indices of scrambling in Japanese. *Brain and Language*, 86(2), 243–271.

Ueno, M. & Kluender, R. (2009). On the processing of Japanese *wh*-questions: An ERP study. *Brain Research*, 1290, 63–90.

Urbach, T. P., DeLong, K. A., & Kutas, M. (2015). Quantifiers are incrementally interpreted in context, more or less. *Journal of Memory and Language*, 83, 79–96.

Urbach, T. P. & Kutas, M. (2002). The intractability of scaling scalp distributions to infer neuroelectric sources. *Psychophysiology*, 39(6), 791–808.

Urbach, T. P. & Kutas, M. (2010). Quantifiers more or less quantify on-line: ERP evidence for partial incremental interpretation. *Journal of Memory and Language*, 63(2), 158–179.

van Berkum, J. J. A., Brown, C. M., & Hagoort, P. (1999). Early referential context effects in sentence processing: Evidence from event-related brain potentials. *Journal of Memory and Language*, 41(2), 147–182.

van Berkum, J. J. A., Brown, C. M., Hagoort, P., & Zwitserlood, P. (2003). Event-related brain potentials reflect discourse-referential ambiguity in spoken language comprehension. *Psychophysiology*, 40(2), 235–248.

van Berkum, J. J. A., Brown, C. M., Zwitserlood, P., Kooijman, V., & Hagoort, P. (2005). Anticipating upcoming words in discourse: Evidence from ERPs and reading times. *Journal of Experimental Psychology: Learning, Memory, and Cognition*, 31(3), 443–467.

van Berkum, J. J. A., Koornneef, A. W., Otten, M. & Nieuwland, M. S. (2007). Establishing reference in language comprehension: An electrophysiological perspective. *Brain Research*, 1146, 158–171.

van Berkum, J. J. A., Zwitserlood, P., Bastiaansen, M. C., Brown, C. M., & Hagoort, P. (2004). So who's "he" anyway? Differential ERP and ERSP effects of referential success, ambiguity and failure during spoken language comprehension. *Supplement to the Journal of Cognitive Neuroscience*, 16.

van Herten, M., Chwilla, D. J., & Kolk, H. H. J. (2006). When heuristics clash with parsing routines: ERP evidence for conflict monitoring in sentence perception. *Journal of Cognitive Neuroscience*, 18(7), 1181–1197.

van Herten, M., Kolk, H. H. J., & Chwilla, D. J. (2005). An ERP study of P600 effects elicited by semantic anomalies. *Cognitive Brain Research*, 22(2), 241–255.

Van Petten, C. & Kutas, M. (1991). Influences of semantic and syntactic context on open- and closed-class words. *Memory and Cognition*, 19(1), 95–112.

Van Petten, C. & Luka, B. J. (2012). Prediction during language comprehension: Benefits, costs, and ERP components. *International Journal of Psychophysiology*, 83(2), 176–190.

Verleger, R. (1990). P3-evoking wrong notes: Unexpected, awaiting, or arousing? *International Journal of Neuroscience*, 55(2–4), 171–179.

Vissers, C. Th. W. M., Chwilla, D. J., & Kolk, H. H. J. (2006). Monitoring in language perception: The effect of misspellings of words in highly constrained sentences. *Brain Research*, 1106(1), 150–163.

Vos, S. H., Gunter, T. C., Kolk, H. H. J., & Mulder, G. (2001). Working memory constraints on syntactic processing: An electrophysiological investigation. *Psychophysiology*, 38(1), 41–63.

Wicha, N. Y. Y., Bates, E. A., Moreno, E. M., & Kutas, M. (2003). Potato not Pope: Human brain potentials to gender expectation and agreement in Spanish spoken sentences. *Neuroscience Letters*, 346(3), 165–168.

Wicha, N. Y. Y., Moreno, E. M., & Kutas, M. (2003). Expecting gender: An event related brain potential study on the role of grammatical gender in comprehending a line drawing within a written sentence in Spanish. *Cortex*, 39(3), 483–508.

Wicha, N. Y. Y., Moreno, E. M., & Kutas, M. (2004). Anticipating words and their gender: An event-related brain potential study of semantic integration, gender expectancy, and gender agreement in Spanish sentence reading. *Journal of Cognitive Neuroscience*, 16(7), 1272–1288.

Wolff, S., Schlesewsky, M., Hirotani, M., & Bornkessel-Schlesewsky, I. (2008). The neural mechanisms of word order processing revisited: Electrophysiological evidence from Japanese. *Brain and Language*, 107 (2), 133–157.

Zhang, Y.-X. & Zhang, J.-T. (2008). Brain responses to agreement violations of Chinese grammatical aspect. *NeuroReport*, 19(10), 1039–1043.

# 25

# Corpus Studies of Syntax

Jerid Francom

## 25.1 Introduction

Modern linguistics is an empirical science whose primary theoretical goal is to understand the structure of the language system and the human capacity to acquire this system. The structure and organization of this system is not accessible to direct evaluation. Therefore, all evidence employed in linguistic inquiry originates from methods which explore the output of this system. Since the 1950s linguistic introspection, in the form of acceptability judgments, has served as the primary source of linguistic evidence for theoretical syntax. Over the last decades, however, other elicitation methods have made important contributions to the field in their own right or as corroborating evidence to provide a more robust understanding of tacit grammatical knowledge. Many of these methods are covered in Chapters 23–24 and 26–27, including behavioral, electro-physical, and neuroimaging approaches.

In this chapter I will focus on another important method for exploring the nature of language and syntactic structure: corpus studies. I will begin contextualizing the role of corpora and corpus studies over the last century with the aim of putting modern corpus studies in perspective with earlier and contemporary trends in the field. I will then provide a sense of the strengths and shortcoming of corpus studies in comparison with other commonly employed methods for studying syntax, with a special focus on acceptability judgment studies. Next I will provide an overview of some key components of conducting a corpus study including a description of what a corpus is, types of corpora and corpus sampling, annotation types, and what kind of data can be extracted from corpora and how it is ana-lyzed. In the course of this discussion, I will attempt to outline the evolving role of corpora in modern linguistic inquiry and frame the outlook for future advances advocating a pluralistic approach to the study of syntactic phenomena through multiple methodological perspectives.

## 25.2  Corpora and Syntactic Investigation

In this section I aim to contextualize the contemporary use of corpora in linguistic investigation and provide on overview of how corpora can be applied in syntactic investigation. First, I will provide the theoretical and methodological backdrop pointing to the evolving role of corpora in language research and syntactic investigation in particular. A key aspect of this discussion will point to the fact that research trends have become increasingly pluralistic given that the strengths and shortcomings of corpus studies and other research methods are often complementary in nature. Then I will highlight how contemporary research can take advantage of both of these methods to address the inherent weaknesses of each approach through concrete studies from the literature.

### 25.2.1  Changing Role of Corpora

Tracing the relationship of theoretical perspectives and methodological approaches over the last century is key to understanding the contemporary use of corpora in syntactic investigation. In the early twentieth century, research in language was based on usage. Whether in anthropology, psychology, or linguistics proper, language researchers adhered to principles of empiricism: that observable language behavior was the primary source of linguistic evidence (Ingram 1989). By mid century a new, rationalist, perspective on language and the mind was taking shape. What became known as the Cognitive Revolution started with a reorientation of linguistics as a study of internal mental states and the mechanisms that aid their acquisition (Chomsky 1959). Tacit linguistic knowledge (competence) was prioritized over "real-world" language usage (performance), which not only signaled a change in theoretical thinking, but also in methodological approach.

Usage data was critiqued as not relevant for the study of competence on a number of fronts: performance errors, inherent in language usage data, could not be distinguished from licit grammatical forms, language usage resources were finite in nature, and therefore would never allow researchers a full view of language creativity, language usage only provided *positive data*, narrowing the scope of analysis to attested structures, and frequency of (co-)occurrence data obtained from corpora bore no relevance to the structural properties of an utterance. Instead it was argued that linguistic introspection (in the form of acceptability judgments) was better equipped for probing linguistic competence by abstracting away from errors present in language performance; allowing researchers to freely probe language creativity and opening the door to investigate syntactic structures unattested in observational data.

Whether some or all the critiques of corpus methods were valid conceptually, it was most certainly the case that language usage resources of the time were rudimentary at best. Corpora were difficult to compile, relatively small in size, and their inspection required human eyes which made analysis prone to error. This early form of corpus studies may be best characterized as what Abercrombie (1965) referred to as a "pseudo-procedure"; a potentially useful methodology, but for practical purposes infeasible. The expediency and efficiency of linguistic introspection compared to corpus studies (especially through informal methods which quickly became commonplace) was undeniable. Given the changing theoretical climate and practical limitations to working with corpora, much of language research, especially in theoretical syntax, turned to introspection as the primary source of linguistic evidence.

Interest in corpora for language research continued, however, primarily in areas where introspection is not a feasible methodology (e.g. language acquisition, historical linguistics) or where the variability associated with language use is the primary focus of investigation (e.g. sociolinguistics, psycholinguistics). This research drove efforts to sustain the development of corpora and refine corpus methods. As early as 1951 the first computerized corpus was developed by Roberto Busa but by the late 60s and into the 70s significant advances in computing and access to electronic media paved the way for landmark corpora such as the *Brown Corpus*, the *Survey of English Usage*, and the *London–Lund Corpus* (see McEnery & Hardie 2012 : 52). These resources marked important gains in the efficiency and reliability of corpora. Sampling practices took on new rigor, increasing the reliability of evidence obtained from corpora. The machine-readable corpus and associated gains in research methods effectively overcame the pseudo-procedure problem; years of manual human inspection could be reduced to seconds on a desktop computer, without the error previously associated with manual human inspection. The use of corpora in language research began to flourish in this resource and methodologically rich environment and would continue to gain momentum.

In the last decades of the twentieth century and into the new millennium, researchers across fields and subdisciplines were increasingly sharing resources, adopting research methods, and building on research findings, including those based on corpora. As syntacticians from across theoretical frameworks came evermore in contact with the tools of each others' trade, more and more researchers began to refine and redefine their investigative practices by scrutinizing standard methodological practices and increasingly combining multiple methodologies to corroborate findings. In the Chomskyan tradition, this effort became known as Experimental Syntax.

The use of corpora increasingly became part of the experimental syntactician's tool belt; albeit as a complementary rather than a primary methodology. This was in large part due to the recognition that observational (corpus) and elicitation (experimental) methods tend to show complementary strengths and weaknesses. The primary strengths of observational data are that they provide access to language as it is used in natural contexts and allow the exploration of complex interactions between linguistic and non-linguistic features. The weaknesses of observational data include the fact that they are finite resources, they provide evidence only from attested use (positive data), and that language use in the wild is often "noisy," complex interactions are difficult to identify and control for which can make the interpretation of results somewhat tentative. Elicited data, including formal acceptability tasks and other commonly used methods in psycholinguistics, provide the researcher the ability to explore attested language use and hypothetical language structures (negative data) and the ability to tightly control the conditions under which evidence is elicited, abstracting away from known and potential confounds in order to observe more precisely a particular phenomenon. Yet the precision of elicited data comes at a cost; the task and/or stimuli used in the experiment may vary in naturalness and furthermore, may unwittingly incorporate linguistic and/or non-linguistic interactions into the experiment which may lead to spurious results.

In recent years, more and more researchers from across theoretical traditions have advocated combining corpus and introspection studies to enhance syntactic investigation on these very grounds.

> Why move from one extreme of only natural data to another of only artificial data? Both have known weaknesses. Why not use a combination of both, and rely on the strengths of each to the exclusion of their weaknesses? A corpus and an introspection-based approach to linguistics are not mutually exclusive. In a very real sense they can be gainfully viewed as being complementary. (McEnery & Wilson 2001: 16)

> While data from corpora and other naturalistic sources are different in kind from the results of controlled experiments (including introspective judgment data), they can be extremely useful. It is true that they may contain performance errors, but there is no direct access to competence; hence, any source of data for theoretical linguistics may contain performance errors. And given the abundance of usage data at hand, plus the increasingly sophisticated search tools available, there is no good excuse for failing to test theoretical work against corpora. (Wasow 2002: 163)

The goal of this section has been to provide insight into the theoretical and practical arguments for and against the use of corpora for linguistic inquiry and provide context for a discussion about the utility of corpus studies in contemporary syntactic research. From early on, from rudimentary beginnings to sophisticated computer-enabled resources, observational data from corpora have played distinct and evolving roles. In contemporary syntactic research, interest in corpus studies has taken on new vigor. This is due in large part to the increased reliability of corpora and corpus methods but is also related to a general tendency across fields and theoretical frameworks to incorporate data from multiple sources as a method for corroborating findings and refining theoretical inquiry.

## 25.2.2 Employing Corpora in Research

In what follows I highlight a number of studies in which observational and experimental studies have been used to complement each other, either through follow-up evidence from another study or within the same study. I've grouped the studies into two main categories: the use of corpus studies to address limitations in elicitation methods and the use of elicitation studies to address limitations of corpus studies.

### 25.2.2.1 Corpus Studies to Enhance Elicitation

Elicitation methods include both online tasks (e.g. self-paced reading) and offline tasks (e.g. acceptability tasks), however, the majority of the discussion will be framed in reference to acceptability studies given that this is the primary focus of this volume. This overview will focus on two general areas where corpus studies can provide key insight: first, by addressing the potential issues with mismatch between natural language use in stimuli creation and task design and second, problems associated with identifying the source(s) of variability arising in acceptability tasks.

#### 25.2.2.1.1 *Addressing Artificialness*

Anyone who has explored corpus data can attest that real-world language is much more diverse than the kind of language one typically has intuitive access to (Aarts 1991). Human intuitions about language can provide a limited view of language possibility and can sometimes lead to constructed example stimuli which may only represent part of a more complex linguistic paradigm (Meurers & Müller 2009). To avoid subjective notions of what language is, a corpus can be consulted to provide a certain level of confirmation, or ecological validation, of what is possible and as such improve descriptive adequacy (Bresnan 2007).

As examples, I will illustrate two particular theoretical claims for which corpus data have provided key counterevidence. The first involves a proposal having to do with the lexical status of a particular idiom *raise hell*. Jackendoff (1997) suggests that this idiom is a lexicalized verbal phrase and therefore cannot be passivized and retain its idiomatic reading.

(1)    Hell was raised by Herodotus. (! = 'cause a serious disturbance')

Riehemann (2001) provides counterexamples extracted from the *New York Times Corpus* where *raise hell* appears in passives (2) and in relative clauses (3) suggesting that the categorical claim of the lexical status of this idiomatic phrase is not borne out.

(2)    So much *hell was raised* that the biologists threw up their hands in surrender.

(3)    Few folks in the Apple speculated on *the hell that would have been raised* by George Steinbrenner if the Yankees had been similarly robbed at Camden Yards.

A second example of using corpus data to externally validate a claim pertains to the Affectedness Constraint (Anderson 1978). This proposal states that a preposed complement in a possessive construction is only allowed when the referent of the complement is affected by the denoted event (4) and disallowed in other contexts (5).

(4)     a. the city's destruction
        b. the boy's removal
        c. the picture's defacement

(5)     a. *the event's recollection
        b. *the problem's perception
        c. *the picture's observation

Bresnan (2007) suggests that language usage data cited in Taylor (1996) contradict this proposal.

(6)     a. Certainly, between the presentation of the information to the senses and *its recollection*, various cognitive processes take place.
        b. Lesson 2: Sound Properties and *Their Perception*
        c. But the standard idea that an event is inseparable from *its observation* is just scientific silliness.

Instead of a categorical constraint hinging on affectedness, the corpus data appear to point to a condition where the preposed possessive nominals (*event's, its*) require adequate discourse context to be topical.

Taken together these examples underscore the fact that subjective notions of what forms language can take can have an influence on the direction of theoretical proposals and that the use of qualitative evidence from corpora can help provide a more realistic understanding of how language is performed in natural communicative contexts. This understanding can then lead to more robust and descriptively adequate theoretical proposals.

Whereas the previous examples highlighted qualitative divergence between constructed and observed language form, some forms of artificialness can have affects on elicitation evidence that are quantitative in nature. Psycholinguistic research has demonstrated that language processing behavior is affected by cues and patterns that are encountered in communicative language experiences. Factors such as frequency, discourse context, event plausibility, pragmatics, and prosody have been cited in the literature as influential in sentence processing. So influential are these factors, that they are standardly controlled for in elicitation tasks to reduce unexplained variability (Gibson & Fedorenko 2013). Here I will touch on frequency and discourse context and illustrate cases where these factors can influence elicited responses in acceptability tasks.

First of all, it is important to make the point that probability of sentence occurrence is not the same as acceptability, as sentence length and lexical frequency conspire to drive down the likelihood of occurrence of some structures, despite the fact that they are perceived as perfectly acceptable (see Chapter 1 for further discussion of this point). Lau, Clark, and Lappin (2016) cite the sentence in (7) as occurring in the *British National Corpus* once, in a corpus of almost 5 million sentences. Nevertheless, it receives high acceptability ratings.

(7)     When the Indians went hunting, whether for animals or for rival Indians, their firepower was deadly.

Although the relationship between sentence frequency and acceptability is clearly not direct, there is a relationship. First, speakers are more likely to produce acceptable sentences than unacceptable sentences (Labov 1972). Second, and more importantly, the influence of the relative frequencies of subsentential linguistic units (Frequency Effects) has been detected in online processing studies at many linguistic levels.

Relative processing costs can influence speaker perception of acceptability. Starting with words, the frequency of individual lexical items (unigrams) can influence acceptability ratings as seen in the contrast between (8) and (9) (Sag, Hofmeister, & Snider 2007).[1]

(8)     Which *letter* did the *judge decide* to *send back immediately*? $\geq$

(9)     Which *epistle* did the *magistrate opt* to *remand forthwith*?

The morphological frequency of lexical items too plays a role in acceptability ratings. Take for instance the following two sentences (Braze 2002).

(10)    The felons *rushed* into the cellblock but couldn't see the warden. $\geq$

(11)    The felons *rushed* into the cellblock couldn't see the warden.

In these examples *rushed* is temporarily ambiguous between past-tense and past-participle readings. Yet, *rushed* appears much more frequently as a past-tense verb than a past-participle leading to a garden-path effect in (11) and not in (10) (MacDonald, Pearlmutter, & Seidenberg 1994). Textbook garden-path sentences, as in (12), are well-known to be found unacceptable for similar reasons.

(12)    The horse raced past the barn fell.

Frequency effects are also found for multiword sequences (n-grams). Arnon and Snider (2010) explored the processing of four-word sequences to explore the relationship between stored and computed forms. They show that there is a phrase-frequency effect for up to four-word sequences.

---

[1] The symbol $\geq$ will be used to show relative acceptability differences.

The more common the word sequence the faster it was recognized in a phrasal-decision task.

In context, these frequent phrasal units can contribute to acceptability differences between structurally similar constructions. In a study surveying the relationship between processing and acceptability of syntactic islands, Hofmeister and Sag (2010) cite the acceptability differences between the following sentences, both of which should be violations of the Complex NP Constraint (see Chapter 9 for discussion of this and other islands).

(13)    How much money are you *making the claim* that the company squandered? ≥

(14)    How much money are you *stating the fact* that the company squandered?

This acceptability difference was noted by Ross (1967), who argued that the *that*-clause in *making the claim* to be a complement of the verb, not of the noun, as it is in *stating the fact*. Notably, however, *making the claim* is a much more frequent collocation (co-occurring pattern) than *stating the fact* suggesting that the collocational frequency difference has led to a structural change (i.e. grammaticalization) (Bybee 2006).

Lexical co-occurrence frequency also is reflected in verb subcategorization preferences. McElree (1993) shows that verbs more often associated with a particular subcategorization frame can influence acceptability judgments. For example, in subordinate clauses intransitive-biased *rushed* is rated less acceptable in transitive contexts and more acceptable in intransitive contexts, while the opposite holds for transitive-biased *watched*.

**Transitive**

(15)    John thought Bill *watched* the ... (preferred) ≥

(16)    John thought Bill *rushed* the ... (non-preferred)

**Intransitive**

(17)    John thought Bill *rushed* for ... (preferred) ≥

(18)    John thought Bill *watched* for ... (non-preferred)

Discourse context can also provide important cues to language processing. In formal as well as informal acceptability tasks, for example, stimuli are often presented without (appropriate) linguistic context which can lead to unexpected variability (see Chapters 2 and 6 for further discussion of the role of context in acceptability experiments).

Wasow and Arnold (2005: 1484–1485) underscore this point:

> Consulting primary intuitions unavoidably involves attempting to assign a meaning and to imagine a context in which the expression under consideration might be used. By leaving all contextual factors up to the

imagination, the use of primary intuitions regarding sentences in isola-tion is arguably more subject to irrelevant interference than an experi-mental method that explicitly controls context.

As noted above, garden-path sentences such as (12) are consistently found unacceptable by informants when presented in isolation. Yet, with an appropriate discourse context, informants find the same construction acceptable.

(19)     The horse that they raced around the track held up fine. The horse that was raced down the road faltered a bit. And *the horse raced past the barn fell.*

Further evidence of the influence of discourse context is found for con-structions which appear to violate the Superiority Condition, as in (21) (see Chapter 5 for discussion of Superiority).

(20)     Who finished what? $\geq$

(21)     What did who finish?

Hofmeister et al. (2013) point to evidence from the Web (in edited contexts) for *wh*-orders which appear to be acceptable under adequately supported discourse contexts.

(22)     What did who know and when did they know it?

(23)     What did who say and who did the asserting?

(24)     What, do you think this is a game? *What rules should who follow?* This shit sandwich is a reality – a competition for survival between all souls …

In sum, relying solely on human intuition to generate experimental mate-rials can be problematic. Consulting corpus data can provide an important step to help externally validate materials used either to forward categori-cal claims or to inform the creation of more authentic stimuli and/or stimulus contexts for presentation in acceptability tasks.

### 25.2.2.1.2 *Exploring Variability*

Formal methods for conducting acceptability tasks have made progress in reducing much of the nuance variability associated with informal accept-ability judgment tasks through the careful design and experimental execu-tion (Schütze 1996; see also Chapter 1). Yet, even addressing some of the known confounds presented in the previous section, elicited responses will always include some degree of unexplained variance. In this section I outline two primary ways that corpora can provide insight into variability associated with acceptability tasks: first, mismatches between informant behavior in acceptability tasks and real-world linguistic behavior and second, investigating complex linguistic relationships that may not have been previously identified.

The objective of modern linguistic inquiry is describing the actual capabilities of the language faculty and not the prescriptive norms associated with conventions of language use. This goal, however, is at times at odds with the methodological instrument of inquiry. Whereas there are important reasons to consult naive language speakers (Spencer 1973), their behavior in elicitation contexts may be conditioned by the context of the experimental session and lead to judgments that do not align with the speaker's own linguistic behavior.

Judgments made by informants may be influenced by prescriptive norms, register, and/or dialect social stigma. Labov (1996: 8) notes that in the case of positive *anymore* elicited responses were "very erratic indeed."

(25)    Cars are sure expensive *anymore*. (Cars are sure *more expensive than they used to be.*)

Labov found evidence that informants who found positive *anymore* unacceptable through elicitation methods freely used the structure in spontaneous conversation, as shown in (26).

(26)    Do you know what's a lousy show *anymore*? Johnny Carson.

Labov (1996: 22) noted that "[i]t is possible that any grammatical pattern that is perceived as regional may be suppressed in introspection, whether or not a social stigma can be detected."

Whereas informants may not be cognizant of their bias toward or against certain language forms, in other contexts the bias is more tangible. For example, code-switching is often associated with strong language attitudes. Badiola et al. (2018) found that bilinguals with negative attitudes to code-switching overall give lower acceptability ratings to code-switching stimuli than bilinguals with positive attitudes toward this language variety. However, Montes-Alcalá (2000: 226) found "attitudes towards code-switching are not a determining factor in the types of code-switching that bilingual individuals produce" as social stigma and negative attitudes did not correlate with code-switching production in a narration task. In these types of contexts, Labov (1996: 7) argues for what he calls the Principle of Validity: "When the use of language is shown to be more consistent than introspective judgments, a valid description of the language will agree with that use rather than with intuitions."

Another source of variability concerns potential linguistic interactions not identified by the researcher from the outset of the experiment. Here corpora can provide investigators a method for investigating potential relationships between linguistic features.

Wasow and Arnold (2005) explore the claim by Chomsky (1955) that the alternation in verb–particle constructions is due to structural complexity of the intervening NP, and not its length (in words).

(27)    They brought [$_{NP}$ all the leaders of the riot] in.

(28)    They brought [$_{NP}$ the man I saw] in.

Chomsky pointed out that his primary intuition about verb–particle alternations is that they are both grammatical, but that (27) was more "natural" than (28). The secondary intuition pointed to the source of this intuition – the more complex the NP, the more chance that the preposition would stay joined to the verb, regardless of the length of the NP.

The authors perform an acceptability and corpus study to explore the contribution of each of these factors. The acceptability study crossed preposition placement and NP object complexity (complex NPs containing verbs, (29) and (30), vs. noncomplex NPs without verbs, (31) and (32)) while holding the lengths of the constituents constant.

(29)    The children took [$_{NP}$ everything we said] in.

(30)    The children took in [$_{NP}$ everything we said].

(31)    The children took [$_{NP}$ all our instructions] in.

(32)    The children took in [$_{NP}$ all our instructions].

Results from an analysis of variance revealed an interaction between NP complexity and particle placement along the lines of Chomsky's intuitions. Statistical significance, however, was only obtained in the by-subjects test. On closer inspection of the findings, it was noted that there was "considerable variation in the responses," in particular for constructions where verb and particle were split by the intervening NP.

To complement this study, and to dig deeper into the source of the response variation and the potential role of constituent length, a corpus study was conducted. Where the acceptability study targeted the role of structural complexity by maintaining NP constituent lengths constant, the corpus study included both NP structure and lexical length as measures of complexity.

A total of 3,268 verb–particle construction tokens were extracted from syntactically parsed corpora representing both written (*The Wall Street Journal, Brown*) and spoken (*Switchboard*) American English corpora. These tokens were annotated for NP structure (complex, noncomplex) and length (in words). Results from a logistic regression suggested length is a better predictor of particle placement than structure. Based on this subsequent evidence, the authors point out that corpus studies provide a necessary perspective to complement intuition about the source of an alternation.

A secondary advantage to corpus studies, exemplified in this case, is that they allow the exploration of gradient, or continuous, variables, such as word length, much more naturally than in an elicitation study, where it is less feasible to create stimuli that differ in a gradient or non-categorical manner (Ford & Bresnan 2010).

### 25.2.2.2  Elicitation to Enhance Corpus Studies

Corpus studies show strengths in allowing researchers to expand the notion of what is possible in language and to explore complex relationships between structures and linguistic and non-linguistic features. This can be a powerful strategy for testing theoretical claims as well as generating new hypotheses. Corpus studies, however, have their limitations which can often be offset through elicitation methods. The gold standard in science, the formal elicitation experiment allows for a more detailed investigation through the use of sophisticated design and appropriate controls to precisely isolate the particular behavior of interest (precision). In contrast to observation studies, elicitation methods also enable researchers to explore unattested forms (negative data) which can provide a more robust understanding of a behavior along one or more dimensions that may not have been previously documented in resources of language use.

### 25.2.2.2.1  *Aiming for Precision*

As mentioned earlier in this section, one of the strengths of corpus data for syntactic research is the ability to explore and identify potentially relevant relationships between linguistic features and syntactic forms that occur in natural communicative settings. On the other hand, a shortcoming of corpus data is the difficultly in separating systematic patterns of interest from the host of complex interactions in which any given utterance is nested. Quantitative approaches and sophisticated statistical methods applied to corpora can provide insight into probable relationships, however, elicitation methods constitute an important step in corroborating and validating evidence extracted from corpora in controlled settings.

In a study which highlights how elicitation can serve to refine corpus predictions, Strunk and Snider (2013) investigated claims concerning constraints on syntactic extraposition addressed by numerous proposals (Subjacency, Barriers, etc.). The basic theoretical notions hold that constituent extraction is directly related to the depth of the embedding of the clause.

In the case of relative clause extraposition, Chomsky (1986) argues that the acceptability of (33) is due to the fact that the relative clause is interpreted as attached to the higher DP clause (*many books with stories*), and not the lower DP clause (*stories*).

(33)    [$_{DP}$ Many books [$_{PP}$ with [$_{DP}$ stories]]] were sold [$_{RC}$ that I wanted to read.]

Nevertheless, evidence from researcher-constructed (34) and usage (35) examples found on the internet appears to challenge the categorical constraint on relative clause extraction. In each of these cases the relative clauses can only be semantically interpreted as attached to the lower, multiply embedded DP.

(34)     [DP Only letters [PP from [DP those people]]] remained unanswered [RC that had received our earlier reply.]

(35)     I'm reading [DP a book [PP about [DP Elliott Smith]]] right now, [RC who killed himself.]

Strunk and Snider (2013) performed a systematic corpus study to follow up on this preliminary evidence. Their study investigated this phenomenon in English as well as German. Given resource (un)availability, the corpus study was performed on a parsed corpus of written German (*Tübigen Treebank of Written German*), from which 2,789 relative clause tokens were extracted and separated into three types: extraposed (movement), integrated (no movement), and edge (where movement was not identifiable). Then the depth of embedding for each type was calculated. Statistical findings suggest that the likelihood a relative clause extraposition is related to the increasing depth of embedding of its antecedent in a gradient, rather than categorical manner.

Although the corpus study proved insightful, the specific nature of extraposition and embeddings required more detailed information than the corpus annotation provided. Specifically, the question remained open as to whether the degree of embedding of extraposed relative clauses was related to high or low NP attachment.

Given annotation limitations of the German corpus and no suitable corpus available for English, the authors turned to an acceptability task to more gain a more precise understanding of the phenomenon for both languages. The experimental design included depth of embedding (*deep, mid, shallow*) and the attachment of the relative clause (*high, low*). High/low attachment preference was coerced by manipulating the semantic cohesiveness between the antecedent and relative clause in terms of animacy and number agreement.

(36)     *Deep-Low:* I consulted [DP1 the diplomatic representative [PP of [DP2 a small country [PP with [DP3 *border disputes*]]]]] early today [RC *which threaten* to cause a hugely disastrous war.]

(37)     *Deep-High:* I consulted [DP1 *the diplomatic representative* [PP of [DP2 *a small country* [PP with [DP3 border disputes]]]]] early today [RC *who threatens* to cause a hugely disastrous war.]

Mid and shallow embeddings were created by manipulating the prepositional phrase as either verbally subcategorized or not.

(38)   *Mid-Low:* I consulted [DP1 the diplomatic representative] [PP about [DP2 a small country [PP with [DP3 *border disputes*]]]] early today [RC *which threaten* to cause a hugely disastrous war.]

(39)   *Mid-High:* I consulted [DP1 *the diplomatic representative* t] [PP about [DP2 a small country [PP with [DP3 border disputes]]]] early today [RC *who threatens* to cause a hugely disastrous war.]

(40)   *Shallow-Low:* I consulted [DP1 the diplomatic representative] [PP of [DP2 a small country [PP about [DP3 *border disputes*]]]] early today [RC *which threaten* to cause a hugely disastrous war.]

(41)   *Shallow-High:* I consulted [DP1 *the diplomatic representative* t] [PP of [DP2 a small country [PP about [DP3 border disputes]]]] early today [RC *who threatens* to cause a hugely disastrous war.]

The overall results from both English and German show two key findings for this discussion. First, there was no significant difference between the acceptability of Deep-High (non-Subjacency violation) and Deep-Low (severe Subjacency violation). Second, there was a significant increase in acceptability for Low over High attachment in both the Mid and Shallow conditions. Taken together, this evidence suggests there is not a categorical but rather a gradient subclause locality effect.

This study highlights the fact that corpus results can be informative and serve to generate predictions that may not otherwise have been considered. It also shows that, although important tools for hypothesis generation, the nature of corpora, or a particular corpus, as in the case outlined here, may not be able to provide a sufficient level of precision. Elicitation studies, such as the acceptability study here, can serve as a follow-up to isolate particular structural configurations in a more controlled environment.

### 25.2.2.2.2   Assessing Negative Data

The finite nature of corpora means that there is always the potential for grammatical/possible structures to appear infrequently or not appear at all. In some cases, these rare/missing structures can pose problems for studying a certain phenomenon as there may be gaps in the paradigm which may be due to grammatical limitations or simply scarce or missing due to the finite nature of the corpus itself. It is a mistake, however, to assume that since a construction is rare or missing it is ill-formed, as language use is affected by a host of factors including avoidance of structures where working memory demands are high or structures where pragmatic contexts licensing the use of the structure are highly specialized in nature (Gibson & Fedorenko 2013).

Hoffmann (2006) conducts a study aimed at better understanding prepositional placement in relative clauses. That is, whether a preposition is stranded, as in (42), or pied-piped, as in (43).

(42)     I want a data source [which]$_i$ I can rely on $_{-i}$.

(43)     I want a data source [on which]$_i$ I can rely $_{-i}$.

Corpus and acceptability studies were performed to try to better understand the factors that condition this alternation. In the corpus study a total of 1,074 relative clause tokens were extracted from the British English component of the *International Corpus of English*. These tokens contained either a preposition without a complement (42) or in which the relativizer was governed by a preposition (43). In addition to preposition placement (*stranded, pied-piped*), the relative clause tokens were coded for various other factors cited in the literature: restrictiveness (*restrictive, non-restrictive*), relativizer type ('that,' *zero*, 'which,' 'who,' 'whom'), containing phrase type ('VP,' 'AdjP,' 'NP'), complexity (*distance between landing and extraction site*), text type (*formality*), and predicate–prepositional relationship (*verb selected, adjunct*). A stepwise logistic regression was performed to assess the relationship between particle placement and the other factors. Results from this analysis showed two categorical distributions. First, the type of relativizer showed categorical distribution, specifically *that/zero* relativizers always appeared stranded and *wh*-relativizers, pied-piped. Second, all *that/zero* stranding cases appeared with prepositions that were semantically selected by the clause predicate (i.e. no adjunct prepositions appeared stranded).

The fact that *that/zero* stranding only occurred in the corpus evidence with predicate-selected prepositions suggested that there was either a semantic constraint at play or an accidental gap in the corpus data. For that reason, an acceptability study was conducted to specifically target the complete prepositional paradigm. Findings from the acceptability study supported the predicate–preposition constraint on stranding detected in the corpus data. However, a post-hoc test directly comparing *that* versus zero relativizers found that the ratings for stranding with *that* were significantly better than with zero relativizers – a nuanced difference that had not been noted before.

This study demonstrates that the combination of a corpus and acceptability study can be used to corroborate findings as well as to help tease apart nuances that might not have been uncovered by either method alone. In this way a corpus study can serve to produce novel predictions, even in cases where key examples do not appear, and with specific predictions in hand, an acceptability study can provide a more detailed understanding of the paradigm by addressing these key contrasts directly through elicitation.

## 25.3   Conducting a Corpus Study

In this section I will step back and look at corpus studies from the vantage point of implementation. The aim is to highlight some of the key concepts that should be taken into account when approaching a corpus study. This will include a discussion on what a corpus is and is not and what sampling and design considerations should be taken into account when compiling and/or selecting a corpus for use in a particular study. I will also provide an overview of the types of evidence that a corpus can be used to produce, including common methods for extracting and analyzing this evidence.

### 25.3.1   Sampling and Design Considerations

A corpus is a type of observational data purposely designed to capture a comprehensive sample of language use in naturalistic contexts of a target linguistic community for language study. In a broad sense all language use is natural, but in a more relevant sense naturalistic text reflects language use in normal, non-elicited communicative functions.[2] It is not simply a collection of texts. A corpus is a purposefully selected set of texts extracted from a target population. A corpus by nature is a finite sample of language. Complete coverage of a linguistic community is typically not feasible; the goal, however, is to attain language samples that best approximate the language usage patterns. The degree to which a corpus approximates the language behavior of a linguistic community is known as *representativeness*.

   The sampling frame of a corpus is key to understanding its potential for providing reliable insight. Various sampling methods are typically employed to obtain representative samples. An intuitive first step is to increase the sample space. A larger sample has a better chance of being representative than a smaller sample, all else being equal. Large samples of language are not sufficient to obtain a representative corpus, however. Language form demonstrates patterns that are contingent on a number of non-linguistic domains (Biber 1993a), dealing with genre, register, text type, and speaker characteristics, primarily, but by hypothesis along a number of other lines that are not explicitly known. A large sample alone cannot avoid the potential for a sample that spans a limited number of these domains and therefore results in a sample that systematically misrepresents a target population. To mitigate this issue corpus designers attempt to identify the relevant domains that comprise the target linguistic community and acquire samples from each. This is known as stratified sampling (Biber 1993b). Given that some domains are more common and plentiful than others, it is ideal to balance the sample with the relative sizes of the domains to better model the population (Atkins, Clear, & Ostler 1992). To fine tune the corpus, the sample should be drawn randomly from the population. Together these measures provide the best practices for capturing a representative language sample.

   A researcher may not need to develop a corpus from scratch and therefore not need to put these steps into practice but being aware of these principles underlying rigorous corpus development is the first step in

---

[2] See Gilquin and Gries (2009 : 5) for a good summary of types of data and their degree of naturalness.

evaluating the potential value of a given corpus for a particular research question. There are two typical mistakes made in selecting a corpus on which to base research that stem from not taking the sampling frame into account. First, a researcher will decide to embark on a corpus study, select a corpus given its popularity as evidenced by citations in the literature, and move straight to analysis. That a corpus may be a relevant sample in one study does not mean that it will be adequate for a different question or purpose.

Second, it is an error to assume that any collection of text is a corpus. A good example of this is using results from a web search engine as the primary source of a corpus study. The internet provides access to very large amounts of textual data and, with careful design considerations, this rich data can be compiled to create a representative corpus for some target population. A search of the web, however, is not an equally adequate resource compared to a rigorously developed corpus. Size is the primary advantage to web searches, but a web search fails the requirement of being purposely designed for language research. No population is identified, let alone domains of that language, and it is surely not random in the appropriate sense.[3]

Sampling considerations are fundamental to sound corpus development and research based on corpora. As in other areas of empirical research, the reliability of the evidence (output) is only as good as the reliability of the data (input). Another consideration to take into account when deciding on the ideal corpus data for a given syntactic investigation is annotation – both linguistic and non-linguistic.

If a corpus is developed in a rigorous way, there should be non-linguistic annotation or metadata associated with the resource (Reppen 2010). This information documents the relevant features concerning the sampling procedure such as date or time period(s), modality(ies), text type(s), speaker(s), etc. These features may be documented in the file names, the header of corpus files, embedded in the files using a markup scheme, maintained in a stand-alone file or files, or stored in a relational database.

At this point it is worth noting two key uses of metadata. On the one hand, as noted above, these non-linguistic features can be used as helpful information to assess the extent to which evidence provided by a corpus can generalize to the target language population. On the other hand, non-linguistic features can be used as criteria either to divide up a corpus into two or more separate samples or to purposely select or develop distinct corpus samples to be considered in relation to one another along one or more dimensions. The division must be purposeful and explicit. For example, a sample which covers a range of time periods, yet the balance of the other non-linguistic features is not accounted for, cannot be considered a reliable corpus for studying change over time.

---

[3] Note, however, that the web and other text collections can be helpful in collecting anecdotal evidence.

Another consideration to take into account when selecting a resource for a corpus study is whether it will be necessary for the resource to be annotated for some level or levels of linguistic information (e.g. lexical, syntactic, semantic, pragmatic, etc.). While it is possible to do some superficial investigation with unannotated, raw running text, most corpus studies of syntax require some level of linguistic annotation. Linguistic annotation augments corpus running text with implicit linguistic information making this information more readily available for extraction.

Meurers and Müller (2009) frame the utility of linguistic annotation in terms of *precision* and *recall*. Take a basic example in which a researcher aims to extract all the verbs that occur in the simple past tense in a running text version of corpus of English. To perform this search, the researcher will need to devise a strategy to identify all the potential morphological variants for the simple past in English. While it is easy for a native speaker to recognize past tense morphology, irregular and/or infrequent verbal forms may not come to mind when formulating the search. If the search parameters do not fully capture the morphological variants, then recall is lowered. If the search captures forms which match the parameters, but are not verbs, then precision is lowered. The best search is one in which precision and recall are high. In our hypothetical search for occurrences of verbs in the simple past, a corpus with linguistic annotation for grammatical category would go a long way to increasing our precision and recall.

There are caveats to keep in mind when working with linguistic annotation. First and foremost, linguistic annotations are inherently theoretically opinionated (Leech 1991). Where there may be a general agreement on how to identify nouns, verbs, and other grammatical categories, consensus breaks down where many competing theoretical formulations exist. This fact can limit the number of resources available for a particular corpus study, if the study depends on features that are tied to a particular formalism. What's more, theoretical formalism often plays a role in determining the particular conventions for encoding annotations, in particular for syntactically parsed corpora. Differences between annotation schemes, such as dependency and constituent parsing, can be reconciled either computationally or through a hybrid approach using computational methods and (semi-)manual engineering (Bick 1997). However, this is often a non-trivial task. For the average syntactician it is often more practical to identify a resource which already explicitly encodes relevant syntactic features for the study at hand.

A second issue concerns the reliability of the annotations themselves. Augmenting a corpus with linguistic annotation information is typically performed automatically using software. State-of-the-art software is largely based on probabilistic models trained on manually annotated data (TnT (Brants 2000), Hunpos (Halácsy, Kornai, & Oravecz 2007), and Stanford PCFG (Klein & Manning 2003)). This software can be applied in ways that significantly increase the reliability of evidence extracted in corpus studies, but also may severely degrade the reliability of the annotations returned if applied in less than ideal situations. The most common error is to assume that reported accuracy for an annotation tool will guarantee this level of accuracy on any target text. Misalignment of sampling frames between the training and target texts leads to the most pronounced and commonly encountered errors in automatic annotation.

A third issue to take into account when working on a study that requires linguistic annotation is the fact that existing annotated corpora and software for performing automatic annotations are skewed toward certain types of linguistic information. Whereas corpora with grammatical category information or phrase structure parsing (or software to automatically perform these types of annotation) may be readily available, there are significantly fewer corpora which are annotated for features such as animacy, givenness, concreteness, and coreference, to name a few. If a study ultimately depends on such information, human intervention will most likely be required. Although manual annotation of an entire corpus is typically not feasible, it may be possible to scale down the annotation to a subset of the corpus by first extracting relevant structures based on existing corpus features. For example, a study aimed at understanding the potential relationship between animacy and the ditransitive alternation may find corpus resources lacking, as animacy is not a feature that is commonly found in existing annotated corpus resources. However, if ditransitives can be identified first, then manual annotation can be applied to this target subset, making the task more feasible.

### 25.3.2   Analysis Strategies

Once a viable corpus, aligning in sampling frame and annotation level with the research question, is in hand, the next step in conducting a corpus study is performing the analysis. This includes extracting the relevant data and then submitting this evidence to evaluation. To frame this discussion, I will outline two general types of approaches to using corpora: *qualitative* and *quantitative*. This distinction is associated with distinct methods for extraction and evaluation.

Data extracted for qualitative study probe the question "what is possible?" Qualitative evidence can be used to confirm or disconfirm categorical theoretical claims as well as generate research questions for further investigation. A basic approach to extract evidence to evaluate a categorical claim is to perform a corpus search for a linguistic type. In cases where the theoretical prediction is the inexistence of a structure, a search returning results can provide important counterevidence. The evidence provided by Riehemann (2001) on the lexical status of idioms such as *raise hell* illustrates this case. In some situations, however, a researcher will want to retrieve the context (linguistic and/or non-linguistic) in which a token occurs to probe the existence of potentially important relationships that have yet to be explored or identified. A concordance, or keyword in context (KWIC), search is commonly employed for this task. The argument made by Bresnan (2007) concerning the proposed Affectedness Constrained suggested that the discourse context plays a key role in the acceptability of preposed complements in possessive constructions. Without consulting the communicative context in which these constructions appear, such observations may go undetected.

The evaluation of qualitative evidence tends to be quite straightforward from a methodological standpoint. The results returned from a search are often inspected manually. When the aim is to test a categorical claim, conclusions can readily be drawn when counterexamples are found. It is important to note that although corpus representativeness is a key consideration in all corpus studies, relevant and strong counterexamples can be found in relatively small and underrepresentative samples. If a counterexample is not found, however, it may be due to an unrepresentative corpus sample or that no counterexample exists. Identifying which of these potential scenarios is at play can be difficult to establish using corpus-based methods alone.[4]

When the aim of the qualitative evaluation is to provide support for intuitions or to explore potentially novel relationships the analysis method is less clearly defined, and conclusions should always be approached as tentative. In these cases, a qualitative corpus approach should be viewed as a preliminary step to refine predictions in preparation for more rigorous, quantitative investigation where exploration of complex relationships and generalizable power is enhanced.

Quantitative evidence, on the other hand, concerns the likelihood of linguistic structures, in other words, "what is probable?" This approach to corpus data aims to gauge the relative frequency of linguistic forms to others. Quantitative evidence can be employed to normalize stimuli for frequency effects in preparation for an elicitation task, or it can be approached as evidence for a dedicated study to either test or refine a hypothesis or to generate novel hypotheses.

The extraction of quantitative evidence tends to be more demanding than in qualitative studies. Instead of searching for linguistic types, as is the case in qualitative analyses, a quantitative analysis aims to gather information about linguistic tokens, that is, individual instantiations of linguistic forms or structures and the potential co-occurring features (linguistic and/or non-linguistic) that relate with the realization of particular structural types. The multifactorial nature of this approach requires search results to be paired with the relevant features of interest. The format of this evidence is often tabular. In many cases this is a multi-step process where preliminary search results are transformed and augmented in

---

[4] See Stefanowitsch (2006) for strategies for assessing negative data.

preparation for evaluation. For example, Wasow and Arnold (2005) performed a corpus study aimed at exploring the role of distinct measures of complexity (structural and word-length) on verb–particle alternations. A syntactically parsed corpus facilitated the extraction of the relevant structures. After this initial search, each of the token structures requires intervention to encode the values for the attributes alternation type, structural complexity type, and constituent length.

Where the importance of a representative corpus and requirements for precision and recall can be relaxed for qualitative analysis, quantitative analysis depends on these characteristics to understand how well the results generalize to the larger population. For this same reason quantitative analysis is rooted in statistics. Language usage is inherently variable and requires sophisticated statistical methods to tease apart the signal from the noise. Statistical approaches and tests vary depending on the goal of the research and the structure of the research design (number of factors, information levels, etc.). If the goal is to test a hypothesis then inferential statistics are employed. Research into phenomena where there is no clear prediction, or the aim is to examine possible relationships (hypothesis generation), employs exploratory analysis methods.

## 25.4　Future Directions

Approaching research through multiple methodological perspectives has increasingly played a role in theoretical linguistics by providing interesting insights to both longstanding and new questions. Yet there is still much to be done on both theoretical and methodological fronts to support even more robust future research.

### 25.4.1　Theory

On the theoretical front, it is becoming clearer that evidence from language use is a valuable tool for generating syntactic predictions, validating, and/or refining syntactic claims. Language usage serves as a needed source to avoid the potential for notions of language form that inform linguistic research to become disconnected from the forms that language takes. This can be in the form of qualitative examples that provide counterexamples to theoretical claims or can come from quantitative evidence which can reveal more complex or nuanced relationships that are not readily available to intuition.

It is becoming clearer that language behavior, and human cognition more generally, has a larger probabilistic component than has been traditionally acknowledged. Throughout a large part of the history of modern linguistic inquiry, the standard methodology for theoretical syntax, acceptability judgments, did not take the influence of previous exposure, working memory limitations, discourse and informational context into account. Evidence presented in this chapter highlights the fact that this has been an oversight and has had the potential to lead theoretical claims and general theorizing astray. This tendency to marginalize language use gained from observation led to increasingly insular syntactic theory, more and more divorced from other areas of syntactic research and language science more generally.

The gap between theoretical positions, however, seems to have been closing in recent years. Researchers have provided important evidence that questions some of the basic tenets of the generative program, such as the categorical nature of grammatical competence (Manning 2003) and the separation between the lexicon and grammar (Langacker 2012). Evidence from multiple sources, including corpus data, suggests that areas that once were considered strong sources of evidence for a categorical competence grammar may not be as convincing as once believed. Evidence from online (i.e. processing) and offline (i.e. acceptability) studies has increasingly shown that "hard" constraints on grammar appear to show more gradience than previously thought. And linguists' own "soft" constraints, in many cases, can be subsumed by constraints conditioned by working memory, probabilistic preferences, etc. In essence, the hard line between functional and formal theoretical frameworks has become more blurred.

How to incorporate the ever more gradient evidence into a model of the language faculty, however, is still an active area of investigation which depends in large part on refining understanding about how evidence from observation and elicitation are related. Clearly, employing usage data in tandem with other sources of evidence is key to further exploring these new avenues of thought. As Ford and Bresnan (2010: 1) point out "[i]t is becoming increasingly accepted that speakers have richer knowledge of linguistic constructions than the knowledge captured by their categorical judgments of grammaticality." Yet different methods provide different measures and it is unclear how the evidence from these different linguistic activities relate (Arppe et al. 2010). In some cases, evidence from multiple sources converge (Hoffmann 2005), but in other cases it diverges (Roland & Jurafsky 2000). But these differences should invite, rather than shut out, further exploration.

### 25.4.2  Methodology

These theoretical gains have been predicated, of course, on vetting evidence from multiple perspectives, but much credit is owed to advances in accessibility to data, increasing computer power and the adoption of more advanced programming approaches, and a wider adoption of rigorous methodological procedures associated with quantitative approaches including experimental controls and statistical evaluation.

Notwithstanding, there are aspects where gains can still be made and issues that need to be addressed.

The increasing access to data has fueled psycholinguistic, computational, and theoretical research. There are more corpus resources available than ever before, yet it is important to point out that language data for most of the world's languages are scarce. Furthermore, even for those languages where there are language resources, many of these resources are based on particular modalities (written), or genres (newswire text), or are not annotated to a sufficient level to provide the substrate for the types of analyses that are necessary to make substantial and meaningful gains in our understanding about the relationship between language use and the language faculty (Meurers & Müller 2009). For those resources that are syntactically annotated, theoretical bias in the annotation scheme can make certain studies infeasible. There has been some effort to stem this limitation by proposing cross-theoretic annotation schemes (Francom & Hulden 2008), but much work is still to be done to address this issue.

In terms of methods, there have been substantial gains in quantitative analysis in language-related fields (Manning & Schütze 1999; Baayen, Davidson, & Bates 2008). Despite these gains, adoption of these methods is increasing but still not the norm in many areas, including corpus analysis (Gries 2015). The strength of corpus data is that it provides evidence from language use in natural communicative settings. Additionally, I have suggested that this is also a shortcoming in some ways. To isolate a particular phenomenon, it is key to attempt to control for aspects which can contribute to noise in the data and can obscure legitimate patterns. Bresnan et al. (2007) is a particularly insightful case study of the dative alternation which outlines a series of issues and proposes strategies to refine corpus research methods which bring analysis practices more in line with those of other quantitative research areas.

Another aspect which should not be ignored is the fact that these methodological advances depend in large part on more technical knowledge than has been previously assumed from language researchers, particularly theoretical linguists. I refer specifically to programmatic approaches. Even for researchers who have worked with corpora for many years, it is much too common to rely on pre-packaged software to carry out the steps for extracting and analyzing multivariate data. There are clear advantages to software of this type, but in the end, it places arbitrary limitations on the researcher. A further benefit to adopting programmatic approaches to linguistic research is that they naturally set the stage for sharing code and increasing the availability of reproducible research. The contents of this chapter have made the case, albeit implicitly, that using corpora supports transparency and accountability in language research. By the same token, programmatic approaches and code sharing further this aim. Open data and extraction and analysis methods that are independently verifiable will inevitably lead to more systematic and organized progress.

## 25.5 Conclusions

The aim of this chapter has been to present corpus studies as an important data source for syntactic investigation. For many years corpus studies have not been an integral part of mainstream theoretical syntax, even actively argued against at times as irrelevant. Recent developments in the experimental syntax program, however, have challenged some of the standard practices for collecting and analyzing linguistic evidence in syntax. In doing so, the methodological and theoretical gap between other areas of language science has begun to close. It is more common than ever before for research in theoretical syntax to incorporate multiple methodologies in the same study – vocabulary and conceptual frameworks merging in the process. Online elicitation methods, adopted from psycholinguistics, have been the most visible new addition to the theoretical syntactician's toolbox. Yet observational data, in the form of corpora, have begun to play a larger role in contemporary syntactic investigation. When applied appropriately, corpus studies serve as an indispensable resource to externally validate categorical claims or serve as a resource to explore and generate more refined hypotheses. Exploiting the strengths and counterbalancing the shortcomings of a range of methods is the hallmark of scientific investigation. Linguistic investigation appears to be experiencing a watershed moment in this respect. In this chapter I hope to have made the case that corpus studies stand to be a vital part of this change.

## References

Aarts, J. (1991). Intuition-based and observation-based grammars. In K. Aijmer & B. Altenberg, eds., *English Corpus Linguistics*. Abingdon: Routledge, pp. 56–74.

Abercrombie, D. (1965). Pseudo-procedures in Linguistics. In D. Abercrombie, ed., *Studies in Phonetics and Linguistics*. Oxford: Oxford University Press, pp. 114–119.

Anderson, M. (1978). NP preposing in Noun Phrases. In *Proceedings of the 8th Annual Meeting of the North East Linguistic Society*. Amherst, MA: GLSA, University of Massachusetts, pp. 12–21.

Arnon, I. & Snider, N. (2010). More than words: Frequency effects for multiword phrases. *Journal of Memory and Language*, 62(1), 67–82.

Arppe, A., Gilquin, G., Glynn, D., Hilpert, M., & Zeschel, A. (2010). Cognitive corpus linguistics: Five points of debate on current theory and methodology. *Corpora*, 5(1), 1–27.

Atkins, S., Clear, J., & Ostler, N. (1992). Corpus design criteria. *Literary and Linguistic Computing*, 7(1), 1–16.

Baayen, R. H., Davidson, D. J., & Bates, D. M. (2008). Mixed-effects modeling with crossed random effects for subjects and items. *Journal of Memory and Language*, 59(4), 390–412.

Badiola, L., Delgado, R., Sande, A., & Stefanich, S. (2018). Code-switching attitudes and their effects on acceptability judgment tasks. *Linguistic Approaches to Bilingualism*, 8(1), 5–24.

Biber, D. (1993a). Using register-diversified corpora for general language studies. *Computational Linguistics*, 19(2), 219–241.

Biber, D. (1993b). Representativeness in corpus design. *Literary and Linguistic Computing*, 8(4), 243–257.

Bick, E. (1997). Turning a Dependency Treebank into a PSG-style Constituent Treebank. In *Proceedings of the Fifth International Conference on Language Resources and Evaluation (LREC'06)*. Paris: European Language Resources Association, pp. 1961–1964.

Brants, T. (2000). TnT: A statistical part-of-speech tagger. In *Proceedings of the Sixth Conference on Applied Natural Language Processing*. Stroudsburg, PA: Association for Computational Linguistics, pp. 224–231.

Braze, D. (2002). Grammaticality, acceptability, and sentence processing: A psycholinguistic study. Doctoral dissertation, University of Connecticut.

Bresnan, J. (2007). A few lessons from typology. *Linguistic Typology*, 11(1), 297–306.

Bresnan, J., Cueni, A., Nikitina, T., & Baayen, R. H. (2007). Predicting the dative alternation. In G. Bourma, I. Kraemer, & J. Zwarts, eds., *Cognitive Foundations of Interpretation*. Amsterdam: KNAW, pp. 1–33.

Bybee, J. (2006). From usage to grammar: The mind's response to repetition. *Language*, 82(4), 711–733.

Chomsky, N. (1955). *The Logical Structure of Linguistic Theory*. New York: Plenum Press.

Chomsky, N. (1959). A review of B. F. Skinner's *Verbal Behavior*. *Language*, 35 (1), 26–58.

Chomsky, N. (1986). *Barriers*. Cambridge, MA: MIT Press.

Ford, M. & Bresnan, J. (2010). Studying syntactic variation using convergent evidence from psycholinguistics and usage. In M. Krug & J. Schlüter, eds., *Research Methods in Language Variation and Change*. Cambridge: Cambridge University Press, pp. 1–29.

Francom, J. & Hulden, M. (2008). Parallel multi-theory annotation of syntactic structure. In *Proceedings of the Sixth International Conference on Language Resources and Evaluation (LREC'08)*. Paris: European Language Resources Association, pp. 2339–2343.

Garnsey, S. M., Pearlmutter, N., Myers, E., & Lotocky, M. (1997). The contributions of verb bias and plausibility to the comprehension of temporarily ambiguous sentences. *Journal of Memory and Language*, 37(1), 58–93.

Gibson, E. & Fedorenko, E. (2013). The need for quantitative methods in syntax and semantics research. *Language and Cognitive Processes*, 28(1–2), 88–124.

Gilquin, G. & Gries, S. T. (2009). Corpora and experimental methods: A state-of-the-art review. *Corpus Linguistics and Linguistic Theory*, 5(1), 1–26.

Gries, S. T. (2015). The most under-used statistical method in corpus linguistics: Multi-level (and mixed-effects) models. *Corpora*, 10(1), 95–125.

Halácsy, P., Kornai, A., & Oravecz, C. (2007). HunPos: An open source trigram tagger. In *Proceedings of the 45th Annual Meeting of the ACL on Interactive Poster and Demonstration Sessions*. Stroudsberg, PA: Association for Computational Linguistics, pp. 209–212.

Hoffmann, T. (2005). Variable vs. categorical effects: Preposition pied piping and stranding in British English relative clauses. *Journal of English Linguistics*, 33(3), 257–297.

Hoffmann, T. (2006). Corpora and introspection as corroborating evidence: The case of preposition placement in English relative clauses. *Corpus Linguistics and Linguistic Theory*, 2(2), 165–195.

Hofmeister, P., Arnon, I., Jaeger, F., Sag, I., & Snider, N. (2013). The source ambiguity problem: distinguishing the effects of grammar and processing on acceptability judgments. *Language and Cognitive Processes*, 28(1), 48–87.

Hofmeister, P. & Sag, I. A. (2010). Cognitive constraints and island effects. *Language*, 86(2), 366–415.

Ingram, D. (1989). *First Language Acquisition: Method, Description and Explanation*. Cambridge: Cambridge University Press.

Jackendoff, R. (1997). *The Architecture of the Language Faculty*. Cambridge, MA: MIT Press.

Klein, D. & Manning, C. D. (2003). Accurate unlexicalized parsing. In *Proceedings of the 41st Meeting of the Association for Computational Linguistics*. Stroudsberg, PA: Association for Computational Linguistics, pp. 423–430.

Labov, W. (1972). Sociolinguistic patterns. *Foundations of Language*, 13(2), 251–265.

Labov, W. (1996). When intuitions fail. In L. McNair, K. Singer, L. Dolbrin, & M. Aucon, eds., *Papers from the Parasession on Theory and Data in Linguistics*. Chicago: Chicago Linguistic Society, pp. 77–106.

Langacker, R. W. (2012). *Essentials of Cognitive Grammar*. Oxford: Oxford University Press.

Lau, J. H., Clark, A., & Lappin, S. (2016). Grammaticality, acceptability, and probability: A probabilistic view of linguistic knowledge. *Cognitive Science*, 41(5), 1202–1241.

Leech, G. (1991). The state of the art in corpus linguistics. In K. Aijmer & B. Altenberg, eds., *English Corpus Linguistics*. Abingdon: Routledge, pp. 20–41.

MacDonald, M. C., Pearlmutter, N. J., & Seidenberg, M. S. (1994). Lexical nature of syntactic ambiguity resolution. *Psychological Review*, 101(4), 676–703.

Manning, C. (2003). Probabilistic syntax. In Bod, J. Hay, & Jannedy, eds., *Probabilistic Linguistics*. Cambridge, MA: MIT Press, pp. 289–341.

Manning, C. & Schütze, H. (1999). *Foundations of Statistical Natural Language Processing*. Cambridge, MA: MIT Press.

McElree, B. (1993). The locus of lexical preference effects in sentence comprehension: A time-course analysis. *Journal of Memory and Language*, 32(4), pp. 536–571.

McEnery, T. & Hardie, A. (2012). *Corpus Linguistics: Method, Theory and Practice*. Cambridge: Cambridge University Press.

McEnery, T. & Wilson, A. (2001). *Corpus Linguistics: An Introduction*, 2nd ed. Edinburgh: Edinburgh University Press.

Meurers, W. D. & Müller, S. (2009). Corpora and syntax. In A. Lüdeling & M. Kytö, eds., *Corpus Linguistics: An International Handbook*. Berlin: Mouton de Gruyter, pp. 920–933.

Montes-Alcalá, C. (2000). Attitudes towards oral and written codeswitching in Spanish–English bilingual youths. In A. Roca, ed., *Research on Spanish in the US*. Somerville, MA: Cascadilla Press.

Reppen, R. (2010). Building a corpus: What are the key considerations? In A. O'Keeffe & M. McCarthy, eds., *The Routledge Handbook of Corpus Linguistics*. Abingdon: Routledge, pp. 31–103.

Riehemann, S. Z. (2001). A constructional approach to idioms and word formation. Doctoral dissertation, Stanford University.

Roland, D. & Jurafsky, D. (2000). Verb sense and verb subcategorization probabilities. In S. Stevenson & P. Merlo, eds., *CUNY-98*. Amsterdam: John Benjamins, pp. 325–345.

Ross, J. (1967). Constraints on variables in syntax. Doctoral dissertation, Massachusetts Institute of Technology.

Sag, I., Hofmeister, P., & Snider, N. (2007). Processing complexity in subjacency violations: The Complex Noun Phrase Constraint. In *Proceedings of the 43rd Annual Meeting of the Chicago Linguistic Society*. Chicago: Chicago Linguistic Society, pp. 215–229.

Schütze, C. T. (1996). *The Empirical Base of Linguistics: Grammaticality Judgments and Linguistic Methodology*. Chicago: University of Chicago Press.

Spencer, N. (1973). Differences between linguists and nonlinguists in intuitions of grammaticality-acceptability. *Journal of Psycholinguistic Research*, 2 (2), 83–98.

Stefanowitsch, A. (2006). Negative evidence and the raw frequency fallacy. *Corpus Linguistics and Linguistic Theory*, 2(1), 61–77.

Strunk, J. & Snider, N. (2013). Subclausal locality constraints on relative clause extraposition. In G. Webelhuth, M. Sailer, & H. Walker, eds., *Rightward Movement in a Comparative Perspective*. Amsterdam: John Benjamins, pp. 99–143.

Taylor, J. R. (1996). *Possessives in English: An Exploration in Cognitive Grammar*. Oxford: Oxford University Press.

Wasow, T. (2002). *Postverbal Behavior*. Stanford, CA: CSLI Publications.

Wasow, T. & Arnold, J. (2005). Intuitions in linguistic argumentation. *Lingua*, 115(11), 1481–1496.

# 26

# Syntax and Speaking

Shota Momma

## 26.1 Introduction

Our syntactic knowledge guides what we say and how we speak. In turn, what we say and how we speak reflect the structure of our syntactic knowledge. Thus, studies of syntax and studies of speaking can be mutually informative, at least in principle. In this contribution, I discuss how syntactic theories are an essential part of theories of speaking, and how studies of speaking may (or may not) inform studies of syntax.

Before going into the main discussion, I would like to introduce the basic architecture of the model of sentence production that is widely accepted in the literature, focusing on syntactic aspects.

## 26.2 Syntactic Processes in Speaking

Traditionally, speaking is viewed as involving a transformation of conceptual representations to articulatory-motor or manual-motor representations (Garrett 1975). Accordingly, models of speaking normally assume that speakers start from pre-linguistic conceptual representations, often referred to as *message representations*. The most extensive discussion, as far as I am aware, is Levelt (1989). According to Levelt, message representation is a multi-component level of representation that includes spatial, kinesthetic, and propositional representations. The most explicitly discussed subcomponent is the propositional representation, which encodes information such as semantic categories (e.g. event, person, manner, place, and so on), function–argument structures, semantic types, and thematic information. Questions such as how speakers build these representations as they prepare utterances remain largely unaddressed, though there is an interesting line of studies that investigates how relational and non-relational components of message representations are prepared in speech planning mainly using eye-tracking during speaking (e.g. Griffin & Bock 2000; Gleitman et al. 2007; see Chapter 23 for further discussion of eye-tracking).

Using (potentially partial) message representations, speakers build some form of grammatical representations. The dominant view in the literature, represented by models like Garrett (1975), Bock and Levelt (1994), and Bock and Ferreira (2013), is that speakers first use thematic representations to build grammatical-functional representations that are similar to the f-structure in Lexical Functional Grammar (Bresnan 1982). This stage of processing is often called the functional level of processing (Bock & Levelt 1994). In the Bock and Levelt model, it is assumed that constituent structures are not yet represented at this stage of processing, but grammatical functional structures (e.g. subject, direct object, indirect object, verb) are represented. Thematic information is used to assign grammatical functions to words (or more precisely, *lemmas*, the mental representations that contain syntactic and semantic information but not phonological information; see Kempen & Huijbers (1983) and Levelt, Roelofs, & Meyer (1999)). How grammatical functions are assigned to lemmas is not entirely clear, but Bock and Levelt (1994) assumed that speakers access the subcategorization information of verbs that encodes which thematic role corresponds to which grammatical functions. Speakers may also use other conceptually encoded information, for example animacy information for grammatical function assignment (McDonald, Bock, & Kelly (1993), among others). Some researchers also argue that speakers may develop a strategy to assign grammatical functions based on the statistical regularity between thematic roles and grammatical functions (e.g. patients tend to get the object function; Iwasaki 2010). It has also been proposed that the subcategorization information of verbs is used only for internal arguments, but not external arguments (Momma, Slevc, & Phillips 2016, 2018).

Once speakers assign appropriate grammatical functions to appropriate lemmas, they then build constituent structures using the functional structures. The exact nature of constituent structure representation is a matter of debate in the literature. Some argue that this level of representation is relatively impoverished. My view (elaborated below) is that constituent structural representation is rich enough to encode arbitrary and subtle constraints of grammar. Traditionally (at least since Garrett (1975)), speakers were assumed to first encode the dominance relation between constituents, independently of the linear order relation (precedence relation), though some argue that dominance and precedence relations are simultaneously represented (e.g. Pickering, Branigan, & McLean 2002). Finally, speakers linearize the constituents encoded in the dominance representation for phonological encoding. After phonological encoding, speakers then convert the phonological representations into motor representations, which results in articulation.

## 26.3 The Nature and Quality of Syntactic Representation in Speaking

In sentence production, speakers construct some sort of syntactic representation of their utterances in real time. Most models of sentence production assume that speakers build hierarchical and abstract representations (Garrett 1975, 1988; Kempen & Hoenkamp 1987; Levelt 1989; Bock & Levelt 1994; F. Ferreira 2000; F. Ferreira & Engelhardt 2006; V. Ferreira & Slevc 2007; Bock & V. Ferreira 2013). But what are the empirical reasons to believe that speakers represent abstract hierarchical structures in real time? This question is central in discussing the relationship between studies of syntax and studies of speaking because syntactic theories are relevant for theories of speaking to the extent that syntactic theories capture the nature of representations that speakers construct in real-time production.

### 26.3.1 Abstractness

First, what is the evidence that speakers construct abstract representations of sentences in real-time production? Syntactic theories typically define structural rules and constraints over abstract categories of syntax (nouns, verbs, prepositions, noun phrases, verb phrases, prepositional phrases, etc.) rather than over specific individual words. For example, phrase structure rules are rules defined over lexical and phrasal categories rather than individual words (except for lexicalized rules). Selectional constraints (specifically, c-selectional constraints, Grimshaw 1990) are defined over syntactic categories rather than over individual words. Constraints on long-distance extractions are typically defined over phrasal categories (e.g. subjacency constraints, Chomsky 1977; *that*-trace constraint, Perlmutter 1968). Thus, in most if not all syntactic theories, syntactic representations are not only hierarchically organized, but abstract. But again, in principle, speakers' real-time representations of their own utterances may or may not be abstract.

Before I discuss evidence for the abstractness of syntactic representations, let me clarify what it means for syntactic representations to be abstract. By abstract syntactic representations, I mean syntactic representations that capture structural generalizations across different surface strings in a manner that is not reducible to other factors. Critically, the issue of whether syntactic representations are abstract is orthogonal to the issue of whether syntactic representation is disconnected from meaning or function, because abstract representations can have meanings and functions. Thus, the view that syntactic representations are intimately tied to meaning and function is perfectly compatible with most syntactic theories (despite occasional claims to the contrary; see Adger (2018) for clarification).

There are three lines of evidence that speakers' real-time representations of their utterances are abstract. The first piece of evidence comes from speech errors. As discussed above, Garrett (1975) (see also Fromkin (1971); Nooteboom (1973)) observed that speakers often exchange words that appear far apart in linear distance. Interestingly, when words are exchanged, the two words involved share the same syntactic category. For example, nouns exchange with nouns but not with verbs, and verbs exchange with verbs but not with nouns. This constraint on word exchange error is known as the syntactic category constraint (Dell, Oppenheim, & Kittredge 2008). The same is true for substitution errors (Fromkin 1971; Nooteboom 1973). There is also some experimental evidence suggesting that lexical competition (the presumed source of exchange and substitution errors) is restricted to words of the same category, even when the two words are closely matched in meaning (Momma, Buffinton, Slevc, & Phillips 2020). The very existence of the syntactic category constraint suggests that the abstract syntactic category is causally involved in controlling what speakers say, even when they err.

The second line of evidence comes from a phenomenon known as *syntactic priming* (also referred to as *structural priming* or *structural persistence* in the production literature). Syntactic priming is a well-established phenomenon in which speakers tend to reuse the structure that they recently encountered when more than one structural alternative is suitable for expressing the same message. For example, Bock (1986) showed that speakers are more likely to describe a picture of an event using passive sentences like (1d) as opposed to active sentences like (1c), after they encountered passive sentences like (1b) compared to (1a).

(1)     a. One of the fans punched the referee. [active prime]
        b. The referee was punched by one of the fans. [passive prime]
        c. Lightning is striking the church. [active target]
        d. The church was being struck by the lightning. [passive target]

Bock (1986) also found that dative alternations such as (2) can be syntactically primed. That is, it was shown that speakers are more likely to use the same dative structure as the structure they encountered in prime sentences like (2).

(2)     a. A rock star sold some cocaine to an undercover agent. [prepositional dative prime]
        b. A rock star sold an undercover agent some cocaine. [double object prime]
        c. The man is reading a story to the boy. [prepositional dative target]
        d. The man is reading the boy a story. [double object target]

Syntactic priming effect has been replicated numerous times, with diverse languages and diverse structural alternations (Japanese scrambling: Tanaka, Tamaoka, & Sakai (2007); Dutch dative alternation: Hartsuiker & Kolk (1998); Control vs. raising in English: Griffin & Weinstein-Tull (2003); English complementizer choice: V. Ferreira (2003); English Spray-Load alterations: Chang, Bock, & Goldberg (2003); noun phrases involving modifications in English: Cleland & Pickering (2003) and in American Sign Language: Hall, Ferreira, & Mayberry (2015); see Pickering & Ferreira (2008) for a review). Importantly, syntactic priming can be observed without any overlap in content or function words between prime and target words in the structure (see, e.g., Bock 1989) although repeating content words, especially the head of primed structures, increases the magnitude of syntactic priming (this additional priming is known as lexical boost in the literature (Cleland & Pickering 2003; Pickering & Branigan 1998). The fact that syntactic priming can be obtained without lexical overlap suggests that the representations of sentences that speakers construct during sentence planning involve abstract syntactic representations (Bock 1989; see Ziegler et al. 2019 for a different view).

Finally, speakers show sensitivity to the grammatical constraints that are hard to define without positing abstract representations. For example, consider the following sentences.

(3)    a. Who do you want to dance with?
       b. Who do you wanna dance with?
       c. Who do you want to dance?
       d. * Who do you wanna dance?

As can be seen in these examples, when *who* is the subject of *dance*, using *wanna* instead of *want to* results in less acceptable sentences (this pattern of acceptability has been noted at least since Lakoff (1970)). Though the robustness of this pattern across different speakers is sometimes questioned (e.g. Wasow & Arnold 2005), it is relatively clear that many adult speakers are sensitive to this constraint (e.g. Karins & Nagy 1993; Zukowski & Larson 2009; Kweon & Bley-Vroman 2011). In the generative tradition, the unacceptability of (3d) is attributed to the presence of a *wh*-trace in between *want* and *to*, which blocks the contraction. In accordance with this acceptability pattern, in an elicited production task, Zukowski and Larson (2009) showed that typical adults produce *wanna* approximately five times more frequently in sentences like (3b) than in the sentences like (3d). To the extent that this constraint is due to the presence of a *wh*-trace intervening between *want* and *to*, this result shows that (adult) speakers are constructing sentence representations involving a *wh*-trace, a textbook case of abstract representation. In a similar vein, prosodic process is conditioned by empty categories. F. Ferreira and Engelhardt (2006) argued that the normally mandatory vowel reduction of *to* as in *to the party* does not occur when the object of *to* is a *wh*-trace or a NP-trace (see also F. Ferreira 1988). Additionally, Franck et al. (2006) reported that the pattern of agreement errors known as *agreement attraction* (see below for more details) is sensitive to the presence of empty categories intervening between the two elements participating in agreement relations. Thus, there are multiple lines of evidence that suggest that various aspects of production behaviors are influenced by abstract syntactic representations. Any theories of production that deny the existence of abstract syntactic representations must explain these data by some other means.

Thus, the syntactic category constraints in speech errors, the lexical independence of syntactic priming, and the effects of empty categories on phonological contraction and prosody, and agreement errors suggest that speakers' real-time representations of sentences are abstract, in the sense that categories of syntax like nouns, verbs, prepositions, noun phrases, verbs phrases, prepositional phrases, and even empty categories, are causally involved in determining what we say and how we speak.

## 26.3.2 Hierarchy

Second, what is the evidence that speakers build hierarchical representations in real-time production? Uncontroversially, sentences can be analyzed as hierarchically organized. Sentences consist of phrases, which consist of smaller phrases, which consist of words, which consist of morphemes, the smallest linguistic units that carry meaning. In line with this observation, varieties of syntactic theories assume that sentences are hierarchically organized (Kaplan & Bresnan 1982; Chomsky 1986, 1995; Pollard & Sag 1994). However, in principle, speakers' real-time syntactic representations may not be hierarchically organized. The fact that sentences can be analyzed as hierarchically organized does not necessarily mean that speakers build hierarchical structures for production or comprehension (e.g. Frank, Bod, & Christiansen 2012).

Nevertheless, there are at least three pieces of evidence that suggest speakers' real-time representations are hierarchically organized. First, Fromkin (1971) observed that speakers frequently make speech errors such as the following (taken from Fromkin, Rodman, & Hyams (2011) and Fromkin (1971)):

(4)     Seymour sliced the salami with a knife. → Seymour sliced a knife with the salami. [phrasal exchange]
(5)     tend to turn out → turn to tend out [word exchange]
(6)     salute smartly → smart salutely [morpheme exchange]

These exchange errors suggest that speakers manipulate phrasal, lexical, and morphemic representations as units when they plan utterances. Exchange errors occur when two planned units are bound to wrong syntactic positions. These errors suggest that speakers, at some stage of production processes, manipulate the representational units that are embedded in bigger-sized representational units. In other words, sentence planning involves processes that are sensitive to different levels of syntactic hierarchy (morphemic, lexical, and phrasal levels).

Second, Garrett (1975) observed that word exchange errors like (5) often occur at a distance, crossing phrasal and sometimes even clausal boundaries. On the other hand, he observed that phonemic exchange errors (e.g. *darn boor* for an intended, *barn door*) and morphemic exchange errors (e.g. *a back trucking out* for an intended, *a truck backing out*) occur locally, mostly involving two phonemes or morphemes belonging to immediately adjacent words. Garrett argued that for an exchange error to occur, two units involved in the exchange must be represented simultaneously in mind. He called this condition that applies to exchange errors *computational simultaneity*. The fact that word exchange errors are relatively unconstrained by linear proximity suggests that linear proximity is not a strong determinant of whether two words are represented simultaneously. On the other hand, linear proximity is a strong determinant of whether two phonemes (and morphemes) are represented simultaneously. From this contrast, Garrett argued that speakers represent sentences hierarchically at the level of syntax but linearly at the level of morphology and phonology.

Finally, speakers produce agreement mostly correctly. Because agreement is indisputably a hierarchy-sensitive relation, the very fact that speakers can do agreement mostly correctly suggests that the production system respects hierarchical relations. If speakers do not represent hierarchical structures in some way, it is unclear how speakers produce correct agreement most of the time. Of course, speakers do occasionally make mistakes in agreement production, especially when a plural noun is close (under some definition of distance) to the singular subject noun in subject–verb agreement (e.g. *the key to the cabinets are rusty*, Bock & Miller 1991). It might seem at first that this type of agreement error suggests that agreement production isn't hierarchical, but even agreement errors are sensitive to hierarchical relations (Bock & Cutting 1992; Vigliocco & Nicol 1998; Franck, Vigliocco, & Nicol 2002; Eberhard, Cutting, & Bock 2005; Franck et al. 2006; though see Gillespie & Pearlmutter 2011). More importantly, regardless of whether agreement *errors* are hierarchy-sensitive, it is clear that non-erroneous agreement production, by and large, shows sensitivity to hierarchy (Bock & Cutting 1992). Thus, the patterns of speech errors, syntactic priming, and agreement production all suggest that speakers represent hierarchical representation during real-time speaking.

### 26.3.3   Quality of Syntactic Representations

So far, I have discussed the (relatively uncontroversial) view that speakers' syntactic representations are hierarchical and abstract. But that does not necessarily mean that the nature of real-time syntactic representations speakers generate is captured by syntactic theories, which are mostly based on acceptability judgment data. Syntactic representations involved in making acceptability judgments and syntactic representations involved in speaking could potentially be mismatched. For example, speakers' representations of sentences may not be as detailed and elaborate as representations involved in acceptability judgment tasks.

Using acceptability judgments, syntacticians have discovered varieties of subtle constraints on sentence structures; e.g. syntactic island constraints (Ross 1967; see also Chapter 9), *that*-trace constraints (Perlmutter 1968; see also Chapter 10), and various other conditions on long-distance extractions, e.g. goal arguments cannot be extracted from double object constructions (Kuroda 1968; Baker & Brame 1972; Merchant 2001). If speakers are sensitive to these subtle constraints, speakers must be able to represent sentence structures that are detailed enough to encode these syntactic constraints. Certainly, even if speakers do obey these constraints, the representations used for making acceptability judgments and the real-time representations used for guiding speaking may not be identical. However, to the extent that speakers obey the same constraints that govern acceptability judgment patterns, there is little motivation to have a different theory of representations for each task (see Phillips & Lewis (2013) for discussion). Thus, syntactic theories offer a representational foundation for theories of speaking, to the extent that syntactic theories capture the nature of speakers' real-time sentence representation that guides their utterances.

It is worth clarifying at the outset that speakers do produce utterances that are generally judged to be unacceptable, often by mistake. For example, speakers use the non-target tense (e.g. *a university that IS celebratING its 50th anniversary a couple of years ago*; taken from the UCLA speech error corpus), use non-target agreement morphology (e.g. *the key to the cabinets ARE rusty*), produce prepositions twice in pied-piped constructions (e.g. *to which we have committed ourselves TO*; taken from the UCLA speech error corpus), produce wrong case-markers in case-marking languages like Japanese, and so forth. All these grammatical errors can be found in naturally occurring speech (Fromkin 1971), and some of these errors can be reliably elicited in experimental settings. For example, subject–verb agreement and pronominal agreement errors can be reliably elicited (Bock & Miller 1991; Bock, Nicol, & Cutting 1999). Case-marking errors can also be experimentally induced (Iwasaki 2010). However, the critical question is not what speakers end up saying, but what speakers' syntactic representations are as they plan their utterances. Many of the errors introduced above can be explained by assuming an imperfect memory or internal repairs of speech. For example, subject–verb agreement and pronominal errors can be attributed to a misretrieval of subject number features when speakers try to encode a verbs' morphological forms; see, for example,

Badecker and Lewis (2007) for a cue-based retrieval model of agreement attraction in production. See also Wagers, Lau, and Phillips (2009) for a review of agreement attraction in comprehension. Case-marking errors can be due to internal repairs of sentences, as acknowledged by Iwasaki. For example, when Japanese speakers use the accusative case for a passive subject (which should receive the nominative case) by mistake, they may be simply starting to produce a scrambled OSV sentence (or a subject-dropped active sentence) and then they repair it into a passive sentence after they have uttered the object noun. Iwasaki argued against this possibility because scrambled OSV sentences are not very frequent in Japanese. But in Iwasaki's data, case-marking errors were also remarkably infrequent (there were 48 case-marking errors out of 2,596 relevant utterances). Certainly, the burden of proof is on the side that argues that what speakers actually said and their representation of their own sentences during planning can dissociate from each other. However, it is premature to conclude, based on speech error data, that speakers represent ill-formed syntactic structures during sentence planning.

More importantly, speakers' errors are not random in kind. As reviewed above, speakers make morphosyntactic errors relatively frequently (e.g. tense errors, agreement errors, case-marking errors), but they rarely violate basic phrase structure constraints (due to the syntactic category constraint introduced above). They also obey more non-obvious constraints like island constraints, the *that*-trace constraint, and some other non-obvious constraints on extractions rather strictly. For example, Pearl and Sprouse (2013) showed that island-violating sentences are vanishingly rare, at least in child-directed speech. Based on the child-directed speech in the *Child Language Data Exchange System* (CHILDES) corpus (MacWhinney 2014), they found precisely zero instances of sentences violating complex NP islands, subject islands, *whether* islands, and adjunct islands. This lack of utterances violating islands means that speakers do not produce sentences that violate island constraints, or at least not frequently enough to appear in the sample Pearl and Sprouse investigated. Certainly, this lack of island violation might reflect simply the lack of opportunities for speakers to speak complex sentences in which island constraints can potentially be violated. However, F. Ferreira and Swets (2005) conducted an experiment in which speakers produced sentences such as the following.

(7)      ? This is the donkey that I don't know where it is from.

This sentence contains a resumptive pronoun, a pronoun that occurs instead of a gap and is coreferential to the filler, in an island context (see Chapter 8, and also Ross 1967; Chomsky 1986; Heestand, Xiang, & Polinsky 2011; Polinsky et al. 2013). In this experiment, speakers were given ample opportunities to violate the island constraint. However, instead of violating the syntactic island, speakers chose to use a resumptive pronoun, at least the vast majority of times. Island-violating utterances with no resumptive pronouns are 1.4 percent without a production deadline and 3.1 percent with a production deadline. Resumptive pronouns are normally judged to be relatively unacceptable. However, unacceptable does not necessarily mean ungrammatical, and a recent study suggests that resumptive pronouns are judged to be better than an island-violating gap in a forced choice task, suggesting that resumptive pronouns inside islands may actually be grammatical in English (Ackerman, Frazier, & Yoshida 2018, but see Heestand et al. 2011; Polinsky et al. 2013). If this view on resumptive pronouns is correct, speakers seem to avoid sentences that are ill-formed due to the violation of island constraints (see Chapters 7 and 8 for extensive discussion of resumptive pronouns).

Speakers also rather rarely violate the *that*-trace constraint (see Chapter 10). For example, Phillips (2013) observed that speakers never violated the *that*-trace constraint in a naturalistic corpus (0 instances of *that*-trace violation in 13 cases of subject extractions from embedded clauses). Experimentally, my collaborator and I found that speakers (n = 52) almost never produced *that* in sentences such as (8), even when they were primed to produce *that* half the time (using a method similar to V. Ferreira 2003).

(8)    Who does the chef think (*that) is splashing the doctor?

Speakers in our experiment produced *that* (violating the *that*-trace constraint) containing *wh*-extractions from the embedded subject position such as in (8) only around 1 percent of the time out of more than 1,400 utterances involving *wh*-extraction from the embedded subject position. This is particularly striking, considering that the production of *that* was syntactically primed half the time. Thus, instances of *that*-trace violations in production are vanishingly rare, in both naturalistic and experimental settings. This rather strict avoidance of *that*-trace violations is not due to a general avoidance of producing *that* in *wh*-sentences. In the same experiment with the same set of participants, we found that speakers produced *that* in sentences containing *wh*-extraction from the matrix subject position such as in (9a) around 50 percent of the time, and they produced *that* in sentences containing *wh*-extraction from the embedded object position such as in (9b) around 7 percent of the time.

(9)    a. Who thinks (that) the monk is splashing the doctor?
       b. Who does the chef think (that) the monk is splashing?

Thus, speakers produce *that* when producing *that* does not result in a violation of grammatical constraints. Note, however, that speakers were much less likely to produce *that* in the sentences containing the extraction from the embedded object position than in the sentences containing the extraction from the matrix subject position. This pattern is consistent with the corpus study by Phillips (2013). Phillips found only 2 instances of *that* production among 161 utterances containing extraction from the embedded object position. Thus, speakers seem to be, for currently unknown reasons, much less likely to produce *that* in utterances containing extraction from the embedded object position, such as in (9b), than in utterances containing extraction from the matrix subject position, such as in (9a) (see Chapter 10 for further discussion of this point). Nevertheless, these results suggest that speakers avoid violating the *that*-trace constraint rather strictly, even when they are encouraged to, via syntactic priming.

Finally, another study that my collaborators and I are currently conducting shows that speakers readily say sentences like (10a) but almost never produce sentences like (10b), according to the observation that an extraction of goal objects in double object constructions is unacceptable (Kuroda 1968; Baker & Brame 1972; Merchant 2001).

(10)     a. Who is the chef giving the book to? [prepositional dative]
         b. *Who is the chef giving the book? [double object dative]

The data collection is still ongoing (n = 24 so far), but we found only 1 instance of sentences like (10b) in 432 trials. In the overwhelming majority of the trials, speakers used the prepositional dative structures such as in (10a). This contrast is unlikely to be due to an artifact of the task or due to a general dispreference of speakers to use double object dative structures in *wh*-sentences. The same speakers in the same experiment, with minimally different picture stimuli, readily produced both types of sentences:

(11)     a. Who is giving the book to the chef? [prepositional dative]
         b. Who is giving the chef the book? [double object dative]

In sum, speakers readily used both prepositional and double object dative structures in sentences with matrix subject extraction, but not in sentences with goal object extractions. Speakers do not produce sentences that violate constraints of long-distance extraction, including island constraints, the *that*-trace constraint, or the constraint on indirect object extraction in double object constructions.

So far, I have argued, perhaps rather optimistically, that the real-time syntactic representations that speakers build during production are isomorphic to representations of sentences described by syntactic theories built on acceptability judgment data. However, I should note that some evidence, mainly from syntactic priming studies, suggests that speakers' syntactic representations are not as detailed as I suggested. For example, Bock, Loebell, and Morey (1990) showed that sentences such as *The wealthy widow drove her Mercedes to the church* syntactically prime the prepositional dative production as much as real prepositional datives, presumably because both of them share the NP–PP sequence. They also showed that locative sentences like *The foreigners were loitering by the broken traffic light* primed passive sentences as much as real passive sentences, presumably because they both contain an auxiliary verb and a *by*-phrase (but see Ziegler, Bencini, Goldberg, & Snedeker 2019). In turn, the findings could be taken to suggest that sentence representation may not be detailed enough to distinguish between arguments and adjuncts or between agentive *by*-phrase and locative *by*-phrase. However, I should note that the fact that a certain tool (e.g. syntactic priming) is insensitive to a certain hypothesized difference is not evidence that the difference does not exist; i.e. the absence of evidence is not evidence for absence (see also the discussion of syntactic priming below).

In this section, I have reviewed the viewpoint that speakers represent abstract hierarchical representations that are detailed enough to encode subtle grammatical constraints. To the extent that this view is correct, syntactic theories provide theories of representations that are an essential part of theories of speaking, in the sense that theories of mental representations are essential for theories of mental processes.

## 26.4 Limitations and Potential Utility of Production Studies in Syntax

So far, I have considered the view that speakers represent abstract hierarchical representations that are detailed enough to encode subtle grammatical constraints in real-time production. Thus, there is little reason to believe that the nature of representations used in acceptability judgment tasks and the nature of representations used in constructing sentences during speaking are different. If this view is right, production data should reflect our syntactic knowledge, and thus production data should be relevant in developing theories of syntax, at least in principle. Next I will discuss how production data may (or may not) be useful in syntactic theorizing.

### 26.4.1 Limitations

Let me start with the limitations of production studies. Perhaps the most obvious limitation is that it is hard to control what people say. This makes it challenging to use production experiments to study varieties of key phenomena in syntactic theories (e.g. *wh*-movement with embeddings, comparatives, sentences involving multiple quantifiers, and sentences involving different types of pronouns and anaphora, among others). Researchers can devise a task that elicits complex sentences, but doing so requires creativity (see, e.g., F. Ferreira & Swets 2005). Also, complex tasks are often subject to criticisms on the basis of external validity (but see Mook 1983). In general, running production experiments on many syntactically interesting phenomena is challenging from a practical perspective.

Furthermore, speaking is a complex behavior that is influenced by a currently unknown number of factors, one of which is syntactic knowledge. This is more or less true for other behaviors like acceptability judgments, but it is likely that the number of factors that influence production behaviors is vastly greater than the number of factors that influence acceptability judgment or comprehension tasks (see also Chapters 1, 4, and 5 for discussion of the factors affecting acceptability). As a result, it is not straightforward to attribute observed differences in production behaviors to a specific cause, especially in non-experimental settings. For example, it may be tempting to infer that a particular sentence structure is not grammatical if one fails to see any instances of such a sentence structure in a naturalistic corpus (see Chapter 25 for related discussion). However, there are many potential reasons why speakers may avoid producing it. For instance, as I reported above, sentences with an embedded object extraction and an overt complementizer are rare in both naturalistic and experimental data. However, this does not mean that the structure is ungrammatical (or less grammatical than some baseline). Indeed, acceptability judgment data suggest that such sentences are likely to be grammatical (Ritchart, Goodall, & Garellek 2016). Speakers can avoid a particular sentence structure for a variety of reasons, and currently, there is no good understanding of what those reasons could be. Thus, making inferences about sentence representations based on production data is risky, likely riskier than making inferences about representations based on acceptability judgment data.

A related issue is that production data are fundamentally ill-suited to test the type of predictions that syntactic theories routinely make; i.e. a certain construction should be ungrammatical. Production data cannot offer definitive evidence that the structure is ungrammatical. Of course, this does not mean that production data should be ignored. The absence of evidence that a structure is grammatical can strengthen independent evidence that a certain construction is ungrammatical. However, there is an in-principle limitation of production data, and without complementary methods such as acceptability judgment, it is not possible to test the predictions of syntactic theories that a certain structure should be ungrammatical.

### 26.4.2  Potential Utilities

Of course, the fact that production studies on syntactically interesting phenomena are difficult does not mean that production studies are irrelevant for the study of syntactic representations. Indeed, production studies can corroborate or challenge insights from syntactic theories and, in the best-case scenario, they may even offer tests for competing theories of syntactic representations (with some caveats).

#### 26.4.2.1 Providing Converging Evidence

Some production studies can offer converging evidence for the basic distinctions and theoretical constructs that most syntactic theories have postulated based on acceptability judgment data. For example, as I discussed above, Fromkin (1971) and Garrett (1975) both showed, by analyzing speech errors, that basic theoretical constructs of syntactic theories, like morphemes, words, phrases, and abstract lexical and phrasal categories do exist as a unit in the speaker's mind, corroborating the acceptability judgment data combined with various constituency tests. Also, the fact that there is a syntactic priming effect (Bock 1986) suggests that phrasal categories are representational units of language. Melinger and Dobel (2005) suggest that simply presenting a verb in isolation is sufficient to obtain a syntactic priming effect for the structure that is strongly associated with that verb, suggesting that verbs encode some category-level syntactic information about their complements, in accordance with most theories of syntax (c-selection; see also Pickering & Branigan 1998). Griffin and Weinstein-Tull (2003), using sentence-recall tasks (cf. Potter & Lombardi 1990), showed that speakers were more likely to recall sentences like *John believed that Mary was nice* than near-synonymous object raising sentences like *John believed Mary to be nice*, after producing another sentence with an object raising construction (e.g. *A teaching assistant reported the exam to be too difficult*) compared to sentences with object control constructions (e.g. *Allen encouraged his roommate to be more studious*). This result corroborates the distinction between object raising and object control structures. Furthermore, Momma et al. (2018) and Momma and Ferreira (2019), using a variant of extended picture word-interference task (Meyer 1996; Schriefers, Teruel, & Meinshausen 1998), showed that speakers plan verbs with different timing when producing sentences with unaccusative verbs compared to when producing sentences with unergative verbs, suggesting that the unaccusative–unergative distinction is relevant at some level of representation (at either a thematic or a syntactic level). Also, as discussed above, speakers rather strictly obey constraints like island constraints, the *that*-trace constraint, and constraints that prohibit extracting goal arguments from double object constructions. These results do not necessarily distinguish between competing syntactic theories and analyses, in the sense that these are basic distinctions and theoretical constructs that most if not all syntactic theories postulate, but they do offer converging evidence that strengthens the foundations of existing syntactic theories.

#### 26.4.2.2 Evaluating Competing Theories of Representations

Production studies may also be able to offer tests for two competing syntactic hypotheses that are hard to evaluate solely on the basis of acceptability judgment data, though with caveats. I introduce three case studies that may potentially be relevant for evaluating competing hypotheses in syntax.

### 26.4.2.2.1 *Passives*

In the syntax literature, how passive sentences should be analyzed is a major topic of research, because it has major consequences for broader theories of syntax, such as Case theory, the theory of movement, theta theory, theories of argument structures, and theories of acquisition. Roughly speaking, there are (at least) two lines of thought. Some propose that passives are derived from active counterparts (Chomsky 1957) or from underlying structures shared between actives and passives (Chomsky 1986) via movement operations. Others argue that passives are formed by lexical rules that change the argument structure of verbs (Freidin 1975; Bresnan 1982; Pollard & Sag 1994).

In the production literature, Bock, Loebell, and Morey (1992) argued that passives are not derived transformationally (see also Branigan & Pickering 2017), based on results from production experiments. In their experiments, speakers read aloud the following types of sentences as prime sentences.

(12)    a. Five people carried the boat.
        b. The boat was carried by five people.
        c. The boat carried five people.
        d. Five people were carried by the boat.

Subsequently, speakers described pictures that can be described by active sentences with an inanimate subject, such as the following:

(13)    The alarm clock awakened the boy.

They measured the proportion of active sentences such as (13) in speakers' responses to the pictures. They found that speakers were more likely to produce active sentences like (13) after the active sentence primes like (12a) and (12c) than after the passive primes like (12b) and (12d). This is a standard syntactic priming effect (Bock 1986). More critically, they found that speakers were more likely to produce active sentences with inanimate subjects like (13) after the primes with inanimate subjects like (12b) and (12c) than primes with animate subjects like (12a) and (12d). In other words, Bock and colleagues found that speakers tend to preserve the mapping between animacy and the surface subject position, regardless of the voice of the prime sentences. I call this the animacy-function priming effect. Bock and colleagues (see also Pickering & V. Ferreira 2008) suggested that, on the transformational account, speakers should show no (or weaker) animacy-function priming effect when the primes are passive sentences. This is because the animate argument (five people) is the underlying object in (12d). Speakers should tend to preserve the mapping between the animacy and object positions, so they should tend to use the animate argument (five people) as an underlying object if the transformational account is correct. This animacy-function priming effect for the deep object position should cancel out with the animacy-function effect for the surface subject position. Contrary to this prediction, their results showed that speakers produce more active sentences with inanimate subjects like (13) after primes like (12b) than (12d). Thus, speakers showed the tendency to preserve the mapping between the animacy and surface subject position, but not the mapping between animacy and the deep object position. Based on this pattern, Bock and colleagues argued that the transformational account of passives cannot explain their production data.

The validity of this argument depends on at least three assumptions, none of which can be false for the argument to hold. First, it was assumed that the passive transformation has a corresponding processing operation that transforms active sentences to passive sentences (in line with the *Derivational Theory of Complexity*, see Fodor, Bever, & Garrett 1974; Berwick & Weinberg 1986; Phillips 1996). Second, it was assumed that an animacy-function priming effect could be obtained for non-subject positions (so that the effect cancels out the competing animacy-function priming effect for the surface subject position). Third, the animacy-function priming effect should be equally sensitive to both levels of representations (underlying and surface representations). If all these assumptions are correct, their data may speak against the movement account of passive sentences. But each assumption can be challenged. This is not to argue that the results from Bock et al. (1992) are irrelevant to syntactic theorizing or should be ignored. Instead, the point is that the assumptions about the relationship between the representational claims and the behavioral effects need to be spelled out and tested independently.

### 26.4.2.2.2 *Syntactic Unaccusativity*
Intransitive verbs can be classified into two subclasses: unergative verbs, whose sole argument is an agent (e.g. *run*), and unaccusative verbs, whose sole argument is a patient (or theme, e.g. *fall*). This basic distinction is not in dispute; there are various signs of unaccusativity across different languages (including in the production data; Momma et al. 2018). The question is whether unaccusative–unergative distinctions are realized not only at the level of semantics, but also at the level of syntax. Kim (2006) showed that speakers were more likely to use passive sentences to describe a picture after prime sentences with unaccusative verbs compared with active transitive verbs. This result suggests that passives and unaccusatives are representationally similar, as syntactic accounts of unaccusative verbs suggest. As Kim admitted, alternative interpretations are possible if one assumes that a repetition of thematic role-grammatical function correspondence or thematic role-linear position correspondence can also

induce a syntactic priming effect. However, if syntactic priming is insensitive to the mapping between thematic structures and linear order, as suggested by Bock and Loebell (1990) (but see Chang et al. 2003), Kim's results may suggest that unaccusative and passive sentences share the same (or similar) syntactic structures above and beyond the difference in thematic structures.

In comparison to Kim (2006), Flett (2006) showed that Spanish speakers tended to reuse postverbal or preverbal subject structures in unaccusative sentences, to the same degree after unergative and unaccusative primes. But this result does not show that unaccusative sentences and unergative sentences are indistinguishable syntactically. It shows that syntactic priming is sensitive to surface word order similarity (Tanaka et al. 2007) and is relatively insensitive to the thematic structure or non-surface syntactic structure. Thus, with an important caveat that the syntactic priming may not be purely syntactic, the result from Kim (2006) might suggest that unaccusatives are syntactically like passives.

### 26.4.2.2.3  *Representation of Ellipsis*

In the syntax literature, there is a debate about the representational nature of ellipsis sites. Some argue that the ellipsis site contains syntactic structure in addition to semantic structure (e.g Chung, Ladusaw, & McCloskey 1995; Merchant 2001). Others argue that only semantic structure is contained in the ellipsis site (e.g. Ginzburg & Sag 2000; Culicover & Jackendoff 2005). Xiang, Grove, and Merchant (2014) tested these possibilities using syntactic priming. In their study, they had speakers read the following sentence fragments:

(14)    a. First Ralph sang a song to Sheila, and then [prepositional dative prime]
        b. First Ralph sang Sheila a song, and then [double object prime]

These fragments of prime sentences were continued with one of the following:

(15)    a. Marcus sang one to her. / Marcus sang her one. [non-ellipsis]
        b. Marcus did. [ellipsis]
        c. Marcus groaned. [neutral control]

In (15a), the continuation again contained the prepositional dative or double object dative structure overtly, and the VP structure matched with the VP structures of the preceding sentences. In (15b) the VP was elided, so there was no overt PD or DO structure. In (15c), the verb was an unrelated verb that did not bear an ellipsis dependency relation to the preceding clause. Xiang et al. found that speakers were more likely to use the structure that they encountered in the initial clause in the non-ellipsis condition and the ellipsis condition, but not in the neutral control condition.

Again, with the important caveat that the syntactic priming may be sensitive to thematic structures, Xiang and colleagues' data may suggest that the ellipsis site contains syntactic representations that cause priming.

### 26.4.2.3 Caveats

Through the discussion of specific production studies, I have argued that production data can be relevant to syntactic theorizing but that the interpretation of these studies depends on the hypotheses about how representational claims connect to behavioral predictions. Such hypotheses can be called *linking hypotheses*, and they can vary independently from representational hypotheses (see Chapter 22 for extensive discussion of this and related issues). This point has long been noted in the comprehension literature (e.g. Miller & McKean 1964; Fodor et al. 1974; Berwick & Weinberg 1986; Phillips 1996; Townsend & Bever 2001; Marantz 2005; Phillips & Lewis 2013). For example, the derivational theory of complexity is a linking hypothesis that claims that more complex structures (e.g. in terms of the number of nodes in syntactic representations or in terms of the number of transformations necessary to derive a sentence, among other potential complexity measures) take more time to compute and thus more time to comprehend. When the derivational theory of complexity (which assumes that the number of transformations is a complexity measure) and transformational theory of passive sentences are combined, it is possible to predict that passive sentences should take more time to understand than active sentences (due to an additional transformation operation). Let's say that this prediction is incompatible with some behavioral data. That would mean that either the representational hypothesis is wrong or the linking hypothesis is wrong (e.g. Berwick & Weinberg 1986). Thus, even when behavioral data go against certain representational hypotheses, it is not always straightforward to make a strong inference about representations. This is especially so when the behavior of interest involves complex processes that are aected by multiple factors, as in the case of sentence production. It is necessary to spell out and test the assumed linking hypotheses before the behavioral data (including both production data and acceptability judgment data) can be used to support or disconfirm representational claims. This difficulty of connecting behavioral data and representational claims may be frustrating to psycholinguists (including myself) because it often prevents them from making a strong claim about representations based on psycholinguistic data. But that does not mean that the problem can be ignored.

### 26.4.3 Other Issues

#### 26.4.3.1 Syntactic Priming as a Privileged Source of Data

Above, I have introduced varieties of syntactic priming studies and their potential utility and limitations in investigating the nature of syntactic representations. In short, syntactic priming can be used as a tool for investigating potential representational similarities between different sentences. In this sense, syntactic priming studies can provide an additional source of data for syntactic theories, provided that the precise cause of syntactic priming can reasonably be identified. I suspect that this claim is rather uncontroversial. However, some researchers have made the stronger claim that syntactic priming should be a privileged source of data for syntactic theories (Branigan & Pickering 2017). In short, Branigan and Pickering argued that syntactic priming should be more privileged than acceptability judgment, because it is implicit, because it is not (or less) affected by parsing factors, and because it can directly examine representations (rather than just whether a sentence is grammatical or not). They argued that acceptability judgment tasks, in comparison, require explicit decision-making tasks, that they involve the source ambiguity problem (explained below), and that they can only assess whether a sentence belongs to a set of grammatical sentences without being combined with constituency tests, which they argued are independently problematic. This claim is particularly relevant to the central theme of this handbook, so let me unpack their argument.

First, Branigan and Pickering claimed that syntactic priming is an implicit effect, but acceptability judgment tasks involve explicit decision-making processes. The syntactic priming effect can indeed be obtained without speakers' awareness (for the clearest demonstration, see V. S. Ferreira et al. (2008)) and it is indeed the case that acceptability judgment tasks require explicit decision making. However, it is not clear how and why implicit methods are better than explicit methods in investigating syntactic representations. Branigan and Pickering noted that the potential decision-making bias might contaminate acceptability judgment results. However, it remains unclear which specific decision-making bias affects the result of which specific acceptability judgment, in a way that is problematic for data interpretation. Of course, if researchers themselves are giving an acceptability judgment, it is important to be aware of potential confirmation bias, but this issue is entirely independent from whether an acceptability judgment task should be used (see Chapters 1 and 4 for discussion).

Second, Branigan and Pickering argued that acceptability judgment tasks invoke what they call the source ambiguity problem, that is, acceptability degradation/improvement can be attributed to some factors other than the grammaticality of sentences. They implied that syntactic priming does not suffer from the same problem. However, the syntactic priming effect, or any other effects on complex behaviors for that matter, do suffer from the same problem. When studying a complex system like human language, it is rarely the case that an experimental effect can be attributed unambiguously to a single cause. As I reviewed above, it is far from clear what causes the syntactic priming effect. It may be due to the repeated thematic role–linear order correspondence (Bock et al. 1990; Chang et al. 2003), repeated linear order of words and constituents (Hartsuiker & Kolk 1998), or a repeated phrase structure sequence (Bock et al. 1990). It is important to be aware that the term syntactic priming as it is often used in the literature refers to a behavioral effect, not a cognitive mechanism. Thus, it is dangerous to make an inference about syntactic representation just because one observes an effect that can be described as "syntactic priming."

Finally, Branigan and Pickering argued that the acceptability judgment task only allows researchers to test whether a sentence belongs to a set of grammatical sentences in a language. That is, they argued that acceptability judgment tasks are a method that determines weak generative capacity. In comparison, they claim that syntactic priming can assess the representations directly, so it is a method that can determine strong generative capacity. This claim is simply false. As pointed out by Gaston, Huang, and Phillips (2017), acceptability judgment tasks are routinely used in assessing representational similarity (ellipsis, coordination), hierarchical relation (binding), and structural locality (*wh*-movement, relativization, topicalization, scrambling, among others).

In sum, syntactic priming can provide an additional source of data for syntactic theories, but it is not clear why syntactic priming should be viewed as a privileged source of data for syntactic theories. A reasonable view, in my opinion, is that which methodology is more suitable depends on what specific question a researcher is trying to answer. Syntactic priming is a good tool for detecting some similarities between two structures (e.g. see the discussion of Kim (2006) above). But it is not a particularly good tool for detecting differences between two structures, because the fact that two sentences prime each other does not mean that they are identical (see the discussion of Bock and Loebell (1990) above). Also, the failure to obtain a syntactic priming effect does not necessarily suggest that two structures are syntactically dissimilar, because syntactic priming is not necessarily sensitive to all aspects of syntactic representations and because there could be various reasons why a syntactic priming effect fails to be observed.

### 26.4.3.2 Breaking Circularity
Acceptability of sentences can be influenced by a variety of factors, including grammaticality, pragmatic naturalness, complexity, and frequency of constructions, among other factors. A critical task for researchers using acceptability judgments is to identify the source(s) of acceptability degradation/improvement. When researchers hypothesize that an acceptability judgment difference is not due to grammatical status, they need to offer an alternative explanation for the acceptability difference. One potential source of acceptability difference is the difference in the frequency of constructions (Greenbaum 1977, 1980; see

Schütze (2016) and Chapters 1, 4 and 25 for discussion). However, the problem is that frequency explanations of acceptability difference are often circular and thus carry little explanatory force, because frequency explanations of acceptability difference need to explain why a certain structure is (in-)frequent to begin with. The same problem holds for frequency explanations of processing difficulties in comprehension. To break this circularity, there needs to be an independent explanation of why certain structures are less frequent than others. Such an explanation necessarily involves theories of speaking. Thus, studies of production can be useful in making a non-circular argument in syntax (and also in sentence comprehension research; see, e.g., MacDonald (2013) for an excellent example in comprehension research).

## 26.5 Conclusion

Theories of speaking seek to capture how speakers use syntactic knowledge during speaking. Thus, understanding the nature of syntactic knowledge is a central part of understanding speaking. In turn, speaking reflects, though imperfectly, the structure of their syntactic knowledge. Thus, production data can be used to test behavioral predictions of syntactic theories, when combined with articulated linking hypotheses that connect representations and behaviors. With the caveats and limitations discussed above, studies of speaking and studies of syntax can be mutually informative.

## References

Ackerman, L., Frazier, M., & Yoshida, M. (2018). Resumptive pronouns can ameliorate illicit island extractions. *Linguistic Inquiry*, 49(4), 847–859.

Adger, D. (2018). The autonomy of syntax. In N. Hornstein, H. Lasnik, P. Patel-Grosz, & C. Yang, eds., *Syntactic Structures after 60 Years*. Berlin: Walter de Gruyter, pp. 153–176.

Badecker, W. & Lewis, R. (2007). A new theory and computational model of working memory in sentence production: Agreement errors as failures of cue-based retrieval. Presented at the 20th Annual CUNY Conference on Sentence Processing.

Baker, C. L. & Brame, M. K. (1972). Global rules: A rejoinder. *Language*, 48(1), 51–75.

Berwick, R. C. & Weinberg, A. S. (1986). *The Grammatical Basis of Linguistic Performance: Language Use and Acquisition*. Cambridge, MA: MIT Press.

Bock, K. (1986). Syntactic persistence in language production. *Cognitive Psychology*, 18(3), 355–387.

Bock, K. (1989). Closed-class immanence in sentence production. *Cognition*, 31(2), 163–186.

Bock, K. & Cutting, J. C. (1992). Regulating mental energy: Performance units in language production. *Journal of Memory and Language*, 31(1), 99–127.

Bock, K. & Ferreira, V. (2013). Syntactically speaking. In V. Ferreira, M. Goldrick, & M. Miozzo, eds., *The Oxford Handbook of Language Production*. Oxford: Oxford University Press.

Bock, K. & Levelt, W. J. (1994). Language production: Grammatical encoding. In M. A. Gernsbacher, ed., *Handbook of Psycholinguistics*. New York: Academic Press, pp. 945–984.

Bock, K., Loebell, H., & Morey, R. (1990). Framing sentences. *Cognition*, 35, 1–39.

Bock, K., Loebell, H., & Morey, R. (1992). From conceptual roles to structural relations: Bridging the syntactic cleft. *Psychological Review*, 99(1), 150.

Bock, K. & Miller, C. A. (1991). Broken agreement. *Cognitive Psychology*, 23(1), 45–93.

Bock, K., Nicol, J., & Cutting, J. C. (1999). The ties that bind: Creating number agreement in speech. *Journal of Memory and Language*, 40(3), 330–346.

Branigan, H. P. & Pickering, M. J. (2017). An experimental approach to linguistic representation. *Behavioral and Brain Sciences*, 40, e282.

Bresnan, J. (1982). *The Mental Representation of Grammatical Relations*. Cambridge, MA: MIT Press.

Chang, F., Bock, K., & Goldberg, A. E. (2003). Can thematic roles leave traces of their places? *Cognition*, 90(1), 29–49.

Chomsky, N. (1957). *Syntactic Structure*. The Hague: Mouton.

Chomsky, N. (1977). On *wh*-movement. In P. Culicover, T. Wasow, & A. Akmajian (eds.), *Formal Syntax*. New York: Academic Press, pp. 71–132.

Chomsky, N. (1986). *Lectures on Government and Binding: The Pisa Lectures* (no. 9). Berlin: Walter de Gruyter.

Chomsky, N. (1995). *The Minimalist Program*. Cambridge, MA: MIT Press.

Chung, S., Ladusaw, W. A., & McCloskey, J. (1995). Sluicing and logical form. *Natural Language Semantics*, 3(3), 239–282.

Cleland, A. A. & Pickering, M. J. (2003). The use of lexical and syntactic information in language production: Evidence from the priming of noun-phrase structure. *Journal of Memory and Language*, 49(2), 214–230.

Culicover, P. W. & Jackendoff, R. S. (2005). *Simpler Syntax*. Oxford: Oxford University Press.

Dell, G. S., Oppenheim, G. M., & Kittredge, A. K. (2008). Saying the right word at the right time: Syntagmatic and paradigmatic interference in sentence production. *Language and Cognitive Processes*, 23(4), 583–608.

Eberhard, K. M., Cutting, J. C., & Bock, K. (2005). Making syntax of sense: number agreement in sentence production. *Psychological Review*, 112(3), 531.

Ferreira, F. (1988). Planning and timing in sentence production: The syntax-to-phonology conversion. Doctoral dissertation, University of Massachusetts, Amherst.

Ferreira, F. (2000). Syntax in language production: An approach using tree-adjoining grammars. In L. Wheeldon, ed., *Aspects of Language Production*. Hove: Psychology Press, pp. 291–330.

Ferreira, F. & Engelhardt, P. E. (2006). Syntax and production. In M. Traxler & M. Gernsbacher, eds., *Handbook of Psycholinguistics*, 2nd ed. Amsterdam: Academic Press, pp. 61–91.

Ferreira, F. & Swets, B. (2005). The production and comprehension of resumptive pronouns in relative clause "island" contexts. In A. Cutler, ed., *Twenty-First Century Psycholinguistics: Four Cornerstones*. Abingdon: Routledge, pp. 263–278.

Ferreira, V. (2003). The persistence of optional complementizer production: Why saying "that" is not saying "that" at all. *Journal of Memory and Language*, 48(2), 379–398.

Ferreira, V. & Slevc, L. R. (2007). Grammatical encoding. In S.-A. Rueschemeyer & M. G. Gaskell, eds., *The Oxford Handbook of Psycholinguistics*. Oxford: Oxford University Press, pp. 453–470.

Ferreira, V. S., Bock, K., Wilson, M. P., & Cohen, N. J. (2008). Memory for syntax despite amnesia. *Psychological Science*, 19(9), 940–946.

Flett, S. (2006). A comparison of syntactic representation and processing in first and second language production. Doctoral dissertation, University of Edinburgh.

Fodor, J. (1983). *The Modularity of Mind*. Cambridge, MA: MIT Press.

Fodor, J., Bever, A., & Garrett, M. (1974). *The Psychology of Language: An Introduction to Psycholinguistics and Generative Grammar*. New York: McGraw-Hill.

Franck, J., Lassi, G., Frauenfelder, U. H., & Rizzi, L. (2006). Agreement and movement: A syntactic analysis of attraction. *Cognition*, 101(1), 173–216.

Franck, J., Vigliocco, G., & Nicol, J. (2002). Subject–verb agreement errors in French and English: The role of syntactic hierarchy. *Language and Cognitive Processes*, 17(4), 371–404.

Frank, S. L., Bod, R., & Christiansen, M. H. (2012). How hierarchical is language use? *Proceedings of the Royal Society of London B: Biological Sciences*, 279, 4522–4531.

Freidin, R. (1975). The analysis of passives. *Language*, 51, 384–405.

Fromkin, V. (1971). The non-anomalous nature of anomalous utterances. *Language*, 47, 27–52.

Fromkin, V., Rodman, R., & Hyams, N. (2011). *An Introduction to Language*. Boston, MA: Cengage Learning.

Garrett, M. F. (1975). The analysis of sentence production. In G. H. Bower, ed., *Psychology of Learning and Motivation*. New York: Academic Press, pp. 133–177.

Garrett, M. F. (1988). Processes in language production. In F. J. Newmeyer, ed., *Linguistics: The Cambridge Survey*, vol. 3: *Language: Psychological and Biological Aspects*. Cambridge: Cambridge University Press, pp. 69–96.

Gaston, P., Huang, N., & Phillips, C. (2017). The logic of syntactic priming and acceptability judgments. *Behavioral and Brain Sciences*, 40,e282.

Gillespie, M. & Pearlmutter, N. J. (2011). Hierarchy and scope of planning in subject–verb agreement production. *Cognition*, 118(3), 377–397.

Ginzburg, J. & Sag, I. (2000). *Interrogative Investigations*. Stanford, CA: CSLI Publications.

Gleitman, L. R., January, D., Nappa, R., & Trueswell, J. C. (2007). On the give and take between event apprehension and utterance formulation. *Journal of Memory and Language*, 57(4), 544–569.

Gold, J. W., Arsenijević, B., Batinić, M., Becker, M., Čordalija, N., Kresić, M., et al. (2018). When linearity prevails over hierarchy in syntax. *Proceedings of the National Academy of Sciences*, 115(3), 495–500.

Greenbaum, S. (1977). Judgments of syntactic acceptability and frequency. *Studia Linguistica*, 31(2), 83–105.

Greenbaum, S. (1980). Syntactic frequency and acceptability. In T. A. Perry, ed., *Evidence and Argumentation in Linguistics*. Berlin: De Gruyter, pp. 301–314.

Griffin, Z. M. & Bock, K. (2000). What the eyes say about speaking. *Psychological Science*, 11(4), 274–279.

Griffin, Z. M. & Weinstein-Tull, J. (2003). Conceptual structure modulates structural priming in the production of complex sentences. *Journal of Memory and Language*, 49(4), 537–555.

Grimshaw, J. (1990). *Argument Structure*. Cambridge, MA: MIT Press.

Hall, M. L., Ferreira, V. S., & Mayberry, R. I. (2015). Syntactic priming in American Sign Language. *PloS One*, 10(3), e0119611.

Hartsuiker, R. J. & Kolk, H. H. (1998). Syntactic persistence in Dutch. *Language and Speech*, 41(2), 143–184.

Heestand, D., Xiang, M., & Polinsky, M. (2011). Resumption still does not rescue islands. *Linguistic Inquiry*, 42(1), 138–152.

Iwasaki, N. (2010). Incremental sentence production: Observations from elicited speech errors in Japanese. In H. Yamashita, Y. Hirose, & J. L. Packard, eds., *Processing and Producing Head-Final Structures*. Dordrecht: Springer, pp. 131–151.

Kaplan, R. M. & Bresnan, J., et al. (1982). Lexical-functional grammar: A formal system for grammatical representation. *Formal Issues in Lexical-Functional Grammar*, 47, 29–130.

Karins, A. K. & Nagy, N. (1993). Developing an experimental basis for determining grammaticality. *Penn Review of Linguistics*, 17, 93–100.

Kempen, G. & Hoenkamp, E. (1987). An incremental procedural grammar for sentence formulation. *Cognitive Science*, 11(2), 201–258.

Kempen, G. & Huijbers, P. (1983). The lexicalization process in sentence production and naming: Indirect election of words. *Cognition*, 14(2), 185–209.

Kim, C. (2006). Structural and thematic information in sentence production. In *Proceedings of the 37th Annual Meeting of the North East Linguistic Society*. Amherst, MA: GLSA, University of Massachusetts.

Kuroda, S.-Y. (1968). Indirect object constructions in English and the ordering of transformations. *Language*, 44, 374–378.

Kweon, S.-O. & Bley-Vroman, R. (2011). Acquisition of the constraints on wanna contraction by advanced second language learners: Universal grammar and imperfect knowledge. *Second Language Research*, 27(2), 207–228.

Lakoff, G. (1970). Global rules. *Language*, 627–639.

Levelt, W. J. (1989). *Speaking: From intention to articulation*. Cambridge, MA: MIT Press.

Levelt, W. J., Roelofs, A., & Meyer, A. S. (1999). A theory of lexical access in speech production. *Behavioral and Brain Sciences*, 22(1), 1–38.

MacDonald, M. C. (2013). How language production shapes language form and comprehension. *Frontiers in Psychology*, 4, 226.

MacWhinney, B. (2014). *The CHILDES project: Tools for Analyzing Talk*, vol. II: *The Database*. Hove: Psychology Press.

Marantz, A. (2005). Generative linguistics within the cognitive neuroscience of language. *The Linguistic Review*, 22(2–4), 429–445.

McDonald, J. L., Bock, K., & Kelly, M. H. (1993). Word and world order: Semantic, phonological, and metrical determinants of serial position. *Cognitive Psychology*, 25(2), 188–230.

Melinger, A. & Dobel, C. (2005). Lexically-driven syntactic priming. *Cognition*, 98(1), B11–B20.

Merchant, J. (2001). *The Syntax of Silence: Sluicing, Islands, and the Theory of Ellipsis*. Oxford: Oxford University Press.

Meyer, A. S. (1996). Lexical access in phrase and sentence production: Results from picture–word interference experiments. *Journal of Memory and Language*, 35(4), 477–496.

Miller, G. A. & McKean, K. O. (1964). A chronometric study of some relations between sentences. *Quarterly Journal of Experimental Psychology*, 16(4), 297–308.

Momma, S. & Ferreira, V. S. (2019). Beyond linear order: The role of argument structure in speaking. *Cognitive Psychology*, 114, 101228.

Momma, S., Slevc, L. R., Buffinton, J., & Phillips, C. (2020). Syntactic category constrains lexical competition in speaking. *Cognition*, 197, 104183.

Momma, S., Slevc, L. R., & Phillips, C. (2016). The timing of verb selection in Japanese sentence production. *Journal of Experimental Psychology: Learning, Memory, and Cognition*, 42(5), 813.

Momma, S., Slevc, L. R., & Phillips, C. (2018). Unaccusativity in sentence production. *Linguistic Inquiry*, 49(1), 181–194.

Mook, D. G. (1983). In defense of external invalidity. *American Psychologist*, 38(4), 379.

Nooteboom, S. G. (1973). The tongue slips into patterns. In V. Fromkin, ed., *Speech Errors as Linguistic Evidence*. Berlin: Walter de Gruyter, pp. 144–156.

Pearl, L. & Sprouse, J. (2013). Computational models of acquisition for islands. In J. Sprouse & N. Hornstein, eds., *Experimental Syntax and Island Effects*. Cambridge: Cambridge University Press, 109–131.

Perlmutter, D. M. (1968). Deep and surface structure constraints in syntax. Doctoral dissertation, Massachusetts Institute of Technology.

Phillips, C. (1996). Order and structure. Doctoral dissertation, Massachusetts Institute of Technology.

Phillips, C. (2013). On the nature of island constraints ii: Language learning and innateness. In J. Sprouse & N. Hornstein, eds., *Experimental Syntax and Island Effects*. Cambridge: Cambridge University Press, pp. 132–158.

Phillips, C. & Lewis, S. (2013). Derivational order in syntax: Evidence and architectural consequences. *Studies in Linguistics*, 6, 11–47.

Pickering, M. J. & Branigan, H. P. (1998). The representation of verbs: Evidence from syntactic priming in language production. *Journal of Memory and language*, 39(4), 633–651.

Pickering, M. J., Branigan, H. P., & McLean, J. F. (2002). Constituent structure is formulated in one stage. *Journal of Memory and Language*, 46(3), 586–605.

Pickering, M. J. & Ferreira, V. (2008). Structural priming: A critical review. *Psychological Bulletin*, 134(3), 427.

Polinsky, M., Clemens, L., Morgan, A., Xiang, M., & Heestand, D. (2013). Resumption in English. In J. Sprouse & N. Hornstein, eds., *Experimental Syntax and Island Effects*. Cambridge: Cambridge University Press, pp. 341–359.

Pollard, C. & Sag, I. A. (1994). *Head-Driven Phrase Structure Grammar*. Chicago: University of Chicago Press.

Potter, M. C. & Lombardi, L. (1990). Regeneration in the short-term recall of sentences. *Journal of Memory and Language*, 29(6), 633.

Ritchart, A., Goodall, G., & Garellek, M. (2016). Prosody and the *that*-trace effect: An experimental study. In *Proceedings of the 33rd West Coast Conference on Formal Linguistics*. Somerville, MA: Cascadilla Proceedings Project, pp. 320–328.

Ross, J. R. (1967). Constraints on variables in syntax. Doctoral dissertation, Massachusetts Institute of Technology.

Schriefers, H., Teruel, E., & Meinshausen, R.-M. (1998). Producing simple sentences: Results from picture–word interference experiments. *Journal of Memory and Language*, 39(4), 609–632.

Schütze, C. T. (2016). *The Empirical Base of Linguistics: Grammaticality Judgments and Linguistic Methodology*. Berlin: Language Science Press.

Tanaka, J., Tamaoka, K., & Sakai, H. (2007). Syntactic priming effects on the processing of Japanese sentences with canonical and scrambled word orders. *Cognitive Studies*, 14(2), 173–191.

Townsend, D. J. & Bever, T. G. (2001). *Sentence Comprehension: The Integration of Habits and Rules*. Cambridge, MA: MIT Press.

Vigliocco, G. & Nicol, J. (1998). Separating hierarchical relations and word order in language production: Is proximity concord syntactic or linear? *Cognition*, 68(1), B13–B29.

Wagers, M. W., Lau, E. F., & Phillips, C. (2009). Agreement attraction in comprehension: Representations and processes. *Journal of Memory and Language*, 61(2), 206–237.

Wasow, T. & Arnold, J. (2005). Intuitions in linguistic argumentation. *Lingua*, 115(11), 1481–1496.

Xiang, M., Grove, J., & Merchant, J. (2014). Ellipsis sites induce structural priming effects. Unpublished manuscript, University of Chicago.

Ziegler, J., Bencini, G., Goldberg, A., & Snedeker, J. (2019). How abstract is syntax? Evidence from structural priming. *Cognition*, 193, 104045.

Zukowski, A. & Larson, J. (2009). Elicited production of relative clauses in children with Williams syndrome. *Language and Cognitive Processes*, 24(1), 1–43.

# 27

# Neuroimaging

William Matchin

## 27.1 Introduction

Recording the brain activity of subjects while they produce or comprehend sentences potentially provides valuable information about syntax. Like event-related potential (ERP) experiments using electroencephalography (EEG) (see Chapter 24), neuroimaging methods are not limited to (nor even require) overt behavioral responses, as the brain signal itself serves as the dependent measure. Neuroimaging methods have an additional benefit when compared to traditional ERPs: spatial precision (hence, neuro*image*). Spatial precision allows the experimenter to compare experimental conditions not only on magnitude or timing but also across brain space. This in turn potentially allows *reverse inference*: inference about the cognitive operations evoked by an experimental manipulation by examining these spatial patterns. While reverse inference is sharply limited by prior confidence in the function of brain areas (Poldrack 2006, 2011), linguistic questions can in principle be answered through this technique. Thus, neuroimaging methods should be of interest to those in search of non-traditional methods, and hopefully new insights, for the study of syntax.

The goal of identifying the localization of syntax is intimately connected to the use of neuroimaging to answer linguistic questions – this is because reverse inference is severely limited by prior confidence in the function of brain regions. To the extent that activation in a "syntax area" of the brain can be used to discriminate among syntactic theories, we must have good confidence in the localization of syntax to begin with. With this in mind, what seem like separate interests – the linguist's interest in using neuroimaging experiments to understand language, and the neuroscientist's interest in spatial localization of language – are inseparable, with progress in the latter question fundamental to progress in the former.

I will first (Section 27.2) introduce the reader to the various neuroimaging methods currently available, including major issues in experimental design, as well as provide a crash course in the cortical neuroanatomy relevant to language. Next (Section 27.3), I will review attempts to localize syntax in the brain through the use of neuroimaging methods. Following this (Section 27.4), I will discuss attempts to use neuroimaging data to adjudicate linguistic questions: the adequacy of syntactic theories, parsing models, and particular structural analyses.

## 27.2   Methods and Neuroanatomy

Functional neuroimaging methods are those that provide images of the brain related to changes in neural activity, in other words, spatial localization of function. There are two classes of such methods: (i) hemodynamic methods, which indirectly measure neural activity via changes in blood flow, and (ii) neurophysiological methods, which directly measure electrical or magnetic waves resulting from neural activity. The most widely used functional neuroimaging techniques, functional magnetic resonance imaging (fMRI), electroencephalography (EEG), electrocorticography (ECoG), and magnetoencephalography (MEG), all record signals associated mainly with the same neurophysiological processes: post-synaptic dendritic activity (Logothetis 2001), facilitating cross-methodological inferences. An overview of these methods is given in Table 27.1. In what follows, I will provide a more detailed overview of the methods, with a particular focus on considerations of experimental design, as well as a brief overview of the brain anatomy relevant to language.

### 27.2.1   Hemodynamic Methods

Hemodynamic methods are used to indirectly assess neural activity by measuring changes in blood flow in the brain. The most widely used neuroimaging technique affording high spatial resolution is functional magnetic resonance imaging (fMRI). fMRI, along with positron emission tomography (PET), has limited temporal resolution but allows precise localization of brain activity measured in small three-dimensional pixels, or *voxels*. While PET has been used in many neuroimaging studies on sentence processing, it has largely been supplanted by fMRI, which is more accurate in both the spatial and temporal dimensions, simpler to administer, and less invasive.

Magnetic resonance imaging (MRI) uses high-strength static magnetic fields, typically at 3 Tesla (3 T), to align hydrogen molecules within the tissue being imaged. Then, three orthogonal gradient magnetic fields (in the x, y, and z directions) are applied, changing the resonance frequency of the molecules within defined regions of tissue and allowing for precise spatial localization. The current resolution of voxels ranges from several millimeters to a fraction of a millimeter in each dimension; current good-

Table 27.1 *Overview of neuroimaging methods*

| Method | Brain signal | Spatial resolution | Temporal resolution |
|---|---|---|---|
| fMRI | Local changes in blood flow (blood-oxygenation level-dependent signal, or BOLD) | Very high (up to ~1 mm³) | Poor (~seconds) |
| EEG (with source localization) | Electrical fields associated with post-synaptic dendritic activity | Moderate (heavily contingent on electrode density, analysis technique, and availability of structural and functional MRI) | Very high (millisecond resolution) |
| MEG (with source localization analysis) | Magnetic fields associated with post-synaptic dendritic activity | High (contingent on analysis techniques and availability of structural and functional MRI) | Very high (millisecond resolution) |
| ECoG | Electrical fields associated with post-synaptic dendritic activity | Very high (up to the millimeter level; dependent on patient availability, electrode grid type, and surgical location) | Very high (millisecond resolution) |

quality standards are 2mm³ for functional imaging and 1mm³ for structural imaging.

MRI is typically used to refer to the use of MR technology to generate anatomical images. fMRI is used to refer to the use of the technology to create a time series of images related to functional brain activity, typically overlaid onto an anatomical image. When neurons fire, they use up energy, and there is increased circulation of hemoglobin to and from these neurons. The rapid change of oxygenation of hemoglobin in active neural tissue has magnetic properties, producing small but detectable changes in the MR signal (the blood oxygenation level-dependent or BOLD signal). This allows the researcher to indirectly detect neural activity via changes in blood flow.

The main limitation of the BOLD signal is its temporal resolution. A typical sampling rate of fMRI (the repetition time, or TR) is 2 seconds, which reflects the time needed to acquire an entire brain volume of data. While researchers have been able to improve the temporal resolution of volume acquisition, the slow speed of the hemodynamic response itself is an in-principle limitation. While cognitive processes and neural firing occur on the order of milliseconds, the typical peak hemodynamic response to a stimulus has a latency on the order of seconds, typically 6–8. This inherently limits inferences regarding the timing of brain activation in fMRI. This is unfortunate, as effects occurring on neighboring regions of a sentence (e.g. the subject, verb, or object of a sentence) are difficult to reliably differentiate.

In fMRI, there are two main types of experimental design: block and event-related (ER). Block designs begin with the rough observation that repeated stimuli produce additive responses to the BOLD signal – e.g. the BOLD response to two sequential tones in auditory cortex can be predicted accurately by summing the expected hemodynamic responses to each tone in isolation. Blocked stimuli, with a typical duration of 20 seconds per block, thus ideally induce a rise in BOLD signal over a few seconds followed by a long period of sustained activation and then a return to baseline. The experiment alternates blocks of stimulation for each condition and "baseline" or rest periods, during which the brain activation in absence of stimulus can be measured. The standard analysis approach is *subtraction*:[1] the magnitude of the BOLD response measured across all voxels in the brain for one condition is subtracted from another condition (i.e. a statistical pairwise contrast). Such comparisons can be done with the rest periods, creating maps of activation for a particular condition relative to "baseline."[2]

Event-related (ER) fMRI involves the rapid, randomized presentation of isolated stimuli from different conditions. ER designs are useful because they avoid the issues of subject habituation and prediction associated with repetitions of stimuli from the same condition, and they are more powerful statistically, as the BOLD signal in a given brain region tends to attenuate with repetition (Grill-Spector et al. 2006). With rapid alternating stimuli from different conditions, the hemodynamic responses will overlap. Thus, a *deconvolution* analysis must be performed, in which the strength of the hemodynamic response associated with each condition within each voxel must be recovered from the combined BOLD signal. An experimenter may assume a canonical hemodynamic response function (HRF) or use more sophisticated techniques to estimate the actual shape of the HRF.

For both of these techniques, statistical analysis is often performed using a general linear model (GLM) in which a set of statistical regressors are added to best account for the data. This typically includes subject motion parameters, behavioral responses, and filters to account for

---

[1] Subtraction should be performed carefully, as the notion of "pure insertion" – that two conditions can be identical but for a minimal difference – doesn't necessary hold, potentially eliciting complex brain responses (Friston et al. 1996).

[2] Many researchers historically and currently assume that a statistical map of a condition vs. rest reflects the brain's response to that condition. However, a critical issue is whether the "baseline" period actually reflects an absence of relevant cognitive processes. Early research by Raichle and colleagues (2001) noticed a consistent pattern of negative activation to a stimulus vs. rest – that is, brain areas more active during rest than during stimulation. Binder and colleagues (1999, 2012) have shown overlap between this "default mode" network and regions involved in conceptual-semantic processing, implying that much of the activity during baseline reflects spontaneous thought with rich conceptual representations. It is critical for neuroimaging experiments of lexical, syntactic, conceptual, semantic, and other levels of representation and processing to potentially account for this issue, e.g. by comparing two experimental conditions to each other rather than to rest.

scanner drift. More recently, many researchers have begun to expand upon comparing gross measures of activation strength among conditions by performing multivariate (or multivoxel) pattern analyses (MVPA; Haxby 2012). MVPA analyses determine whether a computer model can be trained to discriminate the patterns of activity across voxels within a given cortical region (often a sphere or cube of voxels) among conditions. Thus, a given brain area might not be more engaged overall, but the finer-grained pattern of activity might encode information about the stimulus or condition.

There are several additional practical limitations of fMRI. Given the time required to install the subject into the scanner, set up the scanner protocol and acquire calibration and structural data, overall limitations on subject comfort, scanner heating concerns, and financial cost, experiments cannot last much more than 1.5 hours (ideally half that) and must be divided into runs of ~5–10 minutes each. Effective scanning requires the subject not to move their body, particularly their head, otherwise data distortion results, and data are often lost due to subject motion. Finally, subject responses produce brain activity in motor cortex that could contaminate responses in language-related areas. These factors constrain experimental designs; for instance, it is difficult to do studies on overt production or include large amounts of filler items that increase the duration of the experiment.

### 27.2.2   Neurophysiological Methods

In contrast to hemodynamic methods, neurophysiological methods more directly assess neural activity by measuring electrical signals or magnetic waves. This means much more precise temporal resolution, on the order of milliseconds. Historically, neurophysiological methods for use in humans were restricted to electroencephalography (EEG), which has very limited spatial resolution. However, in recent years methodological advances in magnetoencephalography (MEG), intracranial EEG (iEEG) or electrocorticography (ECoG), and cortical localization methods in EEG, allow for much greater spatial precision with neurophysiological data, providing powerful techniques for investigating syntax in the brain.

The most widespread (and affordable) technique is EEG, in which the experimenter places a cap with a number of electrodes (typically 32, 64, or 128) on the head of the subject. The electrodes are sensitive to changes in electrical activity occurring on the scalp, some of which are driven by the brain. However, cortical localization of these signals is greatly hampered by the presence of intervening tissue (e.g. hair, skin, skull, meninges) between the brain and the electrodes that greatly distorts the signal. Additionally, the cortical sources must be aligned parallel to the electrodes in order for the electrical waves to be detected, meaning most signals are derived from gyri (cortical bumps) and preventing the recording of signals from within sulci (cortical grooves) that are oriented perpendicular to the scalp. However, recently researchers have attempted to model these intervening tissues, allowing them to account for the distortion effect and determine more precisely where the signals are generated from. These methods have improved source localization in EEG (see, e.g., Meyer et al. (2015) for an example of EEG source localization in the context of sentence comprehension).

Another technique used for language is magnetoencephalography (MEG). MEG is sensitive to the magnetic fields that are generated orthogonally to electrical waves. Thus, it essentially detects the same underlying neural activity as EEG. However, given the orthogonal orientation of the fields, MEG is mostly sensitive to sulci rather than gyri, giving it complementary neuroanatomical coverage to EEG. The major advantage of MEG over EEG is that magnetic fields, unlike electrical waves, are not distorted by intervening head tissue. Thus, by applying appropriate computational methods the MEG signal can be much more precisely localized to the brain than the EEG signal, particularly when supplemented with the subject's own structural MRI. However, there is still a limit to the spatial precision of MEG, giving it an effective resolution of 2–3 centimeters in the best case. In addition, currently MEG scanners are somewhat rare and expensive to purchase and maintain, particularly so given recent limitations of helium supply, limiting its widespread adoption for language research.

More recently, many studies have used intracranial electrodes (iEEG/ECoG) in order to obtain highly spatially precise measures of neural activity during language tasks. ECoG is impossible to use in healthy subjects, given that it requires surgical opening of the skull to allow electrode implantation onto the cortical surface. However, patients undergoing brain surgery for epilepsy often have electrode grids inserted in order to identify and avoid brain areas critical for language. This affords an opportunity for researchers to present these patients with various language tasks, typically "naturalistic" paradigms such as watching movies or listening to audiobooks. The advantage of ECoG over EEG and MEG is that the location of the electrode is directly on the brain itself, allowing for precise localization to that exact region without sacrificing any temporal information. In addition, depth electrodes can be implanted into sulci, allowing for recordings from both gyri and sulci within the general implanted area.

### 27.2.3   Neuroanatomy of Language

There are three main parts to the human brain: the cerebrum, the brainstem, and the cerebellum; we focus here on the cerebrum, the major structure sitting atop the brainstem and cerebellum.[3] The cerebrum itself is divided into the cortex and subcortex. The cortex consists of a large, thick, and folded sheet of gray matter (cell bodies) that forms the most visible surface of the brain. The folds create the sulci and gyri that form the major anatomical landmarks of the cortex. Underneath this sheet is the corresponding white matter, comprised of myelinated axons, allowing for local and long-range transfer of information among gray matter regions of the cortex. The subcortex consists of pockets of gray matter buried deeper in the white matter of the cortex, chiefly the basal ganglia and thalamus. The thalamus, basal ganglia, and the cortex are interconnected with localized circuit loops running through them (Alexander et al. 1986).

The cortex consists roughly of a fundamental division between sensory-motor cortex and association cortex. Sensory-motor cortex consists of regions specialized for processing a particular modality for perception, motor behavior, or integration of the two (e.g. auditory cortex in the superior temporal gyrus, sensory-motor cortex in the supramarginal gyrus) receiving inputs from subcortical structures connecting to peripheral organs (e.g. retina, cochlea, muscle fibers). Association cortices are nested in-between sensory-motor areas, and are less specialized for a particular modality, likely processing more abstract information such as syntax and semantics (e.g. middle temporal gyrus, angular gyrus). Figure 27.1 illustrates the anatomical regions (left) and functional regions (right) relevant for language that will be discussed in subsequent sections of this chapter.

Regions relevant for abstract linguistic processing have been identified by neuroimaging studies identifying effects independent of modality of presentation, such as auditory speech, orthography, and sign language (Binder et al. 2009; Fedorenko et al. 2010; 2011; Leonard et al. 2012; Huth et al. 2016; Wilson et al. 2018). For instance, a recent fMRI study by Wilson et al. (2018) using MVPA illustrated that association cortex within the temporal lobe, particularly the ventral bank of the superior temporal sulcus and the middle temporal gyrus, did not discriminate between auditory and written language, likely reflecting more abstract processing, whereas surrounding areas did discriminate these modalities. Classical models of language and the brain typically include brain areas such as the posterior superior temporal gyrus (sometimes called Wernicke's area[4]) highly associated with speech perception and phonological processing (Figure 27.1), but most modern models clarify that much linguistic processing at the lexical, syntactic, and semantic levels occurs in association cortex outside of this area (Hickok & Poeppel 2007; Rauschecker & Scott 2009; Bornkessel-Schlesewsky & Schlesewsky 2013; Binder 2017; Matchin & Hickok 2020).

---

[3] We focus on the cerebrum adopting the standard assumption that higher-order faculties rely primarily on the cortex. This assumption is useful for focusing discussion but clearly false in the sense that language behavior, defined broadly, certainly crucially relies on the brainstem and cerebellum to some degree.

[4] The term "Wernicke's area" has historically been poorly defined and has been used to refer to an unusually wide variety of cortical regions (Tremblay & Dick 2016; Binder 2017).

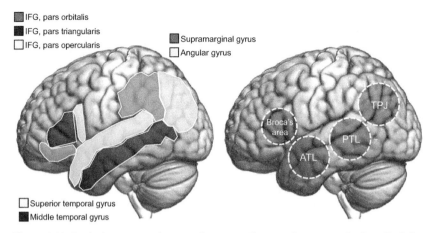

IFG, pars orbitalis
IFG, pars triangularis
IFG, pars opercularis
Supramarginal gyrus
Angular gyrus
Superior temporal gyrus
Middle temporal gyrus

**Figure 27.1** Cortical anatomy relevant to language. The superior temporal sulcus (STS) lies deep in-between the superior and middle temporal gyri. ATL: anterior temporal lobe; PTL: posterior temporal lobe; TPJ: temporal-parietal junction. IFG: inferior frontal gyrus.

## 27.3   Syntax and the Brain: Localization

While the set of cortical regions relevant for language is fairly well established, which regions (if any) are specialized for syntax is a matter of substantial debate, particularly concerning Broca's area (Kaan & Swaab 2002; Grodzinsky & Santi 2008; Rogalsky & Hickok 2011; Bornkessel-Schlesewsky & Schlesewsky 2013; Goucha et al. 2017; Matchin & Hickok 2020). Most experiments using neuroimaging methods to study syntax have attempted to localize syntactic representations or operations (or combinatory processing defined in a more general way) to one or more of the brain regions listed above; to put it bluntly, to find a "syntax area." The idea of localizing syntax in the brain itself involves several potentially invalid assumptions, most crucially that there in fact is a congruous chunk of brain tissue corresponding to syntax (Poeppel & Embick 2005). Even more so, this search has been hampered by a lack of linking hypotheses among competence theories, performance models, and brain activity. Fortunately, recent work has paid closer attention to these issues, and these new developments may lead to greater interaction between linguists and neuroscientists in answering questions of relevance to syntactic theory (Boeckx 2013; Brennan 2016; Goucha et al. 2017).

The rest of this section is divided into two broad categories of studies: (i) *processing complexity* studies aimed at isolating brain responses correlated with well-studied behavioral costs (i.e. reaction time, accuracy) associated with certain structural manipulations such as clausal embedding and non-canonical word order; and (ii) *combinatorial complexity* studies aimed at isolating brain responses correlated with the constituent size or (with some additional assumptions) the number of structure-building operations needed to parse the material. Interestingly, while the two categories focus on two different aspects (roughly, performance and competence), they do converge on brain areas important for syntax.

### 27.3.1  Studies of Processing Complexity

Two of the earliest neuroimaging studies investigating syntax in the brain (Just et al. 1996; Stromswold et al. 1996) performed contrasts that identified brain activations related to " ... 'thinking harder' in the course of sentence comprehension ... " (Just et al. 1996), operationalized as increased reaction times and/or increased error rates for a task such as sentence comprehension (Just & Carpenter 1992). Such studies often use a class of constructions known to induce processing difficulties: long-distance dependencies, which involve a relation between two elements of a sentence that may span an indefinite number of words. One type is known as filler–gap dependencies, which involve apparent displacement between the location of an element (the filler) from another position in the sentence (the gap). Sentence (1) illustrates a common filler–gap dependency, a *wh*-question, in which *which dog* is interpreted as the object of the transitive verb *chase*, after which it normally would appear. The subscript indicates that the filler is interpreted at the appropriate gap position.

(1)     [which dog]$_1$ did the cat chase ___$_1$ ?

Relative clauses are also a common instance of filler-gap dependencies, for example subject-relative (2) and object-relative (3) clauses, in which the head noun phrase modified by the relative clause also serves as an argument of the relative clause verb:

(2)     the reporter that attacked the senator admitted the error

(3)     the reporter that the senator attacked admitted the error

Such constructions have been heavily studied in the experimental literature, in which sentences with relative clauses reduce behavioral performance relative to sentences without relative clauses (such as conjoined actives), and object-relatives increase processing costs relative to subject-relatives (Just et al. 1996; see Gibson et al. 2013 for a review).

Just et al. (1996) compared brain activation during sentence comprehension in the fMRI scanner to three conditions that matched for lexical items and roughly matched for complexity and content of semantic interpretation, but differing on syntactic dimensions and behavioral measures: (i) conjoined active sentences (e.g. *the reporter attacked the senator and admitted the error*), (ii) sentences with subject-relative clauses attached to the main clause subject (e.g. *the reporter that attacked the senator admitted the error*), and

(iii) sentences with object-relative clauses attached to the main clause subject (e.g. *the reporter that the senator attacked admitted the error*). Stromswold et al. (1996), in a PET study, critically compared two conditions: (i) center-embedded object-relative constructions in which the relative clause was attached to the subject of the main clause, (e.g. *the juice that the child spilled stained the rug*) and (ii) right-branching subject-relative sentences, in which the relative clause was attached to the object of the main clause (e.g. *the child spilled the juice that stained the rug*).

Both of these neuroimaging studies found increased brain activation for object-relatives compared to subject-relatives (and in Just et al., increased activation for subject-relatives compared to conjoined actives) in the pars opercularis (the posterior portion of Broca's area) while Just et al. (1996) found additional activation in the pars triangularis (the anterior portion of Broca's area), as well as the posterior temporal lobe (PTL). While some studies using similar structural manipulations report effects in other brain areas, such as the anterior temporal lobe (Den Ouden et al. 2012; Blank et al. 2016), increased activity in Broca's area and the PTL is the most reliable general pattern found across studies, confirmed by a recent meta-analysis (Meyer & Friederici 2016).

Without plausible linking theories, it is difficult to understand what this activation pattern means. Given that syntactic theory in mainstream generative grammar has treated filler–gap dependencies as instances of a grammatical transformation (Chomsky 1957, 1965, 1981, 1995), some authors have interpreted such results as reflecting transformation computations, particularly in Broca's area (Ben-Shachar et al. 2003; Santi & Grodzinsky 2007). Other authors have interpreted these results as reflecting more general syntactic processing mechanisms involved in building basic phrase structure, which may be invoked to handle sentences with non-canonical word order (Makuuchi et al. 2009; Meyer et al. 2012; Wilson et al. 2014). Finally, other authors have highlighted a third possibility: working memory resources needed to maintain information for processing (Just et al. 1996; Stromswold et al. 1996; Caplan et al. 2000; Rogalsky et al. 2008). Many studies have aimed at dissociating between syntactic mechanisms and working memory resources (Caplan et al. 2000; Cooke et al. 2002; Fiebach et al. 2005; Santi & Grodzinsky 2007; Rogalsky et al. 2008; Makuuchi et al. 2009; Meyer et al. 2012; Matchin et al. 2014).

For example, Santi and Grodzinsky (2007) sought to examine effects in Broca's area to filler–gap dependencies as opposed to any kind of long-distance dependency that might induce memory demands, namely anaphoric relations, or overt pronominal expressions that refer to a nominal element for referential interpretation. Sentence (4) illustrates one such anaphoric expression, the relation between a reflexive and its antecedent. Subscripts indicate the coreferential interpretation that obtains, that *herself* refers to *Mary* (as opposed, for instance, to some other person).

(4)    John knows that Mary$_1$ pinched herself$_1$

Santi and Grodzinsky (2007) crossed the factors dependency type (filler–gap vs. anaphoric) and distance (one, two, or three noun phrases intervening between the dependent elements), with the assumption that general memory resources would be taxed for distance regardless of dependency type. By contrast, syntactic transformations are commonly thought to account for the filler–gap dependencies but not anaphoric dependencies (Chomsky 1981), suggesting that a selective distance effect in Broca's area for filler–gap dependencies would reflect a syntactic transformation computation. They in fact found a distance effect for filler–gap dependencies but not anaphoric dependencies in the pars triangularis, suggesting a role specifically for syntactic processing in this region not attributable to more general memory demands.

A key issue overlooked in this study is the processing dynamics of the two constructions. Anaphoric dependencies are typically unpredictable – that is, the reflexive refers to a previously encountered antecedent. For example, in sentence (4), the fact that such a long-distance dependency exists at all is not clear until the anaphoric expression *herself* is encountered. Filler–gap dependencies are different – once the filler is encountered, the gap location is predictable. For example, in sentences (2) and (3), *that* cues the comprehender to the existence of a future noun phrase gap. Behavioral experiments have shown that subjects use this information to actively predict gaps, leading to the so-called *filled-gap effect* (Crain & Fodor 1985; Stowe 1986; Frazier & Flores d'Arcais 1989; see also Chapter 5). Thus, canonical anaphora are processed passively while filler–gap dependencies are processed actively. Given that working memory resources are often invoked to actively maintain information across time and/or linguistic material (Baddeley 1981; Gibson 2000), this suggests that working memory resources are invoked differently for forward-looking dependencies (filler–gap dependencies) and backward-looking dependencies (canonical anaphora), a potentially confounding factor with respect to Broca's area activation.

Interestingly, there is a class of anaphoric dependencies that shares this predictive processing profile – *backward* anaphora, or *cataphora*. In backward anaphora, the anaphor precedes the antecedent, resulting in predictability of the anaphoric dependency, e.g. sentence (5).

(5)    When he$_1$ was fed up, the boy$_1$ visited the girl in the hospital.

Behavioral experiments have shown that subjects expect the gender of the first full noun phrase in these types of sentences to agree with the anaphor, exhibiting a processing cost if this pronoun does not agree, e.g. sentence (6) (van Gompel & Liversedge 2003; Kazanina et al. 2007).

(6)    When he$_1$ was fed up, **the girl** visited the boy$_1$ in the hospital.

Matchin et al. (2014) performed a similar fMRI study to Santi and Grodzinsky (2007) but used backward anaphora, finding a robust effect of distance for backward anaphora in the same subregion of Broca's area that was identified for distance in filler–gap dependencies, the pars triangularis. Thus, the activation profile in this region appears to reflect the processing of long-distance syntactic dependencies generally (e.g. a contribution of working memory resources) rather than a specific syntactic computation.

As a final note, while most processing complexity studies focus on activation in Broca's area, many of these studies report similar (or even more robust) activation in the PTL. The overall similarity of response profile of Broca's area and the posterior temporal lobe pervades the neuroimaging literature on syntax. However, neuropsychological studies aiming to identify correlations between brain damage and language deficits reveal striking differences between these two regions – the posterior temporal lobe is robustly associated with sentence comprehension and syntactic comprehension deficits, while Broca's area damage is not (see Matchin & Hickok (2020) for a review). We will return to this issue below.

Overall, processing complexity studies have provided useful data regarding the brain systems involved in sentence processing, but the relation to syntactic theory remains opaque. This is chiefly because these studies do not spell out the links among syntactic representations and computations, real-time parsing models, and brain signals.

### 27.3.2   Studies of Combinatorial Complexity

Unlike neuroimaging studies of processing complexity, studies of combinatorial complexity focus instead on the representational complexity of the stimulus, regardless of the behavioral data. The informal linking hypotheses are generally of the form (a) that the number of syntactic and/or semantic operations (e.g. phrase structure rules, *Merge*, function application) is correlated with the structural complexity of the stimulus itself, and (b) that the brain signal is also roughly linearly related to the number of operations. For example, starting with the seminal PET study by Mazoyer et al. (1993), many researchers using hemodynamic methods have contrasted sentences or phrases and unstructured word lists (Stowe et al. 1998; Friederici et al. 2000; Humphries et al. 2005; MacSweeney et al. 2006; Rogalsky & Hickok 2008; Fedorenko et al. 2010; Goucha et al. 2015; Matchin et al. 2017; Zaccarella et al. 2017).[5] While the subject may actually perform worse on word lists for tasks such as lexical recall (Matchin et al. 2017), increased activation for sentences is reported broadly and

---

[5] Subjects themselves could impose structure on putatively unstructured sequences of words, thereby complicating the sentences vs. word list contrast. Researchers have tried to limit this issue by using a sequence of nouns rather than scrambling the sentence (e.g. MacSweeney et al. 2006; Rogalsky & Hickok 2008).

Table 27.2 *Stimulus design of Pallier et al. (2011: Table 1). The stimuli were 12-word sequences obtained by concatenating constituents of fixed sizes extracted from natural or Jabberwocky right-branching sentences. In Jabberwocky, all content words were replaced with pseudowords (italics). Examples are only illustrative, because the original stimuli were in French.*

| Condition | Constituent Size | Examples |
|---|---|---|
| C12 | 12 words | I believe that you should accept the proposal of your new associate |
| | | I *tosieve* that you should *begept* the *tropufal* of your *tew viroate* |
| C06 | 6 words | the mouse that eats our cheese two clients examine this nice couch |
| | | the *couse* that *rits* our *treeve fow plients afomine* this *kice bloch* |
| C04 | 4 words | mayor of the city he hates this color they read their names |
| | | *tuyor* of the *roty* he *futes* this *dator* they *gead* their *wames* |
| C03 | 3 words | solving a problem repair the ceiling he keeps reading will buy some |
| | | *relging* a *grathem regair* the *fraping* he *meeps bouding* will *doy* some |
| C02 | 2 words | looking ahead important task who dies his dog few holes they write |
| | | *troking* ahead *omirpant fran* who *mies* his *gog* few *biles* they *grite* |
| C01 | 1 word | thing very tree where of watching copy tensed they states heart plus |
| | | *thang* very *gree* where of *wurthing napy gunsed* they *otes blart trus* |

consistently across left hemisphere language areas, although individual studies vary somewhat (see the review and meta-analysis by Zaccarella et al. (2017)).

The fMRI study by Pallier et al. (2011) is particularly worth reviewing, both for its novelty as well as for the explicit nature of its linking hypotheses. Rather than simply contrasting sentences and word lists, Pallier et al. (2011) parametrically varied the maximum constituent size within 12-word stimuli across six conditions, from unconnected word lists (maximum constituent size = 1) to 12-word sentences (maximum constituent size = 12), as shown in Table 27.2. The linking hypothesis was that neural activity linearly scales with constituent size, such that activity is sustained during the processing of connected constituents and drops back to zero after the completion of a constituent. They convolved this model with a standard HRF to generate quantitative activation predictions for each condition in brain areas involved in structure-building. The results revealed that essentially all left hemisphere language-related regions (except for the pars opercularis) showed a positive correlation of activity with constituent size (Figure 27.2).

Pallier et al. (2011) also used Jabberwocky versions of each level of structure. The term Jabberwocky is taken from the well-known poem of

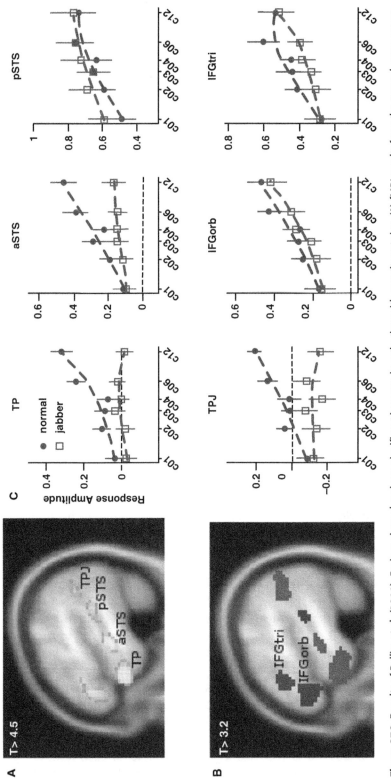

**Figure 27.2** Results of Pallier et al. (2011). Brain regions showing a significant increase in activation with constituent size. (A) fMRI results from the normal-prose group who read sequences with actual French words (group analysis thresholded at T > 4.5, P < 0.05 FWE, spatial extent > 10). (B) Areas in blue show a significant constituent size effect in the Jabberwocky group listening to delexicalized stimuli, whereas regions in red show a significant group by constituent size interaction (reflecting a stronger effect of constituent size in normal prose than in Jabberwocky) (maps thresholded at T > 3.2, P < 0.001 uncorrected, spatial extent > 50). (C) Amplitude of activations across conditions in the six regions of interest (error bars represent ± 1 SEM). Conditions c01 to c12 are organized according to a logarithmic scale of constituent size, thus a line on this graph indicates a logarithmic increase of activation. The fitting lines are from a regression analysis including linear and logarithmic predictors.

that name by Lewis Carroll (1871), which contains sentences that are syntactically well-formed but rendered semantically empty by replacing content words with nonwords. Neuroimaging researchers interested in syntax have used Jabberwocky since Mazoyer et al. (1993) to attempt to dissociate conceptual-semantic from syntactic processes. The assumption is that real sentences involve both conceptual-semantic and syntactic processes, while Jabberwocky greatly reduces conceptual-semantic content. Pallier et al. (2011) found that only some regions showed a correlation with constituent size in Jabberwocky materials: (i) the inferior frontal gyrus, pars triangularis (anterior Broca's area); (ii) the inferior frontal gyrus, pars orbitalis; and (iii) the posterior superior temporal sulcus (pSTS). These regions roughly correspond to the regions typically identified for processing complexity (Broca's area and the posterior temporal lobe). This pattern was essentially replicated by subsequent studies (Fedorenko et al. 2012; Goucha et al. 2015; Matchin et al. 2017).

A separate body of work, mostly performed by Pylkkänen and colleagues, has used MEG to study combinatorial effects in minimal two-word phrasal contexts, e.g. comparing the brain activity occurring at the second word of the phrase *red boat* (i.e. at *boat*) relative to *xkq boat* (see Pylkkänen (2015) for a review). These studies have often reported increased activation for phrasal composition in the left anterior temporal lobe, although the location of significant activation varies across studies and other regions are also sometimes reported, including the ventromedial prefrontal cortex, the posterior temporal lobe, and the angular gyrus.

Thus, combining results across studies, several language-related regions of the left hemisphere have been shown to be sensitive to syntactic structure in sentences with all real words. However, a few key fMRI studies have revealed that only the inferior frontal gyrus and the posterior temporal lobe are sensitive to Jabberwocky structure as well. Less clear is what exactly this sensitivity reflects. Most of these studies did not explicitly articulate the linking hypotheses connecting syntactic and/or semantic operations posited in linguistic theory with online processing models and brain activity.

To address this issue, several authors have also begun to use explicit computational parsing models with assumptions about corresponding neural responses to investigate syntax in the brain (Figure 27.3; Brennan 2016). Rather than performing controlled experiments with carefully selected and balanced materials across conditions, these studies typically present large sections of auditory or written linguistic material taken from published books or podcasts; so-called "naturalistic" designs that are increasingly used in neuroimaging studies. The stimuli are then tagged (typically at the word level) with numerous regressor variables for modeling sensory aspects of the materials (e.g. word length, acoustic power) and

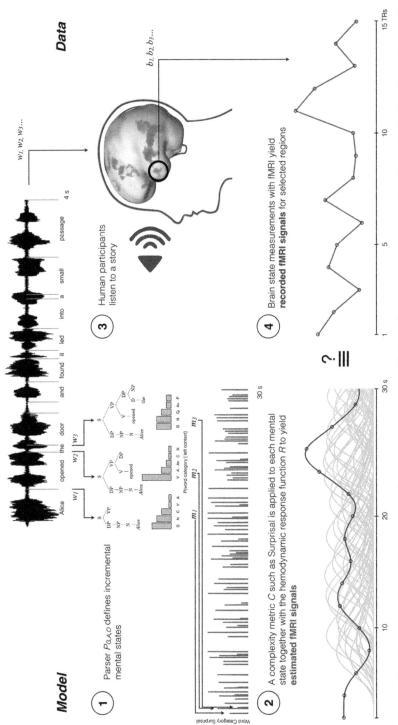

**Figure 27.3** An illustration of the model-based approach (from Brennan 2016). The top of the figure shows a segment of a naturalistic audiobook stimulus. Word boundaries are indicated in blue. (i) The parser defines word-by-word mental states that reflect syntactic constituency and expectations for upcoming words, shown in the gray probability distributions. Here, the grammar G is set to a context-free phrase structure grammar, the algorithm A is set to top-down enumeration, and the oracle O is set to resolve temporary ambiguities to the structures that are ultimately correct. (ii) These mental states are quantified to derive processing predictions by applying the surprisal complexity metric, C, shown in green. This quantity reflects the conditional probability of each word in the stimulus and is higher when words are unexpected. A response function R aligns word-by-word complexity values with fMRI-measured brain signals. The overlapping gray traces show the result of convolving each word's surprisal with the hemodynamic response function. The sum of these, shown in blue, is an estimate of the time-course of fMRI signals that reflect syntactic expectation. (iii) The data for this illustration come from recordings while participants passively listened to the audiobook. (iv) The measured signal from a particular region of interest is extracted (red trace) and correlated against the estimated signal (blue trace) to test how well the estimated fMRI signal aligns with the recorded fMRI signal.

any potentially relevant cognitive aspects, such as lexical, syntactic, semantic, pragmatic, or other dimensions (see, e.g., Wehbe et al. 2014).

These studies (using fMRI, MEG, and ECoG) have largely found effects of parsing complexity in similar regions as controlled experiments, including the anterior and posterior temporal lobe, the angular gyrus/temporal-parietal junction, and the pars triangularis of the inferior frontal gyrus (Brennan et al. 2012, 2016; Wehbe et al. 2014; Brennan & Pylkkänen 2017; Nelson et al. 2017; Bhattasali et al. 2019). Notable differences include less robust activation of the inferior frontal gyrus and occasional bilateral or right-lateralized patterns of activity, unlike what is typically reported in hemodynamic studies of sentence comprehension using controlled stimuli and explicit tasks; that is, left-lateralized activity and Broca's area activation. Right-hemisphere activity and the less robust activation of Broca's area could reflect the underlying reality of syntax and semantics in the brain, supported by authors who have previously argued for a right-hemisphere role in language comprehension, as well as a limited role for Broca's area in comprehension, due to certain patterns of comprehension in aphasia (Hickok 2000; Hickok & Poeppel 2004; 2007; Rogalsky & Hickok 2011). However, it is clear that aphasia overwhelmingly results from left-hemisphere brain damage rather than from right-hemisphere damage generally (Damasio 1992): it is not straightforward how to reconcile these neuroimaging results with this fact. Therefore, in this review we focus primarily on the left, noting that this is an important avenue of further exploration.

## 27.4   Neuroimaging Informs Syntactic Theory

Syntactic theories differ in their structural analyses. Parsing models differ in how they build structure over time. Abstracting across syntactic or parsing theories, the appropriate analysis of particular constructions can be uncertain. Data bearing on these questions can, at least in principle, be obtained from neuroimaging studies. Crucially, this requires adopting specific linking hypotheses regarding how these mechanisms relate to brain activity, and then testing whether different theories and/or models make better predictions about the observed pattern of brain activity in language areas during sentence comprehension.

### 27.4.1   Neuroimaging Informs Syntactic Competence and Performance Models

The goal of assessing alternative syntactic theories and parsing models has been exceptionally undertaken by Brennan, Hale, and colleagues in a series of recent neuroimaging publications (Brennan & Pylkkänen 2017; Brennan et al. 2016; Bhattasali et al. 2019), following the approach detailed in Figure 27.3. Brennan et al. (2016) using fMRI, and Nelson et al. (2017) using ECoG (intracranial EEG), form an excellent complementary pair of studies in this context.

Brennan et al. (2016) sought to address the *competence hypothesis*, first advocated by Chomsky (1965), that the detailed linguistic representations developed by abstracting away from online processing (i.e. competence models) are in fact directly applicable to producing and comprehending sentences (i.e. performance models). Several authors have criticized the competence hypothesis, using certain patterns of psycho- and neuro-linguistic data to motivate the perspective that the detailed syntactic structures posited by theorists may not be routinely used during online sentence processing (or indeed, at all used) (Sanford & Sturt 2002; Culicover & Jackendoff 2006; Ferreira & Patson 2007; Frank & Bod 2011). In order to evaluate the competence hypothesis, they tested whether three broad levels of syntactic representation contributed to the BOLD signal generated from within language-response brain areas (essentially, the functional brain areas outlined in Figure 27.1): (i) linear models (without phrase structure), (ii) phrase structure grammars (without movement and empty categories), and (iii) minimalist grammars (Stabler 1997), incorporating the fullest level of detail typically found in syntactic theories (e.g. Chomsky 1995). These three categories reflect essentially a gradient of complexity, from completely non-hierarchical to heavily detailed hierarchical and transformational representation.

Brennan et al. (2016) first localized language-sensitive regions on an individual subject basis by roughly identifying brain regions responsive to words. They then evaluated the fit of models associated with each level of hierarchical structure to the BOLD signal generated within these areas during sentence comprehension. They found that only language areas of the left temporal lobe, the ATL and PTL, showed effects of both phrase structure grammar as well as minimalist grammars. These results suggest that the detailed structures (including transformations and empty categories) posited in some syntactic theories (Chomsky 1995; Frank 2004) contribute to brain activations within temporal lobe language areas (though notably not Broca's area) during real-time sentence processing. This neuroimaging result converges with a series of psycholinguistic experiments illustrating that representations developed in competence theories contribute to real-time processing dynamics (see Chapter 5 and Lewis & Phillips (2015) for a review).

Brennan et al. (2016) discuss the conflict of their results with those of Frank and Bod (2011) and Frank et al. (2015), who found that hierarchical models of syntactic representation did not provide better fits for eye movements or EEG scalp potentials than linear models. They suggested that the main difference lies in the spatial selectivity of fMRI – only the core language regions of the temporal lobe (ATL and PTL) showed effects of hierarchical representation (including the detailed contributions of transformational grammar), while Broca's area (among other regions) only showed linear effects. This result illustrates a powerful unique appeal of functional neuroimaging, particularly fMRI, over other methods: small but reliable signals associated with intricate grammatical representation can be detected when the signal can be associated with a specific language region.

Importantly, Brennan et al. identified effects of hierarchical syntax in the temporal lobe but not Broca's area. This result breaks the general alignment of neuroimaging effects discussed in the previous sections between Broca's area and the PTL, providing additional evidence in favor of a PTL model of hierarchical syntax (Matchin & Hickok 2020). This result also illustrates the powerful bi-directional possibilities between neuroimaging and linguistic theory: linguistic theory can benefit from spatially specific brain signals in areas known to be important for language, and neuroscience can benefit from the quantitative predictions regarding brain activity generated by competence models and suitable linking hypotheses.

Nelson et al. (2017) sought to address a different but related question: which parsing algorithm builds the structures posited in competence models? They used ECoG to obtain high spatial and temporal resolution data during sentence comprehension, identifying brain regions responding to structural complexity. While they found that the PTL was also responsive to linear, non-hierarchical parsing models, their results converge with Brennan et al. (2016) (as well as a host of other neuroimaging studies) by finding that language areas of the left temporal lobe are sensitive to the hierarchical structure of sentences. Contrary to Brennan et al., they also found that IFG is responsive to hierarchical structure.

Critically, the temporal precision afforded by ECoG allowed them to test subtle differences in timing dynamics posited by different parsing models. They tested three general parsing models: bottom-up parsing, where all the rules of a grammar are applied whenever called for by an incoming word; top-down parsing, where a maximum number of rules are applied in advance of each word; and left-corner parsing, which is a mix of bottom-up and top-down procedures. Their results revealed that different language-sensitive regions were best fit by different models: anterior temporal and inferior frontal regions were best fit by bottom-up and left-corner parsing models, while the PTL was best fit by a top-down parsing model.

Overall, the ECoG study by Nelson et al. (2017) underscores the complexity of human sentence processing, likely incorporating elements of both linear and hierarchical relations as well as both bottom-up and top-down temporal parsing dynamics. Crucially, these effects occurred in nearby yet distinct cortical regions, making the spatial specificity of this neuroimaging technique crucial in revealing this complexity, whereas behavioral methods or EEG analysis at the sensor level might have missed these differential responses by essentially averaging across them.

### 27.4.2    Neuroimaging Informs Structural Analyses

Often the analysis of a particular phenomenon or sentence construction is uncertain and may be difficult to resolve using traditional acceptability judgment methods. Neuroimaging data can in principle bear on the appropriate analysis and have in fact been offered in a few cases using fMRI. I will discuss two: scrambling and head movement. Both cases illustrate the importance of serious considerations of linking hypotheses, incorporating careful assumptions about the performance model in evaluating experimental results.

It is unclear whether certain word order variations exhibited in languages such as German or Japanese, called scrambling (Ross 1967), should also be analyzed as instances of movement (Saito 1989) (see Chapters 12, 16, and 18). Makuuchi et al. (2012) started with the assumption that the pars triangularis of Broca's area specifically processes syntactic movement (as opposed to other long-distance dependencies such as anaphor binding; cf. Santi & Grodzinsky 2007). They performed an experiment similar to that of Santi and Grodzinsky (2007), parametrically manipulating the degree of distance (number of intervening noun phrases) between two kinds of syntactic dependencies in German: movement and scrambling. They observed an overall main effect of distance in several areas, most prominently Broca's area (pars opercularis/triangularis) with a smaller cluster in the middle-posterior temporal lobe, and no interaction with construction type (i.e. the effect of distance was the same for both movement and scrambling within these areas). This is consistent with the fact that previous neuroimaging studies examining effects of processing complexity for both movement and scrambling have identified effects in (roughly) these areas (Ben-Shachar et al. 2003; Santi & Grodzinsky 2007, 2010; Roder et al. 2002; Grewe et al. 2005; Friederici et al. 2006; Obleser et al. 2011). The authors therefore suggested that scrambling is actually an instance of movement.

As discussed in Section 27.3.1, though, the critical assumption of this study – that the pars triangularis is selective for movement – is probably not correct, given distance effects for backward anaphora when the processing profile is matched to filler–gap dependencies (Matchin et al. 2014). Crucially, insufficient attention was paid to the performance model, which acts as a filter between the competence model (syntactic operations) and brain activity (BOLD signal). In all of these constructions (Movement, Scrambling, Backward anaphora), the subject is cued to a dependency and must hold the relevant syntactic representation in memory to resolve it. Broca's area (in particular, the pars triangularis) appears to activate whenever syntactic working memory demands are high, regardless of the specific construction. Scrambling, like other cases of non-canonical word order, likely involves working memory resources needed to link material between positions in a sentence. This means that increased activation in Broca's area for sentences with the scrambling construction does not effectively inform the appropriate linguistic analysis of scrambling.

A series of studies by Shetreet, Friedmann, and colleagues (2010, 2012, 2014) have also used fMRI to address similar questions of linguistic analysis. For instance, Shetreet and Friedmann (2014) addressed the appropriate analysis of head movement. As reviewed in several examples above, movement is an account of apparent displacement, when a linguistic element appears in a distinct position from which it would canonically appear, as in *wh*-questions, relative clauses, and many other constructions. However, since the 80s, mainstream theories in generative grammar have generally distinguished two types of movement: phrasal movement (in which an entire maximal phrasal projection moves) and head movement, in which only the head of a phrase moves, as in yes/no questions in English in which the auxiliary appears at the beginning of the sentence (e.g. *should$_1$ the warship t$_1$ bombard the fortress?*). One question is whether head movement results from the same linguistic mechanisms as phrase movement or whether these two phenomena should be treated distinctly (Chomsky 2001). Shetreet and Friedmann investigated this issue by performing an fMRI study comparing two movement constructions to canonical word order sentences: *wh*-movement (a type of phrasal movement) and verb movement (a type of head movement) in Hebrew. For the effect of *wh*-movement (*wh* > canonical), they replicated previous studies by finding increased activation in left IFG and pMTG. For verb movement, they did not identify this effect, and ROI analyses revealed the same low level of activation in these areas for canonical sentences. Thus, their results suggest distinct linguistic analyses for phrasal and head movement. However, this study suffers from the same flaw as Makuuchi et al. (2012): that increased activation in these areas reflects the movement transformation itself, rather than processing resources required to handle this construction.

Overall, it is clear that while neuroimaging studies have provided some useful information concerning the appropriate analysis of linguistic phenomena, there are few successful examples and many difficulties in doing so. The most pressing obstacle is developing fully fledged processing models for these phenomena and linking hypotheses for brain activity in particular brain systems.

## 27.5 Conclusions

In all, substantial progress has been made in the use of neuroimaging to inform the study of syntax, although this progress has occurred over a long period of time, with recent major breakthroughs. Throughout this entire discussion lies the question of specifying competence models, performance models to implement these mechanisms, and linking hypotheses from these models to brain activation patterns. The approach pursued by Brennan, Hale, and colleagues (among others) has sought to rigorously specify and test the various alternative choices for each of these domains, providing evidence regarding which brain areas are involved in syntax (temporal lobe structures, particularly PTL) as well as the appropriate competence and performance models (e.g. incorporating a high level of grammatical detail such as transformations and testing multiple parsing implementations). Less progress has been made in the way of using reverse inference to inform the appropriate analysis of a linguistic phenomenon. However, progress is certainly possible when specifying the full performance model and brain signal linking theories, and making clear predictions from alternative analyses regarding the magnitude of effects in regions involved in parsing and other domains of cognition, such as processing resources and/or conceptual-semantic processing.

## References

Alexander, G. E., DeLong, M. R., & Strick, P. L. (1986). Parallel organization of functionally segregated circuits linking basal ganglia and cortex. *Annual Review of Neuroscience*, 9(1), 357–381.

Baddeley, A. D. (1981). The role of subvocalisation in reading. *Quarterly Journal of Experimental Psychology*, 33A, 439–454.

Ben-Shachar, M., Hendler, T., Kahn, I., Ben-Bashat, D., & Grodzinsky, Y. (2003). The neural reality of syntactic transformations: Evidence from functional magnetic resonance imaging. *Psychological Science*, 14(5), 433–440.

Berwick, R. C. & Weinberg, A. S. (1984). *The Grammatical Basis of Linguistic Performance: Language Use and Acquisition*. Cambridge, MA: MIT Press.

Bhattasali, S., Fabre, M., Luh, W. M., Al Saied, H., Constant, M., Pallier, C., . . . & Hale, J. (2019). Localising memory retrieval and syntactic composition: an fMRI study of naturalistic language comprehension. *Language, Cognition and Neuroscience*, 34(4), 491–510.

Binder, J. R. (2012). Task-induced deactivation and the "resting" state. *Neuroimage*, 62(2), 1086–1091.

Binder, J. R. (2017). Current controversies on Wernicke's area and its role in language. *Current Neurology and Neuroscience Reports*, 17(8), 58.

Binder, J. R., Desai, R. H., Graves, W. W., & Conant, L. L. (2009). Where is the semantic system? A critical review and meta-analysis of 120 functional neuroimaging studies. *Cerebral Cortex*, 19(12), 2767–2796.

Binder, J. R., Frost, J. A., Hammeke, T. A., Bellgowan, P. S. F., Rao, S. M., & Cox, R. W. (1999). Conceptual processing during the conscious resting state: A functional MRI study. *Journal of Cognitive Neuroscience*, 11(1), 80–93.

Blank, I., Balewski, Z., Mahowald, K., & Fedorenko, E. (2016). Syntactic processing is distributed across the language system. *Neuroimage*, 127, 307–323.

Boeckx, C. (2013). Biolinguistics: forays into human cognitive biology. *Journal of Anthropological Sciences*, 91, 1–28.

Bornkessel-Schlesewsky, I. & Schlesewsky, M. (2013). Reconciling time, space and function: A new dorsal–ventral stream model of sentence comprehension. *Brain and Language*, 125(1), 60–76.

Brennan, J. (2016). Naturalistic sentence comprehension in the brain. *Language and Linguistics Compass*, 10(7), 299–313.

Brennan, J., Nir, Y., Hasson, U., Malach, R., Heeger, D. J., & Pylkkänen, L. (2012). Syntactic structure building in the anterior temporal lobe during natural story listening. *Brain and Language*, 120(2), 163–173.

Brennan, J. R. & Pylkkänen, L. (2017). MEG evidence for incremental sentence composition in the anterior temporal lobe. *Cognitive Science*, 41, 1515–1531.

Brennan, J. R., Stabler, E. P., Van Wagenen, S. E., Luh, W. M., & Hale, J. T. (2016). Abstract linguistic structure correlates with temporal activity during naturalistic comprehension. *Brain and Language*, 157, 81–94.

Buchsbaum, B. R., Baldo, J., Okada, K., Berman, K. F., Dronkers, N., D'esposito, M., & Hickok, G. (2011). Conduction aphasia, sensory-motor integration, and phonological short-term memory – an aggregate analysis of lesion and fMRI data. *Brain and Language*, 119(3), 119–128.

Caplan, D., Alpert, N., Waters, G., & Olivieri, A. (2000). Activation of Broca's area by syntactic processing under conditions of concurrent articulation. *Human Brain Mapping*, 9(2), 65–71.

Carroll, L. (1871). *Through the Looking Glass: And What Alice Found There.* Chicago: Rand McNally.

Chomsky, N. (1957). *Syntactic Structures.* Berlin: Walter de Gruyter.

Chomsky, N. (1965). *Aspects of the Theory of Syntax*, vol. 11. Cambridge, MA: MIT Press.

Chomsky, N. (1981). *Lectures on Government and Binding.* Dordrecht: Foris.

Chomsky, N. (1995). *The Minimalist Program.* Cambridge, MA: MIT Press.

Chomsky, N. (2001). Derivation by phase. In M. Kenstowicz, ed., *Ken Hale: A Life in Language* (Current Studies in Linguistics, 36). Cambridge, MA: MIT Press, pp.1–52.

Cooke, A., Zurif, E. B., DeVita, C., Alsop, D., Koenig, P., Detre, J., ... & Grossman, M. (2002). Neural basis for sentence comprehension: Grammatical and short-term memory components. *Human Brain Mapping*, 15(2), 80–94.

Crain, S. & Fodor, J. D. (1985). How can grammars help parsers. In D. Dowty, D. Kartunnen, & A. M. Zwicky, eds., *Natural Language Parsing:*

*Psycholinguistics, Computational, and Theoretical Perspectives*. Cambridge: Cambridge University Press, pp. 94–129.

Culicover, P. W. & Jackendoff, R. (2006). The simpler syntax hypothesis. *Trends in Cognitive Sciences*, 10(9), 413–418.

Damasio, A. R. (1992). Aphasia. *New England Journal of Medicine*, 326(8), 531–539.

Den Ouden, B., Saur, D., Mader, W., Schelter, B., Lukic, S., Wali, E., ... & Thompson, C. K. (2012). Network modulation during complex syntactic processing. *Neuroimage*, 59(1), 815–823.

Fedorenko, E., Behr, M. K., & Kanwisher, N. (2011). Functional specificity for high-level linguistic processing in the human brain. *Proceedings of the National Academy of Sciences*, 108(39), 16428–16433.

Fedorenko, E., Hsieh, P. J., Nieto-Castañón, A., Whitfield-Gabrieli, S., & Kanwisher, N. (2010). New method for fMRI investigations of language: Defining ROIs functionally in individual subjects. *Journal of Neurophysiology*, 104(2), 1177–1194.

Fedorenko, E., Nieto-Castanon, A., & Kanwisher, N. (2012). Lexical and syntactic representations in the brain: An fMRI investigation with multi-voxel pattern analyses. *Neuropsychologia*, 50(4), 499–513.

Fedorenko, E., Scott, T. L., Brunner, P., Coon, W. G., Pritchett, B., Schalk, G., & Kanwisher, N. (2016). Neural correlate of the construction of sentence meaning. *Proceedings of the National Academy of Sciences*, 113(41), E6256–E6262.

Ferreira, F. & Patson, N. (2007). The "good enough" approach to language comprehension. *Language and Linguistics Compass*, 1, 71–83.

Fiebach, C. J., Schlesewsky, M., Lohmann, G., Von Cramon, D. Y., & Friederici, A. D. (2005). Revisiting the role of Broca's area in sentence processing: syntactic integration versus syntactic working memory. *Human Brain Mapping*, 24(2), 79–91.

Frank, R. (2004). *Phrase Structure Composition and Syntactic Dependencies*. Cambridge, MA: MIT Press.

Frank, S. L. & Bod, R. (2011). Insensitivity of the human sentence-processing system to hierarchical structure. *Psychological Science*, 22, 829–834.

Frank, S. L., Otten, L. J., Galli, G., & Vigliocco, G. (2015). The ERP response to the amount of information conveyed by words in sentences. *Brain and Language*, 140, 1–11.

Frazier, L. & Flores D'Arcais, G. B. (1989). Filler driven parsing: A study of gap filling in Dutch. *Journal of Memory and Language*, 28(3), 331–344.

Friederici, A. D., Chomsky, N., Berwick, R. C., Moro, A., & Bolhuis, J. J. (2017). Language, mind and brain. *Nature Human Behaviour*, 1(10), 713.

Friederici, A. D., Fiebach, C. J., Schlesewsky, M., Bornkessel, I. D., von Cramon, D. Y. (2006). Processing linguistic complexity and grammaticality in the left frontal cortex. *Cerebral Cortex*, 16, 1709–1717.

Friederici, A. D., Meyer, M., & von Cramon, D. Y. (2000). Auditory language comprehension: An event-related fMRI study on the processing of syntactic and lexical information. *Brain and Language*, 74(2), 289–300.

Friston, K. J., Price, C. J., Fletcher, P., Moore, C., Frackowiak, R. S. J., & Dolan, R. J. (1996). The trouble with cognitive subtraction. *Neuroimage*, 4(2), 97–104.

Gibson, E. (2000). The dependency locality theory: A distance-based theory of linguistic complexity. In Y. Miyashita, A. Marantz, & W. O'Neil, eds., *Image, Language, Brain*. Cambridge, MA: MIT Press.

Gibson, E., Tily, H., & Fedorenko, E. (2013). The processing complexity of English relative clauses. *Language Down the Garden Path: The Cognitive and Biological Basis for Linguistic Structure*. Oxford: Oxford University Press.

Goucha, T. & Friederici, A. D. (2015). The language skeleton after dissecting meaning: a functional segregation within Broca's Area. *Neuroimage*, 114, 294–302.

Goucha, T., Zaccarella, E., & Friederici, A. D. (2017). A revival of the Homo loquens as a builder of labeled structures: Neurocognitive considerations. *Neuroscience & Biobehavioral Reviews*, 81(Pt B).

Grewe, T., Bornkessel, I., Zysset, S., Wiese, R., von Cramon, D. Y., & Schlesewsky, M. (2005). The emergence of the unmarked: A new perspective on the language-specific function of Broca's area. *Human Brain Mapping*, 26, 178–190.

Grill-Spector, K., Henson, R., & Martin, A. (2006). Repetition and the brain: Neural models of stimulus-specific effects. *Trends in Cognitive Sciences*, 10(1), 14–23.

Grodzinsky, Y. & Santi, A. (2008). The battle for Broca's region. *Trends in Cognitive Sciences*, 12(12), 474–480.

Halgren, E., Dhond, R. P., Christensen, N., Van Petten, C., Marinkovic, K., Lewine, J. D., & Dale, A. M. (2002). N400-like magnetoencephalography responses modulated by semantic context, word frequency, and lexical class in sentences. *Neuroimage*, 17(3), 1101–1116.

Haxby, J. V. (2012). Multivariate pattern analysis of fMRI: The early beginnings. *Neuroimage*, 62(2), 852–855.

Hickok, G. (2000). The left frontal convolution plays no special role in syntactic comprehension. *Behavioral and Brain Sciences*, 23(1), 35–36.

Hickok, G. & Poeppel, D. (2004). Dorsal and ventral streams: A framework for understanding aspects of the functional anatomy of language. *Cognition*, 92(1–2), 67–99.

Hickok, G. & Poeppel, D. (2007). The cortical organization of speech processing. *Nature Reviews Neuroscience*, 8(5), 393.

Humphries, C., Love, T., Swinney, D., & Hickok, G. (2005). Response of anterior temporal cortex to syntactic and prosodic manipulations during sentence processing. *Human Brain Mapping*, 26(2), 128–138.

Huth, A. G., de Heer, W. A., Griffiths, T. L., Theunissen, F. E., & Gallant, J. L. (2016). Natural speech reveals the semantic maps that tile human cerebral cortex. *Nature*, 532(7600), 453.

Just, M. A. & Carpenter, P. A. (1992). A capacity theory of comprehension: Individual differences in working memory. *Psychological Review*, 99(1), 122.

Just, M. A., Carpenter, P. A., Keller, T. A., Eddy, W. F., & Thulborn, K. R. (1996). Brain activation modulated by sentence comprehension. *Science*, 274(5284), 114–116.

Kaan, E. & Swaab, T. Y. (2002). The brain circuitry of syntactic comprehension. *Trends in Cognitive Sciences*, 6(8), 350–356.

Kazanina, N., Lau, E. F., Lieberman, M., Yoshida, M., & Phillips, C. (2007). The effect of syntactic constraints on the processing of backwards anaphora. *Journal of Memory and Language*, 56(3), 384–409.

Leonard, M. K., Ramirez, N. F., Torres, C., Travis, K. E., Hatrak, M., Mayberry, R. I., & Halgren, E. (2012). Signed words in the congenitally deaf evoke typical late lexicosemantic responses with no early visual responses in left superior temporal cortex. *Journal of Neuroscience*, 32(28), 9700–9705.

Lewis, S. & Phillips, C. (2015). Aligning grammatical theories and language processing models. *Journal of Psycholinguistic Research*, 44(1), 27–46.

Logothetis, N. K., Pauls, J., Augath, M., Trinath, T., & Oeltermann, A. (2001). Neurophysiological investigation of the basis of the fMRI signal. *Nature*, 412(6843), 150.

MacSweeney, M., Campbell, R., Woll, B., Brammer, M. J., Giampietro, V., David, A. S., . . . & McGuire, P. K. (2006). Lexical and sentential processing in British Sign Language. *Human Brain Mapping*, 27(1), 63–76.

Makuuchi, M., Bahlmann, J., Anwander, A., & Friederici, A. D. (2009). Segregating the core computational faculty of human language from working memory. *Proceedings of the National Academy of Sciences*, 106(20), 8362–8367.

Makuuchi, M., Grodzinsky, Y., Amunts, K., Santi, A., & Friederici, A. D. (2012). Processing noncanonical sentences in Broca's region: Reflections of movement distance and type. *Cerebral Cortex*, 23(3), 694–702.

Matchin, W. (2018). A neuronal retuning hypothesis of sentence-specificity in Broca's area. *Psychonomic Bulletin & Review*, 25, 1682–1694.

Matchin, W., Brodbeck, C., Hammerly, C., & Lau, E. (2019). The temporal dynamics of structure and content in sentence comprehension: Evidence from fMRI-constrained MEG. *Human Brain Mapping*, 40(2), 663–678.

Matchin, W., Hammerly, C., & Lau, E. (2017). The role of the IFG and pSTS in syntactic prediction: Evidence from a parametric study of hierarchical structure in fMRI. *Cortex*, 88, 106–123.

Matchin, W. & Hickok, G. (2020). The cortical organization of syntax. *Cerebral Cortex*, 30(3), 1481–1498.

Matchin, W., Sprouse, J., & Hickok, G. (2014). A structural distance effect for backward anaphora in Broca's area: An fMRI study. *Brain and Language*, 138, 1–11.

Mazoyer, B. M., Tzourio, N., Frak, V., Syrota, A., Murayama, N., Levrier, O., ... & Mehler, J. (1993). The cortical representation of speech. *Journal of Cognitive Neuroscience*, 5(4), 467–479.

Meyer, L. & Friederici, A. D. (2016). Neural systems underlying the processing of complex sentences. In G. Hickok & S. A., Small, eds., *The Neurobiology of Language*. Amsterdam: Academic Press, pp. 597–606.

Meyer, L., Grigutsch, M., Schmuck, N., Gaston, P., & Friederici, A. D. (2015). Frontal–posterior theta oscillations reflect memory retrieval during sentence comprehension. *Cortex*, 71, 205–218.

Meyer, L., Obleser, J., Anwander, A., & Friederici, A. D. (2012). Linking ordering in Broca's area to storage in left temporo-parietal regions: The case of sentence processing. *Neuroimage*, 62(3), 1987–1998.

Nelson, M. J., El Karoui, I., Giber, K., Yang, X., Cohen, L., Koopman, H., ... & Dehaene, S. (2017). Neurophysiological dynamics of phrase-structure building during sentence processing. *Proceedings of the National Academy of Sciences*, 114(18), E3669–E3678.

Obleser, J., Meyer, L., & Friederici, A. D. (2011). Dynamic assignment of neural resources in auditory comprehension of complex sentences. *Neuroimage*, 56(4), 2310–2320.

Pallier, C., Devauchelle, A. D., & Dehaene, S. (2011). Cortical representation of the constituent structure of sentences. *Proceedings of the National Academy of Sciences*, 108(6), 2522–2527.

Poeppel, D. & Embick D. (2005). Defining the relation between linguistics and neuroscience. In A. Cutler, ed., *Twenty-First Century Psycholinguistics: Four Cornerstones*. Abingdon: Routledge, pp. 103–18.

Poldrack, R. A. (2006). Can cognitive processes be inferred from neuroimaging data? *Trends in Cognitive Sciences*, 10(2), 59–63.

Poldrack, R. A. (2011). Inferring mental states from neuroimaging data: From reverse inference to large-scale decoding. *Neuron*, 72(5), 692–697.

Pylkkänen, L. (2015). Composition of complex meaning: Interdisciplinary perspectives on the left anterior temporal lobe. In G. Hickok & S. A. Small, eds., *Neurobiology of Language*. Amsterdam: Academic Press, pp. 621–631.

Raichle, M. E., MacLeod, A. M., Snyder, A. Z., Powers, W. J., Gusnard, D. A., & Shulman, G. L. (2001). A default mode of brain function. *Proceedings of the National Academy of Sciences*, 98(2), 676–682.

Rauschecker, J. P. & Scott, S. K. (2009). Maps and streams in the auditory cortex: nonhuman primates illuminate human speech processing. *Nature Neuroscience*, 12(6), 718.

Roder, B., Stock, O., Neville, H., Bien, S., & Rosler, F. (2002). Brain activation modulated by the comprehension of normal and pseudo-word sentences of different processing demands: A functional magnetic resonance imaging study. *Neuroimage*, 15, 1003–1014.

Rogalsky, C. & Hickok, G. (2008). Selective attention to semantic and syntactic features modulates sentence processing networks in anterior temporal cortex. *Cerebral Cortex*, 19(4), 786–796.

Rogalsky, C. & Hickok, G. (2011). The role of Broca's area in sentence comprehension. *Journal of Cognitive Neuroscience*, 23(7), 1664–1680.

Rogalsky, C., Matchin, W., & Hickok, G. (2008). Broca's area, sentence comprehension, and working memory: An fMRI study. *Frontiers in Human Neuroscience*, 2, 14.

Ross, J. R. (1967). Constraints on variables in syntax. Doctoral dissertation, Massachusetts Institute of Technology.

Saito, M. (1989). Scrambling as semantically vacuous A-movement. In M. Baltin & A. Kroch, eds., *Alternative Conceptions of Phrase Structure*. Chicago: University of Chicago Press.

Sanford, A. & Sturt, P. (2002). Depth of processing in language comprehension: Not noticing the evidence. *Trends in Cognitive Sciences*, 6, 382–386.

Santi, A. & Grodzinsky, Y. (2007). Working memory and syntax interact in Broca's area. *Neuroimage*, 37(1), 8–17.

Santi, A. & Grodzinsky, Y. (2010). fMRI adaptation dissociates syntactic complexity dimensions. *Neuroimage*, 51, 1285–1293.

Shetreet, E. & Friedmann, N. (2012). Stretched, jumped, and fell: An fMRI investigation of reflexive verbs and other intransitives. *Neuroimage*, 60 (3), 1800–1806.

Shetreet, E. & Friedmann, N. (2014). The processing of different syntactic structures: fMRI investigation of the linguistic distinction between wh-movement and verb movement. *Journal of Neurolinguistics*, 27 (1), 1–17.

Shetreet, E., Friedmann, N., & Hadar, U. (2010). Cortical representation of verbs with optional complements: The theoretical contribution of fMRI. *Human Brain Mapping*, 31(5), 770–785.

Stabler, E. P. (1997). Derivational minimalism. In C. Retoré, ed., *Logical Aspects of Computational Linguistics*. Berlin: Springer, pp. 68–95.

Stowe, L. A. (1986). Parsing WH-constructions: Evidence for on-line gap location. *Language and Cognitive Processes*, 1(3), 227–245.

Stowe, L. A., Broere, C. A., Paans, A. M., Wijers, A. A., Mulder, G., Vaalburg, W., & Zwarts, F. (1998). Localizing components of a complex task: sentence processing and working memory. *Neuroreport*, 9(13), 2995–2999.

Stromswold, K., Caplan, D., Alpert, N., & Rauch, S. (1996). Localization of syntactic comprehension by positron emission tomography. *Brain and Language*, 52(3), 452–473.

Tremblay, P. & Dick, A. S. (2016). Broca and Wernicke are dead, or moving past the classic model of language neurobiology. *Brain and Language*, 162, 60–71.

van Gompel, R. P. & Liversedge, S. P. (2003). The influence of morphological information on cataphoric pronoun assignment. *Journal of Experimental Psychology: Learning, Memory, and Cognition*, 29(1), 128.

Wehbe, L., Murphy, B., Talukdar, P., Fyshe, A., Ramdas, A., & Mitchell, T. (2014). Simultaneously uncovering the patterns of brain regions involved in different story reading subprocesses. *PloS One*, 9(11), e112575.

Wilson, S. M., Bautista, A., & McCarron, A. (2018). Convergence of spoken and written language processing in the superior temporal sulcus. *NeuroImage*, 171, 62–74.

Wilson, S. M., DeMarco, A. T., Henry, M. L., Gesierich, B., Babiak, M., Mandelli, M. L., Miller, B. L., & Gorno-Tempini, M. L. (2014). What role does the anterior temporal lobe play in sentence-level processing? Neural correlates of syntactic processing in semantic variant primary progressive aphasia. *Journal of Cognitive Neuroscience*, 26(5), 970–985.

Zaccarella, E., Meyer, L., Makuuchi, M., & Friederici, A. D. (2017). Building by syntax: The neural basis of minimal linguistic structures. *Cerebral Cortex*, 27(1), 411–421.

# Index